Also by Carol Sklenicka

D. H. Lawrence and the Child

RAYMOND CARVER

A Writer's Life

Carol Sklenicka

SCRIBNER

New York   London   Toronto   Sydney

SCRIBNER
A Division of Simon & Schuster, Inc.
1230 Avenue of the Americas
New York, NY 10020

First Scribner hardcover edition November 2009

SCRIBNER and design are registered trademarks of The Gale Group, Inc.,
used under license by Simon & Schuster, Inc., the publisher of this work.

For information about special discounts for bulk purchases,
please contact Simon & Schuster Special Sales at 1-866-506-1949
or business@simonandschuster.com.

The Simon & Schuster Speakers Bureau can bring authors to your live event.
For more information or to book an event, contact the Simon & Schuster Speakers Bureau
at 1-866-248-3049 or visit our website at www.simonspeakers.com.

Manufactured in the United States of America

3   5   7   9   10   8   6   4   2

Library of Congress Control Number: 2009027291

ISBN 978-0-7432-6245-3
ISBN 978-1-4391-6058-9 (ebook)

The author gratefully acknowledges permission from the following source to reprint
material in their control: New Directions Publishing Corp. for "A Unison" by William
Carlos Williams, from *The Collected Poems, Volume II, 1939–1962*, copyright © 1948
by William Carlos Williams. Reprinted by permission of New Directions Publishing Corp.

For insert photograph credits, see p. 549.

For Rick

All the stories
never told:
petals shaken
from the rose.

—*R. M. Ryan*

Contents

Introduction   ix

PART I: BEGINNINGS

1. Raymond Junior   3
2. Yakima Valley   10
3. Vocation   21
4. Cigarettes, Beer, Jazz   34
5. Crazy in Love   43
6. Furious Years   60
7. A Story of He and She   74
8. The Athens of the Midwest   87

PART II: SEARCH

9. Grinding and Sharpening   109
10. Were Those Actual Miles?   122
11. Luck   137
12. Reading Mark Twain in Tel Aviv   153
13. The Sixties End   166
14. A Friend in New York   179

PART III: SUCCESS AND DISCONTENT

15. A Story in *Esquire*   201
16. The Illusion of Freedom   218
17. Astounding and Amazing Times   233
18. Drowning   250
19. *Will You Please Be Quiet, Please?*   268

PART IV: RECOVERY

20. Celebrated and Homeless   293
21. Sobriety   311
22. Separation   323
23. Beginning, Again   336
24. *What We Talk About When We Talk About Love*   352
25. *Fires*   376

PART V: TRIUMPH

26. *Cathedral*   397
27. *Where Water Comes Together with Other Water*   413
28. *Ultramarine*   432
29. *Where I'm Calling From*   447
30. *A New Path to the Waterfall*   460

Epilogue   479

Acknowledgments and Sources   491
Works by Raymond Carver   495
Notes on Sources   501
Notes   503
Insert Photograph Credits   549
Index   551

Introduction

We can never know what to want, because, living only one life, we can neither compare it with our previous lives nor perfect it in our lives to come.
> —epigraph to Raymond Carver's *Where I'm Calling From*, quoted from Milan Kundera's *The Unbearable Lightness of Being*

Few American short story writers have been celebrated as Raymond Carver was in the 1980s. Because his spare, colloquial prose hints at something absent and mysterious, critics called him the father of minimalist fiction. Writers and writing teachers revered and imitated his style. Readers loved his grim, often funny, sometimes transcendent stories about the lives of the working poor. He wrote about their money problems, alcoholism, embittered marriages, and disaffected children; about muted, interior crises brought on by bad luck or neglect rather than intent. Carver knew that territory because he lived in it for much of his life.

Carver paid a high price for the experiences that served his art.

When printer's galleys arrived for his first book of short stories, *Will You Please Be Quiet, Please?*, Carver and his wife, who was a schoolteacher, had just been released from their debts by a federal bankruptcy court. Carver drank vodka while he corrected the pages at his dining room table in Cupertino, California.

On the day after the book's publication in March 1976, two of Carver's friends arrived at his house early in the morning. They didn't come to celebrate the book that would become a National Book Award finalist. They came to drive him and his wife to his trial at the county courthouse; he had been charged with lying to obtain unemployment payments. As they all departed, Maryann Carver took a shiny, white book from a stack on their table. The book was dedicated to her, a fruit of their nineteen married years. She would show it to the judge as evidence that her husband was still a man with prospects. She hoped to be able to keep him out of jail. She would explain that he was the victim of unfulfilled dreams and alcoholism.

Indeed, *Will You Please Be Quiet, Please?* was a career-launching book. Carver, then thirty-eight, had published in literary magazines—plus two stories in *Esquire*—but this first book had been a long time coming.

It came almost too late.

Alcohol had ruled Carver's life for longer than he cared to admit. Lying to the state of California was hardly the worst offense Carver had committed as he capitulated to late-stage alcoholism. "Everything," he wrote later, that he and Maryann "held sacred, every spiritual value, [had] crumbled away."

Carver's fate had closed in on him when he suffered an alcoholic withdrawal seizure in the lobby of a clinic where he'd just been detoxified. A doctor told him then that he'd risk irreversible brain damage if he drank again; that first book could be his last. Despite the dire warning, Carver continued to drink, detox, and relapse for another two years. As he became sicker and sicker, he hid the severity of his problem more cunningly from everyone but his family and close friends. These people worried, but they couldn't influence him.

Yet Carver finally turned his life around, becoming one of the rare exceptions in a long line of hopelessly alcoholic American authors. When he finally quit drinking, he made the decision alone. That day of his last drink was the natal day of his new life, the beginning of the decade he described as "gravy"—the sauce that enriches an ordinary meal.

In his eleven sober years, Carver made difficult decisions that changed his work and his circumstances. He relished the rewards, affection, and freedom that came his way. When he died in 1988, *Where I'm Calling From*, a selection of his short stories that the *New York Times* named a favorite book of the late twentieth century, had just been published; he had just completed his third collection of poetry in five years. His work appeared in twenty-two languages and the *Times* of London called him "the American Chekhov." He was a full-time writer, acclaimed by the press and supported by royalties from his books and a generous five-year grant from the American Academy and Institute of Arts and Letters.

In the end, though, Carver measured his own success by what he'd come through and by the work that he believed would survive him. He wasn't a saint, and his sobriety wasn't perfect—he remained a nervous, obsessive, and lovably boyish man addicted to cigarettes and reliant on marijuana. But he credited his productive final years to not drinking: "I'm prouder of that, that I've quit drinking, than I am of anything in my life."

Carver liked to say he had two lives, and sometimes he spoke of two people, Bad Ray and Good Ray, viewing himself with the bemused, kindly detachment he held for his fictional characters. Of course, he was one man with one life. Bad Ray and Good Ray together were messier and more human than his dichotomy supposed.

Carver acknowledged the irrevocable singleness of his life when he selected as an epigraph to his final volume of stories a quotation from Milan Kundera that speaks of the impossibility of knowing "what to want" or of perfecting oneself within one lifetime. Carver became a more confident and luckier man when he stopped drinking, but he didn't become a different man. In recovery, he accepted himself and marveled at his own achievements. His intention to write well remained his true north.

PART I

BEGINNINGS

CHAPTER 1

Raymond Junior

1929–1940, from Arkansas to the Pacific Northwest

> The borderers were a restless people who carried their migratory
> ways from Britain to America. There had been many folk movements
> in their history before the Atlantic crossing, and many more were yet
> to come. The history of these people was a long series of removals—
> from England . . . to the rainbow's end.
> —David Hackett Fischer on the American Scots-Irish[1]

Raymond Clevie Carver was born on May 25, 1938, in Clatskanie, Oregon. His parents, Ella and Clevie Raymond Carver, were Arkansawyers who had come west to find work. Like the Scots-Irish borderers who were their forebears, the Carvers roved in search of economic stability. By the time of Raymond's birth, his twenty-four-year-old father (called C.R. by friends, Raymond at home) had twice migrated between Arkansas and Washington state, participated in a lengthy strike against a sawmill in Washington, and quit a hazardous job at the Grand Coulee Dam. C.R. came to Wauna, Oregon, to work at a sawmill on the bank of the lower Columbia River. He and his pregnant wife arrived there with a clan that included C.R.'s brother and sister and several carloads of aunts, uncles, and cousins. At the end of summer, the others left for better jobs, but C.R., Ella, and Raymond stayed in Wauna for two more years.[2] This rainy, forested country proved to be a haven for the young family.

The Carvers lived in a little wooden house rented from the Crossett-Western Timber Company in Wauna. A doctor could have delivered the baby at their home, but Ella chose to go to the tiny hospital in Clatskanie, twelve miles east, where Dr. James Wooden gave her chloroform during delivery and she enjoyed a requisite ten days of rest. The bill for all that was $45—a hefty sum considering that C.R. earned between $2 and $4 a day at the mill.[3]

The boy's parents thought of him as Raymond Junior but reversed his father's first and middle names on his birth certificate, burying the unusual Clevie (rhymes with Stevie). Raymond made his first appearance in print on the front page of the *Clatskanie Chief* alongside news of a grass fire started by "celebrating workmen with a jug and a few bottles":

> Mr. and Mrs. C. R. Carver of Wauna welcomed a young son born at the Clatskanie hospital on Wednesday. The babe weighed seven pounds, two and three quarters ounces and has been named Raymond, Jr.

There's a folk saying that a well-loved child has many names. By that standard, young Raymond was doted upon. They called him Man and Junior and sometimes Frog or Little Doc. His parents "lived around his desires and wants," one neighbor remembered. "Anytime he cut a tooth, it was a big event." Early in 1939, his parents brought him to a studio for a professional portrait. The result shows a happy, big-headed baby with sparse hair and a sweet smile, seated on a fancy but unraveling wicker stool and wearing a white smock and big shoes.[4]

When he became an author, that cherished son described his father's stay by the Columbia as his "salad days"—the time in C.R.'s youth when he felt proud and happy because he had "a job and a family." Since completing eighth grade in Leola, Arkansas, C.R. had been working as a general laborer. In Wauna he learned the skilled trade of sharpening saw blades. With a little luck—if the Northwest economy improved—he would have a chance at being a good provider for his wife and son. But nothing in his own experience or his family's recent history had given C.R. much reason to hope for such a change of fortune. Indeed, his own father, Frank Carver, hated physical work and had been kicked by every economic downturn in his lifetime. Nonetheless from Omak, Washington, Mary Carver mailed her new grandbaby a handwritten copy of a poem she'd found in a magazine. The poem celebrated a hardworking family that went on for generation after generation accomplishing little of note until, finally, one person rose above the rest to achieve some worldly fame.[5]

For generations, Raymond Carver's ancestors had struggled to survive. On both sides of his family tree, his forebears were descended from so-called Scots-Irish immigrants (lowland Scots and northern English who had displaced the Celtic Irish in Northern Ireland) who began coming to North America in the late 1700s. The people of this migration were "poor and proud" farmers and laborers who crossed the Atlantic primarily for material betterment. Many lacked the religious or political ideals professed by previous immigrants, though they had the fortitude associated with their Calvinist and Methodist religions.[6] Once in the United States, the Carvers (as well as members of other lines of Carver's descent) continued to move, following their relatives in a chain migration toward inexpensive land in the Southeast, Deep South, and West.

When C.R.'s grandfather, Abram Carver, died of brain fever in 1860, his family was at its economic high point, in possession of black slaves and several hundred acres of cotton fields east of the Saline River in Arkansas. Abram's eldest son, Hosea, was a pragmatic fellow who became known as a "turncoat" in family lore: first wounded as a Confederate soldier, he enlisted with the Union when he saw that the South would lose. By marriage to a neighboring farmer's daughter, Hosea increased his land holdings, but when his ninth child, Frank—C.R.'s father—was still a teenager, the family lost all that land during the Depression of 1893.[7] The Carvers became sharecroppers and lumber mill hands, migrating from one sharecropping situation to another within Arkansas. Homesteading farther west was no longer an option, because by then most of the arable land in the United States was already owned. Frank Carver married Mary Green in 1903, and their first child, Fred Edward, arrived that same year. Violet Lavonda followed, and C.R. was a latecomer, born ten years to the day after Fred. The family suffered further deprivation as the cotton-based Arkansas economy collapsed at the end of World War I. Even in hard times, the family raised their own meat and vegetables and had enough to eat. Frank was known for his big appetite and drinking binges. "Aunt Mary wouldn't tolerate alcohol at home," one of his nephews said, "so Uncle Frank occasionally snuck off and drank like an Indian." On one such occasion, the men told the nephew that he was too young to come fishing with them. That night he was awakened by Mary berating the men for drinking themselves sick. "C.R. was a teenager then, drinking right along with the older men."[8]

It was Fred who decided to abandon the economic quagmire of Arkansas. Early in 1929, he and his wife drove to Omak, Washington. Soon he urged his parents to follow. It fell to fifteen-year-old C.R. to drive their old, black Model-T Ford sedan. Frank, who weighed close to three hundred pounds, rode in front. Mary, Violet, her husband, and their month-old baby squeezed into the backseat. Bedding, furniture, luggage, and water for the car's radiator were roped on the top and sides, and Violet hung her baby's diapers to dry in the windows. Over narrow, dusty roads at top speeds of thirty-five miles per hour, the 2,200-mile journey took thirteen days. At

night the whole family crowded into tiny cabins at tourist courts that provided kitchens and cots, but no bedding or meals.*

C.R. and Violet's husband, Bill Archer, joined Fred at the Biles-Coleman
Lumber Company in Omak, where they milled timber and manufactured
apple boxes and coffins. Mary Carver got a job caring for an apple orchard,
and Violet sorted apples at a packing plant. After their hardships in Arkansas, the Okanogan Valley in early summer was paradise regained. Irrigation
nourished apple orchards and farms in this dry country, while lakes, rivers,
and pine forests in the foothills provided some of the best lake and river
fishing and bird hunting imaginable. The state of Washington was sparsely
developed—still rustic—when C.R. arrived, but this western country had
him "around the heart" for the rest of his days.[9]

As a boy, C.R. had wanted to be a railroad engineer, but the Great
Depression narrowed his choices. "I don't think he dreamed much," Carver
wrote of his father. He was "simply looking for steady work at decent pay.
Steady work was meaningful work."[10] C.R. stayed at Biles-Coleman for
most of five years. In December 1935, he drove his parents to Arkansas for
the holidays. While his father took mineral baths for his rheumatism and
his mother visited relatives, C.R. frequented the bars and gambling joints
of Hot Springs. That's when he noticed Ella Casey.

Ella Beatrice Casey was working and rooming in Hot Springs, putting a few
miles between herself and her parents' home in Butterfield. She dressed like
a flapper and bobbed her hair, but her sturdy, country girl's body lacked
the svelte look that went with the clingy dress. About Raymond (as she
always called her husband), Ella later told her son, "He was drunk. I don't
know why I let him talk to me. His eyes were glittery. I wish I'd had a crystal ball."[11]

Like the Carvers, Ella's people had migrated down the East Coast and
across the Southern states before settling in Arkansas. Her parents, Katherine Guyse and William Casey, were first cousins who fell in love as teenagers. When both families opposed their marriage, Katie and Bill eloped
across the Red River to Texas. That accomplished, they returned to Arkansas and stayed there, married for sixty-some years. Bill earned a steady
income, first as an engineer for the Rock Island Railroad and then as a
steam-shovel fireman at a gravel pit.[12]

Ella and C.R. married three weeks after they met, on Christmas Eve. Like

---

* In "My Father's Life," Carver states that C.R. first "walked, hitched, and rode in
empty boxcars" to the West in 1934, but Violet Archer was certain that her brother
made his first trip with the family in 1929.

him, she was twenty-two years old (she two months the elder) and a native Arkansawyer. Her strict Methodist parents were skeptical about the whirlwind romance and shocked when their youngest daughter announced that she would be moving to Washington. Her elder sister, Edna, was already married, and her brother, Sanders, had plans to wed that very week. Fear of being the only child left at home surely spurred Ella's decision to marry the fair-haired fellow from the Northwest, and her preparations for her move dominated the family for the rest of the Christmas season.[13]

When she met her new husband's parents, Ella wore knickers and boots, prompting Mary Carver to wonder if such a fun-loving, fashionable young woman could be content with the rough life they lived in the Northwest. In January, the foursome began the drive to Washington: Mary and Frank, C. R. and Ella. Trouble began when the bride insisted that she and her husband have their own room when they stopped overnight. They were poor working people and Ella's request struck Mary Carver as extravagant. For most of the trip, they camped out. For years to come, Ella complained that she had "slept by the side of the road on her honeymoon."[14]

From the time they arrived in Omak, deep in the winter of 1936, nothing went quite the way Ella had dreamed when she fell in love with C.R. He brought her to live in a tiny cabin that fronted on an alley, and he returned to work across the river at Biles-Coleman. "None of it had made any sense to her, / beginning with the time she left home . . . ," Carver wrote of his mother.[15] Surrounded by her new husband's family, she missed her own family.

Ella hadn't yet adjusted to life in Omak when a new problem arose. As federal works projects began to create jobs, the new, local AFL Lumber and Sawmill Workers Union asked Biles-Coleman for collective bargaining rights, a union-exclusive shop, a forty-hour work week, and a minimum wage of 50 cents an hour. The company refused. In May 1936, C.R. attended a meeting at the union hall where a large majority of the local union members voted to strike.

Men picketed the mill in six-hour shifts. Company operations were curtailed until early June and then resumed with non-AFL workers. The Omak city government and local orchard owners supported the mill owners by blacklisting strikers to prevent their working elsewhere. In June the mill reopened with strikebreakers carried in by the busload from other states, including a contingent who brought their wives from Arkansas. The Carvers and Archers held out against increasing pressure to cross the picket lines and return to work. They received food from commissary trucks sent by AFL organizations in Seattle and Bellingham. The confrontations turned violent, with shootings, a bridge burning, and spikes set in roadways to disable logging trucks. Business people accused strikers of having Socialist and Zionist sympathies, and union speakers accused owners of denying workers' basic human needs.[16]

These were heady times for C. R. Carver. Speakers told audiences that a moral revolution was under way and that in the future, workers would gain greater respect and higher salaries. "Jesus did not take a sawmill and set it in the midst of them and say 'Of such is the kingdom of heaven.' No. He took a little child and set him in the midst of them and commanded the whole world to measure the economic system by its effect on little children," one speaker said. For the rest of his life, C.R. spoke of being one of the holdouts in this strike. Even when the strike was entirely exhausted, he and Fred Carver never returned to work at Biles-Coleman.[17]

Instead C.R. and Fred Carver and Bill Archer joined upward of seven thousand other workers at an audacious project fifty miles southeast of Omak. The Grand Coulee Dam would bring water (electricity was an afterthought) to a vast arid territory—"the biggest thing that man has ever done," folksinger Woody Guthrie called it. Most likely the Carver men did "broom-and-bucket" work, building forms and pouring concrete below the surface of the diverted Columbia River. They received AFL-contract wages of 50 cents an hour with paid overtime. This concrete work—as much as 20,684 cubic yards were poured daily—was dangerous and difficult, whether in the baking summer sun or in the cold winter winds. Rumors of men buried alive in the dam's ten million cubic feet of concrete circulated among workers, but most of the seventy-seven who died during the project fell from great heights or were struck by equipment. In 1937 C.R. listened with a crowd as President Franklin D. Roosevelt extolled the Grand Coulee Dam as the Eighth Wonder of the World. It was, Roosevelt said, "the largest structure, so far as anybody knows, that has ever been undertaken by man in one place." Neither the mystique of the Grand Coulee project nor the president's speech impressed C.R. He never bragged about his own work at the dam, and he complained that Roosevelt hadn't talked about the men who died doing the work there.[18]

The settlements around the dam site were filled with young men and women who had left starving relatives behind on barren farms in the Plains to search for work in the Far West. But the Carver men, older and married, usually left the boom-town entertainments behind to drive fifty miles through the arid foothills and sleep at home. Ella—still a newlywed—looked forward to weekends when she and C.R. could go dancing. But her pleasure in going out was often ruined because her husband got drunk. When his drunkenness began to seem inevitable to Ella, she lost interest in dancing.[19]

• • •

Ella was four months pregnant when she and C.R. moved to Oregon. They drove to the wet, western side of the Cascade Mountains and crossed the Columbia River into Oregon on a high steel bridge at Longview. Old-growth Douglas firs averaging eight feet in diameter and more than three hundred feet tall still covered some of the bluffs and hillsides. At their destination, clear-cutting had removed the trees, leaving a scrubby regrowth laden with ivy and moss. Before all the Columbia dams were completed, this stretch of the river still looked as it did to the early explorers. Sloughs jigsawed the landscape, water oozed and streamed from roadside rocks. Geography and weather combined to make the place feel anachronistic, almost primeval.

The lower Columbia River Valley had once been a densely populated area of aboriginal North America, but the Klatskanies and other native people who lived there were nearly annihilated by malaria epidemics in the nineteenth century. Lewis and Clark's expedition spent four drenched months west of Wauna during the winter of 1805–06. When the Carvers arrived, black smoke billowed from the stacks of steamboats and seagoing log rafts bigger than football fields moved down the river like monstrous sea creatures. Salmon, though in decline, ran bountifully up the Columbia. C.R. once watched three men he knew use a team of horses to pull a gigantic sturgeon out of the river.[20]

Living near the great river and remembering the hardships at Grand Coulee, the Carvers could see the paradoxes inherent in the economic development of the Northwest. In light of such knowledge, Raymond Junior's birth by the side of the great northwestern river seems auspicious. The salmon and the dams, the forests and the sawmills, the orchards and the fragile human settlements of the Columbia Basin would shape this boy just as Arkansas had shaped his parents.

CHAPTER 2

Yakima Valley

1941–1950, Yakima, Washington

I do not envy those whose introduction to nature was lush meadows,
lakes, and swamps where life abounds. The desert hills of Yakima had
a poverty that sharpened perception.
— Yakima High School graduate and
Supreme Court justice William O. Douglas,
Of Men and Mountains[1]

While many American men rushed to enlist when the United States
entered the world war in 1941, C.R. instead moved to Yakima, Washington, where he took a cabin next to his brother Fred's and became a general laborer at Cascade Lumber. He was soon promoted to saw filer, working under Fred. This important job in a critical industry ensured twenty-eight-year-old C.R.'s exemption from military service. Soon Ella and their boy joined him in a little house near the mill. On Easter Sunday 1942, three-year-old Raymond Junior was baptized at the First Methodist Church.[2]

The Yakima Valley, bisected by the Yakima River and cradled by a bend in the Columbia, became the formative place for Carver—the place he kept writing about. "That life and those people whom I knew so intimately made a very large and profound impression on my emotional life, so I still find myself going back to that time no matter how much my circumstances might change. If I have any strengths and can really make a claim in my heart for my fictions, it is with those people," he wrote. Not only the human world of south-central Washington but its natural geography and history shaped Carver and his work. "Yakima has its own particular beauty," Carver felt. "My heart lifts up when I see the Yakima Valley."[3]

To many eyes, it would not deserve such Wordsworthian praise. Located east of the Cascade Mountains in Washington state and west of a desert that hosts an army artillery range and the former Hanford nuclear test site, the

Yakima Valley is a place of contradictions. Wild beauty coexists with unremitting desolation. Human community comes at great cost and often leaves ugliness in its wake. Much of the persistent legend of Raymond Carver—that he had a brutal childhood in an unsavory place—is rooted in interpretations of Yakima and his life there.[4]

When the Carvers arrived in Yakima, its slogan was "Richer Than the Valley of the Nile." The valley had been a desert until someone discovered that the soil was a deep, fertile volcanic ash. Then irrigation began, first from wells and canals and later with water brought down from the lower Cascades. Peach trees bore after two years, and the soil proved perfect for growing hops, the dried flowers used to make beer. The railroad serves the fruit packing sheds and bisects the town. The east side of these tracks where the Carvers lived was almost rural throughout the 1940s. People grew vegetables and kept chickens or pigs in their backyards. Past the edge of town, there were fish in the Yakima River and the creeks and streams that feed it. The north end of the valley and the surrounding hills abounded in elk, deer, cougar, and game birds.

All the Carver kinfolk converged upon Yakima: Grandpap Frank Carver, who at sixty-three had suffered a stroke, Grandmother Mary Carver, Lavonda and Bill Archer and their two boys, Robert and Donald. Bill became primary filer for the night shift, and the Archers purchased a newer house, where Raymond Junior made a second home.[*] Before he could be trusted to remember instructions, Ella would pin a note on his shirt telling Aunt Von when to send him back. In his aunt's kitchen, Raymond made for a cookie jar shaped like a fat lady in a yellow dress, and Uncle Bill told him that the lady baked cookies inside the jar. Otherwise Ella literally kept Raymond on a tight leash. When he grew up, one friend listened in amazement as he egged his mother on to tell stories about his early childhood: "One of them was about taking him into town on a leash. She never broke character because that was her character. If you said, 'A leash!' she said, without irony, 'Well, of course I had to keep him on a leash.' "[5]

When Ella became pregnant again, the C. R. Carvers moved to a house on South Ninth Street where Raymond and the new child could have a bedroom. At this address, for the first time, they had a telephone. James Franklin Carver was born August 18, 1943, at St. Elizabeth Hospital in Yakima. His middle name came from his grandfather Frank. The Carver boys acquired various nicknames, but within the family, their given names

---

[*] The Carver boys called Violet Lavonda Archer "Aunt Von," but the town knew her as Violet. The house at 1114 North Fourth Street where the Archers lived for nearly fifty years has been photographed for documentaries about Carver.

were never shortened. Always they were Raymond and James. For much of his life, Carver would feel fond and protective of his younger brother, sometimes trying to look after him when his parents could not. When he was twelve, for instance, Ray added a note to the bottom of his own Christmas list: "Don't forget James." Later, when Ray and his teenage friends went out, James would ask to come along. If they said no, James would ask them to bring him back a Pepsi. Ray always tried to remember that Pepsi.[6]

A generous, dependable world of friends and relatives surrounded Raymond Junior as a child. The days of wandering and uncertain employment were over. Another family from Arkansas, Buey and Nevel Davis and their children, moved in across from the Archers, and a lifelong friendship began. "When we went across the street to the Archers' place, we never bothered to knock," Buey Davis recalled. "There was no such thing as an invitation to do anything. Our son would be just as apt to go to their place to eat as to come home. If they had something he liked, he'd probably just eat there. It was that kind of an arrangement."[7] This secure world of proud working-class people is vanished and longed for in most of Carver's short stories. In the stories, characters migrate from place to place in a more prosperous and lonelier small-town West, connecting only tangentially with coworkers, neighbors, or people they meet in cafes or bars, living no longer on the wrong side of the tracks but rather in the previous decade's subdivisions. They lack that sense of unity against adversity or a sense of participation in history that some survivors of the Great Depression cherished.

The Carvers weren't regular churchgoers, but, Buey Davis speculated, "There are no Arkansawyers that don't believe in God. I never heard of one that didn't . . . so I can't imagine that they would be atheists." They had James baptized at the First Methodist Church on May 14, 1944. Church records indicate that the Archers and Fred Carver and his wife, Billie, were members, but hold no entries for C.R. or Ella. Nonetheless, a Bible was one of the few books owned by the Carver household, and James Carver remembered, "My father would go to church when I was young. Sometimes he'd be the only one—he'd put on his suit and go. Sometimes I'd go. Just very rarely my mother would go. She believed in God and so forth, but didn't go to church." James did not remember attending Sunday school.[8]

Raymond Junior began first grade at Adams School, east of the tracks and close to the family's house. His report card says that he stood four feet two inches and weighed a solid sixty-nine pounds. Though he was absent about a fourth of the days in the 155-day school year, he received satisfactory marks in every subject. Teacher Alice Piers comments, "Raymond is reading with good speed and expression. He wants to monopolize the conversations here. He interrupts, will have to check that. He wants to do right." Third grade finds Raymond at Jefferson (now Martin Luther King Jr.) School, five inches taller and fifteen pounds heavier. With occasional lapses in music and public speaking, he's still making academic progress, but teacher Hazel Sandberg has a few complaints about his behavior: he argues with his playmates, disturbs others, and needs to mind his own business. He missed half the days of the fourth quarter. By the end of the year, though, he's pronounced "capable of doing very good work."[9]

As the war drew to a close, C.R. took up his boyhood dream of working for the railroad. He'd often lived near enough to the tracks to hear train whistles and rolling boxcars in the night, and in those sounds he heard seductive intimations of another kind of life. With the economy flourishing, his father's health deteriorating, and his own family growing, C.R. must have decided to seize the moment. He got a job with the Northern Pacific Railroad, starting as a fire cleaner with the hope of promotion to engineer.[10] He was thirty-three years old. His appearance also changed during the 1940s. In a photo taken with Raymond Junior in about 1940, his face has a lean, worried look beneath an Irish snap-brim cap, while shots from later in the decade show an impeccably dressed, almost formal, gentleman with thick, wavy blond hair.

In February 1946, Ella and Raymond bought a house that would one day become part of the lore of Carver's childhood because of its backyard toilet. The house was just south of the Yakima County fairgrounds in an area called Fairview, at 1505 South Fifteenth Street. Their land contract for $2,547.20 began with a down payment of $200, called for payments of $25 monthly, and included a clause stating that the property could not be sold to non-Caucasians for a period of twenty-five years. In his essay "My Father's Life," Carver tells how pranksters sometimes moved the outhouse or set it on fire. He illustrates his shame with a story—manuscript notations indicate that it is an invented story—about asking a teacher who offers him a ride home to drop him at another house rather than at the one with a privy. In fact, most houses in Fairview, which has remained outside city limits, lacked an indoor toilet when the Carvers moved there.[11]

James Carver was certain that he and his brother did not feel impoverished as children: "A lot has been written that would make one think that somehow Ray and I were in constant poverty, did without—which was not true. . . . After all, Yakima was mostly fruit pickers. The businesses were fruit warehouses and one lumber mill. There wasn't a great deal of money there. The house we lived in was considered lower-middle class, but Ray and I certainly weren't deprived." And they ate well: "My mother would cook from scratch, fried chicken or roast beef. On Sundays we'd always have a big breakfast of sausage or ham and eggs. That was a tradition. Her cooking was southern country cooking: pies, the whole bit. Canned jams and fruits and jellies."[12]

Fishing occupied the Carvers in the warmer months. When the season opened in April, they joined relatives and thousands of other anglers on Blue Lake, a big reservoir southwest of the Grand Coulee Dam. On these trips, everyone shared cabins, fishing equipment, and food. They caught rainbow trout as big as fifteen inches and over three pounds using an old Arkansas fishing trick of mixing bull's blood from the slaughterhouse with bran and cottage cheese. They'd drop this mixture down the side of the boat in a paper bag weighted with a rock. As the bag disintegrated, fish swarmed to their lines. At night they hid their bucket of blood in their cabin. Both when hunting and fishing, they did illegal things, reusing licenses and such. The Archers owned a substantial fishing craft, while the Carvers had a leaky rubber boat. When Raymond was about six, his aunt said, "he went fishing with his uncle and his dad down in the Columbia River. They'd put the fish they caught in this little pond. After a while, Ray thought those fish needed a bigger body of water, so he takes all the fish and puts them in a bigger pond. When they got ready to go, they couldn't get their fish!"[13]

The Carvers were a happy family, Buey Davis thought, "but they didn't seem to me to do any future planning. It didn't take much money to make them happy." Perhaps that began to change when C.R. gave up his railroading career after less than a year. "He loved the railroad," James remembers. "He was a fireman, and my mother wanted him to quit because he was gone so much of the time. I think he was unhappy about that." He returned to Cascade Lumber as a mill worker, bequeathing his sons the muted dreams and finely honed resentments of a disappointed man. He worked his way up the hierarchy, becoming a filer again in about 1950 and eventually becoming head filer for the division where crates for shipping ammunition and apples were manufactured. Saw filers at Cascade Lumber were skilled workers whose wages were not negotiated by the union, so their earnings and bonuses were a matter of speculation and envy. Nonetheless, one coworker said, "C.R. gave you the impression without saying it that he had been given the short end of the stick."[14]

The Cascade mill, Carver wrote later, was "my entire frame of reference when I was a kid."[15] Just a collection of wooden sheds—not a factory in the modern sense—the mill sat next to ponds where logs were stored and moved, close to the Yakima River. Three men held a triumvirate at Cascade: C.R.'s cousin Tillman Carver, head millwright; Rollie Schlief, head sawyer; and Fred Carver, head filer. The millwrights were in charge of machinery, the sawyers decided how each log would be cut, and the filers kept the blades in perfect condition. Filers were a special breed within the mill because their work was somewhat solitary yet essential to the work and safety of everyone in the mill. The enormous blades had to be changed and inspected after every four hours of use, with each tooth hand sharpened and any damaged points welded. In addition to the usual mill worker's risks of hearing loss and severed fingers and lung problems, saw filers faced hazards particular to them: from inhaled metal particles, from saw guides containing lead, and from grinding wheels containing carbide. Fred Carver lost several fingers at work and Rollie Schlief died instantly when a log carriage he was cleaning slipped backward.[16]

C.R. was a careful worker who avoided accidents. Shop steward Hank Pieti thought that he stood out among mill workers: "He was a deep thinker. He seldom had much to say to anybody, but he was observant of other people's work." As a union officer, Pieti relied "on guys like him to equip me with the knowledge I needed. He had a good mind—he could explain things to you, and he had a good command of the language."[17]

In early May 1948, Frank Carver was hospitalized with another stroke. With his son watching, C.R. shaved his own father's face. "The dying body is a clumsy partner," Carver observed when he recalled the episode in his poem "The Garden." Edwin Frank Carver died on May 11, 1948. He was seventy. His grandson was almost ten. Raymond rode along to the dry cleaner's to pick up the suit his grandfather would be buried in. Viewing of Frank's body, in the fresh suit, preceded a Methodist service conducted by the minister who'd baptized Raymond. Female vocalists sang "Have Thy Own Way, Lord" and "That Old Rugged Cross." Frank's death left a deep imprint on his son and grandson. "What'd I know then about Death?" Carver asks in "Another Mystery." By the time Frank was buried at the Terrace Heights Cemetery east of Yakima, his grandson had received his first lessons. Grandpa Frank and his wife, Mary, had been the hub of the Carver family. Now she lived in a tiny house behind the Archers'.[18]

As he faced changes in his family, Raymond Junior had his own problems. A fifth grader at Jefferson School, he now carried 132 pounds on his five-foot frame. He was a fat boy whose horizontal striped or Hawaiian shirts made him look worse. His *Unsatisfactory* in Handwriting, no surprise to those who've seen his letters, was balanced by As in Spelling and Arithmetic. Still, teacher L. Killgore had a large complaint: "Raymond hasn't developed habits of behavior that we would expect of a boy in the fifth grade.... He does not accept the responsibility of a citizen who has to live with other people."

At the next marking period, Killgore illuminated the nature of Raymond's lapses. The boy "has improved a great deal in writing and shows some improvements in citizenship. He is able to keep his papers off the floor now."

Sixth grade was better. Teacher Willard L. Yoke saw potential in the overweight, messy, often impolite boy: "Raymond does very satisfactory work but is capable of doing excellent work . . . [does not do] nearly what he is capable of . . . reads very well, understands what he reads and retains it." Yoke also noted the usual weaknesses—easily disturbed, trouble keeping to the task at hand, not too considerate of others, makes careless errors in arithmetic—and included a trait that would stay with Ray as an adult and become dear to many of his friends: "has a bad habit of 'giggling' at anything and everything."[19]

C.R. planted roses by the shed where he worked as chief filer for the box division. On a tour of the former Cascade plant in 1997, a retired mill worker pointed out a leggy, untended rose bush climbing a rusty electric tower, remnants of red blooms still hanging on its dry stalks. "That," he said, "is what's left of the rose bush C. R. Carver planted by the old filing room door."[20]

Carver portrays his father's sensitivity in a poem called "The Trestle." He remembers a day when his father drank from a stream and told him he wished that his mother could taste this water. Elsewhere Carver remembered seeing his father stretched out on a bed in the evening reading a Zane Grey Western, "a very private act in a house and family that were not given to privacy." When Raymond asked his father to read to him, he obliged him "by just reading from wherever he happened to be in the book. After a while he'd say, 'Junior, go do something else now.' " On Sunday nights, C.R. let his sons take turns reading with him and falling asleep on the parents' bed. When he looked back at his early life, Carver said, it "exists for me as through a scrim of rain."[21] He glimpsed himself as "a dreamy kid" who checked out books on the Spanish conquistadors, historical novels, books on shipbuilding—anything that caught his fancy.

Like many intelligent people with little schooling, Ray's father mispronounced some of the words he knew. In fact, Carver credits his dad's lapses for his own obsession with finding the right word: "I'd hear words at home, things my dad might say. And I'd repeat these words or expressions and get laughed at by other kids because I was pronouncing the words wrong, and this made me want to get the words right. I just didn't want to be laughed at." A friend of Ray's recalled, "Ray's dad was driving us back from hunting, and there'd been a tremendous rain. The Yakima River was flooded, and Ray's dad looked over and said, 'This is really terrible, look at all the logs and *derbies* over there.' He was trying to say debris. And Ray and I were sitting in the backseat nudging each other and laughing." Another friend remembered that Ray himself often pronounced ephemeral as *e-fem-EAR-e-al* and that his friends used to "give him a rashing over that." The conversations in which C.R. or the boys used such words may have been unusual in Yakima.[22]

Despite his superior sensibilities and skills, C. R. Carver was not a fortunate man. Once, while sitting under a big box elder tree in the Archers' backyard in Yakima, he grumbled about all his bad luck. "No matter what I do, everything just turns sour," he said, extending an arm for emphasis. Right then, his nephew Don Archer said, "a bird crapped right in his hand. And Uncle Raymond never blinked. He just said, 'See what I mean!' "[23]

During the years of Raymond's youth, alcohol became a debilitating problem for his father. C.R. gained weight and walked, Pieti noticed, with "a little bend, like an athlete who's real relaxed." He was never caught drunk or drinking on the job, but Pieti saw him with "some beautiful hangovers, really down. And he was a guy who wanted to be meticulously clean. When he'd show up looking like he'd slept in his clothes, you knew that he'd had a weekend drunk." But Fred Carver protected his younger brother. "Fred was the head filer for the whole mill, so he could help Raymond keep up on bad days. Fred was probably the reason he kept his job as long as he did."[24]

Friends of C. R. Carver's were typically reluctant to categorize his drinking, but Violet Archer acknowledged that her brother "did drink quite a lot. He would be considered an alcoholic now." And the three people who lived in C.R.'s household indicated that his alcoholism hurt them. Ella, interviewed by the BBC some twenty-five years after her husband's death, said, "His beer drinking and such as that, well, other people you can't tell, but with him I could tell. And I used to pour liquor out and water it and everything like that, because I never was a drinker." To an interviewer, Carver recalled that every couple of weeks, his father didn't arrive home as expected after work: "When this happened, it meant he'd gone drinking with friends of his from the sawmill. I still remember the sense of doom and hopelessness that hung over the supper table when my mother and I and my kid brother sat down to eat."[25]

James, possessing the longest retrospect, was irritated by accounts that make it sound like "the whole family was messed up, with my father drunk all the time. That's not true." But he was uneasy when his father drank:

> I hated to see my father drink. So did Ray. I hated alcohol because when my father would drink, he was not like the average person who can take a drink or two and quit. My father would keep drinking until he became intoxicated, and then he became another person. He never—certainly

never—hit me or Ray or abused me, he just became a different person. So I hated alcohol. But he would go for months and months and never touch a drink, never have a beer. He knew that once he started, he could not quit. And I'd say, "Dad, come on, just have *one* drink," but he couldn't do that. But when I think of my father, and I'm sure when Ray thought of our father, it is with nothing but love and affection. If he got too much to drink, it was very unhappy, but that's not what I think of.[26]

One of the unhappy times seems to lie behind Carver's poem "Suspenders," which sketches an excruciatingly dysfunctional scene. Never published in Carver's lifetime, "Suspenders" compresses a number of painful themes: a father's alcoholism, a mother's violence, and a boy's weight problem. In the midst of a tightly enfolded episode of family trouble, the poem's narrator, who is a second-grade boy, takes passive revenge on his father. As the poem opens, the mother is telling the boy that he must wear suspenders to hold up his pants the next day because he has no belt that fits. She threatens to "use" the suspenders on him if he won't "wear them." Then the father complains of the racket going on and asks for a drink of water— because he's hungover, the mother interjects. The boy dips his father a glass of dishwater from the sink. Once the boy's act is discovered, the parents lay their differences to rest by ganging up against the child. When the mother accuses the boy of not loving his father, the son drinks two glasses of the dishwater to prove that he does love him, taking the illness upon himself. The peace that falls is "The quiet that comes to a house / where nobody can sleep."

C.R.'s alcohol consumption and lack of foresight and management combined to keep the family on a payday-to-payday tightrope and magnified differences between C.R. and Ella. To Donald Archer, his aunt and uncle seemed like "a real mismatch because Ella was kind of hard to please and Raymond was real happy-go-lucky." It seems that Ella never felt fully a part of the Carver ménage. She and Billie Carver didn't fish or hunt. Some people found her "odd" or "peculiar." To sustain herself, she relied on work and pride.[27]

"Ella worked everywhere. Everywhere," said Violet Archer, who was head fruit sorter in the same warehouse for twenty-five years. "She didn't have any trouble getting jobs." For Yakima women, a job outside the house was the norm, both during the war and after. When James was a year old, in 1944, Ella worked at the Washington Canners Cooperative. She spoke on a Yakima radio station to urge other women to help in the Food for Victory campaign. A script of the interview, which Ella saved for the rest of her days, offers a glimpse of life at that time. She "mans" two stations at the cannery from seven in the morning until six, while a neighbor babysits her boys. Her favorite job, she says, is splitting peaches, for which "you can make quite a lot more than the hourly wage of 63½ cents."[28]

Ella pursued her work life with remarkable zeal and deep restlessness. She changed jobs frequently, working stretches of a few weeks to a year at cafes, stores, and fruit warehouses. Vi Sullens, Ella's supervisor at a Safeway supermarket, found that Ella "could work at any gall-darned thing, and you could depend on her to work hard, even though she was kind of a peculiar person." Her peculiarity, according to Sullens, was that she kept "so all to herself—she took care of herself and her boys but didn't care much about anybody else. Not everyone liked her. Maybe because she was an Arkansawyer." But Buey Davis noticed, "You could tell by looking at Ella sometimes, she wasn't hearing anything you said. She'd got her mind on something else. That's the way Raymond Junior was, too—kind of." In that respect, Buey came to believe, "Raymond Junior was more like his mother than he was his dad."[29]

C.R.'s drinking binges gave Ella further incentive to work. Her so-called peculiarity, her restlessness and lack of engagement beyond the family, suggest insecurities in her personality that became more pronounced during her children's school years. It seems to have been a double bind for Ella, who became uncomfortable both at home and at work. Typically, spouses of alcoholics are afraid to expose their family situation. Ella's frequent changes of job despite satisfactory work performance may have represented a frustrating cycle of desire for an environment where she could feel appreciated, followed by rejection of new acquaintances as they got close enough to threaten her pretense of a happy home life.

Carver sensed the alienation that drove his mother to seek one job after another, and writes sympathetically of proud women who work for low wages. Waitresses figure often in his fiction, and his unpublished papers include a folder of notes and manuscript scraps for an unfinished work called "Waitress." In one, a waitress recalls the exact moment when a vein first broke in her leg.[30] The boy narrator of "Nobody Said Anything" sees his mother's waitress uniform as an additional character that needs attention in the household, "always hanging in the closet or hanging on the clothesline or getting washed out by hand at night or being ironed in the kitchen."

Ella Carver took pride in her appearance and dressed her boys well when they were small. She got her hair done at a beauty parlor and kept her nails manicured.[31] In snapshots, Ella always looks stylish, dressed in slacks or tailored dresses that accentuate her figure. But in a studio portrait of herself and her boys from about 1950, grooming fails to hide the fact that her face looks tired and a little puffy. At her side, James, still a little boy, has a big grin with missing front teeth and a fringed cowboy shirt. Ray looks over-weight. There's dirt on the cuffs of his white chinos. But he's relaxed, gazing unreservedly at the camera. He has big hands and hair parted on the side, soft and wavy like a teen idol's.

As the 1950s commenced, the Yakima daily papers carried alarming headlines about war in Korea. State selective service boards issued new induction calls, and the military prepared for a theoretical attack on Alaska. Alongside this news were reports of changes in the landscape: for instance, an apparent overpopulation of elk as agriculture encroached on the herd's territory. Nonetheless, optimism was the official tone of public life. In industry and agriculture, white working-class Americans got better wages as labor unions gained power. They bought new cars and new houses, tele-visions, and deep freezes. Most families had a telephone. Children went to decent public schools, where they were expected to finish all twelve grades and become skillful not only at their jobs but as consumers, parents, and citizens. A palpable belief that life was, or ought to be, getting better every year governed people's decisions.

This life was promising but also competitive. The possibility of becom-ing middle class beckoned and pressured the Carvers. Cascade Lumber ran at full capacity. After floods washed out the mill ponds, the sawmill became an industrial operation, with acres of stacked logs flanking the highway through Yakima. The town's population grew to forty thousand, necessitat-ing a larger-format phone book with a more American slogan on its cover: "Fruit Bowl of the Nation." Good times seemed just around the corner.

The summer of his twelfth year marked the close of a very long child-hood, declares the narrator of Carver's early story "Dummy," sending him "ready or not, into the world of men—where defeat and death are more in the natural order of things." Ray turned twelve and began junior high school in 1950. Exhilarating and desperate changes lay ahead for him.

CHAPTER 3

Vocation

1950–1956, Yakima, Washington

Bad Checks, His Mama, and Beautiful Songs
—Carver's playful suggestion of a title
for a collection of his stories[1]

At twelve, Raymond Carver was on his way to becoming a miserable teenager. He was fat, lonely, and inept at school. He was a ringer for the boy he would describe in a poem called "Harley's Swans": "Nobody, then, who could love me, / the fattest kid on the block, except my parents." He asked his family to stop calling him Junior or Frog. He accepted "Doc"—plain Doc, not Little Doc—from his dad, but to everyone else he was Raymond, Ray for short.[2] To his friends, the few he had, he was just Ray.

Years later, Carver told an interviewer that in his teens and twenties he fell into "moods of brooding and depression."[3] It's hard to say now if those moods were more extreme than the next teenager's. Some who knew the Carver family think that Ray exaggerated the difficulty of his youth, while others believe he wrote and spoke about it with unblinking accuracy. His revealing poems and guarded, deliberately chiseled fictions suggest that, like his mother, Ray was on edge much of the time. He was usually watchful and sometimes furtive and manipulative and—at the same time—often needy and grateful for attention. Like most teenagers, he didn't have a lot of perspective on his own situation. He went off by himself, walking or biking, to spend a day fishing and reading and daydreaming. Like the boy in his own story "Nobody Said Anything," he might have masturbated or watched birds fly overhead. He was developing the sensibility of a loner that would serve him well as a writer. Others noticed changes in Ray. Vi Sullens recalled asking Ella, "Is that boy of yours feeling okay? He's just not friendly like he used to be."

Ray's weight problem continued into his early teen years. "He was very heavy, and kids made fun of him," James remembers. "He had a very difficult time. Then he took a series of shots from Dr. Roger Coglon. I don't know what the shots were. All I heard was he was taking these injections to lose weight, and he did lose weight. He lost weight and slimmed down."[4]

James's recollection accords with contemporary medical practice, though tablets were used more commonly than injections. After 1937, researchers shifted from the belief that obesity was caused by endocrine disorders and concluded that the culprit was an imbalance between input of food and output of energy. If counseling was not motivation enough to limit the appetite, medical journals advised, a course of amphetamine sulfate tablets (and related drugs such as dextroamphetamine) might be the best initial treatment. There were side effects even for the most amenable child: restlessness and insomnia, complete loss of appetite, diuresis, a tendency to "facilitate the flow of thought, generally at the expense of concentration," and "a rather fictitious sense of fitness, self-confidence, and well-being." Although the drugs were not known to produce any tolerance or violent cravings, doctors did warn that going off the drugs was likely to produce fatigue, irritability, nervousness, and melancholia.

Ray took up cigarette smoking in his early teens too, a habit that kept weight off and stuck with him for the rest of his life. Most of the adults around Ray smoked and bought their cartons on payday. His parents often got Ray his own carton so he wouldn't mooch from theirs.

During Ray's seventh-grade year, the Carvers bought a house at 1419 Eleventh Avenue South. The new place was on the more prosperous west side of the tracks in a trim neighborhood with sewers and paved streets. Identical to others in its postwar development, theirs was a one-story, four-room box built on a cement slab, under seven hundred square feet, with windows on only two sides. Directly off the living room were two bedrooms—James and Raymond slept in the smaller one—and a bathroom. There was no place to be alone in a house this size except inside one's imagination. Those close quarters figure in Carver's story "Nobody Said Anything." On hot, dry summer nights when James and his friend Larry Davis were about eight, they liked to pitch a tent in the yard and camp, with Ray as their protector. He made up ghost stories, Larry remembered, "Stories good enough to scare the pants off us till we would go in and let Ray have the tent to himself. Ray made up his stories on the spot—they weren't the kind kids pass around." As Larry and James got more and more terrified, Ray piled on more and more details. Monsters and aliens and even cowboys turned up in the same stories, along with plenty of violence and surprise.[5]

Ray drifted through seventh, eighth, and ninth grades at Washington Junior High School with barely a glance at the textbooks. He got Cs in most classes, with a downward trend over the three years: sometimes a B in English, once an A in Music, a string of Ds in Mathematics, Shop, and Physical Education, even one D in English. His ninth-grade report card has an angry circle drawn around the phrase "Absence from classes the greatest cause of failure."[6]

School may have bored Ray, but he avidly soaked up movies, television, magazines, and books. At the Liberty Theatre in 1950, he saw a movie that became his lifelong favorite. *King Solomon's Mines,* based on a novel by H. Rider Haggard and starring Deborah Kerr and Stewart Granger, is a telling choice because it combines an exotic African landscape with a moral dilemma and a complicated love story. Granger is a fatalist, given to speaking lines like these: "And man? He's just meat like everything else. . . . It's all endless and pointless, except in the end one small pattern emerges from it all, the only certainty. One is born, one lives for a time, and one dies." Kerr admits she never loved her husband: "The human heart's a strange thing. When I started on this trip, I was very confused. I thought my motives were so noble . . . It was guilt, and I'm better for knowing it. The nightmares are over."[7] The psychology of love offered by *King Solomon's Mines* seems sophisticated for a thirteen-year-old boy to take in. Perhaps it gave Ray a handle on scenes he had witnessed at home.

While they lived on Eleventh Avenue, the Carvers bought their first television set: a big RCA console model that cost a whopping $500. Though he was devoted to television, more of young Ray's story ideas came from pulp magazines. These magazines arose at the turn of the century and reigned until the midfifties, when they were usurped by comic books and mass-market paperback fiction. With brash, often expressive and beautiful cover illustrations and cheap newsprint pages, pulps propagated the genres of American pop fiction: romance and adventure, mysteries and horror, science fiction, Westerns, and hard-boiled detective stories. Among the authors who got their start by writing for them (for payments of a penny a word or less) were Raymond Chandler, Ray Bradbury, Dashiell Hammett, and Edgar Rice Burroughs. Issues of the pulps were short-lived, but stories like "The Lady from Nowhere" or "The Man Who Made Love to a Corpse" or "A Contract in Kabul" were unforgettable.

Ray owned some books. Classics such as Edgar Allan Poe's tales and Mary Shelley's novel *Frankenstein* survived his many moves, but a dozen volumes from Edgar Rice Burroughs's Tarzan and Martian tales made up the bulk of his collection. He made fun of himself later, quipping to his first interviewers, "My favorite author was Edgar Rice Burroughs, I read all of his books, and most of them five, six and eight times," and admitting that as a boy he wrote stories about "monsters, ants, laboratories, and mad doctors."[8] Burroughs was not such a bad model. In *A Princess of Mars,* a man mysteriously travels to Mars, loves a beautiful woman there, and then just as mysteriously returns to Earth without her. The writing is precise and literate, and the puzzled, Gulliver-like narrator, despite a romantic streak, is a loner and a voyeur who would not be out of place in a Carver story.

Ray also found inspiration closer to home. In June 1947, a small-plane pilot saw nine large, bright objects in a V formation streaking south from Mount Rainier. He said the unidentified crafts, "flat like a pie pan and somewhat bat shaped," moved like "saucers skipping across the water" at more than 1,200 miles per hour. The first people to hear the pilot's account were a skeptical refueling crew at Yakima Airport. News services picked up the story, and in no time, "flying saucers" began to appear all over the country. One night when James and Larry were listening to one of Ray's long, scary yarns, they saw a big blue object coming over the house. That night, Ray ran inside along with the younger boys.[9]

The marital discord that had strained the Carver household during Raymond's childhood began to consume it during his teenage years. Both parents' personalities were distorted by tension and anger, frozen by obstinacy. When the parents were unhappy with each other, their misery inundated the family, gouging channels that would influence Ray's own marriage and shape his writing. In the poem "Mesopotamia," Carver remembers lying in bed as a boy, hearing "a woman crying, / and a man's voice raised in anger, or despair. . . ."

One of Ray's friends compared Ray's home to that of another boy he knew: "The economic circumstances were similar, but there you had a sense of stable family—a mother and father who were content and doing their jobs, settled into their lives. At the Carvers', things seemed as if the whole enterprise might fly apart any minute." C.R.'s coworker Frank Sandmeyer believed the Carvers were like "a bunch of people living together in a house and all of them strangers. There was no communication between them," but Sandmeyer entered the Carver house only once. He was there for twenty or thirty minutes, during which time Ella never spoke to him and C.R. "paced back and forth like somebody that's ready to jump out the door."[10]

Away from home, Ray's father could seem happy-go-lucky, but that trait bothered Ella. Her husband was devoted to his mother, his brother and sister, his sons, and his drinking buddies, perhaps more than to her. The two sometimes kept their own paychecks and argued over who was to pay for what. This method, or lack of method, kept the Carvers in debt for items purchased on layaway and left the big items they wanted most—a new car or good fishing boat or better furniture—beyond their grasp. While Fred and Billie Carver became solidly middle class, the Archers remodeled their house and sent their boys to college, and the Davises' radiator shop prospered, Ella and C. R. Carver sank.[11] In "My Father's Life," Carver quotes his mother's complaint: " 'Money burned a hole in his pocket. He was always doing for others.' "

Ella relied on a bad temper to defend herself. In an interview, she insouciantly described hitting her husband when he came home drunk: "I picked up [the pestle of] that colander that pushed the tomatoes down in a basket, and I hit him with that. It bled and like to scared the boys to death. But he got all right again."[12] Carver lingers over that episode in "My Father's Life": "she hit him between the eyes with a colander and knocked him out. We could see him down there on the grass." Afterward, Carver writes, he would lift the colander and "imagine what it would feel like to be hit in the head with something like that." Another time, Sandmeyer heard, Ella became so disgusted with a couple of fellows who were drinking and playing cards with C.R. that she picked up a chair and ran them right out of the house.

One short story best evokes the conflicts Ray felt in his early teens. First published in 1973 as "The Summer Steelhead" and later as "Nobody Said Anything," the story is about silent, uneasy accommodations to bad situations. To protect their crops from frost, Yakima fruit farmers burned old tires or five-gallon pots filled with oil to raise the temperature around tree branches a few degrees. Both tactics caused a terrific stench and smog. Thus, pollution saved the crops, and, as Carver's story puts it, "you would wake up in the morning with this black ring of stuff in your nose, but nobody said anything." During the 1950s, though, this "smudging" became controversial among growers and town residents.[13]

"Nobody Said Anything" was a germinal story for Carver. It was not autobiographical, he said, but "When I wrote that story I knew . . . I had tapped into something. I knew what it was all about."[14] In it, parents' arguing voices assault a boy who signs himself R. Then the mother starts to cry. R hopes his little brother will wake up and "say something to them so they would feel guilty and stop." The older boy is upset by his mother's tears but quick to take advantage of her distraction. As the mother—her name is Edna, the same as Ella's sister's—hurries to get ready for work, R begs to stay home. He has a stomachache. Reluctantly she agrees, rattling off a stream of loving last-minute instructions: no TV, don't turn on the stove burners . . . try "that medicine." The mischievous R has the TV on before she is even out the door. When she's gone, R snoops for clues about "what they do in bed" before he gathers his fishing gear and sets out for Birch Creek, a sizable ditch that matches Bachelor Creek in Yakima.

Much of "Nobody Said Anything" is a brief picaresque adventure in which R becomes a modern Huck Finn brimming with sexual curiosity and urgency. A woman in a red car stops to give him a ride. She's thin with pimples around her mouth, but the boy detects "nice boobs" inside her sweater. He imagines she might take him home and let him "screw her all over the house." This adolescent, though, is more needy child than ladies' man: "She asks if she can keep her sweater on and I say it's okay with me. She keeps her panties on too." R's struggle with his sexuality is inept, hilarious, and more explicit, especially in the magazine version, than any of Carver's other writing. As R fishes, he postpones thinking about the woman until later, but "right away I got a boner thinking about the boner I would get that night." He worries that he masturbates too often but knows he won't stop. He admits he once tried bestiality. He approached a calf with his shorts off, but when the calf kicked and bawled, he ejaculated in its face. "I thought it was the worst thing I would ever do in my life," R comments, "but now I know better."[15]

At Birch Creek, R and another boy chase, kill, and then cut in half a monstrous fish.* His creel filled with this prize, R returns to his neighborhood at dusk: "I was scared they would start hollering at me for being out after I had stayed in from school." Instead R finds his parents arguing at the kitchen table, expressing not the least concern about his whereabouts:

. . . he said, "What do kids know? You'll see."
    She said, "I'll see nothing. If I thought that, I'd rather see them dead first."

The obscure argument continues, the children somehow, but unclearly, involved. R stands outside, listening and preparing to "march into the house, grinning." A pan burns on the stove and Edna throws the scorched food against the wall. The boy, believing his fabulous fish will eclipse this chaos, enters the room with his offering. His gesture proves disastrous. Edna thinks the boy is showing her a snake and screams for him to take it outside before she throws up. The boy turns to his father, who—incomprehensibly to R—suddenly takes his wife's side. He orders the boy to carry his prize "the hell out of the kitchen and throw it in the goddamn garbage."

---

* When big steelhead showed up in Bachelor Creek, his friend King Kryger said, "Ray would get extremely excited and do anything to catch one. He would chase them and club them and whatever it took, but I don't remember catching many."

"Nobody Said Anything" treats a theme that fascinated Carver: the divided child and divided self. The fish, at first the subject of a simple, brutal yarn, takes on a whole new aspect when the parents look at it. When the parents reject the fish as a monstrosity, the boy identifies with his truncated prize. These parents might as well be throwing their son in the garbage. A closing paragraph in Carver's 1973 magazine version projects an image of the traumatized child who will survive the onslaught of his parents' violence. He will preserve and value himself through his imagination, learn to make himself whole. In this version, as in Christianity and mythology, the fish represents salvation. The boy looks at his grotesque, demeaned fish and thinks, "He looked silver under the porchlight. He was whole again, and he filled the creel until I thought it would burst. I lifted him out. I held him."

Carver's poem "Balsa Wood" parallels "Nobody Said Anything." This time the child finds no escape from the tinderbox of parental emotion and feels "flimsy as / balsa wood." Again there's acrimonious discussion between parents about money, a mother in tears, and a meal ruined on the stove. Then father and son haul a load of garbage—including the ruined breakfast, no doubt—to the dump. The boy knows his father wants to explain something, but the two sit mutely in the car. The boy imagines that they both hear someone—the mother?—crying. In the last lines, Carver remembers feeling he was in two places at once. The parents' estrangement has now inscribed itself as a division in the boy's psyche.

James Carver did not think his brother's stories gave a fair picture of their parents. Because Ray was five years older, James speculated, "perhaps he could recall times that I couldn't when unhappy scenes occurred. I know my mother and brother would get upset when an argument flared up. But, my God, it wasn't something that was a daily occurrence."[16]

Raymond was his mother's confidant. In "My Father's Life," Carver writes that his mother accused her husband of seeing other women, but in a documentary filmed after her husband's and Ray's deaths, Ella stated that her husband "never stepped out" on her.[17] In a late poem called "The Kitchen" (not published in his lifetime), Carver imagines an explicit scenario of his father with another woman. In it a boy comes home and surprises his father drunk and with a woman on his lap. The poem is full of the outraged boy's feelings. While his father and the woman stare at him, the boy, the only one who tries to talk, stutters "with anguish."[18] The poem conveys the boy's inexperience and sense of betrayal by confusing identities: the woman is "not his wife, / nor my mother either." This fracturing of family that the boy feels is further encapsulated by his sense that his father doesn't "recognize his own get." Evidence about C.R.'s extramarital life may be impossible to come by, but one thing is clear: the very idea of his father's infidelity and his mother's violent reactions to it evoked treacherous images and feelings for Carver.

"A little autobiography and a lot of imagination are best" for writing fiction, Carver believed.[19] In early youth, Raymond experienced enough stability and love to allow him to recognize when these qualities were absent. Such knowledge allowed Carver, as a writer, to inhabit even his most degraded characters, to give them a gesture or phrase that makes us regret their lost potential and imagine them better than they are. But he also delights in the petty violence and trickery of characters like the man who cuts his wife's phone cord and smashes her Christmas pies. As that husband departs, he tells himself that he and his wife will have "a serious talk" after the holidays. The inane, brutal simplicity of the scene combined with the narrator's off-center commentary could be a scene from Carver's childhood. It is the view of a child who sees clearly things going wrong around him and has no way to make good sense of them.

In October 1951, Ray's eighth-grade year, Mary Carver died at age seventy. C.R. made the arrangements for his mother's funeral, which was very like the one they'd had for Frank: an open casket for services in the same funeral chapel followed by burial at Terrace Heights. Seven grandnephews served as pallbearers—an indication of the size of the Carver-Green extended family that had settled in the West. Though Mary's progeny were many, none had yet achieved the kind of renown she'd wished for them when she mailed each one a hand-copied inspirational poem in the 1930s.

This death of a second grandparent must have disquieted Ray. In "Another Mystery" he mentions ". . . a time in which relatives departed / this way and that, left and right." The next relative to die was Bill Archer's brother, Olen "Shorty" Archer. He and two drinking buddies slid off the icy Naches Highway into a ditch; then an AWOL soldier, also drunk, plowed into their car. Uncle Shorty's drinking "toots" were infamous, a family standard by which everyone else, including C.R., could be deemed nonalcoholic.[20]

Not long after Grandmother Mary Carver died, Ray's father had a generous idea that probably altered Ray's life. C.R. knew that his elder boy was bored and unhappy. He knew, too, that he could not help his son. He was grieving for his mother, only a few weeks dead, and grieving for his own fugitive youth. He was only forty, but he felt old. He probably feared he was sinking into dependence on alcohol. Frank Sandmeyer, who ran a saw near C.R.'s filing room, remembered the afternoon C.R. asked him a favor: "He said to me, 'I hear you hunt and fish all over this country.' Then he said, 'I've got this boy. I'm going to buy him a shotgun and shells. Will you take him with you? I'll help pay the expense.'" Sandmeyer, who had a daughter and nephews but no son, was glad to oblige.[21]

It is no surprise that characters modeled on Sandmeyer appear in two of Carver's stories. In "Furious Seasons," Frank is "a big man, with a thick quilted jacket zipped up to his chin and a brown duck-bill cap that made him look like a grim umpire." Sandmeyer would pick up Ray before dawn. He'd find him waiting with his gun and a lunch bucket and a big canteen, properly outfitted with a red hat, waterproof boots, and wool coat. If they spoke at all, it was about the weather and the geese. Usually they took the highway south out of Yakima toward Bickleton. They passed "great fields of harvested wheat rolling out toward the dimly outlined hills beyond and broken every so often by a muddy, churned looking field glimmering with little pockets of water."

Before sunrise, they would reach the foothills and head toward the canyons that open out to the Columbia River. Alder Creek Canyon was one of their favorite spots. This landscape was vivid to Carver when he wrote "Furious Seasons":

> The sides of the low bluffs overlooking the river down below were deeply grooved and cut back into the rock, leaving tablelike projections jutting out, marking the high water lines for thousands of years past. Piles of naked white logs and countless pieces of driftwood lay jammed onto the ledge like cairns of bones dragged up onto the cliffs by some giant bird.

The bluffs here formed natural blinds for hunters. At first, Frank recalled, he stayed close to Ray, keeping an eye on him and teaching him to shoot: "He caught on to that shotgun right away. He got to be a good shot with it. I told him about it, how to watch for the birds, how to judge and shoot ahead of them. His dad gave him an account downtown where he could buy his shotgun shells and whatever he needed."

"Distance" pays tribute to Sandmeyer as Carl Sutherland. In the fiction, the boy's father has died. The boy and Sutherland begin to hunt together to "replace a loss they both felt." Even though Ray's father was still alive, Sandmeyer filled a void. He was hardy and strong and fearless, whereas C.R. was unwell and cautious. Divorced, Sandmeyer also represented a model of manhood—free of domestic turmoil and comfortable in the world of guns and danger—that C.R. could only read about in Zane Grey's novels.

With Sandmeyer, Ray developed "a fever for hunting." For five years, the two went bird hunting almost every weekend from October 15 through the end of January. Sandmeyer found Ray "high strung, nervous, impatient, and stubborn. He was just a very impatient person, but he was real good at goals; no problem there." Along with Ray's restlessness, Sandmeyer noticed that Ray drank an inordinate amount of water on these trips, filling up his canteen several times during the day. Both traits might have been related to the weight-loss medication Ray was taking. Fishing, hunting, and simply being outdoors gave Ray freedom from the tension of his family, camaraderie with other males, the pride of skill and success, and an emotional connection with the land. Hunting ducks, geese, and upland game, Carver said, "made a dent in my emotional life, and that's what I wanted to write about."[22] The point of connection, though, was violence. By landing a fish or shooting a duck out of the air, he obliterated some of the frustration and rage of his daily life.

During their drives in the hills, Ray and Frank came across remnants of the people who'd tried to live in this austere land by farming or mining or trading with Columbia River steamers and early railroads. Sandmeyer was intrigued by an abandoned school, but Ray was restless to get on with hunting. Perhaps, too, Ray felt the futility of human undertakings in these buildings left by people whose enterprises had failed. Once in a canyon at the end of a nearly impassable road,

> Ray wanted to get out and chase some of the chukkers around—and there was a two-story house, rough lumber, never been painted, but it had a veranda built. I can't imagine anybody back a hundred years ago building a veranda—there was no mills or towns back then. Inside was an old iron bed. I found a shoe box under the bed. Ray came back, and I took the string off the box, and there was a pair of shoes in there—high-button ladies' shoes with white tops and black bottoms. They'd never been worn. I wish I'd brought them home, but Ray, he took kind of a dim view of it.

Another time, Sandmeyer and Ray came across the ghost town of Alderdale, since inundated by a dam on the Columbia, where they saw old buildings from which "the people just vanished." Sandmeyer's romanticism about old schoolhouses and high-buttoned shoes didn't impress young Ray, but his mentor's curiosity, quick observations of character, and ability to remember details that made for a good yarn showed him the uses a man might make of storytelling.

When Ray was about sixteen, he asked Sandmeyer to take him down into the Yakama Indian Reservation. They didn't have the permit from the tribe required to hunt there, but cut across the fields toward Toppenish Creek just as the poachers do in Carver's story "Sixty Acres." They had wing-shot three or four ducks when "Ray brought down a mallard and went chasing it through the corn patch. He let out a blood-curdling scream. I thought maybe he'd shot himself. He'd made a grab for this crippled mallard duck, and he lacerated one of his fingers all the way down to the bone on a corn husk. He acted like somebody had shot him, he was such a high-strung person."

In the duck-hunting story "Sixty Acres," Carver adopts the perspective of a Yakama Indian man who must chase a couple of kids off his land and lets lavish detail carry the burden of his feeling for nature: "Time, what was time? A bird flying up the valley against the wind until it disappeared. He closed his hand around one of the tall stalks of milkweed that swayed and rustled in the slight breeze that had come up. He snapped its neck, felt the sticky sap ooze into his palm. He looked up when he heard the soft chuckling of ducks over his head; their wings made a rapid, whistling sound as they cut the air. He wiped his hand on his pants and followed them for a moment, watched them set their wings at the same instant and circle once over the creek. Then they flared."[23]

One warm October day, Ray and Sandmeyer went up to Pine Creek. Ray began to climb down toward an outcropping. Sandmeyer warned Ray that the rocks could be "lousy with rattlesnakes." A half hour later, Ray ran screaming back to Sandmeyer:

> "God Almighty!" he said. "I heard some noise around me and above me, and I was setting there, and I looked around and there were so many rattlesnakes I couldn't count them. I just made a wild leap and got out of there. I never had an experience like that before in my lifetime."
>
> "Well, son, your lifetime hasn't been all that long now, has it?" I said to him. That was the spot Ray loved, where the geese fell down in the canyon.

A similar encounter with timber rattlers shows up in Carver's poem "Wenas Ridge." Its narrator, who is hunting grouse with friends and has recently made his girl pregnant, says he felt "more alive then, I thought, than I'd ever be." The life ahead of him will turn out to be a descent "in switchbacks." Every detail of the landscape becomes an impending metaphor: of course, the inevitable snake, when it appears, represents evil and betrayal. Carver's translation of Adam's fall takes place not in a garden but on a dry hillside. Looking back, Carver finds he made an "obscure, criminal pact" there on the ridge: "Praying to Jesus in one breath. / To snake in the other."

• • •

Killing birds in the beautiful, inhospitable terrain of the Columbia River basin as an adolescent helped release Ray from the anxieties of his childhood and gave him the temerity he needed to become a writer. "The Cougar" illustrates how. This poem weaves two stories with a metaphor about Carver's ambitions and drunkenness. In the foreground story, Carver recalls a postreading party in Santa Cruz, California, where two older poets told stories of hunting black bears.[24] Their stories elicit in Carver a sudden, sharp memory of stalking a cougar in a box canyon near the old sawmill town of Klickitat.

At the core of the poem is Carver's younger self: "a nervous, fat, sweating kid . . . but that day I stalked a cougar . . ." The *but* bridging that sentence conveys Carver's wonderment at the impossibility of himself. The self-loathing, fat, and nervous boy becomes a man stalking the largest of the North American cats. And he's right; this is unbelievable. What really occurred, even the poem tells us, is that Ray, "loaded for grouse" and smoking cigarettes, saw cougar tracks and managed for a while to stay upwind of them. He had no chance of killing the cat with his 12-gauge shotgun, but he imagined himself as a man who could face such dangers. "The Cougar" is a fable of self-transformation.

At the barbershop and elsewhere, Ray read outdoor magazines: *Field & Stream, Outdoor Life, Sports Afield*. Alongside black-and-white ads for guns and ammo, gear ("Korean-Type Thermo Boot"), and uranium-discovery instruments ("Currently $150,000 a month is paid by the U.S. Government to people just like you"), between full-color pages hawking cigarettes, liquor, and correspondence courses in taxidermy, ran columns of well-crafted articles and personal narratives. Stories told about hunting game in exotic places, about old dogs who saved the day or new dogs like Hungarian vizslas that might. But most of the copy was about ordinary hunting experiences. Ray began writing down some of the events that had befallen him with Sandmeyer, his dad, and other men. Among Carver's papers is an undated typescript called "A Little Sturgeon."[25] It details how to catch one of these huge fish in the Columbia River by weighting the bait with heavy metal objects like bolts and railroad spikes. It describes his dad with other men, drinking whiskey and coffee from a thermos. An outline projects further topics: keeping the sturgeon in a bathtub after it survives a half day's ride in the car trunk, cooking it, and so forth. Carver's notebooks hold many ideas carried over from those days.

Sandmeyer recalled the conversation when Ray mentioned his writing ambitions. On a bright, cold morning in the mid-1950s, Ray shot three geese before they came back to the car to eat lunch and warm up. As they sat talking, Sandmeyer noticed that Ray was more fidgety and nervous than usual:

Finally, he said, "I'm kind of disappointed. I wrote a story and it didn't sell." And I said, "Well, what did you write?" And he said, "I wrote a story about this wild country, the flight of the wild geese and hunting the geese and everything in this remote country down here. It's not what appeals to the public, they said. I'll have to try something else."

Tentative as it sounds, this was a declaration. Hunting and fishing and family and friends would no longer be the center of Ray's life. He had revised the terms of his engagement with the world. From now on—with one baleful exception—he would live to write.

CHAPTER 4

Cigarettes, Beer, Jazz

1953–1956, Yakima, Washington

The grim frost is at hand, when the apples will fall thick,
almost thunderous, on the hardened earth.
—D. H. Lawrence, *Selected Poems*,
transcribed in one of Carver's notebooks[1]

R ay and his friends at Yakima Senior High School believed they were different from the kids around them, and they could not wait to get out of Yakima. "We would turn the big globe in the school library, measuring with our hands the farthest place from Yakima. It was the coast of Madagascar," Jerry King reminisced, "and we would say that's where we wanted to be."*

Ray's best friends were two boys he'd met in junior high: Jerry King and King Kryger. Jerry King first noticed Ray when he brought "this God-awful-looking black piece of meat" out of his lunch bag. That piece of wild duck, King realized, was Ray's entire lunch. Soon Ray became a fixture at the King family's big, old house downtown, near the library and the theatre where Jerry's dad operated the movie projectors. Ray would lie on a couch in front of the television in the bookshelf-lined den for so many hours that Mrs. King "wondered if he had a brain in his head."[2]

King Kryger first saw Ray carrying another boy in a school-yard fight game called Horse, in which two heavier boys carried two lighter boys on

---

*The high school has been renamed Davis High School. The library there has a corner dedicated to Raymond Carver and his work. The Carver memorial comprises a plaque, some photographs, fishing lures, and other memorabilia, a framed broadside of Carver's poem "The River," and a shelf of his books. The plaque reads "Where I'm Calling From" across the top, as if to say that Carver called to the world from Yakima. The only other alum of the school similarly honored on campus is the late Supreme Court justice William O. Douglas.

34

their shoulders, and the boys on top grappled and tried to "unhorse" each other. The rider on Ray's opponent's shoulders, a recent migrant from Arkansas named Roy Baker, was quick and had a hot temper. The kid Ray carried couldn't get a hold on Baker, but Ray just kept charging. Finally Baker challenged Ray to fight one-on-one after school. When they met, Baker gave Ray a bloody nose and split lip with an upward jab, and Ray got in a few punches. But again, Ray wouldn't give up. Kryger, who was Baker's friend, saw that Ray wasn't going to quit. He was frightened for Ray and got his friends to separate the combatants. From then on, Ray and Kryger were friends. Baker thought he had gotten the best of Ray Carver, because "Ray was big, but not too good a fighter because he was basically meek and mild."[3]

The fellows Ray ran around with cultivated a hoodlum attitude derived from Marlon Brando's 1953 movie *The Wild One*. "We were hood wannabes," King said, "who didn't want to *do* anything bad but badly wanted out of Yakima." They wore their hair greased in either a flattop (also called a Princeton) or an Elvis Presley–like forelock and combed back at the sides into a DA—duck's ass. Shirts were buttoned up to the neck with cigarettes noticeably concealed in the left pocket. The shirt was tucked into denim or white corduroy jeans with legs pegged so tight the wearers could barely get their feet through. These pants rode low on the hips, held precariously by a thin suede belt. In his sophomore class picture, Ray seems to have the look. His boyhood fat is gone, his hair is right, and his pocket shows the outline of a cigarette pack.[4]

But Ray rarely achieved that uniform rebel look. "Ray dressed in early Salvation Army style," classmate Neil Shinpaugh remembered:

He wore these old gray, pleated slacks you'd associate with an older man. Gabardine-type stuff, the kind suits are made of. He had this one ugly plaid shirt—wild, ugly colors in it, just *terrible* colors. For most of us, the thing was to keep our clothes and shoes up, but Ray was dowdy. Wrinkled shirt, wrinkled pants, these unpolished shoes kind of rolled over. His were slip-on loafers, black, with that little bit of elastic in the sides. Even if we went out to a dance at the YMCA, he went in these frumpy old clothes.[5]

Even when Ray owned the right clothes, he looked funny in them. He hunched in his shirts as if he were trapped in them and looked uncomfortable in his body.[6] His face also belied his attempt to look like a hood. His sapphire blue eyes had a mischievous glint, but they didn't look threatening, and his full lips moved more easily toward a smile or a laugh than to a scowl.

"It was a misspent youth," King thought. Cars were at the hub of a culture bent on killing time, but Ray never owned one. He wouldn't have wanted to work on an engine or get a job to support the car. He was seen walking or bicycling around town long past the age when most Yakima boys would rather die than be seen so close to the pavement. But he rode with his friends, especially King, who drove a 1941 Oldsmobile convertible with a '51 engine—he always added the fact of the newer engine—that the boys called Old Leaky.[7] Carver's poem "The Projectile" derives from those years when he and his pals swarmed around looking for kicks. In the poem, "five or six / bozos" lurch along a snowy street, flipping the bird and tossing snowballs and obscenities at other bozos. When the speaker turns his head away, an icy snowball comes through a cracked window to hit him smack on the ear. Carver tells us he cried with the "stupendous" pain while others exclaimed at the *Dumb luck* of this bull's-eye on their friend's ear. Carver fastens his anecdote within a meditation on memory and the ways that pain, humiliation, and chance have become part of his work.

Carver explained that his story "Tell the Women We're Going" also grew out of an aimless cruise around Yakima:

> When I was about sixteen or seventeen years old I had an older friend who ended up doing time in the state penitentiary. He had an old panel truck. We were larking around, drinking beer and smoking cigarettes in the afternoon. We saw these girls on bicycles. And one of these guys who was about three years older than me said, "Let's pick up those girls and rape them." And I thought, Jesus, I didn't sign up for this! Nothing happened that day, I think maybe they pulled up next to them and asked them if they wanted a ride. But much later that emotional thing was still with me so much that I just imagined a story, the extreme situation, out of that summer heat and that feeling of menace that was with me in that park in Yakima.[8]

All the boys and their girlfriends, when they had them, drank alcohol and smoked cigarettes early in high school. Cigarette ads of the day reveal just how prevalent smoking had become: one claims "No Cigarette Hangover"; another, "More Doctors Smoke Camels." When they were juniors, Ray found a rural tavern, the Deerhorn, that would sell him beer, and they tried to list "Deerhorn Teen Club" as one of their activities in the high school annual. If they got a case of beer, they'd bring it to one of their houses where they could drink, play poker, and listen to music for hours.[9]

Ray had grown up listening to country music, the daily fare on Yakima radio and his parents' favorite as well, but he listened to jazz with his friends, Charlie Parker in particular. They heard new 45 rpm releases in listening booths at the record shop and searched for jazz on the radio. At the Playland dance hall north of Yakima, they heard the Dorsey Brothers Orchestra during the midfifties when Jimmy and Tommy Dorsey were reunited. Several times they drove to Seattle for Philharmonic Jazz Series concerts.[10]

For all their poses, Ray and most of his friends were young men who loved words. The homegrown logocentrism that prevailed among them distinguished them in a region where men were supposed to be taciturn. King was quick witted and loved to needle Ray. Ray was good natured, but he'd do a slow burn as King teased him. If he got to the point of real anger, everyone—most of all King—would act surprised. One day when the group was playing poker at Ray's house, Kryger remembered thinking, "God, Jerry's being too rough on Ray, and that's not quite fair, because Ray's kind of stupid."[11]

Ray stayed at the edge of conversations, but he wasn't stupid. He considered himself a "nerd who always hung around the library, half-ashamed to be seen carrying books home." His ironic remarks gave the impression that he knew things the others didn't; like the narrators of the stories he was yet to write, Ray "was there, but he wasn't," Shinpaugh said. "When he said something, even his witticisms, you had to pay attention to catch it."[12]

It's been said that Ray took "bonehead" English in high school. That, according to his twelfth-grade teacher Ben Van Eaton, was not so. In Van Eaton's standard midlevel course where he taught composition and grammar, Ray earned some of the few As he got in high school and wrote "a fine essay on what he saw in jazz." The English teacher sometimes took Ray duck hunting to blinds his family owned along the Yakima River. Another teacher, Roy Hoover, complained in class that he didn't know where to shoot birds, so Ray and Jerry King offered to show him their favorite spots. "Jerry and Ray were both very pleasant fellows to be around. If we talked, it was about where the pheasants were and where they were last week. No deep philosophical discussions." In Hoover's lively American history class, Ray managed to show up most days and earn a few Bs.[13]

Earl Shelton taught Ray and King and Kryger in a class called Radio Production. He asked his students to write news stories, dramatic sketches, and interviews of other students. Ray especially got a kick out of an assignment to cut up interview tapes and rearrange the questions and answers so that meanings were misconstrued to create humor or propaganda. When Shelton noticed the brisk, cross-cut dialogue in Carver's fiction, he wondered "if he hadn't begun to develop his good ear in that class, where he was always a listener and observer." All three boys liked jazz records in the Broadcast Music Incorporated collection donated by a local radio station and were "mentally advanced—they didn't have that silliness other kids had."[14]

If Ray and his cohort knew that they wanted to leave Yakima, they were nonetheless clueless about how to do so. Before the 1962 World's Fair and the Space Needle put Seattle on the map, long before Microsoft and super-coffee and grunge rock, Washington was the most remote of the lower forty-eight states. Many who grew up there were infected by an anomie peculiar to their part of the country. Defining this trait as a tendency to avoid ambition or success (or to disintegrate under the pressure of success; as did the writer Richard Brautigan and the rock star Kurt Cobain), music critic Fred Moody writes, "To be a Northwesterner . . . is by definition to be an underachiever, whether by chance or design. . . . resignation [is] the Mount Rainier of our psychological landscape."[15] Some of Ray's friends joined the military, most commonly the coast guard, while only Jerry King went directly to college. The literary world attracted Ray, but he saw little connection between that and formal education.

On January 25, 1954, a banner headline in the Yakima *Daily Republic* caught Ray's attention: HEMINGWAY BACK FROM JUNGLE; SUFFERS SLIGHT INJURIES IN TWO PLANE CRASHES: NOVELIST ENDS TRIP ON GROUND. The article tells about the Pulitzer Prize–winning novelist's adventures in Italy, Spain, and Africa, noting that Hemingway "lives as dangerously as his hairy chested heroes." It mentions that Hemingway's "short staccato style became a model for a generation of writers." Seeing that article, Carver wrote, was "heady and glamorous stuff" to him then, because the places mentioned "seemed as far away as the moon." Though Ray, at fifteen, had yet to read Hemingway, Papa's fame inspired him, and he "was indebted to him even then, if for the wrong reasons."[16]

At first, Ray associated the problem of writing with the literal act of placing the words on paper. His family didn't own a typewriter, and he watched Ella toil over letters home to Arkansas, unsure of her spelling and sometimes short on legibility as well. Ray's own handwriting continued to be atrocious—his big hands and fingers just didn't cooperate. His three semesters of typing classes may have profited him more than the rest of his high school curriculum.[17]

"I wanted to be right in there with all the rest of the guys. But I also wanted to write," Ray told an interviewer years later. Along with King Kryger, Ray enrolled in a correspondence course offered by the Palmer Institute of Authorship in Hollywood. C.R. paid Ray's initial $25 fee and enrolled James in a drawing course at the same time.[18] The first lesson,

"Essential Elements of a Short Story and How To Develop Them," arrived in a manila envelope addressed to Ray. Imagine the promise of these words:

> In becoming a Palmer student you are taking an important step in establishing yourself in a profession that enjoys the respect and esteem of all classes of people, a profession you may be proud to claim as your own. . . . This may be the vital turning point in the course of your life. . . .

Why People Read

> . . . In a well written story the reader is planted into the shoes of the main character, shares his trials and tribulations, reads his thoughts, feels the thrill of his exciting experiences, worries over his difficulties, and rejoices with him in his success. The reader, for the moment is "taken out of himself" and in the person of the story character, lives a life of adventure, romance and achievement he would like to live if only he had the chance—the wit—and the courage. Many a timid little John Doe "loses himself" in a story of daring deeds such as he would never have the nerve to perform in real life.

Authorship Is a Big, Lucrative Field

> Every year millions of dollars are spent by the John Smiths and Jane Does all over the world for the opportunity of "losing themselves". . . Editors must have thousands of stories to meet the constant demand, and are willing—yes, eager—to pay the writer handsomely who can supply them . . .

Why Not You Too?

> If you have any doubts about your ability to learn to write . . . forget them. All you need to make a good clean start are:
>
> 1. A sincere INTEREST in the work.
> 2. Willingness to WORK and STUDY.
> 3. Enough ENGLISH to write us a good personal letter.
>
> Not much to ask, is it? Yet, with this equipment a great deal—a VERY great deal can be accomplished.

Despite its reliance on capital letters for emphasis, the Palmer course is impressive. A student who actually took it all in, wrote every assignment, and shouldered the task of revising his work according to the instructor's written suggestions would accomplish something akin to a yearlong college course in creative writing. Each lesson was prefaced with a homily like the following by one Barton A. Hebbins:

> Remember, NO person has any greater right to success than YOU. The great success of which you have always dreamed CAN be yours if you but WILL to achieve it and by force of that WILL, keep everlastingly at your studies and your assignments.

The course's sixteen installments covered the technical elements of short story writing and emphasized what would sell to magazines. Lessons were titled: Desire and Opposition, What to Write About, Theme, Motivation, Viewpoint, Plot, Characterization, and so forth. A daunting amount of information and terminology was offered, enough to stymie anyone, let alone a couple of seventeen-year-olds. Still, the lessons offered smart insights, good examples from contemporary magazine fiction, and explicit assignments. Students mailed in these assignments for comment and received them back marked in red pencil.[19]

Ray and Kryger read each other's writing with enthusiasm, but other friends teased them unmercifully. Jerry King, who read one piece before Ray mailed it in, recalled, "He said that somebody's muffler was hotter than—no, the other way—the barrel of a pistol was hotter than a twenty-five-cent muffler on a Saturday night." Roy Hoover, the history teacher, noticed that Ray was always writing something for the Palmer course and worried that it might be a scam.

It really wasn't. The Palmer course hammered on two themes: anyone who worked hard enough and followed the lessons in order and completely could become a professional writer. And a story was finished when it was ready to "sell." Although the pulps were dying, there were many other commercial venues for short fiction in 1955. Ray worked hard at his Palmer Institute writing assignments. He submitted work to outdoor magazines and rented a post office box for his correspondence. He would "stomp in and bring some mail out—rejection slips. And then he'd be pretty depressed." Once, Carver said later, he submitted a story to a magazine's circulation department.[20]

Most of the ultimate strengths of Carver's work are recommended in Palmer's Lesson One. Here Ray read that a good story puts the reader in the shoes of a character, that stories are more popular than novels, and that the secret of good stories is economy in presentation and emphasis. Carver wrote a story about a writer called "Put Yourself in My Shoes"; he never made a successful attempt to write a novel, and he became best known for the severe economy of his style.

• • •

For a long time, Carver once told an interviewer, "it was assumed I would graduate and go to work at the sawmill." As a teenager, Ray often went to school in the morning, then brought his dad lunch and stayed for the afternoon.[21] The two of them were tacit allies against the duress of daily life. Ray's dad covered for him if the school inquired about his absence. Both were loners, one was an active alcoholic, the other beginning to drink. To an inquisitive, observant kid like Ray, the mill offered a fascinating cast of characters. C.R.'s cousin Tillman Carver had a crippled hand that led other workers to abuse him and give him dirty jobs, but despite these disadvantages, he had worked his way up to head millwright. Another figure who intrigued Ray was a deaf mute named Robert Weddle, whom everybody called Dummy. Weddle carried toilet paper rolls in his pockets because one of his tasks was to supply the men's bathrooms; he took a lot of ribbing, some of it delivered with real meanness, from the men and spent a lot of time at the mill ponds, drinking beer and fishing. Carver based his story "Dummy" on Weddle.[22]

Ray never worked at Cascade, nor did he knock himself out to find other jobs in Yakima. He did brief stints as a stock boy at grocery and dime stores and as a picker of apples, cherries, and hops. For the rest of his life, if asked, he would mention that picking hops from vines strung up on high wires was "unimaginably hard work."[23]

In the mid-1950s, as much of the country thrived economically, the Carvers fell behind on payments on the Eleventh Avenue house. In 1955 they sold it and moved into a rented bungalow with a wide porch and large windows that Ray considered the nicest place his family ever lived. Ray converted a downstairs den into his own bedroom and left the second upstairs bedroom to James. His post office was down the street. Yakima's "Nob Hill," where the president of Cascade Lumber lived, was nearby. Beyond that, to the west, began the orchards. On a warm summer night, Ray could stroll happily down the hill toward downtown, feeling lucky, dreaming of love and escape and fame as he watched the moon rise over the Rattlesnake Hills.[24]

Such illusions were brief. A sequence of crises was about to spill over the Carvers like an avalanche, changing them all for years to come. In a flash, it seemed, Cascade Lumber, which had long sheltered the Carvers, suddenly turned against them.

First Fred Carver was dismissed from his job as head saw filer because he opposed changes that a new supervisor wanted to make in the filing system. The company offered Fred a regular filing position, which he had to refuse because he was missing fingers and really couldn't file anymore, as the company well knew. Within weeks of Fred's departure, Ray accompanied his dad to his filing room one day. Before C.R. had begun to work, with his son looking on, a manager brought him a final paycheck and sent him home, jobless. Pieti, who was working in the powerhouse at the time, saw the two Raymond Carvers leave the mill grounds: "I've never forgotten that sight of the father and son walking away that morning. Ray [Senior] was devastated as he walked down the street."

C.R. appealed his firing and the company eventually admitted that they hadn't gone through the correct process and would give him another chance.[25] Before the union investigation was finished, C.R. left Yakima with Fred. They went to Chester, south of Mount Lassen in northern California, where they took jobs at the Collins Pine Company. They told people that they were getting better pay in Chester. C.R. further embellished the tale by mentioning his hopes that he would be promoted to head filer there when Fred retired. C.R. was forty-two years old.[26]

Ella stayed behind in Yakima so that Ray and James could finish out the school year. Forced to get his own spending money, Ray applied for a job as a delivery boy for a pharmacy near his house on Summitview. When owner Al Kurbitz asked Ray if he could change the tire on the delivery car, Ray replied that he'd find another kid to get his hands dirty to do that. Kurbitz felt the same way about manual labor, so he hired Ray.[27]

High school was nearly over for Ray, and with it his aimless youth. "Soon we lumber out of high school . . . ," he wrote on the senior portrait he gave Jerry King. *Lumber* seems to describe Ray's motion in life pretty accurately. Though he scored in the 83rd percentile on an eleventh-grade achievement test, Ray had a C- average on a four-point scale. In a class of 441, he was down in the lower quartile at 337.[28] But he was the first in his family to earn a high school diploma. His father must have been sorry to miss his commencement, and Ray must have missed having him there.

C.R. wrote that he liked his new job at Collins Pine. The work was what he was used to, and Fred was still his boss and protector. Early in June 1956, C.R. asked Ella to pack their gray 1950 Chevy and bring the boys as soon as she could. He had lined up a house for them.[29]

For Ray it wasn't so simple. After all those years of longing to leave Yakima, he now had one good reason to stay.

Her name was Maryann Burk.

CHAPTER 5

Crazy in Love

Summer 1955–Summer 1958, Yakima, Washington,

and Chester, California

. . . I remembered Maryann.
When we were both young.
—Raymond Carver,
"The Windows of the
Summer Vacation Houses"

Ray met Maryann Burk in a Spudnut Shop in Union Gap, Washington, in the summer of 1955. She was fourteen, working her first job as a counter girl for eighty-five cents an hour and hoping for some tips. The first time the tall, slim, curly haired boy of seventeen stopped in with his little brother, she had a premonition. It came to her in these words: "I am going to marry that boy." She rushed to take the brothers' orders before an older woman she worked with could get to them.[1]

That meeting would begin a lifelong story. "Ray and I looked at each other and smiled with delight,"[2] Maryann recounted. The slender, brown-eyed girl soon learned that there was more than fate at work in the boy's frequent returns to the Spudnut. There was the fact that Ray loved doughnuts. There was also the fact that the tall woman in her early forties with whom Maryann worked was Ella Carver.

Spudnuts—doughnuts made of potato flour—were new in Yakima Valley and so was Maryann. The Spudnut Shop's attractions continued to draw Ray even after his mother got into an argument with the boss and quit her job in the middle of the summer. Soon after that, Ray asked Maryann for a date. Ray's earlier foray into romance had ended with him passed out at a dance hall, so Maryann was probably his first serious girlfriend. She looked older than her age; her cousin Irmagene Kulp remembered: "Maryann was tall, about five foot eight. We all wore shorts most of the summer in the dry heat of eastern Washington, and her shapely legs went on forever. She was beautiful, graceful, and intelligent." Like most teenage girls in the fifties, Maryann read romance magazines and listened to popular songs that told her "Love Is a Many-Splendored Thing" for an "Earth Angel" like her. She was primed to fall in love with Ray as soon as he smiled at her. Ray may have been an awkward "doofus" to his friends, but to Maryann he was "as handsome and sophisticated as a guy in a TV ad; the sort who wore those heavy-framed dark glasses while cool jazz played."[3]

But Maryann was not a typical teenage girl. She had lived a more challenging emotional life than many girls her age; she also had more serious ambitions than most girls did in the 1950s. She was to become "The Sensitive Girl" in Carver's poem of that title, a "girl who dreamed / and sang" in a time he "would've died for love." At a private boarding school, Maryann had "learned the right way to hold a teacup," Ray told interviewers. "She'd had religious instruction and gym and such, but she also learned about physics and literature and foreign languages. I was terrifically impressed that she knew Latin. Latin!"[4]

By the time she met Ray, Maryann had moved from one school to another several times and been deeply affected by divorce and its aftermath, but she was eager for new experiences. The more difficulties life threw her, the stronger and more determined she became. One source of her strength was the memory of her early childhood under the protection of her Germanic father; her independent and intellectually restless mother was another.

On both sides, Maryann's grandparents were tough Western homesteaders. Her mother, born Alice Ritchey, completed her high school requirements early and was assigned to memorize long passages of Shakespeare to keep her busy. After some college in Bellingham, Washington, she began teaching school on Burk Road at age nineteen and fell in love with logger and landowner Valentine Burk. As a boy, Val Burk had a passion for baseball and dreamed of a career in sports, but instead took on the farm responsibilities as his older siblings left home. He was a big, fun-loving man with dark eyes, but he had an explosive temper. For Burk and later for his children, the difficulties of rural life were nothing compared to pride in their land. Burk dreamed that someday his descendants would all have houses on his property. Alice did not give up her independence of mind when she married. She left Val once while she was carrying her first child because he had shouted harshly at her younger brother; they reconciled after Bonna Rose (known as Jerry) was born in 1930.[5] She did the farmwork, but her predilection was for learning and conversation, so she returned to the classroom when Jerry started school. Once she accepted a teaching job in a foot-hill town, took Jerry with her, and came home only on weekends.

Maryann Elsie Burk, the second daughter of Alice and Valentine, was born August 7, 1940. Less than two years after Maryann, Amy Edith arrived. A 1945 photograph shows Maryann, looking anxious and responsible, seated behind Amy and holding her protectively. The two sisters, born so close together, were intimate for most of their lives. For them, country girlhood was idyllic. Their father was their "consummate hero—decent, tough, smart, and loyal to the end," Maryann said. But two new daughters did not alleviate Alice's feeling of isolation on the farm. After Jerry left home, Alice divorced Burk. In Maryann's opinion, her mother left Val the final time in part because she was exhausted. Shortly thereafter, Val Burk married Ann, a woman who worked with the haying crew, and they had two daughters together.[6]

As a ninety-two-year-old materfamilias, Alice had one chief regret: "I took Maryann and Amy away from the farm, where they were happy as little girls, and exposed them to a more complicated world." When she was thirty-nine, Alice married James Higinbotham, whom she had known for years; with him, she moved to Wide Hollow near Cowiche, close to her eldest daughter, Jerry, whose husband repaired tanks at the U.S. Army's Yakima firing center.[7]

Amy and Maryann were good students; Maryann skipped third grade and was then three years ahead of Amy in school. But after their mother remarried, Amy began to have discipline problems. When Amy was thirteen, she left the house one night while Alice and her husband were asleep. The girl ran across a field to a neighbor's to telephone Val Burk, who was visiting Jerry. She told him that her stepfather had molested her repeatedly for several years. At first Burk was skeptical, but then he recalled an incident from years earlier that cast suspicion on the man. Burk returned to the house with Amy. Amy remembered that he turned off his headlights as he approached, surprised Alice and her husband asleep in their front room, and beat the other man to within an inch of his life. Before the blow that Amy said would have been the kill, Val Burk pulled his punch. To Amy, Val Burk was like a god come to avenge them: a bull of a man with his eyes flashing, capable of killing the other man but wise enough not to. His anger, to her, was huge and righteous.[8]

Alice divorced Higinbotham and determined to offer Amy and Maryann a new environment. Her sister suggested that Maryann should attend Saint Paul's School for Girls in Walla Walla, the oldest prep school for girls in the Pacific Northwest. Maryann began in March 1955, her sophomore year of high school. Many of the other girls at the Episcopalian school came from wealthy families. Their fathers were presidents of companies, doctors, or owners of silver mines and ranches. Maryann, a scholarship girl, was outgoing and smart and eager to make friends, and soon she did. Only one thing bothered Maryann at Saint Paul's: her lack of spending money.

When Maryann returned to Yakima at the end of her sophomore year, everything had changed. Her mother had moved to a small cabin at Playland Park, had two part-time teaching jobs, and cooked in the evenings at Playland to make ends meet. Alice's pride, she thought later, kept her from sending the girls to their father for the summer or asking him for extra money. That summer Amy worked as a mother's helper, and Maryann took the job at Spudnut.

During the early weeks of their courtship, Maryann found that Ray was "a prodigious reader with a wonderful vocabulary, just like my mother" and that they both loved ancient history. Ray and Maryann were closely watched by her sister Amy and her cousin Irmagene, who found Ray "dark, tall, bashful, reserved, polite, respectful, intelligent," and altogether "a perfect specimen." The younger girls "peeked out the front picture window of Jerry's home to watch them kiss good night after their dates." Ray must have basked in the adoration of a whole family of females. To Irmagene, "Watching Ray was like watching a fly entering a spider's web. He was caught quickly and fast. It worked both ways, though; Maryann was just as enamored with Ray."[9]

As Maryann's fifteenth birthday drew near in August, she worried about how Ray and her father would get along. "If either one had come up short, I would not have been able to take it," she reflected. They celebrated at the big house where Amy was working, and the introduction of Ray and Val went off without a hitch. The Ray that Maryann knew in those days was "poised and sure of himself in a quiet, nice way. He was not shy, but very sweet, like his dad. He could associate with all his father's friends, with my brother-in-law and dad. I saw Ray's ability to associate with men way older than himself as being mature and special."[10]

Ray's family welcomed Maryann, too. She attended a twelfth birthday party for James in mid-August. Ray's father liked to call Maryann by his own mother's name—Mary—and quickly considered her a member of his family. Since the Carvers had a television and Maryann's mother didn't, Maryann would come over to watch Ray's favorite drama, *The Millionaire.* In each episode a messenger delivered someone an anonymous gift of $1 million.

Maryann planned to spend her Spudnut earnings on sweater sets, pleated skirts, and shirtwaist dresses to wear at Saint Paul's, so one of her classmates came to visit and help her shop. Ray set up a double date for the two girls with himself and his pal Dick Moeller. The foursome enjoyed plenty of good times, but one night ended at the police station. Maryann was babysitting her nephews. Dick and Ray brought beer to the house and were making themselves comfortable when they heard Jerry and her husband drive up. With six-packs under their arms, the interlopers slipped out the back door: the girls followed later, after the household was asleep. Then, as Moeller recalled, "we wandered across the railroad tracks and sat in an open boxcar door, our legs dangling over the edge, drinking our beer in that little Podunk town. We saw a cop car—we were probably making noise or throwing beer bottles—and started running, but we got all tangled up in a barbed wire fence and the cops ran us in. They held us a few hours in the local jail and released us." In spite of such shenanigans, both Jerry and Alice approved of Ray.[11]

Carver's 1983 story "Fever" has a similar scene, though the story inflates the number of teenage boys to four and combines two slim babysitters into one fat one who sits, blouse unbuttoned, on the sofa with one of the boys. "Fever" displays Carver's knack for switching point of view to a character different from himself: his story is narrated by a father who comes home early, catches the teenagers red-handed, and sends them and their Rod Stewart album packing.

Before the summer ended, fifteen-year-old Maryann and seventeen-year-old Ray were lovers, she writes in her memoir, *What It Used to Be Like: A Portrait of My Marriage to Raymond Carver*. The start of the school year— Ray's senior year at Yakima Senior High and Maryann's junior year at Saint Paul's—put a two-and-a-half-hour drive between them. Now instead of writing to her girlfriends about Ray, Maryann sent almost daily letters to Ray at his post office box. Equally important to the deepening of Ray's and Maryann's relationship was Ray's growing ambition to be a writer. She read his Palmer course stories and showed them to her sister Jerry, who provided a glimpse of Ray's teenage efforts: "We didn't know many people who dared to say, 'I want to be a writer.' They said, 'I want to be a school-teacher, and I hope I get to write on the side.' They had to toss in that realism, you know, but Ray said, 'I want to be a writer' and made no apologies for it. Jerry noticed that Ray wrote "about relationships between men and women in their thirties and forties, and it just didn't seem to come from his pen. And what I discovered about it over the years was his writing didn't change. He was kind of ageless then, and he stayed that way."[12]

When Ray graduated from high school and prepared to move to California with his mother, he and Maryann were already collaborating on plans to reunite. As Ray drove Ella, James, and their boxes toward his father in California, he must have dreaded the change he'd once yearned for. Indeed, no one in that car could have been too optimistic about this trip. Ray missed Maryann, James was leaving the town where he'd lived his almost thirteen years, and Ella had recently received two worrisome pieces of mail: C.R.'s said he'd been feeling sick after cutting himself on a saw; and an anonymous postcard, also postmarked Chester, said that—as Carver recounted it—"my dad was about to die and that he was drinking 'raw whiskey.' "[13]

Cupped in a gap between volcanic Mount Lassen and the granite Sierra Nevadas, Chester made Yakima look big. Most of the men worked for the power company or for Collins Pine. Cottonwood trees lined Main Street then, along with the Copper Kettle restaurant, a grocery, a two-pump gas station, a classic soda fountain, a gun shop, and, of course, two bars. At the edge of town, Lake Almanor's cold water was known for its rainbow trout and salmon. On the far side of the tiny town they found the mill and then the company trailer where Raymond Senior lived: "I didn't recognize him immediately," Carver wrote in "My Father's Life." "He was skinny and pale and looked bewildered. . . . My mother began to cry. My dad put his arm around her and patted her shoulder vaguely, like he didn't know what this was all about, either."

The family moved into a company house, and C.R. began eating again, but he remained sickly. Ray became a full-time laborer at the mill. He and his dad ate breakfast together and walked into the mill together. This was the first time in his life that Ray had done mill work, and the only thing he liked about the job was the $70 a week he made. As soon as he had a paycheck, he rented himself a tiny apartment above a store in downtown Chester, but the labor of sorting and stacking just-sawed lumber for hours on end left him exhausted.[14] Like many young people before him, Ray discovered that freedom was an unequal exchange for his mother's care. He moved home.

When he had a week off, Ray drove twelve hours in the family sedan to fetch Maryann from Yakima and another twelve hours to bring her back to Chester. That's when she saw how Ella could pamper her sons. Every morning as Ray woke up, Ella gave him a list of choices for breakfast. An incident that occurred in Chester that summer stayed in Maryann's mind as an instance of the Carver family dynamics:

> There were two pieces of cherry pie left in a pie tin. Ray and his mother and James started battling over this pie tin with two pieces of pie. And Ray's father looked at me and I at him, and he just had this bemused smile, as if to say, "Look at them!" They were wrenching the pie tin back and forth at the table—there was no thought of, "You are the guest,

Maryann" or "How can we divide it?" It was flat-out three of us want two pieces. I don't remember who won, but I saw it at the time as Ella putting herself first and teaching her sons the same. Most likely Ray and Ella got the two pieces, probably not James. What she cared about in the world was her two sons—and especially Ray.

Ray's dad, as Maryann came to know him in Yakima and Chester, was "selfless." He was sometimes astonished at how his money just disappeared, but he didn't complain. He would "laugh and say, 'the cartons of milk I've bought would stretch from New York City to Los Angeles.' He always brought home bags of groceries and treats—cheese and grapes and lemons for lemonade. He found money for Ray to buy shotguns and go out on dates or call me long-distance," Maryann recollected.

Ella on the other hand—in Maryann's view—was "a Southern belle. Go see *Gone With the Wind,* watch Scarlett, and you see Ella." While living in the Carver household in Chester, Maryann began to see how the characters of his parents were manifested in Ray. As she came to understand it, "Ella was the perfect mother for Ray, and Raymond was the perfect father, because the son got the sweetness and primary qualities from his dad, but he got—I'm not sure what the right word is—determination and arrogance, a kind of pride or self-possession, from Ella. A wonderful kind of conceit, that's what it was."[15]

Because he was spoiled, Maryann believed, Ray "always wanted more." The things he wanted in those days, when he was eighteen years old in Chester, were fairly simple, and his job enabled him to get them. But at the same time, he was learning that he could not be content with sawmill work.

Maryann brought her summer reading list from Saint Paul's when she came to Chester. She and Ray went together to the Plumas County branch library to find *Madame Bovary* by Gustave Flaubert. She read while Ray was at the sawmill during the day and at night told him the story and read aloud from it to him. The predicament of the large, awkward, mumbling Charles Bovary who is mercilessly teased by schoolmates was familiar to Ray, and so was the hopeless boredom that Emma felt as she endured "the wide solitude of her life." But Flaubert's style, Maryann recalled, was a "small revelation" to Ray. Together they read Chekhov's "The Lady with the Dog" as well as Leo Tolstoy's *Anna Karenina* and Fyodor Dostoyevsky's *Crime and Punishment.*[16]

C.R. got his drinking under control after his family arrived, but he still didn't recover from his undiagnosed illness. Ella waitressed at the Copper Kettle. James began eighth grade in Chester. In *The Crater* yearbook, he's a confident-looking kid with dark hair in a brush cut and sharply arched brows just like his older brother's. He excelled at art. After Maryann took the bus to Yakima at the end of summer, she and Ray wrote letters again. A three-cent stamp was cheaper than a long-distance phone call. Ray wrote Dick Moeller, too, but Dick could not make out Ray's handwriting and brought his letters to Maryann to interpret. Moeller "tried to date her briefly—I don't know where I got the idea that she was free, but I do remember Ray wasn't happy about it." Maryann returned to Saint Paul's School accompanied by Amy, who began ninth grade. Maryann's letters to Ray that fall told him she was studying twelve hours a day, hoping to win a scholarship to study pre-law at the University of Washington. With four National Merit Scholars in her class, she had tough competition.[17]

From the end of the Korean War until 1973, every American male between the ages of eighteen and twenty-six (including, famously, Elvis Presley), was subject to conscription for two years of military service. Between 1953 and 1959, America's draft-induced military inductions averaged 153,000 a year, not a low number. (By comparison, at the height of the Vietnam era, in 1968, 300,000 were drafted.) Those who were disinclined to become army GIs could enlist in the marines, navy, air force, or coast guard or became weekend warriors in a state National Guard or federal Army Reserve unit. As a healthy, unmarried, nonstudent in an ordinary labor job, Ray was ripe to be drafted.

Late in August 1956, Ray passed a medical and dental exam with a doctor in Chester (he weighed 166 pounds, stood 74 inches tall, and had four teeth missing) and joined the California National Guard. He became Private Carver, an E-1 in California National Guard Battery D 170th Antiaircraft Artillery located in Susanville. At the Lassen County Fairgrounds armory, Ray began weekend training with large guns mounted on half-track vehicles. It may be that Ray joined the Guard *not* to sidestep conscription into the regular army (the reason that now seems logical) but rather because he wanted and needed the income or because he liked to shoot guns or thought the experience would serve his writing.

But three months later, Ray was finding sawmill work in Chester and separation from Maryann unbearable. He returned to Yakima and moved in with his Aunt Vonda and Uncle Bill. He contacted Battery A of the 420th Antiaircraft Artillery Battalion of the Washington National Guard in Yakima and persuaded the commander of the 420th to ask his Susanville unit to release him so he could enlist in the Yakima unit. Several pieces of official correspondence between officials in the two states requested "favorable consideration" of the transfer; the California unit released Ray in late November, and those in charge worked to ensure that Private Carver would have a seamless service record.

Before Ray's training could have been much advanced, he withdrew his request to join the Washington National Guard. A lieutenant of the Yakima unit wrote to the California unit that Private Carver "has advised this office that he will be unable to enlist in the Washington National Guard by reason of incompatible employment. He states that his forthcoming employment will necessitate travel outside the continental United States and participation in the National Guard will be impossible." In view of that information, the lieutenant continued, Carver planned to contact the California office "in regard to his discharge." A discharge from his California unit was issued on December 20, but where Ray should have signed his full name, it reads, "EM [Enlisted Man] not available for signature." He couldn't sign it, of course, for the very reason he had requested it. He no longer lived in California. According to a note on his discharge form, Ray "became a member of USAR [Army Reserve] to complete remaining Sv obligation of 5 yrs 8 mo 14 days." In other words, at the end of 1956, Ray was listed on federal military reserve rolls, obligated to apprise Selective Service boards of his whereabouts, and subject to conscription for nearly six years to come.

Ray never spoke of his military episode. His mother saved his discharge paper, his brother recalled that Ray had gone to Guard activities in Susanville, and a file in the California Adjutant General's Office preserves other details given here.[18] Nothing Carver wrote reflects his brief military experiment. Did he slip through gaps of a slipshod peacetime bureaucracy? Or did he cunningly devise a plan that allowed him to avoid further service? Perhaps a little of both. Coordination of records among state National Guard units, federal Army Reserve units, and local draft boards was lax in that pre-computer era. By keeping ahead of the paperwork and muffling his exact location, Ray quietly solved the problem that challenged almost every young American male from the 1950s until the early 1970s.

Ray stretched the truth a good deal when he told the Washington National Guard that he was going to be employed overseas. In fact, he had run into two former Yakima High School football players, Bob Vachon and Larry Berghoff, who were planning a trip to Mexico or Central America. They had not been friends of Ray's before, but they invited him to come with them. Thus began another hazy episode in Ray's eighteenth year. By now Ray had read enough Hemingway to get the idea that adventures in foreign countries might give him good material for writing (as well as a convenient inability to attend National Guard training in any location). Maryann remembered that the threesome, influenced by the film *King Solomon's Mines*, headed for

South America in a beat-up old car, hoping to find diamonds. "He wanted to travel, to see the world, have adventure. At the same time, he wanted me, and he tried to juggle these things, forevermore, really."[19]

A different version circulated in Yakima: Vachon and Berghoff had lined up a deal to run a coffee plantation in Honduras. After they had worked the whole season and finished the harvest, their patron "took the beans to market and never came back." Vachon and Berghoff "made it to the coast and hopped a freighter to bring them home," Neil Shinpaugh remembered. "They were both jaundiced up, malnourished—they'd been big, husky guys, but they were in terrible shape when they got back."[20]

In any case, Ray's part of the trip ended in Guaymas, Mexico, three hundred miles south of Tucson, Arizona. He and his two compatriots got into some kind of a fight—Maryann thought it was over a "monstrosity of a fish" Ray had caught. Berghoff later commented, "Ray and I did not part friends. Enough said." At the end of three weeks, Ray, hungry and dead broke, telephoned his parents from the bus depot in Red Bluff, California. C.R., still unwell, drove to meet him and bought him a big breakfast. Ray's foreign adventure was over, but a legacy of it shows up in one of his first short stories, "The Aficionados."[21] Carver's Mexican tale (like Hemingway's "Hills Like White Elephants") begins with a couple drinking wine in a bodega and holding an awkward, obscure conversation; to himself, the man makes the observation that the "gray humped hills . . . always reminded him of great-breasted reclining women." Then, somewhat like D. H. Lawrence's "The Woman Who Rode Away" with the sexes reversed, the story moves toward a human sacrifice—the woman cuts out her lover-husband's heart with an obsidian knife. An extreme conclusion, but perhaps it foreshadows the mortifying situations men and women put each other through in Carver's later stories.

After resting up at his parents' house in Chester, Ray was back in Yakima again, bunking at the Archers' and making deliveries for Al Kurbitz. Like a lot of eighteen-year-olds, he lived in disjunction and limbo. A man who saw Ray almost daily, Kurbitz's younger partner, Bill Barton, noticed a bit of the "renegade" in Ray and sensed that Ray felt his family had not had a fair deal and that the government, or somebody, owed him something. According to Maryann, Kurbitz offered to pay for Ray's education as a pharmacist if he would return to work for him afterward, but Ray was already determined to be a writer.[22] Ray, then, lived at the center of a number of dilemmas: The only career prospects he had—sawmill work or pharmacy school—did not interest him in the least. He was in love with (and secretly engaged to, Maryann said) a girl who hoped to go to university in Seattle; he had unfinished business with Uncle Sam, but no draft board had his current address. He knew he wanted to be a writer but had suffered miserably in his attempt to live as a free spirit south of the border, got rejections when he sent articles to the outdoor magazines, and did not know what to do with the other stories and poems he was trying to write.

Dick Moeller was the only one of Ray's high school crowd still in Yakima that winter and spring of 1957. The two spent a lot of time together, but when Moeller asked Ray about his father, Ray gave him the impression that C. R. had died in California. Moeller distinctly remembers a day when Ray's uncle allowed them to take out his brand-new Lincoln Premier, a Starmist White two-door hardtop with swept-back tail fins and big white-wall tires and every factory option. "We drove up the old canyon road north of Yakima, and that really thrilled Ray. You could see the smile on his face. Ray loved big cars." Some nights Dick and Ray put on suits and ties so they would look older than their eighteen years and went to the Circus Inn, "a cocktail *lounge,* and we always said we were going there to check out the babes, you know."[23]

As that spring advanced, Maryann came to Ray with news that trumped his other concerns. She thought she was pregnant. One could say that Ray's destiny as a writer was set when he heard this news and proposed marriage. Couples and domestic life became and remained his most profound subjects. Carver makes the point himself in an interview: "Most of what now strikes me as story 'material' presented itself to me after I was twenty. I really don't remember much about my life before I became a parent. I really don't feel that anything happened in my life until I was twenty and married and had the kids. Then things started to happen."[24]

Maryann's mother fumed about Maryann's plan to marry Ray, foreseeing that it would interfere with her career plans. Alice explained, "My sister had offered to pay for her college because Maryann by that time wanted to be a lawyer and would have been a good one." But there seems to have been no hesitation about Maryann's and Ray's decision to marry. In the fifties, before reliable birth control and sexual freedom, it was certainly common for young brides to be pregnant. Maryann and Ray might have married young in any case. During the 1950s, the average age of marriage for American women dropped into the teens and the number of women in college fell lower than it had been before World War II, while the U.S. birthrate soared.[25] Besides, Maryann and Ray were like the couple Carver describes in the story "Distance": "They were kids themselves, but they were crazy in love, this 18-year-old boy and his 17-year-old girl friend when they married, and not all that long afterwards they had a daughter."

Marriage appealed to both Ray and Maryann. Marriage would confer the kind of status Carver mentions in his story "Tell the Women We're Going": as the character Bill thinks, "it made him feel older, having married friends." Confirmation of Maryann's pregnancy by a doctor on the day before their wedding only heightened their enthusiasm.[26] In "Egress," Ray described his feeling: ". . . My wife was pregnant. We were thrilled / beyond measure or accounting for . . ."

Maryann graduated from Saint Paul's on June 1, one of fourteen in the graduating class. Her name does not appear among the list of academic, citizenship, or athletic honors bestowed upon some class members, perhaps because she had postponed her college plans. It would have taken an even bolder girl than Maryann Burk to think of attending university while pregnant in 1957. Few residential colleges of the sort that Saint Paul's girls entered—Wellesley, Mills, and Vassar were typical choices—would have permitted it. Both Ray and Maryann were below the legal age for marriage, so their mothers accompanied them to the Yakima County Courthouse to get a marriage license. At a wedding shower the same night, Ray looked positively ebullient. Handsome in a dark shirt, he winked at a photographer, one arm confidently akimbo, the other around Maryann. Everyone might have suspected that Maryann was pregnant, but she certainly didn't look it. She's thin as a reed in these pictures as she gazes at her intended. The day after the shower, a notice on the society page of the Yakima *Daily Republic* described the event down to "a heart-shaped cake with red roses."[27]

On Friday evening June 7, Maryann and Ray were married at Saint Michael's Episcopal Church. According to Maryann, Ray made all the arrangements for the wedding: "He bought the rings and worked hard on the plans." It was not true, though—as Ray wrote in a 1987 letter—that he attended a high school friend's funeral in the same church the day before his wedding. "Ray was a storyteller. He made that up to create foreshadowing," Maryann said.[28] With a linen and lace sheath dress borrowed from her sister Jerry, Maryann wore a white rosebud corsage. Carrying gloves and wearing a close-fitting feather bandeau in her dark, curly hair, Maryann looked older than her sixteen years. Pictures taken at the church again showed a twinkle in the groom's eye.

Saint Paul's headmistress, Hedwig Zorb, and housemother, Mrs. Fulton, attended the double-ring ceremony. Maryann's older sister, Jerry, stood up with her. Val Burk "gave away" his daughter and paid for flowers, hairstyling, and liquor for the youthful wedding party. Irmagene Kulp remembers that she and Amy were "awestruck with what seemed a storybook courtship and a beautiful wedding." Ray turned to Neil Shinpaugh to be his best man. "Not too many of us were left around there then that ran around with Ray. Seems like it was just a late-minute deal, a whirlwind thing, and I was the one who was handy." Ella and the Archers, along with pharmacist Al Kurbitz and history teacher Roy Hoover and their wives sat on Ray's side of the aisle, but Ray's dad, afraid to leave his job in Chester, was missing from the festivities. Hoover was surprised when Ray invited him to his wedding. He hadn't been aware that Ray *had* a girlfriend; his wife, Marjorie, thought it was "probably the saddest, most poignant wedding I have ever been to in my life . . . because the feeling of caring between families that was missing.[29]

On a honeymoon trip to Seattle, the newlyweds checked into the modest Ray Hotel, but admired the huge red and white neon letters that spelled out *VANCE* on a nicer hotel across the street. That was a name to remember. In one of his notebooks, Carver writes of a man who can recall little about his wedding except that his fingernail kept snagging in his wife's negligee as they made love in a Seattle hotel.[30] That tiny image tells a great deal about Carver: his hypersensitivity to minutiae of the body—he wrote stories about a man with a hair stuck between his teeth and a man whose ear is clogged with wax, and poems about his toes and a numb arm. Maryann recalled that the huge struggle ahead of them began to hit her and Ray while they were in Seattle.

More romantic feeling is evinced in Carver's poem "Woman Bathing," which describes a summer afternoon of making love below a falls on the Naches River west of Yakima. Here the speaker dries his lover with his undershirt, seeing in the outline of her figure the clarity of a Picasso. They laugh, knowing that days like this one are fleeting: "Time is a mountain lion."

The Carvers' family doctor allowed the young couple to live rent-free in a basement below his office in exchange for keeping the office clean. Their apartment had three rooms, linoleum floors, and high windows, just like the one in Carver's story "Distance," where Carver has his character—"the boy"—sit down at the desk in the doctor's private office, put his feet up, and use the telephone and office stationery for personal business, playacting as more jaded couples do in Carver's stories of voyeurism like "Neighbors." Thus Ray and Maryann—teenagers still—imagined what it was like to have a professional office complete with desk and telephone.

Through the summer, Maryann's girlish body grew into a constant reminder of the gravity of their circumstances. She borrowed homemade maternity clothes from Violet Archer's daughter-in-law, who complained that they came back to her in poor condition.[31] The world around Ray and Maryann was changing, too, that fall: in the Carver family's home state of Arkansas, federal troops enforced the Supreme Court–ordered integration of Little Rock Central High School by nine Negro students, and Russia launched two *Sputnik* satellites (one carrying a dog) into space orbit. Jack Kerouac published *On the Road*.

Ray's daily life didn't change, however. He continued working as a clerk and delivery man for the Kurbitz Pharmacies. He wrote poems in longhand. He and Maryann visited Dick Moeller in Seattle and camped in the Cascade foothills. In "The Student's Wife," the character Nan describes in lush detail a camping trip when her husband read aloud to her from Elizabeth Browning and *The Rubiyat:*

> She lay there grinning the whole time, though, burrowed up against his warm body and tracing a finger across his chest while he read in this strong, boyish voice. Then he stood up, tall and white, his giant shadow climbing and dipping on the trunks of the other trees as he fiddled with the lantern . . . stars appeared overhead, sharp and glistening through the openings in the pine trees, and she could hear the swift river on the other side of the clearing. Then they made love.[32]

At Maryann's urging, in the fall Ray signed up for two classes at Yakima Junior College—History of Medieval Europe and Introduction to Philosophy—and he joined a literary club. He got Cs in both classes and picked up a smattering of medieval imagery that would show up later in his stories and poems. In the spring, he would continue with European History Since 1870 and sociology, earning Bs in both classes.[33]

C.R. hadn't attended Maryann and Ray's wedding because he was barely hanging on to his health and his job at Collins Pine. Late in the fall, he finally collapsed at the mill. From California, Ella called Ray and asked him to come help. He rode the bus to Chester, where he found C.R. hospitalized and in the midst of a nervous breakdown. There was little he and his mother could do but take James out of school and drive the whole family back to Yakima, where they knew the doctors and could be close to the wider family. The only time C.R. spoke on the long drive was when Ray "was speeding down a gravel road in Oregon and the car muffler came loose. 'You were going too fast,' he said."[34]

As James saw it decades later, "First my father lost his physical health, then he lost his emotional health." Certainly the work injury C.R. had suffered had something to do with his breakdown, but no clear diagnosis has been reported. James "heard it was a sawtooth cut that got infected and led to blood poisoning." Lead poisoning from filing room tools, with its known symptoms of fatigue and mental deterioration, cannot be ruled out, nor can the effects of depression and alcoholism.

In Yakima, C.R. received electroshock treatments. James and Ella moved into a cabin that Fred and Billie Carver owned, and Ella waitressed at Turf Recreation. James, who turned fifteen that year, worked ten or twelve hours a day picking fruit for a dollar an hour. Still they could not pay the hospital bills. C.R. lived, forever diminished and rarely able to work. Sometimes he and Ella and James received public assistance money, which they all found humiliating; usually they got by on what Ella and James could earn. Ella sold one of her most prized possessions, a Kelvinator Deepfreeze. The freezer had been a bulwark against hard times, kept full of her home-baked pies, along with venison and wildfowl the men had hunted. Its loss—like losing a refrigerator for the unemployed man in "Preservation"—felt like a last mooring giving way. To Ray at the time, his parents' predicament seemed disturbing and disgraceful. After one visit to the little cabin where they and James lived, Ray said, "I'd be ashamed if I cared about them any longer." Ray loved his father dearly, but he must have been angry with him for the weakness—alcoholism or injury or both—that prevented C.R. from being the father that he needed and wanted.[35]

Christine LaRae Carver was born December 2 at Valley Memorial Hospital, named in part for her father and grandfather. During the three days that Maryann stayed in the hospital, Christine's grandfather Clevie Raymond was two floors up in the psychiatric ward. When Ray told his dad that he'd become a grandfather, forty-four-year-old C.R. replied, "I feel like a grandfather."

As the Carver generations realigned, death seemed to prowl the edges of Ray's world. There was his father, a walking ghost it seemed now, whom he never mentioned outside of his family. Tommy Dorsey, the bandleader and sax player, drowned in his own drunken vomit not long after Ray heard him at Playland. In August 1957, Uncle Walter Carver in Arkansas, youngest brother of Ray's grandfather, shot himself with a .22-caliber pistol after he retired from his job as a railroad engineer. Then a man Ray knew, his employer's brother Dr. Ken Kurbitz, fell dead in his bathroom after dinner. To get his body out, a door had to be taken off its hinges. Ray, already developing the writer's habit of storing events for artistic retrieval, made an entry in a spiral notebook: "Removing the door for Dr. Kurbitz." Finding that note years later prompted him to write a poem called "Egress" about a time when, he said, he was young and happy and had no need for death and notebooks. Yet he wrote it down.[36]

Throughout the fall and winter of his first year of marriage, Ray continued to go hunting with Frank Sandmeyer, especially on Sunday afternoons. Maryann noticed that her husband often sat down to work on his poems on

Sunday evenings after a day of goose hunting. These two things—being out in the wild country and traveling within to find the words that sustained him—coincided for Ray. In time he would learn to use words to describe his family life too. Indeed, Carver's story "Distance," based on the winter Ray became a father, records one stage of that interior journey: ". . . he turned up the furnace and helped her bathe the baby. He marveled again at the infant who had half his features, the eyes and mouth, and half the girl's, the chin, the nose. He powdered the tiny body and then powdered in between the fingers and toes."

"Distance" is a classic frame story with a love story nestled inside. A father relates the story to his daughter, "a cool, slim, attractive girl" who has "passed safely through her adolescence into young womanhood." This grown-up daughter asks what it was like "when she was a kid." The father replies by telling her about the young couple who were her parents, calling them simply "the boy" and "the girl." The young couple "were very much in love. On top of this they had great ambitions and they were wild dreamers." Any new parent might recognize the way these two squirm and settle under the weight of their new responsibility. The girl needs to be told the boy loves her, and she flirts with him until he says the thing she wants to hear: "We'll always be together. We're like the Canadian geese, he said, taking the first comparison that came to mind, for they were often on his mind in those days. They only marry once . . ."[37]

When baby Catherine's cries awaken them, the boy and girl take turns rocking her through the small hours of the night. At one point, the boy swears and the girl's voice becomes edgy. The new father's estrangement is further indicated by his random switching of pronouns for the baby: sometimes *it*, sometimes *she*. As dawn nears and the boy puts on his hunting gear, the couple have their first argument. The baby is the cipher—neither knows if she/it is truly sick, neither has any way of knowing, and they are each deeply but differently frightened.

The situation whirls beyond compromise when the girl says: "I don't think you should even consider wanting to go under the circumstance." In that dialogue's inspired hash of verbs, Carver catches the essence of a domestic dilemma: an unfounded fear translates into a pseudo-reasonable demand. The girl's statement produces the opposite effect of what she wants. The boy steps out of the house with these words in his ears: "If you want a family you're going to have to choose. If you go out that door you're not coming back, I'm serious." The boy-husband chooses his family. He cooks bacon and the girl makes waffles. They dance and hold "each other as if there would always be that morning." The story represents what the writer Sherwood Anderson called a "moment of sophistication," when a young man hears "voices outside of himself whisper a message concerning the limitations of life."[38] And so it was, at the end of 1957, that Ray found himself virtually fatherless just as life called upon him to become a father.

Since leaving high school two years before, Ray had been looking for experiences that would make a writer of him. Not long after Christi was born, he proposed moving to Spain for a couple of years with the idea that Maryann could join him there after he found a cheap, sunny village to live in. No doubt Ray's fantasies of having a Hemingway sort of life were a bit far-fetched for a man of his background. As he'd done on the morning of his hunting trip, he would cling to his family. His adventures would be domestic.

To her own amazement, just six weeks after Christine's birth, seventeen-year-old Maryann discovered that she was pregnant. Her second baby was expected in October. By then she would be eighteen.[39]

Maryann understood that if she wanted marriage with Ray to work, she would have to "walk a tightrope between Ray's writing life and our family." She had even promised him that he would never have to choose between her and his writing.[40] At the beginning of June, to prove to Ray that another baby need not impede his dreams, Maryann went to work as a fruit packer. Her sister Jerry took care of Christi while Maryann stood at a conveyer belt and packed layer after perfect layer of cherries into pint boxes.

When she had saved enough money—it took about two weeks—Maryann quit the packing shed and took her earnings to the stationery store to pick up Ray's Father's Day present: his first typewriter.[41]

CHAPTER 6

Furious Years

August 1958–August 1960, Paradise and Chico, California

> . . . There it is
> we'd better acknowledge it and
> write it down that way, not otherwise.
> —William Carlos Williams,
> quoted by Raymond Carver in *Selection*,
> Chico State College, 1960[1]

At the beginning of his twentieth summer, Ray was living in a basement in his hometown with his infant daughter and pregnant wife and working at a boy's job. He owned a typewriter, and his wife admired his poems, but he'd made little other progress toward becoming a writer in the two years since he'd finished high school. By the end of that same summer, he would be enrolled at a four-year liberal arts college preparing to study literature and writing.

Like many pivotal changes in Ray's life, this one was driven by other people's serendipitous decisions. At Saint Paul's School, Maryann's sister Amy decided she'd had enough of boarding school. She wanted to join her former roommate at a public high school in San Mateo, California, and persuaded her mother to drive her there for a visit. Alice needed a fresh start too. She found a teaching job and an apartment in San Mateo, and headed back to Washington to pack.

Reluctant to leave Maryann behind, Alice thought about ways to bring her to California. As she passed through Chico, north of Sacramento at the top of the state's central valley, she was lured by signs pointing uphill toward PARADISE. Paradise, it turned out, was an old sawmill town with a scattering of vacation cottages. While Amy slept in the backseat, Alice saw a one-story, plywood-sided house with big porches at the end of a gravel road. It had a large yard with apple trees where children could play. Alice told Amy she was going to buy this house. She would let Ray and Maryann live there while Ray (and Maryann, she hoped) attended Chico State College. Back in Yakima, Alice cashed in her state teacher's retirement fund to make a down payment on the house in Paradise.[2]

To one generation after another, from Spanish ranchers to forty-niners, Dust Bowl migrants, and wartime defense workers, California had promised a new start, a chance at quick riches. Ray's parents' move there had been disastrous, but Ray still cherished his own version of gold rush dreams. As a teenager, his poem "The Cougar" says, he'd heard that in California there were buffet restaurants where a person could eat all he wanted. Food is Carver's metaphor for economic promise. It was important to Carver and represented other good things as well. One of these was an education; he was ready for that now. The two years since his graduation from high school had driven him toward adulthood and acquiescence. Through the changes, he continued to want to write "anything that involved putting words together to make something coherent and of interest to someone besides myself." He and Maryann believed that education would "open doors for us, help us get jobs so we could make the kind of life we wanted for ourselves and our children. We had great dreams, my wife and I. We thought we could bow our necks, work very hard, and do all that we had set our hearts to do."[3]

Ray gave notice at the pharmacy and borrowed $125 from Bill Barton.[4] He, Maryann, Amy, Alice, and baby Christi left Yakima in an old Chevy coupe with a bad muffler in July. They turned the move into a vacation, stopping at landmarks between the Northwest and California. Their first stop, Maryhill Museum, which Ray called "the strangest museum in the world," sits on a bluff above the Columbia River Gorge. Inside the mad museum built by Sam Hill (son of railroad magnate James J. Hill), the travelers saw Rodin sculptures, Russian icons, and miniature Parisian mannequins made by couturiers to revive their fashion industry after World War II. Outside a sign warns: "Don't walk on the grass as there are rattlesnakes here."[5] From Maryhill, they crossed to Oregon by ferry and drove west on another of Hill's projects, the elegant Columbia River Highway built by Italian stonemasons. By the time Maryann and Ray made the trip, a dam had destroyed the sacred native fishing site at Celilo Rapids. They stopped at the Bonneville Dam visitor center, where tiny speakers feebly emitted the sound of Woody Guthrie singing "Roll On, Columbia, Roll" and a jerky film explained the water cycle with photographs and language that bring to mind Carver's poem "Where Water Comes Together with Other Water."

For thirty years, Carver said, he continued to stop at Bonneville to see the windows that looked into the fish ladders, the sturgeon and trout ponds, and the dam itself. The Columbia River Gorge and the outlandish projects perpetrated there by dreamers and builders like Sam Hill and the U. S. Army Corps of Engineers had great importance in Carver's mind. Although he used but a handful of details about these landscapes and monuments in his work, the ones he chose reveal an ironic cast in his sensibility. As much as he is enchanted by the beautiful, wild country, he is also captivated by the dark oddities of the place.[6] Carver's poem "The Sturgeon" provides one example of the way he imports local details into his work: first, he recollects viewing, with his father, a dead nine-hundred-pound sturgeon "winched up in a corner" at the Central Washington State Fair. His father read aloud to him from a card about the freshwater bottom-feeder that was killed by "exploratory dynamiting" prior to the construction of Dalles Dam. Carver does not need to spell out that he finds it a strange kind of exploration that kills "something left over from another world."

From Bonneville, Ray and his female crew headed into their California future. Maryann, ill with her second pregnancy in two summers, suffered as daytime temperatures hovered above a hundred degrees at the northern end of the Sacramento Valley. As they got close to Chico, they saw grain fields and walnut orchards. This place didn't look like the California they'd seen in magazines and on television. What it resembled was south-central Washington. But the college campus was something else again: with old Italianate and Spanish-style buildings, wide lawns, sycamore and elm trees, and a rocky creek, it had the traditional appeal of a haven dedicated to learning. Ray turned in his application materials, looked inside the library, and decided to stay.

At the edge of Paradise a sign offers this wish: "May You Find Paradise to Be All Its Name Implies." When Alice and the others arrived, they found that her house wasn't ready for occupancy, so they celebrated Maryann's eighteenth birthday, bought "school clothes" for Ray, and saw some stage shows in Reno, Nevada. "Ray was always writing," Alice recalled. Back in Chico, Ray took aptitude tests, met with an advisor, and found a weekend clerking job at Terrace Pharmacy. He registered for classes and paid his tuition: $90 per semester for out-of-state residents (free for Californians), plus a materials-and-service fee of $22 per semester.

Ray wrote a funny, optimistic letter to Barton in Yakima, listing the classes he'd be taking for the year and making fun of himself—"a coward at heart" [and no Hemingway]—for choosing Tennis and General Physical Education rather than Boxing or Wrestling. He'd also be taking English, a speech class, Biology, Art Appreciation, History, and Fine Arts. The college looked good to him "per se" and had an enrollment of three thousand and a "huge" library (sixty-four thousand volumes). He complains that he is writ-

ing on a cigar box because there's wet paint on his desk. He says he's holding Christi, who has the measles, because he woke her up when he yelled at
Maryann to say that playing the radio would wake Christi up.[7]

With a desk in his study and new school clothes, Ray Carver was ready
for college. To get there, he drove down a steep red-rock canyon out of
the pine trees, through oak groves, and into Chico. A new professor that
year whom Ray admired was Dr. Lennis Dunlap (teachers with doctorates
were called "Doctor"), who'd been educated at Vanderbilt University and
the Sorbonne. Dunlap found the English Department "entirely dead." Dr.
Edgar Glenn, who taught Ray in the required freshman speaking and writing course, recalled Ray as "so soft-spoken that he couldn't be heard at the
back of the room."[8]

On October 19, 1958, a month after Ray's school started, Maryann gave
birth to their son at Enloe Hospital near the college campus. Vance Lindsay
Carver, ten and a half months younger than Christine, got his name from
the neon sign that had shone over his parents' honeymoon room in Seattle. But his name derived also from author Vance Bourjaily, whose novel
The Violated came out in 1958. Inevitably, a new baby strained Maryann
and Ray's very limited resources, but—as young and ambitious couples can
do—they took the addition in stride. Ray continued in school. When their
other expenses were paid, they had seven dollars a week left for groceries.
Thus began the years of what Carver later called "ferocious parenting,"
when he and Maryann met themselves "coming and going as we tried to
keep a roof over our heads and put bread and milk on the table."[9]

Vance was one month old and Christi eleven months when Maryann
realized that she would have to go to work in Chico; she spent most of a
rainy November day "pounding the pavements, asking for jobs in a slow
college town that had no industry and many, many students willing to work
for anything." At the end of that day, a former English major aptly called
Mr. Chips (Michael Cippola), owner of Chip's Coffee Shop, hired her even
though he already had enough waitresses. She worked six days a week from
seven in the morning until three. Most nights Maryann and Ray and Christi
and Vance clustered in one room of their thin-walled house to keep warm,
but Ray had a separate study where it was so cold he could see his breath.[10]
Ray and Maryann were not quite alone in their struggle. During vacations
from her teaching position, Alice visited her daughter and her property in
Paradise and helped with the babies.

Ella and C.R. and James came down from Yakima and moved into an
apartment in Chico, the beginning of six rootless years for them. They were
often on the periphery of Ray's life, often flat broke. James was not sure he

remembered all the high schools he attended—they included Chico, Red Bluff, Cottonwood, Eureka, and Fortuna in California, as well as Davis High in Yakima, where they retreated between attempts to settle in California.[11]

During one of those times in Yakima, Frank Sandmeyer had his last glimpse of C.R.:

> It was during a slow season at the mill when they were running a skeleton crew at the box factory. I looked up, and here come Ray Carver [Senior] walking in the back. He just looked at me and didn't stop to talk. He just says "hullo" in a muffled voice and went on walking through the box factory and out to the street. That was a strange thing. The other guys turned around and said, "What's the matter with Ray Carver?" And I said, "God, I don't know." And I never did find out. He must have just wanted to go down there and walk through the place he once worked. Didn't talk to nobody. He just disappeared again, and that's the last time I seen him.[12]

At forty-five, C.R. was now a husk of the father Ray loved and admired. In the two years since he'd left Chester, Carver wrote in "My Father's Life," his father had "lost everything in that time—home, car, furniture. . . . He'd lost his good name . . . and his self-respect was gone." Collins Pine disputed his claim for disability payments. Even if he had been capable of working at his old trade, there were very few jobs open because of a slump in the building industry. Carver didn't write those words about his father until years later, but C.R. cannot ever have been far from his son's mind. One episode that James, then fifteen, recalls, limns the pain the whole family must have experienced:

> We seemed to follow Ray and Maryann. Where they were living, my family would move. There was no reason for us to be in Chico except that Ray and Maryann were there. My mother was a waitress and my father washed dishes. I remember Ray and I going into a restaurant where my father was washing dishes—we saw him working there in the sweat and steam. It was terrible, and it seemed to me he was heartbroken.[13]

By the time Ray reached legal drinking age on May 25, 1959, he and Maryann and their babies had moved into the town of Chico. Ray detailed cars at a gas station and stopped for drinks with a bartender and rodeo cowboy named Billy Brown. The two went fishing together a couple times, and Ray told Billy he was going to write a book. Ray and his dad worked at a mill near the coast for part of the summer of 1959 while Maryann stayed in

Chico to work split shifts at the phone company. When fall classes began, Ray got a minimum-wage job in the campus library. Maryann postponed college to become a full-time telephone operator.[14]

In response to the launching of Sputnik, the National Defense Education Act of 1958 funded low-interest college loans of up to $1,000 per student per year. Ray borrowed $250 when the semester began in September 1959.[15] While Ray had immersed himself in literature and ideas during his first year at Chico, he was more excited about the second year because he would begin upper-level courses such as Shakespeare and Romantic Literature in his English major. But the best thing about the new year was an elective, English 20A, Creative Writing. A new hire, one Dr. John Gardner, was coming from Oberlin College in Ohio to take over the course. Gardner's doctorate from the University of Iowa was in medieval literature, but he was also rumored to be an actual writer of fiction.

No one knew then that in thirteen years this John Gardner would be a flamboyant and successful novelist who appeared on the cover of the *New York Times Magazine* with his long, white hair flowing to the shoulders of a black motorcycle jacket. By then Gardner had declared war between "those age-old enemies, the real and the fake" in his 1978 book *On Moral Fiction*. His novels *Grendel* and *The Sunlight Dialogues* were best sellers, and future generations of writers would esteem his writing guides, *The Art of Fiction: Notes on Craft for Young Writers* and *On Becoming a Novelist*. But those who knew Gardner at Chico might have imagined that he would become an important and influential figure in American literary life. At twenty-six, Gardner was intensely serious about literature and willing to work day and night to practice and inculcate his aesthetics. Three years later, as the college president urged Gardner to leave Chico State, he told him, "Son, I've got you figured for a race horse. What we need around here are more plough horses."[16]

But before that happened, Gardner took Ray and the rest of his Creative Writing class out to meet on the lawn and asked them a few questions. Then, Carver recounted, he "announced that he didn't think any of us had what it took to become writers—as far as he could see not one of us had the necessary *fire*. But he said he was going to do what he could for us . . . we were about to set off on a trip, and we'd do well to hold on to our hats."

These first-day pyrotechnics were meant to intimidate students who weren't serious. Carver stuck. ". . . I'd never laid eyes on a writer. And he was a writer, even though he hadn't published at the time." Gardner thought that writers had to possess particular traits—"verbal sensitivity, accuracy of eye, and a measure of the special intelligence of the storyteller"—and he believed he could help his students develop those traits.[17] Gardner thought, he wrote in *On Becoming a Novelist,* that a novelist needs "almost dae-monic compulsiveness." Gardner had that, even though to Ray he looked like a "square" in his "dark, severe-looking clothes." He was thin with fine facial features, a pale complexion made more dramatic by thick, black, crew-cut hair, and enormous energy. No doubt Carver expected a writer to have the means and discernment to own a stylish car, because he noted with disappointment that Gardner's black four-door Chevrolet with black-wall tires "didn't even have a car radio." More to Ray's taste was the fact that Gardner sat on his desk and chain-smoked in class. Some said Gardner lived on cigarettes and coffee with sugar or was "born with a quicker ratio to the passage of time than the rest of us." Lennis Dunlap and he banded together to enliven the English Department. They began a lecture series— Gardner spoke about modern novelists, but his interests were oceanic. In hopes of helping Gardner keep his job, a journalism professor filmed one of Gardner's lectures.[18] In a seventeen-minute film fragment called *Creative Writing,* Gardner stares straight into the camera, smokes incessantly and talks, without notes,

> about the differences between caricature and character in fiction. Gardner uses his own cartoons, which he draws for us on a chalkboard, to illus-trate the shallowness of caricature, and paintings, by Ken Morrow of the Chico State Art Department, to show the complexities of well-developed character. Along the way, he discusses philosophy, phrenology, ancient astrology, Dostoyevsky, Nietzsche, the Virgin Mary, race, and ax mur-derers. Chillingly, the film ends with Gardner in midsentence—it chatters and chops, the screen turns green, and it's over.[19]

Indefatigable, Gardner had undertaken a translation of *Sir Gawain and the Green Knight* and was planning a biography of Chaucer while at the same time working on several novel manuscripts. While in Chico, he wrote poems, started two magazines, worked in a local theater, and took care of their baby while his wife went to school.

Gardner affected Ray profoundly. Just as Ray had once been initiated into a cult of hunters by Sandmeyer, he now felt himself invited to join the guild of writers. In interview after interview in the 1980s, he praised his first mentor:

> I was simply electrified. . . . He was cut out of different cloth from any-one I'd ever met. He was very helpful . . . and I was at that particular point in my life where nothing was lost on me. Whatever he had to say went right into my bloodstream and changed the way I looked at things . . .

My life was pretty boxed in, but I'd learned things from him and even if I couldn't put these things into practice immediately, the things I learned were longstanding and abiding.[20]

The semester's assignment was to write one story and then revise it until it satisfied Gardner. He rarely lost patience with rereading stories, and by this process he taught Ray that "a writer found what he wanted to say in the ongoing process of *seeing* what he'd said." Gardner favored traditional structures in stories and drew plot diagrams. Carver didn't care for "that side of things" but took from it the lesson that writing was about more than self-expression and that the best writing had always come from a serious attempt to write in a particular form. During the year that Carver studied with him, Gardner and Lennis Dunlap began writing an anthology text called *Forms of Fiction* that included sections of fables, tales, sketches, and yarns as well as short stories.[21] The book came out from Random House in 1962. Its table of contents includes most of the authors who would shape Carver's sense of fiction.[22]

Joan Gardner often came to class with her husband. To her it seemed that "about half of the students were either in wheelchairs or had spent time in prison or in mental hospitals. They thought they had stories to tell, and their counselors had placed them there because it sounded possible. [By contrast,] Ray was a very quiet chap." John Gardner could be harsh and sarcastic about strategies he considered "cheating," by which he meant keeping "necessary information away from the reader in the hope of overcoming him by surprise at the end . . ." For his students, Gardner ordered heavy black binders just like his own to keep their work in. "We carried our stories in those binders, special, exclusive, singled out from others." During this year, too, Ray began using a spiral-bound notepad to write down story situations, scraps of remembered detail, and beginnings of stories; despite using names and locales from Ray's experience, these notes preserve a storyteller's detachment. Ray was not keeping a personal journal; he was keeping a writer's notebook.[23]

Gardner was a crusader for literature who believed that art could have a moral impact. Early in the term, he passed out a reading list of thirty-seven novelists arranged in three groups: Major Figures, Secondary Figures, and Novelists of the Fifties. Except for Faulkner, Hemingway, and Henry James, the major figures are European (Camus, Dostoyevsky, Gide, Kafka, Mann, Proust, Tolstoy) and British (Joyce Cary, Conrad, Forster, Graham Greene, Woolf). "He was amazingly arrogant," Carver recalled. He said "he was there to tell us which authors to read as well as teach us to write." Gardner lugged piles of little magazines and journals into class and talked about each one, emphasizing that *living* authors had written the work on these pages. Hearing this, Ray "felt wild with discovery."[24] That remote world of "authorship" touted in the Palmer correspondence course was suddenly within reach. One of the journals was *Perspective,* edited by Jarvis Thurston, who had taught Gardner. From Gardner's explanation, Carver formed a simple, intensely personal idea of a literary career that stuck with him: one submits work to small journals and eventually finds immortality on college reading lists.

The distance between submission and canonization was almost as much a mystery to Gardner the teacher as it was to Carver the student. He was still trying to break into the literary journals himself. His only publications were two short stories in student magazines, one of which he'd edited. In Gardner's class, Ray wrote "The Aficionados," marking the end of his experiments with outdoor writing and science fiction.[25] In it he reached beyond pulp fiction, but the story retains a kind of mysteriousness that comes from lack of depth: you wonder why people do what they do because the author does not know himself. Still, Gardner recognized Carver's promise and understood that Ray needed a quiet place to work. In fact, as Gardner told the story later, he saw Carver as "brilliant but desperately poor."[26] He invited Ray to use his college office and typewriter on weekends. The gesture gave Ray more than a place to work. It admitted him to the consecrated and private place where Gardner committed words to paper; here, in Ray's mind, he, too, could be a professor and a writer.

The Gardners and Carvers did not become personal friends. Though they both had young families (the Gardners' first child was born in Chico at the end of 1959), there was a five-year difference of age and education between them. Joan Gardner recalled an incident from those days:

> One Sunday morning, John needed a stack of papers from his office and parked behind the building. I waited in the car with Joel and noticed a car with two unattended small children inside in those bouncy, worthless carriers of the time. When John came down, I asked him if he knew whose car and children they were, and he grimaced and bounded back up the steps again. They were Ray's kids, and we took them home with us, offering to take them whenever we could, which we did a few times, but warning Ray not to leave them alone again. I do remember Ray's being more worried that we would tell his wife than he was about the children.

Joan Gardner met Maryann a few times and thought "she seemed as tired as anybody I ever saw." Ray came to the Gardners' apartment for private conferences: "Sometimes he was hangdog when he came in and other times he was the opposite. I did think there was something dangerous about him, in his reluctance to smile."[27] Ray had become terribly thin, too, perhaps from smoking and nervous tension as well as a tight grocery budget.

In conferences, Gardner bore down on Ray: ". . . he took my stories more seriously, read them closer and more carefully, than I had any right to expect. I was completely unprepared for the kind of criticism I received from him." Gardner was sure of himself and a relentless marker of manuscripts. He deleted words, phrases, and sentences and "gave me to understand that these deletions were not negotiable." Items he bracketed were debatable: "We'd discuss commas in my story as if nothing else mattered more at that moment . . ." Sometimes, too, Gardner inserted a word or a sentence "to make clear what I was trying to say." He taught Ray to prefer common words over "pseudopoetic" ones (*ground,* not *earth,* for instance) and showed him the value of contractions. Ray was sensitive to criticism, but Gardner found enough to praise, writing "nice" or "good" in the margin now and then. When he saw those comments, Ray's "heart would lift." Gardner applied a single principle to all stories: "if the words and the sentiments were dishonest, the author was faking it, writing about things he didn't care about or believe in, then nobody could ever care anything about it."[28]

Pat Brice, who also studied with Gardner in Chico, remembers meeting her mentor at the old Hotel Oaks, a faculty hangout near campus, for a conference. He offered her a lesson about dialogue that Carver probably got too. "People are so funny. Listen to them. Go out. Knock on doors. Say you want to rent an apartment. Just listen." Once when Brice told Gardner he looked tired, he replied, "I was up all night writing. But I'm lucid."[29]

Perhaps the most useful thing Carver learned from Gardner was that a serious and passionate writer might also be an unpublished writer. When Carver used Gardner's office, he saw stacks of correspondence from other writers and editors and boxes of manuscripts, including an early version of *Nickel Mountain,* a novel he later published, heaped on the floor beside the desk. Carver was desperate to publish, but the sight of those *stacks* of pages gave him reason to hope and be patient in the years to come. Carver joked later that he snooped through Gardner's manuscripts and stole his titles, "which struck me as awfully good," until Gardner "had to give me a little lecture on the basic proprieties and the like."[30]

Carver would pay tribute to Gardner in a foreword to the latter's *On Becoming a Novelist;* within the text of that same volume, Gardner praises his own mentor at Chico State, the "infuriatingly stubborn perfectionist" Lennis Dunlap: "Night after night for two full years we would work for five, six, seven hours on what sometimes added up to three or four sentences. . . . I came to feel as unwilling as he was to let a sentence stand if the meaning was not as unambiguously visible as a grizzly bear in a brightly lit kitchen." Gardner showed his fiction to Dunlap just as Carver showed his to Gardner. Dunlap's advice, Gardner tells us, was frequently wrong—they were too different in background and experience for it to be otherwise—but he learned from Dunlap that "a writer must take infinite pains" and that "I must figure out on my own what was wrong with my fiction."[31] Likewise, Carver sometimes found his teacher's advice hard to take. Later he told one correspondent that he found Gardner too intellectual and "hard to come up against" and another that he was "haunted" by his influence because they had a difficult love-hate relationship as teacher and student. Carver absorbed "everything from him at the time except his life's blood," he recalled. Later again, he was grateful to Gardner for "putting up with my brashness and general nonsense."[32]

Under Gardner's tutelage, Ray wrote his story "Furious Seasons." Maryann attended the workshop on that story and recalled that Gardner "taught the hell out of it."[33] The story juxtaposes bloody, violent acts with intimate domestic details. In it, one easily recognizes the precision of Carver's later stories, and one also notices an enormous amount of fecund detail, particularly about landscape and weather, that occurs less often in later Carver stories. The construction of the narrative—there are thirteen distinct episodes—is more complex than anything else Carver wrote. "Furious Seasons" concerns a man named Lew Farrell, who is married to a woman named Lorraine. Lew's older sister Iris is staying with him and Lorraine for a few months, waiting for a job to begin in Seattle. Lorraine is reluctant to have her sister-in-law at their house, but Lew sees no alternative. They bring her to Yakima and allow her to sleep on their porch. It gradually emerges that Lew has an incestuous interest in Iris.

Early readers noticed Carver's manipulation of the present and past tenses, which appear to be reversed from their usual functions. The story opens with a scene that sets up a moment of decision: Lorraine leaves the house, and then Lew waits in his living room for Iris to come out of her bath. She tells him she is pregnant. "What are you going to do?" Lew asks her. As he asks the question, Lew feels that his words are "dry, hurrying like old leaves into the dark corners of the room" and knows his sister's breasts are "round and smooth-looking, the nipples like the stems of the warm porcelain fruit on the living room table." Once the old sensuality between brother and sister had been suggested, the story intercuts scenes in Lew's mind with scenes of a hunting trip Lew takes with his older friend Frank. Carver ratchets his cumbersome narrative forward, laying down detail as he peels back layers of emotion until, finally, in the last present-tense scene, he implies that Lew has murdered Iris. The story ends with Lew, who's about to be arrested, holding the tail fin of a sheriff's car. The point of view pulls back to what Frank sees in his rearview mirror:

> Farrell holding onto the tail fin, swaying a little, with the fine impenetrable rain coming down around him. The gutter water rushed over his feet, swirled frothing into a great whirlpool at the drain on the corner and rushed down to the center of the earth.

The last phrase is an inaccuracy of the type Gardner (and eventually Carver) deplored: rainwater does not flow to the center of the earth no matter how disastrous Lew Farrell's moral condition.[34]

It would seem that Carver used all the arrows in his quiver for "Furious Seasons." The core events—incest and murder—may be a beginner's effort to construct an armature of plot for a story that is rich in imagery and attempts to develop character. Young writers, instructed that stories require conflict, often take conflict to mean violence. Despite its excesses, "Furious Seasons" manages to present Lew's mind and history without baldly telling his thoughts. "Furious Seasons" shows the influence of Faulkner, whom Gardner had urged Ray to read. Poe and D. H. Lawrence also lurk in its shadows. Nonetheless, this story disrupts many assumptions about Carver's style and raises questions about his emotional life.

Certainly "Furious Seasons" is tethered by autobiographical impulses. The hunting scenes and the character based on Frank Sandmeyer are familiar, but the incest theme is more complicated. The narrator of a later story, "Distance," says that as a young husband he was "a little in love" with his wife's older sister "just as he was in love with Betsy, the girl's younger sister who was only 15 then." From the time they all moved to California, Amy visited Ray and Maryann often and stayed with them during transitions in her turbulent life. If the violent plot of "Furious Seasons" has a personal basis, it could be in the emotional nexus of Ray's feelings for the Burk sisters. Certainly Carver had no qualms about using the most intimate family material in his stories, but he also felt no restraint about exaggerating that material to make his stories more dramatic. Notes for another story on this subject mention an "affair" with a sister-in-law who had drunk too much beer and a wife learning of the incident at an Independence Day gathering. Like most of Carver's story ideas, that one is sketched out in the third person—it exists in his imagination and isn't about himself. Whatever feelings might have occurred in their youth, Maryann's sisters remained Ray's good friends throughout his life.[35]

• • •

Gardner encouraged his creative writing students to begin a literary magazine. Ray and another English major, Nancy Parke, volunteered to edit it
and were "two of the most harried-looking people on campus" when the
Chico *Wildcat* interviewed them in March 1960. To put out the magazine,
the editors raised money from faculty and friends, but then peculiar things
happened, "like when we found Christi (Ray's two-year-old daughter) eating our best poems," Parke told the newspaper. Ray responded to a question about the magazine's mission: "Some people have asked, you know, if
we're fighting [for] any particular cause. We aren't. Our only intent with
Selection is to publish good writing: good stories and poems. We aren't
devotees of any particular school—San Francisco or Existential or Angry
Young Men—of writing."[36]

Ray was not being vain in that claim. His first issue of *Selection* included
a previously unpublished poem by William Carlos Williams called "The
Gossips." When Ray asked Edgar Glenn to donate to the magazine, Glenn
suggested he write to Williams for a poem, believing "he'd be the sort of
person who would do that—approachable and kindly." The poem appears
with an introduction by one "R.C.": "This tell-it-as-you-see-it belief in
poetry, holding that, chiefly, poetry is communication, as well as feeling, is
underscored in Williams' poetry by a deep sense of human kind. His concentration upon the specific as it relates to and discovers itself in the universal, has been one of the sustaining themes in his poetry for the last 50
years . . ."[37] Ray Carver was defining his taste. At fifty cents apiece, three
hundred copies of *Selection* sold out quickly. Contributors' notes from its
nine writers sketch a group of older students who wrote at Chico, including army veterans and young fathers. At twenty-one, Ray had helped set up
a literary circle and become one of its leaders. Another of them, Jon Remmerde, noticed Ray's focus on his work. When a party went on too long at
Ray's house one night when Ray wanted to write, he simply brought the
guests their coats.[38]

Life was piling up on Ray. His babies were on their feet and running full
tilt. Maryann, approaching her twentieth birthday, was not a kid anymore.
After three years of marriage, motherhood, and work, she was lonely and
eager to see some of their dreams become realities. Her little sister, Amy,
had graduated from high school and was having a good time in the Bay
Area, dating a man who had sports cars and boats; she planned to start college at Chico in the fall. Ella, Raymond Senior, and James had returned to
Yakima, leaving Ray and Maryann on their own with the two toddlers.
When Jerry King stopped to visit, he witnessed a scene that seemed squalid
to him: Ray, having a beer in the middle of the day, tossed crackers across
the room to keep the kids busy while he did his homework. As Ray remem-

bered those years, "My wife and I did not have any money. We did not have any skills. We did have a lot of dreams. When we had the children we were not grown up ourselves. . . ."[39]

Ray felt effaced by the swirl of life around him, a feeling that comes through in a two-page story written about this time. In "The Father," the women of a family cluster around the beribboned bassinet of a baby boy, asking whom he resembles. A little girl says the baby looks like Daddy. The females turn together to stare at the father, who sits with his back to them in another room:

> "Daddy doesn't look like anybody!" Alice said.
>
> "But he has to look like *somebody*," Carol said.
>
> "But he doesn't look like anybody," Phyllis said, wiping her eyes with one of the ribbons. And all of them except the grandmother looked at him again sitting at the table. He had turned around in his chair and his face was white and without expression.

Yet Ray was accomplishing what he'd come to California to do. He was halfway through college. At the end of his second year at Chico State, he had accumulated fifty-nine semester credits and a C-plus grade average (2.83).[40] He was a writer. But he was at a crossroads. The vision of a writer's life that he had formed from his correspondence course no longer seemed credible. He didn't seem to be cut out to write the kind of pulp and popular fiction he'd once admired. John Gardner had inculcated in him the desire to write literature; he had also shown him the near impossibility of earning a living by such writing.

The more difficult Ray's circumstances seemed for writing, the more determined he became. He made adjustments, choosing shorter forms rather than longer ones, embracing the troubles of his life by turning them into stories, but there's nothing in his notes or history to suggest he doubted his vocation. "We thought we could do it all," Ray said. "We were poor, but we thought if we kept working, if we did the right things, the right things would happen."[41]

To keep his sanity, Ray segregated aspects of his life—keeping school, parents, and family separate. Maryann was the only person to whom he confided his secrets, worries, and hopes. Her shoulders were thin, but her willpower was prodigious.

CHAPTER 7

A Story of He and She

August 1960–August 1963, Eureka and Arcata, California

The struggle itself towards the heights is enough to fill a man's heart.
We have to imagine Sisyphus happy.
— Albert Camus, *The Myth of Sisyphus*

In the summer of 1960, Ray and Maryann moved to a town with another promising name, Eureka, on the northern coast of California in redwood country. With hindsight, it appears odd that Ray separated himself from a teacher like John Gardner. It may be that Ray was ready to detach himself from Gardner's gravitational pull and establish his own orbit.

But financial need also motivated the Carvers' move to Eureka. Ray could get good-paying jobs in Humboldt County's lumber mills and finish his bachelor's degree at Humboldt State College in Arcata. After spending most of his life on the dry side of the mountains, he would be living in a damp coastal climate where a favorite local word is *frizzle* (freezing drizzle). Eureka was then the largest California town north of Sacramento, but culturally and geographically it belonged to the Pacific Northwest. Its cloudy coastal skies were then always hazed by smoke from the sawdust burners of dozens of sawmills.

Maryann transferred to the Eureka office of Pacific Telephone. She and Ray rented an apartment briefly and then moved to a ramshackle ranch house at the south edge of town. C.R., who'd partially recovered his health, was a janitor at a mill where his brother filed saws in Fortuna. James and Ray worked there, too, stacking lumber, but Ray later got hired by the Simpson Plywood Mill in Eureka.[1] He made good money working four hours a day, but the job was dangerous. "I had terrible nightmares when he worked on a device the workers called 'the Hog,' which ground up odd-sized poles, sticks, and the odd man that fell into it."[2] Ray disliked the work, but he listened to the other workers, jotting down things he found funny—

like arguments they had over facts such as how many ounces there are in a pound of gold. One night he was put in to replace a Portuguese man whose heart gave out on the job. That year in Eureka was tough on Maryann: "I'd get a paycheck every two weeks, and within half an hour, the money would be gone. By the time I paid the babysitter and all the bills, there was nothing left, and then I'd work another two weeks being dead broke all the time. I worked days, and Ray went to school days and worked in a mill at night."[3]

Eureka had been a flamboyant frontier town, settled by New England seamen and woodsmen. The old waterfront neighborhood called Two Street was still rough when the Carvers arrived. Mill workers had rioted and held off police the year before, and throughout the 1960s, the area's bars, poolrooms, flophouses, and sex trade remained largely beyond police control.[4] That skid row intrigued and frightened Ray; it is the scene of Ralph Wyman's descent to the underworld in his story "Will You Please Be Quiet, Please?"

At Humboldt State College, Forestry Management and Fisheries and Wildlife Management have long been popular majors. The college's Spanish-style buildings stand on a hillside above the town of Arcata at the north end of Humboldt Bay. Ray enrolled in two classes offered by Richard Cortez Day, who had arrived at HSC the year before with a fresh PhD in fiction writing from the University of Iowa. Carver then trailed Day around campus for a week before he "got up the nerve to even speak to him."[5] Whereas Ray credited John Gardner as the teacher who first inspired and intimidated him, teaching him to be tough on himself, Dick Day became both mentor and friend, a partner in the struggle to write well. The Ray Carver who caught up with Day barely resembled the kid who had left Yakima two years before. He had given up attempts to look cool and regarded his earlier look as one of "embarrassing immaturity; oily, carefully combed hair and loud, half-baked ideas about Life and Art."[6] Now Ray had a nondescript short haircut and, Day thought, was "almost invisible as a person. He was tall and thin and stooped. He looked undernourished and weak. He was nervous." He dressed conservatively in slacks and cheap, collared shirts. He could be in a large group, and afterward no one would remember he was there. Horn-rimmed eyeglasses obscured his steady, deep blue, wary eyes. "You didn't really see the eyes unless you looked for them through the glass, and then you'd notice that they were intensely watchful. They weren't missing a thing."[7]

Day taught a "nuts and bolts" writing course. "I asked them to write stories till I got one I thought everyone could learn from to have reproduced for the class." Ray submitted "The Aficionados," one that Gardner had already seen. "I knew," Day recalled, "this was the real thing, and

I thought a teacher of creative writing only gets one writer like this in a lifetime, and I got mine the first time out." Day believed that a real writer needed: a sense of narrative, a skill for using detail to establish a reality, and a voice. A voice was "a real gift, a true sign of whether a person is a writer or not." Right from the start, Ray's voice was "authentic, personal, and compelling." In the months and years ahead, the individuality Day heard in the stories showed itself in Carver's apprehension of unusual perspectives and details. At first Ray "barely participated in the critique sessions and was reluctant to read his own work," Day said. "The fiction he liked to talk about would be Chekhov's or Kafka's or Hemingway's. And the way he liked to talk about it was the way I like to talk about it, which was 'Look what he does here!' Or 'How does he manage to do that?' He was always interested in the ways stories were told."

Day told Carver that he should look closer to home for his material. After that, "he began giving me stories about mill workers, about husbands and wives with children, trapped by poverty, and losing everything little by little." Some of the stories he turned in were "The Father," "Pastoral," and "The Night the Mill Boss Died." The latter two make abundantly clear that the spare, minimalist style for which Carver later became known was distilled from a rich harvest of details. Here is a passage from "Pastoral," a story of an old man on a fishing trip that may reflect Ray's understanding of his father's infirmity:

> He could still see his breath, fogging out in front of him. He held the heavy rod straight ahead of him when he had to push through the bushes or go under the trees with low limbs, cradled up under his arm like it was a lance. . . . he'd imagine himself in the lists coming down on his opponent. The jays at the crowded edge of the woods screaming for him. Then, when it was over, he would sing something as loud as he could. Yell defiance till his chest hurt, at the hawks that circled and circled the meadow . . . The trail was gone and just before he started down the bank to the river, he stepped into a snow drift up over his knees and panicked, clawing up handfuls of snow and vines to get out.[8]

Even when his character was closer to himself, Carver learned to put his details in service of his imagination. As Day explained: "Ray's imagination made those stories out of autobiographical elements, and he's a realistic writer, so everything seemed real. But what happens in life gets a different coloring, a different emphasis, appears out of order, so the story itself has integrity." In "The Night the Mill Boss Died," Carver began with an episode he'd witnessed—a man collapsing from a heart attack at the mill. In

Ray's notebook, the mill keeps running; in his short story, the mill shuts down, leaving the mill worker to spend an evening home alone with his wife. For a setting, he uses a town by a lake that sounds more like Chester than Eureka. Atmosphere permeates the story: wind or rain, reflections and shadows, sounds heard and imagined. The husband is a sensitive, thoughtful fellow who has difficulty saying what troubles him. Though he is inelegant in speech, he carries on a dialogue with himself: "They lay on their sides facing each other, lips almost touching. He wondered if his own breath smelled as clean as hers." He's bothered by the death and by a careless remark he made to the other men, but can say only that he wants to move: "I'd kind of like to go back home and see my folks. Or maybe go up to Oregon. That's nice country." Once his wife has fallen asleep, the man is alone with his malaise. He stares out the window but can see nothing. "He ran his finger across the wet drool on the glass and then pulled the shade." Drool! As if the weather were a monster invading his home. Back in bed, he hears the mill whistle: "It shrilled across the lake and the timber and over the little town and pierced his ears. . . . It kept piercing." Every detail in the atmosphere seems like a personal assault to the man. "He moved closer to her warmth and put his hand on her hip. . . . 'Wake up,' he whispered, 'I hear something outside.' "[9]

At Humboldt, under Professor Thelwell Proctor, Ray developed an affinity for Russian writers: "I read something in a letter by Chekhov that impressed me. . . . it went something like this: Friend, you don't have to write about extraordinary people who accomplish extraordinary and memorable deeds."[10] In the Russians, Ray found more evocative subject matter than the Americans and British offered, from the gritty realism of Dostoyevsky's poor city dwellers to the explorations of marriage and sexual relationships in Tolstoy and the intricacies of loneliness in Chekhov. When Ray named the writers he admired, Chekhov always topped his list.

Carver had Chekhov's 1886 story "The Chemist's Wife" in mind when he drew upon his Humboldt County days to write "The Student's Wife" a couple of years later. Both Chekhov and Carver describe a wife who cannot sleep. In Chekhov's tale, the wife waits on two men who come to the chemist's shop in the early dawn hours. They flirt with her, causing her to declare, "You officers ought to come in oftener from the camp . . . it's awful how dreary it is here." The chemist, oblivious to his wife's unhappiness, snores while she cries bitterly at the story's end. In Carver's rendition, the wife suffers comparably, but turns to her husband for relief that, finally, he cannot provide. The wife's face resembles Maryann's: "She had a smooth-skinned, pale slender face with prominent cheekbones; the cheekbones, she sometimes insisted to friends, half humorously and half fiercely proud, were from her father, who had been one-quarter Nez Perce."[11] The couple in the story have a daughter and a son and live in an apartment building under "a massive blanket of dark clouds." The husband—the student— reads poetry to his wife in bed in a voice that Ray must have wished was his own: "confident, sonorous, pitched low and somber one minute and then rising, clear and sharp the next." The wife drifts off to sleep but wakes up again when the husband turns out the light. From here on, the story lurches forward in a comic mismatch of desires, the wife wanting talk and attention, the husband wanting to sleep. " 'Don't go to sleep before me,' she said. 'I don't want to be awake by myself.' "

But he does go to sleep. She spends her sleepless hours trying to trick herself into sleep, thinking of her dead father, crying, paging through magazines, watching a "baleful" "empty-looking and devastating" sunrise, and at last, praying, "God, will you help us, God?"

"The Night the Mill Boss Died" and "The Student's Wife" are the first among many Carver stories that delicately examine the interior lives of married couples. Together these two form he-she bookends, each coming to a close at a moment when one spouse is asleep and the other is awake and frightened. In both stories, Carver uses a nimble third-person point of view that distributes his imaginative understanding of the story situation between characters.

There is tenderness and fear in these early marriage stories; they convey early warning signs. Though Maryann continued to read some of Ray's course assignments, help him study, and coach him on papers, his level of formal education had bypassed hers. If she had begun college right after she graduated from high school, she would have been finished in 1961. A new decade was beginning, her babies were becoming little children, Ray had become a writer, yet she was still spending her days as a wage slave. She saw no future for herself. Ray was sensitive to Maryann's predicament—after all, he wrote the story about it—but he could not correct the situation. He was nearly consumed by the quest that the two of them had begun together.

Ray saw his work in print for the very first time in the spring of 1961: "Furious Seasons" came out in *Selection* at Chico State, and "The Father" appeared in the Humboldt student magazine, *Toyon*. The next year, he decided to take his degree in General Studies rather than English so he could avoid foreign language requirements. Although Ray wrote some "superb" papers for his literature classes, he asked Day at the end of one course, "How would you feel if I don't turn the paper in?" In reply, Day asked his student how he'd feel about a C. "Ray replied, 'Fine.' Because he was working on a story. So, like anybody with any sense, Ray chose the story." And took the C.[12]

• • •

Family problems sometimes flashed up like wildfire. While Ray and Maryann struggled through a dismal year in Eureka, Amy Burk was working a
secretarial job in the Bay Area and dating a married private detective seven
years older than herself. Maryann and Ray liked Harry Leonard Olliffe, but
Ray believed that Olliffe was divorced.

On May 11, 1961, Ray and Maryann learned that Olliffe had been mur-
dered by his blonde wife, Sally Olliffe. The San Francisco *Chronicle* called
Harry the "Beatnik Cop" because he had worked as an undercover drug
agent with the San Mateo Sheriff's Office. Before she shot her husband,
Sally said, he had asked her to wear her sexiest dress and meet him at the
Red Barn tavern. He wanted her to flirt with strangers while he watched.
When Sally didn't show, Harry came to her apartment, and she shot him
with his own police revolver, which she'd found in a suitcase of his dirty
laundry that he had ordered her to wash. A day later, the *Chronicle* ran a
large photograph of Amy Burk, the "Beatnik Cop's Other Blonde." The
police captain said that Amy was "the nicest, most clean-cut kid we've ever
had to interrogate in a case like this."

Maryann and Ray rushed to Amy's side. More articles on Olliffe's two
blondes followed. Amy told reporters that Harry always treated her "like
a lady" except on one occasion when he beat her after she asked him when
they could be married. People snooped around outside Amy's house at
night and made obscene and threatening phone calls. Someone tossed a
rock with a message attached through a window. Amy, sedated, had hallu-
cinatory nightmares of Harry coming up the stairs, while Ray was too terrified to sleep at all. Maryann, presumably, tried to keep the other two calm.

After Olliffe's funeral, a five-column photograph showed Amy crying
alone on a bench in the cemetery next to his coffin at Golden Gate National
Cemetery. Gradually Amy's grief turned to anger. When Sally went on trial,
Amy attended to "help Sally, if possible." *Chronicle* articles called Sally
"the honey blonde" and Amy "the strawberry blonde." Apparently Sally's
own tale of horror was sufficient for her defense, for Amy was not called to
the witness stand. The jury of six women and six men acquitted Sally Olliffe
on July 19, 1961.[13]

Amy's ordeal suggested to Ray a strange little story, little more than
a twisted joke, really, called "Harry's Death." It's the rare case in which
knowing the background adds coherence to a Carver story. Carver's version omits the cause of Harry's death and focuses on trivia and atmosphere.
A coworker of the deceased Harry says, "Harry was an operator . . . good
with women, if you know what I mean, always had money and lived high
. . . always came out smelling like a rose." The men in the Red Fox where

Harry drank exchange boozy platitudes—"Anybody but Harry"—and take up a collection for a floral spray, which the narrator purchases. When the narrator takes Harry's girlfriend, Little Judith, "to Golden Gate Cemetery to put a pot of flowers on Harry's grave," they cannot locate his plot. In no time, the narrator seduces Harry's Little Judith, marries her, and sails with her to Mexico in Harry's boat. She drowns "accidentally," and the narrator keeps the boat.

Carver published "Harry's Death" some fifteen years later. What prompted him to preserve so slight a piece? The story expresses scorn for this Harry who made such a mess of his own life and death and brought suffering into Ray's family. Perhaps, too, there's anger over the emotion that Amy had expended on the likes of Harry Olliffe. The not-accidental death of Little Judith may represent the death of Amy's youth and first promise. By taking a sarcastic, outsider's view of the soap-opera event that had so engrossed the family, Ray deflates and critiques Amy's extravagant romance. Indeed, "Harry's Death," with its pallid machismo, barroom talk, and choppy prose, marks Carver's good-bye to pulp fiction, and perhaps to Hemingway as well.

The celebrity who had been Ray's first writer hero killed himself with a double-barreled shotgun in Ketchum, Idaho, on July 2, 1961. Like Ray's dad, Hemingway had been depressed by injuries and alcoholism and further damaged by electroshock treatments meant to help him. Carver honored Hemingway for his belief that "fiction must be based on actual experience" and later came to believe it "was not entirely coincidental" that shortly after Hemingway's death, antirealist writing gained ascendancy in American fiction. Hemingway's credo, Carver felt, defined what a writer should do: "his invention, out of his experience, should produce a truer account than anything factual can be."[14]

Another early-1960s event changed the Carvers' lives, too: the U.S. Food and Drug Administration approved an oral contraceptive, Enovid. The little plastic case holding twenty tablets for the month liberated women from fear of pregnancy for the first time in history. Like millions of other women, Maryann felt "free at last."[15] Then John Fitzgerald Kennedy, elected president in November 1960, took the national stage with his wife, daughter, and son. Ray, in Maryann's eyes, was a tall, blue-eyed man of the future like Jack Kennedy. But the future also held menace: race murders and riots in Alabama, Adolf Eichmann's trial and further revelations of Nazi atrocities, the failure of the Bay of Pigs invasion of Cuba, Nikita Khrushchev's ultimatums to Kennedy about Berlin. In response to the Russian threat, Kennedy called up Army Reserve forces and tripled military draft calls. All this anticommunism fortified the defense loan program that helped pay for Ray's education, giving him about $500 a semester. And it reminded him of his unfulfilled military obligation.

One May morning in 1961, "something snapped" in Maryann during a coffee break at the telephone company. She left the building, saying she was ill, and drove to Humboldt State College. She persuaded the registrar to call long-distance for her SAT scores, enrolled in college, and arranged for loans and scholarships to pay her fees. Back in Eureka, she quit her job. She had decided their days of wage slavery had to end, even if that meant taking out more loans.

Nonetheless, their plans had to zig before they zagged. Ray decided to spend a year writing full time, so they headed to a farmhouse on Val Burk's land in Washington for the summer. As Carver's story "How About This?" tells it, their rural experiment was doomed from the start: "All the optimism that had colored his flight from the city was gone now, had vanished the evening of the first day, as they drove north through the dark stands of redwood." Ray had imagined a cozy house with a fireplace. What he found was no electricity, a woodstove, no end of chores, and another man in charge. Worse, Maryann wrote, he learned that "His belief that he could write anywhere *if only he had the time* was simply untrue." They returned to the safer ground of Humboldt State.[16]

Ray took out more student loans himself, quit his mill job, and lined up a comfortable, low-paying job at the college library. "Ray had paperbacks coming out of his pockets," librarian David Palmer said.[17] Like Ray's mother, Maryann had a genius for finding jobs. "You could drop Maryann into any town in the country and within an hour she would have a job," Day believed. In the fall of 1961, she waitressed at Sambo's coffee shop, where a long, curved counter gave Ray the setting for "They're Not Your Husband." On a good day, she made ten dollars an hour in tips alone. From here forward, Ray and Maryann shared a goal: "not to sell out Ray's writing, to not have him get involved in some other career that would make him forget what he really was here on earth to do; that's how he looked at it, and I did, too."[18] To do this, they relied on student loans and her part-time job.

After Harry Olliffe's death, Amy Burk also began college at HSC, where she lived in a dorm and became part of the Carvers' social circle. She took courses with Day, who recalled: "Amy was a blonde, a theater student, who always came to my class a few minutes late. When she entered, all action stopped as every male in the class, and many of the females, gawked at her, and she sashayed to a seat in the front row. She sat down, then lifted her gaze to me with profound innocence."

In Arcata, Ray and Maryann lived in a roomy two-story corner house a few blocks from the water and not far from the college, at 1590 I Street.

Maryann majored in both philosophy and English and again planned to become a lawyer. "She had a keen analytical mind and was a first-rate student, always wrote A papers." Day recalled.[19] Artistic and literary people, faculty and students, stuck together in Arcata, congregating on long, wet winter evenings at bars on the downtown square. "Dick Day could take up a whole evening speaking about Ken Kesey or people he knew from Iowa," Maryann recalled. Day recalled that he'd meet Ray at Tracy's, a storefront all-night cafe "where drunks would land after the bars closed. At midnight or one, we would go down there. Drink coffee and talk about our work."[20] There on the far edge of the west, they harbored a wistful, if ironic, notion that they were at the heart of literary America.

The Carvers became closest friends with two other couples: Day and his wife, Bonnie, and librarian David Palmer and his wife, Charlene, a painter and poet. Whenever anyone had anything to celebrate, a party erupted. At the Palmers' secluded house, parties sometimes lasted all weekend.[21] In a notebook, Carver sketched some literary fantasies and nightmares that these parties spawned: a man slaps his wife to the floor for flirting with another man and she flees to the bathroom; at the end of the night, someone talks about moving to the Left Bank in Paris where they will (collectively) write plays and make movies. Making fun of how far they are from Paris, an ironic late-night talker pictures their movie opening in Arcata, with limousines and lights and "loggers and children under 12 admitted free."[22] Carver's story of drinking and infidelity, "Will You Please Be Quiet, Please?", conveys a darker mood he sometimes felt in Humboldt. Day reminisced, "Things were a tad loose, let's put it that way. There was alcohol relaxing everybody." Anything was possible, and anything could have been imagined. "Ray was a bit jealous of Maryann, because she was much more outgoing than he and, not deliberately, but sort of naturally flirtatious. So that sort of ticked Ray off. But Maryann was loyal to him and his ambitions, and she broadcast that far and wide. She let people know that this guy was something as a writer."

The Carvers were always in a disastrous financial state. They ran a charge account at a market but eventually received a note from the grocer saying "the party's over." But Day felt Ray surmounted his difficulties: "He had a competitive wife, two small children, was trying to get a degree, trying to scrape by. But Ray laughed quite a bit. It was a giggle. Sure, he wrote stories about people for whom it was all up and over, very depressing. But there's a whole lot of difference—the writing of a story is an affirmation, an affirmative action." Notebooks with Chico and Humboldt State logos printed on their covers that Carver saved contain hundreds of pages of story notes and ideas and partial stories in manuscript and typescript, revealing how alive Ray was to the possibilities for stories in everything he saw and heard.[23]

The effort was immense. Day remembers, "Maybe Kafka and Dostoyevsky got to him. It seemed that in his midtwenties, Ray realized that the world was a perilous place, a place where you really couldn't trust anybody. He was apprehensive, sometimes fearful without reason that 'they' (the police, the government, or even the students streaming past his house on their way to the high school) were cooking up mischief. He kept his window shades drawn to the sills, and when I knocked at his door, I would see, at one window or another, his eye at the crack of the blind." Another time, Ray showed up at the Days' house carrying a child-sized suitcase. He said, " 'You've got to help me; they're coming after me.' He wanted me to take him out to where he could hitchhike north. So I said, 'What makes you think they're coming after you, Ray?' He wouldn't say, and as far as I could see, there was no good reason; it was just paranoia. So I talked him into not running away."[24]

Ray's paranoia came from his sensitivity and suggestibility, and was probably exacerbated by drinking. But some of his fears were reasonable. When Army Reserve units were called up during the Berlin Wall crisis in 1961, Ray knew he had failed to complete his Army Reserve obligation or stay in touch with his draft board. At other times, Ray's fears were shameful and confusing even to himself; he could be terrified not just of passing high school students but of his own children.

"Ray was not a natural as a father," in Day's opinion. "At one point, he put a lock on the bedroom door, and sometimes Maryann would go in there in the daytime and find Ray with the covers pulled over his head." According to Maryann, "Ray babysat just a tremendous amount. He preferred that to working. He'd have them draw straws for things they both wanted. He cooked them sloppy joes and tuna melts and rice with brown sugar and milk that they remember better than any three-course dinner I ever served. He spent hours reading to them and teaching them to read and watching Jacques Cousteau with them. He was a teacher to them—he had an encyclopedic mind."[25]

Day never heard Ray mention his parents, and yet Ray's journals hold pages of notes about them, along with aunts, uncles, and grandparents— enough for a family-saga novel if he had found the inclination to shape it. In fact, Ella and C.R. moved to Eureka while Ray and Maryann were in Arcata, pulling James out of school in Yakima just short of graduation. C.R. continued to suffer periods of illness and had trouble holding jobs. Perhaps Ray's parents' bad luck made Ray suspect his own dreams. To James, it looked as if his older brother had gotten away from home just in time, though he credited Ray with lighting a fire under him to read and resume his education later: "He was my mentor. He had me read Tolstoy, Dostoyevsky, and Gorky and all the others. This was in my late teens."[26]

For all his secrets, fears, and peculiarities, Ray wasn't timid about submitting his work to magazines. On the inside cover of an HSC notebook, he listed a dozen addresses of literary journals. John Gardner's teacher, Jarvis Thurston at *Perspective,* offered to publish "Furious Seasons," but then changed his mind with apologies for being behind in his publishing schedule. On a single day in the spring of 1962, Ray got his first acceptance letters from nonstudent magazines: from *Targets* in New Mexico for his poem "The Brass Ring" and from *Western Humanities Review* in Utah for "Pastoral." His payments would be free copies of the magazines.[27]

In the spring of 1962, Ray studied playwriting with John Pauley of the theater department. His projects were ambitious. He adapted for the stage *The Man Who Died,* D. H. Lawrence's parable of a Christ who is resurrected in the flesh and becomes the lover of an Egyptian goddess. His original one-act, *Carnations,* echoes Beckett, Ionesco, and Albee. It has three complicated scenes but was, nonetheless, chosen for performance on campus.[28] *Carnations* differs from the realistic stories Carver had been writing, though it does bring to mind surreal images from his poems. In the play, a baffled American named George Redfeather collides with the symbols and traditions of European literature. Whether the result is a frustrating mess, the literary equivalent of a nervous breakdown, or an intriguing anatomy of the state of Carver's intellect and emotions in his twenty-fourth year, it proves that Ray had been packing every crevice of his brain with books. It shows him thinking about his life by means of literature.

As an allegory, *Carnations* predicts that Ray (aka Redfeather)—shy, passive, loving but distant as a parent and as a son, insecure as a husband, self-accused and self-punished in the world—will survive all forms of internal and external pressure, judgment, and chaos. He will become an artist. This interpretation benefits from the hindsight of knowing what Carver later accomplished. The audience at HSC on Friday, May 11, 1962, had little to go on. The director said he felt that Carver's portrait of a lonely soul "captured the spiritual anguish of our age," while the lead actor found his role difficult and feared the audience would not understand it. Another actor had an insight that applies to much of Carver's early work: "People will be able to identify with the characters, though perhaps they may not want to." The *Lumberjack*'s reviewer was moved by *Carnations:* "These are impressionistic characters . . . frightening because you see yourself exposed on the stage in front of all these people." These student critics noticed qualities in Carver's work that the literary world would not remark for another decade.[29]

As Ray neared completion of his bachelor's degree at Humboldt, he had a busy literary life. Both he and Maryann enthusiastically studied Camus, Sartre, and other European existentialists in an honors seminar with Day.[30] One might wonder how a working-class man at the edge of the Pacific Ocean came to feel an affinity with European intellectuals. In fact, Carver never took a course in American literature, though he read the American modernists as well as the generation just ahead of him: Eudora Welty, John Cheever, Flannery O'Connor. But the specificity of locale, social type, and background in the work of these Americans made them competitors as well as models in Carver's mind. In the Europeans who wrote out of a deeper history of class struggle and disillusionment, Carver responded to a dark inevitability that may be disguised by New World grit and optimism. But the earnest injunctions of existential philosophy weren't a perfect fit for Ray either. He was a materialist and a sensualist and a dreamer. Meeting problems head-on was difficult for him. He had his own strategies for coping with the world. belief in his destiny as a writer; Maryann's faith in him, her buoyancy and her willingness to let Ray be her economic dependent; separation of his life into compartments, a tactic that alcohol abetted; and—finally—the creative act itself and the humor he could find in life when he looked at it with a writer's detachment and intensity.

Ray completed his bachelor of arts degree in February 1963 but stayed in Arcata while Maryann finished her semester. He took Medieval Literature for graduate credit and, with Day as advisor, edited the forthcoming issue of *Toyon*. Just after March 4, 1963, the date William Carlos Williams died, Ray called Day at two in the morning and said, "Bad news. Meet me." At Tracy's Cafe, Ray explained that there was not enough good material to fill *Toyon*, and he would fill it out with his own work, using various names. But as Day recollected the encounter, the editorial situation of *Toyon* was not really the bad news on Ray's mind. What was troubling Ray that night was that both Hemingway and Williams were now dead. Ray confessed to Day that he was not ready to take the place of either one. Perhaps he was kidding, but Day thought not.

Almost half of that 1963 *Toyon*'s text pages were filled with work by Ray Carver and a certain John Vale, identified as "the pseudonym of an HSC student who wishes to remain anonymous." Carver/Vale's three pieces were: "The Aficionados," "Poseidon and Company," and "The Hair." The latter takes to its apparent limit the kind of obsession Carver trademarked in his later stories: it's a Kafkaesque tale about a man with a hair stuck between his teeth. The hair ruins his appetite for breakfast and makes him kick at dogs he sees on the street. It sends him home early from his work in an office. He is sick with the dis-ease of this hair, but reports to his boss that he will be on the job the next morning: "Maybe it was just something he could get used to. He didn't know."[31]

With *Toyon*'s pages filled, Ray was eager to leave Arcata. He asked his faculty friends for advice about his future. Should he attend the Writers' Workshop at the State University of Iowa and study creative writing? Or should he apply to a doctoral program and plan to become a professor? He could see that Gardner's and Day's PhDs hadn't much forwarded their writing careers. They were fine writers and both were struggling—just as Ray was—to get their work into little magazines. When Ray asked his dad for advice, C.R. suggested he "write about some of those fishing trips we took."[32]

One day Ray asked the advice of Jay Karr, who had left Iowa with a master of fine arts degree and was fighting to hang on to his job at Humboldt against the pressures of old-guard faculty, despite having a contract to write a novel for Houghton Mifflin. Karr told Ray that "only if he knew in his gut that life wouldn't be worth living if he didn't go to Iowa, and he was prepared for a protracted period when it might be pretty near not worth living anyway—in every sense except that he would have the freedom to write—then he should go. But if he felt in any way shaky about that, he should take the academic way."[33] Ray took Karr's advice. He applied to the MFA program in poetry at Iowa. What chance did a fellow with a B-minus average in General Studies (that D in General Geology, the Cs in Body Building and World Literature did not help) from an obscure state college have of getting into America's premier writing program?[34]

Iowa Workshop director Paul Engle and his staff understood that talented writers were often imperfect scholars. On the strength of Ray's writing samples, his As in English, and a letter of recommendation from Day, Carver was admitted. Engle offered him a $1,000 fellowship for the year.[35] Ray knew that Maryann could figure out a way to get the rest of the money they needed. Indeed, by now it was clear that much of what he could accomplish depended on her.

CHAPTER 8

The Athens of the Midwest

August 1963–June 1964, Iowa City, Iowa

You are right in demanding that an artist should take an intelligent attitude to his work, but you confuse two things: solving a problem and stating a problem correctly. It is only the second that is obligatory for an artist.

> —Anton Chekhov to Alexei Suvorin, October 27, 1888, transcribed in one of Carver's notebooks

R ay had heard tales about the Writers' Workshop in Iowa City, but he really had little conception of it when he and Maryann and the children, now four and five years old, headed there in August 1963. "Old Faithful," their ten-year-old Chevy, was packed tight. A U-Haul box attached to the roof held the overload. They said their good-byes to Alice and her new husband, Clarence, in Paradise, promising to write and call, knowing they would be gone for at least a year. They'd never been east of Reno. Maryann's mother recalled this version of the journey: "They had thirty-one dollars, an old car, and two kids. Before they were out of town, the battery went dead. So they bought a new battery and started off to Iowa with one dollar. At mealtimes, they stopped somewhere, and Maryann went in and told them she was an expert waitress and would work two hours if they would feed the family. They traveled all the way to Iowa that way."[1]

For westerners of any class, but particularly for a man of Carver's background, the East—"back East"—can seem a suspect and monolithic place. Many native westerners make no more distinction between Cleveland and Boston than an easterner does between Laramie and Boise. Nonetheless, a person who reads books develops an intuitive orientation toward New York as the place named on title pages, the place where writers mail their work to see what the world thinks of it. Literary careers are made in New York City, regardless of where the writers themselves originated. Though he no doubt realized that Iowa was a thousand miles short of New York and directly north of his parents' state of birth, Arkansas, Carver would have felt the import of heading east and imagined that in doing so he approached the powerful people who made the kinds of decisions that could promote or kill his ambitions.

What Carver knew of the Writers' Workshop, besides what his teachers had told him, came from glossy magazines, most of them showing photographs of poet Paul Engle, native Iowan and director of the workshop. Along with catchy lines such as "Iowa, in literate circles, has come to mean not only pigs, but poetry," one phrase occurred frequently in these spreads: "turning out some of America's best writers." The July 1963 *Esquire* listed forty-two former Iowa students and faculty members in its "Structure of the American Literary Establishment"—a third of the names included. Another article blithely explains that "talent" is the primary requisite for admission. Somebody at Iowa, Ray knew, had seen literary talent in the stories and poems he submitted.

Warnings lurked within these pumped-up articles. *Mademoiselle* described the workshop's three degree programs—MA (one year), MFA (two years, with creative thesis), and PhD (longer, with longer thesis)— then reported that "most of the apprentice writers do not achieve careers as professionals." Philip Roth, teaching at Iowa after *Goodbye, Columbus and Five Stories* won a National Book Award in 1960, expressed the opinion that "part of our function is to discourage those without enough talent. A lot of people come for self-expression or therapy."[2]

Yearly more than one hundred students from all over the world were lured to the workshop by Engle's dream of an "alternative between Hollywood and New York . . . a place where the writer can be himself, confronting the hazards and hopes of his own talent, and at the same time he can measure his capacity against a variety of others . . ." As of 1961, at least sixty major works of fiction had been published in the preceding twenty-five years by former workshop students. Among them were Wallace Stegner's *The Big Rock Candy Mountain*, R. V. Cassill's *Pretty Leslie*, Flannery O'Connor's *A Good Man Is Hard to Find and Other Stories*, Walter Tevis's *The Hustler, The Man Who Fell to Earth*, and Thomas Williams's *Town Burning*. The authors of all these books had passed through Iowa City on their way to success in the New York City publishing world.

When the Carvers reached Iowa City, they saw a classic nineteenth-century midwestern town with elm-bowered brick streets on a bend of the Iowa River. In those days, when the town's population was only thirty-three thousand, neither a mall in its center nor a sprawl at its edges disfigured the old town. (Both were in the offing.) On a rise west of the river, the gilt-domed Greek Revival Old Capitol and a cluster of stone and brick edifices gave the campus a hallowed, substantial aspect. From the first pay phone he found, Ray called faculty novelist Vance Bourjaily to say he'd arrived and was in a bad way financially.

Bourjaily invited the Carvers to his home in North Liberty for dinner. They came disheveled and hungry to Vance and Tina Bourjaily's big Victorian house and told Bourjaily that their son was named for him. Christi and Vance played with the three Bourjaily children, and Tina got a meal on the table. As they ate, "Maryann looked out the bay window by our dining table, bleary-eyed and eating her hamburger, at the birdbath where there was a blue jay, and asked, 'Is that a real bird out there?'" Tina thought it was an odd question and thought, too, that "Ray didn't know how to act or dress or anything." She wondered if anyone in Iowa City would think he was a serious writer. And yet she recognized from the difficulties the family had endured in coming to Iowa that Ray "was just obsessed with writing—as if a wild gene were directing him."[3]

Vance Bourjaily showed his guests his writing studio in the barn (a photo of it had appeared in *Life* magazine when *The Violated* was published) and then apologetically directed the Carvers to their lodgings: a tiny trailer at the Hawkeye Trailer Court. For nearly two months, they waited for space in married students' housing. Despite its visual charm, Iowa City's late summer weather was hot and humid and dismal. The constant hiss of cicadas and the surrounding acres of corn and soybeans made the town claustrophobic to a newcomer. Ray missed seeing the ocean. He told Dick Day he hadn't traveled beyond the edge of Iowa City and had no intention of doing so.[4]

Much ink and breath have been expended on the subject of whether imaginative writing can be taught in school. The question remains unanswered, but a class session known as a "workshop" has evolved to attempt the task. Workshops were institutionalized at Iowa because, as Vance Bourjaily put it, "we had to invent a way to teach creative writing." Student manuscripts are the primary subject matter. The professor's and other students' critical minds are the tools with which these manuscripts are "worked" in the shop of the classroom.

Ray wrote both poetry and fiction, so he ambitiously signed up for a workshop in each genre. But his ambition made little impression. Engle led the poetry sessions, assisted by Donald Justice and Mark Strand, then Justice's protégé. Neither Justice nor Strand remembered seeing Ray or reading his poems at Iowa; at the semester's end, he received only one hour of credit for Poetry. But the fiction workshop disappointed Ray even more. Though he preferred Bourjaily, Ray landed in a workshop led by R. V.

Cassill, a highly verbal, academic man who enjoyed intellectual swordplay. In his workshop, student Tom Doherty recalled, "it was kind of a meal to launch into someone's story—not in a mean way, but if they liked something, they got their teeth into it and really analyzed it."

Ray "literally slunked in the corner" of Cassill's classroom. But when Doherty went out for beers with Ray, he realized that Ray had read a lot and was confident about himself as a writer. His conversation revealed his excitement about a Chekhov story or one of Wallace Stegner's novels. Nonetheless, Ray's appearance was not promising. His front teeth were decayed at the edges and he couldn't afford to care about his clothes. He cupped his whole upper body around an ever-present cigarette, sucking it so hard his face caved in. To others, Ray appeared older than his twenty-five years—"as if he'd had a life already," Eric Larsen thought. But his face remained pale and guileless, unformed and boyish, and the frames of his glasses obscured his eyes. "Most of the time"—Doherty again—"his expression was deadly serious, even haunted, with his right eyebrow arched in concentration, but when a grin broke out, it was enormous, and he seemed relieved and grateful. When he was with you, he was *with* you, always focused. He wasn't gazing around the tavern or playing to the crowd. He was a down-to-earth guy who was thrilled that he had discovered writing and wanted to make a go of it."

Carver and poet Kenneth Rosen also compared notes on their fiction workshop experiences over beers at the Airliner Café, a tavern facing the main campus. Both were disgruntled, but their complaints were so different that they weren't able to give each other much comfort. Rosen, then Bourjaily's student, wanted to study "elaborate modernism of the James Joyce variety, and Ray was upset because there wasn't enough emphasis on practical matters such as how to turn stories into cash." Ray's need for money was evident to Rosen from his worn clothing, which smelled of "basements because he had a job shoveling coal or tending oil furnaces." Rosen got the impression that Ray was turning out a lot of work though—several stories a week—and threatening to send them to men's magazines like *Cavalier* in hopes of picking up a few bucks.[5]

Dire as Ray's need for cash always was, his discontent at the workshop had other dimensions. After Gardner had charged his literary sensibilities in Chico, Ray had found a comfortable home for his young vocation in Arcata. At Iowa he felt fierce competition. Even though his story "Furious Seasons" came out in the 1963 issue of *December*, a small but prestigious literary magazine founded by recent Iowa graduates, he felt lost at the workshop. Some students had done a hitch in the military or held other jobs before coming to Iowa City. A few possessed Ivy League educations, accents, sophistication, and wealth the likes of which Ray had barely encountered before. As Rosen noticed, "Iowa presented a self-perpetuating upper-middle-class dynamic; that kind of neurotic exclusiveness that you can never quite put your finger on, but—if you breach it—subtle alarms go off and doors close and faces become blank."

By October Ray had already decided he would leave after one year, which meant stopping with an MA degree without a thesis. He wrote Day that he wanted to find a part-time job and get on with his writing career, explaining that Iowa was a good school, but he would not care to be there longer than necessary. Another letter promises Day reports of "grotesqueries" when they meet again.[6]

The workshop was an amorphous assemblage in the early 1960s, and much was determined by the personalities of faculty and students of a particular year. Members of the workshop tended to feel they'd been chosen for great things. A student from the 1980s, Debra Spark, remembered hearing a young man at the orientation meeting say, " 'Think what would happen to American letters if a bomb dropped on this room.' "[7] Such conceit, to which Ray Carver was no stranger, did not make for the easy camaraderie of equals. The students who came to the nation's flagship writing program were competitive people with fragile egos, and so were their faculty.

The program's sense of specialness was ironically enhanced by its quarters: corrugated steel barracks constructed in the late forties to house the influx of GI Bill students. These huts sat next to the student union on a spot that the Frank Gehry–designed Iowa Advanced Technology Laboratories now occupies. Here faculty and students alike suffered physical discomfort in the name of literature. The barracks were like ovens in summer. When fall and spring rains drummed on the roofs, no one could hear. On the university map, they were labeled "temporaries," but these sheds housed the workshop offices and classrooms for two decades. When Carver came to Iowa, the workshop was in a growth period that would burst forth into a proliferation of writing programs founded by Iowa graduates all over the nation. At the same time, a feud was brewing in the mother school. In 1965 Engle would separate himself from the Writers' Workshop and found the International Writers' Workshop at the University of Iowa. In every way, then, Ray found himself in a pressure cooker environment.

The valve of the academic pressure cooker was the workshop critique session, two hours, once a week. Doherty looked forward to Monday meetings. "We'd be all juiced up because it was our day to actually feel like writers. The rest of the days, you actually had to do the writing." Students submitted typed stories or poems to the teacher in advance, and then, by a process that appeared mysterious, teachers selected pieces for department secretaries to type. Stapled into packets known as "worksheets," the chosen work, printed anonymously in purple ink, reached students' hands, often still damp and scented by duplicating fluid. For the next several days, classmates studied these worksheets, wondered who wrote each piece and— inevitably—asked themselves if it was worse or better than their own work. Ideally, they thought about how it could be improved. If it was their own work, they wondered if anyone would like it or recognize their authorship.[8]

To Joy Williams, who became known for her short stories, novels (*State of Grace*), and environmental essays (*Ill Nature*), Iowa was a "den of vipers" wherein she passed her two years as a student in "a paralysis of awkwardness." All this was part of Engle's vision: "We knock, or persuade, or terrify the false tenderness toward his own work out of the beginning writer. This is the beginning of wisdom." Ray may have been devastated by the experience. During a workshop critique, "the writer kept his head down, like a soldier under heavy fire, listened, and left. So it was really about yourself. And about the writing. Very intense." While the more gregarious students adjourned to a tavern after a workshop, Doherty usually climbed the hill to his dingy apartment on Dubuque Street, feeling let down that the highlight of the week was over, and Ray drove home to his family.[9]

One of Ray's fellow students vividly recalled his presence in a workshop. Novelist Ian McMillan, who grew up in rural upstate New York, recounted:

> In Cassill's workshop, I usually hid and watched. Sometimes I talked to Ray, because he seemed sort of moody and defensive. He struck me as having come from a place like the place I had come from—broken-down rural America, where people were underfed and had bad teeth. When Ray talked, he talked in a peculiar way—short and fast, like a mumble speeded up. When he looked around the class, he looked as if he felt out of place, as I felt out of place.
>
> The degree of Ray's defensiveness showed itself one day when a story of his was discussed in class—it had a boy sleeping on a porch, and there was a goat in the yard. Other stuff happened in the story, too, of course, but when the discussion was over (and I recall that Cassill raised questions about this and that, about the point of the story), Ray had this exaggeration of his out-of-place look on his face. After the class was over, someone stopped and looked down at him—he was still sitting there thinking—and said, "C'mon, Ray, what was the goat doing in the yard?" and Ray responded by looking up at the guy, his face rigid with anger, and saying, "Fuck you! Fuck you!" But it came out as an explosive mumble—that shortness in his voice. He remained sort of obscure, although

you could tell something was going on in his head, as you could tell that writing was important to him.[10]

But Cassill could be generous to students, and Ray surely envied the chosen few. Cassill gave both Doherty and Ted Weesner the word that they should submit stories they'd done for workshop to the new fiction editor of the *Saturday Evening Post*, Rust Hills. Doherty's came back, but Weesner's was purchased for the stunning sum of $1,500 and appeared in an illustrated spread a year later.[11]

In October the Carvers moved into married students' housing at Finkbine Park, a dismal collection of Quonsets (tunnel-shaped corrugated steel dwellings) on the far west side of campus. Stoic through many previous moves, Maryann "did just sit down on the bed and cry" on the cold October day when they moved into their Finkbine quarters with "cement floors, open cupboards in the kitchen, the hot water tank in the middle of the living room floor, a children's room like a cell with two little bunks and a tiny window." The rent was cheap and included utilities, but with out-of-state tuition at $165 a semester for Ray and $310 for Maryann, Ray's fellowship money was spent. On top of that, they had all suffered a flu bug that left five-year-old Christi with a severe kidney infection; Maryann, who had enrolled for a full load of classes and planned to finish her bachelor's degree, dropped out on the first of October to take care of Christi.[12]

By then Maryann was waitressing at the University Athletic Club, an expensive private dining and tennis club, so she was able to afford a secondhand carpet for the chilly floor and a bookcase for their ragged paperbacks. She'd quit smoking, Ray told Day proudly, and become "fat as a butterduck."[13] At the club, Maryann made a record $300 one night after an Iowa-Wisconsin football game. When Ray came to drive her home, they'd stay for a few drinks with the bartender. Joy Williams was—briefly—Maryann's coworker:

I was always getting fired from waitressing jobs, and this was no exception. Maryann was big, beautiful, and so *mature*, I thought. I was a little young for graduate school but I wasn't that young—still I thought I was surrounded by grown-ups, intent, responsible. Everyone had children, small children—everyone was involved in complex, wedded, mysterious lives. What did I know? Nothing. I didn't even drink much in those days. I sensed no desperation, exactly. Ambition, certainly. Ray and Maryann seemed to entertain disarray more than other couples, perhaps, and appeared almost amused by their ill fortune. Maryann brought home whatever money there was to be, and there was never enough of it. Once I recall the phone company arriving and *yanking* the phone from the wall for nonpayment. And the kids were rascals, out of control. They all lived in squalor, actually. But they never wept or wailed about it or dramatized their situation. They weren't full of themselves, that's for sure. They were sweet and hapless, and they loved each other, was the way I saw it. Ray was a great reader. He read more than he wrote, probably.

Sweet, hapless, loving: Maryann's recollection of those days coincides with Williams's: "Ray and I did work some gristly jobs in our time, as we called them, which made the reunions in the evening after work all the more sweet. We commiserated with each other. . . . Laughed and joked and recounted the funny incidents and stories of the day in the salt mines."[14]

Maryann and Ray found congenial neighbors in the other end of their Finkbine hut. Adrian Mitchell, Celia Hewitt, and their daughter became their best friends in Iowa City. Adrian, a British poet and novelist, was visiting Iowa for a year as an instructor; Celia, a sought-after actress in England, was not allowed to work professionally in the United States. To the Mitchells, "Maryann and Ray were friendly from the start. They showed us the ropes—where to pick up bargains, how to spot useful items which departing Finkbiners deposited in the local Dempsey Dumpster." The Carvers and the Mitchells ate together sometimes and their kids played together. When spring arrived, many of the neighbors complained when Sasha Mitchell ran around without clothes, but Maryann and Ray weren't fazed by that or much else.

The Mitchells were invited to faculty parties and heard much of the gossip that circulated there. Adrian knew that Ray had published work in literary journals and regarded him as something between a student and a staff member. From Ray and Maryann's perspective, the Mitchells were worldly, glamorous people. Adrian's first novel, *If You See Me Comin'*, had been published to good reviews in London. He'd won a poetry award from T. S. Eliot and met the Beatles while working as a journalist. They had crossed the Atlantic on the *France* and flown to Iowa City but were out of money when they arrived. Luck struck when they returned to England. Director Peter Brook invited Adrian to write the English version of Peter Weiss's play *Marat/Sade*. It was, Mitchell recalled, "a great hit in London and New York, and for the first time we flew out of debt." Mitchell thought the Carvers had a happy marriage of opposites: "He reminded me of a bear. A thoughtful, amiable, dreaming but often down-to-earth bear. She was like a dancing flame. Earth and fire—yes, sometimes it seemed like that—but they were good friends, and we would have trusted them with our lives."[15]

Joy Williams and Tom Doherty also came over to the Carvers' hut now and then for an evening of talk and drink. On these nights, Doherty saw that Ray and Maryann "had things on their minds—debts and other obligations that weren't fulfilled—things ticking, a lot of them, but he and Maryann were a neat couple. They were in it together. It was like the guys in his stories for whom tomorrow's the last day unless we can come up with something." Maryann was "slight and pretty with a big smile and kind of Roy Rogers eyes, that slightly Asian shape." Doherty remembered a funny thing about one of those nights when they'd all had some drinks: "I was in the bathroom, I was very happy, and I was thinking, 'What a damn shame, they're very talented, and they're such great people, and I am going to have to leave them behind.' I meant I obviously was going to make it, but not all of us could! That was my self-deception at the time. I certainly didn't believe it all the time I was there, but I did that night." Doherty wasn't alone in harboring such a belief; private funds of confidence were almost a necessity for continuing to write every day. As they all found out, there were no sure predictors of success.[16]

Faculty-sponsored events, often in honor of a visiting writer, and student parties in one of the Quonsets or apartments or rooming houses made up the larger social scene. These parties had the kind of fervor that sparks when artistic people emerge from rooms where they work—deeply alone—to seek Dionysian intervals of intense talk, storytelling and gossip, laughter, dancing, alcohol or marijuana, and sexual abandon. Just as Iowa's football players and wrestlers sometimes attracted groupies, Iowa's writers attracted certain women or men on campus; there were opportunities for falling in love and for clandestine or simply gratuitous sex. Ray, married with children, must have, in one of his own phrases, "seen some things," as he looked through the windows of the hothouse.

"Especially in winter," Mitchell remembered, "parties were frequent. We met the same people every time, teachers and students from the Writers' Workshop plus people from the Art Department. There was a lot of booze—huge jugs of gin and vodka sitting on the table—help yourself. A lot of martinis, and, as the snow iced over, the odd fight and some marital squabbles." But Ray did not stand out as a drinker, and he rarely became rowdy. At a party at Douglas Kent Hall's house, the Mitchells played the Beatles' first English-release album, *Please Please Me,* months before the group's first American hits. The album included "Twist and Shout," so Adrian and a few people were shaking it up. Hall remembers trying to do the twist for the first time, while "Ray was standing back, drinking and sidelined by the music and the frenzy."[17]

• • •

The most memorable public event of 1963 was the assassination of John Kennedy in Dallas on November 22. That day became an early memory for Vance Carver, who had just turned five. It was a cold, blustery Friday, and he rode in the car with his dad as he did errands in downtown Iowa City. "Suddenly my dad came out of a store and said we had to go home right away. We went home to the hut and watched the television. We always had a television, usually one that didn't work very well." His parents were very sad. "At times like that, there was something special about my dad that made me want to be with him. He was a big guy, but sensitive."[18]

The evening hours that Maryann worked at the Athletic Club dictated that Ray did a good deal of child care and a certain amount of housekeeping. An essay called "Fires" that Carver composed in 1981 talks about the "oppressive, often malevolent" influence of his children on his writing. In brief, he says that because he never had enough money and always had two children, he chose to write short stories and poems and could not write novels. He acknowledges that he has an "anxious inability to focus on anything for a sustained period of time" (an earlier draft said that span was "rapidly declining"), but then adds that even if he could have concentrated his energy on a novel, he could not have waited several years for the "payoff" on his work. He implies here that "payoff" would be financial, but perhaps he refers as well to recognition.[19]

The dark heart of "Fires" is a two-page anecdote about doing his family's wash at a laundromat in Iowa City. The laundromat was on the corner of Burlington and Gilbert, around the corner from the writers' favorite beer joints. Canadian writer Clark Blaise sometimes chatted with Ray while their clothes spun at this laundromat, as Blaise and his wife, the novelist Bharati Mukherjee, struggled to keep up with their baby's diapers.[20] But Carver is alone in the laundromat epiphany he reports. Maryann is at work, the kids are at a birthday party, and Ray is waiting for a dryer. It's Saturday afternoon and crowded, so he is becoming frantic. Another dryer has stopped, and Carver is moving toward it, ready to replace the other clothes with his own, when the owner of the clothing decides to let it go for another cycle:

> . . . I remember thinking at that moment . . . that nothing could come anywhere close, could possibly be as important to me, could make as much difference, as the fact that I had two children. And that I would always have them and always find myself in this position of unrelieved responsibility and permanent distraction. . . .
>
> Like that it came to me. Like a sharp breeze when the window is thrown open. Up to that point in my life I'd gone along thinking . . . that

things would work out somehow—that everything in my life I'd hoped for or wanted to do was possible.

Is Carver writing fiction here? Could this one moment encompass so much? The essay dramatizes a situation that had smoldered for years. Carver admits in the essay that many writers have overcome "far more serious impediments to their work, including imprisonment, blindness, the threat of torture or death. . . ."

But Carver's pervading complaint is that he does not have control over his life and that it has *always* felt that way. His essay represents the explosion of a man who has had enough, who is, after long deferral, finally striking out. As he explodes, Carver seeks to blame someone who cannot immediately object or argue, someone more helpless than himself: his children. Women in particular have applauded Carver for his forthright statement about the demands of being a parent, glad to hear their similar sacrifices recognized. If the anecdote were about the frustrations of a single day or year, it might be amusing. If it were part of a complex analysis, it might be brave. But Carver burdens his children with more than they deserve. Through this laundromat epiphany, Carver lashes out at his parents' poverty, his truncated youth, his admitted inability to concentrate on longer works, his financial dependence on Maryann (if she weren't at work, he would not have these Saturday chores), his father's alcoholism, and, by extension, his own reliance on drink. More can be said about all this; what seems significant here is Carver's location of his disillusion at that moment in Iowa City. It was his twenty-fifth year. He did not know it, but he was already at the midpoint of his life.

Feeling homesick and poorly housed in Iowa made Ray think about how he wanted to live. In a letter to Day, he sketched a picture of his own ideal life, the one he wanted to create as soon as he finished the master's degree at Iowa: he'd like to be sitting by a stream under a tree "contemplating the things that should be contemplated" and going to the bakery for "big, crumbly pastries." In winter, the seat beneath the tree would be exchanged for one where he could do his contemplating by firelight.[21]

The winter of 1963–64 was exceptionally brutal, even for Iowa. It began before Christmas with a nine-night run of below-zero plunges and four inches of snow. For thirty days in January, temperatures didn't rise above freezing as one blizzard or sleet storm succeeded another. Ray wrote to the Days that he was at the kitchen table wearing several pairs of socks and "hoping my feet don't drop off before spring." To stay warm, he keeps adding additional socks without removing the pairs already on his feet, which feel like "huge sausages." "Old Faithful" was not always running and even when it was its windshield would not defrost, so Maryann leaned her head out the window to see as she drove to and from her shift at the club. Once again, Ray had found the job he liked best, in the library, where he earned minimum wage: $1.25 an hour.[22]

Ray did write in Iowa. On December 8, 1963, he told Day he had finished a story that was still too recent to judge for himself. He didn't know if it was his best or his worst, but he was sure it was his longest. That story had been turned in to Cassill; perhaps it was the one Ian McMillan heard critiqued, perhaps one Ray hoped to send on to the *Post*. In any case, the rough treatment Ray thought he received in workshop did not stymie him. Once out of the spotlight, he turned his resentment back into writing. Iowa winter intensified his solitude and made him glad to stay inside and work. He gave each new story to Maryann to read first. "I just took the pencil and marked out words that weren't needed, as we both learned to do when he was a young student of John Gardner's. It was our favorite thing, when Ray would finish a story, and we would hone in on it." He took about half of Maryann's suggestions, she believed.[23]

Ray had some justification in doubting the workshop criticism. *Carolina Quarterly* had just written him to accept "The Night the Mill Boss Died" for its very next issue, before Christmas. Doherty recalled, "It was just thrilling to get something landed anywhere, and Ray was, that year, one of the few who was actually placing stuff." Despite the miseries he felt at the workshop, Ray had much to celebrate: three stories and two poems in nationally respected publications since he had finished college less than a year before.

Ray and Doherty sometimes showed each other work, and Doherty found Ray's criticism direct and generous:

> He wouldn't bullshit you. If it didn't work for him, he'd tell you and try to give you some hints or suggest what you should read. If he did like it, he just said he was glad he read it. His criticisms were based on how he felt about a story, not any head-trip things. Then, anyway, he was a genuine innocent; there was no calculation beyond what he was enthusiastic about. He wrote and rewrote himself and had a constant preoccupation with whatever he was working out—he liked to roll it through [the typewriter] again and shrink it. We used those yellow second papers, the pulp paper, and I bet he just had wastebaskets full of that stuff.[24]

As the fall semester tailed off into January, Ray and Maryann worked together on his paper about the German poet Rainer Maria Rilke and endured the cold as best they could, mainly by staying indoors. Maryann had often done research for papers in Ray's literature classes when he was immersed in writing a story. She enjoyed the reading and the conversations they could have about the project, but this was the first time she'd drafted a paper for him.[25]

On January 21, a telegram brought the news that Maryann's father, sixty-one-year-old Valentine Burk, had died of a heart attack. He'd had a pulse when he was found unconscious in his car; after a seventeen-mile ambulance ride to the hospital, he was dead.[26]

Immediately Maryann made plans to travel west to attend the funeral. Her aunt May would wire money for train fare. The children would go with Maryann so Ray could finish his classes, go to his library job, and write during the coming break between semesters. The death of Val Burk was an enormous shock to Maryann: "It just broke my heart, took me to the quick, because I was only twenty-three, just a raw thing, and that was the first great loss." Ray drove Maryann and the children thirty miles over ice-glazed roads to board their train. Her mother, Alice Reed, met Maryann in California and kept the children with her there while Maryann flew north for the services in Bellingham. Shortly after the funeral, a pathology report compounded everyone's sense of loss. Carbon monoxide was found in Burk's tissues. A leak in a car he had recently purchased had poisoned him. Had he received oxygen in the ambulance, Maryann believed, he might have lived.[27] Val Burk was survived by his estranged second wife, Ann, and his five daughters: Bonna (Jerry), Maryann, and Amy, and their two half-sisters, Annette and Valla.

Two days after Maryann and the children left, Ray wrote the Days with the news about Maryann's father. He said he was "unbewifed" and gloomy. It was three in the morning on a Friday, and he was slogging away on his Rilke paper. He told Day that he found Cassill too intellectual and "hard to come up against," a phrase he also used to describe John Gardner. He hoped to avoid him the next semester, take the comprehensive exam for his MA in August, and then leave Iowa behind. He found the "scene here really kind of strange" but was glad he had been able to see it for himself. With timidness that comes through on the page, he asks Day if he could apply for a part-time teaching job at Humboldt State; he wants to live someplace where Maryann can finish college.[28]

Even though he had written many pages of fiction recently, Ray took a grade of Incomplete in Cassill's workshop. He would close a semester that had been costly to both his psyche and his family's pocketbook with gentleman's Bs (rarely does a graduate student receive a lower grade) in a mere seven credit hours—three each for his literature class and Cassill's lecture, and one from the poetry workshop. He earned no credits in fiction writing.

After two weeks with her sisters, Maryann flew back to Southern California, where, at her mother's urging, she rested awhile longer. She was emotionally exhausted, especially after learning that her father's death might have been prevented, and could not summon the energy for the long train journey in coach seats with two small children. She was still away when Ray wrote to the Days again on February 12, thanking them for a loan, and saying he'll continue to feel bleak until Maryann returns. In notes jotted about this time, Carver describes a man who is separated from his family and misses fresh foods his wife served. He likes it best when the children are asleep and she fixes them a bite to eat as they talk by themselves. The man reminisces that they had fun then—and that he had fewer problems with his digestive system.[29]

In Maryann's absence, Ray wrote the first draft of a story that would eventually win him national attention: "Will You Please Be Quiet, Please?" Despite some details pulled straight from Ray's and Maryann's lives, in this story Carver, for the first time, puts his working-class characters in the background and gives his young couple middle-class attributes: Marian and Ralph Wyman attended college in Chico, California, married in an Episcopal church, and honeymooned for six weeks in Guadalajara, Mexico. Now they are teachers, home owners, and parents of two in Eureka, California. Marian teaches French and English at the junior college, while Ralph stays on at the high school. Ralph feels encumbered by piles of themes to grade, while Marian cheerfully does the ironing and listens to the radio. Ralph feels "enormously happy" with his domestic life.

But Ralph is a man inclined to emotional disintegration. In college, before he met either Marian or his mentor, Dr. Maxwell ("a handsome, graceful man in his early forties" modeled on Lennis Dunlap), he'd felt he was on the "brink of some kind of huge discovery about himself. But it never came." Instead he joined a fraternity and got drunk every night and "almost had a breakdown." Then, on his honeymoon trip to Mexico, Ralph was secretly appalled by the squalor he saw and "anxious to return to the safety of California." A memory from that trip undermines his feeling for his wife, who was "looking away from him, staring at something toward the horizon."[30]

More than he'd done in his undergraduate stories, Ray apprehends his material as a writer. He relates this moment with detachment ("something from a play"), combining and inventing details from disparate episodes in his own experience (his own trip to Mexico, some view of Maryann, homesickness for California), and yet charges it with the feeling that he'd been abandoned by his wife in the foreign country of an Iowa winter. A later edit of the story replaced the sentence about the horizon with a phrase that emphasizes the narrator's feeling of being left out: "an intensely dramatic moment into which Marian could be fitted but he could not."

From that moment of foreboding, Ralph gives in to his doubts about Marian, for "he had taken it into his head one night at a party that Marian had betrayed him with Mitchell Anderson, a friend." At a faculty party several years before, Marian had gone with Anderson on a last run to the liquor store before closing time. The two did not return for a couple of hours. On the Sunday evening of the story, seemingly out of the blue, Marian asks Ralph if he ever thinks about that night, and he—against his better judgment, promising he won't be angry—urges her to tell him the story. From here, Carver follows his demons through a very dark passage.

Listening to Marian's escapade, Ralph is erotically charged and horrified. She admits that she and Anderson had "a go at it" in his car, though—under Ralph's angry questioning—she insists, " 'He didn't come in me.' " Ralph then leaves the house and spends the night in the bars and poolrooms on skid row in Eureka. His symbolic descent into hell is studded with recognizable places in Eureka; along the way, Ralph trolls through memories and regrets, and suffers visions of avid femininity: pornographic graffiti, visions of Marian copulating with Anderson, "a huge neon-lighted clamshell with a man's legs sticking out."[31] He gets into a poker game and tries to tell the other players about his wife's betrayal. Finally he is assaulted by a "Negro in a leather jacket" and passes out on the street until morning.

Back home, "everything seemed to him open": the phone book, the cupboards, the draperies; the ashtray is full of his wife's cork cigarette ends. He looks at his sleeping wife and then puts his head down on the kitchen table. Ralph's tidy life has come open. "He did not know what to do. Not just now, he thought, not just in this, not just about this, today and tomorrow, but every day on earth." The children wake him with their early morning chatter, but he manages to lock himself in the bathroom before he encounters Marian. Marian knocks on the door and pleads with Ralph to come out, until he speaks the story's now-famous title: "He said, 'Will you please be quiet, please?' " (A similar line of dialogue occurs in Hemingway's "Hills Like White Elephants.") Alone in the bathroom, Ralph "made faces at himself. He tried many expressions. Then he gave it up." He bathes and sneaks into the bedroom. When Marian find him under the covers, he pretends to be asleep. She strokes his back. "He tensed at her fingers, and then he let go a little. It was easier to let go a little." The story concludes quickly, as Ralph responds to Marian's advance: "He held himself, he later considered, as long as he could. And then he turned to her. He turned and turned in what might have been a stupendous sleep, and he was still turning, marveling at the impossible changes he felt moving over him."

The moment of moral decision is suspended here, not so much in the wordless sexual scene but in the question of whether Ralph is asleep or awake; the story proposes—Carver proposes to himself, perhaps—that the reconciliation is an astonishing and marvelous thing, a movement into an open space beyond the simple bourgeois marriage Ralph had before. An "impossible" change has occurred, a paradox. The writing of it is possible. Carver's fear that his smart, vibrant wife could betray him (never mind whether she has actually done so) has been transformed into fiction.

The story is skillfully done, but it is also courageous. Carver, like Ralph, could not decide what face to wear into the world and did not know what to do when things went wrong. The story's faithfulness to this weakness in his character allows Carver to write a strong story about a weak man.

When Maryann and the children returned to Iowa City in mid-February, the family was destitute and had new debts from her trip as well. She took on extra hours at the Athletic Club, and Ray began a new semester. This time he took Modern English Grammar, American Poetry, The Contemporary Novel: Realism and Naturalism, and the fiction workshop with visiting lecturer Bryan MacMahon. MacMahon came to Iowa from County Kerry, Ireland, to replace Bourjaily, who was on leave. Ray decided to join MacMahon's workshop (rather than Cassill's or Holmes's) when he heard him speak on February 10. Rosen recalled that session: "There was a big meeting of all the fiction workshops to get to know the new guy. MacMahon came in and said, 'The first thing I tell any writer when I see his manuscript is to throw away his first page.' To us it sounded terrible, worse than heresy."[32]

Ray, a quiet heretic, was not shocked. He told Day that he "went for" MacMahon after hearing about ten words from him. Two books of MacMahon's short stories had appeared in the United States, and his plays had been produced at Dublin's Abbey Theatre. He was the father of five, headmaster of a school, a student of traditional Irish life, and a hunter and fisherman; in addition, he knew the great Irish story writers Frank O'Connor and Sean O'Faolain. MacMahon told the *Daily Iowan*, "People must have a life of imagination or they will perish. It is necessary for every man."[33] MacMahon was lively and old-worldish. He critiqued stories himself, inviting very little student input. He demonstrated memory devices and advised students to learn a new word every day. MacMahon encouraged Ray, and Ray, in turn, submitted his newer stories for critique. From MacMahon, Ray received four workshop credit hours and a grade of A. He also received—for the first time—the blessing of a mature and successful man of letters.[34]

MacMahon's support for Ray did not, apparently, extend to securing him money for a second year at Iowa, though it made him more willing to stick around. In those days, the workshop was "run out of Paul Engle's back pocket," meaning that Engle personally raised the money and controlled the budget. To request tuition relief or fellowship support, a student had to line up at Engle's office on a particular day and defend his need and answer Engle's questions.[35] Perhaps Ray neglected to figure out the procedure for making his case to Engle. Nonetheless, he was crushed when his name was not among those invited to apply for fellowships. Then, Maryann checked around and confirmed that Ray had more publications than most others in the workshop. On a Friday morning while he was out, she got her hair done, put on a red dress, and scooped up all of Ray's stories—including the incomplete "Will You Please Be Quiet, Please?"—and went to Engle's office and waited to see him. She waited all day:

> I was a bit of a firebrand in those days, especially when it came to my family. I was going to make sure we survived. I was so angry . . . finally around four in the afternoon, Paul Engle showed up. He asked me into his office, but he picked up his mail at the same time. He asked me what was on my mind, but when I started to tell him, he kept reading his mail. So I stopped talking, and after two minutes he noticed that, but I told him it was OK, why don't you just finish reading your mail. He realized of course that he'd been rude and pushed the mail aside and began listening to me.

Engle did not seem to recognize the name Carver, so Maryann mentioned that the Iowa faculty had turned down Tennessee (then Tom) Williams's creative project called *The Glass Menagerie* in 1940 and sent him away without a degree. She told Engle he had "another situation almost exactly like that" with her husband. The parallel she drew to Williams was not exact, but Maryann held Engle's attention. He took the work from her hands and promised to have a faculty member read it over the weekend.[36]

When Ray came home to discover all his work missing, he began to drink and did not sober up all weekend. He was furious because, Maryann explains, "I wasn't to touch works in progress, the kids weren't to touch them." But when he learned where the work was and what Maryann had done, "he was actually pleased." Not unlike Ralph in "Will You Please Be Quiet, Please?" Ray got angry and drunk and, repenting the drinking, forgave those who had offended him.

While Ray was drunk, his stories were with John Clellon Holmes. He, Maryann reports, "went wild over [the work] and came back on Monday raving about Ray's work and passed it around to other powers-that-be." Ray was offered a second chance in the form of a stipend for the following year.[37]

Iowa's outrageous winter was matched by the sudden exuberance of its spring. For people who had been cooped up indoors, spring could be both a celebration and a disappointment, as nature bursts out in color but human dreams remain elusive. Violent acts—suicides, shootings, and rapes "bred in the icy entombment of winter that erupt in the spring," as one graduate put it—are part of folk history in Iowa City.[38] Ray turned his worries on himself and suffered a depression during which he dropped all his courses except MacMahon's workshop. The parties moved out of doors. The jugs of liquor were augmented by kegs of beer. By now, the Beatles had conquered America, just one of many signs that huge social changes were under way in the nation. President Lyndon Johnson was proving himself a bold leader by pushing the Civil Rights Bill through Congress, but he was also increasing the number of American advisory troops in South Vietnam. In the Carver household, Peter, Paul and Mary's "Puff the Magic Dragon" was Christi's favorite song. The kids sang it together loud and often.[39]

In early May, Ray drafted, in a single afternoon, "The Student's Wife," a story filled with empathy for Maryann. While she'd been away in California, he had missed her terribly. In this story, he was able to represent the sadness she felt over the death of her father and the disappointments that she and Ray had suffered. A quieter story than "Will You Please Be Quiet, Please?" it is Carver's first story that convincingly takes a wife's point of view. For the wife's name, he chooses another permutation of Maryann: Nan. Ray said it took "tremendous daring" to write from a woman's point of view, but then he "liked doing it, being able to do it." He was so confident about this story that he mailed it off to *Carolina Quarterly* a day or two after he finished it.[40] In this version of the story, Carver amplifies the sad circumstances of Val Burk's death: Nan's father has died five months before, without family, on the steps of a rooming house in Modoc, Oregon. Also in "The Student's Wife," Nan tells the husband a dream, in which an older couple invites them to go for a ride in a boat that has a front seat just "big enough for three. You and I started arguing about who was going to sacrifice and sit all cooped up in the back. . . . But I finally won out. I squeezed in the back of the boat, but it was so narrow it hurt my legs, and I was afraid the water was going to come in over the sides. And then I woke up."[41]

The sacrifice that turns out to be more painful than anticipated was becoming familiar to Maryann, too, but she was willing to stick it out for another year at Iowa so that Ray could leave with a degree that would help him get professional work. So far he had completed only twelve credits (less than one semester's worth) of thirty required for an MA or sixty for an MFA. She had postponed her education so that he could finish his, and she was more than ready for him to support the family.

The next year at Iowa, Ray might have studied, at last, with Vance Bourjaily or with Nelson Algren or Richard Yates, who visited that year. He might have become friendly with students like Ted Weesner and Andre Dubus, with whom he shared a devotion to careful prose and realistic fiction. He might eventually have finished his course work, turned in a creative thesis, received an MFA degree, and joined the faculty of another creative writing program. Or he might have drawn the attention of a teacher or editor who could give him access to a magazine that paid serious money for a story.

He might have done all that, but he did not. Ray Carver was often impetuous, but that does not explain exactly why he decided to drive west out of Iowa before the beginning of summer. Maryann noted that their friends the Mitchells were going back to England, and "Ray got itchy feet too." MacMahon was returning to Ireland. Students were splitting in all directions, some for a summer of farm or factory labor, others for exotic (to Ray) destinations like Cape Cod, the Catskills, or Europe; some were graduating, going out to see if they had what it took to be a writer in the world. Maryann, like Ray, was homesick for the West and her family. Grief for her father intensified that longing. The thought of spending a hot Midwestern summer and then another Iowa winter in a Quonset hut cannot have been appealing.

The validation of a second fellowship had salvaged Ray's pride, and perhaps he simply could not face another year in an atmosphere he disliked. It would be wrong to conclude that Ray's decision to leave Iowa was self-destructive. He felt, rightly or not, that something in Iowa was destroying *him*. Fear of that drove him to cut his losses. What Ray could take away with him were the short stories he had written during the past year—at the end of his life, he still considered them among his best—and the confidence he had gained by writing them. "The grass must be greener elsewhere and so on," was the best explanation Maryann could come up with years later.

And so off they went, piled into the old Chevy again. "Being in the car, just the four of us, was always a calming, close time," Christine Carver recalled.[42] They headed toward Sacramento, California, where Ray's parents were living and finally collecting a little disability money from Collins

Pine because of Raymond Senior's injury eight years before. Ray believed he could find a job that paid enough to allow Maryann to finish college. In his "Fires" essay, after Carver explains the "baleful" influence of his children on his life and work, he concludes that he had learned that "I had to bend or else break. And I also learned that it is possible to bend and break at the same time."

The compromises Ray made *would* break his spirit. And from that breaking, he continued to make short stories and poems, dredging the depths of his worst experiences and making them over in his imagination. Despite its apparent meanness, his essay "Fires" holds a profound truth. His early marriage, the burden of caring for children, that hard year in Iowa City, and the worse years that would follow—all those things became manifest in his stories.

PART II

SEARCH

CHAPTER 9

Grinding and Sharpening

Summer 1964–December 1966, Sacramento, California

I have not known many survivors.
—James Baldwin,
Nobody Knows My Name:
More Notes of a Native Son,
transcribed in one of
Carver's notebooks

The Carvers were excited to be returning west in June 1964. When they saw the mountains and felt the High Plains air of Wyoming, they bought fireworks at a stand and shot them off to celebrate.[1] They were back in the "home of possibility," as the writer William Kittredge calls it, where "the vast landforms and skies still seem to imply freedom . . . a sense that an expansive, generous life is possible in this open place. You can be anything you can manage—that's the message a lot of us get."[2]

Managing was often a problem. Things began to go wrong when they arrived at C.R. and Ella's in Sacramento and discovered that the U-Haul box on the roof of the car had slipped, jamming the car doors shut. The kids climbed out a window and got help to extricate their parents from the car. When Ray and Maryann saw his parents' faces, they knew they had made a mistake. C.R. and Ella had waited years for a disability settlement from Collins Pine. It was all the money they had in the world, and they were terrified that Ray and Maryann and the children were going to cost them some of it.[3]

Gravitating to the University of California at Davis, Maryann quickly enrolled herself in summer school, got a married students' apartment, and a job as a breakfast-shift waitress.[4] To welcome the Carvers back to California, Amy brought a white poodle puppy that the children named Mitzi. When Ray looked for a full-time job, he learned that his General Studies degree opened no doors, at least not when it was presented by a nervous man who needed dental work and a new wardrobe. He applied for jobs as a civil servant in the federal war on poverty program or an insurance adjuster or underwriter. He turned down an offer from a bill collection agency because he'd want to tell the "poor devils owing money to lie low until the heat was off."[5] By the end of summer, Ray was so discouraged that he felt he should not have left Iowa. There were no jobs that he could tolerate. Believing Ray wanted more professional work, Maryann's mother persuaded someone she knew in Willows, California, to offer him a job teaching high school with a provisional teaching certificate. In midsummer when he signed the contract, this job sounded ideal: it gave him the rest of the summer to write. But as September neared, he "went into a major case of the heebie-jeebies."[6]

Ray left the school district in the lurch. They tried to sue him for breach of contract, but he refused to pick up the registered letters they sent him. As a result of all that, he had a sort of "nervous breakdown." One day he even half packed his car, with the idea of driving back to Iowa. As the last hot days of summer parched the valley, a drunken man showed up at their door at four in the morning trying to kill Ray with a tire iron—a case of mistaken identity. To Ray's mind, that episode represented the whole summer, which he described to several correspondents as one of "mistaken identity, dissolution, evaporation." Through all these three months, his typewriter had been broken down, and he wrote nothing except letters.[7]

Not long after that nadir, Ray was holding down two jobs: full time as a shipping and receiving clerk at Weinstock-Lubin department store, and four hours nightly as a salesman in what he called a "good" bookstore. They moved to a four-bedroom house in Sacramento, where Ray had a study and the kids had bedrooms; all they lacked was furniture. Vance and Christi started school, and Maryann returned to college—not at UC Davis but at the more affordable Sacramento State, which charged a mere $48 per semester. Maryann went to school during the day and began hostessing at a restaurant.[8]

At the bookstore, Ray bought a copy of *The Best American Short Stories of 1964,* then edited by Martha Foley and David Burnett. At the back of the book, he discovered to his "surprise and pleasure" that Foley had included "Furious Seasons," published in *December,* among her several hundred "Distinctive Stories."[9] *December: A Magazine of the Arts and Opinion,* an unlikely vehicle for Carver's first national recognition, is one key to understanding his entire career. The fat annual magazine that had more pages (three hundred) than it had paying subscribers put out its first issue in December 1957 (hence the name). When editor Jeff Marks left Iowa City to become a Chicago postman, he took the magazine with him. Marks often stopped for coffee with an editor named Curtis L. Johnson at the *Encyclopedia Britannica* offices. Tired of doing the magazine, Marks soon "gave" it to Johnson, along with "Furious Seasons," which he'd recently accepted. Johnson named himself editor in chief and became a "one-man operation of gall, grit, and gruesome pride."[10] Johnson's antiestablishment attitude suffused his magazine, and he had a particular fondness for realistic fiction about working-class characters.

Little magazines, or "littles," like *December* served to register the nation's literary activity. As Michael Anania, of the Coordinating Council of Literary Magazines, explains, littles "functioned primarily for writers. Readers were desirable, sometimes even actively sought out, but the impulse behind most is the writer-editor's conviction that there are writers who are not being served by existing publications . . . In contrast, commercial magazines find audiences and financial support and then, almost incidentally, find their writers."[11] Agents and big-magazine editors have long sought new work in littles just as music producers scout new talent on nightclub stages.

After Foley's list came out, Ray and Johnson began to correspond. Johnson admired Ray's "hard-earned sense of human predicaments and of the fears these instill in people without money." By then, Johnson had become proprietary about his magazine, outspoken about politics, and an indefatigable promoter of his writers: "The Vietnam War was going on, and I was one of the few independent littles, one of the few typeset and conventionally bound books with the freedom that mimeo magazines had earlier." Johnson typed out individual letters inviting people to subscribe and submit work, and hustled constantly to keep *December* going.[12]

Soon after Ray was honored in the Foley collection, he quit his bookstore job and began writing at night instead. His crisis was over, he wrote Tom Doherty, barely acknowledging that the vast improvement in his mental state coincided with the recognition of his story and his resumption of writing. Yet suddenly the house that had been too big and unfurnished was a grand place where they had a dog and tree toads hopping around at night. Nor did he mind the dull retail job; it gave him a routine and time to write.[13]

By October Ray had more good news in a letter of acceptance and a $20 payment for "The Student's Wife" at *Carolina Quarterly*.[14] But before Christmas, the whole fragile structure came tumbling down. As Christmas approached, Ray began to dislike his job because he was inept at assembling electric trains and other holiday toys, but catastrophe struck when the whole crew was fired over a theft of cookies from the store. Ray swore he wasn't the culprit. In any case, Ray—who had for a few weeks and for the first time been the family's main wage earner—was out of work. They made light of it; at least, that's what Maryann remembered:

We had this big house that was at least a hundred dollars more than we could afford, and this horrible, mindless poodle that became the topic of the dog story ["Jerry, Molly, and Sam"]. She attacked our laundry and urinated on the living room rug every chance she got. The children loved her and played with her by the hour, dressing her in clothes or pushing her in the doll buggy. But Ray was so funny. We'd just laugh instead of cry. No furniture. But we'd sit there at night and count the urine stains on the rug. We'd never had this happen to us. We couldn't pay the rent or the light bill, and they shut the power off, and we were beaten. Ray was looking for work, and he couldn't find it.[15]

Good humor was not enough to get them through this time. Maryann dropped out of Sacramento State College even though she was close to the end of the semester. Losing a job as a "stock boy," Maryann later said, precipitated the first time Ray "really faced himself—he was shy and sensitive and hated the work anyway . . . it made him withdraw more . . . he was in an awful state."[16]

Ray insisted on driving Maryann to and from work in the evenings. He helped himself to her tip money to buy himself a double whiskey at the bar when he came to pick her up. One night he failed to pick her up and admitted that he'd been out to see a girl he'd met in Davis. When they couldn't pay the December rent, they snuck out of the big house and separated, "the only time we ever had to go home to our parents just to survive," Maryann said. She and the children (and dog) stayed with her mother in Paradise. Christi—who had just turned seven—missed her father and acted out her sadness by eating a whole package of Ex-Lax.[17]

Meanwhile, Ray camped out with his parents in Sacramento, sleeping on the floor of James's bedroom. Carver's story "Night School," according to Maryann, "reflects that time and that mood—not so much the events as the mood."[18] It's an allegory of impotence about a man whose wife, girlfriend, car, and career have all gotten away from him. Spending his last $2 in a bar called the Donner Club, he finds himself talking to two women who are going to night school to learn to read. They'd like to be able to read stories by Hemingway, but so far they are practicing on *Reader's Digest*. Carver steers around scorn in his attitude toward the women, but his narrator knows he's desperate to be hooking up with them. The narrator plans to borrow his father's car to drive the women somewhere, but he can't because his mother has taken the keys away from his father! While he's talking to his father, the narrator hears the two women from the bar cursing him on the sidewalk outside. He looks at his cot and the book he's reading, *Set This House On Fire* by William Styron, and sneaks out a back door to go to his mother's place of work for a free sandwich. After that, he "would go back to the apartment and read the books as if nothing else mattered; until it was all somewhere behind me, and I slept."[19] It must have looked to Ray as if his life was turning out to be too much like his father's.

About this time though, C.R. got a break. Fred Carver found him a saw filing job at a mill in the town of Klamath, on the northernmost coast of California. C.R. had done no skilled work in nearly seven years. He moved north by himself and stayed in a one-room cabin close to the mill. Each day his father worked then "was the most important day of his life," Carver wrote later. After enough of those days, C.R. began to believe he was strong enough to continue working. Ella and James moved to nearby Crescent City, at the edge of the harbor district that had been wiped out by tidal waves in 1964. James went to the mill with his dad. By then, Carver wrote, his father "could do the work and didn't think he had to worry that he'd let anybody down ever again."[20]

The extremity of the Carvers' predicament in late 1964 seemed magnified by changes in American life. Less than a year after Kennedy's death, President Lyndon Johnson had defeated right-wing Republican senator Barry Goldwater of Arizona. Soon the man who had pushed the Civil Rights Act and the war on poverty through Congress was explaining to the country that United States Navy vessels had been attacked by North Vietnamese torpedoes off the coast of Vietnam. Three years later, the authenticity of these attacks was discounted, but in August 1964, President Johnson pressed Congress to pass the Gulf of Tonkin Resolution, which became the basis for the American war in Vietnam that would be under way by the end of the following year and would last for nine years.

While separated from Ray, Maryann visited her sister Amy, who was working at the No Name Bar in Sausalito. She thought about starting her life over there, without Ray. Then two bar customers she'd confided in presented her with a book of Chinese poems. Inside she found $20 and a bus ticket to Sacramento. She used the ticket and reconciled with Ray early in January 1965. She took a waitressing job at a nightclub in Sacramento and cut a deal on weekly rent of a motel room with a kitchenette. Elements of a similar arrangement show up in "Gazebo," where a couple spend the day regretting their lost innocence as they drink, fight, have sex, and make up in the upstairs suite of a motel they are supposed to be managing.

Maryann and Ray fetched the children back from Paradise, and Ray again took care of them while Maryann worked a night shift. By saving her paychecks and living on her tip money, they managed to move into a tiny one-bedroom house that was a step up from the motel. Being separated had shaken them both enough to give them a new start. Ray wrote that he'd been "at absolute zero" but was now better because everything about their circumstances and states of mind had changed. Ray was still uncomfortable and fearful because they were living entirely on Maryann's earnings, but he had seen "the proverbial abyss and had really to take a grip on myself." Clichés mask the exact nature of Ray's troubles and decisions (which are much clearer in his fiction), but he seems to mean that he has decided to stay in his marriage. Neither Ray nor Maryann yet acknowledged that his drinking was not merely a symptom of his frustration but a growing cause of difficulty in itself.[21]

Again, Ray was feeling like a writer. Maryann agreed not to return to college. She would work until Ray found suitable employment because, Ray's "suffering was real. He was totally and utterly temperamental. He wasn't happy unless he was writing."[22] When the Carolina Quarterly with "The Student's Wife," arrived in late January, it seemed to Ray like an "artifact" that he no longer cared much about, but he judged it "a clean story" and was satisfied with his prose. He found fault with the rest of the issue, and pointed out that six of the poems were previously published in other journals. This sort of thing could happen by accident, he conceded, but, "if it's intentional, I condemn the practice."[23]

Finally, in February Ray started a job as a janitor at Mercy Hospital in Sacramento. He started out on the day shift, six days a week, changing beds and mopping floors. He had narrowly missed assignment to the cleanup crew for the morgue and the autopsy room. For the first time in his life, he was saving money, intending to pay off his bill at Iowa so he could return there the following fall. Compared to a year earlier, when he was "living under such a pall," he now felt "decisive and sharp edged." He called his current sense of well-being an "upswing"—as close as he ever came to naming the moods that passed through him.[24] During an upswing, Ray probably used alcohol to calm himself and inflate his belief in his potential. When the Ferris wheel of circumstances and moods brought him down again, the booze was there to blunt the pain and render him oblivious. If that sounds like a vicious cycle, it was.

But Ray did perform day-to-day parental tasks while Maryann was at work. When a car hit Christi while she was riding her bicycle, her dad was the one who took her to get stitches in her leg: "I had a bleeding gash in my calf, but the mother and son who hit me stopped, looked, and then drove on. Dad couldn't get over that people could be like that. We went over that many times."[25] "A Small, Good Thing," the story that Carver eventually wrote about a boy who is killed by a hit-and-run driver as he walks to school, says nothing about the driver's motives and yet disperses huge burdens of guilt and anger among its other characters.

After a few months at Mercy Hospital, Ray switched to the night janitorial shift. He liked the inverted schedule. After he'd slept a few hours, he had the whole day free to write.[26] As Ray told it later, the "first two years went by without a hitch." His life in Sacramento gave him much of the material that would make him a "poet of the working poor" and a "chronicler of blue-collar despair." He never felt that the people he wrote about were "losers and down-and-outers—the waitress, the bus driver, the mechanic; the country is filled with these people. Those lives are every bit as valid as ours. I am drawn to those people. They are good people, like my parents, people doing the best they could."[27] Again he found models in the Russians, especially in Ivan Turgenev's *A Sportsman's Notebook*, where the shape of a day and "simple, reflective, poetic feeling" serves in place of form or plot (as the British story writer V. S. Pritchett wrote) and in Isaac Babel's ruthless depictions of Cossacks, Russians, and Jews at war in 1918. What Babel said of himself might be applied to Carver: "I am the sort of writer who has to keep silent for several years so as then to explode."

Maryann got out of waitressing when she took a job selling encyclopedias door-to-door with the Parents' Magazine Cultural Institute. For an outgoing woman like Maryann, this was "an opportunity to make money, dress well, and use my intelligence, and I went for it," she recalled. "It was such a relief not to have this money worry. I felt like a thousand-pound weight had been lifted off my head." Maryann's natural talents with people were enhanced by the sales formula developed by Parents' charismatic sales director, Werner Erhard.[28]

Unknown to Maryann, Erhard was the assumed name of a former Philadelphia used-car salesman whose early history resembled the Carvers': at eighteen, Jack Rosenberg had married his high school sweetheart. To support his four children, he had worked "a series of dead-end jobs that paid little and offered even less hope for the future," according to one of his biographers. Then Rosenberg discovered he had a "knack for the high-pressure, slick-talking tactics that have long been a hallmark of aggressive auto salesmen in America." He began to make money and, in 1960, he and a girlfriend took new names. By the end of 1962, Erhard was living on the West Coast, working as sales director for Parents' encyclopedia division, and studying the ideas of Zen master Alan Watts and psychologists Carl Rogers and Abraham Maslow. Erhard based his success on having charismatic, interesting, "self-actualizing" people in his sales force. Most of the people who worked for Erhard were "overqualified" for door-to-door selling, but he had no trouble recruiting and keeping them because they formed their own community.[29]

Maryann was then twenty-four years old. The Erhard sales program added to her natural confidence, and in no time she was earning good commissions. At the end of March 1965, she was earning double what Ray made. Ray liked the money but complained about Maryann's late hours. He called it a "wretched life," with no time to do much besides "work, sleep, and gobble down food at appointed hours," but hoped they could stick with it long enough to get out of debt. He was keeping his "shoulder to the boulder," he said, styling himself as Sisyphus.[30] But he enjoyed Maryann's success, especially when he could turn it into a good story. Not every transaction followed Zen principles. Ray told this tale to Dick Day when he stopped at the Carvers' in Sacramento. In Day's retelling, it goes like this:

> Maryann knocked on a door and was invited in by a man. She spread her sales materials on the floor, while he sat on the sofa watching and listening to her spiel. At some point she realized that things weren't quite right; she looked over and saw that he'd opened his fly and was massaging an erection. She stopped talking, then said, "All right, you sonofabitch, pay up," and handed him the contract to sign. He signed it. He'd bought $500 worth of books.[31]

Within months, Maryann was attending meetings with Erhard, who was both her boss and the manager of the Bay Area sales office. On forms completed later, she reported $8,000 in income for 1965; for the same year, Ray reported $3,000. For the Carvers, the total income of $11,000 was a fortune, and, in fact, it did hoist them into the middle class.[32]

As money began to come in, Ray rented an office in someone's home where he could go to write. But soon Ray began to think that what he really would like to do was become a librarian; he was accepted at Western Michigan University's program in library science, the only one in the country, as far as he knew, that did not have a foreign language requirement. Just as that was decided, he began to have second thoughts about abandoning the Iowa Writers' program — "unfinished business or something," he called it. A reminder of what he'd abandoned in Iowa appeared in *Look* magazine in June: an article about Paul Engle's international influence on literature included a picture of Ray and Maryann, the Mitchells, the Holmeses, and Paul Engle himself.[33]

Ray said he knew he had to plan his life carefully in the future, because at twenty-seven, he was "getting too old to make any more wrong moves." He made up his mind to depart for Kalamazoo for the library science program on June 21, leaving Maryann in Sacramento. As the date approached, Ray broke a long dry spell and began to write several hours a day.[34] Instead of going to Kalamazoo, however, he cut his hours at the hospital to weekends and wrote, all day, five days a week. By the time his classes would have started in Michigan, he had mailed out a new fifty-page story and had two more in the works. Next, he determined to reenroll at Iowa in the fall of 1965, where, he believed, he could simultaneously complete his MA in creative writing and a library science degree. This plan, he boldly explained, would qualify him for his ideal job: half teaching and half librarianship.

Ray made and abandoned such plans at least four times while he lived in Sacramento. He was terrified by his inability to earn a living, but he wanted to believe that his real job was writing. When his work won some respect in the world, he did believe it. Whenever he had devised a clear plan for his future—such as the one to study in Kalamazoo—he felt secure enough to trust his writing and whatever it took to keep him writing, including Maryann's income. With that feeling of security, he—with apparent perversity—threw off the new self-forged shackle that would have prevented him from writing. Gradually, though, the cycle would begin again: with no career plan, he would again lose faith in his writing and sink into depression and increased drinking.

Maryann reveled in the money she earned at Parents'. She bought herself dresses at fine clothing stores, joined book and record clubs, and treated herself and Ray to nights out. They ate at the places where she used to wait tables. Her former boss at the Flambé Room had opened a new place, Aldo's Restaurant. In those pre–Julia Child days, Aldo's menu of richly sauced continental dishes was sophisticated. In Carver's 1970 story called "A Night Out," a couple in their late thirties try to have an extravagant evening despite breakthrough strains in their marriage. Wayne is self-conscious and insecure and angry; his wife, Caroline, is eager to impress Aldo and take in the new experience. Baffled by foreign words on the menu, Wayne orders a steak. Wayne refuses to linger after the meal and snubs Aldo, who responds by kissing Caroline's wrist and giving her a rose. The celebration has flopped, and the marriage sustains more damage.

Like the fictional Caroline, Maryann was making conquests. Erhard's sales plan succeeded brilliantly with baby-boom parents eager to buy the best for their school-age youngsters. Maryann earned promotions and raises. They could go to Reno for a day or two. Christine remembered that her parents "would drop us off at a movie theater for all-day Disney movies while they'd go gambling, then they'd pick us up and go to a casino for dinner, and Vance and I would drink a Shirley Temple and a Roy Rogers."[35] On one such trip, Ray lost $100. He'd been reading Dostoyevsky's novella *The Gambler,* which reflects its author's addiction to roulette, and thought its description of the gambling fever was right on the mark. Ray's loss depressed him. He was still a janitor with unpaid loans. The Russian's dramatic binges at the tables in Wiesbaden, Germany, were part of a successful, if chaotic, literary life of the sort Ray was only dreaming about.[36]

Despite setbacks, Maryann and Ray lurched forward with their new arrangement. He wrote. Vance and Christi stayed in Paradise during vacations. Maryann and Ray bought a scarcely used candy-apple red 1962 Pontiac Catalina convertible in which—as she remembered it—Maryann "rode like the wind." Carver's poem "A Summer in Sacramento" mentions being able to afford a car, and comments "a yr ago we wd have taken it / & fled to Mexico." For Ray, running away would always have some appeal. The poem suggests other troubles: a couple without much to talk about when they go out, the man seeing another "girl." In August Ray was still "writing up a storm" and planning to return to Iowa in September after a camping vacation with the whole family.[37]

September came, and Ray again put off a return to Iowa. New debts piled up faster than they could pay down old ones. Mitzi, the mindless poodle, added a litter of puppies to their problems. They had a daily housekeeper and babysitter, but her duties fell on Ray when the young woman ran off to San Francisco. Ray complained of a "three-week hiatus" in his writing, but made use of the experience later in "Fever." After that hiatus, Ray rented a new writing studio and got "under way" again. Five stories and six poems were out to magazines. When school began, with Vance in first grade and Christi in second, Ray tried to write every day. Sometimes, like Myers the writer in "Put Yourself in My Shoes"—he suffered days when "he was between stories, and he felt despicable" or when well-meaning acquaintances told him they'd look for his name on the bestseller lists. Most days, though, he did the lonely trench digging that actual literary life requires and submitted his work to editors.[38]

Ray's letters to Johnson would span many years and comprise the best record of his early literary aspirations. He presented himself as a member of a literary world that had, in actuality, been receding from him since he left Iowa City. Small events became news: he was excited that a librarian at Sacramento State College had ordered magazines he suggested. Ray's vocabulary in these letters is formal, with a dash of country or redneck phrasing, but he slides into contemporary slang when he describes this "swinging" librarian and the "beautiful" possibility of receiving more literary journals.[39] His letters jangle with the effort of a man trying to figure out how to live a confident and literary life. Along with contemporary fiction, he read the lives and correspondence of writers. Some books he admired were the letters of Chekhov, Hemingway's Paris memoir, *A Moveable Feast,* published by Scribner's in 1964, Lawrence Durrell's Mediterranean island books, and a collection of letters between Durrell and Henry Miller.

December accepted the marital novella that Ray began in Iowa, *Will You Please Be Quiet, Please?* His most ambitious work to date was going to appear in the same small-circulation magazine that had published his very first story three years before. Ray and Maryann celebrated the acceptance in a bigger rental house, the nicest place they'd ever lived. Most of the $250 monthly rent came from Maryann's salary.[40] She became manager of the Sacramento office, working directly under Erhard. Both sides of their families descended on their large house for the holidays; Ray expected a "free-for-all," but planned to get through it by making it a "wet Christmas." Still employed as a janitor at Mercy Hospital, he listed his occupation as "porter" in the city directory, and the life he described in letters sounds more like that of a middle-class parent on a career path than that of a working-class guy just trying to stay afloat. In his mind, Ray lived in both these worlds.[41]

After her years of menial jobs, Maryann was thrilled to be doing more interesting work. As a top West Coast sales producer for Parents' in 1966, she won a TV, cash, and further notice by Erhard. She insisted that her relationship with Erhard was "just a work association, no hanky-panky whatsoever, but we did work well together."[42] Nonetheless, Ray could not help but be jealous.

While Maryann was often on the road, Ray was still mopping floors for a few hours a night while getting paid for a full shift. He laughed that his was "a writer's sort of job" and wondered "if he'd ever again have such a wonderful job, writing by day, working so little by night." But that easy job pulled Ray inside the world of infirmity and death he'd glimpsed as a delivery boy for the pharmacy in Yakima. Images of illness inundated him every time he went to work and gave him reasons to feel sorry for himself. Sometimes he was asked to clean up the autopsy room and other times his curiosity drew him there. The sight of a baby's corpse gave him insomnia for several weeks.[43]

Carver shows how the job affected him in "The Autopsy Room," thirty-one lines that convey the essence of his Sacramento experience: a sixteen-line stanza lists the body parts that have been left out for him to clean up, including a dead baby, a huge black man with his organs in a pan next to his head, and a woman's leg. The astonishing sight of the leg leads him into the next part of the poem. Now he is at home, and his wife is trying to comfort him. His hands touch her leg, which is "warm and shapely." But this comfort and the wife's promises of better times ahead are not enough to calm the poet, who senses that "Life / was a stone, grinding and sharpening." To Carver's mind, Sacramento was not the real difficulty. The problem was mortality. Legs now warm would soon be pale. Time was grinding at him every day. He felt this acutely and personally, as if life were sharpening itself upon his body. "Ray always felt that he would die young," Maryann averred. "He just knew, and this is one reason we always put him first."[44]

After a year at Mercy, Ray looked less raw than before, his body no longer rail-thin, his face accruing form. And he was drinking more. J Street, the main route between the Carvers' house on the east side of the American River and the hospital, passed through a neighborhood of elegant older homes, gardens, and palm trees, symbols of successful lives. Also along the route, another symbol beckoned Ray: the neon outlines of martini glasses, complete with olive and swizzle stick, marked bars where he could down a whiskey, listen to a jukebox, and talk to live human beings. Instead of going home after work, he began stopping by the Fireside Lounge on H Street, a smoky bar then frequented by old fellows coming in for boilermakers."[45]

At the time, no one understood that some of Ray's indecision and moodiness was due to increasing dependency on booze. "He functioned, he wrote, he worked," Maryann recalled. "We thought his dad couldn't handle alcohol, but we didn't think we couldn't. And his dad didn't drink a lot, but he couldn't drink very much without showing it. We didn't relate to it at all." Maryann thought the drinking they did then was recreational. "We had a blast. We were like a George Burns–and–Gracie Allen act. We had everybody in stitches." Drinking assuaged Ray's anxieties and resentments and allowed him to have fun, but his need for alcohol became more powerful as it helped him medicate his feelings. Looking back from 1984, Ray theorized that in Sacramento he'd had "too damned many problems with the way my life was turning out. I was too young to be a father . . . Those needs kept me doing odd jobs which didn't fit my personality at all. When all I really wanted to do was write. So that's why drinking took hold at a certain point in my life. If I couldn't find a goal in life anyway, it just might as well have been the bottle."[46]

Despite Maryann's good income and Ray's steady work, the close of 1966 found Ray and Maryann trying to borrow money "right and left." Their outstanding student loans were catching up with them, since they had been out of school for more than two years. A December 6, 1966, letter from Ray to his sister-in-law Amy and her family in Hollywood gives a glimpse of those days. Amy was staying afloat with bit parts in movies and occasional television commercials.[47] She had married another actor, Michael Patrick Wright, and they had a baby daughter named Erin. Ray asked Amy to bring up "a few kilos (or barrels)" of Mary Jane, the not-very-sneaky slang of the day for marijuana.[48] Street pot wasn't very potent then, but a few kilos (he's kidding about the barrels, of course) would have been a pretty large quantity for domestic use.

Amy's husband was coming to Sacramento to be on location for his first movie role. "Built like a tree trunk and subtle as a sledgehammer," he played a gravel pit supervisor and lead stud (in service of giant-breasted actresses Alaina Capri, Karen Ciral, and Haji) in one of director Russ Meyer's hilariously dour faux documentaries of the sexual revolution, *Good Morning . . . and Goodbye!* (1967).[49] Meyer filmed south of Sacramento, at a big ranch house near Snodgrass Slough and Dead Horse Island. Friends heard that Ray worked on the screenplay or, more credibly, that Ray looked at the script and asked "Where's the plot?" and that Meyer replied, "There is no plot."[50]

At the end of 1966 in Sacramento, the clouds of Ray's artistic isolation— his days as a stay-at-home dad and writer, his nights as a janitor—were breaking up. The friendships, compromises, and losses that Ray experienced in Sacramento would affect the rest of his life.

CHAPTER 10

Were Those Actual Miles?

September 1966–June 1967, Sacramento, California

> Torrents replace the usual seasons . . .
> —Barbara Guest, "The Jungle,"
> transcribed in one of Carver's
> notebooks

On a fall afternoon in 1966, poet Dennis Schmitz's students noticed a nervous man hunched against the wall of the temporary building at the edge of the Sacramento State College campus where their seminar met. His face was hidden behind dark glasses and a wreath of smoke. When Schmitz arrived, "the mysterious guy stopped him, mumbled a few quiet words, and offered his hand in greeting. It was the middle of the sixties, the rest of us were wearing our hair long, and the guy just looked out of place," poet Gary Thompson remembered. "In a few minutes, Schmitz came into the room accompanied by the man, and introduced us to Ray Carver, a poet and short story writer who happened to be living in Sacramento, and who wanted to audit our workshop."[1]

Schmitz's lively enthusiasm for poetry was just what Ray had been thirsting for during his two years in Sacramento.[2] Thoughtful, fair haired, and poised, Schmitz was only a year older than Ray, but he had completed more education. Raised on an Iowa farm, Schmitz studied literature at the University of Chicago and became part of a poetry circle led by John Logan, the editor of *Choice* magazine. Shortly after Ray introduced himself to Dennis, the Carvers invited him and his wife, Loretta, to dinner. By Christmas, the two families were close enough that all the Carvers came to a party at the Schmitzes'. Christi and Vance fussed over the three little Schmitz girls, and Maryann braided their hair.[3]

Ray and Dennis could talk all afternoon. They "would extrapolate from stories or do parodies of writers. He enjoyed that kind of cooperative storytelling; it was a way to exaggerate and have fun," Dennis recounted. "Ray had a wonderful sense of humor about the overblown and the trite. He delighted in spun-out jokes and stories that two people could build together." As the exchange progressed, Ray "would lean closer and say, 'No!? Oh, my God! You don't mean it!' He would feed on that, encouraging you to gossip." When Ray talked about his own hard luck, he did so with humor rather than self-pity and added "a compass, a finish, a completion to the thing. So the short story did seem to be his form."[4]

"Maryann wanted to promote Ray's writing and considered it her job to see that he got things done," Loretta Schmitz said:

> She had a big dream that her husband was going to be not a good writer but a great writer, and she was willing to waitress and sell encyclopedias and do all this while he was home dinkering with the short stories! Maryann and I would go for walks or talk into the night. The cost—what she did *cost*! Whether you say her motive was egoism or altruism, she was completely dedicated to having Ray become a great writer. She was tirelessly loyal to that vision and gave the best she had to give. I was a young woman with a writer husband, too, but Dennis was teaching so we could eat.[5]

To Dennis's eye, Maryann's promotion of Ray had "a certain naïveté to it that sometimes made it kind of humorous. She believed fiercely in him, but sometimes she wanted to be on the make without really knowing what that meant." Sometimes Ray found it humorous or became impatient with it, "but he was more than willing to leave the practical jobs to other people." Even though the Carvers were inexperienced, Schmitz felt, they weren't limited by Ray's working-class background. "They were smart and well educated. It was just that they were young and vulnerable and had no coping mechanisms. Neither of them had a solid 'reality principle' or resources from their parents to fall back on." For the next decade, the Schmitz home served as a base camp where the Carvers would come to regroup. They would drive up, Dennis said, "at the most inconvenient times and not seem to realize it. One year Loretta had pneumonia. They never said things were going badly. They would tell extravagant stories, and everyone would laugh like it was the most hilarious thing."[6]

Although Sac State had begun as a sleepy, conservative campus dominated by athletics, the English Club had a hundred members during the sixties, and poetry was hip. Schmitz's poetry class attracted some "wonderfully odd" personalities and became the nucleus of literary activity in Sacramento. After class a "coterie of the truly obsessive" went to the Hornet cafeteria for coffee and more passionate talk about poetry. "Ray was fully formed when he came here," Schmitz said. "The poems were very good. He had made those breakthroughs a short time before I met him."[7]

As the politics, styles, and music of the 1960s seeped into Sacramento, Ray continued to wear what Schmitz called "sort of J. C. Penney's clothing." His appearance was anonymous during a time when others donned extravagant ethnic or counterculture costumes, military surplus gear, or jeans and work shirts. Ray knew about working-class life and he had no desire to simulate it. Ray's poem "On the Pampas Tonight," first published in Sacramento, mentions a president who "barbeques" in Asia (surely a reference to napalm bombing in Vietnam) and says he wishes he could "stand against this nemesis . . ." but when Thompson and others organized antiwar poetry readings, Ray did not participate. The October 1966 draft call was the highest yet, and almost a half million American troops were already in Vietnam. Ray counseled his brother, James, not to register with his selective service board and to carry a fake draft card instead. He studied Thompson's card, trying to determine if it contained hidden numbers.[8]

Admired by students and befriended by Schmitz, Ray found a degree of comfort that he'd been severely missing the previous two years. When the alternative paper the *Levee* produced a poetry issue, Carver contributed five poems. Seen as reports of Ray's Sacramento experience, they are dark but resolute. In "Balzac," Carver portrays the hard labor of writing. His Balzac rises after thirty hours at his desk and looks down from his window at the life on the street: creditors, young couples promenading, empty carriages. Carver considers the artist an observer and servant of the lives he writes about.[9] After "Balzac" appeared in the *Levee,* Ray submitted it to *Carolina Quarterly,* where a graduate student editor named Jack Hicks accepted it. After Hicks became a literature professor in California and a friend of Ray's, he understood how that poem "refigures Ray's own problems with domestic decline and financial disaster." Ray could write vividly about Balzac because, as his Sacramento friend Jim Young observed, "His mind was populated by the books and authors he loved. He went on and on about Dostoyevsky and his gambling. He talked about these people as if he knew them. They illuminated his imagination."[10]

Ray showed his professionalism in his contributor's note for the *Levee*'s poetry issue. Others described themselves in such casual sixties patois as this forgettable line: "Whether I am a poet, only my balloon and me knows." Ray set himself apart with this terse though inaccurate statement: "Raymond Carver graduated from Humboldt State and is now a graduate student at SSC [he was not enrolled]. Formerly published in *West Coast*

Review, the *Beloit Poetry Journal,* the *Western Humanities Review, Discourse,* and others."

Dennis Schmitz and Raymond Carver both pronounced the word *poetry* with an unusual inflection, something like "poi-tree." A minor detail, perhaps, but when either of these men spoke of the beloved subject or about a single "poi-eem," he conveyed a sense that the subject was personal to him. Schmitz and Ray were deeply committed to knowing the poetry of their own time. Some of the American poets influential to them then, Schmitz recalled, were Randall Jarrell, Louis Simpson, and Gary Snyder. In addition, Schmitz introduced Carver to translations of the Italian Cesare Pavese, who wrote both poetry and fiction after World War II.

The poetry that Carver wrote and that he was drawn to is more relaxed and personal than his stories, and some of it gains power though the intimacy established by its tone. He allowed himself to get closer to his subjects in poetry than in stories. Whereas humor, irony, and a third-person distance determine artistic form in the stories, Carver allowed poetry to become the place where he was able to say "I" more easily. There he speaks of his fragility and mortality. Carver's poems "redeemed him," Schmitz wrote. "He could speak in a level voice, directly, in a conversational way that often rises to a tone of reverence, praise, wonderment." And overriding Carver's fears, Schmitz continued, "there is still an astonishment, a surprised gratitude when he survives certain kinds of things."[11]

Thompson believed Ray was probably a prose writer at heart because he "always thought in sentences, rather than in lines and images."[12] His rhythms were based on conversational speech. Carver's early poems are often a bit mysterious. Whereas the stories are chiseled to reveal common experience in everyday language with little explanation of motivations and feelings, the poems use natural and dreamlike imagery to hint at deeper dimensions. In this regard, they more resemble a personal journal than reports spoken directly to readers. To take just one example, the prosaically titled "Trying to Sleep Late on a Saturday Morning in November" begins with some snapshots of the morning: Walter Cronkite reporting on a space launch, and Vance Carver wearing a "space helmet" and "iron boots." By dream logic, the boy's boots remind Carver of frostbitten feet and angling for whitefish on Satus Creek (near Yakima). From there, the poem becomes strange, as the would-be sleeper is likened to a fish on its side in the reeds. An even simpler poem, "Near Klamath," dives inward in its final line as the salmon fishermen "move upstream / slowly, full of love, toward the still pools."

Financed by Maryann's salary, the Carvers were on a binge of living well in 1966 when Ray went over to Sac State to meet the poets.[13] Her red convertible represented their piece of the booming consumer culture. Others might criticize American greed as the engine behind domestic racism and aggressive foreign policies, but the Carvers were still trying to become middle class. After years of scraping by from week to week, they suddenly felt rich—and yet quickly fell further into debt than they'd ever been when they were poor. As that cycle spun, Maryann's work life drew her away from home; the money was enticing, but equally invigorating were the motivational theories she was hearing from Werner Erhard. His sermons about transforming lives and using one's mind to recast experience cannot have been welcome to a man in Ray's situation. Jealous and insecure, Ray spent more time (and money) at the bars or hiding behind closed drapes.

These Sacramento years were, in Maryann's words, "the worst and the best of times . . . a real confrontation with ourselves and the world out there that wasn't academia." One of these confrontations surely took place within their marriage. Specifics about the ripenings and fissures that occurred as they approached a tenth anniversary are largely hearsay or conjecture, memory being unreliable in such matters anyway. Carver's notebooks hint occasionally of infidelities, but the references are oblique, not clearly datable, and usually framed as story ideas. In a January 1966 letter, Carver wrote cryptically: "Things are rather all in a muddle here—mainly my fault. . . ."[14]

Ray had always believed that lust was his "conspicuous cardinal sin," he told a correspondent in the mid-1970s."[15] Whatever his impulses may have been, Ray was tethered by the sexual attitudes of the fifties and did not glide casually into the free-love spirit of the sixties. Hugh Hefner's *Playboy* magazine, begun in 1953, allowed Everyman to be a voyeur, and Russ Meyer's movies did the same. Both Hefner and Meyer "exerted a huge influence on the common man's sexual psyche," Meyer biographer Jimmy McDonough writes. Hefner was on "a quest for that impossible ultimate romantic experience" (his own words) whereas for Meyer, men and women fought a war in which sex was "a momentary truce . . . more wrestling match than any expression of affection."[16] The sexual messages were confusing, and Ray, absorbent as a sponge, copped both attitudes. In his stories, though, infidelity is always a sign of trouble for somebody, rarely an occasion for discovery or liberation. His attitude toward faithless spouses resembles that of Protestant writers a generation older than he, John Updike and John Cheever. In fact, explicit sexual encounters are rare in Carver's published work. And yet as Hicks pointed out, "the jealousy, the anger, the deceit that you see in the stories are only the reverberations of the deeper shock waves. Ray was a master of repression." It's hard to say, with regard to the Sacramento years, whether the faithless couples in his writing come from

Carver's experience or from his fantasies. A comment by Maryann herself steps around the question with as much insight as anyone else is likely to bring to it: "Oh, I saw myself in these stories, of course, but Ray was a fiction writer, and he took liberties, God knows."[17]

Like others who read Carver in the mid-sixties, Thompson thought, "It was scary, how revealing—how raw—those stories could be. The only literary judgment he would make was whether it was true and sincere." Maryann was a storyteller, too, people noticed, so the fact that she didn't contradict a story never meant it had occurred. Hicks said, "Maryann had a good sense of incident and scene. She was an astute reader of his work, and early on he trusted her literary judgment enormously. And later, when memory became a problem for him, she was one of the people who could remember what went on when they were drunk. He trusted her judgment, is the best way to put it."[18]

In Sacramento, Carver became bolder about using the problems of his own life for fiction; along with boldness, though, came a method for objectifying the materials. Schmitz saw that "he was handling hot material with tongs in the sense that those were the problems in his life that he couldn't solve, but he could encompass them in the structure and stylistic manner of a story, propose an ending."[19] The culture provided fuel as well, from the marital quicksand of Edward Albee's *Who's Afraid of Virginia Woolf?* (on Broadway in 1963, a movie in 1966) to singles-only clubs and magazine covers that asked, "Is Marriage Obsolete?" In this period, Carver also began to explore aberrations in relationships. In the poem called "The Man Outside," a husband tells in just six stanzas how he and his wife have moved from fear of a Peeping Tom to exhibitionism and a terrifying mutual fixation. Exhibitionism and voyeurism are themes that will become more prominent in Carver's work during the next ten years, almost a trademark of his stories, an undercurrent of perversity that makes them distinctive.[20]

As he developed those themes, Carver also revealed a segment of American life that had not appeared before in fiction. Jack Hicks, by then conceiving his influential anthology *Cutting Edges: Young American Fiction for the '70s*, found it "absolutely striking, as freshly minted as anything I had read during the period." He attributes this as much to Carver's locales and subjects as to his style:

He wrote about people who lived in post-industrial suburbia—those sort of drifting regions of California. These were people who were running a three-bedroom, two-bathroom house who seemed very nice, but yet were rent by absolute domestic discord and at the brink of bankruptcy. For these people, all of life is temporary and leased. There's no retirement, there's no ownership, no guarantee a relationship will last or a child will grow up. Carver saw something significant in those small tragedies and moments of humor.[21]

The Kafkaesque story called "The Lie," published in *Sou'wester* in 1971, investigates the delicate brutality of a couple's financial and sexual interaction: a wife comes in from work dressed in hat, coat, gloves, sweater, and skirt, and answers a husband's accusation. The story's gambit is not specifying the accusation (infidelity is implied) and focusing instead on the dynamics of the couple's reaction. The wife dramatically denies "the lie" told to the husband by a supposed friend. Then the husband searches his mind for an explanation that will erase the lie: "I began to think about my wife, about our life together, about truth versus fiction, honesty opposed to falsehood, illusion and reality." After thinking about the movie *Blow-Up* and about Tolstoy, the husband remembers a pathological liar he knew in high school. The existence of that person allows the husband to believe that "such a person was my informant."

But just when he reaches this happy conclusion, the wife blurts out a confession—the unspeakable lie is true!—kicks off her shoes, and pulls her sweater over her head. She asks him about his day and strips out of her remaining clothes, ravenously eats cocktail nuts, and calls her husband "my little muzhik."[22] One last time the story turns on itself: the husband says, "I want the truth," and simultaneously becomes a child, crawling to the couch, putting his chin on a cushion next to his wife's body. In the closing paragraph, the wife tells the husband to rest his head on "'mommy's breast" and chides, "'How could you believe such a thing? I'm disappointed in you. Really, you know me better than that. Lying is just a sport for some people.' "[23]

"Ray got jealous of my job and the power and attention I had there," Maryann believed. She had been offered another promotion at Parents': "Werner was going to have me expand into a position that would involve overlaying the human potential movement on the sales work we were doing."[24] The inequality in the Carvers' work lives brought them early to a crossroads that many American couples would face in the next decades. At the time, though, there was no popular rhetoric for discussing what it meant if the wife earned more than the husband. To the contrary, in 1963 *The Feminine Mystique* by Betty Friedan launched a new feminist movement by arguing that American wives were smothered by their husband's superior earning power.

Ray continued—erratically—to look for white-collar work. He turned down a civil service job with the California Department of Employment because he would rather be a librarian. Once he asked Clark Blaise and his wife, Bharati Mukherjee, to help him get a teaching job ("college or intermediary grades") in Calcutta! Apparently Ray felt that teaching in a foreign country would be less frightening than facing high schoolers in California. Ray admitted he didn't know much about India except what he learned from Satyajit Ray's Apu films and *colored* photographs of the country. He told Curt Johnson he was "writing like a streak," but in the meanwhile he was resurrecting his plan to go to Michigan for an MA in library science. He said that he didn't want to teach and might like to work for a publishing house. Johnson replied with the name of Dick Carter, a friend of a friend who worked at Science Research Associates in Palo Alto and might read *December* (where the intermediary friend had published a story) "so that might be of some use."[25] On the basis of this thin connection, Carver mailed off a letter of inquiry about jobs.

Ray's malleable sense of his destiny sounds like a teenager's. Responsibilities had been forced upon him when he was still a boy, and perhaps he remained stuck at that point, convinced he'd done enough when he married the mother of his children. But by early 1967 he knew he was losing his direction, and he began to take measures, drastic measures, to alter his course. When Maryann reviewed decisions she and Ray made, it seemed to her that "I had power within the house on a day-to-day level, but Ray set the ethos or the vision for our lives." At critical junctures, she "would be going full steam ahead on the last vision, and he would all of a sudden abruptly change."[26]

At a bar, in the spring of 1967, Ray met a bankruptcy attorney who offered him a way to get off this spinning world. Maryann was "vehemently opposed to declaring ourselves bankrupt, but Ray was not ashamed at all." She remembered this attorney as "the most myopic person I'd ever seen. His glasses were four inches thick. It was like dealing with a mole." In Maryann's opinion, the bankruptcy was unnecessary; indeed, her credit-based notion of how to get ahead has since become an American norm. "We were both making good money and we were paying our bills. We weren't having any trouble with creditors. But Ray just decided we didn't want to do this anymore."[27]

The creditors, nonetheless, were numerous. Before they filed the bankruptcy papers, they sold Maryann's "faster than the wind" car. She advertised it in the Sacramento *Bee* with this attention-getting tag:

> **MOTHER Must Sell Her Car.** 2nd owner. 62 Pont. Catalina Convert. Exl. Cond., ps, pb, rh, new auto. trans. Premium ww tires. Well cared for, $875. 481-0368, aft. 7.[28]

and sold it to Don Hickey Motors for $525 before the bankruptcy papers were filed on April 14, 1967. Remaining possessions listed were household goods ($300), books and pictures ($25), and a 1962 Corvair ($350). Of course, those figures would be on the low side, for who can prove the value of secondhand goods? The creditors' claims totaled $7,836, about equal to the annual salary Maryann reported for 1965 or about $47,000 in year-2005 dollars. Unpaid college loans made up nearly $5,000 of the debt, with Humboldt State claiming $4,000; Chico State had turned $920 in student loans over to finance companies. Then there were bills totaling $800 from women's clothing stores such as Joseph Magnin's in San Francisco; the Courtesy Charge Association of Long Beach ($100) was no longer courteous, nor was Bankamericard ($268). The phone bill was $80, and gasoline companies claimed $706, but medical care—four doctors' bills totaling $48—had been a bargain. The Sacramento *Bee* demanded payment for the classified ad about the Pontiac ($14). At odds with the Carvers' own valuation of their library, the Book-of-the-Month Club wanted $50 and the Literary Guild $115 for books that had been ordered and not paid for; a claim for $190 in damages to a parked car in an accident Maryann had the previous year had been lodged against the Carvers in small claims court, and the Sacramento Bail Bond Agency presented a bill for $50.[29]

Family members also suffered in the debacle. Ray's mother was owed $100, Amy Burk Wright, $200. Two violet bicycles belonging to the Carver children had been secured by the Dial Finance Company of North Sacramento. Five years later, Carver published "Bicycles, Muscles, Cigarets," about a boy accused of taking another boy's bike and a father who tries to defend his son's honor with his fists. Rare because of the tenderness it shows between father and son, the story may be a convoluted attempt to make amends for the disappearance of those purple bikes during the bankruptcy.

For better or for worse, undergoing bankruptcy, like losing virginity or getting arrested, changes a person. Historically, it has carried considerable social stigma and yet been viewed as a second chance at the American dream, an opportunity for people to reorganize their financial affairs. Ray scoffed at the stigma and embraced the opportunity. He was delighted to be stepping off what seemed to him a terrible treadmill of economic servitude that mirrored his parents' struggles and failures, kept him from advancing in his literary career, and made him dependent on his wife. With the proceedings in process, his whole life, including Maryann's voice, seemed sweet again, as Carver writes in the poem called "Bankruptcy": "Today my heart, like the front door, / stands open for the first time in months."

When Carver wrote about bankruptcy again in his 1972 story "Are

These Actual Miles?" he drilled into some of the episode's darker layers.[30] The fictional Toni and Leo must sell her big red convertible *immediately* so it will not be seized by the court. Toni "is smart and has personality," so she heads out to the used-car dealers' row, hoping to get $900 and telling Leo that she will probably have to go out for drinks with "them" because "that's the way they work." Toni is angry to find herself married to a bankrupt, but Leo has his share of anger, too—and catalogs the way they have been squandering money.

The night of the story, the night Toni is out unloading her convertible, is punctuated by Leo pouring himself Scotch and waters and Toni telephoning in reports on her progress. Altogether, it is a long humiliation for both of them: Toni gets drunk and tells the car buyer why they are desperate to sell the car. Even after she has the check for $625 in her purse, she stays to finish her dinner, telling Leo it is "part of the deal." Leo loathes himself and thinks of suicide while he waits all night for her to come home. After the buyer drops Toni off, she lunges at Leo, tears his shirt, and calls him "bankrupt" and "son of a bitch." He looks around "for something heavy" (to hit her with, one assumes) but lets her stumble off to bed. The typescript of this story shows a tighter connection between bankruptcy and sexuality than the published version does. Leo undresses Toni, inspects her underpants (not mentioning what he finds), and tucks her under the covers. When the buyer returns with Toni's forgotten makeup bag, Leo tries to speak to the man, but all he can get out of his mouth is "Monday." Monday's the day they go to bankruptcy court, the day he will be "home free."

As the next stage of their financial regenesis, Ray and Maryann moved out of their big rented house and took on the management of an apartment complex on Lunar Lane. The typical postwar California buildings—two-story, stucco, with outside unit entrances—were ominously named the Diablo Riviera. Ray and Maryann received a free apartment and $100 a month. Maryann rented apartments, collected rent, and kept accounts; Ray was supposed to take care of maintenance and outdoor work. But Ray would do anything to avoid manual work and was, Thompson thought, "the most mechanically incompetent person I ever met"—nor was he the sort of person who would respond eagerly to emergency calls.

The children liked the Diablo Riviera because the complex had a swimming pool. Maryann and Ray celebrated his twenty-ninth birthday and their tenth wedding anniversary on this riviera. Thompson, too, recalled an afternoon of sunshine and friendship at the poolside that belied the troubles that dominate the official documents and short stories from those ragged times:

It was about one in the afternoon, and they were having a party at their apartment—Amy and her actor husband were there too. I spent all afternoon at their place drinking beer and sitting around—all the doors were open, kids running around, talking about Hollywood. The camaraderie and stories and laughter were adventurous for me, because I had grown up with such different values and I found it liberating to be around the Carvers.

Christine Carver, though, recalls that the apartments also provided the setting for her father's story "The Bridle." That story of rootless urban society and a dreamer from the Midwest who breaks his neck while trying to dive into the swimming pool from a balcony catches the place's diabolical potential, though Ray did not write it for fifteen more years.[31]

On May 29, 1967, four days after his twenty-ninth birthday, Carver received news he called "the best thing that's happened, ever." It was a letter and a contract from Houghton Mifflin letting him know that his story "Will You Please Be Quiet, Please?" had been selected by Martha Foley for the *Best American Short Stories 1967* (*BASS*) collection. He was "bowled over" and in a "state of euphoria" about this news. When Ray looked back at this day, it became the first of three times in his life when "something good" happened to turn him around at a critical time.[32]

With that news in hand, Ray received the welcome information that the University of Iowa had been accredited to offer a degree in library science with no foreign language requirement. Ray's previous workshop credits would count as electives, so Ray optimistically calculated he might acquire the library diploma in two semesters. He could also check out the workshop without expressing a desire to rejoin it. On May 31, he gave notice at Mercy Hospital, where he had been employed for more than two years, the longest he'd ever held a single job in his life. "I don't think there'll be any turning back," he wrote Johnson.[33]

On June 7, 1967, Ray loaded up his gray Corvair to go to Iowa. Maryann and the children would spend the summer in California, where she would work and manage the apartments while the kids stayed in Paradise. Thompson and his seventeen-year-old brother, Bob, en route to their parents' in Michigan, rode with Ray: "We stopped a lot because we couldn't dim the high-beam lights on this Corvair. Ray had an idea about wrapping a blanket over the lights, so we drove eighty miles an hour with this blanket, straight through to Cheyenne. In Cheyenne we slept in a cheesy old downtown hotel by the stockyards, the kind of place Ray had a propensity for."

As they crossed the United States, they heard news of the Six-Day War in the Middle East, during which Israel captured territory in the Sinai Desert, Golan Heights, Gaza Strip, and West Bank. That war, begun June 5 and ended before Ray's classes started in Iowa, would have more impact on Ray than he could have imagined at the time. Back in Iowa City after three years in Sacramento, Ray found digs in a downtown boardinghouse. The Thompson brothers hitchhiked east. In his knapsack, Gary carried a copy of *Best American Short Stories 1967* with his friend Ray's story in it as a gift for his parents.[34]

Alone in the middle of the country, Ray Carver faced his future. On June 13 the court in Sacramento "adjudged" the Carvers bankrupt and discharged them from their debts. A day later, Ray began his library science degree with a clean slate.

Early on his first Saturday morning in Iowa City, he told Maryann later, Ray dreamed that his father was at the doorway of his bedroom, looking at him and saying, "Good-bye, Son." Ray wakened with a start, he said, fearful that something had happened to his father, and then fell back to sleep. It was June 17, 1967.[35]

That same morning, in Crescent City, Ella Carver found that her husband had died in his sleep. Clevie Raymond Carver was fifty-three years old. He had been working again as a saw filer for two years. He seemed healthier than he'd been since 1956. A coroner's autopsy deemed that coronary occlusion (heart attack), cardiovascular disease, and generalized arteriosclerosis caused his death. Confronting what seemed a cruel and sudden loss, the Carvers considered other explanations.[36]

James Carver, who lived with his parents and rode fifteen miles by bus every day with his father to the Simpson Timber mill in Klamath, recounted:

It was a complete shock when my father died. He was trying to lose weight at the time, and I think that contributed to his death. He was not huge, not overweight, but he was heavy and he knew it, and perhaps the doctor had told him that he should lose weight. He seemed to be concerned about it, so he started trying to reduce. For this he was taking all kinds of pills, which was fashionable during that time for weight-reducing. I remember seeing big banners flying, advertising these pills in Crescent City. So he had yellow tablets, green tablets, purple tablets, and they were all lined out. God knows, I don't know, what those pills were. No one inquired.

The night he died, he and I had some whiskey and a seafood dinner that he made—he was a good cook, liked to cook. But he didn't get drunk. He controlled his drinking better as he got older. My mother might have been working at the restaurant there in Crescent City, because I don't remember her there having dinner with us. Then my father just went to bed and didn't wake up.[37]

In "My Father's Life," Carver relates another version of the same night—the version, he says, that he heard from his mother. Ella believed that on the night he died C.R. sat at the kitchen table and finished a bottle of whiskey before he went to bed. She found the bottle "hidden in the bottom of the garbage under some coffee grounds." He snored so loudly that she slept on the couch. When Ella got up in the morning, her husband "was on his back with his mouth open, his cheeks caved in. *Gray-looking,* she said. She knew he was dead—she didn't need a doctor to tell her that. But she called one anyway, and then she called my wife."[38]

When Maryann picked up the phone, Ella told her, "Ray is dead." For an awful second, Maryann thought that Ella was speaking of *her* Ray. Then Ella said, "Mary, what should I do? He's cold!" and Maryann realized she was talking about Raymond Senior. "I was so grateful that she was the widow instead of me that I just took over," Maryann said.[39]

The first thing Maryann had to do, of course, was to contact Ray in Iowa City. Within a few hours the messenger came, wakened Ray, and confirmed the fear raised by his early-morning dream. In notebook jottings, Carver sketched the anguish of a son receiving news of his father's death from a bartender or while in bed with a woman.[40] Shame more than fact emerges from these incomplete scenes, the sort of shame that led Ray to judge himself a lesser man than his father in the last lines of "Photograph of My Father in His Twenty-Second Year."

Ray had been only three days advanced on his plan to become a librarian when his father died. He drove the brights-only Corvair to Dave and Charlene Palmer's in Rockford, Illinois, and they got him to Chicago for a flight home. In Crescent City, Maryann and Ray accompanied Ella and James to Taylor's Mortuary to plan a funeral; Maryann thought she was the only one who went in to see Raymond's body. Carver's poem "My Dad's Wallet" describes a meeting in a dusty undertaker's office where they agreed to transport Raymond's body 512 miles north to Yakima so he could be buried as he wished, near his parents. They paid for embalming and a casket. He no longer owned a suit, so they had to purchase that too, declining the option to save money by burying him without pants. It would all be expensive, but Ella "nodded / as if she understood." They all stared at her husband's worn wallet as Ella extracted his cash to apply it "toward this last, most astounding, trip."

The trip was strange for the family following the hearse as well. "Our car would round a corner," Maryann remembered, "and we'd see the undertaker's hearse, with Raymond's coffin inside, stopped at a drive-in, where the mortician had stopped to eat. Not only did that give us all a sad start, but for Ray, the writer and elder son, it was a dramatic, ironic experience to travel across three states, on the same route with his dad's coffin. He kept saying, in tears, 'I just wish I could go take my dad and bury him.' "[41]

Clevie Raymond Carver's funeral took place at Shaw and Sons in downtown Yakima, late on Thursday morning, June 22, 1967. C.R.'s cousin Robert Green, Claude Sullens from the mill, and two other men carried the casket. They chose "That Old Rugged Cross" for one of the hymns, just as C.R. had done when each of his parents died. "Father's funeral really tore Ray and me up," James remembered. In a manuscript sketch called "The Brothers," Carver wrote that he felt an outpouring of affection for his brother as they stood beside their father's casket. Other notes describe the two brothers: the elder is a college teacher with a marriage on the rocks who is trying to write; the younger always had to work and has not finished school. The younger brother, these notes say, had been most devoted to their father.[42]

Though his own parents had been buried at Terrace Heights Cemetery east of Yakima, Raymond Senior's body was cremated and placed in the mausoleum at that cemetery, as Ella's would be after her death in 1992. In his poem "The Meadow," Carver mourns his father, now "Reduced to a cup of ashes, / and some tiny bones." As the family parted again in California, no one's future was clear. Ella sold her household things and planned a train trip to Arkansas and Texas to visit her family.[43]

Ray had not had a chance to tell his father "good-bye, or that . . . I was proud of him for making a comeback." Nor had Ray taken the chance to make his father proud by showing him his published writing. He'd feared that his father wouldn't "particularly care about, or even necessarily understand, what I was writing in those days." His father, Carver told himself, was not the sort of reader "I imagined I was writing for." Ray was learning to make ruthless use of the material of his own life for fiction, and he never hesitated to show the stories that this method yielded to Maryann, Amy, and others who might see themselves in them, but his parents were a different matter. He kept barriers there.[44] Perhaps he would not have been able to stand disapprobation from his father.

C.R.'s death had an impact on Ray's own drinking. His poems and notes disclose that he was already self-conscious and privately worried about his reliance on alcohol.[45] After his dad died, he tightened his embrace of the very substance that killed his father, as if seeking a way to commune with him, to learn secrets that were in the bottle. A writer and an alcoholic who was acquainted with Carver explained his own case this way:

I was told that before I went to my father's funeral I had been a drinker, but when I returned from it I was an alcoholic. "You had to find out what was in that bottle," a friend said to me. One finds out what there is to find out quite quickly, but I think that perhaps the paramount importance of booze to the parent makes it seem to the child that there was something beyond what the child can really experience, something that would explain why the parent's marriage, family, career, health, and brains were all put in second place.[46]

Ray had missed too much of his summer session to bother returning to Iowa. Bob Thompson drove the bright-beamed Corvair home for Ray. It now lacked a reverse gear, but he got it as far as Lake Tahoe, where its engine blew up at the top of a grade. The multi-lived Corvair stayed in Ray's possession a few more seasons, until it died on Highway 101 a few days before Christmas in 1968. Salvaged by humor and retrospect, it became known as the "car with no reverse gear" and the "car that threw a rod" in Carver's list poem "The Car."

"Iowa for us seems hard on fathers," Ray wrote Johnson, remembering how they got word of Val Burk's death in 1964.[47] In the ten years following his father's death, Ray composed several poems about him: "Bobber," "Forever," "The Meadow," "My Dad's Wallet," "Near Klamath," "Prosser," and "Photograph of My Father in His Twenty-Second Year." The last of these, a declaration of love, closes with a question that would absorb Ray for much of the next decade: ". . . how can I say thank you, I who can't hold my liquor either, / and don't even know the places to fish?"

Such financial solidity as the Carvers gained by declaring bankruptcy had crumbled when they returned to Sacramento after Ray's father's death. Ray saw no future for himself. All he wanted, he wrote on July 6, was to "get off somewhere by myself and write, but that seems to grow daily harder. . . ." Instead, Maryann recalled, Ray renewed his search for a white-collar job and "decided to become head of the family with a vengeance." To Ray this meant conceding that "there were more important things than writing a poem or a story . . . a very hard realization for me to come to. But it came to me, and I had to accept it or die."[48]

CHAPTER 11

Luck

July 1967–July 1968, Palo Alto, California

The more horses you yoke, the quicker everything will go—not the
rending of the block from its foundation, which is impossible, but
the snapping of the traces and with that the gay and empty journey.
—epigraph to Raymond Carver's
  Near Klamath, quoted from Franz Kafka's
  "The Great Wall of China"

That July, Ray finally got some luck. With a referral from Curt Johnson, he went to the offices of Science Research Associates in Palo
Alto, where the textbook publisher was setting up its college department.
Mereda Kaminski, the editor of the junior college series, overheard Carver's voice when he approached the receptionist and recognized "the tone
of a man who had always compromised but just kept hoping." She invited
Ray into her office. He told her he had no professional experience as an editor but volunteered that he had written a small book of poems and some
short fiction. Kaminski thought that showed "dedication and courage." She
described the editorial work, and Ray told her that he was a "fairly fast
learner," so she considered him hired. After another interview to set his salary, Ray was ready to leave Sacramento.[1]

He gave an ultimatum to Maryann: "your marriage or your job." It was
coming up on three years since she had reluctantly withdrawn from college to work full-time; now leaving a job she liked posed an "enormous
dilemma." But the free rent arrangement at the Diablo Riviera apartments
had collapsed since Ray's dad died. Instead the Carvers owed rent and
their electricity had been cut off. Jim Young and Gary Thompson came in
Young's truck to help them move quickly, after dark, "very hush-hush."
Ray left boxes of papers and manuscripts behind during stealthy moves;
perhaps this was one of those times.[2]

137

Ray paid more than he could afford (literally, since they'd borrowed money from Maryann's aunt) to rent a house in Palo Alto and was "turned-on with" his new situation. As his phrase indicates, Ray entered a new cultural zone when he moved to the San Francisco Bay area. SRA's college department office was on University Avenue, across the rail tracks and El Camino Real from Stanford University. The Grateful Dead played at the In Your Ear Club on a nearby corner. It was the summer of long hair, pot, light shows, and concerts by local bands like the Jefferson Airplane and Big Brother and the Holding Company. Kids from all over converged on Haight-Ashbury and Golden Gate Park in San Francisco, ready to "Tune in, turn on, and drop out" with LSD.[3]

But Ray was at the edge of that, hearing the sounds but not living that life. What turned him on in Palo Alto was a white-collar job, fringe benefits, and "a good place to live." They were in a neighborhood of ranch houses with single-car garages close to Highway 101 and its round-the-clock traffic drone. Loma Verde was a busy thoroughfare, too, but the family found it all appealingly conventional. Christi and Vance enrolled in third and fourth grades at a school around the corner, and Vance soon became friends with a boy who lived in a cul-de-sac across the street. Ray drove to work down Middlefield Road beneath overhanging maple trees. This time it really was a new start for the Carvers.[4]

Maryann took courses at Foothill Community College. Ray had a "cottage-den" in a converted garage across the backyard from the house. By Labor Day, he was at work on a long story, "averaging about 10 words a day" because a "platoon of relatives showed up" for the holiday, which caused the shower and bath drains to clog. Offhandedly, Ray mentioned to Johnson that he would probably sign a contract with a literary agency in New York. A month later, he was "one of the nags in the Harold Matson Co. stable," and Matson had sent a group of stories to Houghton Mifflin, the publisher of the Foley anthologies. If that failed, Matson would circulate individual stories to magazines. Ray was tickled by the agency's belief in his work, but Matson had no luck with Carver's stories during the years he represented him. Publishers did not want books of short stories by first-time authors, and commercial magazines were afraid of Carver's strange, underlit domestic tales.[5]

Johnson warned Ray that IBM-owned SRA was a company "where editors are all afraid the coffee machines will replace them." Ray replied with a typical bracketing of his options. He would give SRA a try but might return to the library school in Iowa if he didn't like it. But the trappings of his desk job pleased Ray enormously and he liked the work. SRA had pioneered a product called the Reading Laboratory Series, or "reading box," which allowed students to work at their own level and pace with color-coded cards. Ray had to select readings to interest college students and then condense and edit them for elementary-level readers. It was hard to find ideal materials. To his delight, Ray was expected to spend half his days reading short stories and essays in search of selections for the box. Mereda Kaminski's confidence in Ray was rewarded within a very short time. He knew stories by Chekhov or Maupassant that other editors didn't think of. Within a month, her "editor without experience had become an excellent editor who could compete with the best." She wondered later if the training Carver got at SRA—stripping down texts to make them simpler and shorter—helped him tighten his style.[6]

Once it was clear to Kaminski that Ray could make it as an editor, she introduced him to her husband, Jerry, an editor at another firm who also wrote fiction. Jerry, in turn, introduced Ray to textbook editor Richard Kolbert, who was putting together a junior high textbook. When Ray gave Kolbert copies of his poems, Kolbert requested "Wes Hardin: From a Photograph" for his book. What appealed to him was how Carver's "quirky eye fastens on the bullet hole in the fabled outlaw's hand."[7] Before the book reached print, Bob Dylan issued his album *John Wesley Harding*, the title song of which celebrated the same Texas outlaw as a sort of Robin Hood of the late Wild West.

Dick Kolbert and his young wife, Sylvia, were new to California. Dick was a New Yorker, and Sylvia was German. Ray and Dick liked to talk about books, but they also discovered a common interest in prizefighting, and both were angered that Muhammad Ali had been stripped of his title when he refused to go into military service. It was Ray's conversation, "his intimately low voice, the short phrases, the pauses, the colorful details," that Dick enjoyed most: "He'd get it out, and in a wonderful way that would build suspense. He could make a trip to the grocery store interesting."[8]

Sylvia loved to party, and she always wore hats. Dick noticed that his wife had a particular charm for Ray—"not only what attracted other people, her physical appearance, but her quirky nature and personality delighted him, as did her accent and her foreign manner." Sylvia was drawn to Ray, too:

Ray had blue eyes and curly hair and this grin always on him, his laugh, and full lips. He was so polite to the ladies—the way he offered me something like a glass of wine. He was not really flirtatious. But I had his attention, that's all. And he just adored Maryann. She helped Ray out so much, and he loved her. And she made herself always pretty; even as exhausted as she was, she had a lot of energy.[9]

Not long after they'd all met, the Kolberts and the Kaminskis came to a party at the Carvers' on Loma Verde. Sylvia thought the furniture was sparse—it was "the kind of place that comes with terrible gray drapes," but Maryann "knocked herself out always for guests and for everyone, the kids, too," while Ray talked and talked. Everyone except Mereda, who had a new baby at home, smoked marijuana that night. It was a first for Jerry. "At the end of the evening," Dick recalled, "Jerry became quite concerned when he suddenly realized that pot would impair his driving. The solution was that Ray drove him and Mereda home. Ray, obviously, could smoke grass and drive at the same time!"[10]

Dick Kolbert saw a difference between his two writer friends. "Jerry wrote novels, but he made compromises with life so he could have a good, steady income and provide a home and the usual bourgeois stabilities. Ray, too, had a job, but—and I think Jerry and I both admired this about Ray— you got the sense that writing was more central for Ray. Not that he *meant* to step on other people, he didn't have a bad bone in his body, but he made sacrifices in order to write."[11]

Both Kaminskis thought the relationship between Ray and Maryann was "too poisoned to witness." To them it seemed that she was jealous of Ray's talent and destructive in response to it. But Jerry had alcoholism in his family and was more terrified by Ray's drinking: "I had watched such excess from childhood. In the company of Ray, we drank far too much. I got scared." Dick and Sylvia Kolbert, however, remember nothing of the kind: "Maryann became louder and more talkative when she had a little wine, and she loved to have a good time, but they complemented each other," both agreed. "In the late 1960s, she believed in him, believed his ship would come in. He was willing to give all for his writing, and she understood that."[12]

Palo Alto was then a Mediterranean-style California town with a university in its midst, not yet the hyper-upscale center of world technology. The Stanford Linear Accelerator had begun operating, and some high-tech companies leased land from the university, but the term "Silicon Valley" hadn't yet appeared in print, and Intel Corporation was a year in the future. The street where Ray worked was still part of a quaint downtown with local businesses, movie theaters, and independent bookstores. Scholars and scientists lived quietly here, coexisting with strong literary and counterculture communities.[13]

For some years, novelist Wallace Stegner presided over Stanford's unique writing program, which offered young writers a year's support without degree requirements. Stegner favored outsiders to the literary establishment and took pride in spotting talents who hadn't had much college, such as Tillie Olsen and Robert Stone. Ken Kesey was a Stegner fellow when he wrote

One Flew Over the Cuckoo's Nest and came across LSD. Though the Stanford writers met on the campus just across the tracks from Ray's SRA office, they might as well have been a hundred miles away. Ray didn't drop in there the way he'd done at Sac State, but he did apply for Stegner fellowships. From 1963 until 1971, Ed McClanahan, a friend of Kesey's who worked with Stegner, screened every application for a Stegner fellowship, making first selections before passing them on to a committee. McClanahan recalled turning down Ray's submission one year: "He sent a story about a couple up in Humboldt. It was high on everybody's consideration, but it wasn't that good then. He didn't quite have that touch that came along later."[14]

So Ray remained outside the turmoil, a man with a family who wore ties to work as the West Coast scene burst from private to public significance. There was poetry in the streets and on political platforms and in mimeo magazines; Allen Ginsberg toured college campuses, and Gary Snyder returned to San Francisco after years of studying Zen in Japan. Then there was Richard Brautigan, a writer who, like Carver, had grown up working-class in Washington State and had lived in San Francisco since the tail end of the beat movement. In 1967 his book of very short, whimsical stories, *Trout Fishing in America*, became immensely popular.

In a way, Carver's not being part of all this defined him; he watched the innovators and the experimenters and kept on writing his out-of-step, dark domestic stories. Words were not highly valued in the counterculture: words were the medium of betrayal, the tools the government used to justify an unjust war, the tools corporations used to advertise their wares and justify greed. The most important art forms of the day were movies, art and theater happenings, and rock music. Long, difficult forms were in abeyance. In *Against Interpretation*, Susan Sontag explained that the function of art was transformation, becoming "an instrument for modifying consciousness and organizing new modes of sensibility." The model art product of that new sensibility was "not the literary work, above all, not the novel."[15]

Nonetheless, novels were published. Cormac McCarthy's *The Orchard Keeper* came out in 1965 and Robert Stone's *A Hall of Mirrors* in 1967, but neither drew much notice at the time. Older, iconoclastic writers who opened doorways to sensual experience such as Henry Miller, Lawrence Durrell, Hermann Hesse, and D. H. Lawrence had a following. Novels that approached the moral ambiguities of history or contemporary life with black humor (a critical buzz word of the time)—Joseph Heller's *Catch-22*, Kurt Vonnegut's *Cat's Cradle* and *Slaughterhouse-Five*, or Thomas Pynchon's works—succeeded where traditional social realism seemed ponderous. Norman Mailer and others began writing journalism instead of fiction.

As much as young writers and their creative writing instructors liked to intone that nothing mattered as much as "good writing," there was yawning uncertainty about what that meant. To be known as a "stylist" might fuel an academic career but not book sales. Carver admired authors like Stegner and John Gardner and William Styron who wrote big novels with "content." And yet here was the irony and his dilemma: Carver was uncomfortable with content and was not aware that he had any ideas he could embody in his fiction or develop to the length of a novel.[16]

Most of the stories Carver published before 1971 were domestic or semirural and traditionally realistic. He provided settings and weather and interior thoughts for his characters, and he usually satisfied readers' expectations for some kind of denouement. Later in the tumultuous 1960s, he moved toward a scrubbed-down sort of realism that went hand in hand with his predilection for short stories. He'd read Hemingway's theory of omission in *A Moveable Feast*: "you could omit anything if you knew that you omitted and the omitted part would strengthen the story and make people feel something more than they understood."[17] At the same time, Carver rejected fantastical or experimental modes of fiction of the sort practiced by John Barth, Donald Barthelme, Robert Coover, William Gass, John Hawkes, and others. When Carver wrote Blaise that his "Sometimes a Woman Can Just About Ruin a Man" is "much better" than "Dummy," he signaled a new stage in his fiction.[18] While the magazine version of "Dummy" is rich in details and explorations of feeling by means of imagery, the other story is the kind of spare, interpretation-resistant tale of rootless contemporary life that would one day be called Carveresque.

High with expectations for the release of *The Best American Stories 1967* (*BASS*) at the end of September, Ray was on a roll, hiring a typist (and complaining about her errors), and proffering opinions on matters seemingly beyond his ken. Hearing that *Paris Review* editor George Plimpton was editing an anthology of stories from little magazines, Ray tendered his opinion that Plimpton wasn't "the man for the job."[19]

At long last, on October 24, Ray held the *BASS* volume in his hands. Eleven of the authors' names stood in bold black type on the front of a white dust jacket. *Raymond Carver* floated there between Kay Boyle and MacDonald Harris. *Raymond Carver* appeared again on the back cover. Carver's biographical note telegraphs browsing agents and editors that he is working on his first novel and has a collection of poetry "ready for publication." Ray was "bowled over" by the stories, "including mine, glorybe." He found "Will You Please Be Quiet, Please?" sandwiched with nineteen others, only a few of whose authors' names—Arthur Miller and Joyce Carol Oates, perhaps Henry Roth and Boyle—remain familiar. Ray praised the Boyle and Miller stories.[20] But he kvetched that the publisher hadn't sent him a copy and most bookstores weren't carrying it. If friends hadn't brought it to him, he wouldn't have seen it yet. The Kaminskis were the friends who showed the *BASS* collection to Ray. They hoped to celebrate, but discovered Maryann and Ray in the midst of an "endless screaming fit," so they gave up the thought.[21]

Because of *BASS,* Johnson called Carver his prizewinning author and redoubled his efforts to help him. Sometimes Carver sent original manuscripts to Johnson, warning him, "I never know what's good until I look at something again months later." It was understood between them that Ray would prefer that his agent sell the stories to magazines that paid, but Johnson let Ray know which ones would be welcome at *December,* "a magazine, after all, for which you edit." The 1967 *December,* a double issue, carried two new lines on the masthead: Associate Editor Raymond Carver and Special Editor Gordon Lish. Carver had yet to meet either Johnson or Lish in person.

Johnson sent Ray detailed criticism of his story about a father and son who meet during an airport layover. " 'The Fling,' " Johnson wrote, "needs all the punches shortened just a trifle, in a couple of places quite a lot and the intention looked to. If you ever have a carbon, I'll be glad to go through it with a No. 2 pencil and suggest how and where." Ray told his friend he was "right as rain" about the story and he was "gouging away at it." Johnson brought up a point that went to the heart of Carver's fictional practice at that time:

> First person with you often seems to be kind of a fake first person, one you make up out of whole cloth and don't, somehow, really invest with a narrator's (not your own, necessarily) personality. The "fling" could damn-near well have been told without the frame of the narrator because not enough is, finally, made of the narrator. It seems to me you do better from third person unless—perish forbid—you break down entirely some day and tell it like it really is and come on strong in your own voice.[22]

Only a handful of the thirty stories in Carver's first two collections use first-person narration, and the most effective of these use a character who is very close to Ray ("Nobody Said Anything," "Collectors") or Maryann ("Fat"). Third person gave Carver a mental distance and clarity he needed to turn his experience into fiction. Listen:

> When he was eighteen and was leaving home for the first time, Ralph Wyman . . .

It had been two days since Evan Hamilton had stopped smoking . . .

Earl Ober was between jobs as a salesman.

Fact is the car needs to be sold in a hurry, and Leo sends Toni out to do it.

The telephone rang while he was running the vacuum cleaner.

Johnson's criticism was prophetic. Two stories that have defined Carver as a writer, both written in the 1980s, the title stories of his last two collections, have first-person protagonists who, as Johnson advised, "come on strong" in Carver's own voice: "Cathedral" and "Where I'm Calling From."

With what seems massive understatement, Ray told friends early in December that he'd barely had time to "recall which end is up" since beginning at SRA. Indeed, he had endured the death of his father and a great upheaval in his own way of life. Daily maintenance of business demeanor and production of work to satisfy his supervisors sapped all his energy. Around Christmas, Ray took vacation time with the intention of finishing writing projects he had under way, but instead spent a week visiting Amy and her family in Hollywood, from which trip he was still "recovering" on January 16. After six months in his white-collar job, he wanted a "real" vacation rather than a visit to relatives, he wrote Johnson, but he still couldn't afford one. Johnson, who did take vacations, replied that he was just back from a resort in Mexico where he didn't enjoy himself because he hated seeing headlines in Spanish "about how we are wiping out one Viet village after another and felt low and mean as a dog for being a rich gringo tourist." Johnson complained that he had trouble getting grant support for *December* because of the vogue for experimental stories. He was outraged that more realistic work like Carver's was out of fashion.[23]

Indeed, the January *Saturday Review* panned the Foley collection, citing "a Raymond Carver job" as the worst of a vulgar lot, "hardly more than sophomoric pornography"; reviewer Herbert Mayes remarks that the man's feelings in the story are predictable, while the woman "is the one who should have been explored and explained." That advice may well have influenced Ray. With the miraculous lifting of obstacles that marks his creative periods, Ray reported to Johnson on February 6 that he was "working seriously again, regularly . . ." and determined to apply for fellowships to support his writing and "keep on while I'm hot."[24]

While Ray was busy with his new life in Palo Alto, the English Club at Sacramento State was ready to publish a collection of his poems. They hoped to make a difference in the career of a writer they knew and liked and to make themselves a part of the world of poetry that was so vibrant in those days. They got seed money from the college and fantasized that the proceeds of Carver's book would fund the next book—and so forth into perpetuity.

Ray arranged twenty-six of his poems. Abandoning an earlier title idea ("On the Surface"), he chose "Near Klamath" as the opener and book title. Schmitz paid the campus printer $100 and cautioned him, "Ray isn't like the others. This is different." As the holidays approached, the uncollated pages of Ray's first book languished on a table at the Schmitz house. Finally a crew, including Ray himself, finished the job. Early in 1968, five hundred copies of *Near Klamath* were ready for the world. The chapbook was simply eight sheets of white paper folded within a rich red matte cover. The English Club celebrated and began talking about its next release, Daniel Davis's political poems. Gary Thompson reviewed the book in the campus paper, praising Carver for the "extreme personal nature" of his poems and for not "shouting against the injustices of the world in vague and abstract terms." Ray's friends set up tables to sell *Near Klamath* for 50 cents, but Sac State's jocks and aggies did not rush to buy poetry. "It didn't seem as difficult as it turned out to be," Schmitz reflected. "In any kind of literary publication, the hardest part is distribution. Compared to that, writing is easy." They ended up with extra copies and no profits. Davis was left holding nothing but ironies: "*Near Klamath* did not sell enough, and that was the end of the series. But I got my two pages of fame, because Ray helped me publish a poem in *December* magazine."[25]

Low sales of his first book didn't faze Ray. He retained that ability to soldier on that had pulled him through dozens of disappointments before. Carver always listed *Near Klamath* as his first book, even as the poems reappeared in later collections. His friends saw that as a credit for their efforts—either that or a way for Ray to fatten his résumé. An autographed copy of *Near Klamath* was priced at $7,500 in 2008.[26]

In January 1968, Maryann transferred to San Jose State College, her fourth college in seven years. The semester was barely underway when she saw a poster offering a year abroad through the California State College International Program. She stopped by the program office and persuaded the program director that she and her husband, the published writer, would be an asset to the program. Ray wanted to go to Italy, but the director recommended a less expensive destination offered for the first time in 1968: Tel Aviv, Israel. He offered them an additional $500 in scholarship money and a villa with a view of the Mediterranean Sea in Tel Aviv.[27]

Nine-year-old Vance resisted another move. Life in Palo Alto was as good as he could remember. He played catcher on his Little League team and sometimes both his parents—his dad still in his business clothes—watched him from the bleachers as the afternoon cooled into evening. The baseball diamond on Middlefield Road was scented by eucalyptus trees, a scent Vance would always associate with those days when school was around the corner and his best friends lived nearby.[28]

By May, the trip looked settled except for a question about Ray's draft status, which came into the open when he applied for a passport. Ray admitted to Johnson that he had "fallen out of touch" with his draft board and the Army Reserve after he married, but counted on the "people in charge of the International Program" to resolve it for him. It was resolved, or ignored. The Carvers had tickets to fly to Israel on July 1. Ray took an educational leave from his SRA job. "We were finally going to get to travel . . . and we were incredibly excited, as high as kites," Maryann recalled.[29]

Real life, it is said, happens while you wait for something else. While Ray dreamed of escaping his workaday life and living in a villa by the sea where he could write every day, events—or, rather, people—converged that would change his literary fortunes. After five years of letter writing, his first editor and now friend, Curt Johnson, was coming to a conference on little magazines in Berkeley. Ray planned to meet Johnson at an airport bar and drive him to the conference hotel. He warned Johnson that he'd be "in disguise," wearing a shirt and tie.[30]

Ray and Johnson planned to celebrate the release of "Will You Please Be Quiet, Please?" in a pocket-sized paperback edition of BASS. A cover in Day-Glo colors made the book look like a record album jacket. This pitch to youth culture (though not one story inside portrays that culture), along with Ray's apology for wearing a tie, epitomize the zeitgeist into which Raymond Carver and his story arrived. Purveyors of literature were frantic to reach a generation for whom politics and drugs mattered more than reading. The Tet offensive in Vietnam in January had shown that the U.S. forces were losing the war and irreversibly damaged Lyndon Johnson's presidency. In March LBJ announced that he would not run for president, and the movement against the war muscled up for widespread, often violent confrontations. On April 4, Martin Luther King was shot; exactly two months later, Robert Kennedy would be shot.

In between those two assassinations, on the last Saturday in May, two days after Curt Johnson and Ray Carver finally met, Ray would be thirty, or, as sixties culture put it, over the hill and too old to be trusted.

• • •

Ray and Curt set out in Ray's Corvair, which still lacked a reverse gear. They smoked grass with a friend of Johnson's in Sausalito. Late and drunk, Ray trundled the Corvair and his editor across two bridges to his hotel in Berkeley and got himself back (one more crossing of the bay) to Palo Alto. When Johnson called Ray to retrieve him, he learned that the Corvair's transmission had failed entirely. So he phoned Gordon Lish, the other *December* editor who lived in the South Peninsula.

Johnson and Lish, who then worked for an educational publisher, had discovered their mutual interest in little literary magazines while working at textbook fairs. After jockeying sales tables all day at some educators' convention, they would go out together for drinks. "We had a common enemy then, the Establishment," Johnson recalled. "We were both for the underdog writers." On those nights, "Gordon would talk like crazy." When Lish told him that he'd like to work in New York, Johnson warned him, "New York corrupts those who go to edit there." But Johnson already recognized something that he would never doubt in the decades ahead: "Gordon had infallible taste in fiction. Infallible."[31]

On the day Johnson called him for a ride, Lish, who was separated from his wife, had spent the afternoon with his three young children. In what seemed to Johnson a "luxurious sedan," Lish and his girlfriend, Barbara Works, took Johnson to Johnny Kan's on Nob Hill for a "Wild Turkey-sauced" Chinese dinner during which Lish "ragged a rich Texas redneck at another table into a fury."

Then Lish delivered Johnson to the Carvers' to spend the night. Stirred up from seeing his kids and the restaurant altercation with the Texan, Lish came in to meet the other Palo Alto *December* editor and his wife.[32] Lish told Ray he had read "Will You Please Be Quiet, Please?" He "raved about the story. He was high on it," Maryann recounted. Then Lish told the others that if he had been editing that story, Ralph Wyman wouldn't have stayed with his wife. If he'd written it, Lish told them, the story would have had a different ending. "And I just looked him right in the eye," Maryann said, "and answered, 'Well, that's just the point, Gordon. It isn't your story. You didn't write it.' "[33]

Ray and Lish discovered that their offices were, respectively, at 165 and 220 University Avenue. The three editors met for lunch the next day.[34] Such was the inauspicious beginning of a relationship that would change Ray's life. Within eighteen months, Lish had a new office on Madison Avenue in New York City.

How that came to pass has little to do with Carver and yet a great deal to do with his future. It's also a part of an upheaval that was going on in American culture during the late sixties. In their differences as well as in their similarities, Carver and Lish each disproved Scott Fitzgerald's pronouncement that there are no second acts in American lives. By the time he met Carver, in fact, Lish had already reinvented himself more than once.

Gordon Lish, born in 1934, grew up in Hewlett, on New York's Long Island, where he was ostracized by other children because of his severe psoriasis. His father, Philip, a partner in Lish Brothers, manufactured women's hats. At Phillips Academy he got into a fight with a kid who called him a "dirty little Jew" and was encouraged to drop out. When he was about fifteen, an experimental steroid medication (ACTH) he took for the psoriasis launched him into a hypomanic episode, and he passed some time in a mental hospital—or, as he phrased it, the "bughouse" or "buggybin." Here he encountered poet Hayden Carruth. In 1955, while working as Gordo Lockwood for radio WELI in New Haven, Connecticut, Lish began a correspondence with Carruth. The poet told Lish he lacked ideas and sent him a copy of the *Partisan Review*. Carruth continued to advise Lish for two decades. To alleviate his skin ailments, Lish and his wife migrated to Tucson, where he took Carruth's advice that he attend college.[35]

At the University of Arizona, Lish completed a four-year program in two years, majoring in English and German. Like Carver, Lish was a working father while still in college, and, like Carver, he sought mentors for his literary ambitions. He met a writing instructor, Edward Loomis, who preached classical literary values he'd learned at Stanford. Crushed by Loomis's response to some writing he presented in class, Lish left the room in tears and soon departed Arizona altogether. A decade later, Lish told Loomis that those classroom remarks had trampled on his own intellectual gods—passionate individualists such as Ralph Waldo Emerson and Dylan Thomas and Jack Kerouac. Lish recovered, his faith unshaken. He moved his family to San Francisco because he wanted to meet Dean Moriarty, the fictional hero of *On the Road*.[36] While he waited for that impossible chance, he acquired a teaching credential and exposure to the San Francisco poetry scene, which was flourishing after a local judge's ruling that Ginsberg's *Howl* was not obscene.[37] In 1960, as John F. Kennedy and Richard Nixon ran for president, Lish, now twenty-six, began teaching English at Mills High School in the suburb of Millbrae. He was a stocky, handsome, blond man of medium height, often dressed in tweed or glen plaid jackets. His psoriasis was under control, and his forceful, radio-trained baritone charmed his students. The principal praised the new teacher: "I was impressed by your hustle. I wish I could dilute your vigor with the rest of the faculty, and the mixture would raise the interest level of the entire student body." Other teachers complained that Lish's "pupils get so excited about ideas their voices could be heard in the hall," and responded with pointed disinterest when Lish argued for curricular improvements. The student magazine Lish sponsored drew fire for publishing ostensibly "beatnik" verses.

Outside of school, Lish and fellow teacher Candido Santogrossi worked on a magazine called *Chrysalis Review,* which morphed into *Chrysalis West* and then into their own enterprise, *Genesis West.*[38] The word *shit* in an early issue caught the interest of the Mills High principal. Surveillance of Lish increased. A list of his trespasses accrued: wearing a hat indoors, reciting the pledge of allegiance too quickly, allowing students to ignore duck-and-cover drills, having "funny furniture" and abstract paintings in his house, and recommending the ideas of Emerson. If this list seems far-fetched, keep in mind that some San Mateo County residents had recently demanded that abstract art be banned from their county fair.

Despite testimonials that called him brilliant and inspirational, Lish was denied tenure at the end of his three-year probationary period; two teachers who supported him also left their jobs. After public hearings, a local reporter wrote about the brouhaha for the *Nation.* He predicted that Lish's chances for reinstatement were "about as good as those of a bull in the Barcelona ring." Lish's dismissal changed him: "I haven't told the whole truth since teaching school—and what I got for my folly then were fits of crying and extremely precise directions on the swiftest route back to the safety of civilian life. . . . Every mistake in my life was founded on an effort to be nice. Whereas when I was *good,* the gods gave me the best that it's in them to give."[39]

Lish had multiple interests to consider as he trawled for a new profession. He applied to the University of Chicago Divinity School and corresponded with its dean but turned down a fellowship because he feared he was "all flash and no scholarship." He also declined invitations to teach at Deep Springs, an all-male college in the California high desert, and to edit educational materials in Israel for the African market; he circulated his fiction to Grove Press, the *Partisan Review,* and other publishers, but had no takers. Lish joked that he was waiting for Grace Paley, J. D. Salinger, Bernard Malamud, and Herb Gold (successful Jewish writers of short fiction) "to pitch over and die." In the meantime, his writing of fiction was stalled.[40]

Hearing of Lish's troubles, educational publisher Allen Calvin hired him to write a grammar textbook for his company, Behavioral Research Laboratories. Calvin's project, a programmed text system called *English Grammar,* surely molded its author's editorial habits. Grammar and writing are an *art,* Lish insists, that calls for "a scrupulously precise analysis of the dynamics of the American English sentence." He classifies words by the *work* they do: "a noun's work is to name something." His students must examine the ways in which words perform their work. In short, they learn sentence-level editing. The student who followed the Lish grammar program was guaranteed "a command of the language that will assure him emotional, social, and economic freedom and mobility."[41] Indeed, editing skill would become Lish's own ticket to freedom and mobility.

Lish read prodigiously in search of the fiction he favored, which usually had a controlled, precise situation or voice. Another reason he read so much, he said, was because "Lish is looking for models. It may be his Jewishness, his generation, or his naïveté—and likely all three. So far as Lish is concerned, any man's truth will do . . . Whatever I read I believe. Can you imagine what a muddle that makes of the mind?"[42]

Lish published *Genesis West* until 1965 and through that endeavor met dozens of writers. The idealism of the times and of Lish himself is indicated by a motto on the first issue's title page: A Garden to Grow the World Again. In lieu of the fictional Moriarty he'd been seeking when he drove to North Beach, Lish met his original, Neal Cassady. That meeting came about with the sort of serendipitous luck that seems to have marked both Lish's and Carver's progress. Lish wanted to meet an architecture critic named Alan Temko. Unable to find a listing for that Temko, he dialed another one, who had literary connections of his own. With typical California manners, Philip Temko invited the Lishes to a party where some former-wrestler friends of his from Oregon also turned up. One of these was Ken Kesey, who arrived with the great Cassady in tow. Within days, both Kesey and Cassady appeared at a party in the Lish home in Burlingame.[43] Lish published one of Kesey's stories and signed him on as a fiction editor. The roster of authors whose early work appeared in *Genesis West* testifies to what Johnson called Lish's "superior ability to spot good writers of every stripe": Donald Barthelme, Gina Berriault, Leroi Jones (Amiri Baraka), Tillie Olsen, and Grace Paley. He ran a story by Leonard Gardner ("The Last Picking") six years in advance of Gardner's now-classic novel about small-town California prizefighters, *Fat City*. Before that story came out, Lish contacted Gardner with editorial suggestions:

> He wanted to add a few lines, and he kind of implied, "Do you want to get published or not?" And I said, "I've got the story the way I want it." I really had worked it over. And I said, "I don't like your lines. What you're trying to add seems crude and gross to me. But I don't care if you don't publish it." And Gordon went ahead and did it my way.

When the story appeared, Gardner was surprised to read in the contributors' notes that he was "a California farm boy making his first appearance in print." That, Gardner surmised, "was just Gordon goofing—I'd never been a farm boy."[44] Making Gardner sound like a rustic was an early instance of the way Lish could spin an author's image and materials.

No project Lish undertook was too humble to become the vehicle for his prodigious personality. For the Job Corps, a Kennedy-era program for unemployed young men, he created a boxed set of reading folders called *Why Work*.[45] Instead of gathering already-published materials, Lish sent telegrams to thirty writers he admired. One of these telegrams went to J. D. Salinger, who had been in seclusion for more than a decade. Lish followed his telegram with letters—numerous letters—to Salinger that show Lish inventing himself as a literary impresario. A few months later, he received a telephone call at work from Salinger himself. When he understood who was calling him, Lish reports, "I was grinning so hard that my brain could not have had any room left over in it for one speck of business." As Lish tells it, Salinger said, "I'm calling because I was worried about you." Salinger again refused to write for *Why Work*. But Lish was not unhappy: "I mean, forget that it was animating him all four months later, it worked! had worked!— because there he was, J. D. Salinger, the impeccably reclusive J. D. Salinger, calling me—."[46]

In February 1968, Neal Cassady was found unconscious beside a railroad track in San Miguel de Allende, Mexico. He died soon after. To assist Cassady's widow, Lish tried to interest New York editors in a collection of letters among Cassady, Kerouac, and Ginsberg. In declining the project, one editor promised to try to find a publishing job for Lish in New York, but that would have to wait until Lish's divorce was settled.

Such was the limbo that Lish lived in when he and Johnson and Carver met for a workday lunch. "Not only," Johnson recalled about that meeting, "could Lish spot good writers, he apparently could also establish instant rapport with them." It would be another year, nonetheless—perhaps the strangest year so far for either Carver or Lish—before their friendship caught fire.

Johnson spent the rest of that Monday afternoon at the house with Maryann. She had allowed Christi and Vance to stay home from school "because of the visiting editor," though Johnson couldn't see that he was benefited. In fact, Ray and Johnson had been in the kitchen having an eye-opener drink when the school principal called to ask about the children's absence. "Maryann lied impressively: 'I was just going to call you,' she said. 'I don't know what it is, but they both have low fevers . . .' " When she hung up, Ray asked her, "in a slow and grumpy voice that sounded angry to Johnson, 'Do you always have to make up some story?'" Johnson found that Maryann had "clear opinions on many matters, and she expressed them forcefully. She was brimful of nervous energy and had facial features verging on the beautiful. She talked a lot, and I would guess was as close to a complement to Ray's personality as he was likely to find, strong where he was weak."

For lack of payment, the Carvers' outgoing phone service had been cut off, preventing Johnson from making business calls, but Maryann went ahead with plans to throw a party for Johnson. Gordon Lish did not attend that party, but "they had all kinds of people over," their Palo Alto friends as well as a *Partisan Review* editor who had been at the magazine conference. They bought "steak and booze, and it was terrible because they couldn't afford any of it," Johnson thought. In those days, "Ray and I both drank, but we were young. We didn't feel good when we got up in the morning, but we could function." During his visit, Johnson began to form an impression about Ray's reasons for drinking:

> I don't know that there is ever any explanation for a drunk's being a drunk, but in my opinion, just my theory—he couldn't stand the little hurts that people inflicted on each other; I'm not talking about self-pity— he just wanted to get along so that he could write. That was his consuming interest. And conversation was fine, camaraderie was fine, making love was fine, raising a family was okay, but it interfered with his writing. He just wanted to write. And why he wanted to write is as inexplicable as why he wanted to get drunk. Maybe they have the same root cause. It's likely.[47]

That was hindsight, of course. In June 1968 the Carvers were in a whirl of preparations for their year overseas. Maryann had a list of books to read about Israel, but they were out of date because the Six-Day War had taken place just a year before. Most of their belongings, including that malfunctioning Corvair, were stored at Maryann's mother and stepfather's in Paradise. Clothing, books, and Ray's typewriter were packed. The International Program paid Maryann to shepherd the younger California students going to Tel Aviv.

Finally the four Carvers boarded a jet bound for New York City. Like the horses in the epigraph Ray had chosen for *Near Klamath*, they were snapping the traces of their old lives, setting off on a "gay and empty" journey. The gaiety, for the most part, would be Maryann's and the emptiness would be Ray's.

CHAPTER 12

Reading Mark Twain in Tel Aviv

July–November 1968, Israel

We live lives based upon selected fictions. Our view of reality is con-
ditioned by our positions in space and time—not by our personalities as we like to think. Thus every interpretation of reality is based
upon a unique position. Two paces east or west and the whole picture is changed.

—Lawrence Durrell, *Balthazar,*
transcribed in one of Carver's notebooks

I was away from my sources," Carver would tell friends when he later
bemoaned the difficulties he'd had in Israel.[1] In his eager quest for a change
of scenery and a comfortable place to write, Carver had ingenuously accompanied his family to one of the world's most complicated places. The sheer
foreignness of the Middle East proved overwhelming and dangerous for a
man with Carver's insecurities and propensity to let himself be thrown off
course. Whether he understood much of it or not—it's hard to know—the
political and social maelstrom shocked and overwhelmed him. To know how
Israel affected him, one must look to the poems he wrote about it, as well
as to a handful of letters to Curt Johnson, an incomplete novel called "The
Augustine Notebooks," and some unpublished notes regarding this period.
They share an undertone of uncertainty, fear, and unnamable menace.[2]

Because of Israel's decisive victory in the Six-Day War of 1967, civilian
life in Israel had rarely been safer than during the months that the Carvers (and the California state colleges) were making plans for study in Tel
Aviv. On Israel's twentieth anniversary, in May 1968, decades of anxiety
had been diluted in an ecstatic celebration: "strangers kissed in the streets,
homes were thrown open to out-of-towners, middle-aged matrons joined
with giddy teenagers who danced and sang to the accompaniment of homemade drums."[3] After the holiday, the joyous mood persisted. Though Israel

was still a third-world country, its economy grew 13 percent in 1968. In Tel Aviv, the number of art galleries, theaters, nightclubs, and restaurants doubled and tripled. Slums were cleared and universities expanded. Whereas most immigrants to Israel since 1939 had been refugees, now significant numbers began to come from advanced, affluent countries, seeking not survival but identity and belonging. Nonetheless, unforeseen difficulties and contradictions followed the Six-Day War. The territories that Israel occupied in 1967 were home to one million non-Jews; these areas could be held and settled, perhaps, but they could not be governed in accord with the new nation's ideals of human rights and dignity.[4] Early in June 1968, while the school year was ending in Palo Alto, a mortar attack on Kibbutz Manara at the new Lebanese border presaged the troubles that lay ahead.

Ray began the fifteen-thousand-mile trip from California to Israel with high hopes. He surprised Maryann with his ability to find his way through airports and ride herd on the college students. But when the younger students were dispatched to dormitories at Tel Aviv University, the Carvers got disappointing news. The fabled villa by the Mediterranean Sea at Herzliya—in reality, a house with a small yard—was assigned to six Australian students. A university representative could not explain further, urged Ray to be flexible, and suggested they check into a hotel until new arrangements could be made. To add insult to injury, when Ray opened his typewriter, he discovered it had been badly damaged en route. For three weeks they stayed in the Hotel Sharon and dined in their room on white linen tablecloths with heavy hotel silver. It was the sort of lark they once might have enjoyed, but being cooped up in one room and worrying about the "certain enormity" of the hotel bill muted the fun. A girl staying in the hotel watched the children and took them to the beach while Ray tried to reclaim the villa.[5]

Tel Aviv was hot and humid. It reminded Ray, he said on a postcard addressed to his mother and James at Ella's mother's in Arkansas, of summer in the Midwest.[6] The Carvers had no automobile and were obliged to find their way about a city of 390,000 in crowded buses or *sherut* (shared) taxis. People lived literally on top of one another in both the ancient and new parts of these cities. In 1968 Israel was not a modern country in the Western style, despite its rapidly developing economy. Its Jewish population had grown by two million since 1948, primarily by immigration from 102 countries. These immigrants were precariously united only by Jewish identity and a new national language, Hebrew. English was not widely spoken in Israel in 1968.

Though some writers like to work in a foreign country where they can pass days without hearing English outside of their own heads, Ray, fringe-walker and eavesdropper that he was, hated to be estranged from his native tongue. Since the Hebrew alphabet is non-Roman, he was denied even the pleasure of sounding out and pondering the words on signs and in newspapers. Vance recalled that his father learned a few Hebrew phrases but was too shy to utter more than a mumbled "Shalom, shalom." For ten years, Carver had been working to master literate English and integrate it with American vernacular. In this he'd been nourished by the language of ordinary life around him. Separation from that resource was a true deprivation for him.

To bolster Maryann's application for scholarship money, Ray had said he would attend classes in Tel Aviv, maybe pick up a few credits he could apply to his unfinished master's degree. From what Ray had told him, Dick Kolbert had formed an impression that the country of Israel had invited Ray to be a writer in residence, all expenses paid! Even Curt Johnson, with whom Ray was usually candid, believed that Ray had some formal role in Israel and wondered later if one or both Carvers were Jewish! (They weren't.) Even before he arrived in Israel, Ray decided he'd forgo classes in order to write, travel, and relax as much as possible.[7]

In an unfinished story draft about the trip, Carver's husband character is a Fulbright exchange professor at Tel Aviv University, while the wife character is recovering from a nervous breakdown and does not want to stay in Israel. In other words, Carver reversed the roles. For it was Maryann who had a place at the university and Ray who felt on the verge of a nervous collapse.[8]

In mid-July the Carvers moved into an apartment belonging to a musician who had gone to Canada for two years.[9] At first Ray was optimistic. The place was furnished with paintings, a piano, radios, books in three languages, and a telephone. That last was important because the wait for telephone installation in Tel Aviv was two years. Despite misgivings, Ray signed multiple copies of a one-year lease and an inventory of items in the apartment, including goldfish and a valuable guitar. Still, Ray hedged by asking what would happen if they had to return home due to some unforeseen emergency (and had the Carvers ever known any other kind?). He learned that it would be difficult to hold citizens of another country to the conditions of the lease.[10]

The lease signatures were barely dry when, on July 23, 1968, an El Al Airlines flight bound from Tel Aviv to Rome was diverted to Algiers by hijackers identified with the Popular Front for the Liberation of Palestine. Women, children, and non-Israelis were soon released, but thirty-two Israeli men were held for five weeks and finally exchanged for sixteen Arab prisoners held in Israel. Three more attempts to hijack El Al flights occurred that year before the airline's heightened security procedures—including body searches of passengers, steel-reinforced and locked cockpits, armed undercover air marshals, and combat-trained flight crews—succeeded in making its flights almost impregnable.

Although Ray had resided at twenty-one different addresses in his life, he could not learn to feel at home in Tel Aviv. Some of the reasons remind us that Ray Carver was quite an ordinary man in every way except his talent. He was curious about other people's lives and loved a good story, but he wasn't intellectually curious about other cultures and religions. Though Tel Aviv and the university district were primarily middle class and politically liberal, this was little comfort on their tight budget. He found it an "incredible adjustment to make" and rued giving up his secure income from SRA. American liquor was expensive, and Ray disliked the sweet Israeli wines that he ended up drinking. Nor did Tel Aviv's bustling beach and sidewalk cafes offer the kind of cheap, unobtrusive companionship he wanted. Maryann met other English-speaking students, but their constant debate of Israeli issues wearied Ray. Worse, every Friday brought the Sabbath, which irritated him—"fucking bloody Shabbat begins this afternoon"—by making it difficult to shop for cigarettes or groceries or liquor, travel by bus, or go to the post office.[11]

Ray's stomach turned in the marketplace where unplucked chickens hung by their feet and flies crawled over slabs of butchered beef and mutton. He couldn't bring himself to buy meat. He tried the local food and soon tired of it. At one point, the whole family developed skin rashes that they attributed to a vitamin deficiency. Israeli Amos Elon writes that his country's "notoriously lively bustle and busyness and seemingly limitless vivacity" are "compensatory devices for a morbid melancholy and a vast, permeating sadness. The most casual visitor is not likely to escape this melancholy." Certainly Ray did not escape it. He had become "an America First sort of person" he told Johnson in mid-July. After he'd been overseas for six weeks, he was in "a bad slump" and "a manic-depressive state of mind."[12]

But Christi and Vance found friends in the building, Ray and Maryann became friendly with their neighbors Schlomo and Sima Karlibach, and Ray realized that they were living better than most citizens in Israel. The luxurious apartment of the respected Israeli musician and his wife was more cramped than any place in which the Carvers had resided in years. Like most housing in Tel Aviv, a city then only fifty years old, it was part of a block of closely packed flats with limited ventilation, small, identical balconies, and little privacy. Christi, then ten, minded sharing a bedroom with her nine-year-old brother. Vance was moved by the stories he heard about the Holocaust, and overall he liked Israel. Ray and Maryann took him to hear Leonard Bernstein conduct the Israel Philharmonic Orchestra at a free afternoon rehearsal in Tel Aviv. At the university, some Americans let Vance shoot hoops with them, but he found no one who wanted to play baseball. Outside the apartment building, he threw pop-ups and ran to catch them himself. "People stared because they had never seen anyone do that before."[13]

After a few weeks in the apartment, Ray was still trying to get TWA to pay for the repair of his typewriter and hoping to get himself on a "good schedule" as soon as the children began classes at the American International School. Meanwhile, "pressing business" battered him daily.[14] To get anywhere, he had to take a city bus. Not having a car to drive may, in truth, have been the most severe hardship of life for Ray in Israel. Even more than he was an American, Ray was a Californian, and that meant that he considered it his right to travel by automobile whenever and wherever he wished.

It was by bus, though, that Ray was occasionally hauled out of his malaise and came to know something of Israel. He and Maryann toured Bethlehem and Hebron (safer to visit in 1968 than they would be later) and walked through Jerusalem's Old Jewish and Arab quarters and followed the legendary Via Dolorosa, along which Christ carried his cross from the court of Pontius Pilate to Calvary. The half-mile walk passes through the narrow, covered stone lanes of the Muslim Quarter and ends at the Church of the Holy Sepulchre, a grand shrine of uncertain authenticity. Vance remembered tiptoeing through as an ornately robed priest performed a ritual, but one must take at face value Ray's single sentence report to Johnson: "Jerusalem is an incredible place." From his youth, though, he had been a reader of history. He was particularly fond of stories about Alexander the Great and other eastern Mediterranean military figures.[15]

Walking in Jerusalem, surrounded by a four-thousand-year accumulation of limestone buildings, ruins, and excavations—churches, mosques, synagogues—both impressed and intimidated Ray. As the weeks wore on, he was increasingly angry with Maryann for choosing to study in Israel rather than Florence, Italy. Whereas he had initially focused on the villa, which sounded European to him, he now repeated over and over, "What am I doing in Asia?"[16] If Ray had ever seriously imagined that he was an heir of Hemingway's, this trip proved otherwise. Nonetheless, trace elements of the trip to Israel appear in his writing.

The Middle East shows up in his poems as a subtle, frightening presence, almost invisible. "Seeds" shows how Carver went about miniaturizing complicated emotions within a single exchange. A vendor with a cart pulled by an old horse sells watermelon seeds to Christi. As they stand on a dry roadside, the two men glance at each other nervously, and then a bird's shadow crosses over their hands, "something unseen / between the vendor & myself." The girl opens her hand to offer her father some seeds. He receives her offering as a "blessing."[17] The work that came from Carver's trip to Israel confirms his natural predilection to compress his meanings within the small details of daily life, to express what his friend Chuck Kinder called "the mystery in the mundane."[18] The power of "Seeds" (and what saves it from sentimentality) is in its focus on hands.

The letters Carver wrote to Johnson from Israel are squeezed onto aerograms and partially devoted to requests for news of the publishing world. Ray uses a few lines to critique a manuscript that Johnson has sent him and more lines to comment not very explicitly about an unhappy domestic and marital situation—"reproaches, name-calling, blah, blah, blah" that he blames on both the external situation and being cooped up together too much. Ray had left behind the social life he valued most: drinking and talking with other writers. He could see American movies (Vance recalled that his father took Christi and him to see *Bonnie and Clyde* there), and he could get almost any paperback in the shops downtown. The first one he went into had six copies of the paperback *BASS* containing his own story, but he missed reading the literary magazines and asked Johnson to mail those when he could.[19]

The Carvers had already been in Tel Aviv for a month when Ray learned that the tuition for Christi and Vance at the American International School, which catered to diplomats' children, would be $800 each. With little hope, they applied for scholarships and looked for another school. In August Amy and her two-year-old daughter, Erin, arrived with a welcome supply of American liquor, canned goods, and cigarettes. Amy found a job modeling in ads for Ascot, "Israel's Quality Cigarette," and soon finagled an invitation for all four Carvers to join her at a hotel in Haifa for a photo shoot, giving them a reprieve from the city heat and crowds as well as free, edible meals. Vance remembered the day spent overlooking the harbor, his attention divided between glamorous models and a submarine he could see below. Amy had to smoke all day long. Soon photos of her smoking with other beautiful people in front of picturesque Israeli vistas, her long, blonde hair waving in a breeze or pinned with a flower, appeared on the front page of the *Jerusalem Post* above the legend "they too smoke Ascot, Ascot tastes better—is better!"[20]

When Maryann and Amy—two beautiful, lightly clothed Western women—walked through Old Jerusalem's *shuks,* they provoked comments, gestures, and attempted embraces from the men they passed in the narrow passageways. To that, Ray felt helpless to respond. Even that classic entertainment for tourists, the camel ride, became frightening. While Ray waited behind, a camel driver led Maryann and Amy out of sight and even-tually asked them to dismount and find their own way back to Ray, who was in a panic that they had been sold into slavery—which, to be fair, was rumored to exist in North Africa and Asia at the time. Late in the summer, Ray made a quick trip to Athens and Rome to meet someone; he doesn't say whom. He missed his connection, though, and spent "a day or two" on his own before returning to Israel. Some people wouldn't mind being stuck in Rome, but Ray told Johnson he hadn't known what a homebody he was until then and was glad to return to his "lot in Tel Aviv."[21]

The long siege of vacation time promised to subside when Christi and Vance began at Tabeetha School in September. Founded by Scottish mis-sionary nuns, Tabeetha had served Arab children for a century before Israeli independence and continued to offer English education to students from all over the world. The school was in Jaffa (Yafo in Hebrew), the very old city at the southern edge of Tel Aviv.[22] It cost just $20 a month per child, and Ray liked both the teachers and the physical surroundings much better than he'd liked the AIS. He was frustrated when the kids asked him for help with math problems in pounds and shillings but impressed by the iron-fisted headmistress, Miss Jean B. Rosie. The nuns were strict with their "teeming multicultural band of students," Vance recalled, "and Christi found herself popular with the boys there." From their apartment to Jaffa was less than ten miles, but by bus with a transfer at the old Central Bus Station in the poorest part of the city, it could take Ray and the chil-dren an hour and a half. After a few days, an English parent began driving Vance and Christi to and from school, but Ray still had to take the bus to do marketing.[23]

Unfamiliar surroundings and difficulty working because of his respon-sibilities for the children dropped Ray into a severe depression; he felt he'd backslid ten years. He described his inability to function in Tel Aviv in a poem called "Tel Aviv and *Life on the Mississippi.*" Most of it is a tribute to Mark Twain, who was "all eyes and ears" as he traveled the river. In con-trast, Carver confesses, he is unable to apprehend this new place and instead holds Twain's book "like a wheel." He felt he'd been "sold down river" when he agreed to this trip.[24] Ray's state of mind turned from ennui to para-noia, it seems, when he left his balcony to see the country. "The Mosque in Jaffa" begins at the top of a minaret where a man is pointing out the sights, which run together in his grinning spiel—"market church prison whore-house"—and key phrases from history: "trade worship love murder . . ." Two things stand out in the poem: Ray's unfounded suspicion of the Mus-lim tour guide and Ray's depression. The closing lines tie the two together: both the speaker and the tour guide are running out of time. Ray retained his prejudice against Arabs for years. "All Arabs are insane, all of them," he said whenever the subject came up in the 1970s. Carver recounted that a woman he met had told him that her husband had been dismembered by Arabs in 1949.[25]

Ray talked about pulling up stakes and going home but continued to hope that things would improve. He'd been depressed before; in fact, he may have been depressed before he left the United States, one letter suggests. The contrast between his mood and Maryann's was extreme, another source of difficulty, because this was a high time in her life, "studying at the university, learning Hebrew, and listening to Golda Meir speak, and dancing Jewish folk dances." Her work with Erhard had already set her on a journey of spiritual inquiry; when she looked back at her youth, she would see Israel as "the absolutely perfect place for me given my later interest in spiritual realities. . . ."[26] On the practical side, Ray did not want Maryann to sacrifice a whole semester of college credits. The sooner she got her degree, the sooner she would be supporting the family again.

Ray's resignation and hope evaporated in a single hour, the morning of Wednesday, September 4, at eleven-thirty, when three bombs exploded in waste receptacles in and near the Central Bus Station of Tel Aviv. An elderly man was killed and seventy-one persons, Jews and Arabs, were injured by flying metal from the exploded trash cans. The blasts, audible through much of the city, led to rioting by Jewish citizens. When police sealed off the bus station, the mobs moved into the streets of South Tel Aviv and Jaffa (where Christi and Vance were in school), attacking Arab market stalls and carts and shops. Cars with West Bank or Gaza license plates were overturned. Police controlled the riot within hours. Sixteen Arabs from the newly occupied territories (East Jerusalem and Hebron) were charged with these bus station bombings as well as an earlier series in Old Jerusalem. That night Ray announced to Maryann that he was taking his children and going home. Their experiment in international living was over.

The way Ray internalized Israel changed him and his work. Being in a place where four thousand years of history were piled on top of one another, empire upon empire all turning to dust, reinforced his natural self-involvement and modesty. He had always liked to read history before, but now it overwhelmed him. That is the meaning of the poem titled "Morning, Thinking of Empire," which seems to have nothing to do with empires. It's a poem about a couple eating breakfast in a place above a sea that pounds upon the old town's crumbling walls. The poem is concerned with mortality (greasy coffee "will one day stop our hearts") and unhappiness in marriage ("Surely we have diminished one another"). Ray may have been disappointed in himself and his inability to embrace this exotic adventure, but he knew when he was defeated and turned for home.

Maryann did not want to leave Israel. Through the month of September, they argued about it, and Ray's demand made her feel "as if I had been kicked in the stomach; I was viscerally upset." Then, too, she discerned that Ray's emotions were "deadened" because he was "ignoring his profound grief over his father's death, damaging himself, hardening his carapace of cynicism." Decades later, Vance said that he'd "have gladly stayed the whole year in Israel" and did not fully understand why they'd left.[27] Ray's letter to Johnson—a typed letter, so finally his machine was repaired—on September 23 indicates that he, too, was in despair about the situation: "a heartbreakingly unpleasant experience here, not just in the bitterly dashed hopes dept. but at the life and love counter." His expressions seem intentionally vague, the words of a man who is depressed or one who hopes he will live to regret these words. They are living, he says, in a "trackless wasteland," and he's suffering stomach trouble, head trouble, and a "shattering loss of faith." Loss of faith in what, he does not say. God? Life? Work? Certainly his work is a big part of it. He imagines himself as an old man, humiliated because he has wasted his time "with all this shit and shifting around." And another part of it, clear in the poems and veiled in the letters, is his marriage: ". . . a few more scenes to play yet, but something is going to give." From Chekhov he quotes, "either sit in the carriage or get out."[28]

He and Maryann were much too tightly bound as a couple, as parents, as the most consistent elements in each other's history and dreams to make a decision to separate over this or any other issue. Much more disintegration would occur before either of them came to that pass. Eventually Maryann would come to feel that "Ray could see the seeds in events—he was perceptive, and he did get us out of Israel when the getting was good."[29]

Ray threatened to take his children and go home, but what he actually did—on September 30—was visit the office of a Mediterranean cruise line and make arrangements for a six-day cruise. He persuaded the reservation agent that he was a working journalist who would write about his trip. For this he was given a 10 percent discount on the passage and what he called "first cabin" accommodations. Excited about the trip, he outlined the itinerary in detail to Johnson: their boat would stop at Cyprus, Rhodes, Crete, Corfu, Athens, and Dubrovnik before delivering them to Venice, where they'd rent a car and drive across Europe. They had just enough money left in the budget for the year to do this traveling, to salvage that bit of the romantic writer-in-Europe fantasy, though the schedule would be brisk. Ray closed his letter containing their itinerary by confessing that he felt guilty about having uprooted his family so many times in the past. All he wanted to do now was "settle them, get them their animals, and keep them in one spot."[30] Guilt alone would not be enough to fulfill that wish.

Though their plans happened by accident, the Carvers chose the perfect season to sail on the *Pegasus* through the Mediterranean, and it seems that they had a wonderful time. Ray made up for lost meals with the "unbelievably good" food. When Vance turned ten on October 18, the crew surprised him with a birthday celebration. Their vessel was Greek, but the Carvers traveled under the spiritual flag of one of Ray's favorite authors, Lawrence Durrell, whose books describe Corfu, Rhodes, and Cyprus.[31] On a picture postcard of the Venus of Rhodes, Ray said the cruise was just what they'd needed, with the best Scotch available for nine drachmas (twenty-seven cents). Hundreds of butterflies circled them as they walked in the old town of Rhodes after a warm downpour. "If I'm dreaming this, please don't wake me up."[32]

Carver's novel fragment "The Augustine Notebooks" is set in Rhodes, but its mood is very different from that in the postcard he wrote there. The fragment has two sections dated October 11 and October 18, the very dates the Carvers sailed, and involves a writer named Halprin and an unnamed woman. The couple argue and then decide to abandon their Mediterranean cruise and stay on the island for six months. The man believes he can write a novel if they can avoid being like "broken-down Hemingway characters." Defending his idea to the woman, this Halprin says:

> "My life is half over, more than half over. The only, the only really extraordinary thing to happen to me in, I don't know, years, was to fall in love with you. The other life is over now, and there's no going back. I don't believe in gestures, not since I was a kid, before I married Kristina, but this would be a gesture of some sort. . . . That is, if I pull it off. But I think I might if I stay."[33]

Plainly, Ray shares Halprin's fear that his life is half over. But this fictional couple travels without children, this woman is not the bride of Halprin's youth; Halprin wants to have the nerve to take a chance on himself. Like the reverse side of a fabric, this setup clarifies the pattern on the front. It suggests that Ray craved six months without responsibilities, accompanied by a woman who was herself free to risk this crazy idea of staying in Rhodes. The story's agenda is obvious. One day on each of those islands (where Durrell had spent years) would be torture for a man who felt a year's retreat in a villa by the Mediterranean had been snatched away from him. Of course, he wanted to stay on and on.

Ray probably wavered that day. He might have been tempted to pass up a return to the daily grind of working and trying to make a permanent home in California. He might desperately have wanted to take his half of the family's cash and give himself a fresh start as a writer. Who is to say it would not have been a good idea? But it didn't happen.

Ray meant to keep the vow he'd made in his October 1 letter to Johnson: "no more ill-conceived or half thought-out escapist ventures." He was tormented but dutiful, rebellious but attached. Perhaps he was afraid to be alone. Likewise, Maryann could not choose Ray over the children. Instead they both made difficult compromises, compromises that parlayed or distorted everyone's intentions. The trip to Israel was such a compromise, with Mideast politics brokering the odds against the Carvers. Had it worked out as intended, Maryann would have had her excitement and a year of college, Ray a year off to write, and the children the enrichment of living in a foreign culture.

Carver also wrote a brief synopsis for a Middle Eastern novel. He planned a big story with an opening scene in Rhodes, further scenes in Athens, Jerusalem, and Corfu, and a parallel story (semiautobiographical) that begins in the past and moves into the present. The characters in the novel are to be a "hip, handsome" male professor and his lover whom he met at his college in Sacramento. The professor has it all—job, family, home—but will lose it in the course of the story. His lover is a student activist, the wife of a Jordanian student who belongs to an Arab guerrilla group and works nights at a hospital. The professor has left his wife and children, and the woman has run away from her Jordanian husband. For some reason to do with hashish, the couple will go to the Middle East. After that they will cruise to Rhodes, where the Jordanian husband will show up to kill the professor. A gunfight and a chase scene will occur on the stone streets and battlements of Corfu. The professor will tell the husband that he is writing a book and may put him in the book! The Jordanian will be neither impressed nor dissuaded.

It would be easy to say now that Carver never meant to write a novel, but this outline from 1979 is an attempt in that direction.[34] Even before he went to Israel, novel writing had been on Carver's mind. In a last letter before his departure, he thanked Johnson for trying to get him an advance from an editor and regretted that he did not have one hundred pages of his novel typed.[35] He knew he needed a novel to get a book publication. The calamitous trip to the Middle East had given him the sort of exotic, action material from which he believed novels were made. He'd matured in the shadow of Hemingway; to follow that pattern, he needed to move on from short stories about his youth or couples adrift to something more worldly.

Like Papa, he would write a love story with a foreign setting and an up-to-the-minute conflict. It was not, in truth, such a bad idea.

But of course, he did not write it. One reason for that is also suggested in another note: "Drunkenness, always drunkenness." Those nine-drachma shots of whiskey did wonders for ambition, but little for accomplishment.

In "The Augustine Notebooks," Carver mentions that the legendary statue to Apollo never straddled the Rhodian harbor entrance, although "postcards for sale in the marketplace depicted a gigantic cartoon colossus with boats coming and going between its legs." In his poem "Rhodes," Carver admits that he'd like to stay here, where a colossus waits "for another artist," but he's not bold enough to take on anything like that. If he stayed, he'd "hang out / with the civic deer." This realization seems to refine the one Carver said he had in an Iowa City laundromat four years earlier: he will write about little things, simple things, domestic rather than colossal matters he can encompass in a short story. The domesticated deer are beautiful, "under the assault of white butterflies."

Maryann's memories of the cruise through the islands were simpler. They "sat on a balcony in Corfu and had a lemon-fix, as it was called there, and talked about *Bitter Lemons* and Durrell."[36] A picture snapped as the group embarked at Rhodes would become one of her touchstone images of their happy family: Vance, a sturdy boy with straight-up posture and a quizzical face, fair hair clipped around his ears, leads the procession; Ray, a half step behind, carrying a handful of souvenir bags and a camera (where are *his* pictures?), looks gaunt and determined in short, thick hair, sunshades, long-sleeved white business shirt (smokes and pen in the pocket) over a white T, narrow belt, and dark slacks. Behind them, sweet faced, almost smiling, Christi holds her mother's arm. Maryann, still wearing her dark hair in the pixie style she adopted in Arcata, looks slim, tanned, and relaxed. Both mother and daughter have their eyes on Ray (or the photographer), while Vance and Ray are intent on something off to their right.

From Venice, they took a train to Florence, where they again regretted that they had chosen Israel over Italy for a year abroad.[37] Ray grumbled that traveling with the kids was hard, but they pushed on toward Paris in a current-model Renault rented from Hertz—the first time they'd ever had a new car to drive. From Paris they sent Christi and Vance on a non-stop, over-the-pole flight to Amy in Los Angeles, where they arrived in time to go trick-or-treating. Maryann and Ray stayed in Paris for ten days by themselves before boarding their low-fare Icelandic Airlines prop-plane flight to New York City.

When Ray picked up the threads of his literary correspondence the next spring, he boasted that they'd been on "an odyssey" and a "grand trip." The cruise and the drive had been the best parts of it, he said, apparently forgetting the difficulties with the children.[38] His regret and resentment about Israel seemed forgotten.

And yet in 1984 Ray would explain to an interviewer that his whole life had "gone bust" and he'd begun to turn to alcohol because of this "wacky trip to Israel." As he elaborated his statement to the reporter, he telescoped several events *ad hoc ergo propter hoc*: "I had wanted that villa on the Mediterranean all my life, and at that point I knew I was never going to get it. My writing had done nothing but bring me grief. My wife and I split up . . ."[39]

Ray did not give up writing, nor did he and Maryann separate after that trip. But images tell a truth that calendars can't reveal. The image that stands out here is the villa that he had wanted "all his life"—which needn't have been in Israel or even on the Mediterranean, because what it represented was the opportunity to be a writer; a writer who wrote every day and let nothing, not even himself, stand in his way.

CHAPTER 13

The Sixties End

November 1968–December 1969, Hollywood and San Jose

Great writers and artists ought to take part in politics only so far as
they have to protect themselves from politics.
— Anton Chekhov to Alexei Suvorin, February 6, 1898,
transcribed in one of Carver's notebooks

From New York, Ray and Maryann hopscotched across the Midwest
with stops at the Palmers' in Ohio and the Johnsons' in Chicago. Ray
carried a little case with him, Dave Palmer noticed. "When he opened it, I
saw all these little sample bottles of gin and booze that he must have picked
up on their flights." In both photos taken in front of the Palmers' white
clapboard two-story house, Ray looks like a Midwestern professor in dark
slacks, sport coat, and black turtleneck, and Maryann is sprightly in a mini-
dress and sandals. In one shot, Ray wraps both Maryann and Charlene and
a couple younger Palmers in his wide arm span.[1]

The country to which Ray and Maryann returned after four months was
less idealistic than the one they'd left. While they were traveling in Europe,
a heroine of their youth, Jacqueline Kennedy, had married an elderly Greek
multimillionaire named Aristotle Onassis. Thousands of antiwar demonstrators had converged on Chicago to protest as the Democratic Party convention nominated Vice President Hubert Humphrey to run for president
against Richard Nixon, and a beefed-up Chicago police force responded by
beating demonstrators in full view of TV cameras. Nixon won the election
with an argument that he had a secret plan to end the war in Vietnam. He
called his constituency the Silent Majority.

Squeaking along on the last of their travel money, Ray and Maryann
arrived at Curt and JoAnn Johnson's in the Chicago suburb of Western
Springs. Curt served Scotch, and JoAnn had cookies arranged on a plate
for later; Maryann, hungry and thirsty, munched cookies with her cock-

tail, much to everyone's amusement. Maryann remained ebullient, but Ray was "very, very quiet." When the conversation turned to politics, he grumbled that it all depressed him. Otherwise, Curt recalled, "Ray was always pleasant, but he was depressed on that trip. Most writers shove themselves in your face, but he didn't do that, he just listened and responded with a story to tell. But to draw a picture of him from his prose, you would get the impression that he couldn't do anything. I'm thinking that he saw himself that way. But he was a capable guy except when he was drunk." Curt drove them into the Loop to see the Picasso sculpture and the Art Institute museum, and they went to see Mel Brooks's movie *The Producers*. The Johnsons' gracious home showed Maryann "what could befall a couple who minded their manners and their business well." But Maryann felt no pressure: "I was a young girl, traveling on a wing and a prayer, still in my twenties, en route from Paris with my young husband."[2] For Ray, though, already thirty, the party was over. He was "so goddamned uptight with circumstances—broke, homeless, disillusioned—generally all round poor white attitude," he wrote Johnson afterward, "I must have been the poorest possible company." Johnson agreed that they hadn't had a good time. "Next time will be better. Next time is always better." There would be only a few more face-to-face meetings for Ray and Curt, but they corresponded throughout the 1970s. Combative where Ray was passive, the Iowa Swede with a mustache and pale blue eyes directed his prodigious energy and irascible idealism to many projects. When he got fed up with textbook editing, he freelanced and occasionally worked construction jobs.[3]

The Carvers reunited with Christi and Vance in Los Angeles, arriving completely broke in mid-November to move in with Amy and Michael Wright on Gregory Avenue. There was trouble in the Wrights' marriage. Now twenty-six, Amy juggled her serious acting ambitions with taking care of two-year-old Erin and earning a living. She performed in an episode of TV's *Mannix*, and on stage at the Century City Playhouse and the Stage Society. She did voice-overs and TV commercials—including a Wonder Bread spot—and stints as a dermatologist's receptionist and cocktail waitress. But she refused to do club shows or topless shows, which would have brought easier money. Literally a starving actor at times, Amy had learned some tricks to stretch her food dollars. In a grocery store, she'd switch the labels on meat packages and exit the store with steak for the price of hamburger, or five pounds of hamburger for the price of one. If the cashier noticed, she could feign amazed ignorance well enough to avoid arrest. Then there was the More-Than-You-Can-Eat plan. Amy and Maryann lined their large shoulder-strap purses with plastic bags and filled them as they went down a buffet line. These were crazy and good times. Maryann and Amy sparked each other's hopes, and both believed fervently in Ray's talent.[4]

Amy got Ray a temporary job selling programs with her at the Cinerama Dome Theater. It should have been an easy job—it required only a loud voice, a bit of showmanship, and ability to make change quickly. But Ray failed as a huckster. He'd stand at the edge of the lobby with his stack of programs, sneak a glance about him, and mutter "Programs" so no one could hear. Anyone whose eye happened to fall on him might've thought he had stolen those programs.

Yet L.A. was a lively scene. When Amy's husband was around and they had a little cash, the two couples went dancing at the Whiskey A Go Go with the "beautiful people." The musical *Hair* was in town (they went) and at UCLA, John Wooden coached the best college basketball team in the country. *Open City,* the city's alternative paper, ran a weekly screed of stories and opinion called "Notes of a Dirty Old Man," by Charles Bukowski, then a middle-aged postal worker and little-known poet. Ray liked Southern California so well for a couple of weeks that he thought of settling there.

His enthusiasm faded fast. The Burk sisters shared and fought over everything in their lives, pulling each other out of every kind of jam, but such intimacy had a high price tag. Ray could not write amid so much emotional intensity. Soon he was sick of "futzing around" and could not envision wanting to live in the L.A. area under any circumstances.[5] Even so, Ray observed the interactions of himself and Maryann with Amy and the men in Amy's life. The unsteady, unbreakable axis of those two women may be the ur-story behind Carver's many stories in which two couples function as foils to each other.[*]

Alone, Ray fled to northern California. He picked up the Corvair and his desk typewriter in Paradise, checked in with his brother and the Schmitzes in Sacramento, arranged to resume work at SRA on January 15, and stayed with his mother in Palo Alto. During this jaunt, he found himself in his mother's apartment at three in the morning with a bottle of Old Crow and wishing badly for Johnson's companionship. When he returned to Hollywood on Christmas Eve day, he'd lost both the typewriter—stolen out of the car in Sacramento—and the Corvair, which threw a rod through its engine on Cuesta Grade. He had no luck. He accepted a loan of $300 out of Johnson's *December* account as a "bolt from the blue" that would allow

---

[*] Among these stories are "Neighbors," "What's in Alaska?" "Put Yourself in My Shoes," "Tell the Women We're Going," "What We Talk About When We Talk About Love," "Feathers," "Why Don't You Dance?" and even the posthumously published "What Would You Like to See?" and "Vandals."

him to rent a house and "settle, permanently, and in the northern part of the state." In a Christmas card, Maryann wrote, "We are too conservative for Southern California." In her perfect schoolgirl's script (polar opposite of Ray's barely legible scrawl), she noted good-humoredly that they were so poor they'd applied to the community chest for a food basket and been turned down because they had not resided in the United States for the past sixty days.[6]

In January Maryann returned to classes at San Jose State and the four Carvers moved into an apartment in married students' housing across from Spartan Stadium on a block that's since become a parking lot. The kids walked to school along a street lined with a jarring mixture of palm and maple trees, and Maryann went farther down the same street, past Spartan Liquors, to her classes. Ray set up a grueling schedule for himself. He'd attend library science classes in San Jose and work nights at SRA in Palo Alto, shuttling himself in a "falling-apart 1961 Rambler" borrowed from Maryann's mother. He disburdened himself of his desire to return to Iowa for library studies because San Jose now had an accredited program—"the last word in the library field"—and he'd have his pick of colleges to work in. But—still—the distance between this cup and his lip stretched into a chasm for Ray. He stayed enrolled in the program until the end of 1969, but never finished a degree.[7]

Instead Ray climbed back in the saddle of his literary life. He rented a room in Palo Alto where he could spend weeknights away from the tiny San Jose apartment and try to write. A "metaphysical hole . . . swallowed me up entire last summer as it'd always threatened to do in the past," he confided to Johnson. "There're no answers. Rather there are answers but they're so fucking shocking & uprooting they're hard to entertain." He asked Johnson if he'd ever thought of moving to Greece to live cheaply and write. Adversity fed his work, though, and during the spring he salvaged two new stories out of the past year's wreckage.[8]

Ray kept his work in circulation. Jarvis Thurston, the editor of *Perspective* magazine in St. Louis, took a Carver story for *The Best Little Magazine Fiction,* an anthology that he and Curt Johnson were editing for the publishing company Scott Foresman. Shortly thereafter, Carver submitted "The Fling" and "A Dog Story" to Thurston.[9] "The Fling" had been in Ray's drawer since 1967, but "A Dog Story" was recent. In it a hapless father called Al tries to abandon a dog who urinates on the carpet and chews out the crotches of the family's clothes (she's Mitzi of Sacramento days) and then tries to retrieve it again when his daughter misses the dog. As the story opens, Al believes "that the loss and abandonment of the dog would be the first step toward salvation, a pulling out of the nosedive he felt he was in," but a day later, he "looked upon its loss as the final step in his downfall."

In its original form, the story sketches life with children as an uneasy tightrope between irritation and sentiment. Al the narrator is thirty-one years old (like Carver in 1969) with two young kids. Their mother, Al says, keeps her equanimity most of the time, but once in a while she gets fed up enough to turn on the kids "savagely and slap their faces or the sides of their heads." Al's situation sounds like that "metaphysical hole" Ray told Johnson about. He hates getting up early for a job from which he fears he'll be laid off, drinks too much, and resents his wife because they've moved to a too-expensive house. He's guilty about a lackluster affair he's having with a girl he met in a bar. He sees his flaws and cannot change: "what a weathervane he was . . . a prisoner of the moment . . . It was his great weakness . . . and yet, somehow, his only strength." Al knows he has no moral center. When at last he finds the dog, he lets it walk away. The dog makes the decision that Al cannot make himself: "He didn't feel free, particularly—but neither did he feel captive any longer. He felt—well, nothing." He lives with "one lie thrown after another until he wasn't sure he could untangle them if he had to."[10]

At SRA Ray moved to the advertising department and sometimes traveled to educators' conferences to recruit authors and promote books. The new SRA position taught Ray "how to market his materials six ways to Sunday," Maryann said, but stress, business meals, and travel gave him new excuses and opportunities to drink.[11] Gordon Lish still had an office across the street from Ray's SRA office, but the two rarely encountered each other. Both Lish and Carver corresponded with Johnson, though, and he passed news from one to the other.

In the spring, Amy arrived on the doorstep of the Carvers' tiny apartment with her daughter, Erin. Her husband had departed for Rome with another woman. In late May, the novelist Evan S. Connell (best known for his *Mrs. Bridge* and *Mr. Bridge*) invited Amy to accompany him on a trip to New Mexico. Everyone had hoped this would be a respite for her, but after a week, she suffered a nervous collapse—it would turn out to be her first of several manic episodes—and was hospitalized in San Jose. Maryann quit her waitress job and pressed on toward her college degree, but once again their finances were in a "shambles."[12]

The shambles and attendant stresses were waiting for them when they returned home from a week's vacation in Oregon and a visit to relatives in Yakima. On a Wednesday in July while she and Ray were having an argument, Maryann collapsed, losing consciousness for a quarter of an hour. She underwent tests at the hospital, and two days later was "some better." Both

Ray and she were left "worried and wondering."[13] Johnson, to whom Ray both wrote and spoke about the incident, had his own theory about it: "It's been my experience that sometimes when a woman can't get through to a man that she cares for and tries again and again, it hurts her physically. She just goes down. And I think it was that way about Ray's bouts of depression—and drinking made it worse.[14]

Johnson's theory gains credibility when placed next to two speeches delivered by the wife in "A Dog Story":

> "I didn't ask you to get drunk last night, did I? Don't snap at me, by God. I've had enough of it, I tell you! I've had a hell of a day, if you want to know. And little Alex waking me up at five o'clock this morning getting in with me, telling me his daddy was snoring so loud that you *scared* him. . . .
>
> "Is everybody going crazy?" she said. "I don't know what's going to happen to us. I'm ready for a nervous breakdown. I'm ready to lose my mind. What's going to happen to the kids, then, if I lose my mind?" She slumped against the draining board, her face crumpled and tears rolling off her cheeks. "You don't love them anyway! You never have. It isn't the dog I'm worried about; it's us! It's us!"[15]

With little understanding of what was happening to them, less of what to do about it, Maryann and Ray were devolving into a situation that they would later recognize as codependent and dysfunctional. Without the benefit of such categories—with instead a sixties ambience that celebrated personal freedom, self-expression, and rebellion—they spun out of control. Even without domestic malfunction, the late sixties were difficult times for children to become teenagers, as eleven-year-old Vance and twelve-year-old Christi were then doing. College-student Maryann was looking more like a counterculture person herself, dressed in bell-bottoms and peasant tops. She began to wear her hair long and blonde and looked so youthful that people's eyes focused on her and ignored her daughter, who struggled with her weight just as Ray had done at her age. Opening Christi's diary once in San Jose, Ray read, "Chris is pretty but she is fat," and just broke into tears. Christi often babysat for other families in their apartment building at San Jose State. Once, as her charges played, she began a girls' romance novel in a notebook. After the parents reprimanded her for being inattentive, she gave up the idea of writing a story. Recalling it all right down to the camouflage-patterned cover of her notebook, she said, "That's just typical of how easily I used to give up when something went wrong."[16]

• • •

In the spring, editor George Hitchcock invited Ray to a collating party for his magazine, *kayak*. Hitchcock, a Bay Area icon who would make a difference in Ray's literary life and usher him toward his first teaching job, had published two Carver poems—both of them dangerous speculations about estrangement of self and body—in *kayak* while Ray was in Israel.[17]

At fifty, Hitchcock "carried himself with the exuberance of a very big man," poet Philip Levine recalled. His graying hair "was so thick, long, and wild, it looked as though it had never faced the shears of a trained barber." As politics and art became entwined in the sixties, everyone wanted to get Hitchcock interested in their causes because of his powerful voice and the organizing ability he'd developed in the previous decades. Hitchcock had begun *kayak* after a spell as an associate editor of the *San Francisco Review* that taught him "collective editorship . . . has dreadful drawbacks," and named his magazine *kayak* because he regarded it as a "small watertight vessel operated by a single oarsman." Truly it was. He taught himself printing and solicited work from poets he admired. Unencumbered by coeditors and printers' bills, Hitchcock cultivated his "passionate prejudices" for strongly imagistic and surrealist poetry. Once Hitchcock had designed and printed his magazine's pages, he held a collating party to assemble, staple, and trim the issues. About twenty friends and contributors worked under Hitchock's direction. After the work was done, he served food and drinks. You were supposed to work before you partied.[18]

Invitations to collating days at Hitchcock's house in San Francisco were a perk of getting published in *kayak*. Ray came by himself the first time. When Hitchcock saw that he was a big guy, he assigned him to operate the trimming machine, which required a strong arm. Ray managed the job and was invited back in July. This time Ray brought both Amy and Maryann along, and they met several writers from Santa Cruz who would come to be the Carvers' friends and advocates: poet Mort Marcus, fiction writer and musician James Houston, and memoirist Jeanne Wakatsuki Houston. Marcus had known both Dick Day and Dennis Schmitz as fellow students at Iowa. Jim Houston, operating the stapling machine next to the trimmer, also felt an immediate kinship with Ray, which he soon realized was due to their similar origins—Houston's father had come west from East Texas in the 1930s.

Hitchcock, recently separated from his wife, took a liking to Amy. In the fall of 1969, Amy and Erin lived in Hitchcock's house, in a room he painted yellow for her, while Amy sought theater work in San Francisco and made plans to move to New York City. For a few months, Amy and George and Maryann and Ray were "kind of a family group," and Hitchcock got a close look at the life that Ray drew upon so much for his fiction.

"It *was* shabby lower-middle-class, but not as bad as the stories reveal," he thought. "Ray's world was, visually, let's say, not very attractive, but it was pleasant enough." Maryann was working all the time, usually in restaurants, and the Carver children "stayed in the background, a little sullen and disconnected," it seemed, though once they all played baseball on a Sunday afternoon.[19] But that imitation of American suburban life seemed to recede from Ray's sight faster than he could invent it.

The National Endowment for the Arts, young then, gave Hitchcock an unsolicited $10,000 to advance the "cause of unknown, obscure, or difficult writers." With his bare-bones production methods, Hitchcock stretched his NEA dollars to produce thirty fine-printed poetry books, including *Winter Insomnia* by Raymond Carver. "I can't say that I thought the world of Ray's poems," Hitchcock said much later. "I thought the short stories were a lot better, and I still do—but I liked these poems, or I wouldn't have published them."[20] Kayak Press paid Carver $200 and agreed that Hitchcock would make no changes in the text and the author would have no say in the design. A partial rerun of *Near Klamath* (thirteen poems are reprinted), the *Winter Insomnia* manuscript also included sixteen new poems written during the two years since the earlier book was compiled. Before Carver's book was finished, Hitchcock moved his publishing operation to Santa Cruz, where he had been appointed to teach part-time at the new University of California campus.

The year 1969 seemed to be more than just the closing act of a decade. No hype and spin were required to make the daily news sound extreme; during August, for instance, Charles Manson's cult murdered a houseful of people in Southern California, and four hundred thousand turned up at the peaceful Woodstock Music festival in New York (and a million more wished or claimed they'd been there). The Rolling Stones headlined what was meant to be a West Coast equivalent at the Altamont Speedway. With Hells Angels acting as security guards and bad-quality drugs fueling the mood, four people died (one beaten by the Angels, three by accident). The Stones kept playing, believing that worse chaos would ensue if they stopped. Extremes marked the music that played on the radio and in the background of people's lives. While Simon and Garfunkel and even Bob Dylan (on *Nashville Skyline*) were reflective, harder, more desperate and menacing sounds dominated: "The Star-Spangled Banner" rendered ominous by Jimi Hendrix, "Bad Moon Rising" from Creedence Clearwater Revival, and from the Rolling Stones, "Gimme Shelter" and "Let It Bleed."

American foreign policy and domestic life seemed out of control. "Minds and bodies are being maimed as we watch, a scale model of Vietnam," Joan Didion reported from the Haight district of San Francisco in her essay "Slouching Toward Bethlehem." Nihilism and carpe diem alternated to create a sense that nothing mattered and you could get away with anything. Women went without bras, and men and women alike uttered angry profanities to display minds as unfettered as their bodies. In the movies, glorified outlaws ended up dead in dramatic conflagrations: *Bonnie and Clyde, Butch Cassidy and the Sundance Kid,* and *Easy Rider.*

In much mainstream fiction, the sanitized, middle-class fifties were left behind. Novels published in 1969 included Philip Roth's chronicle of masturbation, *Portnoy's Complaint,* Thomas McGuane's manic, dark *The Sporting Club,* Kurt Vonnegut's antiwar allegory *Slaughterhouse-Five; or, The Children's Crusade: A Duty-Dance with Death.* A young writer, Joyce Carol Oates, won a National Book Award for *Them,* a working-class family saga that closes with the Detroit race riots, but the best seller of the year was Mario Puzo's *The Godfather,* a book both escapist and toweringly metaphorical. Popular nonfiction titles also characterized the era: *Revolution for the Hell of It* (Abbie Hoffman), *I'm OK, You're OK* (Thomas Harris), *Reflections upon a Sinking Ship* (Gore Vidal), and *The Selling of the President 1968* (Joe McGinnis). Two notable first books that were collections of short stories signaled a change in publishing: James Alan McPherson's stories of violent black urban life in *Hue and Cry,* and Leonard Michaels's witty, brisk, and literary *Going Places.*

Gordon Lish, too, sensed "a decision and a change of style" for himself in 1969. Despite Johnson's urging, he hadn't yet called Ray because he was afraid Ray would depress him. In March, as he finished his anthology *New Sounds in American Fiction,* he told Carruth he wished he could go into a line of work "with straightforward violence to it." Lish had typed that letter on his girlfriend's stationery, which featured a halftone screen of her model-perfect face because "fancy letterhead makes it easier for me to write; gives me confidence that I have something to say." Lish elaborated that he felt "uncomfortable in the world"—a "cosmic discomfiture" that was worsening and made him fear he was "disappearing in front of my own eyes."[21]

During a summer of intense turmoil for both of them, Ray and Lish succumbed to Johnson's urging that they get acquainted. They lunched and drank together often. "I like him," Ray reported to Johnson. Their lunches at Lish's apartment were "frugal" and likely to be interrupted by someone at the door inquiring to buy Lish's furniture from him. Sometimes Lish just snacked from Ray's plate as Ray got drunk and they matched dirty stories and tried to think of ways to make money.[22]

Soon Lish announced a new project. He was going to publish a "magnificent magazine" to be called *Journal of American Fiction* with his friend Ray Carver. Johnson accused his two friends of teaming up to compete with him, but he needn't have worried. Ray understood that Lish might bolt at any time. In the elite typeface of an office machine whose *o* printed a solid circle, Carver reported to Johnson: Lish "anxious, like all of us, to change his life. He and Barbara. Much talk about prospects in Europe, money-making schemes, etc."[23] Carver's letters from this period frequently include the disclaimer that he is drunk and use a telegraphic style like that just quoted but are precisely punctuated with their typos corrected.

Both Lish and Carver were excited and envious about Leonard Gardner's *Fat City*. Gardner had taken ten years to write his slim novel about San Joaquin Valley boxers. When the hardcover edition was barely out, Gardner sold movie rights for a rumored $100,000. In an author photo that filled the back dust jacket of a classy Farrar, Straus, and Giroux volume, thirty-five-year-old Gardner looked like a teenage idol. He posed in a denim shirt, just an ordinary fellow in a coffee shop. Within days, Lish had shoplifted (he claimed) a copy from a local bookstore and declared it "damn good."[24] Carver admired the book, too, for its craftsmanship and its truthful and vivid, unsentimental portrayal of the boxers' low-down existence. It was, in short, a book he wished he'd written himself.

Meanwhile, Johnson needed a photograph of Ray for the contributors' notes of the anthology he was finishing up with Jarvis Thurston. On one of their lunch days, Ray got Lish to shoot him with his reliable Polaroid Land camera. For these, Lish insisted that Ray squeeze himself into an old workshirt of his, "à la Leonard Gardner." The session was a success. The photo that appeared in *Short Stories from the Literary Magazines* (with no photo credit line) renders Ray's homely moon face as the shadowed, brooding visage of a man with pointed ears who looks intently from beneath an impressively arched right eyebrow. Unfortunately, something in the background—a candlestick?—looks like a pipe rising out of Ray's shoulder. His shirt collar lies open enough to hint at pectoral muscles.[25]

Decades later, when he looked back at that last summer in California, Lish was hard-pressed to explain his association with Ray Carver. He'd believed he'd had more in common with Johnson than with Carver, and yet for some reason Carver held his attention during that dry season. Lish thought Ray was "below the salt" and found himself physically uncomfortable around the awkward hulk of Ray, and yet he sensed a certain "reciprocity of opposites" between them. Some of his other friendships had soured. He no longer had a magazine as a means of making literary connections and must have sensed that his California decade was about over.

After coming to know the heroes of his youth, men like Kesey and Cassady, he could not play the acolyte to writers he considered lesser beings. Textbook editing bored him excruciatingly; he was three years overdue on a new grammar text for Scott Foresman because he could not find a way to write such a book better than the one he'd already devised in his programmed text for Behavioral Research.[26]

Before the first issue of *Journal of American Fiction* was off the dining room table, Gordon and his new wife, Barbara, were leaving California. They stopped by the Carvers' place in San Jose "in a big flurry," Maryann recalled. From a relative's address on Long Island, Lish wrote Ray to say he might soon have good news for him. "Mysterious," Carver commented. "Don't know what he's up to. Hope he's getting on all right."[27]

He was and he wasn't. He hated New York City: "Lish called once and said NYC is driving him crazy," Johnson wrote Ray. "The edl [editorial] scene and guys in stores—clerks—undressing his wife with their eyes, and such."[28]

During that phone call, Johnson passed along a tip to Lish from a writer named Henry H. Roth, author of *Boundaries of Love and Other Stories*. Roth told Johnson that editor Hal Scharlatt at Dutton and Company was creating a new annual magazine along the lines of the *New American Review*. Roth thought Johnson ought to apply for an editing job there. Johnson had no desire to give up his one-man show at *December*. He told Lish about Scharlatt's project.[29] Lish got a meeting with Scharlatt and learned that his masthead was already filled; Scharlatt mentioned to Lish that *Esquire* magazine was looking to hire a new fiction editor. It seemed that Rust Hills, who had returned to that job at *Esquire* when Bob Brown left it, was tired of the arrangement. On October 16 Lish met with Hills, was encouraged by what he had to say, and the next day mailed an astonishing letter to *Esquire* editor in chief Harold Hayes. The letter blends an old-fashioned courtly style that Lish thought would appeal to Hayes with a brasher tone that suggests what he can contribute to the magazine. In the letter's three parts, Lish summarizes his academic and employment history; he expresses his desire for the job; he sketches the actions he would take during his first year as editor if he were hired.

As he concludes his list of teaching and editing experience, Lish breaks the rhetoric of the job application letter to say:

> The plain fact is, Mr. Hayes, I have earned this job—through great love for the short story and great labor to know it, to make it the province in which my sensibilities live. Reading short fiction is the work I do best, and for this task I have a natural ear. What I mean to say is that I am good

and that there is in me the will to leave a mark as an editor, and I want this job because it represents the best chance for me to be all that it is in me to be. I want this job, and I want it with more eagerness than is becoming to a man of my age because this is the work I was meant to do, and because I have not been doing it.

The third part of the already remarkable performance—for though it is but a letter on well-designed personal letterhead, one easily hears Lish's voice and sees his gestures in its more than four dense pages—includes a list of three dozen story writers from whom Lish would seek submissions for the pages of *Esquire*. The names range from Eudora Welty and John Cheever to Ken Kesey and Grace Paley and, yes, Ray Carver.[30]

Hayes was won over by Lish's letter.[31] On October 24, Lish reported to Johnson that Hills would "move heaven and earth to convince Hayes I'm the right guy for the job." He was to meet Hayes and Hills for dinner the next week but still didn't think he could "hack it in NYC." When the three men ate and drank at The Brussels restaurant and shared incoherent exchanges, Lish sensed tension between Hills and Hayes, who had been in competition for the editorship of the whole magazine. Before he departed for his solitary train ride home, Lish asked, "Do I have the job or don't I?" As Lish remembered it, Hayes then turned to Hills and asked him how much he made. The answer, which Lish suspected was rehearsed, was $15,000. It was far less than Lish needed to support his family and live in New York City. But how could he turn down such a chance?[32]

The only thing left between Lish and the job was an obligatory lunch with publisher Arnold Gingrich. Gingrich, who had "some form of narcolepsy," Lish recalled, "seemed to be sleeping at the table. He believed I was a professor of English from the University of California. He smoked Camels to the nub and had these thick, callused fingers." At some point, he woke up and said, "I hear you are going to do *the* new fiction. Can I count on that?" Lish agreed. He didn't know when the article *the* had been added to his mandate, but he accepted it. He and Barbara moved to Manhattan.

Within days, Ray mailed a few stories to Lish at *Esquire*'s Madison Avenue offices. In a chatty cover letter, he said he'd come to New York City when his fortunes changed and expect a restaurant meal. That first group of stories came back in a flash, with comments that prompted Ray to ask Lish not to critique what he rejected. Stung but undaunted, Ray sent Lish three more stories. All came back, but Lish asked him to prune and resubmit one of them. The one Lish liked was called "Friendship," a story about rape and murder that is one of the most overtly terrifying Carver ever wrote. Even after Carver's pruning, Lish declined "Friendship."[33]

Ray was not discouraged. He had been tirelessly submitting manuscripts to magazines for a decade, working every angle he could devise to form personal connections with editors who might appreciate his work. And now the most unexpected thing had occurred. His drinking buddy and casual friend had been plucked from the vast field of literary aspirants all over America and dropped down inside the fortress of New York City publishing. That, for Ray Carver, was a miracle.

And it was another miracle that his buddy was acting as a true friend, giving his manuscripts serious consideration. As the old decade closed, Ray yearned for new inspiration and discipline. He was ready for a fresh start.

CHAPTER 14

A Friend in New York

January 1970–May 1971, San Jose and Sunnyvale, California

It is not necessary to portray many characters. The center of gravity
should be in two persons: him and her.
— Anton Chekhov to Alexander Chekhov, May 10, 1886,
transcribed in one of Carver's notebooks

Let's soar in seventy," Ray exhorted Lish. Taken with his alliteration, he
wrote Johnson: "Let's swing in seventy." Ray's soaring and swinging
depended on turning out more good writing. He was frantic to begin. On
the first Saturday in January, he was at his SRA office trying to work while
Maryann and Amy met Evan Connell for lunch. He liked Connell, he told
Johnson in a letter that afternoon, but feared a day wasted in "the drinks,
the parking, the bullshitting . . . the this, the that."[1] Some of the best stories
written by American writers arrived on Lish's desk at *Esquire* every day.
Ray was determined that, given privacy and time, he could compete with
the best.

Ray's expectations for the seventies ran from the sublime to the ridiculous. He had his hopes at *Esquire,* he was in the running for a grant from
the National Endowment for the Arts, and Random House editor Joe Fox
was looking at a dozen of his stories. While the stories were out, Ray was
engaged in plan B. "We're gonna get rich, rich," he wrote (echoing Willy
Loman's brother in *Death of a Salesman*) upon receiving a chain letter and
getting copies of it out to sixteen new people the same day. It was, after all,
a literary chain letter: novelists Philip Roth and Russell Banks were on the
list. That chain letter fizzled; Ray's mailbox never overflowed with dollar
bills.[2]

During this time, Maryann waitressed at Brave Bull, a steak house in Los
Altos. One night she served an unusual man who gave her more than a good
tip. He dined alone, but "referred to himself as *we,* as if there were two

people eating." And he was as large as two people. "He was very nice and refined, wore a blue blazer—a *huge* coat. He told me, 'We haven't always eaten like this.' And I was a cultivator of stories then—still am—I drew them out of people." Maryann's customer told her he'd gained a certain number of pounds each year since he'd left the navy. She got him extra butter, extra bread, whatever he wanted, and he kept ordering more. " 'If you don't mind, we'll have two desserts'—that's how he spoke." Back in the apartment in San Jose, still wearing her black waitress dress and white apron, Maryann told Ray all about her obese customer.

That was the beginning of a breakthrough story that Carver wrote soon afterward. He called it "Fat" and told it much as he'd heard it, from the point of view of the waitress. Maryann didn't give Ray the "business about me or the cook or the other waitress hearing the story—he made all that up to create an epiphany, to make it more than just an incident. But I was taken with it all, with the fat man and his manner of speaking."[3] Carver's waitress is so unnerved by the fat man that she spills his water while making his Caesar salad at his table and imagines that she herself has become fat and her husband (Rudy, a cook) has shrunk down to "a tiny thing, hardly there at all."

In early March, Ray read in the evening paper that he'd won a $2,000 NEA grant. A week earlier he'd been promoted to the public relations department at SRA. The grant wasn't enough to replace Ray's job, but it allowed Maryann to quit the Brave Bull. Until she got her bachelor's degree in July, she would be a full-time student, homemaker, and mother with no wage-earning job. She could "enjoy school and homework and writing a paper without being just exhausted." About then, Ray had a chance to buy stock in SRA's parent company, IBM, that was about to split. They might have afforded it with Maryann's income, but she promised him her degree would be a better investment.[4]

Ray got an immediate benefit too. While Maryann was with the children in San Jose, he stayed in Palo Alto four or five nights a week. An English family, hearing of the award-winning writer, offered Ray an apartment in their home. Ray was able to work and get some "reflection time, an amazing nearly forgotten concept."[5]

Kayak Press brought out *Winter Insomnia* in April 1970, the first of many limited editions, broadsides, and holiday cards that Carver allowed artisans to make throughout his career. Hitchcock designed and printed *Winter Insomnia* at his new outpost in Bonny Doon, near the University of California Santa Cruz campus. The handsome book reprints thirteen poems from *Near Klamath*, which is probably why Carver dedicated it to Dennis Schmitz and used the same epigraph from Kafka that had appeared in the earlier book. But differences exist between *Near Klamath* and *Winter Insomnia*. The poet's mind is more alone and often on the edge of despair or madness in the latter book.

One figure in *Winter Insomnia* haunts the poet's mind most chillingly. In "The Current" an old, eyeless, almost motionless creature with a dark mouth enters the poet's dreams. It holds a place in the poet's memory that belongs to Carver's father and to the alcoholism bequeathed him by his father and grandfather. Recovering alcoholics speak of the effect of alcohol on a family as "the elephant in the living room," a sinister, ubiquitous presence that is seldom named or recognized. In "Winter Insomnia" that old fish plays the elephant in the mind of the poet.

Carver considered using the last poem in the book, "Drinking While Driving," as its title piece. The phrase "drinking while driving" itself might serve as a metaphor for the way Ray would steer his life during the seventies. The speaker is happy driving and sharing a bottle with his brother, but also willing to "lie down and sleep forever." Yet the speaker in "Winter Insomnia" is also doomed to stay awake because his mind is "sick." He wishes that the great Chekhov, a doctor as well as a writer, could give him something to make him sleep. In a way, Chekhov answered Carver's plea for help. The Russian doctor's genre, the short story, would serve Carver in several ways in the 1970s. He would learn to use stories as a tool for emotional survival, a means for negotiating the terrifying waters of his own psyche. Taking something that had happened to him or someone he knew and turning it into a story allowed Carver to let his mind be bold and self-protective at the same time. In this manner, he gained some distance from his painful feelings and perceptions. To turn your life's stories into fiction, Carver told the *Paris Review* in 1983, "You have to be immensely daring, very skilled and imaginative and willing to tell everything on yourself. You're told again and again to write about what you know, and what do you know better than your own secrets?"[6]

From his social acquaintance with Ray, Hitchcock took the impression that he "did not take himself all that seriously." Ray's refusal to be ponderous was both a hedge and a strategy, a defensive move for a man who expected nothing and wanted everything. In letters to his closest confidants, Carver talked unabashedly about his hopes and slid over rejections. Ray's capacity to feel elated by any small success kept him going. As he waited to hear from book publishers, for instance, he was excited to have "Sixty Acres" solicited for an anthology of Native American stories, but wondered if they thought he was an Indian.[7] At some level, it was all equal to Ray. If he couldn't get ahead, he was satisfied to keep moving. He was a small-town Northwesterner through and through. Despite his unceasing effort, he really had no idea of how difficult it could be for a person from his circumstances to break into the literary establishment. Ray's (and Maryann's) naïveté probably protected him from the cynicism that desiccates many aspiring writers. He didn't know enough to quit.

Ray shows his doggedness in a series of letters to Jarvis Thurston, editor of *Perspective* in St. Louis. When Thurston recommended Ray for an NEA Discovery award, a couple of his stories were languishing on Thurston's desk. Ray waited eight months to send an inquiry after "A Dog Story" and "The Fling," adding (through gritted teeth, one imagines), "they were mailed last June." Thurston didn't budge, even after Carver had occasion to thank him for the Discovery nomination. On the one-year anniversary of his submission, Ray tried: "I'd be most interested to know if PERSPEC-TIVE is still holding . . ." At fourteen months, saving on postage, Ray typed on a postcard: "To the best of my knowledge you are holding two stories of mine . . ." but still the silence reverberated from St. Louis.[8] By then, Carver was frantic to get all his unpublished stories home so he would be free to submit them to Lish at *Esquire*.

In mid-March SRA flew its new public relations man to an English teachers' convention at the Olympic Hotel in Seattle. As he browsed the book racks in the deserted lobby one night, Ray noticed a couple across the room examining *The Best Little Magazine Fiction, 1970*. William Kittredge, then a struggling writer himself, recounted, "This scruffy fellow came right up to my elbow and tried to look over my shoulder. 'I've got a story in there,' he said."[9]

Kittredge was skeptical until the fellow showed him his story, "Sixty Acres," in the book. Then he recognized Raymond Carver as the author of "Will You Please Be Quiet, Please?" from *Best American Short Stories 1967*. It had rung so "absolutely true" that Kittredge recalled where he'd read it: the Benson Hotel in Portland. The next thing Carver said clinched the new friendship: Carver told Kittredge he admired *his* story in the *Northwest Review*, which "made him one of the few people in the world I had met who'd ever laid eyes on a story of mine." Later, Kittredge reminisced:

> This was indeed the life. We were shy for some moments, then we touched, we shook hands, we talked about a cup of coffee. Wait a minute, he said, why not a beer? I said, why not a drink? A drink would be fine, maybe a couple of drinks, what the hell; all things lay before us. It was that moment between drunks known as Exchanging Credentials. Would you have a drink? Well, maybe, sure.

Already late in his thirties and in his second life when the two met, Bill Kittredge had grown up on a big grain farm in southeastern Oregon. He followed his father's path with one deviation: mornings, before he went to the fields, he read some pages of philosophy or literature. At thirty-three, he left the ranch to study fiction writing at Iowa. When Ray met him, he was teaching at the University of Montana, where poet Richard Hugo directed a writing program that attracted like-minded writers and drinkers.[10]

The story of Kittredge's that Ray knew, "The Waterfowl Tree," is about a city boy whose father wants to show him where he spent his youth. The homecoming turns deadly when the father falls through ice. The son cannot save him. It's hard to think of a short story that would have resounded more for Ray at that time, less than three years after C.R.'s death. Thus, before they'd even lifted glasses together, Kittredge and Carver knew each other. They were both from the inland West whose people—as Carver phrases it in a foreword to his friend's work—"are light-years away from the American Dream . . . whose high hopes have broken down on them and gotten left behind like old, abandoned combines."[11] When Kittredge called Ray's room in the morning, Ray sounded too hungover to go anywhere. Kittredge didn't expect to hear from him again, but he was wrong. The two writers began a regular correspondence; in almost every letter, Ray mentions plans for a trip to Missoula, Montana. It was understood that there'd be serious drinking involved. The drinking to which both Kittredge and Carver devoted themselves *seemed* justified by their aspirations as writers. They gave themselves permission to do whatever they pleased because "anything was forgivable as long as you were writing well."[12]

Despite the continual difficulties and intermittent chaos of their lives, the Carvers never lacked friends and amusements. With Sylvia and Dick Kolbert, for instance, they drove to Jack London State Historic Park north of San Francisco. Ray hadn't read all fifty-nine published volumes of London's work, surely, but he was captivated by his biography. London survived an impoverished boyhood to become a child laborer at twelve, an oyster pirate at sixteen, a sailor on a Pacific schooner at seventeen, and an alcoholic at twenty. An exhibit in the park museum showed some of the six hundred story submissions London made before receiving his first acceptance and $40 from the *Black Cat* magazine in 1899. A year later, he was becoming the most popular American writer in the world.

London claimed he wrote one thousand words a day. At London's former home, Ray saw what London acquired by his labor: hillsides like Tuscany's, trout streams, and redwood groves. The Carvers and Kolberts went on a long hike, Ray and Dick in front talking, Maryann and Sylvia looking at the wildflowers. They peered into the cottage where London wrote and marveled at the four-story stone ruins of his Wolf House, destroyed by fire in 1913. By then, London's kidneys were diseased. At age forty, he was dead. Debate continues about the role of alcohol in London's illness.

"Ray wanted to *touch* everything," Sylvia recalled. He stood at a wrought-iron railing and considered the boulder with London's name scratched into it that sits above his ashes. The Carvers and Kolberts closed their day with wine and dinner, but Ray continued to ponder London's death. He found a used copy of *John Barleycorn,* London's out-of-print "alcoholic memoirs," and began praising London's book about the invisible soul-sickness with which alcohol infects an imaginative man.[13]

As SRA's public relations director, Ray had to give a presentation at an IBM meeting in Tarrytown, New York. He managed to pad a few days in New York City and travel expenses for Maryann into his corporate budget. In the run-up to his departure, he'd sent Lish several notes pleading for a response to stories he was holding at *Esquire*. Surely he'd imagined telling people in the East that he had a story forthcoming in the magazine, but when he and Maryann met Gordon and Barbara Lish at the Russian Tea Room, Lish could offer him no more than a sumptuous lunch. As they sat in the gilt and red Art Deco rooms, served by red-jacketed waiters, Lish told them the history of the landmark restaurant, a place where powerful and famous people came to promote their ideas and celebrate their successes.[14]

Amy was the member of the Carver ménage who had success to celebrate that spring. She was acting on Broadway, playing the warder's wife in Brendan Behan's *Borstal Boy*. Her name appeared (misspelled "Burke") near the bottom of the cast list in the *New York Times* on April 1 next to Clive Barnes's review; *Borstal Boy* won a Tony Award for the Best Play of 1970. After seeing the play, Ray went to his IBM meeting. Maryann stayed in the city until Ray called to insist that she come to Tarrytown. Hiding out in his hotel room, she coached him for his presentation. When the other wives arrived on Saturday, he brought her out for the big buffet.[15]

Some of the political turmoil of 1970 occurred right at Ray's doorstep. On May 1, President Nixon announced that the United States had invaded Cambodia. On campuses all over the country, students clashed with police and National Guard troops. Christi Carver remembered seeing riots near their apartment at San Jose State. Police entered the Stanford campus thirteen times in the spring of 1970 to quash demonstrations. At Jackson State University in Mississippi and Kent State University in Ohio, students were killed. Near the edge of the UC Santa Barbara campus, activists torched the Bank of America building.

That same spring, Maryann tabled her dreams of graduate school in literature. While Christi and Vance spent the summer in Yakima, she joined an accelerated program that allowed her to finish her bachelor's degree and begin teaching high school in the fall. She was offered a job at Los Altos High School, one of the highest-ranked high schools in California. Los Altos students and parents were demanding, but Maryann's department chair, Claire Pelton, saw that she could hold her own academically and assigned her the junior-year American Literature course. The Carvers leased a big, furnished house in Sunnyvale. Twelve-year-old Christi and eleven-year-old Vance went to middle school, where Vance made friends with a neighborhood boy whose father was a physicist at the Stanford Linear Accelerator. All things considered, life was good.[16]

Ray loved all that, of course. But his most fervent hopes were pinned on the stories Lish was holding in New York.

Lish was "beginning to get most of my way with fiction" at *Esquire,* and he wished he had more work he liked to pass along to his superiors. Among the "new fiction" Lish ran in his first year at the magazine were stories by Stanford student Michael Rogers, by his Palo Alto colleague John Deck, and by longtime *December* author Jerry Bumpus. Of course, *Esquire* continued to publish work by established writers, and Lish quickly developed skill at making magazine cuts from longer stories and soon-to-be-published novels.[17]

In July, Lish sent two stories back to Ray—edited but not rejected. One was about a meek man who is changed by a woman's wrong-number call. Carver had called the story "Adventure," but Lish proposed a new title taken from dialogue in the story: "You Will Come Again, Won't You?"[18] The other was "Fat." Lish had marked up both stories with interlinear changes in heavy black ink. He asked Ray to review and retype both stories.

A year earlier, Carver had cringed under Lish's criticism and begged for simple rejections. Now he thanked Lish for taking a pen to his manuscripts. In his glee, Ray compared Lish's work to the corrections he'd received from John Gardner when Ray was his student. The stories were now "first class"[19] Ray told Lish. In "Fat," Lish had removed some personalizing details, changed all the verbs to present tense, and focused on the fat man's fingers. Carver's line "I began to feel sorry for him right away" became "My God, Rita, those were fingers." The story wasn't much shorter, but it had a cooler, more frightening tone. When Ray returned the story, Lish sent it up *Esquire*'s chain of command. Carver reined in his hopes, telling Lish that regardless of what happened at the magazine, he was grateful for "the fine eye you turned on them."[20] "Fat" passed from one editor's desk to another's, through a half dozen readers. When the editors met over drinks after hours, Hayes pressed Lish to explain his taste in stories because "it seemed to Hayes and Gingrich that Lish liked some very peculiar things."[21] Ultimately, they declined "Fat."

Carver and Lish both persevered. In August Ray sent "a new one called 'The Neighbors'—maybe a weak title, maybe a weak story." The story of Bill and Arlene Miller, whose sex life gets a charge from their explorations in their neighbors' apartment, didn't seem weak to Lish. He line edited the manuscript and returned it. Carver reviewed and retyped. Lish combed through it again. He sliced *The* off Carver's title and omitted whole lines of personalizing details. He left Carver's past tense alone but downplayed sexual motives. He added lines that suggest a philosophical bleakness that supersedes the mundane horniness in the story. A longer note on the last page suggests that a bit about dirty pictures should be cut because it "tends to suggest another motive for their desperation to get back inside. Heavier stuff maybe without it. But I don't know. Anyway, consider the thought and see what M. thinks."[22]

Clearly, Lish left final decisions on "Neighbors" to Ray. Just as clearly, he expected that Ray would consult Maryann. Lish's note provides the only available written evidence of the editorial contribution Maryann Carver made to her husband's stories. "Essentially my job was to give Ray feedback he could use when he began revisions," Maryann said.[23] The "pictures bit" stayed in, and the story retained the sexual undercurrent that Carver had written into it, but some dialogue became more oblique. Carver accepted these line edits but worried that the story "feels a little thin now." Before the end of the month, he sought an opinion from Johnson about two "heavily revised" stories and two new stories.[24] He didn't say whether he or Lish had done the revising.

At Lish's suggestion, Ray left the Harold Matson agency for a new agent, Ellen Levine, who was developing her own clientele at Curtis Brown. On a blank sheet at the back of the second "Neighbors" manuscript, Lish declared: "Listen, goddamit if I don't get this one in Esq. & if Brown [ie. Levine] doesn't place Fat & Doctor I'm gonna lay right down & croak. Shit, man, these are *great* stories." As "Neighbors" passed from one skeptical reader to another, Ray reminded Lish to "Hang tough."[25] He saw himself and Lish as allies, both finding their way in new territory.

In Lish's recollection, the process was a little different. He needed "the new fiction" he'd been hired to deliver, and Carver's characters seemed unusual to him: "the particularities [in his stories] delivered a social type hitherto unknown to me. His characters were one step up—they had apartments and a little money." Lish found Carver's characters "grossly inept" and was taken by "their blatant illiteracies, of which Carver himself was unaware." It was, Lish would later claim, merely the raw material of Carver's stories that interested him. Lish believed that his editorial work on Carver's stories was a creative act in its own right for which he deserved acknowledgment.[26]

Ray was turning out new work and revising old work at extraordinary speed. The lure of publication in *Esquire* was surely the greatest spur to this activity, but not the only one. Ray's correspondence with Kittredge, whom he'd begun to regard as a close friend after their one evening together, inspired him, as did George Hitchcock and other Santa Cruz friends. With Christi and Vance away for the summer and Maryann in class at night, he was as well positioned as he'd ever been to work at his writing. To *be* a writer.

Naturally, with everything going so well, Ray had his mind on changing his situation. As soon as something broke for him, he hoped to quit SRA and return to Iowa City to finish his MA and qualify himself to join the English Department at the University of Montana, where he'd asked Kittredge to put in a word for him. SRA had noticed that Ray was abusing his expense account, so he feared his days there were numbered.[27]

When Maryann's mother arrived for a celebration of Maryann's graduation and new career, Ray picked her up at the depot. "I asked Ray to stop at a shopping center so I could buy Maryann an attaché case, because she'd always carried her papers in a box. But he said, 'Oh, she doesn't need one of those. What we really need is some groceries.' " Alice always regretted giving Ray that money, "because it was one more instance of how Maryann never had anything for herself."[28]

One must allow for maternal prejudices, but there's no doubt that Maryann worked incessantly. As she entered her salaried position, Ray was leaving his. Late in August, he accepted a three-month severance package from SRA; he promised the company he would freelance for them but hoped instead to collect unemployment benefits for six months after the severance pay ran out.[29] Thus he'd have the nine months of Maryann's teaching year for full-time writing, vitiated only by some child care and housekeeping.

He had just learned that "Neighbors" was in the hands of Editor in Chief Harold Hayes. Gordon and Barbara Lish came to California on an early September vacation and took Ray and Maryann out to dinner, but Hayes and Gingrich still hadn't decided about "Neighbors."[30] Ray kept waiting through the month as he took his brother, James, to Humboldt County to enroll at College of the Redwoods. For the first time since their father's sudden death three years before, twenty-seven-year-old James felt able to leave his mother on her own. Ella Carver remained in the Bay Area, sometimes in a live-in situation as a nanny and sometimes in her own apartment.[31]

Ray was sick in bed, ears buzzing with cold medicine, when Lish phoned to tell him that *Esquire* would buy "Neighbors." After calling Maryann out of a classroom to tell her, he went straight to work on another story, all the while popping aspirin and blowing his nose. But at that very moment, his typewriter broke, and he began to beat it with his fist and yell at it for letting him down when there was no time to be lost. "I wasn't myself," he explained to Lish. He took the unruly typewriter to the shop and, by hand, assured Lish that he hadn't "backed the wrong horse." When the machine came back, he sent Lish a requested biographical statement, noting that he was presently writing more stories and a novel set in Israel and other parts of the Middle East.[32]

The story would appear the next March or April, and Ray would be paid "good dough" with a promise of "twice that amount" on the next story. Ray told Lish he wanted his byline on the story to read "Raymond" (not Ray) Carver. A successful literary partnership had commenced, but Carver was probably not marked to become the most prominent of the writers whose literary careers were touched by Lish. Levine sent Carver stories to *Playboy* and other magazines that paid, but had only one hit. "Ray's work was not for everyone," Levine recalled. "It was not easy to place at first; it really wasn't."[33]

Ray was thirty-two years old when *Esquire* bought "Neighbors." He wasn't necessarily older than other writers were at this stage in their careers, but he had been away from home, on his own financially and emotionally for fourteen years. During that time, since he first encountered "The Lady with the Lap Dog" on Maryann's high school reading list, he had been learning to write "him and her" stories.

Carver's focus on he-she stories became more intense after *Esquire* purchased "Neighbors." From a television quiz show called *He Said, She Said*—aired for a year beginning in 1969—he and Maryann appropriated a shorthand to refer to the type of story he was writing. This marked the beginning of Carver's bolder approach to his subjects and greater mastery of his craft. And Lish was eager to edit that new work.

When Lish accepted the assignment to bring "the new fiction" to *Esquire,* he walked onto a stage where many of the best American authors of the twentieth century had appeared. From its founding in 1933, *Esquire* had published literary writing by Hemingway and Fitzgerald, who became personal friends of publisher Arnold Gingrich's. During the early 1940s, the magazine catered to soldiers (there were pinups), and its literary cachet declined. In 1952 Gingrich decided to "go for quality again" and hired a phalanx of new editors, including Rust Hills and Harold Hayes. Hills believed that "the kind of fiction a magazine publishes affects its image all out of proportion to the amount of fiction published." By the end of 1957, the centerfold was gone, and in its stead were pages of stories by top-notch authors. Hills and his successor, Robert Brown, introduced writers who hadn't been published commercially before, such as George P. Elliott, Stanley Elkin, John Barth, Terry Southern, Bruce Jay Friedman, and Flannery O'Connor. The magazine continued to provide a market for shorter works and excerpts by established writers such as John Cheever, Bernard Malamud, I. B. Singer, and Vladimir Nabokov."[34]

But as the 1960s advanced, fiction competed for space and prestige in *Esquire* with "New Journalism" that used techniques borrowed from novelists—scene setting, dialogue, class mannerisms, and manipulation of point of view (the list is Tom Wolfe's)—to report current events.[35] New Journalism provided energetic and politicized narratives. Some late-sixties issues of *Esquire* carried no fiction.

Lish had searched the country for a job that could engage his demandingly manic personality, and he'd found it. *Esquire* handed him an opportunity to reinstate fiction and invigorate the magazine. The stakes were high for both Gingrich and Lish when they cobbled together the notion of "new fiction" through that simple misunderstanding over lunch. Lish began reading frantically to see what he could find. He read submissions from writers he already knew, including Carver, and he listened to agents who pressed their writers upon him. He even read the stories in the so-called slush pile. He had a capacity for reading, slept very few hours, and maintained his outsider's belief that the commercial literary establishment sometimes overlooked true literary talent. Under Lish's watch, the door was always ajar for new writers at *Esquire*.*

Lish first appeared on the masthead as fiction editor in the March 1970 issue. He was a demanding and confident editor. Instead of using copy editing marks and notes to authors, he wove his own version through and around the original manuscript, then asked writers to retype their pieces. He was preternaturally skillful at this, as the thousands of manuscript pages he saved over the years prove. After Lish had worked over a manuscript, it would be laborious at best (at least in precomputer days) to restore it to its original state. Although a number of authors over the years refused the changes he proposed, many did not.

---

* Lish told his editors that he'd discovered Carver in the slush pile and Carver reiterated that tale in his essay "Fires."

• • •

Ray told everyone he knew about *Esquire*'s acceptance of "Neighbors." To Joy Williams he sent a letter of congratulations about her first book and went on to say that he was "writing like a streak." He enclosed a copy of *Winter Insomnia*, which had been out for half a year; it looks as if he waited till he had good news about his fiction before writing to fiction colleague (and competitor) Williams. Effusively, he invites Williams and her family to call collect and to come for a visit at the huge Sunnyvale house with "four bedrooms, three baths, etc."[36]

Ray even wrote air mail to his present landlord, Frank Zepezauer, about "Neighbors," taking the occasion to inform him that the Zepezauer cat had sneaked into his house and scratched up a couch. The cat, Ray assured his landlord, would appear in the story (it does, as Kitty). Jack Hicks, by then teaching American literature at the University of California at Davis, came to meet Ray in Sunnyvale and asked to reprint "Neighbors" in an anthology of fiction he was editing. Before Hicks departed, he'd given Ray an advance payment on the story out of his own book advance and asked Ray to compose a few paragraphs about the story.[37]

Ray was champing at the bit to celebrate his success with Kittredge in Missoula, but didn't get there until November, when his mother-in-law was able to stay with Christi and Vance on evenings while Maryann was in classes.[38] Missoula, the town known by the book and movie *A River Runs Through It*, held enormous appeal for Ray.* The ingredients of that appeal were simple: friends, bars, and an old-fashioned downtown where cowboy types coexisted with university and counterculture types. Montana enforced practically no restrictions on the consumption of alcoholic beverages. Open containers were permitted on the street, and there was no law against drinking while driving! The landscape may have reminded Ray of the country around Yakima, but in the 1970s, Missoula's natural beauty was marred by wood smoke from sawmill teepee burners and pollution from a plywood operation in Milltown, five miles upriver.[39]

One must reckon with the drinking and the tricks of memory in any account of Ray's visits to Montana. Ray spent a week there in November, ostensibly to see about getting a job. Back in Sunnyvale on November 18, he wrote to thank the Kittredges for everything, especially for "that party!" He'd never been a guest of honor before, he declared. Missoula became a regular stop in Ray's peregrinations—a source of both sustenance and trouble—for years to come. Besides Kittredge, Carver soon became friendly

---

* With Annick Smith and Robert Redford, Kittredge was a coproducer of the movie based on Norman MacClean's 1976 story.

with James Welch, Jon A. Jackson, James Crumley, and Richard Hugo—all, he said, "real old-time, hardline drinkers too."[40]

Jackson first heard of Carver right after Kittredge met him in Seattle. "Bill said Ray was a smart writer—*smart* was a favorite adjective for us then—and then he told me, 'Jon, I know you like to drink, and I like to drink, but I never met a guy who likes to drink like Ray likes to drink.' " When Ray showed up in the flesh, Jackson encountered a man with

an amiable, disarming, bumbling manner, full of humor and wit, a twinkle in his eye, kind of a tousled little boy look. Physically, he was very soft—flabby and gangly, had no muscle tone, and was hopelessly unathletic. His only sport was fishing. He had somewhat high and pronounced hips, narrow shoulders, soft hands. A real mama's boy, one might think, and perhaps he was.

Drunken fellowship wasn't Missoula's only attraction. They all talked about books, favoring those "smart" books that appealed to a large readership without being unliterary. A lot of Missoula writers scraped by on any kind of work they could get, from screenwriting to construction jobs, so the town lacked the usual university status distinctions. Some of these men wondered why Carver limited himself to domestic subjects because, as Jackson put it, "domestic relations were what you had to put up with—why would you write about that?"[41]

"Competition among us was fierce, but we were all like seventh grade boys, competing in that way. We called it 'the town without pity,' " Kittredge reflected. Carver, for the most part, refused to state his qualms about other writers' work. When he first read one of Crumley's books, he ended his comment about it to Kittredge with an ellipsis: "some of it was very good, some of it . . ."[42] He was generous to a fault when it came to reading friends' manuscripts and promoting them as best he could.

After a year in New York, Lish had extended his influence beyond *Esquire*. He showed "Are You a Doctor?" to editor Betsy Freund at *Harper's Bazaar*. Freund called Carver early in December to buy the story and praise it "to the skies." She wanted to publish within the next two months, but Lish insisted that she wait until after "Neighbors" had appeared in *Esquire*. He wanted Carver to be his own discovery. Freund told Carver that she owed Lish a favor and postponed his *HB* debut until the summer. Meanwhile, Levine sent "Fat" to Freund, who decided she preferred it to "Are You a Doctor?"[43]

"Neighbors" brought Ray his first invitation to give a paid reading, at

American River College in Sacramento. The man who'd invited him, Tom Schmidt, thought that Ray and Maryann had "a strikingly matching look of unhealthiness: pale and bloodless skin, sickly hair—hers bleached in the pre-golden-girl peroxide way, Ray's unfashionably short, greasy, and unwashed. They both chain-smoked with particular fervor." After Ray read six or seven poems and "Neighbors," he chatted with students while Maryann thanked Schmidt profusely. "She told me how grateful Ray was even though he would certainly not be able to tell me that himself." Ray invited Schmidt to come to a *kayak* collating party, insisting that it would be worth the long drive because he would meet "extraordinary people." When Schmidt told Ray that a story of his own had been accepted at *Transatlantic Review,* Ray smiled for the first time since he'd arrived. "We're on our way!" he told Schmidt, who felt that Ray's joy in their mutual good fortune was "pure and complete."[44]

Ray was finishing a story he called "Bummer" (probably an early title for "What's in Alaska?") but he had no complaints as the holidays neared. "I keep checking my pulse, waiting for the roof to fall in," he wrote. When his severance pay stopped, he began collecting $65 a week in state unemployment benefits.[45] With the momentum of his recent success, Ray composed a letter to Jarvis Thurston in St. Louis that belongs in a museum of aggrieved writers' artifacts: laconically, he offers a list of magazines that have recently taken his stories, thanks Thurston again for the NEA grant he steered toward Carver, and "presumes" it would be all right to send elsewhere the two stories Thurston has been holding. Though the stories had been languishing for a year and a half, the names *Esquire* and *Harper's Bazaar* seem to have been magical. Ray received an acceptance from Thurston within the week. Still, publication was distant for those stories. It seems surprising that Carver allowed Thurston to keep them at all.[46]

From Amy in New York came first good and then bad news. She knew the actor James Earl Jones, who might help her get dramatic roles; invited to an *Esquire* party by Lish, she met the poet James Dickey, whose novel *Deliverance* was a best seller at the time. Lish had persuaded his editors to try short poems as "fillers" in place of the sketches they'd used in the past, and Dickey had assumed the title of poetry editor. Ray had hopes that the double connection would help him place poems in *Esquire,* but felt nervous about Amy's involvement with Dickey, who was married."[47] Meanwhile, billboards all over New York City advertised Amy's next play, *Foreplay,* with a picture of her lying nude, facedown, in a circle with two male actors. She was rehearsing to play the rejected wife in the homosexual coming-out story when she suffered a manic break. She saw a psychiatrist who blamed her mental illness on abuse by her mother's second husband but assured her that it would all be worse if she had not witnessed her father's vengeance against the man. By the time Amy arrived at the Carvers' for Christmas, *Foreplay* had opened to bad reviews with another actress in her place.[48] She intended to try Hollywood again after the first of the year.

January 1971 found Ray working hard and in high hopes for his future, even though the holidays he'd looked forward to with such fervor had let him down. Now that he and Maryann were occupying a nice house and could put food on the table, their relatives descended on them "with three bags full of hopelessness and despair." Years ago, he lamented, his parents and James had been the needy cases, "homeless, back and forth on the highway between Washington and Chico-Sacramento." Now they had Amy as well as Maryann's mother, who'd been there since she came to help in November, though she probably didn't borrow money. Ray desperately hoped that someone's luck would change, because he and Maryann were "only holding by our nails anyway." Erin remained at the Carvers while Amy went to New York to get her things. When she returned, she invited Ray and Maryann to dine with her and James Earl Jones. Ray, obviously starstruck, wrote Lish that Jones was "a great good" man and actor. At the moment, though, Amy's hopes were centered on Dickey, who was recommending her for the role of a model in the movie version of *Deliverance*.[49]

When Ray's fellow student from Iowa, Tom Doherty, sent Ray his novel-in-progress based on his tour of duty in Vietnam, Ray offered fingers-on-the-pulse commentary: the supporting characters were vivid, but he had trouble caring about the protagonist. Carver apologized for being a "prick critic" and said Doherty's language was "too literary" and made him "too often conscious of the author behind the scene . . ." With faint, precise brackets and notes on Doherty's first page, he broke up long sentences, cut words, eliminated passive verbs, narrowed the focus. Carver pared "leaned their backs against the cab, monopolizing the available shade" to "leaned against the cab, in the shade." Hoping Doherty wouldn't be angry, Carver explained that Lish did a similar job for him. (In fact, Lish's editing was more determinative.) Carver praised Doherty for the "thrust" behind his two hundred pages, noting that he'd never written anything over fifty pages.[50]

Novel writing and Lish's editing were, in fact, at the forefront of Carver's mind that spring. Ray's novel was "abudding," but he couldn't get started on it. He had finished three stories in the first six weeks of the new year. Levine sent his stories out, but some kept coming back like bad pennies. A story that no one would buy from Carver in the spring of 1971 was "They're Not Your Husband."[51] It joins restaurant material like that in "Fat," with painful scrutiny of Earl and Doreen Ober. Earl is "between jobs as a salesman" and Doreen is a waitress. After Earl overhears another cafe customer say of Doreen, "Look at the ass on that . . ." he pressures her to lose weight. When Doreen has starved herself into a smaller uniform, Earl comes in for coffee again. He cues a man to remark on Doreen's behind: "Don't you think that's something special?"

His move recoils on him. Near the story's end, Earl hears another waitress ask Doreen who he is:

> Earl put on his best smile. He held it, and it broadened until he felt his face pulling out of shape.
>
> But the other waitress was frowning at him, and Doreen began to shake her head . . . They all stared at Earl.
>
> "He's my husband," Doreen said at last, shrugging. She looked at Earl and waited, and then she put the unfinished chocolate sundae in front of him and reached for the coffee pot.*

"They're Not Your Husband" is one of Carver's most self-revealing stories. Its brilliance resides in the subterfuge of its point of view. It conveys compassion for one character (Doreen) by focusing its narrative through a less likable character (Earl). If Earl is something like Ray, then one may see here a sketch of the way Carver's imagination (and perhaps his marriage) worked. Earl's shame leads him from self-pity into bullying and a ridiculous display of his own weakness; but finally — after Earl humiliates himself more publicly — comes a moment wherein Doreen acknowledges that, for better or for worse, he's hers.[52]

About the time Carver was recovering from rejection of that story, Samuel Vaughn at Doubleday returned a manuscript of stories.[53] Ray asked Lish to take a look at it, noting that he was sticking with his title (alas, he does not say what it was) after rejecting "for instance, 'Bad Check, His Mama, and Beautiful Songs.'"[54] His joke title parodies country-and-western song subjects he heard growing up. Indeed, transformed by a generation of ragtag life and education, those are Carver's subjects, too.

Ray had enjoyed almost half a year off from a day job, but the jackals of debt were circling. Again, the biggest debts were from unpaid student

---

* Quoted from *Chicago Review* 24:4 (1973), 107. Changes Lish made in the story before it appeared in Carver's *Will You Please Be Quiet, Please?* sharpened the closing dialogue and image: " 'He's a salesman. He's my husband,' Doreen said at last, shrugging. Then she put the unfinished chocolate sundae in front of him and went to total up his check."

loans. Declaring bankruptcy in Sacramento three years before bought time on some of these but did not erase them. Now that Maryann was working, the collectors were after them again. Ray began doing freelance work under the table for SRA, which wearied him so much that he couldn't write fiction. On top of that, Ray was trying to save his "great good looks" by getting deferred dental work done. At age thirty-one, his teeth hurt so badly that he was "running on codeine, Percodan, and aspirin." In February he had root canals on his two front teeth.[55]

On March 8, 1971, Ray spent most of an unemployment check to take Vance to a closed-circuit broadcast of the heavyweight championship fight between Muhammad Ali and Smokin' Joe Frazier. The next time Ray saw the Kolberts, he narrated the fight for them. Dick recalled: "Listening to Ray was better than having a ringside seat . . . he gave a round-by-round recounting of the fight. I've never been absorbed and rapt like that. I knew the outcome, but Ray was able to achieve suspense."[56]

Vance cherished the action and the crowd and the rare father-son outing. Ray's need for solitude, his many anxieties, and his furtive drinking undoubtedly added to the difficulties most parents confront as their children become teenagers. Ray watched an occasional World Series game with Vance, but his involvement with his children was increasingly sporadic.[57] Both Vance and Christi often felt that their own needs and desires could not compete with their parents' intense attachment to each other and their mutual dedication to whatever they believed might further their father's writing career.

When Johnson included "A Night Out" in *The Best Little Magazine Fiction, 1971* anthology, he again asked Ray for an author photo. Ray found one of himself at about age eleven that he preferred over any portrait of himself as a "tormented writer." He called it "Washington Fats in the good old days." Johnson cropped it to a head shot, explaining that Carver, "whose boyhood picture appears here, is in his thirties." The blurry, badly lit picture does set Ray apart from the other authors, including R. V. Cassill, the teacher who'd frustrated Ray at Iowa, and Joyce Carol Oates in a beehive hairdo.

Uncropped, Ray's chosen image shows him sitting at Wenas Lake with a fishing pole with a dry hillside behind him, squinting into the sun, chubby and unsmiling, summer-bleached forelock ruffled by the wind. It was, he told Johnson, the "only pic of me that I feel is me somehow."[58] When a married man with children and work forthcoming in *Esquire* decides that his preadolescent self is more authentic than his present self, he's surely struggling over his identity. As if to underscore the question of who he was, Ray ordered a negative and six or more copies of "Washington Fats" to give his friends. Kittredge received one, as did Lish.

Maryann's first year of teaching at Los Altos High School went unusually well, and the district renewed her contract. As Claire Pelton had hoped, she was academically solid, innovative, and well liked by students. Maryann encouraged her colleagues to invite her writer-husband to speak to their students. He visited one of Maryann's classes as well as a creative writing class for seniors. According to Pelton, Ray was "arrogant and dismissive" and "laughed at the kids' questions," and she wondered if Maryann faced that kind of attitude at home.[59] Ray's impressions, sent to Lish, diverge so much from Pelton's that one suspects they are not talking about the same event: the girls were "wide-eyed and wet-lipped. . . . This from an old married who's got, next to yours, the only good marriage he knows of."[60]

During the spring of this year, Carver's literary business became entangled with Amy Burk's love affair with poet and novelist James Dickey. Over months or years of their involvement, Dickey spent a lot of money on her, for meals and clothing; according to Amy, Dickey also told Lish that her daughter, Erin Wright, of whom he was fond, was his illegitimate child, in order to secure Lish's help in passing private funds from himself to Amy. Dickey told the *Deliverance* movie director, John Boorman, "John, if I weren't a Baptist and a famous poet, I'd divorce my wife and marry Amy Burk."[61]

Dickey's effort to send money to Amy was connected with *Esquire*'s publication of two poems by Carver in the summer of 1971, though details remain fuzzy. Lish recalled that Carver objected to the arrangement. "Hunter"—fourteen lines of which had already been printed in *Near Klamath*—had seventeen when it filled a small space at the bottom of a page in the July *Esquire*. The new lines, from "Believe in the fingers" to the end, don't sound much like Carver's work and one wonders if Dickey or Lish added them. During this period, Carver worried that Lish had somehow been made uncomfortable by these arrangements for "funds channeled through me to A" and briefly held off on sending more stories to Lish.[62]

Nonetheless, Ray dreamed that all the stories he had out might be bought up by paying magazines at the same time. He also entered the Joseph Henry Jackson Award contest for northern California writers.[63] When Leonard Michaels, one of the judges, phoned him to say that he thought his stories were terrific and offered to show them to his editor at Farrar, Straus and Giroux, Ray considered the $2,000 award his. "Gratuitous kindnesses" like this kept him going, he wrote Kittredge, and headed to Berkeley, where Michaels was a professor in the English Department, to meet his benefactor.[64] Michaels thought Ray looked as conventional as an insurance salesman, but what he liked in his stories was a certain "craziness" and their "sense of humor and the suppression of rationality, so the events in a story would move forward by virtue of a subconscious compulsion." Carver told Michaels that his stories in *Going Places* had influenced his own. Ray couldn't help envying a man like Michaels, who had been able to publish a collection of stories without first writing a novel.[65]

But Ray was mistaken about the award. He received a special commendation and $200, but the big prize went to Santa Cruz novelist Richard Lourie. At a celebration lunch with Lourie, Michaels, and another judge, Al Young (author of *Sitting Pretty*), Ray hid his disappointment, downed stingers, and ate pepper steak. His attitude was, better this than nothing.* Thus Carver saw through things and ignored or made the best of them. On a few occasions, Carver simply awarded himself the Jackson prize. When "A Dog Story" finally appeared in *Perspective*, the contributor's note said that Carver "won last year's Joseph Henry Jackson Award."[66]

In April 1971, Lish made an unusual request of Ray. He asked him to acquire some information about a woman who lived in Burlingame, south of San Francisco International Airport. The woman was Lish's former wife, and the address his former home. Ray's letter doesn't say what Lish wanted to know; he may simply have wanted reports on his children's welfare or on his former wife's activities. Ray declined. In an explanation that's a fair appraisal of his personality, Ray said he was "not very good at offensive maneuvering," though he had no problem with defensive actions where caution, secrecy, and paranoia would be useful. Not to disappoint Lish, Ray offered to hire a private detective for the day's work—about $75, he estimated—without mentioning Lish's name.[67]

That probably ended the episode, but Lish himself later elaborated upon it. He said that he and Carver had made an exchange. Lish needed a reliable, neutral person to keep tabs on his California family. His old friends Cassady and Kesey weren't good candidates (indeed not, as one was dead and the other lived in another state), so he asked Carver to do the job. It was in return for that favor, Lish convinced himself later, that he promised Carver that he would try to sell his writing in New York.[68]

"Neighbors" was scheduled for *Esquire*'s June issue. As Carver waited for that event, he came to the end of ten months of full-time writing during which he had produced the "nucleus" of his first fiction collection.[69] With Lish's help, he was learning to sustain his tone in a story and create a whole-

---

* Young later told Carver that Michaels had voted for Lourie while Young had favored Carver. "Ray said, 'I know, Al, but it's okay.'"

ness of effect, thus to turn solid realistic stories into distinctive magazine stories. Kittredge and Michaels, who both first knew the Carvers during the spring of 1971, understood something similar about Ray and Maryann's collusion in the making of these stories:

> Michaels: "You can imitate a Carver story, but you can't really write one unless you came from where he came from and listened all your life to the way his people talk. The people he dealt with and lived with were all participants in a way in his writing. I imagine Maryann lived through a hell of a lot of that material with him, and I suspect that she *and* Ray paid for those stories with their lives."

> Kittredge: "Ray had grown up in a caste system where Okies and Arkies were viewed with disdain, and he and Maryann were united in wanting to escape that. It may explain the profound bond they formed at an early age. They were partners in the getaway."[70]

The first stage of the escape was almost complete. Together Ray and Maryann had overcome unusual challenges. They had college degrees; Ray was getting paid, if occasionally, for his work; and Maryann had a profession. Now Ray was refining their lives into stories that would be widely read. Desires and fears that had driven them for fifteen years were soon to be replaced by opportunities and dangers more sinister than any they'd met before.

PART III

SUCCESS AND DISCONTENT

CHAPTER 15

A Story in *Esquire*

June 1971–April 1972, Santa Cruz, California

[Gordon Lish is] remarkably smart and sensitive to the needs of a manuscript. He's a good editor too. Maybe he's a great editor. All I know for sure is he's my editor and my friend, and I'm glad on both counts.

—Raymond Carver to *The Paris Review*, 1983

The June issue of *Esquire* arrived at the Carvers' in Sunnyvale early in the afternoon of Wednesday, May 5, 1971. Ray poured himself a glass of Scotch, turned the glossy pages with wonder, and waited to show Mary-ann.[1] In some ways, "Neighbors" had become a commodity, no longer his own. First, there had been Lish's aggressive editing; now the magazine's graphics packaged the story: a subtitle under the byline—"a cup of sugar, an egg, a stick of butter, and thou"—suggested a naughtiness typical of *Esquire*. A full-page illustration faced the second page of the story: a couple dressed in conservative overcoats (the man also wears a dark fedora) in an urban apartment hallway. The top halves of their bodies are unlocking one apartment while the bottom halves—apparently lopped off with pinking sheers—approach an opposite door. The art telegraphed an interpretation of Carver's story: a modern couple, divided and walking away from themselves.[*]

A story by an unknown like himself in *Esquire* "should give hope to every writer in America," Ray wrote Kittredge that same afternoon. At

---

[*] Lish commented on the magazine's presentation of fiction: "Anything that tries to take the reader's eye from the story or makes an effort at representing the story in any other medium strikes me as obnoxious. I mean, how can you make a picture that shows a story? If you can do that, then don't write the story." (John Bowie and Monroe Lerner, "Editor Discusses Fiction in Magazines," *Daily Iowan*, 4-10-74.)

the end of summer, *Harper's Bazaar* ran "Fat" along with a photo (one of those taken by Lish) and a note that said Carver contributed "to *Esquire* and most of the major literary magazines" and was "working on" his first novel. Both claims were premature, but Ray's prospects had never been brighter. He had fourteen or fifteen stories out in the mail.[2] Fifteen others had already appeared in small magazines, usually after numerous submissions.

Yet Ray was ill prepared for success. Like his parents, he was more familiar with bad luck and failure and depression than with recognition. Intimations of success made him nervous and suspicious. One recalls that he left the Iowa Writers' Workshop just after Maryann's intervention had snagged him a new fellowship there. But he could not retreat into failure this time. His work was appearing in prestigious places, and this in itself drew people toward him. Herein, of course, lay the new difficulty. Since he was the same man writing the same sort of stories he'd been writing for ten years, he could not help but suspect that there was something insincere in the attention he was suddenly receiving. So he embraced new opportunities on one level and—it seems—repressed his fear of them on another.

Such doubts, along with the duress of the Carvers' lives—insolvency, frequent moves, a life guided by parental ambition rather than children's needs—meant that Christi and Vance grew up without the stability of neighborhood and nuclear family that were ideals of middle-class life. Counterbalancing that, at least while the children were little, was the extended family made up of Maryann's two sisters, her mother, and Ray's mother. These women formed a safety net that worked well enough—until Christi and Vance became teenagers. Then the frequent moves, financial stress, and parents' frenzied social life disrupted the kids' ties with friends and, in Vance's case, sports teammates. In the early 1970s, Vance thought, his father seemed distant from family life: "I don't know if it was because of his drinking or general restlessness. I happen to believe that my dad was trying more than anything to establish himself as a writer and therefore to be with other writers—hence he had little time anymore for family, even though at heart he was a family-oriented person, because he had family solidarity growing up."[3]

The owners of the Sunnyvale house were expected back on August 1, Ray's unemployment payments had ended, and their phone was disconnected. Nonetheless, Maryann threw a dinner party when the Kittredges came to visit.[4] James B. Hall showed up along with George Hitchcock and several other Santa Cruz writers. Hall was Provost of College V, the yet-unnamed arts college founded in 1965 at UC Santa Cruz. He wanted master artists "walking through the quadrangle so a student could look up and say 'Hey, there he goes . . .' " George Hitchcock held such a position, as did jazz musician Chet Baker and poet William Everson (Brother Antoninus), and novelist Annie Steinhardt, author of *Thunder LaBoom* and *Getting Balled in Berkeley*. Hall found Carver "sufficiently authentic" to fill a visiting artist position, though he seemed "Southern, almost white trash in his attitudes." Hall, who'd grown up on a pig farm in Ohio, saw a similarity between Carver's stories and those of his fellow Ohioan Sherwood Anderson, but it was Maryann who convinced him to hire Ray: "She was a wonderfully warm person. I vividly remember her face and her hair. They had something of a mattress-on-the-floor kind of place, and I felt so sorry for them: married so young, not much money at all, children. There was a kind of cheerful make-do about their lives." Carver liked Hall, the author of *Us He Devours* and a dozen other books, and considered him the best writer in the Santa Cruz area.[5]

Hall offered Ray a job teaching poetry, contingent upon his providing letters of reference. Using his now-illicit SRA phone card, Ray telephoned Day, Schmitz, Lish, and Dickey.[6] Lish's letter praised his discovery lavishly: "Our friendship has been a long one . . . there is no speaking properly to the matter of Ray Carver without mentioning the fineness of his character. I suppose the connection may reside in this: that in whatever task Ray undertakes he does it with all that it's in him to be; he withholds nothing, he gives himself in abundance." Then, perhaps recalling that he is recommending Carver to teach poetry: ". . . my guess is that Ray is by disposition a poet first and finally. He values the well-made thing, the ellipsis, and a shape of decisive beginning and end. He is indeed a carver, onomatologic notion intended . . ."[7] Whether Lish was simply amusing himself or laying it on thick to puff his editorial intentions, his letter won Ray the job.

Ray would teach creative writing one day per week for about $115 per day, enough to augment Maryann's income and provide "social activity and a semblance of life away from the suburbs." In addition, he'd have a private office, free cafeteria meals, and responsibility for a literary magazine. Within days of securing the appointment, Maryann—"a good woman who deserves diamonds," Ray said—took him shopping for a professorial wardrobe. Nervously aware that he might be stepping into the role in some young writer's life that John Gardner had played in his own, he spent most of August reading and boning up to lead classes.[8]

When Kittredge stayed at Ray's house, he noticed a much-thumbed and annotated paperback anthology of fiction about doppelganger figures such as Conrad's "The Secret Sharer," Dostoyevsky's *The Double,* and Ambrose

Bierce's "An Occurrence at Owl Creek Bridge."* As he observed the development of Ray and his work, Kittredge found that doubleness figured deeply in his friend's relation to the world: "I think it was that he was two times too smart and too sensitive for the place he was born into and grew up in. There was one Ray who lived his life and another who watched all of that life." Alcohol may have dulled the pain he felt and given him a false sense of unity, "but writing was the only thing that saved him all along; that allowed him to connect one self with the other. It was a struggle, always, and sometimes he connected artistically but not morally."⁹

A disabling doubleness, understood as a perception that things are not as they appear, affected many realms of American society at this time, from junior high school potheads to the nation's president. In June, military analyst Daniel Ellsberg gave the *New York Times* a cache of top-secret government reports that exposed a history of duplicity in the formulation of Vietnam policies. These documents became known as the Pentagon Papers. President Nixon organized a clandestine team of White House "plumbers" to investigate Ellsberg and plug future leaks. Three years later, discovery of the actions of Nixon's team would lead to his downfall. It was in this political climate that Carver wrote his only story with a clear political theme. "The Man Is Dangerous" is a satirical tale in which a woman describes her son. He tortures a cat, lies pathologically, threatens his mother's life. After delivering a brilliant speech at his high school commencement, the son leaves home never to return and becomes—surprise—*not* a serial killer but a successful politician. When her son becomes president of the United States, the mother fears that he will kill her because she knows his secrets. While it's a minor, one-trick story, it exploits a kind of paranoia that was familiar to Carver's imagination.¹⁰

The kids liked Sunnyvale and the suburbs, and Maryann taught in Los Altos, only minutes from Sunnyvale. Nonetheless, the next house the Carvers rented was in the working-class, vacation, and hippie hamlet of Ben Lomond on the San Lorenzo River northeast of Santa Cruz. The Carvers lived in a tall, wooden vacation house on Hillcrest Drive, itself a narrow gravel loop on the side of a steep hill off Scenic Way. Ray's study overlooked a creek. Dense redwoods, firs, and ferns made the place otherworldly and dark at most hours of the day. Christi and Vance rode a bus down a wind-

---

* Richard Cortez Day recalled owning and losing just such a book and suspected that his star pupil—ever the rascal—had borrowed it and liked it too well to think of returning it.

ing highway to their school. At a nearby stable, Christi took riding lessons and began purchasing her own horse; Vance played senior league baseball. Maryann drove forty miles to work, departing at dawn to cross the Santa Cruz Mountains on Highway 17, a highly trafficked road known for frequent rock slides and accidents in foggy, wet, or icy conditions. Still, she made the best of her commute because it gave her a chance to be alone and "make lesson plans in my head." In January, as the rainstorms intensified, she got financing from the teacher's credit bureau for their first new car, a yellow Datsun station wagon. Sometimes Cat Stevens's hit song "Morning Has Broken" would come on the radio just as she crested the hill above Scotts Valley, "and that's what it would look like out there, the first morning," as the sun rose above the bay. "I'd feel like, now I'm descending, I'm on vacation."[11]

Living in Ben Lomond served Ray's interests more than it did the rest of the family's, but they all hoped that *this* might be the move that would allow them to establish a permanent home and stop moving around. Ray was a half hour from campus and the town of Santa Cruz and close to Bonny Doon, where George Hitchcock held his monthly *kayak* collating parties. The conjunction of Hitchcock and Hall and local talent fueled a lively literary scene.

After a year of solitary writing, Ray threw himself into the literary hubbub at Cooper House Café and other venues. Mort Marcus launched a poetry series at the Immediate Family Restaurant—the restaurant gave free dinners and wine to poets who read. Hundreds of people came, one poet recalled. "We'd all gather together as if it were a Broadway opening. Ray was the generous spirit in the midst of all this—after you read, he would say 'What a wonderful poem!' several times. At these events, he would be very happy and outgoing. Everything was wonderful."[12]

In "The Cougar," Carver calls California "the smorgasboard" where you could eat all you wanted. Indeed, life spread before Ray like a buffet in Santa Cruz. His letters, typed on university letterhead a month before classes started, convey the excitement of a kid in a candy shop. Ray "felt the prestige of a university job," James Houston recognized. "It has a particular draw for working-class people like us, we like to put our suits on and be professors."[13] On a Friday in September with Tanqueray in hand, Ray wrote that he'd just had a drink with Marcus to celebrate his new book, and was headed out for free drinks and a barbeque with Maryann's faculty, then back for a beach party near the Houstons' on Saturday, and a *kayak* collating party on Sunday. Ray blamed the Tanqueray for a couple of tangled sentences. Free or not, the drinks were becoming essential to Ray.[14]

New faculty at College V became friends and embraced the California life quickly. There were parties and potlucks on weeknights as well as weekends, and people consumed a lot of liquor. Lynn Swanger recalled that they had a Hanukkah party, and "Ray and Maryann came—among all the Jews!"[15] For her part, Maryann was impressed that the Swangers could afford to purchase economy-sized half gallons of Scotch and vodka. For the first time, Maryann said, she and Ray drank so much that they suffered "monster" hangovers and dehydration. In Maryann's estimation, "We both never stopped drinking until we were drunk." Every day, whether he was having a beer with students or a cocktail downtown, Ray drank; when he got home, he and Maryann relaxed with a cocktail or wine with dinner or both.[16]

All that drinking did not cancel the Swangers' impression that Ray and Maryann "wanted middle-class things—nice car, nice house, nice Scotch. Maryann got up and drove to school every morning, Ray wrote and had these university connections, and they were buying a horse!" Maryann "was kind of regal, even stunning, and Ray was a very, very rough diamond. He *could not* have dressed Bohemian—would not have suited his personality."[17] Ray's friendship with David Swanger, who had a doctorate from Harvard, stretched the biases of class and geography that tended to make him partial to people of humble background. Swanger was also a "nascent" poet who saw Ray as a "one-man literary machine." He was glad to have Ray read his work; when he wrote *The Poem as Process* in 1974, he included Carver's "Morning, Thinking of Empire" as an example.[18]

To begin a literary magazine at UCSC, Ray telephoned student David Myers, who had edited an undergraduate magazine the year before. They were joined by students John Kucich and Robert L. Wagner and a young professor of American literature, Paul Skenazy. These coeditors planned a magazine with nationwide distribution that would also showcase Santa Cruz talent. Ray suggested calling it *Quarry* after an abandoned marble quarry on campus, which made this name the kind of actuality-based metaphor Ray liked. Gleefully, he sent a call for submissions to his circuit of friends and editors.[19] The committee of five met for long afternoons on campus or around a battered Formica table at Ray's house. Ray's views came out "in brief declarative comments on whether a piece worked or not. He didn't argue much, didn't work hard to defend his opinions, didn't concern himself with line-by-line editing, took pleasure in an enormous range of styles and voices as long as the language sang."[20]

"Ray got a kick out of the editorial meetings at which we defended our selections and attacked everyone else's. He never tried to pull rank," but he did bring in work from his "old-boy network," while the undergraduates demanded that all submissions be considered equally. They made trade-offs rather than compromises. When the student editors resisted the script of a talk by Gordon Lish because of its "flippant, cool style," Ray said they were lucky to get that essay."*[21] The issue that emerged also included prose by Leonard Michaels, Jon A. Jackson, and William Kittredge.[22] It was rounded out with poetry and drawings from a handful of locals, including undergraduate Mark Jarman. When galley proofs arrived, the editorial group was surprised to see that Carver had listed himself as its chairman. He "meekly agreed" to replace *Chairman* with *Advisory* [*sic*]. In early February 1972, *Quarry* number one was ready to distribute, and Ray "ran from office to office excitedly, waving it over his head." Copies sold for one dollar.[23]

Ray served with Hitchcock and Everson on a committee to invite poets to read at UCSC during the 1971–72 school year. Ray's friends Dennis Schmitz, Richard Hugo, James Welch, and Leonard Michaels were all invited to Santa Cruz and hosted at the Carvers' with lavish parties complete with a ham and a full bar."[24] When Michaels was there, he got acquainted with Maryann and found her "strong, bright, forthright, even a little fierce." The iconoclastic but tenured survivor at Berkeley thought her opinions might be dangerous: "A writer's name would come up, and she might say, 'There's nobody home,' meaning the work was shit. Ray never disagreed . . . but he was cautious, diplomatic . . . As far as I could tell, she was right in her judgments. Ray was lucky to have her reading his work, just to keep it free of schmaltz and manipulation."

When Carver's work began to appear in *Esquire*, Michaels heard some of his Berkeley colleagues complain that it was "downbeat." Such comments by "established sensibilities" made Michaels like Ray's work all the more: "It should have been more cheery and optimistic, maybe like Beckett and Kafka. The more people attacked Ray, the more I realized he was an important writer." Snobbery about the short story form also united the saw filer's son from the Northwest and the barber's son from the Lower East Side. Michaels felt, "When you write a short story, you're permitted no mistakes. It has a kind of pure, magical form . . . you can almost count the measure from one end of a Carver story to the other. I'm calling that literary, a sense of style and an ear for the sound of prose."[25]

It was probably Ray who proposed inviting Charles "Hank" Bukowski

---

*Lish's "How I Got to be a Bigshot Editor and Other Worthwhile Self-Justifications," began as a speech that Lish was unable to deliver at the University of Arkansas on October 13, 1971. As William Harrison, the writer who orchestrated Lish's visit to Fayetteville after *Esquire* published some of his stories, recalled in 2006, Lish "was drunk during his visit here. He held a question-and-answer session that he barely managed, and he didn't read a Carver story or anything else. I loved him, but he was a splendid disgrace on that night."

to Santa Cruz in the spring of 1972. Writing, Bukowski once declared, "has to come out like hot turds the morning after a good beer drunk." His work was read not for its craft but for its bluntly told stories of boozing, whoring, and living a proudly illicit life; Bukowski had been "kind of a hero" to Carver when he lived in Arcata.[26] Perhaps Carver wanted Bukowski as a variation from a guest list of established poets that included Galway Kinnell, Lawrence Ferlinghetti, Gary Snyder, and Kenneth Rexroth. Bukowski, then fifty-one and recently retired from his post office job, had just begun making public appearances. On stage he transformed from "a wobbly drunk into a dynamo" who exchanged insults and obscenities with his audience in a gravelly, snarling drone. His readings "weren't so much readings as wild spectacles . . . Half the audience came to worship him, the other half to heckle. Most of them were drunk."[27]

Before Bukowski even arrived, Carver feared that he was getting more than he'd counted on. *Quarry* editor Myers wrote in the campus paper that "Buk" was coming to "piss all over UCSC's middle-class students." Bukowski was already drunk when Ray met him at the airport. At dinner he couldn't keep his hands off Maryann. Ray, "completely sober—and worried," asked Marcus to "stick close and be sure to come to the party after—please." Myers, whom Ray had asked to introduce Bukowski, arrived late, so Ray was forced to do the honors. Then Bukowski found he didn't have his poems with him, so Ray gave Bukowski a book that Myers had lent him.[28] Ray was mortified as Buk performed as anticipated, swilling gin and abusing his audience. He felt responsible for whatever happened and "saw his credibility slipping with his superiors at the university with every insult Bukowski growled."[29]

Because of Bukowski's reputation, none of the faculty wanted to host a party. Ray cajoled his student Diane Smith and her roommate to volunteer their rented house, but he forgot to bring the food and liquor. When Buk came into Smith's house, he demanded, "Where's the booze?" Ray ran out to the liquor store. Bukowski sat on the only furniture—Smith's bed—and held forth all night.

Marcus, who drank little, probably remembered the party as clearly as anyone:

> Bukowski, drinking everything in sight, muttered, bragged, cursed, and, getting drunker by the minute, grabbed the girls and mashed his whiskery face against theirs, or shot his hand to the crotch of their jeans or down their blouses . . . girls screamed and ran from the house . . . more cerebral students sat back and stared straight ahead, probably stoned . . . Ray started drinking.

Bukowski stubbed out cigarettes on the floorboards and spoke to Ray derisively. Soon enough, Ray was drunk too. Finally, he stalked out. When Ray returned, he looked down at Bukowski "but said nothing, his expression caught midway between disgust and pity." Ray was drunker than Marcus had ever seen him: "Something about Bukowski's behavior struck deep inside him . . . I'm convinced he saw in Bukowski's drinking and behavior intimations of his own future, a sort of Mr. Hyde who would be released by his incessant boozing."[30]

Bukowski's memories of his Santa Cruz visit pick up the next morning:

We drank all night. The next morning Carver's banging on my door. He wants breakfast. Big mistake. Greasy eggs and bacon come swimming in their plates and Carver needs just one look. When he comes back from the toilet, I say, "That's ok, Ray, I finished my plate and now I'm gonna eat yours an' then we're gonna go out and find us another bottle." An' we did.

They "escaped to a bar" where Carver confided to his famous guest that his friend Gordon Lish was going to publish "every goddamn short story I send him" in *Esquire*.[31] If Ray thought or said that, his expectations were a bit delusional. Somehow Ray delivered the legendary Buk to the airport for his flight to Los Angeles; later on, when the crazy night became a story, Ray was "much amused that neither of them was fit to drive but somehow they made it."[32]

Carver took revenge with a potent weapon: a five-page monologue poem that lets Carver have his cake and eat it too. In "You Don't Know What Love Is (an evening with Charles Bukowski)," Carver takes possession of Buk's voice and puts his name on the result. Carver said he used "phrases taken directly from" Bukowski during the Santa Cruz visit, including a string of insults against "termites" and "bloodsuckers" who "hang around colleges / and go to poetry readings." The speaker of the poem lists the experiences he's had that make him the only real poet in the room, including one that Carver may have consigned to Buk from his own life: being fired from a stock-boy job for stealing cookies.

Perhaps Carver was remembering the stale cookies he'd been accused of helping himself to at the Weinstock-Lubin Store in Sacramento, pulling a good detail into his poem as his answer to Buk's claim that only he was a real poet.[33] Readers have disagreed about whether the poem is a tribute or a put-down. It's both, but the poem's sheer energy makes the distinction almost irrelevant. Donald Justice, whose workshop Ray attended with so little distinction at Iowa, said it was "a masterpiece of comedy" and "a terrific parody, and if you're a true Bukowski fan and want him to be idolized, you're not going to like the poem."[34]

Magazine making and hosting visiting writers were generally agreeable to Ray, but Hall had hired him to teach. Myers found that "as a classroom teacher, Ray was nothing special. He mimeographed and handed out student work and allowed students to dominate class discussion. Ray said little, but did teach Myers two things: "The first, which he attributed to Kittredge, was that dialogue should be a series of non sequiturs. Human beings do not really respond to one another, Ray believed." The second was that "any passage that invites underlining . . . must be canceled." Myers found Ray impatient with writers like Saul Bellow whom he considered "monologists who like to hear themselves talk. Stories are written in *Other People's Voices* (the title of an anthology he assigned in one course), not the writer's own."[35]

Although Diane Smith (later the author of the novels *Pictures from an Expedition* and *Letters from Yellowstone*) turned in only one short story draft in Ray's fiction seminar, he "was gentle, always tried to be helpful . . . some of the work was so awful, and he was always encouraging. I wrote something about the breath of a horse on a character's hand, and he wrote in his tiny scribble, 'Ahh.'" On Smith's narrative evaluation, he wrote, "'she didn't write as much as *we* would have wished.'" Smith understood that "*we* meant he and I."[36]

Ray's best teaching occurred in private conferences. Robert McDowell, later the founder of Story Line Press, had been walking all night through the fog and redwood trees thinking a nineteen-year-old's "big, wandering thoughts" when he saw Ray on the balcony of his office at about five in the morning. "'Hi, Bob,' Ray said, cheerily, 'want to come up?' I did, and we sat together talking for an hour or more. It was one of the best office hour visits I ever had."[37]

All the students came to realize that Ray drank a lot. Smith stopped by his office about something and saw a bottle in a bag in the bookcase: "it seems like I came in as he was hiding it. 'Oh it's just you,' he said, and he took it out."

The very first time Mark Jarman ever got falling-down sick drunk was at Ray's house:

I was so sick I had to stay the night. I was mortified, but Maryann said, "Oh, don't worry, Mark. This happens to us all the time!" They got me situated in a cot downstairs, and I felt terrible. There was a wind chime in an open window near me, and its sound was just excruciating to me.

When a friend came to see how I was, I told him to take down the wind chime. Later Ray checked on me and said, "You'll be fine. I've lived through this and so will you."

Then he looked in the window and said, "Well, who took this down?" And he put it back up! I have a strong image of Ray being solicitous as he restores the wind chime, putting that small thing in order.[38]

Legends about Ray's drunken behavior began to accrete. Attempting to verify these tales is like playing a game of Clue. Myers once saw him in a convenience store parking lot: "When he rolled down the window to greet me, a stale-smelling cloud filled the space between us as if the air were being let out of his solitude. 'What are you doing here?' I asked. Ray shrugged. 'I needed to get away,' he said." Other former students offered variant details. McDowell believes he and Jarman were the ones who found Ray thus ensconced in his car and that Ray told them he was "fine" and offered them a drink from a bottle in a brown bag, while another said that Ray offered them vodka and orange juice and said, "I'm terrible, but thanks for asking." Perhaps numerous people encountered Ray smoking and drinking in his car. But one should recall that Ray was surrounded by storytellers. Most of his friends and all of his students were on the lookout for material and happy to circulate it.

Unbeknownst to his coterie of writing students, by Thanksgiving Ray was contemplating a move to Montana. With six weeks of teaching experience under his belt and Kittredge's help, he sought a full-time visiting professorship in Missoula. If he got the job and a salary of at least $10,800, he figured Maryann could take a leave of absence and complete a master's degree there. When Ray let Michaels know that the department chair at Montana might be calling him as a reference, Michaels replied that he was trying to secure an appointment for him at UC Berkeley. Then, a few days into the new year, Hall—having received a call from Montana—came to Ray and urged him to stay at UCSC! Hall argued that at UCSC Ray had an easy teaching load at a prestigious university and better weather as well, but he couldn't offer any more money.[39] For the first time in his life, Ray was in demand. Few realized how much he was drinking. On his way home, he'd stop at Paul's Lounge, a bar frequented by workers from the Wrigley chewing gum plant. "He would drink the moment he got out of class. He'd have several drinks, and his whole drinking pattern changed," Maryann reflected later.[40] Maybe that's why Montana pulled him like a magnet.

On January 12, 1972, the University of Montana offered Ray a teaching position. Ray accepted, pending discussion with the family. Maryann had apprehensions about Ray's friends there. She'd heard Ray joke about

Missoula men who left home at eight in the morning, shaved and dressed in fresh-starched shirts "as if they were going off to work, when what they were doing was going off to drink." That worried her, and so did the fact that many of those friends were divorced, "into their second and third wives . . . the slogan was 'another wife, another life.'" That attitude about divorce was in keeping with the seventies' notion of self-fulfillment, but often it became a self-serving adjustment of old-boy values to new feminist ideologies: financially independent women and women without children demanded less commitment from their husbands. Such thinking had no charm for Maryann. She already had children, and she'd been supporting Ray and his artistic career since 1957. She had seen the pain that divorce caused in the lives of her mother and her two sisters and was determined not to put her own family through that trauma.[41]

But Maryann acquiesced to Ray's Montana plan, beginning to look forward to a year off from teaching with time to work on a master's degree. One night in Sacramento, Ray told Gary Thompson, who intended to go to Iowa for an MFA in poetry, "No, we're all going to go to Montana." Thompson didn't realize then that Ray's shyness had not served Ray well at Iowa. "After dinner, Ray and Maryann and my wife and I went to the Carvers' hotel room for more drinks, and Maryann kept saying, 'We're going to Montana, where the men are men and the women are women!' That was sort of her punch line for the evening." The Thompsons were persuaded that Gary should study poetry at the University of Montana instead of Iowa.[42]

The Carver children were a tougher sell. They were determined to return to Sunnyvale, where Chris—then fourteen and no longer answering to Christi—could begin high school with her friends. When she misbehaved, Chris told her parents, "I'm just like Dad. If I'm depressed, I'm depressed. And I'm *depressed*!" As the normal conflicts of a mother and daughter sharpened, Chris identified with her father. In the mirror, she saw that her clear blue gray eyes with a darker margin came from him, as did most of her facial features. Like him, she had an easygoing, passive personality, but also a temper that came out when she was pushed to extremes. Her temper she attributed to being a Burk daughter and a Sagittarius. Both kids longed to live in one place and have longtime friends, but their parents were still searching for the combination of home and jobs that would best support Ray's writing. When Ray explained that they'd never return to Sunnyvale, Chris and Vance said they'd take Missoula over another year in Ben Lomond.[43]

Under redwood trees on the east slope of the Santa Cruz Mountains, winter days can be wet and bone cold. Surprisingly, then, despite a three-week "coughing binge" that forced him to cut down to a half dozen cigarettes a day, Ray showed few signs of seasonal depression during late fall and early winter there. On the contrary, his letters brim with energy and news about his literary life.

After "Neighbors" appeared in *Esquire*, months passed without another sale, but Ray kept up a correspondence with Lish, every month sending his opinions of the new issue of *Esquire*. Lish's reputation was growing. He began signing his internal *Esquire* memos "Captain Fiction"—a name first given him by author Barry Hannah, whom Lish called Commodore Fiction—and the name stuck. He gave talks at colleges and read "Fat" and "Neighbors" as examples of fiction he liked. Or was he subtly appropriating the stories as his own by speaking them in his own voice? In a year-end report to his editors on changes in American fiction, Lish noted that "*our* Raymond Carver—ours because he was uncovered in 'slush' here and because our publication of his 'Neighbors' was his first outing in a national magazine and because I say he's ours—appeared in September *Harper's Bazaar* with a magical and eerie business called 'Fat,' a story that leaves you no peace."[44]

In five paragraphs that Carver wrote about "Neighbors" for Hicks's anthology *Cutting Edges,* Ray sounds less confident about his new work than his editor does. He says that he pared it to its present length from a manuscript that was originally twice as long. Brimming with doubts, he continues:

> I think the story is, more or less, an artistic success. My only fear is that it is too thin, too elliptical and subtle, too inhuman. I hope this is not so, but in truth I do not see it as the kind of story that one loves unreservedly and gives up everything to; a story that is ultimately remembered for its sweep, for the breadth and depth and lifelike sentiment of its characters. No, this is a different kind of story. . . .[45]

Carver seems to be apologizing for what's not in his story, as if he's still receiving sensations from the phantom limbs of his excised words and sentences. The statement is also a challenge to his own artistry, a wish—a prayer?—for stories that would please both Lish and himself.

Ray was writing as a professional now, Maryann thought, but not with his "usual joy." She sensed that "he hoped to write us out of the rat race. . . . He had used up all his reserves . . . it was as if Ray had extracted the new work from his raw nerve ends."[46] One of those new stories configured the rock-bottom days of the Carvers' lives in Sacramento when they were forced to sell their convertible. "Are These Actual Miles?" is about bankruptcy, suspicions of infidelity, and suicidal depression. Ray pushed into new territory with this story, and it proved to be exactly what Lish was waiting for. Late in November, Lish telephoned to say that Gingrich and Hayes were "wild" about the story. Not only that, but Lish planned to include both "Neighbors" and "Miles" in an anthology of fiction from *Esquire* that he was editing for Doubleday.

In "Are These Actual Miles?" Carver created a narrator, Leo, who wants to destroy himself. Lish excised violent details in favor of a more philosophical ennui. Where the published story says that Leo wants to bite the rim off his whiskey glass, the typescript continues that he'd like to grind it slowly in his mouth and swallow it. Lish also cut resonant statements about weather, which had no part in his minimalist aesthetic: "The sun is behind the hills now," Carver had written, "but the heat seems to have increased." For Ray Carver, the fear and pressure of being an ignored, barely published writer had gone away like sun dropping behind the hills, but the fear and pressure he felt internally had only increased.

From Captain Fiction, *Esquire* was getting just what it had bargained for: a shot in the arm to liven up the magazine during the late Nixon-era doldrums. Dozens of authors—among them E. L. Doctorow, José Donoso, Stanley Elkin, George P. Elliott, John Gardner, and James Purdy— approved excerpts that Lish carved from their forthcoming books for publication in *Esquire*. "Gordon would have ferocious attachments to his writers: first Ken Kesey, later Raymond Carver," Herbert Gold remembered. "Gordon may have liked the fact that Carver was weak emotionally, but he was proud of him, he talked about him. He liked to find writers who were different and develop them. There's nothing so strange about this. Writers are eager for publication—every writer will cultivate someone who can be helpful. Any number of writers were nice to Gordon and let him edit."[47] Occasionally authors refused Lish's changes: John Deck, Lish's acquaintance from Palo Alto, withdrew a story rather than accept Lish's rewrite. In 1972 Don DeLillo declined to publish an excerpt that Lish had created from his forthcoming novel.[48]

Lish thrived in New York. He and Barbara had a son, Atticus (after the lawyer in *To Kill a Mockingbird*), and they planned to stay in the city. Lish's essay in *Quarry* explained that lately he had been "encouraged to regard himself with a new seriousness" because of his seat in the New York Establishment. "The system is really pretty good . . . if people like me did not become editors, we might instead become writers—and then look how much worse things would be." Lish remained a maverick. Good editing, Lish contended, is mindless, instinctual. He recognized good writing by the response it invites "from the long muscle that runs down the inside of my thigh." He took Grace Paley and James Purdy as models when he began to impose a style on Carver's stories. Paley's female monologists in "The Used-Boy Raisers" and "An Interest in Life" have a lilting, humorous despair like that Carver also sometimes discovers in ordinary life, while Purdy's realistic marital tales—"Don't Call Me by My Right Name" or "Man and Wife" or "A Good Woman," for instance—exceed Carver's in the sharpness of the scalpel they use to autopsy conventional emotions. Lish was under the influence of Paley and Purdy "in every respect" and admired Purdy's sense of "the dark, the unexplained, the uncanny."[49]

As Lish did his work in New York and Ray did his in Santa Cruz, a buzz about Raymond Carver's stories traveled through the writing community. Acceptances increased. What tipped the balance? Carver's cover letters, on university letterhead, listing previous publications and a 1970 NEA fellowship probably helped, but the stories he circulated, including those Lish hadn't yet touched, were more distinctive too. Carver had gained confidence and maturity as an artist during his year of full-time writing, and he'd learned from Lish. Late in 1971, Ray applied again for a Stegner Fellowship at Stanford University and an Iowa Short Fiction Award at University of Iowa Press. At Iowa he made it into the group of twenty semifinalists out of two hundred entrants.[50] About a Stegner Fellowship, there'd be no word until spring.

Carver nearly emptied out his storeroom with "Are These Actual Miles?" Eleven days before Lish accepted that harrowing interior journey for *Esquire,* Ray sat down to his novel. Myers, his *Quarry* coeditor, recalled that the novel was called *Augustine,* and Ray "used to talk about it all the time." Myers speculates that Carver destroyed "an entire draft" that "would have been a central text in the Carver canon" when he left Santa Cruz.[51] On March 8, 1972, Carver told Johnson that he would soon finish "a long ms— hate to say novel at this point." It seems that he didn't say *novel* again for several years. On June 1, he sent Johnson a short story, calling it "one of the best I've ever done." Somewhere between those two dates, Carver's novel had stalled out on him.[52]

When Carver received galley proofs for "Are These Actual Miles?" from *Esquire* in March, he was dismayed to see that Lish had changed the story's title to "What Is It?" He complained about it to Lish and to several Santa Cruz friends. He and Maryann argued about it too. Maryann "accused [Ray] of being a whore, of selling out to the establishment." She wondered if Lish had Ray's best interests in mind. Ray argued that a major magazine publication was worth the compromise. It was more of a sellout, he told

Maryann, to be a purist who left his stories sitting in a drawer. In his poem, he gave a similar line to Bukowski: "starving is more of a cop-out. . . ."[53] Ray reasoned, too, that he would be able to write more if he had more money.

In the end, Ray accepted Lish's title and the fairly heavy editing that came with it. Maryann remembers that he told her, " 'They're still my stories. . . . I'll change them back, or use original titles if I want to, after they've served their purpose.' "[54] He believed he would have more say in the matter — eventually — when the stories came out as a book collection. To decline a profitable publication offer or to displease his benefactor would have gone against the grain of Ray's upbringing and social class.

Lish's title is flat compared to Carver's, which, as Maryann notes, captures the story's "off-center cruelty" and offers more metaphorical resonance.[55] The story is grotesque in its use of the red convertible as a symbol for Leo and Toni's dreams of a better life; there's parallel grotesquerie in Carver's figuration of the jealousy and self-loathing that bankruptcy engenders in the couple: "Fact is the car needs to be sold in a hurry, and Leo sends Toni out to do it." The suggestion that she will sell her body as well as the car is planted in the vernacular "do it" of the first sentence.

An illustration accompanying "What Is It?" in the May 1972 *Esquire* telegraphed the sexual implications that were understated in the story: a nude woman on a bed dangles like a pair of dice from a car's rearview mirror.[56] Carver's earlier he-she stories deal with almost-forgotten adulteries or revealing encounters, or attempts to ditch troublesome dogs or placate angry parents. Kirk Nesset calls "What Is It?" one of Carver's "darkest, most unsettling stories" because it hints at deliberate betrayals and implacable resentments.[57] In common with "Will You Please Be Quiet, Please?" it has a male protagonist "whose torments, bad as they are, bring them back to the very source of their troubles — to bed — with markedly varying degrees of relief."

In both typescript and published story, the ending scene in a marital bed mirror-images that of "Will You Please Be Quiet, Please?" Leo feels the stretch marks on his sleeping wife's hip. Within that gesture, Leo experiences a dilemma that Ray Carver knew well: Leo and Toni have been through a lot together, known parallel hopes and humiliations; he is helpless to imagine what he would be without her. The word *love* is not used, but it, or something more difficult, is implied by a metaphor that blends the body and the car. "They are like roads, and he traces them in her flesh. He runs his fingers back and forth . . . remembers waking up the morning after they bought the car, seeing it, there in the driveway, in the sun, gleaming." Finally, it's the objectification of the wife that sets this story apart from most of Carver's early stories. We cannot tell "whether Toni still loves

Leo," critic Lucy Morse writes, "for we are limited to Leo's point of view, and have no access to the thoughts of the character who is the main focus of Leo's thoughts."[58] Leo is unable to see beyond his own pain. Toni's behavior might be intended to break through to him, but readers can't be certain. "What Is It?" fit beautifully into a collection of stories from *Esquire* that Lish titled *The Secret Life of Our Times*. While evidence suggests that Maryann sold her car with a classified ad in the Sacramento *Bee,* she has preferred to mystify those who ask about the origin of the story: "People would ask me if such and such really happened, and I would say, 'I'll never tell' and I never would."[59]

Ray had come a long way by allowing his fiction to hold his secrets while he bumbled forward with his improbable life. But his balancing act was becoming more difficult. At Santa Cruz, Mark Jarman noticed that Ray, a large, solid man, had "this funny little handshake where he would only grab you by the tips of the fingers."[60] After a year of teaching and higher-profile publishing, Ray found himself exposed to the world in ways that— as that timid handshake showed—made him uncomfortable. He believed that moving to Missoula would solve those problems.

There was one problem he couldn't leave behind. The elephant in the room, the secret he couldn't face himself, grew bigger by the day.

CHAPTER 16

The Illusion of Freedom

May 1972–September 1972,

Cupertino, California, and Missoula, Montana

> Every day that we fail to live out the maximum of our potentiali-
> ties we kill the Shakespeare, Dante, Homer, Christ which is in us.
> Every day that we live in harness with the woman whom we no lon-
> ger love we destroy our power to love and to have the woman whom
> we merit.
>
> —Henry Miller, *Cosmological Eye,*
> transcribed in one of Carver's notebooks

No sooner had Carver returned the galleys for "What Is It?" to *Esquire* than he received word that Maryann's sister Amy had suffered a manic break in Los Angeles. While preparations were made to move her to a hospital in Santa Cruz, Ray and Maryann made the four-hundred-mile trip south, collected her things, including a pregnant dog, and drove them and her car back north. As soon as they got Amy moved, Chris became very ill, and by April 14, when Carver wrote to Kittredge, they hadn't fig-ured their income taxes.[1]

Amy stayed in Santa Cruz after she was discharged, and the Carvers acquired the "windfall" of an Irish setter and six puppies, certainly a step up from the mindless Mitzie they'd had in Sacramento. They kept Ginger, the bitch, and sold five of her pups for $50 each. The sixth, Mr. Six, became Chris's pet. The puppy's name was just one of the Carver family's quirks and phrases that Chris would cherish later. Others were her dad's prefer-ence for Royal Crown Cola because it carried his initials and his habit of calling "Hello, hello" twice, like a rough chime, whenever he entered the house or called home.[2]

Ellen Levine, Ray's devoted but thus far unsuccessful literary agent, complained that she'd known nothing about the sale of "What Is It?" and believed she'd been double-crossed. The problem, of course, was that Ray routinely showed his work to Lish before he showed it to Levine. Ray placated Levine by mailing her a new story that same afternoon. The next day he submitted three stories directly to Leonard Michaels for *Fiction.* In such matters, Ray erratically tried to get along with everyone. In a pitch to secure financial aid at Montana for Thompson, he wrote that it would be "almost tragic" if Montana offered nothing to Thompson—because, of course, Ray had convinced his friend to turn down a fellowship at Iowa in order to follow him to Montana![3]

Amid such confusion, Ray undertook a "frenzy of poetry composition." First came "Country Matters," followed shortly by "Your Dog Dies" and many of the poems collected in *At Night the Salmon Move.*[4] He wrote "Your Dog Dies" as Chris was grieving for Mr. Six, who had been killed by a car. But then, as Carver wrote the poem, he realized that he was enjoying himself because the dog's death had given him a good poem.

That shock effect disguises the poem's accuracy and honesty. For Carver, as for most writers, there was enormous pleasure in getting the words right. The membrane between the sadness of life and the pleasure of work can become dangerously thin if the writer is freely pulling the materials of his life into his work. The conflict Carver sets up in "Your Dog Dies" continues when a woman screams his name ("both syllables," he writes, so one hears his mother's or his wife's voice saying "Ray-mond"). The writing and the screaming both continue as the poet wonders "how long this can go on."

What is *this*? Perhaps it is the tug of war between his two selves: one that wants to be a good husband and family man, one that wants to write; or one that wants to write exactly as he pleases and another that wants to be a famous writer published in the likes of *Esquire* regardless of the compromises required; or one that wants to be a responsible person and another that wants to be drunk.

Another poem from the spring of 1972, "This Word Love" introduces the theme of Carver's middle stories: how love causes harm. In the poem, *love* begins to consume the paper it is printed on (and, in a later version, to consume the lovers). The poem was important to Carver; he published it in *Poet and Critic* as part of a roundtable exchange with two other poets who commented on one another's work.[5] Ominously, the poem tells us that the word *love* "grows dark, grows heavy." While no amount of testimony from outsiders can explain what goes on in a marriage, neither can the couple themselves be trusted on such matters. All one can be certain of is that the changes in Carver's life strained his marriage. From there it is possible to imagine Maryann's reactions to these changes, her need for reassurance that the sacrifices she had made would not be squandered.

In early May, Ray and Maryann were trying to figure out the logistics of their move to Missoula. Her school district refused her request for a leave of absence. She'd been at Los Altos High School just two years; in the upcoming year, she'd be reviewed for tenure. If she could tough out that process, she would then be able to take a leave without losing her job and eventually be eligible for paid sabbaticals. Ray told Kittredge that he might move to Missoula with Vance while Maryann and Chris stayed in an apartment in Los Altos. Then, if Ray was promised another year at Montana, Maryann would abandon her job and move north.

Then Ray received a letter that threw him into unfamiliar terrain: too many desirable choices. He was offered a Wallace Stegner Fellowship of $4,000 for participation in the Stanford Writing Workshop for the next academic year. Ray was "knocked out" by the chance to join the very selective workshop. For a day, he contemplated taking the best of both worlds by flying between Montana and Stanford every week but soon concluded that to do so would be "lunacy." The day after he heard from Stanford, his wheel of fortune took him a notch higher. UC Berkeley offered him a position teaching two seminars in fiction writing beginning in January 1973.

With regret, Ray broke his contract with the University of Montana. A few years earlier, the family might have taken any chance, moved at a whim, but now he felt "crippled" and cynical even though Missoula pulled at "the deepest part" of his heart. Someone reading his letter to Kittredge might think Ray was in love with a woman in Montana, but that wasn't so. It was the pull of friendship and company and liquor. Bill Kittredge was his best friend. He worried that Kittredge would lose respect for him. He was so eager to talk to Kittredge that it was an effort *not* to call him long distance whenever he'd had a few drinks.[6] Ray longed for days spent in the taverns, days, Kittredge reminisced, "of perfect irresponsibility, long hours when it was possible to believe we were invisible and shatterproof . . . and beautiful in our souls."[7]

Still in their early thirties, Ray and Maryann celebrated their fifteenth wedding anniversary on June 7. Their decision to stay in California—so reasonable on paper—represented a serious attempt to tighten their hold on middle-class life. Ray would teach at UCSC in the fall and at Berkeley in the new year, all the while receiving a Stegner Fellowship. As she commuted between Los Altos and Ben Lomond in her Datsun, Maryann kept her eyes open for their next house.

Western Santa Clara County had changed since 1971 when Intel began selling microprocessor chips. It had become part of Silicon Valley, and housing prices jumped. On the ragged edge of the suburbs near a Kaiser Aluminum plant and the Gate of Heaven Cemetery in Cupertino, Mary-ann found a bright blue ranch house for sale by owner.* It was one of a half dozen houses on a cul-de-sac below Foothill Road. There were no side-walks, and prickly pear cactuses and agaves grew alongside pine trees in the dry roadside soil. The air was scented by grassland hills to the west. Inside, the house had a long, narrow kitchen left of the foyer. Directly ahead, a large living room with a fireplace continued into a family room floored with black-and-white tiles—a good party space—and from there a sliding glass door opened onto a backyard with lemon trees. The bathroom and three small bedrooms occupied the north wing of the house. Beyond the kitchen were separate mother-in-law quarters that could be rented out. A storage room looked ideal for Ray's study. The icing on the cake was the location: 22272 Cupertino Road was in the same consolidated school dis-trict as Sunnyvale. Chris and Vance could attend high school with their junior high school friends.

Ray expected an income of $12,000 for the coming academic year, more than Maryann's salary. The Stegner Fellowship would cover a down pay-ment on the blue house, but they did not have the money yet. One of Mary-ann's teaching colleagues lent them that amount. They got a mortgage from the teachers' credit union and planned to complete the purchase in mid-July.

Ray made a new editorial connection at a corn roast festival near Santa Cruz late in the summer of 1972. Jim Houston was playing upright bass with a bluegrass band called the Red Mountain Boys, while Mort Marcus wandered the grounds with Capra Press publisher Noel Young. They came upon Ray "at peace with the world, sprawled in a meadow with a drowsy grin and a moustache of beer suds . . . while folks stepped over his outstretched legs."[8] Young had owned a printing shop when he met Henry Miller, the author of *Tropic of Cancer* and *Tropic of Capricorn*, in Big Sur, California. In 1969, as "Leon Elder," Young wrote and printed a book about hooking up water heaters to sawed-off wine casks. *Hot Tubs* started a national trend, so Young became a publisher. He operated his Capricorn Books (later Capra Press) in a historic building in Santa Barbara. Under the logo of a long-horned ram, Young published Miller's *On Turning Eighty* and all his subsequent books, as well as volumes by Lawrence Durrell and Anaïs Nin.

---

*The town is named for Joseph of Cupertino, a slow-witted Italian saint known for his levitations.

Young made his best money on lifestyle books (*Free Beaches* followed *Hot Tubs*), but he liked to introduce unknown literary writers to the public and hoped to turn a profit by being the first publisher of writers who might later become big. Carver fit this bill perfectly. Young offered to publish a chapbook of "Put Yourself in My Shoes," one of Carver's favorite stories.

"Put Yourself in My Shoes" is about luck and menace, about the way accidents could determine one's fate. In the story, Myers "was between stories, and felt despicable." Ray borrowed the name (possibly the phrase as well) from his student David Myers, to whom he spoke about the writing of "Put Yourself in My Shoes":

> [Ray told me] that the first sentence of the story had come to him from nowhere. His face, which normally masked his emotions, was boyishly bright with excitement. He was not sure what it meant, but he knew it was the opening sentence of a story. Ray's principle of composition, also a religious principle when you think of it, was to remain open to the remarkable in the ordinary.[9]

In the story, Myers and his wife, Paula, drop in unannounced to visit the Morgans, whose house they'd sublet the year before. The Morgans serve drinks and tell Myers anecdotes they hope he can use in his writing. Concluding a tale about a woman they met overseas, Mrs. Morgan says: "Fate sent her to die on the couch in our living room in Germany." That fatuous attempt to give the story importance sends Myers into a fit of laughter. Edgar Morgan scolds:

> "If you were a real writer, as you say you are, Mr. Myers, you wouldn't laugh," Edgar said as he got to his feet. "You wouldn't dare laugh! You'd try to understand! You'd plumb the depths of that poor soul's heart and try to understand. But you're no writer, sir!"
>
> Myers kept on laughing.

One could ask for no more vivid portrait of Ray and his wife as he saw them in the middle years of their marriage than the one in this story.[10] Myers, who lacks a first name, is polite and fearful, restless in a depressed way, and secretive: "We should call if we're going to do anything like that." Paula is bold and brash and also restless, consciously in quest of adventure: " 'No,' she said, 'That's part of it. Let's not call.' " He lives in his own mind much of the time, but is tenderly curious about her. Paula remembers receiving a holiday card from their former landlords; Myers remembers receiving an insulting letter from them. In their way, both Myerses are childlike; she in her spontaneity, he in his secretiveness: he "looked around for an ashtray. He dropped the match behind the couch."[11]

"Put Yourself in My Shoes" addresses the question of how to keep writing. At the end of the story, Myers has shed his passivity. He is no longer between stories. His wife's "voice seemed to come to him from a great distance. He kept driving. Snow rushed at the windshield. . . . He was at the very end of a story." Myers is at the end of the story he is going to write, the story of his evening at the Morgans' house that the reader has just finished reading. This postmodern gambit in "Put Yourself in My Shoes" makes it unique among the stories in Carver's first three collections.

Such deliberation about a subject for a story (and a point of view) suggests that Carver felt lost during the spring of 1972. In this year of so many successes, he had done much less writing than in the previous year. His new professorial role took time and energy. Submitting everything he wrote to be marked by Lish's persuasive editorial pen also changed his relationship to his own work. With the completion of "Put Yourself in My Shoes," all but one of the stories for Carver's first story collection, *Will You Please Be Quiet, Please?*, had been written and sent out to one magazine or another. It's a difficult fact to hold in mind, because the book did not appear for another five years. The story of the intervening years is complicated, but it does not involve a great deal of new writing on Carver's part.

At the end of June, the Carver family of five—that included their Irish setter—took off for the Northwest in their station wagon. They planned to travel until they could take possession of their own house in Cupertino. A photo of the Carvers seated on a couch at Ray's aunt and uncle's in Yakima shows Christi—at thirteen—eyeing the camera with the cautious independence of a teenager. Although she worried about her weight, she looks lovely and shy, not at all chubby. She's edged behind Maryann's shoulder while Maryann is upright, in a miniskirt, the center of the portrait, half-smiling as if about to speak, one hand on each child's knee. Twelve-year-old Vance slouches, still a boy, slender and tan and bare chested, almost gangly, his hair in a pageboy cut. His hands are moving, and his eyes have closed at the camera flash, giving the impression he'd rather be somewhere else. Ray is here, too, anchoring one end of the couch, a leg crossed into the foreground of the picture; his glasses muddle his expression, but he looks relaxed, with one long arm stretched across the back of the couch, circling the others. His wooly brown hair has grown out of control and his trouser legs are cut wide, but otherwise he is without style in a rumpled, collared, short-sleeved shirt.

Next they drove toward Missoula, where the real vacation was to begin.

Ray was at the wheel with Maryann at his side reading the bestselling biography *Zelda.* Nancy Milford's story of F. Scott Fitzgerald's wife changed the landscape of many American literary lives in the early 1970s, nudging thousands of male writers' wives to think of themselves and wonder if they had sacrificed too much in their unstinting support of their husbands' aspirations. Vance and Chris were squabbling restlessly in the backseat when Ray became "coldly furious," demanded that Maryann and Chris switch places, turned the car around, and declared he was not taking the kids to Missoula.[12] That was only the beginning of a summer of reversals and false recoveries.

The whole family—augmented by Erin and Amy, who had alighted at the Carvers' again, and Maryann's nephew Val Davis—were residing in the new house by the end of July. Home ownership, so far, was making Maryann depressed and anxious. The new house felt crowded, the weather was unbearably hot, and Cupertino felt lonely and suburban compared to Santa Cruz. She and Ray went out by themselves to talk over the situation. Ray was unhappy too. He had written letters to all the magazines that were holding his stories, informing them of his "new, permanent" address, but he didn't feel at home. He hadn't had a hit with *Esquire* for several months. "This is supposed to be the end of the rainbow," he told Maryann, "but I don't see the pot of gold." They left Amy in charge of the household and drove to Monterey for an early celebration of Maryann's thirty-second birthday.[13]

When they returned, nothing had gone wrong. Nor had anything changed. It was still too hot, and the house was still full. Classes at Stanford and Santa Cruz did not begin until September, and there was no plan to get the nephew back to Yakima. Ray announced to Maryann that he'd be glad to drive the boy to Yakima if he could continue from there to go fishing in Missoula. James Crumley and James Welch were expecting him, willing to show him the good places to fish. Thompson would ride along, to help with the driving and give himself a chance to meet Ray's friends—his future teachers—in Missoula. The plan made sense to Maryann, but she hated to see Ray go just then. He was, she remembered telling him, her "piece of *sanity* around here."

To that—Maryann's recollection again—Ray replied that he was facing a crisis in his writing. He told Maryann he'd like to have "the illusion of freedom" in order to work his way through that crisis. To do that, he said, he needed to go to Montana.[14]

One might see a parallel between this "crisis" Carver underwent as he was taken up by Lish and the misgivings that Anton Chekhov felt when his stories began to gain attention: "Formerly, when I didn't know that they read my tales and passed judgment on them, I wrote serenely, just the way I eat blini; now, I'm afraid when I write," Chekhov said in 1886 when Alexei Suvorin of St. Petersberg's *Novoye Vremya* published him. Of Chekhov, "abruptly catapulted from obscurity to celebrity," Janet Malcolm writes: "His letters of the period have a feverish, manic quality. . . . He is alternately boastful and fearful. Chekhov's letters now also begin to express an ambivalence toward writing that was to remain with him. They suggest that the literary artist . . . is doing something unnatural . . . Chekhov would often talk of idleness as the only form of happiness. He said he loved nothing better than fishing."[15] A similar doubt about the value of writing *as work,* a similar tension between literature and idleness, appears in the biographies of many working-class and middle-class writers. Unfortunately, Carver didn't resolve his dilemma as Chekhov had, by slowing down and going at his work with new seriousness. Instead he turned away from it by drinking.

Since the age of nineteen, Ray had been married and writing and moving from one rented house to another. Now he'd *almost* achieved success as a writer, his children seemed almost grown, and he was paying a mortgage instead of rent. No move in the middle of the night would allow him to escape this setup. For a person with Ray's combination of sensibility and selfishness, the prospect of decades ahead without change, surrounded by the same people and responsibilities, might have seemed crushingly boring. He was young for a midlife crisis, but he felt old. When he drank he escaped, briefly, the strictures and duties of his routines. It released him to a land of adventure without boundaries. It gave him that illusion of freedom he craved.

Maryann made no further objections when Ray told her that he needed a trip to Montana because of his writing. On about August 8, she kissed him good-bye several times through the window of her yellow Datsun. Her nephew was in the passenger seat, glad to be going home. Maryann felt— she's never forgotten—a premonition that something was going to happen to Ray on this trip. In Sacramento, Thompson took over the driving for the eight-hundred-mile haul to Yakima, and Ray pulled out a pint of Old Crow. A first drink in midday had become his regular habit. "Ray had a funny sense of humor and ability to draw out a story," Thompson said. "He'd have you cracking up for half a day's drive just telling you all the little adventures of daily life. He would also have manuscripts along he was working on, and sometimes he'd read aloud from these while I drove."[16]

Ray went trout fishing on the Bitterroot River with Welch, Crumley, Kittredge, and Thompson. As a fisherman, "Ray was wonderful," Thompson recalled. "Very graceful; he knew his stuff there." Another tame episode in what turned into a "wild week" began when Kittredge, Carver, and Thompson hatched the idea that Thompson should meet poet Madeline DeFrees, a new member of the faculty. DeFrees, a former nun, resided in a tiny attic room in a boardinghouse. When the three big men—each over six feet and two hundred pounds—came calling, they took up the entire room. DeFrees graciously served them a beer—one beer, divided "into three dainty tea glasses."[17]

At a birthday bash for Bill Kittredge's fortieth birthday, Ray talked to a slim, dark-haired, Wedgewood blue–eyed woman with a prominent smile named Diane Cecily. Cecily, daughter of a U.S. Forest Service supervisor and granddaughter of a doctor in Steamboat Springs, had grown up in Missoula. She'd gone east for college at Vassar, then returned for graduate school at Missoula. When Ray met her, she was the director of publications for the university and completing a thesis about femininity in the novels of Doris Lessing and D. H. Lawrence. Cecily was an accomplished young woman, but her personal life was a mess—"out of control," she said. Her marriage to a student in the Montana writing program had just ended, so she was living alone and spending a lot of time in the bars with Patty Kittredge and Maggie Crumley.[18]

When she met Ray, Cecily was feeling disconsolate, and Ray listened: "I sat down with Ray and proceeded to tell him that there was no hope for relationships in this world . . . and we just established a kind of a real caring. There was an innocence about Ray. He allowed me to laugh and be sentimental. He never had to be sophisticated. He would just hunch his shoulders and laugh. He was liberating." What Cecily remembered most about Ray was "simply his ability to find the wonder. It was very positive wonder—not the bad wonder, but the great wonder."

Ray invited Cecily to meet him for dinner the next night and spent many hours with her during the remainder of his week in Missoula. He told her that he was married but assured her that the marriage was headed toward a breakup, that both he and his wife knew this. Then he lost himself in the enchantment of a new woman. He stayed at her apartment, terribly nervous and hungover, but falling in love nonetheless. As he wrote her later, he'd found their days together "absolutely splendid" and she had gone "right into my bloodstream."[19]

Thompson and Carver left Missoula on a Friday—probably August 18—and drove south all day and all night, 1,200 miles. Ray was in bad shape, taking Valium to calm himself down but still unable to drive. He called Cecily from a pay phone after midnight. A couple of hours later, as they roared through Nevada at eighty miles an hour, a tire blew out on the Datsun. True to the intention he'd stated to Bill Barton when he interviewed for his job at the pharmacy in Yakima years before, Ray got others to do the dirty work. "Some rancher who'd been out all night, drunk as a skunk," pulled over to see what was happening. Ray pulled out his bottle and sat with the rancher in the cab of his pickup while Thompson changed the tire. Ray dropped his chauffeur off in Sacramento about nine Saturday morning and headed toward his family and his new house in Cupertino.[20]

Maryann hadn't expected Ray till Monday. He looked "terrible, worn, and exhausted." He didn't wait long to tell his wife about his trip. First he told her about the blown-out tire, which he attributed to the crash of a meteor at the side of the road. He hadn't been killed, as her premonition had made her fear he would be. But she'd had another fear, that he would fall "desperately in love" with someone in Montana. When everyone else was asleep, she asked him about that, and he told her.[21]

Ray confessed to Maryann that he and the other woman had gotten in over their heads. He explained that he felt he needed to change his life. To an extent, the urgency for change Ray felt must have been the predictable result of wanting to grasp new opportunities for his writing. What he'd longed for during those days when the world seemed "fractured" to him, he told an interviewer in 1985, was "to have some kind of respite. I used to dream of having a week or two to be relieved of pressure. Impossible to find that."[22] In Ray's mind, the pressure was associated with his family; he would have been incapable of admitting that alcohol abuse was part of his problem. He imagined that Cecily could give him the peace he needed.

This was a crisis, as both Maryann and Ray were quick to recognize. They drank and talked and cried and decided that they needed to get away to talk some more. Amy rallied herself and took charge of the children while Maryann and Ray, armed with a supply of vodka and fruit juice, checked into a nearby motel. Maryann found Cecily's address on a slip of paper in Ray's wallet and destroyed it, but his feelings would not be banished that easily.[23]

For three days, neither Ray nor Maryann slept more than a few hours or ate more than a meal a day, Ray wrote Lish. They drank and took Valium. Maryann revealed a onetime infidelity (described as a rape in *What It Used to Be Like*) from seven years before that seemed so "vivid" to Ray that it could have happened the day before. But, Ray insisted, what he felt after three days with Diane Cecily was real love. Both he and Maryann marveled that such a thing had happened so quickly. Over the next weeks, Ray and Maryann kept up a constant dialogue about the "situation" while at the same time preparing themselves and the children for a new school year, and allocating their money to begin paying Maryann's colleague back for the down payment on their house.[24]

Carver dramatized some of the pain they both suffered and inflicted during these weeks in "Gazebo," a story about a couple named Holly and Duane. A passage that was edited out of the published "Gazebo" explains that Duane confessed an affair to Holly because they were so close that she would have guessed anyway: ". . . you can't keep that kind of a thing secret for long. Nor would you want to."[25] As Maryann and Ray did, the couple in "Gazebo" seclude themselves in a motel room (it so happens that Duane has become enamored of a maid in the motel that he and Holly manage) to discuss their problem: "There was this funny thing of anything could happen now that we realized everything had," Duane explains.

In "Gazebo"—and, one imagines, in Maryann and Ray's original discussions—the wife feels shamed and damaged because her husband has "gone outside the marriage." It's hard to tell if Holly is exaggerating her feelings when she tells Duane, "Something's died in me. . . . You've killed something, just like you'd taken an ax to it. Everything is dirt now." The earlier draft of the story pays more attention to the husband's feelings. After an initial fight in which Holly has thrown a glass and said "awful things," and Duane has slapped Holly, Duane asks for forgiveness and believes that Holly "could maybe have weathered it out . . . maybe she was willing to forgive me if not to forget it."[26] The author of "Gazebo" also offers an explanation that was not available to Maryann and Ray in 1972: "When I look back on it, all of our important decisions had been figured out when we were drinking. Even when we talked about having to cut back on our drinking, we'd be sitting at the kitchen table or out at the picnic table with a six-pack or whiskey."[27]

The tie between Maryann and Ray was such that they could not refrain from discussion—some of it acrimonious, no doubt—of their problem for any length of time. Amy took it upon herself to find another place to live, a waitress job at the Cabana, and a night sitter for Erin. When Maryann told her sister how much she admired her courage, Amy replied that her own problems had suddenly looked manageable when she learned about Maryann's. In an extended family that had endured innumerable breakups and breakdowns, illnesses and recoveries, the Carvers' marriage had been a constant. That it might now fail—that it might fail just as Ray's writing talent was gaining recognition—was a shocking thought for everyone.

As his situation in Cupertino ebbed and flowed, Ray wrote letters and made collect calls to Cecily, gradually revealing that his freedom was indeed illusionary. He wouldn't be able to leave his marriage easily but he affirmed that he loved her. She understood this and came to understand, too, that Ray's life had been disorderly before he met her. She loved him, but she was also an analytical person who wanted Ray to be clear about the problems of his marriage. She wanted to know if the conversations between Ray and Maryann were honest and if his feeling for her was really the cause of the trouble. He, in turn, let her know that he wouldn't be able to visit again in 1972 but warned her not to make him any offers she didn't mean because he might turn up at her door "with a suitcase and a box of mss."

In fact, almost the first thing Ray had done was mail Cecily a box of his published writing. He told her he'd taken a bundle of these things to a department store to be packaged and mailed. He'd even asked a clerk to write the address because his handwriting had become shaky of late. He apologized for the heaviness of the package, told Cecily not to feel obliged to comment, and asked her to read some of it only when she felt like it. Despite his modesty, it's obvious that Ray was sending part of himself in that package, eager to hear what his new love made of it all.

About the relationship, Ray stalled for the time being. He told Cecily that he and Maryann had been unhappy together since they lived in Israel four years before. He'd recently feared that he'd lost his ability to love, he told her, but now he loved her. In the early fall, Cecily visited for a week, staying in a motel in Palo Alto, and returned to Missoula filled with optimism. Soon, though, Cecily received a bright bouquet of zinnias and other fall flowers with a card from Maryann. Though Cecily never knew the exact intent of this gesture, she understood that there would be no smooth beginning to a new life with Ray. In October, Ray wrote Lish that there would be no divorce because he and Maryann "care mightily for each other." Both women were alarmed by Ray's drinking. Ray had promised his wife that he wouldn't have any contact with Cecily for three months.[28]

Yet Ray and Cecily corresponded through the fall. She told him the news from Missoula, where the Kittredges, the Crumleys, and others were having marital dramas of their own, with many of the scenes performed in bars. Kittredge had a line that was usually good for a few laughs: "Get your programs quick, the characters are changing."[29] His lighthearted remark emerged from some complex midcentury attitudes about sex and marriage. The availability of divorce and birth control irrevocably changed people's expectations of marriage. By 1970 men and women were looking at fidelity and children as a choice, not a duty or a responsibility. The freedom Ray wanted may have been illusory. His wanting of it was not.

But Ray was not really an independent free spirit in the 1970s mode. He was a needy, old-fashioned, and alcoholic man who thrived on the love of women. He needed to feel loved. He'd needed that when he married Maryann, and he still needed it in 1972. His marriage was stretched thin. Probably, as he told Cecily, he'd felt unappreciated and unloved in Israel and never regained the feeling he craved since. The compromises of publication that he'd experienced with Lish added to his fears that he was not loved unconditionally. Cecily allowed Ray to dream of starting over in a passionate relationship that would sustain his work.

To accept Cecily's love, Ray would have to give up Maryann, and he'd also have to give up whatever self-respect he maintained as a father. Leonard Michaels made this observation about Ray and Maryann: ". . . there were things that I could see about that marriage that suggest to me however bad it may have been, the very badness came out of some tremendously deep, intimate absolute condition . . . I saw they had trouble, and I saw they were deeply—it looked to me permanently—connected."[30]

In letters to Cecily, Ray relived the few days they'd spent together, lingering on simple details, shared conversations, and silences. He called her his little fish. He hoped that they might spend time together in Berkeley, where he intended to get an apartment after Christmas. Since he'd be teaching there several days a week, it would be a natural arrangement, as well as a half step into independence. In the face of all that, Cecily believed she'd found a man who could make her happy, but she also wondered if Ray weren't holding back from her. She wanted to know things that Ray wasn't sure of himself.[31]

During these months, Ray became violently possessive of Maryann. He needed "an illusion of freedom" but could not bear the thought of *her* with another man. As they were getting into the car to leave a bar where a man had smiled at her several times, Maryann writes, Ray "pulled me down and half out of the car [and] banged my head on the pavement. I begged him to stop . . . Three or four hard blows, then he let me go. Somehow I dragged myself up inside the car, and he drove us home."[32]

That night ended with a call to the police (who wouldn't intervene) and black eyes that caused Maryann to miss the first three days of her school year. Extreme episodes of this sort occurred for months, lesser ones for years. Maryann missed work and threatened Ray with a knife or burning cigarettes. One morning he rammed her head into a corner of their bedroom. Chris drove her mother to the emergency room that day but was too embarrassed to come inside with her.[33]

The marriage also became vulnerable to the sort of psychological manipulation that had appeared before in Carver stories—"The Lie" or "Neighbors" or "They're Not Your Husband," for instance—but hadn't, Maryann thought, been part of their daily lives: "Head games and ambiguity were new to us. Neither of us could yet orchestrate subterfuge on a personal level or read the signs of betrayal accurately."[34]

Ray's drinking increased dramatically, too. Maryann warned him, "This has gone way beyond five drinks a day. This is now a round-the-clock preoccupation. You are slowly committing suicide. I want you alive." Maryann was drinking with him during these sessions and when they went out, but she tempered herself on weekdays for the sake of her job. As long as the discussion continued and they could drink together, Ray was still there. He hadn't left her. But the family had changed: "All Ray and I could talk about, hour after hour, day after day, was the crisis. The situation. The turn of events. Heaven help the kids if they needed to interrupt us to ask a question or wanted to tell us about their day at school . . . We wanted to hurry back to the unending drinks and our endless talk."[35]

Ray was unable to write, but he acted his part as up-and-coming author. Just days after his return from Montana, he answered a solicitation from *Antaeus* editor Daniel Halpern by sending him "They're Not Your Husband." Lish had read Carver's "Fat" to Halpern's fiction class at the New School in New York City. "Gordon talked about working on it with Ray," Halpern remembered, "and he said, 'This is the guy. This is the one who is going to emerge from this group of young writers who'll really become an important voice in the short story.' And I have to say he was right. He supported Ray, he loved Ray, and I think he really put Ray on the map."[36] *Antaeus* turned down "They're Not Your Husband" (as did the *New Yorker* and of course *Esquire* itself), but Ray sent along another. If Ray was on the map, the roads were unmarked. He had to keep studying the little magazines and hustling every story.

Carver competed in a literary world bursting with ambitious writers. *The Best American Short Stories 1972* included an excerpt from *The Car Thief*, a forthcoming novel by his Iowa classmate Ted Weesner, but overlooked Carver's "Neighbors." The anthology did list Carver's "Nightschool" in its "Distinctive Short Stories, 1971," in company with "The Song of Grendel" by John Gardner and stories by Kittredge and Michaels. Gardner was on the threshold of a critical triumph with *Grendel*, a short novel about the monster who attacked Beowulf in the Old English saga. Ray asked Lish to put him in touch with Gardner, but nothing came of it then. While emotional chaos reigned at home, Ray learned that "What Is It?" would appear in the 1973 O. Henry Prize collection.

Every such success reminded Ray that he was not writing. When his life soured, Ray's work was "not a refuge or a consolation, but the weathervane of his personal storms, spinning in the wind, pointing nowhere steadily," Maryann said.[36] Ray told Cecily that he thrived on a writing schedule and had proven it in the past. He admitted he could be a wild man, but he was also a "burgher" who wanted an orderly domestic life. He'd become a homeowner but he felt like a man with "a hearth but no slippers . . . or even logs to burn . . ."[38]

Carver drove to Santa Cruz to pick up his mail, including letters from Cecily. On a Wednesday afternoon in October, from his office at UCSC, he complained to Kittredge that he'd had only three hours' sleep and wakened so hungover that he'd needed a shot of blackberry brandy to get going. He swore he'd be professional again by Friday, his teaching day. All he needed to "get straight" was two shots of whiskey and eight hours' sleep. He did not then think he was an alcoholic because he believed alcoholism was something strange and horrible that didn't hit decent, hardworking people like him.[39]

Feeling divided against himself, Ray was strongly drawn to a novel popular with intellectuals of the time, *I'm Not Stiller,* by the Swiss writer Max Frisch. It's about a prisoner named Stiller who insists he is not the man his accusers claim he is. That, in a nutshell, seems to be how Ray Carver felt about himself as he assumed the prestigious position of a Stegner Fellow in the Stanford University Writing Program. For several years, Carver had been an outsider living near the periphery of the 2,300-acre campus. Now he was invited inside. As every variety of chaos swirled around and within him, he drove over to Stanford, entered the sandstone and red tile building, and took a seat at the seminar table.

CHAPTER 17

Astounding and Amazing Times

September 1972–August 1973,

Cupertino, Palo Alto, Santa Cruz, Berkeley

> You can put anything into words, except your own life. It is this impossibility that condemns us to remain as our companions see and mirror us, those who claim to know me, those who call themselves my friends, and never allow me to change, and discredit every miracle (which I cannot put into words, the inexpressible, which I cannot prove)—simply so they can say: "I know you."
>
> —Max Frisch, *I'm Not Stiller,* a novel Carver
> assigned to his students at Berkeley

When Carver declined a full-time teaching job at the University of Montana in favor of the prestigious Stegner Fellowship at Stanford and home ownership in California, he was making an investment in his future as a writer. But the immediate dividend was supposed to be stability for his family. Instead, when the fall academic term began, Carver found himself in geographical and psychological limbo. He had a waiting girlfriend in Montana, an unhappy but devoted wife, two children, a house, and a dog in Cupertino, a current job and office in Santa Cruz, a job for the next term in Berkeley, and, of course, the writing seminar at Stanford in Palo Alto. One imagines he was gravely sorry that he had not taken the job in Missoula where he would be near Cecily as well as Kittredge and his buddies.

The writing seminar Ray joined on an afternoon in late September met around a long table in Building 50 of Stanford's wide inner quadrangle, not far from the imposing mosaic of Christ that memorializes Leland Stanford's son. Many distinctive writers have held Stegner Fellowships: Edward Abbey, Wendell Berry, Ernest Gaines, Ken Kesey, Thomas McGuane, Larry McMurtry, Tillie Olsen, Robert Pinsky, Robert Stone, to name a few in addition to those Stanford program alums Ray already knew in the Bay Area—Evan S. Connell, James B. Hall, Jim Houston, Charlotte Painter, and Al Young. The mood was casual—there was often a jug of wine on the table—but the writers' ambitions were ferocious. Fellowships such as the one that Ray won gave emerging writers an opportunity to concentrate on writing for the better part of a year without course requirements or grades.[1] The teachers of the workshop in 1972 were Richard Scowcroft and William Abrahams. Scowcroft's fifth novel was forthcoming from Atlantic Monthly Press. Abrahams edited the O. Henry Prize short story annuals and had chosen Carver's "What Is It?" for his 1973 collection. Ray wasn't the only fellow with impressive publications. John Batki, for instance, had published a story in the *New Yorker.* Yet Batki found Carver experienced and intimidating; to him Ray seemed "lit up" with intensity, but didn't appear drunk. (Almost everyone, Batki added, used some kind of consciousness-enhancing substance in those days, so it was hard to know.)[2]

Ray may not have appeared drunk, but he was unquestionably in the first full bloom of alcoholism, drinking every day, sometimes all day. He blamed the increase in his drinking on his inability to choose between Diane Cecily and his wife, but—typically—does not attribute enough to the accumulating effects of his condition. It had been five years since his father's death, four since the collapse of his hopes in Israel; alcohol dependency was unraveling his life at a very predictable pace. And Maryann drank, too, ostensibly to stay close to Ray and to deaden the pain of knowing that Ray was in love with Cecily. Ray begged Maryann not to "find someone else." He needed time, he said, and needed her, and yet he didn't cut off the relationship with Cecily. In letters to Cecily, Ray tried to sound as if he were in control of the situation and of his feelings. Maryann saw this for the having-my-cake-and-eating-it-too gambit that it was. Eventually Cecily would as well.[3]

One afternoon at the end of a seminar meeting, novelist Chuck Kinder asked who could give him a lift down El Camino toward his house. Ray offered, and Kinder followed "this big shambling fellow" who "always dressed goofy" to an old Ford Falcon convertible, "just beat to shit, an old rattletrap that looked like if we got in it would collapse around us." There were cigarette butts and manuscripts and paper cups all over. At the shudder of Ray's engine, a bottle of cheap Scotch slid out from under the driver's seat. Ray said, " 'Ooh, look what we have here,' laughing in that way of his . . . 'Maybe we should have us a little drink.' " By the end of a two-mile drive, the half quart was nearly finished. Kinder didn't want Ray to know where he lived, so he got out at the Taco Bell on his corner.

Kinder's house was across a wooden bridge over Matadero Creek, enveloped in foliage under redwood trees, a dark bungalow invisible from the road. Nonetheless, about ten o'clock the next morning, Ray stood on Kinder's porch with two paper sacks. One held magazines and anthologies; the other, ice and a bottle.[4] Ray was networking. The man he'd come to see was a big West Virginian with thick, dark hair and a full beard. Kinder affected the early-seventies look of a "hip, hippie hillbilly" in work boots and coveralls.[5] When Ray asked him if he was working, Kinder said he was just watching TV—in fact, watching old movies and thinking about writing a novel with a main character modeled on his idol, James Dean. By the end of the afternoon, Kinder and Carver were "best buddies."[6]

Kinder had recently sold his first novel, *Snakehunter,* to Knopf. He'd paid little attention to Ray, who mumbled, smoked, and bit on his thumbnail between his rare, astute comments at the seminar. But when Kinder read Carver's work, he was impressed by Ray's ability to discover art in everyday occurrences—what he called "a strange conjunction between accident and art." After the two became friends, Ray was less abashed about speaking in the workshop. Scott Turow, a lecturer at Stanford and later the author of *Presumed Innocent* and other legal thrillers, began to sit in on the workshop because he was "impressed with the authoritativeness with which Ray spoke about fiction" and knew he was influencing Kinder and other friends.[7]

Kinder's friendship was a godsend to Ray. Here was a man who wrote beautiful, lyrical prose—Ray admired his *Snakehunter,* a "ghost story" about a boy trying to make sense of death—and also loved to drink and party in the old boy, down home manner. The two liked nothing better than sitting around a table drinking and telling stories that they proudly called lies. Kinder even remembered sitting at a table with Carver, late at night or early in the morning, joking about what they'd tell each other's biographers: "We'd make up stuff that we'd tell them and joke about it all, but then we'd get serious too. There is literally stuff I've never written about and I'll never tell."[8] As Ray struggled with marriage and family issues, longed to see Cecily in Montana, and maintained his three-point commuting life, he found a psychic home in Kinder's cabin and circuit of bars and friends' houses and apartments.*

No one could claim that the Bay Area in the 1970s was Paris in the

---

* As it turned out, Ray Carver would haunt Kinder for the middle years of his writing career. His long manuscript and shorter published novel *Honeymooners: A Cautionary Tale* are repositories of Carver legends—of Kinder's "ghosts" turned into words. "It would be disingenuous to say my novel is not about Ray and myself," Kinder said. "Those stories aren't utterly journalistic, but emotionally they are true."

1920s, but the party scene that evolved in Palo Alto and then moved (with Kinder) to San Francisco a couple of years later shared some characteristics with Hemingway's moveable feast: alcohol, shaky finances, young talent, and big ambitions. That West Coast writing scene, as Michael Rogers wrote later for *Newsweek,* was "a last call for the grand (if dismaying) big-drinking, bad-behaving, macho tradition of American fiction." Rogers, then an undergrad who attended the seminar, knew Ray then and later, when he became a *Rolling Stone* reporter and novelist. "The bad old days are pretty much gone," Rogers reflected, for reasons ranging from "modern health science to the disappearance of genteel poverty as a viable lifestyle."[9]

Ray made himself at home among Kinder's crowd because, among other reasons, they diverted him from the alcoholic fears and loneliness that were closing down on him. Crossing the creek to Kinder's was like entering another world in the midst of Palo Alto. With a few exceptions, the men who populated this bad-old-days scene were provincials — small-town westerners or Southerners and country boys who brought their working-class backgrounds and literary aspirations to Silicon Valley. One man who became close to Ray was Max Crawford, the most political man in the group. He had a degree in economics and a hitch in the army behind him when his friend and fellow Texan Larry McMurtry suggested him for a Stegner in 1968. Rumor (enhanced by Crawford's 1979 novel *The Bad Communist*) held that Crawford had been involved with the radical Left and the Black Panther Party.[10] By 1972, he was disillusioned with politics and had begun writing novels, including the classics *Waltz Across Texas* and *Lords of the Plain.* Crawford's buddy Michael Köepf ran his own fishing boat in summer and studied writing at San Francisco State College; his novels would include *The Fisherman's Son* and *Save the Whale.* Kentuckians Ed McClanahan (author of *The Natural Man*) and Gurney Norman had been around Palo Alto since Kesey's days. Norman's novel *Divine Right's Trip* appeared in *The Last Whole Earth Catalog.*[11] Others who partied in Palo Alto, some associated with Stanford and others employed by area publishers, were Turow, *Clockers* author Richard Price, poet and social activist Don Paul, freelance writer and editor George Lynn, and novelist Tom Zigal. And then there was Zap Comix cartoonist S. Clay Wilson, an originator of underground comics whose "rough, crazy, coarse, deeply American" drawings led his more famous colleague R. Crumb to call him "the most original artist of my generation."[12] As the "astounding" (Kinder) and "amazing" (Crawford) times unrolled, Ray invited his friends from Santa Cruz and Missoula to Kinder's parties. By means of such connections, augmented by wives and girlfriends, the circle continually shifted and expanded.

Gurney Norman's description of Ray and Maryann suggests why all

these people touched one another's lives so intensely and why Carver—
even if he had not become the most famous member of the group—meant
so much to them:

> It was all of our working-class backgrounds that connected us under-
> neath. When I would have a few beers, I would start telling anecdotes
> about my hillbilly family. Ray need not himself have had much awareness
> of this particular line of thinking—it's just that he *embodied* it. It's cen-
> tral to Ray's total identity. Maryann was also kind of a good old boy . . .
> a very good talker, very smart. I remember her confidence and the qual-
> ity of the conversation. If she'd been at any of those parties without Ray,
> she would have been a strong member of the party, one who really helped
> make the occasion. She seemed like somebody from *home*—as Ray did.[13]

The men who found one another during those evenings in Palo Alto in
1972 were gaining perspective on the places they'd come from and, in most
cases, readying for a move to somewhere else. If they had fellowships at
Stanford and working wives (as Kinder, Crawford, and Carver did), they
could devote their days to reading and writing, liquor, and hangovers. They
projected their vivid, crazy talk onto the surreal, almost narcotic blank page
of Palo Alto. (Price had his fill of that after one semester and headed east
with his work-in-progress about teenage gangs in the Bronx.) For most of
them, California was, as 1962 Stegner Fellow Robert Stone wrote in *A Hall
of Mirrors,* "at the further edge of the bad trips . . . at the western end of
your mind, man."

Carver, Kinder, Crawford, and sometimes Kittredge and Köepf made up
what came to be called the "Beef Trust." They were, Turow said, "slightly
reminiscent of last year's Phillies. They didn't look a bit like writers, more
like truck drivers. They'd come striding across the quad at Stanford elbow to
elbow looking purposeful, if not mean."[14] Like a bunch of fraternity brothers, they gave each other nicknames. Kinder took "Trout" from Brautigan's
Trout Fishing in America; Kittredge, because of his large head and manner
of charging across a room, was "Buffalo"; Carver, for sneakiness regarding money and women, became "Running Dog" or "Dirty Dog." Crawford
became "Rhinestone Commie." Köepf was "Big Fish." Carver and Kinder in
particular teased each other like brothers, though some thought that Kinder,
who was quicker witted than Ray, gave out more ribbing than he received.
He got on Ray's case much as Jerry King had once done in Yakima.[15]

The rivalry among the brotherhood was to see who could become
a famous writer first. Most of them wrote novels and expected that Ray
would have to do that, too, if he wanted to become "rich and famous."

When Lynn defended some "experimental" fiction he was working on by saying, "Ray, writing isn't a fucking horse race," Ray answered with conviction, "Yes it is. It is a horse race." Lynn was sure Ray meant publishing and fame.[16] By the time he came to Stanford, Ray had fallen behind in that race. The box of work he'd mailed to Cecily and the bag of magazines he brought over to Kinder's contained most of his finished work.

"I was never into the myth or the mythos of alcohol and the artist," Ray said. "I was into the alcohol itself. I liked the taste of it."[17] More than the taste, of course, he craved the effect. Nor—another myth—did he get drunk to find story material. "We got drunk and behaved chaotically and even sociopathically," explained Lynn, whose own chaotic life eventually landed him in a federal prison for ten years, "because we were jaded and it amused and entertained us. It allowed us to ventilate suppressed feelings."[18]

Ray, Crawford, and Kinder "could drink all day and not be falling-down drunk by evening," Zigal said. "And we smoked dope, too, which I think probably has not been said a lot. But the truth is there was always some weed around, and we always smoked it."[19] Ray was a big man blessed—or cursed—with a high tolerance for alcohol, meaning that his brain and body were making compensatory adaptations to chronic alcohol exposure. As neuroscientists have shown, an individual's chance of becoming addicted depends on the reaction of the brain's neurons to alcohol. Social circumstances may contribute, but at least half of the factors that determine this reaction are genetic. People who don't get sick from drinking—who "handle their liquor"—are able to send more alcohol to their brains. Their brains respond initially by blocking the binding of glutamate (a neurotransmitter, or "messenger substance") to neuron receptors and by reducing the number of dopamine receptors that are able to respond to other pleasant stimuli (such as food or sexual stimulation). To compensate, alcoholic brains then increase the number and sensitivity of their receptors. Then, drinkers boost their intake in order to achieve the intoxication they enjoyed before, and their inhibitory and excitatory messenger substances become permanently unbalanced.

Such a drinker, in a perverse behavioral adaptation, learns to appear normal while under the influence. This typical pattern leads to physical dependency on alcohol for normal central nervous system function.[20] The whole insidious process is just gradual and baffling enough to allow an alcoholic to ignore what is happening. Most alcoholics are physically dependent before they comprehend what has occurred. When comprehension does begin, it can be too late to change. During his year as a Stegner fellow, Carver inched toward that quandary.

To several observers at the time, it was Maryann who had trouble managing alcohol. She was, McClanahan said, "a very beautiful woman, just a knockout, and she pounded the liquor down right up there with Ray." But she became drunk more easily than Ray. At a fifties costume party, Tom Zigal saw Maryann "so drunk she didn't realize it was a theme party. She said to me, 'I know who you are, I know you.' Her implication was that I was a phony person because of the way I dressed. She was wandering around and not getting it, and Ray was explaining it to her in a very frustrated way." At times, others said, she "was pyrotechnical, regaling us with stories about fights," and "Ray seemed amused by her, because she was so immediately expressive—seemed like he was just sitting back and purring. It was complicated, but something about it suited Ray."[21]

"Maryann's mind was quick, fast as a buzz saw, when she was drunk," Crawford said. "She was easygoing with a husky laugh, and she told her stories *in third person*." Crawford recollected one about a woman who is staying with her kids in a motel cabin while her husband works at a sawmill: "She gets drunk with the motel owner, who seduces her. In disgust with herself, she drops her kids' crayons in the furnace and sets her cabin on fire! She calls her husband, gathers up her kids, and runs to the landlord's place. Her husband arrives in time to see the conflagration of his cabin. He thinks his family has all gone up in flames. But then, as he's weeping, here comes his wife, with lipstick all askew, out of the landlord's cabin." That, Crawford said, "was this knife-in-the-water quality her stories had: the husband doesn't want his family to be dead, but he doesn't want his wife to be alive coming out of this other guy's cabin, either." As Maryann told "this jabbery little thing, this amazing story, there was Ray, just sitting there, and you could tell that the humiliation of the story was terrible for him—but on the other hand, he loved the fucking story, her telling it and making it up."[22]

When she was drunk, Maryann also became flirtatious. But among the inner circle of men, "it was an absolute established fact that it wasn't going to go any further than that." A few stories on the theme have drifted down from those years. In one, Maryann, wearing a skirt, is play-wrestling on a couch with one of the men when the couch tips over and her legs go flying in the air. In another she sits on a man's lap and gets herself a bite on the neck. Some tales involve Maryann behaving provocatively with another man while Ray watches. Whether Ray liked or hated the role of voyeur these scenes assigned him varies with the teller. Michaels described a triangle in *Time Out of Mind*: "In the modern version the husband deliberately creates the triangle. He needs to feel jealousy—his darkest, most exquisite pleasure. At a party in Cupertino, I saw Ray Carver watching me dance with Marianne [sic]. He was sodden drunk, gloomy, and glowering. Who knows what he imagined. I said good night and drove away. I won't be in one of Ray's jealous husband stories."[23]

Michaels's perception of a story in the making seems to accord with Lynn's psychological take on the couple: "She would come on to Crawford or me, usually, while Ray watched, sweating profusely, with a pained expression . . . *clearly* Maryann was an angry woman, angry with Ray about *something,* some attention that he could not or would not give her. There was a kinkiness to their game that showed up in Ray's stories. Both he and she were in great pain together, yet you knew they needed each other desperately." Crawford had a simpler explanation: "The crazy stuff they would do to each other was *booze.* Maryann could be bad on booze, but they loved each other like teenagers. She was such a powerful woman, and he was a funny guy, kind of soft. I've never met anybody like him."[24]

Maryann carried on as the steady earner in the family while Ray cobbled together fellowships, reading and publication fees, and teaching jobs. What she could still manage, Maryann did with more flair than ever. She dressed fashionably. She transformed her hair from a straight, bleached curtain into thick, wavy, honey blonde tresses. She completed a graduate course at Stanford and was awarded tenure at Los Altos High School. At work, Pelton said, she mentioned worries about her children but "never complained about the stark unhappiness of her marriage."[25]

Maryann *was* flirtatious, Ray's former student Diane Smith thought, and "all the men were in love with her. Not only was she smart, funny, gorgeous, and able to drink with the best of them, but she supported Ray." Smith's impression, formed when she returned to the Bay Area with Crawford, was that the tales about Maryann were exaggerated by affection:

> That was a bad generation of men. These men believed our job was to support the great artist that they would one day become. Maryann had the qualities they all desired. Most of us worked at jobs with no future, but she was the model because she was able to hold down a professional job plus waitress at night. One weekend Max and I went to play a round of golf at this nine-hole golf course in Cupertino—Ray played too! Maryann was tending bar at the little club there while we were playing golf.[26]

Köepf echoed Smith's assessment:

> I remember Maryann being like Zelda Fitzgerald. She was a witty woman. It's just horseshit that she was the cause of Ray's drinking, as some people implied later on. She had to hold a job down. She had two kids, she taught

high school, and she had to take care of Ray. Taking care of Ray was not that easy. He was close to a low-rent criminal—in a wonderful, charming way, but he was. He was having a tough time, but he was having fun too. It wasn't good clean fun, but it was fun.[27]

McClanahan and some of the others had a regular Friday night poker game. Ray loved poker, had been playing since high school, but as the night progressed, he would confuse diamonds and hearts in his hand and make stupid bets. On one of these nights, Ray asked if he could write a check for more chips, Lynn recollected. "One guy was already pissed at Ray because he'd persuaded a typist at his office to type Ray's stories, and then Ray paid her with a rubber check. So the answer was no." Ray drove Lynn home after the game:

> A blue light began flashing blocks before we reached my address. Ray halted in front of my apartment. The cops began giving Ray sobriety tests. He failed miserably. To stay out of jail, he would have to give them six hundred dollars bail.
>
> Ray sidled over to me and said, "George, you got any money in the house?" Truth is, I had eight hundred dollars cash that I had received that week for doing freelance work. But I knew damn well if I gave it to Ray, I'd never see it again, and I had a wife working on the switchboard at Stanford and two small boys, so I lied and said no. They drove Ray off in the squad car.
>
> But someone called Maryann, and she went right down and bailed him out. Maybe she was afraid he'd get the *delirium tremens* or maybe it was just the old "enabler" crap, but she never let his ass bounce when he screwed up.[28]

But Maryann couldn't do everything, and her children often felt the strain. Crawford threw a football with Vance during odd moments during parties at the Cupertino house: "He reminded me of my own son. And this poor kid, he'd almost get tears in his eyes. It seemed to me that he'd missed his boyhood."[29]

Vance appreciated Crawford's attentions, but they made little difference in his bitter memories of this "depressing, hard time." In Cupertino, he took up with a guy he'd known in junior high who had been in sports but was now into drugs:

> I was needy of a friend, but hanging around this guy was a bad idea. I smoked pot on and off, as it seemed practically everybody did then,

whether from stable families or struggling ones like ours. My parents didn't inquire about why I didn't go out for baseball again. They just didn't ask. No one was minding the store. I think at Cupertino, the social life and the family life just fused. No possibility of coming home from school to a predictable afternoon.

Our house was in the school district but at the outskirts of town, where they were able to get away with these loud parties. My sister and I could drink and use drugs along with the adults. No one seemed concerned. And then I would go to the school where everyone had an expensive middle-class life, and there was no sympathy for people with chaos at home. I felt very different from the other kids.[30]

Neither Ray nor Maryann could figure out the series of incremental changes required to make their lives simpler and more orderly. While Maryann struggled just to meet the next crisis—indeed, as meeting crises became her way of life—the best thing Ray could imagine for himself was a complete change: an orderly life in another place with another woman. "We had a crisis that lasted for six years; we had an emergency that lasted for six years; we had the Vietnam War in our home for six years," Maryann said. Her comparison may have been apt.[31]

The Vietnam War had been going on since the Carvers were in college, and it was expiring along with their marriage. Since 1970, peace talks had been under way in Paris while President Nixon lowered troop levels and spoke of the "Vietnamization" of the war. Democrats nominated an antiwar candidate, George McGovern, to run against Nixon in 1972. McGovern lost every state except Massachusetts. The war dragged on.

The last American combat troops left Vietnam in March 1973. By then, as a writer of a later generation, David Foster Wallace, remarked, the "brave new individualism and sexual freedom of the 1960s devolved into anomic self-indulgence" for the so-called Me generation of the 1970s. The political focus of the sixties provided a stage for the human scene that fascinated Ray. The seventies focus on self-improvement interested him less, in part because he couldn't take seriously the kind of jargon churned out by most group undertakings, more so because alcohol made him cynical about changing anything, especially himself.

Though he wrote little, Ray did not neglect his literary life, such as it was. He continued to build his ties to Lenny Michaels in Berkeley. The two of them talked about publishing a West Coast edition of the New York–based tabloid called *Fiction*. In September Ray and Maryann joined Michaels (West Coast editor), David Reid (editorial associate), and avant-garde fictionist Donald Barthelme (art director) at the Hotel Durant bar in Berkeley to discuss their plan. Barthelme ordered four martinis before the last call, Ray downed doubles of Smirnoff with grapefruit juice and daydreamed about the next time he'd see Cecily, and Maryann drank Scotch (singles) and—Ray believed—knew exactly where her husband's mind was wandering. In conversations with Reid, Ray exhibited his "vast and miscellaneous" reading, mentioned that Lawrence Durrell was his favorite author, and—though he was seldom a pedant—corrected Reid's pronunciation of "Durrell." In November, Ray participated in a reading at Berkeley's Stuffed Inn to raise money for *Fiction*. His story, he bragged to Cecily, was a big hit. They had a full bar, and readings lasted past midnight. When Jim Houston, reading fifth, paused for a drink of water, the inebriated emcee got up and said "thank you" and tried to introduce the next reader. When it was really over, this same emcee stumbled on his way out the door and dropped his bag of *Fiction* cash, manuscripts, and letters. The dispersing crowd spent an hour recovering items from a rainy street. That, presumably, was a final blow for the western edition, but the New York editors persevered. Carver's "Are You a Doctor?" appeared in their spring issue for 1973.[32]

In December Carver finished teaching at UCSC and prepared to take up his new teaching assignment at Berkeley. He rented unit 303 in the Durant Park Apartments and planned to spend a few nights a week there. The place came with a bed, refrigerator, and some cheap Danish modern furniture. After Christmas, Cecily flew down from Montana to spend her week's vacation with Ray. When he brought her to his apartment, she was surprised to see that it looked completely unlived in. There was none of the usual clutter except some empty bottles and a few books. The bed was made up with one big pillow and one smaller one that belonged to a couch.[33]

"Ray giggled all the time," Cecily remembered. "He simply didn't put on any macho posture at all. If you delighted in something, he was right there delighting in it with you." During the time she was there, Cecily rode with Ray to Cupertino so he could check his mail, which, he said, was not being forwarded properly. They went during the day, while Maryann and the children were at school. "If I'd had even a shard of a brain, his going down while Maryann was teaching and riffling through the mailbox should have alerted me that Ray really hadn't made a complete break with her. But I think, I really didn't want to know."[34]

These were, in any case, lax times. The institution of marriage was up for inspection in those days and constantly discussed in the media, but Cecily was in a more convenient position to think about that than Ray was. If Ray became cynical about his marriage, it was only indirectly because of changing cultural attitudes. The simple clash of his desires against his wish to be a good man was tearing him up. He and Maryann were both instilled with the true-love ideal of fifties' pop songs and by secondhand Protestant morality. The life Ray really craved was the one that would sustain his work, but he no longer knew how to realize that life.

Deception for all was the inevitable result of the mess Ray had gotten himself into. Cecily "believed that Ray was headed for divorce. There was no timetable for that, of course, just Ray's assessment that the relationship had ended in Israel." Still, this visit had not been everything either of them had envisioned. Cecily needed reassurance and found that Ray was unable to give that. She began to understand that he was deeply involved with his wife and relied on her to take care of him. When Cecily first read Carver's stories, too, she was "swayed by the pain of relationships that was so palpable." Only when she read "Neighbors" did she notice that the stories were also humorous and "deliciously wicked."[35] That story opened the door to Carver's literary world for her and may, too, one surmises, have allowed her to become more circumspect about the cunning and lovable author. He was—as many have said—a trickster.

Cecily thought that despite his feeling that his marriage had been unraveling since 1968, Ray was influenced by Maryann's ability "to take adversity and process it. She could take the worst-case scenario and in her recreation of it, it became something optimistic, something that was going to be wonderful and *was* wonderful. Ray had that capacity, too—that was what I knew best in our friendship—but Ray also had the dark spots, the demons and holes in him that didn't see light at the end of any kind of tunnel." In Kinder's view, the Carvers' marriage was not as horrific as Ray's stories make it sound: "It's not utterly a myth, but they'd have an outrageous fight, and by the next morning they could sit around the kitchen table and laugh about it. And reremember it. And Maryann especially would be just howling with laughter no matter how outrageous it had been. Stories come from conflict, and Ray knew that."[36]

Maryann did not know that Cecily had been visiting until her rival had gone back to Montana. That same afternoon, Ray introduced Maryann as his wife at an English Department event. She limited herself to one tall Scotch and water, and they left early. When Maryann came to Ray's apartment, she saw that small second pillow on his bed. This "trivial evidence of betrayal" stunned her, but she continued to believe that "Ray would come off his bender—his latest bender—and pick up his life with me. It just wasn't possible for me to write him off." That night in Berkeley, Maryann realized that "Ray was teaching and juggling, barely, his personal life. That was as much as he could do. I saw that it might get a lot worse before it got better."[37]

In a January 1973 letter, Carver wrote Lish that he didn't know what would happen with the "lady from Missoula." He loved her, he said, but loved "M." too, even though the life at home bothered him.[38] As Carver would make brutally clear when he wrote his essay "Fires," he felt burdened by parenthood all along, but Chris's and Vance's teenage years exhausted his patience and left him embittered. Christine would spend years trying to understand what happened to her dad after he returned from Missoula. Alcoholism, she concludes, was the sole culprit:

> . . . his drinking escalated, and it began undermining every aspect of family and work structure he had, and my childhood as I had known it had changed and was gone forever. But at the time, we didn't recognize the drinking as a serious problem. You cannot blame anybody for what went on. It's part of the disease of alcoholism to put blame on everyone and everything, but my dad was an existentialist, and he would be the first to say that you have to take responsibility for your actions. The compounding problems from the drinking took a toll on everyone. It's tragic how two people in love, with such great ideals and talent, became victims of this disease. The infidelity broke my mother's heart, and my dad suffered horribly as well.[39]

Given the obstacles, Carver's teaching at Berkeley went remarkably well. Michaels promoted Carver as a rising short story writer, and the class was oversubscribed. Still, when Christine Flavin entered Carver's classroom, she thought she had made a mistake. She saw a moonfaced man sitting in a chair desk, "overflowing it a little, wearing jeans with a polyester shirt like you'd find now at Wal-Mart." He looked like a slob, but Flavin and fifteen others stayed on to hear Carver's off-the-cuff anecdotes about the writing life and his own struggles to get published. The class was primarily a poetry-writing workshop and Flavin thought Carver was much too merciful about some druggy writing that deserved to be "blasted."

Carver talked to the class about drinking so often that Flavin later realized he was wrestling with it himself, but at the time, he seemed to be suggesting that when writers drink, smoke, or abuse their bodies, it was "part of the way they got in touch with their inner selves." He handed out a demanding reading list and expected students to turn in reports on the selections. Three of the books were *I'm Not Stiller* by Frisch, *Death on the Installment Plan* by Louis-Ferdinand Céline, and *Stop-Time* by Frank Conroy. Altogether there were about ten books, all of them personal narratives. Carver's "idea seemed to be to get us close to what made us write and function, to the essence of our real lives." They scarcely discussed the books in class, and when Flavin went to Carver because she was bogged down in Céline, he advised, "Don't you worry about the reading, you just write."

When Flavin won one of the English Department's lesser poetry prizes, Carver asked her why she had not submitted to the more-coveted Eisner Prize. "You would have won," he told her, "I was on the board." Novelist Charlotte Painter, who also lectured at Berkeley then, noticed that Ray would sometimes miss a class and then come to school in dark glasses and tell the students, "My mother died." When Painter told him that he'd done this more than once, Ray replied, "Well, my mother died some time ago, but I still miss her!" This was, of course, classic Running Dog Ray behavior. In fact, Ella Carver had yet to suffer her one allotted death and was at that moment residing in Mountain View, California.

When the term ended, Flavin "respected Carver enormously and was moved by his encouragement" but didn't think he knew how to teach. Overall, she thought—and heard from others—that Carver did not fit easily into the department at Berkeley. "He and his wife were very blue collar in appearance; not exactly what the UC faculty had in mind. I heard she showed up at a faculty get-together in white go-go boots, which *they* considered rather lowbrow. But by then I respected the Carvers for not having those pretensions that most of the Berkeley faculty had."[40]

The whole gang came along with Ray to turn in his grades in Berkeley. Who exactly? Maryann remembers that Kittredge was in town, and both Kinder and John O'Brien, another writer with West Virginia roots, recollect the day. Here is O'Brien's version:

> We loaded this big picnic jug with a couple of quarts of vodka and OJ and ice. We kept getting lost. I don't know how long the trip to Berkeley should have taken, but we had drunk the damn cooler dry before we arrived, so we needed more stuff.
>
> Ray stopped at this liquor store in town, and there were Chicanos marching back and forth holding up signs "Don't shop at this store— it sells Gallo products," so Ray pulled away from the curb and said "I won't break a picket line!" Chuck and I were looking at each other—*Ray* wouldn't break a line for booze!
>
> But then Ray pulled over just down the street and said, "Especially when there is another store right here." So we got more vodka and poured more into the cooler. I don't mean to suggest that Ray and Chuck led me into perdition—I was always leading the parade with a banner— but around Ray and Chuck it all became incredibly easy; we were three drunks together.

O'Brien went into the university post office with Ray: "He had his grades in this big manila envelope, and the envelope wouldn't fit into the proper slot! So Ray got down on his knees and began to plead with the slot! 'If you don't accept these, I'm not going to get my money . . .' "[41]

Hundreds of similar incidents and anecdotes, most of them undated if not apocryphal, became part of the lore known as Ray stories, meaning stories about the Ray Carver who was drunk and broke most of the time during the years from 1973 until 1977. "Every night there was something," Kittredge said. "What we loved most was the recalling, the news, telling the story."[42]

After trying it for two years, Ray had decided that teaching was the best white-collar job for him.* He listed his University of California jobs on his résumé and conveniently omitted his failure to complete a graduate degree at Iowa (or anywhere else). And yet Iowa was always there, the unfinished business of his early ambition. Every year he submitted stories to the Iowa Short Fiction Award committee. In 1973 workshop director John Leggett and contest founder William Cotter Murray read the year's 250 entries and sent contenders to an outside judge. "We've got our winner," Leggett forecast to an editor at the press. But judge John Hawkes passed over Carver. Leggett was so surprised by this outcome that he telephoned Carver to apologize; on a hunch "that this guy was so good that we had to do something for him," Leggett offered Carver, a man he'd never met, a job teaching a graduate fiction workshop the next year. The salary was the most Carver had ever been offered. Ray asked for time to think about it.[43]

As he mulled over a one-year relocation to Iowa, Ray, who relished playing literary matchmaker, urged the Stegner directors to give fellowships to Bill Kittredge and Joy Williams. He emphasized to them that the year had been "spiritually enriching" for him. Maybe that was a pun, for without doubt he'd spent most of his money on spirits. To Kittredge, Ray admitted that the best thing about the fellowship was the money.[44] During that Stegner year, Ray continued to win accolades. *The Best American Short Stories 1973* listed both "What Is It?" and "Put Yourself in My Shoes" among the also-rans in the back of the book. William Abrahams told Carver that "The Summer Steelhead," forthcoming in *Seneca Review,* would be in his next O. Henry Prize volume. When Carver announced that to Lish, he added that the fishing story was his own favorite.[45] "They're Not Your Husband,"

---

* Max Crawford believed that Ray's "absolute terror of having to go back to the working class really informs his stories in a way that few literary intellectuals understand. The best thing for him was when he got a white-collar job with a pen holder in his pocket. He loved that."

his little masterpiece about the marriage of an alcoholic salesman and his waitress wife, continued unsold. Finally, Curt Johnson hand-delivered it to the *Chicago Review,* where student editor Douglas Unger accepted it on the spot. It came out late in 1973, accompanied by an ink drawing of the waitress bending over to scoop ice cream and her husband studying her thighs."[46]

Leggett's invitation to teach at Iowa was indeed too flattering for Ray to refuse. He'd be filling in for Vance Bourjaily, a writer he'd long admired and missed studying with at Iowa himself, and he'd have an easy two-course teaching schedule. Despite his relationship with Cecily, Ray spoke of bringing his family with him to Iowa and renting their California house to Joy Williams. He said Maryann would take a leave of absence but later told her he didn't want to uproot her for just one year. When he accepted Iowa's offer at the end of April, Ray postponed telling Hall at UC Santa Cruz, who was expecting him for the next year. He told himself he'd hang on to the position and then recommend Kittredge as his replacement.[47]

Ray's plans were not so much a tissue of lies as a tissue of indecision. Shortly before his thirty-fifth birthday, he told Lish that he'd be giving up the apartment in Berkeley at the end of the spring quarter. He and Maryann, he wrote, had decided to stay together, and he and Cecily would stay friends but not live together. His "soap opera" had "about run its course." By then, Cecily understood that Ray was unable to make decisions: "He was really just trying to figure out what was happening and who *he* wanted to be, not trying to deceive me or Maryann. Unfortunately, with the alcohol, he wasn't giving himself a fair shot at being able to do any of that."[48]

Clarifying—at least to himself—the terms of his involvement with Cecily and moving home did not solve Ray's family problems, because the situation with his teenagers had deteriorated. Ray listed their school suspensions, impudence, and problems with cars, dope, and alcohol among the scourges that tormented him and Maryann.[49] If Ray saw the irony that *his* alcohol consumption was affecting everyone, he wasn't ready to admit to it.

Kittredge won a Stegner Fellowship, but didn't want the job at Santa Cruz, so Ray just kept quiet about it. Liquor bills and other expenses of an incomeless summer loomed, and bill collectors buzzed around about Ray's student loans. He was afraid they would contact Maryann's school or garnish her salary. About seven one morning, Lynn was at his type-writer working on a low-vocabulary version of *Charlotte's Web* when he saw Ray grinning sheepishly at his kitchen window. Lynn declined a drink from Ray's open bottle of vodka and listened as Ray excitedly explained the brainstorm he'd just had that would solve his money problems. He would *commute* between his full-time teaching job in Iowa City and his once-a-week visiting-artist gig in Santa Cruz! Lynn pointed out that even if he could handle such a schedule, it would be expensive. Ray said he'd charge the flights on his credit card.[50]

Cost-effectiveness aside, Ray's plan accommodated his vacillation between Diane Cecily in Montana and Maryann in California. He would, in effect, live nowhere and make money doing so. A year before, Ray had rejected as "lunacy" the notion of a commute between Montana and California, but now he embraced an equally lunatic shuffle. No doubt such a schedule might have been possible for a workaholic. The two universities were on different calendars: Iowa's semester would be a month under way before UCSC's quarter began, Iowa would be on a winter break as the fall quarter closed in California, and so forth. Things were so lax at UCSC, Ray figured, that he needed to make only half of his classes. On top of Iowa's generous salary, $3,000 for a workshop on the occasional Friday in Santa Cruz was pure bonus. Those debts would vanish.

To Noel Young, Ray wrote that it would all work out fine and he'd "be home free" by December.[51] Where was home? It was wherever he found his next bottle of liquor.

CHAPTER 18

Drowning

August 1973–July 1974, Iowa City

> I used to feel that the classical libation was very much a part of life. I drank very happily until I found that I was an alcoholic. I never wrote when I had been drinking. But then there were fewer and fewer days that I could write.
>
> —John Cheever to Christina Robb, 1980[1]

Late in August, Ray departed Cupertino alone in a nine-year-old Ford Falcon convertible, aiming (for the third time in ten years) to make a new start in Iowa City. When he'd driven to the Midwest in 1963 and 1967, once with his family and once without, he was pursuing graduate degrees he never completed. Now he was joining the faculty of the very institution that had failed to recognize his talent a decade before. Other fiction faculty at the workshop would be John Cheever, John Irving, William Price Fox, and program director John Leggett. Ray may have been ambivalent about leaving California, but he hungered to be accepted where he once felt rejected, to be ranked among John Cheever's colleagues. Indeed, as Jim Houston noticed, Ray's "will to write and to fraternize with writers was the driving force of his life."[2]

Ray drove to Iowa by way of Missoula, adding about six hundred miles to the direct route. He arrived drunk and eager to get to the liquor store, Cecily recalled. She began to realize that Ray wasn't just celebrating. "It was turning into a way of living, and it was pretty scary. I saw him changing. And I tried not to look at it that way, tried to make excuses for it, but those excuses weren't working because we didn't have much communication anymore. That was difficult—a difficult thing to watch."[3]

Jon Jackson, now a student at the workshop, who'd been working on a summer construction job and a novel in Montana, would ride with Ray. Nursing hangovers, they loaded up Ray's Falcon, and Jackson announced

250

that if he had to do the driving, there'd be no drinking on the road. "With great round eyes and a look of absolute innocence," Ray agreed. But Ray had a drink caddy set up between the seats and insisted on a stop at the Eastgate Lounge for ice and grapefruit juice. A few miles outside of Missoula, Ray pulled out his half gallon of vodka and poured himself "a wee drinky" to kill his hangover.[4]

Waking early and hungry at a cowboy motel in Sheridan, Wyoming, Jackson saw that Ray had been sick in the night. His breath sounded like "a slow strangling." Jackson found his way to a bar where he could get a breakfast with his morning drinks. The bartender called him to the phone as he was tucking into his eggs. Ray said, "I feel like a hired killer. I'm looking down onto an empty western street, and I don't know what town I'm in." Jackson asked Ray how he'd located him. Ray said he'd opened the Yellow Pages to Taverns.

Ray refused to eat in local restaurants because he didn't intend to pay for his meals. He chose Howard Johnson's and other chain restaurants, where he took pride in stiffing a corporation, forgetting that it was the waitress who paid when customers walked out on a bill. But Ray "left food on his plate. Like a lot of alcoholics, he was getting his sugar from alcohol. I don't think he ever finished a meal in those days."[5] Across Wyoming and Nebraska and Iowa, Ray talked about John Gardner and Isaac Babel and Chekhov. He argued with Jackson, who didn't care much about short stories and wanted to study novel writing at Iowa. "Ray was just elated with Babel's *Red Cavalry* stories, especially the way Babel abandons the story line and moves on to something else. That was important to him."[6]

It may go without saying that Carver and Jackson were drunk when they pulled into Iowa City. Jackson helped Ray move into the Iowa House, a concrete-block hotel on the east side of the river close to where the writers' program barracks used to stand. Ray got room 240, in a corner by the stairs at the end of a long hallway. The television set was bolted to the chest of drawers. Downstairs, a cafeteria overlooking the river served three meals a day and a lounge sold beer, but there was no bar, no hard liquor.

Ray delivered Jackson to his wife and daughter, who took him in after a summer apart. Before dawn the next morning, Jackson was awakened by the sound of Ray in his house. Ray needed help. It seemed—Ray was vague on the details—that a young actor he'd met in a bar had needed a place to crash for the night before taking a bus out of town in the morning. Ray—never averse to a drinking companion for the loneliest hours of the night—had offered his couch. When the handsome black man got to Ray's room, he stripped to leopard-print briefs, made himself comfortable on Ray's single bed, and, it seems, extracted a jar of Vaseline from his bag. Realizing that a misunderstanding was under way, Ray drove to Jackson's.

Jackson suggested that Ray sleep on *his* couch, but Ray feared the intruder would swipe his typewriter. Back at Iowa House, Ray and Jackson jointly failed to evict the drunken, sleepy visitor. They called the campus police, who listened patiently to "wildly conflicting stories" and conferred with Jackson in the hallway. Jackson explained that "Professor Carver" had simply made a mistake and didn't wish to cause the young actor any trouble. The police rousted him and took him to the bus depot.[7]

By August 30, Ray had visited the writing program office in the English-Philosophy Building and returned with a supply of University of Iowa letterhead on which he typed letters to his editors, Gordon Lish and Noel Young. To both he explained that he, the "intrepid and wasted adventurer," would be making just six commutes to visit his family and meet his classes in Santa Cruz. With Young he tried to sort out the muddle he'd created by promising an artist $200 to do linocuts for the Capra chapbook edition of *Put Yourself in My Shoes* while telling Young that the artist would probably do them for free.[8] Ray expected to meet Cheever that very evening at dinner. He'd heard that Cheever had split from his wife, was in Iowa against doctor's orders, and would never make it out alive.[9] If that forecast alarmed Ray, he didn't say so.

Late that afternoon, the living American short story author that Carver most admired came to room 240. Jackson, having stopped for a drink, opened the door to a "pleasant little man in a tweed jacket, flannel trousers, and penny loafers" who held out a glass and said, "Pardon me. I'm John Cheever. Could I borrow some Scotch?" At this, "Ray hurried forward, his lips and eyes all 'o' with awe. 'John Cheever,' he said. 'No, I'm so sorry. I don't have any Scotch. Would you like some vodka?' He hurried back to the dresser to retrieve the huge bottle of Smirnoff's. Mr. Cheever smiled sadly and deigned to join us in vodka. Straight. No ice, no grapefruit juice."[10]

Sixty-one that fall, Cheever still resembled the buoyant fellow pictured on the cover of his recent collection, *The World of Apples*. When those stories came out the previous spring, Cheever had been hospitalized for cardiomyopathy due to alcoholism. In the delirium of withdrawal from drink, he'd thought the hospital was a Soviet prison and thrown a positive review of his book across the room in the belief that he was being forced to sign a confession. When Cheever calmed down, doctors told him he'd kill himself if he drank again. For a few weeks he abstained, lost weight, and gained vitality. Then he decamped to Iowa.[11]

Over Ray's vodka, Cheever and Carver expressed admiration for each other's stories.* The wonderfully urbane and cordial guest even implied that he knew who Jackson was (unlikely) and then inquired, "Where does one get Scotch around here? Is this a dry state?" Indeed, Iowa had a long history of alcohol-control laws, but by 1973 it allowed many of the conveniences a social drinker desires: mixed drinks were served in restaurants, even on Sundays. For packaged goods, Cheever and Carver had to go to the state-run liquor store. Jackson offered to drive Cheever there at nine the next morning. Cheever asked if they could leave at eight forty-five so he could be there when the store opened.[12]

Cheever and Carver walked up the hill from Iowa House to Leggett's for dinner. As their host watched them approach, he saw that "they were fast friends after having just encountered one another. They were the most astonishing pals—this tiny, highly disciplined, Brooks Brothers–suited Cheever immediately affectionate with this great hulking cowpoke of a Carver!"[13]

The two visiting professors occupied identical, oddly shaped rooms on different floors of the Iowa House. Cheever's was just above Carver's and had "the same reproduction of the same painting hanging on the wall," Ray recalled. When department chair John Gerber held a formal dinner, Ray—who could never manage to tie his own necktie—asked Cheever for help. They got the job done over a few drinks in Cheever's room. Soon they developed a routine. "He and I did nothing *but* drink," Carver said of that semester. "I mean, we met our classes in a manner of speaking, but the entire time we were there . . . I don't think either of us ever took the covers off our typewriters." Cheever, born a year before Ray's father, was ahead of his acolyte on the morbid journey toward total alcoholic breakdown. Together they passed afternoons sitting at the bar at the Mill; at Iowa House they drank in the older man's room because Cheever was afraid of getting mugged in the hallway. Since Cheever had no car, Ray took him on a liquor run twice a week. Cheever noted in his journal that Ray was "a very kind man." A tire on Ray's car had an "aneurism," and once they drove on a flat tire. Another day, a cold day, Ray found Cheever pacing in the lobby well before the appointed time, wearing loafers without socks. They got to the store as "the clerk was just unlocking the front door [and] John got out of the car before I could get it properly parked. By the time I got inside the store, he was already at the checkout stand with a half gallon of Scotch." Tales of the two writers making great fools of themselves on

---

* Perhaps Cheever had seen Carver's "What Is It?" in the 1973 O. Henry collection where his own "Jewels of the Cabots" also appeared.

these trips to the liquor store circulated so widely that one suspects that the novice writers found nervous consolation in the addiction that tormented their masters.[14]

Ray's affair with Cecily had lost its momentum, but he called her from Iowa and sometimes put Cheever on the line. "They were wonderful, nonsensical, crazy phone calls, and I guess I knew Ray's drinking was going full speed ahead." Hearing rumors that Ray was seeing other women at Iowa, Cecily put the previous year's dreams behind her. She and Ray remained good friends.[15]

Iowa City in those years was an extraordinary place, more so than it had been when the Carvers lived there a decade earlier. The political battles of the sixties hadn't scarred Iowa much, but the accompanying social and sexual revolution ushered in a time of experimentation and outlandish individuality. It was "the wildest place I have ever lived," said New Englander Tracy Kidder, who has served in Vietnam and reported from Haiti. There were amazing parties with writers that the International Writers' Program (founded by Paul and Hualing Engle) brought in from all over the globe. Downtown, there were bars that catered to every clientele, including one with topless female dancers and another with female impersonators. The Mill and the Deadwood and Joe's Place were bars the "Shoppies" favored. The locals ranged from burned-out druggies to street poets to a man named Ms. Bunch who won a Judy Garland look-alike contest without altering his usual costume. Such a tremendous amount of philandering and illegal drug use and heavy drinking went on that few noticed when an individual was in serious trouble.[16]

But some people did see how much alcohol Ray consumed. When Ray was expected for dinner, Dennis Covington set a bottle of vodka on the kitchen counter just for him. To Covington, Ray never seemed depressed, but his one-liners—"I felt so bad this morning I could barely make it to the liquor store," for instance—gave him away. Nor did Ray seem dangerous, but his anecdotes had a dark side. He chuckled with disbelief when he told about a night when he'd hit Maryann with a chair. Someone had called paramedics because her head was bleeding, but Ray met them at the door and explained there'd been some mistake. Ray talked about Maryann's drinking problem and told drastic (but comical in the telling) tales of incidents such as the one where his drunken wife drove her car into a fire hydrant and created a water fountain. The one time Ray seemed upset was when Maryann called to say that Chris had run away from home.[17]

In those years, especially in Iowa, Ray lived indoors. Once, thinking it would do Ray good to get outside, Covington invited him to ride to the

Mississippi River with him to watch eagles. When he came to fetch Ray, he found him sitting on the floor deep in conversation and vodka with a Czechoslovakian playwright. There was no fresh-air expedition for Carver. But he did make an exception to "stand in a drilling rain on an Iowa morning, fishing for bass at the pond on the Bourjailys' farm," Jackson said. "I know damn well he was desperately hungover, because I was, and I'd been with him the night before. I wanted to quit and go get dry, but Ray loved to fish. So we stayed." He didn't keep his fish, though. "No, he'd give them to you! He'd make a face and say that you could probably clean them better than he could anyway—that he'd just make a mess of it!"[18]

The workshop had more than a hundred graduate students at this time, about forty of whom received financial support from the university. Among the fiction writers were many who went on to become productive writers: T. Coraghessan Boyle, Dennis Covington, Dan Domench, Allan Gurganus, Ron Hansen, Kent Haruf, Jon Jackson, Tracy Kidder, Joanne Meschery, and Mary Swander. On the other hand, competition was intense, and not a few aspirants were sent on to "happier lives" by the harsh critical comments of their classmates. Kidder began his successful career as a journalist when he decided he didn't want to compete with the fiction "hotshots." Poets of the era included Michael Burkard and his wife, Tess Gallagher, Denis Johnson, Tom Meschery, George O'Connell, Michael Ryan, John Skoyles, and Michael Waters.[19]

There was competition to get into Cheever's workshop, and John Irving also had a following, but few of the students knew what to expect from Carver. The route that brought Mary Swander to Carver's class was probably typical: "Leggett had told me about this young writer who had *not* won the Iowa fiction award who was going to come and teach. And I'd looked up his stories and thought they were great. So while the big talent streamed toward Cheever, I ended up in this class that was considered the dregs of the workshop." Fourteen others, mostly men, were waiting for the dregs in a classroom in the English-Philosophy Building when Carver walked in and said, "I don't like this building, do you?" The students dutifully agreed, and Ray moved the class to the back room of the Mill, where they could drink beer and smoke cigarettes as they worked. José Steele objected to the smoking, but Ray retorted, "You can't tell a bunch of writers not to smoke." Then, oblivious to the ironies, he told everybody they needed to get their lives in shape so they could write. "You can't write if you are constipated or drunk," he said, launching into his tale of woe about writing in the car at night when he was young. At the end of this rap, he suggested it would be really nice if someone would invite him home for a dinner. One female student took the hint and became romantically involved with Ray for a while.[20]

It would have been strange if Ray had not found willing women in Iowa City in those politically incorrect days. He charmed women with his tousled boyish manner and his cachet as a workshop lecturer. "Women had to know that he was not a sexual threat," Jackson said. "Any woman looking at him would know, 'He's not going to put the make on me, I have to put the make on him'—and they did! He never talked about it much."[21]

When he was too drunk to teach, Ray scrupulously called each student to cancel class. Still, Swander found Carver's instruction very good. The other men in the room greeted with dull silence a story Swander wrote about a woman who had dementia, but Ray said, "It just ripped my heart out." The anthology of readings for Carver's class contained fifty-six American short stories, only four written by women.[22] But Swander was heartened to discover that Carver could discuss not only those four but many of the other women she read: Eudora Welty, Carson McCullers, Joyce Carol Oates. Shortly after Ray praised Swander's work, she moved up in the workshop's "free-flowing hierarchy" to receive sought-after invitations and a plum teaching assignment. "All of a sudden," she recalled, "I was at this party with an elite group, and I asked Jack Leggett, 'What am I doing here?' And he said, 'You are writing good stories, Mary. Ray says so.' "

Ray wore the same sweater to class every week. In September it had a little hole in the elbow. The hole grew and grew until he could put his whole arm through it in December. That sweater was the least of the problems Ray had arranging his life during the fall semester. There remained the matter of his job in Santa Cruz. He made his first trip in late September. On the Iowa end, he was missed when he failed to show for a dinner invitation he'd accepted at the Kidders'. John Skoyles called Jackson to see what had become of Ray and learned that he was "at his other job—in California." Cheever knew about the secret job and noted in his journal that Ray was planning a tryst with a lover in Denver during a stopover. Legend maintains that Ray smooth-talked an official at United Airlines out of some vouchers for free flights by promising to mention the Friendly Skies in his stories or—alternate version—write an article for the in-flight magazine. Ray's colleague William Price Fox bragged of pulling off a similar coup and may have inspired Ray. In any case, Jackson swore that he saw Ray's free tickets and received the gift of an unused one from Ray.[23]

In California, Chuck Kinder and Bill Kittredge met Ray at the San Francisco Airport. He was always smashed when he arrived, and, more than likely, they'd had a few themselves. Once, as the passengers debarked from

Ray's plane, Trout and Buffalo hid behind a big poster on the concourse and jumped out hollering when Running Dog Ray approached. "Ray fell to his knees in alarm," Kinder recounted, "and his briefcase went flying and broke open when it landed, and all Ray's stuff, including his little pick-me-up pint, scattered everywhere."[24]

Though Ray had planned on meeting his Santa Cruz class half a dozen times in the twelve-week quarter, it's doubtful that he made it that often. Twice he and his pals actually drove to the campus, but, at the last minute, Ray asked the other two to pin a note on the door saying he was ill—as indeed he was. Once, at least, Ray sent Kittredge and Kinder to cover the class for him. On another occasion, Kinder said, "Bill and I even held a sort of office hour in Ray's utterly unused office, and one kid came in and told us he had yet to meet the mysterious Professor Carver all term." Before the end of the quarter, Provost Hall got wind of his professor's absenteeism and let him know the jig was up. One version holds that Maryann called Hall to tender her husband's resignation for him, while another maintains that Hall—himself an Iowa alum—advised Ray that he'd best focus on his opportunities at Iowa.[25]

The Carver-Cheever trips to the liquor store seem to be the most vivid image others have of those two together. And yet Cheever was a man who liked to talk about literature. He cultivated a quasi-aristocratic Boston accent that intensified as he drank and sometimes dropped into an unintelligible mutter peppered with words few literate people could define. Carver said he'd "never heard anyone so eloquent and witty when talking." His shyness pretty well obliterated by round-the-clock drinking, Ray, too, rose to the occasion and gained a reputation for speaking passionately about books and writers. He and Cheever had some mutual convictions about fiction, despite all the differences one could note about their stories and their social spheres. Cheever told Ray, "Fiction should throw light and air on a situation, and it shouldn't be vile. If somebody's getting a blow job in a balcony in a theater in Times Square, this may be a fact, but it's not truth."[26] Cheever believed fiction is "our most intimate and acute means of communication, at a profound level, about our deepest apprehensions and intuitions on the meaning of life and death."[27] Both writers also disdained the so-called experimental fiction of the period.

Still alive despite the dire prognosis with which he'd arrived, Cheever left Iowa in early December, days after being appointed to the American Academy of Arts and Letters. Ray's personal friendship with Cheever never resumed after this separation, but Ray had absorbed heavy real-life lessons as well as literary ones from his friend upstairs. Within the next year, Cheever was scraping the bottom of his alcoholism, unlikely to survive the damage to his brain and general health. Ray could feel himself coming to such an end, too—an impending doom alcoholics know but rarely admit. After Cheever left, Ray confided to his student Dan Domench that from Cheever he'd learned "what alcohol was really all about. Ray said that he was just starting to learn what that meant."[28]

It meant despair. Kidder got a glimpse of that when he told Cheever how much he admired his novel *The Wapshot Chronicle*. Cheever "scowled and answered, 'I don't think anything I've written is worth a shit.'" During the period of his heaviest drinking, Cheever told his daughter, Susan, "everyone who liked me thought I was dying. My reaction was, 'so what.'" As Domench observed, "With such drinking, the drive that once impelled an artist transmutes into a tyrant's mechanism to destroy oneself and family."[29] The dream world of fiction, as Cheever called it in an interview, becomes a nightmare.

The holidays in Cupertino were, Maryann wrote, "horrible." Ray announced that he was returning to Iowa for the entire spring semester—he planned no visits to California this time. Trying to gain some independence, Chris, sixteen, pumped gas at an all-girl station, bought herself a car, and moved in with Amy and her cousin Erin. Maryann objected, but Amy hoped that a change would do her niece good. That left fifteen-year-old Vance with his mother in the big house in Cupertino.[30]

Separated from her husband, Maryann was entirely miserable. A few of her teacher friends saw her as a codependent and realized they could not help her; others were simply tired of hearing about her personal troubles. Yet with a combination of natural exuberance and tremendous willpower, she kept her reputation as a good teacher. She became alarmed for herself when she suffered a couple of alcoholic blackouts. Fearful that she'd be meeting "hollow-eyed ghouls," she attended an Alcoholics Anonymous meeting for professional women and learned that alcoholism could be the "reward" that competent women received for trying to do too much. That tenuous insight was the beginning of recovery for her.[31]

Sometimes Ray spoke of Maryann's sobriety: "He'd say, 'The sobers hate the drunks and the drunks hate the sobers.' He was pondering it," Covington said, "must have been, but he never said anything about having a problem himself." For hours, he talked on the phone to Maryann, Kinder, or Kittredge. When poet Michael Waters noticed his phone cord running under a closet door, he found Ray huddled inside. There was $90 in long-distance calls to California on his bill: "I had to wait for Ray's payday, but he did pay. He knew we had less money than he did."[32]

• • •

Stanley Elkin, then working on *The Franchiser,* his novel about the "man who made America look like America," replaced Cheever on the fiction faculty. Recently diagnosed with multiple sclerosis, Elkin drank very little and tended to intimidate students with his sharp remarks. He and Ray passed like ships in the night, a missed opportunity that Ray would try to remedy in the next decade. For the present, Ray was lonely without Cheever. He moved out of the Iowa House into a suite with a shared kitchen at the Mayflower Apartments. Now he was away from downtown and the center of campus, dependent on his dilapidated convertible that lacked proper tires for snowy streets. When Ray invited three students to his apartment for dinner, he fried ground beef with Hamburger Helper and passed the skillet and the one fork around until they'd eaten every bite.[33]

Maryann began drinking again when she spent a long February weekend with Ray in Iowa. They had dinner at the Covingtons' one night and went to a big, wild party the next. Like Ray, she took to the students with backgrounds similar to their own: Covington, from Alabama, and Domench, from Stockton, California. At the big party, Covington recalled, "Maryann and I, both drunk, were kissing in the kitchen when Ray came in, gestured to show there must be some mix-up, and said, " 'Hey, what's going on here?' He was so playful and funny that he didn't seem like he was jealous or could ever become physically abusive." Covington came by Ray's apartment the next morning and found Maryann rummaging through Ray's underwear drawer. " 'I'm looking to see if Ray's been writing any stories with me in them,' she said. She wasn't surprised to see me walk in," said Covington, "and she just turned and told me what she was doing." To Covington that made perfect sense at the time because their lives were "so disordered and so open."[34]

That same weekend, Maryann discovered "firsthand" that Ray was involved with a woman in Iowa. This time the other woman wasn't a divorcée on the rebound or a dazzled young student, but a married writer with children.[35] Ray's new affair seemed of a piece with a "mythic status" her husband had assumed in Iowa. He was surrounded by students and "everything bizarre he did now became legendary. Ever more flagrant, he somehow still managed to pull things off." Maryann did not see Ray again that semester. She began attending AA meetings in earnest. Ray wrote her love letters promising that things would be different—better—when he returned. He might have believed his promises. She could not.[36]

Curt Johnson was appalled by his award-winning writer's condition when he came to visit him in Iowa. Ray was burrowed into his chair, chainsmoking and telling his elliptical anecdotes in a throaty, mumbling voice.

Every so often, an ash fell and burned his shirt or he got up and made himself another drink. He didn't stumble or slur his speech, but mentally he was "floating and incapacitated." Johnson got angry at some guys who were "ragging" Ray and declared that they didn't know what they were talking about because Ray was one of the great American writers.[37]

Again in the spring semester, Ray taught a workshop and a reading course. One student's workshop notes preserved this homily that sums up what Ray had learned about the writing life since his own unhappy year as a workshop student: "Some people come here and write. Others come and never write, but they go on to teach. This is just a microcosm. You think it's tough? Wait, this is nothing."[38] In his reading course, Ray never delivered a lecture or provided background material. He read to the class or simply assigned a cluster of stories and expected the students to analyze them from a writer's perspective: How does the story work? What can I learn from the story? Once Ray asked the class if they'd read the stories. When they indicated they had, he said he hadn't and read his own "Summer Steelhead" to them instead. By then his classroom demeanor was so poor that one student asked Ray on behalf of the class, "What exactly are we supposed to be learning from this class?"[39]

Dan Domench spent a lot of time with Ray that spring. "Ray's love of writing was the appeal for me," said Domench, who was in his twenties at the time. "I was obsessed with the writing and I hoped it would save me." Domench, one of the few people around who matched Ray's capacity for alcohol, "could go all night drinking with him, right into dawn. He liked that." Ray would call Domench, who lived in a trailer near the Mayflower, at any hour to see if he had anything to drink. "I would walk over at three a.m. in the weird blue predawn light and we would drink." At that hour, they didn't talk much. But they became familiar with each other's menu of liquor-fueled tricks, scams, and betrayals.

Half-Spanish-Basque and half-Irish, Domench thought his two ancestries bequeathed him both the "slow, simmering" and the "hell-bent" varieties of alcoholism, suiting him to become one of a circle of people who loved and protected Ray. Doing that, he witnessed and participated in and enabled actions that, he said, it still hurts to think about. Ray shared his Running Dog nickname with Domench:

> He called me the dog of dogs. The worst he'd ever seen. And then he would laugh. It was true. I was heartless in some areas, heartbroken in others. We were using people, lying, stealing, and sleeping around. Ray was a trickster, but his tricks could be very dark and funny and hurtful. We knew what we were doing. We did it anyway and talked about it.

Perhaps the times and the place—a certain demoralization and burnout that accompanied the war in Vietnam and the Watergate scandal—plus Iowa City's conceit about its own distinction and creativity—encouraged people to tolerate odious behavior. Ray's infectious, deep, rolling belly laugh drew people to him. In turn, Ray loved people who could make him laugh. People took care of them. Domench couldn't imagine a teacher today getting away with what Ray did. Ray could be forgiving too. When others disparaged a workshop administrator for dancing with self-abandon at a party, Ray turned to a student and said, "in a sweet, generous, natural way, 'She's just a beauty.' "[40]

But Domench saw "something western and violent about Ray's descent into the late stages." In Ray's face he saw and recognized rage: "Not anger. Not frustration. Rage. At the core of Ray, there was a rage beyond reckoning. His father and mother put it there and society confirmed it." Domench decided that Babel, the author Carver talked about so much then, offered a key to Ray Carver's fiction: "Ray took the techniques of the *Red Cavalry* stories, the exacting descriptions and the blunt endings, and he pointed them at the working poor and working-class suburbia. He was a war correspondent."

With Domench, Ray dropped his usual mild-mannered generosity about other writers: "When he talked about writing, he was passionate and opinionated." When he did not like someone's writing, he didn't like the person and seemed almost bitter about it. Plausibly, doubts about his *Esquire* publications provoked Ray's sour grapes about literary achievement. How many others, he must have wondered, owed something to unacknowledged help? Was he, like the character in his little fable "The Father," a man who had no expression of his own? Could he, enslaved to alcohol, estranged from his family, and beholden to Lish, still be an artist—the only thing he'd ever wanted to be? Such doubts sabotaged Carver's middle years. One day, though, Domench would understand that their common rage made Ray a necessary teacher for him: "He taught me passion and anger and focus and—Ray's words now—'to outlive the bastards.' He never quit. He had that. That rage transformed into art."[41]

As spring breached Iowa, Ray declared in a letter to Lish that he was in love, elaborating that he had a regular sex life, was eating salads, and had written a dozen poems.[42] The object of his affection was still the married student. She was a talented writer whose husband's career often took him on the road. An admirer of Ray's work and part of his circle of caretakers, she gave Ray the love and concern that had been essential to him all his life. Perhaps she helped him to forestall a total alcoholic collapse that semester.

Still, salads and affection and poetry couldn't reverse Ray's physical and mental dissolution. He looked ten years older than his age, had a wary expression until he'd drunk enough alcohol to bring him relief and laughter. Both his face and his body were bloated. When he wore the hip-hugger jeans and wide leather belts in style in the early seventies, his belly protruded above the belt. His hair was scruffy, his face sprouted sideburns. Continuous inebriation erased the timidity that used to make him look smaller than he really was. Now his big and lumbering presence could and did intimidate people: "I would brace myself whenever Ray walked toward me at a clip," Domench said. One warm, false-spring Iowa night, as Ray drove past Joe's Place, a drunken bartender threw a beer bottle through the ragtop of his Falcon. Domench, then a bartender at Joe's, watched as "Ray got out of his car. He was ready. But that stuff was happening all around us. It's the karma of the drunk."

On the strength of editors who anthologized his stories, Carver's literary career drifted forward while he sank. *The Secret Life of Our Times: New Fiction from Esquire* showcased short stories that Lish had published in his three years at the magazine.[43] The thick, expensive ($12.95) book carried an introduction by Tom Wolfe, who wrote that Lish has "come to New York to turn his bizarre energies loose on this whining, wornout city." Wolfe called Lish's selections literary exercises in a nihilistic style written by people who themselves are unfamiliar with despair. The anthology contains no information about the story writers. It has, however, a crowing autobiographical foreword by Lish. Included are thirty-five stories by both very famous and utterly unknown authors. Carver's two pieces, "Neighbors" and "What Is It?" seem, at least in retrospect, to disprove Wolfe's glib formulation. The basis of Carver's stories in real despair often shows. It is one source of their power.

Both Ellen Levine and Gordon Lish came to Iowa City in the spring. She spoke to Ray's classes and found him "more than ever chain-smoking and jittery" but felt, nonetheless, that "there was warmth between us. We were friends." That was, Levine reflected, "the golden day of publishing: there were ideas in the air and feminism and consciousness-raising were making women think in fresh ways. It was before the conglomerates; there were many opportunities for new writers."[44] But Carver was scarcely a new writer. It had been two years since his last appearance in *Esquire*. Commercially, he had stalled out.

"Captain Fiction," famous for being "suave and well dressed and coifed and so New-York-City" showed up unshaven in a "lumberjack shirt." Still, Lish's reputation and performance were such that "nervous students whose stories were being cavalierly dissected wound up laughing at his jokes about their work" and loathing themselves for it later. Lish talked about himself for an hour before turning to the student manuscripts. Finally he picked up a story, declared it "shit," and went on at length about why he thought so.[45]

Lish admitted that he hadn't finished all the stories and closed by asking Gurganus if he could have his story for *Esquire*. Gurganus balked. He told Lish he had promised to show his story to other editors but that, "if they didn't want it, I would send it right to him. This got a great laugh."[46] When Lish praised an excerpt from Covington's novel-in-progress, Ray urged him to schmooze with Lish, but Covington was disturbed by Lish's rudeness and avoided him.[47]

Ray did not write to Lish again until fall. He had no new fiction to send him, nothing else to say to him.

With the help of his imprudent angels, Ray had survived his return to Iowa. In May Jackson paid Ray $50 for the Ford Falcon and drove it back to Montana. The Falcon's California plates were expired, and Ray was unable to provide a title document; in Missoula, a sheriff warned Jackson to abandon the car because it appeared to be stolen.

Ray rode with Domench to California. They drove a '65 Chevy Malibu convertible that belonged to a woman Domench was seeing. The Covingtons saw them off with a breakfast of grits and eggs. About ten o'clock, Ray and Domench drove away, waving good-bye and reaching for their bottles: "We both started laughing. We were so relieved to be driving away from that normal breakfast table with everyone being so nice to us. Besides, we were already hungover and needed to cut the headache. It was medicine." By now, Ray and Domench had developed some give-and-take in their friendship: "He tried to run the tab on Little America, the truck stop in Wyoming, and was disappointed in me when I paid it. People ran tabs on me when I was bartending. I didn't think it was funny." After that, they discussed it, or Domench paid. On the long drive, they drank, and they shrugged and winced their way through conversations about how to drink better—how to "last." Almost clinically, they talked about strategies and foods that allowed their bodies to take in what they needed to reach their high. From these muttered exchanges, Domench later recognized that he and Ray had both been alcoholics from the first time they took a drink.

Alcohol was barely working for Ray in his thirty-fifth summer. His heart was "empty and sere," his poem "Where Water Comes Together with Other Water" tells us. But he could make the trip, even drive if he had to. Cheever, with his hands that never stopped shaking and his need to drink even after he'd been told by doctors that it would kill him, had shown Ray where this addiction led. Growing up in Yakima, Ray had known older alcoholics, but it unnerved him to see an artist he greatly admired trapped in that endgame. He and Domench talked about what happened when men got to the end of their drinking. It was a way of edging around the question of what would happen to themselves, Domench thought: "We drove across the West drinking day and night and talking about other drunks, drunks worse than us. Malcolm Lowry and Frederick Exley. Bad drunks. Then there were times of terrible silence. I think we each knew we couldn't drink like this much longer. But how to slow down? How is that done? And if you do, then what happens?"

Soon—but when?—alcohol would no longer offer the relief of fantasy or peace or surrender. As alcoholism progresses, pain and fear and guilt grow stronger. When the booze no longer relieves any of the pain, Domench continued, "Death becomes a choice. Dying looks pretty good. You can't imagine a life with your addiction anymore, and you can't imagine a life without it. At this point, it is always the same: the miracle either happens or it doesn't. You get clean or you die."

From the conversations they had during that two-thousand-mile ride, Domench was absolutely convinced that "Ray *was* a moral man. He *craved* dignity." The hours of serious talk and tacit understanding that he and Ray shared on Interstate 80 were accompanied by some hilarious episodes and many bottles of hard liquor. Their talk was interrupted by the forays to find liquor stores. Ray could feel his way through a town, "giving directions like a medium and then, invariably, finding the store right where he'd said it would be." Then there'd be a delay in getting back on the road because Ray made Domench stop at any motel where he could nab free ice out of an outdoor machine.

One morning they got on the road late with only a half pint of liquor between them. They were in a desolate river town in a "dry" county—no liquor stores at all. Finally, they saw

a shack, beer signs in the window, not enough room in it for a pool table, near the road. It wasn't going to open any time soon. Ray got out and walked behind the tavern to a wooden house with a raised porch. He knocked, got let inside, and returned with a bottle of liquor cradled in his arm. An old woman watched from the doorway. She looked at me with pity, turned and went inside. Ray was elated. He said, "Drive, go." I asked how he got the bottle and got only a smile and a shrug. That meant, discussion is over. Ray had an amazing ability to get booze when he needed it.

Late at night, they'd argue about who would get out under the buzzing neon lights of a motel office to sign the register. Ray was sure that somehow they were being tracked by the police. Mornings were no easier. The first drink of the day, however badly needed, would roil the stomach. Like most late-stage alcoholics, Ray spent a long time in the bathroom every morning trying to get ready to face the day. There were lighter moments too. If Ray felt good, he'd start conversations with strangers, a motel maid for instance, "and then find himself tangled up, muttering, half-drunk, laughing, just fumbling around and getting everyone to laugh around him . . . everyone loved it when he was feeling good and being funny like that. It wasn't about quips or fast talk. Something would strike him funny as he was talking to someone, and it would roll on a little."

As they headed up the eastern slope of the Sierra Nevada, Ray said aloud, "Something bad is waiting for me." On the other side, at the Domench home in Stockton, Ray delayed, eating dinner with Domench's parents and talking in the backyard about a big sprawling novel set in Africa that he wanted to write. Ray so charmed Domench's mother that she sent him off with a bouquet of her pink roses for Maryann.

Ray's Cupertino household had changed in the previous four months. His daughter didn't live there anymore. His fifteen-year-old son seemed like a stranger. His wife was sober. Many of his Stanford friends were gone, but Kittredge, just finishing his year as a Stegner fellow, came to see Ray and Maryann. These three were *old* friends in a floating world of itinerant teachers and writers. When Maryann's school year ended, so did her resolve to stay sober: ". . . before long, Bill, Ray, and I were all on the same wavelength—drunk," she wrote later.[48]

In Cupertino, Ray faced a lonely, demoralized summer. He exchanged letters with his lover from Iowa, receiving his billets-doux at George Lynn's address. Only his family understood the gravity of his alcohol problem. Only his family and a few others saw the worst of it. Others found something romantic about the idea of a writer risking everything. As Kittredge put it, "Ray was our designated Dylan Thomas, I think—our contact with the courage to face all possible darkness and survive. We thought he was walking on water there for a while."[49] But Ray was drowning. Booze was defeating him. One night that summer, Domench saw him carrying a *gallon* bottle of vodka propped in his right arm. It was the shape of a regular fifth and yet huge, as if made to serve his large body and a larger addiction. That night, Ray had trouble walking.

When Kittredge returned to Missoula, he took with him a three-car caravan of friends including Kinder, Crawford, and Michael Rogers. A reshuffling of the cast soon followed. Kittredge began living with fiction writer Sara Vogan. Crawford took up with Diane Smith (Ray's former student at Santa Cruz). And—in the switch that most affected Ray—Chuck Kinder and Diane Cecily met, fell in love, and began living together.[50]

Corruption and violence pervaded the live broadcast of current events that new technology enabled in 1974. The world was more with us, late and soon, than ever before. In February a paramilitary group called the Symbionese Liberation Army (SLA) kidnapped newspaper heiress Patricia Hearst from her Berkeley apartment. In May the Los Angeles police killed six members of the SLA in a shoot-out but failed to find Hearst, who had changed her name to Tania. A sixteen-month hunt began for Tania/Hearst, who now seemed cooperative with her captors. By late July, Nixon's guilt in the Watergate scandal was confirmed by tapes he'd recorded in the Oval Office. On August 9, with impeachment and conviction considered inevitable, Nixon resigned. When Gerald Ford became president the same day, he declared, "Our long national nightmare is over." In fact, it was only shifting to another stage.

For a long time, Maryann had seen her husband's drinking and infidelity as part of his embrace of the identity of a "wild writer," but her attitude was changing. When Domench came into the Cupertino house with a bottle of Cutty Sark, he noticed that Maryann was sober and resented his arrival. Another time, Maryann got Ray and Domench to attend an AA meeting with her. They kept chatting with each other and were told to leave if they couldn't keep quiet. They waited outside, smoking and drinking, until Maryann came out of the meeting.[51]

The Carver children's role in their father's life changed, too. Ray, long torn between the demands of his art and the responsibilities of parenthood, now cast his children as villains in the drama of his alcoholism. They complied. "Because of everything I'd seen," Chris remembered, "I didn't accept him as an authority figure anymore. He'd order me around, and I just wouldn't take it. There were some horrible scenes when he was drunk, and he'd batter me up." Lack of self-esteem, her brother Vance thought, caused Chris to look elsewhere for the reassurance she didn't receive at home. "I always felt I could not compete with my immensely talented parents," she said of herself. "They were extremely social, hanging out with their friends for days on end."

Common sense would seem to dictate that all-weekend bashes were a dangerous example for teenagers, but at the time, it seemed to Chris that the worst times came between parties: "[Then] my dad found it hard to cope, and so he drank daily. It was very destructive to his writing and ability to teach. The whole family would get into horrible fights. We'd sit down at the dinner table, and my dad would be drunk and he'd start egging my brother on. He'd have my brother in tears." If Maryann defended Vance, Ray might turn on her too. Overall, Vance believed, his sister's behavior tended to be more overt and absorbing of their parents' interest. Thus he was left free to drift on marijuana or let his schoolwork slide.[52]

There was never enough money to pay the household bills, buy liquor and marijuana, and provide the things that teenagers living in an affluent suburb wanted. The family argued over food, drink, cigarettes, and dope. Ray tried to hide his supplies, and sometimes the kids found his stashes. Food purchased for parties disappeared before the guests arrived. Credit cards were maxed out or used fraudulently, and few businesses would take checks from the Carvers. Now genuinely unemployed, Ray again drew unemployment benefits. In 1970 he'd used that windfall to give himself a year of full-time writing. Now it would take more than an unemployment check to balance the Carver family budget. Only seven years after they'd filed for bankruptcy in Sacramento, Ray was looking to that solution again.

It seems to have been during that difficult summer that Ray saw a newspaper report about some men who'd found a woman's body in a river: "It said that the discovery was made on Friday and the report was made on Monday, and it struck me that this was very odd. It was at least two days." Though he'd been writing next to nothing, Ray felt he needed "to find out how best to tell that story of the fishermen" and "plunged in and just started." The story "went every which way" and grew to sixty or eighty pages. "Maybe it wanted to be something else. I just launched into it. I had no idea where I was going."[53] In Carver's version, four friends pack into a remote part of the Cascade Mountains for their cherished annual fishing trip, only to discover the body of a woman floating in their favorite trout pool. The moral and emotional consequences of the men's decision not to report the body immediately unwind in one of Carver's darker and more complex stories.

Knowing that Ray felt like a dead man himself in those days, one understands the deep sympathy his story extends to the dead woman, the one beyond help.

CHAPTER 19

Will You Please Be Quiet, Please?

September 1974–December 1975,

Santa Barbara and Cupertino, California

And now comes John Barleycorn with the curse he lays upon the imaginative man who is lusty with life and desire to live. John Barleycorn sends his White Logic, the argent messenger of truth beyond truth, the antithesis of life, cruel and bleak as interstellar space, pulseless and frozen as absolute zero, dazzling with the frost of irrefragable logic and unforgettable fact. John Barleycorn will not let the dreamer dream, the liver live . . . And the feet of the victim of such dreadful intimacy take hold of the way of death.

—Jack London, *John Barleycorn: Alcoholic Memoirs*[1]

If you want to know the truth," Carver said when he'd published six books and become a celebrated author, "I'm prouder . . . that I've quit drinking than I am of anything in my life." Such a thing did not happen overnight. It took Ray Carver almost another three years to quit drinking. That would be one way to look at it. Another way would be that it took him thirty years, from the first time he drank as a boy until the last day he drank. But if one wants to specify when Ray and Maryann "hit bottom," when the worst losses and humiliations occurred, the fall of 1974 and following year fit the bill.

Another university, another city, another rented house, a shrinking circle of drinking buddies and acolytes—such were the circumstances of the collapse of all hopes and decencies that Carver describes in a poem called "Next Year." Ray got a job at the University of California campus near Santa Barbara without an interview. Almost as soon as he arrived, his dramatic burnout began.[2]

Though Ray hinted to a couple of friends that he viewed the three-hundred-mile southward removal as a separation from Maryann, she took a leave of absence from Los Altos High School and rented out the family's house on Cupertino Road. Chris and Vance had little choice but to come along. As a visiting writer at UCSB's campus on a bluff by the Pacific, Ray was to teach a couple of creative writing courses and advise the editors of the established student magazine, *Spectrum.* His position at the university was adjunct and temporary, but not without perks. The department held a welcoming party, and Maryann was admitted to a selective doctoral program in English.[3]

At that party, Maryann was reportedly quite flirtatious with a couple of the young professors. But Ray was no saint. Another professor's wife had "a fascinating discussion" with Ray, who seemed "a wonderful man, like a bear," until he startled her by making a pass at her. Maryann called that woman afterward to apologize for Ray's behavior. A writer who admired Ray's work and invited him to his house found that "it was really difficult even to look at him; the booze and the cigarettes were so much there that they seemed like another person with us in the room."[4]

The Carvers leased a house in a subdivision of Goleta near the airport.[5] This house in many ways resembled their own in Cupertino, but Ray never got comfortable in Santa Barbara. The English Department was unsociable, beaches and sunshine dictated the manner of living, and there were few serious whiskey drinkers. One of that few was Capra Press editor Noel Young, who was the hub of a downtown literary scene that poet Lin Rolens thought was "alive with possibility and excess." John Martin operated Black Sparrow Press there, and Lawrence Durrell and Henry Miller came through town, as did Kenneth Rexroth and Gary Snyder. Ray became a regular at the corner table in the Jacques European-Style Family Restaurant on lower State Street, where Young held court and Rolens was often their waitress: "It was a huge scene. These meals that went on for hours . . . they talked about literature and women. They did what they damned well pleased. Horrendous drinking. If you could make it home, it was okay."[6]

Young was talking about publishing a book of Carver's poems to be called *At Night the Salmon Move,* which he and Ray used as an additional excuse to keep drinking throughout the afternoon. On one so-called editorial afternoon as the first day of classes neared, Young sensed that the author grappled with "some invisible torment." Ray recommended that Young read and reprint London's *John Barleycorn* because it " 'deals with *invisible* forces.' " The book that had seized Ray's attention several years earlier combines London's own drinking history with a treatise on alcoholism and a discussion of alcohol-induced depression. London divides drunks into "stupid" men who drink themselves into unconsciousness and "imaginative" ones who receive from John Barleycorn "the pitiless, spectral syllogisms of the white logic." Such a man—superior in his capacities, but unfortunate in his drinking,

> sees through all illusions . . . transvalues all values. God is bad, truth is a cheat, and life is a joke. From his calm-mad heights, with the certitude of a god, he beholds all life as evil. Wife, children, friends—in the clear white light of his logic they are exposed as frauds and shams . . . he sees their frailty, their meagerness, their sordidness, their pitifulness . . . And he knows his one freedom: he may anticipate the day of his death . . . suicide, quick or slow, a sudden spill or a gradual oozing away through the years, is the price John Barleycorn exacts.[7]

After telling Young about London's "great book," Ray left his editor at the table and walked out the back door of the restaurant. Early the next morning, Young got a call from the county jail, where he found Ray dozing behind bars on a cement floor. Young bailed him out and drove him home.[8]

Ray appeared in court on charges of driving while intoxicated and paid a fine of $100. Both Carvers were so out of control that the Youngs avoided inviting them for hot-tubbing and other hippie-era pleasures at their house on Mountain Drive. But Ray showed up without invitation at novelist Thomas Sanchez's Casa Coyote, banged down a bottle of Wild Turkey, and said, "Now we are going to tell each other our life stories." Sanchez replied that that was a college-boy notion, and they were men who told their stories through their work. Next, Ray praised Sanchez's *Rabbit Boss* as the great epic of their generation, but added that he would have written it differently. Unabashed, the author of the four-hundred-plus-page novel told Ray that he could not have written it at all: "You are a sprinter, I am a long-distance runner," Sanchez recollected saying.[9]

Every other week, Ray flew or drove north, stayed overnight at his mother's in Mountain View, and picked up an unemployment check in Santa Clara County, assuming that the state unemployment agency would not know he had a job in Santa Barbara. While there in mid-September, he wrote Lish that his "center" was not holding, admitting that he'd been in jail twice during the first two weeks in Santa Barbara. When both Ray and Maryann were arrested, sixteen-year-old Chris was called to fetch her delinquent parents out of jail. "My mom's drinking wasn't as severe as my dad's, but it was severe," Chris remembered. "You know, you can't really say—it took different forms. His was more physical than hers. A woman's alcoholism tends to be more psychological, because there are tasks at home that she still manages to do no matter what."[10]

One night Maryann and Ray came home to find a note from Chris: she had left for the Bay Area in her Corvair and begged them not to come after her. When her car broke down in King City, a sheriff took her to juvenile hall. When her parents came after her, she persuaded them to let her live with her grandmother in Mountain View. For Vance, too, the move to Goleta proved pivotal. Away from his pothead friends, enrolled in a strange school as he turned sixteen, he plotted to become independent of his family.[11]

By now Ray understood—from being with Cheever, from hearing about AA, from spending a night in jail, and from reading *John Barleycorn*—that "suicide, quick or slow" was the price exacted by addiction to alcohol. He tried to manage his drinking and sometimes succeeded for a few hours. Often enough, he made it to his afternoon fiction writing class. His student Marc Louria, who was also editor of *Spectrum,* "had no idea that Raymond was an alcoholic. There were no outward manifestations of it. He came to class on time—he was disheveled and soft-spoken, but I saw no impairment at all." Ray must have kept the occasional date with his typewriter, too. When Louria came to Ray's house one morning with manuscripts for his issue of *Spectrum,* he asked if Ray might offer him a story. Ray handed him a bunch of pages and said, casually, "I just finished this thing." The story was "So Much Water So Close to Home."[12]

Carver would say in 1984 that he'd almost thrown the story away when he first drafted it and had never been satisfied with it. But he ushered the young editor to his own desk to read it. Already spellbound by the sight of a letter on *Esquire* stationery that lay on his teacher's desk, Louria had a "chilling, overpowering reading experience":

> I was thinking: my God, he's giving me this story to publish. But the penultimate line in his original story was, "For God's sake, Stuart, she was only a child." And the last line was, "Somewhere I heard someone scream. How long could this go on?" I knew he had written a poem with that same kind of ending.
>
> I told Raymond, "This is an incredible story. But you know what? I think you should take out the last line."
>
> He looked at me, and looked at the story and said, "You know, I think you're absolutely right." So he took out a red pencil, and he crossed it out.[13]

Thus one of Carver's most discussed stories appeared in a college magazine.[14] In his biographical note, Louria listed Carver's accomplishments and added, "This editor, for one, regrets that Mr. Carver's yellow Datsun will no longer be seen around these parts." Indeed, the Carvers left UCSB at the end of the fall quarter, before *Spectrum* came off the press.

When Bill Henderson wrote *Spectrum* to ask for nominations for his first *Pushcart Prize: Best of the Small Presses,* Louria nominated Carver's story. Carver later published other versions of "So Much Water . . . ," but eventually restored the version that had appeared in *Spectrum.* It has provided the basis for screenplays of two films, *Short Cuts* and *Jindabyne.*

In the 1970s, mainstream publishers began to reflect the changes that had washed across the American landscape in the 1960s. The business got bigger and faster—more books were published and fewer stayed in print. Shopping mall book emporiums began to replace traditional bookshops and force publishers toward larger wholesale discounts. To stay in play, publishers increased advertising budgets for a selected few books on their lists. They also sought new authors—the young, women, Asians, blacks—and new formats that suited busy people. Novels composed of story-length vignettes, fiction broken into text blocks with generous white space, books with movie tie-ins, and books about popular culture gained popularity. As writers who had attended MFA programs in the 1960s became college teachers, they passed their interest in literary short stories along to their students. This is the wave that Gordon Lish was riding when he turned himself into Captain Fiction. It was only a matter of time until book publishers discovered that short story collections could be marketed for a profit.

Lish called Carver with big news on November 11. Frederic W. Hills, editor in chief at the McGraw-Hill Company, had offered him an imprint to publish books of fiction for McGraw-Hill. Lish, who continued as fiction editor at *Esquire,* had proposed several writers he admired. Hills had selected Carver to be first in the series.

Ray responded to Lish by letter, declaring that he intended to "set the globe afire" now. Twice before in his life, he'd received this kind of exciting news: when the Foley collection chose "Will You Please Be Quiet, Please?" in 1967 and when *Esquire* took "Neighbors" in 1971. They planned to call the book *Put Yourself in My Shoes.* What now appears inevitable then seemed a miracle. Never had Carver expected that the man he'd met first in Palo Alto in 1968 would be the editor of his first book. Even when Lish accepted and revised two of Carver's stories for *Esquire* (and edited "Fat" before it went to *Harper's Bazaar*), Carver could not have predicted that Lish would determine the form his stories would take between hard covers. Ray and Lish agreed that some editing would be necessary, and Ray promised he'd "go after it" or wait to hear what Lish wanted done—"whatever, or both." What Carver wanted most from the book was recognition of his talent. And, he said, he wouldn't mind modest sales and a National Book Award nomination.[15]

The miracle came about because Lish had worked tirelessly to cultivate relationships with book editors who could offer him excerpts of forthcoming novels. Hills was one of these men. A strategic shift at McGraw-Hill also prepared the terrain for a Carver collection. In the midst of a recession that brought the city of New York to the brink of bankruptcy, McGraw-Hill, under Hills's guidance, chose not to join the jostle of publishers who laid down huge amounts of money to generate best sellers (as, for instance, Simon & Schuster had done with Judith Rossner's third novel, *Looking for Mr. Goodbar*) and to concentrate on a selective list of literary fiction writers they could afford. They published Heinrich Böll, Vladimir Nabokov, and Elizabeth Spencer, as well as Canadians Carol Shields and Alice Munro. Carver fit the McGraw-Hill list.[16]

In *What It Used to Be Like*, Maryann alleges that Lish telephoned *her* in Santa Barbara and urged her to free Ray "from the exigencies of his life" so he could fulfill his promise as an artist.[*] Maryann had no intention of doing that when their prospects were finally improving. Instead she and Ray made financial plans to protect whatever money Ray might earn on the book. Their debts had piled up again, even though their combined income in 1974, bolstered by Ray's Iowa and UCSB salaries, had been their highest ever: $23,000. Declaring bankruptcy would give them a clean slate, but in order to hang on to their house in Cupertino, they would have to reside there during the bankruptcy process. That's one reason Ray bolted from his position at UCSB in December; Maryann dropped out of the PhD program, went back to AA and cut back on her drinking, and asked their Cupertino renters to move out before Christmas.[17] In the new year, Ray would keep collecting unemployment benefits and devote himself to preparing a manuscript. She would find some kind of job to tide them over until she returned to Los Altos High in the fall.

Full of his astounding news, Ray flew off on a "reading tour" to Missoula, Iowa City, and Birmingham, Alabama. Lois Welch, then department chair in Montana, sent out publicity and arranged a reception, but Ray didn't arrive until the reading date had passed. Diane Smith picked Ray up at the airport. After squeezing into her Volkswagen, he made a rare first move. "Would it be presumptuous of me to say, should we go get a motel?" Ray mumbled. Smith said it would be. Ray heard her verdict with a squeak, and giggled, "Okay." That was the only time in many meetings that her former teacher ever made a pass at her, Smith said. "Probably we got a drink instead."[18] In Iowa City it was Dan Domench who acted as Ray's

---

[*] Some thirty years later, Lish had no recollection of such a call, but believed that Ray might have "put him up to such a thing."

impresario. A couple hundred people showed up for a disastrous reading. Ray was ill with a sore throat and laryngitis, and Amy had "bucked him up" with hot toddies to get him to the reading—late. Still, he was barely heard. Domench slid down in his seat when Ray dedicated a poem to him. For others, like student Anthony Bukoski, Ray's charm abided. His red face glowed above a colorful cowboy shirt and blue jeans. "He read about twenty minutes, sometimes incoherently. I naïvely thought his showing up like that was artistic and rebellious. . . . [then] Jack Leggett came on stage to ask Ray Carver to quit early, suggesting that Carver could continue another time when he was sober."[19] As Amy hustled Ray out of the auditorium, she remembered to ask program coordinator Hope Landris for "the envelope, please." Ray was desperate for money, and Amy feared that Landris would deny payment for the botched appearance. Ray didn't make it to Alabama.

Back in Santa Barbara, he and Maryann gathered the paperwork for declaring bankruptcy in the U.S. District Court for the Central District of California. That humiliation wouldn't be necessary, Maryann insisted, if Ray would quit "pissing away his earnings" on alcohol. Bankruptcy forms in hand, Vance, Maryann, and Ray retreated to Cupertino for Christmas. In New York, Levine and Hills were working on Carver's book contract, but at the moment there was no money. The last check from UCSB was spent, the unemployment checks were minuscule, the liquor bills were astronomical—$1,200 a month, Ray once bragged disconsolately to George Lynn. Mortgage and tax payments were due. Maryann was on an unpaid leave from the high school, the national economy was dragging. "Ray's drinking," Maryann wrote, "had progressed so dramatically that he couldn't eat." He said he drank wine for the bioflavonoids. His tolerance had reversed, too, because his liver function was compromised. He appeared as drunk as he was.[20]

Two sets of renters had trashed the blue house on Cupertino Road, but Maryann called the extended family together to celebrate.[21] She needed the hullabaloo of a family gathering to restore herself, but Ray, as the many complaints about the holidays in his letters attest, did not relish them as she did. Especially if the liquor-induced White Logic was upon him, he would have seen the relatives as enemies and resented the constant talking, arguing, and milling around. In 1986 Carver published a poem about those Cupertino holidays called "From the East, Light." There's a father hungover and snoring on the couch, a tree knocked over on the rug, and a giftwrapped package containing the mother's suggestion to the father: a rope to hang himself with. That poem, narrated from the perspective of hapless, disappointed children, proves at least that Carver recognized the distress around him.

After Christmas, Maryann turned to the business that had staved off financial collapse for the Carver family time and again. Six nights a week she served cocktails at the Blue Pheasant, a seafood and steak restaurant near a Cupertino golf course. Her tips provided the family's cash flow. They met their mortgage payments, but other collectors were relentless. Maryann surrendered her yellow Datsun to her credit union only to be told that they still owed $900 on it because "excess mileage" and $300 to $400 in needed repairs had lowered its value. After that blow, they proceeded with the bankruptcy plans they'd laid in Santa Barbara. At Mabie Theater in Iowa City, Amy played "a magnificent Lady Macbeth." On the last night of performances, she went into character for the mad scene and failed to return. She was hospitalized and diagnosed with bipolar personality disorder. In the midst of it all, Maryann worked at sobriety, she reports, and Ray became "the neighborhood drunk."[22]

Ray admitted he was a drunk now. He met 1975 with ambition to change his life. He tried to cut back. For the next two years, he would straddle two diverging tracks, one leading toward the bottom of his alcoholism, the other toward recovery and literary success. In January he caught up on correspondence with a crisp note of thanks to Jarvis Thurston for publishing the story he'd been holding for five years; it had "been awhile" since he'd seen the story, Ray quipped. To others he announced his forthcoming book and sought invitations to read. He was "off the sauce" and limiting himself to white wine in the evening, he told Lish on January 24. In February he received McGraw-Hill's $1,500 advance for a book of stories.[23]

Jack Hicks, a professor at UC Davis, invited both Ray and Max Crawford (whose novel *Waltz Across Texas* was just out) to visit his California literature class. When the writers requested a drink before class, they went to 7-Eleven and bought twelve tall Budweisers. As they sat in a field at the edge of campus near the freeway drinking their breakfast, they watched six or eight black-and-white police cars line up. Ray became "totally paranoid" and read for Hicks's class "lickety-split, so terrified that sweat was dripping off his face onto his pages." As it turned out, the police were preparing to raid a house where they believed Patricia Hearst and her SLA captors to be hiding. (Hearst was arrested finally on September 18, 1975, in San Francisco.) Crawford thought it was the reading itself that really terrified Ray: "I had to haul him in there. These things were very difficult for him, things that are easy for other people." The afternoon and evening "fell into advanced disrepair" for all three men. Ray left the Nut Tree Restaurant on Interstate 80 with a sizable pepper grinder under his jacket—a gift for Maryann, a generous thought precariously executed.[24]

In the distant background, the war in Vietnam was in its last days. In April President Ford would order the evacuation of all remaining Americans. Twenty-one years after the French were defeated at Dien Bien Phu and fourteen years after the American military began its involvement in the tiny Southeast Asian country, the war was over.

In March, Lish bought "Collectors" for the August issue of *Esquire*. One of Carver's quirkiest tales, "Collectors" epitomizes the death-in-life strangeness that Carver endured at the end of his drinking. The story develops a situation that was very real to Ray: a man who cannot acknowledge his identity because he's hiding from bill collectors. Yet with absurd hope, the first-person narrator (Slater, evidently) answers his doorbell. A salesman named Aubrey Bell talks about itinerant poets—Auden and Rilke—while setting about to vacuum the carpet, the mattress, even the bed pillow. Bell's allusions give him a certain fallen grandeur that makes him a voice for an abandoned artistic aspect of Slater's character. As he vacuums, the obsessive, intrusive Bell explains, "Every day, every night of our lives, we're leaving little bits of ourselves, flakes of this and that, behind." When a letter comes in through the mail slot, Bell sticks it in his own pocket: "It's for a Mr. Slater, he said. I'll see to it."

Alas, there can be no Mr. Slater. He's a dead man, dead to himself, scooped up by the vacuum cleaner. The story carries a spooky sense that this showdown matters. The narrator has been cleaned out and will have to start over now. The story enacts a spiritual crisis, making consequential symbols of mundane details. One may look to this nine-page story for evidence that Carver understood himself to be finished. No longer was he the writer and man named Raymond Carver: he was a nameless bankrupt and drunk whose wife had little use for him, ready for the dustbin of history. He may have joked about all this to friends, but "Collectors" and a poem called "Miracle" convey the pain he felt over his inepcunity, his second bankruptcy in seven years, his years of "failure and corruption."

For their bankruptcy case, Maryann and Ray filed a list of their debts. The Carvers' creditors included UCSB ($1,744 in alleged overpayment of wages to Ray, $250 for Maryann's registration fees [disputed], and an open account at the faculty club), the University of Iowa Credit Union (a $1,100 loan), Stanford University (for Maryann's tuition), the California Teachers Association ($2,000 loan) and American Federation of Teachers ($650 loan), and a miscellany of providers of services ranging from Shell Oil ($800) to Joseph Magnin's ($500) and Mervyns ($638) department stores. There was a list of

1

Ella Beatrice Casey met Clevie Raymond Carver in Arkansas in 1935 when she was twenty-two. Within weeks they married and moved to the Northwest with his family. Their son Raymond Junior was born in Oregon in 1938, not long before his mother posed for this picture.

Raymond Carver said the stories his father told him kindled his desire to write. When his first son was small, C. R. Carver was learning the skilled trade of saw filing, work that exempted him from military service during World War II.

2

3

At the time of Raymond's birth, his parents lived in a company house
belonging to the Crossett-Western lumber mill in Wauna, Oregon,
by the side of the Columbia River.

4

Neighborhoods were still rural on the east side of Yakima, Washington,
when the Carver family moved there in the early 1940s. Ray visited the pigs
in his aunt Von's yard.

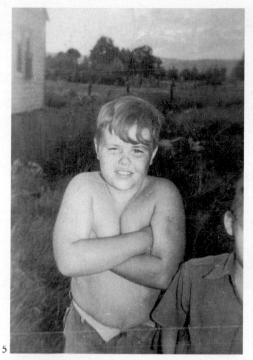

5

6

As a boy, Ray took ridicule from his classmates for being overweight. He resided "in little two-bedroom houses" and spent his days fishing in nearby creeks and ponds. In a late-1940s studio portrait, he posed with his mother and his younger brother, James.

"Don't forget James," Ray wrote in a note to Santa Claus that his mother saved.

8

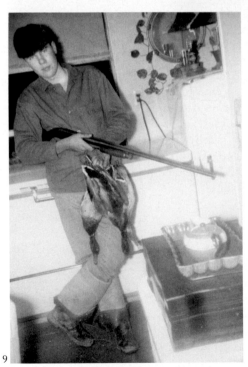

9

At sixteen, Ray had slimmed down and developed a passion for hunting ducks and geese. His mother cleaned the birds and froze the meat in the deep freeze that was one of her most prized possessions.

10

Ray couldn't wait to leave high school and begin to earn money, buy a car, and pursue his writing ambitions. But when graduation day arrived, his parents had problems that threatened to overwhelm his dreams of independence.

11

Ray met Maryann Burk just before her fifteenth birthday in 1955. When they married two years later, a local doctor found them a place to live and their families showered them with household necessities.

Ray and Maryann's first child was born in the same hospital where Ray's father was being treated for a nervous breakdown. Gathered together early in 1958 (left to right) are Ella, James, Ray, Maryann (holding Christine LaRae), and C. R. Carver.

12

13

Ray and Maryann and baby Christine
moved to Paradise, California, in 1958.
At age twenty, he became a freshman at
Chico State College, where he studied
with John Gardner. A second child,
Vance Lindsay, arrived the same year.

14

While Ray studied at Humboldt State
College in the early 1960s, he worked
nights in a sawmill and Maryann
worked days as a phone operator.
Ray published his first stories and
poems in small journals and edited the
college magazine; they both formed
close friendships with
professors and other writers.

15

The Carvers had already lived at eight different addresses when they
packed their old Chevrolet and headed to Iowa City in 1963 so Ray
could study at the prestigious Iowa Writers' Workshop.

At the Iowa Writers' Workshop, conversations moved outdoors on warm days. Here Ray Carver (center of photo with arm akimbo), Celia and Adrian Mitchell (left), and novelist Tom Filer focus attention on Maryann Carver. To the right, poet Paul Engle talks with novelist John Clellon Holmes and his wife, Shirley Holmes. (*Photo © Charlotte Brooks*)

16

17

Maryann Carver's younger sister, Amy Burk, studied theater and acted on stage and in several movies. She lived intermittently in the Carver household while raising her daughter and pursuing her work.

18

Editor Curt Johnson of *December* was first to publish Carver's fiction. Johnson introduced Carver to Gordon Lish shortly after Carver's story "Will You Please Be Quiet, Please?" was selected for *Best American Short Stories 1967*.

With high expectations, Christine, Vance, Ray, and Maryann Carver got passports
in 1968 and planned for a year in Israel, where Maryann would study history
and philosophy while Ray took in a view of the Mediterranean as a full-time writer.

Carver had an easy smile and a rolling laugh that often overcame his customary shyness. He was a fringe-walker who dressed conservatively throughout the sixties and seventies but milled the turmoil he witnessed into stories that captured the disappointments and dislocations of those decades.

Maryann Carver, characteristically stylish and unreserved, posed on a friend's new Cadillac in the mid-1970s.

During the summer of 1969, Ray asked his friend Gordon Lish to take his picture for a story anthology. Aiming for a tough-guy look, Ray borrowed a denim shirt from Lish and left the top buttons undone. A couple of months later, Lish became the fiction editor at *Esquire* magazine.

Gordon Lish became known as Captain Fiction while he was at *Esquire*, where he published three of Carver's breakthrough stories. As a book editor, Lish trimmed and toned the stories collected in *Will You Please Be Quiet, Please?* and *What We Talk About When We Talk About Love* and advanced Carver's career.

27

At thirty, Maryann Carver finished college
and become a high school English teacher, freeing
Ray to concentrate on writing short stories.

28

Underground cartoonist S. Clay Wilson drew the invitation to a party celebrating
the publication of Carver's *Will You Please Be Quiet, Please?* in 1976. Carver is
caricatured at left, resting his arm on a table above a stack of his books. Other
figures are Jon A. Jackson (upper left), dark-haired Diane Cecily (center), blonde
Maryann Carver (upper right), Max Crawford (signing his novel, *The Backslider*),
and Chuck Kinder (prone on floor). (Art © S. Clay Wilson)

The Carvers' house in Cupertino, California, was the site of raucous celebrations and domestic disturbances during the years of Carver's severe alcoholism. By then Ray (in shades) rarely used his backyard office (at left). He posed here with his mother and brother.

29

During his year as a Stegner Fellow at Stanford, Ray met Diane Cecily in Montana and Chuck Kinder in California. He had a love affair with Cecily and became one of Kinder's best friends. Three years later, Cecily and Kinder married each other.

30

Novelist Douglas Unger became part of the Burk-Carver family when he met Amy Burk at the University of Iowa in 1975. The Ungers remained close to both Carvers after Ray and Maryann divorced.

31

After fourteen months of sobriety, Ray began a relationship with poet Tess Gallagher in 1978. That year he brought her to a large Thanksgiving gathering at Chuck Kinder and Diane Cecily's flat in San Francisco.

Carver (third from left) with Tess Gallagher and (left to right) novelists Max Crawford, James Crumley, Chuck Kinder, and Michael Köepf in North Beach, San Francisco.

35

Tobias Wolff, Carver, and Richard Ford read together at the Poetry
Society in London in 1985 after *Granta* magazine dubbed them "dirty
realists." Carver wrote about this photograph and his affection for these
two fellow writers in his essay "Friendship." (*Photo © Allan Titmuss*)

36

Novelist Richard Ford (left) and Carver (second from left) read their fiction
at the University of Saskatoon, Saskatchewan, in 1986 and then joined their hosts,
David Carpenter and Bill Robertson (at right), for a weekend of goose hunting.

37

38

Gary Fisketjon brought Carver a bigger readership with his Vintage Contemporaries trade paperbacks. Fisketjon visited Ray in Port Angeles, Washington, in the fall of 1987 to complete editing of *Where I'm Calling From*.

Vance Carver (left) completed his BA at Syracuse University while his father taught there. He was a graduate student when he visited his father following his lung surgery in October 1987.

Raymond Carver strolls the dock at Port Angeles Boat Haven with
Tess Gallagher in the summer of 1987. Gallagher and Carver married in 1988.
(*Photo © Dale Wittner*)

restaurants up and down Highway 101 that had made the mistake of accepting the Carvers' checks. From Sakura Gardens in Mountain View and Denny's in Salinas to Pea Soup Andersen's in Buellton and the Cattlemen's Inn in Santa Barbara, the bills had rolled in. Hi-Time Liquors in Santa Barbara ($49) and *Playboy* magazine ($10) had claims. The names of utility companies, medical providers, and—casting doubt on Ray's claim that he'd cadged free flights between California and Iowa—United Airlines ($726) appeared.

The sad, dizzying catalog included a culprit familiar from the Carver's 1967 bankruptcy proceedings: student loans. Humboldt State College held a claim against Ray but waived Maryann's debt because she taught in a public school. They owed $500 to Santa Barbara attorneys who had defended them on drunk driving charges, and had promised to pay their bankruptcy attorney $350 out of their federal tax refund. In total, Ray and Maryann reported unsecured debts of $24,390.67, including $5,000 in student loans and disputed claims from the owner of the house they'd leased in Goleta and a real estate agent who'd been involved in the rental of their own house in Cupertino.[25]

One difference from the 1967 bankruptcy filing papers was that the Carvers were able to exempt significant assets: their "homestead" on Cupertino Road, valued at $45,000 with $35,000 still owed; and two retirement annuities: Maryann's $3,027 in California and Ray's $128 in Iowa. In addition, they had household goods such as a piano ($350); a 1966 Ford station wagon ($500); one desk and one manually operated typewriter ("Petitioners' tools of trade," $75); and professional libraries valued at $200. Three dogs rated no cash value, though a note adds that one is an Irish setter.

For a hearing in May, Maryann and Ray flew to Los Angeles. They argued strenuously on the flight back. Maryann writes that she was "utterly saddened by the whole business" and began to hit Ray as he joked about it. Carver's long, harrowing poem "Miracle" (not published in the United States until after Carver's death) describes a couple who get drunk in the airport bar and assume their own battles are a "universal human condition waged." (Indeed, such an assumption makes Carver's early stories dangerously evocative for many readers.) The poem describes a wife who pummels her husband's head until she's worn out. The husband thinks he deserves this beating. When his wife's punches cease, he thinks about their shared history and lifts his plastic drink glass "as if nothing's happened." Afterward, they hold hands (gold wedding bands, $100, exempt), and the husband wonders if anyone could have predicted all this when they cut their wedding cake. His head is ringing like a telephone, he says, but he "can't answer it" because no one is home. The miracle is that they *aren't* dead.[26]

• • •

After Ray wrote their old friends Sylvia and Dick Kolbert with news about his forthcoming book, the Kolberts invited him and Maryann to dinner at their San Francisco apartment. It was the last evening the two couples spent together, Sylvia recounted:

> We had some wine, but Ray said we need to get some more of something before the liquor store closes. Maryann and Dick were having a heavy conversation, so I drove Ray to get the gin or vodka or whatever it was. It was a tiny car, and Ray was very close to me, and maybe he wanted to kiss me, maybe he wanted a little loving.
>
> We came inside and I don't know if Maryann wanted to make Ray jealous or was just very interested in what Dick had to say—they were both very bright. But Ray picked up a heavy glass and threw it at Maryann's face. She ducked, and Dick and I exchanged a look that said, "They have to go." I was so scared, and all of a sudden I saw how Ray had changed. He was in a rage, and Dick and I were frightened.
>
> We made coffee and got them to leave. Maryann seemed okay to drive. She was always very good at handling Ray when he was upset, even this time. She could talk him down and change the subject. I think he loved her almost to the point of obsession.[27]

Though Maryann was not sober all the time herself, she had been learning about alcoholism and following with interest the est (Erhard Seminars Training) movement founded by Werner Erhard, her former boss in the encyclopedia sales business. Explanations and vocabulary acquired from AA and the so-called New Age spiritual movements that were thriving in California at the time, along with Eastern-influenced philosophies and paranormal psychology, helped both Maryann and her daughter cope with their chaotic household. To Ray, this talk of raised consciousness and psychic energy and spiritual awakenings could be laughable and irritating.

Yet Ray knew that no one needed change more than himself. Shortly after their bankruptcy court appearance, Maryann took Ray to a mental health clinic where he began a treatment program connected with Agnews State Hospital in San Jose.* At first, he wrote Dennis Schmitz, begging him to get him out of there. Four days later, Ray was waiting for an exit interview with a physician when, without warning, he crashed to the floor and cracked his forehead open. Maryann found him writhing on a narrow bed, back arched and mouth open, as the clinic staff kept him from choking on his tongue. When the episode passed, Ray's wound was sutured at the hos-

---

* Agnews has since been renovated as part of the Sun Microsystems campus.

pital next door. Maryann accompanied him back to the doctor's office. He learned that he had just undergone an alcoholic seizure.[28]

Sober and detoxed, Ray had experienced an uncommon form of alcohol withdrawal syndrome known as seizure disorder. Many alcoholics experience hallucinations or delirium tremens at this point of withdrawal, but Ray also suffered the equally severe and the less common seizure stage. His central nervous system had adjusted to the constant presence of alcohol in his body by compensating for alcohol's depressive effects on brain function and on communication among nerve cells. Abstinence had cleared his body of alcohol, but his brain remained in a hyperactive state that produced uncontrolled electrical activity. The doctor explained this to Ray and warned him that he must not drink again—ever. If he did, he would develop "wet brain"—permanent brain damage.

From then on, Ray had a death sentence on him. Whichever way he turned—toward the next drink or away from it—he felt doomed. He stayed sober a few days, or so he claimed in letters, but all too soon, in spite of the seizure and dire prognosis, he was drinking again. Then, recollection of the seizure made him afraid to quit drinking again. He now saw the dangers of increased nervous sensitivity known as "kindling" (also the title of one of Carver's posthumous stories) that increases the likelihood of seizures and brain damage, especially to the memory center. With alcoholism's perverse logic, Ray blamed Maryann for the double bind he found himself in: "After that I don't think Ray and I ever spoke naturally in public. His remarks to me had a condescending edge or were icily civil. It was as if he had to demonstrate how justified he was."[29]

Adding to the complexity of the situation was a reshuffling of the group that had migrated to Montana the summer before. On March 22, 1975, Chuck Kinder (one of Ray's best friends) married Diane Cecily (the woman Ray had loved so much that he'd nearly left his family) and moved to an apartment just vacated by Scott Turow (who was departing for Harvard Law School). Enhanced by Cecily's hospitality, the Matadero Road party reconvened in San Francisco. Ray and Kinder introduced their wives and put their own friendship back on easy terms. Soon the two couples developed a friendship like that Kinder embellished in his novel *Honeymooners: A Cautionary Tale*. Nonetheless, Maryann never discarded a conviction that Cecily had been the root cause of Ray's increased drinking and the disintegration of their marriage.[30]

A July vacation plan—Ray and Maryann without the kids; a second honeymoon, so to speak—detoured into a nearly fatal incident. The Carvers would kick off their travels with dinner at the Kinder-Cecilys'. Maryann wore a beautiful white dress. All seemed convivial until Maryann ignited an argument by asking Ray whose bed he planned to sleep in. When Kinder's friend Shorty Ramos dropped by, Maryann began a tipsy flirtation with him. After Ramos departed, things seemed calm. Kinder went to bed. Cecily and Maryann and Ray sat in the living room for a while. Cecily didn't pay attention to Ray's and Maryann's conversation until she saw Ray bristle, grab a wine bottle, and strike the side of Maryann's head. Ray and Maryann ran out into the street. Cecily saw drops of blood on the floor. She followed them outside and found Ray standing on the street. Afraid that he might drive away, she ordered him back to the apartment. With a neighbor's help, Cecily followed the blood trail down the hill and around the block. Maryann cowered in an alley, her white dress soaked with blood. Cecily half walked, half carried her back into the house and dialed 911. While Ray hid in the kitchen, Maryann woke Kinder and said, "Look what Ray did." Kinder held a towel to her neck until an ambulance arrived, followed by police investigators and a general disturbance in the building.

Cecily rode to San Francisco General Hospital with Maryann but was sent home. Doctors told Maryann she'd lost 60 percent of her blood through a severed artery near her ear. Kinder saw her and Ray together for a few minutes the next day: "Maryann went over to him and placed her hands on the back of his head and gently patted him. She didn't say much." Maryann declined to file charges against her husband, and a teacher friend took her to recuperate at her home.[31]

Ray stayed on at the Kinder-Cecilys'. Cecily had "never seen Ray more depressed. Kinder found the bottom of the wine bottle—it looked like "a big, dark glass coin"—on the mantel. By phone Ray apologized to Maryann, and she met him at a motel in Palo Alto to resume their honeymoon trip. Her teacher friend, the one who'd warned her about alcoholism four years before, never spoke to her again. "I had gone through the looking glass," Maryann believed. "The life I actually found myself in was the wrong one, not the one I'd dreamed of, or planned for, or worked so hard to achieve. What I had to do was bring reality around, make things right, get my life with Ray back on track. That's what I believed. Because I had to. Yes, *had* to."[32]

Ray and Maryann set out anew on a trip that proved "uneventful" almost to the end when, once again, "something went wrong," and Maryann found herself in an emergency room with a dislocated shoulder. Her greatest worry was that she would have to return to Los Altos High School with her arm in a sling. That time, Ray promised to stop the physical violence. "He said it was the last time, absolutely, no matter what the psychological provocation or wound."[33]

There were no more trips to the ER. Maryann began to believe that Ray would stop drinking. She even began to hope that he'd get back to the writing for which she felt she had given her youth. It would have been a perfect time for him to do so. The August *Esquire* with the classic photograph of Marilyn Monroe lying nude on red satin on its cover stood out on newsstands; at the center of the issue, on heavy, tinted paper, were Carver's "Collectors" and a story by Harold Brodkey.[34] Carver's first volume of stories was scheduled for publication in February 1976. He expected to receive galley proofs from Lish any day.

Carver and Lish had already debated about titles for the book and individual stories. Lish wanted to call the book *Put Yourself in My Shoes,* but, after polling friends, Ray made a stand for *Will You Please Be Quiet, Please?* Lish selected twenty-two stories (out of at least thirty-four Carver had published) for the book and proposed title changes for several of them.[35] Over Carver's objections, "Cartwheels" became "How About This?" while "A Night Out" first became "Another Rose" and then "Signals." Carver sent Lish the book's dedication page: THIS BOOK IS FOR MARYANN, it read. Every subsequent edition of the book has carried those words.

On September 9, 1975, the Carvers were "released from all dischargable debts" by the bankruptcy court. As Ray told the story later, the creditors' attorney tried to collect only one thing: Ginger the unpedigreed Irish setter. Ginger stayed, and it seemed, for the moment anyway, that Ray's Running Dog era might be over. Maryann returned to teaching at Los Altos High School in the fall of 1975, and her steady paychecks resumed. After the year away, she was assigned to basic-level classes. Her fellow teachers knew she had problems at home and tried to insulate her from some of the stresses at school, but they were burning out on the Carver melodrama.[36]

The timing of events in Ray's life could be uncannily ironic. Chris remembered seeing her father surrounded by his unpaginated proof sheets—long, slick, white pages imprinted with the handsome type of his stories. Ray let his daughter help him "correct and organize the connecting pages," as he drank screwdrivers. "We spent a lot of time together," Chris reminisced. On September 28, Carver finished corrections, mailed two pages of detailed comments, and praised his editor for "a superb job of cutting and fixing."[37] Three days later, a man knocked on the door with a warrant for his arrest. The charge was making a false statement to obtain public money, a violation of the section 2101 of the California Unemployment Insurance Code. As Governor Ronald Reagan finished out his second term, the state implemented his 1971 welfare reform act, a process that included improved cross-checking of employment records against welfare and unemployment insurance claims. Ray had collected unemployment money while employed by several branches of the University of California in 1972 and 1973. His friends had often thought that he was unnecessarily paranoid whenever matters of law enforcement were concerned, but now the authorities really had him. Ray posted $250 bail, pled not guilty, and embarked upon a series of pretrial hearings and postponements—not the ideal program for a man trying to control his anxiety or cut back his drinking.[38]

Lish had worked diligently on *Will You Please Be Quiet, Please?*, shaping the individual stories to make a distinctive collection. In most cases, he first edited photocopies of magazine versions of the stories and then reedited on typescripts made from that first editing. Carver discussed this editing with Lish and ultimately approved it, with reservations. It appears that Carver, hampered by his alcoholism and eagerness to see the book appear, made compromises with Lish. Still, the stories retain their original form, colloquial tone, humor, and characteristic use of quotidian data to present a reality that is both frightening and seductive. As a sound recording engineer might bring up one instrument and play down another, Lish eliminated details that give characters a defining personal history or make settings specific and intimate. Sometimes he changed the emphasis of a sentence and, substituting a few words, made the stories louder and brassier. In others, he enhanced the tones of loss and menace, giving the stories what Clark Blaise (who saw his fellow student as a "dedicated realist" in 1963) called their "ghostly radiance."[39]

The stories Lish cut most severely were early ones such as "The Student's Wife" and "Will You Please Be Quiet, Please?" In the version of "Quiet" published in *December* and *BASS* in 1967, the couple's reconciliation conveys tenderness and psychological compulsion:

> Her eyes were filled and seemed to contain layer upon layer of shimmering color and reflection, thicker and more opaque farther in, and almost transparent on the lustrous surface. Then, as he gazed even deeper, he glimpsed in first one pupil and then the other, the cameo-like, perfect reflection of his own strange and familiar face. He continued to stare, marveling at the changes he dimly felt taking place inside him.

In Lish's revision, Ralph's gaze into Marian's eyes and the telling detail of his reflection there are absent. A three-paragraph (189-word) conclusion, of which the section quoted above is a part, is condensed into the following 93 words:

He tensed at her fingers, and then let go a little. It was easier to let go a little. Her hand moved over his hip and his stomach and she was pressing her body over his now and moving over him and back and forth over him. He held himself, he considered later, as long as he could. And then he turned to her. He turned and turned in what might have been a stupendous sleep, and he was still turning, marveling at the impossible changes he felt moving over him.

Lish did not substantially alter the arc of events or the characters in any of these stories, and yet he substantially refabricated their feeling.

Here is a change from "They're Not Your Husband" that's typical of what Lish did throughout *Will You Please Be Quiet, Please?* Earl Ober watches his wife, Doreen, scoop ice cream. In the *Chicago Review* version, "The white skirt tightened against her hips and crawled up her legs, exposing the lower part of her girdle, the backs of her fleshy thighs, and several dark broken veins behind her knees." After Lish had gone over that sentence twice, the reasons for Earl's discontent were sharper. If the passage was bolder, it was also meaner, coarser, and somewhat diminishing to both characters: "The white skirt yanked against her hips and crawled up her legs. What showed was girdle, and it was pink, thighs that were rumpled and gray and a little hairy, and veins that spread in a berserk display."[40]

Editing that verged on rewriting was already familiar to Lish from his magazine work as well as from ghostwriting. Recently, Hills and McGraw-Hill had hired him to ghostwrite former New Orleans District Attorney Jim Garrison's 1976 *The Star-Spangled Contract,* a fictional account of the assassination of President Kennedy.*

A different situation ensued when Hills sent Lish the manuscript of Vladimir Nabokov's 1974 novel, *Look at the Harlequins!,* for possible first-serial placement in *Esquire.* Hills served as Nabokov's editor, but said, "nobody truly edited Nabokov, whom we called VN." Hills personally delivered the galley proofs of the new novel to Nabokov in Zermatt, Switzerland, and assisted as the author reviewed "every sentence, every comma, every semicolon." While Hills was there,

VN pulled out some twenty pages of edited manuscript and held it up by a corner of the packet, one hand lifting it up in the air as if it were a bag of three-day-old fish.

---

* Lish was aggrieved that Garrison sent him an inscribed copy of the influential book and never acknowledged the extensive work that Lish had performed on his behalf.

"Fred," he said, "who is this fellow Gordon Lish and what is he doing?" Well, *Look at the Harlequins!* is a very witty novel that plays around with a man who has supposedly had a few wives. It has stories within stories. And Gordon had attempted to cut and paste together and reshape sections of the novel to make it look like a straight autobiographical memoir of Vera [Nabokov's wife] by VN, when of course it was nothing of the sort. So after VN held up the sheaf of edited papers, he said, "We simply return it to him and say, 'This is not possible.' "

Lish's insensitivity with Nabokov had not dissuaded Hills from engaging Lish to edit books for McGraw-Hill. The veteran editor admired what Lish had done at *Esquire,* and knew Lish's aggressiveness and rashness were part of his ambition and talent.[41]

When bound galleys reached Ray in October, he responded quickly with a list of essential corrections, "things he didn't want to live with," and began thinking of people who might write blurbs. To Ray's enormous disappointment, John Cheever—released from alcohol rehabilitation and hard at work—declined his request, saying that he admired the "uncommonly steady gait" of Carver's prose but had already given his allotted two blurbs of the season to Saul Bellow and Mark Helprin.[42]

Chuck Kinder and Carver and their wives *motored* (as Maryann liked to say) together to Santa Barbara for Thomas Sanchez's extravagant "Writers' Stampede" party during the full moon of October. At Sanchez's Casa Coyote, guests walked around in awe of the house and grounds purchased with $125,000 of the sum Sanchez received for the film rights to *Rabbit Boss.* Sanchez himself, Kinder recalled, "wore leathers, like the Elvis of American literature." Ray tagged along when Kinder introduced himself to one of their idols, *Fat City* author Leonard Gardner. "They had both read *Fat City,*" Gardner said, "and Ray and I did talk some about writing style and craftsmanship, but it was hard to imagine that Ray was a hell of a good writer off that meeting because he was the kind of guy you had to watch or he'd fall in the pool and drown."

But Ray wasn't too drunk to ask Gardner to read *Will You Please Be Quiet, Please?* Gardner was "blown away" by the book. He found the stories both "wonderful" and "devastating" because "they are about betrayal of the closest loved ones, out of weakness or selfishness or being broke or anger against a situation or poverty or whatever. The people don't assault each other, but they make these quiet betrayals that cause terrible pain." Both Gardner and his partner, writer Gina Berriault, submitted blurbs, and Gardner became the first to describe Carver's vision as "unflinching."[43]

When they were ready to leave Casa Coyote, Kinder and Cecily didn't see their motel mates. As Cecily steered down the winding mountain road, Ray and Maryann came out of the trees and stood in her headlights in the middle of the road like astonished deer. They were holding hands, Kinder recalled, and Ray held a bottle of rum or bourbon he'd stolen:

> The serendipity of it, that they came out of trees just then! Then Diane started hitting on the horn, and I started yelling out the window. When they realized it was us, they said, "Oh, hello, hello," like we always met this way, and clambered into the car.
>
> At one time I wanted it to be the closing image of *Honeymooners*—their voices going on forever. I see it now in my mind's eye, that image of Ray and Maryann like two kids coming out of an enchanted forest, stepping out of a fairy tale.[44]

There is a vacuum at the heart of the family drama that Carver reports in certain poems and in his 1982 essay "Fires." Following is that essay's densest, most difficult passage. It is a truthful (yet passively voiced) confession:

> The time came and went when everything my wife and I held sacred, every spiritual value, crumbled away. It was something we had never seen occur in any other family. . . . It was erosion and we couldn't stop it. Somehow when we weren't looking, the children had got into the driver's seat. As crazy as it sounds now, they held the reins and the whip.[45]

What, one wonders, connects this erosion of spiritual values with children holding a family's reins and whip? One may offer excuses—the parents were young and impoverished, the times were tempestuous, the dreams poorly articulated—but alcoholism is the only thing that adequately accounts for this erosion. In their own ways, Christine and Vance each tried to step aside from the avalanche. They were struggling just to survive and—as teenagers will do—to get attention.

About dawn one morning in October 1975, poet Alan Shapiro was wakened by shouting in his Palo Alto apartment. He found his roommate sitting at the kitchen table with Ray and Maryann and other friends: "Ray's daughter had come looking for them . . . She was accusing Ray of not caring at all about his children and caring only about his work and his writer friends. She said that the family was only valuable to him insofar as it contributed to his career as a writer. Then she stormed out."[46]

When Ray complained about the noise John O'Brien's kids were making as Ray read a story aloud, O'Brien snapped at Ray, "For Christ's sake, Ray, kids are more important than stories." Ray shot back, "That remains to be seen!" On another occasion, O'Brien called Maryann to warn her that Ray was on his way home, drunk and angry at Vance: "He was talking about how dreadful his son was—a little son of a bitch, he said, because his son had just swiped money or talked back maybe. Ray told us he had said 'Come on,' put his fists up and wanted to fight him."[47] In "On an Old Photograph of My Son," a poem unpublished in his lifetime, Carver draws a hateful picture of Vance as a teenage bully. Looking at the 1974 snapshot of Vance fills the father with despair and makes him want a drink. The boy the picture calls up in his father's memory looks like a Greek hero, but is instead a "petty tyrant" with a "contemptuous expression" who orders his mother around while his father does—what? If the poem may be trusted for facts, the father does nothing. He is drunk.

Chris, equipped with the car her mother had helped her buy and her gas station job, had been transferred from regular high school to an alternative classroom. Here she met Mike Pleadwell, who came to talk to the class about poetry. Pleadwell, who went by the name of Shiloh, was five years older than Chris. After high school, he spent three years in the Marine Corps, including service in Vietnam, and completed a course in electronics at a technical school. At the time he met Chris, he was riding a 1952 T-110 Ironhead Triumph motorcycle and looking for work, which was scarce due to the recession. Pleadwell wrote poems that so impressed his former high school writing teacher that he invited him back to speak to his students. When Pleadwell first visited Chris's house, he sat outside under the lemon trees with Ray and "discussed that I had done some weird writings and was questioning things. Raymond and I were in different worlds." For Pleadwell, "Life was crazy—it was all party, that's all it was, and the Bay Area was, shit, damn near on top of it. The Cow Palace, Day on the Green concerts, Fillmore West, and party party party, not to mention free love. That's all life was about. Vietnam and a party."

Pleadwell was an undeniable match for Chris's imagination and vulnerabilities. An ex-marine on a motorcycle might have seemed entirely different from her father, but there were familiar features in his love of parties, interest in poetry, and familiarity with street drugs. "Chris was with me up at Stevens Creek Dam all the time. Christi tried to be a pretty tough girl. She was a pretty tough old girl, I'd say. I'm sure Raymond worried about his daughter."[48]

Ray saw himself in Chris's round face and clear, intense blue gray eyes with dark margins. What's more, he saw himself in her passions and anxieties, in her moods, and in her readiness to experiment with alcohol or drugs. He could not understand how the baby in "Distance" had turned into the teenage girl in "One More Thing." Carver reveals the untenable opposition of his feelings about his children in several poems he wrote during the 1980s. The list poem called "Fear" includes these two items: "Fear of my children's handwriting on envelopes" and "Fear they'll die before I do, and I'll feel guilty."

Vance's earlier dream—so opposite to his parents' pursuits—of becoming a professional athlete still seemed out of reach when he returned to Homestead High School to finish his sophomore year in 1975. Instead of going out for baseball in the spring, he got a job as a janitor at a nearby elementary school. His coworker was a Foothill Community College student who was taking a course in international relations, learning about the Strategic Arms Limitation Talks. Vance "had never met anyone who had such an interest before," he recalled, "and I was inspired." This young man, with his relatively straight lifestyle and determination to complete college, acted as an older brother to Vance. Never "really comfortable under the influence of marijuana," Vance gave up both pot and cigarettes, but "it did take awhile before I could do that." He sequestered himself from his family and—"through an iron will"—taught himself to study. He also began working out in the gym and won respect from the coaches even though his job prevented him from playing competitively.[49]

The rest of the household responded ambiguously (at best) to the new straight-arrow Vance. "We considered him a little weenie and a tattletale then," Pleadwell said. "But I'm the uncle of his daughter and he's the uncle of my daughters, so we don't argue or fight or nothing now."

Christmas 1975—filled with anticipation of Ray's forthcoming book— would be the last celebrated by the Carver family on Cupertino Road. Amy and Erin came from Iowa City, followed by Amy's new love and future husband, Douglas Unger. A University of Chicago graduate who'd also studied in Buenos Aires, Argentina, Unger was a twenty-three-year-old fiction student who was excited to meet the author of a story he'd published in the *Chicago Review*. He got off his plane at San Francisco airport wearing a suit and tie and long, thin goatee. Ray had the shakes when he led Unger to his filthy, rattly Ford wagon and reached for his vodka. On the drive to meet Amy and Maryann at a party in San Francisco, Unger thought that Ray was wondering why his beautiful, sexy, thirty-three-year-old sister-in-law had taken up with him. It soon became clear that Unger was there to take care of them. After the party, Unger drove Ray's car to Cupertino for him. He'd never seen a house "so pockmarked by human conflict— holes in the plasterboard, the carpet and the furniture tattered and over-used." Most mornings, Ray woke everyone by calling out "Hot dough-nuts! Steaming hot cups of coffee!" but when they got to the kitchen, "heart starter" Bloody Marys were the main offering. Ray wanted company, and so commenced a new day.[50]

One morning, thanks to Vance, was more dramatic. At seventeen Vance was, Unger recalled, "fighting for order in a very dysfunctional house, the only one not drinking or on drugs in that whole scene. He was officious and petulant about not getting meals and things he needed, and he bickered with his mom, who had to go to work and often just handed him money and told him to forage for himself." It seems that Vance answered when a former boyfriend of Amy's named Frank telephoned. In what might have been a bid to restore the status quo, Vance said that his aunt was asleep with Unger. Frank, who was "strong and scary" came right over. As Unger tells the story,

> He came in and slapped us awake. I went out, and he said some disparaging words. Ray and Chuck [Kinder] and S. Clay [Wilson] were just goading us on. They wanted to be entertained and wanted to see what scene would occur that would become mythic. I slapped Frank's cigarette out of his mouth and punched him, and he reeled and went over into the Christmas tree behind him, and the tree crushed against the wall.

Once the situation was under control, "Ray got very officious and got Frank out of the house, telling him he didn't belong there anymore, and everyone just drank and laughed, and it became an interesting story." During this commotion, Amy poured a cup of Tide detergent into Frank's gas tank. That was Unger's welcome to the Christmas season and the Burk-Carver family.[51]

The tree was restored, but the house was neither quiet nor joyful during the holidays that year. Chris (now eighteen), with Shiloh and "flying on alcohol and methamphetamines," passed through. When Ray's brother, James, and his wife, Norma, came to Christmas dinner, they found everybody so drunk that they went to eat at a restaurant rather than wait for dinner. Kittredge and Crawford were there, along with James Crumley, in town to interview for a job at the Modern Language Association convention. Crumley recalled that Ella Carver and a woman they called the Queen of California (who rented the apartment attached to the Carver's house) slid merrily in the grease they spilled on the floor as they pulled the turkey out of the oven. "Those people," Crumley said, "had a capacity for degeneracy that I'd never seen, and I've lived pretty rough, broke and criminal. I loved Ray, but he was absolutely defenseless. Could not take care of himself at all. That's how he survived." Crumley placed a cameo of the Carvers in his now-classic detective novel *The Last Good Kiss*:

. . . a passing paperboy told me it was Cupertino. . . . Two houses up the street, a curly-headed guy was standing in his driveway, sucking on the remains of a half-pint as he tried to dodge a barrage of kitchen utensils that flew from an unseen hand inside the house and glittering out into the morning light. He ducked a large spoon and a heavy ladle, chortling and dancing, but a potato masher caught him on the lower lip with a sudden burst of bright blood. As he started weeping, a blond woman in a house-coat rushed outside and led him back inside.

Jack Hicks, also en route to the MLA convention, heard music blaring out the windows of the Carvers' house, let himself in, passed some boys roller-skating in the family room, and found Ray and Maryann in their bedroom having a dispute. Ray didn't look defenseless to Hicks: "His hands were around Maryann's throat. When he saw me, he let go and said, with this put-on Brit accent, 'Hello, old sport.' "[52]

"You never start out in life with the intention of becoming a bankrupt or an alcoholic or a cheat or a thief. Or a liar," Carver said later.[53] As the bottom of his alcoholism sank lower and lower, he had become all of those things.

PART IV

RECOVERY

CHAPTER 20

Celebrated and Homeless

January 1976–June 2, 1977, Northern California

The sea is high again today, with a thrilling flush of wind.
—Lawrence Durrell, *Justine*,
a favorite sentence of Carver's

The holidays waned into early January. One night, Ray was sitting in a rocking chair, and Kinder and Crumley and Crawford were needling him about his first book coming out, because some of them were on second or third books. Ray fell asleep in his chair for a while. Then, Unger remembered, "He woke up with a start and said, 'What's happening to my career?' And everyone laughed and repeated it over and over, 'What's happening to my career? Ha ha!' "[1]

A lot was happening, in fact. In its first issue of the new year, *Publishers Weekly* printed its notice of *Will You Please Be Quiet, Please?*

> Twenty-two mini-stories that explore the depressing emptiness and futility of American life . . . Downbeat but perceptive writing about the inarticulate worlds of Americans . . .[2]

The winter of 1976 was a season of anticipations, celebrations, and regrets for Ray. He began using cream-colored stationery embossed with his name in terra-cotta letters: RAYMOND CARVER. He'd been writing the story of himself and Maryann for many years, and now it seemed to be over. They'd chosen "to live on those edges, to court experiences," Kittredge said. Living on the edge had taken a terrible toll.[3] Soon Ray would be on trial for defrauding the State of California. He might go to prison.

Ray had virtually abandoned his study at home because he couldn't work with his kids around. In a rented room in Los Altos, he labored "slowly, slowly" on pages he hoped might "turn into" a novel, but accomplished little. On Valentine's Day, Ray brought Maryann a homemade valentine, but the family meal degenerated into a fight between Ray and Vance. After her AA meeting that evening, Maryann went to coffee with an unemployed engineer and sympathetic listener named Ross Perkins. Within a few weeks, Perkins and Maryann began a love affair. Blearily, Ray noticed. He agreed with Maryann that something should be done to save their marriage, but postponed action until summer.[4] He was focused on his soon-to-be-published books.

Ray was thrilled with Capra Press's work on *At Night the Salmon Move*. On the marine blue cover, a ribbon of salmon passes through a dark, starry window and circles around the crimson-red title to a vanishing point. Carver dedicated the book to Maryann's sisters, Jerry and Amy. As an author photo, Ray used the one he called "Washington Fats" of his chubby twelve-year-old self with fishing rods. The description of the author also promoted an image of Ray as an average Joe, giving the population of his birthplace (717) and a list of "laboring jobs." In this and future Capra Press books, Carver was sketching the "good guy" personality that would carry him through the 1980s and offsetting the image of himself promoted by Lish as a desperate, brooding fellow from a "sunless post-speech world." Thus Ray saw divisions he'd long felt within himself projected on the screen where public mythologies are made.

With hope that his book would earn him a welcome to the East Coast literary world, Ray had applied for a residency at the Yaddo artists' colony in upstate New York. He would work on his first novel, "already well in progress," he wrote on the application form. Cheever recommended Ray to Yaddo, gilding their Iowa acquaintance to describe Ray as "an industrious teacher, an ambitious writer, and an easy-going companion." A panel made up of Syracuse novelist George P. Elliott and two other writers ranked Carver's submission A, A-, and B+. Yaddo offered Ray a berth from May 10 through June 30.[5]

Ray kept himself busy with preparations for his debut as a national author. He worried over the mailing of review copies, fretted when his agent was out of her office, badgered McGraw-Hill to pay for "hard liquor" for a San Francisco party and a plane ticket for Lish to attend it, proposed reviewers, and set up appearances at bookstores. During these days of anticipation, Maryann augmented her teaching salary with a second job at a mall restaurant near their house to pay off their Christmas bills, and Ray touched his usual suspects for loans so they could make their house payment.

When advance copies arrived, Ray invited Leonard Michaels to a small dinner party, "just a few couples." Michaels and his fiancée, poet Brenda Hillman, arrived late and found the blue house bursting with at least a hundred celebrants. Maryann, looking a bit flustered, stirred enormous pots of spaghetti. Hillman, who'd just come from Iowa City, found the conversation, "sweet, somewhat shallow . . . like wading in a warm sea and never seeing a wave." Ray, very drunk, proclaimed that the best short story writers were John Cheever, Michaels, and himself. The "highlight" of the party came when Hillman got locked in the bathroom:

> We all rose and went to the bathroom door and then immediately, not wasting a minute, began to talk about how to open the door. Some people pushed a little at the door, but most of them wanted to talk. Somehow, after we tried several times to count in unison to three, we made it—one, two, three—and all together we threw ourselves at the door. A really grand occasion in American literary history, all these writers together, drunk, flinging themselves at a bathroom door. It was the best literary conference I ever attended.[6]

The official publication date for *Will You Please Be Quiet, Please?* was March 9, 1977. Carver's trial on charges of making false statements to the state of California was set for March 10. His attorney had entered his not-guilty plea months earlier. As Maryann, Kinder, and Crawford escorted a terrified Ray to his trial at a San Jose courthouse, Kinder "teased him unmercifully, telling him what would happen to him in jail," Crawford said.[7] Ray waived his right to a jury trial, and a deputy DA presented the People's evidence: two papers showing Ray's employment and fourteen computer cards indicating that he'd contemporaneously collected unemployment insurance. Three state employees explained these papers and cards.

Ray avoided the witness stand. His evidence was Maryann. She was, as the court proceedings record, "sworn and examined for the defendant." On the stand, Maryann—in Kinder's words—"saved Ray's bacon." She promised to make restitution. She showed Judge Louis C. Doll a copy of *Will You Please Be Quiet, Please?* and assured the court that her husband intended to improve himself now that his literary work was coming to fruition. She spoke passionately about what it had cost her husband to write. Here is part of the tongue-in-cheek two-page exaggeration of her speech that Kinder created in *Honeymooners*:

> Sir, there will always be those rare individuals who must stare into the darkness of themselves in order to really see for us all. My husband . . . is one of those damned yet blessed individuals who must both suffer and soar because of the gift of that burden. . . . [he] drinks like a fish, and lives about half the time in some parallel world of story. It is because of this

that my husband has a diminished capacity to recognize and act upon
notions of right and wrong in the real world. . . . Sir, I would like to offer
the fiction of our lives into evidence as exhibit A for the defense . . .[8]

Despite Maryann's defense of Ray on artistic grounds, Judge Doll found
him guilty.

From Humboldt, Dick Day wrote to plead that Ray not be sentenced to
prison. "To make talent bear fruit, requires years and years of hard work
in isolation, daily endurance without recognition from the world, and an
absolute persistence in the struggle towards excellence. Such a way of life is
not for the weak or for anyone lacking moral courage."[9] Day was laying it
on pretty thick, but it seems to have worked.

Judge Doll sentenced Ray to ninety days in county jail, then suspended
that sentence and placed him on two years' probation. Ray was ordered to
make restitution to the state for the illegal payments and attend AA once a
week. When the judge asked him for a copy of *Will You Please Be Quiet,
Please?* Ray said he couldn't spare one.[10]

The design of Carver's book embodied Lish's idea of letting work stand
on its own without attention to the author. Black letters on the white dust
jacket said THE STORIES OF RAYMOND CARVER WILL YOU PLEASE BE QUIET,
PLEASE? Teal blue and red orange shadows behind the letters hinted at an
off-key America inside. There was neither a photograph nor a biography of
the author and yet, on the back jacket flap where those items usually appear,
one finds Lish's imprint: "A McGraw-Hill Book in association with Gordon Lish." The front flap was devoted to a fulsome editorial description of
a stark book:

> Here is the short fiction of a literary artist of the first rank, a maker of sto-
> ries that deliver the dark of the American heart. . . . In the sunless, post-
> speech world that Raymond Carver sees, apprehending the grossness of
> our fixed destinies amounts to a kind of triumph, a small but gorgeous
> prevailing against circumstance. Here is the work of the increasingly
> influential Raymond Carver . . . in whose precise rendering on the page
> readers in pursuit of excellence in the national literature may all exult.

Lish was not thinking of a single book when he prepared that copy. He
was thinking of Carver's career—and of his own career. One could even
analyze the statement to show that Lish has buried this "Raymond Carver"
who possesses "vision" behind such a blizzard of extravagant blurbo-
babble that he barely exists.[11]

Much later, Lish would claim that Carver and his stories were his personal creation, a marvelous literary hoax built upon the foundation of Carver's magazine stories.[12] This was not true. But it is true that in 1976 Lish was throwing the considerable skill and momentum he had gained during his five years in New York behind this book.

Novelist and biographer Geoffrey Wolff gave *Will You Please Be Quiet, Please?* an astonishing review in the Sunday *New York Times Book Review*. After describing Carver's people as "bewildered," Wolff praises the uniqueness of Carver's prose: "I would like to believe that having read these stories I could identify him on the evidence of a paragraph. . . ." Wolff perceives both the essential Carver in these stories and the fineness of Lish's editing of them. Ray must have been pleased, too, to read that one of Wolff's favorites was "Nobody Said Anything," a story Lish had never been enthusiastic about. To read that Wolff found it "a perfectly realized story" with "one of the best erotic sequences (unrealized sexuality as usual here) that I have ever read" was a welcome affirmation to Carver's intentions as a writer.[13]

Ray gave a bookstore reading in San Francisco on March 13. The night continued with an "Ides of March Party and Lit'ry Soiree" at the Kinder-Cecilys'. Cartoonist S. Clay Wilson made one of his dense, Rabelaisian drawings as a party invitation — "Bring coke, jokes, dope, hooch, ice, cigarettes, good lookin' ginch and watch your husband, wife, girlfriend, boyfriend, drink, poke, hat and coat . . ." the dialogue balloon said. Events to be celebrated: Carver's two new books, Crawford's second novel, Tim Dekin's book of poems, Cecily's birthday, Kinder and Cecily's first anniversary, and the going-out-of-print of Kinder's *Snakehunter*. Cecily taps a gnarly, shirtless, pointy-eared Carver on the elbow. Near to hand, Ray has his "Holy Vodka" and a stack of books titled *Will You Shut the Fuck Up?* Maryann is the serene blonde in the background, the only figure not extravagantly caricatured.

Ray carried his books and reviews around in his briefcase. He pulled out anything that bolstered his self-esteem and read it aloud. "It sounds comical now, but in those days it was very touching," Alan Shapiro said. "The joke was that he was pulling out papers from the third grade and reading what the teacher said about him. Anything good that happened to him shocked him." The reviews surprised Carver for another reason, too: ". . . I never felt the people I was writing about were so bad off . . . The waitress, the bus driver, the mechanic, the hotel keeper. God, the country is filled with these people. They're good people. People doing the best they could."[14]

Doug Unger and Amy came for the party and were still there when a *Newsweek* photographer shot a photo to accompany the magazine's review. "We were all cheering Ray on to adopt a blue-collar, tough-guy expression, which he did."[15] The result was a review titled "Desperate Characters" and a mug shot of Ray—bloated and hairy, sucking on the fag end of a cigarette, scowling, and captioned "Carver: Pain and occasional horror." The career was launched.

In April, worries about going to jail abated, Ray cut down his drinking and flew east. He'd stop in Iowa City (where people would be reading his book), then go on to Johnson's in Chicago before taking up his residency at Yaddo. Unger persuaded John Leggett that Ray was sober enough to give a reading, but Ray had an attack of nerves as the hour approached, and Amy fixed him martinis. Ray disliked gin, but it was all they had. So Ray was ebullient when he ran into his former UCSC student Mark Jarman: "He introduced his sister-in-law and said, 'Give her a kiss, Mark,' and we looked at each other—it was embarrassing—and gave each other a little peck." Only the people in the front heard Ray read, but Jarman thought, "he read marvelous things—poems for half the reading and some very short stories that seemed like prose poems."[16]

The turnout for the reading was meager, but Unger remembered seeing "the whole crew from those days" at the party that he and Amy hosted afterward: John Irving, Donald Justice, Marvin Bell, Allan Gurganus, Chase Twitchell, Mark Jarman, Jane Smiley, Barbara Grossman, Richard Wiley, T. C. Boyle, Richard Bausch, Michael Henderson. Ray gave Henderson, a solicitor and writer from New Zealand, a pair of boots: "Ray had these strange workmanlike boots, brown leather, thick rubber soles, that didn't fit him; and Michael was going around in dress shoes in the Iowa snow. So Ray, in his cups, just gave Michael the boots, and they fit perfectly!"[17]

That party started Ray on a binge from which even Amy, who had always been able to get him to taper off and eat and sleep, could not divert him. He settled in a curtained basement alcove in her house, quarters he had to share with Erin's pet rabbit. The rabbit spooked Ray. He claimed it kept him awake at night, hopping in the shower stall. The household also included a large dog named Byron, a tiny one called Puppy, and at least seven people. Brendan Ward, an Irish playwright who slept on a broken-legged couch propped up by a copy of *Acting Is Believing,* discovered that the reason Ray "was so affable and interesting and talked nonstop was the vodka bottle under his mattress." He was drinking one fifth of vodka before noon, a second fifth in the afternoon.[18]

Ray carried *At Night the Salmon Move* with him. He read aloud from it and gave away copies. He and a physician friend, Qais Al-Awqati, enjoyed "competitive quotings" of poetry they'd memorized. When Ray recited his own poem about Alexander the Great, "Nobody was letting Ray finish and everybody was jumping in questioning—especially Brendan, who is a historian—and the whole thing ended up going in so many tangents that it was really hilarious except to Ray. He was really angry." By now, Ray was "big and bloated, his nose and whole face red with broken blood vessels," student Robert Pope said. Sometimes he "held forth" to Unger's workshop class. "He looked bad, but he was eerily sincere. Those stories sound just like him—the voice—that sense of underlying urgency."[19]

In hindsight, with the publication of *Will You Please Be Quiet, Please?*, 1976 would seem like the year that began a revival of realism in American short fiction. At Iowa in particular, Carver's work influenced young writers, Pope thought:

> We'd come through the period of experimental writing, and then it died. There was a time of "what do we do now?" and then Ray Carver was latched on to, followed by terms like minimalism and dirty realism. People imitated him and found the way back into high realism, which has little to do with Carver's stories. Something unusual about them marks them as not being standard American realism. The comedy is peculiar. Carver could have fit perfectly into the experimental period, but instead he became this salvation of American literature.[20]

First Ray had to save himself. Unger heard Ray call Yaddo to explain that he was unable to accept its invitation: "He was afraid to go in the condition he was in, and he was incredibly sad about it. He made an excuse that he had to get back to Maryann in Cupertino." He had absorbed the fact of Maryann's affair now, and was "jealous as hell" but felt unable to travel. Then Unger's older brother Steve arrived in Iowa City. Steve Unger was, one could say, the incarnation of the Vietnam War in this extended family. A talented guitarist and folksinger, Steve had dropped out of college in the mid-sixties to pursue a music career. He wound up as a door-gunner on a helicopter in Vietnam. He was discharged from the army after he began to suffer episodes of paranoid schizophrenia.[21]

A Falstaff merrily giving away what was not his to give, Ray used his old faculty ID card to host a farewell lunch at the union. As everyone ate and talked, two university policemen approached the group. "Ray's face went ashen, thinking the jig was up for him," Unger said. But they took Unger aside. They had arrested his brother for uprooting gingko trees in a city park! Voices told Steve to pull up the trees. The police recognized Steve as a psychotic and didn't want to keep him in jail. "In years to come," Unger said, "Ray told the story of how the cops came looking for me while he was shaking in his boots that they were really after him for the cafeteria scam!"

Dire situations became funny stories later, but Ray warned Unger, " 'Madness is catching, Doug! Madness is catching! A person could go crazy in a house like this. You've got to write; you can't be distracted by all this!' "

Ray had been holed up in Iowa when his ninety-year-old grandmother, Katherine Casey, died in Arkansas. Ray's mom, Ella, went to the funeral and visited her sister Edna and brother Sanders. Though Ella arrived all dressed up and in good spirits, the visits did not go smoothly because "there was always a reason why things went wrong for Ella. Issues found her," a niece recalled. Sanders's son, a doctor, examined Ella and diagnosed emphysema. She ignored his advice to quit smoking and returned to California. After her mother's death, Ella's chronic restlessness increased.[22]

When word reached Ray that his daughter and her dog were on their way to Iowa City, he fled town just before she arrived. Back in California, Ray found that Maryann and Perkins were drinking together and his household was a "loony bin." One may get some idea of these dark days from stories of marital collapse such as "One More Thing" in *What We Talk About When We Talk About Love*. Carver later caricatured Perkins as "Mr. Fixit" in "Mr. Coffee and Mr. Fixit" and a longer version, "Where Is Everyone?" To Lish he wrote that he regretted having missed the satisfactions of fatherhood. He jokingly suggested to Maryann that they just turn the house and mortgage over to Chris and Vance, commit some acts of vandalism, and scoot away.[23]

But Ray already was scooting out the door, headed toward Lake Tahoe for a brief experiment in sobriety and mountain living with the writer who'd been his lover in Iowa two years before. That she had three young children, wasn't divorced, and "was used to all the amenities" didn't seem to trouble Ray. Ten days later, he wrote Lish that he hadn't felt so good in years. He loved being in a little town in the Sierras—the first time he'd lived among rugged natural surroundings for decades. He wasn't drinking and had banished "that fucking wolf that's come to sit at the foot of my bed every night now for months." He was writing, too, and planned to join his lover in Palo Alto when she came there on a Stegner Fellowship in the fall.[24]

Only days later, Ray rented a two-room apartment under the eaves of a tall house at 1115 Castro Street in San Francisco. Maryann helped decorate it and explained to Perkins that she would not abandon Ray "when he was so far down." Vance went to Yakima to work in the apple orchards. Chris was eighteen and, it seemed, beyond supervision. Ray worked for $2.35 an hour at Upstart Crow Books in Sausalito. He persuaded the store to stock his books and then grumbled that the distributor of *Will You Please Be Quiet, Please?* was slow to ship them. He took his breaks at the No Name Bar next door.[25]

Sometimes Ray got together with Gina Berriault to talk about short stories. Both Berriault and her partner, Leonard Gardner, became close to Ray then because "even when you see this artist and he can hardly talk, you know what's in there—it's much different from meeting a derelict on the street . . ." Gina had enormous compassion, and she responded to Ray. To Berriault, alone in a corner at a party at the Kinder-Cecilys', Maryann confided her jealousy of Cecily. Gardner reflected,

> Maryann seemed *astounding*. She was a model of maturity and sophistication, able to accept her husband's lover as her best friend, but when she told Gina the story, it was evident that she had gone through real hell over it earlier. Gina was always going to write a short story about that, and she never did it. But Maryann may have pulled it off so well that none of the other three ever realized it was still troubling her. It was a strange, remarkable friendship that those two couples had.[26]

The foursome met with some strange incidents. While picnicking at Ocean Beach, they saw a drowned man who had tattoos all over his arms. That night, Ray and Kinder drew tattoo designs, promising each other they'd have them inked on. "Ray drew a pretty good picture of an anatomical heart, not some valentine heart, and he wrote MARYANN in it."[27]

When Ray lived alone in San Francisco, his physical condition spiraled downhill so quickly that he was willing to be dried out again. He entered the Garden Sullivan Hospital on Geary Street in July. While he was there, Maryann spent the night with Sylvia Kolbert at a friend's house in Sausalito: "I didn't understand what Maryann meant by 'drying out.' I said, 'Is he dying?' and Maryann said, 'He could, he could,' and she sobbed and sobbed and talked for hours and hours. Her whole life came out. And then the next morning she had to go back to where Ray was." Discharged with a toehold on recovery, Ray wrote Lish that he was leaving his past behind; days later, he was "ambitious-edgy, in the best sense."[28] His sobriety lasted until a birthday celebration for Maryann's mother.

Soon Ray was a champagne drunk. His story "Careful" is based on episodes that occurred then. From that story, too, one senses that Maryann and Ray were restoring civility and kindness to their relationship as they began to understand the disease that afflicted them. At his typewriter, too, Ray sought acceptance. He worked on an article called "A Little Sturgeon," in which a boy is supposed to be watching the fishing rods and the river but yearns instead for his father's attention and the drink in his father's thermos: whiskey and coffee. He wishes he were older.[29] Carver was confronting the fact that the lost Eden of his childhood was also the place where he became addicted to alcohol: it was part of the father he mourned.

Carrying their fresh MFAs from Iowa, Amy and her daughter and Unger moved, with Erin, into a flat owned by St. James Episcopal Church across California Street from the Kinder-Cecily flat in San Francisco. Unger worked nights as a bilingual hospital clerk and days as a handyman at St. James, where Amy taught Sunday school. Maryann moved back into the Cupertino house and returned to Los Altos High. Chris and Shiloh had a rented house in Sunnyvale. Vance—now as tall as his dad—began his senior year at Homestead High School, driving a red 1966 Volkswagen Beetle purchased with his summer earnings. He resumed his custodian job, earned high Bs in college-bound classes, and tried to figure out how to give himself a better life. He would be eighteen in October.[30]

Ray planned to stay in the Castro Street apartment.

He'd show his picture in a ratty copy of *Newsweek* to waitresses and tell them he needed someone to cuddle with. Caught stealing books at Upstart Crow, he lost his job (leaving behind unsold copies of his Capra Press books he'd ordered).[31] After his taste of celebrity, Ray's world was empty again. He gave up his apartment. Homeless, he migrated between Cupertino and California Street, between people who loved him and would give him a meal and place to sleep: Maryann, Amy and Doug, Chuck and Diane. Learning of Ray's distress, McGraw-Hill editor Fred Hills asked Ray for a "specific picture" of his financial situation and offered to try to recommend him for an award. Ray hoped that Jack Hicks would hire him at UC Davis for the winter quarter, but neither Hicks nor anyone else could take a chance on Ray now, not even for ten weeks. The only thing he finished during these months was a paranoid paean to vodka he first called "Drink Poem." *Esquire* published it as "Cheers." Lish sent a note warning Ray he ought to take it easy.[32]

Ray's antics as a drunk were insignificant compared to his deteriorating physical condition. Endstage alcoholism involves often irreversible damage to the liver, heart, brain, and other tissues. He was lucky to be alive at all. "I was completely out of control and in a very grave place," Ray said later. "Blackouts, the whole business . . . You might drive a car, give a reading, teach a class, set a broken leg, go to bed with someone, and not have any memory of it later. You're on some kind of automatic pilot."[33]

"We all thought he would keep on drinking until it killed him," Unger said. "And he thought so too." Then Maryann heard about a recovering alcoholic named Duffy whose private residential treatment program offered tools for staying sober. Eugene Duffy Senior, a stone mason from Illinois, had sobered up through AA in 1964 and moved to California to start over.

He bought an old church resort in Calistoga at the north end of Napa Valley and began Duffy's Myrtledale for "problem drinkers seeking recovery." Duffy recommended a four-week stay. It cost $175 a week.[34]

To raise money for another treatment and clear their debts again, the Carvers sold their house. Thanks to the development of Silicon Valley, they took a profit on it despite the considerable damage it had sustained in the four years of their possession.[35] With the closing date on the house sale two months away, Amy, Doug, and Maryann drove Ray to Duffy's. They brought fried chicken, but Ray had no appetite for food or festivity.[36] He drank wine and squeezed Maryann's hand all the way to Calistoga.* At Duffy's they found a meeting space filled with worn couches and chairs. The walls were hung with words: inspirational slogans about sharing strength and hope, posters of the 12 steps of Alcoholics Anonymous. Amy and Unger watched the intake process from a distance while Maryann paid for his first week and tried to speak for Ray, who was drunk and quiet. As he wrote later in "Where I'm Calling From," "Part of me wanted help. But there was another part."[37]

Ray became a newcomer, assigned to the convalescent room. Duffy had experience with treatment programs (much of it as a patient) but no medical license. To newcomers he administered a regime of "hummers"—shots of rot-gut bourbon in water—every three hours for three days. Patients who couldn't hold a glass drank through a straw or had hummers poured into their mouths. The hummer system worked fairly well, unless the alcoholic got too amped up between shots and had a convulsion.[38] In "Where I'm Calling From" it's a fat electrician from Santa Rosa who convulses as he's telling a story: "He was on his back on the floor with his eyes closed, his heels drumming the linoleum."

After a newcomer tapered down on the hummers—Ray accomplished that in just two days—the Duffy system got even simpler: "Don't drink until your ass falls off." Outside was the eucalyptus-scented warmth of northern California autumn, but Duffy's "guests" passed much of their time indoors. There were good, plain meals, three or four meetings a day in the public rooms, and a ride in Duffy's old station wagon for a town AA meeting. Of those others, another fiction writer and Duffy alum wrote, "Excepting alcohol, I could not see any true common denominator among us. But we had all hit a point of powerlessness, of loss of control, so that to one degree or another we had fouled what was of value in our lives." All the talk was about alcohol because, "Ordinary living seemed so distant, its

---

* Calistoga is named after Saratoga Springs, New York, the town nearest the Yaddo artists' colony. Ray had found his way to a retreat after all.

problems so small compared to the one we shared. . . . Alcoholics make each other laugh a lot." They told one another hidden-bottle stories and splendid-advice stories. They talked about the fear of death, and the therapists told them that a quarter of a million Americans died every year of alcoholism, that it complicated many other diseases, played a role in murders, suicides, and highway fatalities. Such conversations allowed the fears that they all felt to be spoken.[39]

Both Ray and Maryann were full of hope and good humor when she came to see him on his first weekend, bringing the mail and meeting the other guests, including an inspirational pair she called "The Winnebago Lovers."

> She was all banged up—one leg useless and bandaged, so her loving husband was entirely solicitous about her maneuvers and the pain she was in. She had bandages on her face as well. It seems they lived in their Winnebago and she fell, drunk, while trying to walk in the Winnebago while her husband was driving it. As a result of that accident, they took themselves to Duffy's, and told this story to a circle of us there. Ray and I could hardly contain ourselves, we were so amused . . . and after we got back to his room, we laughed and laughed and expanded upon the story and circumstances.[40]

A rendering of that pair would become the hospitalized old couple—Ray's archetype of true love—in "What We Talk About When We Talk About Love."* After a week, Ray wrote letters to Dick Day and Gordon Lish, enclosing a Duffy's business card as his temporary address: ". . . finally had to do something about this fucking shit else lay down & pretend I'm dead, which I would have been soon." He'd quit the booze forever, he wrote Day. "*Want* to quit, finally . . . ," he explained.[41]

As recovery proceeds, most alcoholics remember and regret the bad behavior of their drinking days. With a few days of sobriety behind them, they are champing to go back into the world and fix the things that went wrong. Duffy opposed leaving early. Too often a patient in residential treatment plays—as Ray did—"a schizophrenic charade the entire time he is there and then rushes to the first bar he can find." Thus it occurred that days after Ray returned to Cupertino, he announced that his retreat had done him a great deal of good. He said he had learned that he could never again drink hard liquor and would thenceforth limit himself to Andre

---

* The old couple's role is lengthier in the earlier version of the story titled "Beginners."

champagne. By now the family resided in a small rented house close to the one they used to own. As Ray had read in the AA literature and been told at Duffy's, an alcoholic is *"absolutely unable to stop drinking on the basis of self-knowledge."*[42]

Maryann reached her limit in November. She asked Ray to move out:

> He harassed me into the wee hours of every morning, sitting in a chair, drinking in our bedroom, talking incessantly. (At this point in time, he could not cross a street safely without my help.)
>
> . . . my mental barragement (he wasn't personally abusive, he just would not stop talking—he was lonely—and was totally selfish about my lack of sleep that went on day after day until I was a veritable sleepwalker at the high school . . .) began to cause me embarrassment and jeopardy at school, and I had a dream that Ray was carried out of the house in a pine box.[43]

Ray tried to live in an apartment by himself and hated it. Then he asked his brother, James, if he could stay in his Santa Clara apartment while James and his wife were on vacation. Concerned that Ray's drinking, smoking, and partying might lead to damage at their home, James and Norma declined Ray's request. Ray took it hard. He told his friends, "My brother forsook me, he forsook me"—lingering over the biblical phrase as much as he did over the wound. From their mother, James later learned that Ray never forgave him. He would come to regret putting "material possessions before my love for my brother," because Ray "never forgot injustices or mistreatments." It all went back, James thought, to the ridicule Ray received for being overweight as a young boy in school. In late 1976, Ray found aid and comfort with his former secretary at SRA, Jean Coburn. Coburn, as Carver wrote in "Jean's TV," let him transact his "shabby business" from her home. She bought him liquor and gave him money and an old television set. In return, Ray "taught her to drink" and gave her and her son a cameo in "Where I'm Calling From."

Maryann continued to turn to Perkins "because he was so giving to me." When she invited Perkins and his daughters to stay with her, Vance resented the intrusion so strenuously that the Perkins family soon sought other quarters. After the Perkins family's removal, Ray and Maryann "tried to sort out the alcohol problem." He asked if she wanted a divorce. She replied that divorce was the furthest thing from her mind. She "wanted Ray to recover and *live*."[44]

Ray stored his things from the Cupertino Road house in the basement at St. James Church. When Ray (driven by Unger) rushed to the bank to take

out the money from the sale of the house, he found Maryann already there
(with Amy) and the account frozen. A scuffle occurred in the bank lobby,
but the money stayed put and Ray stayed broke. One morning Ray looked
outside and saw the parish ladies preparing a bazaar. His own things were
displayed on the tables—clothing, books, and typewriter. He and Unger
walked along the tables reclaiming Ray's belongings. A few months later,
Amy experienced the first manic break she'd had since meeting Unger and
could no longer work at the church, so they had a street sale of their own.
Carver's "Distress Sale" describes that scene as he saw it from a window
above, awash in sadness and regret, understanding that he "can't help anyone."[45]

Crumley got a glimpse of the terrors that drove Ray before a party at the
Kinder-Cecily apartment. Cecily had told Ray not to start grazing until the
table was set, but when Crumley walked through the kitchen, "There was
Ray with the jar of pickled eggs in his hand and two stuffed in his mouth.
He had this terrified look. He always had that terrified look. It was as if
someone had beaten him. I knew about that kind of terror and that's what
I thought, that someone had once beaten him and put that terror in him."
Drunk enough, Ray turned that terror on others. He didn't write in those
days, but he still tried to manage his career. He telephoned Levine to make
emotional pleas for more promotion of *Will You Please Be Quiet, Please?*,
sometimes adding angry threats. She knew she had already done all that
could be done for the book and later understood that Ray's drinking fueled
his tirades. On December 3, Ray sent two telegrams: one terminated his
relationship with Levine and the other authorized John Sterling of the Paul
R. Reynolds Agency as his new literary agent.[46]

There had been bad Christmases before, but 1976 was the worst ever for
the Carver family. Maryann was sober and "uptight." Ray was jealous of
her continuing association with Perkins. Along with Vance, Chris, and
Ella Carver, the gathered family included Amy and Erin Wright, Doug
Unger, his brother Steve, and his father, Maurice. Ray came over but didn't
stay. As he left the house, he tossed a whole carton of pressed-wood logs
into the fireplace, igniting a blaze that threatened to spread into the room
before Unger doused it with water. Someone shouted to Ray, "That's the
last Christmas you'll ever ruin for us!" That line provided the germ for his
story "A Serious Talk."[47]

On New Year's Eve, Ray returned to Duffy's. By then he was so impressed
by Eugene Duffy that he thought of writing his life story, and he did portray him in the character of Frank Martin in "Where I'm Calling From."

Considered the Babe Ruth of AA speakers, Duffy would yell at people and scare them and insult them to break down their denial that they were alcoholic. That was what Ray needed. Duffy also "fancied himself a writer," his son said, and "learned three new words a day, and wrote stories, so he would have been able to connect with Ray. He would have talked about Jack London."[48]

Duffy's happens to be eleven miles as the crow flies from Jack London's Beauty Ranch. In "Where I'm Calling From," Frank Martin tells the men on the veranda, "Jack London used to have a big place . . . behind that green hill you're looking at. But alcohol killed him. Let that be a lesson to you. He was a better man than any of us. But he couldn't handle the stuff, either." To have the second chance at life that Duffy's offered, Ray would have to disconnect alcohol and writing. He would have to admit that he was an ordinary drunk, part of an undistinguished "we" who were "powerless over alcohol" (step one) until they "made a decision to turn our will and our lives over to the care of God *as we understood Him*" (step three). Emphasis on Higher Power was central at Duffy's. Images of praying hands appeared on business cards and pamphlets. Ray did not trouble himself to define the Higher Power that would take care of him. Asked if he was religious, Carver would reply, "No, but I have to believe in miracles and the possibility of resurrection. . . . Every day that I wake up, I'm glad to wake up."

Unger, Amy, and Kinder came in Unger's truck to retrieve Ray from Duffy's. Amy and Kinder drank some beers on the way. They found Ray waiting by the drained swimming pool. Kinder went to use the bathroom off a room where Ray had his bags ready to go. "I don't know what possessed me," Kinder said, "but I got those empty beer cans out of the truck and stuck them in his pillows and his drawer—just evidence everywhere." Heading south, Ray and Kinder rode in the truck bed, "bouncing around like a pair of field hands because Doug drove like a maniac, talking and smoking some dope." That night, Kinder recalled, "Ray talked about his father and his father's death with such emotion and sadness." The full moon was out in a clear sky by the time they emerged from the tunnel above the Golden Gate Bridge. At that moment, Ray told Kinder, "he was real close to having his last drink."[49]

Alcoholism is a progressive condition. Regardless of how long a person has been abstinent, the drinker's brain reacts to alcohol with the same morbidity that had developed months or years earlier. When Ray drank again, he plummeted to the depths he'd just escaped. He did calamitous things he couldn't remember. When Lish was in town, Ray came to his airport hotel to give him a ride. Finding Lish's room open, Ray and his companion settled in to wait. Lish was furious to find three bottles of champagne on his room service tab. Thus Ray began to apprehend how disastrous the consequences of his blackouts could be.[50]

In March, two literary events converged to prove to Ray that alcohol was ruining him as a writer. First, Cheever published *Falconer,* a novel about an imprisoned heroin addict and murderer. Cheever's picture was on the cover of *Newsweek.* Crawford saw Ray "just looking at it, and you could just tell Ray longed for that kind of recognition so much." Inside the same issue of the magazine was an interview with Cheever about his sobriety conducted by his daughter. *Falconer* became a bestseller. Such glorification of sobriety in connection with a major American writer was surely a first.[51]

Ray had been sober two weeks when the National Book Award judges announced their finalists for 1977. In the fiction category were five books: *Will You Please Be Quiet, Please?* headed the list. Cecily thought that this nomination gave Ray another kick toward sobriety—"That was his old work. He was a contender with no new work coming. He realized if he wanted another chance he would have to stay sober." When Wallace Stegner won the award, Ray called to congratulate him. Stegner told Ray, "You're young, you'll have more opportunities." Ray wasn't sure about that.[52]

Ray slipped again. He couldn't afford to return to rehab, so Amy and Unger administered his hummers. During this hummer time, Unger said, "Ray was in absolute despair . . . We had a fireplace where it was illegal to have a fire, but I could make a fire in a little hibachi thing we had. He would sit in front of that or in front of the TV and just weep." Ray stayed sober for weeks. He attended AA meetings at the church next door and faced his many losses. He found his desire to write blunted and, as he said a decade later, might have "in some subconscious way blamed some of the things that had happened in my family on my wanting to write. I had taken my family on strange odysseys to one place or another trying to find the ideal writing situation, the ideal job, the ideal place to live."[53]

Certainly San Francisco was not the ideal place for him to live in his fragile sobriety. He went to Humboldt County. He found a house behind the Bella Vista Restaurant in McKinleyville, just across the Mad River from Arcata. It belonged to the restaurant owner, one of whose chefs had just moved out. He borrowed money from Maryann for the rent. By early April, he was settled, "living alone, hand-to-mouthing it," three hundred miles from the party life and old associations, close to ocean and woods.[54]

Maryann flew up for a weekend, and, Ray wrote Curt Johnson, "there is every possibility we'll get back together this summer." Even though he was lonely and broke, he wrote John O'Brien, this "self-imposed exile" was the best thing that ever happened. His life had become "unbearably complicated," but now he was on the wagon and writing. At Michael Ryan's suggestion, he applied to teach in the Goddard College low-residency MFA program, but director Ellen Voigt didn't reply. Ray speculated that she'd probably heard about liquor, "telephone abuse," and "prurient interest," when she checked his references.[55] At the end of April, Capra Press offered Ray a $250 advance for a book of stories that had been omitted from the McGraw-Hill volume. In a bizarre letter to Lish, Ray said he had written two plays and was beginning a satirical novel about New York writers and critics that would also defend the "writing tenets, aesthetics, etc. of the 1950's." He thanked Lish for his encouragement over the past year and said he was now "producing like mad."[56]

Perhaps in some fool's paradise of early sobriety Ray was "producing," but his main occupation was his sobriety. He attended AA meetings and guzzled coffee. When Köepf came through intending to spend the night, Ray had all the doors and windows open to the chilly sea air: "He said if he got comfortable he'd want to drink. He had some apprehension that seeing an old friend from the past would tempt him, so I stayed in a motel." When Ray went out for salmon with a one-legged eighty-year-old fisherman, he seemed to bring the man bad luck: on their first trip, his motor blew up and the Coast Guard towed them in; next time, they caught a loose crab pot and lost $150 in gear.[57]

Ray made a foray to San Francisco for the American Booksellers Association (ABA) convention. Both his publishers, Noel Young and Frederic Hills, were there, and Ray knew he needed to grab opportunities provided by his National Book Award nomination. He spent Friday afternoon with Hills, sipping Cokes in North Beach bars and telling about a novel he'd been "fooling on." Hills invited Ray to go out for lunch with him on Sunday. On Saturday, after moving some boxes in Cupertino and arguing with his children, Ray was "fit to be tied." Maryann joined him for a dinner hosted by Young at the St. Francis Hotel. There Ray picked up a glass of wine and went around the bend, blacked out for the rest of the night. He woke "hideously hungover" to learn that he'd fought with Maryann, acted as if he were hearing voices, and arrived by taxi at Unger and Amy's apartment.[58]

Ray's bender continued. He and Maryann weren't speaking when they picked up Hills at his hotel on Sunday. In order to drive, Ray had fortified himself with vodka: "I was drunk and hungover both," he said later. He was dismayed to learn that Hills wanted to have lunch in Sausalito. After an excruciating hour of driving, Ray found himself eating an expense-account lunch at a table overlooking the bay. He was on his second Bloody Mary when Hills told him that McGraw-Hill would bring out a paperback edition of *Will You Please Be Quiet, Please?* in the spring. That news Ray'd had reason to expect. But then, Hills said words that Ray had only dreamed about before. He offered him a $5,000 advance to write a novel. All he'd need, Hills said, was a proposal. Ray promised to send one the next week.[59]

Ray left the table, went to the restroom, and cried. In the fifteen years he'd called himself a writer, no one had offered him money for something he hadn't written yet. He paused at the bar to toss down a double on the rocks. His appetite perked up, and he ate the shrimp on his plate followed by a bowl of strawberries and a cup of coffee. He managed the drive back easily. He and Maryann dropped Hills at the convention hall and pulled the car over so they could hug. Ray drove to a liquor store. Then they invited Unger and Amy to an oyster bar to celebrate Ray's good fortune. At the end of the meal, the Carvers realized they had no money, so Amy wrote a rubber check for the tab. "I ought to write a story called 'Without a Dime,' " Ray told Unger. That was May 29.[60]

Ray stayed in the city for a couple more days and then flew back—alone—to McKinleyville, still drunk when he arrived. He took his last drink of alcohol at the Jambalaya bar in Arcata on Thursday, June 2, 1977.[61]

Ray told people he loved this sentence of Lawrence Durrell's: "The sea is high again today, with a thrilling flush of wind." Perhaps he loved the cadences and sibilance of it, but he must also have loved its promise of a second, fresh beginning. June 3—sun rising behind the chef's house in McKinleyville and moving across the Pacific, offshore wind coming in from the west—became the morning he'd longed for. He woke up and he drank nothing alcoholic. Again the next day he abstained. And the next. The days accumulated. He was very ill, but he was able to say, "I'll always be an alcoholic, but I'm no longer a practicing alcoholic."[62]

On June 5, Ray typed a long letter to thank Hills for having faith in him. "By God, everything *is* coming together, the things in my life *are* falling into place."[63]

This time he was right.

CHAPTER 21

Sobriety

June 1977–December 1977, McKinleyville, California

That which has happened is not necessarily probable. That which has happened is merely history, possible, not art.
— Aristotle, *Poetics*, transcribed in one of Carver's notebooks

On the third day of his new sobriety, Ray mailed Fred Hills and John Sterling a completely implausible plan for a novel. He proposed to tell the story of three German naval heroes who successfully foiled British naval forces in East Africa during World War I . Though the background of his story would be exotic (*"The African Queen* seen from the other side"), Ray would use the three men as point-of-view characters and focus on their histories and conflicts. He assured Hills that he'd been thinking about this novel for about ten years.[1]

Sterling knew that Ray struggled to write short stories, and he soon learned that his client "did not have the novel all worked out in his head," so he had reasonable doubts about his ability to complete a novel "in the grand epic tradition of courage, duty, heroism, sacrifice, and ultimate 'victory' against great odds," as the contract described it. But the beginning agent was delighted to secure the advance money his client needed and thought it would be a fantastic surprise if Carver could write it. He negotiated a contract that totaled more than Hills had offered Ray in Sausalito: $4,000 upon signing, $3,500 upon delivery of a manuscript in September 1978. Though Lish knew about Ray's proposal, there was no talk of involving him as an editor. Sterling was convinced, and Carver's letters of the time support his view, that "Ray had every intention of doing it. It was not cynical or mercenary on his part." In the bright new days of his sobriety, Ray believed he was going to write the book, and Sterling encouraged him. He had a couple of other ideas for novels, too, "more au courant" subjects that would be easier to complete, he said, and he wanted to do them all. The important thing, Ray felt, was that he would now have the time.[2]

With $4,000 on the way, Ray focused his attention on making domestic arrangements that would help him stay away from alcohol. He did not like living alone. Maryann flew up to celebrate their twentieth wedding anniversary—with apple juice, smoked salmon, and fresh oysters—and agreed to stay the summer in the house behind the Bella Vista Restaurant. She returned south for Vance's high school commencement, then set him up to stay with a family in Los Altos for the summer. Right after his mother left, Vance's girlfriend broke up with him, and someone stole the stereo out of his Volkswagen. He worked every day as a union-wage janitor, "while not really understanding what my parents were up to."[3]

What they were up to was trying to salvage their marriage. Ray promised Maryann he would try to be the man she'd fallen in love with. They relaxed, sleeping late and speaking carefully. They no longer believed in speaking without forethought. They had no telephone, so no one could call with an emergency. They bought fishing equipment, folding chairs, and hats, and drove to places where Ray had once fished with his dad and brother and Uncle Fred, stopping for burgers and milkshakes in Fortuna. Or they went north to Freshwater Lagoon and caught enough trout for supper. They were friends again. Some nights, Ray wrote, they were "cheerful . . . dancy," but they were hanging on to each other for dear life.[4]

For years to come, Carver turned over in his mind that time in McKinleyville. His story "Chef's House," narrated by a wife, caught the mood: "I found myself wishing the summer wouldn't end. I knew better, but after a month of being with Wes in Chef's House, I put my wedding ring back on." That actually happened, Maryann said.[5] During the first month of sobriety, Ray went to one or two Alcoholics Anonymous meetings a day. He probably didn't have an AA sponsor, and there's no evidence that he systematically worked the 12 steps, but he needed AA in those early months: "I felt absolutely crazy, nearly, every morning I woke up . . . and felt, too, like I hadn't done any work at all and that what I had done wasn't worth anything, etc."[6]

When interviewers asked Ray if he went to AA to hear the stories, he insisted that the "funny, crazy, sad" stories he heard there "never struck me as material I wanted to use for a story." He had enough of his own drinking stories. In this frightening and lonely passage, he found comfort in being with other recovering drunks and inspiration from the speakers. After a month of sobriety, he began to understand who he might be without alcohol. When Doug Unger and Amy came for a weekend, Unger noticed that he'd become more generous: "Ray had read my work in manuscript when he was drunk and been cruel to it. Up there he took an interest in my new novel."[7]

Ray and Maryann did ordinary things to keep busy. They watched horse races at the county fairgrounds, played bingo in church social halls (and they cheated, as the young couple does in Carver's story "After the Denim"), rode a jet boat up the Rogue River. His boozer's belly receded. He purchased new guns so he'd be ready in case he got a chance to go hunting, which he hadn't done since his children were small. He described these days with satisfaction in letters to Noel Young and other friends but mentioned Maryann infrequently.[8]

Sobriety is a painstaking process; wisdom and self-knowledge do not descend upon a person immediately after taking that last drink. During this time, Ray was of two minds about writing. Part of him didn't care if he ever wrote again. He later told a fellow alcoholic that he could do little more than write letters for the first six months of his sobriety. Was this true? Evidence supports Maryann's recollection that Ray was back at his desk early in the summer: "He wrote immediately after he quit drinking, when he was still shaky and ill from alcohol, though off it."[9] His first business was to correct proofs for *Furious Seasons,* the volume of stories that Capra would publish. Some shuffling occurred before Carver and Young settled on these eight stories: "Dummy," "Distance," "The Lie," "So Much Water So Close to Home," "The Fling," "Pastoral," "Mine," and "Furious Seasons."[10] Young planned a limited hardcover edition (a hundred copies signed by the author) and 1,200 softcovers.

Given the rough water Ray was riding as he finished *Furious Seasons,* it's not surprising that he changed his mind several times about dedicatees for the book. He considered including Lish in the list, then left him out because he feared the book would be an embarrassment. (Lish noticed and complained about the omission.) After several revisions, he sent Young the amended roster that appears in the book:

For Maryann, again; and for Curt Johnson; and Max Crawford, Dick Day, Bill Kittredge, Chuck Kinder, and Diane Cecily; creditors.[11]

Even the punctuation in that dedication reveals indecision and complexity.

Carver completed two new stories in the summer of 1977: "Why Don't You Dance?" and "Viewfinder." Both went to Lish and both were on the path to acceptance at *Esquire.* But Sterling also saw that Ray was "working to extend himself as a writer. I'd get stories that were six pages long, maybe even shorter. They were glimmers and fragments. There was always something in them." Hints of these attempts survive. Carver's letters mention plays, poems, and a fishing piece intended for *Esquire*'s outdoor column that was turning into an essay about alcoholism.[12] Sterling—a veteran of a creative writing class that Lish taught at Yale—knew Ray was sending him things that he hadn't yet shown to Lish: "Ray had great strength, but at the same time he had real gentleness, and it led me to feel that he needed gentleness too. He really did have a sense that he could break."[13]

Carver wrote a sheaf of notes for stories to be called "Drunkenness" or "Humiliations." One page says simply, "Tell it all . . ." Ray underlined that injunction to himself, but he didn't follow it. Perhaps no one could tell it all. The AA program asks recovering alcoholics to make amends to people they have harmed "except when to do so would injure them or others." Perhaps Ray had misgivings about recounting certain episodes from these years when alcohol ruled his life. Or, more likely, he decided that some of those humiliations wouldn't make good stories. He confessed to Lish that no one except Maryann "and maybe you" knew what bad shape he had been in: ". . . an awful lot of wreckage, waste, and ruin back there."[14] His purpose was not confession, but rather—as he would explain in 1986—"to bear witness. . . . every poem or story counts . . . becomes a part of the writer, part of his witness to his time here on earth."[15]

As a drunk, Ray had often laughed and told stories on himself and Maryann. As a sober man, he continued the genre with stories about a practicing alcoholic he called "Bad Ray" or "Bad Raymond" while he worked at living his new persona, the one he called "Good Raymond." Thus, his fascination with double characters—his tendency to see himself double—took new form. "One night in McKinleyville, Ray was sitting in his chair laughing," Maryann recalled vividly:

> It went on for like twenty minutes, and I'd say, "Come on, Ray, what's so funny?" But every time he'd try to tell me, he'd start laughing so hard he couldn't tell me.
>
> Finally, he got it out: "Didn't I run that drinking into the ground, though?" He said it over and over. "Didn't I run that drinking into the ground?"[16]

Ray had made no progress at all on the novel by mid-August when he and Maryann left McKinleyville to go fishing in Montana. "It sounded preposterous, but he did fantasize about writing this historical novel. He *read* a lot of history," Unger said. When Kinder and Cecily came to visit, Ray had sharpened pencils, a stack of yellow legal pads, and a handbook on novel writing by John Braine at the ready. He asked Kinder, then writing his second novel, " 'Where do you start it? What do you do?' " Kinder was sure that his friend's talent was ill suited for writing an exotic novel. He assured Ray that he'd pulled off a tremendous scam in getting an advance for a book he'd never write.[17] Eventually Ray began to tell the story that way himself. When he learned that another author was working on a novel about the German naval episode, he promised Hills an outline for a more contemporary story.[18]

Going to Montana was a risky venture for Ray's sobriety, but he missed his friends. They shared a cabin at Flathead Lake with Bill Kittredge, Sara Vogan, Diane Smith, and Max Crawford. The others held down their drinking in deference to Maryann and Ray. While the rest trolled for pan-sized kokanee, Ray became maniacal about catching big fish and was out there "as illegally as can be, chumming them with canned corn."Ray talked about how much he loved fishing the little inlets and streams around McKinleyville, but Kittredge noticed that Maryann and Ray's relationship had cooled: "During that week, they were amiable, comfortable with each other, but clearly not as connected as they had been." He thought "their relationship was broken."[19]

Ray and Maryann's mutual sobriety had eliminated some of the swings from extreme crisis to tender reconciliation that had long been part of their marriage, but it could not turn time backward. For Maryann, it was the beginning of a new school year—and she was, for the second time in seven years on an unpaid leave, without the professional independence that she'd worked so long to gain. Ray was writing, she was taking graduate courses at Humboldt State in Jungian psychology and Asian philosophy. They spoke of going to live in Europe for a year. As the honeymoon of early sobriety ended, they faced mundane challenges and missed the fury of their old relationship. But they hadn't yet taken account of that with each other.

Early in September, *Esquire* magazine was acquired by Rupert Murdoch and Clay Felker, whose own magazines (*Village Voice, New York,* and *New West*) had also been purchased by the Australian media mogul. Lish wrote Carver that he was quitting *Esquire* to go—well, anywhere else, it seemed. He interrupted an angry letter to tell Carver that he was reading *Furious Seasons*: "In the middle of this shitstorm . . . I am reading the goddamn book and it is goddamn wonderful. Jesus, man, are your stories the stories I want to hear . . . you should read one of your own stories and you'll know what's up with my story right now."[20] In turn, Ray wrote his patron and editor a long statement of praise and thanks, reviewing their nine-year relationship. Lish had made a "single-handed impression on American letters" and had been for him an "ideal reader" who "loomed large in my conscious and unconscious life." He remembered their "wacky" lunches in Palo Alto and Lish's fight to "top of the anthill back there."[21]

Within days Lish had three job offers. He took a position as a book editor at Knopf. As before, his career move would have consequences for Carver's literary development. Lish continued to praise *Furious,* allowing that it "could use a bit of a shaping and pruning, but they are all fine stories and I am very proud of you."[22]

Carver's newest stories went homeless. "Why Don't You Dance?" was submitted to the *New Yorker* at the invitation of Charles McGrath, then a new fiction editor who wanted to "de-stuffify" the venerable magazine. But McGrath couldn't sell editor in chief William Shawn on "Why Don't You Dance?" and wrote a rejection explaining that he'd been a Carver fan for a long time, but this story seemed "a little slight" and "everyone" at the magazine felt that "in the end Carver never did enough with the situation he set up." They wanted to wait for one of Carver's "really first-class efforts." It's the sort of withering and almost-personal *New Yorker* rejection that has brought sadness and hope to many an aspiring author. "Everybody knew that was the code—a casual and dimly enthusiastic line meant they are noticing you and really do want to see your work," Sterling said.[23]

When Ray gave up alcohol, he turned the considerable force of his old fixation onto other objects: first on sobriety per se, then on fishing and writing. Despite the knowledge that alcohol and living beyond their means had kept the family in chaos for half a decade, Ray was frustrated that the troubles continued to proliferate now and feared any exposure to turbulent emotions would trigger him to drink again. Chris and Pleadwell's lives were then, according to Unger, in chaos. Chris had gotten into some legal trouble, so Maryann and Ray brought her to McKinleyville with them. Then Unger and Ray went to ask Pleadwell to leave the house Maryann had rented for him and Chris. They found the floor "covered with dog feces while Shiloh was typing poems and saying something like, I'm a poet too. I have a right to stay here and do this." Ray was furious."[24] Ray complained that he was "too old" for this kind of thing, but Chris remembered that during this "fragile time" her father "was kind to me, good to me . . . more like his old self."[25]

Vance, starting at Foothill Community College, was—according to Unger—"going through a personal psychological crisis. He could be demanding, but not in any criminal way—he was truly left out, and in need."[26] Under emotional duress, Ray and Maryann followed their habitual patterns. For Maryann this meant trying to intervene in crises—she'd had years of practice at that; for Ray it meant keeping his distance from chaos as he got back to work. Dealing with his children had been "harrowing," Ray wrote Lish, but he was proud that he'd managed to stay sober throughout the ordeal. He was—with frequent attendance at AA meetings—trying to make the difficult distinctions called for in the prayer for "serenity to accept the things I cannot change, / Courage to change the things I can, and wisdom to know the difference." At the time, Ray thought Maryann was wasting energy and money on these crises when she should be concentrating on their marriage. "People don't understand how bitter Ray felt," Unger reflected.[27]

When Ray's advance from McGraw-Hill and the magazine sale money were gone, some of it spent on a lawyer for Chris, Maryann became a cocktail waitress at the Red Lion Hotel in Eureka. At thirty-seven, she could wear the uniform miniskirt and low-cut blouse to advantage and could pick up good tips, but this wasn't quite the life she'd hoped for when she took a leave of absence from Los Altos. Ray typed résumés and contacted everyone who might assist him to an academic job. He applied again to Yaddo. He applied for a Guggenheim Fellowship and lined up forceful recommenders to go with his application: Lish, Cheever, Michaels, Geoffrey Wolff. He waited and he wrote.[28]

Good Ray was still capable of a little mischief in the service of his literary career. The curriculum vitae he sent out contained a few stretchers, beginning with his birthdate (changed to 1939), continuing with a self-awarded MFA degree from Iowa (1966, he claimed), and study at Tel Aviv University, and omission of his disastrous spell at UCSB. But it hardly mattered—his work had appeared in more than fifty-seven periodicals and ten anthologies; he had published four books; one of them had been a nominee for the National Book Award. His achievements were remarkable for a man with his liabilities. Some people were beginning to appreciate that. *Antaeus* magazine asked him to contribute to a list of "Neglected Books of the Twentieth Century."[29]

When *Furious Seasons* came out, Ray gave a brief reading at Northtown Books in Arcata, then flew off to a literary festival at Southern Methodist University in Dallas. Two poets who'd known him as Bad Ray in Iowa, John Skoyles and Michael Ryan, got him the Dallas gig. He'd be joining a lineup of heavyweights—Joan Didion, E. L. Doctorow, Donald Justice, and Philip Levine—along with younger writers Richard Ford, Tess Gallagher, Michael Harper, and Michael Waters. Ray knew, Maryann said, "that this trip was going to be an acid test of his commitment to sobriety." Originally she and Ray planned to drive to Texas together; instead she went to the Bay Area to get Chris. While she was there, she told Perkins that she and Ray Carver were definitely back together.[30]

Writers got royal treatment at SMU—Harper was astonished that his student escort drove a Rolls-Royce—and the festival was a wild and frivolous time of little work and much play. There were receptions at the homes of wealthy patrons, open tabs for food and drink at the Hilton, and "women who were there to come on to [male] writers." One pretty undergraduate poet aggressively sought Ray's attention. While Ray may have spent one evening with her, he was soon trying to evade her. Versions of the story feature Ray climbing out of windows and hiding in shower stalls. Richard Crossland, a festival organizer who was supposed to keep an eye on Ray, said, "Ray went missing from a house party. I found him in the yard sitting under a bush, smoking. He called to me in a whisper and asked me to take him to a coffee shop. I think he was still afraid that he would just pick up a drink and be lost." Between bouts of real fright, Ray tried to prove that he could have a good time. One night he insisted that Waters and other friends come upstairs with him to fetch his jacket:

> Everybody had been talking about their conquests and other people's wild affairs. So Ray turned on the light in his room and there hung a black bra on the lamp shade! It was obvious that Ray had contrived this! Everybody started joking and saying, Oh, Ray, you are such a bad boy and so on. And he was like, Oh, gosh, I can't believe you guys saw this.[31]

At Dallas, Ray met a man who would become his close, perhaps closest, friend for the rest of his life. Richard Ford had published a first novel the year before. The native Mississippian was thirty-three, lanky and athletic, and spoke with a drawl that both invited and held off intimacy. Carver thought him "poised and courtly." Like Carver, Ford chose his words with care, had Arkansawyers in his background, and had knocked around the country a bit. Ray thought Ford's first novel, *A Piece of My Heart*, which he'd read the previous summer, was "the best book I've read in years."[32] Over breakfast the two writers talked about fishing and shooting. Ray tasted Ford's grits. Ray thought Ford "emanated confidence" and was "clearly everything I was not!" Soon after the SMU festival, Ray wrote to friends that Ford was his "great friend." To Ford, Ray "seemed friendly but slightly spooked, though not in a way that spooked you." He looked "as if he'd stepped down off a Greyhound bus from 1964, and from someplace where he'd done mostly custodial duties. And he was completely irresistible."[33]

A small crowd turned out for Ray's reading in a large hall. When he brought a glass of water to Ray at the podium, Waters joked that the LSD should kick in shortly. "That's okay, Michael," Ray replied, "as long as there's no vodka in there." Carver read two stories that night, including his new one, "Why Don't You Dance?" Ford described Ray's performance:

hugely hunched over a glaring podium lamp, constantly fiddling with his big glasses, clearing his throat, sipping water, beetling down at the pages of his book as if he'd never really thought of reading this story out loud and wasn't finding it easy. His voice was typically hushed, seemingly unpracticed, halting almost to the point of being annoying. But the effect of voice and story upon the listener was of actual life being unscrolled in a form so distilled, so intense, so *chosen,* so affecting in its urgencies as to leave you breathless and limp when he was finished.

Ford told Carver he thought the story was terrific and said he'd read it "perfectly." Carver grinned and asked, " 'Did you like that? Did you? Oh, Christ, I'm glad to hear that, I really am . . . I hadn't read a story sober in longer than I can remember. Maybe never. I was shaking in my boots . . . But that you liked it means the world to me . . .' "[34]

Poet Tess Gallagher was also in the audience for Ray's reading. At dinner, she saw that Ray loaded up his plate with Southern country food. They soon discovered that they'd both been born to Depression-era migrants to the West and grown up in working-class towns in Washington State. Before the conference ended, Gallagher was a confirmed Carver fan. She bought his books and he inscribed one of them to his "little pal, Tess."[35]

For his participation in the festival, Ray received $1,000, all his expenses, and several T-shirts printed with a typewriter and the names of the guest authors, including himself. He had debuted his new persona. A new cycle of tales began: the Good Raymond stories. This new Ray was a man becoming sure enough of his sobriety to make jokes about alcohol, a nice guy who seldom uttered a discouraging word about another writer and was astonished when good luck came to himself. He had a terrible sweet tooth, drank Coke and ginger ale, and reeked of cigarettes.

From Dallas, Ray wrote an exuberant letter to Maryann and told her that the audience had been "knocked out" by his reading.[36] Before he left Dallas, he visited his mother's prosperous brother, Sanders Casey, who lived in that city. His mood crashed as Crossland drove him to the airport:

Ray was depressed, on the verge of tears, because he thought he'd never make any money as a writer and was utterly incapable of writing anything more than about twenty-five pages. He said he wanted to be successful, even famous, like the other writers he'd met in Dallas who actually earned a living as writers. He had no prospects, couldn't even get a decent teaching job. I told him his stories were terrific, we all thought so, but he'd probably have to write a novel to earn real money. I told him a novel was just a bunch of stories strung together. He didn't talk about his marriage, but I gathered that was on the back of his mind as well. I remember putting my arm on his big shoulder and saying, "You'll figure it out." Little did he know![37]

Waiting for Ray's return to McKinleyville, Maryann opened a note to her husband from the young poet he'd been avoiding at the festival. The letter writer thanked Ray for the wonderful night they'd spent together and asked if she could see him again. When Maryann confronted Ray with this letter, he insisted it wasn't important and he hadn't given out his address. Ray urged Maryann not to spoil things by making a big deal out of it.[38]

Ray was pumped up to write and terrified of discord. Maryann squelched her worries and prepared for Thanksgiving guests. The holidays may have soothed marital tension, but, as Ray told O'Brien, the "influx of ragged and neurotic relatives" interrupted his work. Chris was still there as well. If her presence distracted Ray, he understood that "right now the alternatives [for her] are pretty frightening."[39] Soon after, Chris joined girlfriends at Lake Tahoe, where she expected to find a job. Unger and Amy and her daughter, Erin, left for New York City, where Amy hoped to work in theater again and Unger to finish a novel, *Leaving the Land,* which editor Ted Solotaroff wanted to publish. Maryann kept her restaurant job.

While he was sorting the mail with Maryann, Ray received a white envelope from Gallagher. As Maryann recalled, Gallagher told Ray that she loved his stories and thanked him for letting her pal around with him and his friends in Dallas.[40] To escape Thanksgiving houseguests who would stay till the "foodstuffs have disappeared," Ray hid out at Dick Day's. From there he wrote Lish that he'd stayed sober in Dallas and "didn't fall in love." Full of zest for their new friendship, he asked Ford about jobs and places to stay in the East. He told him that he and Maryann wanted to escape California and their role as parents and hoped that by this time next year they'd be across or out of the country.[41]

Ray was serious about a change of place. He beat the bushes for a teaching job, but few would consider hiring such a legendary and violent drunk. But when Crumley spoke to his friend Les Standiford at the University of Texas in El Paso, he assured him that Ray wasn't just on the wagon but a changed man, sober for the long haul. Standiford returned a message that he'd love to hear from this new Carver. By the end of the year, Ray had asked no fewer than eight people to send letters of reference.[42]

A similar barrage of recommendations, plus a forthright letter from Ray about his recovery and good intentions persuaded poet Ellen Bryant Voigt to hire Ray for the Goddard MFA program in Vermont. The innovative program was strapped for cash: Voigt offered Ray $1,200 and *half* of a

round-trip airfare to lead a two-week workshop in late January followed by
six months of correspondence with six students and meetings with those six
in July. Ray accepted. He would remain in the East after the session ended.
Maryann, he told Ford, would stay in northern California to get Vance and
Chris settled somewhere and finish the courses she was taking at Humboldt
State. She might join him in the spring.[43]

By all accounts the four Carvers had a peaceful Christmas together. It was,
Ray reported, "pleasant, the best I can remember," with "no wildness or
friction, those old conditions," but he was glad everyone had gone home
again." Chris remembered "a beautiful Christmas," but Vance thought his
parents seemed in "a state of standstill, neither happy nor unhappy, just
dazed and ambivalent." Ray gave them the other three numbered, cloth-
bound copies of *Furious Seasons and Other Stories*. In Chris's he wrote,
"For my darling daughter Chris, at Christmas 1977. With all love . . ." His
inscription to Maryann promised love "now and forever."[44] Ray packed for
Vermont. Maryann rented a room in McKinleyville. The interlude behind
the Bella Vista was over.

The two stories Ray composed in McKinleyville may be read in light of
his recovering condition. In "Why Don't You Dance?" a man who drinks
heavily finds himself displaying all of his household furnishing for sale
in his front yard. A young couple just setting up housekeeping comes by
and tries his bed, dances to music on his record player, and gets drunk on
the man's whiskey. "You must be desperate or something," the girl tells
the man. Even as she sets out on her fresh life, the young woman remains
haunted by the man's story.

"Viewfinder" also deals in loss and recuperation. A stranger with hooks
for hands comes to a man's door offering for sale a Polaroid picture of the
man peering out the window of his own house. The photographer, a doppelganger of sorts, notices that the narrator has been abandoned by his family. The narrator climbs on his roof and waves at the photographer, who
waves back with his hooks. Unlike Mr. Slater in "Collectors," this narrator
rises above his empty household. "Viewfinder" exhibits a man recovering
from losses, finding a way to survive, taking a new view.

Nor did those two stories use up all Carver had to say about his months
in McKinleyville. His best-known fictional treatment of that time was
"Chef's House," in 1981. He returned to the subject in the poem "Late
Night with Fog and Horses" and his 1986 story "Blackbird Pie" and again
in two posthumously published stories, "Call If You Need Me" and "What
Would You Like to See?" The latter is an artistically flaccid but richly autobiographical piece in which a husband recounts his last hours with his wife

before a separation. In the night, the husband notices that "something that I had been hearing I didn't hear anymore." A generator has failed, causing the restaurant's frozen salmon to spoil. Marriages, like food, the story suggests, may spoil due to lack of energy.[45]

After Christmas, Ray drove Chris to the airport. In her gift copy of *Furious Seasons*, she read a story called "Distance" wherein she figured as a tiny baby and as a grown daughter asking about her childhood. Vance returned to Los Altos—there was no story for him in that book, and at that time he did not understand his father's work. For a few more nights, Maryann and Ray slept in her single bed in Arcata. Maryann took Ray's sobriety to mean that "he'd come back to me for good." She should have known that an addict never successfully gives up an addiction for someone else, but she needed this hope.

Though Ray and Maryann's story would continue and Ray's relationship with his children would improve, Christmas 1978 was the last time all four of them were together. "Our family was disbanded. That's what it was, a disbanding," Christine Carver reflected decades later.[46]

CHAPTER 22

Separation

January 1978–August 1978, Vermont and Iowa City

Nature reconciles man, that is, makes him indifferent. And in this
world one must be indifferent. Only those who are unconcerned are
able to see clearly, to be just, and to work.
      — Anton Chekhov to Alexei Suvorin, May 4, 1889,
      transcribed in one of Carver's notebooks

At thirty-nine, Ray was parting from his wife and children and everything he found familiar, heading east on a one-way ticket. A rabbi sat
next to him on the long red-eye flight. He spent most of the night talking
to him about facing his mortality and making a new beginning. It was, Ray
wrote Les Gutterman later, "an extraordinary encounter."

Ray arrived at the Goddard College campus without winter clothing. In
Vermont's subzero weather he wore vinyl slip-on shoes that looked like a
doll's and a thin leather safari jacket. He set his feet "carefully in other people's tracks, shaking his head as if the weather were just one more thing in
an astonishing world." By the end of the week, Ray had conquered the elements. He was driving a car that belonged to one of his students, spending
cash borrowed from another, and wearing gloves belonging to poet Barbara
Greenberg. He was so happy to have a job that the weather didn't much
concern him.[1]

Goddard's low-residency MFA program in creative writing was begun
by poet Ellen Bryant Voigt in 1975 to serve writers who couldn't attend
conventional graduate schools. She hired teachers who'd published first
books and were still hungry enough to participate in the residencies and
keep up the correspondence obligations. Faculty for the January 1978 term
included Ray's friends Michael Ryan and Richard Ford and several who
became his friends: George Chambers, Donald Hall, Thomas Lux, Stephen Dobyns, Tobias Wolff, and his brother, Geoffrey. Here Ray found "a

group of peers who were involved in aesthetic discovery and passing it on to their students," Voigt thought. "Ford and the Wolff brothers, especially, respected Ray and said things to him that helped him make his own decisions about his artistic life."[2]

They all lived in a dormitory—men on one floor, women on another—in single rooms. For Ray, who'd been married with children during his college years, this was "a trip to camp," and he was grateful to have the narrow bed, the bathroom shared with other men, and the all-night bull sessions. Students and faculty alike were bold and ambitious, and their intensity led to parties, drinking, and sexual escapades for students and faculty alike. But Ray, Tobias Wolff recalled, "behaved with unusual dignity, frankly, at Goddard."[3] Like many recovering alcoholics, he was on the lookout for big meals and a steady supply of sugar. He loaded his cafeteria trays and smuggled out packets of brownies or doughnuts and stashed them in his desk drawers. When a practical joker replaced his brownies with slices of stale, white bread, he told everyone about the funny trick someone had played on him.[4]

Ray spent his free time hiding, smoking, and pacing or wandering out to a squalid dorm lounge where he "hung out with the old folks" and swapped stories.[5] He polished his Bad Ray stories into a niche genre, a way of acknowledging the damage of those days and stepping away from it. He told his stories, Wolff recalled, "in a hushed voice that made you lean forward . . . He was also a great listener. His curiosity was almost predatory. He listened with his head cocked and a slight squint in one eye, like a man taking aim."[6] Wolff had seen Ray before, at parties in the Bay Area, when, "his skin was chalky, his eyes deep-sunk and watchful . . . in a nervous, narrow way—a narrowness emphasized by thick sideburns that obscured the natural openness of his face." Now Wolff encountered a Ray who "quickly became one of the really great friends" he made later in life. Both Wolff, whose first short story collection, *In the Garden of the North American Martyrs,* would not appear for three more years, and Carver, still shaky in his recovery, thought it miraculous that Voigt had hired them. Ray was drawn to the thirty-two-year-old, mustachioed Wolff: "I remember waking at five one morning, suffering my own anxieties, to find Toby at the kitchen table eating a sandwich and drinking some milk. He looked deranged and as if he hadn't slept in days, which he hadn't."[7]

Ray arrived at Goddard with no money. One of his students was a Chicago teacher named Warren Miller who had been writing without publishing for years. Ray borrowed $100—perhaps more?—from Miller in exchange for reading not only his course assignments but *any* writing that Miller cared to send him. "The guy just emptied out his drawers and sent everything to Ray!" Voigt learned later, "and Ray read and commented on it! And paid him back his money besides! But that was a time when he felt like he had to pay stuff back."[8]

While Ray was at Goddard, the University of Texas in El Paso (UTEP) offered him a full-time position (renewable, if he behaved himself and kept publishing) as a professor. For $16,800 a year, he would teach three writing courses a semester. With a job ethic entirely new to him, he focused on getting himself to El Paso and performing adequately enough there to recover his reputation. Until then, he was homeless and nearly penniless, at the mercy of friends.

Ray's Goddard friends urged him to invite poetry student Linda McCarriston, another nondrinker, to a party at John Irving's home to celebrate the publication of *The World According to Garp*.[9] McCarriston, later the author of *Eva-Mary* and *Little River*, "didn't want to be attached to a writer," because she "wanted to *be* a writer," but she drove Ray to Irving's and they had a "brief, sweet time together":

> We were kind to each other. We talked a lot about drinking and divorce and marriage. He was turning over new leaves, and I assumed our marital situations were similar. He wasn't sophisticated about women, not a smoothie, and I was inexperienced and emotionally impaired myself. He seemed abashed and at the mercy of things around him. We knew we were both from the other side of the tracks, but I don't think either of us had much political consciousness about how a working-class background affected us as writers. I am an alcoholic, but I wasn't in recovery then. I was just staying afloat and dry. Ray at that time was in what AA calls the honeymoon. He was full of gratitude, radiant with it, as if he was overcome by his good luck.

After the party, Ray went home to Hebron, Maine, with McCarriston. Though she and Ray had sidestepped having sex at the party, they felt comfortable enough to do so in Maine. For Ray, though, the occasion was complicated by the discovery of a bat hanging from the ceiling in McCarriston's bedroom. When Ray told friends about his visit to Maine, he focused on how he'd dislodged the bat by tossing a shoe in its general direction. Indeed, a certain gentlemanliness or prudishness usually turned Ray's conversation away from sex, toward domestic humor or conflict. He told Dobyns that he'd been involved with only three or four women in his life and was flattered by McCarriston's interest. He'd felt safe, in a haven of domesticity, for that one weekend but departed before her children returned. To Lish he wrote later that he knew "a lovely woman" in Maine and would have liked to live there or in Vermont.[10]

Of course, Ray also wanted to enjoy the author's perk of a whirl in New York City. *Will You Please Be Quiet, Please?* was forthcoming in a McGraw-Hill trade paperback. He lunched with both Lish and with Sterling, who had just moved to International Creative Management (ICM), but readings Sterling had set up for Ray were canceled when the heaviest and longest snowfall in ninety years paralyzed the Northeast. He, his sister-in-law Amy, and Doug Unger were snowbound in a little apartment on Forty-third Street and Ninth Avenue. Their old Iowa friends Brendan Ward and Qais Al-Awqati came from Columbia University to eat roast chicken with them. Then Steve Unger arrived with his tongue bleeding and his hands cramped up because a VA hospital had overdosed him with Haldol. "Ray was out of his mind with frustration, and incredulous, too, because here we all were, once more—curled up on mattresses on the floor. Ray's mattress was in our miserable little kitchen about half the size of a walk-in closet!"[11]

Ray fled to Richard and Kristina Ford's in Princeton. Kristina taught urban planning at Rutgers; her husband had a Guggenheim Fellowship and worked steadily on a novel. Early one morning, Ray told Ford that he wanted to get himself "set up" as he was, with a good car, a decent house, a room for writing. Ray spoke quietly, "as if bad memories and certain fond hopes congregated then and needed to be sorted through carefully." It suited Ray, too, that the Fords were five years younger than himself, as if, Ford wrote, "he so wanted time given back to him . . . that he willingly *became* my age and at least, when it suited him, assumed my state of being an entreater to the literary world."[12]

In this homeless time, Ray often wrote to his earlier mentors Johnson and Day. He begged Johnson for use of his summer house. There Ray would begin anew, "sober and dead serious about what I want to do, and don't want to do." Between blizzards, he made his way to Chicago, where he and Johnson talked about Lish. Since 1965, Lish had written Johnson some five hundred letters. The stream ended when Johnson accused Lish of holding an "up the ass of the working class, I'm a foreman now" attitude toward writers in a *December* editorial. As Johnson saw it, "Gordon did a lot of good for writers, he did. But he came to think that he knew everything and he only knew about 40 percent of everything. It became pernicious."[13] Carver, for his part, was loyal to Lish and averse to any position that might compromise his publishing opportunities.

For his retreat to Johnson's cabin, Ray bought a used typewriter. On Valentine's Day Johnson drove him across the plains of Illinois to the little town of Elizabeth, where a farmer sold Ray a 1968 Oldsmobile Delta 88 that supposedly had been driven only to Grange meetings. Johnson watched Ray unload his provisions for the week: "an eight-ounce package of Oscar Mayer bologna, a loaf of Wonder Bread, a quart of low-fat milk . . . not even coffee." Johnson loaned him a portable radio, a sweater, and a coat. The cabin's sliding glass doors opened on to a deck and a view down two valleys. There were electric heaters and a woodstove for warmth, for company nothing but black walnut trees and a big white owl. Ray told friends he was settling down to work; "send a letter or a woman" he implored Lish.

Ray, who had always kept the blinds drawn in his houses, felt naked to the elements; he'd be naming that owl before long, he joked in one letter. The place was just too desolate for a newly recovering alcoholic. On the third morning, he had to spend a chunk of his borrowed money on a tow truck. He couldn't get to AA meetings; he couldn't trust the phone to work. After he'd been alone for seven days, he didn't trust himself to stay sober. Maryann phoned from Arcata. She, too, was "abjectly lonely" and had gotten drunk on wine and cried until she "couldn't cry anymore."[14] If he'd believed the car would make it, Ray might have driven straight to California. Instead he locked Johnson's house, mailed him his key, and crossed the Mississippi to Iowa City. His temptation to drink had frightened him. He sent Kinder a postcard of a snowy Midwestern farm scene, inking in paw prints running from the house and over a hill. He was a "dog on the run again."[15]

In Iowa City Ray crashed on Dobyns's couch, then rented a room from a Jordanian man and his American wife on Sweet Briar Avenue. This would be his permanent address, "no question, until summer." He and Dobyns were a "steady twosome" for dinners on the Iowa City circuit. He had written some "gorgeous" poems and had a new story under way (probably "If It Please You," the one about bingo) and T. Coraghessan Boyle surprised him with the news that "Viewfinder" was appearing in the next issue of the *Iowa Review*. Proof sheets mailed to Cupertino had never reached Ray, who knew the same story was forthcoming in *Quarterly West* and tried to finesse the problem by asking *QW* to run "Why Don't You Dance?" instead. "Viewfinder" ended up in *both* magazines. Ray blamed the mixup on Sterling, protesting too much about how ashamed he was and suggesting he should "change his name and start over."[16]

He wouldn't change his identity, of course, but during this Iowa City interlude, Ray continued to perfect those Bad Ray stories that helped him manage the paradoxes of his life. As Dobyns recounted, he would say,

"You know, I remember a funny thing," and then he would be off with some story about how a lawyer had sued him, trying to get his dog because Ray hadn't paid his bill . . . when someone else was telling a story he would burst forth with oddly archaic interjections like, "you don't say" and "think of that." Then he would shake his head and look around in amazement. . . . His whole body would collapse backwards as if he had been struck in the chest with something happy and his face would wrinkle and a high raspy noise would burst out again and again.[17]

By now, Ray was comfortable staying sober while others drank, though in recovery parlance he was sober but not "clean" because he smoked marijuana. Stories were his form of conviviality.*

In a load of forwarded mail that caught up with him in Iowa, Carver received an invitation to Yaddo (already forfeited), a contract from the university in El Paso, and a request for a budget from the Guggenheim Foundation, an indubitable sign that he was in the running for a fellowship. He calculated that he'd need $20,700, including $1,200 for his family, for a year in McKinleyville and Florence, Italy. He began to imagine a "tiny villa" near the Mediterranean.

But Ray was "belly-up" in Iowa City, so broke that he wrote to poet Bruce Weigl in Salt Lake and asked for a loan of $75 or $100; Weigl, a graduate student, couldn't help. Kinder and Cecily bought Ray a plane ticket so he could attend their Ides of March party in San Francisco. As Ray headed back to the city of past humiliations, his hopes had never been higher. Maryann would meet him there, he'd cash in his return flight, and they'd drive to Iowa City in her car. Once they got to El Paso, Ray wanted to support her, as she had long supported him. It would not be good for them to be back in "those old roles," and he hoped Maryann could "go for an advanced degree or two" instead of working.[18]

Maryann drank for the last time ever with friends in Arcata and, slightly hungover, headed south to meet Ray at the Kinder-Cecily party. March 11, 1978, thus became her lifetime AA birthday. Ginger, the Irish setter they'd nearly lost to a lawyer, went to live in Yakima. Maryann's remaining possessions fit in her car. Vance stayed in Arcata. He lived in a dormitory room Maryann had finagled for him at Humboldt State, worked as a busboy, and planned to enroll at HSU for the spring quarter. With friends like Dick Day to look out for him, Maryann believed Vance would thrive in college.[19]

The party at Kinder and Cecily's differed from all the hundreds Ray and Maryann had given or attended during twenty years in California in that they

---

* When Ray regaled Iowa friends with a tale of his flight from Johnson's cabin, he laid stronger emphasis on the failings of the location than on his own fears, describing Johnson's chairs as lawn furniture and complaining that flies filled the house when he turned on the heat. Johnson was not amused.

both stayed sober among a host of old friends and drinking buddies. Ray had regained his confidence, Cecily thought: "He now spoke with authority of things that had always mattered to him: writers, stories, publishers. He returned to the best of Ray that had been there from the beginning, but with a new maturity and confidence that had eluded him in the past."

Ray's new friend Tobias Wolff brought Stanley Elkin, who happened to be attending the Associated Writing Programs (AWP) convention. Leaning on a cane, suffering visibly from his multiple sclerosis, Elkin disdained a chair that Ray offered him and held forth to a crowd of admirers in the dining room. Having been too drunk to keep up with Elkin when they were colleagues in Iowa City, Ray was glad to meet him again as the author of *Will You Please Be Quiet, Please?*[20]

For many of the World War II and baby boomer generations who had partied hard in their youth, the late 1970s became a time for moderation. The two-fisted drinking crowd was aging and the drug scene was menacing. Antics that used to be amusing became embarrassing; hangovers hurt more. The belief that alcoholism is a disease encouraged funding of recovery programs by governments and health insurance companies. Public figures such as former First Lady Betty Ford spoke about their treatment for addictions to alcohol and prescription drugs. In "Alcohol and Poetry: John Berryman and the Booze Talking," Lewis Hyde argued that "ours is a civilization enamored of drugs which deaden the poetry-creature" because alcohol—an anaesthetic—curtails aesthetic power or "the ability to see *creatively*." Geoffrey Wolff recalled "a real sea change in attitudes toward drinking in this era. Whereas before people had somehow admired poets like Lowell and Berryman for their addictions, suddenly they asked, what does that have to do with making poems? Besides, many people were unable to make poems because their lives were just wrecked. Madness was no longer an asset."[21]

President Jimmy Carter, who'd assumed office in 1977, encouraged a sort of national restraint. He worked to reduce the nuclear arsenal, urged strong environmental protections, and repatriated Vietnam-era draft dodgers. As the president extolled moderation, his brother Billy turned up on the cover of *Newsweek* promoting Billy Beer. Billy's venture failed, and he too went to a rehabilitation center.

A less noted event that would affect the Carvers occurred on January 1, 1978, when the 1976 Copyright Act became law in the United States, revising and extending protections for authors that had been in place since 1909. One obscure passage of the new law, which applied to works copyrighted after 1977, revised certain statutory provisions pertaining to renewal of copyrights. It would affect the legacies of authors like Carver whose oeuvre spanned both sides of this date.[22]

• • •

Ray once quipped that the only problem with the drive between California and Iowa City was that the highway passed through Nevada, and he always lost money there. This time he and Maryann almost lost their daughter at Lake Tahoe. They discovered Chris lying on the floor of an apartment, bloated with alcohol poisoning, alone except for her little dog and the rolling screen of a black-and-white TV. Ray was "horrified" to see his addictions refracted to his once-lovely twenty-one-year-old daughter. The next day Maryann put Chris and her dog on a flight to the Bay Area where Ross Perkins, Maryann's former lover and AA friend, and her grandmother would care for her. Ray felt beaten down, almost paralyzed by Chris's grim situation.[23]

Good news awaited Ray in Iowa. The Guggenheim Foundation offered him $16,000 for the next year. Dennis Schmitz and Ellen Bryant Voigt were also winners that year, news Ray proclaimed as eagerly as he did his own. Determined to become a man who kept his promises, he planned to defer the fellowship until after his gig at UTEP. In fact, he requested that his payments begin early, on the first of May, but figured he'd save—saving for the first time in his life—what came in after his UTEP salary commenced.[24] He hoped to stabilize his domestic situation before finding a village where he might live "decently and inexpensively" in Europe. "Now for the other life! The one without mistakes . . ." he wrote Ford when he told him about the fellowship.[25]

After a night in Ray's rented room, Ray and Maryann moved to a housekeeping cottage at the Park Motel west of Iowa City. These were days of contentment, though Ray had his usual doubts about whether the détente could last. Maryann worked on a memoir and applied to the Goddard program. Ray edited her application. On Easter evening they watched a BBC version of *Anna Karenina,* and Ray re-created the scene in a poem called "Marriage." Maryann read Ford's novel *A Piece of My Heart,* and the two of them talked at length about it and about Ray's new friend, "as if you were very close," Ray wrote Ford. Ray gave a *successful* reading at the Writers' Workshop, offsetting the two he'd botched earlier. He ignored the forthcoming due date of the manuscript he'd promised to McGraw-Hill and gratefully wrote "a bunch of poems . . . praise the Lord."[26]

When Maryann's contract for the next year at Los Altos High School arrived, she replied with a letter of resignation. That sealed her commitment to staying with Ray. He, too, had been thinking about their future. He told Maryann they would have to change their manners when they arrived in El Paso. "We would have to stop being so friendly and accessible. . . . We should practice discretion in what we revealed." Maryann took offense. To her it seemed that Ray was getting "precious" over a teaching job. She wasn't sure she wanted to be "dependent on this man, my husband, who suddenly was a hot dog, a snob, after being the town drunk for years." But Ray was no longer anybody's drunk. Free of alcohol, he was seeking the feelings of independence and poise that had eluded him since adolescence. "This is a new time in my life," he told an interviewer from the *Daily Iowan*. "My children are both grown, and I just received a Guggenheim Fellowship."[27]

But there was family, always family, upon which Ray had long depended. Amy and Unger gave up on New York and moved in next door at the Park Motel. Maryann went west to help her sister Jerry get sober. Ray sublet a flat on Lucas Street and began attending AA meetings again. When Maryann returned, she noticed that Ray had lost her college diploma during the move, which to her was a bad omen. Then Ray told her that he no longer wanted her to attend the Goddard program while he was teaching there in the summer. He said it would be uncomfortable for an instructor to have his wife enrolled as a student. It seems he was working on what are known in AA as "boundaries," and he wanted to separate his professional life from his married life.[28] To Lish, Ray declared on May 8, "After this summer, I can't ever again be subject to this gypsy life, no sir."[29]

Having given up alcoholic spirits, Maryann wanted an invigorated intellectual and spiritual life. That Iowa City spring, she and Amy joined a discussion group on the work of philosopher Walter Kaufmann led by novelist William Cotter Murray. Ray sometimes came along for a cup of coffee but never said anything beyond a mutter. "He seemed detached," Murray said. "My own feeling about it was that he was totally a writer; even as he was just walking along, he was composing sentences, and he only tolerated company because he didn't want to go boozing. He needed voices around him and a relationship going on, but nothing demanding." Maryann's and Amy's attraction to a psychic who turned up in Iowa City that year, claiming he could see auras and foretell the future disturbed Ray. He took the view that this psychic was running some kind of sex and drug operation. Dobyns noticed that Ray "was really squeamish about it. He was chipper when Maryann first came, but as all these people closed in, he just got jittery.[30]

A gloss on the situation the Carvers faced may be found in the work of Lois Wilson, wife of AA founder Bill Wilson, who wrote that strained relations "often developed in families after the first starry-eyed period of sobriety was over." In her own case, Wilson recognized that she'd developed self-sufficiency by acting as her husband's "mother, nurse, caretaker, and breadwinner" as well as always thinking of myself on the credit side of the ledger and my alcoholic husband on the debit side . . ." At the same time, Mrs. Wilson's pride was hurt because an AA sponsor had been able to do for her husband what she had "failed to do all our married years."[31]

Flush with his first Guggenheim check, Ray sent $10 to his son, who was completing his first quarter at Humboldt State. In an eight-page reply to his dad, Vance told him about his classes. He'd written a paper on Hemingway's "The Short Happy Life of Francis Macomber" and was getting ready to write his own short story—"that's going to be pretty hard"—about an old cook he worked with at the Eureka Inn. Vance's boyish, oft-corrected penmanship conveyed a disarming keenness for learning and, more than that, a desire to know his father. He liked his English class so much that he was planning to take another in the fall from Ray's own professor, Dick Day. He proposed meeting his parents in Iowa so they could all drive west together: "My Geology teacher said she'll help plan a route so I could stop and identify Geologic features along the way." For the rest of the summer, Vance planned to work at his union-wage janitorial job in Los Altos. He was grateful for "the sanity of knowing where I'll be in the fall." At nineteen, Vance was supporting himself—as, indeed, his parents and grandparents and millions of working-class kids had done before him.[32]

Amy and Maryann organized a big party for Ray's fortieth birthday on May 25. Preparations were elaborate—printed napkins said "from Running Dog to Dandy Dog"—and many workshop faculty attended. Ray later wrote David Swanger that it had been "the happiest occasion of that sort that I can recall. I was sober and starting a new life." When Maryann and Ray celebrated their twenty-first anniversary at a restaurant on June 7, they clinked glasses of Perrier water and promised each other another year.[33]

All too soon, Maryann's mother and her husband paid a visit to Iowa City. Then Vance arrived by bus. Seven people—Ray and Maryann, Alice and Clarence, Amy and Doug, and Vance—now resided in the house Unger was housesitting. Cicadas kept Ray awake and for two solid weeks, loud Christmas carols blared from the house next door. The reveler was novelist Mark Helprin, who was putting himself "in a mood to write winter chapters full of snow and nineteenth-century sleds." One night while taking his garbage out, Helprin saw Ray Carver and another man staring at his house and saying, "I don't know, but it really is weird!" Unger watched Ray pace circles in the borrowed living room: "He was terribly frustrated, weighed down by this barrage of family and having trouble working. 'We're milling, that's all we're doing here, just milling,' he would say. He had the Guggenheim money and his high hopes, but he wasn't getting much work done."[34]

Vance Carver had ridden the Greyhound into the eye of a hurricane. He

needed his father to recognize his change from a troubled teen to a responsible young man. Ray, it would appear, had no help to give. Though his life
had turned around, he remained an anxious alcoholic in early recovery, a
forty-year-old child.

Maryann and Ray's marriage seemed to be crumbling before their eyes.
Maryann saw what she called Ray's "detachment and his disdain" growing
as he entered his second year of sobriety. He told Maryann that their marriage was not large enough to accommodate her ego. She felt that her "ego
had all but disappeared, along with my diploma and a vision of the future."
In her recollection, "Ray was always of two minds about *everything*. In the
same day and the same sentence, there'd be the devoted Ray, the husband
Ray, and then there'd be the other, the one I've called a smart-ass."[35]

Some fifteen years after the hungry Carver foursome arrived on their doorstep in 1963, Vance and Tina Bourjaily invited Ray and his clan out to their
Redbird Farm to meet Mark Helprin, he of the Christmas carols. To the
Bourjailys' surprise, when Doug Unger drove up, he chauffeured a carful
of Carver relatives, but not Ray. The day was a catastrophe. Maryann was
dejected and distraught. Alice accidentally pushed the hamburgers into the
fire. Vance Carver swam a race against Helprin in a quarry pond but lost to
the older man who sprinted daily at a pool. As the afternoon and the wine
waned, hostess Bourjaily and Helprin rode bareback on two of her white
horses. The horses spooked and Tina's horse fell backward on top of her,
causing her severe injuries.[36]

With his family thus occupied, Ray was flying to California. He'd
reached a tipping point. He departed just two days after Vance arrived. But
Ray's frustration and anger had brought him to a moment of crisis almost
as severe as his alcoholism. He understood that sobriety was his only possession. He understood that being around his children or participating in
Maryann's worry about their children could sink him. To stand at a remove
from them was a harsh decision with long-lasting consequences, but perhaps not one that others have a right to question.

As recently as June 3, Ray had written Lish that he and Maryann intended
to meet up in Vermont and drive together to El Paso. Now as he departed
for California on June 23, he told Maryann that he'd be spending the summer without her. And there would be no geological tour for Vance.

In California, Ray led a workshop in Santa Cruz, saw Cecily and other
friends in San Francisco, and his mother, who'd moved to Sacramento. But
he canceled a trip to the Northwest for the Archers' fiftieth wedding anniversary and fishing in Montana. Instead he did what he most needed to do:

drove to the north coast and stayed for a week in a cabin borrowed from Dick Day. Here, close to the place of his sobriety, solitary but not isolated, he could attend AA meetings and gather his wits before his return to Goddard.[37]

Maryann took stock of her own situation. She hadn't forgiven Ray's abrupt departure right after Vance's arrival; she had no reason to stay in Iowa City. On July 20, she wrote Ray describing her hopes for the separation ahead of them: "I shall be your mistress and your muse," she said, and "the wires, the invisible ones, across the miles will *zing* with our telepathy." She closed with a declaration that Ray would be a wonderful teacher and enjoy his "adventure." She was trying, it seems, both to set Ray free and to will him to return to her. She mailed her letter to Vermont. She wouldn't be there, but she still might join Ray in Texas. On July 24, she flew from Iowa to California.[38]

At Goddard for the summer session, Ray again stayed away from parties, but relished his new life. One day he came back from town "looking as if some vicious animal had attacked his head." When Voigt inquired if he'd had a haircut, Ray said,

> Oh, yes, Ellen, I did. It was fantastic! I saw a barber sign up, so I went in and the guy put me right in the chair. He was cutting my hair, an older guy, so I asked him about it. And he said he'd been in this same shop for fifty-five years. So I said, That's really amazing. And I said to him, I said, You know, this is the first time I can ever remember having my hair cut by somebody who was a left-handed barber, and the guy said, "Yeah, I switched about seven years ago after my stroke." And I said, Oh, you did, you switched over after your stroke? That's just really fantastic that you were able to do that. And the barber said, "It's not too bad except for the Parkinson's."

Voigt continued, "Ray didn't care what his head looked like. The haircut was nothing. What's irreplaceable was his delight in it."[39]

Mary Karr, the East Texas native who later wrote *The Liars' Club* (a memoir) and several books of poetry, began her MFA studies at Goddard that summer. "All those short story writers loved poetry," she said. "When you look at their precision and economy of language, you know they were reading poetry." Some women at Goddard objected that the male faculty were sexist, but Karr thought those accusations unwarranted: "I hung out with them all the time, and I never heard anything awful. They were 'guyed-up,' just boyish and silly. I think those guys were a protective circle for Ray, shoring him up and letting him be one of the boys, which I'm sure he'd never really been. A bunch of avuncular, funny, smart, tease-the-shit-out-of-you guys. And he was the one they all revered for his work, the guy they were all imitating."

When she met Ray, Karr noticed he "was very shaky, but had this enormous humility. I think he was still going to AA meetings, but not in Vermont. He was on the marijuana maintenance program as in 'I'm not going to drink but I'm going to be gunched out of my mind.' " Karr and Ray compared their childhoods: "Like me, Ray had read a lot of comic books and we both loved those Tarzan books and trashy things like Jim Thompson's *The Killer Inside Me*."[40]

As Ray left Goddard, he passed Frank Conroy, later director of the Iowa Writers' Workshop. "I'll see you on the trail, Frank," Ray said through his car window. "That's what it was like then," Conroy said. "We were all so broke and living as itinerant storytellers and teachers."

By letter, Ray invited Linda McCarriston to visit him when he got settled in El Paso. She replied that she was involved in a new relationship.[41] Ray's old car got him as far as Van Horn, Texas. Though he'd later claim he'd traded his car for a bicycle, Ray actually covered the last 120 miles of his journey on a Greyhound bus.[42] From a pay phone, he called down a list of UTEP faculty until he got Bruce Dobler. If Dobler hadn't answered, Ray told him later, he would have just gone on to California and skipped the job at El Paso.

By then Maryann was substitute teaching in California. She'd given her teacher's retirement account money to Chris and Pleadwell so they could move to Bellingham, Washington. Chris was pregnant. Maryann supported Chris's wish to keep the baby, believing that motherhood would settle her; Ray was dead set against it. Fearful that conflict over Chris's decision would erupt in El Paso, Maryann told Ray she would join him in December if he would go into marital therapy with her. To that proposal she received no reply. Writing to the Justices to settle an Iowa telephone bill, Ray explained that he and Maryann were living apart. They retained "a strong measure of mutual love and respect," he said, but were "just not able to live together, now."[43]

Raymond and Maryann Carver never lived together again. Their anniversary pledge to another year together was not to be honored, though they didn't divorce for another four years. Who had left whom? In the conventional arithmetic of split-ups, Maryann had failed to show at Ray's place of residence and employment. But in the differential calculus of the Carver marriage, it wasn't that simple. The end of a marriage, like everything within a marriage, affects others but is witnessed firsthand only by the wife and husband. Despite surviving letters, Ray's stories, and Maryann's memoir and statements, an exact calendar of dissolution is impossible to draw.

CHAPTER 23

Beginning, Again

August 1978–December 1979, El Paso and Tucson

> And isn't the past inevitable,
> now that we call the little
> we remember of it "the past"?
> — epigraph to Raymond Carver's
> *Fires*, quoted from "Cows Grazing
> at Sunrise" by William Matthews

Stubborn good intentions and fear of backsliding brought Ray Carver to the University of Texas in El Paso. At first he wished he'd sequestered himself in a New England town where he could be surrounded by clapboard and stone and Yankee solidity. Instead, he found himself in a wedge of Texas bounded by Old Mexico on the south and New Mexico on the north. What the Spaniards called El Paso del Norte is an ancient crossroads, inhabited by Native Americans for ten thousand years, colonized by Spaniards in 1598. When Ray arrived there, it was the most Mexican city in Texas. Outsiders who come to El Paso, it's said, experience sudden upheavals in their lives. Though Ray stayed there less than a year, the West Texas town would be a place of pivotal change for him too.

From the bus station, Bruce Dobler brought Ray to dinner at a writers' conference where he met the man who'd hired him, Les Standiford, and the conference's star guests: editor Theodore Solotaroff, Vance Bourjaily, and Tess Gallagher. Ray "hugged me like a man sinking, like he had come to a raft and pulled up onto it for a breath of air," Gallagher told an interviewer in 1990. Then Ray kept a late-night appointment with a professor whose house he was to lease. As if inspired by Carver's story "Put Yourself in My Shoes," the professor listed the items in the house that Ray was not to disturb. Ray, spooked, told the professor he could keep his $300 deposit and went home with Dobler. Thirteen-year-old Stephanie Dobler ceded her bedroom to Ray; she and her sister called Ray "the Owl" because of his glasses and "tufty" hair.[1]

At conference dinners, Ray chatted with his colleagues, but he left when others began to drink the evening away. At a restaurant in the tourist sector of El Paso's twin city, Juarez, Mexico, Ray asked Gallagher if she thought he was good-looking. He was indeed, she assured him. She took his question to be "naïve and beautifully innocent." He "beamed" when she answered in the affirmative. When Bruce Dobler mentioned to Gallagher that Ray seemed depressed, she offered to talk to him. Bruce and his wife left her alone with Ray while they checked on their daughters at a nearby swimming pool.[2]

A notable change had come over their two guests when they returned: "They seemed very enamored of each other and, amazingly, like a loving couple," Bruce Dobler recollected. At the glamorous reception at a conference sponsor's home, Bourjaily also noticed that "sparks had flown (in the dark, we assume). It was delightful seeing them fall in love and there was the further happiness that Ray was sober and this would help him stay that way."[3]

Like Ray, Tess Gallagher had received a Guggenheim Fellowship for the 1978–79 year. She had stated her view that writing poetry is dangerous in the title poem of her first book, *Instructions to the Double*: "You / could die out there. You / could live forever." Twice divorced, first from a military pilot (whose last name she retained) and then from poet Michael Burkard, she had a second book, *Under Stars,* in press and planned to spend her Guggenheim year working on her next book in a cabin near her parents' home on the Olympic Peninsula. This second serendipitous meeting with Ray radically changed her carefully laid plans.

On Saturday night, Ray invited Tess to the dog races in Juarez. Before they crossed to Mexico, they mailed a jubilant postcard to Kittredge and Smith with the message, in Gallagher's hand, that they were heading to Mexico to make their fortunes. Above the address, Ray printed a phrase he used repeatedly in correspondence from El Paso: "We're going to the dogs!" The evening ended in an emergency room because Gallagher accidentally ripped the lobe of one of her pierced ears.[4] After she departed, Ray announced by letter to both Michael Ryan and Richard Ford that he was missing her "severely."[5]

Ray found himself a used Volkswagen and a town house apartment. Amid a parched, brown volcanic geography, Ray finally had a place to start his new life. El Paso reminded him of Israel, "with Mexicans standing in for Arabs."[6] From his neighborhood near the university, he could see south past an enormous refinery smokestack and the muddy canal of the Rio

Grande toward the shack-covered hills of Juarez, a city of seven hundred thousand with no sewage system beyond the tourist streets.

Ray was often at the Doblers. Their daughters loved Edward Lear's verse "The Owl and the Pussycat" and were charmed that Ray, their owl, and Tess had fallen in love like the elegant fowl and the beautiful feline in the poem. One night, Bruce Dobler asked Ray what had happened that afternoon in their apartment to cause him to fall in love so quickly. Stephanie, who had just turned off the television, overheard the question and lingered to hear the answer. "I was very curious, and I never forgot what Ray said. He said, 'She fucked my socks off.' "[7]

To distract himself after Gallagher left El Paso, Ray went with Bruce Dobler to a bullfight in Juarez. After the third dead black bull left the ring, Ray said the spectacle made him squeamish. Dobler humored him with a story about a veterinarian who performed miracles on the bulls:

> Ray chuckled and took a pained breath to say "I'll try to believe that!" He said bullfighting must be okay because Hemingway loved it.
>
> Then, in a Hemingway voice, Ray said: "It's good here in the afternoon sun. A new matador enters the arena. Some clap, or cheer. It is the right day for this." And we went on in various imitations of Hemingway.[8]

Ray returned for the final *corrida* of the season with Tess, whom he'd invited back to visit.[9] On September 8, after receiving a dozen red roses from Gallagher, Ray wrote Lish: "That Irish lass, I like to have fallen in love with her." Before the month was out, he told Lish that Gallagher would come to live with him in El Paso in January. He'd agreed to stay at UTEP through the spring (teaching two days a week for $10,000) and believed he would "get significant work done yet, before it's over. My life is getting in order, I can tell you that. Yes, sir."[10]

Nonetheless, Ray still suffered periods of anxiety when he was unable to concentrate and would do just about anything to keep busy and avoid the temptation to drink, Dobler said: "We dropped into an arcade one night and got ourselves into a game that had rifles and moving targets (no real bullets). In the car, Ray said, 'We shot the shit out of that, by God we did. Shot the shit out of it.' And looked pleased, smiling, nodding because he'd capped off that event with just the right words." Another night, he drove circles in a parking lot with the Dobler family as they all watched the odometer of their old Chevy turn 100,000 miles.[11]

Furious Seasons was doing "respectably well" for Capra Press and got a handful of reviews. Ann Beattie, whose short fiction, like Carver's, rose to national prominence in 1976, reported in *Canto* that she'd felt "awed and repelled" when she first read "Neighbors" in *Esquire*. She reasonably assumes *Furious Seasons* to be Carver's later work, and surprisingly finds the title story—first published nineteen years earlier—one of the finest in the collection. She notes a quality that consistently defines Carver's stories (though Lish's editing often flattened it): "nature is humanized, and humanity is defined in terms of nature." When she considers two parent-child stories, Beattie notices how uncomfortable that relationship can be in Carver. She notes that for him, as for Hemingway, "marriage—women—has ruined the good times." Unfazed—or vindicated?—by such details, Ray loved this review from "one of the best contemporary fiction writers around. . . ."[12]

The *Village Voice* featured the Capra collection in its "Alternate Currents" column. Reviewer Gary L. Fisketjon observed that "in his salad days" Carver's stories had appeared in *Esquire* and been nominated for a National Book Award, but "those days, alas, seem to be gone." Given that Carver had not written a novel and that no profit-minded major publisher would dare a second book of stories in the absence of a novel, Carver might have spent the rest of his writing career in the minor leagues.

The son of Norwegian mink ranchers in Oregon, Fisketjon had worked on fishing boats as a teen. He recognized Carver's towns that "possess neither the splendor and neuroses of the city nor the purity and boredom of the country." Fisketjon attended Williams College, where he roomed with an aspiring poet named Jay McInerney. After finishing Radcliffe College's publishing course in 1977, he found the New York editorial market wide open. Publishers were "looking around, saying, 'We're all old; we should get some young people.' " At twenty-three, with blond hair to his shoulders, Fisketjon was an editorial assistant to Random House editor in chief Jason Epstein. As he found his way into the literary scene, Fisketjon—like Lish before him—tracked the work of literary writers who were neglected by mainstream publishers. Carver was one of these.

Next Fisketjon telephoned Ray. Was he speaking to Raymond Carver? he asked. A muffled voice said, "No." When Fisketjon identified himself as an editor rather than a debt collector, Ray quickly amended, "This's Raymond Carver."[13] Fisketjon wanted to acquire an expanded edition of *Furious Seasons* for Random House. Carver was willing, but the publishing house soon heard that *Will* had sold only 1,500 copies in paper and decided that there'd be no profit in that venture unless Carver had another book— a novel, for instance—to publish in conjunction with it. Even if Carver had written a novel, his contract with McGraw-Hill was a complication. There was, for the time being, nothing to be done.[14]

From El Paso in the spring, Carver sent Hills, who had just become a senior editor at Simon & Schuster, a new outline of a novel, explaining that he'd decided to drop his World War II story in favor of a contemporary situation.[15] He sketched a love story involving an alcoholic freelance writer in Italy on an assignment, a woman and her former lover (an Arab), and the journalist's wife and children in the States. "This is, fundamentally and finally," Carver wrote, "the story of several loves, in fact, which intersect. It will be a look at love in all its various guises, its very real responsibilities and obligations, its horrors—and rewards." Carver also sent some pages of manuscript.[16] Hills told Ray he had "the nucleus of a wonderful novel," but the bulk of his reply did little to encourage Ray in what he already viewed as a daunting task. Hills's advice was sound enough, but for Ray, always a writer who discovered his story through the writing—at this juncture a very insecure writer—Hill's criticism was dispiriting. Carver sent at least part of his sample to the *Iowa Review* where it appeared late in the year as "The Augustine Papers." Carver never made significant progress on a novel again.[17]

The University of Texas at El Paso was founded as a school of mines in 1913 and had been renamed several times by the time Ray arrived. About half of its ten thousand students were Spanish-speaking, making it the only truly bilingual university in the United States.[18] The thick-walled, tile-ornamented buildings in a style derived from the temples of Bhutan serve well in the windy, hot West Texas climate. Ray's office in a building that backed up against the Franklin Mountains had a big window overlooking the campus and across to Juarez.

Before Carver was hired at UTEP, graduate students had lobbied for a poet. When Standiford announced that Carver—a fiction writer who also wrote poetry—would teach their graduate seminar in poetry, some of them "raised a big stink." They changed their minds when they read Carver's work and planned a party to welcome him. They surmised they'd need a supply of liquor. When Ray arrived at Gary Eddy's house, he asked for a glass of grape juice. "So there's, like, our food allowance spent on cheap booze from Juarez, and we're all sitting around drinking grape juice. That's how we first met," Eddy said. Ray went home early. Soon, though, Ray began inviting some students to his apartment to play poker. They drank his Pepsis and looked at his books, and he took their money. Sobriety had improved his game. He was stone-faced and bet the same way whether his hand was good, bad, or indifferent. "In that ugly apartment with bleached white walls," Ray González said, "Ray would talk a little from behind his screen of cigarette smoke, and that's how I got to know him, in those poker games. He did talk then." After the poker games, students would go with Ray to Winchell's for doughnuts to supply his "major sweet tooth."[19]

"I had to learn to teach sober . . . I had to learn to do nearly everything over again, sober," Carver wrote Johnson at the end of his year in El Paso. Ray told his classes to "read read read!" and introduced them to new writers. "I'm a poet first, and I've published more poetry than fiction," he said. A remarkable number of students who took Ray's poetry classes continued as poets. González credited Ray with instructing him to observe "those details, those images, those experiences that lead to that major moment in a poem" and with understanding his "cultural references to being a Mexican American writer on the border." Ray's critical intuitions were acute, even when swathed in kindness. He might "get frustrated by something he saw in a poem and make an outburst, but he never put people down."[20]

Ray often spent the first segment of a class reading aloud. "He'd be smoking with his hands shaking, and he'd read Maupassant or Babel, but we loved him and forgave him and tried to write stories like his," Vicky Anderson recalled.[21]

For Dagoberto Gilb, another writer then living in El Paso, Carver became a sort of contrary inspiration. Someone told Gilb he should meet Carver because they both wrote about the working class. When Gilb read *Will You Please Be Quiet, Please?*, he thought, "Those stories didn't seem to be about working people. Working people are energetic. They can be dangerous and crazy, but they are not sitting around. I could see where he came from the working class, but he *wasn't* it. His stories were about graduate students' lives, but he smartly made his characters vacuum cleaner salesmen or whatever."

Gilb's own work changed after he read Carver's: "I thought, they want stories about working people. I'm doing the shit, and I'll tell you what it's like." He sent Ray his first short story. When he came by Ray's office, he saw a framed photo of Ray looking "very Northwesterly" in working clothes. "All I could think of," Gilb recounted, "was that *his* job was the job I dreamed about, being a professor. And there he was, as if he were ashamed of it and telling me that he was like me." The encounter between Gilb and Carver lasted only minutes, but Carver liked Gilb's story about heroin-using construction workers so well that he mumbled an offer to recommend Gilb to the Iowa Writers' Workshop. Gilb, who'd never heard of the workshop, "wondered why would I want to go to school? That was my first exposure to this other [academic] universe moving forward in American culture." Gilb, who worked in construction another dozen years before entering the professoriate himself, included the story he'd written for Carver ("Down in West Texas Town") in his PEN/Faulkner finalist collection *The Magic of Blood*.[22] His stories and Carver's share a notable integration of vernacular phrasing with unobtrusively literary sentences.

Ray grew accustomed to El Paso and fond of Juarez. His letters are peppered with references to horse races, dog races, bullfights, and—especially—inexpensive steak dinners in Juarez. He sent postcards of greyhounds jockeyed by monkeys at the Hipódromo y Galgódromo. Evidently Ray got a charge out of hearing Spanish; he addressed friends as *Señor* and wished them *Buenas tardes,* signed letters "*Sr. Ramon,*" and gave out the number of his "*telephono.*" González noticed that his teacher was "curious about the clash of cultures in the border towns, the things you can see there." El Paso fed Ray's imagination, and he wrote several poems on Mexican subjects, including "The Baker" which first appeared in the UTEP newspaper.[23] But Ray wasn't thinking about spending the rest of his life in West Texas. He sought invitations to travel and asked grad students to cover his classes when he was gone. In early October he visited Gallagher—"a wonderful time . . . just what I needed," he wrote Day—and gave a reading at the University of Washington in Seattle. Later the same month, Ray visited Catherine and Tobias Wolff in Phoenix. The Wolffs were vegetarians at the time. When they served dinner, Tobias Wolff recounted,

> Ray pushed all the vegetables out toward the edge of the plate until there was this big hole in the center where he expected the meat to be. Finally I said, "Ray, you have to eat your vegetables because that's what dinner is!" But you could see the flashing sign of a burger joint from our backyard. After Ray left, we found all these Whataburger wrappers under the bed!

While in Phoenix, Ray and a couple of other poets performed for the Rocky Mountain Modern Language Association. Then the presider moved to the next agenda item, the election of a new president. "They elected Ray!" Tobias Wolff recalled. "We were vastly amused at the idea of Ray being president of anything. He resigned on the spot."[24]

In November Ray made a triumphant tour of the Northeast, beginning with a job interview at Syracuse University, from which the novelist George P. Elliott would soon retire.[25] The prospect of a permanent, prestigious position outweighed Ray's earlier dream of living alone and frugally on his Guggenheim in Europe. For despite his sobriety, employment, and Guggenheim checks, Ray had money troubles. His UTEP paychecks were delayed; he borrowed money from colleagues, and owed Dennis Schmitz $300. When his daughter called him at school, he sent Chris $30 (half of what he had on hand) and then learned she was traveling with Shiloh. When she called again from Montana, Ray had students in his office and agreed to send another $30. He regarded the calls as something akin to blackmail and felt there would be "no end to it ever, that awful worry, that horror that hangs just over our heads." He feared that Chris would land in jail "or worse." When she returned to Bellingham, Ray sent her (via Unger) a check for $150 to rent an apartment, warning that he couldn't "do any better, or any more." Unger, then working on salmon boats, and Amy, teaching drama at Whatcom Community College, became a conduit between Ray and Maryann and Chris during these times.[26]

For years, Maryann Carver had remembered to mail a shiny Christmas card from herself and Ray to Mr. and Mrs. Gordon Lish. In 1978 Ray alone signed the card, requesting "for Xmas" the fat, new, pomegranate red and silver-jacketed collection of sixty-one short stories by John Cheever. Ray planned to spend Christmas with Gallagher and her parents in Port Angeles, Washington. He saw his daughter in Bellingham and invited Vance to visit him in El Paso between Christmas and New Year's. When Maryann heard that, Ray invited her to El Paso too. But when Maryann and Vance arrived, Ray was hospitalized with bleeding ulcers. He was released, and the reunion, Maryann wrote, was "bittersweet, splendid and unsettling, joyous and miserable." Ray and Maryann attended an AA meeting together, and all three of them shopped and ate in Juarez. Vance helped Ray collect furniture from a colleague who noticed that the relationship between Ray and his handsome son seemed guarded. Before Maryann left, Ray told her that he could not face marital counseling and was determined to follow through with his plan to live with Gallagher. Maryann saw her husband "hunched over in his car, crying" as she and Vance boarded their plane for California.[27]

Tess Gallagher arrived in El Paso to live with Ray on January 1, 1979. She had been reluctant to leave her solitary cabin, but her Guggenheim Fellowship allowed her to live wherever she chose, whereas Ray intended to fulfill his contract with UTEP. For Gallagher, "That [was the] decisive physical moment of saying, 'I'm with you, Babe!' and then beginning life together." Over five months of courtship by phone and letter, Gallagher had made up her mind to take "a gamble that Ray might make it and actually stay sober, if he had someone who could hold the high ground with him."[28] Gambling metaphors were familiar to Gallagher because her father, Leslie Bond, was a card player who carried a deck of cards in his breast pocket. Born Theresa Jeanette Bond on July 21, 1943, Gallagher had already had her fill of "trying to haul alcoholic men out of the abyss." Her father's "drinking and the quarrels he had with my mother because of it," Gallagher writes, "terrorized my childhood." She was "very frightened" by Ray's alcoholism. "But I also felt he was so amazing; how was he going to keep that going if he didn't have somebody to shelter him a bit?"[29] Gallagher later wondered

if she'd been bluffing when she told Ray she'd leave if he drank again: "...
I was deeply in love, as if my life until then had simply been a rehearsal for
meeting him. There was a way in which all the failed alcoholics in my life
were symbolically delivered by Ray's success. He was drying out for all of
them."[30]

Gallagher wrote a story that parallels the situation she faced when she
moved into the brick-sided ranch house Ray had rented at 553 Ridgemont.
In "At Mercy," a writer named Esther moves in with a professor named
Robert, and learns that Robert's wife has visited their very house only days
before. After hearing Robert's explanation, Esther thinks, "Surely he was
trying to be kind to everyone ... " A day later Esther telephones Robert's
wife and finds her "very calm and assured, not the pitiable woman Robert
had described. ...." The wife tells Esther, " 'I'm his wife. I have a perfect
right to come where he is anytime I want to. I'm the mother of his children
... He asked me to come. What's more, he paid my way.' " When Esther
broaches the subject to Robert a second time and tells him she is thinking of
leaving, he answers, " 'Please don't talk like that ... Esther, I'm with you.' "
Robert promises that his wife will not visit again; they agree not to speak
further of the matter. Esther lies awake, imagining herself on a ship moving
"steadily into deeper waters."[31]

Maryann Carver did receive a phone call from Tess Gallagher in El Paso
asking about the status of the marriage and whether Ray was free. Maryann
recalled that Gallagher said she had confronted Ray with questions about
her visit and that Ray had admitted that he still loved Maryann. Nonetheless, Tess stayed in El Paso, and Maryann—in her own words—"stepped
aside" from the marriage. In a letter, Ray told Maryann, "We've been
through a shipwreck. We can't help each other now. We need help."[32] Gallagher was ready to help Ray. From her early years, she had acquired what
she called a "refugee mentality" that taught her "to be industrious toward
the prospect of love and shelter."[33]

To set up housekeeping, Ray and Tess begged and borrowed furniture
from colleagues. One day Ray brought home an antique dresser missing
a drawer. Tess sent him to look for it. When Ray found the drawer on
the highway, she told him, "You have a lot of bad luck, don't you? That's
going to have to change if you're going to be around me. I don't want to
be around that much bad luck." The couple's first quarrel, which was over
money, became a tale they would recount together. As he left to give a reading in Houston, Ray asked Tess to lend him her credit card. She hesitated.
As a poet and itinerant professor, she survived by making careful decisions
about money. She was taking emotional chances with Ray, but being asked
for her credit card by "a reformed alcoholic with two bankruptcies" (as she

described him to *Vanity Fair*) caused her to dig in her heels. In the end, she tossed the card on the bed, and Ray took it.[34]

Ray and Tess's social scene in El Paso had two poles: Juarez and the Upper Valley section of El Paso. In the gated country-club enclaves of the latter lived several affluent women who took courses at the university and liked to host parties for visiting writers. Especially appreciated were the parties at the home of Sherry, a former nurse who studied writing, and her husband, Herb, a cardiologist, who had a ranchlike spread with a pool and horses. On these occasions, many noticed that Ray and Tess were devoted to each other, and she was protective of him. Gallagher appeared to be so nurturing of Ray that some feminists on the faculty wondered aloud why a writer of her stature would set her own work and career aside to "nurse" him.[35] Parties at Sherry and Herb's place started in the afternoon and slid toward the night as people stayed for more drinks and the kind of wandering, booze-fueled conversation from which Carver built his signature short story "What We Talk About When We Talk About Love."[36] While no one claims that the story is an exact portrait of particular people, fellow travelers from those days agree that Herb was certainly the model for the story's Mel McGinnis. In June 1980, about the time Ray was finishing the story, the original Herb gave up alcohol. After the story appeared in book form, Herb wrote Ray to thank him for his encouragement to become sober.[37]

Gallagher was flamboyant. She wore her dark hair long, often with hats, dressed colorfully, and rode horseback in dramatic attire. One night when a handful of people were talking around the table, Mimi Gladstein recalled, "Walter Taylor looked toward Tess and said, with great love and admiration, 'A red-headed Irish witch is what she is.' " As another party wound down, Eddy reminisced, "Tess sang Irish ghost ballads in Gaelic. It was wonderful, a great moment." Ray took pleasure in Gallagher's success. He bragged that *Instructions to the Double* had sold five thousand copies and was in its third printing (keeping pace with Carver's *Will*)—remarkable sales for a book of poems from a new press. [38]

At the beginning of March, Syracuse University offered Ray a dream job. Beginning in January 1980, he would replace Elliott as a full professor earning $27,000 plus an 11 percent retirement contribution and moving expenses. He'd teach two courses a semester and receive four years' credit toward tenure. His children could enroll tuition-free in any college that admitted them and offered reciprocity with Syracuse; Ray hoped that Vance might be able to go to Stanford or George Washington University.[39]

• • •

Ray had found serenity and good story material in El Paso, but he wrote no new stories there. He did review books for the *Chicago Tribune*, beginning with William Humphrey's novel *My Moby Dick*. His reviews tended to be of the yea or nay variety, declarations of love or expressions of regret that an author has not produced something he can say he admires. Usually he follows the schoolchild's formula of summarizing the story and then announcing his opinion. And yet those reviews, written in first person, reveal the personality of Carver's mind. Books excite him, imitation bores him, and he thinks fishing provides the best metaphor for the human endeavor to create meaning.[40]

UTEP reduced Ray's teaching schedule for the spring semester, but his travel schedule, with Gallagher and without, was daunting. Together they spent spring break in Mexico City. Ray found the city "very beautiful and exciting," but in his 1984 poem "The Young Fire Eaters of Mexico City" he laments the children who fill their mouths with alcohol and breathe out flames to get a few pesos. Damaged by their desperate art, these child artists "have no voice within a year."[41] Ray must have seen himself in those fire-eaters.

Ray was also giving readings all over the country—from Hattiesburg, Mississippi, to Spokane, Washington—and gleefully picking up as much as $1,000 for a day's work. Thus he kept in touch with old friends and made hundreds of new ones. After a reading at Intersection Center for the Arts in San Francisco with his *kayak* publisher, George Hitchcock, a bookseller from San Jose named Lewis Buzbee came up to Ray with a copy of his own first published story; Ray took it graciously and returned a careful critique. When Gallagher left El Paso for a two-week residency in Illinois, Ray wrote Kittredge that he missed her so much that he'd "taken to sitting at her little desk, trying to use her little electric typewriter. I'm going to try on some of her little clothes next."[42]

On May 26, the day after Ray's forty-first birthday, twenty-year-old unmarried Christine Carver gave birth to a baby girl and named her Windy Michelle. "I am a granddad now!" Ray wrote Ford. Maryann had moved from California to Bellingham, so, Ray continued, "my daughter has family in the area, and a community."[43] Behind Ray's excitement and hope, one senses a father's wish to believe that his child is happy and untroubled and won't bring him new complications and responsibilities.

At the end of May, Ray and Tess shipped their household goods to a house she had purchased in Tucson, where she would teach the next year, and decamped to a cabin near Port Angeles, Washington. On a clear day, he could see across the straits and islands to the northern Cascade Mountains, where his wife, daughter, granddaughter, sister-in-law Amy, and Doug Unger lived in the shadow of Mount Baker. His visits to that family were brief, but the landscape they shared was a constant reminder of other proximities.

For most of the summer, Ray and Tess rode the writing conference circuit: Santa Cruz, Aspen, Goddard, and Evansville, Indiana. By midsummer, Ray was feeling "screwy with travel" and wanted to settle down. He was still sober but "trying to smoke myself to death." By letter he confessed to Maryann that he'd felt "completely ungrounded" one night in a Wyoming motel, but managed to not drink.[44] In mid-August he and Gallagher were back on the Olympic Peninsula, where Ray stopped by the Port Townsend Writers' Conference. In a little cabin on the conference grounds, Jim Crumley recalled, he and Ray shared "a huge mound" of cocaine. "We had a very cordial and easy cocaine relationship, because whereas dope and drinking made Ray depressed, cocaine made him happy."[45]

Gary Eddy, who was moving from El Paso to Tucson, agreed to look after Gallagher's house there for her until she and Ray moved in. When Eddy arrived at 2905 East Twenty-third Street, he found that vandals had wrecked the swamp cooler and poured sugar on the carpet and urinated all over it—"just a colorful mess." Without money or tools, Eddy was hard-pressed to make repairs and spent most of the summer "sitting in front of a fan in the living room reading all of Faulkner." When Ray and Tess arrived, they spent a few days at the home of department chair Richard Shelton before braving her house. The Sheltons, who had other guests, recalled "seeing Ray and Tess sitting in the corner with their arms around each other like lost children." Things did not much improve for them in Tucson. They felt "addled" by the heat and looked forward to the snow and freezing wind of Syracuse. Their Tucson backyard had "black widow spiders as big as pansies" and there were "gangs of thugs in every street"; he was afraid to go outside, and he worried that Tess would be mugged when she left to teach.[46]

Yet Ray saw an opportunity in this imprisonment: he had "four months of straight clear road ahead" before he had to move again. He determined to put himself "on a war-footing here and tighten the hatches . . . and just try to work steadily the next four months." He took his mission so seriously that he began an exercise routine for the first time in his life, rising at six every morning to walk in a park while Tess jogged.[47] Shelton thought Gallagher was sometimes bitter about her own life in Tucson, but she was protective of Ray's time . . . she didn't encourage him to go places or encourage people to visit him.[48]

But there were exceptions. When Richard Yates came to Tucson to promote *A Good School* in mid-September, Ray finagled the opportunity to spend most of a day with the writer who'd been his hero since he was stopped "dead in his tracks" by *Revolutionary Road* in 1961. To mention that novel, Richard Ford writes, "is to invoke a sort of cultural-literary secret handshake among its devotees." In person, Ray gave Yates *Will You Please Be Quiet, Please?* Days later, he mailed him *Furious Seasons* as well, noting that he recommended only half of the stories therein: "Dummy," "Distance," "So Much Water So Close to Home," and "The Fling." Ray liked "Dick" Yates very much but noticed that his health was "not so good."[49] Plainly, the encounter reminded Ray that his own days were numbered and hardened his determination to work on stories. He immediately commenced his most productive period of writing in a decade. The first two stories he wrote were "Where Is Everyone?" and "The Calm."

By November 3—seven weeks after spending the day with Yates—Carver said he had seven new stories.[50] By the end of the next spring, he had completed a total of nine, including "Gazebo," "Pie" ("A Serious Talk"), "One More Thing," "If It Please You" ("After the Denim"), "I Could See the Smallest Things," "What We Talk About When We Talk About Love," and "A Small, Good Thing."[51] Except for "A Small, Good Thing," the stories are about marriages breaking down or apart. Within several of them are nostalgic vignettes, like this speech by the wife in "Where Is Everyone?"

> "When I was pregnant with Mike you carried me to the bathroom when I was so sick and pregnant I couldn't get out of bed. You carried me. No one else will ever do that, no one else could ever love me in that way, that much. We have that, no matter what. We've loved each other like nobody else could or ever will love the other again."[52]

"The Calm" takes place in a barbershop. Its narrator listens from the chair as three other men argue about a deer. In the end, this story is also about marriage. Here are the concluding lines as they appeared in the *Iowa Review*:

> But today I was thinking of that place, Crescent City, and my attempt at a new life there with my wife, and how even then, in the chair that morning, I had made up my mind to leave and not look back. I recalled the calm I felt when I closed my eyes and let the fingers move through my hair, the hair already starting to grow again.[53]

One dare not argue that Ray experienced such a precise moment of decision about the end of his old life (and marriage), but surely the story makes a true fiction of a process that had brought him to Tucson, to live with a new woman, and begin writing a new kind of story about his old subject, the he-she of human relationships.

Of these stories written in Tucson, "Where Is Everyone?" stands out as a transition between Carver's earlier and later work. In it he eschews distancing techniques and writes from a male, first-person point of view; by pulling the story close to himself, he's able to show just how fragmented his life has become. The story begins and ends in a single evening when the alcoholic narrator, hoping to crash at his mother's for a few nights, finds her kissing a man on the very sofa where he will sleep:

> . . . during those days, when my mother was putting out to men she'd just met, I was out of work, drinking, and crazy. My kids were crazy, and my wife was crazy and having a "thing" with an unemployed aerospace engineer she'd met at AA. He was crazy too.[54]

In the course of the story's few hours, this unreliable but likable narrator vividly evokes all these characters, recounts the night his father died, and discusses (with humor) his wife's affair with the engineer. The narrator ruminates on the question posed by the title as he drives around, waiting for his mom's boyfriend to leave. The closing scene between mother and son echoes the opening scene of another story dear to Ray's heart, "Nobody Said Anything." As before, the mother makes a bed for her son on the couch and he watches TV with the sound turned down. Like so many of Carver's stories, this one ends with an indeterminate spiritual fear or longing: "A snowy light filled the room. There was a roaring coming at me. The room clamored. I lay there. I didn't move."

To keep up with this outpouring of stories, Ray bought himself a brand-new Smith Corona Coronamatic 2500: "it sounds like a cigar, but it's my first electric typewriter, and my first new typewriter ever," he told friends.[55] The new machine was midsized, big enough for his hands and small enough to carry in a case. He gave his work to a typist for final copies. "Where Is Everyone?" went directly to Kittredge for an issue of Western stories he was editing for *TriQuarterly*. "Pie" and "Gazebo" and "If It Please You" went to Sterling and on to the *New Yorker*. Charles McGrath turned down all three, reporting that the editors had found the first "not quite original or surprising enough," the second "too pat at the end," and the third "very un-Carverlike," though McGrath was impressed by the "depth of feeling" in the story. McGrath remained determined to publish Carver.[56]

In November Ray sent about one hundred manuscript pages to Ford and broke his story binge. The El Paso cardiologist and his wife came for a visit that left Ray tired from an overdose of "drugs and Winchell's doughnuts."[57] Ella Carver came to see her son for Thanksgiving; together they went to the greyhound races, and Ray won $20 on a dog named Bijou Bill.

When George Hitchcock and Marjorie Simon came to read at the Poetry Center in December, Ray withdrew an invitation to dine at his and Tess's house because it wasn't fit for visitors. Ray told Hitchcock he was writing morning and afternoon and did not want to be distracted by beautiful surroundings.[58]

Critics and friends of Carver's have argued about why he returned so often to his old life to find subjects for his fiction. Some say he was obsessed by guilt and wished to make spiritual atonement for the damage his alcoholic years had done to his family and himself. Tobias Wolff rejected that notion. In proceeding with his new life, Wolff said,

> Ray brought along only those things which were going to be useful to him and guilt was not going to be one of them. He put the transgressions of the past to use in his fiction, but I don't think that he felt much guilt about things that had gone bad. He was *boyish,* and one of the features of that boyishness, I think, was that he had a talent for forgiving himself.[59]

And Carver implicitly understood—and had understood when he was sixteen and mailed his first story to a magazine—that nothing mattered more to him than writing. If, during his months of early recovery, he'd had to put his physical health ahead of his writing, he returned now to writing as his means of psychic survival. He did not in a strict sense follow an AA program for making amends to others or making "conscious contact with God." His work was his program. The turbulence and static of family emotion—what he called "milling"—that had driven him out of Iowa City in the summer of 1978 was nonetheless the grain that Ray ground into his art: the grist for his mill. In Tucson, in the third year of his sobriety, he had discovered a way to be apart from his family and still operate the machinery of his art. Or, to use a phrase that Tobias Wolff has applied to his friend's modus operandi, Ray was able to have his cake and eat it too.

Gallagher saw something inexplicably miraculous in Ray's return to daily work:

> Here the word *somehow* has to come in. Because somehow he gradually gathered himself into a place where he lived for the promise of the future, where each day without drinking had a glow and a fervor. Once we were living together and he was steady enough, he took heart from seeing me at my writing . . . The leopard of his imagination pulled down the feathers and blooded flesh of stories fueled by his previous failures and delivered as the result of his recovery.[60]

His sojourn in the Southwest drawing to a close, Ray anticipated holidays in Washington, including a visit with his daughter and granddaughter. Most of all, as the 1980s commenced, Ray looked forward to moving *permanently* to Syracuse, New York. "Maybe I can hang up my guns at long last and come in off the trail," he wrote Lish.[61]

The late 1970s were a promising time for readers and writers and publishers of short stories. *Stories of John Cheever* won the Pulitzer Prize and the National Book Critics Circle Award and became one of the few books of short stories ever to make the *New York Times* bestseller list. Major publishers gambled on story collections by Ann Beattie (*Distortions*), Jayne Anne Phillips (*Black Tickets*), Alice Munro (*The Beggar Maid*), Mary Robison (*Days*), and Barry Hannah (*Airships*). Four of these volumes, including the Cheever, came from Knopf; Robison's and Hannah's were edited by Gordon Lish.

Tess Gallagher had told Ray that he would have to maintain his lucky streak if he wanted to be with her. After writing seven stories in seven weeks, Ray began to hope that he might be able to do just that.

CHAPTER 24

What We Talk About
When We Talk About Love

January 1980–August 1981, Syracuse, New York

Order is an autonomous conquest for each generation, for each discipline of art, for each individual. It is the true quest of every man. It is the secret image that every artist pursues, it is his reason for being, the substance of what he creates. If he does not create an order, he does not create.

> —Michel Seuphor, *Sculpture of This Century*,
> transcribed in one of Carver's notebooks

In the 1980s, Ray Carver applied himself to the creation of order in his art and in his life. One cannot underestimate the urgency this quest held for him. He regarded his sober life after 1977 as "gravy"—an unearned blessing, more than he'd ever counted upon. These years were less dramatic and less amusing to others than his previous existence, but they were critical to his enduring literary reputation. As it would turn out, he wrote about half of his short stories before 1977 and the other half after that date. His relationship with Tess Gallagher and the new habits of work and life that he was able to establish became (to force his metaphor) the plate that held his meat and gravy.

In January 1980, as Jimmy Carter's presidency limped through its final year and Ronald Reagan's first presidential campaign gathered momentum, Ray moved to Syracuse. He lived alone—"if you can call living alone living"—in an apartment sublet, furniture and all, from poet Hayden Carruth (who'd moved in with a girlfriend). "Ray thought Syracuse was at the west edge of Princeton," Carruth said. "He thought it was a major Eastern university." In fact, Syracuse was a solid private university in a small city in northern New York state. Renovations were always in progress, but the city remained rundown. It has notoriously long, damp, "lake effect" winters that blow down off the Great Lakes. For Ray, it was a place where he could work, afford a house, and stay put. Poet Brooks Haxton, then a grad student who lived upstairs, heard two sounds from Ray's quarters: the typewriter going all day long and laughter in the evenings when he spoke to Tess on the telephone. Ray's first phone bill of $218 reminded him of days when such bills were normal for him.[1]

At Syracuse, Ray became an exemplary academic citizen, except for his insistence on smoking in his classroom and office. He sat on the search committee for a "junior" fiction writer and reviewed applications to the master's program, which took only six poets and six fiction writers each fall. Through such tasks Ray put his stamp on the respected writing program, making it, he thought, "one of the better programs in the country." The junior fiction-writer's position went to Tobias Wolff, whose stories were appearing in the *Atlantic Monthly* and other good magazines. Before long, his short stories and his novella, *The Barracks Thief,* would earn him a substantial readership.

Building his writers' empire at SU didn't go to Ray's head. "I always think they're going to find me out and give me a janitor's job instead," he wrote Johnson. He lived "a little like an animal in a cave" and on a typical Saturday night heated a frozen dinner, wrote letters, then smoked a joint and watched TV for half an hour before going to bed.[2] The marijuana helped him sleep; the work kept him going: "I have finished, just about to my satisfaction, a 40-pager I began after I got here," he reported to Day. In the spring, he planned to send a manuscript of about eighteen stories to John Sterling. That forty-pager would eventually, after a long odyssey in the publishing world, emerge as one of Carver's most beloved pieces, "A Small, Good Thing."[3] In it a bland, middle-class couple whose son is hit by a car descend into the hell of a modern hospital. No one can tell them what is happening to their son. There is no reason, the doctor says repeatedly, why the boy hasn't recovered consciousness. Everyone in the story speaks in stilted rhythms and without the vernacular phrases and humor that Carver usually employs. When the parents go home, they receive harassing calls from a baker because the mother has failed to pick up the birthday cake she ordered for her son. The death of the child, who is given no personality whatsoever, brings the parents closer to each other—they "seemed to feel each other's insides now, as though the worry had made them transparent in a perfectly natural way"—and leads them to a reconciliation, a literal breaking of bread, with the angry baker.

When Gallagher visited Syracuse during her spring break, she and Ray found themselves a three-story shingle-sided house with a fireplace and four bedrooms on a steeply sloping lot. It was a mansion compared to the dozens of suburban ramblers and boxlike apartments Ray had inhabited before. Ray told friends he knew this big old house would be a happy one. As "joint tenants with rights of survivorship," Gallagher and Carver purchased the house at 832 Maryland Avenue and assumed a mortgage from the sellers. They would take possession in May. The deed filed with Onondaga County, New York, makes no mention of Carver's marital status and Carver made no effort to secure a divorce from Maryann.[4]

That spring Ray spent a week with Michael Waters and earned $1,000 as a visiting writer at Salisbury State University in Delaware. Sleepless as usual, Ray let Waters's dog out early one morning, not knowing that the dog—Bobby by name—wasn't allowed out on his own. When Bobby was missed, a repentant Ray spent hours cruising the neighborhood and looking for him. That reprise of Carver's earlier dog story "Jerry and Molly and Sam" (wherein a narrator sets out to lose his children's dog) verified Ray's new luck. He found the dog! The mutt sprawled by the fireplace all day, "legs flung open in some canine parody of bliss," as Waters wrote in a poem about the episode. Ray kept imagining Bobby's adventures and saying, "I gave Bobby the best day of his life!"[5]

Carver read three new stories to the Salisbury students: "Why Don't You Dance?" "Gazebo," and "If It Please You." In a video recording of the event, Ray's sideburns are neatly trimmed and he's wearing a jacket and tie. After finishing the second story, he sighs and says, "I didn't realize until I began reading these particular stories that they all seem to have a common concern [sigh] a theme if you will [sigh] a meaning as Flannery O'Connor would say." Carver speaks as if this thought had just now occurred to him and doesn't name the concern. Surely even the young undergraduates in the audience understood, though: these were stories about young love and damaged love, fresh couples and jaded couples, dreams and losses. All had been written since Carver quit drinking in 1977.[6]

As Carver was gathering enough stories for a new book, he learned that John Sterling had resigned his position at the ICM agency and moved to Maine. Undaunted, Carver submitted "Beginners" to *Antaeus* (it was rejected) and then to *TriQuarterly*, which took it for its winter issue.[7] To Lewis Buzbee, who was interviewing Ray by mail, Ray wrote "I think the new stories, some of them, are different yet." Ray delivered his new book manuscript (referred to here as version A) directly into Lish's hands at lunch in New York City.[8] His working title, "So Much Water So Close to Home," implied that everyone is drowning, not only in faraway rivers but near to home. Carver listed the prestigious ICM agency on his title page though he had no longer had a representative there.[9] Lish matched him with an independent agent, Liz Darhansoff, but Carver continued to make most of his own magazine submissions. Ray fretted while Lish read. On May 10, Lish let him know that he wished to publish the stories. He would edit them and seek a contract from Knopf. That same day, a Saturday, Ray wrote Lish a gushing letter of thanks for their past friendship and told him to edit the stories as he knew only he could: "I want them to be the best possible stories . . . Not to worry about money. . . . Be enough, you know, to have Knopf do a book of mine and have you as my editor. So open the throttle. Ramming speed."

Ray wrote that as he left for the funeral of George Elliott, his predecessor at SU, who had died of a heart attack. In his haste, Ray omitted a line from the envelope address. At nine the same evening, he wrote Lish again, worried that the emotional letter would go astray. Again he urged Lish to "put more muscle in the stories" if he saw occasion to do so.[10]

Ray embarked on a summer of travel, beginning with the Midnight Sun Writers' Conference in Fairbanks, Alaska, and family visits in the Northwest. On June 13, as Ray packed for Alaska, a newly edited version of the book arrived from Lish. This—version B—comprised Ray's typescript (A) with Lish's editing in felt-tip marker running through and above the typed lines. Lish had already arranged to have it retyped.[11] "The collection *looks* terrific," Carver wrote Lish, "though I haven't been able to read much more than the title page—which title is fine, I think. Yes."[12] The new title supplied by Lish was *What We Talk About When We Talk About Love*, a line Lish tweaked from dialogue spoken by the cardiologist in the story Ray had called "Beginners":

> ". . . it ought to make us all feel ashamed when we talk like we know *what we were talking about, when we talk about love*." [emphasis added]

Without making changes to version B, Ray mailed Lish a check for the typist who would make a clean typescript based on Lish's own copy of version B. Ray carried the edited pages (version B) with him to Alaska and began waiting to hear if Knopf would offer him a contract.[13]

Once, in a story title, Carver had wondered "What's in Alaska?" He found there endless supplies of free liquor to decline and endless daylight to aggravate his insomnia. Tess brought her father. With them and Geoffrey Wolff and James Welch, Ray went fishing for Arctic char and attended a baseball game at the Solstice. He hit it off with the star of the Midnight Sun conference, English poet Ted Hughes.[14] Across four time zones, Lish called Ray in Fairbanks. Knopf would offer an advance of $5,000 for *What We Talk About When We Talk About Love*.[15] "What an umbrella title!" Ray declared as he spread the news at the conference and beyond. He carried the pages around with him and read "So Much Water So Close to Home" to the group.[16] More than likely, he added his own marks to the typescript during his travels.

From Alaska, Ray, Tess, and her father cruised through the inland passage. Tess went home to Port Angeles with her father. Ray departed for Syracuse.

Carver's book contract from Knopf was waiting for him when he returned alone, with a "dilly of a chest and head cold," to Syracuse. He signed and mailed it back right away. Thus, consulting neither an agent nor an attorney, he entered a binding contract for his book. Embarrassingly, the check he'd sent to cover the retyping of his manuscript had bounced. On Independence Day, he mailed Lish a new check. He fretted that he had yet to receive "the revised collection" that Lish had had retyped while Carver was in Alaska. Because of the holiday, he would now have to wait all weekend before he could read a final typescript based on Lish's editing.[17]

On Monday, July 7 the new typescript (version C) arrived. For the rest of that day and most of that night, until "July 8, 8 a.m."—he dated a letter to Lish that precisely—Carver compared the version (B) he'd received on June 13 with this new and final one (C). The differences between the two astounded Carver. They can be fully comprehended only by means of the kind of page-by-page, story-by-story comparison that Carver himself undertook.

This retyped version C included changes that had not been there on the hand-edited version B. What had happened? It seems most likely that Lish had continued to edit on his own copy of B, overwriting his first round of editing with more extensive changes than the ones Carver had seen. Or, it's possible that Lish had edited on the typescript formed from B to create a second generation of revisions. Or, perhaps he had lost his version of B and reedited, coming out with a more extreme result. Whatever the exact process that occurred, little archival evidence of the differences between versions B and C has become available to scholars. Yet it seems incontrovertible that there were significant differences, because Carver describes them at length in letters to Lish.

Although the precise stages of editing are obscure, comparison of versions A and C shows that whole pages of stories were excised, most notably from "A Small, Good Thing," which also had its title changed to "The Bath." Main characters became nameless. Secondary characters nearly disappeared. Landscapes and weather were gone. Endings that tended toward epiphany vanished. Carver was shocked. He had urged Lish to take a pencil to the stories. He had not expected him to take a meat cleaver to them.[18]

To get an idea of the changes Lish made in two stages of editing, readers may compare the following published works: the version of "So Much Water So Close to Home" that appears in *Where I'm Calling From* (1988) and in *Fires* (1983) with the same title in *What We Talk About* (1981); the story called "A Small, Good Thing" in *Where* and *Cathedral* (1983) with "The Bath" in *What*; "Where Is Everyone?" in *Fires* with "Mr. Coffee and Mr. Fixit" in *What*; and "Distance" in *Fires* with "Everything Stuck to Him" in *What*, and "Beginners" in the *New Yorker*, December 24–31, 2007, with "What We Talk About . . ." in *What*.[19]

After spending all night studying Lish's work, Carver was fatigued and "awash with confusion and paranoia." Confusion is evident throughout the four-page, single-spaced, typed letter that Carver sent Lish. But Carver's decision is clear enough. He begins: "Dearest Gordon, I've got to pull out of this one. Please hear me." He concludes: "Please do the necessary things to stop production of the book. Please try and forgive me, this breach."[20]

Between those two supplications—note how often Carver uses the word *please*—lie more than two thousand words with which Carver attempts to justify his decision and beg and secure Lish's compliance and forgiveness. He praises Lish ("You are a wonder, a genius . . . better than any two of Max Perkins . . .") and he praises the stories ("Even though they may be closer to works of art than the originals and people will be reading them 50 years from now. . . ."). Forgetting his own twenty years of struggle and the love of the two remarkable women who have sustained him, he tells Lish: "This whole new life I have . . . everything, I owe to you for WILL YOU PLEASE."[21]

Those homages paid, he blames himself: ". . . this has to do with my sobriety and with my new-found (and fragile, I see) mental health and well-being." He is direly afraid of losing Lish's "love or regard over this . . . It would be like having a part of myself die, a spiritual part." If that sounds extreme, bear in mind that during his alcoholic years Lish had, to a degree, become the authorial voice within Carver, in effect usurping Carver's authority over his own work. While publication always turns art into a commodity, Lish's heavy editing and Carver's alcoholism combined to make the whole process painfully ambiguous. Carver may have doubted his own authorship.[22]

These new stories, Carver declares, are integral and essential to his recovery from alcoholism: ". . . I've come back from the grave here to start writing stories . . . I'd given up entirely, thrown it in and was looking forward to dying, that release." There are three stories in particular—"A Small, Good Thing," "Where Is Everyone?" and "If It Please You," as well as parts of "What We Talk About When We Talk About Love"—that Carver feels are so deeply connected to his recovered sense of "worth and self-esteem" that he cannot in any way permit them to be published in the severely altered form that Lish has proposed.[23]

Additionally, there is fear. Lish intends to publish *What We Talk About* in the spring of 1981. Many people have read the stories in their original, longer forms. He names Gallagher, Donald Hall, Richard Ford, Tobias Wolff, Geoffrey Wolff, Bill Kittredge, and Thomas McGuane.[24] Some of the stories have appeared in magazines, some have been read to audiences. Trying to be practical, Carver asks if publication of the book could be postponed, because in eighteen months or two years these friends may no longer recall what they read. But hiding or postponing the problem doesn't really appeal to Carver. His letter veers away from that line of thinking, back to frantic alternation between praise for Lish and fear "that if the book were to be published as it is in its present form, I may never write another story, that's how close, God Forbid, some of those stories are to my sense of my regaining my health and mental well-being."[25]

Carver is sure of one thing in addition to his desire to stop publication. He has compared the hand-marked manuscript (B) he received June 13 with the new typescript (C) he received July 7. He has concluded that "the first one is better, I truly believe . . ."[26]

In all his two thousand words, Carver never expresses anger at Gordon Lish. Nor does Carver imply that there is arrogance in Lish's uncommon method of editing a literary text and having it retyped (making the changes less apparent to the eye) without first securing its author's approval. Instead, Carver writes on and on, trying to explain himself with characteristic alcoholic self-blame and need for approval. He even offers to pay Lish for the time he has spent on the misbegotten manuscript and *apologizes* for having signed a contract without seeing the final edit. Carver's is a lovable and awful performance. Nonetheless, Carver is clear: to allow these stories to be turned into Lish's stories would be dishonest. And it would undermine his confidence in his sobriety and ability to write.

Two and a half days later, the evening of Thursday, July 10, Carver wrote Lish a very different kind of letter. In the interim, Carver has changed his mind. Publication is going forward and Carver has been going over the new typescript in detail: "It's a beauty for sure. It's simply stunning, it is, and I'm honored and grateful for your attentions to it. I've been with it since early morning, except for the time I took out to eat and to call you."[27]

The correspondence from Carver that Lish saved gives no indication of how Carver's change of heart came about. Lish has said, "My sense of it was that there was a letter and that I just went ahead." Tess Gallagher has said publicly that Lish informed Carver by telephone that he would not restore the book to its earlier incarnation. She noted that Carver regarded Lish as a friend, but Lish also held the "power of publication access." Carver, she wrote after his death, "felt the book, even at the time of its publication, did not represent the main thrust of his writing, nor his true pulse and instinct in the work."[28] Historian Carol Polsgrove, who first noticed the extent of Lish's editing on Carver's *Esquire* stories, has suggested that Lish may have secured Carver's compliance by threatening to reveal the amount of work he'd done on Carver's earlier stories. John Sterling, who thought Lish was "an astonishing analyst of text," noticed that Lish's attitude toward Ray changed after he left *Esquire* for Knopf: "He began to brag and say that Ray was his creature."[29]

Lish, then forty-six and in his third year at Knopf, was an influential editor in New York. He was known for indefatigable work habits, for maniacal devotion to his writers, for teaching six-hour seminars without bathroom breaks ("urinating is probably the first index of a less-than-literary heart" he told one class), for daily consumption of significant quantities of cigarettes and liquor.[30] It is easy to believe that Lish simply bullied Carver by refusing to cancel his contract and refusing to publish any version of the manuscript but the last one he (Lish) had created. Maryann Carver, on the other hand, believes that Ray might have conceded to Lish's editing because he pitied him: "Ray was no child pitted against Gordon's Svengali presence. He liked Gordon and felt sorry for him, because, as the saying went, Gordon would have given his left ball to have the talent to write the way Ray could. Ray was the original and Gordon could only hack away at and change what Ray put on paper."[31]

And yet Lish's own statements about writing suggest another scenario. In the 1980s Lish was able to act out the passionate feeling he'd long had for fiction on a very large stage. He exhorted his students that "Marriages don't last, friendships don't last, children don't last. Work lasts. Look to your work." Lish had, the *Boston Globe*'s Gail Caldwell writes, "the oratorical skills of a roadshow preacher and the quiet brainpower of a classics scholar." On July 9 or 10, 1980, Lish may have called upon his oratorical skills to persuade Carver that the severely edited July version (C) of *What We Talk About* was a thing of beauty; perhaps he persuaded Carver that earlier versions of the book were sentimental and would embarrass him, or that he would demean himself by canceling the book. "What I cared about as I worked was the making of the beautiful things," Lish would aver two decades later. "Which has the greater value? The document as it issues from the writer or the thing of beauty that was made? What remains is an artifact of power."[32]

Lish's defense of the completed work of art over the expressions and tastes of the artist meshed neatly with Carver's insecurities, especially since Ray and his agent had been unable to place these stories in major magazines. The outpouring of stories he had produced the previous fall seemed to him a gift, something he could not take credit for and did not fully own. If Lish urged him to reread the collection—as Carver's July 10 letter says he has done—and consider it with detachment, Carver must have done so and been persuaded to allow Lish to have his way.

Lish did not think he made a mistake in editing Carver as he did. He believes that the worst he could be charged with is that he was "aggressive" with all his authors. "Carver was not by any means an isolated occasion. For pity's sake, I did it all the time where I felt it was indicated. I believed that I was good enough at this not to have done it in instances where it wasn't required." It was not, he insists, a case of his imposing his personality on the personality of the writer, but rather his "sense of what was and was not acceptable to me in literary form as an editor." Lish has acknowledged that he edited *What We Talk About* more aggressively than Carver's previous book because he felt that there was more to protect in the second book. *Will You Please* had been nominated for a National Book Award, so *What We Talk About* had a shot at something big. Lish has also speculated that Carver, in his post-alcohol work, may have considered himself a "big shot" and written more freely so there was more to edit.[33]

One wonders, too, if Lish's growing sense of himself as an author played a role in his conflict with Carver. He had begun to place his own short fictions in prestigious literary quarterlies. One of these, a monologue called "The Death of Me," describes an impulse that might have driven Lish's bold editing:

> I wanted to be amazing. I wanted to be so amazing. I had already been amazing up to a certain point. But I was tired of being at that point. I wanted to go past that point. I wanted to be more amazing than I had been up to that point. I wanted to do something which went beyond that point and which went beyond every other point and which people would look at and say that this was something which went beyond all other points and which no other boy would ever be able to go beyond, that I was the only boy who could, that I was the only one . . .[34]

Lish rarely let editors change his own work, both he and one of his editors have reported.[35] At the same time, Lish continued to ghostwrite books, including *Coming Out of the Ice* (by Victor Herman, 1979). A novel that Lish edited speaks to all this. In Bette Pesetsky's *Author from a Savage People* (Knopf, 1983), a woman named May Alto ghostwrites books for a man who eventually wins a Nobel Prize with her work. Alto's psychiatrist, appalled when he learns that his patient wrote some of his favorite books, asks her, " 'Have you ever thought that being all these different people may be causing you pain that you are unwilling to recognize?' "[36]

Whatever Carver may have agreed to by phone, he did not utterly acquiesce to Lish in his July 10 letter. He returned the new manuscript (C) with suggestions for changes, asking if Lish still had his copy of the earlier one (B) for comparison. According to Carver's letter, the changes he wanted were "a question of reinstating some of those things that were taken out in the second version." Carver defends in detail sections he wishes to restore in several stories. He is especially concerned about "The Bath," which he says has been reduced from fifteen pages to twelve in the second revision.[37] He wants to reinstate the title "Distance" for the story Lish called "Everything Stuck to Him." Most urgently Carver asked Lish to "jettison" the story now called "Mr. Coffee and Mr. Fixit" because it had already been in *TriQuarterly* and was already slated for the next O. Henry collection. "It was the first story I wrote when I began to write again in Tucson, and I want to leave it where it is, by its lonesome there in this special issue of TRIQUARTERLY." Apart from some requests to change names in stories, Carver got his way on only one significant change, the restoration of this line as the ending of "Gazebo": "In this, too, she was right."[38]

Scholars of Carver's work have been unable to read the edited typescript (B) that Carver thought was "fuller in the best sense."[39] In a letter dated July 14, 1980, Carver asked Lish if he should return this first revised manuscript (B) so Lish could refer to it when he reviewed Carver's comments on the second revised version (C). This B version is not identifiable among Lish's papers at Indiana University or among Carver's in the William Charvat Collection of American Fiction at Ohio State University, though it seems to have been in Carver's possession in Syracuse in July 1980.[40] Scholars William Stull and Maureen Carroll have edited a manuscript based on version A with Carver's original title, "Beginners," which is included in a Library of America volume of Carver's stories. In their edition, they write that Carver's manuscript was "cut and reshaped by Lish in two rounds of close line editing," but they do not catalog the differences between the first and second rounds.[41] The B typescript with Lish's first revisions (and any that Carver might have added himself) would answer questions about Carver's intentions for these stories and his receptivity to Lish's first round of suggestions. A generation of Carver scholars has already made the mistake of assuming that *What We Talk About* represents an extreme minimalist phase in Carver's work from which he began to rebound in his next story collection, *Cathedral*, an interpretation that Carver himself supplied in several interviews. Access to the B typescript would assist scholars in their efforts to analyze the development of Carver's fiction.[42]

Carver concealed his remaining doubts about his forthcoming book in energetic efforts to assist Lish with its promotion. On July 14, the night before he was to fly to Bellingham to see Chris and Windy, he wrote Lish with ideas about magazines that might publish the stories in advance of the book. But he was still worried about the revisions too. "My greatest fear is, or was, having them too pared." Carver's comment about "The Bath" and "Community Center" (which became "After the Denim") surely echoes the argument Lish made to him on the phone:

> I want that sense of beauty and mystery they have now, but I don't want to lose track, lose touch with the little human connections I saw in the first version you sent me. They seemed somehow fuller in the best sense, in that first ed. version . . . please give them another hard look. That's all. That and what I said about Where Is Everyone?—Mr. Coffee, Mr. Fixit. I won't gather that one into the collection. The next collection, not this one.[43]

In each instance, it appears that Lish overrode Carver's wishes.

The final judgment as to Carver's feelings about the entire headache-inducing matter may perhaps be found in the fact that he later republished those three stories in longer forms.[44]

Traveling to Bellingham, Ray stayed in a motel so that he could control his contact with his family. At Ray's expense, his mother flew up from California to see him. Maryann remained in Bellingham, failing to find a permanent teaching position despite strong recommendations from Los Altos, and helping care for Chris's daughter. Ray sent occasional checks to the Bellingham contingent. Jobs were scarce there during the early 1980s, and Maryann substitute taught and waitressed to make ends meet. Amy Wright and Doug Unger got married in San Francisco while touring with their original play *Diaries of Women*. Vance, who worked the season in a salmon cannery near Kodiak Island, planned to transfer to Syracuse University to study international relations. Ray boasted that the IR program at SU was excellent and that Vance would attend tuition-free (a $6,000 value) "seeing as how his Da is on the faculty." Able to offer his son something, Ray had become, at forty-two, a proud father.[45]

Back on Maryland Avenue, Ray and Tess set about making their house a good place to work and entertain. In one sweep they bought a houseful of cream-colored furniture and neutral draperies. The living room was set up for conversation with an L-shaped sofa and a coffee table covered with books and Ray's overflowing ashtray. Ray burned a fire whenever there was a chill in the air. Tobias Wolff admired a couple of their paintings, "one by a Mexican artist, an almost surreal rendering of a drinker at an outdoor cafe, the other a view of a cottage with a white fence." A gray kitten named Blue joined the household. Ray's study was a large room on the top floor where his long oak desk stood beneath a south-facing window. Novelist C. J. Hribal, then Ray's student, worked in an attic window next door that overlooked Ray's roof. "Ray would look up from his typewriter and his cigarette and see me. We'd wave and go back to work, as if we could communicate stories across the void."[46]

In New York in mid-August, Fisketjon joined Lish and Carver for a meal, and Darhansoff renegotiated Carver's contract with Knopf, gaining an increase on royalties for a Vintage paperback edition of *What We Talk About* that Fisketjon would oversee. Lish placed the title story in *Antaeus,* where Ray's earlier version of the same story had been declined. Throughout the fall, Lish and Carver corresponded, seemingly at ease. Carver's letters included ambitious lists of writers he thought might do blurbs—Stanley Elkin, Richard Yates, Ted Hughes, Evan Connell, John Gardner, and John Cheever. Half-seriously he listed Samuel Beckett, Jorge Luis Borges, and Gabriel García Márquez. Not only had he put aside his scruples about Lish's editing, he'd taken on Lish's hope that this new book would give him a seat at the table with some of the world's great writers. But Carver balked when Lish sent the galleys for the book with a note asking Carver to sign off on them without reading them. He read them but found nothing to alarm him except the omission of the title story from the table of contents. They fixed that. Lish urged Carver not to worry so much.[47]

Ray had soon finished a new, long story, sent it to Ford, and replied gratefully to his friend's criticism, saying he would look to see "what can be done, squared up" in it.[48] "Vitamins" drew upon the time in Sacramento when Maryann sold encyclopedias: "Jesus, I never thought I'd grow up to sell vitamins," the wife in the story says. "Door-to-door vitamins." Alone among Carver's stories, "Vitamins" has several black characters and uses contemporary social context as a resonator for the narrator's desperation.

At "a spade bar in a spade neighborhood" the narrator and a friend with whom he's starting an affair encounter a black man named Nelson who is just returned from Vietnam. As the narrator and his friend depart, Nelson—a man who has no illusions—issues a dire warning: "It ain't going to do no good. Whatever you do, it ain't going to help none!"[49]

When Ray came to give a reading at Columbia University on December 8, he met Lish and Fisketjon for lunch. Afterward Fisketjon sent Ray to his friend Jay McInerney's to pass the time until the evening. Things hadn't been going well for twenty-five-year-old McInerney when the "hulking, but slouching" figure of his favorite living author filled his doorway. His mother had died, his wife had left him, and, fired from his job as a fact-checker at the New Yorker, he couldn't afford his expensive New York life. Ray enthusiastically tried cocaine with McInerney that afternoon, and the two embarked upon "a talking jag where we talked about everything under the sun and loved the sound of our own voices." Racing uptown by subway, they barely made it in time for Ray to speed read "Put Yourself in My Shoes" to a small audience. Ray saw that McInerney was dissipating his energy in New York. He urged him to study fiction writing at Syracuse. "I had some resistance," McInerney recalled. "I felt I was in the center of the media and publishing world . . . it's easy to confuse that with the literary world." That same night, not fifty blocks from where Carver gave his reading, Mark Chapman hid in an alcove at the Dakota building to shoot and kill forty-year-old Beatles icon and pacifist John Lennon.[50]

Bound galleys of What We Talk About went out in mid-December. Soon after, New York Times Book Review editor James Atlas invited Carver to write "something" about short stories, intentionally leaving the assignment vague. Soon Carver had twenty-three pages of "somethings" and was worried that he'd told too much about himself. He showed a draft of the piece to Lish, who discouraged Carver from submitting it to Atlas. Despite Lish's reservations, Carver trimmed his pages and Atlas accepted them. The matter settled, Carver wrote Lish that the essay was a "boost to my confidence" and made him feel "two inches taller." He hoped Lish would see his way to share his pride, but Lish did not. Stricken by Lish's displeasure and prepublication anxiety, Ray suffered a recurrence of the ulcer trouble he'd had in El Paso two years before. The Book Review ran "A Storyteller's Shoptalk" on Sunday, February 15, 1981.[51]

When he reprinted the essay in Fires in 1983, Carver changed its title to "On Writing." In it Carver offers his ars poetica for the short story, taking his stand for realism and accurate language, rejecting experimentation ("tricks") for its own sake. An often-quoted passage in the essay states Carver's belief in the power of simple, realistic details:

It's possible, in a poem or a short story, to write about commonplace things and objects using commonplace but precise language, and to endow those things—a chair, a window curtain, a fork, a stone, a woman's earring—with immense, even startling power. It is possible to write a line of seemingly innocuous dialogue and have it send a chill along the reader's spine—the source of artistic delight . . .

Taken whole, the essay provides a fine gloss on Carver's stories. Read with knowledge of the battle and compromise Carver has just undergone with Lish, it emits some ambiguity. Carver says he is "dumbfounded" when writers apologize for publishing work that could have been better if only they had not been rushed. Excuses and apologies bother Carver; "Don't complain, don't explain," he advises. And that, perhaps, is the surest explanation to be found for Carver's own acquiescence and reticence about the editing of *What We Talk About,* a book that he believed would have been better in the first revised form he received from Lish in June of 1980.[52]

Nonetheless, as he completed his fourth year of sobriety, gratitude became a keynote of Ray's response to life. To Dan Domench, his former Iowa City student and partner in drunken adventures who had quit drinking late in 1978, Ray wrote, "We beat that cancer. What can they do to us now? Half my friends, at least half, are fighting it right now or are gone under with it. You and me, we have blessings galore to count."[53] A long letter to his sister-in-law Amy Unger acknowledges that he feels "deferred anguish" and "sorrow" for "that gone life and my part in it" for which he can never make amends. If he died now, though, "it would be all right in that every day I have now is a real gift, and I look on it as a gift, another blessing." He's grateful, too, "to still have your abiding love. And Doug's. And Maryann's. Good lord, I am a lucky man to be so well loved and I mean that." Ray had good words for his children, too, telling Kittredge that Chris was doing "okay" and Vance was a "prince of a fellow." In fact, Vance was doing splendidly at Syracuse, earning As and planning to spend the 1981–82 academic year living with a French family and studying in Strasbourg.[54]

During his first academic year at Syracuse, Vance reminisced in his essay, "C'est Complet, Monsieur, C'est Complet" that he was "thrilled" to be near his father "and able to befriend him sober" after the strife between them in the 1970s. Though Vance, like all visitors, was discouraged from dropping by the house while Ray and Tess were working, he often went out with his dad. On April 1, for instance, Ray met Vance for dinner at his dormitory and a classroom screening of *The Battle of Algiers*. When Vance took Tobias Wolff's survey course in the short story, he said to Wolff, "My dad's really good, isn't he?" Wolff said, " 'Vance, your dad is one of the greatest short story writers who ever lived!' And that had some meaning for him because he was learning about this art form that his father pursued so single-mindedly. He could see him in this landscape of art."[55]

Ray invited Vance to visit him while he was in residence at the Province-town Fine Arts Works Center on Cape Cod in March. John Skoyles dined with Ray, Vance, and Richard Ford:

> Vance asked Ray a very simple question, something like "Does a writer mail out his stories?" and Ray furrowed his brow and answered him very seriously! It suggested they weren't familiar with each other on that level and Ray *obviously* was very attached to the boy and had invited him down here to stay with him. He wanted us to meet him. We all talked about Mexican baseball, which interested Richard at the time. And Ray invited his son into the conversation—it wasn't a literary conversation. Ray was obviously making a great rapprochement.

Ray also took seriously his mentoring tasks at Provincetown. For Maria Flook he line edited an entire story and then proposed that she change a "long Carver-imitation title" to "Clean." He amused everyone with his insatiable hunger for a snack food called Fiddle Faddle. When Skoyles brought Ray to his house, they found Skoyles's desk laden with items returned by an ex-lover. As he listened to the story of the broken affair, Ray sorted through the boxes. He said, " 'I think Little Tess might like a couple of these things,' and I said, 'Help yourself, Ray.' And he did."[56]

Indeed, Tess collected clothes and accessories, as photographer Annie Leibovitz noticed when she took her picture for a *Life* magazine piece on poets: "There were masks all over her house and coat racks full of clothes," Leibovitz writes. "She wanted to get dressed up . . . When you were with Gallagher you were in her world and you could see the way her imagination worked." Leibovitz's color spread of Tess in a silver gown lying on the bare back of a Palomino horse appeared in *Life* in company with iconoclastic images of other poets including Richard Hugo in boxer shorts next to his hospital bed, Philip Levine lifting weights, and Galway Kinnell swimming. Tess posted a copy of the portrait outside of her office at the university.[57]

The book that Gordon Lish created from Raymond Carver's stories—17 stories in a mere 150 pages—was dazzling to behold. Its neon-bright dust jacket flashed the words of the title in yellow on a magenta ground within concentric rectangles of acid green and cobalt blue. The author's name appears in hot pink, perhaps the only color that could match the extreme hype of Lish's copy on the inside flaps, much of it referencing the story Carver wanted to omit, "Mr. Coffee and Mr. Fixit." There's no photograph of the author in or on the book, which is dedicated to Tess Gallagher.

One of the first reviews of *What We Talk About* appeared in the *Chicago Tribune*. Editor John Blades devoted the front page of his Bookworld section to the short story, bracketing Tim O'Brien's review of Carver's book with an essay on the difficulties of the form by Harry Mark Petrakis and a review of *The Collected Stories of Caroline Gordon*. O'Brien, whose novel *Going After Cacciato* had recently won a National Book Award, wrote: "Carver uses the English language like a whittler's knife . . ." O'Brien compares Carver's stories to Hemingway's and notes that their fictions require readers to "perform acts of imagination and deduction" and define the "moral aboutness" of the stories.[58]

Anatole Broyard, a regular and often prickly reviewer for the daily *New York Times*, loathed what O'Brien praised. "'Mr. Coffee and Mr. Fixit,'" he asserts, "is written in faux-naïf Hemingway sentences as they might be spoken by an illiterate person." Michael Wood took on a larger question that lurks behind such differences of opinion. Beginning with Chekhov and Joyce, Wood writes, "the notion of crisis in fiction has become questionable," leaving the contemporary story to offer not moments of illumination or decision but rather "invisible" or "false" crises and "gleams of promised meaning."[59] Wood's review appeared on the most valuable literary real estate in North America: the front page of the *New York Times Book Review*. Two columns of type flanked Thomas Victor's full-length photograph of a big-shouldered and surly-looking Carver in jeans and a sweater (his Clarks Wallabees shoes do mitigate that tough-guy look). Ray's wooly hair is trimmed and his sideburns are gone. A steely, troubled stare displaces his old horn-rimmed glasses. Wood declares Carver "a master" of the Joycean and Chekhovian genre. He finds Carver's America "helpless, clouded by pain and loss of dreams, but . . . not as fragile as it looks . . ." Still, Wood expresses reservations: "Popular Mechanics" exemplifies "the unkindness and condescension of some of these stories . . . He is imitating himself here, turning his intuitions into a program . . ." Such "slickness" was not, Wood believes, present in Carver's earlier book. It can't have been lost on Carver that several of Wood's examples of imitation and slickness come from passages where Lish's editing had prevailed.

When the *Times* appeared, Lewis Buzbee, then selling books at Printers' Inc. in Palo Alto, got a call from Ray's mother. She asked him to hold copies for her and soon presented herself to pick them up: "Ella was a real Carver-country character — and she was completely thrilled to see her son's picture on the front page."[60]

Ella might well have been proud, too, to see the materials of her troubled life transfigured in her son's art. *Time* magazine noticed that Carver's tales echo country music (the kind Ray grew up hearing on the family radio) in their concern with "adultery, separation, D-I-V-O-R-C-E and the rage that ordinary folks experience" and face with "numbed endurance." For Robert Tower, writing in the *New York Review of Books,* Carver's stories are "low-rent tragedies involving people who read *Popular Mechanics* and *Field and Stream,* people who play bingo, hunt deer, fish, and drink." This reviewer and most of the others, regardless of whether they actually like the stories, are at pains to define who the characters are. Whether they call them "ordinary" or "working class" or "country" or part of a "vast population that most often eludes or falls through the net of our fiction," these reviewers all seem slightly baffled by Carver's people. When they praise Carver for not condescending to his characters, one senses that they themselves can't imagine *not* condescending to them. Nobody they know, one senses, plays bingo or goes fishing. Thus, at the same time these reviews welcomed Raymond Carver into the literary world, they hinted at the difficulties a man like himself might face in that world.

Carver was most surprised by a review by James Atlas, who had solicited his essay "On Writing." Writing for the *Atlantic Monthly* under the title "Less Is Less," Atlas says that Carver's "lackluster manner and eschewal of feeling become tiresome" and contrasts the "minimality" of "savage parables so prevalent in fiction now" with the descriptive richness and lively agitation of sixties writers such as Styron and Updike. Not only that, Atlas makes a palpable hit when he observes: "Carver's first collection was more robust, more 'literary,' and displayed a mastery of colloquial American idioms reminiscent of Ring Lardner or Sherwood Anderson. This new book, half as long, seems thin, diminished . . . his reticence now seems stubborn, willed." Unknowingly, one assumes, Atlas pointed a finger at Lish's editing. The qualities he disliked in *What We Talk About* are, to an uncanny extent, the ones introduced by Lish. Paradoxically, Carver felt personally betrayed by Atlas. "What an education all this has been, from start to finish. And it's not over yet!" Carver wrote to Day on the date Atlas's attack was published.[61]

Ray's close friends, the ones he'd worried would be puzzled or displeased by Lish's editing, knew that Lish was an aggressive editor and assumed that Ray had embraced the changes they saw in the stories. Some, including certainly Gallagher and Hall, encouraged Carver to publish his earlier versions. Hall especially missed the husband's attempt to pray that was cut from "After the Denim," the closing scene of "Tell the Women We're Going," and the meeting with the baker—"that little communion of lost humans"—cut from "The Bath." Hall invited Carver to publish the earlier versions in an issue of *Ploughshares* he would soon edit. Carver himself would speak of these later incarnations as "expansions" rather than the restorations they truly were. According to Gallagher, Ray chose not to speak about his disagreement with Lish because "he never wanted to cause harm to Gordon Lish." Indeed, Gallagher continues, "I don't know what the significance of Lish's role is/was because Ray didn't ultimately accept it, as we know from his letter . . . When you know the whole story, you grieve for both of them, you really do."[62]

Still, there remains the question that Lish himself would have one ask: Which book, the one Carver begged to retrieve or the one Lish construed out of it, is the more beautiful? *What We Talk About When We Talk About Love* has many partisans. Probably because of Lish's editing—the whole book reworked in the space of a few weeks—this volume has a devastating economy of mood. One cannot deny—indeed there is no reason to deny—the powerful impact of the collection. For a long time, fiction writer Charles Baxter kept a copy on his desk "as an example of what I did not want to do. . . . I loved the book. But I hated it too."[63] By paring the stories as he did, Lish formed a book that is stronger than its parts. His arrangement of stories and imposition of a uniform tone and attitude gave some of these stories the intensity of poems. Edgar Allan Poe had argued a short story writer should "deliberately subordinate everything in the story—characters, incident, style, tone—to the bringing out of a single, preconceived effect." Lish was able to give the entire collection of seventeen stories a single effect—to make a snowman out of a snowdrift. Comparing the way Lish honed the endings of four stories from the middle of the book—"The Bath," "Tell the Women We're Going," "After the Denim," and "So Much Water So Close to Home"—reveals that in each case Lish's version ends with a held breath and a suggestion of imminent violence.

For some readers *What We Talk About When We Talk About Love* is the quintessential Carver text, the ur-text of a literary style that came to be known as minimalism.* The *Saturday Review* calls its prose "as sparingly clear as a fifth of iced Smirnoff." Indeed, there is something inebriating in the experience of reading *What We Talk About*. Leonard Michaels also thought that alcohol contributed to the manner of these stories: "Certain moments in Ray's stories, where he focuses very hard on virtually nothing,

---

* Lish finds offensive the formulation that he is the "godfather of minimalism," noting that he has edited or instructed many successful authors whose work is not minimalist, from Barry Hannah and Harold Brodkey to Lily Tuck and Elizabeth Strout.

are reminiscent of an inebriated struggle to see the immediate environment. There is a kind of rage that is held in check or suddenly expressed in a brutal or mindless way by the story's action as a whole, or by the narrator."[64]

Christine Carver, remembered the day her father's new book arrived in the mail:

> I read the first story and the next and was so emotionally charged that I read every story and literally could not put it down until it was finished. That collection charges you with anxiousness. Every story is so tense, yet there is something to it. It's the love for the characters in some way — there's not one character that you can downright despise. They are all human. You know what I'm saying? That's another thing about my dad. He stayed true to his characters.[65]

In the marketplace, *What We Talk About* was a winner. By early May, fifteen thousand hardcover copies had sold, impressive for a story collection, and additional printings were under way. Vintage paid $20,000 for paperback rights.[66] "It's a strange and astounding life," Ray declared to numerous correspondents. The success of this book filled Ray's mailbox with letters from old friends. Yet there remained one person from his past whom Ray longed to meet again: John Gardner. In April, while in New York City to give a reading at the 92nd Street YMHA with Ann Beattie, Ray met writers Harold Brodkey and Ellen Schwamm. Ray mentioned his debt to Gardner, and Schwamm offered to arrange a meeting. On May 3, Tess and Ray drove to Ithaca, New York, to dine with Gardner and his current wife, Liz Rosenberg, at the Brodkey-Schwamms'. The two writers took "honest and simple delight in each other's company," Rosenberg recalled. Gardner invited Ray to read at SUNY Binghamton in the fall.[67]

Ray and Tess planned to vacation in New York City for a week in mid-May. They would borrow a friend's apartment and have time for museums, plays, and long dinners. As they rode the train along the Hudson River from Syracuse to the city, Ray began drafting a story. In New York, he sequestered himself in a room of the apartment and continued to write. At week's end, to his own surprise, he'd completed a first draft of a story he would call "Cathedral." His idea for this story came from the recent visit to Syracuse by Jerry Carriveau, whom Gallagher had worked for when she was a graduate student in Seattle. Gallagher had served as a reader and typist for Carriveau, who was blind, while he was an administrative intern for the Seattle police. For one assignment, she drew outlines of fingerprint types on textured paper and guided Carriveau's hand to touch these as she described them. In a 1976 application to Yaddo, Gallagher proposed to write a series of poems using metaphors of fingerprinting and blindness.[68]

When Jerry Carriveau visited Syracuse, Ray poured him a couple of drinks while they smoked and chatted about television and religion, but Carriveau is certain that they did *not* watch a documentary about cathedrals or even turn on the television, or draw anything together. When McInerney visited Syracuse a few days later, Ray told him anecdotes about the blind guest and his own discomfort and surprise. "He was expecting the guy to be wimpy and pathetic," McInerney thought. "It intrigued him that the blind man was feisty—as if a three-legged dog had come to visit."[69]

In the story Carver wrote, the narrator is nervous about his wife's blind friend, Robert. Jealous and fearful, he comforts himself by denigrating others. He's especially bothered that Robert served as confidant to his wife during her earlier marriage. Robert had "touched his fingers to every part of [my wife's] face, her nose—even her neck!" and his wife "never forgot it. She even tried to write a poem about it."[70] Like Robert in the story, Carriveau is a garrulous and confident man with a strong, throaty chain-smoker's voice. He chooses not to hide his eyes (over which he has little muscular control) with dark glasses. He believes that many of the hardships of blindness derive from sighted peoples' fears and prejudices.[71] In "Cathedral," Carriveau found, "Raymond played around with my character so much that a friend of mine would not recognize me there." He noted that Carver borrowed phrasing from tapes he'd sent Tess over the years, but invented most of the dialogue: "Never in my life have I used the word 'Bub'!" Carriveau declared. The ending of the story was also pure invention:

> I am not good at following pen scratchings or hand movements and would not have been able to do so on a paper bag with a subject as complicated as a cathedral. But I think that in the story Raymond was trying to get across that blind people can, through logic, have a sort of visual reference in their minds. I appreciated that. Blindness is many people's worst fear. In revealing that fear in the narrator, Raymond shows that both men are willing to go beyond their usual boundaries for communication.[72]

Carver felt "a rush" as he drafted the story. Gallagher provided Ray with information about the fingerprint drawings she and Carriveau had done and urged him to write "a fully ecstatic ending." Unlike the Lish-edited stories in *What*, "Cathedral" lifts off at the end in a classic epiphany: the sighted narrator and the blind man together draw a cathedral on heavy paper. Carver called the story "Cathedral" and asked Darhansoff to send it to the *Atlantic Monthly*. It took daring for Carver to send a new story there while Atlas's negative review of him in that very magazine was on the news-stands, and it gave him particular satisfaction when the magazine bought the story on July 10 for $2,000. Thus he answered the criticism of the "min-imality" of his style with the "opening up" that occurs in "Cathedral." It seems that the success of *What We Talk About* influenced *Atlantic* fiction editor C. Michael Curtis to recommend purchase of "Cathedral" despite reservations he had about Carver's writing. In an interoffice memo, Cur-tis advised that the magazine "should" take the story because it is "unusual and surprisingly powerful," though he disliked Carver's "stylized repeti-tions."[73] To Ray, this acceptance was all the sweeter because it came to him with no assistance from Lish.

Carver himself thought that "Cathedral" was "totally different in concep-tion and execution from any stories that have come before." The first-person narrator in this story is a typical bumbling, addictive character with a load of human stains: prejudices, blunt-mindedness about his wife's concerns and needs, a large appetite for food, drink, and marijuana. Unlike most of the stories in *What We Talk About,* however, "Cathedral" is not primarily con-cerned with marriage problems (though they are part of its underpinning). When Tobias Wolff read "Cathedral," he felt "weightless, filled with a sense of profound, inexplicable joy. Blessed, and conscious of it, I understood that I was in the presence of a masterpiece." Wolff praises the way Carver imper-ceptibly leads readers to apprehend "the fear that drives the narrator's harsh-ness and cruel humor" until "the apparently minimal terms of the story have become the foundations of a soaring act of artistry and hope."[74]

Over time, as Carver faced interviewers who asked pointed questions about the development of his fiction, he spoke of "Cathedral" as a pivotal story for him:

> When I began writing that story I felt that I was breaking out of some-thing I had put myself into, both personally and aesthetically. I simply couldn't go on any farther in the direction I had been going in *What We Talk About When We Talk About Love* . . . Oh, I *could* have, I suppose, but I didn't want to. Some of the stories were becoming too attenuated. I didn't write anything for five or six months after that book came out. I literally wrote nothing except letters.[75]

In this explanation of the change in his work, Carver's omission of any mention of Lish's role skews the facts of the matter and throws undue emphasis on "Cathedral." As we have seen, he had completed "A Small, Good Thing," also a transcendent and affirmative work, much earlier.

While *What We Talk About* was in production, he had written "Vitamins." And it was only a month (not five or six) between the publication date of *What* and his composition of "Cathedral."

If Carver adjusted his memory to shape a narrative about the evolution of his stories, the world conspired to make it true. The *Atlantic* got "Cathedral" into print quickly. Ray was learning that writing well and writing independently were the best revenge he could take against Lish's grandiosity and vagaries of the literary establishment. He'd been brooding about how to gain control over the disposition of his work for months. He informed Darhansoff that henceforth he'd submit stories to magazines himself. He felt he would be able to write a story more easily if he could decide where to send it. Ray's instinct seems to have been correct. *Esquire* accepted "Vitamins" just days after he mailed it there. The success of *What* (orchestrated, for worse or better, by Lish) had unlocked doors for Carver. He was more than ready to walk through them.

Ray was also learning to take the benefits of his success on his own terms. At a summer gig in Milwaukee, Wisconsin, where he'd been invited by novelist Sara Vogan, he discovered that if he just taught his UW-M classes and didn't socialize he could be productive away from home. He was tickled to reside in an elegant three-story colonial house with a view of Lake Michigan, a house built, he believed, by a "beer baron" (shades of Jay Gatsby) and now owned by "a deconstructionist."[76] The house, the lake view, and the proximity to respected academic intellectuals were part of the "astounding life" that seemed to have come to him out of the blue. Poet Al Young from California got a close look at his friend's life on the "come-back trail" when he stayed with Ray in his mansion. Young noticed that Ray had the "poor man's habit" of keeping all his things spread out where he could see them, but was also a "neatnik" who liked to vacuum and keep the place in order. Every day he told Young he thought he'd been saved. "He'd say, 'All these great things are happening to me and all I have to do is not have a drink.' "

Young saw a different side of Ray's AA training when Vogan, drunk, fell and injured herself during a party. Young asked Ray to speak to Vogan about her drinking. Reluctantly, Ray accompanied Young to her apartment:

> Ray looked very irritated . . . he liked to hang around in his robe and pajamas and work, but he put on his clothes and we went to Sara's place. She was marking papers and drinking vodka and grapefruit juice, not looking good. I mean this was an hour and a half after she had been dropped back from the hospital. And Ray said, "Sara, you saw the shit that I've gone through. Why should you put yourself through that? I see all the signs." And she looked up and she blinked at us.

She went to the john and Ray turned to me and said, "She's drunk."
I said, "What do you mean?" And Ray explained, "She can't tell she's
drunk. The way she's sweating, she's in very bad shape. I've said all I can
say. I'm going home to work, Al." He *was* very concerned, but he knew
you couldn't talk to someone who was drunk.[77]

Ray did counsel friends who indicated they were concerned about their
own drinking. He urged Curt Johnson, a binge drinker, to give up alcohol
if,

it's fucking you up any, getting in the way of your writing. . . . And the
only thing that works is AA . . . It's hard, hard, God knows, to ask for
help, to admit powerlessness over the stuff, but it's no disgrace. What is a
disgrace is when you do like I did, drink and piss away my brains and my
talent, and bring the whole house down around me.[78]

Ray stepped forward again when Michael Rogers, a novelist and *Rolling
Stone* writer who'd known Ray at Stanford, had a life-threatening alcohol-
withdrawal seizure. Rogers told Ray he couldn't find a sponsor, "couldn't
identify with any of these people, they don't have this writing thing, etc.,
etc. I think Ray was sympathetic to that. He operated as, and I thought of
him as, my sponsor. When people at meetings asked me if I had a sponsor
I always said, Yes."[79]

Yet there was one person that Ray was helpless to help: his daughter,
Christine. For a while her difficulties were so extreme that Amy Unger
dared to suggest that Ray should move her to Syracuse. Ray replied that he
thought about Chris's situation from morning till night, but, he reasoned in
a long, sorrowful, and determined letter, Chris had to make her own decisions. He'd already offered to help her financially if she wanted to make
changes in her living arrangements, but he feared she'd have to face her
alcoholism first. In any case, he would not bring her to New York: "We all
have to do what we can, and when we can't do anything else, or the impossible, we have to say so. My heart broke all to pieces years ago." Bringing
Chris to New York, Ray feared, would cause him to quit writing and start
drinking again.[80]

Ray wrote that letter to Amy from the Yaddo artists' community in Saratoga Springs, New York, where he was a guest in July and August. Here
Ray had a bedroom in the fifty-five-room stone mansion built by financier
Spencer Trask and his wife, Katrina, as well as a private work cabin in the
woods adjoining the Saratoga horse-racing track. Ray described the routine
to several correspondents: at breakfast he picked up a traditional laborer's

lunch box with a thermos clamped in its lid and was off to his studio for the rest of the day. After a day alone, he joined the other guests—musical composers and visual artists as well as writers—for a hearty dinner in the baronial dining room. He returned to his studio in the evenings, too, as author Julia Alvarez recalls:

> Some of the guests were talking about escaped convicts at supper, so I was apprehensive . . . but I headed out to my cabin after supper and worked till late. I was headed back to the main house in the dark, feeling a little jittery, when out of some dark bushes a big hulking figure emerged. I gasped and cried out something like, "Who are you?"
>
> "I'm Raymond Carver," he said. Oh, my God, I was so relieved. I told him I thought he was the murderer everyone was talking about. It was too dark to know what his face did, but I thought I heard him chuckle. Afterwards, I'd read any new Carver story looking for that scene to appear because it was such a Raymond Carver moment.

Perhaps, Alvarez speculated, Ray was afraid of convicts, too, because he drove his car the short distance between the mansion and his writing studio.

While Ray was at Yaddo, "Cathedral" came out in *Atlantic*'s September issue. Ray sent a copy home with Don Justice and wrote innumerable letters about it to his friends but didn't flaunt it to other Yaddo guests. He was busy "wrestling" with a difficult new story (probably "Chef's House") and an essay about the early influences on his writing that he would call "Fires."[81]

". . . I'm writing this at a place called Yaddo . . . it's afternoon, early August," Carver announces in that essay. "Every so often, every twenty-five minutes or so, I can hear upwards of thirty thousand voices joined in a great outcry. This wonderful clamor comes from the Saratoga race course." He goes on to explain how the sounds of the nearby horse races have stimulated a short story he's working on. After the crowd has roared, he tells us, "I feel spent, as if I too had participated." Though horse races took place daily while Ray was at Yaddo, and though Ray loved to watch and bet on the horses, he didn't break his writing stride to attend a race until the final two days of his residency.[82]

At forty-three, Carver wasn't playing any hunches. He was placing his bets on himself.

CHAPTER 25

Fires

September 1981–October 1982, Syracuse

And really we writers aren't human beings but bundles of *témoignage,*
words scribbled on paper. Every good death should incite us. Every
good sorrow should teach us to keep feeling, keep working! The only
real way to love the world, I guess.
— Lawrence Durrell to Richard Aldington, October 4, 1961

As his work was read and celebrated by more people, Ray was able to
reduce the professional debt he'd long felt to Lish and the emotional
debts he felt toward members of his family. In his new life, he could be—
was encouraged to be—a writer before all else. Tess Gallagher had been
drawn to the writer, hearing his stories first and then coming to know the
man. In the fall of 1981, Carver mailed Gordon Lish a copy of a letter by
Lawrence Durrell (quoted above), saying that something in it "struck" him.
Perhaps that something was Durrell's romantic notion that writers may
achieve immortality through their words.[1] Increasingly, Ray tried to subordinate everything to the demands of his writing.

From Alaska, where he worked all summer as a salmon egg processor,
Vance wrote his father to ask if they could go fishing together before he flew
to France. To Ford, Ray speculated that Vance might be bored with "watching me sit around and smoke dope." They didn't fish, but Ray helped Vance
with his travel preparations. In letters, Ray grumbles that Vance's visit kept
him from his work; in those same letters, he tells about Vance's studies and
exudes pride in having a son who is "well and happy" in France.[2]

Vance cherished a memory of the day Ray saw him off for Europe from
JFK Airport. When his father noticed that Vance wasn't wearing a watch,
he stripped off his own and said, " 'Well, here, son, take mine . . . Don't
lose it. Good-bye son. Take good care now. I love you.' "[3] Vance lived with
a French family and took classes at Syracuse University's study center in

Strasbourg. Ray sent him long, encouraging letters, expressing joy in his progress—his "quantum leaps—self-confidence, self-esteem, the feeling of being able to *get on with it,* whatever the task might be." Ray praised Vance's plan to work in Europe for the summer rather than return to Alaska "to work a killer job up there in that lonesome part of the world."[4]

After seeing his son off to France, Ray completed the essay about influences that he'd begun at Yaddo. "Fires" remains the most read and admired of the handful of essays Carver wrote. In its twelve pages, Carver discusses influences on his work, emphasizing the difficulties of writing while trying to take care of a young family. Readers who know about those "ferocious years of parenting" that Carver described have applauded his honesty and praised him for talking about a subject that women had long understood but often not spoken about.[5] Only incidentally does Carver also acknowledge the *desire* that drove him and Maryann: "We had great dreams, my wife and I. We thought we could bow our necks, work very hard, and do all that we had set our hearts to do. But we were mistaken." Carver wrote this as his dreams were, after all, coming true. His sense that he was mistaken seems to mean that his marriage did not survive into these better days.

But he doesn't write that. What he does write is that his two children have been a "heavy and often baleful influence" on his life and his writing. *Baleful* is a Middle English word meaning deadly; evil; harmful; or, at least, sorrowful; wretched. It is a poetic word that occurs often in *Beowulf* and in John Gardner's novel *Grendel.* It is a word few people would use about their own children. Carver blames his children over and above other interferences such as poverty and alcoholism. Indeed, he claims he would not have been poor or alcoholic without these burdensome children. In the essay, he seems to lack either a political perspective or the personal humility to analyze other factors that contributed to the breakdown of his family. As we have seen, in interviews and letters, Ray did discuss how his alcoholism contributed to the collapse of his family, but here, in what would become a widely read publication, he chose not to do that.

It is shocking to compare some of the statements in "Fires" with the many warm, concerned letters Ray wrote to both Vance and Christine during the 1980s. "Fires" is an example of what Vance refers to as "the Raymond Carver dichotomy," which he has come to understand in this way: "On the one hand, he loved his family dearly. On the other hand, when stress levels boiled over, he could despise us, find us burdensome, or 'baleful.' . . ." One can only speculate about why Carver wrote and published such things about his children in 1981, when his life was going well and his children, aged twenty-three and twenty-four, were no longer under his roof (though still needing financial help). Was he carried away by the opportunity to unburden himself of old resentments? Conversely, perhaps writing nonfiction limited the working of his imagination that, in fiction, led him to compassionate revelations about other people.

Another answer is suggested by consideration of the development of Carver's writing. He composed "Fires" at the same time he began to write stories that he would publish independently of Gordon Lish.[6] He may have needed to put up defensive walls to ensure that he would never again take on responsibilities that kept him from his work. In the 1980s, Vance points out, his father continued to write about subjects from his "old personal repository of alcoholism, self- and family alienation, grief and fear accumulated during his 'Bad Raymond Days.' Why? Because that was his way of gradually processing and coming to terms with his past life of pain, frustration, and — destruction. He was not somebody who would go see a professional about his demons." In short, Vance argues, putting into writing — with little qualification — the hostilities he harbored from his years as a practicing alcoholic was his method of holding at bay or exorcising those feelings.[7] In 1982, with five years of sobriety behind him, the method seemed to work for him, despite its shortfalls as therapy for his family.

It was a story in this mode of emotional housekeeping — "Chef's House" — that Carver sent to Charles McGrath at the *New Yorker,* from whom he'd recently received a fan letter about "Cathedral." William Shawn, the magazine's editor in chief, "just fell in love with it," McGrath said. They set the story in type right away because they found it "nearly perfect the way it is." Payment for "Chef's House" would be at least $1,250, perhaps more depending on the magazine's word-rate formula.[8] Cracking the *New Yorker* meant a lot to Carver. When the placement of "Chef's House" was a fait accompli, he mailed a copy of the manuscript to Lish. In late November, just before "Chef's House" appeared in the magazine, Gallagher also sold a story to the *New Yorker* and they celebrated with chocolates and ginger ale. When Maryann Carver read "Chef's House," she felt "almost offended that they could call it fiction. All he was doing was writing an account of what happened there . . . though, in fact, there were a few changes."[9]

Next Carver sent Donald Hall the long version of "A Small, Good Thing," restored and again revised after Lish's pruning of it into "The Bath," and Hall gladly included it in the issue of *Ploughshares* he was editing.[10] For his next story, Carver sifted his repository of memories more selectively to produce a long, nimble, complicated monologue based on his stay at Duffy's recovery facility. Narrated by a recovering alcoholic named J.P., "Where I'm Calling From" is an ambitious story with a half dozen important characters, intersecting time frames, and a tentative but fully earned hopeful ending. The *New Yorker* accepted "Where I'm Calling From" before Christmas. Again, the magazine's editorial suggestions were minimal, though Shawn required that the words *fucking* and *fart* be excised. Working with Ray by telephone was an intense process, McGrath recalled. "He liked as much as I did to work on sentences, length of passages, at a very painstaking level, which is where Ray's stories occur. He would get nervous and just lock on to even a question about a comma. We couldn't get on to the next point until we had dealt completely with the one in hand. I don't think I've met a writer with such ferocity of concentration." Before "Where I'm Calling From" appeared, the *New Yorker* had purchased a third Carver story, "The Bridle." About that story, McGrath said, "We talked about the bridle, the theme of restraint, and at the last minute he thought it was too heavy and backed off a little bit."[11]

At Syracuse, Ray's daily life ran smoothly. His salary was good—$29, 903 for the academic year of 1981–82—and his two classes a semester attracted students who admired his work and embraced his idiosyncrasies as a teacher. Even though his new life lacked scandalous deeds or brushes with the law, writing students added to the cycle of legends about their mentor. The smallest things he did or said became "Good Raymond" lore that circulated along with the still-vivid "Bad Raymond" legends. Ray's mild manner kept peace among the notoriously backbiting and self-involved young writers. He was "a great coaxer of stories; whatever was there that was any good, he would find it." He read each story carefully and was always willing to meet with students privately. Once Robert O'Connor asked, " 'Ray, did you get my story?' and he said, 'You know, you're one of my favorite writers, Bob, but this isn't one of my favorite stories.' He didn't humiliate me publicly."[12]

Ray's primary mission at Syracuse was to lead workshops in fiction, but he also taught courses on topics such as Form and Theory of American Contemporary Short Fiction. Reading assignments for these courses were substantial,[13] but Ray's classroom method was ad hoc. When a diligent PhD student inquired, "So far we haven't talked about any form and I don't remember us ever discussing theory, so I'd like to know, when will we get to it?" Ray parried: "What I'm allowing you to do in the class is— you *form* your own *theory*." Ray couldn't lecture and preferred listening over talking, but as he spoke about a book he loved, McInerney said, "eventually there would come a moment when the nervousness would lift off of him as he spoke about writing that moved him." Not every book he assigned moved him to eloquence. After a class read *Of the Farm* by John

Updike, Hribal said, "We were trying to guess what he liked about it, and Ray opened the class (holding his hand behind his head with his cigarette between his fingers) by saying, 'Jeez, I read this years ago and I hadn't read it again till last week. You know, it's not very good, is it?' We were relieved because we weren't wrong."[14]

Ray also taught by the example of his present life. Before McInerney moved to Syracuse to study with Ray in the fall of 1981, he'd "thought of writers as luminous madmen who drank too much and drove too fast and scattered brilliant pages along their doomed trajectories." Ray taught him an essential trade secret: to write, "you had to survive, find some quiet, and work hard every day." McInerney figures Ray saved him "a year of further experimentation with the idea that the road of excess leads to the palace of wisdom. I'd already done a fair amount of destructive stuff, and he encouraged me to write about that."[15]

To Gallagher, as program coordinator, and to Ray, as senior fiction writer, fell the job of inviting and hosting guest writers. Every so often, Hribal recalled, "Ray would telephone from next door and say something like Allen Ginsberg's in my living room—come have coffee. And sure enough, there he'd be, just as Ray said, eating Danishes and drinking coffee, wearing a tweed jacket with his pen in the front pocket." During the years Ray lived in Syracuse, there was a visiting writer almost every week during the academic term, including such luminaries as Saul Bellow, Joyce Carol Oates, and John Cheever. Often the visitors stayed overnight at Ray and Tess's house so the program budget, which Tess administered, could be used to pay the writers.

The second week of November 1981 may have been the high point of Carver's own career on the reading circuit. As John Gardner's guest, he gave a reading at SUNY Binghamton and spent the night at Gardner's farmhouse. Gardner, then forty-eight, had become a prominent and controversial literary figure. He wore his white hair to his shoulders, dressed in dirty jeans and a motorcycle jacket, and, according to one observer, looked "something like a pregnant woman trying to pass for a Hells Angel." Another said Gardner's presence induced "a feeling of benign sorcery in the air." Gardner's *On Moral Fiction* had shifted fiction from an academic, postmodern style toward more realistic, character-driven concerns, but at the time Carver visited, Gardner drank heavily and his personal life was in turmoil. Though Ray and Gardner had dined together in the spring, this overnight visit by Tess and Ray with Gardner and Liz Rosenberg, was the real beginning of their friendship. When he got home, Ray wrote Fisketjon: "Beats all I ever saw or heard of, this life . . . reading for Dr. John Tuesday night at Binghamton . . . and him saying he couldn't have done it better himself, which I of course took as great praise."[16]

Asked how it felt to be successful after years of struggle, he said, "I don't know about having 'arrived' . . . truth to tell, it's never occurred to me. No, you're always trying to get the work done. That's what counts. If I don't have a half-finished story in the drawer at all times, I'm a little anxious."[17] Back from well-paid reading jaunts to Binghamton and Dallas, Ray and Tess were in their "respective places and stations—she downstairs in her study, me up here in mine. Working, praise be. In the old days, I'd about as soon be dead as to be caught at home on a Saturday night." By the end of 1981, Ray had succeeded in establishing order in his own life and holding the chaos of others' lives at bay. No longer did he send out holiday blues letters filled with vain resolutions that next year will be better. His stories were going to big-circulation magazines, and literary quarterlies, including the *Paris Review* and *Poetry*, were soliciting his poems. "My God, my cup over flows, and overflows, again and again," he told Fisketjon with amazement.[18]

With so much to look forward to, Ray was ready to make a new start on the business side of his career too. Ford had recommended that he sign on with his own literary agent, Amanda Urban of International Creative Management (ICM). Despite the disagreement he and Lish had had over *What We Talk About*, he did not plan to change editors. Instead he would have a powerful, independent agent to buttress him. He announced his decision in a letter to Lish on January 21, insisting that it would not affect their friendship. "Maybe it's a flaw in me I need this change, but I do need it," he wrote to Darhansoff, who was stunned and perplexed by Carver's defection, but aware that it must have had something to do with his relationship to Lish. To her request for her $500 commission on the renegotiated contract for *What We Talk About*, Carver answered with a refusal so flashing that it stands out among all his archived correspondence. He told her that he didn't care about money and would prevent anything from ever happening with film rights to any of the stories in that book if she claimed the commission. Then he carbon-copied the letter to Lish, urging him to make Darhansoff be reasonable and adding, "There is a mean streak in me, about to show itself if she persists in this course." Darhansoff didn't think the $500 was worth fighting over. She relinquished any unsold rights to Ray's work to ICM but remained the agent of record for *What We Talk About*, which—a quarter century after publication—continued to earn about $5,000 annually in royalties.[19]

During the early months of 1982, professional travel gave Ray an opportunity to visit with old friends. Chuck Kinder now taught at the University of Pittsburgh, where he and Cecily resituated their literary parties and kept close to Kinder's West Virginia roots. He worked on a novel about the complicated friendship of the old foursome: Maryann and Ray Carver, Cecily and Kinder. He began his story with his rendition of a disastrous anniversary dinner shared with the Carvers. Kinder read that "absolute kernel of the book" to Ray, who "shook his old woolly head" and called his friend a thief and an outlaw. Kinder's manuscript figured in a movie (*Wonder Boys* based on the novel by Kinder's student Michael Chabon) before it saw print as *Honeymooners: A Cautionary Tale.*

John Gardner invited Ray to Binghamton again after he and Rosenberg selected "Cathedral" for the *Best American Short Stories 1982.* That story, more than Carver's earlier work, met Gardner's ideal of moral fiction and put their friendship on a footing of mutual admiration. Nonetheless, Gardner didn't feel comfortable enough with Ray to reveal his personal life. At the time Gardner was living with Susan Thornton but still married to Rosenberg, whom he regarded as his intellectual partner. Before Ray and Tess arrived, he asked Thornton to move out and pretended that he and Rosenberg had not separated. It seems unlikely that Gardner's ménage would have shocked Ray, who was, after all, still married to Maryann and living with Tess. But Thornton complied for the weekend and expressed her own outrage to Gardner right after Ray and Tess's departure. Gardner in turn asked her to marry him in the autumn, just as soon as he could divorce Rosenberg.[20]

At the University of Akron, Robert Pope ran a tape recorder during Ray's session with his students. Ray advised the students to listen to editors because "nine times out of ten, a suggestion is worthwhile. The other times, if it doesn't feel right, stay away from it. Don't do it. Stick to your guns." He praised Solotaroff's work on his essay "Fires" and spoke about Maxwell Perkins's genius in helping Thomas Wolfe give coherent form to his overlong manuscripts and Fitzgerald's excision of a first chapter from Hemingway's *The Sun Also Rises.* He mentioned the "vast liberties" Ezra Pound took as European editor for *Poetry.* Writing something good, Carver concluded, is "like building a fantastic cathedral. The main thing is to get the work of art together. You don't know who built those cathedrals, but they're there." That, in a nutshell, was Lish's view of *What We Talk About.* Carver could say all that more easily now that he had completed his own cathedral—his story by that name—by himself.

"Nobody could be fake around Ray Carver," Pope said of Ray's visit to Akron. "Everything broke down and became personal." Ray persuaded everyone to tell a story of "serious electrocution or shock that ended with the phrase 'and that's when I became a writer.' " When a drunk staggered in front of Pope's car, Ray growled, "There but for the grace of God go I." When Pope took Ray to his departure flight, the waiting plane "was a converted two-prop mail plane with four or five windows. I said, 'Ray you don't have to get on that plane, we'll make a different reservation.' But he said, 'Oh, no, no problem.' And he climbed on it and we saw him sitting in a window looking over a manuscript. Didn't blink an eye and off he flew."[21]

Carver contracted with Knopf for a new collection of short stories to be published in the fall of 1983. Lish would be the editor. "What do you think of my new agent? I think she's an ace," Carver wrote Lish when negotiations were under way. Urban secured an advance of $22,500 for a book that Carver planned to call *Cathedral*—a more than fourfold increase over the hardcover advance for *What We Talk About*.[22] Four of the stories were already prominently published; Ray had reason to feel confident that his higher profile and Urban's clout would allow him to withstand editorial pressure from Lish. His greatest concern was to produce enough good stories. "My stories are changing now," he'd told the Akron students. "I couldn't write those same stories again, for better or for worse." The new stories would have "more affirmation," not because he'd decided on that but because "It's just happening."[23]

Besides the story collection for Knopf, Carver was preparing a new book for Capra Press. Since *At Night the Salmon Move* and *Furious Seasons* were both almost sold out, Noel Young proposed combining them into one volume and adding new pieces to make "a kind of Carver reader" to be called *Fires*. The advance was under $1,000, but Ray wanted to keep his less commercial work in print. He rearranged the poems and added thirteen that were not in his earlier collections. He republished the long versions of "Distance" and "So Much Water So Close to Home" from *Furious Seasons* and also took the opportunity to include "Where Is Everyone?" (from which Lish had carved "Mr. Coffee and Mr. Fixit").[24]

Carver must have realized all this shuffling and reshuffling would confuse even the most earnest scholars. Whether for his own peace of mind or theirs, in an "Afterword" to *Fires* he explains that he'd "rather tinker with a story after writing it, and then tinker some more, changing this, changing that, than have to write the story in the first place. . . . I think by nature I'm more deliberate than spontaneous, and maybe that explains something." He explained, too, that "Distance" and "So Much Water" had been "largely rewritten for the Knopf book" but neglected to mention that the rewriting had been done by Lish. "After some deliberation, I decided to stay fairly close to the versions as they appeared in the Capra Press book . . . they have been revised again, but not nearly so much as they once were. But how long can this go on? I suppose there is, finally, a law of diminishing returns. But I can say now that I prefer the latter [in other words, earlier] versions of the stories, which is more in accord with the way I am writing short stories these days."[25]

With this return to one of his first publishers and those declarations about revisions, Carver put the whole awkward story of Lish's editing behind him and moved optimistically forward to write and publish stories in his own way. He was restaking his claim to his work and moving forward without sacrificing his relationship to Lish. He was, again, having his cake and eating it too.

Perhaps not cake, this time, but chocolates and more chocolates. When Ray finished his spring semester, he joined Gallagher at the University of Zurich where she was a guest lecturer. Reaching Zurich on May 13, Ray gave a reading and savored the praise of an eighty-four-year-old who had eulogized James Joyce in 1941. He explored the city's literary associations, making a visit to the Joyces' grave site and having coffee at the Café Odeon, famously the hangout of Joyce, Lenin, and Tristan Tzara and now a gay bar. But Ray's favorite locale in the Swiss city was the Confiserie Sprüngli, a shop that sold handmade chocolates of every configuration. To stateside friends, Ray sent Sprüngli's postcards declaring that he was "mainlining" chocolate and would need to go to a rehab facility for chocolate withdrawal when he returned.[26]

Next, Ray and Tess headed toward Venice by way of Lucerne and Geneva. His poem "Reading," set at Lake Geneva, meditates on the mysterious life of a man who sits calmly in the window of a château with a view of Mont Blanc, all the while hiding out from his worries about his mother, his children, and "the clear-eyed woman he once loved / and her defeat at the hands of eastern religion" (as Ray saw Maryann's interest in esoteric philosophies). Carver writes about this man in the window as if he were someone else, imaging the doubleness of his own life. From Venice, they went to Strasbourg to meet up with Vance. Then Ray and his son spent two days in Paris.[27]

At six feet, four inches, twenty-three-year-old Vance had grown taller than his father, but in other ways he resembled Ray. Like him, Vance had an unsophisticated face and carried his large body with a slight stoop. His wavy hair was then a lighter shade of brown than Ray's, and his clear eyes less intensely blue, but the resemblance remained striking. There were contrasts as well. The son was athletic, loose-jointed and comfortable in his large body, and health-conscious in his habits. Given a choice, he would walk a mile rather than drive. He had become a reader and linguist with a

serious interest in literature, but his intellectual curiosity was more socio-
logical than literary.

In Paris Ray and Vance celebrated their reunification as father and son,
as well as Vance's success as a student at Syracuse and Ray's as a writer
and recovering alcoholic. "We were both rebuilding productive lives and
looking to the future with promise and optimism," Vance said. They were
a team, Vance able to speak French and Ray able to pay the bills. They
viewed Impressionist paintings in the Jeu de Paume and the sarcophagus of
Napoleon at Les Invalides. Mostly they enjoyed "walking together in the
spring weather and stopping in cafes, just watching the world go by. We
ate meals on the sidewalk, watching the animated street life, the jugglers
and flame spitters." On their final afternoon, Ray suggested a visit to the
Cimetière du Montparnasse where many writers are buried, among them
Guy de Maupassant and Jean-Paul Sartre.[28] To a western American used to
country cemeteries with simple markers and occasional stone angels, the
resting place of the French intellectual elite is a grandiose spectacle. Massive stone tombs and sculptures honor the once-wealthy or famous dead.
Most are meticulously groomed for curious posterity, but some crooked,
unkempt monuments bear a notice of payments in arrears and imminent
eviction. One cannot see the cemetery without imagining its effect upon
Carver in 1982, just as he was beginning to think of himself as a prominent
man.

A guard showed Ray and his son about the cemetery. Ray wondered
about a flat tombstone bearing the names of Charles Baudelaire, his mother,
and his stepfather. With grins and shrugs, the guard explained that it was
"a Baudelaire sandwich." Ray recounts the cemetery visit in a poem called
"Ask Him," that describes the son as reluctant, bored, and resigned. But
Vance writes of feeling "tickled" to be with his father even if he wouldn't
have proposed to see a cemetery. He thinks his father was "harking back to
the days of my childhood and adolescence, when I wasn't as interested in
the arts as my parents." The poem, Vance writes, indicates Carver's "artistic
penchant for embracing something negative."

The poem, though, serves its own unities. It sets up a duality between
the dark curiosity of the poet and the sunny humor of the guard. Carver
presents *himself* as the odd man out who can't speak French and has a morbid interest in dead writers. He envies the "untroubled" existence of his
son and the guard who can "talk and joke together / in the French language
under a fine sun." As they part, the narrator directs his son to ask the guard
if he wishes to be buried in this cemetery. The guard stares in disbelief and
walks away to (the poet imagines) eat his lunch and drink his wine in the
sunshine. Carver gives his blessing to those—like the son—who walk in

the sun. Writing about the same day, Vance remembers a different question posed by his father:

> . . . my father asked me to ask our guide how one could be buried there. I looked at him puzzled. "What did he mean by this? Why was he asking such a question?" . . . I asked the old man, who was walking next to us, *"Qu'est-ce qu'on fait pour être enterré ici?"* The old man stopped, fixed his gaze on me, and said with total seriousness. *"C'est complet monsieur, c'est complet"* ("We have no more room, sir; we are full"). . . . my equally serious father fell silent and motionless when I translated. The next morning we returned to Strasbourg.[29]

Vance stayed on in Europe for summer school and travel, for which Ray gave him $1,500. Before he caught his flight home from Zurich, Ray stocked up at Confiserie Sprüngli—nothing to declare in his suitcase except chocolates, he joked; Switzerland appealed to the "burgher" in him. He said he'd like to return as the "Tobler Chocolate Chair in Short Fiction."

Back in the states, Ray had to face clouds that had formed on his horizon. Some months earlier, Maryann had raised the possibility of his obtaining a divorce. She believed a divorce might begin to alleviate some of the pain and the suffering she had endured without relief since Ray's trip to Montana in August 1972, but could not bear to get the divorce herself and end the marriage. An attorney Maryann met had advised her to file for a divorce in Washington, a community-property state in which she had a right to half of her husband's assets. This attorney also urged serving divorce papers to Ray as he gave a reading at the Centrum conference in Port Townsend that summer. On reflection, Maryann decided that "suing Ray for divorce would kill him if he reacted by a return to drinking" and chose not to take such a meretricious and "mean-spirited" action against the love and marriage she considered the great endeavor of her life. She again suggested that Ray file against her. "He didn't get back to me for three or four months. When he finally did go to see the divorce lawyer, he told me, he didn't hear a word the lawyer said. Instead he stared out the window and thought about our little house in Paradise where we started out, all four of us living in one room much of the time to keep warm, except when he went to his study."[30]

Except for that initial visit to a lawyer, Ray had taken no further steps toward a divorce before he left for Europe. Knowing he would have to face it when he returned probably accounted for the fears that shadow his poems about Lake Geneva and Paris. During the three and a half years that Ray had lived openly with Tess Gallagher, Maryann had viewed herself as a "literary Cinderella, living in exile for the good of Carver's career." She saw that Gallagher provided Ray with financial stability he needed to further his writing. Though Maryann had never met Gallagher, she sensed that Ray—now older and more cautious—did not have the kind of fervent emotional tie to the poet that he had felt in his earlier relationship with Diane Cecily. As for Ray, one reason for his hesitation to divorce had been, as he told Leonard Michaels, a friend of both Carvers, that he was "bothered by the thought of another man 'buttering Maryann's toast.' "[31]

In June 1982, as the Carvers' twenty-fifth wedding anniversary passed without celebration and Ray's career was at last on a steady upward trajectory, neither spouse could sidestep the inevitable. The lawyer Ray had consulted, James M. Baker of Syracuse, recommended "abandonment" as the "least offensive grounds" for a New York state divorce. On June 19, 1982, Maryann testified later, "Ray called me and promised to pay me four hundred dollars a month for as long as *we both agreed* I needed it. He also promised other special assistance (medical benefits, travel to son's college graduation, etc.) as needed and help for the children (transportation, college expenses, clothes for grandchildren, holiday help—Christmas, Easter, Valentines and the like)." Maryann's average yearly income from 1978 through 1981 was, by her own report, $5,500. Ray's income reported to the IRS over the same period averaged $18,000; for 1981, he reported a total income of $67,000 from teaching and royalties. The handful of deductions he took on his federal return included $3,350 in alimony, one dependent child (Vance), travel to promote his work ($7,965), and agent's commissions ($3,320).[32]

On June 23, Ray's attorney sent Maryann a letter outlining the informal financial arrangement she had agreed to on the phone. He reminded Maryann that their agreement was not legally binding and counseled her to "rethink" it "if you do not trust Ray to provide you with financial assistance on a voluntary basis."[33] The divorce was under way. At the end of July, Ray wrote Ford that he and Maryann had a "long and good conversation on the phone" a week earlier and were proceeding with the divorce. But the situation was "fluid" and all in all it was "the goddamnedest time . . ." Unger remembered some of the deliberations:

> Ray would phone me and ask what's going on, has she gotten the papers yet? Will she sign them? And Amy would be telling Maryann not to sign the papers, no way she should, it was a terrible deal for herself and the family. And then I would tell Ray, I think Maryann wants something guaranteed for life. The only time in my life I ever betrayed Ray Carver was then. I also told Maryann not to sign. I told her, I love Ray, but I think you are a fool to sign away everything in this way.

What Maryann and her advisors had to consider was the possibility that the work Carver had done while they were married might generate significant income in the future. Among the assets she might have claimed were royalties on the three books of stories and two major books of poems that he'd published during their marriage, as well as a movie option and renewal rights on the story collections. If she were to claim an interest in that work, she might one day pass that interest on to their children. Maryann also had to decide whether to ask the court to set alimony payments or to trust Ray to help her as needed. Both Ray and Maryann must have hoped that Maryann, who'd earned more than Ray during the years they resided together, would get back on her feet financially when the economy improved in the Northwest. Since 1980, though, her income had been so precarious that she qualified for $80 worth of food stamps a month.[34]

Ray was in Syracuse when his lawyer presented his proposals to Maryann. He worked on stories and read Gardner's new novel, *Mickelsson's Ghosts.* "Time and again I just found myself giving over to the book, going with it, wherever, I didn't care," he wrote his first mentor. On June 18, John Cheever died of kidney cancer, soon after publishing the short novel *Oh, What a Paradise It Seems,* which Carver thought "very bad," though he believed Cheever's stories would be read in the next century. Cheever, seventy when he died, had been sober seven years. Shortly before, Carver had written a story called "The Train," whose protagonist is Miss Dent from Cheever's "The Five-Forty-Eight." He dedicated it to Cheever.[35]

During the summer, while Maryann debated whether to accept Ray's voluntary support or go to court for a more substantial settlement, Ray resided a hundred miles across the water from her in Freshwater Bay west of Port Angeles. He and Tess had rented a cabin there for two months, hoping to enjoy the beach and mild weather. The house had no telephone. Ray needed some quiet to work on stories for his next Knopf collection, promised for the fall, but the business of his literary life followed him everywhere now. To cite just one example, the *Paris Review* declined the interview Carver had completed with Buzbee, and Ray urged Buzbee to submit it to the *New England Quarterly.* Soon after that, Mona Simpson, an editorial assistant at the *Paris Review* and a friend of McInerney's, wrote Ray that the magazine had asked *her* to interview him in the fall.[36]

Ray and Tess were barely settled in their summer residence when Tess's father learned he had lung cancer. Leslie Bond, who had smoked from the age of nine, had lost twenty-two pounds, but refused to see a doctor until Tess persuaded him to go. By then the malignancy—"the big C," Ray called it in letters—had metastasized to his ribs and nothing could be done medically. Bond's cancer gave Ray the nudge he needed to quit smoking, which he commenced to do on July 14. He was so nervous, he said, that he couldn't hold a pen in his hand and was barely able to operate the typewriter.[37]

As the summer advanced, Tess took care of her father all day and much of the night (her short story "The Lover of Horses" draws upon these months), and Ray worked as if "there's no tomorrow." Indeed, he wrote Lish, he feared that might be the case, because his effort to quit smoking on his own was a bust. He might have to "clinic up," he thought: "It's got me licked, like the alcohol once did."[38] The summer went from bad to worse when Chris Carver had an automobile accident; Chris had a broken collarbone, her baby had a concussion, her car was totaled, and she had to move in with Maryann. That was, Ray explained to Ford, an "explosive" and "debilitating" situation for Maryann. To help Chris gain some independence, Ray bought her a car and made a down payment on a house trailer for her. Meanwhile, Ray's mother had embarked upon another move in what was becoming her obsessive pattern. This time she left Bellingham, where she'd hoped that Maryann would be a companion to her, for Sacramento, where her son James resided. And James, usually so reliable, had been laid off of his job and had to borrow some money from Ray. Even Vance, thriving in Europe, needed extra money to get home.[39]

"Everybody wants some of my bacon," Ray groused to Leonard Michaels.[40] But Ray's complaints weren't just about money. "Almost every time we were together privately or spoke by phone," Vance recalled, "he immediately expressed his concerns for my mother and sister, and often for my grandmother as well. He grieved for them that their lives had not turned out better or rebounded as well as the two of ours had. He felt anguish that theirs resembled those of the characters in his stories." By 1982, Ray had more money than any of the others, but he didn't have enough money to help everyone, especially when their needs seemed beyond satisfaction. He felt "like an old stick of wood being worked at by carpenter ants, army ants, red stinging ants."[41]

In the midst of this season of "horrors," so distracted he couldn't read, Ray embarked upon an exhilarating spree of story writing. He'd finished three new stories by the end of July, including "The Compartment" and a "33-pager" (probably "Fever"). By the middle of August, he had completed six, enough to fill out the new collection. When he'd promised a new book to Lish, Ray had half-expected to miss his November due date. Instead, at the end of summer he had fourteen or fifteen stories finished. He planned to "diddle around" with them and send them to magazines before surrendering them to Lish.[42]

Not every story found quick acceptance. Though the *Atlantic* purchased

"Feathers" for $3,000 after it passed from one editor's desk to another's for months, "Careful," a story that revolves around an alcoholic whose estranged wife is trying to help him clear the wax from his ears (as an addict he is metaphorically deaf), struck the *Atlantic*'s editors as "too bleak." When "Feathers" appeared in the same magazine's August issue, a subscriber inquired why Ivy League–educated readers should be expected to respond to the insignificant lives of Carver's characters.[43]

One story from Ray's troubled, productive summer is particularly revealing of the way he milled his life into fiction. "The Compartment" is about a morose engineer named Myers (the name Carver also used for his two writer-protagonists) on vacation in Europe. He has been disappointed by Venice and Milan, and now he's riding a train to visit his son in Strasbourg. These geographical details come directly from the trip Ray took in May. With those toeholds in actuality, Carver wove a story that distills his doubts and fears about parenthood. Myers is terrified of seeing his son after six years of estrangement. Reviewing their parting, he "shook his head as if it had happened to someone else. And it had. He was simply not the same person. These days he lived alone and had little to do with anybody outside of his work." Myers envies another passenger's ability to sleep on the train as he sits awake worrying about how to greet his son. As the train approaches Strasbourg, Myers discovers that an expensive watch he has brought for his son is missing from his coat pocket. Then, Myers decides that "he didn't want to see the boy after all. He was shocked by the realization and for a moment felt diminished by the meanness of it." As Myers thinks about that, he produces a deluge of resentments that seem to rationalize his decision: he will not get off the train. He will stay on the train and ride—alone—to Paris.

At the end of the story, Myers wanders into the second-class car. As he lingers there, afraid to ask if the train is headed to Paris, imagining his son "wondering what happened to his father," the coach he's standing in is delinked from the one that holds his compartment and suitcase. Where he expected to find his old place, he finds instead "small, dark-skinned men who spoke a language Myers had never heard before." He has, in short, left his old life behind and does not know where he's going. But—and here is the touch that distinguishes the story—when Myers finds himself detached, he is no longer angry. He takes a backward-facing seat offered him by the jovial strangers: "He was going somewhere, he knew that. And if it was the wrong direction, sooner or later he'd find it out." In this detached state, Myers finds the sleep that eluded him. With that dying note, the story ends.

"The Compartment" embraces separation, the unknown, perhaps death. It seems to speak from the darkest regions of Carver's experiences during the summer of 1982 as he witnessed Leslie Bond's suffering from lung cancer, the end of his long marriage to Maryann, and the problems of his mother, brother, and daughter. Though in daily life Ray now had a good relationship with his own son, the story posits his inability to maintain the relationships of his earlier life. Revealingly, "The Compartment"'s turning point occurs when Myers finds that he has nothing to *give* his son because the watch he bought for him had been stolen.

Ray had given Vance the watch off his own wrist when he departed for Europe. He probably wrote "The Compartment" at about the time he wired Vance $1,000 to get himself home from Europe, an act he described with a bit of swagger to Ford: "he was fucking stranded over there and no way back. This on top of the $1,500 I gave him when I was over there." As much as Ray might have missed his $2,500, that sentence also declares that he is a man who can afford to have a son in Europe. "The Compartment" may be seen as a bold artistic decision to take the idea of not getting off the train to its limit. It may be that Ray, like Myers, feared that he could not love his son sufficiently. Very possibly, with an alcoholic's self-loathing, he knew and hated to admit that he had damaged those he loved.

Ray sent "The Compartment" to Rust Hills at *Esquire*. Hills first accepted the story and then changed his mind. He objected to the story's lack of dialogue and felt cheated because the father and son never meet. Hills recommended that Carver rewrite the story to include a meeting of father and son and thus make his contribution on "one of the great themes of literature and incidentally one of the great preoccupations of *Esquire*." Carver declined to change his story.[44]

Hills wasn't the only editor who encountered a new intransigence in Carver. On August 11, Carver wrote a long letter, almost a rant, to Lish about his new book. He worries that he and Lish will disagree about his new stories, which are "fuller" than those in his earlier books. Carver demands full control over the editing of these stories:

> . . . I can't undergo the kind of surgical amputation and transplant that might make them someway fit into the carton so the lid will close. There may have to be limbs and heads of hair sticking out. My heart won't take it otherwise. . . . we're going to have to work very closely together on this book—the most important of them all for me, at every stage . . . the last book passed as if in a dream for me. This one can't go that way and we both know it.[45]

Ray's backbone was strengthened by praise he was receiving for "The Bridle" in the *New Yorker* and "A Small, Good Thing" in *Ploughshares* where a note on the story's first page erroneously stated, "This story is expanded and revised from *What We Talk About When We Talk About Love*."[46] When "A Small, Good Thing" took first place in the O. Henry Award volume, Carver again said he'd *expanded* "The Bath" into this celebrated new story. With that face-saving lie he covered his debt to Lish and worked the soil for the theory that his new "fuller, more generous stories" emerged organically from his experience. It's likely he had come to believe in that paradigm himself, for he indeed felt that he was breaking out of an enclosure into freedom.[47]

Before leaving the West Coast, Ray planned to drive Tess to a poetry festival in Portland and then travel up the Columbia River to Yakima to visit Violet and Bill Archer. It would do him good, he wrote Ford, to see these "very old and very dear" relatives as well as his "growing-up country." He names the places he'll drive through as if they were mantras—Bonneville Dam, Deschutes River, Celilo Falls, and Snoqualamie Pass. He ended the summer with a float trip down the Yakima River with Maryann's nephews.[48]

Tess stayed with her father when Ray returned to Syracuse on September 1. Leslie O. Bond died on October 6, survived by his wife, Georgia Morris Bond, two sons, and two daughters.[49] Tess stayed on to help her mother and to supervise the building of her house in a development east of Port Angeles.

Ray's nerves were in a terrible state all fall. He didn't like sleeping alone and was frantic with worry over his work and his divorce. Köepf mailed him emergency packages of marijuana from California, but nothing calmed his anxieties. To Lish, Ray wrote that he was afraid Maryann would "fight him" and expected to hear any minute if his divorce "is going to be a white-man's divorce or if we are going to turn into beasts." Vance stayed with Ray until he found housing for the school year. His year abroad had been a personal and educational triumph. "Not only could I graduate on time," he recalled, "but I had a newfound love of French that has served me all of my life." Sadly, even though Ray was wild with loneliness, he was unable to find much comfort in his son's presence. The situation was complicated when Vance invited French friends to visit him in Syracuse. Ray felt that he was "living like a fugitive in my own house, holed up here in my room."[50]

Just as the tension in his own life had stretched him to a breaking point, Ray learned that John Gardner had perished in a motorcycle accident. It happened on the clear, dry afternoon of Tuesday, September 14, on a country road beside the Susquehanna River. Gardner was forty-nine. Ray had planned to attend his wedding to Thornton the very next Saturday. On the night of Gardner's death, Ray "came into the classroom looking shaken to his bones," a student recalled, "and said he couldn't possibly teach. It was awful." Ray made calls to mutual friends and sent flowers but "just couldn't go to his funeral," he wrote Maryann. "That is, I chose not to go." He gave the *Chicago Tribune* a reminiscence of Gardner and read the same piece at a memorial service for Gardner at SUNY Binghamton. Afterward, Ray described to his fiction workshop, "how Gardner's father, partially paralyzed and unable to speak, sat there in his wheelchair with tears streaming down his face." It was, O'Connor felt, typical of Carver to notice the man's "combination of being paralyzed and in terrible turmoil on the inside."[51]

Ray no longer slept, he told Lish in early October: "I just squat in a corner for a half hour or so, then go in and brush my teeth, wash my face, make coffee." During the month ahead, he sent the manuscript of *Cathedral* to Lish and the manuscript of *Fires* to Young. He taught the graduate fiction workshop and his "form your own theory" course. The final book on the reading list for the latter was *Best American Short Stories 1982* edited by Gardner and including "Cathedral." On top of that, Ray (along with Gallagher and Tobias Wolff) was undergoing tenure review at Syracuse; Ray was optimistic that he'd be awarded that guarantee of future employment but complained of having to fill out forms with "things published when I was a child, asking people to write letters on my behalf, etc."[52]

While seeing to those mundane academic matters, Ray accepted a lucrative project from movie director Michael Cimino, Oscar-winning director of *The Deer Hunter*. Cimino had an unsatisfactory script for a life of Dostoyevsky and the backing of producer Carlo Ponti. Cimino, who admired *What We Talk About*, wanted Carver to doctor the script. He paid Ray's expenses for a meeting in New York, where Ray learned the "astonishing" secret that the original screenplay had been written by deported Soviet dissident and Nobel laureate Aleksandr Solzhenitsyn. The screenplay, he thought, was "ponderous, boring, and inconsistent with everything I know about D's life." Gallagher did research, and together they wrote a new screenplay, mailing scenes and revisions across the country and reading them aloud to each other on the phone. They completed a 219-page screenplay in two months. Ray chose Dostoyevsky's last-minute reprieve from the firing squad as the focal moment of his screenplay, because, Tobias Wolff felt, "he had been there himself . . . had come very close to suffering not only physical death but also moral and spiritual annihilation."[53]

Ray was finishing the Dostoyevsky screenplay when Unger came to Syracuse to write a screen treatment based on Carver's stories for director Richard Pearce. "Ray would sneak around the house, keeping quiet, while I was upstairs in my room typing away. And I'd go nuts because I could hear him sneaking," Unger recalled. "At lunchtime he would make some soup and put a tray down by the door without even knocking, so I'd open the door and almost stumble over it because he didn't want to disturb me! In the evening he would do notes and hand them to me by noon the next day."[54]

Neither movie was ever made. Ponti pulled out of the Dostoyevsky project, but Capra Press published a section of the script in 1985. The Pearce project, "Talk About Love," one of several attempts to make feature films based on Carver's stories during his lifetime, also came to naught.

Ray's anxiety crested as the date for Maryann's response to the court summons closed in on her. On her side, Maryann was haunted by the words of the lawyer who had wanted her to sue Ray for divorce. He'd said "her life was like a bag of doorknobs that wouldn't open any doors." That hurt her feelings and her pride. She'd been there when Raymond Carver began to invent his future, and she trusted him to be there for her when she needed help. She declined cautionary advice. "Ray says he'll send money every month and I believe him," she told Unger. On September 20, Ray had shown himself as good as his word. Though the divorce wasn't yet final, he sent Maryann $2,000 to cover the five months since they'd made their agreement by phone in June, a smaller check for Chris, and the news that Vance was doing "*very* well" and "dating a lot of girls." If others thought she was a fool to sign away her claims on Ray's success, she saw it differently. She signed the papers agreeing to Ray's terms of voluntary support.[55]

On October 18, 1982, Justice Donald Miller of the Supreme Court of the State of New York, County of Onondaga, granted Plaintiff Raymond Carver a divorce from Defendant Maryann E. Carver.

PART V

TRIUMPH

Cathedral

October 1982–December 1983,

Port Angeles, Washington, and Syracuse, New York

. . . a writer who has some special way of looking at things and who gives artistic expression to that way of looking: that writer may be around for a time.

—Raymond Carver, "On Writing," 1981[1]

Relieved by the amiable terms of his divorce and flush with movie money, Ray went shopping for a car. As he told the story, he dropped into a Mercedes-Benz dealership wearing his bedroom slippers and test-drove a big 1983 pewter gray 300D sedan. Without bargaining, he told the salesman he'd take it. When the skeptical manager asked Ray how he'd pay for it, Ray said he'd use cash if that was all right.

Anecdotes about Ray and his automobile proliferated. The car, one student noted with Fitzgeraldian resonance, was "the color of money." Ray crowed to Dick Day, "I don't drive anyplace anymore, I motor," but he nearly motored right into Bob O'Connor as his tires squealed onto Euclid Avenue in Syracuse. To Lish, who was taken aback by the extravagance, Ray replied that his fifty-two-year-old sister-in-law (Jerry Davis) had had two heart attacks, so "Why save it? Fuck saving. Spend." In buying this car, Ray had leaped into a new idea of himself and seemed the happier for it, Gallagher told Fisketjon. In Port Townsend, the Welches took pictures of Ray and Tess and each other cavorting on the hood of the Mercedes, but when Ford told Ray that his "leather" seats were vinyl, Ray fulminated, "Next time you see me, I'll have leather seats or I'll have a different car . . . I paid for leather seats. I want them." Novelist Russell Banks, who owned a used Mercedes, knew that for Ray the car was a working-class boy's affirmation that he'd arrived: "We talked about it, the feeling that in middle age we were each able to afford a car that our fathers should have owned but couldn't."²

Carver's completion of *Cathedral* was another sign that he'd reached the autonomy and ripeness of middle age. When he turned in the manuscript in late October, he repeated his request that Lish "help me with this book as a good editor, the best . . . but not as my ghost." He encouraged Lish to make final decisions about cover art and arrangement of stories, but "the matter of the text . . . has to be mine."³ Lish sent an edited copy of "Where I'm Calling From" as a sample of what he considered minimal and neces-sary editing. "To do less than this would be, in my judgment, to expose you too greatly." Lish and Carver skirmished some about "The Bridle," which Lish especially disliked, but in the end Carver took most of his editor's sug-gestions, which were indeed minor.⁴ Ray seems to have been entirely confi-dent that the book would be well received.

Ray's Mercedes was not the only sign of the freedom and plenitude Carver had achieved since moving to Syracuse. With only one dissenting (and secret) vote, the English Department recommended him for tenure. The review committee, which included McInerney, reported that "students are impressed—in some cases transformed—by the integrity of his dedi-cation to the craft of fiction . . ." No one questioned either his claim to an MFA degree from Iowa or a 1939 birthdate. Gallagher (whose MFA was legit) was also granted tenure. Ray felt that they'd pulled a coup—"They opened the gate a crack and we bounded in," he wrote Day.⁵ Gallagher was honored in the department as a poet and as Carver's partner. Professor Paul Theiner was amused by the talks Gallagher gave to introduce visiting writ-ers: "With no self-consciousness, she gave lengthy introductions about her-self and how she met the person." Writer Alice Sebold, who was raped as an undergraduate at Syracuse, found an intrepid supporter in Gallagher, who accompanied her to court hearings and urged her to write about her trauma. "Tess was my first experience of a woman who inhabited her weirdness, moved into the areas of herself that made her distinct from those around her, and learned how to display them proudly. . . . What Tess had was met-tle," Sebold later wrote. Esteemed poet Hayden Carruth found Tess intel-ligent, talented, and a good teacher, and was especially appreciative of what she had done for Ray:

> There was no question that Ray was in love with Tess. He was the kind
> of guy who couldn't tie his own shoes. He was awkward and bumbling,
> didn't quite know anything about practical life. He was reinventing his
> style and his language and to some extent his imagination and his mem-
> ory. Before Tess moved here, he was doing that in a somewhat fumbling

and timorous way. After she came and set up the house for them, Ray was happy.[6]

In the two years he'd known them, McInerney had watched Ray and Tess go from being grateful for any attention to feeling that they had to protect their privacy. One night he stopped by with Mona Simpson, who had come to Syracuse to interview Ray for the *Paris Review*: "It wasn't that late, maybe eleven o'clock. I thought I'd introduce Mona to Ray. It was like a Carver story—we could see that they were home, but they pretended not to be. The next day, Tess told us about these thoughtless people who'd banged on their door after midnight! Soon after, a kind of psychedelic handmade 'No Visitors, Please' sign appeared on their door." McInerney didn't admit that he and Simpson had been the offending duo.[7]

Though Ray was finally divorced, he and Gallagher did not rush to marry. In 2001, Gallagher told an interviewer that she had "wanted a relationship without the legal aspect, after the collapse of two marriages. I thought—if it lasts, it's going to last for other reasons, and I'm not going to have us held together by laws." As for children, Ray once told Amy Unger that he and Tess might have a child together. Tess later told a reporter that Ray was willing to have a child with her, but she chose against it in favor of their relationship and their work: "I think I did exactly the right thing for both of us, and that did mean some sacrifice on my side of the ledger," she said.[8]

On December 16, 1982, after Gallagher returned to Syracuse from Port Angeles, Ray wrote a will. He bequeathed $5,000 each to Maryann, Christine, and Vance Carver. The remainder of his estate, including "ownership of all literary, dramatic, and cinematic works and properties of any kind and nature written and created by me . . ." he bequeathed to "Theresa J. Gallagher, if she survives me, and if she does not survive me, then to my children, me surviving, in equal shares. . . ." He named Gallagher executrix of this will, with Tobias Wolff as her substitute if she were unable to serve. Wolff, grateful for the gesture of trust, had "a sinking feeling" about the prospect of someday being called upon to fulfill the role. The will granted the executrix authority to complete and publish manuscripts that might be left unfinished at Carver's death.[9]

For both Ray and Tess, 1982 had been a year of extreme tensions and losses and remarkable gains. As it wound down, it appeared that Ray had brought to his life the orderliness and integrity that he'd long needed. Motoring in the Mercedes, Ray and Tess reached Port Angeles before Christmas and moved into her new house of wood and glass, which she named Sky

House. Here they had two studies, two bathrooms, the Olympic Mountains behind, and the deep sea channel out front. Tess photographed Ray standing beneath the house's knotty-pine ceiling beams. His face, with its puggish nose and a slight dimple in his chin, looks youthful, thin, and healthy. His arched right eyebrow conveys a skeptical, perhaps jocular, mood; a smile plays on his full lips. His hair, graying, is neatly trimmed. He's removed his glasses, leaving his countenance open and his eyes serious, serene.

Ray liked these homemade pictures so well that he asked Lish to use one on the jacket of his new book. "I think all my wonderful and lasting qualities shine through," he told Lish. Was Ray kidding, to speak of himself in that way, to Lish of all people?[10]

Probably not. Ray was beginning an eight-month leave of absence from Syracuse. He had good reasons for confidence. He could think of himself as a writer in the mode described by Durrell—"a bundle of *témoignage*"— a witness, a man who turned his troubles into words.

After being on the move and away from the Northwest for a quarter of a century, Ray began to make himself a home in Port Angeles. The town occupies a narrow shelf between the Pacific Ocean and the rain forests and glaciers of the Olympic Mountains. Its harbor, the deepest natural seaport north of San Francisco, is protected by a sand spit called the Ediz Hook. Before the decline of logging industries, the shore here was lined with timber-processing plants—sawmills, plywood manufacturers, pulp and paper mills. Ships loaded timber for export to Asia and naval vessels passed by on their way to Whidbey Island.

Theresa Bond Gallagher was born and raised in Port Angeles. In 1983, her mother, Georgia Bond, brothers Morris and Thomas, an aunt, two uncles, and several nieces and nephews resided in the vicinity. Tess had moved around a lot in her own life but always returned there for holidays and summer retreats. Though Port Angeles had a library, a bookstore, and a community college, in pre-internet days it was well removed from cultural commerce. At the very beginning of his retreat, as Ray was establishing routines and prospecting his imagination for his next work, he had a severe reaction to cocaine he took with a visiting acquaintance. An emergency room doctor warned him never to try it again. To Lish he joked that God was protecting him by keeping him away from expensive drugs.[11] While Ray could find an ironic blessing in a trip to the emergency room, he was astonished by the next gift of fortune.

On January 10, the American Academy and Institute of Arts and Letters in New York City offered Carver a Strauss Living award of $35,000 annually, tax-free, for at least five years. The endowment for this award, designated for writers of English prose who were "on the verge of public recognition," came from the recently deceased editor in chief at the Knopf publishing company, Harold Strauss, and his wife, Mildred Strauss. Holders of the Living were—as Ray gleefully told many correspondents—forbidden to hold paying jobs or receive income exceeding $1,000 per year from sources other than the sale of written work. Not only that, but the award was renewable for another five years, perhaps indefinitely. Indeed, Ray imagined that he would never again have to work for a university or teach a class.

Ray was flabbergasted by the award. "But there *can't* have been a mistake made—it's in the papers, right?" he wrote Carruth. To celebrate, he and Tess took the ferry to Victoria, spent two nights at the Empress Hotel, and munched on watercress sandwiches (which he didn't care for) and cakes (more to his taste) at high tea. Before the end of January, Ray received his first monthly check from the academy in the amount of $2,916.67.[12] Receiving this money also made Ray feel "something resembling guilt" when he watched television or even sat down with a book, because he'd "wasted so many years." He steadied himself by reading a lot of poetry. "It's where I started, and it's good for my soul."[13]

The Academy swore Ray to secrecy about the award until public announcements were made. Ray tried to keep mum but soon heard his secret from Fisketjon, who had heard it from Lish, who had heard it from a publicist at Knopf. After that, why not tell? "The Millionaire knocked on my door . . ." he wrote a select crowd of friends, referring to the mid-1950s television series that had been his favorite. Within days he resigned from Syracuse University and began lobbying for Unger to be his temporary replacement. Gallagher would keep her position for the time being, and they would keep their house in Syracuse, but Ray was giddy with the thought that he might live anywhere in the world that took his fancy.[14] Cynthia Ozick also received a Strauss Living. Members of the Academy-Institute's official jury were Elizabeth Hardwick, Donald Barthelme, Philip Roth, and Irving Howe.[15]

Ray was already committed to work with Cimino and Joann Corelli on an original screenplay with the working title of *Wagons East*. He hoped to polish off the project quickly, but it required several drafts and many meetings with Cimino, who continued to raise questions long after Ray had lost interest in the project. The script—whose final title was *Purple Lake*—was never filmed. Cimino's letters to Carver indicate that Ray had complained that the script work was distracting him from his plan to write a novel.[16] Ray was also pulled away from his desk in Port Angeles by reading engagements, for which he could now command "big bucks."[17] Early in February he planned to fly to California to meet with Cimino in Hollywood, visit his mother in Sacramento, and give a reading at Stanford.

A few days before his departure, while Ray was fishing, Gallagher took a call from San Francisco writer Marjorie Leet who asked if Carver would tape-record a short story for her. She wanted to produce a series of short story readings for National Public Radio and needed someone prominent— someone like Carver—to do her pilot. When Leet offered $100 up front and another $150 if she got funding for her idea, Gallagher replied that Ray no longer read for less than $1,000. A few hours later, Leet's phone rang. "Marjorie Leet? This is Raymond Carver. I like your idea. I'll do it."

Arriving early at Ray's Palo Alto hotel room, Leet asked Ray to omit profanity from his reading of "What We Talk About When We Talk About Love," and he proved agile at making substitutions. For "Son of a bitch, your days are numbered," he pronounced, "Doctor, your days are numbered" in a way that sounded more menacing than what he'd written originally. Ray told Leet about Tess—"You'd like her, she wears hats!"—and gave her a list of writers to contact for her project. Leet soon found herself recording a writer she'd never heard of named Tobias Wolff who was, Ray assured her, "one of the best short story writers in America." Within weeks, Leet had also signed up Ann Beattie (who told her "I would walk through fire to do anything Ray Carver said"), Leonard Michaels, Leonard Gardner, Al Young, and Grace Paley. When V. S. Pritchett heard her Carver tape, he liked it enough to endorse her project. *Tell Me a Story* aired on more than a hundred public radio stations during the next eleven years.[18]

In downtown Palo Alto, for old times' sake, Ray checked out the locations of his and Lish's former offices. "We made the right move when we left Palo Alto," he wrote his editor. The letter's humor blurred more serious business. Lish had just asked Ray to offer a blurb for his first novel, *Dear Mr. Capote.* One can only imagine Lish's lack of amusement when Ray wrote on Travelodge stationery that he had asked Gallagher to read a few pages of the book and issue a comment on his behalf.[19] In going public as an author, Lish had moved to the other side of the publishing world. Poet and editor Daniel Halpern, who had known Lish from the early 1970s, speculated:

> Gordon said something to me early on, which I'll never forget. He said, "I will never write, because I respect writers too much and I know I don't have the talent." But Gordon's positive editorial effects ended, to my mind, when he crossed over. He became something different after that point. Yet at *Esquire* he was one of the great editors of his era and one of the great supporters of fiction, and should be celebrated for that.[20]

Cathedral was already in production when Carver reminded Lish that he wanted the text to remain exactly as it was when he'd approved it the previous November. Clearly, Carver was worried that Lish would amputate and rewrite as he'd done on *What We Talk About*. For the cover, Carver had imagined a single spire against a blue sky, but the final design was more in keeping with the jacket fronts of Carver's earlier hardcover books: a grayish beige abstract design suggestive of a stained-glass window pattern. The book is dedicated to Tess Gallagher and in memory of John Gardner. The presence of an author photograph on the back cover signaled a break with the earlier Lish-edited volumes. A disgruntled Ray had agreed to use one of him standing in an airport rather than Gallagher's portrait. "Probably more appropriate anyway as I've spent so much time on the road these last few years. I'll see you in May. Love, Ray." That is the last correspondence from Carver preserved in Lish's archives.[21]

Ray returned to New York in May. In the four months he'd been out west, he'd finished two drafts of the screenplay for Cimino, worked on Kittredge's story manuscript and seen it accepted by Graywolf Press, and reworked Mona Simpson's interview with him that was now forthcoming in the *Paris Review*. He had read submissions in fiction for Yaddo (where he was now a board member), been on the road to give readings, and made a trip to Bellingham, Washington, to attend a Harold Pinter play directed by Amy Unger and visit his daughter and granddaughter. Missing from the listing of activities that Carver sent his friends is any mention of new stories or poems.

On that trip to Bellingham, Ray broke his usual habit of getting a motel room to stay with Chris, who had recently learned she was pregnant with her second child. Remnants of such a visit appear in his poems, all revealing his love and concern for a daughter who appeared to possess some of his own weaknesses. Chris, who didn't read those poems until later, cherishes a memory of this time:

> We didn't have a TV, but Shiloh saw one at a sale down the street for $20 and Dad gave us the money to buy it. Dad was thrilled with our daughter, Windy. He had always been the one to get up first at our house, but this time I got up and made coffee. I wore a sweater that my mom had given to me, and he said, "Oh, you just look gorgeous in it," and I said "Thank you, it's Mom's." We were just so tight, then, we were. Later it wasn't that way, after his new relationship and more than that the changes in his life—his high-rolling literary life on the East Coast.[22]

Honors and celebrations occupied Ray in the month of May. First, he attended Vance's graduation from Syracuse University with a major in

International Relations and minor in French. Then at the American Academy and Institute of Arts and Letters annual ceremonial in New York City, the Strauss Living award was officially bestowed upon him. Donald Barthelme composed the Academy-Institute's citation praising Carver's stories for presenting "with great force and effect the quiddity of what are called ordinary lives" in a voice that is "strong, original, and full of truth, an extraordinary example of literature's ability to make itself new." Tess Gallagher accompanied Ray to the luncheon before the ceremony. In addition, he invited Richard Ford, Tobias Wolff, Michael Cimino, his agent Amanda Urban, and editors Gordon Lish and Gary Fisketjon. This was the first awarding of Strauss Livings. The audience uttered a series of gasps as first the amount, then the duration, and finally the tax-free status were announced.[23]

For this big occasion, Ray and Tess stayed at the "swank" Upper East Side Carlyle Hotel. Affording such a luxury tickled Ray: "He'd laugh and quote his 'version of the Pinter line, 'a person feels like he has a chance in a room like this,'" Unger recalled. While in New York, Ray sat down for reading and interview sessions with a fiction aficionado from Missouri named Kay Bonetti. Carver recorded "Fat," "A Serious Talk," and his personal favorite, "Nobody Said Anything" for Bonetti's American Audio Prose Library and then took her questions. In the readings, Ray's deadpan delivery brings out the humor in his stories. His answers to Bonetti's probing questions are halting but not really hesitant. Often Bonetti, whose clear mid-South inflections offset Carver's muttered cogitations, pushes Ray for details and gladdens him with her appreciation for his stories. The Bonetti recording proves (as no written and revised interview could) that Ray had learned to speak in generalities about his art and personal history, but was at his best when he talked about the genesis of particular stories. In describing how an overheard line may become the germ of a story, Ray told Bonetti, "I have not written the story for it yet, but I heard someone say not too long ago, 'He was so sick before he died.' And that set up a whole conjuring of feeling in me because I have known people this would fit."[24]

As his poems tell us over and over, Ray thought often about death. "Maybe," Gallagher has said, "there was something even at a subconscious level that had made him aware that he was not going to be with us that long."[25] He was afraid of it, of course, but he was also a bit tantalized, and he'd learned to fight that feeling with something akin to the Alcoholics Anonymous slogan "one day at a time."

One can hear, though, in Bonetti's 1983 recordings, a certain fragility in Carver's breathing. The voice, cloaked in cigarette smoke, comes in short, shallow exhalations.

• • •

On May 25, 1983, his forty-fifth birthday, Carver worked on a poem that brings the fear of death that was natural to his sensibility into full orchestration with his new embrace of life. In "Where Water Comes Together with Other Water" Carver offers a song of gratitude for his new life on the West Coast, contrasting it with the drought in his heart ten years before. He had been, in Gallagher's words, "a creature of rooms," but returning to the Northwest "reattached him to his childhood." Certainly the house that Tess had built gave him an ideal vantage point. From his desk he could look out across the strait and down to the beach and west along the shore to the smokestacks and lights of Port Angeles. Nor did Ray have to move far from his desk to envelop himself in the natural world. Morse Creek runs at the edge of that neighborhood, accessible by an old railroad trestle and a streamside trail. Here a person can sit on a boulder in the shade and watch the water make its way to the ocean a half mile away.[26]

Ironically, the shorefront golf course and housing development where Ray and Tess lived is one of several likely culprits in the depredation of the creeks' spawning habitat. In a poem called "Its Course," Carver pays homage to his stream's natural history: "It used to flow yonder, where those houses are," an old-timer tells the poet, remembering how the salmon coming in "made a noise like water boiling." Those salmon runs had declined when Ray lived there, but winter steelhead still ran. After Ray heard the local history, he went home to write about the stream. Like many of Carver's best poems from the 1980s, this one enfolds its observations on the natural world with philosophical musings and a premonition of death.[27]

The Cambridge-based literary journal *Granta* gave British readers a new spin on American fiction with its 1983 issue titled *Dirty Realism,* including Carver's story "The Compartment," Ford's "Rock Springs," Bobbie Ann Mason's "Still Life with Watermelon," and Tobias Wolff's "The Barracks Thief." Editor and American expat Bill Buford offered his thoughts on the "peculiar and haunting" *new* American fiction that lacks the epic ambitions of Norman Mailer or Saul Bellow as well as the self-conscious experimentalism of John Barth or Thomas Pynchon. The fiction Buford admired is "a curious, dirty realism about the belly-side of contemporary life . . . [that] makes the more traditional realistic novels of, say Updike or Styron seem ornate, even baroque in comparison."[28]

Carver liked Buford and tolerated being classed a "dirty realist" in gratitude for the attention Buford brought to his work in Britain, but he found its American cognate, "minimalist," diminishing and trivializing. Minimalism—a term borrowed from the visual and musical arts—has been a bugaboo to Carver's critics as well, who have never agreed about what it means or who, besides Carver, should be included in the category. Nonetheless, the term has been identified with Carver to the extent that it popped up on the game show *Jeopardy!* where the following clue caught popular understanding of the word: "The stories of Raymond Carver typified this style whose name indicates it does the most with the 'least.' "[29]

Ushered into *Esquire* by Lish's promise to bring "*the* new fiction" to Arnold Gingrich in 1969, then introduced to England in 1983 as part of a *new* wave of American fiction, Carver shortly became the poster boy for a *new* era in the short story. An article in *Coda,* the newsletter of Poets & Writers, Inc., announced a renaissance for short fiction and led off with a quotation from Carver. The attention and accolades Carver was receiving gave him every reason to hope for good reviews and a shower of awards for his forthcoming books. The *Fires* miscellany appeared first, in two handsome editions, a bright red hardcover and a paperback with a photograph of orange flames on the front. Sales of the Capra Press book were slow, but Fisketjon, who had reluctantly taken on the job of managing editor for the Vintage line of mass-market paperbacks at Random House, snapped up reprint rights. Ray promoted *Fires* at Printers Inc. bookstore in Palo Alto, where his fan Lewis Buzbee sold books. It was a memorable evening in a friendship that was soon to be strained to a breaking point. Over pot and popcorn at Buzbee's house, they celebrated the acceptance of Buzbee's interview with Carver at the *New England Review* and laughed uncontrollably about a bumper sticker that Ray thought represented the story of his second act: "New Hope for the Dead." Ray told his hosts, both writers, to "keep working, keep fighting to find our own voice. He told us that what we were trying to do was crucial."*[30]

* When Buzbee read Mona Simpson's Carver interview in the *Paris Review,* he discovered that nearly half of the questions and answers from the interview he had conducted with Ray—the one that had been declined by the *Paris Review* and had since been accepted by the *New England Review*—appeared verbatim in the pages credited solely to Simpson. Ray explained in a letter to Buzbee that he had noticed the overlap in the proofs and asked the *PR* to credit Buzbee, but that hadn't happened. When Buzbee's lawyer threatened to sue, *PR* publisher George Plimpton telephoned to ask him not to pursue a lawsuit. Buzbee said he could never forget the exact words of the final call: "Who the fuck do you think you are? You're just a little shit on the West Coast. You don't own everything that comes out of your typewriter!" Buzbee replied, "I work in a bookstore for five dollars an hour. My words are all I do own." Ultimately *PR* listed Buzbee as coauthor with Simpson on all reprintings of the interview.
When *NER* asked Buzbee to replace the purloined questions and replies with new material, Ray telegrammed that he'd been advised not to speak to Buzbee until the "unhappy matter" was settled. Ray complained of feeling "like a ping-pong ball." In

• • •

Cathedral would be published early in September. Ray filled the waiting time with intermittent work on the Cimino screenplay, fishing, and visiting. A plentiful salmon run that summer lured him out on the strait in the early-morning hours to catch his limit, but the difficulties of depending on others for rides made Ray think about buying his own boat. A local seafood processor filleted, smoked, and vacuum-packed his fish. Sometimes Ray's old and new lives blended smoothly. Unger recalled a visit that summer during which Amy and Tess got along happily: "It was a great time, the galleys for *Cathedral* were sitting on the table, the galleys to my novel were coming in, and we knew we'd all be together in Syracuse soon. We were all excited, just enjoying ourselves. Amy liked Tess at that point, except for a qualm that she might be betraying Maryann by liking Tess." The most important news from his family was that Christine Carver gave birth to Chloe Alice Carver, his second grandchild, on August 13, 1983.

To promote *Cathedral,* Carver's picture appeared in *Vanity Fair*'s "fame or infamy" nominations section. He posed on the beach below Sky House in a necktie, business shirt, and trench coat, a big brown hand covering the right side of his face—a man willing to be halfway in the spotlight of fame.[31] He ended the summer by driving with Chuck Kinder from California to Pittsburgh. The days in the Mercedes gave Kinder and Carver a chance to talk and joke around and revisit the days when they were Trout and Running Dog in the Bay Area—absent the drinking binges. In fact, part of Carver's agenda for the trip was to influence his old friend to limit his own consumption. It seemed a good omen for both writers when they turned on the television set in their room in Reno and heard novelist E. L. Doctorow compare writing a novel to taking a long car trip at night in the fog: you can see only the portion of the road ahead that is illuminated by your head-lights, but you can make the whole trip that way if you have a map. Somewhere in Utah, Ray first acquired a copy of *Newsweek* with his photo and a review of *Cathedral.* The review disappointed Ray, Kinder recalled, and he was especially miffed that it gave his real age. Trying to get Ray's mind off the review, Kinder joked about walking out on the check:

> I was still razzing Ray when he went to pay the tab with a credit card. I said to the waitress, "Are you sure that's his credit card? How do you know?" Then I shoved the *Newsweek* toward her, with the page opened to the photo of Ray. She was an older lady with a beehive hairdo. She

---

the matter of the mix-up at *PR,* Buzbee believes that Ray "never stepped up to do anything. He got foggy about it and apparently allowed it to happen."

looked at the photo and then at Ray and back to the photo and said, "What'd he *do*?!"[32]

It has been said, repeatedly, that the stories in *Cathedral* are fuller and more generous than Carver's previous work. That belief is largely based on comparison of these stories with the Lish-edited stories *What We Talk About When We Talk About Love*. A truer reckoning may be made between those stories as they existed before their editing in the summer of 1980 and the stories printed in *Cathedral*. Comparing thus, one finds that *Cathedral* is a book of richer perspective and more complex humor than the previous one. It lacks the raw pain and meanness and nihilism of stories like "Tell the Women We're Going" or "One More Thing." On the subject of marriage, the newer stories offer a touch of tender regret where before there had been bitterness. A drunken or an unemployed husband figures in many of the stories in *Cathedral*, but he exhibits kindness and forgiveness toward the wife and sees himself with blessed irony. Take "Fever," the story of a man caring for his children after his wife has left him. The story scrambles elements from the Carvers' marriage beyond identification, but it ends in acceptance: "He understood it was over, and he felt able to let her go. . . . something that passed. And that passing—though it had seemed impossible and he'd fought against it—would become a part of him now, too, as surely as anything else he'd left behind."

Cathedral's first reviewers were less than unanimous about the book's uplifting qualities. In the *Newsweek* review that bothered Ray, David Lehman asserted (with no apologies to Bob Dylan) that Carver's "bewildered, inarticulate, and terminally passive people" reside "on desolation row" where their lives are "unrelieved by humor and unredeemed by heroism or love." Other *Newsweek* writers visited Carver in "Port Angeles, Ore." [sic] where he drove them about nervously in his Mercedes and said, "I'm not interested in the criticism that my fiction is bleak . . . I care for the people I write about. Alienation may emerge from my characters. But it's not a program I've cooked up." The weekly's spread was accompanied by a photo of Ray sitting awkwardly (clad in sport jacket and street shoes) on the beach at Port Angeles, sort of a Brobdingnagian version of that earlier and more at-ease picture of himself fishing, circa 1950.[33]

For the second time, a review of Carver's work appeared on the cover of the *New York Times Book Review*, a valuable thing in itself, but Irving Howe's hedged, patronizing praise did not convey the enthusiasm he'd earlier expressed in his postcard to Carver. Having once attacked Leonard Michaels's stories for their focus on "urban trauma and blithe depravity" and "minimal method," Howe now offered a similar complaint about

Carver: "It's a meager life that Mr. Carver portrays, without religion or politics or culture, without the shelter of class or ethnicity, without the support of strong folkways or conscious rebellion." Meanwhile, in the daily *Times*, Anatole Broyard, not seeing a connection between unemployment or alcoholism and an empty wallet, asks why the couple in "Preservation" don't fix their refrigerator or why the man in "Careful" doesn't get himself to a doctor.[34]

Richard Eder, writing for the *Los Angeles Times*, gets what Howe's earnestness and Broyard's orneriness cause them to miss: "Carver is more than a realist; there is in some of these stories a strangeness, the husk of a myth." Josh Rubins, in the *New York Review of Books*, grasps the real, mundane issues faced by Carver's people: "Will or won't an alcoholic fall off the wagon? More than any other writer, Carver captures the simultaneous delicacy and brutality of that dreaded slip." Rubins credits Carver for illuminating "certain American lives—somewhere between urban and rural, often rootless and culturally impoverished, on the unraveling fringes of erstwhile industrial prosperity."[35]

Sales of *Cathedral* were excellent for a story collection. Eight weeks after publication, it was in its third printing and had sold seventeen thousand copies. As of August 1984, Carver's agent had sent him checks totaling $41,000 in payment for *Cathedral*. In addition, translation rights were purchased by twelve foreign publishers.[36] In the wake of *Cathedral*'s success, Knopf president and editor in chief Robert Gottlieb observed, "Twenty years ago the conventional wisdom held that a publisher should shudder when an author said, 'You've done three of my novels. Now I want a collection of stories.' That is no longer the case." Gottlieb dated the burgeoning interest in short fiction to the success of *The Stories of John Cheever* and noted that many fine writers—he cited Carver and Ozick—were doing their major work in shorter forms. This explanation has merit, but credit is also due to the indefatigable efforts of Gordon Lish, the energizer who brought "the new fiction" to *Esquire* in 1969, and to the tens of thousands of stories being composed in the nation's thousands of creative writing classrooms, which were in effect training readers as well as writers. Douglas Unger, intimate with Ray's milieu before the so-called renaissance, credited the zeitgeist: "Our culture finally caught up to Ray's style and subjects. The disillusionment of the seventies and eighties now suddenly found itself reflected in his work."[37]

Lish, the editor of the enormously successful book, found himself appalled by how avidly Ray responded to his own success. What Lish saw as conceit and reckless enjoyment, other friends saw as a natural counterpoint to the deprivations Ray had suffered in his earlier years. "He was like a child at Christmas with every good review or piece of good news,"

Unger reminisced. "He'd want to come over and play, share his gift, his success."

Theater director Molly Fowler encountered Ray's boyish glee as she sat reading a new book—*Cathedral*—in the lobby of the Gramercy Park Hotel in New York City and was disturbed by a man in a yellow shirt looming over her. He asked, "What's that book you're reading? May I see it?" When she reluctantly showed him, he said, "Well, I'm Raymond Carver, I'm the author of that book. If you give it to me, I'll sign it for you. What's your name?" Then Ray explained that he was meeting with Michael Cimino and that Cimino had told him, "There's a girl out there in the lobby reading your book," and so he'd come to see for himself.[38]

"Ray was very happy that fall," recalled Unger, who had come to teach at Syracuse. He'd take us all to dinner at Pascale, a fine restaurant. Jay and Merry [McInerney] and Amy and I would sit around the table having such a good time, talking about our work and telling stories, laughing—it was a high time."

Ray tried to spend one evening a week at the Ungers. He and Amy and Erin would have time alone together to talk freely about their mutual family before Doug arrived. "Ray was astonished," Unger recalled, "at financial difficulties Maryann was having. Amy didn't want to be in the go-between position, yet she felt there were terrible needs in the family and felt it was her job to speak to Ray about them." Vance was enrolled in a master's degree program in European integration at American University in Washington, DC. Ray mentioned his son's studies proudly and often in letters to friends, but he felt, Unger said, that he'd already given him enough financial help. "No parent helped Ray through college, and he just flat-out didn't want to give Vance more money."[39]

Vance was sitting in front of his apartment in DC when he first read *Cathedral* and saw how his father had used some details about their relationship in "The Compartment." He fought back tears and shook his head with anger, wondering why his father had "taken an experience that ultimately cemented our reconciliation and, instead, turned it into such a dark, unsettling story?" Vance telephoned Ray in Syracuse and asked his question. Ray was caught off guard but assured Vance "it's nothing to take too seriously or get upset about. It's just a good story is all . . . of course, we had a fine time on that trip together." Vance acceded to his father's explanation, but the hurt remained.[40]

In November, for "one reason and another," as Carver put it, he and Lish parted ways. Gottlieb would serve as Carver's editor at Knopf, and Fisketjon would continue as the editor of his Vintage paperback editions. "Being around Ray and Gordon in the early 1980s was like watching a marriage go bad," Fisketjon reflected. "It seemed like Gordon Lish was the one guy who couldn't be happy about Ray's success. He couldn't enjoy it and had to fight it. It was a case of strong affection polluted for reasons of ego and frustration."[41]

Whatever the merits of Lish's editing had been for Carver, he now—with emotional and domestic support from Gallagher, with career direction from Amanda Urban, and with the security of his grant income—stood on his own as an artist. Nonetheless, as Fisketjon also observed, "Ray didn't forget people who had done him kindnesses. He would have retained his gratitude for Gordon over the years." Gratitude would not have been enough for Lish. He believed he'd been a creator of Carver's work and credit for anything less irritated him.[42] Lish began telling associates in New York that he had changed some of Carver's stories so much that they were more his than Carver's. Roy Blount Jr. was surprised when, in 1980, Lish showed him Carver typescripts that he had "drastically slashed and scribbled on," explaining that Carver was an alcoholic whose work required such rewriting. Lish's "casual—or, rather, pointed—indiscretion" shocked Blount as "a violation of editor-author confidence."[43]

When Ray sat down to tackle the mirage of his novel that fall, he found himself writing a memoir about his father that Tom Jenks, then at *Esquire,* solicited from him. Ray drafted "My Father's Life" quickly, feeling that it was coming to him "very directly" and able to see clearly through what usually seemed a "rainy scrim" between himself and his childhood. It is a rough, little-adorned piece of memory writing, powerful in its clarity and simplicity, that signals Carver's recent confidence in himself. He wrote it so soon after his final break with Lish that one is tempted to call it a coming-of-age and naming ritual, an assumption of manhood. It dwells on the fact that both he and his father were called by the same name—Raymond—and in important ways *are* the same.

Ray saved a manuscript and six typescripts of the memoir, leaving scholars a glimpse of his composition process. The manuscript begins with warm-up lists, just a few details or dialogue phrases to a page, and then begins to roll on its sixth page with the legend of his father's migration from Arkansas to Washington. Its details, chosen as much for their sound and color as for accuracy, remain the same throughout successive drafts. In the third typescript, Gallagher's handwriting appears in the margins. Some of Gallagher's interpolated sentences survive into the fourth typescript where they are crossed out again by Carver's hand. In other instances, Carver took Gallagher's additions and suggestions: the sentence "I doubt it" added to the third paragraph; the phrase "in their beautiful voices out of my childhood" added to the closing paragraph. These editorial comments do not constitute, as Lish's did, a usurpation. They are the kinds of comments a teacher makes on a student's manuscript, intended to provoke revision by the author. More important, Carver's responses to this editing exhibit integrity. He rejects many proposed changes, especially those that tend toward generalization or an alteration of fact, and accepts those that refine detail or move the story forward with greater coherence. On the back of one page, Gallagher inscribed a list of questions that she thinks are insufficiently answered in Carver's draft, for the most part psychological questions that push for meaning. Gallagher's editorial work is extremely personal, at once coldly objective and warmly involved. It seems clear that Carver sought such advice and just as clear that he had no scruples about rejecting it. After five years, working together as fellow artists had become part of the intimacy that Ray and Tess shared.[44]

Before Thanksgiving, Ray stepped away from his literary concerns to travel deeper into the West than he'd been in many years. He flew to Washington State and then went hunting for elk and deer in the Olympic Range with Morris Bond. They traveled on horseback and made their wilderness camp in a forest where they could smell snow in the offing. Ray's poem "Elk Camp" tells how far that trip took him from Manhattan. He doesn't, according to the poem, shoot an elk. He looks at the stars, smells a forest as if for the first time, and realizes that he wouldn't mind if he never read a book again. Better yet, he realizes that he's too far in the wilderness to respond to anyone's pleas for help. Out there, he's free because "nothing / mattered more than anything else."[45]

As he closed out 1983 in snowbound Syracuse, Ray was beginning to comprehend the freedom that the Strauss Award permitted him. Perhaps, he speculated, he and Tess might live in Switzerland for six months of every year. (Chocolate beckoned!)[46] *Cathedral* continued to gather attention and accolades, including nominations for a National Book Critics Circle Award and a Pulitzer Prize. Writing for the *Wall Street Journal* a couple of months after *Cathedral*'s debut, Helen Dudar reflects the aura that had begun to form around Raymond Carver in an article called "A Storyteller in Touch With the Angels": "When he appears at New York bookshops to read his fiction, the crowds are large, young, intense and prepared to buy." To those who find Carver's stories depressing, Dudar writes that "lamenting the bleakness of his world" is like "complaining that Chekhov is a downer. Successful fiction, fiction that sheds even a glimmer of light on how we make our way through life, is not at heart depressing."[47]

That was not the last time that Carver's name would be linked with Chekhov's.

CHAPTER 27

Where Water Comes Together
with Other Water

January 1984–May 1985, Port Angeles

From the vantage of his poetry, Ray's life took on pattern and reason and gratitude. . . . Perhaps in the blunt-nosed zigzag of poems he
could attain elevation without the sleek evasions of elegance, irony or
even the easy exit of transcendence. . . .
                              —Tess Gallagher, Introduction to *All of Us*[1]

In what was probably Lish's last letter to his former author, the editor told
Ray that more than twenty thousand hardcover copies of *Cathedral* had
been shipped out to bookstores. "Wonders never cease," Lish concluded.[2]
And as the books sold, Ray's modest fame brought him stacks and stacks
of mail.

That mail included books sent by editors who hoped he'd write a blurb,
and requests to give readings for fees the supplicants are embarrassed to
name. People invited Ray to lead workshops, to judge writing contests, and
to evaluate professors applying for tenure. They asked him to authorize
translations of his work or advise translators about idiomatic phrasing; to
permit the making of low-budget films based on his stories ("this will be
my very first dramatic film," begged one plaintiff, "something I will use as
a portfolio piece"); to allow the adaptation of a short story into a play; to
contribute to magazines and anthologies; and to archive his papers at university libraries. In addition, there was fan mail. Readers sent thanks and
encouragement and praise, often accompanied by gifts of their own work—
recorded songs and slides of paintings as well as manuscripts—that they
hoped Ray would like.

Perhaps the most remarkable thing about the avalanche of correspondence that came Ray's way is that he personally—and politely—answered

413

much of it. Most difficult to refuse were requests for help from other writers. Authors seeking promotional comments made ingenious, if ludicrous, pleas:

> . . . the style of my novel is not unlike and uninfluenced by your own work . . . while I would not slap you with a paternity suit for my novel, you do bear some responsibility for it.

And so did editors:

> You can help us verify the American enterprise of the short story in two ways . . . we would like you to review this collection for an appropriate publication. That way you, too, will have taken a concrete, active interest not so much in this specific book . . . but for the short story form itself.[3]

Indeed, the wonder of Ray's success "verified" the short story and the trajectory of his own life. He found himself enormously pleased (and surely as often amused) by all this. He had not, as the phrase goes, gotten above his raising, and he remembered how much he'd once craved publication and attention and sales himself. He remembered that the distinguished William Carlos Williams from the distant East had sent him a poem when he launched a magazine at obscure Chico State College.

A factor behind the huge number of requests Ray received was the phenomenal growth of degree-granting programs and summer workshops in poetry, fiction, and "creative nonfiction" writing all over the country. Headlining a guest writer whose name was recognizable beyond academic circles could be a huge draw for these enterprises. Carver was particularly sought after because his style was seductive to beginning writers. Longtime *New Yorker* editor Charles McGrath believes he became

> a bellwether for a whole generation, the most widely imitated writer I ever saw. When I first got to the *New Yorker* the influence was Salinger, next was Donald Barthelme, then Ann Beattie, then Carver. And the proof of Carver's brilliance was the difference between what he did and what all his imitators did. American fiction got stuck in a huge rut for years because of Ray, but that wasn't his fault! What he did looks easier than it is.[4]

Alluding to Tolstoy's remark that all the modern Russian writers "came out of Gogol's overcoat," Jay McInerney commented in 1990, "You look at all the short story writers younger than Ray, and there's hardly one that you might say didn't come out of Carver's overcoat. . . . There's an extended family of writers who were so touched by his work that they feel like they were his friends."[5]

To celebrate the issue of *Ploughshares* he edited, Ray gave a benefit reading at Harvard on February 2, 1984. As gifts to donors, Ray signed copies of *Cathedral* donated by Knopf and raised nearly $3,700 for the four-year-old magazine. That night Stephen Dobyns noticed that Ray had "changed entirely from the nervous, anxious person I had known in '78." A magazine photographer was "climbing all around Ray, and even that didn't seem to faze him. He took himself more seriously, not in a conceited way, but because he was aware that other people took him seriously."[6]

The calm with which Ray met the public masked a growing discontent. He had done little concentrated work since the completion of *Cathedral.* The problem was "too much commerce of all sorts" in Syracuse, including the pressure of serving on the search committee for his own replacement.[*] Ray considered renting an apartment or hotel room in Syracuse, but instead bought a sixty-day round-trip plane ticket to the coast, left his Mercedes in Syracuse, and moved into Sky House. After he'd spent two long winter nights there, he confided to Mark Jarman that he felt "unable to fix my concentration on anything. . . . I've put too much pressure on whatever gifts I may have for the last eighteen months . . . I'm walking on thin ice." He'd made a mistake, Ray confided to Tobias Wolff, in not having a new project under way when *Cathedral* came out.[7]

Early on February 21, Ray stopped expecting himself to write a novel. He wrote a poem. He wrote another the next morning. Writing these poems was like catching fish: "There's a bite on here every morning around five to five-thirty. . . ." Most of them are poems of the moment, brief stories of longing and acceptance and happiness, reports of a man seeking to represent himself by means of the things he observes and the thoughts that pass through his mind. Catching these poems transformed Ray's despair to excitement and turned his thoughts toward fishing. He looked at boats for sale, and invited friends to consider his place their fishing lodge come summer. He hoped to buy a house in Seattle and to begin, in the fall of 1984, dividing his time between the city and the peninsula.[8]

The run of poems continued through Tess's spring break visit to Port

---

[*] In the end, the department promoted Tobias Wolff to Ray's former slot and installed Douglas Unger in Wolff's on the strength of the warm reception of Unger's first novel, *Leaving the Land.* Carver explained all this to several longtime friends who applied for the job, declaring he'd never again sit on such a committee.

Angeles in March. At the end of March Ray bought a fire-engine red Jeep wagon. He continued to catch poems in the mornings, sometimes two a day. "Keepers . . . I'm not into catch and release. I just start clubbing them into submission when I get them near my boat." He felt "quietly thrilled and happy." He decided to let his return ticket expire and stay in Washington until he had one hundred of the "little darlings."⁹

After Ray had been in Port Angeles seven weeks, East Coast publicity in the form of journalist Bruce Weber, a former student of Ford's, came west to profile him for the *New York Times Magazine*. Weber found "a large man, with hair in the throes of going gray, a pudding face, the beginnings of jowls . . . wearing a patterned polyester shirt, with an oversized, way-out-of-style collar, blue jeans, and slippers that are coming apart. More than anything, he looks kind." To Weber, Ray seemed cautiously exuberant about "a life that is, at long last, serene, prosperous and productive." Despite his plans to buy a fishing boat, Ray told Weber he generally stayed at his desk from before dawn until late afternoon, left his phone unplugged, avoided social distractions, and had been fishing only once during the past winter."¹⁰

Ray wrote a short poem, "Interview," about Weber's visit, describing how an intense memory of Maryann interrupted his talk about himself. Such poems, indeed all of Carver's poems, have complicated his reputation for readers who prefer to see him solely as a short story writer. Because Carver's poems include imagery from dreams, associate freely among anecdotes, and name feelings that don't occur in the aesthetic of his fiction, they may read like diary or journal entries. But such pragmatic reading does the poems an injustice. The best of his poems, like his short stories, exhibit his particular genius for choosing a tiny incident or mundane detail that becomes what T. S. Eliot called an objective correlative: "a set of objects, a situation, a chain of events" that immediately evokes the particular emotion the artist wishes to represent with "complete adequacy of the external to the emotion."¹¹

"The Hat," for instance, recalls a scene Ray witnessed in Mexico City five years before: a man and a bear chained together. The man strikes the bear with an iron bar until it ". . . snaps and weaves in a poor dance." Then the man takes off his hat and sends it through the crowd for tips. The poet freezes when he finds the hat in his own hand, then tosses in some money. To that point, the poem is a report, albeit one freighted with easy prey for symbol hunters; but in its last stanza, "The Hat" leaps to a different scene: the poet, in bed with his lover, covers his face with her long hair. Subtle parallels suggest themselves, urging the reader to speculate that the entwined lovers resemble the bear and his keeper. That's all. Nothing is spelled out and the poem ends: "I close my eyes, the hat / appears. Then the tambourine. The chain."

• • •

Like Gordon Lish, Gary Fisketjon had an instinct for recognizing good fiction and wasn't afraid to pursue it aggressively: "I know I'm interested in a manuscript when I go from one page to the next, and that counts for more than you would want to imagine," he said. He believed he differed from Lish in preferring to publish writers who have already found their voice and a direction. Another difference between the editorial practices of Lish and Fisketjon, in part a generational difference, was that Fisketjon believed writers ought to be able to live by their writing. "Gordon missed that half of it," Fisketjon commented. "He didn't care about the selling. But if I know something is good, I will figure out a way to sell it."

To that end, since becoming managing editor at Vintage, Fisketjon had been trying to figure out a better way to package literary fiction, which seldom sold enough in hardcover to pay writers a living wage and then—if it went to paperback at all—made a poor showing in the drugstore and grocery store venues that carry "rack-sized" mass-market editions. The mass-market format Vintage edition of *What We Talk About When We Talk About Love* had sold an extraordinary fifty thousand copies. A matching reprint of *Fires,* with a delicate drawing of a boy with a fishing pole on its cover, had also surpassed expectations. Weber called the *Fires* pocketbook "an industry testament to the interest [Carver's] work has spawned . . ." But Fisketjon was not satisfied with simply trying to boost sales of the mass-market paperbacks. He wanted to change the way contemporary fiction was packaged and marketed. He had already surprised his publisher with good sales for a set of Don DeLillo's novels in larger paperbound or "trade" editions whose uniform designs made them identifiable. Now he decided to build on that idea and Carver's name recognition with a trade-sized series of uniform editions by various authors. *Cathedral* would be first on his list.[12]

Once again, Ray Carver was friendly with the right editor at the right time. Alongside *Cathedral,* Fisketjon would issue reprints of other literary books that hadn't yet reached the audience they deserved. McInerney's *Bright Lights, Big City* would be a paperback original in the same series. Fisketjon's books, at $4.95 priced lower than hardcovers and higher than mass-markets, would have big, clear typefaces and wide page margins but still be small enough to slip into a briefcase or handbag. They would remind baby boomer readers of reprinted classics by Franz Kafka and Hermann Hesse they'd read in college. The oxymoronic series title he chose—Vintage Contemporaries—implied that these contemporary works were already classics. Fisketjon would release the first books in the series in September 1984.

Ray blurbed McInerney's novel, declaring it was the last such comment he'd ever write. Then he wrote just one more, for C. J. Hribal's *Matty's Heart*.[13] Reviewing *Selected Letters* by Sherwood Anderson for the *New York Times Book Review*, Carver quotes trenchantly from Anderson's remarks about literary fame: "Fame is no good, my dear . . . Take it from me" and "If I could work the rest of my life unknown, unnoticed by those who make current opinion, I would be happier." Carver writes about Anderson with a self-assurance that was lacking in the reviews he'd written earlier for the *Tribune*. In thinking about Anderson he seems to be thinking about himself and the ways history handles writers. Anderson, he says, wrote about "the underbelly of small town life in mid-America . . . better, and with more fidelity and sympathy, than any American writer before him—and *most of them* since his time" [emphasis added].[14]

While he was thinking about Anderson's career, Ray learned that *Cathedral* was a finalist for the Pulitzer Prize in fiction, to be announced in mid-April. He did not win—like the National Book Award, the Pulitzer went to William Kennedy's *Ironweed*. His months—and his poetry writing—in Port Angeles had settled him and reconciled him to his own gifts. In "For Tess," one of the poems he wrote that spring, he describes an afternoon spent fishing on Morse Creek. He hadn't caught a thing that day, but he was so happy that he rested by the side of the creek and just listened to the wind and the water. He imagines that he has died there. He doesn't mind being dead until he thinks of Tess: "I opened my eyes then and got right up / and went back to being happy again." Carver would place that message of gratitude to Tess at the end of his next collection of poems, *Where Water Comes Together with Other Water*.

Ray drove east in his Jeep in April, stopping in Montana and Pittsburgh, to join Gallagher in Syracuse. He accompanied her to New York City for a reading to mark the publication of her third major collection of poetry. *Willingly*, dedicated to him, includes poems about her father and his death, which she describes with fearless precision in "Accomplishment." At forty, Gallagher understood that grief and the uses of grief were to be important subjects for her. Poems "are the best and oldest forms we have for attending and absolving grief, for bringing it into a useful relationship to those things we are about to do toward a future," she wrote in an essay that same year.[15]

"Raymond Carver: A Chronicler of Blue-Collar Despair" was the title the *New York Times Magazine* gave Weber's cover-story profile of Carver. Some of the text recaps the plausible but exaggerated story of Carver's life as he told it himself, from his pretend 1939 birthdate to his sacrifice of writing in favor of putting milk on the table for his kids or, at best, writing on a scratch pad in the car. But the framing of Weber's article accelerated Carver's version of his background to the velocity of myth. Readers who got beyond the headline learned that Weber did not identify Carver with despair. To Weber, a Carver character is "shabby, not empty, and excruciatingly ordinary," and Carver himself a moralist who shows why "decent men and women, dealt crummy circumstances in a plentiful world, behave badly in their intimate battles with selfishness." Weber's fundamentally correct but highly burnished image of Carver as the patron saint of struggling individuals brought Carver new readers in the 1980s.

These were years of glorified self-interest, the era of Yuppies and dual-income, no-kids couples. President Reagan was reelected. People like Carver's characters, who "yearn for serenity rather than achievement," and "don't get the little they want," were hit by a decline in unionized blue-collar jobs. For some readers who'd been with Carver from the beginning, his new prominence was puzzling. Curt Johnson, for one, wished that Carver were more political: "As it was, they sold his stories of inadequate, failed, embarrassed and embarrassing men, many of them drunkards, all of them losers, to Yuppies. His people confirmed the Yuppies in their sense of superiority."[16]

Johnson's comment points to something about the art and finances of the eighties and the perception of Carver's work in that context. In 1982, New York City had been nearly bankrupt, and the rest of the nation in an economic recession. When the booming Reagan economy emerged, new money infused the art and literary worlds. While corporate types rode in limousines, the lower end of the economy still suffered. AIDS and crack-cocaine plagued at-risk populations and further contributed to poverty and crime. In the arts, a "double bind of elitism and populism" emerged. The sometimes sinister relationship of money and the arts was epitomized, Peter Schjeldahl reflects, by an effort to sell, as folk art, "the crudely lettered, pleading cardboard signs wielded by the homeless who then teemed the city's streets."[17]

By analogy, if the down-and-out characters in Carver's stories are like the homeless, it might be argued that Carver and his followers and backers were turning them into commodities. Editors like Fisketjon and his friend Morgan Entriken at Simon & Schuster rode the economic wave that created prosperity for some players in the literary sideshow of that art scene. A leftist critic, Nicolaus Mills, points out that the art hero of the 1980s "was not the starving painter living in a Greenwich Village walkup. The new art hero was the promoter who knew how to make art pay." Ray hadn't set out to be part of this phenomenon, but his work was grandfathered into it, and his reputation gained momentum from it. In the process, he became subject to the criticism that he had sold out. And yet common sense says that Ray would not have cared about all that. If he had sold out, it was when he failed to stop the publication of *What We Talk About*. He was his own man now. If he relished his comforts, it was because he had spent so many years doing without a reliable car or home of his own, depending on his wife's earnings, writing bad checks, and hiding from bill collectors.

With his status as a fiction writer at a new high, Ray stopped writing his very salable short stories and wrote poems, somewhat to his agent's and editor's frustration. Hubris and perversity? Desire to write as he chose—and to reveal himself—permitted by the safety net of the Strauss Living? The urge that drove him to write poems was a mixture of all of these, but it was certainly *not* a calculated effort to increase his readership or sales. Nonetheless, most of these new poems found publication easily. Jonathan Galassi, then at Random House as well as poetry editor of the *Paris Review*, heard about Ray's spate of poems from Fisketjon and selected ten of Ray's outpouring for *PR*'s thirtieth-anniversary issue.

Ray was "horribly busy" when his former student Mary Bucci Bush sent him her Syracuse doctoral thesis (a collection of short stories) to read, but he read it, gratis, and sent his note of approval to her examination committee. To Bush's chagrin, her pages came back sans the required thesis binder she'd searched all over to find! Ray kept it, he told her, as his "fee" and planned to "stick about seventy new poems in it" to give to Fisketjon. Fisketjon offered $3,000 to acquire *Where Water Comes Together with Other Water* for clothbound publication by Random House in the spring of 1985. Thus, after six years of correspondence and friendship with Carver, Fisketjon established himself as the primary editor of Carver's book-length works.[18]

"My Boat," a poem Ray wrote in Port Angeles in the spring of 1984, announces that he's ordered a boat. There will be room for all his friends on this boat, he says, naming several dozen of them (the list varied slightly in different publications, but the Ungers were the only "family" ever included) before adding capaciously (and coyly), "All my friends! They know who they are." The boat Ray actually owned in 1984 was a used Bayliner runabout. Henry Carlile, the author of poems collected in *Running Lights* and *Rain*, went salmon fishing on the Bayliner after he met Ray at the Centrum conference in July. At the marina where Ray's used boat was moored, Carlile saw instantly that "Ray didn't know enough about boat handling and seamanship to be out on salt water, or any water for that matter. His mooring ropes were granny-knotted and tangled and too small. . . . I doubted that Ray had all the Coast Guard required equipment aboard, but I didn't ask."

". . . No one was more fun to fish with," Carlile found. "Catch a fish, or lose one, he'd yell and get so excited his hands would shake." At the end of the day, Carlile got worried again: "We were heading in, fast—too fast. . . . I kept searching nervously for flotsam—a saw butt, deadhead or floating log—that could punch a hole in our hull and sink us." They approached the harbor just as a big freighter was leaving it: "Ray correctly set a course to pass astern, but as we approached the freighter's considerable wake I saw, too late, that he had no intention of slowing down." They hit the wake at full throttle and "were instantly airborne, slamming back into the water with a bone-jarring crash. Ray chopped the throttle and turned and looked at me. 'Jesus!' he said, wide-eyed."[19]

When poets Mark Strand and Charles Wright visited, they caught five salmon while Ray "steered the boat and saw to their bait." That must have been an exceptional day, because Ray generally preferred—Carlile again—to keep the best fishing opportunities for himself: "Ray's competitiveness was well known to his fishing companions, and tolerated. There was nothing malicious about it. He was like a big kid who simply couldn't help himself, and we indulged him." After Strand and Wright left with their fish, Ray went home, napped, and then went out on his boat again, by himself, to catch the biggest fish of his lifetime. It was, he crowed in a letter to Curt Johnson, a twenty-four-pound king—"as big as a small person . . . an infant anyway."[20]

Another visitor to Port Angeles in 1984 was Haruki Murakami, who had recently translated a book of Carver's stories into Japanese. The book, titled *Where I'm Calling From,* was selling well in Japan and Ray was curious to know why.[21] Murakami's own fiction was not then available in English, so Ray could not have understood how deeply he had influenced his thirty-five-year-old Japanese counterpart. Murakami regarded Carver as "without question the most valuable teacher I ever had and also the greatest literary comrade." Carver served smoked salmon and black tea to Murakami and his wife, Yoko. When Ray drank from a teacup, Murakami thought, he "looked as though he was doing the wrong thing in the wrong place." Murakami audio-taped the meeting, but Ray's speech was so hesitant and quiet that the recording sounded "like little more than a badly done wire-tap." Ray's "massive physical size" surprised Murakami even more than his voice:

He sat on the sofa with his body crouched up as if to say that he had never intended to get so big, and he had an embarrassed expression on his face. Even the movements of his face were excessive; each time he laughed or became perplexed, his expression changed drastically and abruptly. It was not so much that his expressions were extreme as that the effort involved was so great that his movements became exaggerated as well. I had never met up with such a physically imposing writer. And it was also the first time I had met one with such an unassuming and gentle air.

The Murakamis stayed only two hours but invited Carver and Gallagher to visit them in Japan. Back home, the enormously productive Murakami began his breakthrough novel, *Hard-boiled Wonderland and the End of the World,* which appeared in Japan in 1985. His translation of Carver's *At Night the Salmon Move* appeared the same year.[22]

Summer visitors and salmon fishing were distractions Ray could deal with easily given the knowledge that he didn't have to return to teaching for many semesters to come. He took further contentment from the fact that both his children were doing well. Vance, now twenty-five, had completed a summer program in Europe and was studying French in Aix-en-Provence. Christine, twenty-six, was also "fine," attending college classes, attending Alcoholics Anonymous meetings with her mother, and taking steps to manage her own life. Ella Carver, now seventy-one, continued to worry him, particularly since she'd decided to follow Ray to Port Angeles. Ray couldn't resist his mother when she set her mind on something, so he helped her find a house to rent and gave the landlord a deposit. Then the three of them—Ray, Ella, and Tess—went to visit relatives in Bellingham. In a letter sent to Chris just after that visit, Ray asked his daughter to send him (in a book mailer) some "good weed like you sent me last spring."[23]

Ray had barely returned to Port Angeles when he learned that his father's older brother, Fred Edward Carver, aged eighty-one, had died in Sacramento. At the funeral in Yakima, relatives noticed Ray's Mercedes and his well-fitting suit, and they noticed that he "had a pad in his hand when we were all gathered around the backyard laughing and talking, and he was so interested in what everybody said. He was always writing notes on his little pad—you could see his mind was always going."[24]

Ray and Tess closed out the summer with a trip to the Oregon Shakespeare Festival and a detour through Ray's birthplace, Clatskanie, Oregon. Ray autographed his books at the library, found the building where he'd been born, and signed a log of babies who'd been delivered by "Doc" Wooden. The *Clatskanie Chief*'s Deborah Steele Hazen caught up with Ray and Tess in a booth of the Camel Room at Hump's (Humphrey's) Restaurant. Tess and Hazen talked more than Ray did, but Hazen, who heard later about Carver's alcoholism, recognized Ray as a man who'd been through spiritual hell." Hazen mailed the famous native son a copy of his birth announcement. "I made the front page of the paper in 1938, and then, forty-six years later, there I am on the front page once more," he replied. "I like that kind of circularity. Life is a mystery."[25]

Did anyone in Clatskanie tell Ray that the Indian word *tlats-kani,* from which the town derives its name, signifies a system of waterways and portages by which native people traveled? If so, he could not have overlooked the echo of that concept and, indeed, of the place itself in his forthcoming book of poems. His choice to visit his birthplace now (rather than on dozens of previous drives up and down Interstate 5) confirmed his new roots in the West. "The places where water comes together / with other water" are "holy places," for Carver. At the edge of Clatskanie, the 1,210-mile-long Columbia River carries water from Omak and Yakima—indeed from a quarter-million square miles of the West. This is the only stretch of the river itself, one historian writes, that still looks as it did to the early explorers. Here in his native landscape, he must have sensed that the disparate sources of his self and work were "coming together" like the springs and rills and creeks and streams that feed the Columbia.

Ray returned east for the launch of Vintage Contemporaries. Lorraine Louie's design for *Cathedral* became the prototype for the entire VC line. Uniform spines with bold lettering (C A R V E R in white against a red field) invited buyers to collect these books and display them on their shelves. An illustration for the 1984 edition conveyed the surreal and dangerous psychology of Carver's prose: the head of a peacock whose fierce red eye and iridescent feathers belied the trim Victorian house behind it. A grid of pixels on each volume alluded to the comics: Roy Lichtenstein paintings for readers.[26] Fisketjon rolled out his series with dinners and nightclub parties and a major sales push. Vintage Contemporaries filled Manhattan bookstore windows. There were sidewalk sandwich boards, posters, and display bins. For Ray, the rollout began with a dinner at Café de Bruxelles, where he shared a big table with VC authors Crumley, McInerney, and McGuane, and editor Tom Jenks. After dinner, as the rest of the "distinctly male crowd" prepared to move on to a nightclub, "Ray, amid teasing about running off somewhere to see a woman, put himself in a taxi and headed for his hotel room alone. . . . there was no doubt he meant to keep himself out of trouble," Jenks said. Indeed, Ray did have a date with a woman—he and Tess had a standing arrangement to telephone each other at ten on evenings when they were apart. Still, Jenks noticed, Ray "was fair game for the friendly taunts that followed him into the cab."[27]

For several weeks, *Cathedral* and *Bright Lights, Big City* alternated in the first and second places in the *Village Voice*'s idiosyncratic bestseller list. Carver's blurb appeared prominently on the front cover of his student's book. By the end of 1986, *Bright Lights, Big City* had sold three hundred thousand copies and a movie was in the works. McInerney, who had been living on a $6,000 doctoral fellowship and a part-time job as a liquor store clerk in Syracuse, left grad school. If Ray felt any envy about the success that had come so quickly for his thirty-year-old student, he never revealed it. "Ray was proud of Jay," Unger said, "but any of us who knew him up close would not have wanted what Jay had. . . . There were a lot of students that Ray thought really had what it takes to be a writer."[28]

When Bert Babcock, a limited-editions publisher and dealer in rare books, met Carver in 1982, he speculated that Ray's manuscripts and correspondence might be worth $25,000 or $30,000. Ray replied, "That's $25,000 more than I thought," indicating that he might have donated them to Syracuse University. The archive project languished until November 1984, when Babcock made three trips to Syracuse to appraise the papers. Ray gave him access to fourteen boxes in the basement at Maryland Avenue, and Babcock inventoried the manuscripts within the boxes. Most of these pages had accumulated since 1977, but the collection includes notebooks and other items from earlier dates. "Most of what is valuable these days I used to throw away," Ray explained to Kittredge, "and then much was lost in the various moves." Nonetheless, Ray was amused by the whole notion that the detritus of his literary endeavors might command—he and Babcock began to hope—six figures. While Babcock worked in the basement, Ray stayed in his study with the phone off the hook. He made no effort to control what papers Babcock included. He invited Babcock to go through unsorted boxes in his closets. It seemed to Babcock that Ray was not concerned about the completeness ("integrity") of his archive or successive versions of given stories or poems. After gathering Carver's papers, Babcock found that research libraries were faced with more archives available for purchase than they could afford. Former president Richard Nixon's attempt to take massive deductions for his own donated papers had led the IRS to rule that authors could not value their own archives at more than the cost of paper and ink. In order to keep the collection whole (rather than sell off individual items more profitably), Babcock had to find a middleman who was willing to purchase it and then donate it to a library. As a result, Carver's papers would stay in his Syracuse basement until late 1986. During those years, Carver's reputation increased, and he stored more papers in his Syracuse basement, though others remained in Port Angeles.

Babcock's early interest in Carver secured an important resource for scholars. Babcock sold the archive to Charles Apfelbaum, who further sorted and studied it for a few months before reselling its five thousand pages, including seven hundred pages of incoming correspondence, to the

William Charvat Collection of American Fiction at Ohio State University, at a reported price of $95,000. The archive includes typescripts of ten stories from Carver's later-disputed *What We Talk About When We Talk About Love* collection, all in versions longer than those that appeared in the book after Lish's editing. The acquisition did *not* include a typescript with editing marks or any correspondence between Carver and Lish relating to *What*. While explanations for this omission might be proposed, at the least it indicates that Carver did not intend to mark a trail that would invite future scholars to investigate Lish's editing of his books.[29]

The first inklings of respect from the official literary world that Ray Carver received as a young man had come from the annual anthologies called *Best American Short Stories*. That process came full circle when Houghton Mifflin invited Carver to edit the 1986 *BASS*. Series editor Shannon Ravenel would send her 120 favorite stories to Ray, and he would read his magazines with an eye out for stories that excited him. When he read a story that stirred him "to put it by for later," he wondered if Ravenel would choose that story as well. Thus he was ever, and still, the boy from Yakima, wondering how he measured up against the world beyond his ken.[30]

A similar revolution of fortune occurred when Science Research Associates, where Ray had twice worked and once been terminated, included "Neighbors" and "Photograph of My Father in His Twenty-second Year" in a textbook for junior-college students.[31]

In Port Angeles, writing poems and spending hours out of doors, Ray began to feel at home in the world. Perhaps only during his early boyhood and the first years of his marriage had he felt so grounded. He came east to be with Tess when she was teaching in Syracuse or to ply the literary trade in New York, but a date to return west was usually on his calendar. He invited friends old and new to fish with him in Port Angeles. Ray sometimes sent those who didn't come to Port Angeles padded packages that looked and felt like books. Inside his friends found vacuum-sealed packets of smoked salmon.

Though he acquired many new admirers and made new friends during the eighties, and an uncanny number of people considered him a dear friend, Ray's significant relationships continued to be with his ever-vexing family, with Tess Gallagher, and with writers who shared his love of storytelling and outdoor life. Richard Ford, now living in Missoula, where Kristina Ford was a city planner, remained one of his closest friends. Henry Carlile also became a confidant. When Carlile told Ray about marital problems he was having, "Ray didn't say anything. He smoked and looked out over the water. He'd been there. And he knew something I wasn't able to face yet." When Carlile and his wife separated, Ray "phoned to check up on me and wrote frequently. He took my grief seriously and assured me that it was possible to mend even after such a terrible loss." When Ray visited Carlile in his half-empty Portland home, he encouraged him to make a fresh start. "I think Ray felt a lot of guilt about his old life. . . . He remembered what it was like to have a part of his life end, and it brought us close."[32]

The winter holidays again raised the specter of the sort of archetypal family conflicts that most challenged Ray's sobriety and ability to live with paradoxes.

On December 14, 1984, in Port Angeles, Ray typed a long letter to Amy Unger. In it he unloaded long-simmering feelings about his family and money. He didn't even plan to reread this letter before he mailed it to her, he told Amy. The gist of this angry letter is that Ray no longer feels financially responsible for Maryann Carver. He repeats and underlines the phrase "I am no longer responsible" several times in the letter and insists that his emotional relationship with Maryann is over. "Tess is my wife now, in everything but name," he wrote. Since their voluntary divorce agreement, Ray had continued to send money to Maryann. According to Ray's letter, he had sent her a "wad" of money in November, bringing his 1984 payments to more than $5,000.[33] That he also provided substantial support to his mother and to his son further aggravated Ray's feeling that too much was expected of him. Though he also provided occasional sums to Chris, he adds that "she asks me for less, or nothing at all and so . . . she tends to get less than anyone. . . ."

Even though she had chosen not to pursue a more aggressive divorce settlement, Maryann believed she had a right to a portion of the proceeds from works written while they were married that continued to bring Ray success and income. She regarded his work as "family business." Of course, no one had ever expected that his writing income would amount to more than a professor's salary. The Strauss Living and the success of *Cathedral* in both hardcover and Vintage Contemporaries created the impression that his income had skyrocketed.

Maryann had dated other men since her separation from Ray, and in August 1984 she had married Laurent Girard, with whom she had been living for the past year. She married Girard, a Canadian, she said later, so he could continue working in the United States and probably would not have gotten married if the Immigration Department had not been pressuring Girard. Despite her marriage, Maryann's financial situation remained precarious. She owed estate taxes on the Burk family land she had inherited and had borrowed money to build a house on that property. "Mary-ann and I don't share any of the same dreams any longer, we don't value the same things, or set the same store by things, or even agree on much of anything," Ray wrote Amy, adding that he finds this "lamentable" and wishes they might someday "meet as friends and be comfortable in each other's company."[34]

In the past day, Ray told Amy, he had taken his mother out to dinner and given her a check, mailed Chris a check, and wired money to Vance in France. All of it, he confided to Amy, was making him resentful. He had decided that "everybody goes off the payroll next month, or rather, this month." Amy was "heartbroken" by the accusatory tone of Ray's letter to her, even though he had concluded it by saying he didn't want to "dump on her" but feared that she and Doug thought he could give his family more. When Amy explained her feelings, he telephoned to apologize, but Amy wondered if Gallagher had coached Ray in the composition of his uncharacteristically hard-line letter. Certainly Ray's feelings vacillated. He flinched from conflict and wanted everyone to thrive. Just the day before, he'd written his daughter, "Tell me how you are. You are on my mind tonight, and if you had a telephone I'd call you up. How are the kids?" Indeed, Unger recalled, "Ray always had a soft spot for Chris and wanted to help, but understood that there were times when he was killing her by helping, and that hurt him."[35]

Gallagher is not the only person who might have urged Ray to turn down requests for money. After listening to Ray's complaints about his family's demands, Carlile once "suggested as gently as I could that he might be part of the problem. 'You need to cut them off,' I told him. 'In the end, it's no good for anyone. It just creates guilt and resentment.' I resisted using the clichés codependent or enabler. 'I know, I know,' Ray said. But he went on giving until the end. He couldn't have done otherwise."[36]

Like many a father, Ray tended to blame his daughter's troubles on her boyfriend. Once when Ford and Carver were together in Provincetown, Ray was so agitated about his daughter's situation that, Ford writes, he said, "'I swear to God, Richard, I could put a contract out on this biker. I'd do it. I would. You know?' He looked at me, looked deviled by events. 'I'd kill him myself if I didn't know I'd get caught.'" Ford, who knew that Ray "liked to think I was a fierce man," told Ray he'd do the job himself if Ray would buy him a plane ticket to the West Coast. Instead of carrying out the preposterous plan, Ford and Carver wrote a story about it, in this case an eight-page movie treatment. In it a forty-year-old sportswriter travels to the rural Northwest, clumsily murders his friend's daughter's boyfriend, drives around with the daughter and her child for several days, talking about friendship and the dead boyfriend, and in the end leaves them in an all-night cafe. The sportswriter's act of perverse generosity is silent— he never tells his friend what he had done. In a closing scene, the father introduces his friend to his daughter and their eyes meet with shocked recognition. The movie was never made. No bikers were harmed.[37]

Ray planned to spend the winter and spring of 1985 in the West, as he'd done the two previous years. For the first quarter he and Gallagher rented a house near the University of Washington in Seattle, where she would be a visiting professor. Christine and her daughters, Windy and Chloe, visited him there in late January while he was correcting the bound galleys for his poetry collection, *Where Water Comes Together with Other Water*. Ray read the title poem to Chris and she responded with great enthusiasm. But when she read the whole book, two poems in it offended her, "My Daughter and Apple Pie" and "To My Daughter." The latter is an extended wish that his daughter not drink. He ends with advice: "It will kill you. Like it did your mother, and me. / Like it did." The middle of the poem refers to her drunk driving incident two years earlier. Now she felt exposed and hurt by what seemed to her a public betrayal. "When I first read 'Fires,' I told him, 'Dad, it's just not fair. People read your work. And some of those people know me. *My* professors, for instance. It's not right that they have this impression of me.' " But "Fires" had been about her youth. These poems opened fresher wounds. Chris recalled a phone conversation:

> I told him that it was impossible not to take something like this personally. He asked me somewhat sheepishly, "Is this going to affect our relationship?" and I replied, "I don't know, Dad. Maybe it will. Do you want it to? You need to realize that it is very important to me."
>
> At that point, he paused. He thought. It was a pivotal place for us. He was trying at this time to have a new relationship with our family. Finally, he said, "I'm sorry. I think you are right." And he stopped writing that way.[38]

Carver abided by his intention not to publish any more poems specifically about Chris, but the two offending ones stayed in the forthcoming book, and "To My Daughter" was reprinted in a British collection in 1987. He also continued to write about his family's requests for money in other poems and short stories. Of course, Ray knew, too, that an alcoholic is always "recovering," never "recovered." Gratitude and vigilance for his own recovery made him anxious over his daughter's.

Ray followed his phone call with Chris with a long letter of explanation. After apologizing for an "offense" the poems have given, Ray explained that he "had to write them." He reassured Chris that he didn't blame her for the problems he wrote about. As an artist, he explained, he had to bear witness to how things looked from his angle and couldn't shun things that were "'ugly' or unseemly" because doing so might leave him nothing to say: "I can't be any different than I am. . . . I hope you won't think ill of me ever because of what I write, or have written. But if you do, if it ever comes to more than just 'wishing I hadn't written this or that' . . . tell me; somehow we can still be friends and love each other."[39]

Marion Ettlinger took Carver's photograph for the dust jacket of *Where Water Comes Together with Other Water*. The striking result shows Ray's large, hairy forearms and hands as columns of flesh emerging from his dark sweater, nearly as prominent as his unflinchingly stare.* Future commercial editions of Carver's work would feature Ettlinger photographs. In Ettlinger's lens, anyway, Ray Carver knows what he's about. Printed on the covers of book after book, this photo would be the iconic representation of the author Raymond Carver. In an early poem Carver identified with his father, a man who wanted "to pose bluff and hearty for his posterity" but whose eyes and hands revealed timidity. Ettlinger's photos, and Ray's endorsement of the persona they convey, show how far his life and work had brought him. Ettlinger has said that Ray was aware of the impression he made during the photo shoot: "As gentle a guy as he was, he knew he could look really menacing, so he was great to photograph in that way."[40]

Still, this confident man needed marijuana to bring himself to rest in the evenings. Unlike many recovering alcoholics, Ray's craving for alcohol was apparently not awakened by other drugs. Stoned, Ray could step back from himself—ease his worried mind, as the song says—and entertain the doubleness of self that he'd felt so often in his life. Nowhere was this more evident than in his poetry.

By the time *Where Water Comes Together with Other Water* was published in May, Carver had accumulated enough poems for another book. These 1985 poems are longer and calmer in their meditations than any Carver had written before. About a visit to a place where he and Maryann had once lived, Carver writes in "Where They'd Lived" that cold air near a motel window "put its hand over his heart." That anthropomorphic image of "cold" touching with a "hand" is typical of the way Carver approaches a statement of feeling through a literal detail. "I loved you . . . / Before loving you no longer," he concludes.

Whether he no longer loved Maryann or, as some close friends privately

---

* Critics have favored "unflinching" to describe Carver's work ever since Leonard Gardner first used the word in his comment on *Will You Please Be Quiet, Please?*

believed, always loved her, during the spring of 1985, he and she began to speak often, as friends. She recalled that they "started talking every day, and he wrote an enormous batch of poems—he would call me and ask, 'How about this?' and read me something like 'A Poem Not Against Songbirds.' That's when we were just able, you know, to talk every day. He was out here and he had money."[41]

For 1984, Ray reported $36,000 in Schedule C income from his writing, after what seem reasonable deductions of $23,000 for expenses (agent's commissions, travel, and office costs). That, in addition to $35,000 from the Strauss Living gave him upward of $70,000. Out of that $8,000 went to federal income taxes. He took exemptions for the support of his mother and Vance (though Ella also had Social Security and Vance had student loans) and listed $4,800 in alimony payments to Maryann. Ray probably had about $40,000 a year to live on. Not great riches, to be sure, but sufficient for a full-time writer whose needs were expanding but not extravagant.[42]

Even as he prepared for an eight-day USIA-sponsored trip to Australia in early March, Ray longed to be back in his "little port, this safe haven" of Port Angeles. Sometimes, he said, he and Tess were like ostriches hiding their heads from the "heavy traffic" of the East Coast. Australia surprised him, though. He liked its remoteness and he had fun, including a $200 win at the horse races in Melbourne. When Picador's 447-page *Stories of Raymond Carver* came out Down Under, Ray was deluged by fan mail from Australian readers.[43]

By the time Gallagher's term at the University of Washington ended in March, Ray had decided that the one-bedroom Sky House lacked the privacy needed by two writers working day in and day out. To keep up the pace and intensity they both preferred, they would need more space. In Port Angeles they found a two-story clapboard Victorian with a picket fence and fruit trees set on a bluff above a plywood factory and the marina where Ray kept his boat. It must have been built by people of means around the turn of the century, for it is the most substantial house in a neighborhood of small houses and weedy yards that resembles the south Yakima tracts where Ray grew up. Gallagher and Carver purchased the house jointly for $72,500 in April 1985. Ray chose an upstairs room with a window facing the strait to become his workplace.[44]

Ray made a round of readings to promote *Where Water Comes Together with Other Water.* In New York City, he appeared at the 92nd Street Y on a bill with Irish novelist Edna O'Brien, and heard actor Stephen Lang read his story "What Is It?" at Symphony Space. At Harvard, he read "Careful" and had the audience "howling" with laughter over the man whose ear is plugged with wax. His schedule looked grueling, with stops in the Midwest as well, but Tobias Wolff noticed that Ray lapped up attention paid to him with "unfeigned childish delight. It didn't seem to wear him down at all." There's a saying of Chuang Tzu's that fit Ray, Wolff thought: " 'Good fortune is as light as a feather, but few can carry it.' Ray could."[45]

Ray was back in Port Angeles for the first week of May, at his post overlooking the harbor. His desk and his chair were the only furniture in his house.

CHAPTER 28

Ultramarine

May 1985–September 1987, Port Angeles and Syracuse

Hemingway did his work, and he'll last. Any biographer who gives him less than this, granting the chaos of his public and personal life, might just as well write the biography of an anonymous grocer or a woolly mammoth. Hemingway, the writer—he's still the hero of the story, however it unfolds.

> —Raymond Carver, in a review
> of two biographies of Hemingway[1]

In the last five years of his life, Ray Carver completed and readied for publication seven short stories and 204 poems. The Strauss Living award enabled him to work on whatever he wanted, and Fisketjon, his friend and editor, was happy to publish the poems at Random House.[2] All three major books he published in these years were dedicated to Tess Gallagher, and both poetry books close with poems written for her. "I'm grateful to you, you see. I wanted to tell you," is the last line of *Where Water Comes Together with Other Water*. *Ultramarine* concludes with a long poem called "The Gift" that makes more explicit the nature of Ray's gratitude to Tess. Writing in first person, Carver portrays himself and Tess in conversation about a night just past when neither slept well. They are "calm and tender" with each other,

> As if we knew what the other was feeling. We don't,
> of course. We never do. No matter.
> It's the tenderness I care about. That's the gift . . .

With almost a decade of sobriety behind him, Gallagher wrote, "Ray's face lost an almost bloated vagueness it had carried when I'd first met him.

The jawline firmed up and the muscled places, where humor and a sense of confident well being had come together, seemed to restore a youthful mischief to his looks."³ He also bought better clothes, dressed more carefully, learned to look comfortable in a suit and tie, and allowed Tess to keep his wavy salt-and-pepper hair neatly trimmed.

Some have speculated that Gallagher influenced Ray's outpouring of poems during the 1980s or that he wrote poems when he was stuck in his fiction. Gallagher herself called poetry "the spiritual current out of which he moved to write the short stories." But the poems were not merely a means to the short stories. They exist, as Stephen Dobyns puts it, "to define moments of emotion and wonder" and to celebrate "small occasions of fragile contentment, of time lived instead of time passing." These moments are understood to represent more than themselves, but don't demand interpretation. They are, Dobyns continues, "not critic's poems" but "reader's poems."⁴

While Carver was writing poems, Gallagher, inspired by him, had turned her hand to short fiction.⁵ Her version of her blind friend Jerry Carriveau's visit to Syracuse appeared in the *Ontario Review* in 1983, and magazines from *Antaeus* to the *New Yorker* published Gallagher's fiction as well as Carver's. Ray told Amy Unger that he worked with Tess on her stories, some of which hinged on situations from their shared lives. "He'd go over my stories very closely," Gallagher said, praising Ray's abilities to make deletions and general comments. All their work together was, she said, "an extraordinary collaboration of hearts and imaginations."⁶ In her story "King Death," a woman lives alone in Tucson when her husband, a salesman and recovering alcoholic, is transferred to another city. "Beneficiaries" explores a woman's jealousy of her husband's children by a former marriage. "Turpentine" shares details with Carver's "Where I'm Calling From" and, like his "Vitamins," focuses on a door-to-door saleswoman.

In 1985, Gallagher gathered her stories into a collection that was accepted for publication by Ted Solotaroff at Harper & Row. When Solotaroff first read the manuscript, he told Gallagher he wanted to present her work as "stories by the poet Tess Gallagher rather than as stories by someone from the same stable as Ray Carver." She agreed to that but then sent "a story about a blind man who is invited to their home and who the husband becomes very spooked by. I said to Tess, 'If we include this, it will completely undo any attempt I can make to keep your fiction separate from Ray's because "Cathedral" is very well known.'" Solotaroff recalled that Gallagher, "got very angry and said, 'Ray doesn't have a right to that material. The blind man was my friend, not Ray's,' as though that settled the matter."*[7]

By the mideighties Carver and Gallagher worked closely on many projects. Their screenplay about Dostoyevsky, which Ray originally contracted to write by himself, appeared as a jointly authored excerpt in a Capra Press Back-to-Back edition. Like many writers who are first readers for other writers, Gallagher sometimes made her suggestions by simply adding words. Ray "credited Tess with inspiring him," Tom Jenks observed, "not as a collaborator or even as an editor, but as someone who could give him a nudge and set an idea into motion."[8]

On May 9, Ray and Tess went to England for a book tour arranged by *Granta* editor Bill Buford and Carver's two British publishers, Picador and Collins Harvill. After his arrival at the Sheraton Belgravia Hotel, still jet-lagged, Ray gave a videotaped interview to David Sexton for the *Literary Review*. Looking pale in a white shirt under bright lights, Ray told Sexton he'd started writing with "very low expectations" and, with his work now translated into twenty-some languages, still found it strange to talk about "Carver stories." Richard Ford and Tobias Wolff were also touring England. Carver's essay "Friendship" finds its starting point in a photograph taken by Allan Titmuss after a reading the three friends and fiction writer Elizabeth Tallent gave at the National Poetry Centre. Carver meditates on the dream that friendship might be a "permanent thing" and ruefully reminds himself that such things last only to a point: "Chances are that two of the three friends in this picture will have to gaze upon the remains—the *remains*—of the third friend, when that time comes . . . the only alternative to burying your friends is that they will have to bury you."[9]

Ted and Virginia Solotaroff also saw Ray and Tess in London. When they visited the Victoria and Albert Museum together, the Solotaroffs thought that Ray and Tess seemed like innocents abroad: "Ray was kind of 'oh gosh' while Tess was more like 'I wonder what that costs,'" Ted said. He found Ray "extremely sober and self-contained, careful in what he said and yet inordinately proud of this English tweed jacket he was wearing." Gallagher, on the other hand, was "kind of starstruck by tapestries and things that were ornate, material things that were obviously worth a lot of money rather than antiquities *per se*."[10]

---

* Gallagher has published the two stories together with commentary emphasizing her friendly competition with Carver: "He was like the cat that swallowed the mouse whole, after he wrote his story. He knew I had intended to write about it but he didn't let that stand in his way."

Ray went with Tess to Ireland, where she knew several Irish poets and musicians. "Never, under any circumstances, rent a car and drive it in Ireland," Ray cautioned McInerney afterward. Part of the difficulty was the Irish hospitality of music and drinks. Ray didn't want to be in the pubs and often excused himself for an early night's rest. He did write a poem, "The Schooldesk," about a rainy day in a cottage near Lough Arrow in County Sligo where Tess had visited annually since 1968.[11] And he relished a tour of the James Joyce Museum in an old Martello Tower overlooking Dublin Bay, the setting for the opening scene of *Ulysses*. Afterward, Ray visited with eighty-five-year-old Sean O'Faolain and his wife. The novelist and short story writer had known "everybody, inc. Joyce," Ray noted. Literary reminiscences interested Ray as he began to think of himself as a man of letters in the process of creating his own legacy. Among friends, Carver and Gallagher sometimes said to one another, "We're out there in history now, Babe."[12]

Ray truncated his trip to Ireland by four days, was stranded in Holland by an air-traffic controllers' strike that caused him to miss Fisketjon's wedding, and arrived back in Port Angeles on June 6, grateful to be home. He and Tess immediately set about making their new household, buying furniture, hiring a gardener, getting things cleaned, repaired, and painted. Tess's brother, Morris Bond stacked fireplace wood in their basement and helped Ray launch his boat. By the end of June, Ray was nearly settled in the house on B Street, though he had to replace his marijuana stash, which was lost during the move.[13] Ray and Tess gained solitude from their two-house arrangement, even as they both maintained desks in both houses. Ray's mother, living in Port Angeles since the previous summer, had now decided she'd be happier in California. After clearing out her house, she spent a night with Ray and Tess and drove herself back to the care of James in Sacramento. Before she left, Ray arranged to give her a sum of money semiannually and hoped that this would provide her with enough financial security to settle down and stay out of his hair. Tess noticed that Ella's annual moves "inadvertently guaranteed that she would have the attention and resources of her two sons for a concentrated two-month period each year."[14]

Ella's "sad odysseys" soon became material for the first short story Carver had written in three years. "Boxes" encompasses frustration, compassion, and acceptance in its narrator's relationship to his seventy-year-old mother who suffers a severe case of "the grass is always greener on the other side" syndrome. Most of the story takes place during a single evening when the mother, on the verge of leaving a rented house in Washington to move to an apartment in California, asks her son and his friend to help eat the

food in her refrigerator. The mother fries a chicken. Jill, who's known the
son only a few months, tries delicately to reason with the mother. The son
knows there's no point in doing so. When Jill tells the mother "your son is
worried sick about you," the mother responds, "How do you think I must
feel?" During dinner, the son/narrator reflects on the year his mother has
lived in his town. Once he listened to her complaints on the phone while
watching a man working on a utility pole. Only a safety belt keeps the
man from falling to his death. It's the kind of detail that serves Carver as an
objective correlative for an emotion without standing out as imagery. The
mother has no safety belt. The son asks what he can do to help:

> "Honey, you can't do anything," she said. "The time for doing any-
> thing has come and gone. . . . I wanted to like it here. I thought we'd go on
> picnics and take drives together. . . . You're always busy. You're off work-
> ing, you and Jill. You're never at home. Or else if you are at home you
> have the phone off the hook all day. Anyway, I never see you," she said.

Ella Carver was hurt and angered by "Boxes." She told an interviewer that
she threw it across the floor when she first read it. Like the couple in "Are
These Actual Miles?" who so value their red convertible, the mother in
"Boxes" believes her happiness depends on possessions and surroundings:
"All I want is a house and a town to live in that will make me happy. That
isn't a crime, is it?" she demands.

The mother makes her departure. A few days later she calls from California. Things are not as perfect as she remembered there. The son listens,
helpless:

> I don't know why, but it's then I recall the affectionate name my dad
> used sometimes when he was talking nice to my mother—those times,
> that is, when he wasn't drunk. . . . "*Dear*," he'd say. He called her "dear"
> sometimes—a sweet name. . . .
> The word issues from my lips before I can think what else I want to
> say to go along with it. "Dear." I say it again. I call her "dear." "Dear, try
> not to be afraid," I say.

In this moment, the son grows up. He becomes his father. The story could
end here. Had Lish edited it, it might have ended sooner, with raw frustration. But Carver builds on that moment of internal quietus. Again he tells
us what the son sees through his window as he talks. He sees someone driving up to a house down the street. A porch light comes on. The two people embrace and go inside. In a few minutes the porch light goes off again.

Through that image, Carver shows that the son understands his mother's loneliness. And the story has one more dimension. At its beginning and end, Jill pages through the Sears catalog for curtains. She has moved into the son's house and she thinks it needs curtains. The son doesn't "care five cents for curtains." But he doesn't tell Jill that. He's content that this woman, who has had plenty of troubles of her own, is making a home with him.[15]

Vance Carver, having completed an internship in a European Economic Community law office in Brussels, was back in Washington, DC, to finish his master's degree at American University. There he married Ingeborg (Inge) Behrend, a German airline attendant he'd met in Aix-en-Provence the previous summer. After Vance received his degree in July, he and Inge moved to Germany, where Vance began teaching at the American military base in Wiesbaden and studying German. Their only child, Jennifer Vanessa Carver, was born in Germany on September 11, 1985. From then on, Vance would be financially independent of his father. For the next seventeen years, he would live and work in Germany.

Christine continued at Whatcom Community College, taking general courses and training to be a medical assistant. She turned to her father when her car's transmission blew up, when her bills were overdue, or she wanted to send her daughters to dance lessons or camp. During the daytime, Ray could put his family's concerns out of mind, but in late evening "it begins to pick at me and worry me. . . . Guilt, I guess . . ." At the end of September, Ray mailed his daughter some postcards and a check, optimistically qualifying his gift by adding, "when you get rich, and I'm old and impoverished, you can help me out."[16]

By July 1, Ray was going to his desk every morning, not writing anything new but shaping his next book of poems. He took his title and epigraph from "Mt. Gabriel" by Irish poet Derek Mahon:

> . . . sick with exile, they yearn homeward now, their eyes
> Tuned to the ultramarine, first-star-pierced dark
> Reflected on the dark, incoming waves . . .[17]

Ultramarine—the deepest, richest, most precious blue—here represents the way Carver has come to see himself, as an artist working between the blue darkness above and the blue water below. He's a solitary soul reporting on his passage through this life: "I lay in the channel of sleep. Attached / to this world by nothing more than hope . . ." ("Spell"). In *Ultramarine* Carver is determined not to reject any subject. The poem called "What

You Need for Painting" serves as a manifesto for the book. Shaped from a letter by Renoir, the poem lists tools and colors—including rose madder, raw umber, white lead, ivory black, and ultramarine—before coming to its closing lines:

> Indifference to everything except your canvas
> The ability to work like a locomotive
> An iron will.

Those are the things Carver sought and to a degree achieved in his Port Angeles years, years that offered less melodrama than his drinking years but needful sustenance for his work. In the poems he was remaking himself and his art, inventing forms that allowed him to make quick, deep dives into the heart of material. Another entry in "Stupid," a poem that moves between smoking marijuana, a winter storm, and his family's need for money, breaks out with this rhetorical declaration: "So what / if he'd rather be remembered in the dreams of strangers?" That doubleness of being that he felt even as a boy now emerges in a new form as he lives in the present and contemplates his life as history. Many of these poems end with death. So frequently does he end a poem with death that it may be seen as a poetic device for closure. Ray's fixation on death was not so much a death wish (he'd had that, and finished with it when he quit drinking) as an attitude of acceptance.

After entertaining a parade of summer visitors, Ray stayed in Port Angeles to fish and write when Tess returned to Syracuse in the fall. His fishing, especially when Tess wasn't along, often led to mishaps. Carlile had given Ray a copy of the classic reference *Chapman Piloting, Seamanship & Small-Boat Handling,* but Ray never read the book. He knew a couple of fishing knots and those were the ones he used, appropriately or not. When his tackle needed attention, such as cleaning or spooling with line, he took it into a shop.

Carlile bought the boat-handling guide for Ray after hearing a story from Morris Bond about a day when he refused to go out with Ray because he could smell a gas leak. Even a spark from the ignition could have blown up the boat, and Ray lit a lot of cigarettes. But Ray left Morris on the dock and headed past Ediz Hook until he ran out of gas. He sat and fished as a strong tide pushed the boat along. He didn't radio the Coast Guard for help because he knew they'd cite him for a safety violation. After he slammed into a big red buoy and nearly capsized, some fishermen saw Ray's predicament and towed him. Ray made Bond promise not to tell Tess what had happened. A telltale red streak on the side of Ray's boat probably gave him away.[18]

The red buoy came to be known as "Ray's buoy" among friends who were awed by his survival on the water. Often, too, Ray repeated the injunction not to tell Tess what had happened. As Bond said later, "Ray was a funny fisherman. He'd drag anything that glittered. His string of lures looked like Las Vegas. We hollered at him one time, 'Hey, Ray, you are fishing the wrong way, fish with the tide!' About that time he hauled in a thirty-pounder. He was an unconscious fisherman!" Ray "caught fish despite himself," Carlile thought.[19]

As much as he loved the West, Ray told a correspondent, he also missed the East. When he got there, though, the season became "long" and "trying." First, there were complications stemming from one of Amy Unger's manic episodes. Then both Ray and Tess succumbed to bouts of flu and laryngitis. Despite illness, Ray made several trips to New York City to give readings. He also wrote a review of biographies of Ernest Hemingway by Peter Griffin and Jeffrey Meyers. Carver praises the intimacy of Griffin's work on Hemingway's early years, but finds Meyers's book "depressing": "The reader is battered with one display after another of mean-spiritedness and spite, of vulgar and shabby behavior." Among the behaviors Carver singles out is Hemingway's disinheritance of his sons. Carver quotes Meyers's suggestion that it might have been good for Hemingway's reputation if he'd been killed in one of his accidents and "gone out in a literal blaze of glory . . . before he began to decline and waste away."[20]

In January 1986, Carver again gave his serious attention to fiction. He promised Knopf a new book of short stories to be edited by Gottlieb. This commitment he regarded as "being back in harness"—as opposed to the freedom of writing poems that he'd enjoyed since he turned in *Cathedral* in 1983. "I like a harness, by the way—I think it's the thing for me," he wrote Tobias Wolff. Better yet, Knopf would, he said, "line his pockets." At his house on B Street, he canceled a steelhead fishing trip and began spending ten to twelve hours a day at his desk. Soon two stories were under way.[21]

At the same time, Ray completed his selections for *Best American Short Stories 1986* and wrote a defense of realistic fiction to introduce the collection. All the stories he chose, as he sees them, have to do "with family, with other people, with community." One of these was "Bad Company" from Gallagher's forthcoming book of stories. Though he doesn't say so in the introduction, loyalty to his friends—friends who were good writers—counted with Ray. To him, helping a friend was simply passing on his good luck.[22]

The most impassioned passage of his introduction is about luck:

Once in a great while lightning strikes. . . . It may hit the man or woman who is or was your friend, the one who drank too much, or not at all, who went off with someone's wife, or husband, or sister, after a party you attended together. The young writer who sat at the back of the class and never had anything to say about anything. The dunce, you thought. The writer who couldn't, not in one's wildest imaginings, make the list of top ten possibilities.

Ray had been all the people he lists—the drunk and the teetotaler, the philanderer, the dunce. He knew that there was no assurance that the best writers enjoy the most success. But he'd also been the one that lightning struck. So he believed that it was all right to help his friends. Who else would? And why not, especially if he also helped a few good writers he'd never heard of before? Thus, he balanced the odds, had his cake and ate it, too, and tried to keep everyone happy. Lightning strikes, he continues, "But it will never, never happen to those who don't work hard at it and who don't consider the act of writing as very nearly the most important thing in their lives, right up there next to breath, and food, and shelter, and love, and God."

Ray rarely went in for philosophical talk. Experience had taught him that "luck" and "fun" ought not to be questioned. And yet another part of him did believe, had to believe, that luck came to those who deserved it. That he deserved it. And that the making of stories was a worthy thing to devote one's life to. Closing his introduction, Carver hopes that readers will find in these stories "nothing less, really, than beauty given form and made visible in the incomparable way only short stories can do."[23]

Another anthology was also in the works. Jenks asked Ray to coedit a follow-up collection to Robert Penn Warren and Albert Erskine's 1954 volume, *Short Story Masterpieces*. Jenks's proposal for *American Short Story Masterpieces* fetched a $100,000 advance from Delacorte/Dell, which owned the precursor. Narrowing the field to American work from the past thirty-three years, Carver and Jenks chose stories that had "a strong narrative drive, with characters we could respond to as human beings. . . ." Using Jenks's proposal as a template, Ray wrote the introduction. The American writers Ray respected most are in this book.[24] For his own contribution, Ray took Jenks's suggestion of the rarely anthologized "Fever." But it was Ray who proposed Richard Brautigan's story "1/3, 1/3, 1/3," a piece of dark humor about extraordinary ambition. In it a welfare mother, sawmill's night watchman, and a drifter who owns a typewriter, all living under "a black rainy toothache sky" in the rural Northwest, set out to write a novel. As writer, editor, and typist they each intend to get a third of the profits: they are "sitting there in that rainy trailer, pounding at the gates of American literature." Was not that more or less how Ray had begun?[25]

Now many of those gates opened easily for him. "Boxes" appeared in the *New Yorker* in February 1986, followed in April by "Whoever Was Using This Bed." The magazine offered him a first-look contract and $700 honorarium in exchange for right of first refusal on all of his stories for the year. Next he wrote "Intimacy." Most of that story is a pyrotechnical monologue delivered by a former wife whose manner of speaking strikingly resembles Maryann's. It is seen as a tribute to Maryann by some readers, by others as an outrageous betrayal of her. But most can agree that it shows that Maryann Burk Carver retained a vibrant hold on her former husband's imagination.[26] She herself sidesteps the question of the story's source: "I was so deep in that relationship, and he was too, that pat clichés don't cut it. We'd been in it forever . . . It takes a story like 'Intimacy' to say what the psychologists merely hint at. Our emotions were so real, and raw, and overwhelming, we strongly affected each other always, together or apart."[27]

Vance and Inge and their year-old daughter, who flew cheaply because Inge worked for Lufthansa Airlines, stayed with Ray in Port Angeles for several days in February. After they departed, Ray received word that his brother, James, was behind on his house payments because of medical expenses for his wife and that his cousin Robert Archer was dying of brain cancer. In March, Tess was taken ill. Ray confided to his daughter that it had been "a hard business" for Tess. After a surgical procedure, she stayed at her mother's for the several weeks of her recovery, explaining to friends that Ray was writing stories and seemed baffled when she was ill.[28]

While Tess was still recovering, Ray drove south to see Carlile and give a reading at Portland State. He checked Carlile's medicine cabinet for pharmaceuticals that might help him get through the reading but found nothing to his taste. Then, sensing that he might be getting a cold, he "chugged down an alarming number of vitamin C tablets" to give the virus a preemptive strike. Instead, the pills struck Ray with a massive case of diarrhea. "It was nip and tuck," Carlile recalled, "whether Ray would make his reading, but a couple of heavy hits of Pepto-Bismol saved the day." To a packed room, including a group from Clatskanie, Ray read "Whoever Was Using This Bed." Perhaps Gallagher's recent surgery had prompted this story that combines elements of Carver's early and late styles. There's an ominous wrong-number caller (as in "Are You a Doctor?") and a wife who can't get back to sleep and likes to tell her dreams (as in "The Student's Wife"). During sleepless predawn hours, the couple sit up at the foot of their bed and discuss scenarios for their deaths. The wife asks her husband to promise he'll "pull the plug" if she is ever dependent on life-support machines. The husband, in contrast, resolves that "As long as people can stand the sight of me . . . don't unplug anything. Let me keep going, okay? Right to the bitter end. Invite my friends in to say good-bye." The story's title refers to the bed as seen by a couple seated at the foot of it: "It looks like whoever was using this bed left in a hurry. . . . We're into something now, but I don't know what, exactly."

What they're into is mortality: looking at the world, as they're looking at their bed, and seeing themselves absent. Dead and gone. Carlile brooded about this story. He knew that Tess and her mother were worried about Ray's chain-smoking. After the reading, Carlile told Ray about some close calls he'd had recently on his motorcycle: "I've never liked the damned things," Ray said. "I lost John Gardner to a motorcycle, and I don't care to lose another friend that way." Carlile offered Ray a deal: "I'll sell my motorcycle if you promise to give up smoking." Ray agreed. A couple of months later, Carlile phoned Ray. When Tess answered, he told her, "Tell Ray he can quit smoking now. I sold my bike." Carlile could tell that Tess knew nothing of his pact with Ray. When Carlile explained, Tess "was overjoyed. But in the background, Ray said, 'I did not!' " Carlile read Ray a letter in which he'd promised to quit as soon as he finished his book of stories. Ray laughed and said, "Well, I lied. But I got you to sell your motorcycle, didn't I?"[29]

After an April trip to New York, Ray's daughter flew over from Bellingham for a weekend visit and Ray gave her start-up money for a business idea. Chris planned to sell sodas to motorists waiting in line to cross the border into Canada when the Expo 86 world's fair opened in Vancouver in May. Ray asked Chris what she thought of "Blackbird Pie" as a title for a story. "I said, well, let's remember the nursery rhyme ["Sing a Song of Sixpence"] and I reminded him of it, about how the crows came and nipped off her nose and this and that. And he used that title."[30]

"Blackbird Pie" turned out to be the final piece of a six-story suite, all using first-person narration and drawing upon family material. "Intimacy," declined by the New Yorker, was slated for Esquire's August fiction issue. "Menudo," appeared in Granta early in 1987. When Charles McGrath sent "Blackbird Pie" around at the magazine's editorial office, "Everyone thought Ray was going off in a new and terrifically exciting direction." The New Yorker ran "Blackbird Pie" on July 7, 1986. The run of stories stopped in May. Ray had worked his typewriter so hard that he had to send it in for repairs.[31] He did not write any more stories that year, and he did not turn in a manuscript for an all-new collection to Knopf in the fall of 1986, as he had hoped, or even in the spring of 1987, as he had promised. Though Ray had willingly taken the "harness" of a commitment to a new book of stories, he lost interest, or balked, or was dissatisfied with the results of his further efforts after six months.

Yet these stories possess a new subtlety and seriousness, as well as a different narrative tone, that cause one to wish Carver had been able to continue in this vein. "Blackbird Pie" is Carver's last stalking of the subject matter that had absorbed his attention for all his writing years, the "he-she" story (unless one counts the weaker and somewhat redundant stories posthumously collected in *Call If You Need Me,* whose dates of composition and place in the development of Carver's work are still uncertain). "Blackbird Pie" is the story of a night when a wife leaves her husband. At the beginning of the story, she slides a letter under the door of the locked study where the husband is working. Then some horses appear in the yard of the couple's rented house. A sheriff investigates. In the end, a rancher collects his horses, and the departing wife catches a ride to the bus depot with him. The situation draws upon the days Ray and Maryann lived in McKinleyville in 1977. At the end of the story, the now-unmarried narrator, who is a history buff, says, "I'm outside history now—like horses and fog." He means that he no longer exists in relationship to his wife, so there will be no more to say unless "my wife writes more letters, or tells a friend who keeps a diary, say."

What separates "Blackbird Pie" from Carver's other attempts to tell the history of his first marriage is its voice. Its first-person narrator is loquacious, a bit fatuous about his accomplishments, and emotionally distant and unreliable. His speech has a certain evasive courtliness reminiscent of the vacuum cleaner salesman in "Collectors" or Myers in "Compartment." This narrator/husband insists that the letter slid under his door, which he has not read in its entirety, cannot have been written by his wife, "or if she *did* write it, [is] then discredited by the fact that she didn't write it in her own handwriting." It is, as critic Randolph Runyon notes, "a story based on an obvious impossibility" and thus takes its lineage from Kafka, Calvino, Borges—writers who use fabulist propositions to psychological purposes.[32]

The impossible textual puzzle of the letter from the wife that is not in her handwriting becomes solvable when one realizes that the husband is unable to read his wife's handwriting because of alcoholism or another form of illness and self-absorption that has paralyzed him emotionally. The story clothes a well-worn truth: people change and are no longer recognizable to their own spouses. Through the lens of biography, one sees that Ray stayed married to his first sweetheart through two decades of extreme change until he barely recognized her as the woman he'd married.[33] Before that marriage was legally ended, he began an intense relationship with another strong woman who saw to his domestic arrangements and supported his artistic work and mirrored him even more in that she was a successful writer herself. Did she also change, or did Carver fear she would change in ways that would make her unrecognizable to him?

"Blackbird Pie" is a symbol hunter's delight: horses, fog, men wearing uniforms and cowboy hats, a wife in high heels on a rural road, a husband who cannot bestir himself to investigate a noise outside his room. As Runyon suggests, "Blackbird Pie," might be interpreted as "a testament to the pressure that builds when two writers inhabit the same household."[34] As such it is a recognition that the kind of love Mel the cardiologist and all of Carver's earlier couples desire—submersion in the other—cannot be sustained. In his poems Carver indicates several times that in his relationship with Gallagher he did not expect to bridge the chasm of otherness that separates individuals. He valued the knowledge that he was loved without expecting to know everything about his beloved. The end of "Blackbird Pie" sums up this change in Ray's emotional expectations: "That's when it dawns on me that autobiography is the poor-man's history. And I am saying good-bye to history. Good-bye, my darling."

Carver was increasingly professional about his personal history. He collected and resold his own small-press broadsides, holiday cards, and books and saved his manuscripts, page proofs, and galleys. When Ralph Sipper, a rare books and manuscripts dealer from Santa Barbara, offered to purchase such materials, Ray replied that he was saving the versions of the stories that would make up his new book "as I go along, and not feeling self-conscious about it." Sipper spent a day with Ray in August and paid $3,750 for five or six story manuscripts, which eventually ended up in the Charvat Collection.[35]

Ray attended two very different reunions in 1986. In May, he was one of the stars among four hundred writers who attended a fifty-year jubilee celebration of the Iowa Writers' Workshop. Director Frank Conroy told Ray that they considered him an alum even though he'd never finished his degree. Program administrator Connie Brothers procured a cake to celebrate Ray's forty-eighth birthday, but before the candles could be lit, she noticed that a big chunk had been cut from it! The culprit was never identified, but strong suspicion rested on Ray. At the jubilee, Ray appeared on a panel with Bob Shacochis and T. Coraghessan Boyle, but few heard what Ray said despite an admonishment from Tess, who reportedly called out "Speak up, dear!" from her place in the audience. "Ray was just a big lunk of a man," Shacochis said. "You knew he'd be more comfortable in jeans than in that good suit he was wearing. Being with him was like sitting on an old sofa that you've been comfortable sitting on all your life." Ray himself sprawled in an easy chair in the Iowa Union, chain-smoking and laughing with those who came up to say hello. Departing from Iowa, Ray and Tess shared a taxi with poet Kenneth Rosen. Rosen was amazed that his awkward former classmate had become a "silver-haired, dignified personage—he shook your hand like Abraham Lincoln." He was equally impressed by Gallagher:

> She had a large, oval Irish face and reddish hair and painted eyebrows. She went up to the counter to purchase their tickets and pulled out two credit cards and paid for the tickets separately. When she received the paperwork, she signed one set with her right hand and one with her left hand! Writing simultaneously and imitating Ray's handwriting. Every writer needs a Tess Gallagher. Formidable woman. I am not making this up. I saw it happen. She was writing simultaneously *in different hands.*[36]

Ray's star status at the jubilee was offset by his obscurity at the thirtieth reunion of his Yakima High School class. He attended on a whim, in part because his mother had just migrated from Sacramento to Yakima. When he ran into his buddies Dick Moeller and Jerry King at a poolside party, Ray said, "Let's get the hell out of here. I never liked any of these people in high school, and I don't think I like them now!" They went to a cafe where King and Tess drank martinis and Ray stuck to club soda. Tess did the talking, telling about her Sky House and their travels, so they didn't really grasp how well known Ray was until the emcee of the Saturday night dinner-dance gave the answer to this trivia quiz question: "Which classmate has become an internationally known poet?"[37]

With his short story spree behind him, Ray turned his attention to some serious fall fishing. About the fish he was selfish and competitive, hogging the best spot on the boat, using the last of the bait supply, and slacking off on his turn to run the boat. An accomplished fisherwoman herself, Tess often outfished Ray. He had trouble hanging on to his fishing boats and owned a total of four during the 1980s. He traded in an older Bayliner runabout for a fine brand-new runabout with good seats and a Yamaha outboard, but sold it back to the dealer at a loss to help Maryann meet a loan payment.[38] He chose his next boat—a classic Carver—for its name, but then lent it to Morris Bond for his commute to a winter logging job. The Carver broke up when Bond struck an underwater obstruction. Ray's last boat was his worst—the 1978 Olympic hardtop had a host of mechanical problems that kept it in the repair shop. "The previous owner had seen Ray coming and grossly overcharged him," Carlile said.[39]

When Ray and Tess rode with Carlile on the first morning of the Port Angeles Salmon Derby on Labor Day weekend of 1986, Carlile reminded Ray to keep his line away from the trolling motor. The water was crowded. As they tacked away from the path of an oncoming boat, Ray began to yell, "I've got one." But Carlile soon discovered that Ray's line had tangled around his propeller. Afraid his motor had been damaged, he yelled, "Goddamit Ray!"

Ray looked stunned, as if he'd been slapped, and Carlile instantly regretted his outburst. Ray dropped out of that derby and stayed in his study for the evening. Ray's deep reaction to Carlile's flash of temper calls to mind his reaction, years earlier, when Jim Crumley caught Ray stuffing his mouth with pickled eggs meant for a party. Being caught or reprimanded took him straight back to some buried childhood scene. Carlile also realized, later, that Ray didn't enjoy fishing in the morning because it made him "feel guilty for spending time away from his desk."[40]

Now past the midpoint of his five-year Strauss Living award, Ray felt urgency about all of his work. Gallagher remembered saying to herself, "This velocity is killing. If we go any faster, I will fall apart from the sheer energy it takes to keep up with the demands of the day."[41] Ray had always said he didn't expect to live a long life. As he approached fifty, he urged Maryann to see a doctor for a checkup (and send him the bill) because, "We are about late middle age now—old people in the eyes of the young. We don't have all that much longer left . . ."[42]

CHAPTER 29

Where I'm Calling From

September 1986–September 1987, Port Angeles

[On Cézanne's paintings:] As if these colors could heal one of indecision once and for all. The good conscience of these reds, these blues, their simple truthfulness, it educates you . . . You also notice, a little more clearly each time, how necessary it was to go beyond love, too; it's natural, after all, to love each of these things as one makes it: but if one shows this, one makes it less well; one judges it instead of saying it . . . It may be that this emptying out of love in anonymous work, which produces such pure things, was never achieved as completely as in the work of this old man . . .

—Rainer Maria Rilke, *Letters on Cézanne*[1]

On September 7, 1986, Ray confided to Carlile that he wasn't working. The resulting lassitude in turn prompted him to think about traveling to exotic destinations or buying new cars or houses. Ten days later, he complained again to Carlile that the fishing had been terrible (salmon runs declined sharply in the late 1980s) and that he needed a "shrink" to help him deal with his mother. "Let them get my couch ready. Let the doctor prepare to listen carefully, he may never hear such a story again," Ray wrote.[2] Whether Ray's depressed and distracted state of mind were due to middle age, exhaustion, worry, or a change in his relationship to his work is hard to know. A writer experiences and needs fallow times. Burdened with this disappointment in himself, Ray moved about for most of the fall season, traveling for pleasure or to promote *Ultramarine* and Tess's books, and, no doubt, wondering what to do next. He was moving away from writing about alcoholism and married couples, and had made strides in his craft that would, in turn, lead him to new subjects.

In late September, Ray and Richard Ford traveled to Saskatchewan, where they gave readings at the university in exchange for two days of goose hunting. Writer David Carpenter had dreamed up this unusual gig when he interpreted Carver's story "Distance" in *Fires* to mean "Will somebody please take me goose hunting, please?" Their plans were hampered by hurricane-force rains that clogged the roads with sticky mud and prevented the hunting guide from digging blinds. Ray, smoking a joint, saw Carpenter's anxiety and reassured him: " 'I'm excited. Richard here is excited. I feel I'm on some sort of adventure.' " Carpenter, three friends, and Carver and Ford stayed in a shabby, drafty motel. Up before dawn, Ray used a small filter he carried with him to make cup after cup of coffee for everyone. The hosts brought doughnuts. After a day of lying facedown in the mud and leaping up to shoot as the geese flew over, Ray was "close to exhaustion" and limping from a pulled groin muscle, blisters, and a swollen big toe. But on a fruitless drive in search of a Coke, Ray spotted a gravel road with a ditch beside it. Footsore as he was, he got excited about hunting from that spot the next morning, when he borrowed Ford's gun and killed four geese. Carpenter could see that Ray had been a good hunter: "He became youthful again, babbling and repeating himself." As Ray said good-bye, he got choked up and asked if he and Ford could come again the next year.[3]

Worse for the wear after the hunting trip, Ray flew east with Gallagher for most of the autumn. In Chicago, they gave a reading to benefit *Poetry* magazine. Tickets for the fund-raising event were $100; at Ray's request the sponsors sent complimentary tickets to his first editor, Curt Johnson, who had mixed feelings about his friend's celebrity. "Ray deserved it, sure, of course he did, but so did so many other good writers. And I think Ray knew that."[4]

With celebrity, Ray found, came a boatload of inaccurate statements that circled through the journalistic world. One magazine piece imparted the misinformation that Richard Ford was Carver's former student and that Charles Bukowski had recently spent a wild night at his Port Angeles home. But when *People* magazine made an appointment to profile him and Gallagher as a couple, Ray agreed. "Why not? It's all a big carnival, or circus, anyway," he told Unger. *People*'s effort produced a blueprint for a modern-romance version of Ray and Tess's partnership that would survive for years after. "Having been with Tess as long as I have," Carver told the interviewer, "I can't imagine living with someone who is not a writer and not understanding of what a writer requires." Especially Ray noted that he appreciated having someone who wouldn't fool him about his work, "who knows what your best is and when you haven't gone as far as you can." Typically, *People* was intrigued that Carver and Gallagher were unwed and owned separate houses. Tom Jenks spent several days with Ray and Tess in both Syracuse and Port Angeles before he wrote a profile for *Vanity Fair,* and his details ring true: they all stayed at Ray's house, where on a Sunday afternoon Tess played the piano and Ray smoked and read. In the evening, Ray made espresso and listened to the day's accumulation of messages on the answering machine. After the lights were out, he recalled, "I would hear them in their room, laughing. They had a good thing, for each of them." In his article, Jenks concluded, "One feels between them an accumulation of gentleness and strength, a concert of energies. They seem joined by fate and careful of it."[5]

Home by the fire again in early December, Ray read Douglas Unger's new novel, *El Yanqui,* and wrote Unger that he was "thinking strongly about you tonight, hombre." After sealing the letter, he intended to put a log on the fire, take a shower, and get into his pajamas. The past six weeks of "hither and yonning" had been "wearing, or wearying," and he was relieved to stop flying in airplanes and talking about himself. *Ultramarine* had already gone into a second printing. He still lacked the stories needed to make up the new collection he had promised to give Knopf in January.[6]

On December 26, 1986, Ray set up court in a suite at the Bellingham Holiday Inn to celebrate Christmas with his first family. "My dad was caught up in many dilemmas during his last ten years," his daughter wrote in 2004. "Tess and her family—or our family; old friends and work friends—new ones; old writing themes—new ones. These dichotomies ate him alive literally because he was so emotionally attracted to what had been and what was now . . . That [his emotional vulnerability] is one reason he was so beloved by so many—the secret to his success."[7] Chris's analysis comes from a sensibility very like her father's. She suffered his weaknesses and deeply empathized with him. Not only that, she had been especially close to her father during 1986 as she worked to maintain her sobriety and establish an independent life. In July she had driven to Sacramento to help her grandmother Ella make her move to Yakima, taking that burden from Ray and James (briefly). Ella came to Bellingham for Christmas. Ray's arrival in Bellingham was preceded by a flood of mail-ordered gifts on Maryann's doorstep: a smoked turkey, cheeses and sausages and hams, fruitcakes and sweets for all to eat; wind chimes and a ceramic sandpiper for Maryann, a mirror painted with butterflies for Chris, toys from the Smithsonian Museum gift shop for Windy and Chloe. Other gifts went to Vance and his family in Germany. For Chris's daughters, the best gift was seeing Grandpa Ray himself, a man whose largesse and accommodations (a swimming pool and restaurant meals paid for with a stroke of a pen) made him seem a veritable Santa Claus.

According to Maryann, she and Ray had exchanged Christmas gifts every year since 1955, regardless of their marital status. Some years they met briefly; other times their contact was by mail and telephone. But perhaps because Maryann's husband had returned to Canada in November, or perhaps because Ray had written those purgative and transcendent new stories about his family, he invited Maryann to meet him for lunch. In the restaurant parking lot, Ray walked to her car, where they hugged and exchanged gifts. At forty-eight, Ray reminded Maryann of her own father at the same age: "full of life and 'mature handsome' " to her eye. She gave her former husband a figure of a standing nude female "with a gorgeous body" carved in oak. When Ray released a deep breath, his lungs sounded "like valves of a dirigible release." With nervous tension, Ray fiddled with the loose end of a fabric belt that Maryann wore. Neither of them commented when he pulled the belt off and stuffed it in his sport coat pocket.

At an upstairs cantina table in Dos Padres restaurant, they drank Perriers with lime and relaxed into the winter afternoon. They didn't touch, according to Maryann, until she slipped her shoes off to stretch her legs: "Then he reached under the table and I lifted my feet into his hands." He released her feet; they sipped more Perriers and continued a conversation about their children and Ray's work. "Besides our children, that was the important thing. His work had been our business . . . even with all the emotional scars, his work justified so much of what we'd put ourselves through." Maryann told Ray about her new business partnership with a logger who would harvest firewood from her property. When Maryann experienced a compelling extrasensory perception that her dog, who was at a veterinary hospital, wanted her to come to him, she excused herself. As Maryann recalled in her memoir, Ray's acquiescence was "slightly hesitant in that appealing way some men have." The dog died shortly after she arrived at the hospital.[8]

As unemployment in Washington State reached an all-time high in the late 1980s, Ray's Bellingham family's financial crises and urgent appeals to him continued, but middle-aged Ray and Maryann had "come through" (to borrow a phrase from D. H. Lawrence) the highs and lows of their long love affair and found a way to be friends. Scholars may ask if "Intimacy" and "Blackbird Pie" are autobiographical stories. In turn, one may wonder if those stories provided a catharsis to Ray and Maryann.

On December 13, Ray had decided to unplug the phone and get back to work. Then the holidays with their usual duties and pleasures intervened. The trip to Bellingham must have been emotionally demanding. Ray's intention to get back to work, held at bay all fall, became his new year's resolution. During his fall travels, he'd been chastened and inspired by reading Rainer Maria Rilke's *Letters on Cézanne*. The German poet's letters to his wife, Clara, are about artistic vocation, his own and Cézanne's. Ray was impressed that Rilke and his wife sometimes lived apart in order to do their work. He must also have been moved by the German poet's description of work habits of the painter who developed "a taste for work" in his fortieth year, "but then to such an extent that for the next thirty years he did nothing *but* work." According to Rilke, Cézanne even missed his mother's funeral so as not to interrupt his work.[9]

Thus, Ray barreled into 1987 with intentions of doing six months' work in six weeks. After reading *Chekhov* by French biographer Henri Troyat (translated by Michael Henry Heim), he began a historical fiction based on the death of Chekhov. At first he called it "The Mortician" or "Room Service" or "Champagne." Then it became "The Errand" and finally "Errand."[10]

Carver followed Troyat's account closely, cherry-picking episodes that would build up to the scene that most intrigued him: Chekhov's death. Altogether, he used about a dozen sentences closely paraphrased from Heim's translation, Carver wasn't worried, apparently, about his debt to Troyat and Heim; instead, he believed, "I couldn't stray from what happened, nor did I want to." Carver devotes the first half of his story to exposition of Chekhov's final illness, beginning with a hemorrhage in a Moscow restaurant. He adds details to emphasize the elegance and costliness of the restaurant where Chekhov dined with his publisher. For all Carver lifted from Troyat, the second half of "Errand" bears the signature of his own style and way of looking at an episode.

"Errand" circumnavigates the scene of Chekhov's death at age forty-four as a cinematographer might, adopting the views of Chekhov's wife, Olga, a doctor, and a waiter. More specifically, Carver zooms in on what might be called the stage props and stage business of the scene. He adds that very Carverian implement, a telephone, which Chekhov's doctor uses to order champagne. "A tired-looking young man whose blond hair was standing up" delivers the champagne. This waiter overhears the "ferocious, harrowing sound" of the dying man who "panted ferociously for breath" in the other room. When he returns after Chekhov's death, interrupting Olga's solitude with her husband's corpse, she gives him an *errand* to bring a mortician.

For four quietly spectacular paragraphs Carver runs his imagination of the scene into the future—to the completion of the errand that the boy has, in the story's real time, not yet begun. Someone—is it Olga or the waiter?—daydreams the movements of those four paragraphs. Then Carver closes his story:

But at that moment the young man was thinking of the cork still resting near the toe of his shoe. To retrieve it he would have to bend over, still gripping the vase. He would do this. He leaned over. Without looking down, he reached out and closed it into his hand.

With a gesture known to no one except the waiter, this ending presents a restoration of order. Carver makes a point of saying that the young man's name has not survived and "it's likely he perished in the Great War." With it, he reminds us that unnoted moments define the quality of famous lives, and insists upon the importance of forgotten people.[11]

"Errand" went first to Charles McGrath at the *New Yorker*, who recognized that Ray was again doing something different. The story required more editing than any of Carver's stories because the magazine's fact-checking department (which does review fiction) "had to move him off of Troyat, but on the other hand, they had to stick to the historical record, and it was frustrating for Ray because this didn't leave him much room to move." Ray fiddled a lot with his ending, too, which didn't initially revolve around the cork: "It took a long time and it was a great feeling when Ray got it finally right." Gallagher has said that she proposed to Carver that the waiter pick up the cork at the end of the story and has published a typescript page that shows emendations in Carver's hand and in her own.[12] Either Carver or Gallagher might have found a hint for closing the story in this piece of advice from Raymond Chandler: "They [readers of detective fiction] thought they cared nothing about anything but the action. The things they really cared about, and that I cared about, were the creation of emotion through dialogue and description; the things they remembered, that haunted them, were not for example that a man got killed, but that in the moment of his death he was trying to pick a paper clip up off the polished surface of a desk."[13]

When the editing of "Errand" was going on, Ray saw his doctor for a physical—"lab work, chest x-rays, the works"—and had extensive work done on his teeth. With his ivories ready for the cameras and his health certified, he completed plans for two European trips, one to the Continent in April and another to Britain in June.

In February, Christine sent her father copies of a paper she'd written on Matisse and a midterm take-home exam. "My heart moved," he wrote her, "when I saw those folders with your name on them, and the college class title and number . . ." But Ray was, after all, a teacher and a parent, so his praise was followed by advice. He tactfully suggested that she—like Vance and Tess—needed to keep a dictionary handy to check her spelling. And he suggested a way to improve the "expression" of her ideas: "When something feels complex or complicated to you, write it out carefully and thoughtfully, several different times if necessary, until it flows smoothly and expresses exactly what you want it to communicate and nothing else."[14] One could hardly wish for more sensible writing advice!

While his daughter flourished, Ray's mother sank. The situation had been "nightmarish" since Ray and Ella had a "serious falling-out" in Bellingham at Christmas. Now Ella wanted to leave Yakima and return to Sacramento. Jerry King and James Carver both tried to help, but nothing pleased Ella, who was—in Ray's opinion—"clear crazy." Her situation grieved him, and he felt like "an orphan." To King he explained that he could send her money, but couldn't "make her happy or fundamentally change her life in any way." But the real problem was that Ella Carver believed she had given the best years to her kids—perhaps she had—and was now expecting her reward. In her view, Ray was getting paid not to work, so why couldn't he find more time for his mother? According to Maryann Carver, Ella and Ray had always been close and always argued viciously. In the past, calm had been restored when Ella and Ray both "ran out of gas," and that continued to be the case now that their dependencies were reversed.[15]

During the time Ray and Ella were estranged, Ann Beattie chose "Boxes" for the 1987 *BASS* collection out of all the fine stories Carver had published in the past year. If Ray understood that his family was troubled when they recognized themselves in the things he published, it didn't seem to stop him. "Let go, let God," the AA slogan for detachment, was serving him well. Several of his new poems, "Suspenders," for instance, sketched—and presumably revisited—an abusive episode from his childhood in which his mother whipped his legs with the suspenders he refused to wear.

After he finished "Errand" and a short prose memoir for *Poetry* magazine, Ray began reeling in a poem a day, as he'd done for the previous three winters. One of them, called "Poems," includes an ominous line: "It's true my lungs / have heated up like ovens."

Everyone urged Ray to quit smoking, especially Tess Gallagher. In a poem from this period, "The Painter & the Fish," a painter is angered by words spoken to him by his wife on the telephone. "Who could sleep if your woman sneered / and said time was running out?" he asks. The painter leaves his studio and walks off his anger in the rain, stopping to watch an electrical storm and men at a lumber mill. Still feeling desperate, he sees a fish jump from the water and stand on its tail. At this sign, he decides he will quit smoking—and never talk on the telephone again! Invigorated, the painter goes back to work, determined to keep going until he has painted everything that's on his mind. In real life, Ray couldn't quit cigarettes. When he had quit drinking, he meant to preserve his brain for writing. For him the same logic was no help in quitting smoking. Smoking tobacco and marijuana calmed him. He tried to enjoy a pipe, but what was in his hand most often was a low-tar cigarette brand called Now 100. He lived in that *now*. He wrote fellow recovering alcoholic Dennis Covington that if he had a stroke right that very day, he would die a happy man.[16]

After Valentine's Day, Ray scratched out a five-page letter to Maryann in reply to a "sweet" and "thoughtful" card she'd sent him. He'd mailed cards to Chris and her girls, but been too late to order flowers for Maryann, he apologized. Instead he sent her three new anthologies that included his stories. The original idea for one of those stories, he mentions (without naming it), had come from a story she told him. There's nothing private or even surprisingly personal about the letter, but it's friendly and it shares concerns (about Vance, for instance) that only parents could share. A paragraph of the letter is devoted to his difficulties with publishers, another to travel plans. Mainly it's a missive from a man who has a lot on his shoulders. He's tired, and he's grateful for the comfort that had come to him with his former wife's "good warm note."[17]

Tired. Worried. Alone. Complicated. Busy. These are words that recur in Carver's correspondence from the early months of 1987. Counting "Errand," he had only seven of the dozen stories he owed Knopf. A series of personnel changes came to his rescue. The previous summer, Gary Fisketjon had left his position at Random House and Vintage to become editorial director at Atlantic Monthly Press, which had been purchased by his friend Carl Navarre. Initially, Carver planned to stick with Knopf—the premier American publisher of fiction. But then Knopf president Gottlieb moved to the *New Yorker,* where he replaced William Shawn. Ray felt abandoned at Knopf without Gottlieb. After some agonizing, Carver decided to switch to Atlantic Monthly. His agent, Amanda Urban, undertook negotiations. Several rounds of FedExed letters and phone calls later, it was concluded in May that Atlantic Monthly Press would publish Carver's next book in the spring of 1988. This book would contain his own selection of a dozen or more stories from his previous works to make up a book with his seven new stories. "Gary! I'm really pleased—I couldn't be happier! . . . Yippee!" he wrote Fisketjon.[18]

While most of that negotiation was going on, Ray was on the road, again. As Lane Lecturer at Stanford, he read "Elephant" to an SRO crowd in Kresge Auditorium, carrying off this return to the scene of old embarrassments with great aplomb. "People who previously did not have good things to say about Ray," Al Young noted, "now gave him a standing ovation, happy to bask in his glory." Ray spied Young in the crowd and bore down upon him with a "long, long hug." Ray said, " 'Man, it means everything to see you here' . . . and that was our farewell."[19]

Ray traveled deeper into his past with readings at UC Davis, where Jack Hicks was his host, and Sacramento State University, where he stayed with Dennis and Loretta Schmitz and had breakfast with his brother, James. Hicks found Ray "amused by these august literary occasions in the 1980s. We had little secrets that the adoring lit crowd never knew. He was glad to have those safely packed away, but also accepting that those days had been part of his journey." Dennis Schmitz introduced Ray at Sac State by elevating him to a literary pantheon: "Shelley says, 'We lack the power to imagine what we know.' Ray Carver is one of those who has the power, one of those writers who has revived the short story form in our time, I think—with his vision as much as with his craft. Ray." Those who heard Ray read "Errand" one night and "Whoever Was Using This Bed" the next noticed that these stories shared a concern with the subject of fatal illness. "It was uncanny," Loretta Schmitz said. "I didn't think he looked well, and then he read these stories and I wondered if he had some kind of premonition. I really wondered, I did."[20]

European travel, broken by a return to Port Angeles in May, occupied Ray and Tess for most of the spring. On both trips Gallagher kept a diary, which she later published. For a week in Paris, Ray was entertained and feted by his French editor, Olivier Cohen. "I'll be glad to get home!" Ray told Tess in a note that she pasted into her journal on the fifth day; he added a promise to walk with her on the beach when he got there. After going out by himself in a futile search for bacon and eggs on a Sunday morning, Ray told Tess that he had "new respect for Vance living . . . where English isn't spoken."[21]

From Paris, they went to Germany, staying near Vance and his family's apartment. Ray found it a "rest and relief" to be in Wiesbaden. Vance had yet to find a stable job. That this should have bothered his father seems a little ironic. Vance was then only twenty-eight; Ray had not stayed in one job for more than a year until he went to Syracuse—at age forty-one. But after a childhood remembered as baffling and chaotic, Vance valued stability. Meanwhile, he taught American and European history courses at the air force base in Wiesbaden and took full care of Jennifer when Inge flew Lufthansa's international routes. Vance considered a job as a researcher for "the company" (CIA). He passed on that, but the scofflaw father was amused and surprised by the thought of his son as a spy. In Wiesbaden, Inge cooked Ray those scrambled eggs he'd been craving, and they all toured along the Rhine in a rented Mercedes. In the Casino at Wiesbaden, Ray and Tess played roulette in the very room where Dostoyevsky had won and lost

3,000 rubles in 1865. Tess won a 175-deutsche mark jackpot—which Ray inflated to 350 DM or 500 DM on postcards home.

In Zurich, a friend secured them entry to Thomas Mann's archives and Mann's large study with its fine mahogany desk, parquet floor, couch, and easy chairs. They opened Mann's books and handled his fountain pens and Asian figurines. "Who couldn't work well with a study like this?" Ray wrote on a postcard, before grumbling that Zurich had "more Japs than Swiss" and more gays than straight people. Tess's journal indicates that Ray felt anxious about getting meals at specific times and taking a nap in the afternoon. Those difficulties were somewhat offset for him by the availability of Swiss chocolate. After making their third visit to the cemetery where James Joyce is buried and studying several funerary sculptures there, they dined at Kronenhalle, which Joyce had frequented. Lectures and meetings with publishers in Rome and Milan closed the trip at the end of April. Weary of media attention and foreign food and foreign languages, Ray gratefully retreated to Port Angeles.

"Errand" appeared in the *New Yorker* the day Ray and Tess arrived in London for the second phase of their European spring. They had rented a small flat near Holland Park for a month. While Tess spent a week in Ireland, Ray made a book tour in Scotland with his publisher, Christopher MacLehose. In London his social life ranged from a black-tie event at a British arts society to a meeting with Sir V. S. Pritchett and an informal, home-cooked dinner (chicken with ginger) with Salman Rushdie and Marianne Wiggins. Rushdie admired Carver's work, considering him "a great writer" and "a poet of inclusion, of capaciousness."

At the end of the month, they were back in Paris for Ray's reading at Maison des Écrivains. A photograph taken by a stranger with Tess's camera shows the couple at Les Deux Magots, the cafe where Sartre and Camus once drank. Ray, looking solemn, wears dark shades and a brown leather flight jacket that Tess gave him for his forty-ninth birthday. She called it his "Camus jacket." When the Fords joined them in Paris, Richard noticed that Ray didn't seem to feel like walking anywhere and "looked thin and kind of gaunt." He feared "something was amiss" with his friend.[22]

People came from all over the country to fish for salmon with Ray Carver during the summer of 1987. In July, so many other visitors arrived that Ray and Tess slept at her mother's house and left their own houses to the guests. Olivier Cohen and Maya Nahum came from France, while Ford, Kittredge, Robert Stone, and Geoffrey Wolff and his family traveled from within the States. Ray's boat sank when he put it in the water, so he chartered two commercial boats to take everyone out. Among all the experienced fishermen, it fell to Cohen, wearing borrowed rose-colored sunglasses, guts wrenched with seasickness and ambivalence about killing wildlife, to hook a whopping forty-pound king salmon. Ray caught nothing.

When the fishing party reconvened at Ray's house for broiled salmon, the storytelling began. Following a run of anti-English tales, Gallagher rejoined that "Sir V. S." [Pritchett] had been very kind to them in England. Her brother Morris Bond interrupted another writer's Scotch-propelled, angst-ridden discourse with a tale about an airline pilot he'd taken on an elk hunt. "You could see the mischief on Ray's face," as he watched the others listen to Bond, Geoffrey Wolff recalled. "Morris was a fantastic tale-spinner, and this thing went on for many paragraphs of bloody detail. He told how the would-be hunter had fired at the elk a dozen times and hit him only once with a gut-shot before Bond killed the elk by clubbing it with the butt of his rifle." When Ray recounted it all later, he added, "So much for angst and identity crisis." After the elk-hunt story, Cohen announced that he and Nahum were animal lovers and must excuse themselves. Before the night ended, Ray decisively urged one guest to go to bed rather than pour himself another drink. Ray's authority as a drunk ensured that his suggestion was taken.

"I've never seen a man happier to be alive and among friends," Geoffrey Wolff recalled, "and he and Tess were manifestly crazy about each other. He kept marveling aloud, 'The goddam wheel of fortune, isn't it something!'" Still, Ray didn't like to hear just how capricious luck could be. When Wolff described his recent open-heart surgery, Ray interrupted, "'Oh, Jesus, Geoffrey, I don't want to hear about that!'" He countered worries with humor. When Tess was in the hospital with a general anesthetic for a biopsy in late summer, Ray reported that "she counts her pain pills, afraid I've had my big bear's fist in there!" Tess's doctors found nothing to worry about and her lab reports were negative.[23]

In August Ray complained that the waters near Port Angeles were too crowded to enjoy the fishing. A trip to a resort in Ketchikan, Alaska, paid for by *GQ* magazine disappointed him, too, because the people they shared a boat with hogged the best spots on board. Nonetheless, Ray brought home plenty of salmon and four halibut, as well as an obligation to write a two-thousand-word article about the trip.[24] Ray carried Ford's *Rock Springs,* just published by Fisketjon at Atlantic Monthly Press, with him to Alaska. He admired the stories and declared the book "gorgeous." Ray was equally pleased to know that his own new book would be as finely designed as Ford's. "How proud I am of Richard! And you," he wrote Fisketjon. "Good for all of us, is what I say."[25]

• • •

Christine Carver, now twenty-nine, moved into the town of Bellingham and began a bachelor's degree program at Western Washington State University in the fall of 1987. Ray sent her a check for tuition ($120) and "outfits" for school and praised her decision to separate "from that dreadful life out there. Good. . . . Be brave. Do it now, without fail, do you hear?" The rest of his letter to his daughter explains that both he and Tess are "wild with a sense of urgency to get to our desks and stay at our desks . . . Our real life, as it were." For that reason, he continues, he must postpone visits with her and Vance.[26] It's easy to imagine that his children felt shortchanged by his decision, since most of their father's letters were filled with tales of out-of-town guests and long-distance travel.

Ray's manuscript was due on the first of September. All summer he'd been thinking about which stories to reprint along with his seven uncollected stories and making minor editorial changes in all the stories. Initially, he and Fisketjon talked about choosing only a dozen stories from Carver's four previous collections. When Fisketjon came to Port Angeles in early September, he delivered good news. The Franklin Library would publish a leather-bound, gold-edged edition of the book, each copy to be signed by the author. Ray and his editor, two guys from small-town Oregon, celebrated Fisketjon's birthday, fished, and went over the manuscript together. They decided to expand the book to include thirty of the earlier stories, giving them a larger canvas to show how Ray's work had evolved. In the final count there were twelve stories from *Will You Please Be Quiet, Please?* two ("Distance" and "So Much Water So Close to Home") in versions from *Fires,* eight from *What We Talk About When We Talk About Love* (as edited by Lish), and eight from *Cathedral.* For a while Carver wanted to replace "Careful" with "Compartment," but he ultimately decided to omit the story that had so troubled Vance.[27]

The volume of thirty-seven selected and new stories would be called *Where I'm Calling From.* These, Ray told Maryann, were stories he felt "he could live with. And yes, be remembered by." In an introduction for the deluxe edition, he emphasizes that the stories were written over a twenty-five-year span, and concludes that "any writer will tell you he wants to believe his work will undergo a metamorphosis, a sea change, a process of enrichment if he's been at it long enough." Fisketjon agreed: "The main reason Ray and I wanted to do a 'new and selected' with *Where I'm Calling From* was to show how steadily his work had evolved and to shuck the moronic 'minimalist' label." Fisketjon, who had read many of Carver's stories in their earlier magazine versions, said, "*Where I'm Calling From* is the definitive edition of Ray's stories. Those are the stories that Ray wanted to restore."[28]

While making the selections for *Where I'm Calling From,* Carver had been on a streak of writing poems, "big, fat misshapen things, some of them." Writing these poems, "makes me glad always," he told Kittredge, because he feared that "that part of me will go away somehow, or that I'll forget how to do it." Some of these long, meditative poems are "a clutter up from the depths" of his memory like "Another Mystery," wherein he recalls his grandfather's and father's deaths and teeters on the edge of predicting his own. Others, like "The Offending Eel," extrapolate their meditations on luck and mortality from a line in his reading (the story of an old, drunken prince who choked on a dish of eels). These big poems are expansive not only in shape but in vision. Here one encounters a writer who is looking over the geography of his life from the peak of his experience, looking with the detachment of one who no longer expects to change anything and yet finds life fascinating in all its details.[29]

The *People* profile of Ray and Tess ran with a picture of them posed, like Grant Wood's farmers in *American Gothic,* before a steep gable of Ray's house on B Street. There was no pitchfork, but Tess wore an all-American-looking sweater patterned with large stars. Yet when that picture was published, the house on B Street no longer fulfilled Ray's dreams. He was tired of his noisy neighborhood and the old-fashioned house. Ever since the Fords had purchased a large home on acreage above Missoula, Ray had been on the lookout for something similar. In September, as he and Tess were preparing to depart for Syracuse, he found what he wanted in a development at the base of the Olympic Mountains east of Port Angeles. Trees screened the front of the house from the road. From its backyard the land sloped to Morse Creek. This 3,500-square foot, two-story, four-bedroom house was exactly what he wanted. His offer of $217,000 was accepted. He would complete the paperwork by mail and become its owner at the end of December.[30]

This was the house of a lifetime, a "luxury" house, Ray said. He and Tess would call it Ridge House. Tess could have her piano here, and there would be plenty of space and privacy for them both while her house remained a workplace and guesthouse. Ray would install bookshelves in the master bedroom suite—it had a fireplace—and turn that into his study. Working in a room like this—a room reminiscent of Thomas Mann's *arbeitszimmer* in Zurich—would be just the sort of thing he needed to steady himself for the years of writing ahead.

While the Fisketjons were visiting, Ray took his editor out on the strait in his boat. Cruising along west of Port Angeles, they noticed a group of people congregated above them on the bluffs. Fisketjon wondered what was going on.

"I think they're planting somebody up there," Ray answered.[31]

CHAPTER 30

A New Path to the Waterfall

September 1987–August 1988, Syracuse and Port Angeles

"Don't weep for me,"
he said to his friends. "I'm a lucky man. . . ."
—Raymond Carver, "Gravy"

As was his habit, Ray stayed in Port Angeles when Tess returned to Syracuse in September. Though his biggest dilemma might be whether to write or go fishing, he felt restless and disoriented even as he worked assiduously on *Where I'm Calling From*. Since early August, Ray had been bothered by a cough—bronchitis, he assumed—that didn't go away. As he looked toward the autumn, it seemed that Syracuse would be only a stopover before another goose hunt in Saskatchewan, then a tour of Japan, then a trip to New York City. When these travels were completed—each exciting in itself but wearing in the whole—he would move into his new house in Port Angeles.[1]

In the second week of September, Ray's plans were overturned by a dash of red in his sputum. Coughing up blood (hemoptysis), a persistent cough, and a wheeze in breathing are the early symptoms experienced by most lung cancer patients, but Ray's lungs had looked clear in a chest x-ray just six months earlier. Absolute diagnosis of malignancy requires a tissue analysis. Ray returned to Syracuse to be with Tess and became a patient at the SUNY Upstate Medical Center in Syracuse. Images revealed a dark, isolated tumor, but no definite diagnosis could be made. Ray was scheduled for surgery on Thursday, October 1, 1987 at St. Joseph's Hospital.[2]

His autumn would not be spent shooting geese with the Fords and traveling to Japan to sleep in the extra-large bed the Murakamis had built just for him. It would not be spent writing a novel or completing a new collection of poems. He could only hope that he'd recover his health in time to oversee the publication of the new and selected stories in *Where I'm Call-*

ing From.[3] During these days of uncertainty, Ray learned that, due to his productivity and success during the past five years, the awards committee of the American Academy and Institute of Arts and Letters had decided not to renew his Strauss Living. His last check would be issued in December. The committee passed the awards on to Diane Johnson and Robert Stone. In his five-year tenureship of a Strauss Living, Ray had published four major books and became a regular contributor to the *New Yorker* and big-circulation magazines; his career was in full flower.

Doctors recommend surgery for lung cancer only when they believe that the surgeon will be able to remove every cancer cell from the body and only if they deem the patient strong enough to survive a highly invasive thoracotomy. In addition, physicians must predict whether the patient will be able to breathe adequately after the removal of a partial or entire lung. In many cases, despite advanced imaging techniques, a surgeon must make a final decision about removing a tumor only when the chest cavity is already opened.

Even as his surgery approached, Ray did not give up cigarettes. He had been smoking tobacco for forty of his fifty years, and marijuana for at least twenty of those. These were the addictions, solaces, crutches—call them what you will—that he would not forgo despite the pleas of Tess Gallagher and all the others who loved him and had long worried over his health. Richard Ford, who flew in to spend the Sunday before the surgery with Ray, reflected: "Once he had penetrated the necessary nervousness, he seemed resolved. . . . [The cancer] didn't surprise him. He just hated it." Early in the week, Ray mailed Maryann money for a new dress and shoes and left signed checks with Amy Unger in case his daughter and former wife needed to buy plane tickets to attend his funeral. Then he turned his financial affairs over to Tess. When he met the Ungers for lunch on the day before he was to enter the hospital, Ray "was terribly frightened, couldn't eat at all," Unger recalled. "He ordered soup and when it came, he said. 'I'm looking at this soup and I'm thinking I'm in the soup.' He said that twice. He smoked in the restaurant that day and persuaded Amy to sneak cigarettes into the hospital for him."[4]

He left those cigarettes tucked into the fold of his bedsheet when they took him to the operating room. "He was joking with us," recalled Unger, who took shifts at the hospital along with Amy and Tess. "He said there was the old life, and then there had been the new life. There he was lying on the gurney, a blue shower cap on his head, and he said, 'Well, I'm on to the next new life.' Then they wheeled him out of the room."

The operation lasted into the afternoon. Ray knew his surgeon, Suras V. Pradhan, through a mutual friend, physicist Kameshwar Wali. Ray had found further comfort in the rumor that Pradhan's daughter admired his stories. When Ray regained consciousness, he looked "crazed and wild-eyed" and was unable to speak because of the ventilator. Amy soothed him with the AA slogan "Let go and let God." Dr. Pradhan came in and reported that he had removed one lobe of Ray's left lung and shaved down the adjoining lobe. The surgeon was so exhausted that he had to lean against a cabinet to keep standing, but he believed he had removed all of the cancerous tissue. The Ungers brought Ray a portable tape player and some classical and jazz tapes and stayed until he was comfortable for the night.

When the Ungers came the next morning, they found Ray awake and irritated because the boom box was stuck on one song that was driving him to distraction. But he was so grateful for the outcome of his surgery that he was able to leave the smuggled cigarettes unlit. He vowed never to smoke again. A couple of days later, Amy and Doug were alone with Ray when an oncologist came to recommend that he follow up his surgery with a course of radiation treatments. Like the bewildered parents in his story "A Small, Good Thing," Ray tended to be squeamish and incurious about medical procedures. He listened politely as the specialist explained the pros and cons, including a risk that radiation might burn his remaining lobes. "After the guy left, Ray said, 'Is he trying to sell me an air conditioner for the trunk of my car? I've had enough.' So he decided not to do it and never revisited his decision."[5]

By the end of October, Ray was editing proofs for *Where I'm Calling From.* "He was high," Unger recalled. "He was very satisfied with the new collection. He talked about doing a series of stories based on the biographies of writers he admired—Kafka, de Maupassant, Hemingway." He complained that Tess had no time to do anything except meet her classes and submit insurance forms. At the same time, Ray was completing the paperwork to purchase his new house in Port Angeles. He tired easily and wrote his letters by hand on a notepad in his lap.[6]

From a conversation he had with Tess shortly after the operation, Stephen Dobyns understood that "the prognosis was not good. There was a chance he might survive, but Ray felt more comfortable without the information of what was happening. Not talking about it was a way to put it out of his head."[7] Ray heard exactly what he wished to hear when he and Tess saw Dr. Pradhan for a postsurgical follow-up on October 23. To a colleague who'd offered to talk to him about his own oncological experience, Ray replied that his surgeon "got it all, and there isn't a trace left, and radiation may do me more harm than good now." On the same day, he wrote Dave Carpenter that he was "well away on the road to complete recovery, and for that I'm infinitely grateful." He asked to be counted in for a week of Saskatchewan goose hunting the next fall.[8]

Ray Carver believed in luck, in fate, in events that befell without rhyme or reason. For him, a reprieve from lung cancer was another in a line of miraculous occurrences that extended back to meeting Maryann Burk and John Gardner, to getting published in *Esquire* and having Gordon Lish as his editor, then to finding the strength to not drink, and forward to living with Tess Gallagher and winning the Strauss Living award. He recovered with enthusiasm. He went walking with Kamesh Wali, did his exercises, and smoked very little. He took his cannabis in brownies.[9] Life continued to compensate him for his losses.

Though his Strauss Living would not be renewed, Carver would be honored as a "Literary Lion" by the New York Public Library at the library's annual fund-raising event. In 1987, twenty-six prominent writers were deemed "Lions" (a reference to the stone lions at the Fifth Avenue entrance of the library) and prominent donors paid $1,500 a head to attend. Ray looked sharp in his black tie and gold lion medallion, but he was not well. Robert Stone, who slapped Ray on the back and then regretted it, was alarmed at the amount of weight Ray had lost. A high point of the evening was seeing Jacqueline Kennedy Onassis, though Tess was the one who got to sit by the former first lady. But Ray, whose literary reputation was much on his mind as he faced his mortality, found a greater thrill in being lionized alongside Harold Pinter and Stanley Elkin as well as previous Lions Sir Stephen Spender, whose literary memory reached back to the late 1920s, and eighty-three-year-old storytelling master and Nobel laureate Isaac Bashevis Singer. After cocktails in the library's marble corridor, trumpeters announced dinner, which was served in the special-collection rooms where Ray's correspondence with *Antaeus,* the *New Yorker,* and other publications would one day be archived. Seated with donors from the R. J. Reynolds Tobacco Company, Ray reportedly turned down an after-dinner cigarette by saying, "No, thanks, I've done my part for you boys."[10]

A poignant sidebar to the story of Ray's recovery emerges in his letters to his mother. Following his surgery, Ray seemed to be pleading for a loving letter from Ella that neither complains nor asks for money. After the Literary Lions gala, he wrote her with simple details: he had used a wheelchair in the airports and spent a lot of time resting in his hotel room before going "out to this big dinner with lots of famous writers." He wore a tuxedo, he told her, and they hung a red sash around his neck. "It was a very big occasion."[11] Along with his boyish report, Ray sent his mother a clipping from the November 13, 1987, *New York Times,* including a photo of Ray happily conversing with fellow Lion Roy Blount Jr. Ray looks thin, but he's laughing as if he's just pulled off a terrific coup; the camera caught him with his middle finger extended—flipping the bird at anyone who might question his luck. Mrs. Onassis appears in a separate frame on the same page. This was a picture of success that Ella Carver could appreciate: her Raymond attending the same party as Jackie Kennedy. Yet Ella penciled a note of more basic motherly concern at the top of her letter from her famous son: "Ray's letter in a wheelchair."[12]

Ray's confidence grew throughout the fall. In New York City, Marion Ettlinger had come to his hotel room to photograph him. Hair now more gray than brown, he posed in his leather jacket and deemed the result "not so bad for a man recovering from major surgery." Ray looks lean and self-assured in the portrait that would appear on the cover of *Where I'm Calling From* and go on to become an iconic image of Carver.[13]

By December, Ray's euphoria was obvious to all who knew him. He was consumed by plans for the future. Fisketjon and Amanda Urban collaborated to secure him a three-book contract with Atlantic Monthly Press as well as an editorial advisory position at the publishing house. The three books were to include one volume of poems, a collection of stories, and a novel or memoir. One reason for offering Carver an editorial position was to try to get him on the publisher's health plan.[14] Ray typed an ebullient four-page list of places to photograph for Bob Adelman, who planned a book of pictures about Carver's earlier life. The letter included a paragraph about courting Maryann at Playland, when she'd lived there with her mother and sister three decades earlier.[15]

At a holiday party given by the Dobynses, Ray was vigorous enough to dance. His one and a half remaining lungs seemed to be enough. He had gifts for everyone, including a whole ham for Steve Unger. Someone took a picture of Ray with Steve, "hamming it up." But the real ham act of the evening was Ray's gift to Amy: a framed print of Ettlinger's photo of himself. Before going home, Ray pulled Doug Unger aside to offer him some serious advice: "I was drinking again and Ray reminded me about what he'd been through and urged me to quit. He was worried." For Christmas dinner, Ray and Tess joined the Wolff family and then said good-bye to them for a year. They were headed to Berlin, where Tobias Wolff would complete his memoir *This Boy's Life*.[16]

With much to celebrate, Ray and Tess spent New Year's Eve in Port Angeles. *Amplitude,* a collection of Gallagher's new and selected poems, had just been published and was getting enthusiastic reviews. Early in 1988, Ray wrote Maryann: "It's a gift, this life, on loan . . . live it to its fullest, drink deeply from it as much as we're able." He mailed Maryann two of the Ettlinger portraits signed by the photographer, but, defeated by the logistics of getting them framed, suggested she could find inexpensive frames for them there. He chastised Maryann for spending the Christmas money he'd sent her ($300) on other people, urged her to take care of her health, and offered to pay for a physical exam for her. He told her he'd been glad to hear about the kids' Christmas and suggested she sell some of her property to pay her debts. "Time for everybody to paddle their own boat now," he wrote. "Time for good things to happen to Maryann and not everything — time and money — drained away." Ray was talking to himself, while also warning Maryann that his gifts to her were going to end. He told her that he hoped Ella's brother Sanders, "a rich man with two Texas-style Cadillac convertibles," would take over his mother's maintenance. "My poor mother is crazy," Ray concluded. "It's a heartbreaker, but I don't know what I can do."[17] The ending of his Strauss Living gave Ray reason to stop helping everyone. His decision to guard his own health and resources and let Tess manage his finances made it a necessity.

Ray was ready to work on his next collection of poems, but first, he had to move into his luxury house. The task was almost overwhelming even with hired help. He wrote Maryann that he felt as if their move had taken months and he was "*so* eager to resume my work and feel like a writer again." In fact, Tess managed things so that Ray could move into his study, upstairs at the back of the house, before anything else was set to rights. Bookshelves were installed to hold all the editions of his work in dozens of languages. He had a fireplace and leather sofa, a mahogany desk, and a swivel chair in front of the Smith Corona he continued to use even as his contemporaries embraced word processors. He kept his study uncluttered, displaying just a few favorite objects — photographs of Chekhov and of Tess, a jade Buddha from Tess, the oak figurine from Maryann, a vase of fresh flowers. From a deck just outside, he heard only water and birdsong. He saw down Morse Creek Canyon to the strait and across to Victoria.[18]

In his new quarters, Ray reviewed final proofs of *Where I'm Calling From,* finding little to change except some characters' names. Atlantic Monthly produced a distinctive volume, nearly four hundred pages, with a tasteful illustration of an American colonial house on the front and Ettlinger's magisterial portrait of Carver on the back. His epigraph, from Milan Kundera — "We can never know what to want, because, living only one life, we can neither compare it with our previous lives nor perfect it in our lives to come" — sounds a note of acceptance from Carver, who so often stated that he'd lived two lives.

Next Ray turned out a brief introduction to the Franklin edition of *Where.* As he labored to sign *ten thousand* title sheets to be bound into that edition, he received word that both the Quality Paperback and Book-of-the-Month clubs had purchased *Where* for their spring lists. For his annual hand-printed holiday cards, which he didn't send out till January, he chose "Music," a blithe verse about the passionate affairs of Franz Liszt: "Music. Music! / Everybody grew more famous," the final lines read. Fame and reputation were on Carver's mind as he finished his major story collection, but perhaps more telling were the new poems he would write in 1988. "Lemonade," for instance, ponders a chain of innocuous circumstances that led to the drowning of the young son of the handyman who built Carver's new bookshelves.

In February, Ray suffered terrible headaches. Thanking his daughter for a Valentine's card, he wrote that his "nerves were bad" and he rarely answered the phone because there were "several hundred (thousands?) of people" he didn't want to talk to. He told Chris he'd been thinking about her "a great deal lately" and urged her to write him a letter. To his mother, he reported, "Nothing but rain here. We are trying to survive. Sometimes it's hard." On February 23, he and Tess consulted with a Port Angeles lawyer, Nathan Richardson, to review Washington State laws on joint ownership of property. Richardson reviewed the wills Gallagher and Carver had signed in New York in 1982 and deemed them consistent with their present wishes. Then Ray signed a power of attorney giving Gallagher the authority to make decisions for him if he were incapacitated. Ray and Tess explained to Richardson that they were preparing for a trip to New York.[19]

Because their own house was rented out, they stayed with the Walis on their two-day trip to Syracuse to consult with doctors. Ray was advised that he should have either surgery or radiation. After deliberation, they decided to return west for treatment. On February 26, they went to Virginia Mason Clinic in Seattle where Ray had an MRI of his brain and brain stem in preparation for radiation therapy. To one friend in whom he confided, Ray promised that he would never smoke or drink again.

Lung cancer spreads, or metastasizes, when cancer cells break off from the lung and move through the bloodstream to other places in the body. When the metastasis occurs in the brain and spinal cord, a persistent headache is generally followed by weakness, seizures, a decrease in alertness, and other signs of neurological breakdown. According to statistics published in 2000, the five-year survival rate for lung cancer patients whose disease has metastasized to the brain ranges between 1 and 2 percent. If Ray knew this, he gave no indication of it to his friends or family. According to account statements from the clinic, Ray attended four office consultations before he began intermediate-level brain radiation treatments on March 14. Tess wrote to the Dobynses that another tumor had occurred, but she did not say where it was. She also said that Ray had declined to have an operation.[20]

If Tess understood the gravity of Ray's condition, as it appears she did, she honored his desire not to speak of it to others. To one correspondent, Ray mentioned "health problems" and to another "things are a bit hectic— even difficult here." Only to his closest friends did he hint that his cancer had flared up, but the doctors were hopeful that he could defeat it.[21]

During this time, Ray had a close call of another sort. One day in March he "began to feel a fearfulness about his sobriety," Gallagher records, and set out to drive to an AA meeting in a town near Port Angeles. Unable to find the meeting, he called Gallagher from a tavern pay phone. He'd ordered a drink, he said, but hadn't yet lifted it to his lips. She asked him to leave the drink on the bar and come home. He did. Later she understood that the pressure in his head renewed the "shame and helplessness of his drinking days" and "caused his brush with the old compulsion to drink."[22]

Once Ray had hoped to buy a condo in Seattle. Now he and Tess rented a furnished apartment near the hospital for the seven weeks he would receive treatments. They spent four nights a week there and caught the ferry back to Port Angeles on Friday mornings. To make up for lost time, Ray worked on Sundays. In Seattle, they made the best of things by going out to movies and using the Jacuzzi at the apartment. Tess stopped at the Elliott Bay Book Co. for volumes of the Ecco Press edition of Chekhov's stories, which they read together during these weeks. When Vance wanted to fly in for a visit, Ray explained that Tess was taking care of everything and giving him what he needed: "privacy and solitude and the ability (and will) to do what work I can and try to keep my head above water." On April 5, halfway through his radiation treatments, Carver received a check for $67,500, his payment due upon signing a three-book contract with Atlantic Monthly Press. The final two weeks of radiation proved very fatiguing. By then Ray's face was noticeably swollen as a result of intracranial pressure and medications.[23]

Before the radiation ended, Ray told Maryann, Vance, Chris, Ella, and James about the brain tumor. Word reached some friends as well. After Carlile wrote to say he wished he'd heard the news directly from his dear friend, Ray answered that he and Tess had decided not to tell anyone the location of the tumor simply because they couldn't face the distress that others would feel when they heard such news. Ray insisted that he was not dwelling on thoughts of death and, in fact, did not even want to be reminded of such thoughts. Besides, he further insisted, his doctors believed his tumor was nearly dissolved and the cancer eradicated from his body. To Tobias Wolff's expression of concern, he replied that "everybody has high hopes, especially me" and that he was lining up a reading tour for the year

2000. He also praised Wolff for *This Boy's Life*, which Fisketjon had let him read in manuscript.[24]

On April 22, while Tess was away for a few days, Ray invited Maryann and Chris and her daughters to join him at the Four Seasons Hotel for lunch. When Ray entered the lobby, Maryann thought he was the most tragic sight she'd ever seen: "I saw him—his features—only in the middle of his face [because] it was so swollen. He had this big coat on, and a scarf around his neck, and a cap to cover his loss of hair from the radiation treatments." Despite his condition, Ray "matter-of-factly took his hat off to show us what he looked like. He was unashamed. He put on a real party for the little girls." When Maryann said grace at the beginning of the meal, Ray joined right in, because, she thought, "He was a consummate survivor. If praying would help now, he would pray." In the afternoon Maryann showed him the dress she'd purchased with money he sent her before his surgery and then accompanied him to his radiation treatment. When they had some quiet minutes together, she held his head in her hands and gave him a Reiki healing treatment. "My hands got hot, and I was holding the exact part of his head where he was daily being zapped with radiation treatments. . . . He kept saying, 'This feels so good, oh, this feels so good.'" According to Maryann, Ray wrote her letters throughout the year of his illness, called her on their anniversary in June, and mailed her a copy of the Franklin Library edition of *Where I'm Calling From*. His inscription, as she later read it to an interviewer, said:

> To Maryann, my oldest friend, my youthful companion in derring-do, my mid-year companion in the same, my wife and helpmate for so long, my children's mother, this book is a token of love, and some have claimed obsession. In any event, this is with love always, no one knows, do they, just absolutely no one. Yours, Ray. May 1988.[25]

Ray's feelings for his former wife were no secret even from friends of his who'd never met her. "Everybody knew that Ray always loved Maryann," Fisketjon said. "It was evident." Kittredge, who'd known them both, understood that Ray felt guilt and sorrow toward Maryann because, he left "with all the success" while she had to "stand out in the rain." As he didn't hesitate to write in "The Offending Eel," Carver sometimes thought their life together had driven her mad. In the end, Kittredge emphasized, Ray took his "deepest feelings, and used them to make art in ways that were partly a payment back to Maryann and at the same time another story."[26]

At the end of May, Maryann wrote Ray a letter that "organized our whole life together from my point of view, hoping that he would live and put it in a novel. . . . He wrote back that it was the kind of letter he liked to get, with a beginning, a middle, and end. You know, a real story. He was pleased."[27]

Still bloated and bald from treatments and steroid medications, Ray purchased a toupee and prepared for a trip east that was too beguiling to pass up. His wig looked like a helmet of straight, brown hair. "He knew it wasn't becoming and wore it as he'd wear a hat," Doug Unger said. In Hartford, Connecticut, he accepted an honorary doctor of letters degree from the University of Hartford. Tess and her mother, the Ungers, and other friends heard him speak to the college graduates about the word *tenderness* as it is enacted in Chekhov's novella *Ward No. 6.* Gallagher had worked on the talk with him, using her new Apple computer so that they could revise manuscripts without sending them out to a typist. The prose of the Hartford speech moves in a rhythm that sounds more like Gallagher's than Carver's, but there's a definite Carver touch in his valedictory paragraphs: ". . . words, the right and true words, can have the power of deeds. . . . Pay attention to the spirit of your words, your deeds. That's preparation enough. No more words."[28] Pleased and bemused by his doctorate, Ray joked that his new business cards would read "Dr. R. C. Carver, Narratologist."

His next stop was New York City. Carver's visit was heralded—as it were—by a front-page review of *Where I'm Calling From* in the May 15 *New York Times Book Review.* Reviewer Marilynne Robinson rejects the notion that Carver is a minimalist and asserts that he "stands squarely in the line of descent of American realism." His stories "create meaning through their form," and he should be "famous for the conceptual beauty of his best stories and disburdened of his worst . . ." In a brief interview printed alongside the review, Ray declared that he would beat his cancer: "I have books to write. The next one is a book of poems."[29]

Ray invited the Ungers, the Schweitzers, and the Walis, as well as Gary Fisketjon and Amanda Urban, to attend his induction as a member of the American Academy of Arts and Letters. When Vance Carver got a last-minute flight from Germany to attend the occasion, Ray treated him to a room near his own at the St. Regis. Until then, Vance had not realized how sick his father was or how devastating cancer could be. "Of course, my dad knew that his days were numbered. He just didn't let on to the inevitable," Vance recalled. "And I thought maybe, just maybe, he was going to get better. I know he really wanted to live."[30]

Induction into the prestigious AAAL followed naturally from Carver's honorable completion of the Strauss Living. John Updike, seconded by Stanley Elkin and Joyce Carol Oates, nominated Carver for membership.

It had been just twelve years since his first commercial book publication, eleven since he'd quit drinking; he was the youngest of five writers chosen in 1988. Carver's short stories, Updike wrote, had "given new definition and impetus to the form." To an exhibit of manuscripts by new academicians, Carver contributed sixteen versions of the first page of "Errand." He barely had the stamina to get through the induction ritual and reception, which were held in the academy's grandiose limestone quarters at Audubon Terrace, on the Upper West Side beyond Harlem. Chiseled above the academy's bronze doors are mottos meant to inspire men like Ray Carver:

ALL PASSES. ART ALONE UNTIRING STAYS TO US.
BY THE GATES OF ART WE ENTER THE TEMPLE OF HAPPINESS.

And so, during this week in New York, Ray embraced the happiness that his art had brought him. He signed copies of *Where I'm Calling From* at several bookstores, including the Charles Scribner's Sons shop in the building on Fifth Avenue at Forty-eighth Street where once upon a time Maxwell Perkins had edited Fitzgerald and Hemingway. Hundreds of people lined up to shake Ray's hand and get his autograph. He signed for hours and became so warm that he pulled off his toupee and set it on the table. "He kept saying, 'Can you believe this? Isn't this amazing? Who would have thought this?' He was proud of all the attention, and he was so good with all those people," Unger said. "Finally they had to shut the bookstore down."[31]

Throughout his visit to the East Coast, Ray let it be known that he had beaten his cancer and was now recovering from the symptoms of radiation. He was "one of the luckiest men around," he told Gail Caldwell of the *Boston Globe*.[32] If Ray cringed at becoming an object of sympathy and consternation, in his own way he also subscribed to the view that mind might triumph over body. Gallagher's statements confirm this: "Ray kept working, planning, believing in the importance of the time he had left," she writes, "and also believing that he might, through some loop in fate, even get out of this." Nonetheless, rumors of darker purposes have persisted. Perhaps Ray showed this brave face to the world because he did not want his publisher to break his three-book contract, or because he was in a tenuous situation regarding health insurance coverage. Deception was aided by the fact that most of Carver's friends and associates were his own age or younger, too young to believe that cancer could take down someone like themselves.

For Ray, the strain of public appearances and the pretense that he was feeling better must have been considerable. Unger noticed that he had a package of small cigars in his hotel room and felt these indicated that Ray had given up in his battle against his cancer. When Ray saw Qais Al-Awqati, he asked his physician friend if he knew of any other medical approach that might help him. Al-Awqati telephoned Ray's clinic for a report and learned the extent of the disease. "Then I called some friends at Sloan-Kettering, who said there wasn't anything significant that could be done. So I wasn't able to help him in any way." Before Vance departed, Tess spoke to him privately. "She said that if I wished to say something to my dad, now was the time. She told me my father was very ill."[33]

On the night before his fiftieth birthday, with Tess at his left ready to take over if his breath failed him, Ray read to several hundred people at Elliott Bay Book Co. in Seattle. As Ray seated himself before the microphone, the audience of hundreds took in that he hadn't been well. A respectful, almost reverent hush set in, followed by an outburst of applause. Ray began to read "Elephant." Over the sound system, you could hear him draw a breath. "You weren't sure he would make it; was he strong enough? But the story took over," Rick Simonson recalled. "People listened intensely, there was then laughter, more and more of it. With the laughter, Ray's voice gained strength. It was a great reading, plain and pure."[34] Next Ray and Tess flew to Anaheim for the American Booksellers Association convention. He joined Ford and David Leavitt and Carolyn See to promote their new books. Apologizing that he was unable to read something long or new, Ray made his way through "Why Don't You Dance?" in a "controlled, airy" voice, taking shallow breaths that gave out before the ends of his short sentences. The audience laughed heartily during this elegiac story of a man giving away all his possessions to a young couple. Perhaps as he read, Ray remembered that he'd received a mere $35 for that story when it first went into print.

At a rooftop party hosted by Atlantic Monthly Press, Ray chatted with Toni Morrison (at the ABA to promote *Beloved* in paperback) and invited her to come salmon fishing. Ray passed up a Vintage Contemporaries lunch in Newport Beach. Fisketjon recalled that both he and Ford were shocked by the way Ray looked at the ABA convention. "Richard had thought they were all going to go fishing in Alaska that summer. He still had that hope."[35]

On June 1, James Carver made his first visit to Port Angeles. "He'd invited me to come fishing many times, and we stayed in touch about our mother, because she was so unsettled, but I'd never been able to make the trip." Ray drove to pick James up at the airport:

> I felt so sorry for him. He was bloated and ungainly from the cortisone treatments. I stayed at his house, but Tess was protective of his time. He wasn't stoned on morphine or anything. He was entirely lucid. But we didn't have a whole lot of time to talk alone. I just did not know Tess very

well. To me she was a stranger, and I did not feel the freedom to talk as
brothers talk about things. I don't know if Tess meant to interfere. I know
she was there every moment.

When James left, he carried with him a box of autographed copies of his
brother's books. "For me, it was a very sad trip," James said. He sensed that
he would not see his brother again.[36]

For three decades, Raymond Carver had been writing poems about death.
Now he would grasp the subject close to himself. No one could provide a
truer description of events that befell him next than the scenes Carver offers
in several poems beginning with "What the Doctor Said":

> he said it looks bad in fact real bad
> he said I counted thirty-two of them on one lung . . .

"Them"—or *they*—were tumors on Ray's right lung and on the remainder of his left lung. He received this news from his Port Angeles doctor on
Monday, June 6. Ray and Tess decided to tell no one about the return of the
carcinoma to his lungs.[37] With virtually no hope of extending his survival
by medical means, they chose, as she put it, "to keep our attention on the
things we wanted to do." They wanted to have a wedding.

On June 17, Ray called his brother from Reno, Nevada, to tell him that
he had just married Tess. "Then, he said he'd cashed his chips. He told me
the tumors had returned. So we talked a little bit. That was the last time I
talked to him."[38] When the newlyweds returned from Reno, they held a
reception for local friends and returned to work on Ray's final poetry collection. "Proposal" tells about their decision to marry. It's a simple story,
two pages only, about how they'd both rebounded after the doctor's fatal
pronouncement—"time pressing down on us like a vise"—to "needing / a
celebration, a joining, a bringing friends into it. . . ."

They'd flown to Reno, been married by Minister W. Eckroat at the
Heart of Reno Wedding Chapel ("the world's oiliest minister," Ray said
afterward), and stayed in a suite at Bally's. Before leaving Port Angeles,
they'd purchased rings and told Tess's family, a few close friends, and
Amanda Urban where they were headed. They invited the Fords to be
witnesses, but they couldn't make it, so two strangers did the job instead.
The ceremony was tape-recorded and someone took a picture of the newlyweds with Tess's camera. In it, Tess gazes calmly at the man who by then
looked to her "like a very tender Buddha." Ray wears dark glasses and a
huge snap-brimmed cap. For Tess, the wedding was followed by a three-

day winning streak at roulette. On the morning of their departure, she left Ray standing "with our luggage, his arms heaped with wedding flowers which had been wired to us by friends abroad," while she placed one more bet on the wheel. Her luck held. Her hands full of money, she ran back to Ray's arms.[39]

On June 27, Ray had chest x-rays in Seattle; no additional treatments were recommended. On June 30, he and Gallagher met with attorney Richardson to discuss revisions to their wills in light of their recent marriage. As he had done in his 1982 will, Ray left $5,000 each to Vance, Christine, and Maryann; he added a new bequest of $1,500 for his mother. He gave outright ownership of the balance of his real and literary estate and all responsibilities of managing these to his wife, Theresa J. Gallagher. In the event that Gallagher were unable to serve in that capacity, he appointed Richard Ford (rather than Tobias Wolff, whom he had named in 1982) to serve as "alternate personal representative" and "literary personal representative." At this meeting, Richardson later testified, "Carver and Gallagher each expressed their mutual wish that any remaining literary rights of Raymond Carver owned by Theresa Gallagher as survivor would after her death pass to Carver's two children." Richardson recalled that he asked Carver if he wished to set up a trust to ensure that his children would succeed Gallagher. Carver said no. Then Carver and Gallagher asked Richardson to prepare new wills for them to sign.[40]

"Our having married," Gallagher wrote, "anchored us in a new way."[41] Now all things tended toward completion of Ray's final book. Alfredo Arreguin arrived with a painting secured to the top of his car. In the vivid, intricate patterns of *The Hero's Journey*, the Northwest's totemic salmon toil upstream against rapids to spawn and return peacefully across the sky in another, less visible form of being. Inspired by Arreguin's painting, Tess proposed a line from an earlier Carver poem for the book's title: *A New Path to the Waterfall*. Ray kept writing. In what can only have been rapid succession, he composed five more poems and one so-called fragment about his impending death: "Cherish," "Gravy," "No Need," "Through the Boughs," "After-glow," and "Late Fragment." Four of them are addressed to Tess or about Tess. In these final days they cleaved closely to each other, holding steady against their lonely expectation of Ray's death. Ray had his reasons for lying about his condition to his family and to the public, but he no longer lied to himself. He told Tess, "I want to keep both feet in life right to the end."[42]

Perhaps it was true, as he wrote in the best known of these poems, that he regarded the ten years since he'd quit drinking as "pure gravy"—as bonus years he'd never expected to have. His best work in fiction had always been marked by tremendous receptivity to the lives of others. His characters were people to him, not abstract and distant figures. To write about them as convincingly as he did, he had learned to join his receptivity with detachment. And so, faced with his final subject, his death, he called upon that capacity for detachment. With heartbreaking boldness and steadiness, "No Need" and "After-glow" describe the world from which the poet knows he'll soon be absent.

"Late Fragment," an elegy for himself that has been reprinted so often it can no longer be read as a fragment, asks and answers a question with disarming psychological honesty. What he wanted from his life, Carver tells us, was the knowledge that he was loved. And indeed, he had been loved— as a son and brother and friend, as a father, twice as a husband, and finally as an author.

Ray complained that no one in Port Angeles could remember such rainy, windy weather as they had in June 1988. As he and Tess saw their way clear to completing his book, they allowed a few visitors to come to Ray's Ridge House. Richard Day barely recognized the skinny kid who'd been his student thirty years earlier in the "grotesque figure of the dying man" until they sat out on Ray's deck and exchanged bizarre tales as they'd always done. Then the evening became "a prolonged, enchanted time-out." Neither man mentioned the reason for Day's visit. "Tess was on Ray like a viper about his smoking," Day said, but when she left them alone, Ray asked him for a cigarette.[43]

Kameshwar and Kashi Wali came next, flying in from Syracuse for a week. Ray drove them to view Mount Olympia from Hurricane Ridge and to the hot springs at Sol Duc. When Tess's neighbors held a Fourth of July bonfire party on the beach, Ray attended. He even left his work to ride the ferry across to Victoria for high tea at the Empress Hotel with the Walis. Before the Walis departed, Dennis and Loretta Schmitz, who were vacationing in the Northwest, also arrived. Although they'd wondered if this might be a last visit, they were stunned by Ray's condition. To them, Ray seemed extremely nervous. "He was unable to stop flipping the TV channels and watching the screen, trying to follow the news of an Iranian passenger plane shot down by the U.S. Navy." After the Walis cooked an Indian dinner, Ray relaxed enough to turn on a video—it was *El Cid*—and laugh a little. Dennis reminded Ray of a morning when he'd made a steep, risky climb from a Sonoma coast beach where they were camped just to get coffee. These two poets knew each other's minds intimately. They both understood that Schmitz saw that morning climb as a metaphor for Ray's last climb: "The climb was hard and he went up and away from us without our knowing," Schmitz wrote later.[44]

During the summer of 1988, Christine Carver was pregnant with her third child, whose father she had met in her logic class at Western Washington University. Ray mailed her $300 for her college tuition and asked her please to finish her summer class. That check was followed by another a few days later, $200 designated for "summer outfits." On July 15, he sent her a note on a plain postal card congratulating her on moving into a house and asking for her new telephone number. By phone he told her he would come to Bellingham on August 2, following the close of her summer session.[45]

When Vance Carver came to see his father in Port Angeles on July 14, they went out alone together. Ray appeared more ill to Vance now than he'd looked in May. After a lunch of fish and chips, they took a ride in a rowboat on the harbor. Then Ray felt some distress in his stomach and went home to bed. At the airport the next day, Ray squeezed his son's hand so tightly that it hurt and then said, with tears in his eyes, that he had wanted to see Vance's daughter grow up. Back in Bellingham, Vance told Christine that their father's eyes looked yellow and his stomach was upset. From that information, Christine began to fear that her father's whole body was now failing him. She immediately wrote her father and offered to come to Port Angeles. She received no reply to that letter.[46]

Amy and Doug Unger realized that Ray's condition was grave on July 19, when Ray called with condolences after a house where they were staying in Idaho burned to the ground, destroying Unger's novel in progress and killing their two dogs. When Doug asked Ray how he was, Ray answered, "I'm thinking about those dogs." His voice was very, very whispery, and Unger understood that his remark about the dogs was code, his way of saying he wasn't going to make it. "He tried to give us moral support, but he just had no strength for it."[47]

Tess confided to Ray that she felt anxious about an eventual meeting with Maryann, "about how she might behave, and also my own behavior." In reply, Ray reminded Tess that when he had met fourteen-year-old Maryann, she was like an angel. He asked Tess to "keep in mind that she was once like an angel, and so could you please treat her that way?"[48]

Maryann has described three identical postcards she received in her last envelope from Ray:

Nothing was written on them. The postcards showed a picture of two hands in prayer, a Rodin sculpture. I remembered when we were in Paris. We had lost ourselves in the Rodin museum, going back repeatedly . . .

Ray and I had seen that sculpture of two white feminine-shaped hands in prayer. Two porcelain-white praying hands.

This was how he told me he wasn't going to make it.[49]

Despite everything, Ray continued giving shape to—finding, as it were—*A New Path to the Waterfall*. Gallagher arranged the book in six sections, including poems that first appeared in magazines in the sixties or in Carver's early collections *Near Klamath* and *Winter Insomnia*.[50] To complete the book, they interspersed Carver's poems with quotations from other writers. A few of the never-before-published poems that Gallagher included in *A New Path to the Waterfall* disturbed members of Ray's family. Critics may well wonder if Carver intended to publish or collect them while Maryann, Ella, and Vance were still living. These questionable inclusions are "The Kitchen," "Suspenders," "The Offending Eel," "On an Old Photograph of My Son," and, possibly, "Miracle." And yet Ray's relationship to his family was as complicated as a tangled fishing line. As Maryann has said, "Ray did what he needed to do to write captivating stories and poems; profit, personal catharsis, and hurt to family members were secondary considerations at best." Because Ray was "so decent and loyal" in private, she continued, his publications could shock and deliver a sense of betrayal to those who loved him.[51]

A New Path to the Waterfall, published in the summer of 1989, includes fifteen versified passages from Chekhov, two from authors on fishing, six poems by other poets, fifty Carver poems (sixteen published years before but uncollected). Arreguin's painting is reproduced on the book's endpapers. Reviewer Elizabeth Benedict describes the book accurately as "Carver's scrapbook during the last year of his life."[52] Gallagher's introduction ameliorates the book's hodgepodge quality by telling the story of Ray's last year and explaining the arrangement of the book. Its last section, in any case, stands on its own, made fiercely coherent by its subject: an author "roaring" in the face of his death, as one of his quotes from Chekhov puts it:

To scream with pain, to cry, to summon help, to call generally—all that is described here as "roaring." In Siberia not only bears roar, but sparrows and mice as well. "The cat got it, and it's roaring," they say of a mouse.

When the book was finished to his satisfaction in mid-July, Ray was loath to give up his mornings and evenings to other people. He asked Gallagher not to tell the guests they were finished, because he needed her with him. "So," she writes, "the book as a pretext allowed us a few more precious mornings with each other before what would be the final onset of his illness."[53]

Ray's decision to keep quiet about his condition forced him to tell some whoppers that were also fantasies. He postponed a visit from rare book dealer Ralph Sipper by announcing that he and Tess were about to depart on a long trip to Russia, and that Tess did not feel he should sell any more materials just now. "This summer will not be a summer for doing business of any sort whatsoever," he concluded. His last letter to Stephen Dobyns, dated July 9, mentions that he's been "feeling very housebound" and might go to London and Amsterdam in August. All over the country, other friends of Ray's went on naïvely hoping that their friend who had survived so many other things might also beat lung cancer. Chuck Kinder planned to fly west to see Ray after a two-week stay at Yaddo. Even those who suspected differently found reasons for hope in Ray's letters. On the same day he wrote Dobyns about Amsterdam, Ray invited the Fords to a fishing resort in Alaska where they could have their own boats and bait boys to clean up after them. "The later in August it gets, the better the fishing," Ray urged.[54]

Of course, no one knew exactly how long Ray might live. Neither statistics nor medical imaging machines can make exact predictions about a determined human spirit. As Tess wrote, "The insistent nature of Ray's belief in his own capacity to recover from reversals during the course of his illness gave us both strength." He and Tess even talked seriously—to the point of phoning travel agents—about making a trip to Russia to visit Dostoyevsky's and Tolstoy's houses and Chekhov's grave. Imagining themselves in Russia "was a kind of dream-visit that lifted our spirits," Gallagher wrote. She compared it to Chekhov's reading of railway timetables during the last days of his life.[55]

When he and Tess realized a literary pilgrimage to Russia was too complicated and difficult, they decided to go by themselves to an Alaskan fishing lodge. Before they departed, they made an appointment to sign their new wills at Nathan Richardson's law office in Port Angeles on August 1.

While they were away, Ford and Fisketjon telephoned Ray's house from the Fords' in Montana. No one answered, but "none of us took that to mean the worst," Fisketjon said. By then, Ray and Tess were in Seattle, their fishing trip cut short when Ray's disease forced him to enter Virginia Mason Clinic on July 23. Gallagher has not chosen to write about these days in any detail. Medical bills show that for the week Ray remained in the hospital, he underwent tests on his chest, abdomen, heart, kidneys, liver, bile ducts, and pancreas, including the placement of a stent. He was discharged on July 30. Tess's Aetna insurance, to which Ray was now entitled as a spouse, paid the charges for that hospitalization.[56]

Tess arranged a white Cadillac to carry them home to Port Angeles. The local hospice set up a hospital bed for Ray in the living room and saw to his pain medications. On the morning of August 1, Tess called Richardson's office to say that Ray was too ill to come in to complete their wills. Richardson agreed to drive to Ridge House with witnesses so Ray could sign his there. By phone, Richardson advised Gallagher that he "would put a paragraph in the will regarding discussions during the June 30th conference about the disposition of Carver's literary interests after Gallagher's death." In the midafternoon, Richardson arrived with his wife, Norma, and Dorothy Catlett, who had often worked as a secretary for Ray and Tess. According to Richardson, he and Carver held a conversation about the clauses of the will and Richardson read him the paragraph he had inserted that day. In a shaky but legible hand, Ray signed his last will.[57]

In "My Death" (April 1984), Carver wrote that he hoped he'd be lucky enough to be allowed time "to say goodbye to each of my loved ones. . . . and take that memory with me." It didn't happen that way. Ella Carver later said she had left several phone messages for Ray during the weeks prior to his death. When he called back, his voice was weak, but he told his mother he wanted to hear her voice. At the end of July, Ella telephoned Tess's mother and said she wanted to visit. Mrs. Bond reportedly told Ella that she wouldn't be able to do her son any good.[58] Asleep in the mansion at Yaddo, Chuck Kinder woke at 3:00 on the morning of August 2 to find himself frightened of the dark. He turned on all the lights and didn't fall asleep until the sun rose. He saw no one all day. When he went to the porch to meet friends for dinner, "they both looked up to me as I approached and I knew. I said, 'It's Ray, isn't it?' "[59]

On the night of August 1, Ray and Tess watched a videotape of *Dark Eyes,* an Italian movie based on Chekhov's story "The Lady with the Pet Dog." Because she had slept very little in the past few days, Tess asked Jack Estes, a teacher at Olympic Peninsula College, to sit with Ray for part of the night. Before she left the living room, Tess and Ray kissed three times and said they loved each other. Several times during the next few hours Estes helped Ray move himself and his oxygen supply between the hospital bed and the couch. Though Ray was in pain and couldn't stay comfortable in any position, his spirits were good. The two men conversed a little about Chekhov and about movies. Ray fell asleep, but Estes kept awake, listening to Ray's breath.

Early the next morning, Ray's breathing became more labored. Estes woke Tess. She held Ray and spoke to him quietly, but he did not answer or open his eyes. Just after sunrise on August 2, 1988, Raymond Carver died.[60]

Epilogue

All those qualities you sensed about Raymond Carver, that he was
a man who would do the decent, the right and generous thing—that
was how he was.

—Tess Gallagher, *Soul Barnacles*[1]

Throughout the day Carver died, friends and family picked up their telephones and learned of his passing. Even those who had seen how ill he
was were surprised that his death occurred as soon as it did.

Ray's people set their daily lives aside and busied themselves with travel
arrangements and more telephone calls. Tess's mother and sisters and brothers converged to help her. There was no time for indecision. A funeral at
home and burial at Ocean View Cemetery in Port Angeles were scheduled
for Thursday, August 4, just two mornings after Ray's death.

Vance Carver traveled farthest and was the first to arrive from beyond
Port Angeles. His wife had managed to get him a seat on the next flight
from Frankfurt to Vancouver, then on to Seattle and Port Angeles. He had
never attended a funeral before.

At Ridge House, Vance found his father's body dressed in a good suit
and fine shoes, laid out on his large bed in the dining room. Tess told
Vance that keeping the deceased's body at home in this way was an Irish
tradition, a wake. That night, Vance slept in Tess's other house by the
water.[2]

Richard Ford was not surprised to see Ray's body present at home. He
recognized this custom of American country Southerners, the people of
Arkansas and Missouri who were his and Ray's and Tess's ancestors.[3]

Even so, for Gallagher, whose father's services had been held in a funeral
parlor six years earlier, the choice to keep Ray at home appears to have been
entirely personal. In "Wake," one of her grieving poems collected in *Moon
Crossing Bridge*, the poet asks herself: "Did I want to prove how surely /
I'd been left behind?"[4]

• • •

479

In New York, Ray's editor, Gary Fisketjon, thinking that Ray was still fishing in Alaska, was shocked to learn that he'd died. He and Carver's agent, Amanda Urban, flew west the next morning. The Fords picked them up at the airport and brought them to Ridge House where they found Mona Simpson and the Ungers and other out-of-town visitors standing around in the front yard, disconcerted by Ray's corpse in the house. Tess and her mother sat inside, near the fireplace. "Everyone was distraught, in catatonic shock," Fisketjon remembered.[5]

Relatives arrived by car from other parts of Washington State, including Ray's aunt Violet Archer and Maryann's sister Jerry Davis from Yakima. Maryann, wearing a rose-colored crepe dress that she'd bought with money Ray sent before his surgery, arrived with her half sister. Christine, seven months' pregnant, flew to Port Angeles. Many other friends and relatives, including Diane Cecily, Bill Kittredge, Chuck Kinder, Tobias Wolff, and Ray's mother and brother, could not travel to Port Angeles on such short notice.[6]

The gathering at Ridge House was private. Family and friends spoke their words of remembrance, grief, and consolation in the room where Ray's unembalmed body was laid out. Some read his poems. "We all had appropriate things to say," one mourner recalled, "and given the fact that it was, shall we call it, an extended family, there were extenuating things expressed." On that day, as he'd been on many days past, "Ray was the calm center of a nutty life," another mourner thought. In his "Late Fragment," Ray wrote that he was grateful "to feel beloved." Those who loved him showed their grief in many ways, from masking their emotions with jokes to outright hysteria. Vance was consumed by sadness, because "we had worked hard to become better friends, and then suddenly he becomes gravely ill and dies." At the funeral, he felt torn between Gallagher and his mother's family, between trying to keep the day running smoothly and consoling those who hadn't been forewarned of Ray's death.[7]

From notes he'd jotted down on a scratch pad at his hotel, Richard Ford spoke at length about his dear friend: "Ray reposed everything he knew and could discover and make up about himself—everything he thought might be useful or pleasing or revealing of life—in his work," Ford said. "Most notably, into his work he wrote everything he knew or could sense of human frailty and everything he could figure out or say to offer that frailty consolation . . . He employed himself, the way he employed verbs and nouns . . . And because he did and did so wonderfully, *we knew him*! We felt . . . *increased*."[8]

• • •

Vance and several other men placed Ray's body in a casket for the drive to Ocean View Cemetery, where loggers and fishermen and war veterans lie beneath simple stones in the midst of a splendid landscape. Just months earlier, from the water below this very cemetery, Ray and Fisketjon had noticed a funeral. "It could be worse, Gary," Ray had said then. "It could be you or me they're planting up there."

Later Gallagher turned Carver's resting place into a literary shrine like those she and Ray had seen in Zurich and Paris. Visitors to Carver's grave now find a bench alongside three large slabs of black granite. The stone over Ray reads RAYMOND CARVER with his dates of birth and death, the words "Poet, Short Story Writer, Essayist," and his poem "Late Fragment." Another slab to the right is prepared for Theresa Bond Gallagher Carver. It is one of the few places where Carver's widow has appended his last name to hers. Her legal name is Theresa J. Gallagher. A center stone carries his poem "Gravy" and a photograph of Gallagher and Carver together, her dark hair enveloping his head.

After the interment, mourners returned to Ridge House for food and drink. Townspeople brought casseroles and pies, and Tess invited visitors to come upstairs to see Ray's study. Keeping her promise to Ray, Tess included Maryann in her invitation to return to the house; nonetheless, Maryann's sorrow for Ray's death was exacerbated by the feeling that she and her family had been excluded from hearing news of him during the final weeks of his illness. Their feelings were further exacerbated when members of Gallagher's family monitored their access to Ray's study.[9] For Maryann and Christine and others who belonged, as it were, to Ray's earlier life, this visit to his spacious, comfortable, fully furnished home was a revelation of the financial success Ray had begun to find in recent years.

While Ray's close friends and family were burying him, his death had become a public event. On the morning of August 3, obituaries of Carver appeared in the *New York Times,* the *Seattle Times,* and hundreds of newspapers that reprinted an Associated Press report. On the following Sunday, book review editors further regretted the early death of "perhaps the most influential, respected and widely imitated of contemporary short-story writers" and celebrated his recent work for "moving into more expansive territory, beyond 'minimalism' " (*Chicago Tribune*).

The *Times* (London) published a review cum eulogy of Carver's last seven stories (published separately in England) with a headline that was destined to attach itself to his reputation for years to come: "The American Chekhov; Elephant and Other Stories by Raymond Carver." Writing for the venerable newspaper, Peter Kemp noted that "Errand," Carver's story of Chekhov's death, offers an "uncannily authentic slant" on the famous event. He called Carver "the Chekhov of Middle America."

"Errand" courts the yoking of the two writers' names that Kemp's review established.[10] Despite the differences between the late-nineteenth-century Russian and the mid-twentieth-century American, Kemp's epitaph has become a key element in the longevity of Carver's reputation in a literary world with a short memory. At one extreme, Carver is classified as the exemplar of minimalism. At the other, he is called upon to be America's answer to the inventor of the modern short story whose prose works comprise fourteen volumes.

In this fog of cliché and hyperbole, it's useful to know that, accurately enough, Kemp found Carver Chekhovian because he reveals "the strangeness concealed behind the banal," "extracts a poetry of the prosaic," and "irradiates the melancholy" of his stories with "sardonic ventriloquism."[11]

The *Times* eulogist also observed that the narrator of Carver's story "Elephant" gives money to "feckless and disaster-prone members of his family" as "a kind of expiation for his own former irresponsibility." That narrator understands that he won't escape his obligations to his family. His acceptance makes him walk down the road whistling and swinging his arms. Ray's own letters and his family's memories of his last years suggest that he made peace with his frustrations about his family.

Two other late stories use fallen leaves as an image for responsibilities. In "Menudo," an unfaithful husband obsessively rakes leaves, trying to create order in a neighborhood where marriages are falling apart. At the end of "Intimacy," another man notices piles of leaves in front of his former wife's residence: "Somebody ought to make an effort here. Somebody ought to get a rake and take care of this."

Carver's recent success and the secrecy surrounding his final illness left a good deal of business for somebody to take care of. As designated by his will, that person was Tess Gallagher.

In 1978, when he won a Guggenheim Fellowship and started teaching in El Paso, Raymond Carver was dead broke. He'd never worked at one job for more than eighteen months, and he'd never made enough money on his writing to consider himself a full-time writer. Maryann, his primary support for years, had resigned her teaching job. His children were living hand-to-mouth on the money they could make doing service jobs or manual labor.

Ten years later, Carver was the full or joint owner of three houses, two newer automobiles, and a ten-year-old boat. Additionally, he had savings accounts totaling nearly $215,000.[12] His financial solvency—and his indisputable ascent from the class he'd called the "working poor" to the professional middle class—was a notable achievement. During the same time, he had given his son financial help toward a master's degree and provided a monetary safety net for Maryann, his daughter and her children, and his own mother.

This solvency was part of what he meant in calling the years since he'd quit drinking "pure gravy." The unknown factor in any attempt to assess the value of Carver's estate is the value of his literary work. *Where I'm Calling From* was well on its way to earning out its advances, but he owed McGraw-Hill for an unwritten novel and had completed only two of three books promised to Atlantic Monthly Press.

In giving copyrights to all of his published and unpublished work to Gallagher, Carver merely gave her the opportunity to protect and extend his reputation. Success was not assured. Along with that opportunity came the time-consuming and delicate job of keeping Carver's work and reputation alive for future readers—becoming the keeper of his immortality. She understood the gravity of the mission he'd given her.

For some days after Ray's death, his mother, former wife, and children heard nothing regarding his estate. When official notice that Carver had left them only cash bequests reached Ella, Maryann, and Christine, they were still reeling from a death that was, for them, sudden.[13] Ray had always been there for these three women in times of extreme need. His mother was simply devastated to learn that the monthly checks she'd counted on for several years were no longer assured.

While Carver's estate was tied up in probate, his literary legacy grew. "Gravy" appeared in the *New Yorker* on August 29. Friends and associates organized additional memorial services for Carver in a chapel in Syracuse, a church in New York City, and Legends nightclub in London. Among the speakers were Douglas Unger, Kameshwar Wali, Ted Solotaroff, Christopher MacLehose, and Salman Rushdie. At the fall meeting of the American Academy and Institute of Arts and Letters, John Updike read a tribute to Carver.

When friends or fans came to visit Tess Gallagher in Port Angeles, she usually showed them Ray's study and invited them to sit before his typewriter and write him a note. Sometimes she gave them a piece of Ray's clothing or let them wear his leather jacket or his bathrobe. In the pockets of these garments, the friends found small cigars, joints, and notebooks. She spoke of maintaining Ray's Ridge House as it was when he died, as a museum and tribute to his work and perhaps as a retreat for other writers.[14]

Vance Carver, who had been closest to Tess, returned to Germany, where he became a military intelligence analyst employed by the U.S. Air Force. Christine Carver, anxious to establish good relations with Tess, wrote her letters (copied to Richard Ford and Gary Fisketjon) to ask if her father had made any ongoing financial provisions for her and to invite her to be a godmother to her new baby.

She received no reply. Heidi LaRae Carver was born October 18. By strange happenstance, as she waited for the school bus with her daughters Windy and Chloe one morning, Christine found an envelope from her father on the ground. Mailed the month before he died, it contained a check for $250 to use for summer clothes and pizza. By phone Christine asked Gallagher if the check could be cashed and learned that it could not because Carver's estate was in probate. She was disappointed that Gallagher did not offer to send a replacement check.[15]

When Ray and Maryann divorced in 1982, he promised her financial help (in his attorney's words) "for as long as you two feel you need financial assistance." Unfortunately for Maryann, this promise was not legally binding. Even so she filed a claim against Carver's estate, requesting back payment of support based on their $400-a-month agreement in 1982. She further explained that even when Ray had not paid her $400 a month, he made "repeated reassurances" to her that both she and their children would be "taken care of." Since his will had made no provision for her future support, she claimed ownership of "an undivided one-half interest" in the property owned by herself and Ray on the date of their divorce. She stated that in conversations with Carver she had been "lulled into a false sense of security by what I now know to be misrepresentations of his intentions toward me and our children." It had been her belief that she would be rewarded in Carver's estate plans for supporting him during their marriage and for not demanding alimony in their divorce settlement.

The same attorney who represented Maryann in her claim against Carver's estate also filed a petition on behalf of Christine and Vance (who soon withdrew himself from the action) for a declaration of their rights under Carver's will. Christine asked the court for a legal interpretation of the paragraph that Nathan Richardson had inserted on the afternoon of Carver's death: "I express my desire to my spouse . . . my intention that ultimately, after her death, the then remaining interest which had been owned by me at my death . . . pass to my two children."

Christine expressed her belief in the following statement: "My father was dying at the time he made his last Will, but none of us were told . . . Because he was so critically ill, and was heavily medicated to reduce his pain, it was probably not possible for him to get in touch with either me or my mother . . . I feel that his estate plan would have been more clearly and adamantly stated had he had any of his family around him during those last days."

These two legal disputes generated hundreds of pages of documents and thousands of dollars in legal fees for the two Port Angeles attorneys who represented Carver's estate and the Carvers. A Seattle reporter wrote that Gallagher's savings had been "siphoned away to such an extent that ownership of one of their two houses was threatened."[16] Judge Grant Meiner issued an oral opinion that neither Ray's promises to Maryann nor the clause expressing his "desire" and "intention" were legally binding. Gallagher was granted full discretion to use and dispose of Carver's literary property as she saw fit. She was not obligated to follow the "desire" or "intention" expressed in Carver's will.

Gallagher told the reporter she was "glad that Ray did not have to go through those things I did. But he knew I could and he was right. I'm pretty sturdy in all areas."[17] Maryann accepted a $5,000 payment (in addition to Carver's $5,000 bequest) from Gallagher in exchange for releasing her and Carver's estate from a sweeping list of claims and liabilities "now or in the future" and "unknown, unforeseen, and unexpected" on behalf of herself and her heirs.

Although Christine considered appealing the county court's interpretation of her father's will, she accepted a $5,000 payment (over and above the bequest) instead. Much of the money she received went to lawyer's fees. Upon receiving their specific bequests from their father's estate, both she and her brother also signed broad release documents drafted by Gallagher's attorney to waive "any and all claims" against Carver's estate and Gallagher. Ella Carver did likewise when she received her $1,500 payment.[18]

By the end of 1989, Christine Carver felt that she had been "disinherited" by her stepmother. Vance Carver and his wife and daughter continued to maintain cordial relations with Gallagher. Ella Carver kept in touch with both Tess and Maryann, though it concerned her that Tess spoke ill of Maryann and Christine while Maryann never complained to her about Tess. On Tess's advice, Ella sold her letters from Ray to Ohio State University, but she received no financial help from Tess. She lived frugally in public housing for the elderly in Sacramento and, at seventy-eight, worked as a "grandmother" aide in an elementary school. "It's too bad," James thought, "that Ray didn't see how settled our mother was in her last years."[19] Ella Carver died of cancer in 1993.

· · ·

The challenges to Carver's will took place in Gallagher's hometown, in the Clallam County Superior Court. While these actions were going on, she remained a member of the faculty in Syracuse and was occupied with seeing Carver's last books translated and published all over the world, as well as with the preparation of films and books about Carver.

In February 1990, after the legal disputes relating to Carver's will had been quelled, filmmaker Robert Altman read a collection of Carver's stories during a transatlantic flight. He immediately asked his attorney to acquire rights to option Carver's stories and began talking to Frank Barhydt about cowriting a screenplay.

Gallagher welcomed Altman's offer of $10,000 for an option on several Carver stories and one poem. Altman's lawyers sent the necessary paperwork, including a requirement that renewal rights to these stories be specifically included in the option. At this point, Gallagher learned that by U.S. Copyright law, the right to renew copyrights on literary works published before 1978 is automatically inherited and shared by a writer's spouse and children, regardless of what the writer's will has directed. This meant that Christine and Vance had each inherited 25 percent of the renewal rights to every poem and story that Carver had published before January 1978. (By bizarre coincidence, this was very close to the date of Carver's last drink as well as to the breakup of his marriage to Maryann.)

Even though Christine and Vance had signed waivers of their rights to Carver's literary work in 1989, Altman's legal advisors insisted upon a specific assignment of renewal rights.[20] From here on, the story becomes murky. In July 1990, Gallagher asked Christine and Vance to sign new documents to correct a "technical defect" in the 1989 waiver, and she offered them each $2,000 to do so. They both recall that she mentioned that Carver's work would go into the "public domain" if this were not completed.[21] Something about Gallagher's urgency in this matter aroused Christine's suspicion. Both she and Vance attempted to get advice from attorneys but apparently did not learn that they already owned the renewal rights under discussion.

Vance signed the document, but Christine, in the middle of final exams to finish her bachelor's degree, delayed. Gallagher telephoned her several times. Christine recalled that she asked Gallagher why she urgently needed this document if she already owned all Carver's literary rights. She also recalled that she asked if there was a possibility of a movie to be made from her father's works. Gallagher later disputed Christine's recollections.

Fearing that Christine would complicate her management of Carver's estate or that Altman would withdraw his offer, Gallagher increased her pressure. At Gallagher's request, Amanda Urban discussed the issue with

Christine by telephone. Gallagher then offered Christine another $1,000 to sign over the rights. Vance urged his sister to sign, too, explaining that he believed Tess would honor "the essence of Dad's will" by leaving royalties to himself and Chris when she made a new will.[22]

Christine signed the release on August 9, 1990.

The importance of the renewal rights depended on many things: whether Altman would go forward with plans to make a film, how many pre-1978 stories he would want to use, how much he would pay for those rights, and how much the resultant film would earn.[23] Beyond Altman's concerns, the value of the rights depended on how much interest there would be in these stories during their renewed term of copyright. That was something no one could predict.

Although Altman's initial option lapsed, two years later he renewed it and then paid Gallagher $225,000 (less commissions) for the rights to nine stories and one poem that he adapted for *Short Cuts*. Seven of those stories were copyrighted before 1978.

When *Short Cuts* was released in 1993, Christine wondered if Gallagher's concern with the renewal rights to Carver's early stories had been connected to the making of this film. Understanding that movies are often more profitable than books, she secured *pro bono* representation by Seattle intellectual property attorney Matthew Geyman. Geyman argued that Christine had been mistakenly or perhaps fraudulently persuaded to sell her rights and filed a lawsuit on her behalf against Gallagher in early 1995. Gallagher also hired a Seattle attorney and spent a good deal of the money she'd acquired from the film to defend her ownership of the renewal rights to Carver's work. The suit was set for a jury trial in January 1997. Legal documents, including lengthy depositions with Christine Carver and Tess Gallagher, indicate that the trial's arguments might have boiled down to a question of what was said in a phone call between Christine and her stepmother more than six years earlier. Days before the trial, Christine accepted a payment reported to be "about the price of a good used car" to settle out of court. The undisclosed amount was determined after an analysis of income from Carver's pre-1978 works for the six years following his death. In accepting the settlement, Christine abandoned her suit to recover renewal rights.[24]

After spending a few years in California, Christine and her daughters and several grandchildren, including one named Shyloh Raymond Carver, have settled in Washington State near Maryann Burk Carver. For her memoir of her marriage to Raymond Carver, Maryann chose the title *What It Used to Be Like*, a phrase from the Alcoholics Anonymous Big Book. Maryann has continued her studies in religion and philosophy while trying to maintain her inherited land and assist her family by substitute teaching, working at a health food and vitamin shop, and delivering pizzas. After a career as head English instructor and translator at Deutsche Bundesbank, Vance Carver returned to the United States in 2002 and began teaching high school–level French, German, and political science. His daughter, Jennifer, works for Lufthansa Airlines.

Gallagher has published books of poetry, fiction, and translations since 1988. She has divided her time between Port Angeles and County Sligo, Ireland, the home of storyteller and artist Josie Gray, a man she described as her "intermittent companion." Carver is a presence in her 2006 collection of poems, *Dear Ghosts,* where she writes, "Our life apart / has outstripped the mute kaleidoscope / of the hydrangea and its seven changes."[25]

Gallagher completed renewal of Carver's pre-1978 copyrights in her own name in 2005. Under her oversight Carver's work remains in print around the globe. In addition, she has shepherded the publication of several posthumous collections, including the miscellaneous collections *No Heroics, Please* and *Call If You Need Me* (which include early work and five stories left unfinished at Carver's death) and the variorum collected edition of Carver's poems, *All of Us.* An Australian film company bought film rights to "So Much Water So Close to Home" from Gallagher and Altman in 2003, the year Gallagher renewed that story's copyright, and released *Jindabyne* in 2008.

Though sales of Carver's books have fallen off in the twenty years since his death, his influence abides. He is, as he liked to say, "out there in history." Under Gallagher's stewardship, his major books have remained in print and websites in several languages have fostered discussions of his work. Ray's laugh has been posted on one website. His work has found new readers by means of anthologies for students. John Updike selected "Where I'm Calling From" for *The Best American Short Stories of the Century.* Debate about Lish's influence on his work has flared up in the media from time to time; a Library of America edition collects his stories and reprints earlier versions of stories that Lish trimmed. The International Raymond Carver Society, founded in 2005, promotes critical study of his work.

Carver's dearest friends—too many to list again—have continued to reflect him in their own work and retell their stories of the mischievous Ray. Some of those friends have become esteemed men and women of letters, garlanded with honors as Ray was in his final year. Many more have remained at their desks, well known, unknown, or forgotten writers who, out of fervent belief in the power of fiction and poetry to restore our lonely lives, have turned out their work regardless of the poor odds for wider success.

"I don't know what I want, but I want it now," Carver wrote in a pocket notebook. Perhaps a writer never knows exactly what he wants, but Carver had followed his impatience and yearning where it led him, into some very dark places, and then beyond, toward that elusive goal he'd glimpsed in his youth—a writer's life. Another notebook entry that Tess Gallagher found after Carver's death gives what may be his own modest assessment of his life: "Whatever this was all about, this was not a vain attempt—journey."[26] He had made stories that would last.

Acknowledgments and Sources

Raymond Carver was, as one of his friends said "a story-catcher." In writing this biography, I have been privileged to catch stories from hundreds of Carver's relatives, friends, and colleagues. Among the first to share their knowledge and recollections were Nevel and Buey Davis, Jerry King, Dick Moeller, and Frank Sandmeyer in Yakima. James Carver, Maryann Burk Carver, Amy Burk Unger, Christine Carver, and Vance Carver all set aside initial reservations to speak to me about Ray, as did Violet Archer, Donald Archer and Gloria Archer, Mavis (Jack) Green, Vivian Bachman Mosley, Edith Guise, and Franklin Casey provided invaluable family records. Richard Cortez Day, Loretta Schmitz, and Dennis Schmitz offered me their reminiscences of long friendships with the Carvers. The following people also added to my understanding of Carver's early years: Pamela Allen, Roy Baker, Charles William Barton, Larry Berghoff, Clark Blaise, Herb Blisard, Bettina Bourjaily, Vance Bourjaily, David Boxer, Eleanor Bronson, James Callaway, Todd Collins, Daniel Davis, Larry Davis, Tom Doherty, Lennis Dunlap, Joan Gardner, Edgar Glenn, Fred Green, Douglas Kent Hall, Ada Hazen, Deborah Steele Hazen, Gerald Helland, Roy and Marjorie Hoover, Jay Karr, Ruth King, King Kryger, Irmagene Kulp Zacher, Eric Larsen, Ian McMillan, Adrian Mitchell, Dick Moeller, Bharati Mukherjee, Charlene and David Palmer, Cassandra Phillips, Hank Pieti, Alice Ritchey Burk Reed, Jon Remmerde, Kenneth Rosen, Tom Schmidt, Earl Shelton, Neil Shinpaugh, Ben Short, Giles Sinclair, Kathy Starbuck, Vi Sullens, Liggett Taylor, Gary Thompson, Benjamin Van Eaton, Ted Weesner, James Whitehead, Joy Williams, and James Young. Thanks to Hugh Davies, Raymond Shore, Ben Short, and Dale Sparber for information about saw filing and Cascade Lumber.

For generous recollections of Carver's professional struggles, I am particularly grateful to George Hitchcock and Marjorie Simon, Gordon Lish, James D. Houston, Curtis L. Johnson, Richard Kolbert, Sylvia Kolbert, William Kittredge, Morton Marcus, Leonard Michaels, and David and Lynn Swanger, as well as to James B. Hall, Jack Hicks, Mereda and Gerald Kaminski, Ellen Levine, Paul Skenazy, Annie Steinhardt, Al Young, and Frank Zepezauer, and to Carver's former students Mark Jarman, John Kucich, Robert McDowell, David Myers, and Diane Smith. Carver's gift for friendship, with but a few exceptions, became all the more accommodating during his years of heavy drinking. Those who helped recreate those years in my imagination include, above all, Diane Cecily and Chuck Kinder and Douglas Unger, as well as Max Crawford, Dan Domench, Frederic W. Hills, Jon A. Jackson, Michael Köepf, and George Lynn. In addition, I am grateful for contributions from Porter Abbott, Qais Al-Awqati, Steve Allaback, John Batki, T. Coraghessan Boyle, Anthony Bukowski, Dennis Covington, Sue Parsons Crawford, James Crumley, Eugene Duffy Jr., Robert and Liisa Erickson, Blair Fuller, Leonard Gardner, Brenda Hillman, Rust Hills, Judy Hudson, Tracy Kidder, Patricia Kittredge, John Leggett, Richard Lourie, Graham Macintosh, Ed McClanahan, Gurney Norman, Becky and John O'Brien, George O'Connell, Nancy Packer, Charlotte Painter, Don Paul, Claire Pelton, Michael Pleadwell, Robert Pope, David Reid, John Ridland, Michael Rogers, Lin Rolens, Michael Ryan, Thomas Sanchez, Richard Scowcroft, John Skoyles, Lynn Stark, Peter Steinhart, John Sterling, Scott Turow, Brendan Ward, Michael Waters, Lois and James Welch, Don Williams, Steven Clay Wilson, Judy Young, and Tom Zigal, along with Carver's former students Christine Flavin, Marcus Louria, and Mary Swander.

To this already full boat of friends and associates, Carver added a host of others during the last decade of his life. My thanks go to all of the following: Patricia Aakhus, Julia Alvarez, Bert Babcock, Russell Banks, John Blades, Roy Blount Jr., Connie Brothers, Henry Carlile, David Carpenter, Pat Esslinger-Carr, Jerry Carriveau, Hayden Carruth, Frank Conroy, Richard Crossland, Sally Daniels, Liz Darhansoff, Nicholas Delbanco, Bruce Dobler, Lisa Dobler, Stephanie Dobler, Stephen and Isabel Dobyns, Gary Fisketjon, Dagoberto Gilb, Mimi Gladstein, Barbara Greenberg, Leslie Gutterman, Daniel Halpern, Barry Hannah, Stratis Haviaras, Robert Hedin, DeWitt Henry, Jim Heynen, Tony Hoagland, Tom Jenks, Jean and Donald Justice, Mary Karr, Christopher Kennedy, Carol Lipson, Linda McCarriston, Charles McGrath, James Mortenson, William Cotter Murray, Jack Myers, William Pitt Root, George Saunders, Bob Shacochis, Alan Shapiro, Richard and Lois Shelton, Ralph Sipper, Theodore Solotaroff, Tony Stafford, Les Standiford, David Steingass, Mark Strand, Walter Taylor, Paul Theiner, Leslie Ullman, Ellen Bryant Voigt, Bruce Weigl, Geoffrey and Priscilla Wolff, and Tobias and Catherine Wolff. And as before, Carver continued to attract students and admirers, many of whom shared memories with me: Vicky Anderson, Mary Bucci Bush, Lewis Buzbee, Lee Merrill Byrd, Gary Eddy, Maria Flook, Martha Geis, Ray González, Cecelia Hagen, Brooks Haxton, C. J. Hribal, Christopher Kennedy, David Lazar, David Leavitt, Jay McInerney, Robert O'Connell, and Jeff Schiff.

Librarians throughout the United States and Canada were tireless in their efforts to assist me. My greatest debts are to Geoffrey Smith, Elva Griffith, Rebecca Jewett, and Eileen Kunkler at the William Charvat Collection of American Fiction of the Rare Books and Manuscripts Library at Ohio State University; Breon Mitchell, Saundra Taylor, and Christopher Harter of the Lilly Library at Indiana University; and David McCartney at the University of Iowa. In addition, I'd like to thank the special collections librarians at the John Hay Library of Brown University, the University of Calgary, the University of California Santa Cruz, Chico State University, Humboldt State University, Michigan State University, Northwestern University, Sacramento State University, the University of Saskatchewan, Syracuse University, Texas Tech University, the University of Texas at El Paso, the University of Virginia, and Whitman College. I found additional materials at the American Academy of Arts and Letters, the Bancroft Library at Berkeley, the Howard Gotlieb Archival Research Center at Boston University, Semm Library at the College of William and Mary, the California Center for Military History, Cornell University Library, the University of Chicago's Regenstein Library, the Berg Collection of the New York Public Library, Hollins University Archives, the Little Maga/Zine Collection of the San Francisco Public Library, the Greene Library at Stanford University, Memorial Library Special Collections at the University of Wisconsin Madison, and the Golda Meir Library Special Collections at the University of Wisconsin Milwaukee. The Yakima Public Library, the Tacoma Public Library's Northwest Room, the Washington State Library, and Sacramento Public Library provided essential materials, as did the public recorders of Yakima and Clallam counties in Washington, Onondaga County in New York, and Santa Clara County in California. Local historical museums in Arkansas and Oregon and Washington have also been helpful. Last but not least, my thanks to the librarians at my two home library systems, Milwaukee County Libraries and the Sonoma County Libraries, who called upon Interlibrary Loan Services to find me almost any book or newspaper I requested.

Other writers and observers have kindly shared information or impressions with me, particularly Pamela Allen, Jun Amano, Thomas Bontly, Ralph Brave, Robert Dana, Sam Halpert, Eveline Lamige, John Magee, Carol Polsgrove, Philippe Romon, Moshe Ron, Barry Silesky, and Bruce Weber, as well as Keith Abbott, Blake Bailey, Bruce Betz, Kay Callison Bonetti, Pat Brice, Matt Brown, Wayne Carver, Brian Evensen, Marjorie Leet Ford, Richard and Kristina Ford, Molly Fowler, Adrian Frazier, Herbert Gold, Allan Gurganus, Nancy Hamilton, Elizabeth Hardwick, Jim Harris, William Harrison, Deborah Steele Hazen, John Irving, Sandra

Kleppe, Edward Loomis, Bret Lott, Anne Mansbridge, D. T. Max, Mark Maxwell, Jimmy McDonough, Patrick McGilligan, James Alan McPherson, Katharine Ogden Michaels, Louisa Michaels, Lucy Morse, Kirk Nessett, Bette Pesetsky, Liz Rosenberg, Philip Roth, George Saunders, Rick Simonson, and Allan Titmuss. Sandra Lee Kleppe and the International Raymond Carver Society provide a vibrant platform for discussion of Carver's work.

I am grateful to the Lilly Library at Indiana University for Everett Helm Visiting Fellowships in support of my research in its collections; to the Wisconsin Arts Board for a travel award; and to the Corporation of Yaddo for residencies that allowed me time and peace of mind for writing. For their hospitality, I thank especially Violet Archer, Terrie and Bill Cornell, Janyce and Richard Day, Diana and Gary Fisketjon, Diane Cecily and Chuck Kinder, Carol Polsgrove, Loretta and Dennis Schmitz, and George Hitchcock and Marjorie Simon. At Scribner, I am grateful to Susan Moldow, Roz Lippel, Nan Graham, Jessica Manners, Katie Rizzo, Jay Schweitzer, Phil Bashe, Elisa Rivlin, Erich Hobbing, and Rex Bonomelli.

No book is completed alone. I could not have gone the distance on this one without friendship, conversation, and commentary from friends Martha Bergland, Rae Brown, Melanie Campbell, Robin Coffman, and Carol Polsgrove. For keen and judicious reading of successive versions of my manuscript, I can never thank enough Deborah Denenholz Morse and Deborah Robbins. Annette Brass, Flora Coker, Dan and Paige Conley, Joan Fagan, Kate Fenton, Judith Harway, Lisa Hiller, C. J. Hribal, Marsha Huff, Paul Ingram, Mae Joy, Joe Kennedy, Alexis Lynn, Hongshen Ma, Betty Madonna, Henry Navas, Irina Nedelcu-Erickson, Jay Rogoff, K. C. Ryan, and Stephanie Turner refreshed my enthusiasm from time to time. My children, Katherine Snoda Ryan and Robert Lewellin Ryan, have been encouraging and curious. My husband, Rick Ryan, has been passionate, sensible, and loyal to me and this book when others doubted it could be finished. I dedicate it to him.

And for bringing it to publication, all credit goes to the enthusiasm and insight of my agent, Sandra Dijkstra, and the perseverance and wisdom of my editor at Scribner, the incomparable Colin Harrison.

Works by Raymond Carver

BOOKS (FIRST AMERICAN EDITIONS)

Near Klamath (poems). Sacramento: English Club of Sacramento State College, 1967.

Winter Insomnia (poems). Santa Cruz: Kayak Books, 1970.

At Night the Salmon Move (poems). Santa Barbara: Capra Press, 1976.

Will You Please Be Quiet, Please? (stories). New York: McGraw-Hill, 1976.

Furious Seasons and Other Stories. Santa Barbara: Capra Press, 1977.

What We Talk About When We Talk About Love (stories). New York: Knopf, 1981.

Fires: Essays, Poems, Stories. Santa Barbara: Capra Press, 1983.

Cathedral (stories). New York: Knopf, 1983.

Dostoevsky: A Screenplay (with Tess Gallagher). Santa Barbara: Capra, 1985.

Where Water Comes Together with Other Water (poems). New York: Random House, 1985.

Ultramarine (poems). New York: Random House, 1986.

Where I'm Calling From: New and Selected Stories. New York: Atlantic Monthly, 1988.

A New Path to the Waterfall (poems). New York: Atlantic Monthly, 1989.

No Heroics, Please: Uncollected Writings. Edited by William L. Stull. Foreword by Tess Gallagher. New York: Vintage Books, 1992.

All of Us: The Collected Poems. New York: Knopf, 1998.

Call If You Need Me: The Uncollected Fiction and Other Prose. Edited by William L. Stull. Foreword by Tess Gallagher. New York: Vintage Books, 2001.

Raymond Carver: Collected Stories. Edited by William Stull and Maureen Carroll. New York: Library of America, 2009.

SHORT STORIES

Carver published almost all of his stories in magazines and often published the same story in more than one magazine. Then he revised or restored stories in successive books. The following list gives an overview of this history for Carver's seventy-two published stories. *Raymond Carver: Collected Stories* includes versions of his work previously unavailable in book form. Composition dates given in the second column are surmised from archival sources. A key to abbreviations appears on pages 501–2.

SHORT STORIES
(IN APPROXIMATE ORDER OF COMPOSITION)

Titles	Time of composition	Magazine publications	First book publication	Subsequent book publications
The Aficionados	1959	*Toyon* 1963 (as John Vale)	*NHP*	*CIYNM*
Furious Seasons	1960	*Selection* 1961; *December* 1963	*FS*	*NHP, CIYNM*
The Father	1960–61	*Toyon* 1961; *December* 1968	*Will*	
The Hair	1960–63	*Toyon* 1963; *Sundaze* 1972	*NHP*	*CIYNM*
The Cabin (Pastoral)	1960–63	*Western Humanities Reviews* 1963; *Indiana Review* 1982; *Granta* 1984	Pastoral, *FS*	The Cabin, *Fires*
Poseidon and Company	1960–63	*Toyon* 1963; *Ball State Teachers College Forum* 1964	*NHP*	*CIYNM*
The Ducks (The Night the Mill Boss Died)	1960–63	The Night the Mill Boss Died, *Carolina Quarterly* 1963	The Ducks *Will*	
Little Things (Mine) (Popular Mechanics)	1960–63	Mine, *Playgirl* March 1978; Little Things, *Fiction* 1978	Mine, *FS;* Popular Mechanics, *Love*	Little Things, *Where*
What Do You Do in San Francisco (Sometimes a Woman Can Just About Ruin a Man)	1960–63	Sometimes a Woman Can Just About Ruin a Man, *Colorado State Review* 1967	What Do You Do in San Francisco? *Will*	What Do You Do in SF? *Where*
Will You Please Be Quiet, Please?	1964	*December* 1966	*Will*	
The Student's Wife	1964	*Carolina Quarterly* 1964	*Will*	*Where*
The Third Thing That Killed My Father Off (Dummy)		Dummy, *Discourse* 1967	*FS*	The Third Thing That Killed My Father Off; *Love; Where*

Titles	Time of composition	Magazine publications	First book publication	Subsequent book publications
Harry's Death		*Eureka Review* 1975–76; *Iowa Review* 1979	*Fires*	
Bright Red Apples		*Gato Magazine* 1967	*NHP*	*CIYNM*
Sixty Acres		*Discourse* 1969	*Will*	
How About This? (Cartwheels)	1967	Cartwheels, *Western Humanities Review* 1970	How About This? *Will*	
Sacks (The Fling)	1967	The Fling, *Perspective* 1974	The Fling, *FS*	Sacks, *Love*
Signals (A Night Out)	1969	*December* 1970	Signals, *Will*	
Jerry and Molly and Sam (A Dog Story)	1969	A Dog Story, *Perspective* 1972	Jerry and Molly and Sam, *Will*	
Neighbors	1970	*Esquire* June 1971	*Will*	*Where*
Tell the Women We're Going (Friendship)	1969	Friendship, *Sou'wester,* 1971	Tell the Women We're Going; *Love*	
Fat	1970	*Harper's Bazaar* Sept. 1971	*Will*	*Where*
The Lie		*Sou'wester* 1971; *Playgirl* May 1978	*FS*	*Fires*
Night School (Nightschool)		Nightschool, *North American Review* 1971	Night School, *Will*	
The Idea	1970	*Northwest Review* 1971–72	*Will*	
Why, Honey? (The Man Is Dangerous)		*Sou'wester* 1972	Why, Honey? *Will*	Why, Honey? *Where*
Nobody Said Anthing (The Summer Steelhead)	1970	Seneca Review 1973	Nobody Said Anything, *Will*	Nobody Said Anything, *Where*
Are You a Doctor?	1970	*Fiction* 1973	*Will*	

Titles	Time of composition	Magazine publications	First book publication	Subsequent book publications
The Pheasant	1971	*Occident* 1973; *New England Review* 1982	Metacom Press chapbook	*Fires*
Are These Actual Miles? (What Is It?)	1971	What Is It? *Esquire* 1972	What Is It? *Will*	Are These Actual Miles? *Where*
What's in Alaska?	1971	*Iowa Review* 1972	*Will*	*Where*
Bicycles, Muscles, Cigarets	1971	*Kansas Quarterly* 1973	*Will*	*Where*
They're Not Your Husband	1971	*Chicago Review* 1973	*Will*	*Where*
Put Yourself in My Shoes	1971–72	*Iowa Review* 1972	Capra Press chapbook	*Will; Where*
So Much Water So Close to Home (several versions)	1974	Longer version, *Spectrum* 1975; abridged version, *Playgirl* April 1976	Longer version, *FS*; short version, *Love*	Longer version, *Fires* and *Where*
Distance (Everything Stuck to Him)		Distance, *Chariton Review* 1975; *Playgirl* 1978	Distance, *FS*; Everything Stuck to Him, *Love*	Distance, *Fires* and *Where*
Collectors		*Esquire* August 1975	*Will*	*Where*
Why Don't You Dance?	1977	*Quarterly West* 1978; *Paris Review* 1980	*Love*	*Where*
Viewfinder (View Finder)	1977	*Quarterly West* 1978; *Iowa Review* 1978	*Love*	*Where*
Where Is Everyone? (Mr. Coffee and Mr. Fixit)	1979	Where Is Everyone? *Triquarterly* 1980	Mr. Coffee and Mr. Fixit, *Love*	Where Is Everyone? *Fires*
The Calm	1979	*Iowa Review* 1979	*Love*	*Where*
A Serious Talk (Pie)	1979	Pie, *Playgirl*; *Missouri Review* 1980	*Love*	*Where*
I Could See the Smallest Things (Want to See Something?)	1979	Want to See Something? *Missouri Review* 1980	I Could See the Smallest Things, *Love*	

Titles	Time of composition	Magazine publications	First book publication	Subsequent book publications
Gazebo	1979	*Missouri Review* 1980	*Love*	*Where*
What We Talk About When We Talk About Love (Beginners)	1979	What We Talk About, *Antaeus* 1981; Beginners, *New Yorker*, December 24–31, 2007	What We Talk About, *Love*	What We Talk About, *Where*
One More Thing	1979	*North American Review* 1981	*Love*	*Where*
After the Denim / If It Please You	1979	If It Please You, *New England Review* 1981	After the Denim, *Love*	*If It Please You*, Lord John Press chapbook
A Small, Good Thing (The Bath)	1979–80	The Bath, *Columbia* 1981; A Small, Good Thing, *Plough-shares* 1982	The Bath, *Love*	A Small, Good Thing, *Where*
Vitamins	1980	*Granta* March 1981; *Esquire* October 1981	*Cathedral*	*Where*
Cathedral	May 1981	*Atlantic* September 1981	*Cathedral*	*Where*
Chef's House	1981	*New Yorker* November 30, 1981	*Cathedral*	*Where*
Careful	1982	*Paris Review* 1983	*Cathedral*	*Where*
Where I'm Calling From	1982	*New Yorker* March 15, 1982	*Cathedral*	*Where*
The Bridle	1982	*New Yorker* July 19, 1982	*Cathedral*	
Feathers	1982	*Atlantic* September 1982	*Cathedral*	*Where*
The Train	1982	*Antaeus* 1983	Cathedral	
Preservation	1982	*Grand Street* 1983	*Cathedral*	
The Compartment	1982	*Granta* June 1983; *Antioch Review* 1983	*Cathedral*	
Fever	1982	*North American Review* 1983	*Cathedral*	*Where*

Titles	Time of composition	Magazine publications	First book publication	Subsequent book publications
Boxes	1985	*New Yorker* February 24, 1986	*Where*	
Whoever Was Using This Bed		*New Yorker* April 28, 1986	*Where*	
Menudo		*Granta* 1987	*Where*	
Elephant		*New Yorker,* June 9, 1986	*Where*	
Blackbird Pie		*New Yorker,* July 7, 1986	*Where*	
Intimacy		*Esquire* August 1986	*Where*	
Errand	1986	*New Yorker,* June 1, 1987	*Where*	
Kindling		*Esquire* July 1999	*CIYNM*	
What Would You Like to See?		*Guardian* June 24, 2000	*CIYNM*	
Dreams		*Esquire* August 2000	*CIYNM*	
Vandals		*Esquire* October 1999	*CIYNM*	
Call If You Need Me		*Granta* 1999	*CIYNM*	

Notes on Sources

I conducted interviews in person and by telephone over a period of years, beginning as early as 1994 and continuing until the book was completed in 2009. A few interviews were conducted entirely by email, and many interviewees responded to further questions by phone or mail. Therefore, all oral and written communications to me are simply noted as "to CS." When I haven't indicated otherwise, readers may assume that information came from the source mentioned in my text, from multiple sources that agree, or (in a very few cases) from a source that preferred not to be named. While my quotations from Carver's letters are necessarily brief, I have acquired factual information from them, so the dates of relevant correspondence are given in the endnotes. Carver's correspondence is widely scattered and much of it remains in private collections. The primary archive for his papers is the William Charvat Collection of American Fiction at Ohio State University. Stories and poems by Raymond Carver mentioned in the text are not cited in the notes except in cases where I quoted from a version of a story or poem that differs significantly from that in his major collections. The following abbreviations have been employed:

AoU	*All of Us: Collected Poems*
Brown	John Hay Library, Brown University
Cathedral	*Cathedral*
Charvat	Raymond Carver Papers, William Charvat Collection of American Fiction, Rare Books and Manuscript Library, Ohio State University Libraries
CIYNM	*Call If You Need Me*
CLC	Christine LaRae Carver
Conversations	Gentry, Marshall, and William Stull, eds. *Conversations with Raymond Carver.* Jackson: University of Mississippi Press, 1990
Country	Adelman, Bob. *Carver Country.* NY: Charles Scribner's Sons, 1990
CS	Carol Sklenicka
FS	*Furious Seasons and Other Stories*
Halpert	Halpert, Sam. *Raymond Carver: An Oral Biography.* Iowa City: University of Iowa Press, 1995
Lilly	Lilly Library, Indiana University
Love	*What We Talk About When We Talk About Love*
Kind	*To Write and Keep Kind*, directed by Jean Walkinshow, KCTS Seattle, 1992, included in Criterion Collection of *Short Cuts* by Robert Altman
MBC	Maryann Burk Carver

n.d.	no date
NHP	*No Heroics, Please*
RC	Raymond Carver
RR	Stull, William and Maureen Carroll, eds. *Remembering Ray: A Composite Biography of Raymond Carver.* Santa Barbara: Capra Press, 1993
SB	Gallagher, Tess. *Soul Barnacles: Ten More Years with Ray.* Edited by Greg Simon. Ann Arbor: University of Michigan Press, 2000.
VLC	Vance Lindsay Carver
What	Carver, Maryann Burk. *What It Used to Be Like: A Portrait of My Marriage to Raymond Carver.* NY: St. Martin's Press, 2006
Where	*Where I'm Calling From*
Will	*Will You Please Be Quiet, Please?*

Notes

PART I: BEGINNINGS

Chapter 1: Raymond Junior

1. David Hackett Fischer, *Albion's Seed: Four British Folkways in America* (NY: Oxford U P, 1989), 759.
2. had come to Wauna with a clan: Violet Archer to CS.
3. Clatskanie hospital and mill salary: Ada Hazen to CS; Ruth Schwegler to CS. Sometimes the mill operated only two or three days a week.
4. neighbor: Ada Hazen to CS.
5. "My Father's Life," *CIYNM*, 84; poem: Mavis Green to CS.
6. "poor and proud": Fischer, *Albion's Seed.*
7. Carver ancestors: Mavis (Jack) Green and Connie Carver, first cousins of RC's, traced the Carver lineage to the Stories Creek area of what was then Caswell County in North Carolina, where three Carver brothers settled before 1780. Two generations later, after trying Alabama and Mississippi, Abram Carver homesteaded near the Saline River in Arkansas.
8. drinking: Mavis Green to CS; RC bore an uncanny resemblance to his grandfather Frank: "It was almost weird seeing him in motion," Green reported after seeing a videotape of RC.
9. traveling west and life in Omak: Violet Archer to CS; "around the heart": "The Trestle," *AoU*, 137.
10. "simply looking": "My Father's Life," *CIYNM*, 77.
11. "He was drunk": Ibid., 78.
12. Casey ancestors: Vivian Mosely to CS; Edith Guyse to CS; Franklin Casey to CS.
13. marriage: Vivian Mosely to CS.
14. trouble: Mavis Green to CS; "slept by the side of the road": Violet Archer to CS.
15. "None of it": "My Dad's Wallet," *AoU*, 89.
16. Strike: Violet Archer to CS; Omak, *Chronicle*, 5-19-36 and 7-14-36.
17. one of the holdouts: Hank Pieti to CS.
18. C.R. listened: "My Father's Life," *CIYNM*, 78.
19. Commute: Violet Archer to CS; dancing: Alice (Ritchey) Reed to CS.
20. C.R. once watched: "The Sturgeon," *AoU*, 252.

Chapter 2: Yakima Valley

1. William O. Douglas, *Of Men and Mountains* (San Francisco: Chronicle Books, 1990), 41.
2. Baptismal Register, First Methodist Church, Yakima.
3. "That life": *Kind;* "My heart": *Conversations*, 135.
4. Bob Adelman's photographs in *Carver Country* portray Yakima (as well as Arcata and Sacramento) as bleak places. An aged outhouse pictured as belonging to 1515 South Fifteenth Street, the address RC mistakenly gave Adelman, is on the verge of collapse. Rather than conveying the nostalgia RC suggests in a letter to Adelman, the pictures selected for the book imbue the scenes with an austerity that matches or perhaps even surpasses that of Carver's stories.

5. leash: Judy Hudson, 8-6-07.
6. Christmas list: James Carver to CS; Pepsi and names: Jerry King to CS.
7. "When we went". Buey and Nevel Davis to CS.
8. "There are no Arkansawyers": Buey Davis to CS; church: James Carver to CS.
9. report card: Courtesy of James Carver.
10. railroad: James Carver to CS; Polk City Directory.
11. Documents regarding the Fairview house at the Yakima County courthouse show that it was located at 1505 South Fifteenth, not, as often reported, 1515. The Carvers maintained an interest in the house for eight years, before selling it to another couple by land contract.
12. James Carver to CS, 9-26-96 and 1-15-97.
13. fishing: Violet Archer to CS.
14. happy family: Buey and Nevel Davis to CS; "He loved the railroad": James Carver to CS; saw filers: Hank Pieti to CS. U.S. Department of Labor Bureau of Labor Statistics reported that average weekly earnings of production workers in the lumber and wood industry for 1947 was $44. Saw filers often earned 50 percent more.
15. "frame of reference": RC to Bob Adelman, 12-13-87, *Country*, 45.
16. Cascade mill: Violet Archer to CS; Pieti to CS; Raymond Shore to CS; hazards: Dale Sparber, North Cascades Sawfilers' Association; Hugh W. Davies, University of British Columbia.
17. Pieti to CS.
18. Shaw and Sons funeral directors to CS.
19. Report cards: Courtesy of James Carver.
20. rose bush: Ben Short, Boise-Cascade tour, 09-97.
21. RC's early life and reading: *Conversations*, 114; bed: Reed to CS.
22. "words": *Conversations*, 173; Mispronunciations: Jerry King and Dick Moeller to CS.
23. "a bird crapped": Donald Archer to CS.
24. alcohol: Pieti to CS; Fred protected: Raymond Shore to CS.
25. C.R. considered alcoholic: Violet Archer to CS; "his beer drinking": *Dreams Are What We Wake Up From*, BBC, 1989; *Conversations*, 32–33.
26. "I hated to see": James Carver to CS.
27. "odd" or "peculiar": Buey and Nevel Davis to CS; "mismatch": Donald Archer to CS.
28. Radio station KIT, Yakima, WA, aired 9-15-44. Transcript courtesy of James Carver.
29. "so all to herself": Vi Sullens to CS; "You could tell": Buey Davis to CS.
30. "Waitress": Charvat.
31. Alice Reed to CS.

Chapter 3: Vocation

1. RC to Gordon Lish, n.d. c. 1971.
2. "My Father's Life," *CIYNM*, 77.
3. *Conversations*, 167–68. MBC reported that Ray "told me long after we were married that from an early age, before I had ever met him, as a teenager he'd considered suicide several times" (Halpert, 65).
4. "that boy": Vi Sullens to CS; "shots": James Carver to CS.
5. Yakima County holds no record of the house purchase. There may have been an unrecorded land contract with the previous owner. Vern Schlief told Frank Sandmeyer that he had tried to purchase the house but found that too many back payments were owed on it; ghost stories: Larry Davis to CS.
6. Washington Junior High School report cards, courtesy of James Carver.
7. Screenplay of *King Solomon's Mines* by Helene Deutsch.
8. Carver's childhood library: www.whitman.edu/english/carver/childbooks.html; "favorite author": *Conversations*, 4.
9. "flying saucers": Bill Bequette, *East Oregonian*, 6-26-47; blue object: Larry Davis to CS.

10. "economic circumstances": King Kryger to CS; "like a bunch": Frank Sandmeyer to CS.
11. Davises, Archers, Sandmeyer, Pieti, and Kryger to CS.
12. colander: *Kind.*
13. "Two Schools of Thought Argue on Smudge Pots," *Yakima Morning Herald,* 5-7-50.
14. *Conversations,* 61.
15. Quotations from "The Summer Steelhead" in *Seneca Review.* The bestiality passage was removed from "Nobody Said Anything" in *Will* and *Where;* In about 1974, RC told George Lynn he thought it unmanly to masturbate.
16. James Carver to CS.
17. confidant: MBC, *What,* 90; Ella: *Kind.*
18. "The Kitchen": This poem, plus three others that deal with extremely personal and revealing subjects from Carver's childhood and first marriage, first appeared in the posthumous volume called *A New Path to the Waterfall.*
19. *Conversations,* 41.
20. Violet Archer to CS.
21. Frank Sandmeyer to CS. Further narration by Sandmeyer in this chapter was given in interviews with CS.
22. "dent": *Conversations,* 33.
23. "Sixty Acres," *Discourse* 12 (1969), 117–127; the passage is shortened in *Will.*
24. The poets were Keith Wilson and John Haines. The poem was first published in a 1973 issue of *CutBank* that also included poems by Haines and Wilson.

Chapter 4: Cigarettes, Beer, Jazz

1. Several of RC's college notebooks in the Charvat archives include pages of brief quotations that RC copied by hand from his reading.
2. "big globe" and "piece of meat": Jerry King to CS; "wondered if he had a brain": Ruth King to CS.
3. Fight scene: King Kryger, Jerry King, Roy Baker, and Larry Davis to CS.
4. Hoodlum look: Jerry King and Dick Moeller to CS.
5. "early Salvation Army style": Neil Shinpaugh to CS.
6. uncomfortable in his body: King Kryger to CS.
7. "misspent youth": Jerry King to CS.
8. RC to Bruce Weber, 1984, quotation condensed from taped comments.
9. King and Moeller to CS.
10. jazz: King Kryger; Playland: RC to Bob Adelman, 12-13-87, rpt. *Country.*
11. All of Ray's Yakima friends were storytellers, but two made careers based on language. Jerry King became a leading disk jockey for station WLS in Chicago, and King Kryger earned a PhD in nineteenth-century English literature and became an editor.
12. "nerd": *Newsweek* review of *Where,* 6-6-88, 70; "was there, but he wasn't": Neil Shinpaugh to CS.
13. Benjamin Van Eaton to CS; Roy and Marjorie Hoover to CS.
14. Earl Shelton to CS. Shelton was lured to Yakima from southern Missouri by a $3,800 salary, but "something about Yakima didn't make you want to stay."
15. Moony, Fred, "Reluctant Rock Stars: Screaming Trees Found Fame and Fortune and Wished They Hadn't," *Seattle Weekly,* 5-1-96, 20+.
16. "Hemingway Back from Jungle; Suffers Slight Injuries in Two Plane Crashes." *Yakima Daily Republic,* 1-25-54: 1–2; "was indebted": "Coming of Age, Going to Pieces," *CIYNM,* 276.
17. typewriter: *Conversations,* 34; three semesters: Yakima Valley Community College transcript.
18. "I wanted": "Carver: To Make a Long Story Short," *Newsweek,* 6-6-88, 70; Palmer course: Kryger to CS and James Carver to CS.
19. Palmer Institute of Authorship (Hollywood, California, 1955). I acquired a set of the

lessons and assignments from poet Lewis Turco who also took the course in the mid-1950s while serving in the U.S. Navy.

20. worked hard: MBC, *What*, 22; post office box: Dick Moeller to CS; circulation department: *Conversations*, 34.

21. "it was assumed": *Conversations*, 34; lunch: Pieti to CS.

22. Robert Weddle: Pieti to CS; Pieti thought it likely that C. R. Carver planted black bass in Cascade's mill ponds, "because they certainly arrived there. Prior to that, all we caught in those ponds were huge carp that we'd sell to black people."

23. hops: *Yakima Herald-Republic*, First Person interview form, completed by RC in 1988; RC to Adelman, *Country*, 25.

24. the address was 3415 Summitview (not, as RC states, 1501): *Country*, 29; bedroom: James Carver to CS; post office: Moeller to CS.

25. The Carver brothers' separation from Cascade Lumber: Pieti to CS and Violet Archer to CS. The firing of Fred and C.R. Carver occurred while Cascade president James Bronson was engaged in preliminaries to merge his company with the Boise Payette Corporation. The merger brought together Cascade's timber acreage in the Cascades with the Idaho company's capital. In 1957 the Yakima mill became part of a much larger corporation called Boise Cascade and entered a new era. The box factory was shut down, and manufacture of a new product—plywood—took its place. Strangely enough, the company replaced C.R. as head box-factory filer with a man who, in Pieti's opinion, "was going from real bad to a lot worse. He set up a liquor cabinet in there."

26. In "My Father's Life," Carver writes that his father quit his job in Yakima and moved to Chester for higher pay and a promise of promotion. Then he says that he really thinks his father was restless and adds that C.R.'s parents had died a year before, within six months of each other—quite an exaggeration given that Frank and Mary Carver died in 1948 and 1951 respectively.

27. Kurbitz: Bill Barton to CS. Barton co-owned two pharmacies with Al Kurbitz.

28. High school grade point average reported on Yakima Valley Community College transcript; SCAT score reported on Humboldt State College transcript.

29. James Carver to CS; also MBC, *What*, 26–27.

Chapter 5: Crazy in Love

1. MBC, *What*, 4.

2. "smiled with delight": MBC to CS.

3. passed out: RC to Adelman, 12-13-87, *Country*, 25; "Maryann was tall": Irmagene Kulp Zacher to CS; "doofus": Jerry King to CS; handsome: MBC, *What*, 9.

4. RC in *Conversations*, 34–35.

5. Alice Ritchey Reed to CS, hereafter cited as Alice Reed. Mrs. Reed died November 9, 2000, at age ninety-four. She was married to her third husband, Clarence L. Reed, for thirty-seven years, until his death in 1998.

6. Burk family: MBC to CS and Alice Reed to CS.

7. Alice Reed to CS.

8. Abuse by stepfather: Amy Burk Unger to CS; Alice Reed to CS; Douglas Unger to CS.

9. "prodigious reader": MBC to CS; "dark, tall": Irmagene Zacher to CS.

10. "If either one": MBC to CS.

11. Babysitting and police story: Moeller to CS; see MBC, *What*, 31 for another version.

12. lovers: MBC, *What*, 17; Ray's ambition: Halpert, 61; Jerry Davis: *Dreams Are What You Wake Up From*, (video) directed by Daisy Goodwin, BBC, 1989.

13. "My Father's Life," *CIYNM*, 81; MBC writes that at this time C.R. suffered from chronic diarrhea, anxiety, and depression (*What*, 28).

14. RC at mill: MBC to CS; apartment: James Carver to CS; RC's earnings: report by RC on military enlistment form.

15. Carver family in Chester: MBC to CS and MBC, *What*, 31.

16. MBC, *What*, 33.

17. Moeller to CS; James Carver to CS; MBC, *What,* 27–36.
18. California Military Department, Office of the Adjutant General; additional background from Susanville National Guard Armory; the Washington National Guard reports "no record at all" on RC; discharge record courtesy of James Carver.
19. Halpert, 57.
20. A different version: Shinpaugh to CS.
21. "monstrosity": Halpert, 58; Larry Berghoff to CS; "one of his very first stories": MBC to CS.
22. Charles William Barton to CS; MBC to CS; also, MBC, *What,* 41.
23. Dick Moeller to CS.
24. "Most of what": *Conversations,* 113; see also MBC, *What,* 41–49.
25. Alice Reed to CS; marriage and birthrate: William Manchester, *The Glory and the Dream* (Boston: Little, Brown, 1973), vol. 2, 955.
26. MBC, *What,* 49.
27. Saint Paul's School archives, Penman Memorial Library, Whitman College; Violet Archer to CS; Loretta Archer to CS; Yakima *Daily Republic,* 6-6-57.
28. RC to Adelman, 12-13-87; MBC to CS.
29. Yakima *Daily Republic,* 6-10-57; Irmagene Kulp Zacher to CS; Neil Shinpaugh to CS; Marjorie and Roy Hoover to CS.
30. Hotels: MBC, *What,* 61–62; fingernail episode: Charvat.
31. Loretta Archer to CS.
32. "The Student's Wife," *Carolina Quarterly* 17: 1 (fall 1964), 19–29. The quoted passage does not appear in later versions of the story.
33. Yakima Valley Community College transcript.
34. RC in "My Father's Life" gives the date of February 1957; MBC writes that C.R. migrated between Yakima and Chester during most of 1957. Both RC and MBC write that C.R. was in the hospital in December 1957 when CLC was born, which dates C.R.'s breakdown to late 1957; "During the entire trip": "My Father's Life," *CIYNM.*
35. CR's illness: James Carver, Alice Reed, MBC, Donald Archer, Loretta Archer, and Violet Archer to CS.
36. Uncle Walter: family history by Mavis Green; death of Dr. Kurbitz: Charles W. Barton to CS, and Mrs. Al Kurbitz to CS.
37. "Distance" quoted from *FS;* Sandmeyer remembered a morning when RC came to his house to go hunting and then decided to return home to his wife.
38. Anderson, "sophistication," *Winesburg, Ohio.* Anderson's story "The Untold Lie" especially warrants comparison with RC's "Distance."
39. MBC, *What,* 81; Maryann had been breast-feeding Christine and did not believe she could become pregnant (Alice Reed and CLC to CS); Ray suggested that they might go abroad to find a legal abortion, but Maryann refused (*What,* 82).
40. MBC, *What,* 65.
41. Packing cherries, first typewriter: MBC, *What,* 82–83.

Chapter 6: Furious Years

1. The lines are from "A Unison," *Collected Poems of William Carlos Williams,* volume 2, 1939–1962 (NY: New Directions, 1988), 157.
2. Alice Reed to CS. The house was located at 840 Roe Road. In "John Gardner: The Writer as Teacher," RC omits his mother-in-law's role.
3. "anything": "John Gardner: The Writer a Teacher," *CIYNM,* 107; "open doors": "Fires," *CIYNM,* 97.
4. According to RC's account in "John Gardner: The Writer as Teacher," he borrowed money from Barton before he moved. Barton recalls that it happened later, when Ray mailed him a copy of something he had published in Chico and asked for a loan toward his further education. Barton received one $25 repayment from Ray and then never heard from him again. Carver's personal essays tend to sharpen dramatic movement at the expense of factual precision. Two more examples occur in the first sentence of the

Gardner piece: Ray says that he and his wife moved to California with "two baby children" and then "found an old house." In fact, Maryann was pregnant with the second baby and the house was already designated for them.

5. RC to Bob Adelman, 12-13-87, *Country,* 33. All quotations about the Columbia River sites are from this source.

6. Here one still finds juxtapositions so fabulous that they would suit Garcia Márquez's Columbia rather than Raymond Carver's. At North Bonneville, a yellow "goose crossing" is posted in front of a powerhouse whose turbines have prevented billions of wild fish from migrating to the ocean; and, deep inside the dam at Bonneville, a "Fish Count" chart reports on the number of fish swimming upstream, but neglects to mention the decline in these numbers since the inception of the dams. In the gift shop a few steps away, salmon-themed souvenirs are in good supply.

7. RC to Barton, 9-10-58. The listed courses, confirmed by Carver's Humboldt State College transcript, make up a full load.

8. Lennis Dunlap to CS; Edgar Glenn to CS.

9. Vance Bourjaily to CS (RC told him his son was named for him); an uncle of Ella Carver's was named Samuel Houston Vance Guyse; "ferocious parenting": "Fires," *CIYNM,* 97.

10. MBC to CS.

11. James Carver to CS.

12. Frank Sandmeyer to CS.

13. James Carver to CS.

14. Billy Brown's story was passed to me by his nephew, Matt Brown, who teaches American literature at Chico State University. His uncle recognized his former buddy's picture on a copy of *Cathedral;* summer: MBC, *What,* 106–110 and MBC to CS.

15. NDEA loans: RC bankruptcy papers, courtesy of Ralph Brave.

16. Barry Silesky, *John Gardner: Literary Outlaw* (Chapel Hill: Algonquin, 2004); college president: "American Night Writer," *Chico News and Review,* 1-22-04.

17. "Fires," *CIYNM,* 103.

18. Carver believed that Gardner's ideas about fiction had not changed a great deal between the year he had him as a teacher and the years when he began publishing them in his two handbooks and *On Moral Fiction.* Barry Silesky writes that Gardner was at work on all three books years before they were published; "daemonic compulsiveness": Gardner, *On Becoming a Novelist,* 62; "thin": Lennis Dunlap to CS; "born . . .": Nicholas Delbanco, "In Memoriam: John Gardner," *New York Times Book Review,* 10-19-82; Pat Brice, "Memories of John Gardner," 2004.

19. film fragment: Metzger, "American Night Writer," *Chico News and Review,* 01-04.

20. *Conversations,* 141.

21. "John Gardner: The Writer as Teacher," *CIYNM,* 110; Lennis Dunlap to CS.

22. *The Forms of Fiction* included these stories: Katherine Ann Porter, "The Witness"; Ernest Hemingway, "After the Storm"; James Thurber, "The Unicorn in the Garden"; Nathaniel Hawthorne, "Wakefield"; Franz Kafka, "A Country Doctor"; Mark Twain, "Baker's Bluejay Yarn"; Sherwood Anderson, "Death in the Woods"; William Faulkner, "Spotted Horses"; Edgar Allan Poe, "Ligeia"; Isak Dinesen, "Sorrow-Acre"; Ivan Bunin, "The Gentleman from San Francisco"; Fyodor Dostoyevsky, "The Peasant Marey"; Leo Tolstoy, "Three Deaths"; Guy de Maupassant, "The Piece of String"; Anton Chekhov, "A Trifling Occurrence"; James Joyce, "The Sisters"; Katherine Mansfield, "The Fly"; Luigi Pirandello, "War"; Isaac Babel, "The Story of My Dovecot"; John Steinbeck, "The Chrysanthemums"; Liam O'Flaherty, "Two Lovely Beasts"; Peter Taylor, "The Fancy Woman"; Flannery O'Connor, "A Good Man Is Hard to Find"; Stephen Crane, "The Blue Hotel"; Joseph Conrad, "The Secret Sharer"; Lionel Trilling, "Of This Time, of That Place"; Henry James, "The Jolly Corner"; D. H. Lawrence, "The Fox"; Herman Melville, "Benito Cereno"; Thomas Mann, "Death in Venice."

23. students: Joan Patterson Gardner to CS; "cheating" and "binders": "John Gardner: The Writer as Teacher," *CIYNM,* 110–112; Chico State College notebook at Charvat.

24. Reading list: Charvat; "arrogant": "Fires," *CIYNM*, 103; "authors to read": "John Gardner: The Writer as Teacher," *CIYNM*, 111.
25. MBC, *What*, 84.
26. "brilliant but desperately poor": Liz Rosenberg to RC, 12-30-82.
27. Joan Gardner to CS.
28. "John Gardner: The Writer as Teacher" and "Fires," *CIYNM*.
29. Pat Brice to CS. Gardner encouraged Brice to take chances in her writing and directed her to seek out authors like Isak Dinesen and the early Truman Capote, declaring he would turn her into a Gothic writer.
30. *Conversations*, 4.
31. Gardner, *On Becoming a Novelist*, 18–19.
32. grateful to Gardner: RC to Gordon Lish (n.d. circa 1970) and RC to Richard Cortez Day, 1-24-64, and in "Fires," *CIYNM*, 104.
33. Halpert, 61.
34. The water motif in "Furious Seasons" foreshadows "So Much Water So Close to Home."
35. Notes: Charvat.
36. *The Wildcat*, Chico, California, 3-18-60, 4.
37. *Selection*, number 1, spring 1960, 2. "The Gossips" was first collected in Williams's *Pictures from Brueghel.*
38. Remmerde to CS.
39. Jerry King to CS; *Conversations*, 123.
40. RC's Humboldt State College transcript.
41. *Conversations*, 123.

Chapter 7: A Story of He and She

1. Employment and residence information from Fortuna and Eureka City Directories and telephone books, confirmed by author's interviews with Violet Archer and James Carver.
2. Fortuna: James Carver to CS; Simpson Timber: MBC to CS. Blood cancers in former Simpson mill employees have been reported at a rate sixteen times normal, and dioxin, a carcinogenic chemical, was present in the "Woodlife" preservative applied to Simpson products, though workers did not know this at the time. ("Forgotten But Not Gone: Dioxin Pollution Threatens Humboldt Bay," 6-1-02, www.wildcalifornia .org/html/publications-article-17.shtml and "Eureka Waterfront Site to Be Cleaned of Dioxin," 2-21-08, www.humboldtbaykeeper.org/ERSimpson022108.htm.)
3. RC's notes: Charvat; Halpert, 62–63.
4. Eureka: *California: A Guide to the Golden State* (NY: Hastings House, 1954), 253-254.
5. *Conversations*, 5.
6. "The Student's Wife," *Carolina Quarterly* 17:1 (fall 1964), 22. Revised in *Will* to: "He did not remember very much, he thought. What he did remember was very carefully combed hair and loud half-baked ideas about life and art, and he did not want to remember that."
7. Day to CS. Further citations to author's interviews with Day occur in text.
8. "Pastoral," *Western Humanities Review* 17:1 (winter 1963), 33–42.
9. "The Night the Mill Boss Died," *Carolina Quarterly* 16:1 (winter 1963), 34–39.
10. "letter by Chekhov": *Conversations*, 46–47.
11. This and subsequent quotations from "The Student's Wife," from *Carolina Quarterly* 17:1 (fall 1964), 19–29. A different version (without the last seventeen paragraphs of the magazine version) appears in *Will*. RC finished the story in 1964.
12. Day to CS; RC took required courses in health and music, first-year French, a sociology elective called "Marriage," Proctor's Russian literature, and world literature with Day, who regarded his literature courses as an opportunity to study "the Greeks through Absurd Theater, including some of the writers Ray was interested in."
13. Olliffe: San Francisco *Chronicle*, articles in section A, 5-12 to 5-19 and 7-6 to

7-20-61; Superior Court Records, San Mateo County, California; RC terrified: RC to Clark Blaise, 10-12-65.

14. RC quotes EH's *Men at War* in "Coming of Age, Going to Pieces," *CIYNM,* 277.
15. "free at last": MBC, *What,* 143.
16. MBC, *What,* 144–154.
17. David Palmer to CS; in the spring of 1963, Ray worked at the mill again to pay off new debts.
18. MBC to CS.
19. Day to CS; MBC, *What,* 158.
20. Kesey, San Francisco; MBC, *What,* 158; Tracy's: Day to CS.
21. David and Charlene Palmer to CS.
22. Notebook: Charvat.
23. disastrous: Charlene Palmer to CS; difficulties: Day to CS; Notebooks: Charvat.
24. Richard Cortez Day, "Introduction," to Raymond Carver, *Carnations: A Play in One Act* (Vineburg, CA: Engdahl Typography, 1992); "Kafka" and suitcase: Day to CS.
25. MBC to CS.
26. James Carver to CS.
27. *Conversations,* 36.
28. It is not the case, as William L. Stull asserts in his "Afterword" to the play, that Ray was enrolled in Day's seminar on existentialism while working on *Carnations.* According to Carver's transcript, the seminar occurred the following fall.
29. Bob Graham, HSC *Lumberjack,* May 18, 1962.
30. At Iowa, both Day and John Gardner had studied recent European literature with Ralph Freedman, an enthusiastic scholar who was himself a novelist.
31. *Toyon* 9 (1963), 30.
32. Gardner's first published story, "A Little Night Music," appeared in *Northwest Review* shortly after Carver left Chico. Day was having better luck with his stories at the time; he later published a novel, *When in Florence* (NY: Doubleday, 1986), and the story collection *Something for the Journey* (Spokane: Eastern Washington University Press, 2005). "My Father's Life," *CIYNM,* 84.
33. Jay Karr, "The Most Unhappy Man," *RR,* 28; Karr to CS.
34. As he waited to hear from Iowa, Ray lived alone in Berkeley, where Dave Palmer had found him a job at the University of California Biology Library. He lived on his own—for the first time—until the family joined him for the summer.
35. RC said the fellowship was $500 (*Conversations,* 35), but MBC reports $1,000 (Halpert, 63), perhaps $500 per semester.

Chapter 8: The Athens of the Midwest

1. Alice Reed to CS.
2. Background on the Iowa Writers' Workshop drawn from *A Community of Writers: Paul Engle and the Iowa Writers' Workshop,* ed. Robert Dana (Iowa City: U of Iowa P, 1999); *Seems Like Old Times: Iowa Writers Workshop Golden Jubilee,* ed. Ed Dinger (Iowa City: U of Iowa P, 1986); *The Workshop: Seven Decades of the Iowa Writers' Workshop,* ed. Tom Grimes (NY: Hyperion, 1999); David Myers, *The Elephants Teach: Creative Writing Since 1880* (Englewood Cliffs, NJ: Prentice-Hall, 1996); David Boroff, "The Muses Meet in Squaresville," *Mademoiselle,* November 1961; Calvin Kentfield, "State University of Iowa," *Holiday,* November 1963; T. George Harris, "Poet Grower to the World," *Look,* 6-1-65; Rust Hills, "The Structure of the American Literary Establishment," *Esquire,* July 1963; Maureen Howard, "Can Creative Writing Be Taught in Iowa?" *The New York Times Magazine,* 5-25-86; Saul Maloff, "Writers at Work in Iowa," *Publishers Weekly,* 7-4-86; and archives of the University of Iowa.
3. Bettina Bourjaily to CS; Vance Bourjaily to CS.
4. missed seeing the ocean: RC to Day, 10-18-63; Tom Doherty to CS; "a life already": Eric Larsen to CS.

5. Kenneth Rosen to CS.

6. Kathy Salyer (later married to workshop director George Starbuck) to CS, 2-24-03; RC to Dick and Bonnie Day, 10-18-63 and 2-12-64.

7. Debra Spark, "Recollection," *The Workshop: Seven Decades of the Iowa Writers' Workshop*, ed. Grimes, 72.

8. Doherty to CS.

9. "vipers": Joy Williams to CS; "head down": Donald Kent Hall to CS; "feeling let down": Doherty to CS.

10. Ian McMillan to CS. In 1986 RC told McMillan that the atmosphere there when they were students had been "too tense and too competitive and in a way almost destructive."

11. Weesner to CS; Doherty to CS.

12. MBC to CS.

13. RC to Day, 10-18-63.

14. Joy Williams, 9-27-03; MBC to CS.

15. Adrian Mitchell to CS; "Theater, Poetry, and Bars Appeal to English Woman," *Daily Iowan*, 12-11-63.

16. Doherty to CS.

17. Adrian Mitchell to CS; Hall to CS.

18. VLC to CS.

19. He wrote the essay at the request of Ted Solotaroff and Steven Berg for a volume they edited called *Influences*. On December 12, 1981, he submitted it to Daniel Halpern for *Antaeus*, and it appeared first in that magazine. He was still making revisions to it in June of 1982 as it went to press. "Fires" is reprinted in *Fires, NHP*, and *CIYNM*.

20. Clark Blaise to CS.

21. RC to Day, 10-18-63.

22. RC to Day, 12-8-63; MBC to CS.

23. MBC to CS.

24. Doherty to CS.

25. RC took Contemporary European Literature from professor and novelist Ralph Freedman. His notebook from that course is archived at Charvat; MBC, *What*, 178.

26. MBC to CS.

27. MBC to CS; Alice Reed to CS.

28. RC to Day, 1-24-64.

29. MBC to CS; RC to Dick and Bonnie Day, 2-12-64; notes: Charvat.

30. Quoted from "Will You Please Be Quiet, Please?" *December* 8:1 (1966), 9–27.

31. avid femininity: Kirk Nesset, *The Stories of Raymond Carver* (Athens: Ohio U P, 1995), 23–26, discusses Ralph's "fear of the uncontrollably feminine."

32. MBC to CS; RC to Day, 2-12-64; Rosen to CS.

33. MacMahon (1909–1998) had published two books of stories in the United States when he came to teach at Iowa: *The Lion Tamer* and *The Red Petticoat*. From the Writers' Workshop he received $4,000 for the semester; he worked on his second novel while there. Weesner later visited MacMahon in Ireland, but apparently Carver did not. Weesner to CS; Curt Sylvester, "Imagination Is His Byword," *Daily Iowan*, 2-22-64, and University of Iowa archives.

34. Descriptions of MacMahon: Weesner to CS and Eric Larsen to CS; newer stories: Douglas Kent Hall to CS.

35. "Engle's back pocket": Charles Wright, "Improvisations on Donald Justice," *A Community of Writers*, ed. Robert Dana (Iowa City: U of Iowa P, 1999), 186.

36. MBC, Halpert, 65–66. Douglas Kent Hall, a student assistant to Engle, noticed that Engle "was always difficult when you went to him for money because he tried to make it go as far as it would." (Hall to CS); Tennessee Williams completed his BA in the Theatre Department in 1938, under the skeptical eye of Professor E. C. Mabie, but Mabie passed over the playwright for a scholarship that would have allowed him to return to Iowa for a master's with a creative thesis. Williams did not begin *The Glass Menagerie* until later, though at Iowa he had talked about writing "a tragedy of middle-class stagnation" (Lyle Leverich, *Tom: The Unknown Tennessee Williams* [NY: Crown, 1995], 231–65).

37. Halpert, 65–67; MBC to CS.
38. Calvin Kentfield, "State Univerity of Iowa," *Holiday,* November 1963, 88.
39. "Puff": MBC to CS.
40. Drafting of story: RC to Day, 10-18-64; "daring": RC to Bruce Weber, 1984.
41. "The Student's Wife," quoted from *Carolina Quarterly* 17:1 (fall 1964), 19–29.
42. CLC to CS.

PART II: SEARCH

Chapter 9: Grinding and Sharpening

1. MBC to Ralph Brave.
2. William Kittredge, Introduction, *The Portable Western Reader* (NY: Penguin, 1997), xix; Kittredge describes his own drive west from Iowa City where he attended the Writers' Workshop from 1964 to 1966.
3. U-Haul box: MBC to Ralph Brave; disabilty: MBC, *What,* 186.
4. MBC to Brave.
5. "poor devils": RC to Doherty, 1-14-65.
6. Teaching job: MBC, *What,* 188–189.
7. "nervous breakdown" and disastrous summer: RC to Doherty, 7-22-64 and 9-n.d.-64 and RC to Dick Day, 10-18-64.
8. RC to Doherty, 7-22-64. The house was at 2845 Berkshire Way in Sacramento. Sacramento background from Ralph Brave, Dennis and Loretta Schmitz, Gary Thompson, Jim Young, Aldo Bovero, and others; Brave conducted a group interview with Dennis Schmitz, Thompson, Young, and Quentin Duvall on 6-18-98; MBC spoke to Ralph Brave, 8-9-98.
9. *The Best American Short Stories 1964,* ed. Martha Foley and David Burnett (NY: Houghton Mifflin, 1964), 352.
10. The first editors were Richard Schechner, Deborah Trissel, and Louis Vaczek, followed by Marks and then by Johnson, according to *TriQuarterly* 34 (1979), 693; "gall . . .": *Chicagoland* magazine, 1969; Johnson to CS.
11. Michael Anania, "Of Living Belfry and Rampart: On American Literary Magazines Since 1950," *The Little Magazine in America: A Modern Documentary History,* eds. Elliott Anderson and Mary Kinzie (Yonkers, NY: Pushcart Press, 1978), 6–23.
12. Curt Johnson, "Short Cut: Raymond Carver and the Writer's Life," *Stony Hills: New Reviews of the Small Press,* 5:1 (May 1994); Johnson to CS: *December* archive, Brown.
13. RC to Doherty, 9-n.d.-64.
14. RC to Day, 10-18-64.
15. MBC to Ralph Brave, 8-9-98; MBC to CS.
16. MBC to Ralph Brave, 8-9-98.
17. girl: MBC, *What,* 199; snuck out: MBC to Ralph Brave.
18. MBC to Ralph Brave. RC's letters mention domestic trouble less explicitly. In fact, Ray kept the car when he and Maryann separated. In "Night School," the car that's with the absent wife functions as a symbol of the narrator's impotence. That theme becomes more obvious in "Are These Actual Miles?"
19. Quotations from "Nightschool," *North American Review,* fall 1971, 48–50. Some of the lines quoted and the name Donner Club are excised from the version of this story printed as "Night School" in *Will.* In the book version, "We think he's homo," becomes "We think he's home."
20. James Carver to CS; "My Father's Life," *CIYNM,* 83.
21. Family reunited: MBC to CS; the tiny house: 2641 Matheson Way, Sacramento; "at absolute zero": RC to Blaise, 1-13-65; "proverbial abyss": RC to Doherty, 1-14-65.
22. "Raymond Carver: The Sacramento Years," Sacramento *News & Review,* 8-13-98.
23. RC to Blaise, 1-27-65.

24. New job, "upswing": RC to Blaise, 2-20-65.
25. CLC in Halpert, 79.
26. RC to Johnson, 12-14-65.
27. *Conversations*, 74, 92.
28. Halpert, 70; MBC to Brave.
29. "knack": Pressman, Steven, *Outrageous Betrayal: The Dark Journey of Werner Erhard from est to Exile* (NY: St. Martin's Press, 1993); "success": W. W. Bartley III, *Werner Erhard: The Transformation of a Man: The Founding of est* (NY: Clarkson N. Potter, 1978).
30. "wretched life": RC to Blaise, 3-27-65; Sisyphus: RC to Doherty, 4-27-65.
31. Day to CS.
32. middle class: The federal poverty line for a family of four in 1965 using "low-cost" food prices was $4,000. Generally, multiply 1965 dollars by six to calculate year 2005 dollars.
33. RC to Doherty, 4-27-65; RC told Johnson about the *Look* photo on 8-13-65.
34. RC to Blaise, 5-4-65.
35. Halpert, 79.
36. RC to Blaise, 3-27-65.
37. "rode like the wind": MBC to Brave; RC to Blaise, 6-28-65; The model year dates of the cars the couple looks at in the poem ('71, '72) are either a mistake or an attempt to update the poem, first published in *At Night the Salmon Move* in 1976. "Writing up a storm": RC to Johnson, 8-13-65.
38. RC to Blaise, 9-10-65.
39. RC's letters to Johnson, Brown.
40. The large rental house was located at 2642 Larkspur Lane in Sacramento.
41. "free-for-all": RC to Blaise, 12-20-65.
42. Halpert, 70–71; MBC, *What*, 205–6.
43. "writer's sort of job": Dennis Schmitz "Secret Places," *Poet News*, September 1988; "baby's corpse": MBC to CS.
44. "die young": MBC to CS.
45. Fireside Lounge: Jim Young to Ralph Brave, 6-18-98.
46. "in stitches": MBC to Ralph Brave, 8-9-98; problems: *Conversations*, 74.
47. Amy: Obituary, *Bellingham Herald*, 6-29-03; Douglas Unger to CS.
48. RC to Amy and Michael and Erin Wright, 12-6-66.
49. "Built like a tree": Jimmy McDonough, *Big Bosoms & Square Jaws: The Biography of Russ Meyer, King of the Sex Film* (NY: Crown, 2005), 19–20.
50. "plot": Jim Young to Ralph Brave, 6-18-98; Jim Young to CS; shooting location: Jimmy McDonough to CS. The John Moran–scripted and Meyer-directed movie is weirdly like a graphic-novel version of Carver's stories. Its four men and four women who are linked by lust and hostility cruise through the Sacramento Valley from one tryst to the next in vehicles (from a gold Caddy convertible to an Arkansas hillbilly pickup) that sum up their personalities. A voiceover promises "an adult motion picture that explores the deepest complexities of contemporary life as applied to love and marriage in these United States. All of the characters are identifiable, perhaps even familiar . . . losers in a game all of us play, high rollers that always crap out." When auteur Robert Altman crafted *Short Cuts* from eight Carver short stories, he relied on a similar (though more intricate) method to interconnect the stories.

Chapter 10: Were Those Actual Miles?

1. Gary Thompson, "Walking Home from 57th Street," *Richer Lives: A Tribute to Dennis Schmitz*, ed. Quinton Duval (West Sacramento, 1977), 1–4; Gary Thompson to CS. David Palmer knew Dennis Schmitz and suggested that Ray look him up.
2. MBC, *What*, 204.
3. Dennis and Loretta Schmitz to CS.

4. Dennis Schmitz to CS.
5. Loretta Schmitz to CS. "Interviews are weird," Loretta cautioned. "I don't necessarily agree with everything I say. Extroverts get carried away with an audience."
6. Dennis and Loretta Schmitz to CS.
7. "coterie," int. Young, 4-28-00. Dennis Schmitz, Gary Thompson, and Jim Young to CS.
8. Thompson to CS.
9. A 1983 revision adds lines: Balzac, his brain "sizzling," decides to write one more scene. The addition makes the theme clearer but regrettably effusive. In Sacramento, when Carver conceived the poem, he knew the loneliness of a desperate writer and dared not romanticize it.
10. Jack Hicks to CS; Jim Young to CS.
11. Schmitz, "Secret Places," *Remembering Ray*, 49–52.
12. Thompson is the author of *To the Archaeologist Who Finds Us* and other collections.
13. MBC to Ralph Brave, 6-18-98.
14. "the worst and the best": MBC to Brave; "muddle": RC to Blaise, 1-21-66.
15. "conspicuous": RC to Lish, 4-15-77.
16. McDonough, *Big Bosoms & Square Jaws*, 12, 78.
17. "repression": Hicks to CS; "saw myself": MBC to Halpert (tape).
18. Thompson to Ralph Brave; Thompson to CS; Jack Hicks to Brave, 7-8-98.
19. Schmitz to Ralph Brave.
20. David Boxer and Cassandra Phillips's article "Will You Please Be Quiet, Please?: Voyeurism, Dissociation, and the Art of Raymond Carver" lays the groundwork for all future discussions. "Through many of the stories of RC is woven a double strand of voyeurism and dissociation. The term 'voyeurism' is used advisedly here, to mean not just sexual spying, but the wistful identification with some distant, unattainable idea of self. Dissociation is a sense of disengagement from one's own identity and life, a state of standing apart from whatever defines the self, or of being unselfed." *Iowa Review* 10:3 (summer 1979), 75.
21. Hicks to Brave; ten years hence, the kids who grew up in that postindustrial suburbia would become the core of Carver's readership.
22. A *muzhik* is a Russian peasant; the word occurs often in the stories of Isaac Babel, which Carver greatly admired. Colloquially, it may simply mean a male person of lower class or notable masculinity.
23. "The Lie," *Sou'wester* (winter 1971); the story appeared again in *Playgirl* in 1978.
24. MBC to CS; MBC, *What*, 205–6.
25. RC to Johnson, 10-8-66 and 10-14-66.
26. MBC to Brave.
27. MBC to Brave.
28. Sacramento *Bee* classifieds, 4-11-67, courtesy of Beth Daugherty, Sacramento Public Library.
29. MBC and RC filed identical lists of their debts with the U.S. District Court for the Eastern District of California except for an additional loan of $111 owed to a finance company on Ray's statement. Court records courtesy of Ralph Brave.
30. The story appeared as "What Is It?" in *Esquire*, May 1972 and again in *Will;* Carver returned to his original title when he included the story in *Where*.
31. Thompson to CS; CLC to CS.
32. *BASS*: RC to Doherty, 5-29-67. RC explained the "very profitable" financial arrangements for British and American editions (about a 2 percent royalty per author); three times: RC to Lish, 11-11-74.
33. RC to Johnson, 5-31-67.
34. Thompson to CS, 7-20-01.
35. MBC to Philippe Romon, 4-17-03.
36. autopsy: death certificate, Del Norte County, CA.
37. James Carver to CS, 10-23-04.
38. "My Father's Life," *CIYNM*, 77–86.

39. MBC to CS, 8-10-03, the similar conversation that Carver records in his essay is drawn, MBC believes, from her memoir that Carver read in manuscript.
40. RC's dream reported by him to MBC; notebook jottings: Charvat.
41. MBC to Romon to CS.
42. "The Brothers," Charvat.
43. Franklin Casey to CS.
44. "My Father's Life," *CIYNM*, 83–84.
45. RC made at least one attempt to write fiction about the days surrounding his father's death. In eight unpublished manuscript and typescript pages archived at Charvat called "Drinking's Funny," he approaches this material through the voice of the dead man's daughter-in-law. In the story the father and son, Hank Sr. and Hank Jr., drink together, over the objections of Hank Sr.'s wife, who is named Ella or Bea.
46. Blair Fuller to CS.
47. Corvair: Thompson to CS; "hard on fathers": RC to Johnson, 6-26-67.
48. future: RC to Blaise, 7-6-67; MBC to Halpert, 71; "hard realization": RC to Bruce Weber, *Conversations*, 91.

Chapter 11: Luck

1. Mereda Kaminski to CS.
2. "your marriage or": Halpert, 70; Young to CS, 4-28-00; lost papers: Bert Babcock to CS, 10-29-01.
3. "turned-on": RC to Blaise, 8-8-67.
4. Their address was 886 Loma Verde, Palo Alto; RC to Blaise, 8-8-67; VLC to CS.
5. MBC, *What*, 211; RC to Johnson: "cottage-den," 8-12-67; "averaging" and "platoon," 9-6-67; Matson: 10-1-67.
6. IBM: Johnson to RC, 8-10-67; "Chekhov": MBC, *What*, 211; M. Kaminski to CS, 12-4-02.
7. Gerald Kaminski to CS; Richard Kolbert to CS.
8. R. Kolbert to CS; Sylvia Kolbert to CS.
9. S. Kolbert to CS.
10. S. Kolbert to CS; R. Kolbert to CS.
11. R. Kolbert to CS.
12. G. Kaminski to CS; S. Kolbert to CS.
13. Thanks to Gurney Norman and Deborah Denenholz Morse for impressions of Palo Alto in the 1960s.
14. Max Crawford, Richard Scowcroft, Nancy Packer, and Ed McClanahan to CS; *The Uncommon Touch*, ed. John L'Heureux (Stanford, CA: Stanford Alumni Association, 1986); Jackson J. Benson, *Wallace Stegner: His Life and Work* (NY: Viking Penguin, 1996).
15. Susan Sontag, *Against Interpretation* (NY: Farrar, Straus & Giroux, 1966).
16. The outpouring of novels written by women influenced by feminism (*Diary of a Mad Housewife* by Sue Kaufman, *Memoirs of an Ex-Prom Queen* by Alix Kates Shulman, *Fear of Flying* by Erica Jong) brought domestic subjects back into the mainstream. But in the late 1960s, domestic novels like Richard Yates's *Revolutionary Road* or Evan S. Connell's *Mrs. Bridge* and *Mr. Bridge* were not much read outside of writing schools.
17. "Hunger Was Good Discipline," *A Moveable Feast* (NY: Scribner's, 1964).
18. RC to Blaise, 7-6-67.
19. RC to Johnson, 10-14-67.
20. RC to Johnson, 10-24-67; a second title, "A Child's Christmas in Utah," appears under RC's name in the list of distinguished stories at the back of the book. That story's rightful author was Wayne Carver.
21. Early the next year, when Johnson accepted a piece of Kaminski's novel for *December,* Ray told Johnson that this acceptance had "come at an important and critical juncture" for him. Kaminski thought about dropping out and going to Mexico to write but never did. "My friendship with Ray had no valor in it. When the news of his death

came, I wondered whether if I had been a better friend I might have influenced him to drink less, smoke less, and perhaps live longer. I have never stopped missing him." (G. Kaminski to CS, 12-4-02).

22. Johnson to RC, 11-11-67; RC to Johnson, 11-16-67.
23. understatement: RC to Bharati Mukherjee and Clark Blaise, 12-10-67; "recovering": RC to Johnson, 1-16-68; headlines: Johnson to RC, 2-19-68.
24. Herbert R. Mayes, "Trade Winds," *Saturday Review of Literature*, January 27, 1968, 12; RC to Johnson, 2-6-68.
25. English Club: Schmitz to CS; Schmitz's own first book, *We Weep for Our Strangeness*, was forthcoming; printer: Gerald Helland to CS; "500 copies": Schmitz to Brave, 7-18-98; "Review," *The Hornet*, n.d.; ironies: Daniel Davis to CS.
26. The leftover copies and original metal plates for *Near Klamath* have disappeared; $7,500: Joseph the Provider bookseller, Santa Barbara.
27. RC to Doherty, 3-26-68; RC to Johnson, 4-15-68.
28. VLC to CS.
29. RC to Johnson, 5-16-68; Halpert, 71.
30. RC to Johnson, 5-16 and 5-20-68.
31. Johnson to CS, 12-19-01.
32. Curt Johnson, "Short Cut: Raymond Carver and the Writer's Life." *Stony Hills: News and Reviews of the Small Press* (issue 13, May 1994), 4–7; Johnson to CS.
33. MBC to CS, 12-14-03.
34. Johnson, "Short Cut."
35. Sources on Lish: "Gordon Lish Interviews Gordon Lish," *Genesis West* 3, nos. 1 & 2, rpt. *December* 10, no. 1 (1968), 191–96; "How I Got to Be a Big Shot Editor," *Quarry* 1 (1971); D. T. Max, "The Carver Chronicles," *The New York Times Magazine*, August 9, 1998; Hayden Carruth, Brian Evenson, Edward Loomis, Herbert Gold, and Leonard Michaels to CS; Carol Polsgrove, *It Wasn't Pretty, Folks, But Didn't We Have Fun?* (NY: Norton, 1995), 239; Lish archive, Lilly.
36. Crying: Loomis to CS; to meet Dean Moriarty: "I love a man who was once so green and open that he assumed Dean was real," writes David Bowman, who attended Lish workshops in 1991: "Lashed by Lish," *Salon*, www.salon.com/media/1998/09/01media. html.
37. Lawrence Ferlinghetti and Nancy J. Peters, *Literary San Francisco* (San Francisco: City Lights/Harper & Row, 1980).
38. Candido Santogrossi was denied tenure at Mills High School along with Lish.
39. Lish at Mills High School: Donovan Bess, "The Man Who Taught Too Well," *The Nation*, 6-15-63, 507+; Leslie Santogrossi to CS; dismissal changed him: Lish, "How I Got to Be a Big Shot Editor."
40. Lish to CS: Lish to Carruth, 6-61 and 6-20-62.
41. *English Grammar* (Palo Alto: Behavioral Research Laboratories, 1964).
42. Lish to Carruth, 9-28-67.
43. Gordon Lish to CS.
44. Leonard Gardner to CS, 10-11-02. *Genesis West* 1 (spring 1963), 269–279.
45. Job Corps was a Kennedy-era program within the Office of Economic Opportunity. Inspiration for *Why Work* and a second series called *A Man's Work* came from Reed Whittimore, then consultant in Poetry for the Library of Congress. Lish himself proposed asking authors to write motivational pieces for the disadvantaged young men in Job Corps. Among the authors who contributed were: Kay Boyle, Hayden Carruth, Evan S. Connell, Stanley Elkin, George P. Elliott, William H. Gass, Herbert Gold, Grace Paley. James T. Farrell, the author of *Studs Lonigan* and forty other books, objected to changes Lish had made in his story's dialogue and insisted that its byline be changed to read "based on a story by James T. Farrell." Lish himself contributed a story called "The Last Fly Ball."
46. Gordon Lish, "A Fool for Salinger," *Antioch Review* 44 (fall 1986), 413.
47. Johnson to CS.

Chapter 12: Reading Mark Twain in Tel Aviv

1. "away from my sources": Unger to CS.
2. "The Augustine Notebooks," *CIYNM*, 167–74.
3. celebration: Amos Elon, *The Israelis: Founders and Sons* (NY: Penguin, 2d ed., 1991), 4.
4. Elon, 254.
5. MBC to Halpert; RC, "The Arab Question," Charvat.
6. RC to Ella Carver, postmark in Hebrew.
7. Kolbert to CS; Johnson to CS.
8. "The Arab Question."
9. Apartment 5 at 17 Hoffien Street in Ramat-Aviv rented for $100 a month and was just a block from the campus gate. Thanks to Moshe Ron for firsthand research in Tel Aviv.
10. "The Arab Question."
11. "incredible": RC to Bruce Weber; RC to Johnson, 8-23-68.
12. skin rashes: Unger to CS; Elon, 199; RC to Johnson, 8-23-68.
13. VLC to CS.
14. RC to Johnson, 8-23-68.
15. MBC to CS, 8-8-03; Halpert, 71–72; VLC to CS.
16. Walking in Jerusalem: RC to Johnson, 7-17-68; "Asia": Douglas Unger to CS.
17. Carver published "Seeds" twice in 1970 but not again in his lifetime.
18. Halpert, 37.
19. RC to Johnson, 7-17-68; VLC to CS, 8-1-05.
20. RC to Johnson, 8-23-68; Douglas Unger to CS; VLC to CS.
21. camel ride: Unger to CS; trip: RC to Johnson, 8-23-68.
22. The population of Jaffa was then about a third Arab and two-thirds newly arrived Sephardic Jews from Africa and Middle Asia. Its old winding streets had just been turned into artists' quarters and restaurants, and there are views of the sea from its towers and ramparts. Carver's poem "Morning, Thinking of Empire" is set there.
23. Tabitha school: RC to Johnson, 9-68; math: RC to Bruce Weber, 84; VLC to CS.
24. "backslid": RC to Johnson, early September; Twain: Richard Kolbert to CS.
25. George Lynn to CS.
26. Halpert, 71.
27. "kicked": MBC to CS; "deadened": MBC, *What*, 219; VLC to CS.
28. RC to Johnson, 9-23-68.
29. MBC to Philippe Romon, 4-17-03.
30. RC to Johnson, 10-1-68.
31. RC to Tom Doherty, 4-21-69; RC to Joy Williams, 4-21-69 These two letters are almost identical, which was often the case with letters RC sent to different correspondents on the same day.
32. RC to Johnson, 10-16-68.
33. *CIYNM,* 167–174.
34. Notes toward novel: RC to Lish, 10-21-70, and RC to Johnson, 11-6-70; RC told R. Kolbert that he was writing a novel set in the Mideast (R. Kolbert to CS). Thanks to Frederick W. Hills for showing me RC's outline for the novel.
35. RC to Johnson, ("Friday") 6-14-68. The editor was Henry Plotnik at Regnery Press.
36. MBC to CS.
37. RC to Johnson, postcard, 10-24-68.
38. RC to Doherty, 4-21-69; RC to Joy Williams, 4-21-69.
39. *Conversations,* 69–70; RC told Bruce Weber that a "villa on the Mediterranean was what I'd been looking for since I was 14 years old" (RC to Weber, 1-84).

Chapter 13: The Sixties End

1. Charlene and Dave Palmer to CS.
2. cookies: MBC to CS; RC depressed: Johnson to CS; "young girl": MBC to CS.

3. poor company: RC to Johnson, 5-1-69; next time: Johnson to RC 5-25-68 (apparently misdated). Johnson was a talented writer himself, as evidenced by Stanley Elkin's selection of one of his short stories for the 1980 *BASS* volume; his own December Press backlist includes a dozen titles (fiction and nonfiction) by Johnson and his selected work is compiled in *Salud* (Ellison Bay, WI: Cross†Roads Press, 2007).
4. *The Bellingham Herald,* 6-03; eulogy for Amy, Michael Wright, 8-8-03; Douglas Unger to CS.
5. RC to Johnson, 12-29-68.
6. RC to Johnson, 12-29-68; MBC to Johnson, 12-19-68.
7. RC to Johnson, 2-26-69; San Jose State University records, consulted 5-24-05; the School of Library and Information Science preserved no documentation on RC.
8. RC to Johnson, 2-26-69; RC to Johnson, 6-19-69. In 1984, RC told Bruce Weber he didn't write for a year and a half after coming home from Israel, another exaggeration.
9. Thurston and *Perspective* archives, Olin Library, Washington University in St. Louis.
10. "A Dog Story," *Perspective* (winter 1972), 36, 44, 45.
11. "how to market": MBC to CS.
12. RC to Johnson, 6-2-69. Connell, who had not known Amy long, later drew some details for his novel *Double Honeymoon* from the experience; at the time of her breakdown, the reclusive and scholarly Connell extricated himself from the relationship but remained friendly, even promising Maryann that he would recommend Ray for a fellowship; "shambles": RC to Johnson, 6-26-69.
13. RC to Johnson, 7-11-69.
14. Johnson to CS.
15. "A Dog Story," *Perspective* (winter 1971), 43–44.
16. MBC to CS; CLC to CS.
17. RC to Johnson, 5-1-69.
18. Levine: foreword to *One-Man Boat: The George Hitchcock Reader,* Robert McDowell and Joseph Bednarik, eds. (Ashland, OR: Story Line Press, 2003); *kayak*: Hitchcock to CS; Hitchcock in sixties: Morton Marcus to CS.
19. Hitchcock and Amy: RC to Johnson, 8-15 "Friday" [1969]; Hitchcock to CS.
20. Hitchcock to CS.
21. Lish to Carruth, 3-4-69; Lish to Carruth, 3-11-69.
22. RC to Johnson, 6-26-69, 7-11-69; Lish to Johnson, 8-6-69; Johnson to Lish, 8-20-69.
23. Mention of the magazine comes in Johnson's article as well as in two letters: Lish's letter of 10-17-69 to Harold Hayes, and RC to Johnson in late August; Lish confirmed that the plan was serious in a telephone conversation with the author in 2002; RC to Johnson, [June] Thursday, 19th [1969].
24. Lish to Carruth, 8-2-69; Lish to Johnson, 8-6-69.
25. RC to Lish, 2-23-70; *Short Stories from the Literary Magazine,* Jarvis Thurston and Curt Johnson, eds. (Glenview, IL: Scott Foresman, 1970).
26. Paragraph based on Lish's correspondence to Carruth and Johnson, author's conversations with Lish, and Lish archive at Lilly.
27. MBC to CS; RC to Johnson, 11-6-69.
28. Johnson to RC, 10-12-69.
29. Johnson to CS; Johnson to Lish, 11-9-69.
30. Here is the full list from Lish's letter to Hayes dated 10-17-69: "Ben Maddox, Tillie Olsen, William H. Gass, Ken Kesey, Rosalind Drexler, Joyce Carol Oates, John Deck, Stanley Elkin, James Purdy, David Godfrey, H. W. Blattner, Edward Loomis, Ivan Gold, David R. Bunch, Bruce Jay Friedman, Robert Coover, John Graves, John Hawkes, Leonard Gardner, Grace Paley, Thomas E. Conners, Jonathan Strong, Marguerite Young, Arthur Miller, Evan S. Connell, Leonard Michaels, Edward Stewart, John Hawkes [sic], Leslie Fiedler, John Zeugner, Bernard Malamud . . . [a comment on Malamud is omitted], Ray Carver, Eudora Welty, John Halverstadt, Terry Southern, and to exceed my allotment for majesty itself, John Cheever."
31. Carol Polsgrove, *It Wasn't Pretty, Folks, But Didn't We Have Fun? Esquire in the Sixties,* 239–241.

32. Lish to Johnson, 10-24-69 and Lish to Johnson ("Dear Eel") undated. Lish claimed he'd prefer to retreat to Vermont or the Southwest, because "this merchandized, packaged, substance-free shit is getting to me," but he did want the *Esquire* job and told Johnson: "When Lish sells out he sells out nasty."

33. The stories RC sent likely included "A Night Out" and the two languishing at *Perspective* ("A Dog Story" and "The Fling"), but Ray had few compunctions about sending out already published work, so it's probable that most of his previous stories except the widely distributed "Will You Please Be Quiet, Please?" made a round trip to Lish's office. Cover letters: RC to Lish, 11-23-69; in Portola Valley, Lish had been selling off the household goods from his first marriage; rejects: RC to Lish, 12-4-69. "Friendship" remained something of a black sheep in Carver's oeuvre. It was turned down by *Esquire, Hudson Review, New American Review, Evergreen Review, Transatlantic Review,* and even *December* before Carver placed it in *Sou'wester* (a dauntless lit-mag published by Southern Illinois University at Edwardsville). Editors passed over it for both *Will* and *FS.* With its tone much altered by Lish, it finally appeared between hard covers as "Tell the Women We're Going" in *Love.*

Chapter 14: A Friend in New York

1. RC to Johnson, [1-3]-70.
2. RC to Lish, 11-5-69; RC to Johnson, [12-69].
3. MBC to CS.
4. MBC to CS.
5. "reflection": RC to Johnson, 2-27-70.
6. *Conversations,* 41.
7. Hitchcock to CS; RC to Johnson, 2-27-70; apparently the editors learned that Carver was not a Native American; the book, *The Way: An Anthology of American Indian Literature,* eds. Shirley Hill Witt and Stan Steiner (NY: Knopf, 1974) includes nothing from Carver.
8. Thurston papers, Olin Library, Washington University in St. Louis.
9. Johnson, Curt, ed., *Best Little Magazine Fiction, 1970* (NY: New York U P, 1970).
10. Kittredge, *Hole in the Sky;* "Bulletproof," *RR;* Halpert, 15–16; Kittredge to CS.
11. RC, Foreword to Kittredge's *We Are Not in This Together* (Saint Paul, MN: Graywolf Press, 1984).
12. Kittredge, "Bulletproof."
13. S. Kolbert to CS.
14. MBC to CS.
15. MBC to CS.
16. MBC to CS; Los Altos High School: Claire Pelton to CS; VLC to CS.
17. Lish to Carruth, 1-14-71; Lish papers, Lilly.
18. RC to Johnson, 7-26-70; "You Will Come Again . . ." became "Are You a Doctor?"
19. RC to Lish, 7-15-70.
20. RC to Lish, 7-20-70.
21. "Fat" passed: memos, Lish collection, Lilly; "It seemed": Polsgrove, 240.
22. Manuscripts in Lish collection, Lilly Library, Indiana University.
23. MBC, *What,* 238; MBC may have manuscripts in her private collection that she has not shown to researchers.
24. RC to Johnson, 7-26-70. In the same letter, Carver also mentioned a story called "The Man Outside," which may have been an early version of "The Idea."
25. Lish collection, Lilly; RC to Lish, 7-15-70.
26. Lish to CS. Of his own dealings with Lish at about that time, James B. Hall recalled, "It was clear that Lish was trying to 'invent' (no better word) a 'school' of writers, and his intention, apparently, was to ride upwards towards publisher status on and by their work." (J. B. Hall to CS.)
27. RC to Kittredge, "Friday," 8-[14]-70.
28. Alice Reed to CS.

29. RC to Lish, 8-20-70; RC to Kittredge, 9-2-70.
30. RC to Kittredge, 9-2-70; RC to Johnson, 9-1-70, and "Thursday," probably 9-17-70.
31. RC to Johnson and RC to Kittredge, 9-17-70; James Carver to CS.
32. "horse": RC to Lish, [9-70].
33. "dough": RC to Joy Williams, "Thursday," [10-70]; Ellen Levine to CS, 9-28-04.
34. *Esquire: The Best of Forty Years,* compiled by the editors of *Esquire* (NY: David McKay Co., 1973); Rust Hills, introduction, *Great Esquire Fiction: The Finest Stories from the First Fifty Years,* ed. L. Rust Hills (NY: Penguin, 1983); *Smiling Through the Apocalypse: Esquire's History of the Sixties,* Harold Hayes, ed. (NY: McCall, 1969).
35. Tom Wolfe and E. W. Johnson, eds., *The New Journalism* (NY: Harper and Row, 1973).
36. RC to Williams, "Thursday," likely October 1970.
37. Frank Zepezauer to CS; Jack Hicks to CS.
38. RC to Kittredge, 11-2-70.
39. At the time, RC was working on "Nobody Said Anything," wherein poor air quality from orchard smudge pots in Yakima serves as a metaphor for moral compromises. Milltown Dam has been a Superfund site since 1987 because of high arsenic content in local water due to copper mining farther upriver.
40. RC to Johnson, 4-24-71.
41. Jon A. Jackson to CS, 8-19-02.
42. Kittredge to CS, 8-16-02; RC to Kittredge, 4-19-[71].
43. RC to Kittredge, 12-12-70; RC to Johnson, 12-12-70; RC to Lish, 2-4-71 and 2-22-71.
44. Tom Schmidt to CS.
45. RC to Kittredge, 12-12-70 and 12-20-70; RC to Johnson, 12-12-70.
46. RC to Thurston, 12-16 and 12-23-70; it's possible their letters had crossed in the mail.
47. RC to Lish, 12-12-70.
48. Douglas Unger to CS; Amy Burk to CS. The play by Robert M. Lane opened at the Bijou on December 1. *New York Times* 10-31 and 12-11-70.
49. RC to Lish, 1-n.d.-71; Henry Hart, *James Dickey: The World as Lie* (NY: Picador, 2000), 474; RC to Kittredge, 2-10-71.
50. RC to Doherty, "Sunday," c. 1971 or 1972. Content indicates early 1971; Tom Doherty, edited ms. titled "Snapshots from the Field."
51. RC to Lish, "Sunday," 2-n.d.-71.
52. RC discussed the story as an early example of his use of frames, or "people looking *through* something at someone else" as a method of detachment from his own feelings. (*Conversations,* 155).
53. Claudia Ansorge, who wrote the rejection letter for Vaughn, praised "The Summer Steelhead" and "Neighbors" but found "Fat" and other stories wanting (Ansorge to RC, 3-10-71).
54. RC to Lish, n.d.
55. RC to Kittredge, 2-10-71; RC to Lish, "Friday" n.d., spring 1971.
56. Richard Kolbert to CS.
57. VLC to CS.
58. RC to Johnson, "Monday," [April 1971]; RC to Lish, 4-1-71.
59. Claire Pelton to CS.
60. RC to Lish, undated.
61. Amy Burk Unger, quoted by Hart, 464–65, 474.
62. Carver retained the additional three lines of "Hunter" in later publications of the poem, including *AoU.* Lish to CS; RC to Lish, n.d.
63. RC to Kittredge, "Monday," 3-15-71; he entered the seven stories he considered his best in 1971, three of which Lish had edited: "Neighbors," "Are You a Doctor?" "Fat," "Nightschool," "A Dog Story," "The Summer Steelhead," and "What's in Alaska?" according to the Joseph Henry Jackson Award archive, Bancroft Library, UC Berkeley.
64. Michaels phoned: RC to Joy Williams, 5-24-71; "gratuitous": RC to Kittredge, 3-15-71.

65. Halpert, 18; Al Young and Leonard Michaels to CS.
66. The magazines where RC listed himself as a Jackson Award winner (technically true, because of the special commendation) were published in the Midwest; he didn't do so in West Coast publications.
67. RC to Lish, "Friday" n.d., likely May 1971; Lish to CS.
68. Lish to CS.
69. RC to Bruce Weber, 1984.
70. Halpert, 23; LM to CS; Kittredge to CS.

PART III: SUCCESS AND DISCONTENT

Chapter 15: A Story in *Esquire*

1. *Conversations*, 50.
2. RC to Kittredge, 5-5-71.
3. VLC to CS.
4. RC to Johnson, 7-6-71; RC to Kittredge, 7-9-71; Kittredge to CS.
5. Hall to CS; RC to Johnson, 5-10-71.
6. RC to Kittredge, 7-9-71.
7. Lish to Hall, 7-8-71.
8. "social activity": RC to Kittredge, 7-9-71; "diamonds": RC to Lish, 7-13-71; nervous: Amy Burk to Kittredge, 8-4-71.
9. Kittredge to CS.
10. "The Man Is Dangerous" appeared in *Sou'wester* late in 1972; it became "Why, Honey?" in *Will*.
11. MBC to CS.
12. Marcus to CS; Swanger to CS. A photograph of local authors taken at Cooper House includes: John Deck, William Everson, James B. Hall, George Hitchcock, James D. Houston, Morton Marcus, Annie Steinhardt (the only female), Peter S. Beagle, Nels Hanson, Stephen Levine, Robert Lundquist, Lou Mathews, Victor Perera, Mason Smith, and T. Mike Walker.
13. James D. Houston to CS.
14. RC to Kittredge, 9-7-71.
15. David Swanger to CS.
16. MBC, *What*, 242.
17. Lynn and David Swanger to CS.
18. Swanger, David, *The Poem as Process* (NY: Harcourt Brace Jovanovich, 1974), 114–116.
19. David Gershom Myers, "Between Stories," *Philosophy and Literature* 22:2 (October 1998), 457–67; Kucich to CS.
20. Skenazy, preface to *Quarry West* 31(1993). After it first few issues, *Quarry* editors learned of a Canadian literary journal by the same name and appended *West* to their title.
21. "Ray got a kick": Myers, "Between Stories," 460; "old-boy network": Kucich to CS; "flippant": Paul Skenazy to CS; Lish in Arkansas: William Harrison to CS.
22. The first publication of Michaels's signature story "Murderers" occurred in *Quarry*.
23. RC to Johnson, 11-17-71; "meekly": Myers, "Between Stories"; "ran": Skenazy, preface to *Quarry* 31 (1993).
24. Swangers to CS; Thompson to CS.
25. Halpert, 23; Michaels to CS.
26. *Conversations*, 36.
27. "wobbly": Neeli Cherkovski, *Hank: The Life of Charles Bukowski* (NY: Random House, 1991), 233; "spectacles": Jim Christy, *The Buk Book, Musings on Charles Bukowski* (Toronto: ECW Press, 1997).
28. Myers never saw his book again.

29. *Conversations,* 192; in this 1987 interview Carver said he was "in his early twenties" when Bukowski came to his house, but he was actually thirty-three. Bukowski reading: Myers to CS; Diane Smith to CS; Marcus, "All American Nightmares," *RR,* 62–65.

30. "On the other hand," Marcus admits, "this is said with a good deal of hindsight and may be just literary balderdash." (*RR,* 64)

31. Robert Gumpert, "Pen and Drink," *Charles Bukowski: Sunlight Here I Am, Interviews and Encounters 1963–1993,* ed. David Stephen Calonne (Northville, MI: Sun Dog Press, 2003), 271–72.

32. Houston to CS.

33. In *Ham on Rye,* Bukowski writes that he was fired from "Mears-Starbuck" for fighting on the job, not for stealing cookies.

34. Halpert, 33.

35. Myers, "Between Stories."

36. Smith to CS.

37. Robert McDowell to CS.

38. Mark Jarman to CS.

39. RC to Kittredge, 11-20-71; RC to Kittredge, 12-1-71.

40. Paul's: Geoffrey Dunn, *RR,* 68–69; Halpert, 74.

41. wives: Halpert, 74; "divorce": MBC, *What,* 228.

42. Thompson to CS. Maryann was probably repeating something Ray had said to her.

43. MBC, *What,* 269; CLC to CS; RC to Kittredge, 1-21-72.

44. Lish report on 1971 fiction titled "Changes," Lilly; in his essay "Fires," RC also implied that Lish had first found his work in the slush pile (*CIYNM,* 105).

45. *Cutting Edges: Young American Fiction for the 70s,* ed. Jack Hicks (NY: Holt, Rinehart and Winston, 1973), 528–529.

46. MBC, *What,* 252.

47. Herbert Gold to CS; Gold, too, learned that Lish could take a proprietary view of others' work when Lish heavily edited his story "A Death on the East Side" for *Esquire.* When the story was chosen for the 1972 *BASS* collection, Gold restored his own version.

48. Deck to CS; DeLillo to Lish, 9-14-72, Lilly.

49. *Quarry* 1 (winter 1971–72): 45–55; Lish to CS.

50. University of Iowa Press archives; Joyce Carol Oates chose *The Burning and Other Stories* by Jack Cady for the 1972 Iowa prize.

51. Myers, "Between Stories." Myers suggests that Carver had Augustinian qualities. It's worth noting, too, that Bob Dylan's 1968 album *John Wesley Harding* includes the apocalyptic song called "I Dreamed I Saw St. Augustine."

52. RC to Johnson, 6-1-72.

53. Houston, 10-17-00; RC to Lish, n.d. [likely 3-72].

54. MBC, *What,* 240.

55. MBS on title: Halpert 75.

56. The illustration is by David Wilcox.

57. "darkest": Kirk Nesset, *The Stories of Raymond Carver: A Critical Study* (Athens: Ohio U P, 1995), 20.

58. Lucy Morse, "In Raymond Carver's 'Are These Actual Miles?' Is the American Consumerist Culture Devouring the Sacredness of the Object and the Self?" Unpublished paper, University of York, 2004.

59. MBC, *Kind.*

60. Jarman to CS.

Chapter 16: The Illusion of Freedom

1. RC to Kittredge, 4-12-[72].

2. MBC, *What,* 241; "windfall": RC to Lish, 4-25-72; CLC to CS.

3. RC to Kittredge, 4-14-[72]; Thompson to CS.

4. MBC, *What,* 241.

5. The version published in *Poet and Critic* lacked five lines that appear at the end of it in *AoU*, 235. RC is critical of both other poems and finds "plain awful" two lines by Christine Zawadiwsky wherein a woman promises to save a man by means of her "affectionate vagina."
6. Stanford and Montana: RC to Kittredge, 5-12 and "Friday" both likely 1972.
7. Kittredge, "Bulletproof," *RR*, 88.
8. Young, "Happy Hour with Ray," *RR*, 96.
9. Myers, "Between Stories," 464; Carver repeated the name in "The Compartment" and "Kindling."
10. Chuck Kinder to CS.
11. The leasing of the house on Wright Avenue in Sunnyvale lies behind the story "Put Yourself in My Shoes," but the Carvers never met the Zepezauers, who owned the house, which suggests that one of Carver's most beloved and self-conscious stories is pure invention. According to the Zepezauers, the Carvers left their house in good order, though a neighbor recalled helping Ray install a new backsplash to conceal damage from a stove fire. (Frank Zepezauer and James Carter to CS.)
12. MBC, *What*, 251.
13. "end of the rainbow": MBC, *What*, 253.
14. MBC, *What*, 254.
15. Malcolm suggests that Chekhov's "Kashtanka," which is about a performing dog, can be read as a parable of the successful artist's alienation and tragic longing to return to a previous life of abuse and privation; *Reading Chekhov: A Critical Journey* (NY: Random House, 2001).
16. MBC, *What*, 254; Thompson to CS.
17. DeFrees could not recall the occasion when I spoke to her in 2004, but Thompson is certain it occurred.
18. Diane Cecily to CS.
19. Diane Cecily to CS.
20. Thompson to CS.
21. MBC, *What*, 255.
22. *Conversations*, 125.
23. MBC, *What*, 256.
24. For three days: RC to Lish, 8-22-72; over the next weeks: MBC, *What*, 257.
25. Typescript for *Love*, Lilly.
26. Typescript for *Love*, Lilly.
27. "Gazebo," *Where*, 143.
28. Cecily to CS, 11-20-03; RC to Lish, 10-23-72.
29. Kittredge: MBC, *What*, 278,
30. Michaels: Halpert, 22.
31. Cecily to CS.
32. MBC, *What*, 258.
33. MBC, *What*, 272; Scott Turow in Halpert, 49; John O'Brien to CS.
34 MBC, *What*, 257.
35. MBC, *What*, 273–74.
36. Daniel Halpern, 9-27-04.
37. MBC, *What*, 244.
38. Cecily to CS.
39. RC to Kittredge, "Wednesday," 10-12-72; "alcoholism": RC in *Kind*.

Chapter 17: Astounding and Amazing Times

1. The Stegner Fellowship had no requirements other than participation in a twice-weekly seminar. Since the program began, fiction seminars had been led by two cofounders, Wallace Stegner and Richard Scowcroft. In 1972, Stegner who'd recently won the Pulitzer Prize for his novel *Angle of Repose*, was retired from teaching; Scowcroft was in his final year as program director.

2. John Batki to CS; his story "Strange-Dreaming Charlie, Cow-Eyed Charlie" won first place in the 1972 O. Henry contest and was part of a quartet of stories, three published in the *New Yorker* and a fourth in *Fiction #2*.
3. MBC, *What*, 273; Cecily to CS.
4. Halpert, 35–37.
5. D. Johnson, "The Real Wonder Boy," *Mobylives* www.mobylives.com/Kinder .interview.
6. Halpert, 35–37; Johnson, "The Real Wonder Boy."
7. Chuck Kinder, *Snakehunter* (NY: Knopf, 1973); "mystery": Halpert, 37; Turow to CS.
8. Kinder to CS.
9. Michael Rogers, *Newsweek* Web Exclusive Section, Arts & Entertainment, 6-28-01.
10. Max Crawford to CS; Sue Crawford to CS; Peter Steinhart to CS. S. Crawford confirmed only that *she* once went to the Panthers' Oakland office to help get a publication ready for press.
11. Köepf to CS; Norman to CS. Norman's novel was one of the first to let the material its characters watched on television blur into its story, something Kinder and Carver did too.
12. R. Crumb, Introduction to *The Art of S. Clay Wilson* (Ten Speed Press, 2006).
13. Norman to CS.
14. Turow: Halpert, 48.
15. nicknames: Kinder, 12-7-02; ribbing: Köepf to CS.
16. rivalry: Köepf to CS; Lynn to CS.
17. RC in *Kind*.
18. Lynn to CS. George Lynn, who had completed an MFA at the University of North Carolina in Greensboro with ambitions to become a fiction writer, probably took the hardest fall from the grandiose attitudes that prevailed during the group's glory days. He returned to his native Alabama and a series of teaching jobs and marriages. After years of addiction, he became sober but landed in federal prison at the age of fifty for possession of homemade bombs (which he'd been making as part of his plan to break his fifth wife out of prison) and attempted shooting of a police officer who had been trying to stop him for a traffic violation. "My precipitous decline in physical and mental health was masked by the fabulous time we had in California," Lynn wrote. "That was the bait that drew me to a hedonistic fury from which I never recovered short of prison. Years after the men and women I knew in Palo Alto had settled down to reasonable lives and careers, I continued to seek the elation of those libertine nights and days. I had lost all sense of purpose for my life, and did not recover it until 2002."
19. Tom Zigal to CS.
20. Andreas Heinz, "Staying Sober," *Scientific American Mind*, April/May 2006, 57–61; Karen Bellenir, *Alcoholism Sourcebook*, 1st ed. (Detroit: Omnigraphics, 2000).
21. Zigal to CS; "pyrotechnical": Ed McClanahan to CS; "amused": Peter Steinhart to CS.
22. Max Crawford to CS.
23. Flirtatious Maryann: McClanahan to CS; M. Crawford to CS; Zigal to CS; Lynn to CS; jealous Ray: Michaels, *Time Out of Mind* (NY: Riverhead, 1999), 114.
24. Lynn to CS; Crawford to CS.
25. MBC to CS; *Excalibur*, LAHS, 1971, 1972; graduate course: Office of the Registrar, Stanford University; "never complained": Claire Pelton to CS.
26. Diane Smith to CS.
27. Köepf to CS.
28. Lynn to CS.
29. M. Crawford to CS.
30. VLC to CS.
31. MBC, *Kind*.
32. David Reid to CS; Cecily to CS.
33. RC to Lish, 1-12-73; Cecily to CS.
34. Cecily to CS.
35. Cecily to CS.

36. Cecily to CS; Kinder to CS.
37. MBC, *What*, 276.
38. RC to Lish, 1-12-73.
39. CLC to Halpert, 83.
40. Christine Flavin (then Christine Coonrod) to CS; Charlotte Painter to CS.
41. John O'Brien to CS.
42. Kittredge to CS.
43. 250 entries: *Daily Iowan*, 12-20-73; Leggett to CS; William Cotter Murray to CS; Halpert, 9–11; RC to Noel Young, 8-30-[73].
44. RC to Kittredge, 2-13-73; RC also had hopes that the seminar teacher William Abrahams, also an editor at Doubleday, would publish a collection of his stories.
45. RC to Lish, 5-16-73; perhaps RC wanted to remind Lish that some editors liked his fuller, more personal stories.
46. *Chicago Review* 24: 4 (1973), 101–107.
47. RC to Kittredge, 4-24-73.
48. RC to Lish, 5-16-73; Cecily to CS.
49. RC to Lish, 5-16-73.
50. Lynn to CS.
51. RC to N. Young, 8-30-[73]; according to former Iowa Workshop director John Leggett, the usual salary offered at the time was between $15,000 and $20,000 per semester.

Chapter 18: Drowning

1. *Conversations with John Cheever*, ed. Scott Donaldson (Jackson: U P of Mississippi, 1987), 216.
2. Houston to CS.
3. Cecily to CS.
4. Jon A. Jackson, *Ridin' with Ray* (Santa Barbara: Neville Books, 1995), 12; all details about the road trip to Iowa are drawn from Jackson's memoir, supplemented by his interviews with CS.
5. Jackson, *Ridin'*, 14.
6. Jackson to CS.
7. Jackson, *Ridin'*, and Jackson to CS.
8. Capra Press correspondence, Lilly.
9. RC to Lish, 8-30-73.
10. Jackson, *Ridin'*, 19.
11. Scott Donaldson, *John Cheever: A Biography* (NY: Random House, 1988), 268–69.
12. Jackson, *Ridin'*, 20.
13. Leggett to CS.
14. necktie: RC interviewed by Scott Donaldson, 10-23-84 (Semm Library, College of William and Mary); The Mill: T. C. Boyle to CS; "aneurism": Tracy Kidder to CS; rooms, typewriters, hallway, store: *Conversations*, 39–40, but the liquor store stories exist in many variants; Cheever's journal, courtesy of Blake Bailey.
15. Cecily to CS.
16. Kidder to CS; Robert Pope to CS.
17. Covington to CS. A different version appears in MBC, *What*, 258.
18. eagles: Covington to CS; fishing: Jackson to CS.
19. "happier lives": Mary Swander to CS; Kidder to CS.
20. dregs: Swander to CS; home for dinner: George O'Connell to CS.
21. Jackson to CS.
22. *How We Live: Contemporary Life in Contemporary Fiction*, eds. Penney Chapin Hills and L. Rust Hills (NY: Macmillan, 1968).
23. Swander to CS; sweater: John Skoyles to CS; Cheever's journal, courtesy of Blake Bailey; tickets: Jackson to CS.
24. Kinder to CS; Halpert, 17.

25. Kinder to CS; Hall was able to cancel Carver's appointment without alerting any one else at the university to Ray's double-dipping. (Hall to CS.)

26. *Conversations,*142.

27. Cheever in *Conversations with John Cheever,* 77.

28. Dan Domench to CS. Further information from Domench in the text comes from email and telephone conversations.

29. Kidder to CS; *Conversations with John Cheever,* 126.

30. MBC, *What,* 280; Halpert, 85; VLC to CS.

31. MBC, *What,* 281.

32. the "sobers": Covington to CS; Michael Waters to CS.

33. skillet: Kidder to CS.

34. Covington to CS.

35. "firsthand": MBC, *What,* 292.

36. MBC, *What,* 281-282, 286, 292.

37. incapacitated: Johnson to CS; Johnson angry: Kidder to CS.

38. Notes by Bejou Merry from 5-5-74, rpt. *Seems Like Old Times,* ed. Ed Dinger (Iowa City: University of Iowa Press, 1986).

39. Swander to CS.

40. forgiving: George O'Connell, 7-19-06.

41. Some of what Domench learned from Carver may be found in his ongoing audio book series, *The Speedway 6.*

42. RC to Lish, 3-19-74; the poems *might* have included "At Night the Salmon Move," "Rhodes," "Tel Aviv and *Life on the Mississippi,*" "Poem for Hemingway and W. C. Williams," or "A Summer in Sacramento." All of these made their first appearance in RC's 1976 collection *At Night the Salmon Move.*

43. *The Secret Life of Our Times* (New York: Doubleday, 1973). Among those included, indicating the breadth of Lish's taste: John Barth, Thomas Bontly, Jorge Luis Borges, Richard Brautigan, Jerry Bumpus, John Deck, Don DeLillo, John Gardner, William Harrison, John Irving, Vladimir Nabokov, Joyce Carol Oates, James Purdy, Michael Rogers, Joy Williams. At Doubleday the book's editor was a young novelist named Bill Henderson; over lunch, Henderson and Lish conceived the annual Pushcart Prize series to celebrate small presses and magazines.

44. Ellen Levine to CS.

45. "suave": Gurganus, 10-17-05; lumberjack shirt, nervous: Boyle to CS; shit: Covington. After Boyle recovered from the trauma of the workshop, he mailed Lish a story about Lassie. With a change of title from "A Boy and His Dog" to "Heart of a Champion," it became Boyle's first slick publication. Lish "got his fingers on the story a little" — but Boyle restored most of it (except the title, which he approved) when he included it in his first story collection.

46. For Gurganus, the drama continued through another act. His agent sent all his unpublished stories to Lish, who kept three for the holiday issue. After changing their titles, he sent Gurganus "revisions performed, not in pen or pencil, but in a wide black magic marker. Whole thirds of the stories had been Xed out, and sample sentences of what should replace the missing passages had been sketched along the margin. I thought at the time that he was a frustrated writer who didn't know how to start a story and therefore built his on the backs of others." With counsel from Elkin, Gurganus refused to "malform" his stories to meet Lish's "careless self-imposing suggestions." Lish even warned Elkin against taking Gurganus's side. In the end, Gurganus wrote Lish, "If I sell out at this age, all the suspense will be gone. Write your own stories, not mine." Gurganus had no regrets and sold stories elsewhere, but, he admitted, he'd been "tempted by the career-making promise of having three stories in the visible December issue." Lish to Elkin, several letters, 5-73; Gurganus to CS. In 2002 Lish described Elkin to CS as "a writer, the real thing, the most underrated writer in America."

47. Covington to CS, 7-03-06.

48. MBC, *What,* 281.

49. Lynn to CS; Kittredge to CS; Domench to CS.
50. Halpert, 42–43; Kinder and Cecily to CS.
51. Domench to CS.
52. Halpert, 85; VLC to CS; CLC to CS.
53. RC to Bruce Weber, 1-84; the story might also have been suggested by frequent "body dumpings" that occur in Yakima County, Washington, or even by Charles Bukowski's story of necrophilia, "The Copulating Mermaid of Venice, Calif." RC told Weber that he lived in Sunnyvale when he read the article. Other indications place the story later. Sandra Kleppe notes the story's correlation to murders of women in Washington State: "Women and Violence in the Stories of Raymond Carver," *Journal of the Short Story in English* 46: (spring 2006), 119–123.

Chapter 19: *Will You Please Be Quiet, Please?*

1. Jack London, *John Barleycorn: Alcoholic Memoirs* (NY: Oxford, 1989), 188.
2. Michaels recommended RC for the position.
3. "adjunct" and "welcoming": Porter Abbott to CS.
4. Abbott to CS; booze and cigarettes: Allaback to CS.
5. The address in Goleta was 6253 Parkhurst Drive.
6. unsociable: John Ridland to CS; literary scene: Lin Rolens and David Dahl to CS. Rolens is coauthor with Noel Young (as Leon Elder) of a book Carver later owned, *Waitress: America's Unsung Heroine* (Santa Barbara: Capra, 1985).
7. Noel Young, "Happy Hour with Ray," *RR; John Barleycorn*, 7–8.
8. Young, "Happy Hour"; RC to Johnson, 9-22-74.
9. Judy Young to CS; Thomas Sanchez to CS.
10. "center": RC to Lish, 9-13-74; jail: MBC, *What*, 282; CLC to CS.
11. Halpert, 85–86; VLC to CS.
12. Marc Louria to CS.
13. never satisfied: RC to Weber, 1-84; last line: Louria to CS.
14. In *Playgirl* (April 1976) this line appeared at the end: "I begin to scream. It doesn't matter any longer." In *Fires* Carver restored the *Spectrum* version. It's likely that *Playgirl* was already considering the story when Carver gave it to *Spectrum*.
15. RC to Lish, 11-11-74.
16. Frederic W. Hills to CS; "Enthusiasm and Timing Were S&S's Keys to Success for Looking for Mr. Goodbar," *Publishers Weekly*, 11-10-75, 32–34.
17. Telephone call: MBC, *What*, 283; Bankruptcy No. BK-75-05915, District Court of the U.S. for Central District of California (Los Angeles).
18. Lois Welch to CS; Diane Smith to CS.
19. Domench to CS; Anthony Bukoski to CS; Amy Burk, as told to Douglas Unger.
20. MBC, *What*, 283; Lynn to CS.
21. MBC, *What*, 284; Halpert, 143.
22. Datsun: bankruptcy filing; Ray Heffner, "Except for Lady Macbeth Production Seemed Wrong," Iowa City *Press-Citizen*, 2-22-75; Unger to CS; MBC, *What*, 284.
23. RC to Lish, 01-24-75.
24. Hicks to CS; Crawford to CS.
25. Bankruptcy filing. $20,000 then would be about $60,000 in 2006 dollars or double Maryann's salary, a high amount even if measured by later years' soaring levels of personal credit card debt.
26. "Miracle," *AoU*, 242–245.
27. Sylvia Kolbert to CS.
28. D. Schmitz to CS; MBC, *What*, 284–86.
29. MBC, *What*, 286–287; RC to Lish, 5-21-75; RC to Young, 5-22-75; MBC writes that RC drank brandy on the very evening he was released from the mental health facility.
30. Cecily to CS; Kinder to CS; MBC, *What*, 249; MBC to CS; Kinder, *Honeymooners: A Cautionary Tale* (NY: Farrar, Straus, and Giroux, 2001).
31. MBC to CS; Kinder to CS.

32. Cecily to CS; Kinder to CS; Maryann: Halpert, 43–45.
33. MBC, *What*, 287–89.
34. Brodkey's story was "His Son, in His Arms in Light, Aloft" and the magazine cover carried the line "New Fiction by Harold Brodkey" near Monroe's left foot; at this time Carver's name would not have boosted sales.
35. Omitted stories included: "Furious Seasons"; "Dummy" / "The Third Thing That Killed My Father Off"; "Distance"; "The Lie"; "So Much Water So Close to Home"; "The Fling"; "Pastoral" / "The Cabin"; "Harry's Death"; "Mine" / "Popular Mechanics"; "The Pheasant"; and "Friendship" / "Tell the Women We're Going."
36. Halpert, 84.
37. RC to Lish, 9-28-75.
38. Case M773636 County of Santa Clara, California; RC repeated the scam in 1974 but apparently was not caught.
39. Lish archive: Lilly; Blaise to CS.
40. "TNYH," *Chicago Review* 24 (1973) 4: 101.
41. Frederic Hills to CS.
42. RC to Lish, 5-21-75; Cheever to Lish, 10-6-75; Cheever to RC, 10-7-75.
43. Kinder to CS; Sanchez to CS; Leonard Gardner to CS.
44. Kinder to CS; Cecily to CS.
45. "Fires," *CIYNM*, 100.
46. Alan Shapiro to CS.
47. John and Rebecca O'Brien to CS.
48. Michael Pleadwell to CS.
49. VLC to CS.
50. Douglas Unger to CS.
51. Unger to CS.
52. Chris "flying": Unger to CS; James Carver to CS; James Crumley to CS; *The Last Good Kiss* (NY: Random House, 1978), ch. 7; Hicks to CS.
53. *Conversations*, 38.

PART IV: RECOVERY

Chapter 20: Celebrated and Homeless

1. Unger to CS.
2. *Publishers Weekly*, 1-5-76.
3. "to live on those edges": Halpert, 148.
4. RC to Johnson, "Saturday" [Feb. 1976, dated by Johnson]; MBC, *What*, 290–294.
5. Corporation of Yaddo archives, NYPL and Yaddo.
6. Michaels to CS; Hillman to CS.
7. "teased": Crawford to CS; proceedings of case M773636 County of Santa Clara, California.
8. Kinder, *Honeymooners*, 283. MBC's testimony is not part of the court record.
9. Richard C. Day to Mr. Ochoa (probation officer), 3-16-76; David Swanger also wrote on Carver's behalf.
10. Kinder to CS.
11. In his second anthology of fiction from *Esquire, All Our Secrets Are the Same* (NY: Norton, 1976), Lish included Carver's "Collectors." His foreword attacked "Barth, Barthelme & Co." and posited that these thirty-eight stories were boulders launched in defense of "the huge utility of literature."
12. Lish would claim: D. T. Max, "The Carver Chronicles," *New York Times Magazine*, 8-09-98.
13. *New York Times Book Review*, 3-7-76, 2.
14. briefcase: Alan Shapiro to CS; RC never felt: *Conversations*, 92.
15. Unger to CS; *Newsweek*, 4-26-76.

16. martinis: Unger to CS; "kiss": Jarman to CS. One story he read that night was "The Father," which has as its closing words, "his face was white and without expression."
17. Unger to CS.
18. Unger to CS; Brendan Ward to CS.
19. Alexander poem: Qais Al-Awqati to CS; big and bloated: Robert Pope to CS.
20. Robert Pope to CS; Ann Beattie's *Distortions* and *Chilly Scenes of Winter* were published later in 1976; other books full of details that seemed realistic that year included Stanley Elkin's *The Franchiser,* Lisa Alther's *Kinflicks,* Tom Robbins's *Even Cowgirls Get the Blues,* and Ron Kovic's memoir of a working-class man's experience in Vietnam, *Born on the Fourth of July.*
21. Unger to CS.
22. Vivian Mosely to CS; Franklin Casey to CS; Caroline Berry to CS.
23. fled: Unger to CS; RC to Lish, 6-3-76.
24. RC to Lish, 6-13-76.
25. MBC, *What,* 295; Upstart Crow: RC to F. Hills, 6-17-76.
26. Gardner to CS.
27. Halpert, 45, and Kinder to CS.
28. MBC, *What,* 295; Sylvia Kolbert to CS; RC to Lish, 7-20-76; RC to Lish, 7-26-76.
29. RC enclosed a poem called "The Sturgeon" with a letter to Lish dated 8-17-76. He says it "dropped out of the typewriter" while he was working on the article, but actually his poem of that title appeared in a small journal in 1967. Likely he hoped to republish it in *Esquire.*
30. Unger to CS; VLC to CS.
31. *Newsweek* photo: Kinder to CS; books: Lewis Buzbee to CS.
32. Hicks to CS; Hills to RC, 8-3-76; Lish to RC. n.d.-76.
33. *Conversations,* 38.
34. Halpert, 90; MBC, *What,* 296; Eugene Duffy Jr. to CS.
35. In June 1980, the house sold for $101,405.
36. In addiction, the neural pathway called the *nucleus accumbens* loses sensitivity to basic pleasures (Anahad O'Connor, *New York Times,* 8-3-04, D-1).
37. MBC, *What,* 298; Unger to CS.
38. Eugene Duffy Jr. to CS.
39 Blair Fuller, "Until a Morning Came," *Quest* (May/June 1978), 41–45; RC read Fuller's essay.
40. MBC to CS.
41. RC to Lish, 9-27-76; RC to Day, 9-29-76.
42. "charade": Fuller, "Until a Morning Came," 44; *Alcoholics Anonymous* 3d ed. (NY: AA World Services, 1976), 39–42.
43. MBC, Answers to Interrogatories, 5-4-89, Superior Court, Clallam County, WA.
44. James Carver to CS; "forsook": Kinder to CS; MBC, *What,* 302.
45. Unger to CS.
46. Crumley to CS; Levine to CS.
47. *Conversations,* 41.
48. Eugene Duffy Jr. to CS; "Gone Fishing," Charvat.
49. Halpert, 46–47; Kinder to CS.
50. RC to Lish, 3-4-[77]; Kinder to CS; Kittredge to CS.
51. In the same year, Lewis Hyde published his important essay, "Alcohol and Poetry: John Berryman and the Booze Talking," in *American Poetry Review.*
52. Ray learned he was nominated on March 22; the other nominees in fiction were MacDonald Harris, *The Balloonist;* Ursula K. Le Guin, *Orsinian Tales;* Cynthia Propper Seaton, *A Fine Romance;* Wallace Stegner, *The Spectator Bird.* Fiction judges were Erskine Caldwell, George P. Elliott, and Orville Prescott. Carver saved his unused ticket for the award ceremony held in New York City on April 13; Cecily to CS; Kinder to CS.
53. Unger to CS; *Conversations,* 175.
54. The address was 1131 Henry Lane, later behind the Six Rivers Brewery; "hand-to-mouthing": RC to Johnson, 5-9-77; ocean and woods: RC to M. Ryan, 4-3-77.

55. RC to Johnson, 5-9-77; RC to O'Brien, 5-23-77; RC to M. Ryan, 4-3-77 and 7-5-77.
56. RC to Lish, 4-15-77.
57. Köepf to CS; RC to O'Brien, 5-23-77.
58. RC to N. Young, 6-2-77.
59. *Conversations,* 89; Fred Hills to CS. To Hills, Ray seemed "worn out, maybe a bit ragged, whether from lack of sleep or a hangover, but reasonably articulate and certainly not drunk."
60. *Conversations,* 39, 89–90; F. Hills to CS; MBC, *What,* 305; Unger to CS.
61. *Conversations,* 39 and 89–90; neither version mentions hummers, so it could be that he went cold turkey this last time. He told interviewers he "felt terrible physically" and "was sick for four days." On 6-2-81 he wrote Day that he'd taken his last drink exactly four years ago at the Jamabalaya.
62. Durrell: Skoyles to CS; *Conversations,* 38–39.
63. RC to Frederic Hills, 6-5-77.

Chapter 21: Sobriety

1. RC to Frederic Hills, 6-5-77.
2. John Sterling to CS; F. Hills to CS.
3. RC missed his son's graduation just as C.R. missed Ray's; VLC to CS; MBC, *What,* 307.
4. "ring": Halpert, 76; "Gone Fishing or Closing In," Charvat.
5. Halpert, 77.
6. RC to Mr. Hallstrom, 9-17-86, published in *Country,* 105–107.
7. *Conversations,* 39, 77, 115; Unger, 11-14-03.
8. RC to O'Brien, 7-9-77; RC to Young, 6-10-77 and 7-20-77; RC to Lish, 9-3-77.
9. RC to Mr. Hallstrom; MBC to CS.
10. Proposed and excluded were RC's "A Summer Steelhead" (already published in revised form as "Nobody Said Anything" in *Will*), "Friendship," "Harry's Death," and the poem "You Don't Know What Love Is." Young vetoed the violent "Friendship." (Capra archives, Lilly.)
11. RC to Lish, 9-3-77 and 9-27-77; Lish to RC, 9-17-77; *FS* ms., Lilly.
12. RC to Lish, 4-15-77 and 7-24-77.
13. Sterling to CS.
14. notes: Charvat; confessed: RC to Lish, 9-27-77.
15. *Conversations,* 175.
16. MBC to CS.
17. The handbook was *Writing a Novel* (London: Methuen, 1974); Unger to CS; Kinder to CS.
18. On August 12 a *New York Times* article described a novel-in-progress by William Stevenson about the German East African led by Lettow-Vorbeck. Hills wrote Stevenson that he had National Book Award nominee Carver under contract for a novel on "precisely this subject." The veteran journalist and author of eight books was not dissuaded. His *Ghosts of Africa* came out in 1980; promised Hills: RC to Sterling, 11-22-77.
19. Kittredge to CS, and Halpert, 54; Smith to CS; MBC, *What,* 308.
20. Lish to RC, 9-21-77.
21. RC to Lish, 9-27-77.
22. Lish to RC, 10-1-77; at this time "Why Don't You Dance?" was titled "Why Don't You Sit Down?"
23. McGrath to Gail Hochman (Paul R. Reynolds, Inc.), 12-2-77; McGrath to CS; Sterling to CS.
24. Unger to CS; trouble: RC to Swanger, 11-23-77 and CLC to Halpert, 87.
25. "too old": RC to Johnson, 11-3-77; CLC to Halpert, 87.
26. VLC to author, 10-1-06; Unger, 8-6-06.
27. RC to Lish, 9-27-77; Unger to CS.
28. RC to Johnson, 1-17-78.

29. For *Antaeus* RC chose Gina Berriault's *The Mistress and Other Stories,* John Clellon Holmes's *Get Home Free,* Ella Leffland's *Mrs. Munck,* James Salter's *A Sport and a Pastime,* and Wallace Stegner's *Big Rock Candy Mountain.* The list appeared in *Antaeus* 27.
30. MBC, *What,* 310; intended to drive: RC to O'Brien, 7-9-77; told Perkins, *What,* 310.
31. Rolls Royce: Michael Harper to CS; women: Michael Waters to CS; Ray missing: Richard Crossland to CS; black bra: Waters to CS.
32. Ford, "Good Raymond," *New Yorker,* 10-5-98, 70; RC, "Friendship," *CIYNM,* 119; "best book": RC to M. Ryan, 7-21-77.
33. RC to O'Brien, 11-22-77; Ford on RC "Good Raymond," 70.
34. Good Raymond, 72.
35. Tess Gallagher, "The Ghosts of Dreams," *RR,* 103–104; "Instead of Dying," *The Sun* (December 2006), 26.
36. MBC to CS.
37. Crossland, 5-10-07.
38. MBC, *What,* 310; MBC to CS.
39. relatives: RC to John O'Brien, 11-22-77; Chris: RC to Swangers, 11-23-77.
40. MBC to CS.
41. RC to Lish, 12-1-77; RC to Ford, 11-25-77.
42. Les Standiford to CS; the referees were Richard Day, Donald Justice, Jack Leggett, Gordon Lish, Leonard Michaels, Josephine Miles, Michael Ryan, and David Swanger; all except Lish were employed by universities.
43. Voigt to RC, 11-7-[77]; RC to Ford, 11-25-77, 12-30-77; MBC has said RC decided to spend the winter in the East after seeing John Cheever speaking on *The Dick Cavett Show* (Halpert, 117).
44. "pleasant": RC to Sterling, 1-7-78; "no wildness": RC to Swanger, 12-29-77; CLC to Halpert, 87; VLC to CS; MBC, *What,* 311–312.
45. Gallagher writes in her introduction to *Call If You Need Me*: "The closing image of spoilage recalls Ray's story 'Preservation' in its suggestion that relationships, like food on the thaw, are perishable, and beyond a certain point, you can't get them back."
46. MBC, *What,* 312; CLC to CS.

Chapter 22: Separation

1. RC to Leslie Gutterman, 10-8-78; Stephen Dobyns, *RR,* 108–109; Barbara Greenberg to CS.
2. Voigt to CS.
3. Tobias Wolff, "Appetite," *RR,* 243, and T. Wolff to CS.
4. Dobyns, *RR,* 109–113.
5. RC to Ford, 3-3-[78].
6. T. Wolff, *RR,* 244.
7. Friendship, *CIYNM,* 120.
8. Dobyns to CS.
9. Irving: RC to Day, 1-31-78; Linda McCarriston: Dobyns to CS.
10. McCarriston to CS; RC to Lish, 8-25-78.
11. RC to Bruce Weigl, 2-18-78; D. Unger to CS; Brendan Ward to CS.
12. Ford, "Good Raymond."
13. accused: *December* 15: 1–2 (1973), 274; Johnson to CS.
14. Johnson, "Short Cut," *Salud,* 131–132; car: RC to Day, 2-16-78; "letter or woman": RC to Lish, 2-17-78; owl: RC to O'Brien, 2-16-78; abjectly lonely: MBC, *What,* 314.
15. RC to Johnson, 2-25-78; RC to Bruce Weigl, 2-18-78; Kinder to CS.
16. address: RC to Lish, 2-23-78; RC to Ford, 3-3-78; blamed Sterling: RC to Andrew Grossbardt and Bruce Weigl, 5-8-78.
17. *RR,* 109–113.
18. RC to Amy Burk and D. Unger, 3-8-78; "old roles": RC to M. Ryan, 11-21-77; loan: RC to Weigl, 2-28-78.

19. MBC, *What,* 315–316; Humboldt State College became a university in 1972.
20. Cecily and Kinder to CS; RC n.d. to Ford; T. Wolff to CS.
21. Hyde: *American Poetry Review* 4 (1976), 4; Geoffrey Wolff to CS. The National Institute on Alcohol Abuse and Alcoholism was founded in 1971.
22. The 1976 Copyright Act extends protection for up to seventy-five years from the date of publication (twenty-eight years plus a renewal term of forty-seven years, or for the author's lifetime plus fifty years).
23. MBC, *What,* 316 and MBC to CS.
24. RC to Day, 3-21-78; there were 292 awards altogether, including one to Tess Gallagher, but RC mentioned just himself, Schmitz, and Voigt in a letter to Day. Guggenheim Foundation to RC, 3-15-78 and 4-10-78; Guggenheim Foundation to CS, 1-2-07. The foundation accepted Ray's report on his accomplishments as a fellow on 5-23-79, confirming that he'd been receiving money that year.
25. RC to Unger and Amy Burk, 3-8-78; Europe: RC to Day, 3-21-78; RC to Ford, 3-21-78 and 4-15-78.
26. RC to Ford, 5-1-78; poems: RC to Swanger, 1-15-78.
27. MBC, *What,* 318–319; *Conversations,* 8.
28. MBC, *What,* 319; and, though he hadn't dedicated himself to the sexual circus at Goddard before, he was aware of opportunities there and especially hoped to see McCarriston again (RC to Lish, 4-15-78 and 8-25-78).
29. RC to Lish, 5-8-78.
30. MBC annotated her textbook and passed her notes along to Murray who kept the book for years because her notes were so interesting. Murray to CS; Murray to RC, 10-6-[78]; Dobyns to CS.
31. *How Al-Anon Works for Families and Friends of Alcoholics* (NY: Al-Anon Family Groups, 1995), 139.
32. VLC to RC, 5-15-78.
33. RC to Swanger, 11-30-80; MBC, *What,* 319–321.
34. Unger to CS; Helprin to CS.
35. MBC to CS.
36. V. Bourjaily, B. Bourjaily, Helprin, and D. Unger to CS.
37. RC to Lish, 6-3-78 and 6-8-78; RC to Swanger, 7-12-78.
38. MBC, *What,* 323; MBC to RC, 7-20-78; in *What,* MBC compares a farewell letter she wrote to RC to the wife's letter in his story "Blackbird Pie."
39. Dobyns, *RR,* 112; Ellen Bryant Voigt to CS.
40. Mary Karr, 11-11-03; Karr to Halpert (unpublished interview).
41. McCarriston to CS.
42. RC to M. Ryan, 8-30-78; Bruce Dobler to CS.
43. MBC, *What,* 323; RC to Jean and Donald Justice, 9-7-78.

Chapter 23: Beginning Again

1. Gallagher to Halpert; Bruce Dobler to CS; Stephanie Dobler to CS.
2. Gallagher to Halpert; Bruce Dobler to CS.
3. B. Dobler to CS; Vance Bourjaily to CS.
4. RC and TG to Kittredge and Smith, 8-26-78; Greg Simon, preface, *Soul Barnacles,* by Tess Gallagher (Ann Arbor: University of Michigan Press, 2000), ix. Tom Jenks, "A Literary Love Story," *Vanity Fair,* 1986, www.narrativemagazine.info/pages/r_t.htm.
5. RC to Ryan, 8-30-78; RC to Ford, 8-31-78.
6. RC to Ryan, 8-30-78. His town house was #153 at 6938 Alto Rey.
7. B. Dobler to CS; Stephanie Dobler to CS.
8. Bruce Dobler to CS.
9. Patricia Dobler memorialized the occasion in her poem "Juarez 1978," *Collected Poems* (Pittsburgh: Autumn House, 2005), 182.
10. RC to Lish, 9–8-78 and 9-21-78; Ford reminded Ray that leaving UTEP would make it impossible for him to go someplace better (Halpert, 101).

11. Bruce Dobler to CS; See Dobler, "Odometer," *Collected Poems*, 183.

12. Young to RC, 1-30-79; Ann Beattie, "Carver's *Furious Seasons*," *Canto* 2:2 (summer 1978), 178–182; RC to Young, 9-29-78.

13. Gary Fisketjon, "Normal Nightmares." *Village Voice*, 9-18-78, 132–134; Fisketjon to CS.

14. The McGraw-Hill paperback, despite its attractive trade format and a "New and Noteworthy" listing in the *Times*, got a slow start. At first the book was handled by the college division, which meant trade bookshops received only a 20 percent discount and were reluctant to stock it. Sales picked up when the book became available at a 40 percent discount (Buzbee to CS). By February 1980, 5,000 copies had sold and the book was in its second printing. A third printing was ordered in the summer of 1982 (Timothy Yohn of McGraw-Hill to RC, 2-8-80 and 7-14-82). Sterling to Fisketjon, 3-5-79; RC to Fisketjon, 9-24-79; Fisketjon to RC, 9-24-78.

15. Hills did not move RC's contract with him when he became a trade book editor at Simon & Schuster. RC still owed a novel to McGraw-Hill.

16. F. Hills to RC, 4-27-79 and four-page typescript by RC called "Outline for a Novel" in Hills's archives.

17. Hills recalled that RC sent him forty to fifty pages, but these have not survived (Hills to CS).

18. Jon Manchip White, *A World Elsewhere* (NY: Thomas Crowell, 1975), 274.

19. UTEP offered an MA with creative writing option, not an MFA; Gary Eddy to CS; stone-faced: Eddy to CS; bleached: Ray González to CS; Winchell's: Jeff Schiff to CS.

20. RC to Johnson, 5-8-79; "poet first": González to CS; continued as poets: González is the author of *Consideration of the Guitar: New and Selected Poems* (Rochester: BOA Editions, 2005); Schiff of *Burro Heart* (DuBois, PA: Mammoth Books, 2004).

21. Vicky Anderson to CS.

22. Dagoberto Gilb, 9-13-04; *Magic of Blood* (Albuquerque: U of New Mexico P, 1993).

23. Letters to Day, Ryan, O'Brien, Ford; UTEP *Prospector,* 12-14-78.

24. RC to Day, 10-18-78; T. Wolff to CS.

25. William Penn to RC, 10-12-78 and 2-6-79; Paul Theiner to CS; Halpert, 101.

26. RC to Amy Burk and D. Unger, 9-21-78 and 11-29-78.

27. RC to Lish, 12-11-78; Xmas plans: RC to Ford, 11-n.d.-78; Bellingham: Unger to CS; ulcers: MBC to CS; colleague: Mimi Gladstein to CS; Ray told her: MBC, *What,* 324–325.

28. "decisive physical moment": "An Afternoon with Tess Gallagher," interview by Melvin Sterne, *Carve Magazine* (www.carvezine.com), accessed 8-3-03; "a gamble": Gallagher, "Instead of Dying," *The Sun* (December 2006), 26.

29. "trying to haul": Gallagher, "My Father's Love Letters," *A Concert of Tenses: Essays on Poetry* (Ann Arbor: U of Michigan P, 1986), 4, 10; "he was so amazing": Mick Brown, "Untold Stories," London *Telegraph,* 7-15-00.

30. bluffing: Gallagher, "Instead of Dying," 27.

31. Gallagher, "At Mercy," *The Lover of Horses* (NY: Harper & Row, 1982).

32. phone call: MBC to CS; shipwreck: MBC, "Triumph."

33. Gallagher, "My Father's Love Letters," 10.

34. Tom Jenks, "A Literary Love Story," *Vanity Fair,* 1986, posted http://narrative magazine.info/pages/r–t.htm. Jenks, "Literary Love Story."

35. devoted: V. Anderson, 2-22-07; feminists: Gladstein.

36. In early drafts of the story, the cardiologist who holds forth about love is named Herb. Carver changed his name to Mel just before publication; RC to Lish, 7-10-80.

37. Anderson, Gladstein, and Walter Taylor to CS; RC to Lish, 7-10-80; Herb to RC, 2-22-82.

38. Gladstein to CS; Anderson to CS; Eddy to CS; bragged to Day, 2-15-79.

39. RC to Day, 4-2-79; RC to Swanger, 8-30-79.

40. RC's book reviews are collected in *CIYNM*.

41. Mexico: RC to Lish, 2-1-79.

42. RC to Kittredge, 5-21-79; Buzbee, "New Hope for the Dead," *RR,* 114.

43. RC to Ford, 5-28-79.
44. RC to Johnson, 7-25-79; MBC, *What*, 329–330.
45. Crumley to CS.
46. Eddy; Lois and Richard Shelton, 10-7-03; dislike of Tucson: RC to Day, RC to Kittredge, RC to Johnson, 8-22-79; RC to Swanger, 8-30-79.
47. "four months": RC to Kittredge, 8-22-79; war footing: RC to Swanger, 8-30-79; exercise: RC to Lish 9-12-79.
48. R. Shelton to CS.
49. RC to Yates, 9-17-79; "Dick": RC to Day, 9-17-79.
50. RC to Hitchcock and Simon, 11-3-79; for his main character in "One More Thing," Carver borrowed initials from Gallagher's U of Arizona colleague L. D. Clark. "He told me he just liked the sound of the name when he first heard it" (Clark to CS).
51. Evidence in RC's correspondence indicates that the first seven stories listed, beginning with "Where Is Everyone?" were written in Tucson.
52. "Where Is Everyone?" *Fires*.
53. *Iowa Review* 10:3 (summer 1979), 37.
54. *Fires,* 173.
55. RC to Ford, 10-12-79; RC to Swanger, 11-3-79; RC to Hitchcock/Simon, 11-3-79.
56. McGrath to Sterling, 11-16 and 11-30-79.
57. Halpert, 101–102; "doughnuts": RC to T. Wolff, 11-16-79; a fictionalized version of the doughnut scene appears as the chapter "Donut Joy" in the novel *Nixoncarver* by Mark Maxwell (NY: St. Martin's Press, 1998), who heard about it from a son of the cardiologist.
58. Ella: RC to Burk and Unger, 11-26-79; Hitchcock and Simon to CS.
59. *Kind*.
60. Gallagher, "Instead of Dying," 26.
61. RC to Lish, 5-21-79.

Chapter 24: *What We Talk About When We Talk About Love*

1. "living alone": RC to Covington, 1-15-80; Carruth to CS; Haxton to CS; phone bill: RC to Day, 2-15-80. Ray's address was 1604 Westmoreland Avenue.
2. "janitor's job": RC to Johnson, 2-15-80; "one of the better programs": RC to Swanger, 2-27-80; Saturday night: RC to Covington, 4-26-80.
3. RC to Day, 2-15-80; my conclusion that the story was "A Small, Good Thing" is based on papers in the Lilly Library; it's possible, though seems less likely, that the story was an earlier version of "What We Talk About When We Talk About Love" called "Beginners," which RC mailed to Sterling on 2-12-80. Rust Hills declined "Beginners" for *Esquire* on 2-25-80, advising that it needed to be compressed.
4. RC to Covington, 4-26-80; Onondaga County Archives.
5. Waters to CS. Waters's poem "Raymond Carver" appears in his book *Darling Vulgarity* (Rochester, NY: BOA Editions, 2006).
6. The video recording, which Waters possesses, preserves a longer version of "Gazebo" that had not been published. "Why Don't You Dance?" follows the *Quarterly West* text; "If It Please You" became "After the Denim" but later appeared in its original length in a chapbook.
7. RC to Halpern, 4-14-80; RC to Lish, 4-29-80; RC to Lish, 7-1-80; Jonathan Brent of *TriQuarterly* to RC, 6-13-80.
8. Buzbee to RC, 4-8-81 and RC to Buzbee, 4-13-80; lunch: RC to Day, 5-15-80.
9. title page: Lilly.
10. RC to Lish, 5-10-80; RC to Lish, 5-10-80, 9 pm.
11. Lish's papers are housed at Lilly. In my opinion, this first revised manuscript is not identifiable among the Lilly holdings. It is not absolutely clear from Carver's 6-13-80 letter to Lish whether he is referring to his version A with Lish's interlineated hand editing or a retyped version. In either case, I refer to the edited version Carver received on 6-13-80 as version B. Stull and Carroll, according to an unsigned article in the *New*

Yorker (12-24 and 12-31-07), believe that Lish "had cut the original manuscript by 40 percent."

12. RC to Lish, 6-13-80.
13. RC to Lish, 6-13-80.
14. James Welch to CS; G. Wolff to CS; RC to Swanger, 6 [sic, likely 8]-7-80.
15. RC to Liz Darhansoff, 1-30-82; Darhansoff renegotiated the contract, regaining some rights, in the fall.
16. "umbrella": RC to M. Ryan, 8-1-80; pages: G. Wolff to CS; read: John Morgan to CS.
17. contract: RC to Fisketjon, 6-29-80; bounced check: RC to Lish, 7-4-80.
18. Gallagher writes that Ray's Knopf editor asked him to remove drinking from the stories in *Love* and that she advised Ray to "get rid of that editor" ("Instead of Dying," 27). Lish remained the editor; the excisions he ultimately made did not focus on drinking. Carol Polsgrove first reported the severity of Lish's editing of Carver in 1995; further research was done by Brian Evenson (unpublished) and the issue was widely publicized by D. T. Max's "The Carver Chronicles," *New York Times Magazine*, 8-9-98.
19. An indication of the difficulty of determining how many versions once existed is the fact that a photograph of the last page of the edited manuscript offered with "Beginners" in the *New Yorker* (12-24-07 and 12-31-07) differs from the version in *Love*. See also Stull and Carroll's comparisons posted at http://www.nytimes.com/packages/pdf/Carver.pdf and their Note on the Texts included in *RC: Collected Stories*.
20. RC to Lish, 7-8-80, 8:00 a.m.
21. RC to Lish, 7-8-80.
22. RC to Lish, 7-8-80.
23. RC to Lish, 7-8-80.
24. "Where Is Everyone?" was Ford's favorite story in the entire collection. In a letter dated 2-15-80 he wrote RC that "all the details and half-told events . . . give the story great gravity . . . just immense tenderness and survivor intelligence there."
25. RC to Lish, 7-8-80.
26. RC to Lish, 7-8-80.
27. RC to Lish, 7-10-80.
28. "My sense": Max; Gallagher, lecture on Northwest Writers, University of Washington, 7-19-01; Peter Monaghan reports that Gallagher told him she was "livid" and Carver was "ashamed" about the editing but "too depleted by his fight with alcoholism to object . . ." ("Tess Gallagher Shares Her Passions for Poetry, the Precision of Language, and the Prose of Raymond Carver," *Chronicle of Higher Education*, 6-13-97, B8–B9; "felt the book": "A Nightshine Beyond Memory," *Soul Barnacles*, 239–240.
29. Polsgrove to CS; Sterling to CS.
30. Gail Caldwell, "Treating Writing Like Life and Death: Gordon Lish—a Man of Absolutes—Leaves His Students Mesmerized," *Boston Globe*, 3-6-88; "Captain Fiction: Super-teacher Gordon Lish," *Boston Globe*, 3-7-88.
31. MBC to CS.
32. Lish to CS.
33. Lish to CS.
34. *The Selected Stories of Gordon Lish* (Toronto: Somerville House, 1996).
35. Lish accepted some editing by William Abrahams on his first novel, *Dear Mr. Capote*. Lish laughed at theories he's heard about why he edited Carver as he did. As an example, he offered, "I am a New York Jew who would have liked to, or who did, inhabit the big-boned Northwestern man. You could say that." (Lish to CS.)
36. Pesetsky—whose novel was a fictional venting of her experience as a woman writer and ghostwriter of nonfiction—appreciated Lish's editing: "He could pull the best out of you as a writer . . . convince a writer to move past personal shields and not hold back . . . Gordon was a line editor—a rare bird today—and didn't hesitate to say when writing was bad and needed reworking." (Pesetsky to CS.)
37. "A Small, Good Thing" is thirty printed pages in *Cathedral*, so Lish had already cut it severely in his first revision.
38. RC to Lish, 7-10-80. MBC associated the line "she was right" with a statement she

made to Ray in 1979: "I said, 'In the words of the song "Frankie and Johnny," Ray, you were my man, and you did me wrong.' " RC gave her a copy of the original manuscript of "Gazebo" (MBC to CS).

39. RC to Lish, 7-14-80.
40. The 80,000 items Lish placed at the Lilly Library have not been fully arranged and catalogued.
41. The "original" version of the story called "Beginners" identified by Stull and Carroll matches one that Carver submitted to *TriQuarterly* before he submitted his book manuscript to Lish. *TriQuarterly* accepted the story, but Carver later withdrew it; *Antaeus* then published the Lish-revised (C) "What We Talk About When We Talk About Love." (Northwestern University Special Collections).
42. Stull skirted the issue in his essay for *The Dictionary of Literary Biography* when he wrote that Carver's "best-known collection emerges as his least representative book" and noted that over the next two years Carver "restored and expanded the work he had pared down under the influence of editor Lish."
43. RC to Lish, 7-14-80.
44. For most of the stories Carver republished after 1981, it's difficult to determine if Carver used any of Lish's first-revision changes.
45. RC to Ryan, 8-1-80; RC to Swanger, 8-7-80.
46. *Writers at Work: The Paris Review Interviews*, seventh series, ed. George Plimpton (NY: Viking, 1986), 299; T. Wolff to CS; the painting *Aunt Margaret's House* by Susan Lytle, was reproduced on the cover of *Ploughshares* 9:4 edited by Carver; Hribal to CS.
47. Darhanoff to RC, 1-30-82; *Antaeus* 40/41; RC to Lish, 8-17-80 and 10-6-80.
48. Ford to RC, 1-80; RC to Ford, 2-4-81.
49. Political correctness notwithstanding, usage of "spade" by whites to refer to blacks was not uncommon in the 1970s. More disturbing are Carver's occasional uses of "nigger" in unpublished letters to Lish and to friends he considered "good old boys."
50. Halpert, 133–134; McInerney to CS.
51. RC to Lish, 1-19-81 and 1-30-81; ulcers: RC to Swanger, 11-30-80.
52. Carver discussed the making of *Love* with several interviewers. He explained that he had "pushed and pulled those stories in all directions" to "suit a conception of the book as a whole" and did not mention Lish's role at all. He told Bonetti that the long version of "So Much Water" was written first and that he preferred it. See Bonetti, American Audio Prose Library and *Conversations*, 44.
53. RC to Domench, 11-7-80.
54. RC to Amy Unger, 3-3-81; RC to Kittredge, 1-14-81; VLC to CS.
55. VLC, "C'est Complet, Monsieur, C'est Complet," *Frankfurter Allgemeine Zeitung*, 12-4-01, L-2 (trans. Inge Carver and Vance Carver). RC to Amy Unger, 3-3-81; T. Wolff to CS.
56. Skoyles to CS; Flook to CS.
57. RC wrote Lish that the *Life* article aroused a "rumpus" among the poets who were not included, RC to Lish, 9-19-80; "Eleven American Poets," *Life,* 4-81; Annie Leibovitz, At Work (NY: Random House, 2009), 50, 52–55, 223; portrait posted: Hayden Carruth to CS.
58. O'Brien, *Chicago Tribune*, 4-5-81. O'Brien uses similar techniques in *The Thing They Carried.*
59. Broyard, *New York Times,* 4-15-81; Wood, *New York Times Book Review,* 4-26-81.
60. Buzbee to CS.
61. James Atlas, "Less Is Less," *Atlantic Monthly* 247:6 (June 1981), 96–98; RC to Day, 6-2-81.
62. Hall to RC, 1-1-81; "A Conversation with Tess Gallagher," *Artful Dodge* 38–39 (College of Wooster, n.d.), 15–16.
63. Baxter, *The Missouri Review* 31:1 (spring 2008).
64. Donald Newlove, *Saturday Review* 8:77 (4-81); Lish to CS; Michaels to CS.
65. CLC to CS.
66. RC to O'Brien, 5-13-81; RC to Day, 6-2-81.

67. Rosenberg to CS; Brodkey remembered quite a different evening. "Whenever Carver tried to talk to Gardner, Gardner changed the subject or moved across the room or addressed me or went into another room even when Carver was in mid-speech to him. . . ." Brodkey also believed that Gardner disliked Carver's stories and envied his success. (*New Yorker*, 9-13-93, 119). In a letter to the editor printed by the *New Yorker* in January 1994, Rosenberg and Gallagher vociferously disputed Brodkey's description of the meeting.

68. RC to Unger, 3-31-81; RC to Carruth, 6-10-81; Gallagher, *SB*, 213; Gallagher to McInerney, 6-4-81; Gallagher report to Yaddo Committee on Admissions, 1976.

69. Carriveau to CS; McInerney to CS.

70. In his "Author's Foreword" to *Where*, Carver claimed—inaccurately—that he wrote no stories for two years before waking up one day to write "Cathedral."

71. Carriveau found that glasses were uncomfortable on his nose and caused him to bump into things. When he was in law school, a professor urged the students to make eye contact in the courtroom. He asked the professor how he could do that and learned that every eye in the room was on him when he stood up to speak. A photograph of Carriveau, taken after RC's death, appears in *Carver Country*.

72. Carriveau to CS.

73. Darhansoff to CS; Riccardo Duranti, "A Conversation with Tess Gallagher," *Cattedrali*, 98; Curtis memo, 7-80 (Howard Gotlieb Research Center, Boston U).

74. *Conversations*, 44; T. Wolff, *You've Got To Read This*, eds. Ron Hansen and Jim Shepard (NY: Perennial/HarperCollins, 1994), 136–37.

75. *Conversations*, 101.

76. Literary theorist Kathleen Woodward and her husband, Herbert Blau, a founder of the San Francisco Actors Workshop, owned the house at 2685 Lake Drive. UW-Milwaukee paid Ray $4,000 for leading a workshop and giving one public reading.

77. Young to CS; Vogan, the author of *In Shelly's Leg* and *Loss of Flight*, died at the age of forty-three in 1991.

78. RC to Johnson, 8-12-81.

79. Rogers to CS.

80. RC to Amy Unger, 8-19-81.

81. RC to Johnson, 8-12-81; Alvarez to CS; RC to Köepf, 8-21-81.

82. RC to Köepf, 8-21-81.

Chapter 25: *Fires*

1. Durrell continues, "A poet's death is never wholly sad, in the sense of a life unlived—because the work is there, like the aftertaste of a wine of high vintage." From a published letter by Durrell to Aldington about the death of Aldington's ex-wife, poet H. D., that RC mailed to Lish on 11-9-81. *Literary Lifelines*, eds. Ian S. MacNiven and Harry T. Moore (NY: Viking, 1981).

2. RC to Ford, 8-11-81; RC to Lish, 9-16-81.

3. VLC, "C'est Complet."

4. RC to VLC, 2-21-82.

5. See Tillie Olsen, *Silences* (NY: Delacorte, 1978); Bonetti, American Audio Prose Library, 1983.

6. In "Fires," RC also distances himself from Lish by neglecting to mention that he knew him in Palo Alto before Lish became the editor of *Esquire*, allowing readers to believe that Lish picked his work out of his slush pile.

7. VLC, "C'est Complet."

8. Though Shawn retained final say, several new fiction editors had come on board at the *New Yorker* after William Maxwell retired in 1976. Carver was a late arrival at the venerable magazine, finding acceptance after other so-called minimalists such as Ann Beattie, Mary Robison, and Bobbie Ann Mason. Another writer that McGrath brought in was the Canadian Alice Munro. Ben Yagoda, *About Town: The New Yorker and the World It Made* (NY: Da Capo, 2000), 389–90.

9. RC to Lish, 10-6-81; celebrated: RC to Domench, 11-21-81; MBC, "To Write and Keep Kind."

10. Hall to RC, 11-30-81.

11. Charles McGrath to Sam Halpert.

12. salary: Paul Theiner to RC, 5-11-81; Robert O'Connor to CS.

13. In "Form and Theory" (a title inherited from the university catalog) Carver assigned collections by Cheever, Elkin, Barry Hannah, Max Schott, Jean Thompson, Ursula Le Guin, Anderson, Hemingway, Frank O'Connor, Flannery O'Connor, Isaac Singer, Joyce Carol Oates, Mark Helprin, Evan Connell, John Updike, and Ann Beattie; "Masters of European Short Fiction" included Maupassant, Chekhov, Turgenev, Joyce, Kafka, Babel, Dineson, Lawrence, Ian McEwan, and Nabokov; "The Novella" required twenty-five novellas by authors ranging from Dostoyevsky and Mann to W. H. Gass, Andre Dubus, and Barry Hannah; for "The Writer as Critic," students read V. S. Pritchett, Mary McCarthy, Malcolm Cowley, John Gardner, Flaubert, Tolstoy, Eudora Welty, and Gass. In addition, Ray handed out a page of recommended reading for fiction writers. Besides the great standard realist story collections, it included books by Richard Brautigan, Leonard Michaels, Borges, and Gabriel García Márquez.

14. "theory": O'Connor to CS; McInerney, "Raymond Carver, Mentor," RR; Hribal to CS.

15. McInerney, "Raymond Carver, Mentor," RR; McInerney to CS.

16. "pregnant": Stephen Singular, "The Sound and Fury Over Fiction," New York Times Magazine, 7-8-79; "benign sorcery": Barry Silesky, John Gardner: Literary Outlaw (Chapel Hill: Algonquin, 2004), 290; turmoil: Susan Thornton, On Broken Glass: Loving and Losing John Gardner (NY: Carroll & Graf, 2000); RC to Fisketjon, 11-14-81.

17. Lewis Buzbee, "Acts of Faith & Foolhardiness, Raymond Carver Talks About His Writing," The Bloomsbury Review 12 (1992), 1+.

18. RC to Fisketjon, 11-14-81.

19. RC to Darhansoff, 1-29-82 and 2-4-82; Darhansoff to RC, 1-30-82; RC to Lish, 1-21-82 and 2-5-82; Darhansoff to CS.

20. Thornton, On Broken Glass, 152–153.

21. Pope to RC, 1-14-81; Conversations, 11–23; Pope to CS.

22. RC to Lish, 4-1-82; contract: Charvat.

23. RC to Blaise, 4-12-82; Conversations, 20–21.

24. RC omitted "Dummy," "The Fling," "Mine," and "Furious Seasons"; the first three had been published in shorter versions with different titles in Love, while the latter dated to his student days.

25. Young proposed the book in January and Carver completed the table of contents and afterword in September. In September he withdrew "A Small, Good Thing" from the set, saving it instead for Ploughshares and his forthcoming Knopf book. Quotations from "Afterword" to Fires (Santa Barbara, CA: Capra Press, 1983), 189.

26. RC to Carruth, 5-31-82; RC to Day, 5-19-82; RC to Kittredge, 5-21-82.

27. RC to Carruth, 5-31-82; "Reading," AoU, 77–78; VLC, "C'est Complet."

28. VLC, "C'est Complet"; VLC, 8-6-07.

29. VLC, "C'est Complet"; in fact, since that day many new dead, including Jean-Paul Sartre, Eugene Ionesco, and Susan Sontag, have been interred at Montparnasse.

30. MBC to CS.

31. MBC, "Triumph" (written 1998); "fervent": MBC to CS; Michaels to CS.

32. Superior Court of Washington, Clallam County, Case #892000272, May 1989.

33. James M. Baker to MBC, 6-23-82.

34. RC to Ford, 7-30-82; Unger to CS; foodstamps: MBC to Superior Court of Washington, Clallam County, May 1989.

35. RC to Gardner, 6-22-82; Conversations, 13.

36. RC to Buzbee, 5-30-82; Mona Simpson to RC, 6-21-82.

37. RC to Lish, 8-2-82; RC to Fisketjon, 8-11-82; RC to Ford, 7-30-82; RC to Buzbee, 7-14-82.

38. RC to Lish, 8-11-82.

39. RC to Ford, 7-30-82; RC to Ford, 8-9-82; RC to Fisketjon, 8-11-82.

40. Michaels to CS.
41. "C'est Complet"; stick: RC to Ford, 8-9-82.
42. RC to Ford, 7-30-82; RC to Ryan, 9-11-82; RC to Lish, 8-11-82.
43. *Atlantic* archives, Gotlieb Library, Boston University.
44. Rust Hills to RC, 9-5-82 and 8-30-82.
45. RC to Lish, 8-11-82.
46. *Ploughshares*, 8:2, 3. Hall soon urged RC to find places to publish the earlier versions of every story that had been damaged by Lish's editing.
47. Hall to RC, 9-7-82; *Conversations*, 28–29; in the interview, RC said he wrote "A Small, Good Thing" in January 1981, but manuscript evidence shows it was actually finished in the spring of 1980. Gallagher "never allowed 'The Bath' to be published in anthologies of Ray's work at home or abroad, but only inside the book *What We Talk About . . .*" (John Marshall, "Carver's Widow, Scholar Both Discount Controversy," *Seattle Post-Intelligencer*, 09-03-98).
48. RC to Ford, 8-9-82; Lynn Bonsen to CS.
49. *Peninsula Daily News* (Port Angeles, WA), 10-7-82, A10.
50. marijuana: RC to Köepf, 9-3-82; divorce: RC to Lish, 9-41-82; abroad: VLC to CS; "fugitive": RC to Lish, 9-4-82.
51. Gardner: Silesky, 318–28; student: David Lazar to CS; RC to MBC, 9-20-82; fiction workshop: Robert O'Connor to CS. The English Department at SUNY Binghamton sounded out RC about replacing Gardner at a rumored salary of $100,000 a year. Ray considered that offer, waiting for details, but kept his bird-in-the-hand at Syracuse. (RC to Lish, 10-25-82.)
52. RC to Lish, 10-3-82; RC to Swanger, 9-29-82.
53. secret: RC to Swanger, 9-29-82; RC to Day, 11-18-82; RC, *Dostoyevsky: A Screenplay*; Wolff, "Appetite," *RR*, 247.
54. Unger to CS; RC to Amy Burk Unger, 4-13-82.
55. MBC to CS; Unger to CS; RC to MBC, 9-20-82. Contradictions seem inherent in the subject, but further information on the divorce proceedings may emerge as more of MBC's and RC's private papers are placed in public archives.

PART V: TRIUMPH

Chapter 26: *Cathedral*

1. *CIYNM*, 87–88.
2. student: David Lazar; RC to Day, 11-18-82; RC to Lish, 11-5-82; Gallagher to Fisketjon, 10-19-82; Ford, "Good Raymond"; Banks to CS.
3. RC to Lish, 10-29-82.
4. Lish to RC, 11-19-82.
5. RC to Day, 11-18-82.
6. Theiner to CS; Alice Sebold, *Lucky* (NY: Scribner, 1999), 124; Carruth, 11-12-03.
7. McInerney to CS.
8. Melvin Sterne, "An Afternoon with Tess Gallagher," *Carve Magazine*, 2001 (www.carvezine.com); D. Unger to CS; John Marshall, "Tess Without Ray," *Seattle Post-Intelligencer*, 12-18-90; Katherine Griffin, "Childless by Choice," *Health:* 10.
9. December 16, 1982, will: Clallam County records; T. Wolff, 1-10-07.
10. Photos: Charvat; RC to Lish, 3-18-83.
11. RC to Lish, 1-4-83. Several friends of Ray's corroborated this report of a reaction to cocaine.
12. RC to Carruth, 1-25-83; American Academy and Institute of Arts and Letters to RC, 1-7-83.
13. *Conversations*, 54; RC to Fisketjon, 2-9-83 and 3-26-83.
14. RC to Covington, 1-11-83; RC to McInerney, 1-13-03; RC to Unger 1-18-83.
15. *New York Times,* 1-19-83; Howe to RC, 12-15-82.

16. Cimino and Corelli to RC, 2-83 through 9-84 (Charvat); RC to Ford, 3-31-83.
17. RC to Lish, 2-23-83.
18. Marjorie Leet Ford to CS; "What He Talked About When We Talked About Love," *San Francisco Examiner Image,* 10-3-93, 18–21.
19. In the end, editor William Abrahams thanked Carver for his "very thoughtful" comment, but the whole blurb was not used; a later collection of Lish's stories reprints two words from it—"brilliant, insane."
20. Halpern to CS; Halpern named Theodore Solotaroff at *New American Review* and Charles Newman at *TriQuarterly* as the other two great magazine editors of the 1970s.
21. Lish to RC, 3-22-83; RC to Lish, n.d. [spring 1983].
22. CLC to CS.
23. Archives of the American Academy of Arts and Letters; Fisketjon to CS.
24. Carlyle: RC to Buzbee, 5-25-83; Pinter: Halpert, 122; American Audio Prose Library (www.americanaudioprose.org). Bonetti's interview is included in the Criterion DVD of the movie *Short Cuts.* Only a portion of the interview appears in *Conversations.*
25. Gallagher, "A Small Place to Stand," *Doubletake* 8:3 (summer 2002), 112.
26. Gallagher and Port Angeles: *Kind*; Richard Zahler, "Singers of Unsung Songs," *Seattle Times/Seattle Post-Intelligencer,* 3-9-86.
27. Washington Water Resource Inventory Area 18 Watershed Plan, Entrix, Inc., 2000; Carver's title word "course" makes a pun between water course and golf course.
28. *Granta* 8 (1983). *Granta* had published "Vitamins" in a previous issue.
29. The term is discussed by Adam Meyer in *Raymond Carver* (NY: Twanyne Publishers, 1995) and by Robert Rebein in Hicks, *Tribes, and Dirty Realists: American Fiction After Postmodernism* (Lexington: University Press of Kentucky, 2001).
30. *RR,* 116–117; RC to Buzbee, 9-7-83, 9-21-83, 12-1-83; Buzbee to CS. Simpson explained to Sam Halpert that her taped interview with RC had been inaudible (Charvat.)
31. *Vanity Fair,* September 1983, photo by Bonnie Schiffman.
32. RC to Ford, 8-11-83; Kinder to CS.
33. *Newsweek,* 9-5-83.
34. Howe, "Stories of Our Loneliness," *New York Times Book Review,* 9-11-83; Broyard, "Diffuse Regrets," *New York Times,* 9-5-83.
35. Eder, "Pain on the Face of Middle America," *Los Angeles Times,* 10-2-83; Rubins, "Small Expectations," *New York Times Book Review,* 11-24-83.
36. Sales information: Helen Dudar, "A Storyteller in Touch with the Angels, *Wall Street Journal,* 11-14-83 and Charvat; foreign sales included German (10,000 DM), French (40,000 FF), and Arabic ($300). A Japanese edition of seven earlier stories brought $1,500.
37. Judith Applebaum, "Paperback Talk," *New York Times,* 10-2-83; Halpert, 122.
38. Lish to CS; Unger to CS; Fowler to CS.
39. Unger to CS.
40. VLC, "C'est Complet."
41. Fisketjon to CS.
42. Fisketjon to CS.
43. Blount to CS.
44. *RR,* 114; "My Father's Life": Charvat.
45. RC to Buzbee, 9-21-83.
46. RC to Swanger, 12-26-83.
47. Dudar, *Wall Street Journal,* 11-14-83.

Chapter 27: *Where Water Comes Together with Other Water*

1. *AoU,* xxvii.
2. Lish to RC, 2-7-84.
3. Entreaties: Charvat.
4. McGrath to CS.

5. Halpert, 141.
6. *Ploughshares*: DeWitt Henry to CS; Dobyns to CS.
7. RC to Jarman, 2-11-84. RC wrote Jarman to cancel a scheduled visit to Vanderbilt University, where his former student now taught; RC to T. Wolff, 3-5-85.
8. RC owed the novel to McGraw-Hill; if he'd written it, he would probably have bought out that contract and allowed Urban to place the book at Knopf or elsewhere; poems: RC to Unger, 3-20-84; fishing: RC to Ford, 2-23-84.
9. RC to Ford, 3-31-84.
10. Bruce Weber, "Raymond Carver: A Chronicler of Blue-Collar Despair," *New York Times Magazine*, 6-24-84.
11. T. S. Eliot, "Hamlet and His Problems," *The Sacred Wood: Essays on Poetry and Criticism* (NY: Knopf, 1930).
12. Vintage Contemporaries: Fisketjon to CS; "industry testament": Weber, "Blue-Collar Despair"; a second Vintage Contemporaries edition, designed when Fisketjon no longer oversaw the imprint, featured a construction worker with his lunch bucket and a drink on its cover.
13. last such comment: RC to Fisketjon, 3-12-84. About *Bright Lights, Big City*, RC wrote, "A rambunctious, deadly funny novel that goes right for the mark—the human heart"; about *Matty's Heart*: "Our literature is healthier, and wiser, with the publication of this first collection of short fiction by C. J. Hribal. It's an impressive book, and I read it with pleasure."
14. "Fame Is No Good. Take It from Me," *New York Times Book Review*, 4-22-84 (rpt. *CIYNM*).
15. Gallagher, *Willingly* (Graywolf, 1984); "The Poem as a Reservoir for Grief," *A Concert of Tenses*, 117.
16. "yearn for serenity": Weber, "Blue-Collar Despair"; Johnson, *Salud*, 134–35.
17. Schjeldahl described a "do-it-yourself art scene" that lasted from 1981 until 1987 in "That Eighties Show," *New Yorker*, 1-24-05.
18. RC to Bush, 7-7-84; Bush to CS. Bush's stories won a PEN/Algren prize and led her to a publisher for her first book, *A Place of Light*.
19. Carlile, "Fishing With Ray" (unpublished memoir).
20. poets: RC to Anne Truitt, 7-17-84; "competitiveness": Carlile, "Fishing with Ray."; biggest fish: RC to Johnson, 9-11-84. Johnson was one of dozens of longtime correspondents with whom RC kept up as his literary fame grew. Agreeing to recommend Johnson for a Guggenheim Fellowship, Ray told his first editor that he wished he could take him salmon fishing.
21. The Japanese book was a collection of five stories from *Love* and two from *Cathedral* including "Cathedral" and "Where I'm Calling From." It was not the same collection that Knopf published in English under the title *Where I'm Calling From* in 1988. Carver received $1,500 for the translation rights and another $3,500 when some of the stories appeared in Japanese magazines.
22. Murakami, "A Literary Comrade," *RR*, 130–135; Jay Rubin, *Haruki Murakami and the Music of Words* (London: Harvill, 2002).
23. family: RC to Ford, 3-31-84 and 7-30-84; "good weed": RC to CLC, 8-6-84 and 9-17-84.
24. Violet and Gloria Archer to CS.
25. Hazen to CS, 11-15-96; *Clatskanie Chief*, 8-30-84, 8-11-88, 11-6-03, and 5-23-07.
26. Fisketjon, 5-26-07; Joann Davis, "A Talk with Editor Gary Fisketjon," *Publishers Weekly*, 9-21-84; Gliterary Life." Since 1989, when Fisketjon was no longer at Vintage, the press has reissued Carver's books with covers that associate Carver with working-class life and drinking. The reissued *Cathedral* has a literal-minded drawing of a man alone in front of a television with his bottle. There's an outline of a cathedral on the clumsily glowing TV screen.
27. The first series also included reprints of Crumley's *Dancing Bear*, McGuane's *Bushwacked Piano*, Peter Matthiessen's *Far Tortuga*, and Paule Marshall's *The Chosen Place, The Timeless People*; after dinner: Jenks, "Shameless," *RR*, 141.
28. McInerney to CS; Unger to CS.

29. Charvat Collection: Bert Babcock to CS; RC to Kittredge, 7-11-85; Charles Apfelbaum to CS; Geoffrey Smith to CS, 1-9-08.
30. RC to Ravenel, 11-3-84 and *Best American Short Stories 1986* (NY: Houghton Mifflin, 1986), xii.
31. James Burl Hogins, *Literature* 3d ed. (Chicago: SRA, 1984), 460–461.
32. Carlile to CS.
33. RC to Amy Unger, 12-14-84.
34. RC to Amy Unger, 12-14-84.
35. RC to Amy Unger, 12-14-84; RC to CLC, 12-13-84; Unger to CS.
36. Carlile, "Fishing With Ray."
37. Ford, "Good Raymond," 76.
38. CLC to CS.
39. RC to CLC, n.d.
40. Jesse Oxfeld, "Q & A: Marion Ettlinger," mediabistro.com, 11-21-03.
41. MBC to CS.
42. IRS forms from Clallam County Superior Court records, case No. 89-2-00027-2.
43. Australia: RC to T. Wolff, 3-9-85; RC to Ungers, 3-9-85 and 3-14-85.
44. Purchase of 602 S. "B" Street: Clallam County records.
45. Itinerary: RC to Bush, 4-17-85; "careful": *Conversations*, 131; T. Wolff to CS.

Chapter 28: *Ultramarine*

1. "Coming of Age, Going to Pieces," *New York Times Book Review*, 11-17-85; rpt. *CIYNM*, 276–285.
2. Fisketjon to CS.
3. "Ray's face": Gallagher, *Carver Country*, 18.
4. "spiritual current": Gallagher, Introduction, *AoU*, xxiii; Dobyns: *RR*, 111.
5. "A Concert of Tenses: An Interview with Jeanie Thompson," *A Concert of Tenses*, 40.
6. D. Unger to CS; Stull and Carroll, "Two Darings," *SB*, 7.
7. Theodore Solotaroff to CS; *Cattedrali:* 90–92; Jerry Carriveau, the blind man's "original" said he had read Carver's story but not Gallagher's.
8. Stull and Carroll's "Two Darings" reproduces the final page of "Errand" with Gallagher's editing. Although her handwriting in black ink is eerily reminiscent of Lish's, her changes are minor. Stull and Carroll are overreaching to claim in their caption that her notation suggested the story's ending action, which is already evident in the typescript just above Gallagher's note (*SB*, 8); Jenks, 2-10-08.
9. "Friendship," *CIYNM*, 118.
10. Solotaroff to CS.
11. Ireland: RC to McInerney, 7-7-85; Gallagher, *SB*, 51; "A Conversation with Tess Gallagher," *Artful Dodge* 38/39, 19.
12. "out there in history": Carlile to CS. Gallagher quotes RC's use of the phrase in "Raymond Carver, 1938 to 1988," *SB*, 58.
13. two houses: RC to Ford, 6-25-85 and 7-1-85.
14. Gallagher, *Country*, 14.
15. The character Jill is a practical woman who "grooms dogs for a living." That detail might have been suggested by Frank Sandmeyer, the fisherman RC knew and still visited in Yakima, whose daughter, Arlene Brown, was in the pet-grooming business and invented a hair dye for dogs (Sandmeyer to CS).
16. "Guilt": RC to Ford, 6-25-85; RC to CLC, 9-24-85.
17. "Mt. Gabriel," *Antarctica* (Dublin: Gallery Press, 1985).
18. Carlile, "Fishing With Ray."
19. Bond in *To Write and Keep Kind*; Carlile, "Fishing With Ray."
20. Carver's attack on Meyers's book prompted the prolific biographer to write the book review editor about the "irresponsible attempt to butcher" his book. When Carver's posthumous collection *No Heroics, Please* came out in 1992, Christopher Lehmann-Haupt of the *New York Times* thumped Carver's Hemingway review for confusing

"his disapproval of Mr. Meyers's critical attitude toward his subject with disappointment that Hemingway's life eventually went sour" (*New York Times,* 7-6-92).

21. "harnass": RC to T. Wolff, 1-28-86; canceled: RC to Carlile, 1-26-86.
22. RC to Macauley, 10-14-84; established story writers in RC's *BASS* volume included Donald Barthelme, Ann Beattie, Frank Conroy, Richard Ford, Thomas McGuane, Alice Munro, Grace Paley, Joy Williams, and Tobias Wolff. Some names, now familiar, were then little known: Charles Baxter, James Lee Burke, Ethan Canin, and Amy Hempel, for instance. Newcomers included Tess Gallagher, David Michael Kaplan, David Lipsky, Christopher McIlroy, Jessica Neely, Kent Nelson, and Mona Simpson.
23. *Best American Short Stories 1986* (Boston: Houghton Mifflin, 1986).
24. Jenks to CS. Carver told Jenks this was the largest advance he'd ever received for a single book. The authors were Donald Barthelme, Gina Berriault, Vance Bourjaily, Evan S. Connell, Andre Dubus, Stanley Elkin, Richard Ford, Tess Gallagher, Leonard Michaels, Flannery O'Connor, Grace Paley, James Salter, Joy Williams, Tobias Wolff, and twenty-two others.
25. Thanks to the encyclopedic David Reid for wondering, in his review of *NHP* for the *Los Angeles Times,* if RC recognized himself in Brautigan's small masterpiece (*Los Angeles Times,* 7-19-92).
26. After reading "Intimacy," Ford surprised himself by saying, " 'Jesus, Ray, I read your story about Maryann.' It's unlike me because I recognize and I insist in my own work that direct correlations between life and what gets represented in stories are impossible, untrue. And I didn't even know Maryann . . . this remark just leapt out of my mouth. And he said in a very guarded way, 'That wasn't about Maryann.' And then I thought to myself . . . well, that's right" (Halpert, 159–160).
27. Halpert, 142.
28. RC to Ford, 2-20-86; RC to Carlile, 3-17-86; RC to CLC, 2-27-86, 3-2-86, 3-11-86, and 3-30-86; James Carver to CS.
29. Carlile, "Fishing With Ray."
30. CLC, 2-9-04.
31. RC to Ralph Sipper, 5-24-86.
32. Randolf Paul Runyon, *Reading Raymond Carver* (Syracuse University Press, 1992).
33. Maryann Burk Carver, who notes that the letter the husband receives in the story sounds like the long letter she had written to Ray in the summer of 1978, believes the story's metafictional devices simply represent "a little psychological denial" by the "utterly baffled" husband who "won't read the letter because that way it can't become part of his reality—his history . . ." (MBC, *What,* 323). In the story the husband asserts that his wife never underlined words for emphasis. In fact, Maryann often did that. More oddly, underlining occurs throughout "Blackbird Pie." It might be read as another sign of the phenomenon I am calling *folie à deux* or codependency of marriage.
34. Runyon continues, "One of them finds himself writing a story about a man who refuses to believe the obvious that his wife is capable of producing such a text" (*Reading Raymond Carver,* 198–199).
35. RC to Sipper, 6-5-86 and 8-28-86; Sipper to CS.
36. Iowa Jubilee: Brothers, Shacochis, and Rosen to CS.
37. martinis: King to CS; Sky House: Moeller to CS; emcee: Liggett Taylor to CS.
38. boats: Carlile, "Fishing With Ray"; loan payment: RC to VLC, 5-16-86.
39. Carlile, "Fishing With Ray"; Gallagher sold the *Olympic* on eBay for $3,500 to dredging ship Captain Roy Delay, who planned to christen the boat "Carver," according to the *Seattle Post-Intelligencer,* 10-7-04.
40. Carlile, "Fishing With Ray."
41. "velocity": "A Small Place to Stand," *Doubletake* 29 (summer 2002), 112.
42. RC to MBC, 1-18-88.

Chapter 29: *Where I'm Calling From*

1. RC to Ford, 11-3-86 recommends *Letters on Cézanne,* ed. Clara Rilke, trans. Joel Agee (NY: North Point Press, 2002).
2. RC to Carlile, 9-7-86 and 9-17-86. The latter letter rpt. in *Carver Country.*
3. David Carpenter, *RR,* 166–186; Carpenter to CS.
4. Johnson to CS.
5. *People,* 11-23-87; Jenks to CS; Jenks, "A Literary Love Story."
6. RC to Unger, 12-12-86; RC to Bruce Weigl, 11-24-86.
7. CLC to CS, 1-30-04.
8. MBC, *What,* 336–341.
9. Rilke, *Letters on Cézanne,* 32.
10. intentions: RC to Carlile, 2-12-87; "On Errand," *No Heroics, Please,* 197–198; Henri Troyat, *Chekhov,* trans. Michael Henry Heim (NY: E. P. Dutton, 1986); titles: American Academy of Arts and Letters archives.
11. Janet Malcolm discusses biographical versions of Chekhov's death in *Reading Chekhov: A Critical Journey* (NY: Random House, 2001), 57–74, noting that some details Carver invented for his fiction were later appropriated by Philip Callow for his 1998 biography of Chekhov.
12. McGrath to Halpert, 1990, and to CS; Gallagher in *To Write and Keep Kind* and *SB,* 8.
13. *The Raymond Chandler Papers,* eds. Tom Hiney and Frank MacShane (NY: Grove Press, 2000), 87. Thanks to Curt Johnson for sending me the quotation.
14. physical: RC to VLC, 3-3-87; "My heart moved": RC to CLC, 2-18-87.
15. RC to Jerry King, 10-28-86 and 2-17-87; RC to Kittredge, 1-9-87; MBC, *What,* 32.
16. In her "European Journal," Gallagher notes that their small room at Hotel des Saints Peres had "a place for Ray to smoke, so we need only one room" (*SB,* 15). RC to Covington, 10-6-86.
17. RC to MBC, 2-15-87.
18. Fisketjon to CS; RC to Fisketjon, 5-30-87.
19. Al Young to CS.
20. Hicks to CS; audiotape, recorded 2-26-87, Sacramento State University archives; Loretta Schmitz to CS.
21. "European Journal," *SB,* 15–55, is the primary source for reports on RC's travels.
22. Rushdie, *Imaginary Homelands* (NY: Viking, 1991), 340–42; Ford: Halpert, 179.
23. G. Wolff to CS; Carlile to CS; RC to Kittredge, 8-4-87.
24. RC did not complete an article about Ketchikan.
25. RC to Ford, 8-4-87; RC to Fisketjon, 8-16-87.
26. RC to CLC, 7-27-87, 7-23-87, and 7-28-87.
27. RC to Fisketjon, 8-16-87 and 9-6-87; Fisketjon, 2-22-08.
28. MBC, *What,* 330; "On *Where I'm Calling From,*" *CIYNM,* 199–202; Fisketjon to CS.
29. RC to Ford, 8-4-87; RC to Kittredge, 8-4-87; the following poems, all published in *A New Path to the Waterfall,* appear to have comprised this streak: "Another Mystery," "Letter," "Nearly," "The Offending Eel," "On an Old Photograph of My Son," "One More," "Out," "The Painter and the Fish," and "Summer Fog."
30. RC to Ford, 8-87; purchase of "Ridge House": Clallam County records; *People* photograph by Dale Wittner of Seattle.
31. Fisketjon to CS.

Chapter 30: *A New Path to the Waterfall*

1. RC to Ford, 8-4-87; RC to Carlile, 8-26-87.
2. dark, isolated tumor: from a friend's diary 9-22-87; according to Ford, "it was never ascertained that he had lung cancer until he had the surgery" (Halpert, 180).
3. extra-large bed: Rubin, 100; although the guidelines for the Livings describe the awards as "renewable," no author has yet received a Living more than once.

4. Ford to Halpert, 180; D. Unger to CS; RC to Ella Carver, 10-30-87.
5. D. Unger to CS.
6. "high": D. Unger to CS; insurance: RC to Carlile, 11-15-87; house: RC to Carlile, 12-12-87.
7. A letter from Gallagher to the Dobynses dated 4-5-88 refers to the fall conversation.
8. "got it all": RC to Charles Watson, 10-25-87. Chemotherapy was not used for lung cancer treatment in 1988; later studies have concluded that radiation therapy is not a useful treatment for tumors in the lungs. RC to Carpenter, 10-25-87.
9. brownies: Dobyns to CS.
10. *New York Times*, 11-13-87; Stone: Halpert, 132; donors: Paul Andrews, "Raymond Carver's Gravy Years," *Seattle Times Pacific Magazine*, 7-30-89.
11. RC to Ella Carver, 10-30-87, 11-6-87, and 11-16-87.
12. *New York Times*, 11-13-87; RC to Ella Carver, 11-16-87.
13. confidence: RC to D. Carpenter, 11-16-87; photo: RC to MBC, 1-18-88.
14. Fisketjon to CS. As Gallagher's unmarried domestic partner, RC was not, it turned out, eligible for health care coverage through her employer.
15. RC to Adelman, 12-13-87; the paragraph about MBC was omitted from *Carver Country*, which includes Adelman's photographs and the rest of RC's letter.
16. Halpert, 191; Unger to CS.
17. RC to MBC, 1-18-88; MBC said that RC paid her $350 in September and $300 in December of 1987. In 1988 he sent her another $300. According to her, the total amount she received from him after 1983 was $6,850. Clallam County Superior Court, case 89-2-00027-2.
18. RC to MBC, 1-18-88; Mick Brown, "Untold Stories," *London Telegraph*, 7-15-00; MBC, *What*, 341.
19. RC to CLC, 2-17-88; account statements from Virginia Mason Clinic; affidavit of Richardson to Clallam County Superior Court, 5-18-89.
20. Without seeing detailed medical records and physician's notes, no one could judge the impact of such a decision on RC's chances of survival. Surgery is not a common procedure for metastasized lung cancer. In her introduction to *A New Path to the Waterfall*, Gallagher writes that Carver declined recommendations of brain surgery from several doctors.
21. "difficult": RC to Shannon Ravenel, 3-20-88; cancer: RC to Carlile, 3-20-88.
22. *SB*, 209.
23. apartment: RC to Carlile, 3-20-88; Chekhov: Rick Simonson to CS; privacy: RC to CLC, 4-3-88; fatiguing: RC to T. Wolff, 5-5-88; contract: International Creative Management to RC, 04-05-88.
24. RC to Carlile, 3-20-88, 4-4-88, and 4-27-88; high hopes: RC to T. Wolff, 5-5-88.
25. Halpert, 193–94; MBC, *What*, 332, 339; MBC interviewed by Halpert.
26. Fisketjon to CS; Halpert, 151.
27. MBC interviewed by Halpert.
28. Unger to CS; "Meditation on a Line from Saint Teresa," *CIYNM*, 123–125; RC to Wolff; 5-5-88; narratologist: RC to T. Wolff, 5-5-88.
29. Stuart Kellerman, *New York Times Book Review*, 5-15-88.
30. VLC to CS.
31. Halpert, 190; Unger to CS.
32. Caldwell, "An Epitaph to Raymond Carver," *Syracuse Post-Standard*, 08-05-88.
33. Al-Awqati to CS; VLC to CS.
34. Simonson to CS.
35. ABA: Buzbee, *RR*, 117; tape recording, Michigan State University Library; Fisketjon to CS.
36. James Carver to CS.
37. *AoU*, 314.
38. James Carver, 2-14-97.
39. "Proposal," *AoU*; State of Nevada marriage certificate; Gallagher, *SB*, 220–221; "Buddha": *Kind*; photograph, *RR*, 47.

40. Richardson affidavit, 5-18-89. Richardson said that Gallagher wished her nieces and nephews to receive her literary rights after Carver's death if she predeceased Carver.
41. *AoU*, 314.
42. Paul Andrews, "Epilogue: RC, Northwest Literary Giant, Is Dead at Age 50," *Seattle Times*, 8-3-88.
43. weather: RC to Carlile 6-26-88; Day to CS; Halpert, 196.
44. D. and L. Schmitz to CS; *RR*, 51–52.
45. RC to CLC, 6-24-88, 6-27-88, and 7-15-88; CLC to CS.
46. VLC to CS; CLC to CS. In her story "A Box of Rocks," Gallagher explores the moral dilemma of a husband who has chosen to keep his wife's sister from visiting his wife on her deathbed: "Whatever happened, he would be the one who had to remember, and that would be punishment enough if, later, he felt he'd been wrong. One thing was clear. He had kept his wife from painful affairs that might have consumed and unsettled her when her life ought to be calm and in order." *At the Owl Woman Saloon* (NY: Scribner, 1997), 113.
47. D. Unger to CS.
48. *Words Like Distant Rain: A Conversation Between Tess Gallagher and Jakuchō Setouchi* (Spokane: Eastern Washington U P, 2006).
49. MBC, *What*, 333.
50. William L. Stull, the editor of *All of Us: The Collected Poems of Raymond Carver*, provides detailed notes on the publication history of each poem in that volume.
51. Gallagher added seven more of RC's poems to the book as she prepared it for publication after RC's death (Gallagher to Ford, 12-7-88).
52. *New York Times Book Review*, 7-9-89.
53. RC to Dobyns, 7-9-88; *AoU*, 319.
54. RC to Sipper, 6-22-88; RC to Dobyns, 7-9-88; RC to Ford, 7-6-88.
55. *AoU*, 311.
56. Fisketjon to CS, 4-25-08; account statement, Virginia Mason Clinic, Clallam County courthouse.
57. white Cadillac: L. Schmitz to CS, 1-20-00; Richardson affidavit and Last Will and Testament of RC, 8-1-88.
58. Ella Carver to Ruth King, 9-8-88.
59. Kinder to CS.
60. *Dark Eyes:* Andrews, "Raymond Carver's Gravy Years," *Seattle Times Magazine*, 8-89; Estes: quoted by Jim McKeever, "Carver Asked to Go Back to His Home to Die," *Syracuse Herald-American*, 3-20-94; Estes email to CS; *AoU*, 317.

Epilogue

1. *SB*, 59.
2. VLC, 6-29-08.
3. Halpert, 177.
4. Tess Gallagher, "Wake," *Moon Crossing Bridge* (Saint Paul, MN: Graywolf Press, 1992), 5.
5. Fisketjon to CS.
6. Ella came to Washington the following week, staying three days with Maryann in Bellingham and three days with Tess and her mother in Port Angeles. She could not bring herself to go to the cemetery or Ray's house (Ella Carver to Ruth King, 9-8-88).
7. VLC to CS.
8. Unpublished remarks used by permission of Richard Ford.
9. Donald Archer to CS; MBC to Sam Halpert, 4-13-92.
10. Gallagher notes that Ray claimed a "right-of-love" in his appropriation of Chekhov's prose for *A New Path to the Waterfall* (*AoU*, 315).
11. Peter Kemp, "The American Chekhov: Elephant and Other Stories by Raymond Carver," *Sunday Times* (London) 8-7-88 (http://find.galegroup.com).

12. Information regarding Carver's will and probate, records of Superior Court of Clallam County, Washington.
13. CLC believes she should have been called to say good-bye to her father while he was in the hospital in Seattle during the week preceding his death.
14. Andrews, "Epilogue."
15. CLC to CS, 2-9-04; CLC deposition to court, 3-22-96.
16. John Marshall, "Tess Without Ray: Poet Gallagher Weathers Storm Over Carver's Death," *Seattle Post-Intelligencer,* 12-18-90, C1.
17. Marshall, "Tess Without Ray."
18. Information regarding the 1988–1989 court actions drawn from records of case numbers 88-4-00184-7 and 89-2-00027-2, Superior Court of Clallam County, Washington.
19. Ella Carver to Ruth King, letters dated 9-8-88 though 8-13-92; James Carver to CS.
20. The issue had come to prominence because of the so-called *Rear Window* problem created by the Supreme Court's 1990 decision in *Stewart v. Abend.*
21. The works would have gone into public domain only if the owners of the renewal rights neglected to file for them in the appropriate year. Altman was following an industry-wide custom in asking to deal with only one copyright holder (Gallagher) who in turn would assign him the expectancy rights for renewal terms.
22. Clallham County Superior Court, case number 95-2-00704-2; VLC to CLC, 7-30-90. Evidently, both Gallagher and a military attorney had explained the renewal rights to Vance; he does not mention a movie in the works.
23. Altman's preference for pre-1978 stories was due to the fact that filmmaker Jill Godmilow had previously optioned many of the later stories.
24. The suit laid emphasis on whether Christine had a right to know that a movie was in the works when she signed her release, and thus hinged upon whether Gallagher should have volunteered that, whether Christine had inquired about it, and (if she did inquire) whether Gallagher answered sufficiently. Gallagher maintained that the assignment of renewal rights was needed simply to remedy a technical defect in the Carver children's 1990 release of rights. Information drawn from records of case number 95-2-00704-2 ("Complaint for Rescission and Damages"), Clallam County, Washington.
25. "A Small Place to Stand," *Doubletake* (summer 2001), 112; "Sixteenth Anniversary," *Dear Ghosts,* (Saint Paul, MN: Graywolf Press, 2006), 135.
26. Notebook: *The Writer's Life,* Carol Edgarian and Tom Jenks, eds. (New York: Vintage, 1997).

Insert Photograph Credits

1, 15: Courtesy of James Carver

2: Courtesy of Vivian Mosely and James Carver

3: Courtesy of Edvard Evenson and Evenson Timberland Agency and Deborah Steele Hazen

4, 11: Courtesy of Violet Lavonda Archer

5–9, 12–13, 29: Courtesy of James Carver and the William Charvat Collection of American Fiction, Rare Books and Manuscripts Library at the Ohio State University Libraries

10: Photo by Kennell-Ellis Artist Photographers, courtesy of Jerry King

14, 23: Courtesy of Charlene Palmer

16: Charlotte Brooks, photographer, *Look* magazine collection, Library of Congress, Prints and Photographs Division (LC-L9-64-1866 QQ #2A)

17, 38: Courtesy of the Estate of Amy Burk Unger

18: Courtesy of the Estate of Curtis L. Johnson

19–22: Courtesy of Maryann Burk Carver

24, 32–34: Courtesy of Diane Cecily

25: Photo by Gordon Lish, courtesy of Brown University Special Collections

26: Photo credited to "S. Beckett," courtesy of Gordon Lish

27: Photo from 1972 *Excalibur,* courtesy of Los Altos High School

30: Photo by Michael Rogers, courtesy of Diane Cecily

31: Courtesy of Douglas Unger

36: Photo by Peter Nash, courtesy of David Carpenter

37: Photo by Anne Mansbridge, courtesy of Gary Fisketjon

Index

Note: works by Raymond Carver are indicated by the title followed by type of work in parentheses; i.e., (poems); (story).

Abbey, Edward, 233
Abrahams, William, 234, 247
"Accomplishment" (Gallagher), 418
Acting Is Believing (Ward), 298
Adelman, Bob, 464, 486
"Aficionados, The" (story), 52, 75–76, 85
"After-glow" (poem), 473, 474
"After the Denim" (story). *See* "If It Please You" or "After the Denim"
Against Interpretation (Sontag), 141
Agnews State Hospital, 278–79, 278n
Airships (Hannah), 351
Al-Awqati, Qais, 298, 326, 470–71
Albee, Edward, 127
"Alcohol and Poetry: John Berryman and the Booze Talking" (Hyde), 329
alcoholism. *See also* Carver, Ray: ALCO-HOLISM
  AA and making amends, 314
  alcoholic seizure, 279
  awareness of impending doom, 258
  Bukowski and, 207–9
  C. R. Carver and, 5, 6, 8, 17–18, 19, 48
  Carver's circle in Missoula and, 190–91
  Carver's circle in Palo Alto and, 237–38
  Cheever and, 250, 252–58, 263–64, 308
  "elephant in the living room," 181, 217
  end stage, physical damage, 302
  Exchanging Credentials, 182
  Hemingway's, 80
  high tolerance, genetics, and, 238
  hitting bottom, 264
  honeymoon of early sobriety, 315
  Jack London and, 183–84, 269–70, 307
  "kindling," 279
  nutrition diminished by, 251, 274
  pain, fear, guilt and, 264
  professional women and, 258
  as progressive condition, 307
  serenity prayer, 317
  wet brain, 279

Alfred A. Knopf publishers, 316, 351, 359
  Carver promises new book (1986), 439, 442–43, 449, 454
  Carver released from book contract (1987), 454
  Gottlieb as Carver's editor, 410
  Harold Strauss at, 401
  Lish at, 316, 351, 359, 383
  publication of *All of Us*, 413, 488
  publication of *Cathedral*, 383, 389
  publication of *What We Talk About When We Talk About Love*, 355, 363
Algren, Nelson, 105
Ali, Muhammad, 139
All of Us: The Collected Poems, 413, 488
Altman, Robert, 486, 488
Alvarez, Julia, 375
American Academy and Institute of Arts and Letters, x
  Carver's induction, 469–70
  Strauss Living award to Carver, 400–401, 404, 461
  Strauss Living award to Johnson and Stone, 461
  Strauss Living award to Ozick, 401
  Updike's tribute to Carver, 483
American Audio Prose Library, 404
American culture and social change
  1950s, stability and prosperity, 20
  1955, racial equality, space race, and Kerouac, 55–56
  1960s, birth control/sexual revolution, 80
  1963, 173–74
  1964, 104
  1968, 166
  1969, 171, 173–74
  1970, political turmoil, 184
  1970s, attitudes about marriage, 243–44
  1970s, Baby Boomers in, 329
  1970s, divorce and birth control, 229
  1970s, doubleness of, 204

American culture and social change (*cont.*)
    1970s, end of Vietnam War, 242, 276
    1970s, Me generation, 242
    1970s, social and sexual revolution, 254
    1974, technology, Watergate, and
        Hearst kidnapping, 266
    1980, 352
    1980s, 419
    Kennedy years, 80–81
    New Age spiritual movements, 278
    San Francisco counterculture, 138
    shooting of John Lennon, 364
American fiction
    antirealist writing, 80
    Carver's defense of realism, 439
    Carver's influence, 299, 341, 406,
        414–15, 417
    Carver's introduction to *Short Story*
        Masterpieces and, 440
    Copyright Act of 1976, 329, 486
    experimental, 257, 299, 364
    Fisketjon and marketing, 417
    Gardner's *On Moral Fiction* and, 380
    Granta issue: *Dirty Realism,* 405
    imagistic and surrealist, 172
    late 1970s, short fiction and, 351
    mainstream fiction (1969), 174
    mainstream publishers (1970s), 272
    minimalism, ix, 351, 369, 369n, 405–6,
        408–9, 481, 482
    new fiction, 177, 185, 186, 188, 189, 406
    realism, 102, 105, 111, 141, 215, 282,
        299, 364, 380, 439, 469
    short story renaissance, 409
    Updike on Carver's short stories, 470
    West Coast writing scene, 236
American River College, Sacramento, 192
Amplitude (Gallagher), 464
Anania, Michael, 111
Anderson, Sherwood, 58–59, 203, 418
Anna Karenina (Tolstoy), 49
"Another Mystery" (story), 15, 28, 459
Antaeus magazine, 231, 317, 354, 363, 463
Apfelbaum, Charles, 424
Arcata, California, 74–75, 81–83, 85, 86,
    90, 164, 208, 308, 310, 317, 322, 327,
    328
Archer, Donald (cousin), 11, 17, 18
Archer, Olen "Shorty," 28
Archer, Robert (cousin), 11
Archer, Violet Lavonda "Von" Carver
    (aunt), 5, 6n, 11, 11n, 12, 14, 17, 25,
    50, 55, 392, 480
Archer, William (uncle), 5, 6, 7, 8, 11, 12,
    14, 25, 28, 50, 55, 392, 441
"Are These Actual Miles?" (story),

    130–31, 213–14, 215, 436. *See also*
    "What Is It?"
"Are You a Doctor?" (story), 191, 243, 441
Aristotle, 311
Arreguin, Alfredo, 473, 476
Art of Fiction, The: Notes on Craft for
    Young Writers (Gardner), 65
"Ask Him" (poem), 385–86
Atlantic Monthly
    "Cathedral" in, 372, 373, 375
    "Feathers" in, 390
    Tobias Wolff published in, 372
    What We Talk About . . . review, 368
Atlantic Monthly Press, 234, 457
    ABA convention party (1988), 471
    Carver's three-book deal, 464, 467, 483
    Fisketjon at, 454
    Where I'm Calling From, 454, 458–59,
        465
Atlas, James, 364, 368
"At Mercy" (story), 344
At Night the Salmon Move (collected
    poetry), 219, 269, 294, 298, 383
    author photo, 294
    dedication, 294
"Augustine Notebooks, The" (incomplete
    novel), 153, 162, 215
Author from a Savage People (Pesetsky),
    361
"Autopsy Room, The" (poem), 119–20

Babcock, Bert, 424–25
Babel, Isaac, 115, 251, 261
Bad Communist, The (Crawford), 236
"Bad Company" (Gallagher), 439
Baker, Chet, 203
Baker, James M., 387
Baker, Roy, 35
Baldwin, James, 109
"Balsa Wood" (poem), 27
"Balzac" (poem), 124
bankruptcy
    1967, 129–31, 133, 195
    1967, list of debts, 130
    1967, sale of car, 129–30
    1974, 273, 274, 275, 281
    1974, list of assets and debts, 276–77
"Bankruptcy" (poem), 130
Banks, Russell, 179, 397–98
Barhydt, Frank, 486
Barracks Thief, The (Wolff), 353
"Barracks Thief, The" (Wolff), 405
Barth, John, 142, 189
Barthelme, Donald, 142, 150, 243, 401,
    404, 414
Barton, Charles William, 42, 61, 226–27

"Bath, The" (story), 361, 362, 368–69, 378, 392
  comparison of versions, 357
Batki, John, 234
Baudelaire, Charles, 385
Bausch, Richard, 298
Baxter, Charles, 369
Beattie, Ann, 338–39, 351, 370, 402, 414, 453
Beckett, Samuel, 207
Beggar Maid, The (Munro), 351
"Beginners" (story), 354, 355
  comparison of versions, 357, 361
Behan, Brendan, 184
Behavioral Research Laboratories, 149
Bell, Marvin, 298
Bellingham, Washington, 44, 99, 335, 343, 346, 362, 389, 403, 422, 442, 449, 450, 453, 458, 475
Bellow, Saul, 210, 284, 380, 405
Benedict, Elizabeth, 476
"Beneficiaries" (Gallagher), 433
Ben Lomond, California, 204, 205, 212, 220
Berghoff, Larry, 51–52
Bernstein, Leonard, 157
Berriault, Gina, 150, 284, 301
Berry, Wendell, 233
Berryman, John, 329
Best American Short Stories (BASS)
  1964, 110
  1967, 132, 133, 142–43, 144, 146, 158, 182, 272, 282
  1972, 231
  1973, 247
  1982, 382
  1986, 425, 439–40
  1987, 453
Best American Short Stories of the Century (Updike, ed.), 488
Best Little Magazine Fiction, The (Thurston and Johnson, eds.), 169, 182, 195
"Bicycles, Muscles, Cigarets" (story), 130
Bierce, Ambrose, 203–4
Big Rock Candy Mountain (Stegner), 88
Biles-Coleman Lumber Company, 6, 7
"Blackbird Pie" (story), 321, 442, 443–44, 450
black humor, 141
Black Tickets (Phillips), 351
Blades, John, 367
Blaise, Clark, 96, 128, 142, 282
Blount, Roy, Jr., 411, 463
"Bobber" (poem), 136
Bond, Georgia Morris, 392, 400, 478, 480

Bond, Leslie O , 343, 388–89, 390–91, 392
Bond, Morris, 400, 412, 435, 438, 445, 457
Bonetti, Kay, 404
Boorman, John, 196
Borstal Boy (Behan), 184
Boundaries of Love and Other Stories (Roth), 176
Bourjaily, Tina, 89, 333
Bourjaily, Vance, 63, 89, 90, 102, 105, 248, 255, 333, 337
"Boxes" (story), 435–37, 441
  in *BASS 1987,* 453
Boyle, Kay, 142, 143
Boyle, T. Coraghessan, 255, 298, 327, 444
Bradbury, Ray, 23
Braine, John, 314
"Brass Ring, The" (poem), 84
Brautigan, Richard, 38, 141, 237, 440
Brice, Pat, 69
"Bridle, The" (story), 132, 379, 391, 398
Bright Lights, Big City (McInerney), 417, 423–24
  Carver blurb, 418
Brodkey, Harold, 281, 369n, 370
Brook, Peter, 94
Brothers, Connie, 444
"Brothers, The" (sketch), 135
Brown, Billy, 64
Brown, Bob, 176, 189
Broyard, Anatole, 367, 409
Buford, Bill, 405, 434
Bukoski, Anthony, 274
Bukowski, Charles, 168, 207–9, 210, 448
"Bummer" (story), 192
Bumpus, Jerry, 185
Burk, Amy Edith (sister-in-law). *See* Unger, Amy Burk
Burk, Annette, 99
Burk, Bonna Rose "Jerry" (sister-in-law). *See* Davis, Bonna Rose "Jerry" Burk
Burk, Valentine (father-in-law), 44–45, 54, 81, 99, 136, 193
Burk, Valla, 99
Burkard, Michael, 255, 337
Burnett, David, 110
Burroughs, Edgar Rice, 23–24
Bush, Mary Bucci, 420
Buzbee, Lewis, 346, 354, 367, 388, 406, 406n

Caldwell, Gail, 470
California State College International Program, 145, 152
Calistoga, 303, 303n
Call If You Need Me (posthumous collection), 443, 488

"Call If You Need Me" (story), 321
"Calm, The" (story), 348
Calvin, Allen, 149
Camus, Albert, 74, 85
Capra Press, 221, 251, 269, 294, 309, 313, 338, 383, 394, 406, 434
"Car, The" (poem), 136
"Careful" (story), 408, 430, 458
Carlile, Henry, 420–21, 425–26, 427, 438–39, 441, 442, 445–46
Carnations (play), 84–85
Carolina Quarterly, 98, 104, 111, 114, 124
Carpenter, David, 448, 462
Carriveau, Jerry, 370–71, 433
Carroll, Maureen, 361
Carruth, Hayden, 148, 174, 352, 398, 401
Carter, Dick, 129
Carter, Jimmy, 329, 352
Car Thief, The (Weesner), 231
Carver, Abram (great-great-grandfather), 5
Carver, Billie (aunt), 12, 18, 25, 57
Carver, Chloe Alice (grandchild), 428, 449, 484
Carver, Christine LaRae "Christi" or "Chris" (daughter), 57, 61, 63, 89, 105, 110, 112, 118, 122, 131, 132, 138, 151–52, 190
    adolescence, 171, 184, 245, 254, 266
    auto accident (1982), 389
    bailing parents out of jail, 270
    in Ben Lomond, 204–5, 212
    births of daughters, 346, 407, 484
    Christmas (1976), 306
    in Cupertino, 221
    dislocation and moving, 212
    education, 343, 437, 452–53, 458
    family photo, 223
    father's first book of stories and, 281
    father's illness and death, 466, 467, 475
    father's relationship with, 195, 202, 248, 254, 266, 285, 300, 316, 320, 322, 377, 403, 422, 426, 427, 428–29, 437, 442, 449, 452–53, 458, 475
    father's wake and burial, 480
    father's will and challenges to Gallagher's control, 399, 473, 483–85, 486–88
    financial problems, 437, 442
    hit by car, 114–15
    job at all-girl gas station, 258
    leaves home, 258, 271
    life following father's death, 484–85, 488
    in Los Angeles, 167
    Mediterranean cruise and European tour (1968), 164

Mike Pleadwell (Shiloh) and, 286, 288, 302, 342–43, 427
Mr. Six, dog of, 218, 219
in poems, reaction to, 428–29
pregnancy, first, 335
Sunnyvale house, 185
in Tel Aviv (1968), 156–57, 158, 159
What We Talk About, reaction to, 370
in Yakima, 185
Carver, Clevie Raymond "C.R." (father), 3, 4
    alcoholism, 5, 6, 8, 17–18, 19, 48, 133–34
    appearance, 13, 48
    birth of Raymond Junior, 3
    burial in Yakima, 134–35
    in Chico, California, 63–64
    Collins Pine Company, 42, 48, 56
    death of, 133–36, 183
    disability settlement, 105–6, 109
    as disappointed man, 14, 64
    dreams of railroad job, 6, 13, 14
    financial problems, 24–25
    fishing and, 14
    Grand Coulee Dam worker, 8
    health issues, 48, 52, 64, 83
    loss of Cascade Lumber job, 42
    meets and marries Ella Casey, 6–7
    migration from Arkansas to Oregon, 3, 5–6, 6n
    mispronunciation of words, 16–17
    move to Eureka, California, 83–84
    nervous breakdown, 56–57
    personality and character, 49
    pessimism and bad luck of, 4, 17
    Ray and Sandmeyer, 28–39
    Ray's relationship with, 6, 41, 52, 57, 86, 135. *See also* "My Father's Life"
    Ray's wedding and, 55
    religion and, 12
    in Sacramento, 105–6, 109
    as sawmill worker, 3, 7–8, 10, 14–15, 20, 41–42, 48, 56, 113, 133
    sensitivity of, 16
    troubled marriage and home life, 8, 17, 18, 19, 24, 25, 134
    as union man, 7–8
    in Yakima, 11, 56–57, 72
Carver, Ella Casey (mother), 3, 7, 10
    appearance, 6, 19–20
    birth of James, 11
    birth of Raymond Junior, 3
    Carver family's move to California (1955), 47–48
    in Chico, California, 63–64
    Christmas (1975), 288

Christmas (1976), 306
Christmas (1986), 449, 453
in Crescent City, California, 113, 133
emphysema of, 300
estrangement from Ray (1986–1987),
    453
in Eureka, California, 83–84
family background, 6–7
husband's drinking and marital discord,
    8, 17, 18, 19, 24, 25, 56, 57, 134
jobs held by, 18–19, 43, 49, 57
life following death of C.R., 187–88,
    246
meets and marries C.R., 6–7
mother's death, 300
in Mountain View, California, 246, 270,
    271
in Palo Alto, 168
personality and character, 6, 7, 18, 19,
    49
in Port Angeles, Washington, 422
Ray's childhood and, 11, 27
Ray's illness and death and, 463, 466,
    467, 478, 480
Ray's wedding and, 55
Ray's will and, 473, 483, 485
Ray's writing and, 38, 367–68, 436,
    463–64
religion and, 12
return to Arkansas (1967), 135
in Sacramento, 105–6, 109, 389, 402,
    435
sale of letters from Ray, 485
visit to Ray (1979), 349–50
in Yakima, 9–47, 56–57, 72, 445, 449
Carver, Frank (grandfather), 4, 5, 7, 11, 15
Carver, Fred Edward (uncle), 5, 6, 8, 10,
    12, 14–15, 25, 41–42, 57, 113, 422
Carver, Heidi LaRae (grandchild), 484
Carver, Hosea (great-grandfather), 5
Carver, Ingeborg Behrend (daughter-in-
    law), 437
Carver, James Franklin (brother), 441, 453
    appearance, 50
    baptism, 12
    birth, 11
    Carver family's move to California
        (1955), 47–48
    in Chester, California, 49–50
    in Chico, California, 63–64
    childhood, Ray and, 13–14, 22, 46,
        83–84
    Christmas (1975), 288
    in Crescent City, California, 113
    education, 187
    in Eureka, California, 83–84

father's death, 135
father's drinking and, 17–18
father's health and, 56
financial problems, 389
jobs held by, 57
Ray's illness and death and, 467,
    471–72, 480
Ray's will and, 485
refuses to let Ray stay at home, 305
in Sacramento, California, 109–10, 112,
    435
Vietnam War and, 124
in Yakima, 11, 13–14, 22, 46, 72
Carver, Jennifer Vanessa (grandchild), 437,
    441, 455, 488
Carver, Maryann Burk (first wife)
    AA meetings and sobriety, 258, 259,
        266, 273, 275, 278, 294, 306, 315,
        327, 343, 422
    alcohol use and abuse, 140, 166–67, 206,
        231, 234, 239–41, 243, 258, 259, 265,
        268–69, 328
    appearance, 43–44, 54, 95, 139, 152,
        164, 166, 171, 192, 206, 246
    average yearly income, 387
    birth of daughter Christi, 57
    birth of son Vance, 63
    as breadwinner, 112, 113–14, 115, 117,
        119, 125–26, 128, 173, 212, 240, 275,
        281, 317, 320, 482
    Burk and Carver family in Bellingham,
        Washington, and, 44, 99, 335, 343,
        346, 362, 389, 403, 422, 442, 449,
        450, 453, 458, 475
    in Chico, California, 61–63, 68, 72
    Christmas (1976), 306
    cigarettes and, 192
    collapse (1969), 170–71
    college degree (1970), 180, 185
    courtship and wedding, 43–55
    crisis intervention of, 242, 316–17
    Cupertino house, 220–21, 227, 258, 273,
        274–75, 302, 303
    death of Ray's father and, 134
    Diane Cecily and, 279, 301
    divorce from Ray, 386–88, 394
    divorce from Ray, financial problems
        and, 410, 426–27
    divorce from Ray, relationship
        following, 449–50, 454, 458, 461,
        464–65
    domestic violence, 230, 279–81, 289
    editorial contribution to Ray's work,
        179–80, 186, 198, 207, 215
    education, interruptions of, 93, 105,
        112, 114, 170, 185, 273

Carver, Maryann Burk (first wife) *(cont.)*
  est movement and, 278
  family and childhood, 44–46
  family photo, 223
  father's death, 99
  financial success, 117, 118, 119
  first new car, 205
  first pregnancy, 53
  flirtatiousness, 239–40, 259, 269, 280
  at Foothill Community College, 138
  goes to see Engle to fight for Ray's
    fellowship, 103
  graduate study, 240, 315
  Gurney's description, 237
  honeymoon trip, Seattle, 55
  at Humboldt State College, 81–86
  intellect and academic achievement, 44,
    45, 46, 49, 50, 53
  in Iowa City, 93–95
  jobs held by, 63, 81, 87, 93, 96, 102, 109,
    110, 112, 113, 115, 123, 170, 179–80,
    240, 317, 362, 488
  Laurent Girard, second marriage to,
    426, 450
  leaves Erhard job for Ray, 137
  life following Ray's death, 487–88
  life following separation from Ray, 362
  love affair with Ross Perkins, 294, 299,
    300, 305, 306, 317
  management of Diablo Riviera
    apartments, 131–32, 137
  marriage disintegration, 227–32, 234,
    242, 244, 265–67, 279
  marriage separation, reconciliation, and
    failure, 78, 112–13, 305, 315–35, 343
  married life, 59, 72–73, 112–13, 140,
    143, 160–61, 163, 240
  Mediterranean cruise and European
    tour (1968), 161–65
  meeting with Lish, 151–52
  meets Ray Carver, 42, 43
  memoir, 488
  New York City trip (1970), 184
  in Palo Alto (1967–1968), 137–38, 140,
    143, 145
  personality and character, 44, 94, 139,
    151–52, 203, 207, 239–41
  Pontiac Catalina, 118, 126, 129–30
  poverty of marriage years, 87, 93–94,
    102, 112, 137, 152, 167, 168
  Ray and McKinleyville, 312–15
  Ray's alcoholism, codependence, and
    enabling, 171, 239–41, 258
  Ray's bitterness at financial support,
    426, 427
  Ray's fraud charges and, ix–x, 295–96

Ray's illness and death and, 467,
    468–69, 475–76
  Ray's infidelity and, 227–30
  Ray's Montana plan and, 211–12
  Ray's summer trip (1971) and, 224–26
  Ray's wake and burial, 480
  Ray's will and suit for payment, 399,
    473, 483–85
  at Sacramento State College, 110
  sales job and Werner Erhard, 115–16,
    117–18, 119, 125–26, 128
  at San Jose State, 145, 169, 170, 171
  second pregnancy, 59
  at Stanford University, 240
  story "Fat" and, 179–80
  as subject of Ray's writing, 42, 43, 44,
    54, 55, 127, 143, 198, 441, 450
  support for Ray's writing, 59, 73, 81,
    82, 98–99, 114, 123, 139, 147, 168,
    172, 192, 281, 378
  teaching, as substitute, 335
  teaching, Los Altos High School, ix–x,
    185, 196, 205, 220, 240, 281, 315, 330
  in Tel Aviv (1968), 153–62
  at UC Davis, 109
  at UC Santa Barbara, 269–71
Carver, Mary Green (grandmother), 4, 5, 6,
    7, 11, 15, 28
Carver, Norma (sister-in-law), 288
Carver, Raymond
  appearance, 12, 13, 15, 20, 35, 75, 90,
    122, 124, 139, 164, 166, 192, 195,
    203, 206, 234, 245, 246, 256, 262,
    367, 421–22, 432–33, 456, 469, 471
  assets at death, 482–83
  Bad Ray and Good Ray, xi, 314, 317,
    319, 324, 327–28, 379
  as boxing fan, 175, 195
  cigarettes and, x, 22, 36, 192, 340, 347,
    353, 389, 404, 442, 445, 449, 453–54,
    461
  cocaine use, 347, 364, 400
  death, x, 478
  depression experienced by, 86, 104, 117,
    156, 159, 160, 167, 171, 202, 213, 244
  doubleness vs. unity of self, 203–4, 219,
    232
  fishing, hunting, and, 225, 255, 316,
    412, 420–21, 422, 438–39, 445–46,
    447, 448, 456–57
  grave as literary shrine, 481
  Gurney's description, 237
  on luck, 439–40, 457, 463
  marijuana use, x, 120–21, 140, 147, 238,
    328, 335, 392, 406, 422, 429, 448,
    454, 461, 463

military service, 50–51, 80–81, 83, 146
music, jazz, and, 36–37, 38
as myth and legend, 288, 294, 409, 419
number of residences during lifetime,
    156
obituaries and eulogizing of, 481–82,
    483
personality and character, x, 12–13,
    16, 19, 21, 22, 30, 37, 46, 49, 63, 67,
    68–69, 84, 85, 90, 92–93, 94, 114,
    126, 139, 153–62, 167, 168, 181–82,
    191, 196, 203, 217, 229, 261, 398–99,
    414, 439, 444–45
poker playing, 241, 340
premonition of dying young, 120, 404,
    405, 446, 455
quirks and habits, 218, 373
relationship with his children, 58, 63,
    72–73, 83, 96, 105–6, 114, 195, 202,
    241–42, 245, 248, 266, 284–86, 300,
    316–17, 320, 321–22, 330, 332,
    342–43, 346, 363, 365, 376–77,
    390–91, 403, 410, 422, 426, 458
sexual attitudes of, 126
success vs. bad luck and failure, 202
wake, burial, eulogies, 479–82
ALCOHOLISM, ix, x, 135–36, 170
    AA and other drunks, 373–74
    AA slogan and, 453, 462
    alcoholic seizure, 279
    attempts to control drinking (1975),
        275
    benders and binges, 298–300, 309
    blackouts, 302, 308
    blaming and, 234, 240, 279
    Carver on his addiction, 238, 289
    as champagne drunk, 301–2, 304–5, 308
    Cheever and, 250, 252–58
    Crumley on, 306
    denial, 232
    deteriorating physical condition, 251,
        274, 302
    drinking as symptom and cause of
        problems (1964–1965), 114, 117
    drying out, Garden Sullivan
        Hospital, 301
    DWI and other arrests, 270
    dying days and near slip, 467
    effect on writing, 164, 225, 308
    erosion of values and family discord,
        285, 374, 377
    financial price of, 274
    full bloom, daily drinking, 229–32, 234,
        243, 245–47, 248, 249
    hitting bottom, 268–89
    at Humboldt State College, 83

increasing dependency, 120, 126, 204
in Iowa City, 103–4
Jackson on Carver, 191
Johnson on Carver, 152, 167
last drink, 310
late-stage, x, 250–67
Maryann as codependent and enabling,
    171, 239–41, 258
Missoula, Montana, and, 190, 225–26
Palmer on Carver, 166
in Palo Alto (1967–1968), 140, 147,
    151–52
paranoia and, 83
physical dependency and, 238
rage and violence, 230, 261, 262, 278,
    279–81, 286
"Ray stories" (1973–1977), 247, 259
at Sacramento, escalation, 205–6, 209,
    210–12
shakes, 287
sobriety and, x–xi, 268, 308, 309, 311,
    312–22, 331, 334, 343, 352–70, 378,
    383
sobriety and gratitude, 365
as sponsor for Michael Rogers, 374
sweet cravings after quitting, 319, 324,
    340, 349, 366, 384
as theme in work, ix, 18, 181, 276, 277,
    321, 370, 409
treatment programs, 278–79, 278n,
    302–4, 306–7
trip to Israel and, 165
1938–1955 (FAMILY AND EARLY YEARS), 3–9,
    10–20, 21–33
    baptism, 10
    birth, 3, 4, 422–23
    at Blue Lake, 14
    books owned, 23–24
    childhood friends, 12, 16–17, 26n,
        34–35, 37
    Columbia Basin as formative, 9, 10–20
    extended family, 11, 12, 15, 28
    family discord, 23, 24
    as fat child, 15, 20, 21–22, 32
    father and, 41, 52, 57
    father's drinking and, 17–18
    fishing and hunting, 14, 26n, 28–33
    grandfather's death, 15
    grandmother's death, 28
    jobs in Yakima, 41, 42
    lower-middle-class childhood, 13–14
    mother, closeness with, 27
    movies, television, magazines, and
        books during, 23, 24
    as much loved child, 4
    names for, 4, 12, 21

1938–1955 (*cont.*)
  obsession with the right word, 16–17
  religion and, 12
  Sandmeyer and, 28–33, 57, 64, 71
  schooling, 12–13, 15–16, 23, 34–38,
    34n, 42
  Scots-Irish heritage, 3, 4–5
  as teenager, 21–33, 34–42
  Wauna, Oregon, 3–4
  weight loss drugs and, 22, 30
  wordplay and, 37
  in Yakima, 4–42
1955–1964 (MARRIAGE, PARENTHOOD, AND
    COLLEGE YEARS), 43–106
  American social/cultural change and,
    55–56, 80–81, 104
  Arcata, California, and, 74–75, 81–83,
    85, 86, 90
  arrival in Iowa City, 89
  birth of daughter Christi, 57
  birth of son Vance, 63
  Carver family's move to California,
    47–48
  at Chico State College, 61–73
  completes undergraduate degree, 85
  courtship and wedding, 43–55
  death of Val Burk and separation from
    Maryann, 99–102
  as deliveryman for Kurbitz, 42, 52, 56
  education grants, 65
  in Eureka, California, 74–81
  "ferocious parenting," 63, 377
  financial problems, 55, 75, 82, 87, 90,
    93–94, 102
  first apartment, 55–56
  honeymoon trip, Seattle, 55
  at Humboldt State College, 74–86
  Iowa City housing, 89, 93–95
  University of Iowa Writers' Workshop,
    86, 89–106
  jobs, miscellaneous, 62, 64–65, 90, 98
  jobs, sawmill, 48, 49, 50, 64–65, 74–75
  Kennedy assassination and, 96
  leaves Iowa for Sacramento, 105–6
  Maryann as confidant, 73
  Paradise, California, 61–62
  parents' proximity to, 63–64, 83–84
  rural experiment, 81
  signs of problems in marriage, 78
  trip to Mexico, 51–52
  at Yakima Junior College, 56
1964–1971 (SEARCHING YEARS), 109–98
  alcohol use, 114, 117, 120, 126, 135–36,
    140, 147, 151–52, 156, 164, 168, 190
  American social/cultural change and,
    127, 138, 166, 171, 173–74, 184

artistic isolation, 121
auditing Schmitz course, 122–24
bankruptcy, ix, 129–31, 133, 195
Cupertino house, 258
degree in library science and, 116–17,
    129
Dennis Schmitz and, 122–24, 125
desire for vacation and travel, 144
family's poodle, Mitzi, 109, 112, 118,
    169
father's death, 133–36
financial problems, 112, 114, 118, 120,
    136, 137, 152, 167, 168, 195
in Hollywood and San Jose
    (1968–1969), 166–78
University of Iowa library science
    program, 132–33
as janitor, Mercy Hospital, 114, 115,
    119, 132
job loss, Christmas 1964 (cookie-
    stealing incident), 111–12, 209
jobs, miscellaneous, 109–10, 114, 115,
    119
job search and loss of direction, 128,
    136
Las Vegas trip, 117–18
library science courses in San Jose, 169
Lish and publication of writing, 179–98
management of apartments, 131–32,
    137
marital problems, 112–13, 140, 143, 161
Mediterranean cruise and European
    tour (1968), 161–65
"nervous breakdown," 110
in Palo Alto (1967–1968), 137–52
photo by Lish, 175
rented places to write, 116, 169, 180
return to Writers' Workshop
    considered, 116, 117
in Sacramento (1964–1967), 109–36
in San Jose and Sunnyvale (1970–1971),
    179–98
at SRA, 137–39, 146, 168, 169, 170, 179,
    180, 182, 187, 195
Stegner Fellowship, 141, 233–38
Sunnyvale house, 185, 190, 193, 202
in Tel Aviv (1968), 145, 153–62
unemployment benefits, ix, 187, 192,
    195
University of Montana, Missoula and,
    217
vague ambitions, 187
1971–1975 (SUCCESS AND DISCONTENT),
    198–289
  alcohol dependency, 229–32, 243,
    245–47

alcoholism, escalation of drinking and, 205–6, 209, 210–12, 231–32

alcoholism, hitting bottom, 268–89

alcoholism, late-stage and, 250–67

alcoholism, treatment, 278–79

bankruptcy, second, 273, 274, 275, 276–77, 281

"Beef Trust" and nicknames, 237, 257

Ben Lomond house, 205–6, 212, 220

Bukowski and, 207–9

Christmas (1975), 286–89

Chuck Kinder and, 234–38, 235n

Cupertino house, ix, 221, 223, 224, 227, 233, 265–67, 273, 274–75, 287

Diane Cecily and, 226, 228–30, 231–32, 234, 235, 238, 243–45, 248, 250, 254, 387

domestic violence by, 230, 279–81, 289

family photo, 223

financial problems, 202, 267, 273, 274, 276–77

first book of short stories, 272–74

Iowa Writers' Workshop teaching position, 247, 248–49, 250–63

John Cheever and, 252–58

marital crisis, 227–28, 230

marital disintegration, 227–32, 234, 242, 243–44, 265–67

marriage, end of, 333–35

middle-class/white-collar jobs, 247, 247n

reading at UC Davis, 275–76

reading tour and drunkenness, 273–74

Sanchez's party (1974), 284–85

in Santa Cruz (1971–1972), 198–220

sexual affairs, 255–56, 259, 261–62

Stegner Fellowship and Stanford, 215, 220 21, 232, 247

as teacher, 210, 245 46, 255–56, 260

UC Berkeley and, 211, 220, 233, 243, 245–47

UC Santa Barbara and, 268–71

UC Santa Cruz and, 203–17, 220, 232, 233, 243, 248, 249, 256–57

unemployment benefits and fraud charges, 267, 270, 273, 274, 281–82

University of Montana and, 211–12, 220, 223–26

1976–1982 (RECOVERY), 293–394

alcoholism benders and binges, 298–300, 309

alcoholism treatment, Myrtledale, 302–4, 306–7

average yearly income, 387

Burk and Carver family in Bellingham, Washington, 335, 343, 346, 389

cabin near Port Angeles, 346 47

Christmas (1976), 306

Christmas (1977), 321, 322

divorce, 386–88, 394

drying out, 301

financial problems, 310, 317, 324–25, 328, 342–43

"Fires" written (1981), 377–78

fortieth birthday, 332

fraud charges and, 293, 295–96

friendship with Ford, 318, 324, 326, 330, 366

Gardner's death and, 392–93

Goddard College and, 309, 320–21, 323–25, 334–35

Guggenheim Fellowship, 317, 330

as homeless, 302, 325, 326

home life and turmoil, 294, 306, 309, 316–17, 320, 332–33, 389

in Iowa City (1978), 327–33

job at Upstart Crow Books, 300

at Johnson's summer house, 326–28, 328n

in Lake Tahoe with Iowa lover, 300

Linda McCarriston and, 325, 335

loss of belongings, 305–6

marital separation, reunion, final break, 299, 300, 305, 312–15, 323–35, 343

in McKinleyville, 308–10, 312–15, 320–21

movie projects, 393–94

in New York City (1981), 370

Provincetown Fine Arts Works Center and, 366

reading at SMU, 317–20

rootlessness and beginning the sobriety process (1976–1977), 293–310

San Francisco apartment, 300–302

short story collections, 293–94

sobriety, 334–35, 343, 352–70, 378, 383

stories of summer 1977, 313

success and, 370, 376–93

summer travel and Alaska (1980), 355

Switzerland, Italy, France (1983), 384–86

Syracuse house, 354, 363, 380, 392

Syracuse University and, 342, 345, 351, 352–71, 379–92

Tess Gallagher and, 319, 320, 336–51, 353–54, 355–56, 386–87

in Tucson, 346–51

UTEP and, 320, 325, 330, 335, 336–46

visiting writer and short-term jobs, 354, 373

writing conferences (1979), 347

1976–1982 (*cont.*)
  Yaddo and, 294, 298, 299, 317, 328,
    374–75, 377
  Yakima trip (1982), 392
  in Zurich (1983), 384
1982–1988 (FINAL YEARS), 397–478
  Alaska trip planned, aborted (1988),
    477
  archive project, 424–25
  Australia trip, 430
  BASS 1986, Carver edits, 425, 439
  bitterness over family, 426, 427
  boats owned by, 420–21, 438–39,
    445–46, 456–57, 459
  book tour, England/Ireland (1985),
    434–35
  book tour, Scotland (1987), 456
  Cathedral publication/praise, 407–10,
    412
  Christmas (1984), 426
  Christmas (1986), 449–50
  Christmas (1987), 466
  coediting *Short Story Masterpieces*, 440
  criticism of, selling out, 419–20
  daughter, visit to (1983), 403
  death, thoughts/premonitions, 404, 405
  discontent and lack of writing, 415
  European travel (1987), 455–56
  fame and, 399, 407–8, 409–10, 412,
    413–14, 416, 418–19, 430, 431, 448,
    456, 463–64, 469
  fiftieth birthday, 471
  financial gifts to family, 435, 442, 450,
    458, 461, 465, 475
  as guest writer, 414
  health check-up (1987), 452
  honorary degree and speech, 469
  honors and celebrations, 403–4, 463
  income, 401, 430, 467
  Jeep wagon, 416, 418
  Kinder cross-country trip (1983),
    407–8
  Lish, end of relationship, 402–3, 409,
    410–11
  lung cancer and, 460–78
  marriage to Tess Gallagher, 472–73
  Maryann, relationship with, 426, 427,
    429–30, 449–50, 454, 458, 461,
    464–65, 468–69
  Mercedes, 397–98, 399, 408, 415, 422
  mother, estrangement from, 453
  movie projects, 401–2, 403, 407, 427–28
  People magazine profile, 448, 459
  personal papers sold, 444
  photo, Paris (1987), 456
  poetry writing, 415–18

  in Port Angeles, 399–400, 401, 405, 408,
    415, 416, 420, 425–26, 430, 431, 435,
    438, 439, 447, 449, 450, 454–59,
    464–66, 471–72, 474–78
  project for NPR, 402
  readings, 401–2, 415, 439, 441, 447,
    454–55, 456, 471
  Ridge House, study in, 465
  Ridge House purchase, 459, 462, 465
  Saskatchewan hunting trip (1987),
    447–48
  in Seattle, 428, 467, 477
  short stories (1987–1988), 451–52
  sobriety and, 432–33
  Strauss Living award, 400–401, 404,
    412, 426, 432, 446, 461, 465
  Syracuse house, 401
  Syracuse University and, 398, 400, 401,
    407, 415, 415n, 439, 448
  Tess Gallagher and, 398–99, 418,
    433–35, 434n, 447–49, 457, 459,
    460–78
  trip to birthplace, 422–23
  Ultramarine and short story spree,
    437–44
  Vanity Fair profile, 448–49
  wills of, 399, 466, 473, 478
  Writer's Workshop reunion, 444–45
  writes "My Father's Life," 411–12
  Yaddo and, 403
  Yakima class reunion (1986), 445
  in Zurich (1987), 456
WRITING. *See also* American Academy
    and Institute of Arts and Letters;
    "Fires" (essay); *specific publishers*;
    specific titles
  alcoholism as theme, ix, 18, 181, 276,
    277, 321, 370, 409
  ambitions, 33, 38–39, 47, 52–53, 59, 60,
    64, 82, 118, 237–38
  as American Chekhov, 481–82
  autobiography and imagination as
    approach, 28, 71, 76, 127
  "Bad Check, His Mama, and Beautiful
    Songs" as joke title and subject, 194
  bankruptcy as theme, 130–31
  "Beef Trust," 237
  book reviews for *Chicago Tribune*, 346
  book reviews for *NYTBR*, 418, 432,
    439
  British publishers, 434
  as "bundle of *témoignage*," 376, 400
  byline as "Raymond," 188
  "Carveresque" writing, 142
  characters, Carver on, 297
  characters, Lish on, 186–87

characters, Weber on, 419
characters, working-class, lonely, or wandering, 12, 100
Cheever and Carver on fiction, 257
childhood in, 13, 14, 20, 21, 22, 32, 36
chronicler of blue-collar despair, ix, 115, 418
collating parties for *kayak* and, 172, 205
composition process, 411, 470
conflict with breadwinning and parenthood, 63, 73, 76, 96–97, 136, 170, 219, 245, 266, 285–86, 377–78, 428–29
Copyright Act of 1976 and, 486–88
correspondence with Curtis Johnson, 111, 118–19, 136, 146, 153, 158, 159, 161, 163, 164–65, 167, 169, 171, 175, 308, 326, 341, 353, 421
correspondence with William Kittredge, 187, 196–97, 201, 218, 220
crisis of 1971, 224–25
Day's mentorship, 75–86
death in, 15, 28, 57, 119, 405, 422, 438, 442, 459, 472, 473
debut as national author, 294–95, 298
despair as basis, 262
development of his work, 204, 362, 372–73, 378, 383, 408, 442–43
dialogue, 37–38
divided self in, 27
dysfunctional families in, 18, 25–27
early influences, 24
on editors and editing, 382
Ettlinger photographs, 429, 464
fallow period (1986–1987), 447, 450, 451
father as subject, 6, 6n, 13, 16, 18, 25, 27–28, 57, 64, 134, 136
Fiction magazine and, 242–43
final book, 473–76 (*see also New Path to the Waterfall, A*)
first book, 144–45 (*see also Near Klamath*)
first book of short stories, ix, x, 272–73, 275, 281, 282, 284, 293 (*see also Will You Please Be Quiet, Please?*)
first paid reading, 191–92
first poems in print, 84
first short stories published, x, 78
first typewriter, 59
first work in print, 78
fishing and hunting in, 29–33, 57, 71
Fisketjon as primary editor, 420, 432, 458–59, 464
foreign rights and translations, 421, 430
Gallagher's stewardship of Carver's

work and challenges to his will, 482–89
Gardner's mentorship, 65–73, 74, 185, 203
groundbreaking aspects of, 127–28
Hemingway's influence, 38, 51
Hemingway's theory of omission and, 142
he-she stories, 179, 188, 194, 201–2, 216, 222, 348–49, 443
Hitchcock on, 172–73
honored as "Literary Lion," 463
ideal life envisioned by, 97
image cultivated, 294
independence from Lish, 378
interior lives of married couples in, ix, 78, 100, 127–28
Iowa City interlude (1978) and, 327
Jack London and, 183–84
Johnson's criticism and help, 143–44, 248
landscape of Columbia River, Yakima Valley, and other locations used in, 9, 10, 29, 31, 38, 61–62, 70, 356, 405
Library of America volume, 361
as lifelong storyteller, 22
Lish and publication of writing, 146, 147, 151–52, 176–78, 179–98, 189n, 194n, 201, 213, 214, 215, 223, 230, 272, 281, 282, 313, 339, 411
Lish's editing of *What We Talk About When We Talk About Love,* 354–62, 368–69
literary circle of friends, 187, 190–91, 205–6, 207, 211–12, 220, 234, 236, 237, 242–43, 269, 288, 294, 323–24, 337–38, 358, 380–81, 397–98, 420–22, 425–26, 434, 435, 441, 456–57, 474–75, 488–89
literary influences, 49, 67, 71, 76, 77, 83, 84, 85, 115, 118–19, 124, 125, 142, 162, 163–64
in longhand, 38, 56
loss of Joseph Henry Jackson Award, 196–97
loss of joy in, 213–14
loss of papers and manuscripts, 137
love causes harm theme, 219
marriage depicted in, ix, 230, 312, 321–22, 339, 348–49, 408
Maryann as subject, 43, 44, 54, 55, 127, 143, 198, 441, 450
Maryann's editorial contribution, 179–80, 186, 198, 207
"metaphysical hole" and, 169, 170
Mexican trip in, 52

WRITING. (*cont.*)
minimalism and, ix, 299, 369, 369n,
405–6, 408–9, 469, 481, 482
Missoula, Montana, and, 190–91, 220
mother as subject, 7, 19, 435–37, 453
"mystery in the mundane," 235
narrative voice, 76, 210, 443
NEA grant, 180, 215
new typewriter (1979), 349
notebooks, 32, 34, 57, 82–83, 87, 100,
109, 122, 134, 179, 218, 311, 323, 489
novel attempt, never written, 293
novel fragment, 163–64, 188, 193, 215
novel proposal, 311
novel proposal abandoned, 340
objective correlative, 416, 436
Palmer Institute of Authorship and,
38–40
papers at Ohio State University, 361,
424–25, 444
paranoia and, 204
photo for 1971 and 1976 anthologies
("Washington Fats"), 195–96, 294
photo of Carver by Thomas Victor in
NYTBR, 367
places to write: offices and apartments,
68, 69, 116, 169, 180, 243, 294
poems about his daughter, 428–29
poems on Israel, 153, 157–58, 160
as poet, 125, 219, 413, 415–18, 420, 425,
433, 438, 459, 466
as "poet of the working poor," 115
point of view, 47, 71, 78, 104, 143–44,
372, 442, 443
political theme, 204
posthumous Carver documentaries,
collections, and movies, 486–89
pulp fiction, influence of, 23, 80
readings, 297, 298, 317–20, 342, 354,
364, 370, 380, 381, 401–2, 412, 415,
430–31, 439, 441, 447, 454–55, 456,
471
realism/dirty realism and, 76, 84, 105,
142, 144, 198, 282, 299, 364, 405–6,
409, 439, 469
recording of, 404
represented by Amanda Urban (ICM),
381, 383, 454, 464
represented by Ellen Levine, 186, 188,
193, 218–19
represented by Harold Matson Co.,
138, 186
represented by John Sterling, 306, 354
(*see also* Sterling, John)
represented by Liz Darhansoff, 355,
363, 371–72, 373

Sandmeyer as character, 29
sawmill and workers in, 41
screenplays, 393–94, 401–2, 403, 407,
427–28, 434
sexuality and, 26, 126–27
short stories vs. novel, 40
sobriety and, 313–22, 341, 348, 350,
352, 354, 378, 383
sour grapes and, 261
stories about two couples, 168, 168n
style, 40, 70, 76, 139
submission of work, 84, 118, 169,
177–78, 179, 181, 182, 188, 193, 202,
219, 231, 349, 354, 355, 371–72, 373,
389–90
subordination of everything to writing
(1981–1982), 376–93
success and, 215, 224–25, 231, 247, 262,
272–74, 381, 407–12, 413–31
symbolism in, 27, 31–32, 61, 84, 101,
112, 181, 216, 444
as teenager, 38–40
temperament and, 114
Tess Gallagher and, 432, 433, 434, 434n,
473
Tess Gallagher's stewardship of work
and challenges to his will, 399, 466,
473, 482–89
themes from alcoholic years, 350
title suggestion, 21
in Tucson, productivity after meeting
Yates, 348–50
typing of, 38
as "unflinching," 429, 429n
Updike on Carver's short stories, 470
videotaped interview (1985), 434
voyeurism and exhibitionism themes,
55, 127
will revision, June 30, 1988, 477
as working writer, 62, 72, 81, 129, 165,
187
work kept from his parents, 135
writer-in-Europe fantasy, 161
at Writers' Workshop, Iowa, 98 (*see
also* University of Iowa)
on writing, 364–65
writing as vocation, xi, 117
writing trends of the 1960s and,
141–42
Yakima Valley and, 10–11
Carver, Shyloh Raymond (great-
grandchild), 487
Carver, Tillman (cousin), 14, 41
Carver, Vance Lindsay (son), 63, 89, 96, 110,
118, 122, 138, 146, 151–52, 190, 343
adolescence, 171

at American University, 410, 437
appearance, 384
in Ben Lomond, 204–5, 212
Christmas (1976), 306
in Cupertino, 221, 241–42, 258
daughter born, 437
dislocation and moving, 212
family photo, 223
father's illness and death, 467, 469, 471,
    475
father's relationship with, 195, 202,
    241–42, 248, 266–67, 286, 294, 322,
    332–33, 365–66, 376–77, 384–86,
    389, 391, 392, 410, 422, 437
father's wake and burial, 479
father's will and, 399, 473, 483–85, 486
at Foothill Community College, 316
in France, 376–77, 384–86
at Humboldt State College, 328, 332
independence and sobriety, 286, 300,
    312, 332
life following father's death, 484, 485,
    488
in Los Angeles, 167
marriage and employment in Germany,
    437, 441, 449, 455
Mediterranean cruise and European
    tour (1968), 162, 164
post-graduate studies, 422
Sunnyvale house, 185
at Syracuse University, 362–63, 365–66,
    403–4
in Tel Aviv (1968), 156–57, 158, 159, 161
in Yakima, 185
Carver, Walter (uncle), 57
Carver, Windy Michelle (grandchild), 346,
    362, 403, 428, 449, 484
Carver Country (documentary), 486
Cascade Lumber, 10, 14, 20, 41–42
Casey, Edna (aunt), 7
Casey, Katherine (grandmother), 6, 300
Casey, Sanders (uncle), 7, 300, 319, 465
Casey, William (grandfather), 6
Cassady, Neal, 150, 151, 176, 197
Cassill, R. V., 88, 89–90, 93, 98, 99–100,
    195
Catch-22 (Heller), 141
Cathedral (story collection), 362, 389, 393,
    439, 458
    author photo, 403
    Carver's promotion of, 407
    comparison of stories also in *Love*, 357,
        408
    completion of manuscript, 398
    dedication, 403
    dust jacket, 403

Harvard benefit and, 415
Knopf advance for, 383
Lish as editor, 383, 393, 398, 403
publication date, 407
Pulitzer finalist, 418
reviews, 407–8, 412
sales, 409, 423
success of, 412
Vintage Contemporaries edition, 417,
    423
"Cathedral" (story), 144, 370–72, 373, 375,
    378, 433
    in *BASS 1982*, 382
Cat's Cradle (Vonnegut), 141
Cecily, Diane, 226, 266, 284–85, 297, 302,
    308, 314, 328, 381–82
    affair with Carver, 226, 228–30,
        231–32, 234, 235, 238, 243–45, 248,
        250, 254, 387
    Carver's death and, 480
    Carver's violence and, 280
    marriage to Chuck Kinder, 279
Céline, Louis-Ferdinand, 245
Chambers, George, 323
Chandler, Raymond, 23, 452
Cheever, John, 85, 126, 177, 189, 250, 253n,
    259, 263–64, 284, 294, 308, 317, 363,
    380, 388, 409
Cheever, Susan, 258
"Chef's House" (story), 312, 321, 375, 378
Chekhov (Troyat), 451
Chekhov, Anton, 49, 76, 77, 87, 90,
    118–19, 139, 161, 179, 181, 224–25,
    251, 323, 367, 412, 467, 469, 476, 478
"Chemist's Wife, The" (Chekhov), 77
"Cherish" (poem), 473
Chester, California, 42, 48
Chicago Review, 248, 287
Chicago Tribune, 346, 367
    Carver's reminiscence of Gardner, 393
Chico State College, 60, 78, 414
Choice magazine, 122
Cimetière du Montparnasse, Paris, 385
Cimino, Michael, 393, 401, 404, 410
Cippola, Michael, 63
Clatskanie, Oregon, 3, 422–23, 441
Clockers (Price), 236
Cobain, Kurt, 38
Coburn, Jean, 305
cocaine
    Carver's use of, 347, 364, 400
    1980s and, 419
Coda, 406
Coglon, Roger, 22
Cohen, Olivier, 456–57
"Collectors" (story), 143, 281, 321, 443

College of the Redwoods, 187
Collins Pine Company, 42, 48, 64, 105–6, 109
Columbia University, 364
Coming Out of the Ice (Herman), 361
"Community Center" (story), 362
"Compartment, The" (story), 389, 390–91, 405, 410, 443, 458
Confiserie Sprüngli (chocolates), 384, 386
Connell, Evan S., 170, 179, 234, 363
Conrad, Joseph, 203
Conroy, Frank, 245, 335, 444
Coover, Robert, 142
Copyright Act of 1976, 329, 486–88
Corelli, Joann, 401
Cosmological Eye (Miller), 218
"Cougar, The" (story), 32, 61, 205
"Country Matters" (poem), 219
Covington, Dennis, 254–55, 259, 263, 454
Crawford, Max, 236, 237, 240, 247n, 265–66, 275, 288, 294, 295–96, 297, 315
Creative Writing (film), 66
Crescent City, California, 113, 133–34, 348
Crime and Punishment (Dostoyevsky), 49
Crossett-Western Timber Company, 3
Crumb, R., 236
Crumley, James, 191, 224, 225–26, 229, 288, 294, 306, 320, 347, 423, 446
Cupertino, California, 221, 221n, 224, 258, 287
    Carver's blue house, ix, 221, 223, 224, 227, 233, 258, 265–67, 273–75, 287, 302, 303
"Current, The" (poem), 181
Curtis, C. Michael, 372
Cutting Edges: Young American Fiction for the '70s (Hicks, ed.), 127, 213

Darhansoff, Liz, 355, 363, 371–72, 373
Davis, Bonna Rose "Jerry" Burk (sister-in-law), 44, 45, 47, 54, 59, 99, 294, 331, 397, 480
Davis, Buey, 12, 14, 19, 25
Davis, Daniel, 145
Davis, Larry, 22
Davis, Nevel, 12, 25
Davis, Val, 224
Day, Bonnie, 82
Day, Richard Cortez, 75, 78, 81, 82, 83, 85, 86, 89, 91, 93, 97, 99, 100, 102, 116, 172, 203, 204n, 296, 304, 320, 326, 332, 334, 342, 397, 474
Days (Robison), 351
Dear Ghosts (Gallagher), 488
Dear Mr. Capote (Lish), 402

Death of a Salesman (Miller), 179
"Death of Me, The" (Lish), 360
Death on the Installment Plan (Céline), 245
December magazine, 90, 110–11, 119, 129, 143, 144, 145, 147, 168, 176, 185, 282
Deck, John, 185, 214
DeFrees, Madeline, 226
Dekin, Tim, 297
Delacorte/Dell publishers, 440
DeLillo, Don, 214, 417
Deliverance (Dickey), 192, 193, 196
Dickey, James, 192–93, 196, 203
Didion, Joan, 174, 317
"Distance" (story), 29, 53, 55, 58–59, 71, 286, 313, 322, 348, 361, 383, 448, 458
    comparison of versions, 357
Distortions (Beattie), 351
Divine Right's Trip (Norman), 236
Dobler, Bruce, 335, 336–37, 338
Dobyns, Stephen, 323, 325, 327, 331, 433, 462, 464, 466–67, 477
    on Bad Ray stories, 327–28
Doctorow, E. L., 214, 317, 407
"Dog Story, A" (story), 169–70, 171, 182, 197
Doherty, Tom, 90, 92, 93, 95, 98, 111, 193
Doll, Louis C., 295–96
Domench, Dan, 255, 259, 260–61, 263, 266, 273–74, 365
Donoso, José, 214
"Don't Call Me by My Right Name" (Purdy), 215
Dorsey, Tommy, 57
Dostoyevsky, Fyodor, 49, 77, 83, 117–18, 124, 203, 393, 434, 455–56
Dostoevsky: A Screenplay (Carver with Gallagher), 393, 434
Doubleday books, 194, 214
Douglas, William O., 10, 34n
"Down in West Texas Town" (Gilb), 341
"Drinking While Driving" (poem), 181
"Drink Poem" or "Cheers" (poem), 302
Dubus, Andre, 105
Dudar, Helen, 412
Duffy, Eugene, 302–3, 306–7, 378
"Dummy" (story), 20, 41, 142, 313, 348
Dunlap, Lennis, 63, 66, 69–70, 100
Durrell, Lawrence, 119, 141, 161–65, 221, 243, 269, 376, 400
Dylan, Bob, 139, 173, 408

Eddy, Gary, 340, 347
Eder, Richard, 409
"Egress" (poem), 54, 57
Eisner Prize, 246

"Elephant" (story), 454, 482
    Carver reads at Elliott Bay Book Co.,
        471
Eliot, T. S., 416
"Elk Camp" (poem), 412
Elkin, Stanley, 189, 214, 259, 329, 363, 463,
    469
Elliott, George P., 189, 214, 294, 342, 345,
    355
Elliott Bay Book Co., 467, 471
Ellsberg, Daniel, 204
Elon, Amos, 156
El Yanqui (Unger), 449
Emerson, Ralph Waldo, 148, 149
Engle, Hualing, 254
Engle, Paul, 86, 88, 89, 91, 92, 103, 116, 254
English Grammar (Lish, ed.), 149–50
Entriken, Morgan, 419
Epstein, Jason, 339
Erhard, Werner, 115–16, 117–18, 119, 126,
    128, 278
"Errand" (story), 451–52, 454, 455, 456,
    470, 482
Esquire magazine, x, 88, 207
    Carver's work and, 179
    Hills requests story changes, 391
    Jenks at, 411
    Lish as fiction editor, 147, 176–78, 179,
        201n, 213, 231, 359
    as literary magazine, 188–89
    Murdoch acquires, 315
    Nabokov and Lish, 283–84
    poems by Carver in, 196
    publication of "Cheers," 302
    publication of "Collectors," 276, 281
    publication of "Intimacy," 442
    publication of "My Father's Life," 411
    publication of "Neighbors," 188, 190,
        191, 197, 201–2, 213, 272, 339
    publication of "What Is It?," 214
    publication of "Vitamins," 373
Estes, Jack, 478
est movement, 278
Ettlinger, Marion, 429, 464
Eureka, California, 74–75
Everson, William, 203, 207
"Everything Stuck to Him" (story), 361
    comparison of versions, 357
existentialism, 85, 245
Exley, Frederick, 264

Falconer (Cheever), 308
"Fat" (story), 143, 179–80, 185–86, 191,
    193, 202, 213, 231, 272
    recording of, 404
Fat City (Gardner), 150, 175

"Father, The" (story), 73, 76, 261
Faulkner, William, 71
"Fear" (poem), 286
"Feathers" (story), 168n
Felker, Clay, 315
Feminine Mystique, The (Friedan), 128
Ferlinghetti, Lawrence, 208
"Fever" (story), 47, 118, 389, 408, 440
fiction. See American fiction
Fiction magazine, 219, 242–43
Fires (collected writings), 383, 393, 406,
    458
    Carver's Afterword, 383–84
    comparison of stories also in Love, 357
    Vintage Press edition, 406, 417
"Fires" (essay), 96–97, 106, 189n, 245, 285,
    375, 377–78, 428
    Solotaroff's editing, 382
Fischer, David Hackett, xi
Fisherman's Son, The (Köepf), 236
Fisketjon, Gary L., 339, 363, 380–81, 397,
    401, 404, 406, 410–11, 419, 420, 435,
    457, 459, 468, 471, 477, 481, 484
    at Atlantic Monthly Press, 454
    Carver's induction into AAAL, 469
    as Carver's primary editor, 420, 432,
        458–59, 464
    Carver's wake and burial, 480
    Vintage Contemporaries and, 417, 423
Fitzgerald, F. Scott, 148, 188, 224, 382
Fitzgerald, Zelda, 240
"Five-Forty-Eight, The" (Cheever), 388
Flaubert, Gustave, 49
Flavin, Christine, 245, 246
"Fling, The" (story), 143, 169, 182, 313,
    348
Flook, Maria, 366
Foley, Martha, 110, 111
Foothill Community College, 138, 286
Ford, Betty, 329
Ford, Gerald, 266, 276
Ford, Kristina, 326, 425, 456
Ford, Richard, 317–19, 323, 324, 326, 330,
    337, 349, 358, 363, 366, 381, 397,
    404, 405, 425, 427, 447, 448, 456–57,
    461, 471, 472, 477, 484
    Carver's wake and burial, 479, 480
    Carver's will and, 473
"Forever" (poem), 136
Forms of Fiction (Gardner and Dunlap), 67
"For Tess" (poem), 418
Fowler, Molly, 410
Fox, Joe, 179
Fox, William Price, 250, 256
Franchiser, The (Elkin), 259
Frankenstein (Shelley), 23

Franklin Library, 458
Freund, Betsy, 191
Friedan, Betty, 128
Friedman, Bruce Jay, 189
"Friendship" (story), 177, 434
Frisch, Max, 232, 233, 245
"From the East, Light" (poem), 274–75
"Furious Seasons" (story), 29, 70–71, 78, 84, 90, 111, 313
    among "Distinctive Stories," *BASS 1964,* 110, 111
    dedication, 313
Furious Seasons (story collection), 313, 315, 316, 317, 338–39, 348, 383
    as Christmas gift to family, 321
    inscription to Maryann, 321
    reviews, 339

Gaines, Ernest, 233
Galassi, Jonathan, 420
Gallagher, Tess, 255, 317, 337, 358
    background, 400
    Carruth on Tess and Ray, 398–99
    Carver and, 336–51, 353–56, 386–87, 399, 422, 425, 433–35, 434n, 447–49, 453, 457, 459
    Carver's dedications to, 367, 403
    Carver's grave as literary shrine, 481
    Carver's illness and death, 460–78
    Carver's poems about, 418, 432
    on Carver's poetry, 413
    Carver's wake and burial, 479–82
    Carver's writing and, 368, 370–71, 433, 473
    death of her father, 388–89, 392
    editorial contribution to Carver's work, 411–12
    England, Ireland trips, 434–35, 456
    Guggenheim Fellowship, 337, 343
    health issues, 441, 457
    income from Ray's copyrights, 487
    letter to Carver, 320
    life following Ray's death, 488
    marriage to Carver, 472–73
    meets Carver, first time, 319
    People magazine profile, 448, 459
    personality and character, 366, 398
    phone call to Maryann regarding Ray's marriage, 344
    photo by Annie Leibovitz, 366
    poetry collections by, 418, 464, 479, 488
    in Port Angeles, Washington, 343, 346, 356, 388, 399–400, 405, 430, 445, 464–66, 471–72, 474–78, 479–81, 483
    posthumous Carver documentaries, collections, and movies, 486–89

    promotion of books, 447
    Rosen on, 445
    short fiction by, 433–34, 434n
    stewardship of Carver's work and challenges to his will, 399, 466, 473, 482–89
    Syracuse house, 354, 401
    Syracuse University and, 380, 393, 398, 415, 438, 448, 460, 496
    at University of Washington, 428
    at University of Zurich, 384
    Vanity Fair profile, 448–49
    Yaddo and, 371
Gambler, The (Dostoyevsky), 117–18, 455–56
Gardner, Joan, 67, 68
Gardner, John, 65–73, 74, 75, 84, 86, 90, 98, 99, 142, 185, 203, 214, 251, 363, 377, 388, 442
    appearance, 380
    Carver's friendship with, 380–81, 382
    Carver's reading at SUNY Binghamton and, 380–81
    death of, 392–93
    meeting with Carver (1981), 370
Gardner, Leonard, 150–51, 175, 284, 301, 402, 429n
    Will You Please Be Quiet, Please and, 284
Garrison, Jim, 283, 283n
Gass, William H., 142
"Gazebo" (story), 113, 228, 348, 349, 354, 361
Genesis West magazine, 149, 150
Gerber, John, 253
Getting Balled in Berkeley (Steinhardt), 203
Geyman, Matthew, 487
"Gift, The" (poem), 432
Gilb, Dagoberto, 341
Gingrich, Arnold, 177, 186, 188–89, 214
Ginsberg, Allen, 141, 148, 151, 380
Girard, Laurent, 426, 450
Gladstein, Mimi, 345
Glass Menagerie, The (Williams), 103
Glenn, Edgar, 63, 72
Goddard College, 309, 320–21, 323–25, 330, 334–35
Godfather, The (Puzo), 174
Going After Cacciato (O'Brien), 367
Going Places (Michaels), 174, 197
Gold, Herb, 149, 214
González, Ray, 340, 341
Goodbye, Columbus and Five Stories (Roth), 88
Good Man Is Hard to Find and Other Stories, A (O'Connor), 88

Good Morning . . . and Goodbye! (film), 121
Good School, A (Yates), 347
"Good Woman, A" (Purdy), 215
"Gossips, The" (Williams), 72
Gottlieb, Robert "Bob," 409, 410, 439, 454
GQ magazine, 457
Grand Coulee Dam, 8
Granta, 434, 442
    issue: *Dirty Realism*, 405
"Gravy" (poem), 460, 473, 481, 483
Gray, Josie, 488
Graywolf Press, 403
"Great Wall of China, The" (Kafka), 137
Green, Robert, 135
Greenberg, Barbara, 323
Grendel (Gardner), 65, 231, 377
Grossman, Barbara, 298
Guggenheim Fellowship
    Carver receives, 330, 332, 482
    Carver's application, 317, 328
    Richard Ford receives, 326
    Tess Gallagher receives, 337, 343
Gurganus, Allan, 255, 263, 298
Guthrie, Woody, 8, 61

Haggard, H. Rider, 23
"Hair, The" (story), 85–86
Hall, Donald, 323, 358, 378
Hall, Douglas Kent, 95
Hall, James B., 202, 203, 205, 234, 248, 257, 368
Hall of Mirrors, A (Stone), 141, 237
Halpern, Daniel, 231, 402
Hammett, Dashiell, 23
Hannah, Barry, 213, 351, 369n
Hansen, Ron, 255
Hard-Boiled Wonderland and the End of the World (Murakami), 422
Hardwick, Elizabeth, 401
"Harley's Swans" (poem), 21
Harold Matson Co., 138, 186
Harper, Michael, 317
Harper & Row, 433
Harper's Bazaar, 191, 192, 202, 213, 272
Harris, MacDonald, 142
Harris, Thomas, 174
Harrison, William, 207n
"Harry's Death" (story), 79–80
Haruf, Kent, 255
Harvard University, 415, 430
"Hat, The" (poem), 416
Hawkes, John, 142, 247
Hayes, Harold, 176–77, 186, 187, 189, 214
Hazen, Deborah Steele, 422

Heller, Joseph, 141
Helprin, Mark, 284, 332
Hemingway, Ernest, 38, 51, 52, 59, 76, 80, 101, 119, 157, 163–64, 188, 236, 339, 367, 382, 432, 439
Henderson, Michael, 298
Herman, Victor, 361
Hesse, Hermann, 141, 417
Hewitt, Celia, 94
Hicks, Jack, 124, 126, 127, 190, 213, 275, 289, 302, 455
Higinbotham, James, 45
Hillman, Brenda, 294–95
Hills, Frederic W., 272, 273, 274, 283–84, 302, 309, 310, 311, 315, 339–40
Hills, Rust, 93, 176, 177, 189, 391
"Hills Like White Elephants" (Hemingway), 52, 101
Hitchcock, George, 172, 180, 181, 187, 202, 203, 207, 346, 350
    collating parties for *kayak*, 172, 205
    NEA grant and publication of *Winter Insomnia*, 173
Hoffman, Abbie, 174
Holmes, John Clellon, 104, 116
Honeymooners: A Cautionary Tale (Kinder), 235n, 279, 285, 295–96, 382
Hoover, Marjorie, 55
Hoover, Roy, 37, 55
Houghton Mifflin, 86, 132, 138
Houston, James, 172, 205, 221, 234, 243, 250
Houston, Jeanne Wakatsuki, 172
"How About This?" (story), 81
    original title, 281
Howe, Irving, 401, 408–9
Howl (Ginsberg), 148
Hribal, C. J., 363, 380, 418
Hue and Cry (McPherson), 174
Hughes, Ted, 355, 363
Hugo, Richard, 183, 191, 207, 366
Humboldt State College, 74–86, 99, 277, 296, 315, 328
Humphrey, Hubert, 166
Humphrey, William, 346
"Hunter" (poem), 196
Hustler, The (Tevis), 88
Hyde, Lewis, 329

"I Could See the Smallest Things" (story), 348
"If It Please You" or "After the Denim" (story), 327, 348, 349, 354, 358, 368, 369
If You See Me Comin' (Mitchell), 94
Ill Nature (Williams), 92

I'm Not Stiller (Frisch), 232, 233, 245
I'm OK, You're OK (Harris), 174
Instructions to the Double (Gallagher),
    337, 345
International Raymond Carver Society,
    488
*In the Garden of the North American
    Martyrs* (Wolff), 324
"Intimacy" (story), 441, 442, 450, 482
Iowa City, Iowa, 88–89, 97–98, 104, 133
    Carver and Burks in, 332
    Carver and Cheever at Iowa House,
        251–53, 259
    Carver at Mayflower Apartments, 259
    Carver interlude (1978), 327–32
    Carver's reading tour in, 273–74
    Levine and Lish visit Carver in, 262–63
    social and sexual revolution in, 254
Iowa Review, 327, 348–49
Iowa Short Fiction Award, 215, 247
Ironweed (Kennedy), 418
Irving, John, 250, 255, 298
Israel, 153–62
    American International School, 157,
        159
    Amy Burk visits, 158–59
    Carver in International Program, Tel
        Aviv, 145, 153–62
    Carvers at Hotel Sharon, 154
    Carvers in Haifa, 158
    Carvers tour Bethlehem, Hebron, and
        Jerusalem, 157
    Ray's prejudice against Arabs, 160
    Ray's typewriter damaged, 154, 157
    Six-Day War, 132–33, 152, 153
    Tabeetha School, 159
    terrorism and war in, 154, 155–56, 160
    as third-world country, 154
"Its Course" (poem), 405

Jack London State Historic Park, 183–84
Jackson, Jon A., 191, 207, 250–52, 255,
    256, 263
Jackson State University, 184
Jarman, Mark, 207, 210–11, 217, 298, 415
Jarrell, Randall, 125
Jenks, Tom, 411, 423, 434, 440, 448
"Jerry, Molly, and Sam" (story), 112, 354
"Jewels of the Cabots" (Cheever), 253n
Jindabyne (film), 488
Job Corps, 151
John Barleycorn (London), 184, 268, 269
Johnson, Curtis L., 111, 118, 128, 137, 138,
    143–44, 147, 150, 151, 155, 166–67,
    168, 170, 174, 248, 259–60, 298,
    308–10, 419

    on Carver's celebrity, 448
    Carver's letters to, 111, 118–19, 136,
        146, 153, 158, 159, 161, 163, 164–65,
        167, 169, 171, 175, 308, 326, 341,
        353, 421
    Carver's use of summer house, 326,
        328n
    on Lish, 326
    on Ray's drinking, 152
Johnson, Denis, 255
Johnson, Diane, 461
Johnson, JoAnn, 166–67
Johnson, Lyndon B., 104, 113, 146
Jones, James Earl, 192, 193
Jones, Leroi (Amiri Baraka), 150
Joseph Henry Jackson Award, 196–97
Journal of American Fiction, 175, 176
Joyce, James, 367, 384, 435, 456
Justice, Donald, 89, 209, 298, 317, 375

Kafka, Franz, 76, 83, 137, 180, 207, 417
Kaminski, Gerald, 139, 140, 143
Kaminski, Mereda, 137, 139, 140, 143
Karr, Jay, 86
Karr, Mary, 334–35
Kaufmann, Walter, 331
kayak magazine, 172, 192, 205, 346
Kemp, Peter, 482
Kennedy, John F., 80, 96, 148
Kennedy, Robert, 146
Kennedy, William, 418
Kent State University, 184
Kerouac, Jack, 56, 148, 151
Kesey, Ken, 82, 140–41, 150, 176, 177, 197,
    214, 233, 236
Kidder, Tracy, 254, 255, 256, 258
Killer Inside Me, The (Thompson), 335
Killgore, L., 15–16
Kinder, Chuck, 234–38, 235n, 244, 246,
    256–57, 258, 265–66, 279, 284–85,
    288, 294, 295–96, 297, 301, 302, 307,
    314–15, 327, 381–82, 407–8
    Diane Cecily and, 266
    Ides of March party (1978), 328–29
    Ray's violence and, 280
    at Yaddo, and Carver's death, 477,
        478
King, Jerry, 34–35, 36, 37, 38, 40, 72, 237,
    445, 453
King, Martin Luther, 146
"King Death" (Gallagher), 433
King Solomon's Mines (film), 23, 51
Kinnell, Galway, 208, 366
"Kitchen, The" (poem), 27–28, 476
Kittredge, William, 109, 182–83, 190, 198,
    202, 203, 207, 210, 211, 225–26, 229,

231, 232, 237, 246, 247, 248, 256–57,
258, 265–66, 288, 315, 337, 346, 349,
358, 365, 403, 456–57, 459, 468, 480
Carver's letters to, 187, 196–97, 201,
218, 220
Knopf. *See* Alfred A. Knopf publishers
Köepf, Michael, 236, 237, 240–41, 392
Kolbert, Richard, 139, 140, 155, 183–84,
195
Kolbert, Sylvia, 139, 140, 183–84, 195
Korean War, 20
Kryger, King, 26n, 34–35, 37, 38, 40
Kucich, John, 206
Kulp, Irmagene, 46, 54
Kundera, Milan, ix, xi
Kurbitz, Al, 42, 52, 55
Kurbitz, Ken, 57

labor unions, 7, 20
"Lady with the Dog, The" (Chekhov), 49,
188, 478
Landris, Hope, 274
landscape
in Carver's later stories, 70
Columbia River Valley and Carver, 9,
29, 61–62
in "Furious Seasons," 29, 70
in "Its Course," 405
Lish's editing and removal from "The
Bath," 356
Pacific Northwest and Carver, 38
in "Sixty Acres," 31
in "The Sturgeon," 62
in "Wenas Ridge," 31–32
in "Where Water Comes Together with
Other Water," 61
Yakima Valley and Carver, 10, 31
Lang, Stephen, 430
Larsen, Eric, 90
Last Good Kiss, The (Crumley), 288–89
"Last Picking, The" (Gardner), 150
Last Whole Earth Catalog, The, 236
"Late Fragment" (poem), 473, 474, 480,
481
"Late Night with Fog and Horses"
(poem), 321
Lawrence, D. H., 34, 52, 71, 84, 141, 450
Leaving the Land (Unger), 320, 415n
Leavitt, David, 471
Leet, Marjorie, 402
Leggett, John, 247, 248, 250, 253, 256, 274,
298
Leibovitz, Annie, 366
"Lemonade" (poem), 466
Letters from Yellowstone (Smith), 210
Letters on Cézanne (Rilke), 447, 451

Levee newspaper, 124
Carver's contributor's note in, 124–25
Levine, Ellen, 186, 188, 193–94, 218–19,
262, 274, 306
Levine, Philip, 172, 317, 366
Liars' Club, The (Karr), 334
"Lie, The" (story), 128, 230, 313
Lish, Atticus, 214
Lish, Barbara Works, 147, 175, 176, 177,
184, 187, 214
Lish, Gordon, 143, 147–52, 170, 203, 231,
273n, 326
asks Carver for blurb, 402
asks Carver to keep tabs on former
wife, 197
as "Captain Fiction," 213, 262–63, 272
Carver and, in California, 147, 170,
174–76, 187, 402
Carver and, in New York, 184, 404
Carver breaks from, 378, 410–11
Carver's first short story collection and,
272–73, 281, 282, 294–95, 296–97
Carver's letters to, 229, 245, 247, 248,
252, 261, 270, 272, 275, 300, 301,
304, 309, 315, 316–17, 325, 338, 343,
376, 391, 393, 397, 400, 403
Carver's loyalty to, 326
on Carver's success, 409
Cathedral, editing of, 383, 393, 398,
403
editorial contribution to Carver's work,
185–87, 194n, 196, 201, 214, 215,
216, 223, 230, 261, 272, 281, 282,
339, 354–62, 368, 378, 411, 488
at *Esquire*, 176–78, 182, 185–89, 189n,
201n, 213, 214, 262, 276, 313, 406
on fiction, 359–60
ghostwriting and editorial revisions by,
283–84, 283n, 361
Halpern on, 402
idea of letting work stand on its own,
296
image of Carver cultivated by, 294
imprint at McGraw-Hill, 272
at Knopf, 316, 351, 359, 383, 401
life in New York, 214–15
papers at Indiana University, 361
photo of Ray by, 175
quits *Esquire*, 315
script of talk, 207, 207n
*What We Talk About When We Talk
About Love*, editing and versions
of, 354–62, 366–67, 372, 382, 383,
384, 403
Literary Review, 434
little magazines or "littles," 111, 146, 169

"Little Sturgeon, A" (undated typescript), 32, 301–2
Logan, John, 122
London, Jack, 183–84, 268, 269, 307
Look at the Harlequins! (Nabokov), 283–84
Looking for Mr. Goodbar (Rossner), 273
Loomis, Edward, 148
Lords of the Plain (Crawford), 236
Los Altos High School, 185, 196, 240, 269, 273, 280, 281, 315, 330
Louria, Marc, 271–72
Lourie, Richard, 197
"Lover of Horses, The" (Gallagher), 389
Lowell, Robert, 329
Lowry, Malcolm, 264
Lux, Thomas, 323
Lynn, George, 236, 238, 240, 241, 248, 265, 274

MacClean, Norman, 190n
MacLehose, Christopher, 456, 483
MacMahon, Bryan, 102–3
Madame Bovary (Flaubert), 49
Magic of Blood, The (Gilb), 299
Mahon, Derek, 437
Mailer, Norman, 141, 405
Malamud, Bernard, 149, 189
Malcolm, Janet, 224–25
"Man and Wife" (Purdy), 215
"Man Is Dangerous, The" (story), 204
Mann, Thomas, 456, 459
"Man Outside, The" (poem), 127
Man Who Died, The (Lawrence), 84
Man Who Fell to Earth, The (Tevis), 88
Marat/Sade (Weiss), 94
Marcus, Mort, 172, 205, 208, 221
marijuana
    Carver's use of, x, 120–21, 140, 147, 238, 267, 328, 335, 353, 392, 406, 422, 429, 435, 448, 454, 461, 463
    Carver's circle of friends and, 140, 147, 238, 392, 406
    in "Cathedral," 372
    at Iowa Writers' Workshop, 95
    in 1960s, 138
    in "Stupid," 438
Marks, Jeff, 110–11
"Marriage" (poem), 330
Martin, John, 269
Maryhill Museum, 61
Maslow, Abraham, 115
Mason, Bobbie Ann, 405
Matty's Heart (Hribal), 418
Maupassant, Guy de, 139, 385
Mayes, Herbert, 144

McCarriston, Linda, 325, 335
McCarthy, Cormac, 141
McClanahan, Ed, 141, 236, 241
McCullers, Carson, 256
McDowell, Robert, 210
McGinnis, Joe, 174
McGovern, George, 242
McGrath, Charles, 316, 349, 378, 414, 442, 452
McGraw-Hill Company, 272, 273, 275, 283, 302
    advance to Carver for novel, 310, 330, 339–40
    authors on list, 273
    Lish as editor, 272, 283–84
    publication of *Will You Please Be Quiet, Please,* 272–73, 281, 294–95, 310, 326
McGuane, Thomas, 174, 233, 358, 423
McInerney, Jay, 339, 364, 371, 380, 398, 399, 410, 414–15, 417, 423
McInerney, Merry, 410
McKinleyville, California, 308–10, 316, 320–21, 443
McMillan, Ian, 92–93, 98
McMurtry, Larry, 233, 236
McPherson, James Alan, 174
"Meadow, The" (poem), 135, 136
Meir, Golda, 160
"Menudo" (story), 442, 482
Meschery, Joanne, 255
Meschery, Tom, 255
"Mesopotamia" (poem), 24
Meyer, Russ, 121
Michaels, Leonard, 174, 196–97, 198, 207, 211, 219, 230, 231, 239, 240, 242, 245, 294–95, 317, 369–70, 402, 408
Mickelsson's Ghosts (Gardner), 388
Midnight Sun Writers' Conference, 355
Milford, Nancy, 224
Miller, Arthur, 142, 143, 179
Miller, Henry, 119, 141, 218, 221, 269
Miller, Warren, 324–25
Mills, Nicolaus, 419
minimalism. *See* American fiction
"Mine" (story), 313
"Miracle" (poem), 276, 277, 476
Missoula, Montana, 183, 190–91, 220, 223, 250
    Carver's "reading tour" in, 273
    Carver's summer trip (1971), 224–26
    Kittredge return (1974), 265–66
Mitchell, Adrian, 94, 95, 116
Moeller, Dick, 47, 50, 53, 56, 445
Moody, Fred, 38
Moon Crossing Bridge (Gallagher), 479

"Morning, Thinking of Empire" (poem), 160, 206
Morrison, Toni, 471
Moveable Feast, A (Hemingway), 119, 142
"Mr. Coffee and Mr. Fixit" (story), 300, 361, 367, 383
    comparison of versions, 357
Mrs. Bridge and *Mr. Bridge* (Connell), 170
"Mt. Gabriel" (Mahon), 437
Mukherjee, Bharati, 96, 128
Munro, Alice, 351
Murakami, Haruki, 421–22
Murdoch, Rupert, 315
Murray, William Cotter, 247, 331
"Music" (poem), 466
"My Boat" (poem), 420
"My Dad's Wallet" (poem), 134, 136
"My Daughter and Apple Pie" (poem), 428
"My Death" (poem), 478
Myers, David Gershom, 206, 208, 210, 211, 222
"My Father's Life" (essay), 6n, 13, 25, 27, 48, 64, 134, 411–12
My Moby Dick (Humphrey), 346
Myth of Sisyphus, The (Camus), 74

Nabokov, Vladimir, 189, 273, 283–84
Nahum, Maya, 456–57
Nation, 149
National Book Awards
    Joyce Carol Oates for *Them*, 174
    Philip Roth wins, 88
    Tim O'Brien wins, 367
    Wallace Stegner wins, 308
    Will You Please Be Quiet, Please nominated, ix, 308, 309, 360
National Defense Education Act, 65
National Endowment for the Arts (NEA)
    Carver and grant, 179, 180, 192, 215
    Discovery award, 182
    grant to Hitchcock, 173
Natural Man, The (McClanahan), 236
Navarre, Carl, 454
Near Klamath (collected poems), 144–45, 173, 180–81, 196, 476
    epigraph, 137, 152
"Near Klamath" (poem), 125, 136
"Neighbors" (story), 55, 168n, 186, 187, 188, 190, 191–92, 197, 201–2, 213, 230, 231, 244, 262, 272, 339
    Carver on, 213
Nesset, Kirk, 216
New England Quarterly, 388
New England Review
    Carver interview, 406, 406n
new fiction. *See* American fiction

New Journalism, 189
New Path to the Waterfall, A (collected poems), 473–76
    Gallagher's introduction, 476
    publication date, 476
    reviews, 476
New Sounds in American Fiction (Lish, ed.), 174
Newsweek
    Cathedral review, 407–8
    Will You Please Be Quiet, Please review, 298
New Yorker magazine, 231, 234, 316, 349, 414, 463
    "Blackbird Pie" in, 442
    Bob Gottlieb at, 454
    "Boxes" in, 441
    "The Bridle" in, 379, 391
    "Chef's House" in, 378
    "Errand" in, 452, 456
    "Gravy" in, 483
    offers Carver a first-look contract, 441
    "Where I'm Calling From" in, 379
    "Whoever Was Using This Bed" in, 441
New York Public Library
    Carver as "Literary Lion," 463
    Carver's correspondence and other publications in, 463
New York Times
    Cathedral review, 409
    named *Where I'm Calling From* a favorite book of 1988, x
New York Times Book Review
    Carver's "A Storyteller's Shoptalk," 364
    Carver's review of Hemingway biographies, 432, 439
    Carver's review of Sherwood Anderson, 418
    Cathedral review, 408–9
    What We Talk About When We Talk About Love review, 367
    Where I'm Calling From review, 469
    Will You Please Be Quiet, Please review, 297
New York Times Magazine, 416
    Carver article, 418–19
"Next Year" (poem), 268
Nickel Mountain (Gardner), 69
"Night Out, A" (story), 117, 195
    published as "Signals," 281
"Night School" (story), 112–13, 231
"Night the Mill Boss Died, The" (story), 76–77, 78, 98
nihilism, 174
Nin, Anaïs, 221

Nixon, Richard, 148, 166, 184, 204, 242, 266, 424
Nobody Knows My Name (Baldwin), 109
"Nobody Said Anything" (story), 19, 21, 22, 25–27, 143, 297, 349
recording of, 404
No Heroics, Please: Uncollected Writings (posthumous collection), 488
"No Need" (poem), 473, 474
Norman, Gurney, 236
description of Ray and Maryann, 236–37
Northwest Review, 182

Oates, Joyce Carol, 142, 174, 195, 256, 380, 469
O'Brien, John, 246–47, 285–86, 308, 320, 367, 430
Ocean View Cemetery, 481
O'Connell, George, 255
O'Connor, Flannery, 85, 88, 189, 354
O'Connor, Frank, 102
O'Connor, Robert, 379, 397
O'Faolain, Sean, 102, 435
"Offending Eel, The" (poem), 459, 468, 476
Of Men and Mountains (Douglas), 10
Of the Farm (Updike), 379–80
Oh, What a Paradise It Seems (Cheever), 388
O. Henry Prize short story annuals, 231, 234, 247, 253n, 361, 392
Ohio State University, William Charvat Collection of American Fiction, 361, 425, 444
Olliffe, Harry Leonard, 79–80
Olliffe, Sally, 79
Olsen, Tillie, 140, 150, 233
Omak, Washington, 4, 5–6, 7
"On an Old Photograph of My Son" (poem), 286, 476
Onassis, Jacqueline Kennedy, 166, 463, 464
On Becoming a Novelist (Gardner), 65, 66
Carver's foreword, 69
One Flew Over the Cuckoo's Nest (Kesey), 141
"One More Thing" (story), 286, 300, 348, 408
"1/3, 1/3, 1/3" (Brautigan), 440–41
On Moral Fiction (Gardner), 65, 380
Ontario Review, 433
"On the Pampas Tonight" (poem), 124
On the Road (Kerouac), 56, 148
On Turning Eighty (Miller), 221

"On Writing" (essay), 368, 397
originally published as "A Storyteller's Shoptalk," 364–65
Open City newspaper, 168
Orchard Keeper, The (McCarthy), 141
Ozick, Cynthia, 401, 409

Painter, Charlotte, 234, 246
"Painter and the Fish, The" (poem), 453
Paley, Grace, 149, 150, 177, 215, 402
Palmer, Charlene, 82, 134, 166
Palmer, David, 81, 82, 134, 166
Palmer Institute of Authorship, 38–40
Palo Alto, California, 137–38, 140, 143, 145, 147, 151–52. *See also* Stanford University
apartment for writing, 180
Lish and Carver's offices in, 147, 170, 402 (*see also* Science Research Associates [SRA])
party and writing scene, 236–38
Paradise, California, 386
Parents' Magazine Cultural Institute, 115, 117
Paris Review, 142, 381, 388, 399
Carver interview, 181, 201, 399, 403, 406, 406n
Carver's poetry in, 420
Parke, Nancy, 72
Partisan Review, 148, 149, 152
"Pastoral" (story), 76, 84, 313
Paul, Don, 236
Pauley, John, 84
Pavese, Cesare, 125
Pearce, Richard, 393, 394
Pelton, Claire, 185, 196
People magazine, 448, 459
Perkins, Maxwell, 382
Perkins, Ross, 294, 300, 305, 306, 317, 330, 470
Perspective magazine, 84, 169, 182, 197
Pesetsky, Bette, 361
Petrakis, Harry Mark, 367
Phillips, Jayne Anne, 351
"Photograph of My Father in His Twenty-Second Year" (poem), 134, 136
Picador publishers, 430, 434
Pictures from an Expedition (Smith), 210
Piece of My Heart, A (Ford), 318, 330
"Pie" or "A Serious Talk" (story), 348, 349
Piers, Alice, 12–13
Pieti, Hank, 15, 42
Pinsky, Robert, 233
Pinter, Harold, 463
Pleadwell, Mike, 286, 288, 302, 316, 335, 427

Plimpton, George, 142, 406n
Ploughshares, 368–69, 378, 391–92, 415
Poe, Edgar Allan, 23, 71, 369
Poem as Process, The (Swanger), 206
"Poem Not Against Songbirds, A" (poem),
    430
Poet and Critic, 219
Poetics (Aristotle), 311
Poetry magazine, 381, 382, 448
Ponti, Carlo, 393
Pope, Robert, 299, 382–83
Port Angeles, Washington, 343, 356, 388,
    401–2, 464
    cabin near Port Angeles, 346–47
    house on B Street and fishing trips, 430,
        431, 435, 438, 439, 447, 449, 450,
        454–59
    Ridge House, 459, 462, 465, 471–72,
        474, 479, 480, 481, 483
    Sky House, 399–400, 405, 407, 408, 415,
        416, 420, 430, 445
Portnoy's Complaint (Roth), 174
"Poseidon and Company" (story), 85
Pound, Ezra, 382
Pradhan, Suras V., 461–62
"Preservation" (story), 57
Pretty Leslie (Cassill), 88
Price, Richard, 236, 237
Princess of Mars, A (Burroughs), 24
Pritchett, V. S., 115, 402, 456, 457
Proctor, Thelwell, 77
"Projectile, The" (poem), 36
"Proposal" (poem), 472
"Prosser" (poem), 136
Provincetown Fine Arts Works Center,
    366
Pulitzer Prize, 418
pulp fiction, 23, 80
Purdy, James, 214, 215
Pushcart Prize: Best of the Small Presses
    (Henderson, ed.), 272
Put Yourself in My Shoes (chapbook), 252
"Put Yourself in My Shoes" (story), 40,
    118, 168n, 222–23, 247, 336, 364
Puzo, Mario, 174
Pynchon, Thomas, 141

Quarry magazine, 206–7, 208, 214
Quarterly West, 327

Rabbit Boss (Sanchez), 270, 284
Ramos, Shorty, 280
Random House, 179, 339, 420
    acquisition of *Where Water Comes
        Together with Other Water*, 420
    acquisition of *Ultramarine*, 432

Vintage Contemporaries, 417, 423
Vintage Press editions of Carver, 406,
    410, 417
Ravenel, Shannon, 425
Raymond Carver: Collected Stories, 430
"Reading" (poem), 384–86
Reagan, Ronald, 281, 352
realism. *See* American fiction
Red Cavalry (Babel), 251, 261
Redford, Robert, 190n
Reed (Burk), Alice Ritchey (mother-in-
    law), 44–45, 46, 47, 53, 60–61, 62,
    99, 112, 187, 332, 333
Reed, Clarence, 87, 332
Reflections upon a Sinking Ship (Vidal), 174
Reid, David, 242–43
Remmerde, Jon, 72
Revolutionary Road (Yates), 347
Revolution for the Hell of It (Hoffman),
    174
Rexroth, Kenneth, 208, 269
"Rhodes" (poem), 164
Richardson, Nathan, 466, 477, 478, 484
Rilke, Rainer Maria, 98–99, 447, 451
"River, The" (poem), 34n
River Runs Through It, A (film), 190, 190n
Robison, Mary, 351
Rock Island Railroad, 6
"Rock Springs" (Ford), 405
Rock Springs (Ford), 457
Rogers, Carl, 115
Rogers, Michael, 185, 236, 265–66
Rolens, Lin, 269
Roosevelt, Franklin D., 8
Rosen, Kenneth, 90, 445
Rosenberg, Liz, 370, 380, 382
Rossner, Judith, 273
Roth, Henry, 142, 176
Roth, Philip, 88, 174, 179, 401
Rubins, Josh, 409
Running Lights and *Rain* (Carlile), 420
Runyon, Randolph, 443
Rushdie, Salman, 456, 483
Ryan, Michael, 255, 309, 323, 337

Sacramento, California
    Carver and family in (1964–1967),
        109–36
    Carver's brother in, 109–10, 112, 435
    Carver's parents in, 105–6, 109–10, 112,
        389, 402, 435
Sacramento State College, 110, 122,
    123–24, 141
    Carver reads at, 455
    English Club publishes Carver poetry
        collection, 144–45

Saint Paul's School for Girls, 45–46, 54
Salinger, J. D., 149, 151, 414
Salisbury State University, 354
Sanchez, Thomas, 270
    "Writers' Stampede" party, 284
Sandberg, Hazel, 13
Sandmeyer, Frank, 28–33, 57, 64, 71
San Francisco Review, 172
San Francisco State College, 236
San Jose State College, 145, 169, 170, 171,
    184
Santogrossi, Candido, 149
Sartre, Jean-Paul, 385
Saturday Review, 144
Save the Whale (Köepf), 236
Scharlatt, Hal, 176
Schjeldahl, Peter, 419
Schlief, Rollie, 14, 15
Schmidt, Tom, 192
Schmitz, Dennis, 122–24, 125, 127, 145,
    168, 172, 180, 203, 207, 278, 330,
    342, 455, 474–75
Schmitz, Loretta, 122, 123, 168, 455, 474
"Schooldesk, The" (poem), 435
Schwamm, Ellen, 370
Science Research Associates (SRA), 129,
    137–39, 146, 168, 169, 170, 179, 180,
    182, 187, 195, 305
    includes Carver's work in textbook,
    425
    Reading Laboratory Series, 138–39
Scots-Irish, 3, 4–5
Scott Foresman publishers, 169
Scowcroft, Richard, 234
Scribner's, 119, 470
Sculpture of This Century (Seuphor), 352
Sebold, Alice, 398
Secret Life of Our Times, The (Lish, ed.),
    217, 262
See, Carolyn, 471
"Seeds" (poem), 157–58
Selected Letters (Anderson), 418
Selected Poems (Lawrence), 34
Selection magazine, 60, 72, 78
Selling of the President 1968, The
    (McGinnis), 174
Seneca Review, 247
"Sensitive Girl, The" (poem), 44
"Serious Talk, A" (story), 306
    recording of, 404
Set This House on Fire (Styron), 112
Seuphor, Michel, 352
Sexton, David, 434
Shacochis, Bob, 444–45
Shapiro, Alan, 285, 297
Shawn, William, 316, 378, 454

Shelley, Mary, 23
Shelton, Earl, 37
Shelton, Richard, 347
Shinpaugh, Neil, 35, 37, 52, 54
Short Cuts (film), 487
Short Stories from the Literary Magazines
    (Lish and Thurston, eds.), 175
Short Story Masterpieces (Carver and
    Jenks, eds.), 440
    Carver's introduction, 440
"Signals" (story), 281
Simon, Marjorie, 350
Simon & Schuster, 273, 340, 419
Simonson, Rick, 471
Simpson, Louis, 125
Simpson, Mona, 388, 399, 403, 406n, 480
Simpson Plywood Mill, 74–75
Singer, I. B., 189, 463
Sipper, Ralph, 444, 477
Sitting Pretty (Young), 197
"Sixty Acres" (story), 31, 181, 182
Skoyles, John, 255, 256, 366
Slaughterhouse-Five (Vonnegut), 141, 174
"Slouching Toward Bethlehem" (Didion),
    174
"Small, Good Thing, A" (story), 114–15,
    348, 353, 372–73, 391–92, 462
    comparison of versions, 357
    Lish's edit, 356–57, 358, 378, 392
    reprinted without changes, 378, 391–92
Smiley, Jane, 298
Smith, Annick, 190n
Smith, Diane, 208, 210, 240, 266, 273, 315,
    337
Snakehunter (Kinder), 235, 297
Snyder, Gary, 125, 141, 208, 269
Solotaroff, Theodore, 320, 336, 382,
    433–34, 483
Solotaroff, Virginia, 434
Solzhenitsyn, Aleksandr, 393
"Sometimes a Woman Can Just About
    Ruin a Man" (story), 142
"So Much Water So Close to Home"
    (story), 271–72, 313, 348, 354, 356,
    369, 383, 458
    comparison of versions, 357
    film rights, 488
    Pushcart Prize and, 272
    screenplays based on, 272
"Song of Grendel, The" (Gardner), 231
Sontag, Susan, 141
Soul Barnacles (Gallagher), 479
Southern, Terry, 189
Southern Methodist University, 317–20
Sou'wester magazine, 128
Spark, Debra, 91

"Spell" (poem), 437
Sporting Club, The (McGuane), 174
Sportsman's Notebook, A (Turgenev), 115
Standiford, Les, 336
Stanford University, 138
  Carver and Writing Workshop, 220, 233–38
  Carver reads at, 454
  Maryann Carver at, 240
  writing program, 140–41
Star-Spangled Contract, The (Garrison), 283, 283n
State of Grace (Williams), 92
Steele, José, 255
Stegner, Wallace, 88, 90, 140, 142, 308
Steinhardt, Annie, 203
Sterling, John, 306, 311, 313–14, 316, 326, 349, 353, 354, 359
"Still Life with Watermelon" (Mason), 405
Stone, Robert, 140, 141, 233, 237, 456–57, 461, 463
Stop-Time (Conroy), 245
Stories of John Cheever (Cheever), 351, 409
"Storyteller's Shoptalk, A" (essay), 364
Strand, Mark, 89, 421
Strauss, Harold and Mildred, 401
Strout, Elizabeth, 369n
"Student's Wife, The" (story), 56, 76, 77–78, 104, 111, 114, 441
  Lish's editorial work on, 282
Stull, William, 361
"Stupid" (poem), 438
"Sturgeon, The" (poem), 62
Styron, William, 112, 142, 405
Sullens, Claude, 135
Sullens, Vi, 19, 21
"Summer in Sacramento, A" (poem), 118
"Summer Steelhead, The" (story), 247, 260
Sun Also Rises, The (Hemingway), 382
Sunlight Dialogues, The (Gardner), 65
SUNY Binghamton, 370, 380–81, 382, 393
SUNY Upstate Medical Center, 460
"Suspenders" (poem), 18, 453, 476
Swander, Mary, 255, 256
Swanger, David, 206, 332
Swanger, Lynn, 206
Syracuse University, 342, 345, 351, 352–53, 370–71
  Carver leave of absence, 400
  Carver resigns, 401
  Carver's salary, 379
  Carver teaching at, 352–70, 379–92, 398
  guest writers, 380
  Jay McInerney at, 380, 398, 424

tenure review for Gallagher, Wolff, and Carver, 393
Tess Gallagher and, 380, 393, 398, 415, 438, 448, 459, 460, 486
Tobias Wolff at, 415n
Unger replaces Carver, 401, 407, 410, 415n

Tallent, Elizabeth, 434
Targets magazine, 84
Tel Aviv. See Israel
"Tel Aviv and Life on the Mississippi" (poem), 159–60
Tell Me a Story (NPR series), 402
"Tell the Women We're Going" (story), 36, 54, 168n, 368, 369, 408
Temko, Alan, 150
Tevis, Walter, 88
Theiner, Paul, 398
Them (Oates), 174
"The Trestle" (poem), 16
"They're Not Your Husband" (story), 193–94, 230, 231, 247–48
  Lish's edit, 283
This Boy's Life (Wolff), 464, 468
"This Word Love" (poem), 219–20
Thomas, Dylan, 148, 265
Thompson, Bob, 131–32, 136
Thompson, Gary, 122, 124, 127, 131–32, 137, 145, 212, 219, 224, 225–26
Thompson, Jim, 335
Thornton, Susan, 382
"Through the Boughs" (poem), 473
Thunder LaBoom (Steinhardt), 203
Thurston, Jarvis, 84, 169, 175, 182, 192, 275
Time Out of Mind (Michaels), 239
Titmuss, Allan, 434
Tolstoy, Leo, 49, 77, 414
"To My Daughter" (poem), 428
Tower, Robert, 368
Town Burning (Williams), 88
Toyon student magazine, 78, 85–86
"Train, The" (story), 388
Transatlantic Review, 192
TriQuarterly, 349, 354, 361
Trout Fishing in America (Brautigan), 141, 237
"Trying to Sleep Late on a Saturday Morning in November" (poem), 125
Tuck, Lily, 369n
Tucson, Arizona, 346–51
Turgenev, Ivan, 115
Turow, Scott, 235, 236, 279
"Turpentine" (Gallagher), 433
Twain, Mark, 159
Twitchell, Chase, 298

Ultramarine (collected poems), 432,
    437–38
  promotion of, 447
  sales, 449
Unbearable Lightness of Being, The
    (Kundera), ix
Under Stars (Gallagher), 337
Unger, Amy Burk (sister-in-law), 45, 46,
    50, 54, 60, 99, 109, 113, 179, 258,
    274, 294, 306, 312, 399
  abuse by mother's husband, 45, 192–93
  acting career, 167–68, 184, 192, 193,
    275, 320
  belief in Ray's talent, 168
  bipolar disorder, 275
  Carver's alcoholism and, 307, 308, 309,
    365
  Carver's illness and death, 461, 462, 475
  Carver's induction into AAAL, 469–70
  Carver's letter about family, 426, 427
  Carver's reading in Iowa City and,
    298–300
  Carver's success and, 410
  Christmas (1975), 287–88
  at Cupertino house, 224, 228
  daughter Erin born, 120
  George Hitchcock and, 172
  at Humboldt State College, 81
  in Iowa City with the Carvers (1978),
    331
  James Dickey and, 192–93, 196
  manic episodes, 170, 218, 306, 439
  marriage to Douglas Unger, 287–88,
    362
  marriage to Michael Wright, 120–21,
    132, 167, 170
  MFA from Iowa, 302
  murder of Harry Olliffe and, 79–80
  NYC apartment, 326
  in San Francisco, 302
  on Tess Gallagher, 407, 427
  trip to Israel, 158–59
  at Whatcom Community College, 343
Unger, Douglas, 287–88, 297–99, 302, 303,
    305–9, 312–14, 316, 317, 320, 326,
    331, 332, 333, 343, 362, 365, 449
  on the Carver divorce, 387
  Carver's illness and death, 462, 469,
    470, 475
  Carver's induction into AAAL,
    469–70
  Carver's memorial service and, 483
  Carver's wake and burial, 480
  on Carver's writing, 409
  Carver urges Syracuse to hire, 401
  drinking by, 464

  first novel, 415n
  marriage to Amy Burk, 287–88, 362
  on McInerney's success, 424
  screen treatment of Carver's stories,
    393–94
  Syracuse University and, 407, 410
  on Tess Gallagher, 407
Unger, Maurice, 306
Unger, Steve, 299, 306, 326, 464
University of Akron, 382, 383
University of Arizona, 148
University of California, Berkeley, 211,
    220, 233, 243, 245–47
University of California, Davis, 109, 190,
    275, 455
University of California, Santa Barbara,
    184
  Carver teaching at, 268–71
  Spectrum student magazine, 269,
    271–72
University of California, Santa Cruz, 173,
    180, 202, 203–17, 220, 243, 248,
    256–57, 333
  Carver and literary magazine, *Quarry*,
    206–7
  visiting poets, 207–9
University of Hartford, 469
University of Iowa
  Carver in library science program,
    132–33, 169
  Carver in Writer's Workshop, 86,
    87–106, 114, 116, 117, 132, 193, 212,
    231
  Carver reading at, 298–300, 330
  Carver's influence on young writers,
    299
  Carver teaching graduate fiction
    workshop, 247, 248–49, 250–63
  famous writers and, 255
  fiction faculty (1973), 250, 259
  International Writers' Workshop, 91,
    254
  MFA program, 86, 212
  Writers' Workshop, 87, 88, 335, 341
  Writers' Workshop reunion (1986),
    444–45
University of Montana, 183, 211–12, 217,
    219, 273
University of Pittsburgh, 381–82
University of Texas, El Paso (UTEP), 320,
    325, 330, 335, 336–46
University of Washington, Seattle, 428
University of Wisconsin, Milwaukee, 373
University of Zurich, 384
Updike, John, 126, 379–80, 405, 469, 470,
    483, 488

Urban, Amanda, 381, 383, 404, 454, 464, 469, 472, 486
  Carver's wake and burial, 480
Us He Devours (Hall), 203

Vachon, Bob, 51–52
"Vandals" (story), 168n
Van Eaton, Ben, 37
Vanity Fair, 448
Vaughn, Samuel, 194
Victor, Thomas, 367
Vidal, Gore, 174
Vietnam War, 104, 111, 113, 124, 144, 146, 166, 173–74, 184, 204, 242, 276, 299
"Viewfinder" (story), 313, 321, 327
Violated, The (Bourjaily), 63, 89
"Vitamins" (story), 363–64, 373, 433
Vogan, Sara, 266, 315, 373–74
Voigt, Ellen Bryant, 309, 320–21, 323, 324, 330, 334
Vonnegut, Kurt, 141, 174

Wagner, Robert L., 206
"Waitress" (story), 19
"Wake" (Gallagher), 479
Wali, Kameshwar, 461, 463, 474, 483
Wali, Kashi, 474
Wallace, David Foster, 242
Wallace Stegner Fellowship, 215, 220, 221, 232, 236, 237, 247, 248, 265, 300
  famous recipients, 233
Waltz Across Texas (Crawford), 236, 275
Wapshot Chronicle, The (Kidder), 258
Ward, Brendan, 298, 299, 326
Ward No. 6 (Chekhov), 469
Washington State, 6, 38
  peculiar anomie of residents, 38
"Waterfowl Tree, The" (Kittredge), 183
Waters, Michael, 255, 258, 354
Watts, Alan, 115
Wauna, Oregon, 3
Weber, Bruce, 416
Weddle, Robert, 41
Weesner, Ted, 93, 105, 231
Weigl, Bruce, 328
Weiss, Peter, 94
Welch, James, 191, 207, 224, 225–26, 397
Welch, Lois, 273, 397
Welty, Eudora, 85, 177, 256
"Wenas Ridge" (poem), 31–32
"Wes Hardin: From a Photograph" (poem), 139
Western Michigan University, 116
Western Washington State University, 458
Whatcom Community College, 343, 437

"What Is It?" (story), 215–17, 218, 219, 231, 234, 247, 253n, 262, 430
What It Used to Be Like: A Portrait of My Marriage to Raymond Carver (M. Carver), 47, 227, 273, 487
"What's in Alaska?" (story), 168n, 192, 355
"What the Doctor Said" (poem), 472
"What We Talk About When We Talk About Love" (story), 168n, 304, 304n, 345, 348, 358
  comparison of versions, 357
What We Talk About When We Talk About Love (story collection), 300, 372, 420, 458
  blurbs for, 363
  Darhansoff as agent of record, 381
  dust jacket, 366–67
  reviews, 367–68, 369–70
  sales, 370, 417
  versions A, B, C, and Lish's editing, 354–62, 368, 425
  Vintage Press edition, 363, 370, 381, 417
"What Would You Like to See?" (story), 168n, 321–22
"What You Need for Painting" (poem), 438
Where I'm Calling From (selected stories), 454, 458–59, 460–61
  Carver's editing of proofs, 462
  comparison of stories also in *Love*, 357
  earnings, 483
  epigraph, ix, xi
  Ettlinger photograph, 464
  Franklin Library edition, 458, 465, 468
  inscription to Maryann, 468
  in Japan, 421
  New York Times favorite book of 1988, x
  promotion of, 470–71
  Quality Paperback and BOMC editions, 465–66
  reviews, 469
"Where I'm Calling From" (story), 144, 303, 305, 306, 307, 378–79, 398, 433
  in *BASS of the Century*, 488
"Where Is Everyone?" (story), 300, 348, 349, 358, 383
  comparison of versions, 357
"Where They'd Lived" (story), 429
"Where Water Comes Together with Other Water" (poem), 61, 263, 405
Where Water Comes Together with Other Water (poetry collection), 418, 420
  author photo, 429
  poems about his daughter, 428–29
  promotion of, 430–31
  publication date, 429

"Whoever Was Using This Bed" (story),
      441–42, 455
Who's Afraid of Virginia Woolf? (Albee),
      127
"Why Don't You Dance?" (story), 168n,
      313, 316, 321, 327, 354
   Carver reads at ABA convention, 471
Why Work (Lish, ed.), 151
Wiggins, Marianne, 456
Wiley, Richard, 298
Williams, Joy, 92, 93–94, 95, 190, 247, 248
Williams, Tennessee, 103
Williams, Thomas, 88
Williams, William Carlos, 60, 72, 85, 414
Willingly (Gallagher), 418
"Will You Please Be Quiet, Please?"
      (story), 75, 82, 100–102, 103, 104,
      146, 147, 182, 216
   in *BASS 1967,* 132, 142–43
   Lish's editorial work on, 282–83
Will You Please Be Quiet, Please (story
      collection), ix, x, 119, 194n, 223,
      274, 281, 282, 300, 306, 341, 345,
      348, 429n, 458
   author readings, 298–300
   blurbs for, 284
   Carver's readings, 297
   dedication, 281, 367
   Lish's editorial description, 296
   Lish's editorial work on, 282–83
   Lish's support for, 297
   Newsweek review, 298
   NYTBR review, 297
   PW review, 294
   trade paperback, 326
Wilson, Bill, 331
Wilson, Lois, 331–32
Wilson, S. Clay, 236, 288, 297
"Windows of the Summer Vacation
      Houses, The" (poem), 43
Winter Insomnia (collected poems), 173,
      180–81, 190, 476
"Winter Insomnia" (poem), 181
Wolfe, Tom, 189, 262, 382
Wolff, Catherine, 342
Wolff, Geoffrey, 297, 317, 323, 324, 329,
      358, 456–57
Wolff, Tobias, 323, 324, 329, 342, 350, 353,
      358, 363, 372, 393, 402, 404, 405,
      415, 431, 439, 464, 467–68, 480
   Carver's will and, 399, 473
"Woman Bathing" (poem), 55
"Woman Who Rode Away, The"
      (Lawrence), 52

Wonder Boys (film), 382
Wood, Michael, 367
World of Apples, The (Cheever), 252
World War II, 10, 18–19
Wright, Charles, 421
Wright, Erin, 120, 158, 167, 170, 172, 196,
      224, 228, 258, 287, 298, 306, 320,
      410
Wright, Michael Patrick, 120–21, 132, 167,
      168, 170

Yaddo artists' colony, 294, 298, 299, 303n,
      317, 328, 371, 374–75, 377, 477
   Carver on board of, 403
Yakama Indian Reservation, 30–31
Yakima *Daily Republic,* 38, 54
Yakima, Washington, 10–11, 190
   Adams School, 12
   Carvers and Burks in, 9–50, 170–71,
      185, 224, 392, 422
   Carver's class reunion (1986), 445
   Carver's youth in, 9–47, 264
   C. R. Carver buried in, 134–35
   fruit business in, 13, 19
   impact on Ray, 181
   Jefferson School, 13, 15
   Maryann Burk in, 43, 46
   Raymond Carver's jobs in, 41
   Vance Carver in, 300
   Washington Junior High School, 20,
      21, 23
   William O. Douglas on, 10
   women working in, 18–19
   Yakima High School, 10, 34–38, 34n,
      42
Yates, Richard, 105, 347–48, 363
Yoke, Willard L., 16
"You Don't Know What Love Is (an
      evening with Charles Bukowski)"
      (poem), 209–10
Young, Al, 197, 234, 373, 402, 454–55
Young, Jim, 124, 137
Young, Noel, 221–22, 249, 252, 269, 309,
      313, 393
"Young Fire Eaters of Mexico City, The"
      (poem), 346
"Your Dog Dies" (poem), 219
"You Will Come Again, Won't You?"
      (story), 185

Zelda (Milford), 224
Zepezauer, Frank, 190
Zigal, Tom, 236, 238, 239
Zorb, Hedwig, 54

ANATOMICAL CHART COMPANY

ATLAS of PATHOPHYSIOLOGY

THIRD EDITION

ANATOMICAL CHART COMPANY

ATLAS of PATHOPHYSIOLOGY

THIRD EDITION

 Wolters Kluwer | Lippincott Williams & Wilkins
Health

Philadelphia • Baltimore • New York • London
Buenos Aires • Hong Kong • Sydney • Tokyo

Staff

Executive Publisher
Judith A. Schilling McCann, RN, MSN

Clinical Director
Joan M. Robinson, RN, MSN

Art Director
Elaine Kasmer

Editorial Project Manager
Deborah Grandinetti

Clinical Project Manager
Beverly Ann Tscheschlog, RN, MS

Editors
Margaret Eckman, Diane Labus, Gale Thompson

Clinical Editor
Anita Lockhart, RN, MSN

Copy Editor
Karen Comerford

Design Assistant
Kate Zulak

Illustrators
Anatomical Chart Company: Dawn Gorski, Marguerite Aitken, Diane Abeloff, Liana Bauman, Ernie Beck, Michael Carroll, Carl Clingman, Birck Cox, Ruth Daly, Leonard Dank, Brian Evans, Robert Fletcher, Claudia Grosz, Fred Harwin, Tonya Hines, William Jacobson, Keith Kasnot, Jeanne Koelling, Lik Kwong, Mark Lefkowitz, Noah Lowenthal, Lena Lyons, Kimberly Martins, Marcelo Oliver, David Rini, Linda Warren, William Westwood, Christine Young, Bot Roda, Jacalyn B. Facciolo

Associate Manufacturing Manager
Beth J. Welsh

Editorial Assistants
Karen J. Kirk, Jeri O'Shea, Linda K. Ruhf

AP3E010609-071214

Library of Congress Cataloging-in-Publication Data
Atlas of pathophysiology.—3rd ed.
    p. ; cm.
    Includes bibliographical references and index.
    ISBN 978-1-60547-152-5 (alk. paper)
  1. Physiology, Pathological—Atlases.   I. Lippincott Williams & Wilkins.
II. Title: Pathophysiology.
   [DNLM: 1. Pathology—Atlases. 2. Physiology—Atlases. QZ 17
A880398 2010]
   RB113.A87 2010
   616.07022′2—dc22
                         2009004793

CONTENTS

Contributors and consultants   *vi*

Foreword   *vii*

PART I   **CENTRAL CONCEPTS**   **1**

CELLS, HOMEOSTASIS, AND DISEASE   2
CANCER   6
INFECTION   13
GENETICS   21
FLUIDS AND ELECTROLYTES   28

PART II   **DISORDERS**   **37**

CARDIOVASCULAR DISORDERS   38
RESPIRATORY DISORDERS   80
NEUROLOGIC DISORDERS   118
GASTROINTESTINAL DISORDERS   160
MUSCULOSKELETAL DISORDERS   218
HEMATOLOGIC DISORDERS   246
IMMUNOLOGIC DISORDERS   266
ENDOCRINE DISORDERS   280
REPRODUCTIVE DISORDERS   304
RENAL DISORDERS   356
SKIN DISORDERS   380
SENSORY DISORDERS   406

APPENDIX   **431**

TYPES OF CARDIAC ARRHYTHMIAS   432

Glossary   *436*

Selected references   *443*

Index   *444*

Contributors and consultants

Marsha L. Conroy, RN, BA, MSN, APN
Nurse Educator
Chamberlain College of Nursing
Columbus, Ohio

Kim R. Davis, RN, MSN
Nurse Manager, MICU and SICU
Ralph H. Johnson VA Medical Center
Charleston, S.C.

Jennifer L. Embree, RN, MSN, CCRN, CCNS, CNABC
Chief Clinical Officer
Dunn Memorial Hospital
Bedford, Ind.
Faculty
Indiana University School of Nursing–IUPUI
Indianapolis

Bernadette Madara, EdD, APRN, BC
Professor of Nursing
Southern Connecticut State University
New Haven

Phyllis Magaletto, RN, MS, APRN, BC
Instructor of Medical-Surgical Nursing
Cochran School of Nursing
Yonkers, N.Y.

Richard R. Roach, MD, FACP
Assistant Professor of Internal Medicine
Kalamazoo Center for Medical Studies
Michigan State University
Kalamazoo

Barbara L. Sauls, EdD, PA-C
Clinical Professor
Department of Physician Assistant Studies
King's College
Wilkes-Barre, Pa.

Donna Scemons, MSN, MA, PhD(C), FNP-BC, CNS
President
Healthcare Systems, Inc.
Castaic, Calif.

Qiang Shen, MD, PhD
Postdoctoral Scientist
University of California, Davis Medical Center
Sacramento

Deborah Skoruppa, RN, MSN, NP-C
Assistant Professor
Del Mar College
Corpus Christi, Tex.

Jennifer K. Sofie, MSN, FNP, ANP
Assistant Adjunct Professor
Montana State University
Bozeman

Allison J. Terry, RN, MSN, PhD
Director — Center for Nursing
Alabama Board of Nursing
Montgomery

Daniel T. Vetrosky, PA-C, MEd, PhD(C)
Assistant Professor
University of South Alabama
Mobile

Sarah Yuan, MD, PhD
Professor and Director of Research
University of California, Davis Medical Center
Sacramento

FOREWORD

Students seeking to probe and master the secrets of the human organism need to be well versed in many fields before they can begin to understand the marvelous physiologic workings of the body. Likewise, students must also study myriad malfunctions before actually becoming a participant in the healing arts. *Atlas of Pathophysiology,* Third Edition, offers a broad overview of pathophysiology while providing sufficient detail to help the learner understand the principles involved. The atlas format adds the power of visual representation to further enhance learning.

Because every discipline involves a unique language, the opening chapters provide a concise review of the vocabulary of pathophysiology. Part I, "Central concepts," lists and explains the key terms used in the basic disciplines of cancer, infection, genetics, and fluid and electrolyte disorders. Provided in a tabular format, these lists elegantly summarize concepts that students and instructors can reference while building a fundamental knowledge base. The chapter on infectious diseases condenses information on the pathophysiology of over 30 infections, ranging from bacterial to viral to protozoal. The chapter on genetics explores twelve common genetic disorders. The final chapter on concepts clearly explains fluid, electrolyte, and acid-base disorders.

In Part II, wonderful, full-color illustrations make this volume stand out. The illustrations review essential anatomical structures, vividly depict the changes caused by disease, illuminate pertinent pathology, and clarify and simplify difficult to understand terms. Obviously, visual learners will appreciate and remember the elegant drawings.

The team of authors has drawn on their depth of experience in patient care and teaching medical professionals to compile an impressive array of topics. The 12 chapters encompass all the major organ systems of the body, covering an array of conditions that specifically address the concerns of neonates, surgical patients, orthopedics, and the broad field of internal medicine. The book covers nearly 200 conditions, each presented with concisely written text and accompanied by a clinically accurate, brilliant illustrations.

Building on the success of previous editions, this third edition not only updates the information from previous editions, including the latest reported medical treatments and lists of related complications, but also covers eight new commonly encountered disorders—achalasia, intestinal obstruction, neurogenic bladder, oral cancer, contact dermatitis, corneal ulcers, ectropion and entropion, and ocular melanoma.

Atlas of Pathophysiology, Third Edition, fills the need for a factual text for students and a valuable reference for practitioners already providing patient care. Its illustrations can easily be shared with patients as an aid to understanding their disorders. The contributors and consultants are to be commended for their vision and the success of their labor.

Dale Bieber, MD, MS
Associate Clinical Professor
University of Iowa
Iowa City

PART I

CENTRAL CONCEPTS

CELLS, HOMEOSTASIS, AND DISEASE

The cell is the smallest living component of a living organism. Organisms can be made up of a single cell, such as bacteria, or billions of cells, such as human beings. In large organisms, highly specialized cells that perform a common function are organized into tissue. Tissues, in turn, form organs, which are integrated into body systems.

CELL COMPONENTS

Cells are complex organizations of specialized components, each component having its own specific function. The largest components of a normal cell are the cytoplasm, the nucleus, and the cell membrane. (See *Cell components.*)

Cytoplasm

The cytoplasm consists primarily of a fluid in which the tiny structures that perform the necessary functions to maintain the life of the cell are suspended. These tiny structures, called *organelles,* are the cell's metabolic machinery. Each performs a specific function to maintain the life of the cell. Organelles include:

• *mitochondria* — spherical or rod-shaped structures that are the sites of cellular respiration — the metabolic use of oxygen to produce energy, carbon dioxide, and water (They produce most of the body's adenosine triphosphate, which contains high-energy phosphate chemical bonds that fuel many cellular activities.)

• *ribosomes* — the sites of protein synthesis

• *endoplasmic reticulum* — an extensive network of two varieties of membrane-enclosed tubules: rough endoplasmic reticulum, which is covered with ribosomes; and smooth endoplasmic reticulum, which contains enzymes that synthesize lipids

• *Golgi apparatus* — synthesizes carbohydrate molecules that combine with protein produced by the rough endoplasmic reticulum and lipids produced by the smooth endoplasmic reticulum to form such products as lipoproteins, glycoproteins, and enzymes

• *lysosomes* — digest nutrients as well as foreign, obsolete, or damaged material in cells (A membrane surrounding each lysosome separates its digestive enzymes from the rest of the cytoplasm. The enzymes digest nutrient matter brought into the cell by means of endocytosis, in which a portion of the cell membrane surrounds and engulfs matter to form a membrane-bound intracellular vesicle. The membrane of the lysosome fuses with the membrane of the vesicle surrounding the endocytosed material. The lysosomal enzymes then digest the engulfed material. Lysosomes digest the foreign matter ingested by white blood cells [WBCs] by a similar process, *phagocytosis.*)

• *peroxisomes* — contain oxidases, enzymes that chemically reduce oxygen to hydrogen peroxide and hydrogen peroxide to water

• *cytoskeletal elements* — a network of protein structures that maintain the cell's shape and enable cell division and migration

• *centrosomes* — contain centrioles, short cylinders adjacent to the nucleus that take part in cell division

• *microfilaments and microtubules* — enable movement of intracellular vesicles (allowing axons to transport neurotransmitters) and formation of the mitotic spindle, the framework for cell division.

Nucleus

The cell's control center is the nucleus, which plays a role in cell growth, metabolism, and reproduction. Within the nucleus, one or more nucleoli (dark-staining intranuclear structures) synthesize ribonucleic acid (RNA), a complex polynucleotide that controls protein synthesis. The nucleus also stores deoxyribonucleic acid (DNA), the double helix that carries genetic material and is responsible for cellular reproduction or division.

Cell membrane

The semipermeable cell membrane forms the cell's external boundary, separating it from other cells and from the external environment. The cell membrane consists of a double layer of phospholipids with protein molecules embedded in it. These protein molecules act as receptors, ion channels, or carriers for specific substances.

CELL DIVISION

Each cell must replicate itself for life to continue. Cells replicate by division in one of two ways: mitosis (produces two daughter cells with the same DNA and chromosome content as the mother cell) or meiosis (produces four gametocytes, each containing half the number of chromosomes of the original cell). Most cells divide by mitosis; meiosis occurs only in reproductive cells. Some cells, such as nerve and muscle cells, typically lose their ability to reproduce after birth.

CELL FUNCTIONS

In the human body, most cells are specialized to perform one function. Respiration and reproduction occur in all cells. The specialized functions include:

• *movement* — the result of coordinated action of nerve and muscle cells to change the position of a specific body part, contents within an organ, or the entire organism

• *conduction* — the transmission of a stimulus, such as a nerve impulse, heat, or sound wave, from one body part to another

• *absorption* — movement of substances through a cell membrane (for example, nutrients are absorbed and transported ultimately to be used as energy sources or as building blocks to form or repair structural and functional cellular components)

• *secretion* — release of substances that act in another part of the body

• *excretion* — release of waste products generated by normal metabolic processes.

CELL TYPES

Each of the following four types of tissue consists of several specialized cell types, which perform specific functions.

- *Epithelial cells* line most of the internal and external surfaces of the body. Their functions include support, protection, absorption, excretion, and secretion.
- *Connective tissue cells* are present in skin, bones and joints, artery walls, fascia, and body fat. Their major functions are protection, metabolism, support, temperature maintenance, and elasticity.
- *Nerve cells* comprise the nervous system and are classified as neurons or neuroglial cells. Neurons perform these functions:
  - generating electrical impulses
  - conducting electrical impulses
  - influencing other neurons, muscle cells, and cells of glands by transmitting impulses.

  Neuroglial cells support, nourish, and protect the neurons. The four types include:
  - *oligodendroglia* — produce myelin within the central nervous system (CNS)
  - *astrocytes* — provide essential nutrients to neurons and assist neurons in maintaining the proper bioelectrical potentials for impulse conduction and synaptic transmission
  - *ependymal cells* — involved in the production of cerebrospinal fluid
  - *microglia* — ingest and digest tissue debris when nervous tissue is damaged.
- *Muscle cells* contract to produce movement or tension. The three types include:
  - *skeletal (striated) muscle cells* — extend along the entire length of skeletal muscles. These cells cause voluntary movement by contracting or relaxing together in a specific muscle. Contraction shortens the muscle; relaxation permits the muscle to return to its resting length.
  - *smooth (nonstriated) muscle cells* — present in the walls of hollow internal organs, blood vessels, and bronchioles. By involuntarily contracting and relaxing, these cells change the luminal diameter of the hollow structure and thereby move substances through the organ.
  - *striated cardiac muscle cells* — branch out across the smooth muscle of the chambers of the heart and contract involuntarily. They produce and transmit cardiac action potentials, which cause cardiac muscle cells to contract.

AGE ALERT
In older adults, skeletal muscle cells become smaller and many are replaced by fibrous connective tissue. The result is loss of muscle strength and mass.

PATHOPHYSIOLOGIC CONCEPTS
The cell faces a number of challenges through its life. Stressors, changes in the body's health, disease, and other extrinsic and intrinsic factors can alter the cell's normal functioning.

Adaptation
Cells generally continue functioning despite changing conditions or stressors. However, severe or prolonged stress or changes may injure or destroy cells. When cell integrity is threatened, the cell reacts by drawing on its reserves to keep functioning, by adaptive changes, or by cellular dysfunction. If cellular reserve is insufficient, the cell dies. If enough cellular reserve is available and the body doesn't detect abnormalities, the cell adapts by atrophy, hypertrophy, hyperplasia, metaplasia, or dysplasia. (See *Adaptive cell changes,* page 4.)

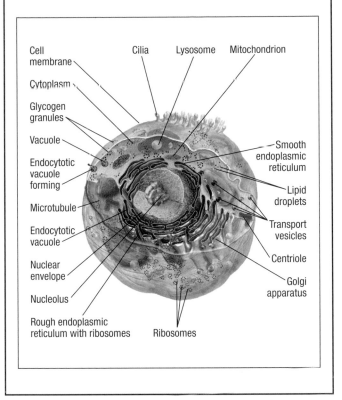

CELL COMPONENTS

Atrophy
Atrophy is a reversible reduction in the size of a cell or organ due to disuse, insufficient blood flow, malnutrition, denervation, or reduced endocrine stimulation. An example is loss of muscle mass after prolonged bed rest.

Hypertrophy
Hypertrophy is an increase in the size of a cell or organ due to an increase in workload. It may result from normal physiologic conditions or abnormal pathologic conditions. Types include:
- *physiologic hypertrophy* — reflects an increase in workload that isn't caused by disease (for example, the increase in muscle size caused by hard physical labor or weight training)
- *pathologic hypertrophy* — an adaptive or compensatory response to disease; for example, an adaptive response is thickening of heart muscle as it pumps against increasing resistance in patients with hypertension. An example of a compensatory response is when one kidney enlarges if the other isn't functioning or present.

Hyperplasia
Hyperplasia is an increase in the number of cells caused by increased workload, hormonal stimulation, or decreased tissue. Hypertrophy and hyperplasia may occur together and are commonly triggered by the same mechanism. Hyperplasia may be *physiologic, compensatory,* or *pathologic.*
- *Physiologic hyperplasia* is an adaptive response to normal changes — for example, monthly increase in the number of uterine cells in response to estrogen stimulation after ovulation.

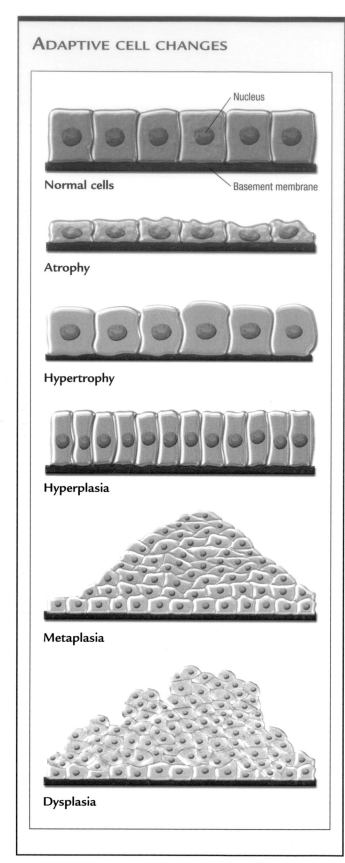

Normal cells

Nucleus

Basement membrane

Atrophy

Hypertrophy

Hyperplasia

Metaplasia

Dysplasia

factors — for example, acromegaly, in which excessive growth hormone production causes bones to enlarge.

Metaplasia

Metaplasia is the replacement of one mature cell type with another differentiated cell type that can better endure the change or stressor. It's usually a response to chronic inflammation or irritation.

- *Physiologic metaplasia* is a normal response to changing conditions and is generally transient. For example, in the body's normal response to inflammation, monocytes migrate to inflamed tissues and transform into macrophages.
- *Pathologic metaplasia* is a response to an extrinsic toxin or stressor and is generally irreversible. For example, after years of exposure to cigarette smoke, stratified squamous epithelial cells replace the normal ciliated columnar epithelial cells of the bronchi. Although the new cells can better withstand smoke, they don't secrete mucus or have cilia to protect the airway. If exposure to cigarette smoke continues, the squamous cells can become cancerous.

Dysplasia

In dysplasia, deranged cell growth of specific tissue results in abnormal size, shape, and appearance. Although dysplastic cell changes are adaptive and potentially reversible, they can precede cancerous changes. Common examples include dysplasia of epithelial cells of the cervix or the respiratory tract.

Cell injury

Injury to any cellular component can lead to disease as the cells lose their ability to adapt. Cell injury may result from any of several intrinsic or extrinsic causes:

- *toxins* — may be endogenous or exogenous (common endogenous toxins include products of genetically determined metabolic errors and hypersensitivity reactions; exogenous toxins include alcohol, lead, carbon monoxide, and drugs that alter cellular function)
- *infection* — may be caused by viruses, fungi, protozoa, or bacteria
- *physical injury* — disruption of a cell's structure or the relationships among the organelles (for example, two types of physical injury are thermal and mechanical)
- *deficit injury* — loss of normal cellular metabolism caused by inadequate water, oxygen, or nutrients.

 CLINICAL TIP
Oxygen deficiency is the most common cause of irreversible cell injury and cell death.

Injury becomes irreversible when the cell membrane or the organelles can no longer function.

Cell degeneration

Degeneration is a type of sublethal cell damage that generally occurs in the cytoplasm and doesn't affect the nucleus. Degeneration usually affects organs with metabolically active cells, such as the liver, heart, and kidneys. When changes in cells are identified, prompt health care can slow degeneration and prevent cell death. Unfortunately, many cell changes are unidentifiable, even with the use of a microscope, and early detection of disease is then impossible. Examples of reversible degenerative changes are cervical dysplasia and fatty changes in the liver. Examples of irreversible degenerative diseases include Huntington's chorea and amyotrophic lateral sclerosis.

- *Compensatory hyperplasia* occurs in some organs to replace tissue that has been removed or destroyed — for example, regeneration of liver cells when part of the liver is surgically removed.
- *Pathologic hyperplasia* is a response to either excessive hormonal stimulation or abnormal production of hormonal growth

Cell aging

During the normal process of aging, cells lose both structure and function. Atrophy may reflect loss of cell structure, hypertrophy or hyperplasia, or lost function. Signs of aging occur in all body systems. Aging can proceed at different rates depending on the number and extent of injuries and the amount of wear and tear on the cell.

Cell death

Cell death may be caused by internal (intrinsic) factors that limit the cell's life span or external (extrinsic) factors that contribute to cell damage and aging. When stress is severe or prolonged, the cell can no longer adapt and it dies. Cell death may manifest in different ways, depending on the tissues or organs involved. It can involve apoptosis or necrosis.

● *Apoptosis* — genetically programmed cell death — accounts for the constant cell turnover in the skin's outer keratin layer and the lens of the eye. It's characterized by a series of events including chromatin condensation, membrane blebbing, cell shrinkage, and DNA degradation. It's controlled by autodigestion.

There are five types of necrosis:

● *Liquefactive necrosis* occurs when a lytic (dissolving) enzyme liquefies necrotic cells. This type of necrosis is common in the brain, which has a rich supply of lytic enzymes.

● *Caseous necrosis* occurs when necrotic cells disintegrate but the cellular pieces remain undigested for months or years. Its name derives from the resulting tissue's crumbly, cheeselike (caseous) appearance. It commonly occurs in pulmonary tuberculosis.

● *Fat necrosis* occurs when lipase enzymes break down intracellular triglycerides into free fatty acids. These free fatty acids combine with sodium, magnesium, or calcium ions to form soaps. The tissue becomes opaque and chalky white.

● *Coagulative necrosis* commonly follows interruption of blood supply to any organ — generally the kidneys, heart, or adrenal glands — except the brain. It inhibits activity of lysosomal lytic enzymes in the cells, so that the necrotic cells maintain their shape, at least temporarily.

● *Gangrenous necrosis,* a form of coagulative necrosis, typically results from a lack of blood flow and is complicated by an overgrowth and invasion of bacteria. It commonly occurs in the lower limbs as a result of arteriosclerosis or in the GI tract. Gangrene can occur in one of three forms:

– dry gangrene — occurs when bacterial invasion is minimal. It's marked by dry, wrinkled, dark brown or blackened tissue on an extremity.

– moist (or wet) gangrene — is accompanied by liquefactive necrosis, which is extensive lytic activity from bacteria and WBCs that produces a liquid center in affected area. It can occur in the internal organs as well as the extremities.

– gas gangrene — develops when anaerobic bacteria of the genus *Clostridium* infect tissue. It's more likely to follow severe trauma and may be fatal. The bacteria release toxins that kill nearby cells, and the gas gangrene rapidly spreads. Release of gas bubbles from affected muscle cells indicates that gas gangrene is present.

Necrotic cells release intracellular enzymes, which start to dissolve cellular components, and trigger an acute inflammatory reaction in which WBCs migrate to the necrotic area and begin to digest the dead cells.

HOMEOSTASIS: MAINTAINING BALANCE

Every cell in the body participates in maintaining a dynamic, steady state of internal balance, called *homeostasis.* Pathophysiology results from changes or disruption in normal cellular function. Three structures in the brain are primarily responsible for maintaining homeostasis of the entire body:

● *medulla oblongata* — the part of the brain stem associated with vital functions, such as respiration and circulation

● *pituitary gland* — regulates the function of other glands and, thereby, the body's growth, maturation, and reproduction

● *reticular formation* — a network of nerve cells and fibers in the brain stem and spinal cord that helps control vital reflexes, such as cardiovascular function and respiration.

Each structure that maintains homeostasis through self-regulating feedback mechanisms has three components:

● *sensors* — cells that detect disruptions in homeostasis reflected by nerve impulses or changes in hormone levels

● *CNS control center* — receives signals from the sensor and regulates the body's response to those disruptions by initiating the effector mechanism

● *effector* — acts to restore homeostasis.

Feedback mechanisms exist in two varieties:

● *positive* — moves the system away from homeostasis by enhancing a change in the system

● *negative* — works to restore homeostasis by correcting a deficit in the system and producing adaptive responses.

DISEASE

Although *disease* and *illness* are often used interchangeably, they aren't synonyms. *Disease* occurs when homeostasis isn't maintained. *Illness* occurs when a person isn't in a state of perceived "normal" health. A person may have a disease but not be ill all the time because his body has adapted to the disease.

The cause of disease may be intrinsic or extrinsic. Genetic factors, age, gender, infectious agents, or behaviors (such as inactivity, smoking, or abusing illegal drugs) can all cause disease. Diseases that have no known cause are called *idiopathic.*

The way a disease develops is called its *pathogenesis.* A disease is usually detected when it causes a change in metabolism or cell division that causes signs and symptoms. How the cells respond to disease depends on the causative agent and the affected cells, tissues, and organs. Without intervention, resolution of the disease depends on many factors functioning over a period of time, such as extent of disease and the presence of other diseases. Manifestations of disease may include hypofunction, hyperfunction, or increased mechanical function.

Typically, diseases progress through these stages:

● *exposure or injury* — target tissue exposed to a causative agent or injury

● *latency or incubation period* — no signs or symptoms evident

● *prodromal period* — signs and symptoms generally mild and nonspecific

● *acute phase* — disease reaches full intensity, possibly with complications; called the *subclinical acute phase* if the patient can still function as though the disease weren't present

● *remission* — a second latency phase that occurs in some diseases and is commonly followed by another acute phase

● *convalescence* — patient progresses toward recovery

● *recovery* — return of health or normal functioning; no signs or symptoms of disease remain.

CANCER

Cancer refers to a group of more than 100 different diseases characterized by DNA damage that causes abnormal cell development and growth. Malignant cells have two defining characteristics: first, they can no longer divide and differentiate normally and, second, they can invade surrounding tissues and travel to distant sites within the body. In the United States, cancer is the number one cause of death in people younger than age 85 and accounts for more than half a million deaths each year.

CAUSES

The healthy body is well equipped to defend itself against cancer. Only when the immune system and other defenses fail does cancer prevail. Current evidence suggests that cancer develops from a complex interaction of exposure to carcinogens and accumulated mutations in several genes. Researchers have identified approximately 100 cancer-related genes: oncogenes or tumor suppressor genes.

Oncogenes provide growth-promoting signals, thereby causing one or more characteristics of cancer cells when overexpressed or mutated.

Proto-oncogenes are genes that can be converted to oncogenes by transforming cells or contributing to tumor formation. *Tumor suppressor genes* are growth-suppressing genes that inhibit tumor development.

Both types of these cancer-related genes can be inherited or acquired. Common causes of acquired genetic damage are viruses, radiation, environmental and dietary carcinogens, and hormones. Other factors that interact to increase a person's likelihood of developing cancer are age, genetics, nutritional status, hormonal balance, and response to stress.

RISK FACTORS

Cancer is recognized as a multistage disease involving multiple, distinct changes in cell genotype and phenotype.

Many cancers are related to specific environmental factors (air pollution, tobacco and alcohol, occupation, and radiation) and lifestyle factors (sexual practices and diet) that predispose a person to develop cancer. Accumulating data suggest that some of these risk factors initiate carcinogenesis, others act as promoters, and some both initiate and promote the disease process. In addition, age and genetics can also determine a person's risk of cancer.

Air pollution

Environmental factors such as air pollution have been linked to the development of cancer, particularly lung cancer. Many outdoor air pollutants — such as arsenic, benzene, hydrocarbons, polyvinyl chlorides, and other industrial emissions as well as motor vehicle exhaust — have been studied for their carcinogenic properties. Indoor air pollution, such as cigarette smoke and radon gas, also poses an increased risk of cancer. In fact, indoor air pollution is considered to be more carcinogenic than outdoor air pollution.

Tobacco and alcohol

A cigarette smoker's risk of lung cancer is more than 10 times greater than that of a nonsmoker's by late middle age. Tobacco smoke contains carcinogens that are known to cause mutations. The risk of lung cancer from cigarette smoking correlates directly with the duration of smoking and the number of cigarettes smoked per day. Research also shows that a person who stops smoking decreases his risk of lung cancer.

Although the risk associated with pipe and cigar smoking is similar to that of cigarette smoking, some evidence suggests that the effects are less severe. Smoke from cigars and pipes is more alkaline. This alkalinity decreases nicotine absorption in the lungs and is also more irritating to the lungs, so that the smoker doesn't inhale as readily.

Inhalation of secondhand smoke, or passive smoking, by nonsmokers also increases the risk of lung and other cancers. Use of smokeless tobacco, in which the oral tissue directly absorbs nicotine and other carcinogens, is linked to an increase in oral cancers that seldom occur in persons who don't use the product.

Alcohol consumption is commonly associated with cirrhosis of the liver, a precursor to hepatocellular cancer. The risk of breast and colorectal cancers also increases with alcohol consumption. Heavy use of alcohol and cigarette smoking synergistically increases the incidence of cancers of the mouth, larynx, pharynx, and esophagus. It's likely that alcohol acts as a solvent for the carcinogenic substances in smoke, thus enhancing their absorption.

Occupation

Certain occupations that expose workers to specific substances increase the risk of cancer. For example, persons exposed to asbestos are at risk for a specific type of lung cancer, called *mesothelioma*. Asbestos also may act as a promoter for other carcinogens. Workers involved in the production of dyes, rubber, paint, and beta-naphthylamine are at increased risk for bladder cancer.

Radiation

Exposure to ultraviolet radiation, including sunlight (UVB) or tanning booths (UVA), causes genetic mutation in the P53 control gene. Sunlight also releases tumor necrosis factor alpha in exposed skin, possibly diminishing the immune response. Ultraviolet sunlight is a direct cause of basal and squamous cell cancers of the skin. The amount of exposure to ultraviolet radiation also correlates with the type of cancer that develops. For example, cumulative exposure to ultraviolet sunlight is associated with basal and squamous cell skin cancer, and severe episodes of burning and blistering at a young age are associated with melanoma.

Ionizing radiation (such as X-rays) is associated with acute leukemia, thyroid, breast, lung, stomach, colon, and urinary tract cancers as well as multiple myeloma. Low doses of radiation can cause DNA mutations and chromosomal abnormalities, and large doses can inhibit cell division. Ionizing radiation can also enhance the effects of genetic abnormalities. Other compounding variables include the part and percentage of the body exposed, the person's age, hormonal balance, use of prescription drugs, and preexisting or concurrent conditions.

Sexual practices

Sexual practices have been linked to specific types of cancer. The age of first sexual intercourse and the number of sexual partners are positively correlated with a woman's risk of cervical cancer. Furthermore, a woman who has had only one sexual partner is at higher risk if that partner has had multiple partners. The suspected underlying mechanism here involves virus transmission, most likely human papilloma virus (HPV). Of the approximately 70 types of HPV, types 6 and 11 are associated with genital warts. HPV is the most common cause of abnormal Papanicolaou (Pap) tests, and cervical dysplasia is a direct precursor to squamous cell carcinoma of the cervix, both of which have been linked to HPV (especially types 16 and 31).

Hormones — specifically, the sex steroid hormones estrogen, progesterone, and testosterone — have been implicated as promoters of breast, endometrial, ovarian, or prostate cancer.

Diet

Numerous aspects of diet are linked to an increase in cancer, including:

- obesity
- high consumption of dietary fat
- high consumption of smoked foods and salted fish or meats and foods containing nitrites
- naturally occurring carcinogens, such as hydrazines and aflatoxin, in foods
- carcinogens produced by microorganisms stored in foods
- low fiber diet.

It's also important to note that childhood obesity may increase the risk of cancer development in later life. Obesity is a prominent risk factor for breast, colon, and prostate cancers. Because cancer is a disease of abnormal cell proliferation, the increased total number of cells in the body associated with obesity undergo a greater number of cell divisions, thereby increasing their susceptibility to abnormal changes and an increased risk of cancer development.

Age

Age is a major determinant in the development of cancer. The longer men and women live, the more likely they are to develop the disease. For example, because of the long natural history of common cancers, prostate cancer may take up to 60 years to become invasive, while colon cancer may take as long as 40 years to develop into an invasive stage. Possible explanations for the increased incidence of cancer with advancing age include:

- *altered hormonal levels,* which may stimulate cancer
- *ineffective immunosurveillance,* which fails to recognize and destroy abnormal cells
- *prolonged exposure to carcinogenic agents,* which is more likely to produce neoplastic transformation
- *inherent physiologic changes and functional impairments,* which decrease the body's ability to tolerate and survive stress.

Genetics

Genes, through the proteins they encode, are the chemical messages of heredity. Located at specific locations on the 46 chromosomes within the cell's nucleus, genes transmit specific hereditary traits.

Most cancers develop from a complex interplay among multiple genes and between genes and internal or external environmental factors. Phenomenal progress has been made in the fields of cancer genetics and cytogenetics that has established specific chromosomal changes as diagnostic and prognostic factors in acute and chronic leukemias, as diagnostic factors in various solid tumors, and as indicators for the localization and characterization of genes responsible for tumor development.

Moreover, in the past 25 years, research has identified and characterized many of the genetic alterations that lead to tumor transformation at the chromosomal and molecular cell level. The Human Genome Project, started in 1988 to identify the entire sequence of human DNA, has helped to increase knowledge about genetics and cancer carcinogenesis. The Philadelphia (Ph) chromosome was the first chromosomal anomaly caused by translocation implicated in a human disease (chronic myelocytic leukemia [CML]). However, it's important to note that not all mutated genes always lead to disease.

As previously discussed, two sets of genes, oncogenes and tumor suppressor genes, participate in the transformation of a normal cell into a malignant cell; however, because multiple, successive changes in distinct cellular genes are required to complete the entire process, the human cell rarely sustains the necessary number of changes needed for tumor transformation. Gene mutations are either *inherited* from a parent (hereditary or germline mutation) or *acquired* (somatic mutation). Inheritance accounts for about 10% of all cancers. Acquired mutations are changes in DNA that develop throughout a person's lifetime. Carcinogenic agents, such as radiation or toxins, commonly are able to damage cellular genes, which are present in the cancer cell genome, thereby triggering cancer development.

Hereditary genes

Genes implicated in hereditary cancer include:

- *mutation of the adenomatous polyposis coli (APC) suppressor gene,* which is altered by somatic mutations in colonic epithelial cells, permitting the outgrowth of early colonic polyps
- *familial adenomatous polyposis (FAP) or APC,* which acts as an autosomal dominant inherited condition in which hundreds of potentially cancerous polyps develop in the colon and rectum
- *familial cutaneous malignant melanoma gene,* on the distal short arm of chromosome 1
- *expression of the N-myc oncogene* in neuroblastoma, with amplification of this oncogene associated with rapid disease progression in children
- *loss of regulation of N-myc gene expression,* which is also a pivotal factor in the development of retinoblastoma, the most common pediatric intraocular tumor
- *germline mutation of the P53 gene,* which is mapped to the short arm of chromosome 17 and is associated with Li-Fraumeni syndrome, an extremely rare familial cancer syndrome that increases susceptibility to breast cancer, soft tissue sarcomas, brain tumors, bone cancer, leukemia, and adrenocortical carcinoma
- *human epidermal growth factor receptor-2 (HER-2)/neu protooncogene,* which is involved in regulation of normal cell growth. Gene amplification or HER-2/neu overexpression, which occurs in 25% to 30% of human breast cancers and to varying degrees in other tumor types, produces activated HER-2/neu receptors and stimulates cell growth. Tumors positive for the

HER-2/neu gene are associated with poor clinical outcomes, shortened disease-free survival, more rapid cancer progression, and poor response to standard clinical interventions.

Gene mutations

Gene mutations have also been linked to inherited tendencies toward common cancers, including colon cancer and breast cancer. The BRCA 1 gene normally helps to restrain cell growth. Researchers have found that families who carry inherited mutations of breast cancer susceptibility genes may also have an increased risk of other cancers, for example, women with an altered copy of the BRCA 1 breast cancer susceptibility gene (located on chromosome 17q21) have increased susceptibility to ovarian cancer as well. Moreover, BRCA 2, a second breast cancer susceptibility gene mapped to chromosome 13q, may account for a significant number of hereditary breast cancers not associated with BRCA 1.

PATHOPHYSIOLOGIC CONCEPTS

The characteristic features of cancer are rapid, uncontrollable proliferation of cells and independent spread from a primary site, the site of origin, to other tissues where it establishes secondary foci (metastases). (See *Histologic characteristics of cancer cells*.) This spread occurs through circulation in the blood or lymphatic fluid, by unintentional transplantation from one site to another during surgery, and by local extension. Thus, cancer cells differ from normal cells in terms of cell size, shape, number, differentiation, function, and ability to travel to distant tissues and organ systems.

Cell growth

Typically, each of the billions of cells in the human body has an internal clock that tells the cell when it's time to reproduce. Mitotic reproduction occurs in a sequence called the *cell cycle*. Normal cell division occurs in direct proportion to cells lost, thus providing a mechanism for controlling growth and differentiation. These controls are absent in cancer cells, and cell production exceeds cell loss. The loss of control over normal growth is termed *autonomy*. This independence is further evidenced by the ability of cancer cells to break away and travel to other sites in the body.

Normal cells reproduce at a rate controlled through the activity of specific control or regulator genes. These genes produce proteins that act as "on" and "off" switches. There is no generalized control gene; different cells respond to specific control genes. In cancer cells, the control genes fail to function normally. The actual control may be lost, or the gene may become damaged. An imbalance of growth factors may occur, or the cells may fail to respond to the suppressive action of the growth factors. Any of these mechanisms may lead to uncontrolled cellular reproduction.

Hormones, growth factors, and chemicals released by neighboring cells or by immune or inflammatory cells can influence control gene activity. These substances bind to specific receptors on the cell membranes and send out signals causing the control genes to stimulate or suppress cell reproduction.

Substances released by nearby injured or infected cells or by cells of the immune system also affect cellular reproduction. For example, interleukin, released by immune cells, stimulates cell proliferation and differentiation, and interferon, released from virus-infected and immune cells, may affect the cell's rate of reproduction.

Additionally, cells that are close to one another appear to communicate with one another through gap junctions (channels through which ions and other small molecules pass). This communication provides information to the cell about the neighboring cell types and the amount of space available. The nearby cells send out physical and chemical signals that control the rate of reproduction. Cancer cells fail to recognize the signals about available tissue space. Instead of forming only a single layer, cancer cells continue to accumulate in a disorderly array.

Cell differentiation

Normally, during development, cells become specialized — that is, they develop highly individualized characteristics that reflect their specific structure and functions. As the cells become more specialized, their reproduction and development slow down. Eventually, highly differentiated cells become unable to reproduce, and some — skin cells, for example — are programmed to die and be replaced.

Cancer cells lose the ability to differentiate; that is, they enter a state, called *anaplasia*, in which they no longer appear or function like the original cell. Anaplasia occurs in varying degrees. The less the cells resemble the cell of origin, the more anaplastic they are said to be. As anaplastic cells continue to reproduce, they lose the typical characteristics of the original cell. Some anaplastic cells begin functioning as another type of cell, possibly beginning to produce hormones. Anaplastic cells

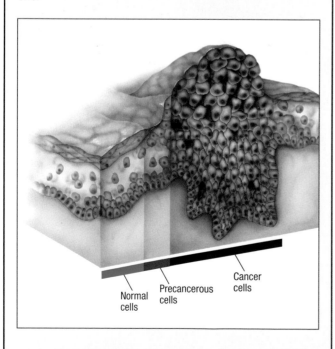

HISTOLOGIC CHARACTERISTICS OF CANCER CELLS

Cancer is a destructive (malignant) growth of cells, which invades nearby tissues and may metastasize to other areas of the body. Dividing rapidly, cancer cells tend to be extremely aggressive.

Normal cells

Precancerous cells

Cancer cells

of the same type in the same site exhibit many different shapes and sizes. Mitosis is abnormal, and chromosome defects are common.

Intracellular changes

The abnormal and uncontrolled proliferation of cancer cells is also associated with numerous changes within the cancer cell itself. These changes affect cell components as follows:
• *cell membrane* — affects the organization, structure, adhesion, and migration of the cells. Impaired intercellular communication, enhanced response to growth factors, and diminished recognition of other cells causes uncontrolled growth and greatly increases metabolic demand for nutrients.
• *cytoskeleton* — disrupts protein filament networks, including actin and microtubules. Normally, actin filaments exert a pull on the extracellular organic molecules that bind cells together. Microtubules control cell shape, movement, and division.
• *cytoplasm* — becomes fewer in number and abnormally shaped. Less cellular work occurs because of a decrease in endoplasmic reticulum and mitochondria.
• *nucleus* — becomes pleomorphic (enlarged and misshapen) and highly pigmented. Nucleoli are larger and more numerous than normal. The nuclear membrane is often irregular and commonly has projections, pouches, or blebs and fewer pores. Chromatin may clump along the outer areas of the nucleus. Chromosomal breaks, deletions, translocations, and abnormal karyotypes are common and seem to stem from the increased mitotic rate in cancer cells.

Tumor development and growth

Typically, a long time passes between the initiating event and the onset of the disease. During this time, cancer cells continue to develop, grow, and replicate, each time undergoing successive changes and further mutations.

For a tumor to grow, an initiating event or events must cause a mutation that will transform the normal cell into a cancer cell. After the initial event, the tumor continues to grow only if available nutrients, oxygen, and blood supply are adequate and the immune system fails to recognize or respond to the tumor.

Two important tumor characteristics affecting growth are location of the tumor and available blood supply. The location determines the originating cell type, which in turn determines the cell cycle time. For example, epithelial cells have a shorter cell cycle than connective tissue cells. Thus, tumors of epithelial cells grow more rapidly than do tumors of connective tissue cells.

Tumors need an available blood supply to provide nutrients and oxygen for continued growth and to remove wastes, but a tumor larger than 1 to 2 mm in size has typically outgrown its available blood supply. Some tumors secrete tumor angiogenesis factors, which stimulate the formation of new blood vessels, to meet the demand.

The degree of anaplasia also affects tumor growth. Remember that the more anaplastic the cells of the tumor, the less differentiated the cells and the more rapidly they divide.

Many cancer cells also produce their own growth factors. Numerous growth factor receptors are present on the cell membranes of rapidly growing cancer cells. This increase in receptors, in conjunction with the changes in the cell membranes, further enhances cancer cell proliferation.

Important characteristics of the host that affect tumor growth include age, sex, overall health status, and immune system function.

AGE ALERT
A person's age is an important factor affecting tumor growth. Relatively few cancers are found in children, and the incidence of cancer correlates directly to increasing age. This suggests that numerous or cumulative events are necessary for the initial mutation to continue, eventually forming a tumor.

Certain cancers are more prevalent in females; others, in males. For example, sex hormones influence tumor growth in breast, endometrial, cervical, and prostate cancers. Researchers believe that sex hormones sensitize the cell to the initial precipitating factor, thus promoting carcinogenesis.

Overall health status is also an important characteristic affecting tumor growth. As tumors obtain nutrients for growth from the host, they can alter normal body processes and cause cachexia. Conversely, if the person is nutritionally depleted, tumor growth may slow down. Chronic tissue trauma has also been linked with tumor growth because healing involves increased cell division. Therefore, the more rapidly cells divide, the greater the likelihood of mutations.

Metastasis

Between the initiating event and the emergence of a detectable tumor, some or all of the mutated cancer cells may die. The survivors, if any, reproduce until the tumor reaches a diameter of 1 to 2 mm. New blood vessels form to support continued growth and proliferation. As the cells further mutate and divide more rapidly, they become more undifferentiated, and the number of cancerous cells soon begins to exceed the number of normal cells. Eventually, the tumor mass extends and invades the surrounding tissues. When the local tissue is blood or lymph, the tumor can gain access to the circulation. When access is gained, tumor cells that detach may travel to distant sites in the body, where they can survive and form a new tumor in the secondary site. This process is called *metastasis*. (See *How cancer metastasizes*, page 10.)

Dysplasia

Not all cells that proliferate rapidly go on to become cancerous. Throughout a person's life span, various body tissues experience periods of benign rapid growth such as during wound healing. In some cases, changes in the size, shape, and organization of cells leads to a condition called *dysplasia*. Exposure to chemicals, viruses, radiation, or chronic inflammation causes dysplastic changes that may be reversed by removing the initiating stimulus or treating its effects. However, if the stimulus isn't removed, precancerous or dysplastic lesions can progress and give rise to cancer.

Localized tumor

Initially, a tumor remains localized. Recall that cancer cells communicate poorly with nearby cells. As a result, the cells continue to grow and enlarge, forming a mass or clumps of cells. The mass exerts pressure on the neighboring cells, blocking their blood supply, and subsequently causing their death.

How cancer metastasizes

Cancer cells may invade nearby tissues or metastasize (spread) to other organs. They may move to other tissues by any or all of the three routes described below.

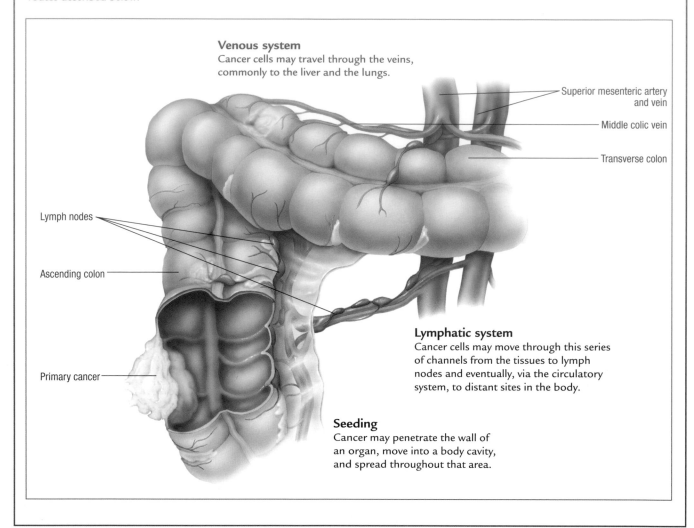

Venous system
Cancer cells may travel through the veins, commonly to the liver and the lungs.

Superior mesenteric artery and vein

Middle colic vein

Transverse colon

Lymph nodes

Ascending colon

Primary cancer

Lymphatic system
Cancer cells may move through this series of channels from the tissues to lymph nodes and eventually, via the circulatory system, to distant sites in the body.

Seeding
Cancer may penetrate the wall of an organ, move into a body cavity, and spread throughout that area.

Invasive tumor

Invasion is growth of the tumor into surrounding tissues. It's actually the first step in metastasis. Five mechanisms are linked to invasion:
- *cellular multiplication* — By their very nature, cancer cells multiply rapidly.
- *mechanical pressure* — As cancer cells grow, they exert pressure on surrounding cells and tissues, which eventually die because their blood supply has been cut off or blocked. Loss of mechanical resistance opens the way for cancer cells to spread along the lines of least resistance and occupy the space once filled by the dead cells.
- *lysis of nearby cells* — Vesicles on the cancer cell surface contain a rich supply of receptors for laminin, a complex glycoprotein that's a major component of the basement membrane. These receptors permit the cancer cells to attach to the basement membrane, forming a bridgelike connection. Some cancer cells produce and excrete powerful proteolytic enzymes; other cancer cells induce normal host cells to produce them. These en-

zymes, such as collagenases and proteases, destroy the normal cells and break through their basement membrane, enabling the cancer cells to enter.
- *reduced cell adhesion* — Cancer cells' adhesion decreases, likely the result of deregulation of cell adhesion receptors.
- *increased motility* — Cancer cells secrete chemotactic factors that stimulate motility. Thus, they can move into adjacent tissues and into the circulation, and then to a secondary site. Finally, cancer cells develop fingerlike projections called *pseudopodia* that facilitate cell movement.

Metastatic tumor

Metastatic tumors are those in which the cancer cells have traveled from the original or primary site to a second or more distant site. Most commonly, metastasis occurs through the blood vessels and lymphatic system. Tumor cells can also be transported from one body location to another by external means, such as surgical instruments or gloves.

Invasive tumor cells break down the basement membrane and walls of blood vessels, and the tumor sheds malignant cells into the circulation. Most of the cells die, but a few escape the host defenses and the turbulent environment of the bloodstream. From here, the surviving tumor mass of cells travels downstream and commonly lodges in the first capillary bed it encounters. When lodged, the tumor cells develop a protective coat of fibrin, platelets, and clotting factors to evade detection by the immune system. Then they become attached to the epithelium, ultimately invading the vessel wall, interstitium, and the parenchyma of the target organ. To survive, the new tumor develops its own vascular network and, when established, may ultimately spread again.

The lymphatic system is the most common route for distant metastasis. Tumor cells enter the lymphatic vessels through damaged basement membranes and are transported to regional lymph nodes. In this case, the tumor becomes trapped in the first lymph node it encounters. The consequent enlargement, possibly the first evidence of metastasis, may be due to the increased tumor growth within the node or a localized immune reaction to the tumor. The lymph node may filter out or contain some of the tumor cells, limiting their further spread. The cells that escape can enter the blood from the lymphatic circulation through plentiful connections between the venous and lymphatic systems.

Typically, the first capillary bed, whether lymphatic or vascular, encountered by the circulating tumor mass determines the location of the metastasis. For example, because the lungs receive all of the systemic venous return, they're a frequent site for metastasis.

SIGNS AND SYMPTOMS
In most patients, the earlier the cancer is found, the more effective the treatment is likely to be and the better the prognosis. Some cancers may be diagnosed by a routine physical examination, even before the person develops any signs or symptoms. Others may display some early warning signals. (See *Cancer's seven warning signs.*)

Unfortunately, a person may not notice or heed cancer warning signs. These patients may present with some of the more common signs and symptoms of advancing disease, such as fatigue, cachexia, pain, anemia, thrombocytopenia and leukopenia, and infection. Unfortunately, these signs and symptoms are nonspecific and can be attributed to many other disorders.

DIAGNOSTIC TESTS
A thorough history and physical examination should precede sophisticated diagnostic tests. The choice of diagnostic tests is determined by the patient's presenting signs and symptoms and the suspected body system involved. Diagnostic tests serve several purposes, including:
- establishing tumor presence and extent of disease
- determining possible sites of metastasis
- evaluating affected and unaffected body systems
- identifying the stage and grade of tumor.

Useful tests for early detection and staging of tumors include screening tests, X-rays, radioactive isotope scanning (nuclear medicine imaging), computed tomography (CT) scanning, position emission tomography (PET) scanning, endoscopy, ultrasonography, and magnetic resonance imaging

---

CANCER'S SEVEN WARNING SIGNS

The American Cancer Society has developed a simple way to remember the seven warning signs of cancer. Each letter in the word *CAUTION* represents a possible warning sign that should prompt an individual to see his health care provider.

C hange in bowel or bladder habits

A sore that doesn't heal

U nusual bleeding or discharge

T hickening or lump in the breast or elsewhere

I ndigestion or difficulty swallowing

O bvious change in a wart or mole

N agging cough or hoarseness

(MRI). The single most important diagnostic tool is the biopsy for direct histologic study of the tumor tissue.

- *Screening tests* are perhaps the most important diagnostic tools in the prevention and early detection of cancer. They may provide valuable information about the possibility of cancer even before the patient develops signs and symptoms. Examples of screening tests are mammograms, Pap tests, and fecal occult blood tests.
- *X-rays* are most commonly ordered to identify and evaluate changes in tissue densities. The type and location of the X-ray are determined by the patient's signs and symptoms and the suspected location of the tumor or metastases.
- *Radioactive isotope scanning* involves the use of a specialized camera, which detects radioactive isotopes that are injected into the bloodstream or ingested. The radiologist evaluates their distribution (uptake) throughout tissues, organs, and organ systems. This type of scanning provides a view of organs and regions within an organ that can't be seen with a simple X-ray.
- *CT scanning* evaluates successive layers of tissue by using a narrow beam X-ray to provide a cross-sectional view of the structure. It can also reveal different characteristics of tissues within a solid organ.
- *PET scans* use radioisotope technology to create a picture of the body in action. Computers construct images from the emission of positive electrons (positrons) by radioactive substances administered to the patient. Unlike other diagnostic methods that simply create images of how the body looks, PET scans provide real-time imaging of the body while it functions. To study cancer spread, PET scans involve injecting the cancer patient with a small amount of radioactive glucose. Cancerous cells metabolize sugar more quickly than healthy cells, and this process can be viewed on the scanned image. The three-dimensional PET scan pictures show malignancies as having a greater concentration of sugar.
- *Endoscopy* provides a direct view of a body cavity or passageway to detect abnormalities. During endoscopy, the health care provider can excise small tumors, aspirate fluid, or obtain tissue samples for histologic examination.
- *Ultrasonography* uses high-frequency sound waves to detect changes in the density of tissues that are difficult or impossible

to observe by radiology or endoscopy. Ultrasound helps to differentiate cysts from solid tumors.

- *MRI* uses magnetic fields and radio frequencies to show a cross-sectional view of the body organs and structures.
- *Biopsy,* removing a portion of suspicious tissue, is the only definitive method to diagnose cancer. Biopsy tissue samples can be taken by curettage, fluid aspiration, fine-needle aspiration, dermal punch, endoscopy, and surgical excision. The specimen then undergoes laboratory analysis for cell type and characteristics to provide information about the grade and stage of the cancer.

Some cancer cells release substances that normally aren't present in the body or are present only in small quantities. These substances, called *tumor markers* or *biologic markers,* are produced either by the cancer cell's genetic material during development and growth or by other cells in response to the presence of cancer. Markers may be found on the cell membrane of the tumor or in the blood, cerebrospinal fluid, or urine. Tumor cell markers include hormones, enzymes, genes, antigens, and antibodies.

Unfortunately, several disadvantages of tumor markers may preclude their use alone. For example:
- By the time the tumor cell marker level is elevated, the disease may be too far advanced to treat.
- Most tumor cell markers aren't specific enough to identify one certain type of cancer.
- Some nonmalignant diseases, such as pancreatitis or ulcerative colitis, are also associated with tumor cell markers.
- Perhaps the worst drawback, the absence of a tumor cell marker doesn't mean that a person is free from cancer.

TUMOR CLASSIFICATION

Tumors are initially classified as benign or malignant depending on their specific features. Typically, benign tumors are well differentiated; that is, their cells closely resemble those of the tissue of origin. Commonly encapsulated with well-defined borders, benign tumors grow slowly, often displacing but not infiltrating surrounding tissues and, therefore, causing only slight damage. Benign tumors don't metastasize.

Conversely, most malignant tumors are undifferentiated to varying degrees, having cells that may differ considerably from those of the tissue of origin. They're seldom encapsulated and are typically poorly delineated. They rapidly expand in all directions, causing extensive damage as they infiltrate surrounding tissues. Most malignant tumors metastasize through the blood or lymph to secondary sites.

Malignant tumors are further classified by tissue type, degree of differentiation (grading), and extent of the disease (staging). High-grade tumors are poorly differentiated and are more aggressive than low-grade tumors. Early-stage cancers carry a more favorable prognosis than later-stage cancers that have spread to nearby or distant sites.

TREATMENT

The number of cancer treatments is constantly increasing. They may be used alone or in combination (multimodal therapy), depending on the type, stage, localization, and responsiveness of the tumor and on limitations imposed by the patient's clinical status. Cancer treatment has four goals:
- *cure* — eradicating the cancer and promoting long-term patient survival

- *control* — arresting tumor growth
- *palliation* — alleviating symptoms when the disease is beyond control
- *prophylaxis* — providing treatment when no tumor is detectable, although the patient is known to be at high risk of tumor development or recurrence.

Cancer treatment is further categorized by type according to when it's used:
- *primary* — to eradicate the disease
- *adjuvant* — in addition to primary, to eliminate microscopic disease and promote a cure or improve the patient's response
- *salvage* — to manage recurrent disease.

Any treatment regimen can cause complications. Indeed, many complications of cancer are related to the adverse effects of treatment.

Surgery, once the mainstay of cancer treatment, is now typically combined with other therapies. It may be performed to diagnose the disease, initiate primary treatment, or achieve palliation and is occasionally done for prophylaxis.

Radiation therapy uses high-energy radiation to treat cancer. Used alone or in conjunction with other therapies, it aims to destroy dividing cancer cells while damaging normal cells as little as possible. Two types of radiation are used to treat cancer: *ionizing radiation* and *particle beam radiation.* Radiation therapy has both local and systemic adverse effects, because it affects both normal and malignant cells.

Chemotherapy includes a wide range of antineoplastic drugs, which may induce regression of a tumor and its metastasis. It's particularly useful in controlling residual disease and as an adjunct to surgery or radiation therapy. It can induce long remissions and sometimes effect cure. As a palliative treatment, chemotherapy aims to improve the patient's quality of life by temporarily relieving pain and other symptoms.

Every dose of a chemotherapeutic agent destroys only a percentage of tumor cells. Therefore, regression of the tumor requires repeated doses of drugs. The goal is to eradicate enough of the tumor so that the immune system can destroy the remaining malignant cells. Unfortunately, chemotherapy also causes numerous adverse effects.

The most commonly used types of chemotherapeutic agents are:
- alkylating agents and nitroureas
- antimetabolites
- antitumor antibiotics
- plant (Vinca) alkaloids
- hormones and hormone antagonists.

Hormonal therapy is based on studies showing that certain hormones can inhibit the growth of certain cancers.

Biotherapy, also known as *immunotherapy,* is treatment with agents known as *biologic response modifiers.* Biologic agents are usually combined with chemotherapy or radiation therapy and are most effective in the early stages of cancer. Many types of biotherapy are still experimental; their availability may be restricted, and their adverse effects are generally unpredictable.

The U.S. Food and Drug Administration has approved several new promising drugs for treatment of cancer. For example, rituximab — a monoclonal antibody — is effective to treat relapsed or refractory B-cell non-Hodgkin's lymphoma.

The major types of biotherapy agent classifications include interferons, interleukins, hematopoietic growth factors, and monoclonal antibodies.

INFECTION

Infection is the invasion and multiplication of microorganisms in or on body tissue that cause signs, symptoms, and an immune response. Such reproduction injures the host by causing cell damage from toxins produced by the microorganisms or from intracellular multiplication or by competing with host metabolism. Infectious diseases range from relatively mild illnesses to debilitating and lethal conditions: from the common cold through chronic hepatitis to acquired immunodeficiency syndrome. The severity of the infection varies with the pathogenicity and number of the invading microorganisms and the strength of host defenses.

For infection to be transmitted, these factors must be present: causative agent, infectious reservoir with a portal of exit, mode of transmission, a portal of entry into the host, and a susceptible host.

CAUSES

Microorganisms that are responsible for infectious diseases include viruses, bacteria, fungi, mycoplasmas, rickettsia, chlamydia, spirochetes, and parasites.

Viruses

Viruses are subcellular organisms made up only of a ribonucleic acid (RNA) nucleus or a deoxyribonucleic acid (DNA) nucleus covered with proteins. They're the smallest known organisms, so tiny that only an electron microscope can make them visible. Independent of the host cells, viruses can't replicate. Rather, they invade a host cell and stimulate it to participate in forming additional virus particles. Some viruses destroy surrounding tissue and release toxins. Viruses lack the genes necessary for energy production. They depend on the ribosomes and nutrients of infected host cells for protein production. The estimated 400 viruses that infect humans are classified according to their size, shape, and means of transmission, such as respiratory, fecal, oral, and sexual.

Retroviruses are a unique type of virus that carry their genetic code in RNA rather than the more common carrier DNA. These RNA viruses contain the enzyme reverse transcriptase, which transcribes viral RNA into DNA. The host cell then incorporates the alien DNA into its own genetic material. The most notorious retrovirus known today is human immunodeficiency virus.

Bacteria

Bacteria are simple one-celled microorganisms with a cell wall that protects them from many of the defense mechanisms of the human body. Although they lack a nucleus, bacteria possess all the other mechanisms they need to survive and rapidly reproduce.

Bacteria can be classified according to shape — spherical cocci, rod-shaped bacilli, and spiral-shaped spirilla. They can also be classified according to their need for oxygen (aerobic or anaerobic), their mobility (motile or nonmotile), and their tendency to form protective capsules (encapsulated or nonencapsulated) or spores (sporulating or nonsporulating).

Bacteria damage body tissues by interfering with essential cell function or by releasing exotoxins or endotoxins, which cause cell damage.

Fungi

Fungi have rigid walls and nuclei that are enveloped by nuclear membranes. They occur as yeast (single-cell, oval-shaped organisms) or molds (organisms with hyphae, or branching filaments). Depending on the environment, some fungi may occur in both forms. Found almost everywhere on earth, fungi live on organic matter, in water and soil, on animals and plants, and on a wide variety of unlikely materials. They can live both inside and outside their host.

Mycoplasmas

Mycoplasmas are bacterialike organisms, the smallest of the cellular microbes that can live outside a host cell, although some may be parasitic. Lacking cell walls, they can assume many different shapes ranging from coccoid to filamentous. The lack of a cell wall makes them resistant to penicillin and other antibiotics that work by inhibiting cell wall synthesis.

Rickettsia

Rickettsia are small, gram-negative, aerobic bacterialike organisms that can cause life-threatening illness. They may be coccoid, rod-shaped, or irregularly shaped. Rickettsia require a host cell for replication. They have no cell wall, and their cell membranes are leaky; thus, they must live inside another, better protected cell. Rickettsia are transmitted by the bites of arthropod carriers, such as lice, fleas, and ticks, and through exposure to their waste products. Rickettsial infections that occur in the United States include Rocky Mountain spotted fever, typhus, and Q fever.

Chlamydia

Chlamydia are smaller than rickettsia and bacteria but larger than viruses. They depend on host cells for replication and are susceptible to antibiotics. Chlamydia are transmitted by direct contact such as occurs during sexual activity.

Spirochetes

Spirochetes are an atypical type of bacteria that have a helical shape, and the length is many times its width. They have filaments wrapped around the cell wall that propel the spirochete in a corkscrew motion. Spirochetes occur with Lyme disease and syphilis.

Parasites

Parasites are unicellular or multicellular organisms that live on or within another organism and obtain nourishment from the host. They take only the nutrients they need and usually don't kill their hosts. Examples of parasites that can produce an infection if they cause cellular damage to the host include helminths (such as pinworms, roundworms, and tapeworms) and arthropods (such as mites, fleas, and ticks). Helminths can infect the human gut; arthropods commonly cause skin and systemic disease.

RISK FACTORS

A healthy person can usually ward off infections with the body's own built-in defense mechanisms, which include:
- intact skin
- normal flora that inhabit the skin and various organs
- lysozymes secreted by eyes, nasal passages, glands, stomach, and genitourinary organs
- defensive structures such as the cilia that sweep foreign matter from the airways
- a healthy immune system.

However, if an imbalance develops, the potential for infection increases. Risk factors for the development of infection include weakened defense mechanisms, environmental and developmental factors, and pathogen characteristics.

Weakened defense mechanisms

The body has many defense mechanisms for resisting entry and multiplication of both exogenous and endogenous microbes. However, a weakened immune system makes it easier for these pathogens to invade the body and launch an infectious disease. This weakened state is referred to as immunodeficiency or immunocompromise.

Impaired function of white blood cells (WBCs), as well as low levels of T cells and B cells, characterizes immunodeficiencies. An immunodeficiency may be congenital or acquired. Acquired immunodeficiency may result from infection, malnutrition, chronic stress, or pregnancy. Diabetes, renal failure, and cirrhosis can suppress the immune response, as can such drugs as corticosteroids and chemotherapy.

Regardless of cause, the result of immunodeficiency is the same. The body's ability to recognize and fight pathogens is impaired. People who are immunodeficient are more susceptible to all infections, are more acutely ill when they become infected, and require a much longer time period to heal.

Environmental factors

Other conditions that may weaken a person's immune defenses include poor hygiene, malnutrition, inadequate physical barriers, emotional and physical stressors, chronic diseases, medical and surgical treatments, and inadequate immunization.

Good hygiene promotes normal host defenses; poor hygiene increases the risk of infection. Unclean skin harbors microbes, offering an environment for them to colonize, and is more open to invasion. Frequent body washing removes surface microbes and maintains an intact barrier to infection, but it may damage the skin. To maintain skin integrity, lubricants and emollients may be used to prevent cracks and breaks.

The body requires a balanced diet to provide the nutrients, vitamins, and minerals needed for an effective immune system. Protein malnutrition inhibits the production of antibodies, without which the body is unable to mount an effective attack against microbe invasion. Malnutrition has been shown to have a direct relationship to the incidence of nosocomial infections.

Dust can facilitate transportation of pathogens. For example, dustborne spores of the fungus aspergillus transmit the infection. If the inhaled spores become established in the lungs, they're notoriously difficult to expel. Fortunately, most persons with intact immune systems can resist infection with aspergillus, which is usually dangerous only in the presence of severe immunosuppression.

Developmental factors

Extremely young and old people are at higher risk for infection. The immune system doesn't fully develop until about age 6 months. An infant exposed to an infectious agent usually develops an infection. The most common type of infection in toddlers affects the respiratory tract. When young children put toys and other objects in their mouths, they increase their exposure to a variety of pathogens.

Exposure to communicable diseases continues throughout childhood, as children progress from daycare facilities to schools. Skin diseases, such as impetigo, and lice infestation commonly pass from one child to the next at this age. Accidents are common in childhood as well, and broken or abraded skin opens the way for bacterial invasion. Lack of immunization also contributes to incidence of childhood diseases.

Advancing age, on the other hand, is associated with a declining immune system, partly as a result of decreasing thymus function. Chronic diseases, such as diabetes and atherosclerosis, can weaken defenses by impairing blood flow and nutrient delivery to body systems.

Pathogen characteristics

A microbe must be present in sufficient quantities to cause a disease in a healthy human. The number needed to cause a disease varies from one microbe to the next and from host to host and may be affected by the mode of transmission. The severity of an infection depends on several factors, including the microbe's pathogenicity, that is, the likelihood that it will cause pathogenic changes or disease. Factors that affect pathogenicity include:
- *specificity* — the range of hosts to which a microbe is attracted (Some microbes may be attracted to a wide range of both humans and animals, while others select only human or only animal hosts.)
- *invasiveness* (sometimes called *infectivity*) — ability of a microbe to invade and multiply in the host tissues (Some microbes can enter through intact skin; others can enter only if the skin or mucous membrane is broken. Some microbes produce enzymes that enhance their invasiveness.)
- *quantity* — the number of microbes that succeed in invading and reproducing in the body
- *virulence* — severity of the disease a pathogen can produce (Virulence can vary depending on the host defenses; any infection can be life-threatening in an immunodeficient patient. Infection with a pathogen known to be particularly virulent requires early diagnosis and treatment.)
- *toxigenicity* (related to virulence) — potential to damage host tissues by producing and releasing toxins
- *adhesiveness* — ability to attach to host tissue (Some pathogens secrete a sticky substance that helps them adhere to tissue while protecting them from the host's defense mechanisms.)
- *antigenicity* — degree to which a pathogen can induce a specific immune response (Microbes that invade and localize in tissue initially stimulate a cellular response; those that disseminate quickly throughout the host's body generate an antibody response.)
- *viability* — ability to survive outside its host. Most microbes can't live and multiply outside a reservoir.

STAGES OF INFECTION

Development of infection usually proceeds through four stages. (See *Stages of infection*.)

PATHOPHYSIOLOGIC CONCEPTS

Clinical expressions of infectious disease vary depending on the pathogen involved and the body system affected. Most of the signs and symptoms result from host responses, which may be similar or extremely different from host to host. During the prodromal stage, a person will complain of some common, nonspecific signs and symptoms, such as fever, muscle aches, headache, and lethargy. In the acute stage, signs and symptoms that are more specific provide evidence of the microbe's target. However, some diseases produce no symptoms and are discovered only by laboratory tests.

The inflammatory response is a major reactive defense mechanism in the battle against infective agents. Inflammation may be the result of tissue injury, infection, or allergic reaction. Acute inflammation has two stages: vascular and cellular. In the vascular stage, arterioles at or near the site of the injury briefly constrict and then dilate, causing an increase in fluid pressure in the capillaries. The consequent movement of plasma into the interstitial space causes edema. At the same time, inflammatory cells release histamine and bradykinin, which further increase capillary permeability. Red blood cells and fluid flow into the interstitial space, contributing to edema. The extra fluid arriving in the inflamed area dilutes microbial toxins.

During the cellular stage of inflammation, WBCs and platelets move toward the damaged cells, and phagocytosis of the dead cells and microorganisms begins. Platelets control any excess bleeding in the area, and mast cells arriving at the site release heparin to maintain blood flow to the area.

SIGNS AND SYMPTOMS

Acute inflammation is the body's immediate response to cell injury or cell death. The cardinal signs of inflammation include:

- *redness (rubor)* — dilation of arterioles and increased circulation to the site; a localized blush caused by filling of previously empty or partially distended capillaries
- *heat (calor)* — local vasodilatation, fluid leakage into the interstitial spaces, and increased blood flow to the area
- *pain (dolor)* — pain receptors stimulated by swollen tissue, local pH changes, and chemicals excreted during the inflammatory process
- *edema (tumor)* — local vasodilatation, leakage of fluid into interstitial spaces, and blockage of lymphatic drainage
- *loss of function (functio laesa) of a body part* — primarily a result of edema and pain.

CLINICAL TIP
Localized infections produce a rapid inflammatory response with obvious signs and symptoms. Disseminated infections have a slow inflammatory response and take longer to identify and treat, thereby increasing morbidity and mortality.

Fever

Fever follows the introduction of an infectious agent. An elevated temperature helps fight an infection because many microorganisms are unable to survive in a hot environment. When the body temperature rises too high, body cells can be damaged, particularly those of the nervous system.

Diaphoresis (sweating) is the body's method of cooling itself and returning the temperature to normal for that individual.

STAGES OF INFECTION

Stage 1
Incubation
- Duration can range from instantaneous to several years.
- Pathogen is replicating, and the infected person becomes contagious, thus capable of transmitting the disease.

STAGE II
Prodromal stage
- Host makes vague complaints of feeling unwell.
- Host is still contagious.

Stage III
Acute illness
- Microbes actively destroy host cells and affect specific host systems.
- Patient recognizes which area of the body is affected.
- Complaints are more specific.

Stage IV
Convalescence
- Begins when the body's defense mechanisms have contained the microbes.
- Damaged tissue is healing.

Artificial methods to reduce a slight fever can actually impede the body's defenses against infection.

Leukocytosis

The body responds to the introduction of pathogens by increasing the number and types of circulating WBCs. This process is called *leukocytosis*. In the acute or early stage, the neutrophil count increases. Bone marrow begins to release immature leukocytes, because existing neutrophils can't meet the body's demand for defensive cells. The immature neutrophils (called *bands* in the differential WBC count) can't serve any defensive purpose.

As the acute phase comes under control and the damage is isolated, the cellular stage of the inflammatory process takes place. Neutrophils, monocytes, and macrophages begin the process of phagocytosis of dead tissue and bacteria. Neutrophils and monocytes are attracted to the site of infection by chemotaxis, and they identify the foreign antigen and attach to it. Then they engulf, kill, and degrade the microorganism that carries the antigen on its surface. Macrophages, a mature type of monocyte, arrive at the site later and remain in the area of inflammation longer than the other cells. Besides phagocytosis, macrophages play several other key roles at the site, such as preparing the area for healing and processing antigens for a cellular immune response. An elevated monocyte count is common during resolution of any injury and in chronic infections.

Chronic inflammation

An inflammatory reaction lasting longer than 2 weeks is referred to as chronic inflammation. It may follow an acute process. A poorly healed wound or an unresolved infection can lead to chronic inflammation. The body may encapsulate a pathogen that it can't destroy in order to isolate it. An example of such a pathogen is mycobacteria, one of the species that cause tuberculosis; encapsulated mycobacteria appear in X-rays as identifiable spots in the lungs. With chronic inflammation, permanent scarring and loss of tissue function can occur.

DIAGNOSTIC TESTS

Accurate assessment helps identify infectious diseases, appropriate treatment, and avoidable complications. It begins with obtaining the patient's complete medical history, performing a thorough physical examination, and performing or ordering appropriate diagnostic tests. Tests that can help identify and gauge the extent of infection include laboratory studies, radiographic tests, and scans.

Most commonly, the first test is a WBC count and a differential. An elevation in the overall number of WBCs is a positive result. The differential count is the relative number of each of five types of WBCs — neutrophils, eosinophils, basophils, lymphocytes, and monocytes. This test recognizes only that an immune response has been stimulated. Bacterial infection usually causes an elevation in the counts; viruses may cause no change or a decrease in normal WBC level.

Erythrocyte sedimentation rate may be done as a general test to reveal that an inflammatory process is occurring within the body.

To determine the causative agent, a stained smear from a specific body site is obtained. Stains that may be used to visualize the microorganism include:
- *Gram stain* — identifies gram-negative or gram-positive bacteria
- *acid-fast stain* — identifies mycobacteria and nocardia
- *silver stain* — identifies fungi, legionella, and pneumocystis.

Although stains provide rapid and valuable diagnostic information, they only tentatively identify a pathogen. Confirmation requires culturing. Growth sufficient to identify the microbe may occur in as quickly as 8 hours or as long as several weeks, depending on how rapidly the microbe replicates. Types of cultures that may be ordered are blood, urine, sputum, throat, nasal, wound, skin, stool, and cerebrospinal fluid, but any body substance can be cultured.

A specimen obtained for culture must not be contaminated with any other substance. For example, a urine specimen must not contain debris from the perineum or vaginal area. If obtaining a clean urine specimen isn't possible, the patient must be catheterized to make sure that only the urine is being examined. Contaminated specimens may mislead and prolong treatment.

Additional tests that may be requested include magnetic resonance imaging to locate infection sites, chest X-rays to search the lungs for respiratory changes, and gallium scans to detect abscesses.

TREATMENT

Treatment for infections can vary widely. Vaccines may be administered to induce a primary immune response under conditions that won't cause disease. If infection occurs, treatment is tailored to the specific causative organism. Drug therapy should be used only when it's appropriate. Supportive therapy can play an important role in fighting infections.
- *Antibiotics* work in a variety of ways, depending on the class of antibiotic. Their action is either bactericidal or bacteriostatic. Antibiotics may inhibit cell-wall synthesis, protein synthesis, bacterial metabolism, or nucleic acid synthesis or activity, or they may increase cell-membrane permeability.
- *Antifungal drugs* destroy the invading microbe by increasing cell-membrane permeability. The antifungal binds sterols in the cell membrane, resulting in leakage of intracellular contents, such as potassium, sodium, and nutrients.
- *Antiviral drugs* stop viral replication by interfering with DNA synthesis.

The overuse of antimicrobials has created widespread resistance to some specific drugs. Some pathogens that were once well controlled by medications are again surfacing with increased virulence. One such pathogen is that which is known to cause tuberculosis.

Some diseases, including most viral infections, don't respond to available drugs. Supportive care is the only recourse while the host defenses repel the invader. To help the body fight an infection, the patient should:
- use universal precautions to avoid spreading the infection
- drink plenty of fluids
- get plenty of rest
- avoid people who may have other illnesses
- take only over-the-counter medications appropriate for his symptoms, with full knowledge about dosage, actions, and possible adverse effects or reactions
- follow the health care provider's orders for taking prescription drugs, and be sure to complete the medication as ordered and not share the prescription with others.

DISORDERS

See *Common infectious disorders,* pages 17–20, which describes a variety of infectious disorders.

COMMON INFECTIOUS DISORDERS

DISORDER	CHARACTERISTICS
Bacterial infections	
Anthrax	Bacterial infection characterized as cutaneous, inhalational, or intestinal. • Diagnosis confirmed by isolation of *Bacillus anthracis* from cultures of blood, skin, lesions, or sputum. • Signs and symptoms directly related to the location of infection. Cutaneous anthrax is characterized by a small, elevated, itchy lesion, which develops into a vesicle and then a painless ulcer, along with enlarged lymph glands. Inhalational anthrax is characterized by flulike symptoms initially, followed by severe respiratory difficulty and shock. With intestinal anthrax, fever, nausea, vomiting, and decreased appetite occur, which progress to abdominal pain, hematemesis, and severe diarrhea.
Chlamydia	Sexually transmitted infection caused by *Chlamydia trachomatis.* • Disease pattern depends on the individual infected and the site of infection.
Conjunctivitis	Bacterial or viral infection of the conjunctiva of the eye. • Culture from the conjunctiva identifies the causative organism. • Associated with hyperemia of the eye, discharge, tearing, pain, and photophobia.
Gonorrhea	Sexually transmitted infection caused by *Neisseria gonorrhoeae,* a gram-negative, oxidase-positive diplococcus. • After exposure, epithelial cells at infection site become infected and the disease begins to spread locally. • Disease pattern depends on the individual infected and the site of infection.
Listeriosis	Infection caused by weakly hemolytic, gram-positive bacillus *Listeria monocytogenes.* • Primary method of person-to-person transmission is neonatal infection in utero or during passage through an infected birth canal. • Disease may cause abortion, premature delivery, stillbirth, or organ abscesses in fetuses. • Neonates may have tense fontanels due to meningitis, be irritabile or lethargic, have seizures, or be comatose.
Lyme disease	Infection caused by spirochete *Borrelia burgdorferi.* • Transmitted by ixodid tick, which injects spirochete-laden saliva into the bloodstream or deposits fecal matter on the skin. • After 3 to 32 days, spirochetes migrate outward, typically causing a ringlike rash, called *erythema chronicum migrans.* • Spirochetes disseminate to other skin sites or organs through the bloodstream or lymphatic system. • Spirochetes may survive for years in joints, or they may die after triggering an inflammatory response in the host. • As infection progresses through three stages, neurologic symptoms and impairment worsen.
Meningitis	Meningeal inflammation caused by bacteria, viruses, protozoa, or fungi. The most common types are bacterial and viral. • Disease occurs when infecting organisms enter the subarachnoid space and cause an inflammatory response. The organisms gain access to the cerebrospinal fluid, where they cause irritation of the tissues bathed by the fluid. • Characteristic signs include fever, chills, headache, nuchal rigidity, vomiting, photophobia, lethargy, coma, positive Brudzinki's and Kernig's signs, increased deep tendon reflexes, widened pulse pressure, bradycardia, and rash.
Otitis media	Inflammation of the middle ear caused by a bacterial infection. • Disease is commonly accompanied by a viral upper respiratory infection. • Viral symptoms occur, generally followed by ear pain.
Peritonitis	Acute or chronic inflammation of the peritoneum caused by bacterial invasion. • Onset commonly sudden, with severe and diffuse abdominal pain. • Pain intensifies and localizes in the region of infection.
Pertussis (whooping cough)	Highly contagious respiratory infection usually caused by the nonmotile, gram-negative coccobacillus *Bordetella pertussis* and, occasionally, by the related similar bacteria *B. parapertussis* or *B. bronchiseptica.* • Transmitted by direct inhalation of contaminated droplets from a patient in an acute stage. It may also spread indirectly though soiled linen and other articles contaminated by respiratory secretions. • After approximately 7 to 10 days, *B. pertussis* enters the tracheobronchial mucosa, where it produces progressively tenacious mucus. • Known for its associated spasmodic cough, characteristically ending in a loud, crowing inspiratory whoop. Complications include apnea, hypoxia, seizures, pneumonia, encephalopathy, and death.

(continued)

DISORDER	CHARACTERISTICS
Bacterial infections *(continued)*	
Pneumonia	Infection of the lung parenchyma that's bacterial, fungal, or protozoal in origin. ● The lower respiratory tract can be exposed to pathogens by inhalation, aspiration, vascular dissemination, or direct contact with contaminated equipment. When inside, the pathogen begins to colonize and infection develops. ● Bacterial infection initially triggers alveolar inflammation and edema, which produces an area of low ventilation with normal perfusion. Capillaries become engorged with blood, causing stasis. As alveolocapillary membranes break down, alveoli fill with blood and exudates, causing atelectasis, or lung collapse.
Salmonellosis	Disease caused by a serotype of the genus *Salmonella,* a member of the *Enterobacteriaceae* family. ● Most common species of *Salmonella* include *S. typhi,* which causes typhoid fever; *S. enteritidis,* which causes enterocolitis; and *S. choleraesuis,* which causes bacteremia. ● Nontyphoidal salmonellosis usually follows ingestion of contaminated dry milk, chocolate bars, pharmaceuticals of animal origin, or contaminated or inadequately processed foods, especially eggs and poultry. ● Characteristic symptoms include fever, abdominal pain or cramps, and severe diarrhea with enterocolitis.
Shigellosis	Acute intestinal infection caused by the bacteria shigella, a member of the *Enterobacteriaceae* family. It's a short, nonmotile, gram-negative rod. ● Transmission occurs primarily through the fecal-oral route. ● After an incubation period of 1 to 4 days, shigella organisms invade the intestinal mucosa and cause inflammation. Symptoms can range from watery stools to fever, cramps, and stools with pus, mucus, or blood.
Tetanus	Acute exotoxin-mediated infection caused by the anaerobic, spore-forming, gram-positive bacillus *Clostridium tetani.* ● Transmission occurs through a puncture wound that's contaminated by soil, dust, or animal excreta containing *C. tetani,* or by way of burns and minor wounds. ● After *C. tetani* enters the body, it causes local infection and tissue necrosis. It also produces toxins that then enter the bloodstream and lymphatics and eventually spread to central nervous system (CNS) tissue. ● Disease is characterized by marked muscle hypertonicity, hyperactive deep tendon reflexes, and painful, involuntary muscle contractions. Severe muscle spasms can last up to 7 days.
Toxic shock syndrome (TSS)	Acute bacterial infection caused by toxin-producing, penicillin-resistant strains of *Staphylococcus aureus,* such as TSS toxin-1 or staphylococcal enterotoxins B and C. It can also be caused by *Streptococcus pyogenes.* ● Menstrual TSS is associated with tampon use. ● Nonmenstrual TSS is associated with infections, such as abcesses, osteomyelitis, pneumonia, endocarditis, bacteremia, and postsurgical infections. ● Signs and symptoms include fever, hypotension, renal failure, and multisystem involvement.
Tuberculosis	Infectious disease transmitted by inhaling *Mycobacterium tuberculosis,* an acid-fast bacillus, from an infected person. ● Bacilli are deposited in the lungs, the immune system responds by sending leukocytes, and inflammation results. After a few days, leukocytes are replaced by macrophages. Bacilli are then ingested by the macrophages and carried off by the lymphatics to the lymph nodes. Macrophages that infest the bacilli fuse to form ephithelioid cell tubercles, tiny nodules surrounded by lymphocytes. ● Caseous necrosis develops in the lesion, and scar tissue encapsulates the tubercle. The organism may be killed in the process. ● If the tubercles and inflamed nodes rupture, the infection contaminates the surrounding tissue and may spread through the blood and lymphatic circulation to distant sites.
Urinary tract infection	Infection most commonly caused by enteric gram-negative bacilli. ● Results from microorganisms entering the urethra and then ascending into the bladder. ● Commonly causes urgency, frequency, and dysuria.
Viral infections	
Avian influenza	An influenza A virus that typically infects birds. ● Reported symptoms in humans include fever, cough, sore throat, and muscle aches. ● Virus could progress to eye infections, pneumonia, and acute respiratory distress.

DISORDER	CHARACTERISTICS

Viral infections *(continued)*

Cytomegalovirus infection	A DNA virus that's a member of the herpes virus group. ● Transmission can occur horizontally (person-to-person contact with secretions), vertically (mother to neonate), or through blood transfusions. ● The virus spreads through the body in lymphocytes or mononuclear cells to the lungs, liver, GI tract, eyes, and CNS, where it commonly produces inflammatory reactions.
Herpes simplex virus (HSV)	HSV is an enveloped, double-stranded DNA virus that causes both herpes simplex type 1 and type 2. ● Type 1 HSV is transmitted via oral and respiratory secretions; type 2 HSV is transmitted via sexual contact. ● During exposure, the virus fuses to the host cell membrane and releases proteins, turning off the host cell's protein production or synthesis. The virus then replicates and synthesizes structural proteins. The virus pushes its nucleocapsid (protein coat and nucleic acid) into the cytoplasm of the host cell and releases the viral DNA. Complete virus particles capable of surviving and infecting a living cell are transported to the cell's surface. ● Characteristic painful, vesicular lesions are usually observed at the site of initial infection.
Herpes zoster	Caused by a reactivation of varicella-zoster virus that has been lying dormant in the cerebral ganglia or the ganglia of posterior nerve roots. ● Small, painful, red, nodular skin lesions develop on areas along nerve paths. ● Lesions change to vesicles filled with pus or fluid.
Human immunodeficiency virus (HIV) infection	An RNA retrovirus that causes acquired immunodeficiency syndrome (AIDS). ● Virus passes from one person to another through blood-to-blood and sexual contact. In addition, an infected pregnant woman can pass HIV to her baby during pregnancy or delivery as well as through breast-feeding. ● Most people with HIV infection develop AIDS; however, current combination drug therapy in conjunction with treatment and prophylaxis of common opportunistic infections can delay the natural progression and prolong survival.
Infectious mononucleosis	Viral illness caused by the Epstein-Barr virus, a B-lymphotropic herpes virus. ● Most cases spread by the oropharyngeal route, but transmission by blood transfusion or during cardiac surgery is also possible. ● The virus invades the B cells of the oropharyngeal lymphoid tissues and then replicates. ● Dying B cells release the virus into the blood, causing fever and other symptoms. During this period, antiviral antibodies appear and the virus disappears from the blood, lodging mainly in the parotid gland.
Monkeypox	Rare disease caused by the monkeypox virus, which belongs to the orthopoxvirus group. ● In humans, monkeypox causes swollen lymph nodes, fever, headache, muscle aches, backache, exhaustion, and a papular rash with lesions that eventually crust and fall off.
Mumps	Acute viral disease caused by an RNA virus classified as *Rubulavirus* in the *Paramyxoviridae* family. ● Virus is transmitted by droplets or by direct contact. ● Characterized by enlargement and tenderness of parotid gland and swelling of other salivary glands.
Rabies	Rapidly progressive infection of the CNS caused by an RNA virus in the *Rhabdoviridae* family. ● Transmitted by the bite of an infected animal through the skin or mucous membranes or, occasionally, in airborne droplets or infected tissue. ● The rabies virus begins replicating in the striated muscle cells at the bite site. ● The virus spreads along the nerve pathways to the spinal cord and brain, where it replicates again. ● The virus moves through the nerves into other tissues, including into the salivary glands.
Respiratory syncytial virus	Infection of the respiratory tract caused by an enveloped RNA paramyxovirus. ● The organism is transmitted from person to person by respiratory secretions or by touching contaminated surfaces. ● Bronchiolitis or pneumonia ensues and, in severe cases, may damage the bronchiolar epithelium. ● Interalveolar thickening and filling of alveolar spaces with fluid may occur. ● The virus is more common in winter and early spring.

(continued)

DISORDER	CHARACTERISTICS

Viral infections *(continued)*

Rubella	An enveloped positive-stranded RNA virus classified as a rubivirus in the *Togaviridae* family. • Transmitted through contact with the blood, urine, stool, or nasopharyngeal secretions of an infected person. It can also be transmitted transplacentally. • The virus replicates first in the respiratory tract and then spreads through the bloodstream. • Characteristic maculopapular rash usually begins on the face and then spreads rapidly.
Rubeola	Acute, highly contagious paramyxovirus infection that's spread by direct contact or by contaminated airborne respiratory droplets. • Portal of entry is the upper respiratory tract. • Characterized by Koplik's spots, a pruritic macular rash that becomes papular and erythematous.
Smallpox	Acute contagious virus caused by the variola virus, a member of the *Orthopoxvirus* family. • Transmitted from person to person by infected aerosols and air droplets. • The incubation period, which is usually 12 to 14 days, is followed by the sudden onset of influenzalike symptoms including fever, malaise, headache, and severe back pain. • Two to 3 days later, the patient may feel better, however, the characteristic rash appears, first on the face, hands, and forearms and then after a few days progressing to the trunk. Lesions also develop in the mucous membranes of the nose and mouth, then ulcerate and release large amounts of virus into the mouth and throat.
Varicella (chickenpox)	Common, highly contagious exanthem caused by the varicella-zoster virus, a member of the herpes virus family. • Transmitted by respiratory droplets or contact with vesicles. In utero infection is also possible. • Characterized by a pruritic rash of small, erythematous macules that progresses to papules and then to clear vesicles on an erythematous base.
Viral pneumonia	Lung infection caused by any one of a variety of viruses, transmitted through contact with an infected individual. • The virus first attacks bronchiolar epithelial cells, causing interstitial inflammation and desquamation. • Virus invades bronchial mucous glands and goblet cells and then spreads to the alveoli, which fill with blood and fluid. In advanced infection, a hyaline membrane may form.

Fungal infections

Histoplasmosis	Fungal infection caused by *Histoplasma capsulatum,* a dimorphic fungus. • Transmitted through inhalation of *H. capsulatum* spores or invasion of spores after minor skin trauma. • Initially, infected person may be asymptomatic or have symptoms of mild respiratory illness, progressing into more severe illness affecting several organ systems.

Protozoal infections

Toxoplasmosis	Infection caused by the intracellular parasite *Toxoplasma gondii,* which affects both birds and mammals. • Transmitted to humans by ingestion of tissue cysts in raw or undercooked meat or by fecal oral contamination from infected cats. Direct transmission can also occur during blood transfusions, organ transplants, or bone marrow transplants. • When tissue cysts are ingested, parasites are released, which quickly invade and multiply within the GI tract. The parasitic cells rupture the invaded host cell and then disseminate to the CNS, lymphatic tissue, skeletal muscle, myocardium, retina, and placenta. • As the parasites replicate and invade adjoining cells, cell death and focal necrosis occur, surrounded by an acute inflammatory response, which are the hallmarks of this infection. • After the cysts reach maturity, the inflammatory process is undetectable and the cysts remain latent within the brain until they rupture. • In the normal host, the immune response checks the infection, but this isn't so with immunocompromised or fetal hosts. In these patients, focal destruction results in necrotizing encephalitis, pneumonia, myocarditis, and organ failure.
Trichinosis	Infection caused by the parasite *Trichinella spiralis* and transmitted through ingestion of uncooked or undercooked meat that contains encysted larvae. • After gastric juices free the larva from the cyst capsule, it reaches sexual maturity in a few days. The female roundworm burrows into the intestinal mucosa and reproduces. • Larvae then travel through the lymphatic system and the bloodstream. They become embedded as cysts in striated muscle, especially in the diaphragm, chest, arms, and legs.

GENETICS

Genetics is the study of heredity — the passing of physical, biochemical, and physiologic traits, both healthy and pathogenic, from biological parents to their children. In this transmission, mistakes or mutations can cause susceptibility to disease, disability, or death.

Genetic information is carried in genes, which are strung together on the deoxyribonucleic acid (DNA) double helix to form chromosomes. Every normal human cell (except reproductive cells) has 46 chromosomes, 22 paired chromosomes called *autosomes,* and two sex chromosomes (a pair of X's in females and an X and a Y in males). A person's individual set of chromosomes is called his *karyotype.* The human genome has been under intense study for about 15 years to determine the structure of each gene in the genome and its location within each of the 23 chromosomes comprising the set of human chromosomes. In May 2006, scientists announced the completion of the entire genome sequence. The sequence consists of more than 3 billion pairs of DNA bases. Decoding the genome will enable people to know who's likely to get a specific inherited disease and enable researchers to eradicate or improve the treatment of many diseases.

For many reasons, not every gene is expressed in every cell. Genetic principles are based on studies of thousands of individuals. Those studies have led to generalities that are usually true, but exceptions occur. Genetics remains an inexact science.

GENETIC COMPONENTS

Each of the two strands of DNA in a chromosome consists of thousands of combinations of four nucleotides: adenine (A), thymine (T), cytosine (C), and guanine (G), arranged in complementary triplet pairs (called *codons*), each of which represents an amino acid; a specific sequence of triplets represents a gene. The strands are held together loosely by chemical bonds between adenine and thymine or between cytosine and guanine. The looseness of the bonds allows the strands to separate easily during DNA replication. The genes carry a code for each trait a person inherits, from blood type to eye color to body shape and a myriad of other traits.

DNA ultimately controls the formation of essential substances throughout the life of every cell in the body. It does this through the genetic code, the precise sequence of AT and CG pairs on the DNA molecule. Genes control not only hereditary traits, transmitted from parents to offspring but also cell reproduction and the daily functions of all cells. Genes control cell function by controlling the structures and chemicals that are synthesized within the cell.

TRANSMITTING TRAITS

Germ cells, or gametes, are one of two classes of cells in the body; each germ cell (ovum or sperm) contains 23 chromosomes (called the *haploid* number) in its nucleus. All the other cells in the body are somatic cells, which are *diploid;* that is, they contain 23 *pairs* of chromosomes.

When human ovum and sperm unite, the corresponding chromosomes pair up, so that the fertilized cell as well as every somatic cell of the new individual has 23 pairs of chromosomes in its nucleus.

Germ cells

The body produces germ cells through a type of cell division called *meiosis.* Meiosis occurs only when the body is creating haploid germ cells from their diploid precursors. Each of the 23 pairs of chromosomes in the diploid precursor cell replicates and undergoes two cell divisions, so that, on completion, each new germ cell (ovum or sperm) contains one set of 23 chromosomes.

Most of the genes on one chromosome are identical or almost identical to those on its mate. The location (or locus) of a gene on a chromosome is specific and doesn't vary from person to person. This allows each of the thousands of genes on a strand of DNA in an ovum to join the corresponding gene in a sperm when the chromosomes pair up at fertilization.

Sex chromosomes

Only one pair of the 23 pairs of chromosomes in each cell is primarily involved in determining a person's sex. These are the sex chromosomes; the other 22 chromosome pairs are called *autosomes.* Females have two X chromosomes and males have one X and one Y chromosome.

Each germ cell produced by a male contains either an X or a Y chromosome. When a sperm with an X chromosome fertilizes an ovum, the offspring is female (two X chromosomes); when a sperm with a Y chromosome fertilizes an ovum, the offspring is male (one X and one Y chromosome). Extremely rare errors in cell division can result in a germ cell that has no sex chromosome or has two sex chromosomes. After fertilization, the zygote may have an XXX, XYY, XO, or XXY karyotype and still survive. Most other errors in sex chromosome division are incompatible with life.

Mitosis

The fertilized ovum — now called a *zygote* — undergoes a kind of cell division called *mitosis.* Before a cell divides, its chromosomes replicate. During this process, the double helix of DNA separates into two chains; each chain serves as a template for constructing a new chain. Individual DNA nucleotides are linked into new strands with bases complementary to those in the originals. In this way, two identical double helices are formed, each containing one of the original strands and a newly formed complementary strand. These double helices are duplicates of the original DNA chain.

Mitotic cell division occurs in five phases: *interphase, prophase, metaphase, anaphase,* and *telophase.* The result of every mitotic cell division is two new daughter cells, each genetically identical to the original and to each other. Then, each of the two resulting cells divides, and so on, eventually forming a many-celled human embryo. Thus, each cell in a person's body (except ovum or sperm) contains an identical set of 46 chromosomes that are unique to that person.

TRAIT PREDOMINANCE

Each parent contributes one set of chromosomes (and therefore one set of genes) so that every offspring has two genes for every locus on the autosomes. Some characteristics, or traits, such as eye color, are determined by one gene that may have many variants (alleles). Others, called *polygenic* traits, require the interaction of two or more genes. In addition, environmental factors may affect how genes are expressed, although the environmental factors don't affect the genetic structure.

Variations in a particular gene — such as brown, blue, or green eye color — are called *alleles*. A person who has identical genes on each member of the chromosome pair is *homozygous* for that gene; if the alleles are different, the person is said to be *heterozygous*.

Autosomal inheritance

On autosomes, one allele may be more influential than another in determining a specific trait. The more powerful, or *dominant*, gene product is more likely to be exhibited in the offspring than the less influential, or *recessive*, gene product. Offspring will exhibit a dominant allele when one or both chromosomes in a pair carry it. A recessive allele won't be exhibited unless both chromosomes carry identical copies of the allele. For example, a child may receive a gene for brown eyes from one parent and a gene for blue eyes from the other parent. The gene for brown eyes is dominant, and the gene for blue eyes is recessive. Because the dominant allele is more likely to mask the recessive allele, the child is more likely to have brown eyes.

Sex-linked inheritance

The X and Y chromosomes aren't literally a pair because the X chromosome is much larger than the Y, with more genetic material. The male has only one copy of the genes on the X chromosome. Inheritance of those genes is called *X-linked*. A man will transmit one copy of each X-linked gene to his daughters and none to his sons. A woman will transmit one copy to each child, whether male or female.

Inheritance of genes on the X chromosome is different in another way. Females have two X chromosomes in each of their cells; however, only one X chromosome is active in each cell because of a process called *X inactivation*. X inactivation occurs during early embryogenesis in the female, and the X that's inactivated in each cell is random. In some cells, the X the female received from her mother is inactivated, and in other cells the X she received from her father is inactivated. For this reason, at the cellular level a heterozygous female will express the recessive gene in some cells and the dominant gene in others.

Multifactorial inheritance

Multifactorial inheritance is inheritance that's determined by multiple factors, including genetic and possible nongenetic (environmental), each with only a partial effect. The genetic factor may consist of variations for multiple genes: some that provide susceptibility and some that provide protection. Examples of environmental factors that may contribute to such a trait are nutrition, exposure to teratogens or carcinogens, viral infections, exposure to oxidants, and intake of antioxidants.

PATHOPHYSIOLOGIC CONCEPTS

Autosomal disorders, sex-linked disorders, and multifactorial disorders result from changes to genes or chromosomes. Some defects arise spontaneously, whereas others may be caused by environmental agents, including mutagens, teratogens, and carcinogens.

Environmental teratogens

Teratogens are environmental agents (infectious toxins, maternal systemic diseases, drugs, chemicals, and physical agents) that can harm the developing fetus by causing congenital structural or functional defects. Teratogens may also cause spontaneous abortion, complications during labor and delivery, hidden defects in later development (such as cognitive or behavioral problems), or neoplastic transformations.

Environmental mutagens and carcinogens

A permanent change in genetic material is a *mutation,* which may occur spontaneously or after exposure of a cell to a mutagen, such as radiation, certain chemicals, or viruses. Mutations can occur at any location in the genome.

Carcinogens are environmental agents, such as cigarette smoke, indoor and outdoor air pollution, and preservatives in certain foods, that may cause cancer.

Every cell has built-in defenses against genetic damage. However, if a mutation isn't identified or repaired, the mutation may produce a trait different from the original trait and may be transmitted to offspring. Mutations may have no effect; some may change expression of a trait, and others may change the way a cell functions. Many mutagens are also carcinogens because they alter cell function. Some mutations cause serious or deadly defects, such as congenital anomalies or cancer.

Autosomal disorders

In single-gene disorders, an error occurs at a single gene site on the DNA strand. A mistake may occur in the copying and transcribing of a single codon through additions, deletions, or excessive repetitions.

Single-gene disorders are inherited in clearly identifiable patterns that are the same as those seen in inheritance of normal traits. Because every person has 22 pairs of autosomes and only 1 pair of sex chromosomes, most hereditary disorders are caused by autosomal defects.

Autosomal dominant transmission usually affects male and female offspring equally. Children of an affected parent have a 50% chance of being affected. Autosomal recessive inheritance also usually affects male and female offspring equally. If both parents are affected, all their offspring will be affected. If both parents are unaffected but are heterozygous for the trait (carriers of the defective gene), there's a 25% chance with each pregnancy that the child will be affected. If only one parent is affected and the other isn't a carrier, none of the offspring will be affected but all will carry the defective gene. If one parent is affected and the other is a carrier, 50% of their children will be affected. Autosomal recessive disorders may occur when no family history of the disease exists.

Sex-linked disorders

Genetic disorders caused by genes located on the sex chromosomes are termed *sex-linked disorders*. Most sex-linked disorders are controlled by genes located on the X chromosome, usually as recessive traits. Because males have only one X chromosome, a single X-linked recessive gene can cause disease to be exhibited in a male. Females receive two X chromosomes, so they can be homozygous for a disease allele, homozygous for a normal allele, or heterozygous.

Most people who express X-linked *recessive* traits are males with unaffected parents. In rare cases, the father is affected and the mother is a carrier. All daughters of an affected male and a noncarrier female will be carriers. Sons of an affected male and a noncarrier female will be unaffected, and the unaffected sons aren't carriers. Unaffected male children of a female carrier don't transmit the disorder.

Characteristics of X-linked *dominant* inheritance include evidence of the inherited trait in the family history. A person with the abnormal trait must have one affected parent. If the father has an X-linked dominant disorder, all his daughters and none of his sons will be affected. If a mother has an X-linked dominant disorder, each of her children has a 50% chance of being affected.

Multifactorial disorders

Most multifactorial disorders result from the effects of several different genes and an environmental component. In *polygenic inheritance*, each gene has a small additive effect, and the effect of a combination of genetic errors in a person is unpredictable. Multifactorial disorders can result from a less-than-optimum expression of many different genes, not from a specific error.

Some multifactorial disorders are apparent at birth, such as cleft lip, cleft palate, congenital heart disease, anencephaly, clubfoot, and myelomeningocele. Others don't become apparent until later, such as type 2 diabetes mellitus, hypertension, hyperlipidemia, most autoimmune diseases, and many cancers. Multifactorial disorders that develop during adulthood are commonly believed to be strongly related to environmental factors, not only in incidence but also in the degree of expression.

Chromosome defects

Aberrations in chromosome structure or number cause a class of disorders called *congenital anomalies*, or birth defects. The aberration may be loss, addition, or rearrangement of genetic material. If the remaining genetic material is sufficient to maintain life, an endless variety of clinical manifestations may occur. Most clinically significant chromosome aberrations arise during meiosis. Meiosis is an incredibly complex process that can go wrong in many ways. Potential contributing factors include maternal age, radiation, and use of some therapeutic or recreational drugs.

Translocation, the relocation of a segment of a chromosome to a nonhomologous chromosome, occurs when chromosomes split apart and rejoin in an abnormal arrangement. The cells still have a normal amount of genetic material, so usually there are no visible abnormalities. However, because of the potential for these individuals to produce unbalanced gametes, the children of parents with translocated chromosomes may have serious genetic defects, such as monosomies or trisomies.

During both meiosis and mitosis, chromosomes normally separate in a process called *disjunction*. Failure to separate, called *nondisjunction*, causes an unequal distribution of chromosomes between the two resulting cells. If nondisjunction occurs during mitosis soon after fertilization, it may affect all the resulting cells. If nondisjunction occurs later during embryogenesis, a portion of the cells may be abnormal, resulting in *mosaicism*, which is the presence of two or more cell lines in the same person. Gain or loss of chromosomes is usually caused by nondisjunction of autosomes or sex chromosomes during meiosis. The incidence of nondisjunction increases with parental age.

The presence of one chromosome fewer than the normal number is called *monosomy* for that particular chromosome; an autosomal monosomy is nonviable. The presence of an extra chromosome is called a *trisomy* for that particular chromosome. A mixture of both abnormal and normal cells results in mosaicism. The effect of mosaicism depends on the proportion and anatomic location of abnormal cells.

GENETIC DISORDERS

Genetic disorders are commonly classified by pattern of inheritance, as shown in the accompanying chart. (See *Common genetic disorders*, pages 24 to 27.)

COMMON GENETIC DISORDERS

DISORDER	PATHOPHYSIOLOGY	SIGNS AND SYMPTOMS

Autosomal recessive disorders

DISORDER	PATHOPHYSIOLOGY	SIGNS AND SYMPTOMS
Cystic fibrosis Inborn error in a cell-membrane transport protein. Dysfunction of the exocrine glands affects multiple organ systems. The disease affects males and females. It's the most common fatal genetic disease in white children.	Most cases arise from the mutation that affects the genetic coding for a single amino acid, resulting in a protein (cystic fibrosis transmembrane regulator [CFTR]) that doesn't function properly. This mutant CFTR resembles other transmembrane transport proteins, but it lacks the phenylalanine at position 508 in the protein produced by normal genes. This regulator interferes with cyclic adenosine monophosphate (cAMP)–regulated chloride channels and transport of other ions by preventing adenosine triphosphate from binding to the protein or by interfering with activation by protein kinase. The mutation affects volume-absorbing epithelia in the airways and intestines, salt-absorbing epithelia in sweat ducts, and volume-secretory epithelia in the pancreas. Mutations in CFTR lead to dehydration, which increases the viscosity of mucous gland secretions and consequently obstructs glandular ducts. Cystic fibrosis has varying effects on electrolyte and water transport.	• Chronic airway infections leading to bronchiectasis • Bronchiolectasis • Exocrine pancreatic insufficiency • Intestinal dysfunction • Abnormal sweat-gland function • Reproductive dysfunction
Phenylketonuria (PKU) Inborn error in metabolism of the amino acid phenylalanine. PKU has a low incidence among Blacks and Ashkenazic Jews and a high incidence among people of Irish and Scottish descent.	Patients with classic PKU have almost no activity of phenylalanine hydroxylase, an enzyme that helps convert phenylalanine to tyrosine. As a result, phenylalanine accumulates in the blood and urine, and tyrosine levels are low.	Treatment includes early diagnosis and avoidance of phenylalanine in the diet; however, if left untreated, these signs and symptoms can occur: • By age 4 months, signs of arrested brain development, including mental retardation • Personality disturbances • Seizures • Decreased IQ • Macrocephaly • Eczematous skin lesions or dry, rough skin • Hyperactivity • Irritability • Purposeless, repetitive motions • Awkward gait • Musty odor from skin and urine excretion of phenylacetic acid
Sickle cell anemia Congenital hemolytic anemia resulting from defective hemoglobin molecules. In the United States, sickle cell anemia occurs primarily in persons of African and Mediterranean descent. It also affects populations in Puerto Rico, Turkey, India, and the Middle East.	Abnormal hemoglobin S in red blood cells becomes insoluble during hypoxia. As a result, these cells become rigid, rough, and elongated, forming a crescent or sickle shape. The sickling produces hemolysis. The altered cells also pile up in the capillaries and smaller blood vessels, making the blood more viscous. Normal circulation is impaired, causing pain, tissue infarctions, and swelling. Each patient with sickle cell anemia has a different hypoxic threshold and different factors that trigger a sickle cell crisis. Illness, exposure to cold, stress, acidotic states, or a pathophysiologic process that pulls water out of the sickle cells precipitates a crisis in most patients. The blockages then cause anoxic changes that lead to further sickling and obstruction.	• Symptoms of sickle cell anemia don't develop until after age 6 months because fetal hemoglobin protects infants for the first few months after birth • Chronic fatigue • Unexplained dyspnea on exertion • Joint swelling • Aching bones • Severe localized and generalized pain • Leg ulcers • Frequent infections • Priapism in males *In sickle cell crisis:* • Severe pain • Hematuria • Lethargy
Tay-Sachs disease Also known as *GM₂ gangliosidosis*, the most common lipid-storage disease. Tay-Sachs affects Ashkenazi Jews about 100 times more often than the general population.	The enzyme hexosaminidase A is absent or deficient. This enzyme is necessary to metabolize gangliosides, water-soluble glycolipids found primarily in the central nervous system (CNS). Without hexosaminidase A, lipid molecules accumulate, progressively destroying and demyelinating CNS cells.	• Exaggerated Moro's (startle) reflex at birth and apathy (response only to loud sounds) by age 3 to 6 months • Inability to sit up, lift head, or grasp objects; difficulty turning over; progressive vision loss • Deafness, blindness, seizures, paralysis, spasticity, and continued neurologic deterioration (by age 18 months) • Recurrent bronchopneumonia

DISORDER	PATHOPHYSIOLOGY	SIGNS AND SYMPTOMS

Autosomal dominant disorders

Marfan syndrome

Rare degenerative, generalized disease of the connective tissue that results from elastin and collagen defects. The syndrome occurs in 1 of 20,000 individuals, affecting males and females equally. Approximately 25% of cases represent new mutations.

Marfan syndrome is caused by mutation in a single gene on chromosome 15, the gene that codes for fibrillin, a glycoprotein component of connective tissue. These small fibers are abundant in large blood vessels and the suspensory ligaments of the ocular lenses. The effect on connective tissue is variable and includes excessive bone growth, ocular disorders, and cardiac defects.

- Increased height, long extremities, and arachnodactyly (long, spiderlike fingers)
- Defects of sternum (funnel chest or pigeon breast, for example), chest asymmetry, scoliosis, or kyphosis
- Hypermobile joints
- Myopia
- Lens displacement
- Valvular abnormalities (redundancy of leaflets, stretching of chordae tendineae, or dilation of valvulae anales)
- Mitral valve prolapse
- Aortic regurgitation

X-linked recessive disorders

Fragile X syndrome

The most common inherited cause of mental retardation. Approximately 85% of males and 50% of females who inherit the fragile X mental retardation 1 (FMR1) mutation will demonstrate clinical features of the syndrome. It's estimated to occur in about 1 in 1,500 males and 1 in 2,500 females. It has been reported in almost all races and ethnic populations.

Fragile X syndrome is an X-linked condition that doesn't follow a simple X-linked inheritance pattern. The unique mutation that results consists of an expanding region of a specific triplet of nitrogenous bases: cytosine, guanine, and guanine (CGG) within the gene's DNA sequence. Normally, FMR1 contains 6 to 49 sequential copies of the CGG triplet. When the number of CGG triplets expands to the range of 50 to 200 and repeats, the region of DNA becomes unstable and is referred to as a premutation. A full mutation consists of more than 200 CGG triplet repeats. The full mutation typically causes abnormal methylation (methyl groups attach to components of the gene) of FMR1. Methylation inhibits gene transcription and, thus, protein production. The reduced or absent protein product is responsible for the clinical features of fragile X syndrome.

Postpubescent males with fragile X syndrome commonly have distinct physical features, behavioral difficulties, and cognitive impairment. Other signs and symptoms include:
- Prominent jaw and forehead and a head circumference exceeding the 90th percentile
- Long, narrow face with long or large ears that may be posteriorly rotated
- Connective tissue abnormalities, including hyperextension of the fingers, a floppy mitral valve (in 80% of adults), and mild to severe pectus excavatum
- Unusually large testes
- Average IQ of 30 to 70
- Hyperactivity, speech difficulties, language delay, and autisticlike behaviors

Females with fragile X syndrome tend to have more subtle symptoms, including:
- Learning disabilities
- IQ scores in the mental retardation range
- Excessive shyness or social anxiety
- Prominent ears and connective tissue manifestations

Hemophilia

Bleeding disorder; severity and prognosis vary with the degree of deficiency, or nonfunction, and the site of bleeding. Hemophilia occurs in 20 of 100,000 male births. Hemophilia A, or classic hemophilia, is a deficiency of clotting factor VIII; it's more common than type B, affecting more than 80% of all hemophiliacs. Hemophilia B, or Christmas disease, affects 15% of all hemophiliacs and results from a deficiency of factor IX. There's no relationship between factor VIII and factor IX inherited defects.

Abnormal bleeding occurs because of specific clotting factor malfunction. Factors VIII and IX are components of the intrinsic clotting pathway; factor IX is an essential factor, and factor VIII is a critical cofactor. Factor VIII accelerates the activation of factor X by several thousand times. Excessive bleeding occurs when these clotting factors are reduced by more than 75%.

Hemophilia may be severe, moderate, or mild, depending on the degree of activation of clotting factors. A person with hemophilia forms a platelet plug at a bleeding site, but clotting factor deficiency impairs the ability to form a stable fibrin clot. Delayed bleeding is more common than immediate hemorrhage.

- Spontaneous bleeding in severe hemophilia
- Excessive or continued bleeding or bruising
- Large subcutaneous and deep intramuscular hematomas
- Prolonged bleeding in mild hemophilia after major trauma or surgery, but no spontaneous bleeding after minor trauma
- Pain, swelling, and tenderness in joints
- Internal bleeding, commonly manifested as abdominal, chest, or flank pain
- Hematuria
- Hematemesis or tarry stools

(continued)

DISORDER	PATHOPHYSIOLOGY	SIGNS AND SYMPTOMS

Polygenic (multifactorial) disorders

DISORDER	PATHOPHYSIOLOGY	SIGNS AND SYMPTOMS

Cleft lip and cleft palate
May occur separately or together. Cleft lip with or without cleft palate occurs twice as often in males as in females. Cleft palate without cleft lip is more common in females. Cleft lip deformities can occur unilaterally, bilaterally or, rarely, in the midline. Only the lip may be involved, or the defect may extend into the upper jaw or nasal cavity. Incidence is highest in children with a family history of cleft defects.
	During the 2nd month of pregnancy, the front and sides of the face and the palatine shelves develop. Because of a chromosomal abnormality, exposure to teratogens, genetic abnormality, or environmental factors, the lip or palate fuses imperfectly. The deformity may range from a simple notch to a complete cleft.
	   A cleft palate may be partial or complete. A complete cleft includes the soft palate, the bones of the maxilla, and the alveolus on one or both sides of the premaxilla.
	   A double cleft is the most severe of the deformities. The cleft runs from the soft palate forward to either side of the nose. A double cleft separates the maxilla and premaxilla into freely moving segments. The tongue and other muscles can displace the segments, enlarging the cleft.
		• Obvious cleft lip or cleft palate
		• Feeding difficulties due to incomplete fusion of the palate

Neural tube defects
Serious birth defects that involve the spine or skull; they result from failure of the neural tube to close at approximately 28 days after conception. The most common forms of neural tube defects are spina bifida (50% of cases), anencephaly (40% of cases), and encephalocele (10% of cases). Spina bifida occulta is the most common and least severe spinal cord defect. The incidence of neural tube defects varies greatly among countries and by region in the United States. For example, the incidence is significantly higher in the British Isles and low southern China and Japan. In the United States, North and South Carolina have at least twice the incidence of neural tube defects as most other parts of the country. These birth defects are also less common in Blacks than in Whites.
	Neural tube closure normally occurs at 24 days gestation in the cranial region and continues distally, with closure of the lumbar regions by 28 days.
	   Spina bifida occulta is characterized by incomplete closure of one or more vertebrae without protrusion of the spinal cord or meninges.
	However, in more severe forms of spina bifida, incomplete closure of one or more vertebrae causes protrusion of the spinal contents in an external sac or cystic lesion (spina bifida cystica). Spina bifida cystica has two classifications: myelomeningocele (meningomyelocele) and meningocele. In myelomeningocele, the external sac contains meninges, cerebrospinal fluid (CSF), and a portion of the spinal cord or nerve roots distal to the conus medullaris. When the spinal nerve roots end at the sac, motor and sensory functions below the sac are terminated. In meningocele, less severe than myelomeningocele, the sac contains only meninges and CSF. Meningocele may produce no neurologic symptoms.
	   In encephalocele, a saclike portion of the meninges and brain protrudes through a defective opening in the skull. Usually, it occurs in the occipital area, but it may also occur in the parietal, nasopharyngeal, or frontal area.
	   In anencephaly, the most severe form of neural tube defect, the closure defect occurs at the cranial end of the neuroaxis and, as a result, part or the entire top of the skull is missing, severely damaging the brain. Portions of the brain stem and spinal cord may also be missing. No diagnostic or therapeutic efforts are helpful; this condition is invariably fatal.
		Signs and symptoms depend on the type and severity of the neural tube defect:
		• Possibly, a depression or dimple, tuft of hair, soft fatty deposits, port wine nevi, or a combination of these abnormalities on the skin over the spinal defect (spina bifida occulta)
		• Foot weakness or bowel and bladder disturbances, especially likely during rapid growth phases (spina bifida occulta)
		• Saclike structure that protrudes over the spine (myelomeningocele, meningocele)
		• Depending on the level of the defect, permanent neurologic dysfunction, such as flaccid or spastic paralysis and bowel and bladder incontinence (myelomeningocele)

DISORDER	PATHOPHYSIOLOGY	SIGNS AND SYMPTOMS
Disorders of chromosome number		
Down syndrome (trisomy 21) Spontaneous chromosome abnormality that causes characteristic facial features, other distinctive physical abnormalities (cardiac defects in 60% of affected persons), and mental retardation. It occurs in 1 of 650 to 700 live births.	Nearly all cases of Down syndrome result from trisomy 21 (three copies of chromosome 21). The result is a karyotype of 47 chromosomes instead of the usual 46. In 4% of patients, Down syndrome results from an unbalanced translocation or chromosomal rearrangement in which the long arm of chromosome 21 breaks and attaches to another chromosome. Some affected persons and some asymptomatic parents may have chromosomal mosaicism, a mixture of two cell types, some with the normal 46 and some with an extra chromosome 21.	• Distinctive facial features (low nasal bridge, epicanthic folds, protruding tongue, and low-set ears); small open mouth and disproportionately large tongue • Single transverse crease on the palm (Simian crease) • Small white spots on the iris (Brushfield's spots) • Mental retardation (estimated IQ of 20 to 50) • Developmental delay • Congenital heart disease, mainly septal defects and especially of the endocardial cushion • Impaired reflexes
Trisomy 18 syndrome Also known as *Edwards' syndrome,* it's the second most common multiple malformation syndrome. Most affected infants have full trisomy 18, involving an extra (third) copy of chromosome 18 in each cell, but partial trisomy 18 (with varying phenotypes) and translocation types have also been reported. Full trisomy 18 syndrome is generally fatal or has an extremely poor prognosis. Most trisomic conceptions are spontaneously aborted; 30% to 50% of infants die within the first 2 months of life, and 90% die within the first year. Most surviving patients are profoundly mentally retarded. Incidence ranges from 1 in 3,000 to 8,000 neonates, with 3 to 4 females affected for every 1 male.	Most cases result from spontaneous nondisjunction meiotic, leading to an extra copy of chromosome 18 in each cell.	• Growth retardation, which begins in utero and remains significant after birth • Initial hypotonia that may soon cause hypertonia • Microcephaly and dolichocephaly • Micrognathia • Short and narrow nose with upturned nares • Unilateral or bilateral cleft lip and palate • Low-set, slightly pointed ears • Short neck • Conspicuous clenched hand with overlapping fingers (commonly seen on ultrasound in utero as well) • Cystic hygroma • Choroid plexus cysts (also seen in some normal infants)
Trisomy 13 syndrome Also known as *Patau's syndrome,* it's the third most common multiple malformation syndrome. Most affected infants have full trisomy 13 at birth; a few have the rare mosaic partial trisomy 13 syndrome (with varying phenotypes) or translocation types. Full trisomy 13 syndrome is fatal. Many trisomic zygotes are spontaneously aborted; 50% to 70% of infants die within 1 month after birth, and 85% by the first year. Only isolated cases of survival beyond 5 years have been reported in full trisomy 13 patients. Incidence is estimated to be 1 in 4,000 to 10,000 neonates.	Approximately 75% of all cases result from chromosomal nondisjunction. About 20% result from chromosomal translocation, involving a rearrangement of chromosomes 13 and 14. About 5% of cases are estimated to be mosaics; the clinical effects in these cases may be less severe.	• Microcephaly • Varying degrees of holoprosencephaly • Sloping forehead with wide sutures and fontanel • Scalp defect at the vertex • Bilateral cleft lip with associated cleft palate (in 45% of cases) • Flat and broad nose • Low-set ears and inner ear abnormalities • Polydactyly of the hands and feet • Club feet • Omphaloceles • Neural tube defects • Cystic hygroma • Genital abnormalities • Cystic kidneys • Hydronephrosis • Failure to thrive, seizures, apnea, and feeding difficulties

FLUIDS AND ELECTROLYTES

The body is mostly liquid — various electrolytes dissolved in water. Electrolytes are ions (electrically charged versions) of essential elements — predominantly sodium (Na^+), chloride (Cl^-), oxygen (O_2), hydrogen (H^+), bicarbonate (HCO_3^-), calcium (Ca^{2+}), potassium (K^+), sulfate (SO_4^{2-}), and phosphate (PO_4^{3-}). Only ionic forms of elements can dissolve or combine with other elements. Electrolyte balance must remain in a narrow range for the body to function. The kidneys maintain chemical balance throughout the body by producing and eliminating urine. They regulate the volume, electrolyte concentration, and acid-base balance of body fluids; detoxify and eliminate wastes; and regulate blood pressure by regulating fluid volume. The skin and lungs also play a vital role in fluid and electrolyte balance. Sweating results in loss of sodium and water, and every breath contains water vapor.

FLUID BALANCE

The kidneys maintain fluid balance in the body by regulating the amount and components of fluid inside and around the cells.

Intracellular fluid

The fluid inside each cell is called *intracellular fluid*. Each cell has its own mixture of components in the intracellular fluid, but the amounts of these substances are similar in every cell. Intracellular fluid contains large amounts of potassium, magnesium, and phosphate ions.

Extracellular fluid

The fluid in the spaces outside the cells, called *extracellular fluid*, is constantly moving. Normally, extracellular fluid includes blood plasma and interstitial fluid. In some pathologic states, it accumulates in a so-called *third space*, the space around organs in the chest or abdomen.

Extracellular fluid is rapidly transported through the body by circulating blood and between blood and tissue fluids by fluid and electrolyte exchange across the capillary walls. It contains large amounts of sodium, chloride, and bicarbonate ions, plus such cell nutrients as oxygen, glucose, fatty acids, and amino acids. It also contains carbon dioxide (CO_2), transported from the cells to the lungs for excretion, and other cellular products, transported from the cells to the kidneys for excretion.

The kidneys maintain the volume and composition of extracellular fluid and, to a lesser extent, intracellular fluid by continually exchanging water and ionic solutes, such as hydrogen, sodium, potassium, chloride, bicarbonate, sulfate, and phosphate ions, across the cell membranes of the renal tubules.

Fluid exchange

Four forces act to equalize concentrations of fluids, electrolytes, and proteins on both sides of the capillary wall by moving fluid between the vessels and the interstitial fluid. Forces that move fluid out of blood vessels are:
- hydrostatic pressure of blood
- osmotic pressure of interstitial fluid
  Forces that move fluid into blood vessels are:
- oncotic pressure of plasma proteins
- hydrostatic pressure of interstitial fluid.

Hydrostatic pressure is higher at the arteriolar end of the capillary bed than at the venular end. Oncotic pressure of plasma increases slightly at the venular end as fluid is drawn into the blood vessel. When the endothelial barrier (capillary wall) is normal and intact, fluid escapes at the arteriolar end of the capillary bed and is returned at the venular end. The small amount of fluid lost from the capillaries into the interstitial tissue spaces is drained off through the lymphatic system and returned to the bloodstream.

Acid-base balance

Regulation of the extracellular fluid environment involves the ratio of acid to base, measured clinically as pH. In physiology, all positively charged ions are acids and all negatively charged ions are bases. To regulate acid-base balance, the kidneys secrete hydrogen ions (acid), reabsorb sodium (acid) and bicarbonate

---

ALTERATIONS IN TONICITY

ALTERATIONS	PATHOPHYSIOLOGY	CAUSES
Isotonic	• Intracellular fluids and extracellular fluids have equal osmotic pressure, but there's a dramatic change in total body fluid volume. • No cellular swelling or shrinkage exists because osmosis doesn't occur.	• Blood loss from penetrating trauma • Expansion of fluid volume if a patient receives too much normal saline
Hypertonic	• Extracellular fluid is more concentrated than intracellular fluid. • Water flows out of the cell through the semipermeable cell membrane, causing cell shrinkage.	• Administration of hypertonic (>0.9%) saline • Hypernatremia from severe dehydration • Sodium retention from renal disease
Hypotonic	• Decreased osmotic pressure forces some extracellular fluid into the cells, causing them to swell. • In extreme hypotonicity, cells may swell until they burst and die.	• Overhydration

ions (base), acidify phosphate salts, and produce ammonium ions (acid). This keeps the blood at its normal pH of 7.35 to 7.45. Important pH boundaries include:
- < 6.8 incompatible with life
- < 7.2 cell function seriously impaired
- < 7.35 acidosis
- 7.35 to 7.45 normal
- > 7.45 alkalosis
- > 7.55 cell function seriously impaired
- > 7.8 incompatible with life.

PATHOPHYSIOLOGIC CONCEPTS

The regulation of intracellular and extracellular electrolyte concentrations depends on these factors:
- balance between intake of substances containing electrolytes and output of electrolytes in urine, feces, and sweat
- transport of fluid and electrolytes between extracellular and intracellular fluid.

Fluid imbalance occurs when regulatory mechanisms can't compensate for abnormal intake and output at any level from the cell to the organism. Fluid and electrolyte imbalances include edema, isotonic alterations, hypertonic alterations, hypotonic alterations, and electrolyte imbalances. Disorders of fluid volume or osmolarity result. Many conditions also affect capillary exchange, resulting in fluid shifts.

Edema

Despite almost constant interchange through the endothelial barrier, the body maintains a steady state of extracellular water balance between the plasma and interstitial fluid. Increased fluid volume in the interstitial spaces is called *edema*. It's classified as localized or systemic. Obstruction of the veins or lymphatic system or increased vascular permeability usually causes localized edema in the affected area, such as the swelling around an injury. Systemic, or generalized, edema may be due to heart failure or renal disease. Massive systemic edema is called *anasarca*.

Edema results from abnormal expansion of the interstitial fluid or the accumulation of fluid in a third space, such as the peritoneum (ascites), pleural cavity (hydrothorax), or pericardial sac (pericardial effusion).

Tonicity

Many fluid and electrolyte disorders are classified according to how they affect osmotic pressure, or tonicity. (See *Alterations in tonicity*.) *Tonicity* describes the relative concentrations of

MAJOR ELECTROLYTES

ELECTROLYTE	CHARACTERISTICS
Sodium	• Major extracellular fluid cation • Maintains tonicity of extracellular fluid • Regulates acid-base balance by renal reabsorption of sodium ion (base) and excretion of hydrogen ion (acid) • Facilitates nerve conduction and neuromuscular function • Facilitates glandular secretion • Maintains water balance
Potassium	• Major intracellular fluid cation • Maintains cell electrical neutrality • Facilitates cardiac muscle contraction and electrical conductivity • Facilitates neuromuscular transmission of nerve impulses • Maintains acid-base balance
Chloride	• Mainly an extracellular fluid anion • Accounts for two-thirds of all serum anions • Secreted by the stomach mucosa as hydrochloric acid, providing an acid medium for digestion and enzyme activation • Helps maintain acid-base and water balances • Influences tonicity of extracellular fluid • Facilitates exchange of oxygen and carbon dioxide in red blood cells • Helps activate salivary amylase, which triggers the digestive process
Calcium	• Indispensable to cell permeability, bone and teeth formation, blood coagulation, nerve impulse transmission, and normal muscle contraction • Plays a vital role in cardiac action potential and is essential for cardiac pacemaker automaticity
Magnesium	• Present in small quantities, but physiologically as significant as the other major electrolytes • Enhances neuromuscular communication • Stimulates parathyroid hormone secretion, which regulates intracellular calcium • Activates many enzymes in carbohydrate and protein metabolism • Facilitates cell metabolism • Facilitates sodium, potassium, and calcium transport across cell membranes • Facilitates protein transport
Phosphate	• Involved in cellular metabolism as well as neuromuscular regulation and hematologic function • Phosphate reabsorption in the renal tubules inversely related to calcium levels (an increase in urinary phosphorous triggers calcium reabsorption and vice versa)

DISORDERS OF FLUID BALANCE: HYPOVOLEMIA

CAUSES	PATHOPHYSIOLOGY	SIGNS AND SYMPTOMS	DIAGNOSTIC TEST RESULTS	TREATMENT
Hypovolemia is an isotonic disorder. Fluid volume deficit decreases capillary hydrostatic pressure and fluid transport. Cells are deprived of normal nutrients that serve as substrates for energy production, metabolism, and other cellular functions. Hypovolemia results from these causes: *Fluid loss* • Hemorrhage • Excessive perspiration • Renal failure with polyuria • Surgery • Vomiting or diarrhea • Nasogastric drainage • Diabetes mellitus with polyuria or diabetes insipidus • Fistulas • Excessive use of laxatives; diuretic therapy • Fever *Reduced fluid intake* • Dysphagia • Coma • Environmental conditions preventing fluid intake • Psychiatric illness *Fluid shift from extracellular fluid* • Burns (during the initial phase) • Acute intestinal obstruction • Acute peritonitis • Pancreatitis • Crushing injury • Pleural effusion • Hip fracture	Decreased renal blood flow triggers the renin-angiotensin system to increase sodium and water reabsorption. The cardiovascular system compensates by increasing heart rate, cardiac contractility, venous constriction, and systemic vascular resistance, thus increasing cardiac output and mean arterial pressure (MAP). Hypovolemia also triggers the thirst response, releasing more antidiuretic hormone and producing more aldosterone. When compensation fails, hypovolemic shock occurs in this sequence: • decreased intravascular fluid volume • diminished venous return, which reduces preload and decreases stroke volume • reduced cardiac output • decreased MAP • impaired tissue perfusion • decreased oxygen and nutrient delivery to cells • multiple organ dysfunction syndrome.	• Orthostatic hypotension • Tachycardia • Thirst • Flattened jugular veins • Sunken eyeballs • Dry mucous membranes • Diminished skin turgor • Rapid weight loss • Decreased urine output • Prolonged capillary refill time	• Increased blood urea nitrogen • Elevated serum creatinine level • Increased serum protein, hemoglobin, and hematocrit (unless caused by hemorrhage, when loss of blood elements causes subnormal values) • Rising blood glucose • Elevated serum osmolality (except in hyponatremia, where serum osmolality is low) • Serum electrolyte and arterial blood gas analysis may reflect associated clinical problems resulting from the underlying cause of hypovolemia or the treatment regimen • Urine specific gravity > 1.030 • Increased urine osmolality • Urine sodium level < 50 mEq/L	• Oral fluids • Parenteral fluids • Fluid resuscitation by rapid I.V. administration • Blood or blood products (with hemorrhage) • Antidiarrheals as needed • Antiemetics as needed • I.V. dopamine (Intropin) or norepinephrine (Levophed) to increase cardiac contractility and renal perfusion (if patient remains symptomatic after fluid replacement) • Autotransfusion (for some patients with hypovolemia caused by trauma)

electrolytes (osmotic pressure) on both sides of a semipermeable membrane (the cell wall or the capillary wall). The word *normal* in this context refers to the usual electrolyte concentration of physiologic fluids. Normal saline solution has a sodium chloride concentration of 0.9%.

• *Isotonic* solutions have the same electrolyte concentration and therefore the same osmotic pressure as extracellular fluid.

• *Hypertonic* solutions have a greater than normal concentration of some essential electrolyte, usually sodium.

• *Hypotonic* solutions have a lower than normal concentration of some essential electrolyte, also usually sodium.

Electrolyte balance

The major electrolytes are the cations sodium, potassium, calcium, and magnesium and the anions chloride, phosphate, and bicarbonate. The body continuously attempts to maintain intracellular and extracellular equilibrium of electrolytes. Too much or too little of any electrolyte will affect most body

Disorders of fluid balance: Hypervolemia

CAUSES	PATHOPHYSIOLOGY	SIGNS AND SYMPTOMS	DIAGNOSTIC TEST RESULTS	TREATMENT
Hypervolemia is an abnormal increase in the volume of circulating fluid (plasma) in the body. It results from these causes: *Increased risk for sdium and water retention* • Heart failure • Hepatic cirrhosis • Nephrotic syndrome • Corticosteroid therapy • Low dietary protein intake • Renal failure *Excessive sodium and water intake* • Parenteral fluid replacement with normal saline or lactated Ringer's solution • Blood or plasma replacement • Excessive dietary intake of water, sodium chloride, or other salts *Fluid shift to extracellular fluid* • Remobilization of fluid after burn treatment • Intake of hypertonic fluids • Intake of colloid oncotic fluids	Increased extracellular fluid volume causes this sequence of events: • circulatory overload • increased cardiac contractility and mean arterial pressure (MAP) • increased capillary hydrostatic pressure • shift of fluid to the interstitial space • edema Elevated MAP inhibits secretion of antidiuretic hormone and aldosterone and consequent increased urinary elimination of water and sodium. These compensatory mechanisms usually restore normal intravascular volume. If hypervolemia is severe or prolonged or the patient has a history of cardiovascular dysfunction, compensatory mechanisms may fail, and heart failure and pulmonary edema may ensue.	• Rapid breathing • Dyspnea • Crackles • Rapid, bounding pulse • Hypertension • Jugular vein distention • Moist skin • Acute weight gain • Edema • S$_3$ gallop	• Decreased serum potassium and blood urea nitrogen • Decreased hematocrit due to hemodilution • Normal or low serum sodium • Low urine sodium excretion • Increased hemodynamic values	• Treatment of underlying condition • Oxygen administration • Use of thromboembolic disease support hose to help mobilize edematous fluid • Bed rest • Restricted sodium and water intake • Preload reduction agents and afterload reduction agents • Hemodialysis or peritoneal dialysis • Continuous arteriovenous hemofiltration • Continuous venovenous hemofiltration

systems. (See *Major electrolytes,* page 29, and *Normal electrolyte values,* page 29.)

Electrolyte imbalances can affect all body systems. Too much or too little potassium or too little calcium or magnesium can increase the excitability of the cardiac muscle, causing arrhythmias. Multiple neurologic symptoms may result from electrolyte imbalance, ranging from disorientation or confusion to a completely depressed central nervous system. Too much or too little sodium or too much potassium can cause oliguria. Blood pressure may be increased or decreased. The GI tract is particularly susceptible to electrolyte imbalance:
• too much potassium — leads to abdominal cramps, nausea, and diarrhea
• too little potassium — leads to paralytic ileus
• too much magnesium — leads to nausea, vomiting, and diarrhea
• too much calcium — leads to nausea, vomiting, and constipation.

Acid-base imbalance

Acid-base balance is essential to life. Concepts related to imbalance include:
• *acidemia* — arterial blood pH less than 7.35, which reflects a relative excess of acid in the blood. The hydrogen ion content in extracellular fluid increases, and the hydrogen ions move to the intracellular fluid. To keep the intracellular fluid electrically neutral, an equal amount of potassium leaves the cell, creating a relative hyperkalemia.
• *alkalemia* — arterial blood pH greater than 7.45, which reflects a relative excess of base in the blood. In alkalemia, an excess of hydrogen ions in the intracellular fluid forces them into the extracellular fluid. To keep the intracellular fluid electrically neutral, potassium moves from the extracellular to the intracellular fluid, creating a relative hypokalemia.
• *acidosis* — a systemic increase in hydrogen ion concentration. If the lungs fail to eliminate CO_2 or if volatile (carbonic) or nonvolatile (lactic) acid products of metabolism accumulate,

DISORDERS OF ELECTROLYTE BALANCE

ELECTROLYTE IMBALANCE	SIGNS AND SYMPTOMS	DIAGNOSTIC TEST RESULTS
Hyponatremia	• Muscle twitching and weakness • Lethargy, confusion, seizures, and coma • Hypotension and tachycardia • Nausea, vomiting, and abdominal cramps • Oliguria or anuria	• Serum sodium <135 mEq/L • Decreased urine specific gravity • Decreased serum osmolality • Urine sodium >100 mEq/24 hours • Increased red blood cell count
Hypernatremia	• Agitation, restlessness, fever, and decreased level of consciousness • Muscle irritability and convulsions • Hypertension, tachycardia, pitting edema, and excessive weight gain • Thirst, increased viscosity of saliva, and rough tongue • Dyspnea, respiratory arrest, and death	• Serum sodium >145 mEq/L • Urine sodium <40 mEq/24 hours • High serum osmolality
Hypokalemia	• Dizziness, hypotension, arrhythmias, electrocardiogram (ECG) changes, and cardiac and respiratory arrest • Nausea, vomiting, anorexia, diarrhea, decreased peristalsis, abdominal distention, and paralytic ileus • Muscle weakness, fatigue, and leg cramps	• Serum potassium <3.5 mEq/L • Coexisting low serum calcium and magnesium levels not responsive to treatment for hypokalemia usually suggest hypomagnesemia • Metabolic alkalosis • ECG changes, including flattened T waves, elevated U waves, and depressed ST segment
Hyperkalemia	• Tachycardia changing to bradycardia, ECG changes, and cardiac arrest • Nausea, diarrhea, and abdominal cramps • Muscle weakness and flaccid paralysis	• Serum potassium >5 mEq/L • Metabolic acidosis • ECG changes, including tented and elevated T waves, widened QRS complex, prolonged PR interval, flattened or absent P waves, and depressed ST segment
Hypochloremia	• Muscle hyperexcitability and tetany • Shallow, depressed breathing • Usually associated with hyponatremia and its characteristic symptoms, such as muscle weakness and twitching	• Serum chloride <96 mEq/L • Serum pH >7.45, serum CO >32 mEq/L (supportive values)
Hyperchloremia	• Deep, rapid breathing • Weakness • Lethargy, possibly leading to coma	• Serum chloride >108 mEq/L • Serum pH <7.35, serum CO <22 mEq/L (supportive values)
Hypocalcemia	• Anxiety, irritability, twitching around the mouth, laryngospasm, seizures, positive Chvostek's and Trousseau's signs • Hypotension and arrhythmias due to decreased calcium influx	• Serum calcium <8.5 mg/dl • Low platelet count • ECG changes: lengthened QT interval, prolonged ST segment, and arrhythmias
Hypercalcemia	• Drowsiness, lethargy, headaches, irritability, confusion, depression, apathy, tingling and numbness of fingers, muscle cramps, and convulsions • Weakness and muscle flaccidity • Bone pain and pathological fractures • Heart block • Anorexia, nausea, vomiting, constipation, dehydration, and abdominal cramps • Flank pain	• Serum calcium >10.5 mg/dl • ECG changes: signs of heart block and shortened QT interval • Decreased parathyroid hormone level • Calcium stones in urine
Hypomagnesemia	• Nearly always coexists with hypokalemia and hypocalcemia • Hyperirritability, tetany, leg and foot cramps, positive Chvostek's and Trousseau's signs, confusion, delusions, and seizures • Arrhythmias, vasodilation, and hypotension	• Serum magnesium <1.8 mEq/L • Coexisting low serum potassium and calcium levels

DISORDERS OF ELECTROLYTE BALANCE (continued)

ELECTROLYTE IMBALANCE	SIGNS AND SYMPTOMS	DIAGNOSTIC TEST RESULTS
Hypermagnesemia	• Central nervous system depression, lethargy, and drowsiness • Diminished reflexes; muscle weakness to flaccid paralysis • Respiratory depression • Heart block, bradycardia, widened QRS, and prolonged QT interval • Hypotension	• Serum magnesium >2.5 mEq/L • Coexisting elevated potassium and calcium levels
Hypophosphatemia	• Muscle weakness, tremor, and paresthesia • Tissue hypoxia • Bone pain, decreased reflexes, and seizures • Weak pulse • Hyperventilation • Dysphagia and anorexia	• Serum phosphate <2.5 mg/dl • Urine phosphate >1.3 g/2 hours
Hyperphosphatemia	• Usually asymptomatic unless leading to hypocalcemia, then evidenced by tetany and seizures • Hyperreflexia, flaccid paralysis, and muscular weakness	• Serum phosphate >4.5 mg/dl • Serum calcium <8.5 mg/dl • Urine phosphorus <0.9 g/24 hours

hydrogen ion concentration rises. Acidosis can also occur if persistent diarrhea causes loss of basic bicarbonate anions or the kidneys fail to reabsorb bicarbonate or secrete hydrogen ions.

• *alkalosis* — a bodywide decrease in hydrogen ion concentration. An excessive loss of CO_2 during hyperventilation, loss of nonvolatile acids during vomiting, or excessive ingestion of base may decrease hydrogen ion concentration.

• *compensation* — the lungs and kidneys, along with a number of chemical buffer systems in the intracellular and extracellular compartments, work together to maintain plasma pH in the range of 7.35 to 7.45.

Buffer systems
A buffer system consists of a weak acid (one that doesn't readily release free hydrogen ions) and a corresponding base such as sodium bicarbonate. These buffers resist or minimize a change in pH when an acid or base is added to the buffered solution. Buffers work in seconds.

The four major buffers or buffer systems are:
• carbonic acid–bicarbonate system
• hemoglobin-oxyhemoglobin system
• other protein buffers
• phosphate system.

When primary disease processes alter either the acid or base component of the ratio, the lungs or kidneys (whichever isn't affected by the disease process) act to restore the ratio and normalize pH. Because the body's mechanisms that regulate pH occur in stepwise fashion over time, the body tolerates gradual changes in pH better than abrupt ones.

Renal mechanisms
If a respiratory disorder causes acidosis or alkalosis, the kidneys respond by altering the processing of hydrogen and bicarbonate ions to return the pH to normal. Renal compensation begins hours to days after a respiratory alteration in pH. Despite this delay, renal compensation is powerful.

• *Acidemia* — Kidneys excrete excess hydrogen ions, which may combine with phosphate or ammonia to form titratable acids in the urine. The net effect is to *raise* the concentration of bicarbonate ions in the extracellular fluid and restore acid-base balance.

• *Alkalemia* — Kidneys excrete excess bicarbonate ions, usually with sodium ions. The net effect is to *reduce* the concentration of bicarbonate ions in the extracellular fluid and restore acid-base balance.

Pulmonary mechanisms
If acidosis or alkalosis results from a metabolic or renal disorder, the respiratory system regulates the respiratory rate to return pH to normal. The partial pressure of carbon dioxide in arterial blood ($Paco_2$) reflects CO_2 levels proportionate to blood pH. As the concentration of the gas increases, so does its partial pressure. Within minutes after the slightest change in $Paco_2$, central chemoreceptors in the medulla that regulate the rate and depth of ventilation detect the change and respond as follows:

• *acidemia* — increased respiratory rate and depth to eliminate CO_2.

• *alkalemia* — decreased respiratory rate and depth to retain CO_2.

DISORDERS
Fluid and electrolyte balance is essential for health. Many factors, such as illness, injury, surgery, and treatments, can disrupt fluid and electrolyte balances. (See *Disorders of fluid balance: Hypovolemia*, page 30; *Disorders of fluid balance: Hypervolemia*, page 31; and *Disorders of electrolyte balance*, pages 32–33.)

Acid-base disturbances can cause respiratory acidosis or alkalosis or metabolic acidosis or alkalosis. (See *Disorders of acid-base balance*, pages 34 and 35.)

DISORDERS OF ACID-BASE BALANCE

DISORDER AND CAUSES	PATHOPHYSIOLOGY	SIGNS AND SYMPTOMS	DIAGNOSTIC TEST RESULTS	TREATMENT
Respiratory acidosis				
• Airway obstruction or parenchymal lung disease • Mechanical ventilation • Chronic metabolic alkalosis as respiratory compensatory mechanisms try to normalize pH • Chronic bronchitis • Extensive pneumonia • Large pneumothorax • Pulmonary edema • Asthma • Chronic obstructive pulmonary disease (COPD) • Drugs • Cardiac arrest • Central nervous system (CNS) trauma • Neuromuscular diseases • Sleep apnea	When pulmonary ventilation decreases, partial pressure of carbon dioxide in arterial blood ($Paco_2$) increases and carbon dioxide (CO_2) level rises. Retained CO_2 combines with water (H_2O) to form carbonic acid (H_2CO_3), which dissociates to release free hydrogen (H^+) and bicarbonate (HCO_3^-) ions. Increased $Paco_2$ and free H^+ ions stimulate the medulla to increase respiratory drive and expel CO_2. 　As pH falls, 2,3-diphosphoglycerate (2,3-DPG) accumulates in red blood cells, where it alters hemoglobin (Hb) to release oxygen. The Hb picks up H^+ ions and CO_2 and removes them from the serum. As respiratory mechanisms fail, rising $Paco_2$ stimulates kidneys to retain HCO_3^- and sodium (Na^+) ions and excrete H^+ ions. 　As the H^+ ion concentration overwhelms compensatory mechanisms, H^+ ions move into cells and potassium (K^+) ions move out. Without enough oxygen, anaerobic metabolism produces lactic acid.	• Restlessness • Confusion • Apprehension • Somnolence • Asterixis • Headaches • Dyspnea and tachypnea • Papilledema • Depressed reflexes • Hypoxemia • Tachycardia • Hypertension/hypotension • Atrial and ventricular arrhythmias • Coma	Arterial blood gas (ABG) analysis: $Paco_2$ > 45 mm Hg; pH <7.35 to 7.45; and normal HCO_3^- in the acute stage and elevated HCO_3^- in the chronic stage	*For pulmonary causes* • Removal of foreign body obstructing the airway • Mechanical ventilation • Bronchodilators • Antibiotics for pneumonia • Chest tubes for pneumothorax • Thrombolytics or anticoagulants for pulmonary emboli • Bronchoscopy to remove excess secretions *For COPD* • Bronchodilators • Oxygen at low flow rates • Corticosteroids *For other causes* • Drug therapy • Dialysis or activated charcoal to remove toxins • Correction of metabolic alkalosis • I.V. sodium bicarbonate
Respiratory alkalosis				
• Acute hypoxemia, pneumonia, interstitial lung disease, pulmonary vascular disease, or acute asthma • Anxiety • Hypermetabolic states, such as fever and sepsis • Excessive mechanical ventilation • Salicylate toxicity • Metabolic acidosis • Hepatic failure • Pregnancy	As pulmonary ventilation increases, excessive CO_2 is exhaled. Resulting hypocapnia leads to reduction of H_2CO_3 excretion of H^+ and HCO_3^- ions, and rising serum pH. 　Against rising pH, the hydrogen-potassium buffer system pulls H^+ ions out of cells and into blood in exchange for K^+ ions. H^+ ions entering blood combine with HCO_3^- ions to form H_2CO_3, and pH falls. 　Hypocapnia causes an increase in heart rate, cerebral vasoconstriction, and decreased cerebral blood flow. After 6 hours, kidneys secrete more HCO_3^- and less H^+. 　Continued low $Paco_2$ and vasoconstriction increases cerebral and peripheral hypoxia. Severe alkalosis inhibits calcium (Ca^+) ionization, increasing nerve and muscle excitability.	• Deep, rapid breathing • Light-headedness or dizziness • Agitation • Circumoral and peripheral paresthesias • Carpopedal spasms, twitching, and muscle weakness	ABG analysis showing $Paco_2$ < 35 mm Hg; elevated pH in proportion to decrease in $Paco_2$ in the acute stage but decreasing toward normal in the chronic stage; normal HCO_3^- in the acute stage but less than normal in the chronic stage	• Removal of ingested toxins, such as salicylates, by inducing emesis or using gastic lavage • Treatment of fever or sepsis • Oxygen for acute hypoxemia • Treatment of CNS disease • Having patient breathe into a paper bag • Adjustments to mechanical ventilation to decrease minute ventilation

DISORDER AND CAUSES	PATHOPHYSIOLOGY	SIGNS AND SYMPTOMS	DIAGNOSTIC TEST RESULTS	TREATMENT
Metabolic acidosis				
• Excessive acid accumulation • Deficient HCO_3^- scores • Decreased acid excretion by the kidneys • Diabetic ketoacidosis • Chronic alcoholism • Malnutrition or a low-carbohydrate, high-fat diet • Anaerobic carbohydrate metabolism • Underexcretion of metabolized acids or inability to conserve base • Diarrhea, intestinal malabsorption, or loss of sodium bicarbonate from the intestines • Salicylate intoxication, exogenous poisoning or, less frequently, Addison's disease • Inhibited secretion of acid	As H^+ ions begin accumulating in the body, chemical buffers (plasma HCO_3^- and proteins) in cells and extracellular fluid bind them. Excess H^+ ions decrease blood pH and stimulate chemoreceptors in the medulla to increase respiration. Consequent fall of partial pressure of $Paco_2$ frees H^+ ions to bind with HCO_3^- ions. Respiratory compensation occurs but isn't sufficient to correct acidosis. Healthy kidneys compensate, excreting excess H+ ions, buffered by phosphate or ammonia. For each H^+ ion excreted, renal tubules reabsorb and return to blood one Na^+ ion and one HCO_3^- ion. Excess H^+ ions in extracellular fluid passively diffuse into cells. To maintain balance of charge across cell membrane, cells release K^+ ions. Excess H^+ ions change the normal balance of K^+, Na^+, and Ca^+ ions, impairing neural excitability.	• Headache and lethargy progressing to drowsiness, central nervous system (CNS) depression, Kussmaul's respirations, hypotension, stupor, and coma and death • Associated GI distress leading to anorexia, nausea, vomiting, diarrhea, and possibly dehydration • Warm, flushed skin • Fruity-smelling breath	• Arterial blood pH <7.35; $Paco_2$ normal or < 35 mm Hg as respiratory compensatory mechanisms take hold; HCO_3^- may be < 22 mEq/L • Urine pH < 4.5 in the absence of renal disease • Elevated plasma lactic acid in lactic acidosis • Anion gap >14 mEq/L in high anion gap metabolic acidosis, lactic acidosis, ketoacidosis, aspirin overdose, alcohol poisoning, renal failure, or any disorder caused by accumulation of organic acids, sulfates, or phosphates • Anion gap 12 mEq/L or less in normal anion gap metabolic acidosis from HCO_3^- loss, GI or renal loss, increased acid load, rapid I.V. saline administration, or other disorders characterized by HCO_3^- loss	• Sodium bicarbonate I.V. for severe high anion gap • I.V. lactated Ringer's solution • Evaluation and correction of electrolyte imbalances • Correction of underlying cause • Mechanical ventilation to maintain respiratory compensation, if needed • Antibiotic therapy to treat infection • Dialysis for patients with renal failure or certain drug toxicities • Antidiarrheal agents for diarrhea-induced HCO_3^- loss • Position patient to prevent aspiration • Seizure precautions
Metabolic alkalosis				
• Chronic vomiting • Nasogastric tube drainage or lavage without adequate electrolyte replacement • Fistulas • Use of steroids and certain diuretics (furosemide [Lasix], thiazides, and ethacrynic acid [Edecrin]) • Massive blood transfusions • Cushing's disease, primary hyperaldosteronism, and Bartter's syndrome • Excessive intake of bicarbonate of soda, other antacids, or absorbable alkali • Excessive amounts of I.V. fluids; high serum concentrations of bicarbonate or lactate • Respiratory insufficiency • Low serum chloride • Low serum potassium	Chemical buffers in extracellular and intracellular fluid bind HCO_3^- in the body. Excess unbound HCO_3^- raises blood pH, depressing chemoreceptors in the medulla, inhibiting respiration and raising $Paco_2$. CO_2 combines with H_2O to form H_2CO_3. Low oxygen limits respiratory compensation. When blood HCO_3^- rises to 28 mEq/L, the amount filtered by renal glomeruli exceeds reabsorptive capacity of the renal tubules. Excess HCO_3^- is excreted in urine, and H^+ ions are retained. To maintain electrochemical balance, Na^+ ions and water are excreted with HCO_3^- ions. When H^+ ion levels in extracellular fluid are low, H^+ ions diffuse passively out of cells and extracellular K^+ ions move into cells. As intracellular H^+ ion levels fall, calcium ionization decreases, and nerve cells become permeable to Na^+ ions. Na^+ ions moving into cells trigger neural impulses in the peripheral nervous system and the CNS.	• Irritability, picking at bedclothes (carphology), twitching, and confusion • Nausea, vomiting, and diarrhea • Cardiovascular abnormalities due to hypokalemia • Respiratory disturbances (such as cyanosis and apnea) and slow, shallow respirations • Possible carpopedal spasm in the hand caused by diminished peripheral blood flow during repeated blood pressure checks	• Arterial blood pH >7.45; HCO_3^- > 26 mEq/L • Low potassium (< 3.5 mEq/L), calcium (< 8.9 mg/dl), and chloride (< 98 mEq/L)	• Cautious use of ammonium chloride I.V. (rarely) or hydrochloride to restore extracellular fluid hydrogen and chloride levels • Potassium chloride (KCl) and normal saline solution • Discontinuation of diuretics and supplementary KCl • Oral or I.V. acetazolamide

PART II

DISORDERS

AORTIC ANEURYSM

A thoracic aortic aneurysm is an abnormal widening of the ascending, transverse, or descending part of the aorta. Aneurysm of the ascending aorta is the most common type and has the highest mortality. An abdominal aneurysm generally occurs in the aorta between the renal arteries and the iliac branches.

Causes

Aneurysms commonly result from atherosclerosis, which weakens the aortic wall and gradually distends the lumen. Other causes include:
- age and family history
- fungal infection (mycotic aneurysms) of the aortic arch and descending segments
- bicuspid aortic valve
- congenital disorders, such as coarctation of the aorta or Marfan syndrome
- inflammatory disorders
- trauma
- syphilis
- hypertension (in dissecting aneurysm).

AGE ALERT
Ascending aortic aneurysms, the most common type, are usually seen in hypertensive men under age 60. Descending aortic aneurysms, usually found just below the origin of the subclavian artery, are most common in elderly men with hypertension. They may also occur in younger patients after traumatic chest injury or, less commonly, after infection.

Pathophysiology

First, degenerative changes create a focal weakness in the muscular layer of the aorta (tunica media), allowing the inner layer (tunica intima) and outer layer (tunica adventitia) to stretch outward. The outward bulge is the aneurysm. The pressure of blood pulsing through the aorta progressively weakens the vessel walls and enlarges the aneurysm. As the vessel dilates, wall tension increases. This increases arterial pressure and dilates the aneurysm further.

Aneurysms may be *dissecting*, a hemorrhagic separation in the aortic wall, usually within the medial layer; *saccular*, an outpouching of the arterial wall; or *fusiform*, a spindle-shaped enlargement encompassing the entire aortic circumference.

A false aneurysm occurs when the entire wall is injured, with blood contained in the surrounding tissue. A sac eventually forms and communicates with an artery or the heart.

COMPLICATIONS
- Cardiac tamponade if aneurysm ruptures

Signs and symptoms

Ascending aneurysm
- Pain, the most common symptom of thoracic aortic aneurysm
- Bradycardia

- Murmur of aortic insufficiency
- Pericardial friction rub (caused by a hemopericardium)
- Unequal intensities of the right carotid and left radial pulses
- Difference in blood pressure between the right and left arms
- Jugular vein distention

Descending aneurysm
- Pain, usually starting suddenly between the shoulder blades; may radiate to the chest
- Hoarseness
- Dyspnea and stridor
- Dysphagia
- Dry cough

Abdominal aneurysm
Although abdominal aneurysms usually don't produce symptoms, most are evident as a pulsating mass in the periumbilical area. Other signs include:
- systolic bruit over the aorta
- tenderness on deep palpation
- lumbar pain that radiates to the flank and groin.

CLINICAL TIP
Pain caused by a dissecting aortic aneurysm:
- may be described as "ripping" or "tearing"
- commonly radiates to the anterior chest, neck, back, or abdomen
- usually has an abrupt onset.

Diagnostic test results
- Echocardiography shows the aneurysm and its size.
- Anteroposterior and lateral abdominal X-rays show aortic calcifications present in abdominal aortic aneurysms; posteroanterior and oblique chest X-rays will show widening of the aorta and mediastinum in thoracic aortic aneurysms.
- Computed tomography scan shows the effects on nearby organs.
- Aortography shows the size and location of the aneurysm.
- Complete blood count reveals decreased hemoglobin levels.

Treatment
A dissecting aortic aneurysm is an emergency that requires prompt surgery and stabilizing measures. Treatment includes:
- antihypertensives such as nitroprusside
- negative inotropic agents to decrease force of contractility
- beta-adrenergic blockers
- oxygen for respiratory distress
- opioids for pain
- I.V. fluids
- possibly, whole blood transfusions.

Dissecting aneurysm

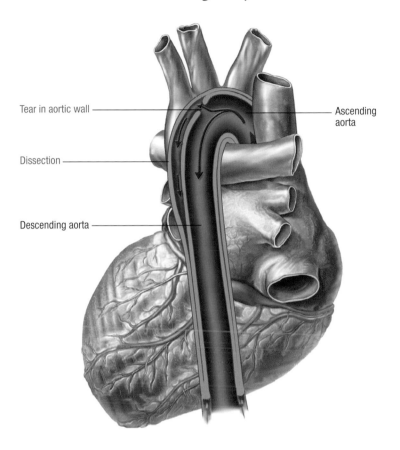

Tear in aortic wall

Ascending aorta

Dissection

Descending aorta

Fusiform aneurysm

False aneurysm

Saccular aneurysm

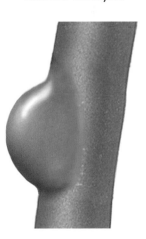

CARDIAC ARRHYTHMIAS

Abnormal electrical conduction or automaticity changes heart rate and rhythm. Arrhythmias vary in severity — from mild, producing no symptoms, and requiring no treatment (such as sinus arrhythmia, in which heart rate increases and decreases with respiration) to catastrophic ventricular fibrillation, which mandates immediate resuscitation. Arrhythmias are generally classified according to their origin (ventricular or supraventricular). Their effect on cardiac output and blood pressure, partially influenced by the site of origin, determines their clinical significance. (See the appendix Types of cardiac arrhythmias.)

Causes

Each arrhythmia may have its own specific cause. Common causes include:

- congenital defects
- myocardial ischemia or infarction
- organic heart disease
- drug toxicity
- degeneration or obstruction of conductive tissue
- connective tissue disorders
- electrolyte imbalances
- hypertrophy of heart muscle
- acid-base imbalances
- emotional stress.

AGE ALERT
Electrocardiogram changes that occur with age include:
- longer PR, QRS, and QT intervals
- lower amplitude of QRS complex
- leftward shift of QRS axis.

Pathophysiology

Altered automaticity, reentry, or conduction disturbances may cause cardiac arrhythmias. Enhanced automaticity is the result of partial depolarization, which may increase the intrinsic rate of the sinoatrial node or latent pacemakers, or may induce ectopic pacemakers to reach threshold and depolarize.

Ischemia or deformation causes an abnormal circuit to develop within conductive fibers. Although current flow is blocked in one direction within the circuit, the descending impulse can travel in the other direction. By the time the impulse completes the circuit, the previously depolarized tissue within the circuit is no longer refractory to stimulation; therefore, arrhythmias occur.

Conduction disturbances occur when impulses are conducted too quickly or too slowly.

COMPLICATIONS
- Impaired cardiac output

Signs and symptoms

Signs and symptoms of arrhythmias result from reduced cardiac output and altered perfusion to the organs and may include:

- dyspnea
- hypotension
- dizziness, syncope, and weakness
- chest pain
- cool, clammy skin
- altered level of consciousness
- reduced urinary output
- palpitations.

Diagnostic test results

- Electrocardiography detects arrhythmias as well as ischemia and infarction by showing prolonged or shortened intervals, elevated or depressed T waves, premature contractions, or absence of waves.
- Blood tests reveal electrolyte abnormalities, such as hyperkalemia or hypokalemia and hypermagnesemia or hypomagnesemia, as well as drug toxicities.
- Arterial blood gas analysis reveals acid-base abnormalities, such as acidemia or alkalemia.
- Holter monitoring, event monitoring, and loop recording show the presence of an arrhythmia.
- Exercise testing detects exercise-induced arrhythmias.
- Electrophysiologic testing identifies the mechanism of an arrhythmia and the location of accessory pathways; it also assesses the effectiveness of antiarrhythmic drugs, radiofrequency ablation, and implantable cardioverter-defibrillators (ICDs).

Treatment

Follow the specific treatment guidelines or protocols for each arrhythmia. Treatment generally focuses on the underlying problem and may include:

- antiarrhythmic medications
- electrolyte correction
- oxygen
- correction of acid-base balance
- cardioversion
- radiofrequency ablation
- ICD
- pacemaker
- cardiopulmonary resuscitation.

Sinus node arrhythmias
- Sinoatrial block
- Sinus bradycardia
- Sinus tachycardia

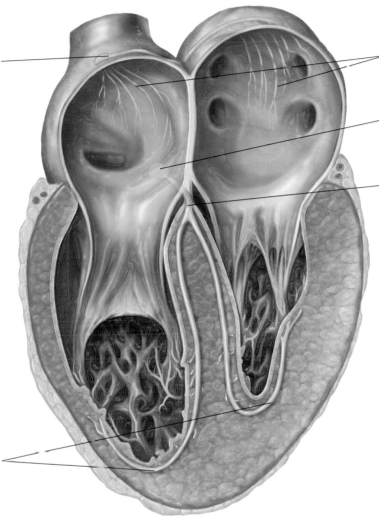

Atrial arrhythmias
- Premature atrial contractions
- Atrial fibrillation
- Atrial flutter

Atrioventricular (AV) blocks
- First-degree AV block
- Second-degree AV block
- Third-degree AV block

Junctional arrhythmia
- Junctional rhythm

Ventricular arrhythmias
- Premature ventricular contractions
- Ventricular fibrillation
- Ventricular tachycardia

CARDIAC TAMPONADE

Cardiac tamponade is a rapid, unchecked rise in pressure in the pericardial sac that compresses the heart, impairs diastolic filling, and limits cardiac output. The rise in pressure usually results from blood or fluid accumulation in the pericardial sac (pericardial effusion). Even a small amount of fluid (50 to 100 ml) can cause a serious tamponade if it accumulates rapidly.

Causes

- Idiopathic
- Effusion (due to cancer, bacterial infections, tuberculosis or, rarely, acute rheumatic fever)
- Traumatic or nontraumatic hemorrhage
- Viral or postirradiation pericarditis
- Chronic renal failure requiring dialysis
- Drug reaction (procainamide, hydralazine, minoxidil, isoniazid, penicillin, or daunorubicin)
- Heparin- or warfarin-induced tamponade
- Connective tissue disorders
- Postcardiac surgery
- Acute myocardial infarction

Pathophysiology

In cardiac tamponade, the progressive accumulation of fluid in the pericardial sac causes compression of the heart chambers. This compression obstructs filling of the ventricles and reduces the amount of blood that can be pumped out of the heart with each contraction.

Each time the ventricles contract, more fluid accumulates in the pericardial sac. This further limits the amount of blood that can fill the ventricular chambers, especially the left ventricle, during the next cardiac cycle.

The amount of fluid necessary to cause cardiac tamponade varies greatly; it may be as little as 50 to 100 ml when the fluid accumulates rapidly or more than 2,000 ml if the fluid accumulates slowly and the pericardium stretches to adapt. Prognosis is inversely proportional to the amount of fluid accumulated.

COMPLICATIONS
- Decreased cardiac output
- Cardiogenic shock
- Death if untreated

Signs and symptoms

- Elevated central venous pressure (CVP) with jugular vein distention
- Muffled heart sounds
- Pulsus paradoxus
- Diaphoresis and cool, clammy skin
- Anxiety, restlessness, syncope
- Cyanosis
- Weak, rapid pulse
- Cough, dyspnea, orthopnea, tachypnea

CLINICAL TIP
Cardiac tamponade has three classic features, known as Beck's triad, that include:
- elevated CVP with jugular vein distention
- muffled heart sounds
- pulsus paradoxus.

Diagnostic test results

- Chest X-rays show a slightly widened mediastinum and possible cardiomegaly. The cardiac silhouette may have a goblet-shaped appearance.
- Electrocardiography (ECG) detects a low-amplitude QRS complex and electrical alternans, an alternating beat-to-beat change in amplitude of the P wave, QRS complex, and T wave. Generalized ST-segment elevation is noted in all leads.
- Pulmonary artery catheterization detects increased right atrial pressure, right ventricular diastolic pressure, and CVP.
- Echocardiography reveals pericardial effusion with signs of right ventricular and atrial compression.

Treatment

- Supplemental oxygen
- Continuous ECG and hemodynamic monitoring
- Pericardiocentesis
- Pericardectomy
- Resection of a portion or all of the pericardium
- Trial volume loading with crystalloids
- Inotropic drugs, such as isoproterenol or dopamine
- Posttraumatic injury: blood transfusion, thoracotomy to drain reaccumulating fluid, or repair of bleeding sites may be needed
- Heparin-induced tamponade: heparin antagonist protamine sulfate to stop bleeding
- Warfarin-induced tamponade: vitamin K to stop bleeding

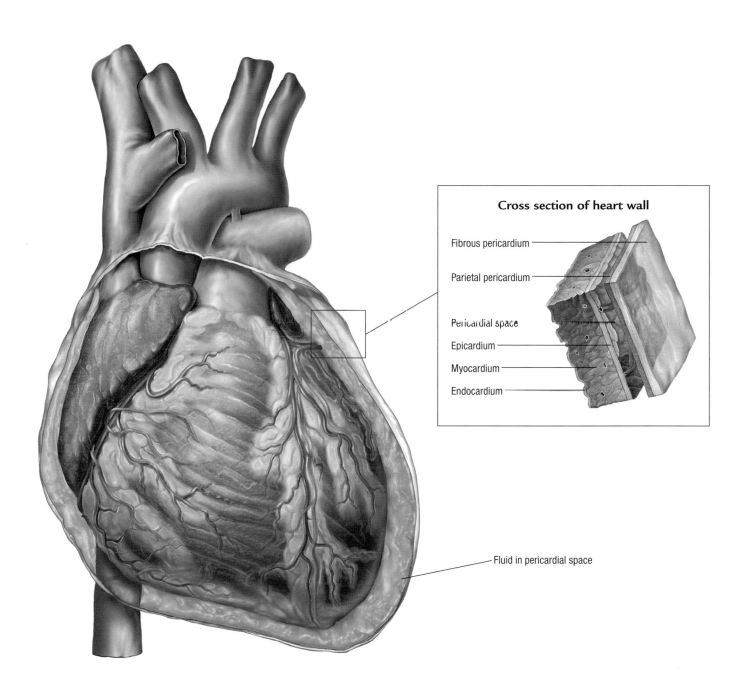

Cross section of heart wall

Fibrous pericardium

Parietal pericardium

Pericardial space

Epicardium

Myocardium

Endocardium

Fluid in pericardial space

CARDIOMYOPATHY

Cardiomyopathy is classified as dilated, hypertrophic, or restrictive.

Dilated cardiomyopathy (DCM) results from damage to cardiac muscle fibers; loss of muscle tone grossly dilates all four chambers of the heart, giving the heart a globular shape.

Hypertrophic cardiomyopathy (HCM) is characterized by disproportionate, asymmetrical thickening of the interventricular septum and left ventricular hypertrophy.

Restrictive cardiomyopathy (RCM) is characterized by restricted ventricular filling due to decreased ventricular compliance and endocardial fibrosis and thickening. If severe, it's irreversible.

Causes

Most patients with cardiomyopathy have idiopathic disease, but some are secondary to these possible causes:
- Viral infection
- Long-standing hypertension
- Ischemic heart disease or valvular disease
- Chemotherapy
- Cardiotoxic effects of drugs or alcohol
- Metabolic disease, such as diabetes or thyroid disease

Pathophysiology

In DCM, extensive damage to cardiac muscle fibers reduces contractility in the left ventricle. As systolic function declines, stroke volume, ejection fraction, and cardiac output fall.

COMPLICATIONS
- Heart failure
- Emboli
- Syncope
- Sudden death

In HCM, hypertrophy of the left ventricle and interventricular septum obstruct left ventricular outflow. The heart compensates for the decreased cardiac output (caused by obstructed outflow) by increasing the rate and force of contractions. The hypertrophied ventricle becomes stiff and unable to relax and fill during diastole. As left ventricular volume diminishes and filling pressure rises, pulmonary venous pressure also rises, leading to venous congestion and dyspnea.

COMPLICATIONS
- Pulmonary hypertension
- Heart failure
- Sudden death

In RCM, left ventricular hypertrophy and endocardial fibrosis limit myocardial contraction and emptying during systole as well as ventricular relaxation and filling during diastole. As a result, cardiac output falls.

COMPLICATIONS
- Heart failure
- Arrhythmias
- Emboli
- Sudden death

Signs and symptoms

- Shortness of breath
- Peripheral edema
- Fatigue
- Weight gain
- Cough and congestion
- Nausea
- Bloating
- Palpitations
- Syncope
- Chest pain
- Tachycardia

Diagnostic test results

- Chest X-rays show cardiomegaly and increased in heart size.
- Echocardiography reveals left ventricular dilation and dysfunction or left ventricular hypertrophy and a thick, asymmetrical intraventricular septum.
- Cardiac catheterization shows left ventricular dilation and dysfunction, elevated left ventricular and, commonly, right ventricular filling pressures, and diminished cardiac output.
- Thallium scan usually reveals myocardial perfusion defects.
- Cardiac catheterization reveals elevated left ventricular end-diastolic pressure and, possibly, mitral insufficiency.
- Electrocardiography usually shows left ventricular hypertrophy, ST-segment and T-wave abnormalities, Q waves in leads II, III, aV_F, and in V_4 to V_6, left anterior hemiblock, left axis deviation, and ventricular and atrial arrhythmias.

Treatment

- Treatment of underlying cause
- Control of arrhythmias
- Angiotensin-converting enzyme inhibitors, diuretics, digoxin (not used in HCM), hydralazine, isosorbide dinitrate, beta-adrenergic blockers, antiarrhythmics, and anticoagulants
- Revascularization
- Valve repair or replacement
- Heart transplantation
- Lifestyle modifications, such as quitting smoking; avoiding alcohol; eating a low-fat, low-salt diet; and restricting fluids
- Ventricular myotomy or myectomy
- Mitral valve repair or replacement

TYPES OF CARDIOMYOPATHY

Dilated

Hypertrophic

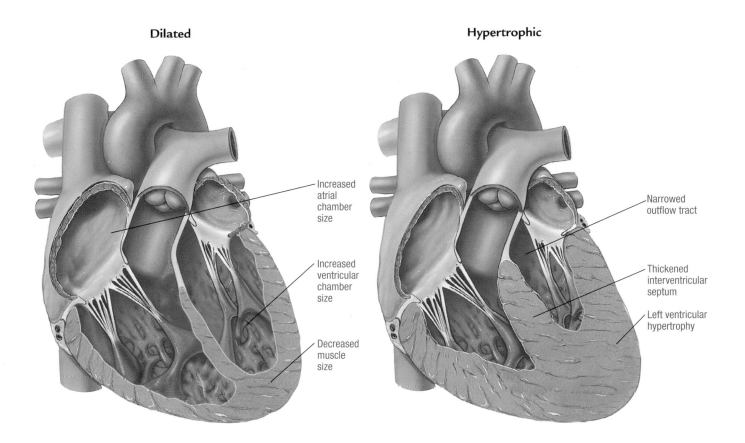

Increased
atrial
chamber
size

Increased
ventricular
chamber
size

Decreased
muscle
size

Narrowed
outflow tract

Thickened
interventricular
septum

Left ventricular
hypertrophy

Restrictive

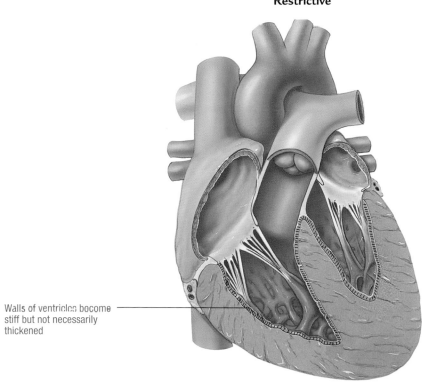

Walls of ventricles become
stiff but not necessarily
thickened

Congenital defects

The most common congenital defects of the heart are atrial septal defect (ASD), coarctation of the aorta, patent ductus arteriosus (PDA), tetralogy of Fallot, transposition of the great arteries, and ventricular septal defect (VSD). Causes of all six defects remain unknown, although some have specific clinical associations.

ATRIAL SEPTAL DEFECT

An opening between the left and right atria permits blood flow from the left atrium to the right atrium rather than from the left atrium to the left ventricle. ASD is associated with Down syndrome.

Pathophysiology

Blood shunts from the left atrium to the right atrium because left atrial pressure is normally slightly higher than right atrial pressure. This difference forces large amounts of blood through a defect that results in right heart volume overload, affecting the right atrium, right ventricle, and pulmonary arteries. Eventually, the right atrium enlarges, and the right ventricle dilates to accommodate the increased blood volume. If pulmonary artery hypertension develops, increased pulmonary vascular resistance and right ventricular hypertrophy follow.

COMPLICATIONS
- Right-sided heart failure
- Heart rhythm abnormalities
- Pulmonary hypertension

Signs and symptoms
- Fatigue
- Early to midsystolic murmur, low-pitched diastolic murmur
- Fixed, widely split S_2
- Systolic click or late systolic murmur at the apex
- Clubbing of nails and cyanosis with a right-to-left shunt
- Palpable pulsation of the pulmonary artery

COARCTATION OF THE AORTA

Coarctation is a narrowing of the aorta, usually just below the left subclavian artery, near the site where the ligamentum arteriosum joins the pulmonary artery to the aorta. Coarctation of the aorta is associated with Turner's syndrome and congenital abnormalities of the aortic valve.

Pathophysiology

Coarctation of the aorta may develop as a result of spasm and constriction of the smooth muscle in the ductus arteriosus as it closes. Possibly, this contractile tissue extends into the aortic wall, causing narrowing. The obstructive process causes hypertension in the aortic branches above the constriction and diminished pressure in the vessel below the constriction.

Restricted blood flow through the narrowed aorta increases the pressure load on the left ventricle and causes dilation of the proximal aorta and ventricular hypertrophy.

As oxygenated blood leaves the left ventricle, a portion travels through the arteries that branch off the aorta proximal to the coarctation. If PDA is present, the remaining blood travels through the coarctation, mixes with deoxygenated blood from the PDA, and travels to the legs. If the ductus arteriosus is closed, the legs and lower portion of the body must rely solely on the blood that circulates through the coarctation.

COMPLICATIONS
- Rupture of the aorta
- Stroke
- Cerebral aneurysm

Signs and symptoms
- Heart failure
- Claudication and hypertension
- Headache, vertigo, and epistaxis
- Blood pressure greater in upper than in lower extremities
- Pink upper extremities and cyanotic lower extremities
- Absent or diminished femoral pulses
- Possible murmur
- Possibly, chest and arms more developed than legs

PATENT DUCTUS ARTERIOSUS

The ductus arteriosus is a fetal blood vessel that connects the pulmonary artery to the descending aorta, just distal to the left subclavian artery. Normally, the ductus closes within days to weeks after birth. In PDA, the lumen of the ductus remains open after birth. This creates a left-to-right shunt of blood from the aorta to the pulmonary artery and results in recirculation of arterial blood through the lungs. PDA is associated with premature birth, rubella syndrome, coarctation of the aorta, VSD, and pulmonic and aortic stenosis.

Pathophysiology

The ductus arteriosus normally closes as the neonate takes his first breath but may take as long as 3 months in some infants.

In PDA, relative resistance in pulmonary and systemic vasculature and the size of the ductus determine the quantity of blood that's shunted from left to right. Because of increased aortic pressure, oxygenated blood is shunted from the aorta through the ductus arteriosus to the pulmonary artery. The blood returns to the left side of the heart and is pumped out to the aorta once more.

Increased pulmonary venous return causes increased filling pressure and workload on the left side of the heart as well as left ventricular hypertrophy and possibly heart failure.

COMPLICATIONS
- Chronic pulmonary hypertension
- Cyanosis
- Left-sided heart failure

Signs and symptoms
- Respiratory distress with signs of heart failure in infants
- Gibson murmur
- Thrill palpated at left sternal border
- Prominent left ventricular impulse
- Corrigan's pulse
- Wide pulse pressure
- Slow motor development and failure to thrive

Atrial septal defect

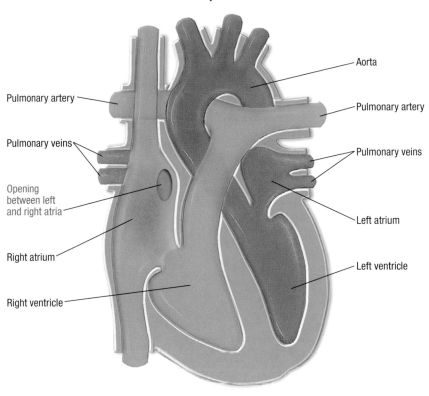

Pulmonary artery

Pulmonary veins

Opening
between left
and right atria

Right atrium

Right ventricle

Aorta

Pulmonary artery

Pulmonary veins

Left atrium

Left ventricle

Coarctation of the aorta

Narrowing
of the aorta

Patent ductus arteriosus

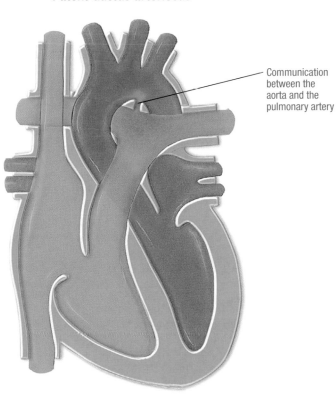

Communication
between the
aorta and the
pulmonary artery

TETRALOGY OF FALLOT

Tetralogy of Fallot is a combination of four cardiac defects: VSD, right ventricular outflow tract obstruction, right ventricular hypertrophy, and an aorta positioned above the VSD (overriding aorta). This defect is associated with fetal alcohol syndrome and Down syndrome.

Pathophysiology

Unoxygenated venous blood entering the right side of the heart may pass through the VSD to the left ventricle, bypassing the lungs, or it may enter the pulmonary artery, depending on the extent of the pulmonic stenosis. The VSD usually lies in the outflow tract of the right ventricle and is generally large enough to permit equalization of right and left ventricular pressures. However, the ratio of systemic vascular resistance to pulmonic stenosis affects the direction and magnitude of shunt flow across the VSD.

COMPLICATIONS
- Endocarditis
- Stroke

Signs and symptoms
- Cyanosis or "blue" spells (Tet spells)
- Clubbing of digits, diminished exercise tolerance, dyspnea on exertion, growth retardation, and eating difficulties
- Squatting to reduce shortness of breath
- Loud systolic murmur, continuous murmur of the ductus
- Thrill at left sternal border
- Right ventricular impulse and prominent inferior sternum

TRANSPOSITION OF GREAT ARTERIES

The aorta rises from the right ventricle and the pulmonary artery from the left ventricle, producing two noncommunicating circulatory systems. This defect is associated with VSD, VSD with pulmonic stenosis, ASD, and PDA.

Pathophysiology

The transposed pulmonary artery carries oxygenated blood back to the lungs, rather than to the left side of the heart. The transposed aorta returns unoxygenated blood to the systemic circulation rather than to the lungs. Communication between the pulmonary and systemic circulations is necessary for survival. In infants with isolated transposition, blood mixes only at the patent foramen ovale and at the PDA, resulting in slight mixing of unoxygenated systemic blood and oxygenated pulmonary blood. In infants with concurrent cardiac defects, greater mixing of blood occurs.

COMPLICATIONS
- Heart failure
- Arrhythmias

Signs and symptoms
- Hypoxemia, cyanosis, tachypnea, and dyspnea
- Gallop rhythm, tachycardia, hepatomegaly, and cardiomegaly
- Murmurs of ASD, VSD, or PDA; loud S_2
- Diminished exercise tolerance, fatigue, and clubbing

VENTRICULAR SEPTAL DEFECT

VSD is an opening in the septum between the ventricles that allows blood to shunt between the left and right ventricles. However, the defect is usually small and will close spontaneously. VSD is associated with Down syndrome and other autosomal trisomies, renal anomalies, prematurity, fetal alcohol syndrome, PDA, and coarctation of the aorta.

Pathophysiology

In neonates with a VSD, the ventricular septum fails to close completely by 8 weeks' gestation. VSDs are located in the membranous or muscular portion of the ventricular septum and vary in size. Some defects close spontaneously; in other defects, the septum is entirely absent, creating a single ventricle.

A VSD isn't readily apparent at birth because right and left pressures are approximately equal and pulmonary artery resistance is elevated. Alveoli aren't yet completely opened, so blood doesn't shunt through the defect. As the pulmonary vasculature gradually relaxes, between 4 and 8 weeks after birth, right ventricular pressure decreases, allowing blood to shunt from the left to the right ventricle. Initially, large VSD shunts cause left atrial and left ventricular hypertrophy.

COMPLICATIONS
- Right ventricular hypertrophy
- Heart failure
- Endocarditis

Signs and symptoms
- Failure to thrive
- Loud, harsh systolic murmur (along the left sternal border at the third or fourth intercostal space), palpable thrill
- Loud, widely split pulmonic component of S_2
- Displacement of point of maximal impulse to left or down
- Prominent anterior chest, cyanosis, and clubbing
- Liver, heart, and spleen enlargement
- Diaphoresis, tachycardia, and rapid, grunting respirations

Diagnostic test results
- Chest X-ray reveals cardiomegaly and ventricular and aortic enlargement.
- Electrocardiography may be normal or may reveal ventricular hypertrophy or axis deviation.
- Echocardiography detects the presence and size of a defect.
- Fetal echocardiogram can reveal a defect before birth.
- Cardiac catheterization confirms the diagnosis and damage.
- Arterial blood gas analysis reveals hypoxemia and acid-base disturbances.
- Atrial balloon sepostomy (for transposition of the great arteries)

Treatment
- Surgery
- Medications, such as diuretics, angiotensin-converting enzyme inhibitors, indomethacin (for PDA), and prostaglandin
- Oxygen therapy
- Antibiotic prophylaxis
- Atrial balloon septostomy (for transposition of the great arteries)
- Treatment of complications

Tetralogy of Fallot

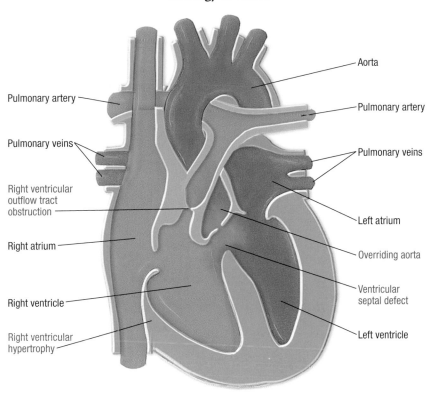

Aorta

Pulmonary artery

Pulmonary artery

Pulmonary veins

Pulmonary veins

Right ventricular outflow tract obstruction

Left atrium

Right atrium

Overriding aorta

Ventricular septal defect

Right ventricle

Left ventricle

Right ventricular hypertrophy

Transposition of great arteries

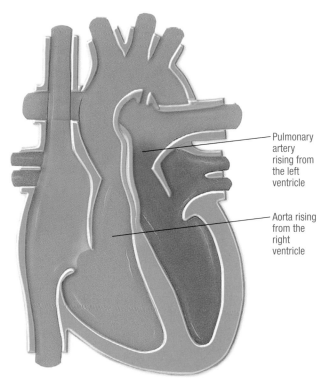

Pulmonary artery rising from the left ventricle

Aorta rising from the right ventricle

Ventricular septal defect

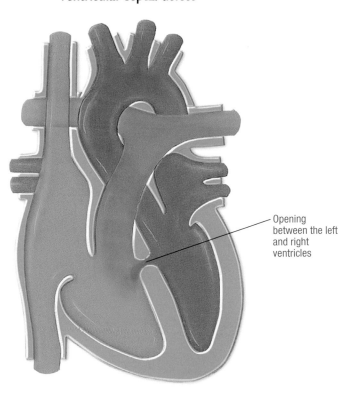

Opening between the left and right ventricles

CORONARY ARTERY DISEASE

Coronary artery disease (CAD) results from the narrowing of the coronary arteries over time because of atherosclerosis. The primary effect of CAD is a diminished supply of oxygen and nutrients to myocardial tissue because of decreased blood flow.

AGE ALERT
The lifetime risk of CAD after age 40 is 49% for men and 32% for women. As women age, their risk increases.

Causes
- Atherosclerosis (most common)
- Dissecting aneurysm
- Infectious vasculitis
- Syphilis
- Congenital abnormalities

Pathophysiology
Fatty, fibrous plaques progressively occlude the coronary arteries, reducing the volume of blood that can flow through them and leading to myocardial ischemia.

As atherosclerosis progresses, luminal narrowing is accompanied by vascular changes that impair the ability of the diseased vessel to dilate. The consequent precarious balance between myocardial oxygen supply and demand threatens the myocardium distal to the lesion. When oxygen demand exceeds what the diseased vessel can supply, the result is localized myocardial ischemia.

Myocardial cells become ischemic within 10 seconds after coronary artery occlusion. Transient ischemia causes reversible changes at the cellular and tissue levels, depressing myocardial function. Within several minutes, oxygen deprivation forces the myocardium to shift from aerobic to anaerobic metabolism, leading to accumulation of lactic acid and reduction of cellular pH. Without intervention, this sequence of events can lead to tissue injury or necrosis.

The combination of hypoxia, reduced energy availability, and acidosis rapidly impairs left ventricular function. As the fibers become unable to shorten normally, the force of contractions and velocity of blood flow in the affected myocardial region become inadequate. Moreover, wall motion in the ischemic area becomes abnormal and each contraction ejects less blood from the heart. Restoring blood flow through the coronary arteries restores aerobic metabolism and contractility.

COMPLICATIONS
- Angina pectoris
- Myocardial infarction

Signs and symptoms
- Angina (pain may be described as burning, squeezing, or tightness that radiates to the left arm, neck, jaw, or shoulder blade)
- Nausea and vomiting
- Cool extremities and pallor
- Diaphoresis caused by sympathetic stimulation
- Fatigue and dyspnea
- Xanthelasma (fat deposits on the eyelids)

AGE ALERT
The older adult with CAD may be asymptomatic because the sympathetic response to ischemia is impaired. In an active older adult, dyspnea and fatigue are two key signals of ischemia.

Diagnostic test results
- Electrocardiography shows ischemic changes during anginal episode.
- Stress testing detects ST-segment changes during exercise or pharmacologic stress.
- Coronary angiography reveals the location and degree of coronary artery stenosis or obstruction, collateral circulation, and the condition of the artery beyond the narrowing.
- Myocardial perfusion imaging with thallium-201 may be performed during treadmill exercise to detect ischemic areas of the myocardium.
- Stress echocardiography shows abnormal wall motion in ischemic areas.
- Electron-beam computed tomography identifies calcium deposits in coronary arteries.
- Cardiac catheterization reveals blockage in the coronary arteries.
- Lipid profile shows elevated cholesterol levels.

CLINICAL TIP
The lipid profile consists of these components:
- low-density lipoprotein (LDL) — "bad" lipoprotein, carries most of the cholesterol molecules
- high-density lipoprotein (HDL) — "good" lipoprotein, removes lipids from cells
- apolipoprotein B — major component of LDL
- apolipoprotein A-1 — major component of HDL
- lipoprotein a — one of the most atherogenic lipoproteins.

Treatment
- Drug therapy: angiotensin-converting enzyme inhibitors, thrombolytics, diuretics, glycoprotein IIb/IIIa inhibitors, nitrates, beta-adrenergic or calcium channel blockers; antiplatelet, antilipemic, antihypertensive drugs
- Coronary artery bypass graft (CABG) surgery
- "Keyhole" or minimally invasive surgery, an alternative to traditional CABG
- Angioplasty
- Atherectomy
- Stent placement to maintain patency of reopened artery
- Lifestyle modifications to limit progression of CAD: stopping smoking, exercising regularly, maintaining ideal body weight, and eating a low-fat, low-sodium diet

CORONARY ARTERIES

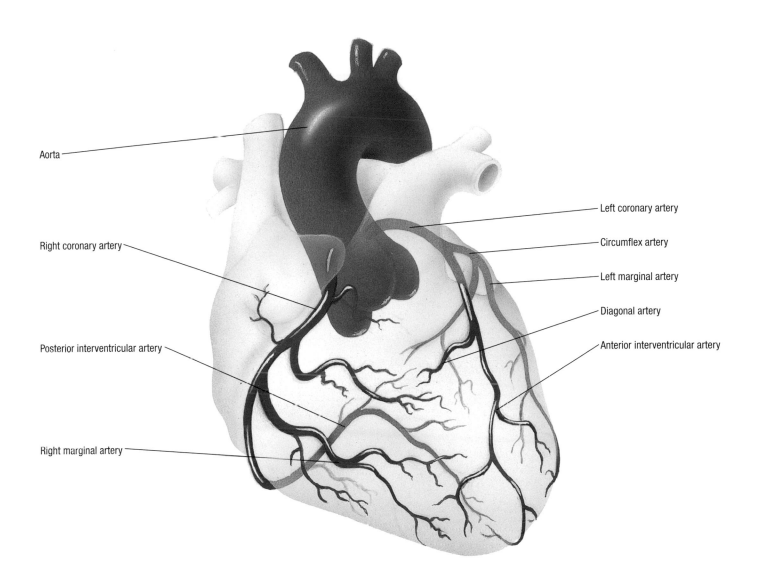

Aorta

Right coronary artery

Posterior interventricular artery

Right marginal artery

Left coronary artery

Circumflex artery

Left marginal artery

Diagonal artery

Anterior interventricular artery

CORONARY ARTERY AND ATHEROSCLEROSIS

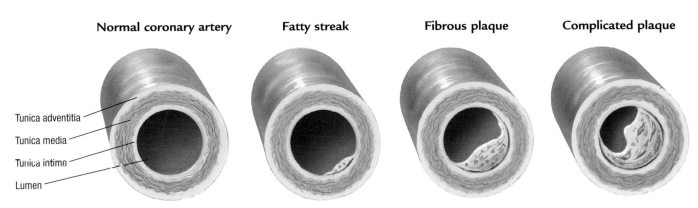

Normal coronary artery **Fatty streak** **Fibrous plaque** **Complicated plaque**

Tunica adventitia

Tunica media

Tunica intima

Lumen

DEEP VEIN THROMBOSIS

An acute condition characterized by inflammation and thrombus formation, deep vein thrombosis (DVT) mainly refers to thrombosis in the deep veins of the legs. Without treatment, this disorder is typically progressive and can lead to potentially lethal pulmonary embolism. DVT commonly begins with localized inflammation alone (phlebitis), which rapidly provokes thrombus formation. Rarely, venous thrombosis develops without associated inflammation of the vein.

Causes
- Idiopathic
- Endothelial damage
- Accelerated blood clotting
- Reduced blood flow, stasis

Predisposing risk factors
- Prolonged bed rest
- Trauma, especially hip fracture
- Surgery, especially hip, knee, or gynecologic surgery
- Childbirth
- Hormonal contraceptives such as estrogens
- Age over 40
- Obesity

Pathophysiology
A thrombus forms when an alteration in the epithelial lining causes platelet aggregation and consequent fibrin entrapment of red and white blood cells and additional platelets. Thrombus formation is more rapid in areas where blood flow is slower, because contact between platelets increases and thrombin accumulates. The rapidly expanding thrombus initiates a chemical inflammatory process in the vessel epithelium, which leads to fibrosis (narrowing of the blood vessel). The enlarging clot may occlude the vessel lumen partially or totally, or it may detach and embolize to lodge elsewhere in the systemic circulation.

COMPLICATIONS
- Pulmonary embolism
- Chronic venous insufficiency

Signs and symptoms
- Vary with site and length of the affected vein (may produce no symptoms)
- Pain or tenderness
- Fever, chills
- Malaise
- Edema and cyanosis of the affected arm or leg
- Redness and warmth over the affected area
- Palpable vein
- Surface veins more visible
- Lymphadenitis

CLINICAL TIP
Some patients may display signs of inflammation and, possibly, a positive Homans' sign (pain on dorsiflexion of the foot) during physical examination.

Diagnostic test results
- Duplex Doppler ultrasonography reveals sluggish blood flow.
- Impedance plethysmography shows a difference in blood pressure between the arms and the legs.
- Impedance phlebography shows decreased blood flow.
- Coagulation studies reveal an elevated prothrombin time in the presence of a hypercoagulable state.

Treatment
The goals of treatment are to control thrombus development, prevent complications, relieve pain, and prevent recurrence of the disorder. Treatment includes:
- bed rest with elevation of the affected arm or leg
- warm, moist soaks over the affected area
- analgesics
- antiembolism stockings
- anticoagulants (initially, heparin; later, warfarin)
- streptokinase
- simple ligation to vein plication, or clipping
- embolectomy and insertion of a vena caval umbrella or filter.

Deep veins of leg

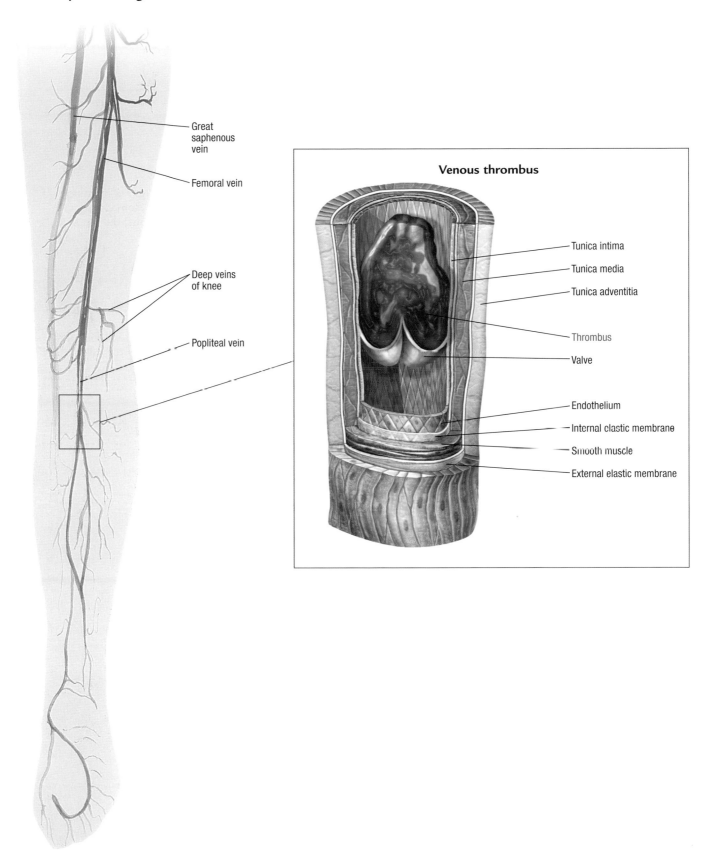

Great
saphenous
vein

Femoral vein

Deep veins
of knee

Popliteal vein

Venous thrombus

Tunica intima

Tunica media

Tunica adventitia

Thrombus

Valve

Endothelium

Internal elastic membrane

Smooth muscle

External elastic membrane

ENDOCARDITIS

Endocarditis, also known as *infective* or *bacterial endocarditis,* is an infection of the endocardium, heart valves, or cardiac prosthesis resulting from bacterial or fungal invasion.

Causes
- I.V. drug abuse
- Prosthetic heart valves
- Mitral valve prolapse
- Rheumatic heart disease

Other predisposing conditions
- Congenital abnormalities — coarctation of aorta, tetralogy of Fallot
- Subaortic and valvular aortic stenosis
- Ventricular septal defects
- Pulmonary stenosis
- Marfan syndrome
- Degenerative heart disease
- Syphilis
- Prior history of endocarditis
- Pregnancy
- Arteriovenous dialysis catheters

Native valve endocarditis (non-I.V. drug abusers)
- Streptococci, especially *Streptococcus viridans*
- Staphylococci
- Enterococci
- Fungi (rare)

I.V. drug abusers
- *Staphylococcus aureus*
- Streptococci
- Enterococci
- Gram-negative bacilli
- Fungi

Prosthetic valve endocarditis (within 60 days of insertion)
- Staphylococcal infection
- Gram-negative aerobic organisms
- Fungi
- Streptococci
- Enterococci
- Diphtheroids

Pathophysiology
In endocarditis, bacteremia — even transient bacteremia following dental or urogenital procedures — introduces the pathogen into the bloodstream. This infection causes fibrin and platelets to aggregate on the heart valve tissue and engulf circulating bacteria or fungi that flourish and form friable, wartlike vegetative growths on the valves, the endocardial lining of a heart chamber, or the epithelium of a blood vessel.

COMPLICATIONS
- Left-sided heart failure
- Valvular stenosis
- Myocardial erosion
- Vascular insufficiency

Signs and symptoms
- Malaise, weakness, fatigue
- Weight loss, anorexia

- Arthralgia
- Intermittent fever, night sweats, chills
- Valvular insufficiency
- Loud, regurgitant murmur
- Suddenly changing murmur or new murmur in the presence of fever
- Splenic infarction — left upper quadrant pain radiating to left shoulder, abdominal rigidity
- Renal infarction — hematuria, pyuria, flank pain, decreased urine output
- Cerebral infarction — hemiparesis, aphasia, other neurologic deficits
- Pulmonary infarction — cough, pleuritic pain, pleural friction rub, dyspnea, hemoptysis
- Peripheral vascular occlusion — numbness and tingling in an arm, leg, finger, or toe

Diagnostic test results
- Positive blood cultures identify the causative organism.

CLINICAL TIP
Three or more blood cultures in a 24- to 48-hour period (each from a separate venipuncture) identify the causative organism in up to 90% of patients. Blood cultures should be drawn from three different sites with at least 1 to 3 hours between each draw.

- Complete blood count shows normal or elevated white blood cell counts.
- Blood smear shows abnormal histiocytes (macrophages).
- Erythrocyte sedimentation rate is elevated.
- Anemia panel reveals normocytic, normochromic anemia.
- Urinalysis shows proteinuria and microscopic hematuria.
- Serum rheumatoid factor is positive in about one-half of all patients after endocarditis is present for 6 weeks.
- Echocardiography (particularly, transesophageal) identifies valvular damage.
- Electrocardiogram shows atrial fibrillation or other arrhythmias.
- Chest X-ray shows the presence of pulmonic emboli.

Treatment
- Penicillin and an aminoglycoside, usually gentamicin

CLINICAL TIP
Any patient who's susceptible to endocarditis, such as those with valvular defects or another predisposing factor, should have prophylactic antibiotics prior to dental or other invasive procedures.

- Bed rest
- Aspirin or acetaminophen for fever and aches
- Sufficient fluid intake
- Corrective surgery, if refractory heart failure develops or if damage to heart structures occurs
- Replacement of an infected prosthetic valve

Normal heart wall

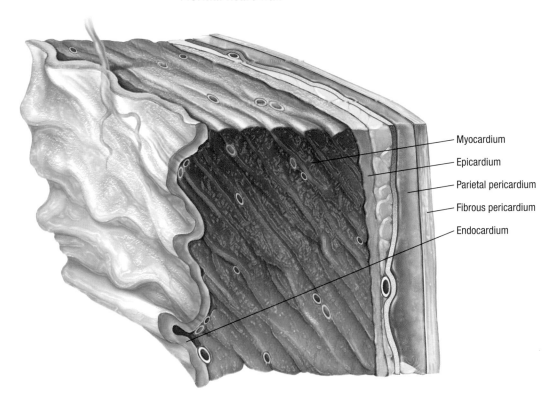

Myocardium
Epicardium
Parietal pericardium
Fibrous pericardium
Endocardium

Endocarditis

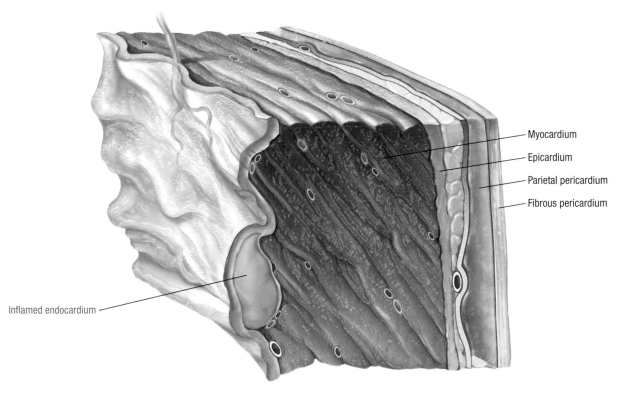

Inflamed endocardium

Myocardium
Epicardium
Parietal pericardium
Fibrous pericardium

HEART FAILURE

A syndrome rather than a disease, heart failure occurs when the heart can't pump enough blood to meet the metabolic needs of the body. Heart failure results in intravascular and interstitial volume overload and poor tissue perfusion.

Causes

Abnormal cardiac muscle function
- Myocardial infarction (MI)
- Cardiomyopathy

Abnormal left ventricular volume
- Valvular insufficiency
- High-output states: chronic anemia, arteriovenous fistula, thyrotoxicosis, pregnancy, septicemia, and hypervolemia

Abnormal left ventricular pressure
- Hypertension
- Pulmonary hypertension
- Chronic obstructive pulmonary disease
- Aortic or pulmonic valve stenosis

Abnormal left ventricular filling
- Mitral valve stenosis
- Tricuspid valve stenosis
- Constrictive pericarditis
- Atrial fibrillation
- Hypertension

Pathophysiology

Heart failure may be classified according to the side of the heart affected or by the cardiac cycle involved.
- *Left-sided heart failure:* decreased left ventricular contractile function. Cardiac output falls, and blood backs up into the left atrium and then into the lungs.
- *Right-sided heart failure:* ineffective right ventricular contractile function. Blood backs up into the right atrium and into the peripheral circulation.
- *Systolic dysfunction:* left ventricle can't pump enough blood out to the systemic circulation during systole; the ejection fraction falls. Blood backs up into the pulmonary circulation, pressure rises in the pulmonary venous system, and cardiac output falls.
- *Diastolic dysfunction:* left ventricle can't relax and fill during diastole. The stroke volume falls.

All causes of heart failure eventually reduce cardiac output and trigger compensatory mechanisms that improve cardiac output at the expense of increased ventricular work.
- Increased sympathetic activity enhances peripheral vascular resistance, contractility, heart rate, and venous return. It also restricts blood flow to the kidneys, causing them to secrete renin, which, in turn, converts angiotensinogen to angiotensin I to angiotensin II — a potent vasoconstrictor.
- Angiotensin causes the adrenal cortex to release aldosterone, leading to sodium and water retention and an increase in circulating blood volume. If the renal mechanism persists unchecked, it can aggravate heart failure.
- The increase in end-diastolic ventricular volume causes increased stroke work and volume during contraction, stretching cardiac muscle fibers. The muscle becomes stretched beyond optimum limits and contractility declines.

In heart failure, the body produces counterregulatory substances (prostaglandins, atrial natriuretic factor, and brain natriuretic peptide [BNP]) to reduce the negative effects of volume overload and vasoconstriction.

When blood volume increases in the ventricles, the heart makes these compensations:
- *Short-term:* As the end-diastolic fiber length increases, the ventricular muscle dilates and increases the force of contraction
- *Long-term:* Ventricular hypertrophy increases the heart muscles' ability to contract and push its volume of blood into the circulation.

With heart failure, compensation may occur for a long time before signs and symptoms develop.

 COMPLICATIONS
- Pulmonary edema
- MI
- Decreased perfusion to major organs

Signs and symptoms

Left-sided heart failure
- Dyspnea, orthopnea, paroxysmal nocturnal dyspnea
- Nonproductive cough, crackles
- Hemoptysis
- Tachycardia; S_3 and S_4 heart sounds
- Cool, pale skin

Right-sided heart failure
- Jugular vein distention
- Hepatojugular reflux and hepatomegaly
- Right upper quadrant pain
- Anorexia, fullness, nausea
- Weight gain, edema, ascites, or anasarca
- Dyspnea, orthopnea, paroxysmal nocturnal dyspnea

Diagnostic test results

- Chest X-rays show increased pulmonary vascular markings, interstitial edema, or pleural effusion and cardiomegaly.
- Electrocardiography shows hypertrophy, ischemic changes, or infarction and may also reveal tachycardia and extrasystoles.
- BNP assay, a blood test, may show elevated levels.
- Echocardiography reveals left ventricular hypertrophy, dilation, and abnormal contractility.
- Pulmonary artery monitoring typically shows elevated pulmonary artery and pulmonary artery wedge pressures, left ventricular end-diastolic pressure in left-sided failure, and right atrial pressure or central venous pressure in right-sided failure.
- Radionuclide ventriculography reveals an ejection fraction less than 40%; in diastolic dysfunction, the ejection fraction may be normal.

Treatment

- Treatment of the underlying cause, if known
- Angiotensin-converting enzyme inhibitors (for patients with left ventricular dysfunction) digoxin, beta-adrenergic blockers, diuretics, nitrates, morphine, or oxygen
- Dobutamine, milrinone, nesiritide
- Lifestyle modifications to reduce risk factors
- Coronary artery bypass surgery, angioplasty, or heart transplantation

TYPES OF HEART FAILURE

Right-sided heart failure

Ineffective right ventricular contractility

⬇

Failure of right ventricular pumping ability

⬇

Decreased cardiac output to lungs

⬇

Blood backup into right atrium and peripheral circulation

⬇

Weight gain, peripheral edema, engorgement of liver and other organs

Left-sided heart failure

Ineffective left ventricular contractility

⬇

Failure of left ventricular pumping ability

⬇

Decreased cardiac output to body

⬇

Blood backup into left atrium and lungs

⬇

Pulmonary congestion, dyspnea, activity intolerance

⬇

Pulmonary edema and right-sided heart failure

NORMAL CARDIAC CIRCULATION

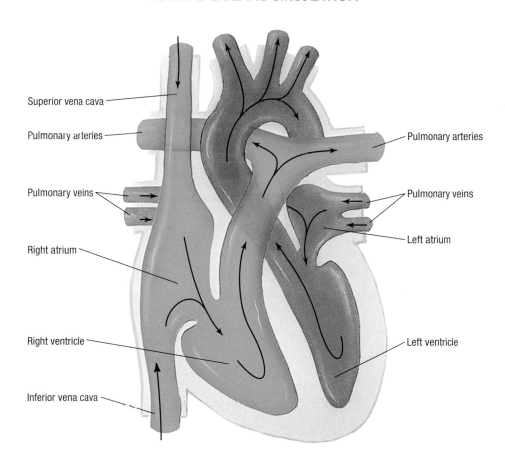

Superior vena cava

Pulmonary arteries

Pulmonary veins

Right atrium

Right ventricle

Inferior vena cava

Pulmonary arteries

Pulmonary veins

Left atrium

Left ventricle

HYPERTENSION

Hypertension, an elevation in diastolic or systolic blood pressure, occurs as two major types: *primary* (idiopathic), which is the most common, and *secondary*, which results from renal disease or another identifiable cause. Malignant hypertension is a severe, fulminant form of either type.

Causes

Risk factors for primary hypertension
- Family history
- Advancing age
- Race (most common in blacks)
- Obesity
- Tobacco use
- High intake of sodium or saturated fat
- Excessive alcohol consumption
- Sedentary lifestyle, stress

Causes of secondary hypertension
- Excess renin
- Mineral deficiencies (calcium, potassium, and magnesium)
- Diabetes mellitus
- Coarctation of the aorta
- Renal artery stenosis or parenchymal disease
- Brain tumor, quadriplegia, head injury
- Pheochromocytoma, Cushing's syndrome, hyperaldosteronism
- Thyroid, pituitary, or parathyroid dysfunction
- Hormonal contraceptives, cocaine, epoetin alfa, sympathetic stimulants, monoamine oxidase inhibitors taken with tyramine, estrogen replacement therapy, nonsteroidal anti-inflammatory drugs
- Pregnancy

Pathophysiology

Arterial blood pressure is a product of total peripheral resistance and cardiac output. Cardiac output is increased by conditions that increase heart rate or stroke volume, or both. Peripheral resistance is increased by factors that increase blood viscosity or reduce the lumen size of vessels.

Several mechanisms may lead to hypertension, including:
- changes in the arteriolar bed causing increased peripheral vascular resistance
- abnormally increased tone in the sympathetic nervous system that originates in the vasomotor system centers, causing increased peripheral vascular resistance
- increased blood volume resulting from renal or hormonal dysfunction
- arteriolar thickening caused by genetic factors, leading to increased peripheral vascular resistance
- abnormal renin release, resulting in the formation of angiotensin II, which constricts the arteriole and increases blood volume.

Prolonged hypertension increases the workload of the heart as resistance to left ventricular ejection increases. To increase contractile force, the left ventricle hypertrophies, raising the oxygen demand and workload of the heart.

The pathophysiology of secondary hypertension is related to the underlying disease.

COMPLICATIONS
- Stroke
- Myocardial infarction
- Heart failure
- Arrhythmias
- Retinopathy
- Encephalopathy
- Renal failure

Signs and symptoms
- Generally produces no symptoms
- Serial blood pressure readings classify hypertension:
  – Prehypertension: Systolic blood pressure greater than 120 mm Hg but less than 140 mm Hg or diastolic blood pressure greater than 80 mm Hg but less than 90 mm Hg
  – Stage 1 hypertension: Systolic blood pressure greater than 139 mm Hg but less than 160 mm Hg or diastolic blood pressure greater than 89 mm Hg but less than 100 mm Hg
  – Stage 2 hypertension: Systolic blood pressure greater than 159 mm Hg or diastolic blood pressure greater than 99 mm Hg
- Occipital headache
- Epistaxis possibly due to vascular involvement
- Bruits
- Dizziness, confusion, fatigue
- Blurry vision
- Nocturia
- Edema

Diagnostic test results
- Serial blood pressure measurements show elevation.
- Urinalysis shows protein, casts, red blood cells, or white blood cells, suggesting renal disease; presence of catecholamines associated with pheochromocytoma; or glucose, suggesting diabetes.
- Blood chemistry reveals elevated blood urea nitrogen and serum creatinine levels suggestive of renal disease, or hypokalemia indicating adrenal dysfunction.
- Excretory urography may reveal renal atrophy, indicating chronic renal disease.
- Electrocardiography detects left ventricular hypertrophy or ischemia.
- Chest X-rays show cardiomegaly.
- Echocardiography reveals left ventricular hypertrophy.

Treatment
- Lifestyle modifications to reduce risk factors
- Diuretics
- Angiotensin-converting enzyme inhibitors
- Alpha-receptor blockers
- Alpha-receptor agonists
- Beta-adrenergic blockers
- Treatment of underlying cause
- Nitroprusside or an adrenergic inhibitor such as propranolol

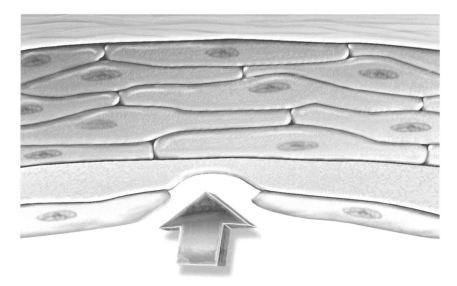

Increased intra-arterial pressure damages the endothelium.

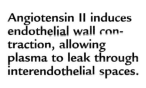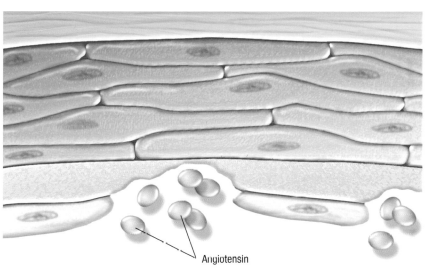

Angiotensin II induces endothelial wall contraction, allowing plasma to leak through interendothelial spaces.

Angiotensin

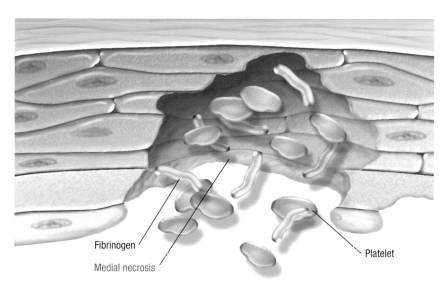

Plasma constituents deposited in the vessel wall cause medial necrosis.

Fibrinogen

Medial necrosis

Platelet

MITRAL VALVE PROLAPSE

Mitral valve prolapse is also called *systolic click-murmur syndrome* and *floppy mitral valve syndrome*. It's probably a congenital abnormality.

Causes
- Autosomal dominant inheritance
- Inherited connective tissue disorders, such as Marfan syndrome, Ehlers-Danlos syndrome, and osteogenesis imperfecta
- Genetic or environmental interruption of valve development during week 5 or 6 of gestation

Pathophysiology
The cusps of the mitral valve are enlarged, thickened, and scalloped, possibly secondary to collagen abnormalities. The chordae tendineae may be longer than usual, allowing the cusps to stretch upward.

COMPLICATIONS
- Mitral regurgitation
- Infective endocarditis
- Arrhythmias

Signs and symptoms
- Commonly produces no symptoms
- Late systolic regurgitant murmur
- Midsystolic click
- Palpitations, arrhythmias, tachycardia
- Light-headedness or syncope
- Fatigue, especially in the morning; lethargy; weakness
- Dyspnea, hyperventilation
- Chest tightness, atypical chest pain
- Anxiety, panic attacks, depression

CLINICAL TIP
The high incidence of mitral valve prolapse (3% to 8% of adults) suggests that it may be a normal variant. It occurs more often in women than in men. Although severe sequelae may occur (such as ruptured chordae tendineae, ventricular failure, emboli, bacterial endocarditis, and sudden death), mortality and morbidity are low. Most affected persons experience no physical limitations. The psychological effects of the diagnosis may be more disabling than the disease process itself.

Diagnostic test results
- Echocardiography reveals mitral valve prolapse with or without mitral insufficiency.
- Electrocardiography (resting and exercise) is usually normal but may show atrial or ventricular arrhythmia.
- Holter monitor detects arrhythmias.

Treatment
- Corresponds to degree of mitral regurgitation
- In the presence of regurgitation, antibiotic prophylaxis before invasive procedures to prevent infective endocarditis
- Beta-adrenergic blockers
- Measures to prevent hypovolemia, such as avoidance of diuretics, because hypervolemia can decrease ventricular volume, thereby increasing stress on the prolapsed mitral valve
- Surgical repair or valve replacement

Cross section of left ventricle

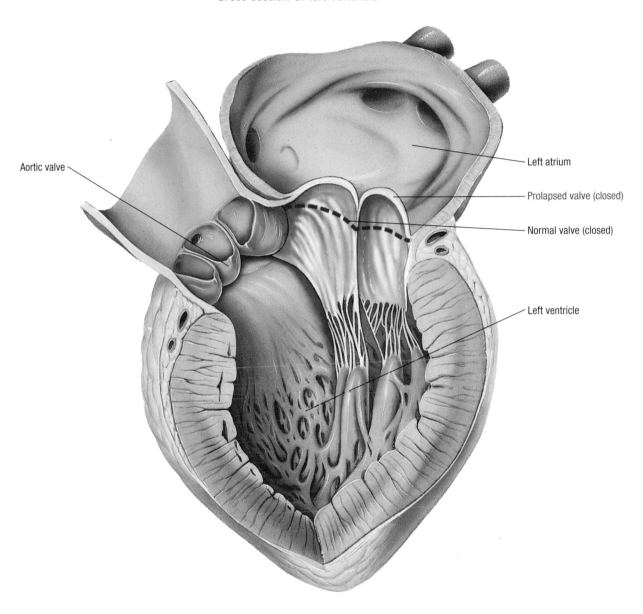

Aortic valve

Left atrium

Prolapsed valve (closed)

Normal valve (closed)

Left ventricle

MYOCARDIAL INFARCTION

In myocardial infarction (MI), a form of acute coronary syndrome, reduced blood flow through one or more coronary arteries initiates myocardial ischemia and necrosis. (See also "Coronary artery disease," page 50.)

Causes
- Thrombosis
- Coronary artery stenosis or spasm

Predisposing risk factors
- Family history of heart disease
- Atherosclerosis, hypertension, diabetes mellitus, obesity
- Elevated serum triglyceride, total cholesterol, and low-density lipoprotein levels
- Excessive intake of saturated fats, carbohydrates, or salt
- Sedentary lifestyle, tobacco smoking
- Drug use, especially cocaine and amphetamines

Pathophysiology
If coronary artery occlusion causes prolonged ischemia, lasting longer than 30 to 45 minutes, irreversible myocardial cell damage and muscle death occur.

Occlusion of the circumflex branch of the left coronary artery causes a lateral wall infarction; occlusion of the anterior descending branch of the left coronary artery , an anterior wall infarction. True posterior or inferior wall infarctions generally result from occlusion of the right coronary artery or one of its branches.

Right ventricular infarctions can also result from right coronary artery occlusion, can accompany inferior infarctions, and may cause right-sided heart failure. In ST-elevation (transmural) MI, tissue damage extends through all myocardial layers; in non-ST-elevation (subendocardial) MI, damage occurs only in the innermost and, possibly, the middle layers.

All infarcts have a central area of necrosis surrounded by an area of potentially viable hypoxic injury, which may be salvaged if circulation is restored or may progress to necrosis. The zone of injury is surrounded by viable ischemic tissue.

The infarcted myocardial cells release cardiac enzymes and proteins. Within 24 hours, the infarcted muscle becomes edematous and cyanotic. During the next several days, leukocytes infiltrate the necrotic area and begin to remove necrotic cells, thinning the ventricular wall. Scar formation begins by the 3rd week after MI; by the 6th week, scar tissue is well established.

The scar tissue that forms on the necrotic area inhibits contractility. Compensatory mechanisms try to maintain cardiac output. Ventricular dilation may also occur in a process called *remodeling*. MI may cause reduced contractility with abnormal wall motion, altered left ventricular compliance, reduced stroke volume, reduced ejection fraction, and elevated left ventricular end-diastolic pressure.

COMPLICATIONS
- Arrhythmias
- Cardiogenic shock
- Heart failure
- Valve problems

Signs and symptoms
- Persistent, crushing substernal chest pain that may radiate to the left arm, jaw, neck, or shoulder blades
- Cool extremities, perspiration, anxiety, restlessness
- Shortness of breath
- Fatigue and weakness
- Nausea and vomiting
- Jugular vein distention

CLINICAL TIP
Signs and symptoms of MI in women may be different or less noticeable than MI in men and may include abdominal pain or "heartburn," clammy skin, light-headedness, and unusual or unexplained fatigue.

Diagnostic test results
- Serial 12-lead electrocardiography (ECG) reveals ST-segment depression or elevation. An ECG also identifies the location of MI, arrhythmias, hypertrophy, and pericarditis.
- Serial cardiac enzymes and proteins show a characteristic rise and fall — specifically, CK-MB, the proteins troponin T and I, and myoglobin.
- Complete blood count and other blood tests show elevated white blood cell count, C-reactive protein level, and erythrocyte sedimentation rate due to inflammation.
- Blood chemistry shows increased glucose levels following the release of catecholamines.
- Echocardiography shows ventricular wall motion abnormalities and detects septal or papillary muscle rupture.
- Chest X-rays show left-sided heart failure or cardiomegaly.
- Nuclear imaging scanning identifies areas of infarction and viable muscle cells.
- Cardiac catheterization identifies the involved coronary artery and provides information on ventricular function and volumes within the heart.

Treatment
- Assessment of patients with chest pain in the emergency department within 10 minutes of symptom onset
- Oxygen
- Nitroglycerin
- Morphine
- Aspirin
- Continuous cardiac monitoring
- I.V. fibrinolytic therapy
- Glycoprotein IIb/IIIa receptor blockers
- I.V. heparin
- Percutaneous transluminal coronary angioplasty with or without stent placement
- Atropine, lidocaine, transcutaneous pacing patches or a transvenous pacemaker, a defibrillator, and epinephrine
- Beta-adrenergic blockers, angiotensin-converting enzyme inhibitors, and magnesium sulfate

TISSUE DESTRUCTION IN MYOCARDIAL INFARCTION

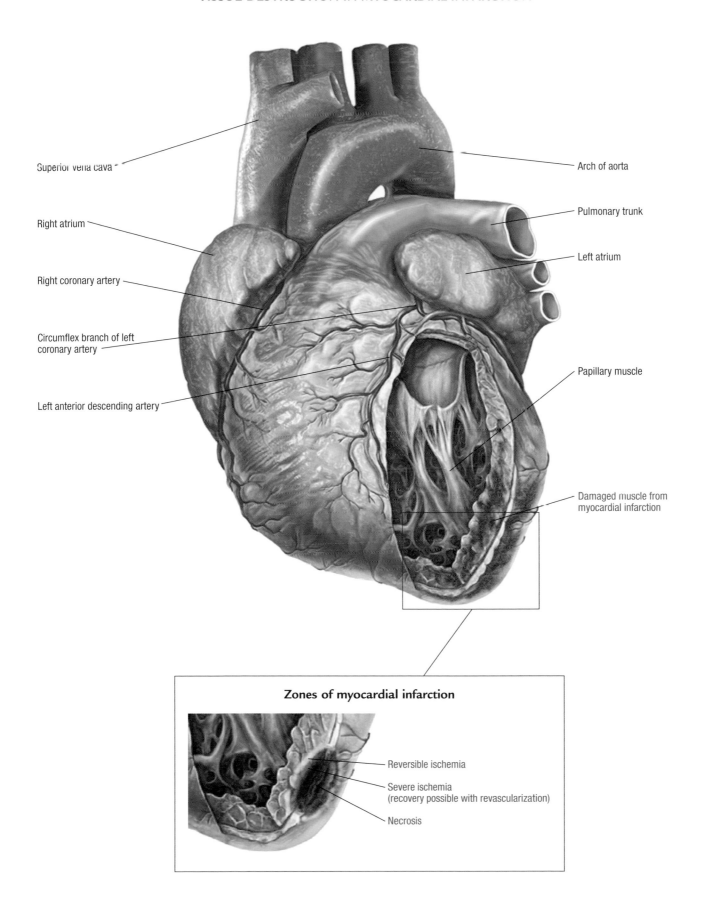

Superior vena cava

Right atrium

Right coronary artery

Circumflex branch of left
coronary artery

Left anterior descending artery

Arch of aorta

Pulmonary trunk

Left atrium

Papillary muscle

Damaged muscle from
myocardial infarction

Zones of myocardial infarction

Reversible ischemia

Severe ischemia
(recovery possible with revascularization)

Necrosis

MYOCARDITIS

Myocarditis is focal or diffuse inflammation of the cardiac muscle (myocardium). It may be acute or chronic and can occur at any age. In many cases, myocarditis causes neither specific cardiovascular symptoms nor electrocardiogram abnormalities, and recovery is usually spontaneous without residual defects.

Causes
- Infections: viral, bacterial, parasitic-protozoan, fungal, or helminthic (such as trichinosis)
- Hypersensitive immune reactions, such as acute rheumatic fever or postcardiotomy syndrome
- Radiation therapy or chemotherapeutic agents
- Toxins, such as lead, chemicals, or cocaine
- Chronic alcoholism
- Systemic autoimmune disorders, such as systemic lupus erythematosus and sarcoidosis

Pathophysiology
Damage to the myocardium occurs when an infectious organism triggers an autoimmune, cellular, or humoral reaction; noninfectious causes can lead to toxic inflammation. In either case, the resulting inflammation may lead to hypertrophy, fibrosis, and inflammatory changes of the myocardium and conduction system. The heart muscle weakens, and contractility is reduced. The heart muscle becomes flabby and dilated, and pinpoint hemorrhages may develop.

COMPLICATIONS
- Left-sided heart failure (occasionally)
- Cardiomyopathy (rare)
- Recurrence of myocarditis
- Chronic valvulitis
- Arrhythmias
- Thromboembolism

Signs and symptoms
- Fatigue, dyspnea, palpitations
- Fever
- Chest pain or mild, continuous pressure or soreness in the chest
- Tachycardia, S_3 and S_4 gallops
- Murmur of mitral insufficiency, pericardial friction rub
- Right-sided and left-sided heart failure (jugular vein distention, dyspnea, edema, pulmonary congestion, persistent fever with resting or exertional tachycardia disproportionate to the degree of fever, and supraventricular and ventricular arrhythmias)

CLINICAL TIP
To auscultate for a pericardial friction rub, have the patient sit upright, lean forward, and exhale. Listen over the third intercostal space on the left side of the chest. A pericardial rub has a scratchy, rubbing quality. If you suspect a rub and have difficulty hearing one, have the patient hold his breath.

Diagnostic test results
- Blood testing shows elevated levels of creatine kinase (CK), CK-MB, troponin I, troponin T, aspartate aminotransferase, and lactate dehydrogenase. Also, inflammation and infection cause elevated white blood cell count and erythrocyte sedimentation rate.
- Antibody titers are elevated, such as antistreptolysin-O titer, in rheumatic fever.
- Electrocardiogram illustrates diffuse ST-segment and T-wave abnormalities, conduction defects (prolonged PR interval, bundle-branch block, or complete heart block), supraventricular arrhythmias, and ventricular extrasystoles.
- Chest X-rays show an enlarged heart and pulmonary vascular congestion.
- Echocardiography demonstrates some left ventricular dysfunction.
- Radionuclide scanning identifies inflammatory and necrotic changes characteristic of myocarditis.
- Laboratory cultures of stool, throat, and other body fluids identify bacterial or viral causes of infection.
- Endomyocardial biopsy shows damaged myocardial tissue and inflammation.

Treatment
- No treatment for benign self-limiting disease
- Antibiotics
- Antipyretics
- Restricted activity
- Supplemental oxygen therapy
- Sodium restriction and diuretics
- Angiotensin-converting enzyme inhibitors
- Beta-adrenergic blockers
- Digoxin
- Antiarrhythmic drugs, such as quinidine or procainamide
- Temporary pacemaker
- Anticoagulants
- Corticosteroids and immunosuppressants
- Cardiac assist devices or heart transplantation

Normal heart wall

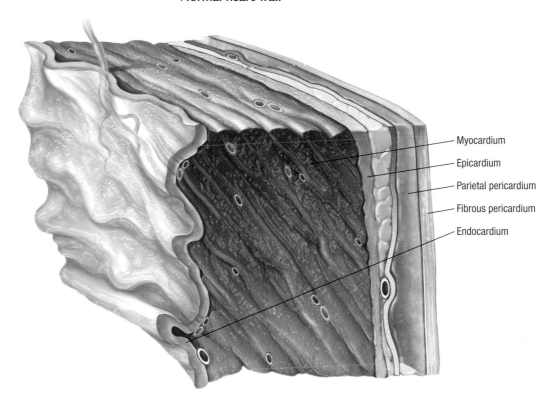

Myocardium

Epicardium

Parietal pericardium

Fibrous pericardium

Endocardium

Myocarditis

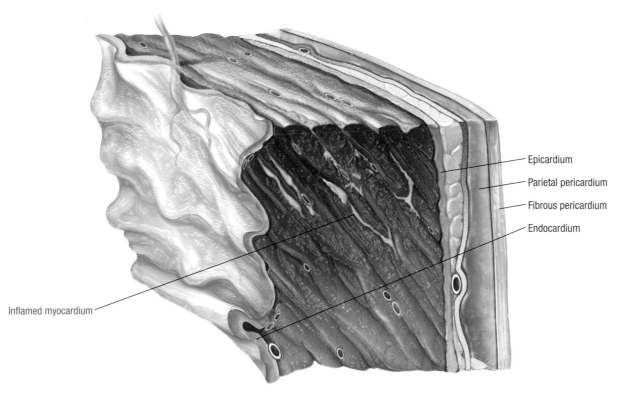

Epicardium

Parietal pericardium

Fibrous pericardium

Endocardium

Inflamed myocardium

PERICARDITIS

Pericarditis is inflammation of the pericardium – the fibro-serous sac that envelops, supports, and protects the heart. Acute pericarditis can be fibrinous or effusive, with purulent, serous, or hemorrhagic exudate. Chronic constrictive pericarditis is characterized by dense fibrous pericardial thickening. The prognosis depends on the underlying cause but is generally good in acute pericarditis, unless constriction occurs.

Causes
- Bacterial, fungal, or viral infection
- Neoplasm
- High-dose radiation to the chest
- Uremia
- Hypersensitivity or autoimmune disease
- Previous cardiac injury, such as myocardial infarction, trauma, or surgery
- Drugs, such as hydralazine or procainamide
- Idiopathic factors
- Aortic aneurysm
- Myxedema

AGE ALERT
Pericarditis most commonly affects men ages 20 to 50, generally following respiratory illness. It can also occur in children.

Pathophysiology
Pericardial tissue damaged by bacteria or other substances releases chemical mediators of inflammation (prostaglandins, histamines, bradykinins, and serotonin) into the surrounding tissue, thereby initiating the inflammatory process. Friction occurs as the inflamed pericardial layers rub against each other. Histamines and other chemical mediators dilate vessels and increase vessel permeability. Vessel walls then leak fluids and protein (including fibrinogen) into tissues, causing extracellular edema. Macrophages already present in the tissue begin to phagocytize the invading bacteria and are joined by neutrophils and monocytes. After several days, the area fills with an exudate composed of necrotic tissue and dead and dying bacteria, neutrophils, and macrophages. If the cause of pericarditis isn't infection, the exudate may be serous (as with autoimmune disease) or hemorrhagic (as seen with trauma or surgery). Eventually, the contents of the cavity autolyze and are gradually reabsorbed into healthy tissue.

Chronic constrictive pericarditis develops if the chronic or recurrent pericarditis makes the pericardium thick and stiff, encasing the heart in a stiff shell and preventing proper filling during diastole. Consequently, left- and right-side filling pressures rise as stroke volume and cardiac output fall.

COMPLICATIONS
- Pericardial effusion
- Cardiac tamponade
- Shock
- Cardiovascular collapse

Signs and symptoms
- Pericardial friction rub
- Sharp and (commonly) sudden pain, usually starting over the sternum and radiating to the neck, shoulders, back, and arms
- Shallow, rapid respirations
- Mild fever
- Dyspnea, orthopnea, tachycardia
- Heart failure
- Muffled, distant heart sounds
- Pallor, clammy skin, hypotension, pulsus paradoxus, jugular vein distention
- Possible progression to cardiovascular collapse
- Fluid retention, ascites, hepatomegaly
- Pericardial knock in early diastole along the left sternal border produced by restricted ventricular filling
- Kussmaul's sign (increased jugular vein distention on inspiration caused by restricted right-sided filling)

CLINICAL TIP
The pain in pericarditis is commonly pleuritic, increasing with deep inspiration and decreasing when the patient sits up and leans forward, pulling the heart away from the diaphragmatic pleurae of the lungs.

Diagnostic test results
- Twelve-lead electrocardiography reveals diffuse ST-segment elevation in the limb leads and most precordial leads that reflect the inflammatory process. Downsloping PR segments and upright T waves are present in most leads. QRS segments may be diminished when pericardial effusion exists. Arrhythmias, such as atrial fibrillation and sinus arrhythmias, may occur. In chronic constrictive pericarditis, there may be low-voltage QRS complexes, T-wave inversion or flattening, and P mitral (wide P waves) in leads I, II, and V_6.
- Blood testing reveals an elevated erythrocyte sedimentation rate as a result of the inflammatory process and a normal or elevated white blood cell count, especially in infectious pericarditis. C-reactive protein may be elevated.
- Blood cultures identify an infectious cause.
- Antistreptolysin-O titers are positive if pericarditis is caused by rheumatic fever.
- Purified protein derivative skin tests are positive if pericarditis is caused by tuberculosis.
- Echocardiography shows an echo-free space between the ventricular wall and the pericardium and reduced pumping action of the heart.
- Chest X-rays show an enlarged cardiac silhouette with a water bottle shape caused by fluid accumulation if pleural effusion is present.
- Chest or heart magnetic resonance imaging shows enlargement of the heart and signs of inflammation.

Treatment
- Bed rest as long as fever and pain persist
- Treatment of the underlying cause, if it can be identified
- Nonsteroidal anti-inflammatory drugs, corticosteroids
- Antibacterial, antifungal, or antiviral therapy
- Partial or total pericardectomy
- Diuretics
- Pericardiocentesis

Normal heart wall

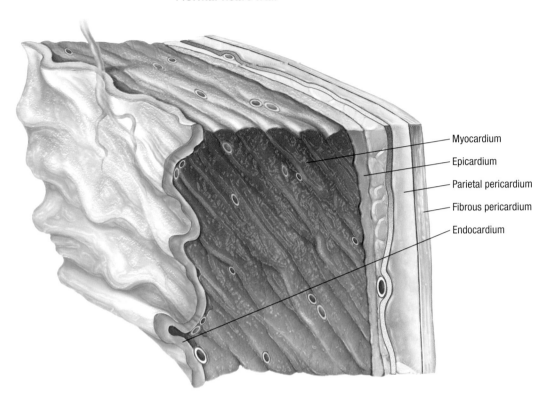

Myocardium

Epicardium

Parietal pericardium

Fibrous pericardium

Endocardium

Pericarditis

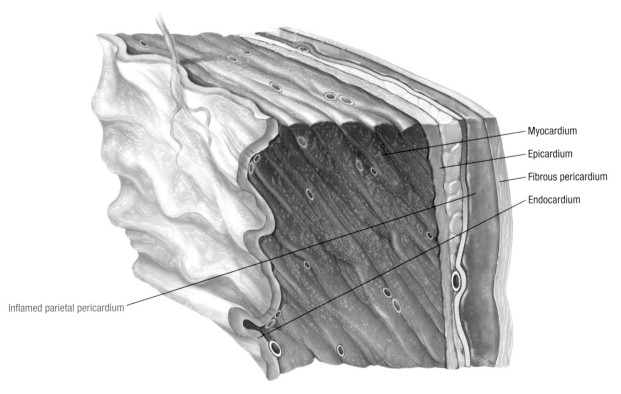

Myocardium

Epicardium

Fibrous pericardium

Endocardium

Inflamed parietal pericardium

RAYNAUD'S DISEASE

Raynaud's disease is one of several primary disorders characterized by episodic spasms of the small peripheral arteries and arterioles, precipitated by exposure to cold or stress. This condition occurs bilaterally and usually affects the hands or, less often, the feet. It's benign, requires no specific treatment, and has no serious sequelae. Raynaud's *phenomenon,* however, is secondary to any of several connective disorders — such as scleroderma, systemic lupus erythematosus, or polymyositis — and progresses to ischemia, gangrene, and amputation. Distinguishing between the two disorders is difficult because some patients experience mild symptoms of Raynaud's disease for several years and then develop overt connective tissue disease, especially scleroderma.

AGE ALERT
Raynaud's disease is most prevalent in females, particularly between puberty and age 40.

Causes
Raynaud's disease
● Unknown; family history is a risk factor
Raynaud's phenomenon
● Connective tissue disorders, such as scleroderma, rheumatoid arthritis, systemic lupus erythematosus, or polymyositis
● Pulmonary hypertension
● Thoracic outlet syndrome
● Arterio-occlusive disease
● Myxedema
● Trauma
● Serum sickness
● Exposure to heavy metals
● Long-term exposure to cold, vibrating machinery (such as operating a jackhammer), or pressure to the fingertips (as in typists and pianists)

Pathophysiology
Raynaud's disease is a syndrome of episodic constriction of the arterioles and arteries of the extremities, resulting in pallor and cyanosis of the fingers and toes. Several mechanisms may account for the reduced digital blood flow, including:
● intrinsic vascular wall hyperactivity to cold
● increased vasomotor tone due to sympathetic stimulation
● antigen-antibody immune response (most likely because abnormal immunologic test results accompany Raynaud's phenomenon).

COMPLICATIONS
● Ischemia
● Gangrene
● Amputation

Signs and symptoms
● Bilateral blanching (pallor) of the fingers after exposure to cold or stress:
– Vasoconstriction or vasospasm reduces blood flow
– Cyanosis caused by increased oxygen extraction resulting from sluggish blood flow
– Spasm resolves, and fingers turn red (rubor) as blood rushes back into the arterioles
● Cold and numbness
● Throbbing, aching pain, swelling, and tingling
● Trophic changes (as a result of ischemia), such as sclerodactyly, ulcerations, or chronic paronychia

Diagnostic test results
● Antinuclear antibody (ANA) titer identifies autoimmune disease as an underlying cause of Raynaud's phenomenon; further tests must be performed if the ANA titer is positive.
● Doppler ultrasonography shows reduced blood flow if the symptoms result from arterial occlusive disease.

Treatment
● Avoiding triggers, such as cold, and mechanical or chemical injury
● Smoking cessation and avoidance of decongestants and caffeine to reduce vasoconstriction
● Calcium channel blockers, such as nifedipine, diltiazem, and nicardipine
● Alpha-adrenergic blockers, such as phenoxybenzamine or reserpine
● Biofeedback and relaxation exercises to reduce stress and improve circulation
● Sympathectomy or amputation

Pallor due to decreased or absent blood flow

Cyanosis due to capillary dilation

Rubor due to excessive hyperemia resulting from reactive vasodilation

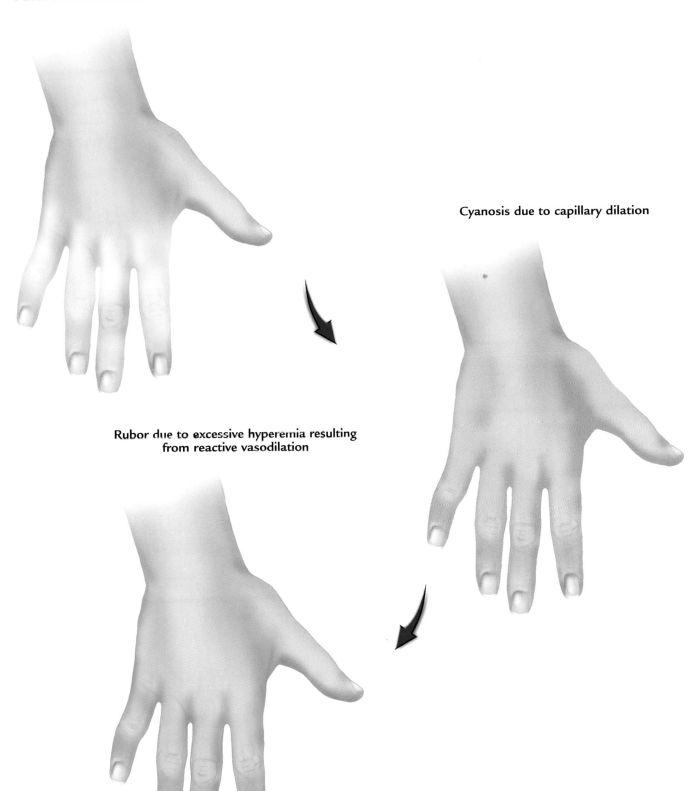

RHEUMATIC HEART DISEASE

A systemic inflammatory disease of childhood, acute rheumatic fever develops after infection of the upper respiratory tract with group A beta-hemolytic streptococci. It mainly involves the heart, joints, central nervous system, skin, and subcutaneous tissues, and commonly recurs. Rheumatic heart disease refers to the cardiac manifestations of rheumatic fever and includes pancarditis during the early acute phase and chronic valvular disease later. Cardiac involvement develops in up to 50% of patients.

Rheumatic fever tends to run in families, lending support to the existence of genetic predisposition. Environmental factors also seem to be significant in the development of the disorder.

Causes

Rheumatic fever is caused by group A beta-hemolytic streptococcal pharyngitis.

Rheumatic fever appears to be a hypersensitivity reaction to a group A beta-hemolytic streptococcal infection. Because few persons (3%) with streptococcal infections contract rheumatic fever, altered host resistance must be involved in its development or recurrence.

Pathophysiology

The antigens of group A streptococci bind to receptors in the heart, muscle, brain, and synovial joints, causing an autoimmune response. Because the antigens of the streptococcus are similar to some antigens of the body's own cells, antibodies may attack healthy body cells.

Carditis may affect the endocardium, myocardium, or pericardium during the early acute phase.

COMPLICATIONS
- Chronic valvular disease
- Pericarditis
- Pericardial effusion

Signs and symptoms
- Polyarthritis or migratory joint pain
- Erythema marginatum
- Subcutaneous nodules
- Chorea
- Streptococcal infection a few days to 6 weeks before onset of symptoms
- Fever
- New or worsening mitral or aortic murmur
- Pericardial friction rub
- Chest pain, commonly pleuritic
- Dyspnea, tachypnea, nonproductive cough, bibasilar crackles, edema

Diagnostic test results
- During the acute phase, complete blood count reveals an elevated white blood cell count and an elevated erythrocyte sedimentation rate.
- Hemoglobin and hematocrit are decreased because of suppressed erythropoiesis during inflammation.

- C-reactive protein is positive, especially during the acute phase.
- Cardiac enzyme levels are increased in severe carditis.
- Antistreptolysin-O titer is elevated in 95% of patients within 2 months of onset.
- Throat cultures show the presence of group A beta-hemolytic streptococci; however, they usually occur in small numbers.
- Electrocardiography shows a prolonged PR interval.
- Chest X-rays show normal heart size or cardiomegaly, pericardial effusion, or heart failure.
- Echocardiography detects valvular damage and pericardial effusion, measures chamber size, and provides information on ventricular function.
- Cardiac catheterization provides information on valvular damage and left ventricular function.

CLINICAL TIP
Jones Criteria for diagnosis require either two major criteria or one major criterion and two minor, plus evidence of a previous group A streptococcal infection.
Major criteria
- Carditis
- Migratory joint pain
- Sydenham's chorea
- Subcutaneous nodules, usually near tendons or bony prominences of joints, especially the elbows, knuckles, wrists, and knees
- Erythema marginatum
Minor criteria
- Fever
- Arthralgia
- Elevated acute phase reactants
- Prolonged PR interval

Treatment
- Prompt treatment of all group A beta-hemolytic streptococcal pharyngitis with oral penicillin V or I.M. benzathine penicillin G; erythromycin for patients with penicillin hypersensitivity
- Salicylates
- Corticosteroids
- Strict bed rest for about 5 weeks
- Sodium restriction, angiotensin-converting enzyme inhibitors, digoxin, and diuretics
- Corrective surgery, such as commissurotomy, valvuloplasty, or valve replacement for severe mitral or aortic valvular dysfunction that causes persistent heart failure
- Secondary prevention of rheumatic fever, which begins after the acute phase subsides:
– monthly I.M. injections of penicillin G benzathine or daily doses of oral penicillin V or sulfadiazine
– continued treatment, usually for at least 5 years or until age 21, whichever is longer
- Prophylactic antibiotics for dental work and other invasive or surgical procedures

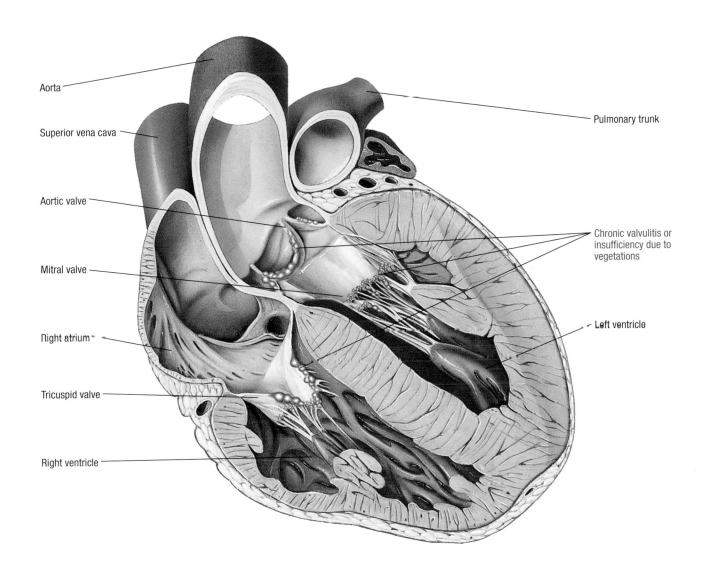

Aorta

Superior vena cava

Aortic valve

Mitral valve

Right atrium

Tricuspid valve

Right ventricle

Pulmonary trunk

Chronic valvulitis or insufficiency due to vegetations

Left ventricle

SHOCK

Shock is a clinical syndrome that leads to reduced perfusion of tissues and organs and organ failure. Shock can be classified into three categories: distributive (neurogenic and septic), cardiogenic, and hypovolemic.

Causes

Neurogenic shock
- Spinal cord injury, spinal anesthesia
- Vasomotor center depression
- Severe pain
- Medications
- Hypoglycemia

Septic shock
- Gram-negative bacteria, gram-positive bacteria
- Viruses, fungi, rickettsiae, parasites, yeast, protozoa, mycobacteria

Cardiogenic shock
- Myocardial infarction (MI), most common cause
- Heart failure, cardiomyopathy
- Pericardial tamponade
- Pulmonary embolism

Hypovolemic shock
- Blood loss (most common cause)
- GI fluid loss, renal loss, fluid shifts
- Burns

Pathophysiology

Each type of shock has three stages.

Compensatory stage: When arterial pressure and tissue perfusion fall, compensatory mechanisms are activated to maintain cardiac output and perfusion to the heart and brain. As the baroreceptors in the carotid sinus and aortic arch sense a drop in blood pressure, epinephrine and norepinephrine are secreted to increase peripheral resistance, blood pressure, and myocardial contractility. Reduced blood flow to the kidney activates the renin-angiotensin-aldosterone system, causing vasoconstriction and sodium and water retention.

Progressive stage: When compensatory mechanisms can't maintain cardiac output, tissues become hypoxic. Cells switch to anaerobic metabolism and lactic acid accumulates, producing metabolic acidosis. Tissue hypoxia promotes the release of endothelial mediators, leading to venous pooling and increased capillary permeability. Sluggish blood flow increases the risk of disseminated intravascular coagulation (DIC).

Irreversible (refractory) stage: Inadequate perfusion damages cell membranes, lysosomal enzymes are released, and energy stores are depleted, leading to cell death. Lactic acid continues to accumulate, increasing capillary permeability and the movement of fluid out of the vascular space, further contributing to hypotension. Perfusion to the coronary arteries is reduced, causing myocardial depression and a further reduction in cardiac output. Circulatory and respiratory failure occur.

COMPLICATIONS
- Kidney or brain damage (cardiogenic and hypovolemic)
- Liver damage (cardiogenic)
- Respiratory or cardiac failure (septic)

Signs and symptoms

Compensatory stage
- Tachycardia, bounding pulse, tachypnea
- Reduced urinary output
- Cool, pale skin (or warm, dry skin in septic shock)

Progressive stage
- Hypotension
- Narrowed pulse pressure; weak, rapid, thready pulse
- Cold, clammy skin; cyanosis, shallow respirations

Irreversible stage
- Unconsciousness and absent reflexes
- Rapidly falling blood pressure; weak pulse
- Slow, shallow or Cheyne-Stokes respirations

Diagnostic test results

- Hematocrit is reduced in hemorrhage or elevated in other types of shock caused by hypovolemia.
- Blood, urine, and sputum cultures identify the organism responsible for septic shock.
- Coagulation studies may detect coagulopathy from DIC.
- Complete blood count reveals increased white blood cell count and erythrocyte sedimentation rate.
- Blood chemistry reveals elevated blood urea nitrogen and creatinine levels; and elevated serum glucose (in early stages).
- Serum lactate increases secondary to anaerobic metabolism.
- Elevated cardiac enzymes and proteins indicate MI as a cause of cardiogenic shock.
- Arterial blood gas analysis reveals respiratory alkalosis.
- Urine specific gravity will be elevated in response to the effects of antidiuretic hormone.
- Chest X-rays will be normal in early stages; pulmonary congestion may be seen in later stages.
- Electrocardiography may show arrhythmias, ischemic changes, and an MI.
- Echocardiography reveals valvular abnormalities.

Treatment

- Identification and treatment of the underlying cause
- Maintaining a patent airway, oxygen and mechanical ventilation, and continuous cardiac monitoring
- I.V. fluids, crystalloids, colloids, or blood products

Neurogenic shock
- Vasopressor drugs

Septic shock
- Treatment with drotrecogin alfa (Xigris) antibiotics, and inotropic and vasopressor drugs

Cardiogenic shock
- Inotropic drugs, vasodilators, diuretics
- Intra-aortic balloon pump therapy
- Thrombolytic therapy or coronary artery revascularization
- Ventricular assist device
- Heart transplantation

Hypovolemic shock
- Pneumatic antishock garment

MULTIORGAN SYSTEM EFFECTS OF SHOCK

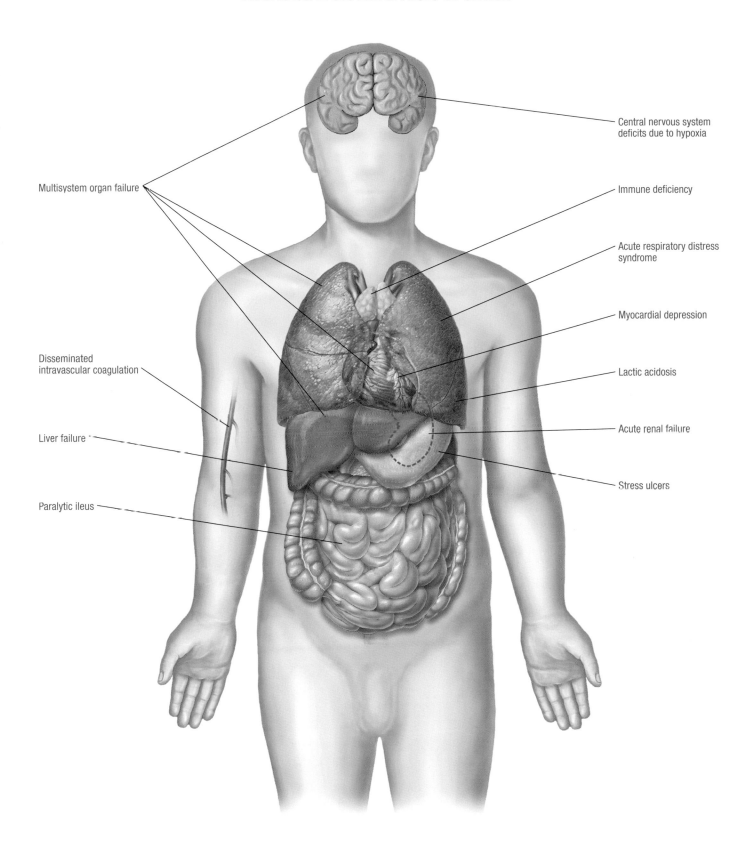

Central nervous system deficits due to hypoxia

Immune deficiency

Acute respiratory distress syndrome

Myocardial depression

Lactic acidosis

Acute renal failure

Stress ulcers

Multisystem organ failure

Disseminated intravascular coagulation

Liver failure

Paralytic ileus

VALVULAR HEART DISEASE

In valvular heart disease, three types of mechanical disruptions can occur: stenosis, or narrowing, of the valve opening; incomplete closure of the valve; or prolapse of the valve.

Causes
The causes of valvular heart disease are varied and differ for each type of valve disorder.

Mitral stenosis
- Rheumatic fever
- Congenital anomalies

Mitral insufficiency
- Rheumatic fever
- Mitral valve prolapse
- Myocardial infarction
- Severe left ventricular failure
- Ruptured chordae tendinae
- Marfan syndrome

Aortic insufficiency
- Rheumatic fever
- Syphilis
- Hypertension
- Endocarditis
- Marfan syndrome

Aortic stenosis
- Congenital
- Bicuspid aortic valve
- Rheumatic fever
- Atherosclerosis

Pulmonic stenosis
- Congenital
- Rheumatic fever (rare)

Pathophysiology
Pathophysiology of valvular heart disease varies according to the valve and the disorder.

Mitral stenosis: Structural abnormality, fibrosis, or calcification obstructs blood flow from the left atrium to the left ventricle. Left atrial volume and pressure rise, and the chamber dilates. Greater resistance to blood flow causes pulmonary hypertension, right ventricular hypertrophy, and right-sided heart failure. Inadequate filling of the left ventricle causes low cardiac output.

COMPLICATIONS
- Pulmonary edema
- Atrial fibrillation
- Pulmonary hypertension
- Right-sided heart failure
- Emboli
- Stroke

Mitral insufficiency: An abnormality of the mitral leaflets, mitral annulus, chordae tendineae, papillary muscles, left atrium, or left ventricle can lead to mitral regurgitation. Blood from the left ventricle flows back into the left atrium during systole, and the atrium enlarges to accommodate the backflow. The left ventricle also dilates to accommodate the increased volume of blood from the atrium and to compensate for diminishing

cardiac output. Ventricular hypertrophy and increased end-diastolic pressure raise pulmonary artery pressure.

COMPLICATIONS
- Endocarditis
- Heart failure
- Emboli
- Stroke
- Arrhythmias

Aortic insufficiency: Blood flows back into the left ventricle during diastole, causing fluid overload in the ventricle, which dilates and hypertrophies. The excess volume causes fluid overload in the left atrium and, finally, the pulmonary system.

COMPLICATIONS
- Left-sided heart failure
- Pulmonary edema

Aortic stenosis: Over time, left ventricular pressure rises to overcome the resistance of the narrowed valvular opening. The added workload increases the demand for oxygen, and diminished cardiac output causes poor coronary artery perfusion.

COMPLICATIONS
- Ischemia of left ventricle
- Left-sided heart failure
- Arrhythmias
- Endocarditis

Pulmonic stenosis: Obstructed right ventricular outflow causes right ventricular hypertrophy, resulting in right-sided heart failure.

COMPLICATIONS
- Heart failure
- Right ventricular hypertrophy

Signs and symptoms
The clinical manifestations vary according to valvular defects and the severity of the defect. The patient may be asymptomatic.

Common to all valvular disorders
- Dyspnea, weakness, fatigue

Mitral stenosis
- Orthopnea
- Palpitations, right-sided heart failure, crackles, jugular vein distention
- Atrial fibrillation
- Diastolic thrill, loud S_1, opening snap-diastolic murmur

Mitral insufficiency
- Palpitations, angina, tachycardia
- Left-sided heart failure, pulmonary edema, crackles
- Split S_2; S_3; holosystolic murmur at apex
- Apical thrill

Aortic insufficiency
- Palpitations, angina, syncope
- Cough
- Pulmonary congestion, left-sided heart failure
- Quincke's sign

HEART VALVES

Normal view

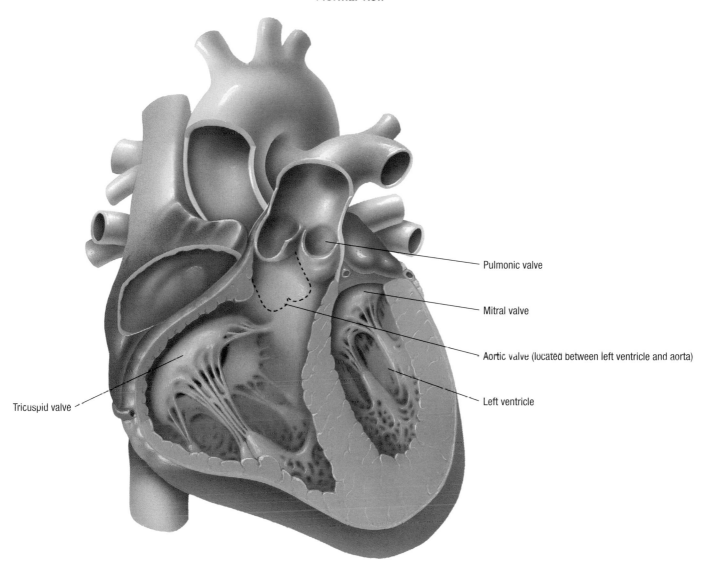

Pulmonic valve

Mitral valve

Aortic valve (located between left ventricle and aorta)

Left ventricle

Tricuspid valve

Superior view of the heart

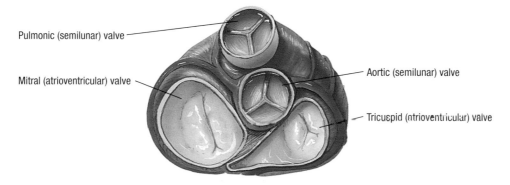

Pulmonic (semilunar) valve

Mitral (atrioventricular) valve

Aortic (semilunar) valve

Tricuspid (atrioventricular) valve

- Pulsus biferiens, visible apical pulse
- S_3 and blowing diastolic murmur at left sternal border

Aortic stenosis
- Palpitations, angina, arrhythmias
- Syncope
- Pulmonary congestion, left-sided heart failure
- Diminished carotid pulses, systolic thrill (carotid)
- Decreased cardiac output
- Systolic ejection murmur that radiates to neck, S_4

Pulmonic stenosis
- Commonly produces no symptoms
- Syncope, chest pain, right-sided heart failure
- Systolic murmur at left sternal border, S_2 split

Diagnostic test results

Diagnostic test results vary with the type of valvular disease that's present. Cardiac catheterization, chest X-ray, echocardiography, and electrocardiography are the standard diagnostic tools used to detect valvular heart disease.

Mitral stenosis
- Cardiac catheterization reveals diastolic pressure gradient across the valve; elevated left atrial and pulmonary artery wedge pressures (PAWP) with severe pulmonary hypertension; elevated right-sided heart pressure with decreased cardiac output; and abnormal contraction of the left ventricle.
- Chest X-ray shows left atrial and ventricular enlargement, enlarged pulmonary arteries, and mitral valve calcification.
- Echocardiography reveals left atrial and ventricular enlargement, enlarged pulmonary arteries, and mitral valve calcification.
- Electrocardiography (ECG) detects left atrial hypertrophy, atrial fibrillation, right ventricular hypertrophy, and right axis deviation.

Mitral insufficiency
- Cardiac catheterization reveals mitral regurgitation with increased left ventricular end-diastolic volume and pressure, increased atrial pressure and PAWP, and decreased cardiac output.
- Chest X-ray shows left atrial and ventricular enlargement and pulmonary venous congestion.
- Echocardiography shows abnormal valve leaflet motion and left atrial enlargement.

- ECG may show left atrial and ventricular hypertrophy, sinus tachycardia, and atrial fibrillation.

Aortic insufficiency
- Cardiac catheterization reveals reduction in arterial diastolic pressure, aortic regurgitation, other valvular abnormalities, and increased left ventricular end-diastolic pressure.
- Chest X-ray shows left ventricular enlargement and pulmonary vein congestion.
- Echocardiography shows left ventricular enlargement, alteration in mitral valve movement, and mitral valve thickening.
- ECG shows sinus tachycardia, left ventricular hypertrophy, and left atrial hypertrophy in severe disease.

Aortic stenosis
- Cardiac catheterization reveals pressure gradient across valve and increased left ventricular end-diastolic pressures.
- Chest X-ray shows valvular calcification, left ventricular enlargement, and pulmonary vein congestion.
- Echocardiography shows thickened aortic valve and left ventricular wall, possibly coexisting with mitral valve stenosis.
- ECG shows left ventricular hypertrophy.

Pulmonic stenosis
- Cardiac catheterization reveals increased right ventricular pressure, decreased pulmonary artery pressure, and abnormal valve orifice.
- ECG shows right ventricular hypertrophy, right axis deviation, right atrial hypertrophy, and atrial fibrillation.

Treatment
- Digoxin, anticoagulants, nitroglycerin, beta-adrenergic blockers, diuretics, vasodilators, angiotensin-converting enzyme inhibitors
- Low-sodium diet
- Oxygen
- Prophylactic antibiotics for invasive procedures, such as dental cleanings, endoscopies, and other procedures where the risk of introducing bacteria into the bloodstream is present
- Cardioversion
- Open or closed commissurotomy
- Annuloplasty or valvuloplasty
- Prosthetic valve for mitral or aortic valve disease

Normal atrioventricular valve

Normal semilunar valve

Stenotic atrioventricular valve

Stenotic semilunar valve

Insufficient atrioventricular valve

Insufficient semilunar valve

VARICOSE VEINS

Varicose veins are dilated, tortuous veins, engorged with blood and resulting from poor venous valve function. They can be primary, originating in the superficial veins, or secondary, occurring in the deep veins.

Causes

Primary varicose veins
- Congenital weakness of valves or vein wall
- Prolonged venous stasis or increased intra-abdominal pressure, as in pregnancy, obesity, constipation, or wearing tight clothes
- Standing for an extended period of time
- Family history

Secondary varicose veins
- Deep vein thrombosis
- Venous malformation
- Arteriovenous fistulas
- Venous trauma
- Occlusion

Pathophysiology

Veins are thin-walled, distensible vessels with valves that keep blood flowing in one direction. Any condition that weakens, destroys, or distends these valves allows the backflow of blood to the previous valve. If a valve can't hold the pooling blood, it can become incompetent, allowing even more blood to flow backward. The increasing volume of blood in the vein raises pressure and distends the vein. As the veins are stretched, their walls weaken and lose their elasticity, and they become lumpy and tortuous. Rising hydrostatic pressure forces plasma into the surrounding tissues, resulting in edema.

People who stand for prolonged periods may also develop venous pooling because there's no muscular contraction in the legs, forcing blood back up to the heart. If the valves in the veins are too weak to hold the pooling blood, they begin to leak, allowing blood to flow backward.

COMPLICATIONS
- Phlebitis
- Leg ulcers

Signs and symptoms

- Dilated, tortuous, purplish, ropelike veins, particularly in the calves
- Edema of the calves and ankles
- Leg heaviness that worsens in the evening and in warm weather
- Dull aching in the legs after prolonged standing or walking
- Aching during menses

AGE ALERT

As a person ages, veins dilate and stretch, increasing susceptibility to varicose veins and chronic venous insufficiency. Because the skin becomes friable and can easily break down, ulcers caused by chronic venous insufficiency may take longer to heal.

Diagnostic test results

CLINICAL TIP

Manual compression test detects a palpable impulse when the vein is firmly occluded at least 8″ (20.3 cm) above the point of palpation, indicating incompetent valves in the vein.

Trendelenburg's test (retrograde filling test) detects incompetent valves when the vein is occluded with the patient in the supine position and the leg is elevated 90 degrees. When the person stands (still with the vein occluded), the saphenous veins should fill slowly from below in about 30 seconds.

- Photoplethysmography characterizes venous blood flow by noting changes in the skin's circulation.
- Doppler ultrasonography detects the presence or absence of venous backflow in deep or superficial veins.
- Venous outflow and reflux plethysmography detects deep vein occlusion; this test is invasive and not routinely used.
- Ascending and descending venography demonstrates venous occlusion and patterns of collateral flow.

Treatment

- Treatment of underlying cause (if possible), such as abdominal tumor or obesity
- Antiembolism stockings or elastic bandages
- Regular exercise
- Injection of a sclerosing agent into small to medium-sized varicosities
- Surgical stripping and ligation of severe varicose veins
- Phlebectomy (removing the varicose vein through small incisions in the skin)

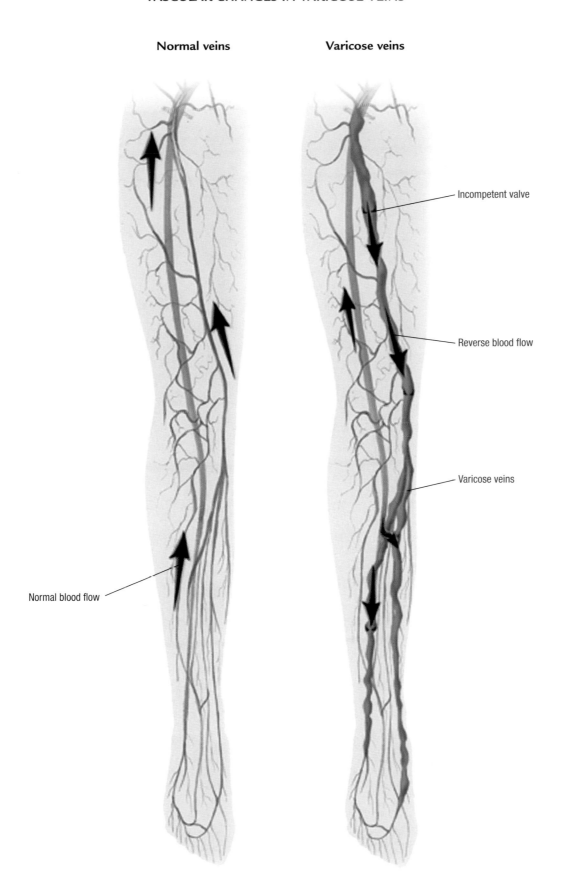

Normal veins

Varicose veins

Incompetent valve

Reverse blood flow

Varicose veins

Normal blood flow

ACUTE RESPIRATORY DISTRESS SYNDROME

Acute respiratory distress syndrome (ARDS) is a form of pulmonary edema that can quickly lead to acute respiratory failure. Also known as *adult respiratory distress syndrome, shock lung, stiff lung, white lung, wet lung,* or *Da Nang lung,* ARDS may follow direct or indirect injury to the lung. However, diagnosis is difficult; death can occur within 48 hours of onset if ARDS isn't promptly diagnosed and treated.

Causes

- Injury to the lung from trauma
- Sepsis
- Trauma-related factors, such as fat emboli, sepsis, shock, pulmonary contusions, and multiple transfusions
- Aspiration of gastric contents, viral pneumonia
- Anaphylaxis
- Drug overdose
- Idiosyncratic drug reaction to ampicillin or hydrochlorothiazide
- Inhalation of noxious gases (nitrous oxide, ammonia, chlorine)
- Near drowning
- Oxygen toxicity
- Coronary artery bypass grafting
- Hemodialysis
- Leukemia
- Acute miliary tuberculosis
- Pancreatitis
- Thrombotic thrombocytopenic purpura
- Uremia
- Venous air embolism

Pathophysiology

Injury in ARDS involves both the alveolar epithelium and the pulmonary capillary epithelium. Damage can occur directly (by aspiration of gastric contents or inhalation of noxious gases) or indirectly (from chemical mediators released in response to systemic disease). The causative agent triggers a cascade of cellular and biochemical changes. After it's initiated, this agent triggers neutrophils, macrophages, monocytes, and lymphocytes to produce various cytokines — which promote cellular activation, chemotaxis, and adhesion — and inflammatory mediators, including oxidants, proteases, kinins, growth factors, and neuropeptides, which initiate the complement cascade, intravascular coagulation, and fibrinolysis.

These cellular events increase vascular permeability to proteins, increasing the hydrostatic pressure gradient of the capillary. Elevated capillary pressure, such as results from fluid overload or cardiac dysfunction, greatly increases interstitial and alveolar edema, which is evident on chest X-rays as whitened areas in the lower lung. Alveolar closing pressure then exceeds pulmonary pressures, and the alveoli begin to collapse.

Exudative phase

During the exudative phase, or phase 1, fluid accumulates in the lung interstitium, alveolar spaces, and small airways. This causes the lungs to stiffen, impairing ventilation and reducing oxygenation of the pulmonary capillary blood, which results in reduced blood flow to the lungs. Platelets begin to aggregate and release substances (serotonin, bradykinin, and histamine), which attract and activate neutrophils.

Proliferative phase

During the proliferative phase, or phase 2, the released substances inflame and damage the alveolar membrane and later increase capillary permeability. Additional chemotactic factors released include endotoxins, tumor necrosis factor, and interleukin-1. The activated neutrophils release several inflammatory mediators and platelet aggravating factors that damage the alveolar capillary membrane and increase capillary permeability, allowing fluids to move into the interstitial space.

Next, as capillary permeability increases, proteins, blood cells, and more fluid leak out, increasing interstitial osmotic pressure and causing pulmonary edema.

The resulting pulmonary edema and hemorrhage significantly reduce lung compliance and impair alveolar ventilation.

Then, mediators released by neutrophils and macrophages also cause varying degrees of pulmonary vasoconstriction, resulting in pulmonary hypertension. The result of these changes is a mismatch in the ventilation-perfusion ratio. Although the patient responds with an increased respiratory rate, sufficient oxygen can't cross the alveolar capillary membrane. Carbon dioxide continues to cross easily and is lost with every exhalation.

Finally, pulmonary edema worsens and hyaline membranes form. Inflammation leads to fibrosis, which further impedes gas exchange. Fibrosis progressively obliterates alveoli, respiratory bronchioles, and the interstitium. Functional residual capacity decreases, and shunting becomes more serious. Hypoxemia leads to metabolic acidosis. At this final stage, the patient develops increasing partial pressure of arterial carbon dioxide ($PaCO_2$), decreasing pH and partial pressure of arterial oxygen (PaO_2), decreasing bicarbonate levels, and mental confusion. The end result is respiratory failure.

COMPLICATIONS
- Metabolic and respiratory acidosis
- Cardiac arrest

Signs and symptoms
- Rapid, shallow breathing and dyspnea
- Increased rate of ventilation
- Intercostal and suprasternal retractions
- Crackles and rhonchi
- Restlessness, apprehension, and mental sluggishness
- Motor dysfunction
- Tachycardia
- Respiratory acidosis
- Metabolic acidosis

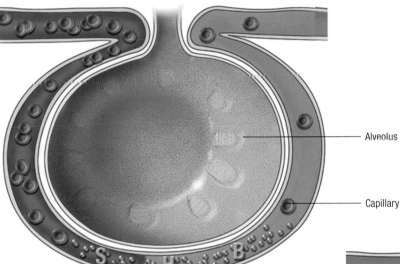

Alveolus

Capillary

Phase 1. Injury reduces normal blood flow to the lungs. Platelets aggregate and release histamine (H), serotonin (S), and bradykinin (B).

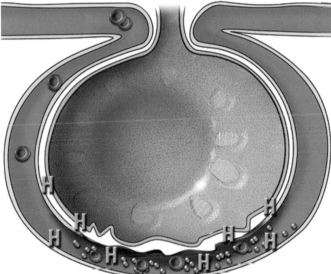

Phase 2. Those substances, especially histamine, inflame and damage the alveolocapillary membrane, increasing capillary permeability. Fluids then shift into the interstitial space.

Phase 3. As capillary permeability increases, proteins and fluids leak out, increasing interstitial osmotic pressure and causing pulmonary edema.

Diagnostic test results

• Arterial blood gas (ABG) analysis with the patient breathing room air initially reveals a reduced Pao_2 (less than 60 mm Hg) and a decreased $Paco_2$ (less than 35 mm Hg). Hypoxemia, despite increased supplemental oxygen, is the hallmark of ARDS; the resulting blood pH reflects respiratory alkalosis. As ARDS worsens, ABG values show respiratory acidosis evident by an increasing $Paco_2$, (over 45 mm Hg), metabolic acidosis evident by a decreasing bicarbonate level (less than 22 mEq/L), and a declining Pao_2, despite oxygen therapy.

CLINICAL TIP

It's important to understand how ARDS differs from acute lung injury. Both have an acute onset, and patients have bilateral infiltrates on frontal chest radiograph and pulmonary artery wedge pressure (PAWP) less than or equal to 18 mm Hg or no clinical evidence of left atrial hypertension. The difference with ARDS is that the Pao_2 is less than or equal to 200 mm Hg regardless of positive end-expiratory pressure (PEEP) level; with ALI, the Pao_2 is less than or equal to 300 mm Hg regardless of PEEP level.

• Pulmonary artery catheterization may show a PAWP of 12 to 18 mm Hg, and pulmonary artery pressure may show decreased cardiac output.
• Serial chest X-rays in early stages show bilateral infiltrates; in later stages, long fields with a ground-glass appearance and "white outs" of both lung fields.

• Chest computed tomography reveals bilateral opacities, pleural effusions, and decreased lung volume.
• Sputum analysis, including Gram stain and culture and sensitivity, identifies causative organisms.
• Blood cultures identify infectious organisms.
• Toxicology testing reveals possible drug ingestion.

Treatment

Therapy is focused on correcting the causes of ARDS and preventing progression of hypoxemia and respiratory acidosis. Treatment includes:
• intubation and mechanical ventilation
• humidified oxygen
• PEEP
• pressure-controlled inverse ratio ventilation
• high-frequency ventilation
• airway pressure release ventilation
• liquid ventilation
• inhaled nitric oxide
• permissive hypercapnia
• sedatives, opioids, and neuromuscular blockers
• high-dose corticosteroids
• sodium bicarbonate
• I.V. fluid administration or fluid restrictions
• vasopressors
• antimicrobial drugs
• diuretics
• correction of electrolyte and acid-base imbalances
• prone positioning
• extracorporeal membrane oxygenation
• surfactant administration.

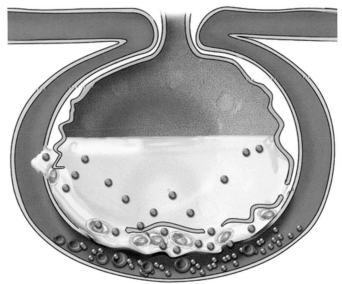

Phase 4. Decreased blood flow and fluids in the alveoli damage surfactant and impair the cell's ability to produce more. As a result, alveoli collapse, impeding gas exchange and decreasing lung compliance.

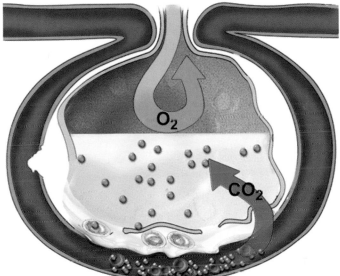

Phase 5. Sufficient oxygen can't cross the alveolocapillary membrane, but carbon dioxide (CO_2) can and is lost with every exhalation. Oxygen (O_2) and CO_2 levels decrease in the blood.

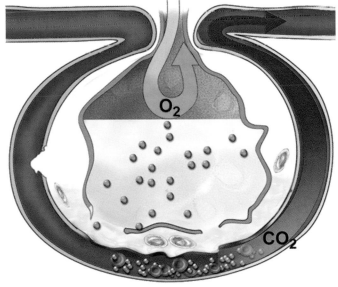

Phase 6. Pulmonary edema worsens, inflammation leads to fibrosis, and gas exchange is further impeded.

ASTHMA

Asthma is a reactive airway disorder characterized by inflammation and episodic airway obstruction. Such obstruction results from bronchospasms, increased mucus secretion, and mucosal edema. Although it's a chronic disorder, patients can suffer from acute exacerbations.

Causes

Asthma may result from sensitivity to extrinsic or intrinsic allergens. Extrinsic, or atopic, asthma begins in childhood; typically, patients are sensitive to specific external allergens. Many patients with asthma, especially children, have both intrinsic and extrinsic asthma.

Extrinsic allergens
- Pollen, air pollution
- Animal dander
- House dust or mold
- Kapok or feather pillows
- Food additives, including sulfites and some dyes
- Noxious fumes, tobacco smoke

Patients with intrinsic, or nonatopic, asthma react to internal, nonallergenic factors.

Intrinsic allergens
- Irritants
- Emotional stress and anxiety
- Respiratory infections
- Endocrine changes
- Temperature or humidity variations
- Coughing or laughing
- Genetic factors

Pathophysiology

In asthma, bronchial linings overreact to various stimuli, causing inflammation and smooth-muscle spasms that severely constrict the airways. When the hypersensitive patient inhales a triggering substance, abnormal antibodies stimulate mast cells in the lung interstitium to release histamine and leukotriene. Histamine attaches to receptor sites in the larger bronchi, where it causes swelling in smooth muscles. Leukotriene attaches to receptor sites in the smaller bronchi and causes swelling of smooth muscle there. It also causes fatty acids called prostaglandins to travel by way of the bloodstream to the lungs, where they enhance histamine's effects.

Histamine stimulates the mucous membranes to secrete excessive mucus, further narrowing the bronchial lumen. On inhalation, the narrowed bronchial lumen can still expand slightly, allowing air to reach the alveoli. On exhalation, increased intrathoracic pressure closes the bronchial lumen completely. Mucus fills the lung bases, inhibiting alveolar ventilation. Blood, shunted to alveoli in other lung parts, still can't compensate for diminished ventilation.

COMPLICATIONS
- Status asthmaticus
- Respiratory failure

CLINICAL TIP

When status asthmaticus occurs, hypoxia worsens, expiratory flow slows, and expiratory volumes decrease. If treatment isn't initiated, the patient begins to tire. Acidosis develops as arterial carbon dioxide increases. The situation becomes life-threatening when no air movement is audible on auscultation (a silent chest) and partial pressure of arterial carbon dioxide ($Paco_2$) rises to over 70 mm Hg.

Signs and symptoms
- Sudden dyspnea, wheezing, and tightness in the chest
- Coughing that produces thick, clear, or yellow sputum
- Tachypnea, along with use of accessory respiratory muscles
- Rapid pulse
- Profuse perspiration
- Hyperresonant lung fields
- Diminished breath sounds

Diagnostic test results
- Pulmonary function tests reveal low-normal or decreased vital capacity, and increased total lung and residual capacities.
- Serum immunoglobulin E levels may increase from an allergic reaction.
- Sputum analysis indicates the presence of Curschmann's spirals (casts of airways), Charcot-Leyden crystals, and eosinophils.
- Complete blood count with differential reveals an increased eosinophil count.
- Chest X-rays may show hyperinflation with areas of atelectasis.
- With arterial blood gas analysis, partial pressure of arterial oxygen and $Paco_2$ are usually decreased, except in severe asthma, when $Paco_2$ may be normal or increased, indicating severe bronchial obstruction.
- Skin testing identifies specific allergens.
- Bronchial challenge testing evaluates the clinical significance of allergens identified by skin testing.
- Electrocardiography shows sinus tachycardia during an asthma attack or right axis deviation and peaked P waves (indicating cor pulmonale during a severe attack that resolves after the attack).

Treatment
- Identification and avoidance of precipitating factors
- Desensitization to specific antigens
- Low-flow humidified oxygen
- Inhaled steroids such as triamcinolone acetonide
- Leukotriene inhibitors such as montelukast sodium
- Long-acting bronchodilators such as formoterol
- Mast cell stabilizers, such as cromolyn sodium or nedocromil sodium
- Aminophylline or theophylline
- Short-acting bronchodilators, such as albuterol or levalbuterol
- Oral or I.V. corticosteroids
- Mechanical ventilation
- Relaxation exercises

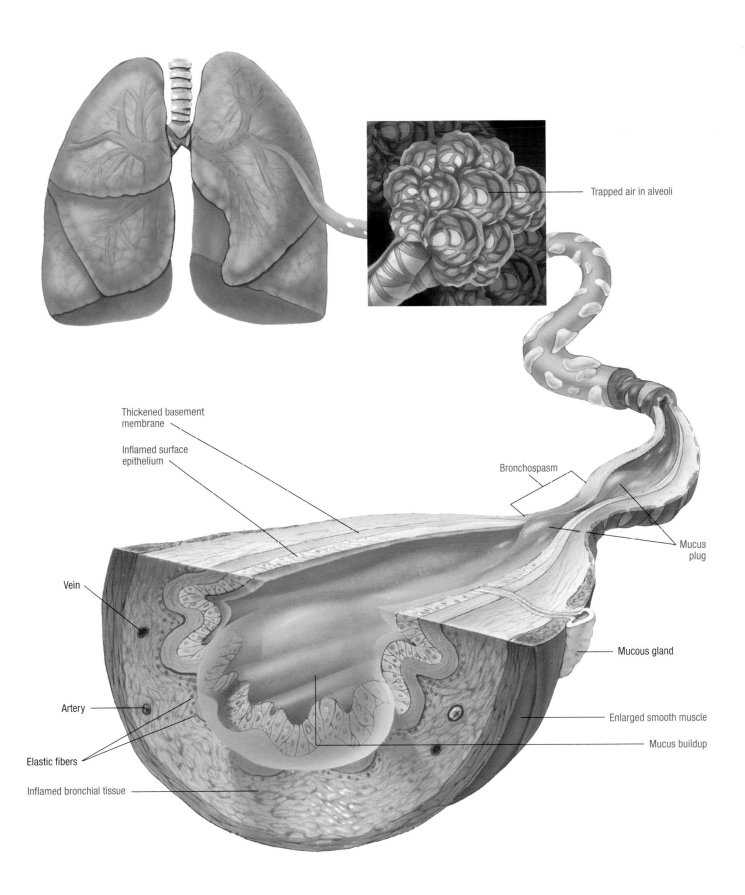

Trapped air in alveoli

Thickened basement membrane

Inflamed surface epithelium

Bronchospasm

Mucus plug

Vein

Mucous gland

Artery

Enlarged smooth muscle

Mucus buildup

Elastic fibers

Inflamed bronchial tissue

CHRONIC BRONCHITIS

Bronchitis is acute or chronic inflammation of the bronchi caused by irritants or infection. The distinguishing characteristic of bronchitis is obstruction of airflow. In chronic bronchitis, a form of chronic obstructive pulmonary disease, hypersecretion of mucus and chronic productive cough are present during 3 months of the year for at least 2 consecutive years.

AGE ALERT
Children of parents who smoke are at higher risk for respiratory tract infection, which can lead to chronic bronchitis.

Causes
- Cigarette smoking
- Exposure to irritants
- Genetic predisposition
- Exposure to organic or inorganic dusts
- Exposure to noxious gases
- Respiratory tract infection

Pathophysiology
Chronic bronchitis develops when irritants are inhaled for a prolonged time. The irritants inflame the tracheobronchial tree, leading to increased mucus production and a narrowed or blocked airway. As the inflammation continues, changes in the cells lining the respiratory tract increase resistance in the small airways, and severe imbalance in the ventilation-perfusion ($\dot{V}/\dot{Q}$) ratio decreases arterial oxygenation.

Chronic bronchitis causes hypertrophy of airway smooth muscle and hyperplasia of the mucous glands, increased numbers of goblet cells, ciliary damage, squamous metaplasia of the columnar epithelium, and chronic leukocytic and lymphocytic infiltration of bronchial walls. Hypersecretion of the goblet cells blocks the free movement of the cilia, which normally sweep dust, irritants, and mucus away from the airways. Accumulating mucus and debris impair the defenses and increase the likelihood of respiratory tract infections.

Additional effects include narrowing and widespread inflammation within the airways. Bronchial walls become inflamed and thickened from edema and accumulation of inflammatory cells, and smooth-muscle bronchospasm further narrows the lumen. Initially, only large bronchi are involved, but eventually all airways are affected. Airways become obstructed and close, especially on expiration, trapping the gas in the distal portion of the lung. Consequent hypoventilation leads to a $\dot{V}/\dot{Q}$ mismatch and resultant hypoxemia and hypercapnia.

COMPLICATIONS
- Pneumonia
- Lung cancer

Signs and symptoms
- Copious gray, white, or yellow sputum
- Dyspnea and tachypnea
- Cyanosis
- Use of accessory muscles
- Pedal edema
- Jugular vein distention
- Weight gain due to edema or weight loss due to difficulty eating and increased metabolic rate
- Wheezing, prolonged expiratory time, and rhonchi
- Pulmonary hypertension

Diagnostic test results
- Chest X-rays show hyperinflation and increased bronchovascular markings.
- Pulmonary function studies indicate increased residual volume, decreased vital capacity and forced expiratory flow, and normal static compliance and diffusing capacity.
- Arterial blood gas analysis reveals decreased partial pressure of arterial oxygen and normal or increased partial pressure of arterial carbon dioxide.
- Sputum analysis reveals many microorganisms and neutrophils.
- Electrocardiography shows atrial arrhythmias; peaked P waves in leads II, III, and aV_F and, occasionally, right ventricular hypertrophy.

Treatment
- Smoking cessation
- Avoidance of air pollutants
- Antibiotics
- Bronchodilators
- Adequate hydration
- Chest physiotherapy
- Ultrasonic or mechanical nebulizers
- Corticosteroids
- Diuretics
- Oxygen therapy

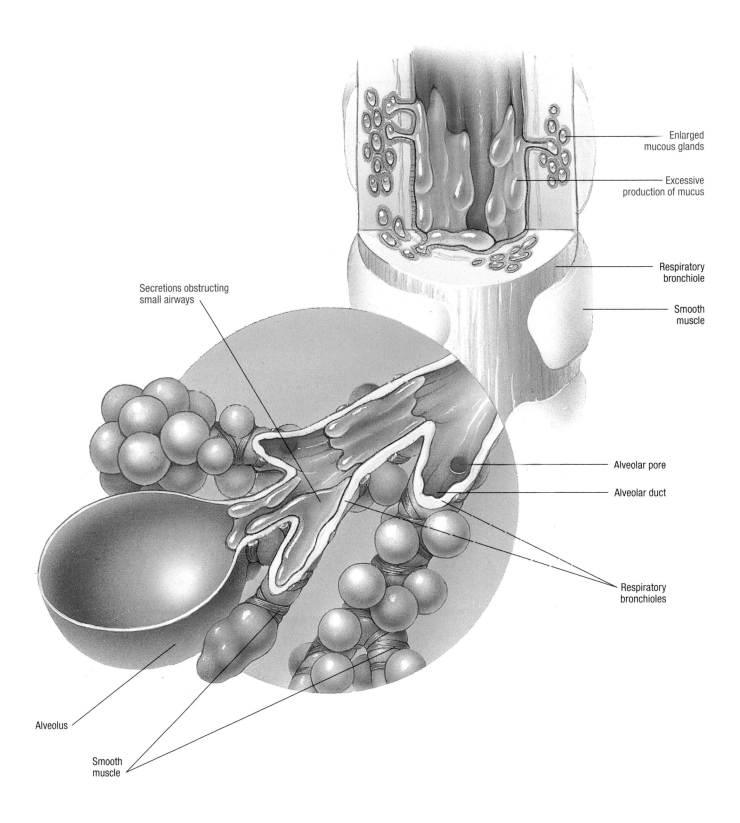

Enlarged
mucous glands

Excessive
production of mucus

Respiratory
bronchiole

Smooth
muscle

Secretions obstructing
small airways

Alveolar pore

Alveolar duct

Respiratory
bronchioles

Alveolus

Smooth
muscle

CYSTIC FIBROSIS

In cystic fibrosis, dysfunction of the exocrine glands affects multiple organ systems. The disorder is characterized by chronic airway infection leading to bronchiectasis, bronchiolectasis, exocrine pancreatic insufficiency, intestinal dysfunction, abnormal sweat gland function, and reproductive dysfunction. Cystic fibrosis is accompanied by many complications and has a median survival rate of 31 years. The disease affects males and females and is the most common fatal genetic disease in children of European ancestry. There are more than 30,000 patients with cystic fibrosis in the United States.

Causes

Inherited as an autosomal recessive trait, the responsible gene, on chromosome 7q, encodes a membrane-associated protein called the cystic fibrosis transmembrane regulator (CFTR). The exact function of CFTR remains unknown, but it appears to help regulate chloride and sodium transport across epithelial membranes.

Pathophysiology

Most cases of cystic fibrosis arise from the mutation that affects the genetic coding for a single amino acid, resulting in a protein (CFTR) that doesn't function properly. CFTR resembles other transmembrane transport proteins, but it lacks the phenylalanine in the protein produced by normal genes. This regulator interferes with chloride channels regulated by cyclic adenosine monophosphate, and with other ions, by preventing adenosine triphosphate from binding to the protein or by interfering with activation by protein kinase.

The mutation affects volume-absorbing epithelia (in the airways and intestines), salt-absorbing epithelia (in sweat ducts), and volume-secretory epithelia (in the pancreas). Lack of phenylalanine leads to dehydration, which increases the viscosity of mucous gland secretions and leads to obstruction of glandular ducts. Cystic fibrosis has a variable effect on electrolyte and water transport.

COMPLICATIONS
- Nasal polyps
- Cor pulmonale
- Cholecystitis
- Pneumothorax
- Rectal prolapse
- Bowel obstruction

Signs and symptoms
- Thick, sticky secretions and dehydration
- Chronic infections
- Dyspnea and paroxysmal cough
- Failure to thrive: poor weight gain, poor growth, distended abdomen, thin extremities, and poor skin turgor
- Crackles and wheezes
- Bulky, greasy stools
- Obstruction of small and large intestines; biliary cirrhosis

Diagnostic test results

The Cystic Fibrosis Foundation has developed certain criteria for definitive diagnosis:
- Two sweat tests (to detect elevated sodium chloride levels) using a pilocarpine solution (a sweat inducer) and presence of an obstructive pulmonary disease, confirmed pancreatic insufficiency or failure to thrive, or a family history of cystic fibrosis.

AGE ALERT
The sweat test may be inaccurate in very young infants because they may not produce enough sweat for a valid test.

- Chest X-rays show an enlarged chest cavity and decreased lung markings, reflecting destruction of lung tissue.
- Stool specimen analysis indicates the absence of trypsin, suggesting pancreatic insufficiency.

These test results may support the diagnosis:
- DNA testing can locate the presence of the Delta F 508 deletion (found in about 70% of patients with cystic fibrosis, although the disease can cause more than 100 other mutations). It allows prenatal diagnosis in families with a previously affected child.
- Pulmonary function tests reveal decreased vital capacity, elevated residual volume due to air entrapments, and decreased forced expiratory volume in 1 second.
- Liver enzyme tests reveal hepatic insufficiency.
- Sputum culture reveals organisms that cystic fibrosis patients typically and chronically colonize, such as *Staphylococcus* and *Pseudomonas.*
- Serum albumin measurement helps assess nutritional status.
- Electrolyte analysis assesses hydration status.

Treatment
- Diet with increased fat and sodium or salt supplements
- Pancreatic enzyme replacement
- Breathing exercises, chest percussion, and postural drainage
- Inhaled bronchodilators
- Antibiotics such as azithromycin
- Transplantation of heart or lungs
- Mucus-thinning drugs such as dornase alfa
- Positive expiratory pressure devices
- Flutter valves
- High-frequency chest compression vest

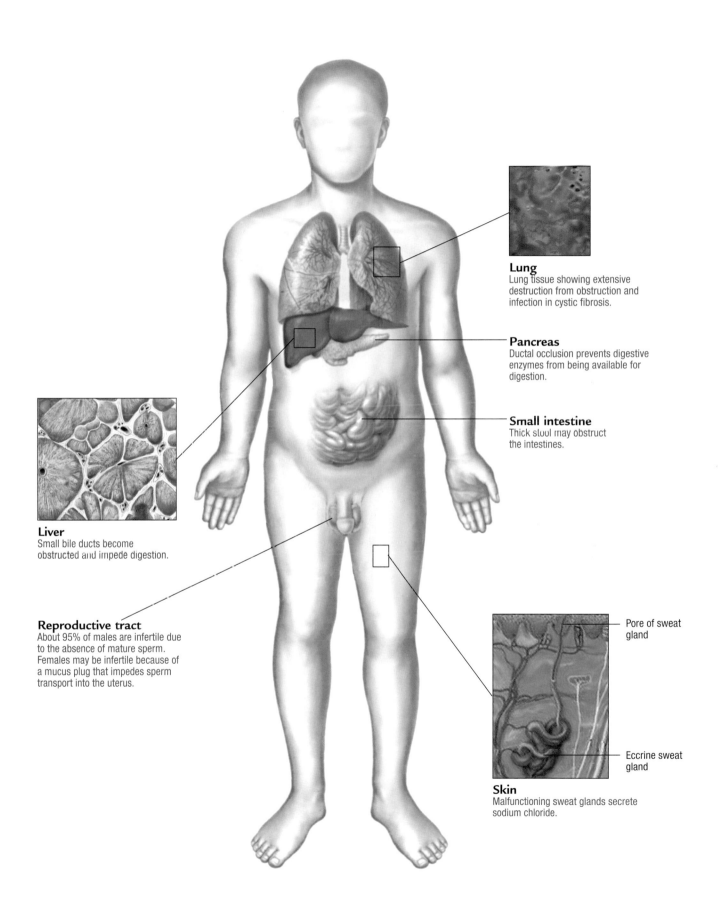

Lung
Lung tissue showing extensive destruction from obstruction and infection in cystic fibrosis.

Pancreas
Ductal occlusion prevents digestive enzymes from being available for digestion.

Small intestine
Thick stool may obstruct the intestines.

Liver
Small bile ducts become obstructed and impede digestion.

Reproductive tract
About 95% of males are infertile due to the absence of mature sperm. Females may be infertile because of a mucus plug that impedes sperm transport into the uterus.

Pore of sweat gland

Eccrine sweat gland

Skin
Malfunctioning sweat glands secrete sodium chloride.

EMPHYSEMA

Emphysema, a form of chronic obstructive pulmonary disease, is the abnormal, permanent enlargement of the acini accompanied by destruction of alveolar walls without fibrosis. Obstruction results from tissue changes rather than mucus production, which occurs in chronic bronchitis. The distinguishing characteristic of emphysema is airflow limitation caused by lack of elastic recoil in the lungs.

AGE ALERT

Aging is a risk factor for emphysema. Senile emphysema results from degenerative changes that cause stretching without destruction of the smooth muscle. Connective tissue isn't usually affected.

Causes
- Cigarette smoking
- Deficiency of alpha$_1$-antitrypsin

Pathophysiology

Primary emphysema has been linked to an inherited deficiency of the enzyme alpha$_1$-antitrypsin, a major component of alpha$_1$-globulin. Alpha$_1$-antitrypsin inhibits the activation of several proteolytic enzymes; its deficiency is an autosomal recessive trait that predisposes a person to emphysema.

In emphysema, recurrent inflammation is associated with the release of proteolytic enzymes from lung cells. This causes irreversible enlargement of the air spaces distal to the terminal bronchioles. Enlargement of air spaces destroys the alveolar walls, which results in a breakdown of elasticity and loss of fibrous and muscle tissue, making the lungs less compliant.

The alveolar septa are initially destroyed, eliminating a portion of the capillary bed and increasing air volume in the acinus. This breakdown leaves the alveoli unable to recoil normally after expanding and results in bronchiolar collapse on expiration. The damaged or destroyed alveolar walls can't support the airways to keep them open. The amount of air that can be exhaled passively is diminished, trapping air in the lungs and leading to overdistention. Hyperinflation of the alveoli produces bullae and air spaces adjacent to the pleura.

COMPLICATIONS
- Respiratory failure
- Cor pulmonale

Signs and symptoms
- Tachypnea
- Dyspnea
- Barrel chest
- Prolonged expiration and grunting
- Crackles and wheezing on inspiration
- Decreased breath sounds
- Hyperresonance
- Clubbed fingers and toes
- Decreased tactile fremitus
- Decreased chest expansion
- Chronic cough with or without sputum production
- Accessory muscle use
- Mental status changes, if carbon dioxide retention worsens
- Anorexia and cachexia

Diagnostic test results
- Chest X-rays in advanced disease show a flattened diaphragm, reduced vascular markings at the lung periphery, overaeration of the lungs, a vertical heart, enlarged anteroposterior chest diameter, and a large retrosternal air space.
- Pulmonary function studies indicate increased residual volume and total lung capacity, reduced diffusing capacity, and increased inspiratory flow.
- Arterial blood gas analysis usually reveals reduced partial pressure of arterial oxygen and a normal partial pressure of arterial carbon dioxide until late in the disease process.
- Electrocardiography shows tall, symmetrical P waves in leads II, III, and aV$_F$; a vertical QRS axis and signs of right ventricular hypertrophy are seen late in the disease.
- Complete blood count usually reveals an increased hemoglobin level late in the disease when the patient has persistent, severe hypoxia.

Treatment
- Avoidance of tobacco smoke and air pollution
- Bronchodilators, such as beta-adrenergic blockers, albuterol, and ipratropium bromide
- Antibiotics
- Flu vaccine to prevent influenza
- Pneumovax to prevent pneumococcal pneumonia
- Adequate hydration
- Chest physiotherapy
- Oxygen therapy
- Mucolytics
- Aerosolized or systemic corticosteroids
- Lung volume reduction surgery
- Lung transplantation

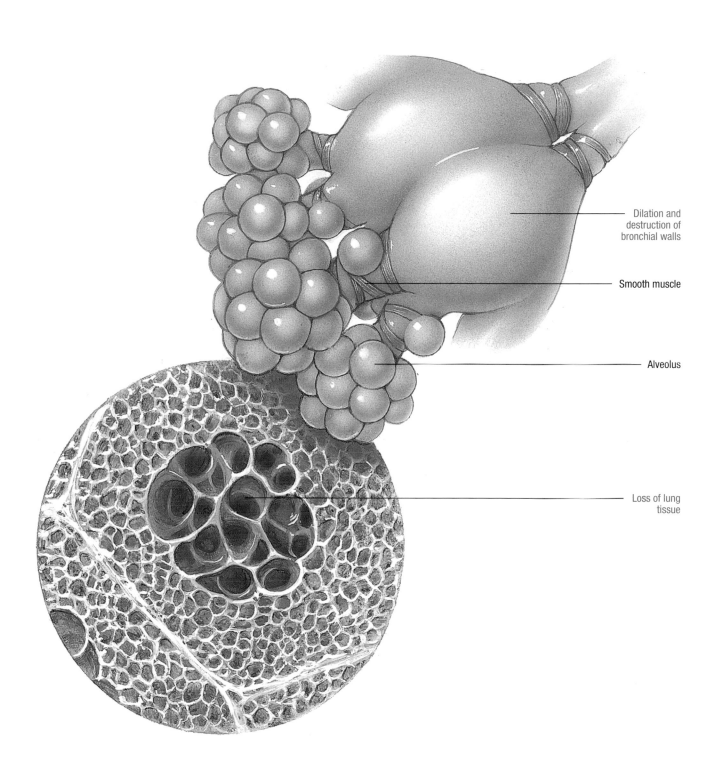

Dilation and destruction of bronchial walls

Smooth muscle

Alveolus

Loss of lung tissue

FAT EMBOLISM SYNDROME

Fat embolism syndrome is a rare but potentially fatal problem. The syndrome involves pulmonary, cerebral, and cutaneous manifestations and occurs 24 to 48 hours postinjury.

AGE ALERT
Young men with fractures are at an increased risk for developing fat embolism syndrome.

Causes
- Fractures of the pelvis, femur, tibia, or ribs
- Orthopedic surgery

Pathophysiology
Bone marrow from a fractured bone or other injured adipose tissue releases fatty globules that enter the systemic circulation through torn veins at the injury site. These fatty globules travel to the lungs, where they form an embolus that blocks pulmonary circulation. Lipase breaks down the trapped fat emboli into free fatty acids.

This process causes a local toxic effect that damages the epithelium, increases capillary permeability, and inactivates lung surfactant. The increased capillary permeability allows protein-rich fluid to leak into the interstitial space and alveoli, increasing the workload of the right side of the heart and causing pulmonary edema. The decreased surfactant causes alveolar collapse, a decrease in functional reserve capacity, and ventilation-perfusion mismatch, leading to hypoxemia. Platelet aggregation on fat, normal injury-related platelet consumption, and platelet dilution through I.V. crystalloid administration all contribute to thrombocytopenia, petechiae and, possibly, disseminated intravascular coagulation.

COMPLICATIONS
- Respiratory distress

Signs and symptoms
- Petechiae
- Increased respiratory rate
- Dyspnea
- Accessory muscle use
- Mental status changes
- Jaundice
- Fever

Diagnostic test results

CLINICAL TIP
Gurd's criteria are used to diagnose fat embolism syndrome. At least one major and three minor criteria are required for diagnosis. Major criteria include:
- petechiae in a "vest" distribution
- hypoxia, with a partial pressure of arterial oxygen (PaO_2) less than 60 mm Hg
- pulmonary edema
- change in level of consciousness.

Minor criteria include:
- tachycardia, with a heart rate greater than 110 beats/minute
- pyrexia, with a temperature higher than 103° F (39.4° C)
- retinal changes
- fat in urine or sputum
- unexplained drop in hematocrit or platelet count
- increasing erythrocyte sedimentation rate
- jaundice
- renal changes.

- Arterial blood gas analysis reveals PaO_2 less than 60 mm Hg; partial pressure of arterial carbon dioxide initially decreases and later increases.
- Chest X-ray is normal initially but later shows patchy areas of consolidation to complete "white out," if the condition progresses.
- Complete blood count shows decreased platelets and decreased hemoglobin levels.

Treatment
- Supplemental oxygen
- Endotracheal intubation and mechanical ventilation
- I.V. fluids such as crystalloids (avoid colloids)
- Coughing and deep breathing

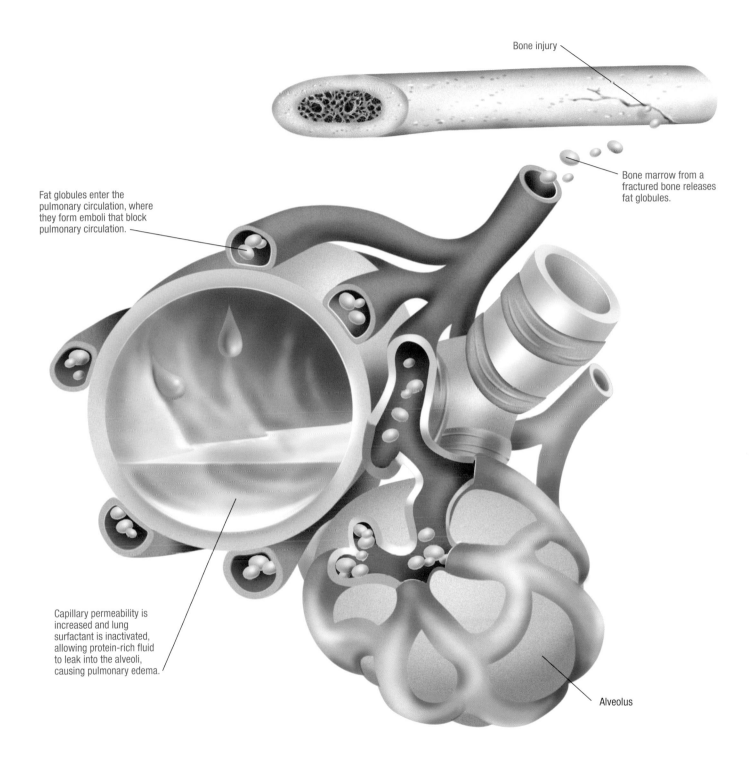

Bone injury

Bone marrow from a fractured bone releases fat globules.

Fat globules enter the pulmonary circulation, where they form emboli that block pulmonary circulation.

Capillary permeability is increased and lung surfactant is inactivated, allowing protein-rich fluid to leak into the alveoli, causing pulmonary edema.

Alveolus

IDIOPATHIC PULMONARY FIBROSIS

Idiopathic pulmonary fibrosis is a chronic and usually fatal interstitial pulmonary disease. Once thought to be a rare condition, it's now diagnosed with much greater frequency. Survival is estimated at 3 to 5 years after diagnosis. Idiopathic pulmonary fibrosis has been known by several other names over the years, including *cryptogenic fibrosing alveolitis, diffuse interstitial fibrosis, idiopathic interstitial pneumonitis,* and *Hamman-Rich syndrome.*

AGE ALERT
Idiopathic pulmonary fibrosis occurs most commonly in people between ages 50 and 70.

Causes
Unknown

Pathophysiology
Idiopathic pulmonary fibrosis reflects the accumulation of excessive fibrous or connective tissue in the lung parenchyma. It's the result of a cascade of inflammatory, immune, and fibrotic processes in the lung. Despite many studies, the stimulus that begins the progression remains unknown. Speculation has revolved around viral and genetic causes, but no good evidence has been found to support either theory. However, it's clear that chronic inflammation plays an important role. Inflammation develops the injury and the fibrosis that ultimately distorts and impairs the structure and function of the alveolocapillary gas exchange surface. The lungs become stiff and difficult to ventilate, and the diffusion capacity of the alveolocapillary membrane decreases, leading to hypoxemia.

COMPLICATIONS
- Respiratory failure
- Heart failure
- Pulmonary embolism
- Pneumonia
- Lung cancer

Signs and symptoms
- Dyspnea and rapid, shallow breathing
- Dry, hacking cough
- Fatigue
- End-expiratory crackles and bronchial breath sounds
- Clubbed fingers and toes
- Cyanosis
- Pulmonary hypertension
- Profound hypoxemia and severe, debilitating dyspnea in advanced disease
- Chest pain

Diagnostic test results
Diagnosis begins with a thorough patient history to exclude any of the more common causes of interstitial lung disease, such as:
- environmental or occupational exposure — coal dust, asbestos, silica, beryllium
- connective tissue diseases — scleroderma, rheumatoid arthritis
- drug use — amiodarone, tocainide, crack cocaine.
    Tests that help to confirm the diagnosis include:
- lung biopsy — shows mixed areas of normal tissue, interstitial inflammation, fibrosis, and honeycombing
- chest X-ray and high-resolution computed tomography — show a pattern of diffuse interstitial lung disease, with fibrosis and honeycombing
- pulmonary function tests — reveal decreased total lung volumes.

Treatment
- Oxygen therapy
- Corticosteroids
- Immunosuppressants, such as cyclophosphamide and azathioprine
- Colchicine
- Pulmonary rehabilitation
- Lung transplantation

    Because idiopathic pulmonary fibrosis generally responds poorly to treatment and because drug therapies cause so many adverse reactions, research studies are currently aimed at learning which factors may improve the patient's response to treatment. The chances of a positive response to therapy and extended survival seem to be best for young female patients with less-than-average dyspnea and hypoxemia, more normal lung function, and no history of smoking. Evidence of inflammation (lymphocytes in bronchoalveolar lavage fluid, circulating immune complexes, and positive response to corticosteroids) also seems to predict a better outcome. Indicators of a poor prognosis are irreversible lung destruction and fibrosis (severe hypoxemia, decreased diffusing capacity for carbon monoxide, and neutrophils and eosinophils in bronchoalveolar lavage fluid).

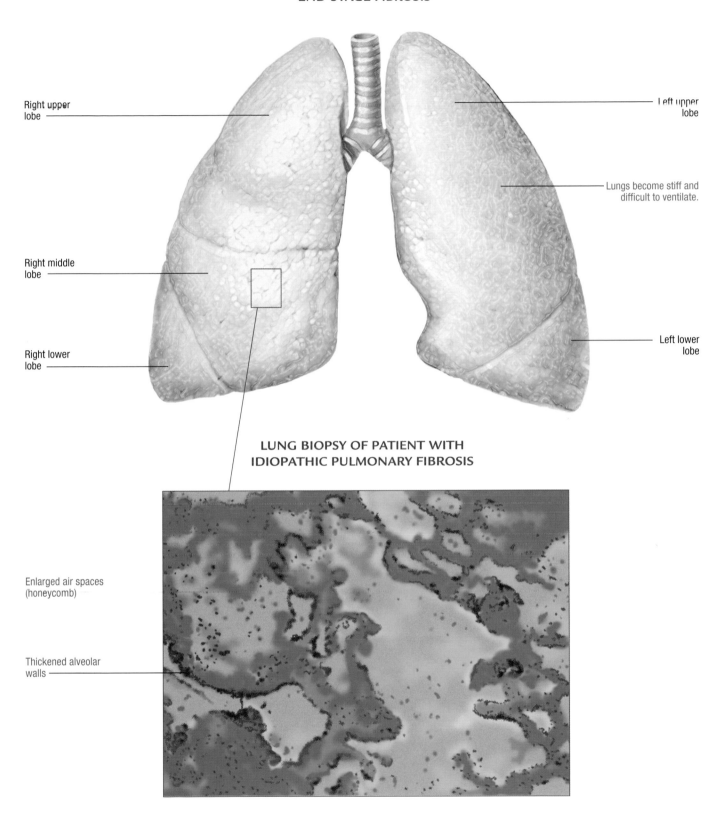

Right upper lobe

Left upper lobe

Lungs become stiff and difficult to ventilate.

Right middle lobe

Right lower lobe

Left lower lobe

LUNG BIOPSY OF PATIENT WITH IDIOPATHIC PULMONARY FIBROSIS

Enlarged air spaces (honeycomb)

Thickened alveolar walls

LUNG CANCER

Lung cancer is the leading cause of cancer death among men and women.

AGE ALERT
Lung cancer is fairly rare in people younger than age 40. The average age at diagnosis is 60.

The two main types of lung cancer are small-cell lung cancer (SCLC) and non–small-cell lung cancer (NSCLC). If the cancer has features of both, it's called *mixed small-cell/large-cell cancer.*

About 20% of all lung cancers are SCLC. Although the cancer cells are small, they can multiply quickly and form large tumors that spread to the lymph nodes and to other organs, such as the brain, liver, and bones. Therefore, treatment must include drugs that kill this widespread disease. SCLC is extremely rare in someone who has never smoked.

The remaining 80% of lung cancers are NSCLC, which includes three subtypes. The cells in these subtypes differ in size, shape, and chemical makeup. They include:
- *squamous cell carcinoma,* which is commonly linked to a history of smoking and tends to be found centrally, near a bronchus
- *adenocarcinoma,* which is usually found in the outer region of the lung
- *large-cell undifferentiated carcinoma,* which can appear in any part of the lung and tends to grow and spread quickly. (This type of cancer has a poor prognosis.)

Causes
- Tobacco smoke
- Carcinogenic industrial and air pollutants (asbestos, uranium, arsenic, nickel, iron oxides, chromium, radioactive dust, coal dust, radon)
- Familial susceptibility

Pathophysiology
Lung cancer begins with the transformation of one epithelial cell of the airway. The bronchi, and certain portions of the bronchi, such as the segmental bifurcations and sites of mucus production, are thought to be more vulnerable to injury from carcinogens.

As a lung tumor grows, it can partially or completely obstruct the airway, resulting in lobar collapse distal to the tumor. A lung tumor can also hemorrhage, causing hemopty-

sis. Early metastasis may occur to other thoracic structures, such as hilar lymph nodes or the mediastinum. Distant metastasis can occur to the brain, liver, bone, and adrenal glands.

COMPLICATIONS
- Phrenic nerve paralysis
- Tracheal obstruction
- Esophageal compression
- Pleural effusion

Signs and symptoms
- Cough, hoarseness, wheezing, dyspnea, hemoptysis, and chest pain
- Fever, weight loss, weakness, and anorexia
- Bone and joint pain
- Cushing's syndrome
- Hypercalcemia
- Hemoptysis, atelectasis, pneumonitis, and dyspnea
- Shoulder pain and unilateral paralysis of diaphragm
- Dysphagia
- Jugular vein distention and facial, neck, and chest edema
- Piercing chest pain, increasing dyspnea, and severe arm pain

Diagnostic test results
- Chest X-ray shows an advanced lesion, including size and location.
- Sputum cytology reveals possible cell type.
- Computed tomography (CT) scan of the chest delineates tumor size and relationship to surrounding structures.
- Bronchoscopy locates tumor; washings reveal malignant cell type.
- Needle lung biopsy confirms cell type.
- Mediastinal and supraclavicular node biopsies reveal possible metastasis.
- Thoracentesis shows malignant cells in pleural fluid.
- Bone scan, bone marrow biopsy, and CT scan of the brain and abdomen reveal metastasis.

Treatment
- Lobectomy, wedge resection, or pneumonectomy
- Video-assisted chest surgery
- Laser surgery
- Radiation
- Chemotherapy

Right lung — Anterior view

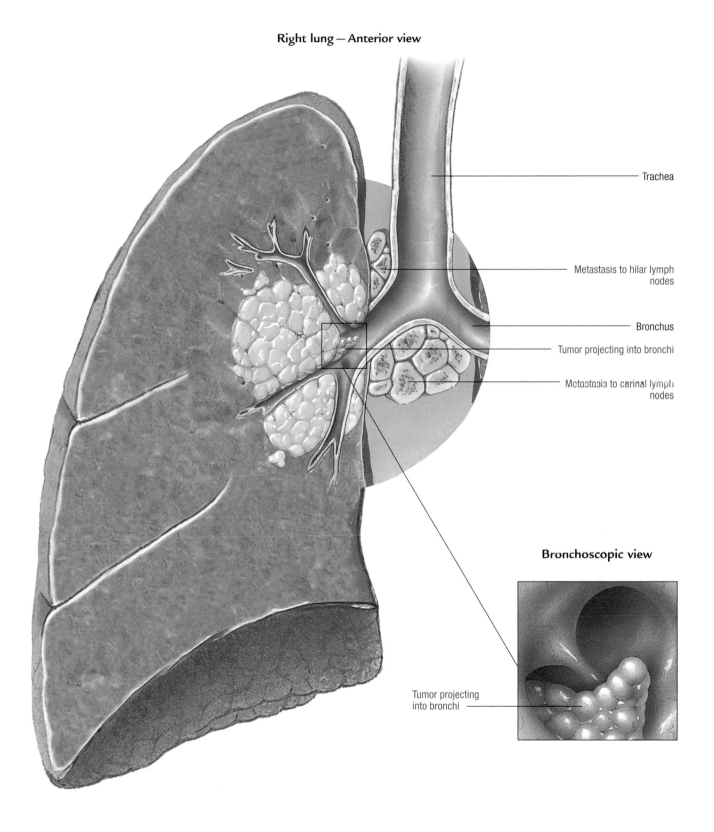

Trachea

Metastasis to hilar lymph nodes

Bronchus

Tumor projecting into bronchi

Metastasis to carinal lymph nodes

Bronchoscopic view

Tumor projecting into bronchi

PLEURAL EFFUSION

Pleural effusion is an excess of fluid in the pleural space. Normally, this space contains a small amount of extracellular fluid that lubricates the pleural surfaces. Increased production or inadequate removal of this fluid results in transudative or exudative pleural effusion. Empyema is the accumulation of pus and necrotic tissue in the pleural space.

Causes

Transudative pleural effusion
- Heart failure
- Hepatic disease with ascites
- Peritoneal dialysis
- Hypoalbuminemia
- Disorders causing expanded intravascular volume

Exudative pleural effusion
- Tuberculosis (TB)
- Subphrenic abscess
- Pancreatitis
- Bacterial or fungal pneumonitis or empyema
- Malignancy
- Pulmonary embolism with or without infarction
- Collagen disease such as systemic lupus erythematosus
- Myxedema
- Chest trauma

Empyema
- Idiopathic infection
- Pneumonitis
- Carcinoma
- Perforation
- Esophageal rupture

Pathophysiology

The balance of osmotic and hydrostatic pressures in parietal pleural capillaries normally results in fluid movement into the pleural space. Balanced pressures in visceral pleural capillaries promote reabsorption of this fluid. Excessive hydrostatic pressure or decreased osmotic pressure can cause excessive amounts of fluid to pass across intact capillaries. The result is a *transudative pleural effusion,* an ultrafiltrate of plasma containing low concentrations of protein.

Exudative pleural effusion results when capillary permeability increases with or without changes in hydrostatic and colloid osmotic pressures, allowing protein-rich fluid to leak into the pleural space.

Empyema is usually associated with infection in the pleural space.

COMPLICATIONS
- Atelectasis
- Infection
- Hypoxemia

Signs and symptoms
- Characteristically related to underlying pathologic condition and how quickly effusion develops
- Dyspnea
- Pleuritic chest pain
- Fever
- Malaise
- Displaced point of maximum impulse, based on size of effusion
- Decreased breath sounds
- Dullness over the effused areas (doesn't change with breathing)

Diagnostic test results
- Chest X-ray shows radiopaque fluid in dependent regions.
- Computed tomography scan will show the location of the pleural effusions.

Diagnosis also requires other tests to distinguish transudative from exudative effusions and to help pinpoint the underlying disorder. The most useful test is thoracentesis, in which analysis of aspirated pleural fluid shows:
- transudative effusions — lactate dehydrogenase (LD) levels less than 200 International Units and protein levels less than 3 g/dl
- exudative effusions — ratio of protein in pleural fluid to serum of 0.5 or more, LD in pleural fluid of 200 International Units or more, and ratio of LD in pleural fluid to LD in serum of 0.6 or more
- empyema — acute inflammatory white blood cells and microorganisms
- empyema or rheumatoid arthritis — extremely decreased pleural fluid glucose levels.

In addition, if a pleural effusion results from esophageal rupture or pancreatitis, fluid amylase levels are usually higher than serum levels. Aspirated fluid may be tested for lupus erythematosus cells, antinuclear antibodies, and neoplastic cells. It may also be analyzed for color and consistency; acid-fast bacillus, fungal, and bacterial cultures; and triglycerides (in chylothorax). Cell analysis shows leukocytosis in empyema. A negative tuberculin skin test strongly rules against TB as the cause. In exudative pleural effusions in which thoracentesis isn't definitive, pleural biopsy may be done. It's particularly useful for confirming TB or malignancy.

Treatment
- Thoracentesis
- Chest tube insertion
- Pleurodesis (injection of a sclerosing agent such as talc)
- Decortication
- Rib resection
- Parenteral antibiotics
- Oxygen therapy
- Pleuroperitoneal shunt
- Pleurex catheter

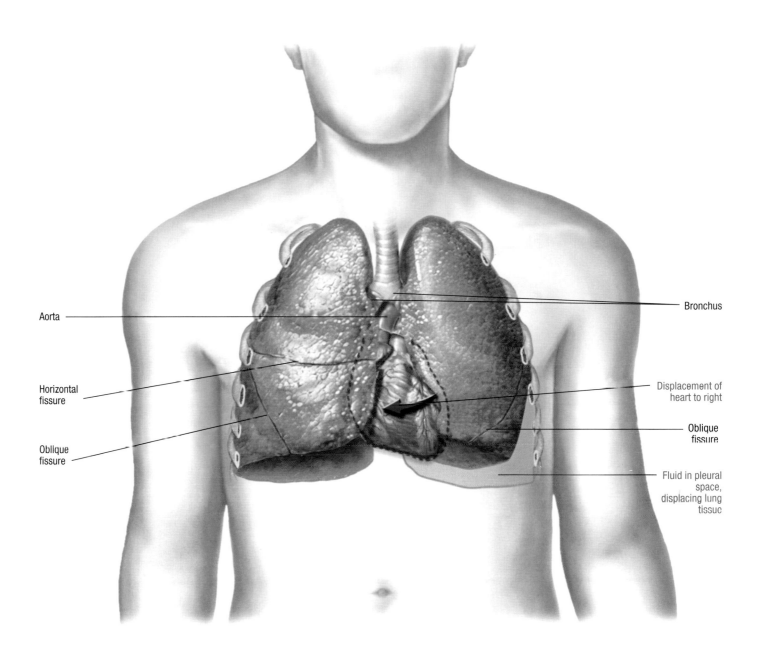

Aorta

Horizontal
fissure

Oblique
fissure

Bronchus

Displacement of
heart to right

Oblique
fissure

Fluid in pleural
space,
displacing lung
tissue

PNEUMONIA

Pneumonia is an acute infection of the lung parenchyma that commonly impairs gas exchange. The prognosis is generally good for people who have normal lungs and adequate host defenses before the onset of pneumonia.

Pneumonia is commonly classified according to location: *bronchopneumonia* involves distal airways and alveoli; *lobular pneumonia,* part of a lobe; *lobar pneumonia,* an entire lobe. It can also be classified according to the causative agent, such as gram negative or gram positive, viral, bacterial, or the specific organ responsible such as pneumococcal pneumonia. Nosocomial pneumonia occurs during hospitalization for another condition.

AGE ALERT
Older patients and very young patients are at greater risk for pneumonia.

Other patients at greater risk are those who are immunocompromised, malnourished, or hospitalized in an intensive care unit; smokers or alcohol abusers; and those with a chronic condition such as cardiovascular disease.

Causes
Primary
- Inhalation or aspiration of a pathogen, including pneumococcal, viral, and mycoplasmal pneumonia
Secondary
- After initial damage from a noxious chemical or other insult (superinfection)
- Hematogenous spread of bacteria from a distant focus

Pathophysiology
In bacterial pneumonia, an infection initially triggers alveolar inflammation and edema. This produces an area of low ventilation with normal perfusion. Capillaries become engorged with blood, causing stasis. As the alveolocapillary membrane breaks down, alveoli fill with blood and exudate, resulting in atelectasis.

In viral pneumonia, the virus first attacks bronchiolar epithelial cells. This causes interstitial inflammation and desquamation. The virus also invades bronchial mucous glands and goblet cells. It then spreads to the alveoli, which fill with blood and fluid. In advanced infection, a hyaline membrane may form.

In aspiration pneumonia, inhalation of gastric juices or hydrocarbons triggers inflammatory changes and inactivates surfactant over a large area. Decreased surfactant leads to alveolar collapse. Acidic gastric juices may damage the airways and alveoli. Particles containing aspirated gastric juices may obstruct the airways and reduce airflow, leading to secondary bacterial pneumonia.

COMPLICATIONS
- Septic shock
- Hypoxemia
- Respiratory failure
- Empyema or lung abscess
- Bacteremia
- Endocarditis
- Pericarditis
- Meningitis

Signs and symptoms
- Coughing
- Sputum production
- Pleuritic chest pain
- Shaking chills
- Fever
- Wide range of physical signs, from diffuse, fine crackles to signs of localized or extensive consolidation and pleural effusion
- Dyspnea
- Tachypnea
- Malaise
- Decreased breath sounds

Diagnostic test results
- Chest X-rays identify infiltrates that confirm the diagnosis.
- Sputum specimen, Gram stain, and culture and sensitivity tests differentiate the type of infection.
- White blood cell (WBC) count indicates leukocytosis in bacterial pneumonia, and a normal or low WBC count in viral or mycoplasmal pneumonia.
- Blood cultures reflect bacteremia and are used to determine the causative organism.
- Arterial blood gas levels vary, depending on the severity of pneumonia and the underlying lung state.
- Bronchoscopy or transtracheal aspiration allows the collection of material for culture.
- Pulse oximetry shows a reduced oxygen saturation level.

Treatment
- Antimicrobial therapy (varies with causative agent)
- Humidified oxygen therapy
- Mechanical ventilation
- High-calorie diet and adequate fluid intake
- Bed rest
- Analgesics
- Positive end-expiratory pressure to facilitate adequate oxygenation in patients on mechanical ventilation for severe pneumonia

TYPES OF PNEUMONIA

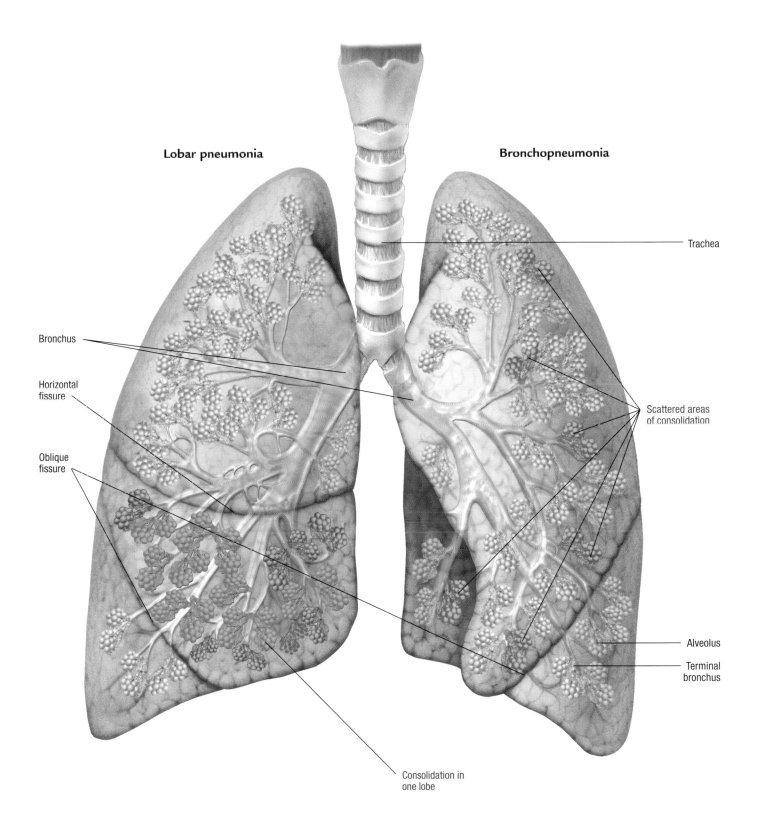

Lobar pneumonia

Bronchopneumonia

Trachea

Bronchus

Horizontal
fissure

Oblique
fissure

Scattered areas
of consolidation

Alveolus

Terminal
bronchus

Consolidation in
one lobe

PNEUMOTHORAX

Pneumothorax is an accumulation of air in the pleural cavity that leads to partial or complete lung collapse. When the air between the visceral and parietal pleurae collects and accumulates, increasing tension in the pleural cavity can cause the lung to progressively collapse. The amount of air trapped in the intrapleural space determines the degree of lung collapse. Venous return to the heart may be impeded to cause a life-threatening condition called *tension pneumothorax*. Pneumothoraces are usually classified as primary spontaneous, secondary spontaneous, traumatic, or tension.

Causes

Primary spontaneous pneumothorax
● Unknown
● Rupture of a bleb or a bulla

AGE ALERT
Primary spontaneous pneumothorax most commonly affects tall, thin men between ages 20 and 40.

Secondary spontaneous pneumothorax
● Chronic obstructive pulmonary disease
● Asthma
● Cystic fibrosis
● Tuberculosis
● Whooping cough

Traumatic pneumothorax
● Traumatic chest injury
● Penetrating chest trauma (stab wound, gunshot)
● Blunt chest trauma (blow from a motor vehicle accident)
● Iatrogenic chest trauma, resulting from puncture of the lung during needle aspiration lung biopsy, thoracentesis, or central venous catheter placement

Tension pneumothorax
● Lung collapse forced by excessive pressure

Pathophysiology

A rupture in the visceral or parietal pleura and chest wall causes air to accumulate and separate the visceral and parietal pleurae. Negative pressure is destroyed, and the elastic recoil forces are affected. The lung recoils by collapsing toward the hilus.

Open pneumothorax results when atmospheric air (positive pressure) flows directly into the pleural cavity (negative pressure). As the air pressure in the pleural cavity becomes positive, the lung collapses on the affected side, resulting in decreased total lung capacity, vital capacity, and lung compliance. Imbalances in the ventilation-perfusion ratio lead to hypoxia.

Closed pneumothorax occurs when air enters the pleural space from within the lung, causing increased pleural pressure, which prevents lung expansion during normal inspiration.

Tension pneumothorax results when air in the pleural space is under higher pressure than air in the adjacent lung. The air enters the pleural space from the site of pleural rupture, which acts as a one-way valve. Air is allowed to enter into the pleural space on inspiration but can't escape as the rupture site closes on expiration. More air enters on inspiration, and air pressure begins to exceed barometric pressure. Increasing air pressure pushes against the recoiled lung, causing compression atelectasis. Air also presses against the mediastinum, compressing and displacing the heart and great vessels. The air can't escape, and the accumulating pressure causes the lung to collapse. As air continues to accumulate and intrapleural pressures rise, the mediastinum shifts away from the affected side and decreases venous return. This leads to decreased cardiac output, which causes hypotension.

COMPLICATIONS
● Fatal pulmonary and circulatory impairment

Signs and symptoms
● Sudden, sharp pleuritic pain exacerbated by chest movement, breathing, or coughing
● Asymmetrical chest wall movement
● Shortness of breath and respiratory distress
● Hypotension
● Cyanosis
● Decreased vocal fremitus
● Absent breath sounds and chest rigidity on the affected side
● Tachycardia
● Subcutaneous emphysema
  Tension pneumothorax produces the most severe respiratory symptoms, including:
● decreased cardiac output, hypotension, and compensatory tachycardia
● tachypnea
● lung collapse
● mediastinal shift and tracheal deviation to the opposite side
● distended jugular veins.

Diagnostic test results
● Chest X-rays confirm the diagnosis by revealing air in the pleural space and, possibly, a mediastinal shift.
● Arterial blood gas analysis may reveal hypoxemia, possibly with respiratory acidosis and hypercapnia. Partial pressure of arterial oxygen levels may decrease at first but typically returns to normal within 24 hours.

Treatment
● Bed rest
● Observation
● Oxygen
● Chest tube insertion
● Thoracostomy
● Analgesics
● Surgery

EFFECTS OF PNEUMOTHORAX

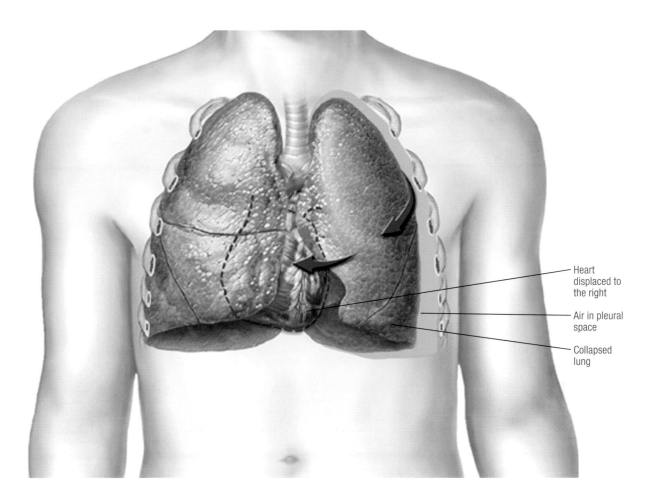

Heart displaced to the right

Air in pleural space

Collapsed lung

TENSION PNEUMOTHORAX

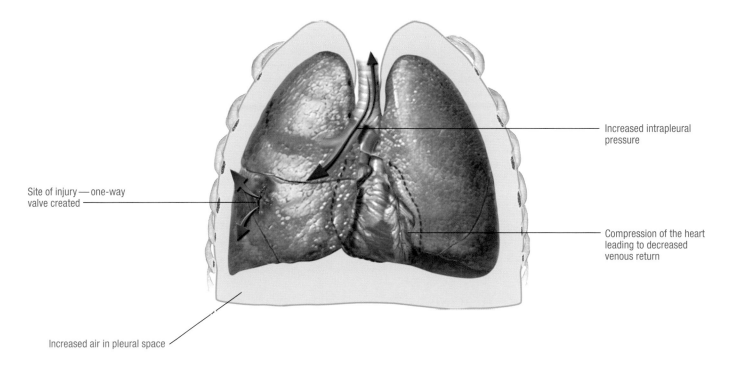

Site of injury — one-way valve created

Increased intrapleural pressure

Compression of the heart leading to decreased venous return

Increased air in pleural space

PULMONARY EDEMA

Pulmonary edema is an accumulation of fluid in the extravascular spaces of the lungs. It's a common complication of cardiac disorders and may occur as a chronic condition or may develop quickly and rapidly become fatal.

Causes
Left-sided heart failure
- Arteriosclerosis
- Cardiomyopathy
- Hypertension
- Valvular heart disease

Predisposing factors
- Barbiturate or opiate poisoning
- Cardiac failure
- Excessive volume or too-rapid infusion of I.V. fluids
- Impaired pulmonary lymphatic drainage
- Inhalation of irritating gases
- Mitral stenosis and left atrial myxoma
- Pneumonia
- Pulmonary veno-occlusive disease

Pathophysiology
Normally, pulmonary capillary hydrostatic pressure, capillary oncotic pressure, capillary permeability, and lymphatic drainage are in balance. When this balance changes, or when the lymphatic drainage system is obstructed, fluid infiltrates into the lung and pulmonary edema results. If pulmonary capillary hydrostatic pressure increases, the compromised left ventricle requires increased filling pressures to maintain adequate cardiac output. These pressures are transmitted to the left atrium, pulmonary veins, and pulmonary capillary bed, forcing fluids and solutes from the intravascular compartment into the interstitium of the lungs. As the interstitium overloads with fluid, the fluid floods the peripheral alveoli and impairs gas exchange.

If colloid osmotic pressure decreases, the hydrostatic force that regulates intravascular fluids (the natural pulling force) is lost because there's no opposition. Fluid flows freely into the interstitium and alveoli, impairing gas exchange and leading to pulmonary edema.

Lymphatic vessels may be blocked by edema or tumor fibrotic tissue or by increased systemic venous pressure. Hydrostatic pressure in the large pulmonary veins rises, the pulmonary lymphatic system can't drain into the pulmonary veins, and excess fluid moves into the interstitial space. Pulmonary edema then results from the accumulation of fluid.

Capillary injury and consequent increased permeability may occur in acute respiratory distress syndrome (ARDS) or after inhalation of toxic gases. Plasma proteins and water leak out of the injured capillary and into the interstitium, increasing the interstitial oncotic pressure, which is normally low. As interstitial oncotic pressure begins to equal capillary oncotic pressure, the water begins to move out of the capillary and into the lungs, resulting in pulmonary edema.

COMPLICATIONS
- Respiratory and metabolic acidosis
- Cardiac or respiratory arrest

Signs and symptoms
Early stage
- Dyspnea on exertion, paroxysmal nocturnal dyspnea, and orthopnea
- Cough
- Mild tachypnea
- Increased blood pressure
- Dependent crackles
- Jugular vein distention
- Tachycardia

Later stages
- Labored, rapid respiration
- More diffuse crackles
- Cough producing frothy, bloody sputum
- Increased tachycardia, arrhythmias, and thready pulse
- Cold, clammy skin and diaphoresis
- Cyanosis
- Hypotension

Diagnostic test results
- Arterial blood gas analysis usually reveals hypoxia with variable partial pressure of arterial carbon dioxide, depending on the patient's degree of fatigue. Respiratory acidosis may occur.
- Chest X-rays show diffuse haziness of the lung fields and, usually, cardiomegaly and pleural effusion.
- Pulse oximetry reveals decreasing arterial oxygen saturation levels.
- Pulmonary artery catheterization identifies left-sided heart failure and helps rule out ARDS.
- Electrocardiography shows previous or current myocardial infarction.

Treatment
- High concentrations of oxygen
- Diuretics, such as furosemide or bumetanide
- Positive inotropic agents, such as digoxin or inamrinone
- Vasopressors
- Arterial vasodilators such as nitroprusside
- Antiarrhythmics
- Morphine
- Mechanical ventilation
- Noninvasive ventilation using continuous positive airway pressure, bilevel positive airway pressure, and positive end-expiratory pressure

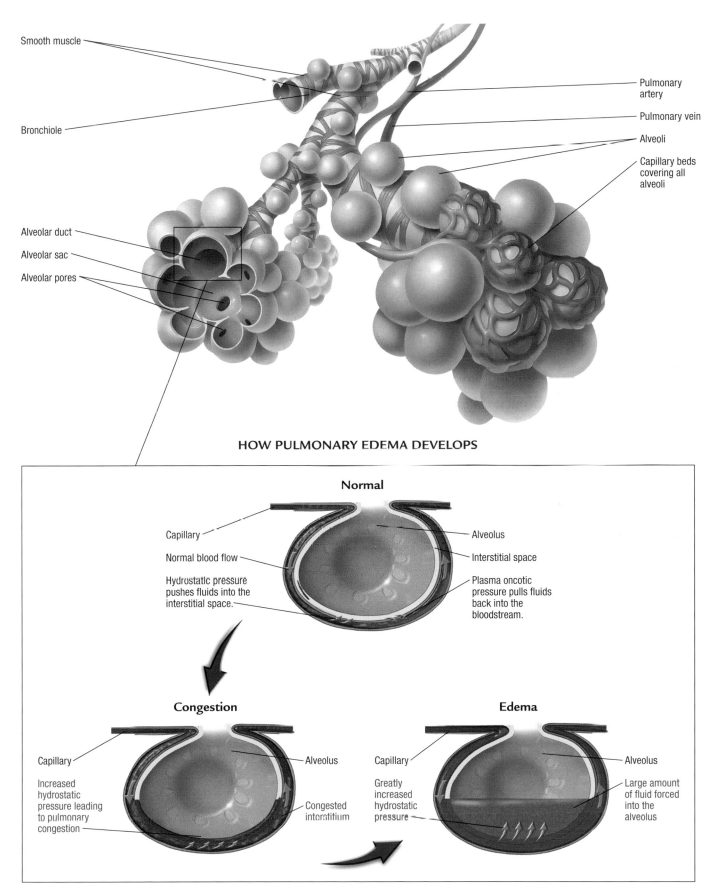

NORMAL ALVEOLI

Smooth muscle

Bronchiole

Alveolar duct

Alveolar sac

Alveolar pores

Pulmonary artery

Pulmonary vein

Alveoli

Capillary beds covering all alveoli

HOW PULMONARY EDEMA DEVELOPS

Normal

Capillary

Normal blood flow

Hydrostatic pressure pushes fluids into the interstitial space.

Alveolus

Interstitial space

Plasma oncotic pressure pulls fluids back into the bloodstream.

Congestion

Capillary

Increased hydrostatic pressure leading to pulmonary congestion

Alveolus

Congested interstitium

Edema

Capillary

Greatly increased hydrostatic pressure

Alveolus

Large amount of fluid forced into the alveolus

PULMONARY EMBOLISM

A complication of patients in the health care facility, pulmonary embolism is an obstruction of the pulmonary arterial bed by a dislodged thrombus, heart valve vegetation, or foreign substance. It strikes about 6 million adults each year in the United States, resulting in 100,000 deaths.

Causes
- Dislodged thrombi, originating in leg veins (most common)
- Conditions that cause increased blood coagulability, such as cancer and hormonal contraceptives
- Surgery
- Long periods of inactivity
- Some medical conditions, such as stroke and myocardial infarction
- Injury to the vein

Predisposing factors
- Obesity
- Some cancers, such as pancreatic, ovarian, and lung
- Smoking
- Pregnancy and childbirth
- Vascular injury and I.V. drug abuse

CLINICAL TIP

A triad of deep vein thrombosis (DVT) formation is stasis, endothelial injury, and hypercoagulability. Risk factors include long car or plane trips, cancer, pregnancy, hypercoagulability, and prior DVT or pulmonary emboli.

Pathophysiology
Thrombus formation results directly from vascular wall damage, venostasis, or hypercoagulability of the blood. Trauma, clot dissolution, sudden muscle spasm, intravascular pressure changes, or a change in peripheral blood flow can cause the thrombus to loosen or fragmentize. Then the thrombus — now called an embolus — floats to the heart's right side and enters the lung through the pulmonary artery. There, the embolus may dissolve, continue to fragmentize, or grow.

If the embolus occludes the pulmonary artery, it prevents alveoli from producing enough surfactant to maintain alveolar integrity. As a result, alveoli collapse and atelectasis develops. If the embolus enlarges, it may clog most or all of the pulmonary vessels and cause death.

Rarely, the emboli contain air, fat, bacteria, amniotic fluid, talc, or tumor cells.

COMPLICATIONS
- Pulmonary hypertension
- Cor pulmonale

Signs and symptoms
Total occlusion of the main pulmonary artery is rapidly fatal; smaller or fragmented emboli produce symptoms that vary with the size, number, and location, as follows:

- dyspnea
- anxiety
- pleuritic chest pain
- tachycardia
- productive cough (sputum may be blood-tinged)
- low-grade fever
- pleural effusion.
  Less common signs include:
- massive hemoptysis
- splinting of the chest
- leg edema and pain
- cyanosis, syncope, and distended jugular veins
- pleural friction rub
- signs of circulatory collapse (weak, rapid pulse and hypotension)
- signs of hypoxia (restlessness and anxiety).
- right ventricular S_3 gallop and increased intensity of a pulmonic component of S_2
- crackles and a pleural rub may be heard at the embolism site.

Diagnostic test results
- Chest X-ray may show areas of atelectasis, elevated diaphragm and pleural effusion, prominent pulmonary artery and, occasionally, the characteristic wedge-shaped infiltrate suggestive of pulmonary infarction
- Lung scan shows perfusion defects in areas beyond occluded vessels.
- Pulmonary angiography reveals the location of the emboli.
- Electrocardiography may show right axis deviation (extensive embolism); tall, peaked P waves (right bundle-branch block); depression of ST segments and T-wave inversions (indicative of right-sided heart strain); and supraventricular tachyarrhythmias. A pattern sometimes observed is S_1, Q_3, and T_3 (S wave in lead I, Q wave in lead III, and inverted T wave in lead III).
- Arterial blood gas measurements may show decreased partial pressure of arterial oxygen and partial pressure of arterial carbon dioxide.
- If pleural effusion is present, thoracentesis may rule out empyema, which indicates pneumonia.

Treatment
Treatment is designed to maintain adequate cardiovascular and pulmonary function during resolution of the obstruction and to prevent recurrence of embolic episodes. Because most emboli resolve within 10 to 14 days, treatment may consist of:
- oxygen therapy and fibrinolytic therapy
- anticoagulation with heparin
- embolectomy
- vasopressors and antibiotics
- vena caval ligation, plication, or insertion of a device to filter blood returning to the heart and lungs, to prevent future pulmonary emboli.

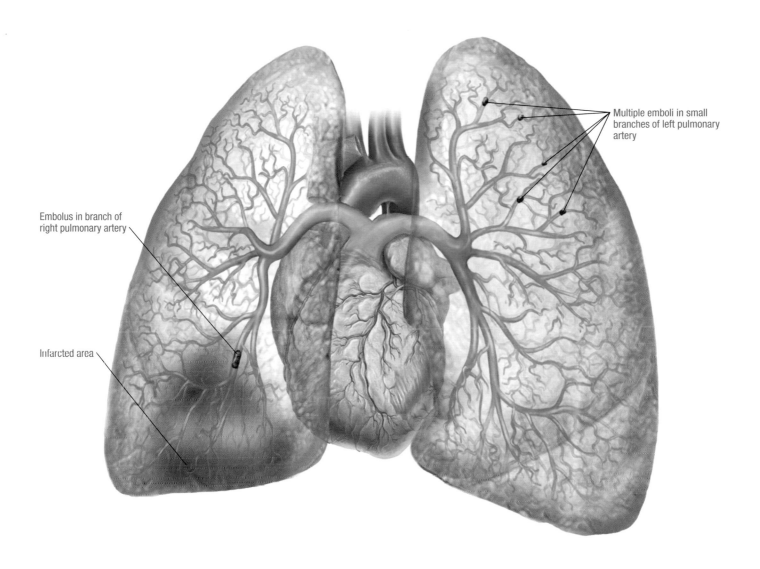

Multiple emboli in small
branches of left pulmonary
artery

Embolus in branch of
right pulmonary artery

Infarcted area

PULMONARY HYPERTENSION

Pulmonary hypertension is a mean systolic pulmonary artery pressure (PAP) above 25 mm Hg at rest and 30 mm Hg during exercise. Primary or idiopathic pulmonary hypertension is characterized by increased PAP and increased pulmonary vascular resistance.

AGE ALERT
Primary pulmonary hypertension is most common in women ages 20 to 40 and is usually fatal within 3 to 4 years.

Secondary pulmonary hypertension results from existing cardiac (patent ductus arteriosus or atrial or septal defect) or pulmonary disease (rheumatic valvular disease or mitral stenosis), or both. The prognosis in secondary pulmonary hypertension depends on the severity of the underlying disorder.

Causes
Primary pulmonary hypertension
- Unknown, but may include:
- hereditary factors
- altered immune mechanisms.
Secondary pulmonary hypertension
- Conditions causing alveolar hypoventilation include:
- chronic obstructive pulmonary disease
- sarcoidosis
- diffuse interstitial pneumonia
- malignant metastases
- scleroderma
- obesity
- kyphoscoliosis.
- Conditions causing vascular obstruction include:
- pulmonary embolism
- vasculitis
- left atrial myxoma
- idiopathic veno-occlusive disease
- fibrosing mediastinitis
- mediastinal neoplasm.

Pathophysiology
In primary pulmonary hypertension, the smooth muscle in the pulmonary artery wall hypertrophies for no known reason, narrowing or obliterating the artery or arteriole. Fibrous lesions form around the vessels, impairing distensibility and increasing vascular resistance. Pressures in the left ventricle, which receives blood from the lungs, remain normal. However, the increased pressures generated in the lungs are transmitted to the right ventricle, which supplies the pulmonary artery. Eventually, the right ventricle fails (cor pulmonale).

Alveolar hypoventilation can result from diseases caused by alveolar destruction or from disorders that prevent the chest wall from expanding to allow air into the alveoli. The resulting decreased ventilation increases pulmonary vascular resistance. Hypoxemia resulting from this ventilation-perfusion mismatch also causes vasoconstriction, further increasing vascular resistance and resulting in pulmonary hypertension.

COMPLICATIONS
- Cor pulmonale
- Cardiac arrest

Signs and symptoms
- Shortness of breath, increasing dyspnea on exertion, fatigue and weakness, and chest pain
- Cough and hemoptysis
- Cyanosis, Raynaud's phenomenon, and syncope
- Ascites
- Jugular vein distention and reduced carotid pulse
- Restlessness and agitation, decreased level of consciousness, confusion, and memory loss
- Decreased diaphragmatic excursion and respiration
- Possible displacement of point of maximal impulse
- Peripheral edema
- Easily palpable right ventricular lift
- Palpable and tender liver
- Tachycardia
- Systolic ejection murmur
- Split S_2; presence of S_3 and S_4 sounds
- Decreased or loud, tubular breath sounds

Diagnostic test results
- Arterial blood gas analysis reveals hypoxemia.
- Chest X-ray shows enlargement of main and hilar pulmonary arteries, narrowing of peripheral arteries, and enlargement of right atrium and ventricle.
- A chest computed tomography scan may show abnormal lung vessels or blood clots.
- Electrocardiography in right ventricular hypertrophy shows right axis deviation and tall or peaked P waves in inferior leads.
- Cardiac catheterization reveals mean PAP above 25 mm Hg or an increased pulmonary artery wedge pressure if the underlying cause is left atrial myxoma, mitral stenosis, or left-sided heart failure.
- Pulmonary angiography detects filling defects in pulmonary vasculature.
- Pulmonary function studies show decreased flow rates and increased residual volume (underlying obstructive disease) or reduced total lung capacity (underlying restrictive disease).
- Radionuclide imaging detects abnormalities in right and left ventricular functioning.
- Open lung biopsy determines the type of disorder.
- Echocardiography shows ventricular wall motion and possible valvular dysfunction, right ventricular enlargement, abnormal septal configuration consistent with right ventricular pressure overload, and reduction in left ventricular cavity size.
- Perfusion lung scanning shows multiple patchy and diffuse filling defects.

Treatment
- Treatment of the underlying cause
- Oxygen therapy
- Fluid restriction
- Digoxin, diuretics, vasodilators, pulmonary vasodilators, calcium channel blockers, beta-adrenergic blockers, bronchodilators, and anticoagulants; endothelin receptor antagonists such as bosentan
- Pulmonary thromboendarterectomy
- Lung or heart-lung transplantation

NORMAL PULMONARY ARTERY

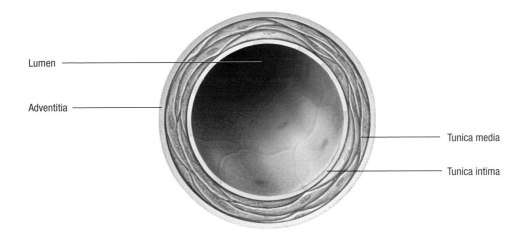

Lumen

Adventitia

Tunica media

Tunica intima

EARLY PULMONARY HYPERTENSION

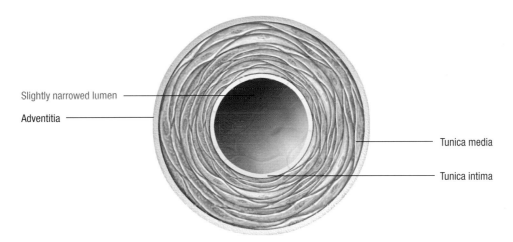

Slightly narrowed lumen

Adventitia

Tunica media

Tunica intima

LATE PULMONARY HYPERTENSION

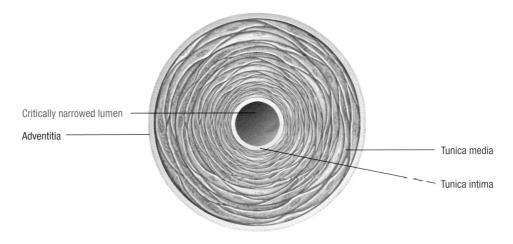

Critically narrowed lumen

Adventitia

Tunica media

Tunica intima

SARCOIDOSIS

Sarcoidosis is a multisystem, granulomatous disorder that characteristically produces lymphadenopathy, pulmonary infiltration, and skeletal, liver, eye, or skin lesions.

AGE ALERT
Sarcoidosis affects twice as many women as men. Onset usually occurs between ages 30 and 50.

Causes

Exact cause unknown

Possible contributing factors

• *Hypersensitivity response* (possibly from T-cell imbalance) to such agents as atypical mycobacteria, fungi, and pine pollen
• *Genetic predisposition* (suggested by a slightly higher incidence of sarcoidosis within the same family)
• *Chemicals,* such as zirconium and beryllium, which can lead to illnesses resembling sarcoidosis, suggesting an extrinsic cause for this disease

Pathophysiology

An excessive inflammatory process is initiated in the alveoli, bronchioles, and blood vessels of the lungs. Monocyte-macrophages accumulate in the target tissue, where they induce the inflammatory process. CD4+ T lymphocytes and sensitized immune cells form a ring around the inflamed area. Fibroblasts, mast cells, collagen fibers, and proteoglycans encase the inflammatory and immune cells, causing granuloma formation. Organ dysfunction results from the accumulation of T lymphocytes, mononuclear phagocytes, and nonsecreting epithelial granulomas, which distort normal tissue architecture, causing alveolitis.

COMPLICATIONS
• Pulmonary fibrosis
• Pulmonary hypertension
• Cor pulmonale

Signs and symptoms

Initial symptoms of sarcoidosis include arthralgia (in the wrists, ankles, and elbows), fatigue, malaise, and weight loss. Sarcoidosis is characterized by formation of granulomatous tissue leading to pulmonary fibrosis. Other clinical features vary according to the extent and location of the fibrosis:

• *Respiratory* — breathlessness, cough (usually nonproductive), and substernal pain; wheezing; pulmonary hypertension and cor pulmonale (in advanced pulmonary disease)
• *Cutaneous* — erythema nodosum, subcutaneous skin nodules with maculopapular eruptions, and extensive nasal mucosal lesions
• *Ophthalmic* — anterior uveitis (common) and glaucoma
• *Lymphatic* — bilateral hilar and right paratracheal lymphadenopathy and splenomegaly
• *Musculoskeletal* — muscle weakness, polyarthralgia, pain, and punched-out lesions on phalanges
• *Hepatic* — granulomatous hepatitis (usually asymptomatic)
• *Genitourinary* — hypercalciuria
• *Cardiovascular* — arrhythmias and, rarely, cardiomyopathy
• *Central nervous system (CNS)* — cranial or peripheral nerve palsies, basilar meningitis, seizures, and pituitary and hypothalamic lesions producing diabetes insipidus

Diagnostic test results

• Arterial blood gas analysis shows a decreased partial pressure of arterial oxygen.
• Chest X-rays show bilateral hilar and right paratracheal adenopathy, with or without diffuse interstitial infiltrates.
• Lymph node, skin, or lung biopsy shows noncaseating granulomas with negative cultures for mycobacteria and fungi.
• Pulmonary function tests show decreased total lung capacity and compliance and reduced diffusing capacity.

CLINICAL TIP
A positive Kveim-Stilzbach skin test supports the diagnosis. In this test, the patient receives an intradermal injection of an antigen prepared from human sarcoidal spleen or lymph nodes from patients with sarcoidosis. If the patient has active sarcoidosis, a granuloma develops at the injection site in 2 to 6 weeks.

Treatment

• No treatment for asymptomatic sarcoidosis
• With ophthalmic, respiratory, CNS, cardiovascular, or systemic symptoms or destructive skin lesions: systemic or topical steroids, usually for 1 to 2 years, but possibly lifelong
• With hypercalcemia: low-calcium diet and avoidance of direct exposure to sunlight

Normal lungs and alveoli

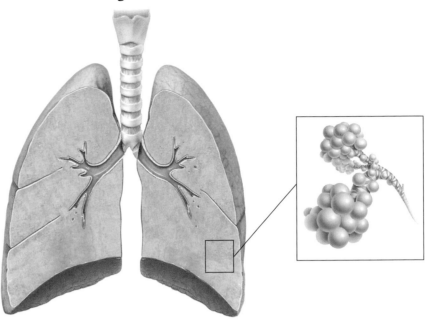

Granulomatous tissue formation

Alveolitis

SEVERE ACUTE RESPIRATORY SYNDROME

Severe acute respiratory syndrome (SARS) is a serious form of pneumonia, resulting in acute respiratory distress and, in some cases, death. In February 2003, the World Health Organization (WHO) identified SARS as a global health threat and issued an unprecedented travel advisory. Over the next few months, the illness spread to more than two dozen countries in North America, South America, Europe, and Asia before the outbreak was contained.

Causes

- New member of the Coronaviridae family (the same family causing the common cold)

Pathophysiology

The virus spreads primarily by close human contact. Droplets containing SARS-associated coronavirus (SARS-CoV) can be released into the air when an infected person coughs or sneezes. Some specific medical procedures performed on SARS patients can also release virus-containing droplets into the air. Touching a SARS-CoV–infected surface and subsequently touching the eyes, nose, or mouth may also lead to infection.

In general, coronaviruses are a group of viruses that have a halo or crownlike (corona) appearance when viewed under a microscope. These viruses are a common cause of mild to moderate upper respiratory illness in humans and are associated with respiratory, GI, liver, and neurologic disease in animals.

COMPLICATIONS

- Respiratory failure
- Liver failure
- Heart failure
- Myelodysplastic syndromes
- Death

Signs and symptoms

Stage 1: A flulike syndrome begins 2 to 7 days after incubation, lasting 3 to 7 days, and is characterized by:

- fever (greater than 100.4° F [38° C])
- fatigue
- headaches
- chills
- myalgias
- malaise
- anorexia
- diarrhea (in some cases).

Stage 2: The lower respiratory phase begins 3 or more days after incubation and is characterized by:

- dry cough
- dyspnea
- progressive hypoxemia
- respiratory failure (requiring mechanical ventilation).

Diagnostic test results

The SARS virus may be detected in a patient's nasopharyngeal or oropharyngeal secretions, blood serum, or stool. The WHO has developed three types of diagnostic tests for SARS:

- A reverse transcription polymerase chain reaction test to detect ribonucleic acid of SARS-CoV. Two tests on two different specimens must be positive.
- Serum tests to detect antibodies immunoglobulin (Ig) M and IgG.
- A cell culture test.

Additional testing may include:

- arterial blood gas analysis, which reveals hypoxemia.
- chest X-ray or chest computed tomography (CT) scan, which identifies the presence of pneumonia or acute respiratory distress syndrome but may also reveal no abnormalities; X-ray and CT scan frequently show focal interstitial infiltrates that may progress to a more patchy, generalized distribution.
- complete blood count, which reveals a low white blood cell count, low lymphocyte count, and low platelet count.
- serum chemistries, which typically show elevated lactate dehydrogenase, alanine aminotransferase, and creatine kinase. Sodium and potassium levels may be low.

Treatment

- Respiratory isolation
- Antibiotics
- Steroids
- Supplemental oxygen
- Mechanical ventilation
- Chest physiotherapy

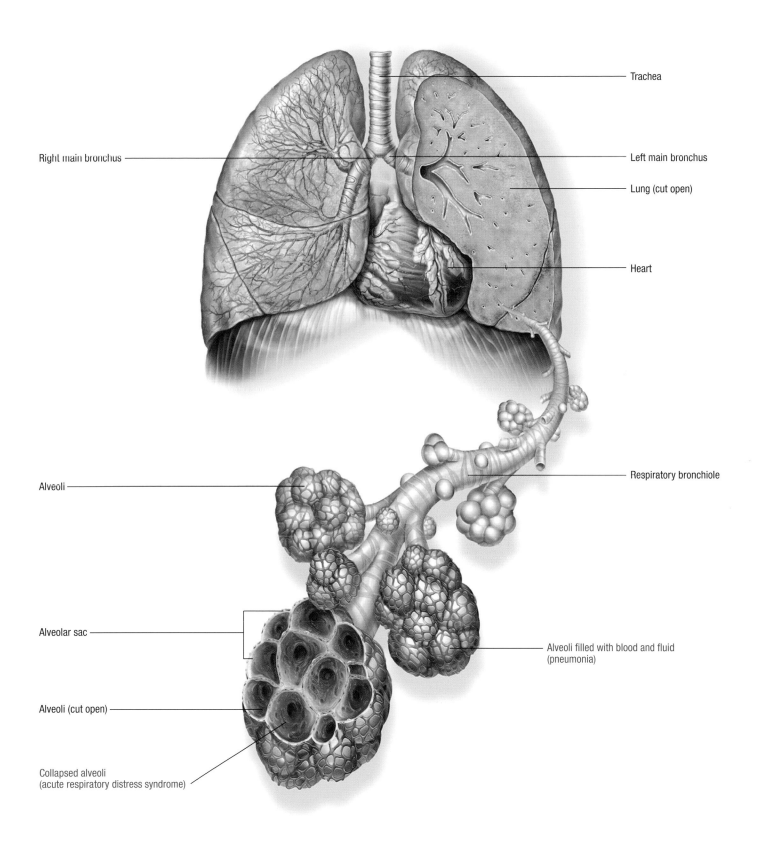

Trachea

Right main bronchus

Left main bronchus

Lung (cut open)

Heart

Respiratory bronchiole

Alveoli

Alveolar sac

Alveoli filled with blood and fluid
(pneumonia)

Alveoli (cut open)

Collapsed alveoli
(acute respiratory distress syndrome)

TUBERCULOSIS

An acute or chronic infection caused by *Mycobacterium tuberculosis*, tuberculosis (TB) is characterized by pulmonary infiltrates, formation of granulomas with caseation, fibrosis, and cavitation. People who live in crowded, poorly ventilated conditions and those who are immunocompromised are most likely to become infected. In patients with strains that are sensitive to the usual antitubercular agents, the prognosis is excellent with correct treatment. However, in those with strains that are resistant to two or more of the major antitubercular agents, mortality is 50%. The incidence of TB has been increasing in the United States secondary to homelessness, drug abuse, and human immunodeficiency virus (HIV) infection. Globally, TB is the leading infectious cause of morbidity and mortality, generating 8 to 10 million new cases each year.

Causes

TB develops after inhaling droplets sprayed into the air from a cough or sneeze by a person infected with *M. tuberculosis*. Although the primary infection site is the lungs, mycobacteria commonly exist in other parts of the body. A number of factors increase the risk of infection, including:
- gastrectomy
- uncontrolled diabetes mellitus
- Hodgkin's disease
- leukemia
- silicosis
- HIV infection
- treatment with corticosteroids or immunosuppressants.

Pathophysiology

After exposure to *M. tuberculosis*, roughly 5% of infected people develop active tuberculosis within 1 year; in the remainder, microorganisms cause a latent infection. Transmission of active disease is by droplet nuclei produced when infected persons cough or sneeze. The host's immune system usually controls the tubercle bacillus by killing it or walling it up in a tiny nodule (tubercle). However, the bacillus may lie dormant within the tubercle for years and later reactivate and spread. Persons with a cavitary lesion (large, granulomatous lesion) are particularly infectious because their sputum usually contains 1 million to 100 million bacilli per milliliter. If an inhaled tubercle bacillus settles in an alveolus, infection occurs, with alveolocapillary dilation and endothelial cell swelling. Alveolitis results, with replication of tubercle bacilli and influx of polymorphonuclear leukocytes. These organisms spread through the lymph system to the circulatory system and then throughout the body.

Cell-mediated immunity to the mycobacteria, which develops 3 to 6 weeks later, usually contains the infection and arrests the disease. If the infection reactivates, the body's response characteristically leads to caseation — the conversion of necrotic tissue to a cheeselike material. The caseum may localize, undergo fibrosis, or excavate and form cavities, the walls of which are studded with multiplying tubercle bacilli. If this

happens, infected caseous debris may spread throughout the lungs by the tracheobronchial tree. Sites of extrapulmonary TB include the pleurae, meninges, joints, lymph nodes, peritoneum, genitourinary tract, and bowel.

COMPLICATIONS
- Respiratory failure
- Pneumothorax
- Hemorrhage
- Pleural effusion
- Pneumonia
- Liver involvement from drug therapy

Signs and symptoms

After an incubation period of 4 to 8 weeks, TB usually produces no symptoms in primary infection but may produce nonspecific symptoms, such as:
- fatigue and weakness
- anorexia, weight loss
- night sweats
- low-grade fever
- adenopathy
- malaise
- anxiety.

Physical examination may reveal crackles, decreased breath sounds, and clubbing of the fingers and toes.

In reactivation, symptoms may include a cough that produces mucopurulent sputum, occasional hemoptysis, and chest pain.

Diagnostic test results

- Chest X-ray shows nodular lesions, patchy infiltrates (mainly in upper lobes), cavity formation, scar tissue, and calcium deposits.
- Tuberculin skin test reveals infection at some point but doesn't indicate active disease.
- Stains and cultures of sputum, cerebrospinal fluid, urine, drainage from abscesses, or pleural fluid show heat-sensitive, nonmotile, aerobic, acid-fast bacilli.
- Computed tomography scan or magnetic resonance imaging allows the evaluation of lung damage and may confirm the diagnosis.
- Bronchoscopy shows inflammation and altered lung tissue. It may also be performed to obtain sputum if the patient can't produce an adequate sputum specimen.

Treatment

Antitubercular therapy is the main treatment. Daily doses of multiple drugs may include combinations of rifampin, isoniazid, pyrazinamide, and ethambutol. After 2 to 3 weeks of continuous medication, the disease generally is no longer infectious, and the patient can resume his normal lifestyle while continuing the medication.

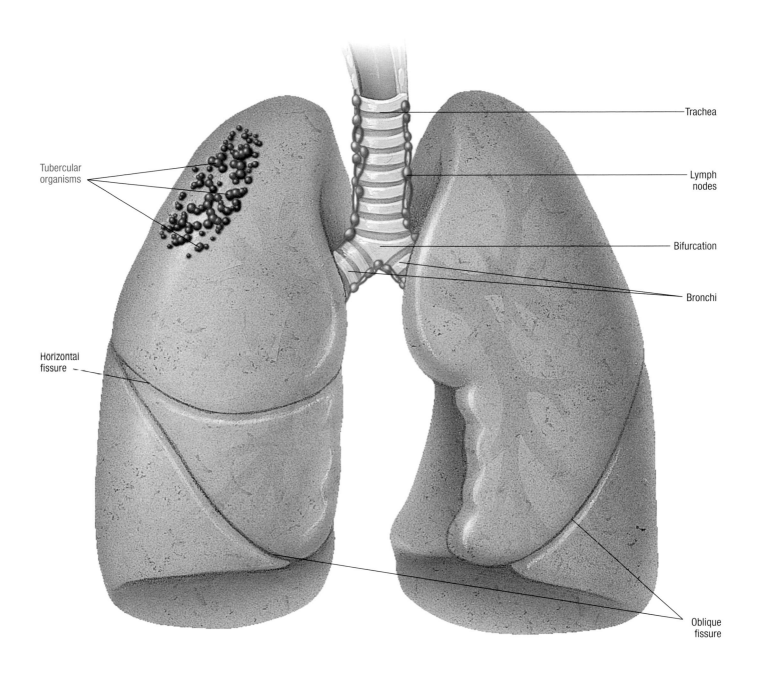

Tubercular organisms

Trachea

Lymph nodes

Bifurcation

Bronchi

Horizontal fissure

Oblique fissure

Upper respiratory tract infection

Upper respiratory tract infection (also known as the *common cold* or *acute coryza*) is an acute, usually afebrile viral infection that causes inflammation of the upper respiratory tract. It's the most common infectious disease. Although a cold is benign and self-limiting, it can lead to secondary bacterial infections.

Causes

About 90% of colds stem from a viral infection of the upper respiratory passages and consequent mucous membrane inflammation; occasionally, colds result from a mycoplasmal infection. Over 100 viruses can cause the common cold. Major offenders include:
- rhinoviruses
- coronaviruses
- myxoviruses
- adenoviruses
- coxsackieviruses
- echoviruses.

Pathophysiology

Infection occurs when the offending organism gains entry into the upper respiratory tract, proliferates, and begins an inflammatory reaction. Acute inflammation of the upper airway structures, including the sinuses, nasopharynx, pharynx, larynx, and trachea, are seen. The presence of the pathogen triggers infiltration of the mucous membranes by inflammatory and infection-fighting cells. Mucosal swelling and secretion of a serous or mucopurulent exudate result.

COMPLICATIONS
- Otitis media
- Sinusitis
- Secondary infections (pneumonia, streptococcal pharyngitis, bronchitis, croup)

Signs and symptoms

After a 1- to 4-day incubation period, the common cold produces:
- pharyngitis
- nasal congestion
- coryza
- sneezing
- headache
- burning, watery eyes.
  Additional effects may include:
- fever
- chills
- myalgia
- arthralgia
- malaise
- lethargy
- hacking, nonproductive, or nocturnal cough.

As the cold progresses, clinical features develop more fully. After a day, symptoms include a feeling of fullness with a copious nasal discharge that commonly irritates the nose, adding to discomfort.

Diagnostic test results

No explicit diagnostic test exists to isolate the specific organism responsible for the common cold. Consequently, diagnosis rests on the typically mild, localized, and afebrile upper respiratory symptoms. Diagnosis must rule out allergic rhinitis, measles, rubella, and other disorders that produce similar early symptoms.

Treatment

The primary treatments — aspirin or acetaminophen, fluids, and rest — are purely symptomatic because the common cold has no cure.

Other treatments may include:
- decongestants
- throat lozenges
- steam.

COMPLICATIONS OF THE COMMON COLD

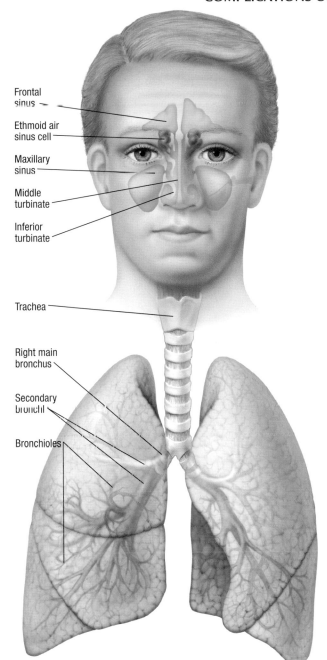

Frontal sinus

Ethmoid air sinus cell

Maxillary sinus

Middle turbinate

Inferior turbinate

Trachea

Right main bronchus

Secondary bronchi

Bronchioles

Sinusitis

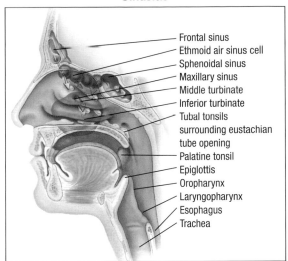

Frontal sinus
Ethmoid air sinus cell
Sphenoidal sinus
Maxillary sinus
Middle turbinate
Inferior turbinate
Tubal tonsils surrounding eustachian tube opening
Palatine tonsil
Epiglottis
Oropharynx
Laryngopharynx
Esophagus
Trachea

Rhinitis

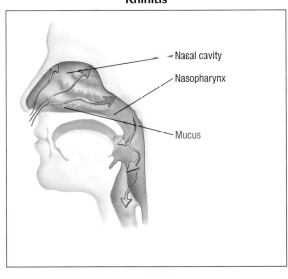

Nasal cavity
Nasopharynx
Mucus

Bronchitis

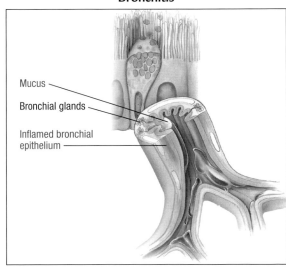

Mucus
Bronchial glands
Inflamed bronchial epithelium

Otitis media with effusion

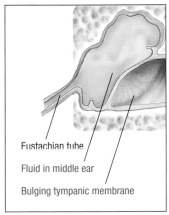

Eustachian tube
Fluid in middle ear
Bulging tympanic membrane

Acute otitis media

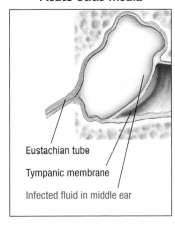

Eustachian tube
Tympanic membrane
Infected fluid in middle ear

ACCELERATION-DECELERATION INJURIES

Acceleration-deceleration cervical injuries (commonly known as *whiplash*) result from sharp hyperextension and flexion of the neck that damages muscles, ligaments, disks, and nerve tissue. The prognosis for this type of injury is usually excellent; symptoms usually subside with treatment of symptoms.

Causes
- Motor vehicle and other transportation accidents
- Falls
- Sports-related accidents
- Crimes and assaults

Pathophysiology
The brain is shielded by the cranial vault (hair, skin, bone, meninges, and cerebrospinal fluid), which intercepts the force of a physical blow. Below a certain level of force (the absorption capacity), the cranial vault prevents energy from affecting the brain. The degree of traumatic head injury usually is proportional to the amount of force reaching the cranial tissues. Furthermore, unless ruled out, neck injuries should be presumed present in patients with traumatic head injury.

In acceleration-deceleration cervical injuries, the head is propelled in a forward and downward motion in hyperflexion. A wedge-shaped deformity of the bone may be created if the anterior portions of the vertebrae are crushed. Intervertebral disks may be damaged; they may bulge or rupture, irritating spinal nerves. Then the head is forced backward. A tear in the anterior ligament may pull pieces of bone from cervical vertebrae. Spinous processes of the vertebrae may be fractured. Intervertebral disks may be compressed posteriorly and torn anteriorly. Vertebral arteries may be stretched, pinched, or torn, causing reduced blood flow to the brain. Nerves of the cervical sympathetic chain may also be injured.

A complex arrangement of ligaments holds the vertebrae in place. Some of the ligaments are barely a centimeter long, and all are only a few millimeters thick. In a whiplash injury, ligaments may be badly stretched, partially torn, or completely ruptured (arrows). Injuries of neck muscles may range from minor strains and microhemorrhages to severe tears. The anterior longitudinal ligament, running vertically along the anterior surface of the vertebrae, may be injured during hyperextension. The posterior longitudinal ligament, running on the posterior surface of the vertebral bodies, may be injured in hyperflexion. The broad ligamentum nuchae may also be stretched or torn.

Closed trauma is typically caused by a sudden acceleration-deceleration or *coup/contrecoup* injury. In coup/contrecoup, the head hits a relatively stationary object, injuring cranial tissues near the point of impact (coup); then the remaining force pushes the brain against the opposite side of the skull, causing a second impact and injury (contrecoup). Contusions and lacerations may also occur during contrecoup as the brain's soft tissues slide over the rough bone of the cranial cavity. In addition, rotational shear forces on the cerebrum may damage the upper midbrain and areas of the frontal, temporal, and occipital lobes.

COMPLICATIONS
- Nerve damage
- Numbness, tingling, or weakness

Signs and symptoms
Although symptoms may develop immediately, they're commonly delayed 12 to 24 hours if the injury is mild. Whiplash produces moderate to severe anterior and posterior neck pain. Within several days, the anterior pain diminishes, but the posterior pain persists or even intensifies, causing patients to seek medical attention if they didn't do so before. Whiplash may also cause:
- dizziness and gait disturbances
- vomiting
- headache, nuchal rigidity, and neck muscle asymmetry
- rigidity or numbness in the arms.

Diagnostic test results
- X-ray of the cervical spine will determine that vertebral injury hasn't occurred.

CLINICAL TIP
In all suspected spinal injuries, assume that the spine is injured until proven otherwise. Any patient with suspected whiplash or other injuries requires careful transportation from the accident scene. To do this, place him in a supine position on a spine board and immobilize his neck with tape and a hard cervical collar or sandbags.

Until an X-ray rules out a cervical fracture, move the patient as little as possible. Before the X-ray is taken, carefully remove any ear and neck jewelry. Don't undress the patient; cut clothes away, if necessary. Warn him against movements that could injure his spine.

Treatment
- Immobilization with a soft, padded cervical collar for several days or weeks
- Ice or cool compresses to the neck for the first 24 hours, followed by moist, warm heat thereafter
- Over-the-counter analgesics, such as aspirin, acetaminophen, or ibuprofen
- Muscle relaxants
- In severe muscle spasms, short-term cervical traction

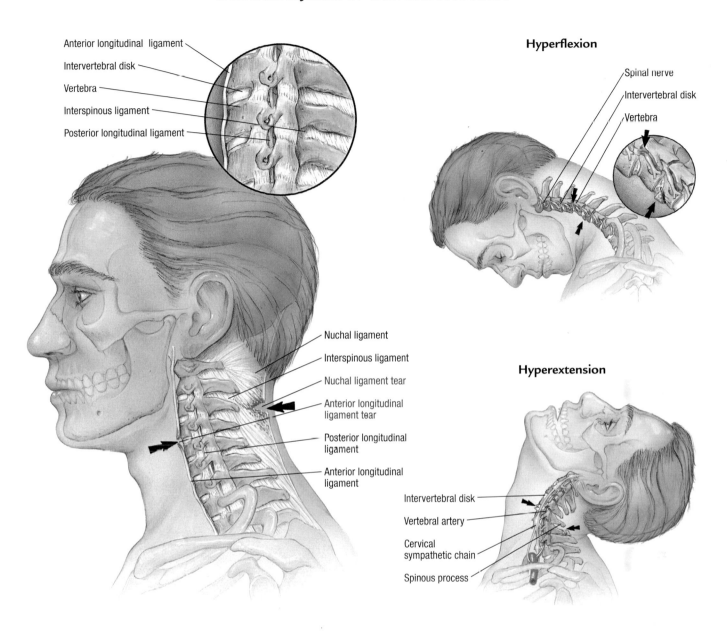

Anterior longitudinal ligament

Intervertebral disk

Vertebra

Interspinous ligament

Posterior longitudinal ligament

Nuchal ligament

Interspinous ligament

Nuchal ligament tear

Anterior longitudinal ligament tear

Posterior longitudinal ligament

Anterior longitudinal ligament

Hyperflexion

Spinal nerve

Intervertebral disk

Vertebra

Hyperextension

Intervertebral disk

Vertebral artery

Cervical sympathetic chain

Spinous process

Muscle injury

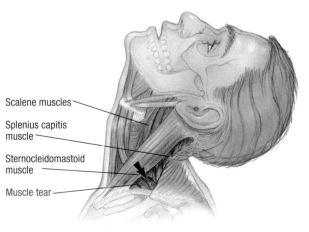

Scalene muscles

Splenius capitis muscle

Sternocleidomastoid muscle

Muscle tear

ALZHEIMER'S DISEASE

Alzheimer's disease is a progressive degenerative disorder of the cerebral cortex, especially the frontal lobe. It affects approximately 5 million Americans; by 2030, that figure may reach 7.7 million. It's the seventh-leading cause of death in the United States.

AGE ALERT
Alzheimer's disease typically affects adults older than age 65, but some cases have been reported in individuals as young as in their late 30s.

The disease has a poor prognosis. Typically, the duration of illness is 8 years, and patients die 2 to 5 years after the onset of debilitating brain symptoms.

Causes
- Exact cause unknown

Possible contributing factors
- Genetic patterns
- Beta-amyloid plaque development
- Inflammatory and oxidative stress processes
- The role of estrogen in the brain

Pathophysiology
The brain of a patient with Alzheimer's disease has three characteristic features: *neurofibrillary tangles* (fibrous proteins), *neuritic plaques* (composed of degenerating axons and dendrites), and *neuronal loss* (degeneration).

Neurofibrillary tangles are bundles of filaments found inside neurons that abnormally twist around one another. Abnormally phosphorylated tau proteins accumulate in the neurons as the characteristic tangles and ultimately cause neuronal death. In a healthy brain, tau provides structural support for neurons, but in patients with Alzheimer's disease this structural support collapses.

Neuritic plaques (senile plaques) form outside the neurons in the adjacent brain tissue. Plaques contain a core of beta-amyloid protein surrounded by abnormal nerve endings or neurites. Overproduction or decreased metabolism of beta-amyloid peptide leads to a toxic state causing degeneration of neuronal processes, neuritic plaque formation, and eventually neuronal loss and clinical dementia.

Tangles and plaques cause neurons in the brain of the patient with Alzheimer's disease to shrink and eventually die, first in the memory and language centers and finally throughout the entire brain. This widespread neuron degeneration leaves gaps in the brain's messaging network that may interfere with communication between cells, causing some of the symptoms of Alzheimer's disease.

COMPLICATIONS
- Injury from wandering, violent behavior, or unsupervised activity
- Pneumonia
- Malnutrition and dehydration
- Aspiration

Signs and symptoms
Mild
- Disorientation to date
- Impaired recall
- Diminished insight
- Irritability
- Apathy

Moderate
- Increased disorientation (time and place)
- Fluent aphasia
- Difficulties with comprehension
- Impaired recognition
- Poor judgment
- Trouble performing activities of daily living (ADLs)
- Aggression
- Restlessness
- Psychosis
- Sleep disturbances
- Dysphoria

Severe
- Unable to use language appropriately
- Memory only to the moment
- Needs assistance with all ADLs
- Urinary and fecal incontinence

Diagnostic test results
- Neuropsychologic evaluation shows deficits in memory, reasoning, vision-motor coordination, and language function.
- Magnetic resonance imaging or computed tomography scan reveals brain atrophy at later stages of the disease.
- Positron emission tomography scanning shows decreased brain activity.
- EEG shows evidence of slowed brain waves at later stages of the disease.

Treatment
- Cholinesterase inhibitors, such as tacrine, donepezil, rivastigmine, and galantamine
- Memantine (Namenda), and N-methyl-D-aspartate receptor antagonist
- Behavioral therapy
- Nonsteroidal anti-inflammatory drugs
- Cholesterol-lowering drugs
- Estrogen

TISSUE CHANGES IN ALZHEIMER'S DISEASE

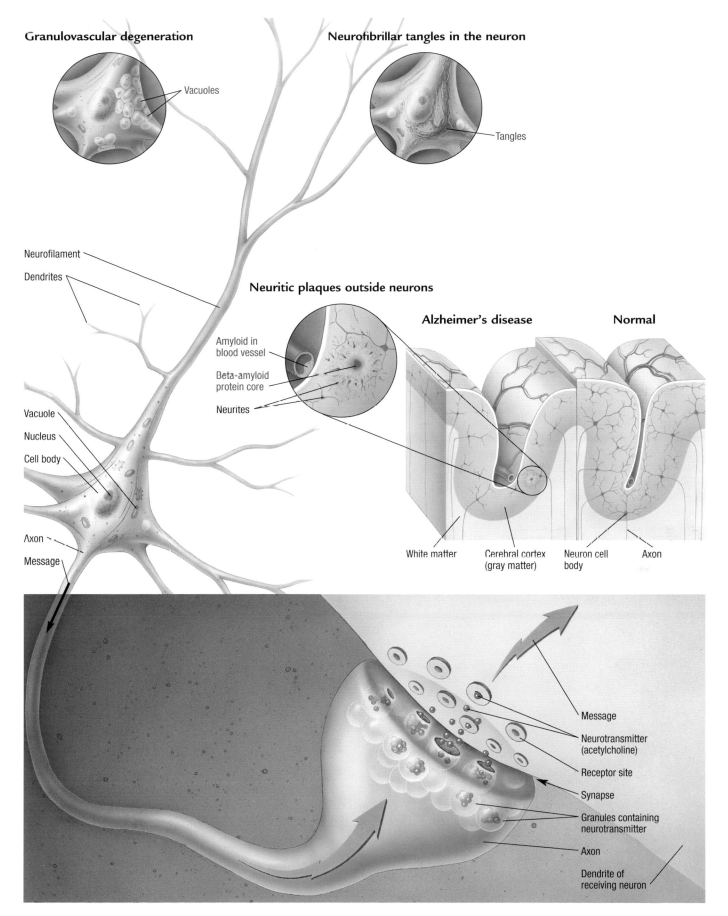

Granulovascular degeneration

Vacuoles

Neurofibrillar tangles in the neuron

Tangles

Neurofilament

Dendrites

Neuritic plaques outside neurons

Amyloid in
blood vessel

Beta-amyloid
protein core

Neurites

Vacuole

Nucleus

Cell body

Axon

Message

Alzheimer's disease

Normal

White matter

Cerebral cortex
(gray matter)

Neuron cell
body

Axon

Message

Neurotransmitter
(acetylcholine)

Receptor site

Synapse

Granules containing
neurotransmitter

Axon

Dendrite of
receiving neuron

Amyotrophic lateral sclerosis

Commonly called *Lou Gehrig's disease,* after the New York Yankees first baseman who died of this disorder, amyotrophic lateral sclerosis (ALS) is the most common of the motor neuron diseases causing muscular atrophy. A chronic, progressively debilitating disease, ALS may be fatal in less than 1 year or continue for 10 years or more, depending on the muscles affected. More than 30,000 Americans have ALS; the disease affects three times as many men as women.

AGE ALERT
The average age of ALS onset is mid-50s but can range from the late teen years to the 80s.

Causes

The exact cause is unknown. A genetic (familial ALS [FALS]) link is seen in 10% of all ALS cases. A specific gene mutation in an enzyme known as *superoxide dismutase 1* has been identified in about 20% of FALS cases. Over 90% of cases of ALS occur randomly with no identifiable cause and no risk factors, and is referred to as sporadic ALS. Several theories have been proposed that explain why motor neurons die, including:

- glutamate excitotoxicity
- oxidative injury
- protein aggregates
- axonal strangulation
- autoimmune-induced calcium influx
- viral infections
- deficiency of nerve growth factor
- apoptosis (programmed cell death)
- trauma
- environmental toxins.

Pathophysiology

Current research suggests an excess accumulation of glutamate (an excitatory neurotransmitter) in the synaptic cleft. The affected motor units are no longer innervated, and progressive degeneration of axons causes loss of myelin. Some nearby motor nerves may sprout axons in an attempt to maintain function but, ultimately, nonfunctional scar tissue replaces normal neuronal tissue.

COMPLICATIONS
- Pneumonia
- Pressure ulcers
- Weight loss
- Acute respiratory distress syndrome

Signs and symptoms

- Fasciculations, spasticity, atrophy, weakness, and loss of functioning motor units (especially in forearms and hands)
- Impaired speech, chewing, and swallowing; choking; drooling
- Difficulty breathing, especially if the brain stem is affected
- Muscle atrophy
- Reactive depression

Diagnostic test results

- Electromyography shows abnormalities of electrical activity in involved muscles.
- Muscle biopsy shows atrophic fibers interspersed between normal fibers.
- Cerebrospinal fluid analysis by lumbar puncture reveals elevated protein levels.
- Nerve conduction studies show normal results.

Treatment

- Riluzole
- Baclofen or diazepam
- Trihexyphenidyl or amitriptyline
- Physical therapy
- Percutaneous feeding tubes
- Tracheostomy
- Speech therapy

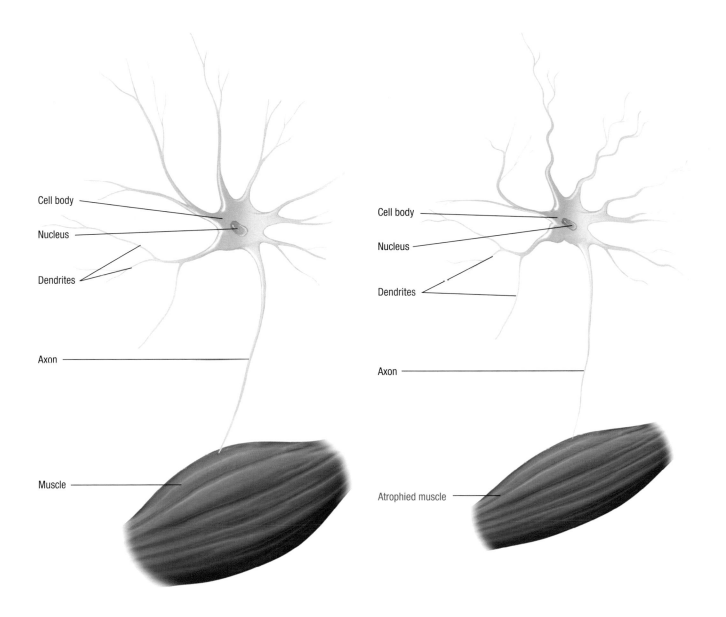

Normal nerve cell and muscle

Cell body

Nucleus

Dendrites

Axon

Muscle

Amyotrophic lateral sclerosis–affected nerve cell and muscle

Cell body

Nucleus

Dendrites

Axon

Atrophied muscle

ARTERIOVENOUS MALFORMATION

Arteriovenous malformations (AVMs) are tangled masses of thin-walled, dilated blood vessels between arteries and veins that aren't connected by capillaries. AVMs are common in the brain, primarily in the posterior portion of the cerebral hemispheres. Abnormal channels between the arterial and venous system mix oxygenated and unoxygenated blood and thereby prevent adequate perfusion of brain tissue.

AVMs range in size from a few millimeters to large malformations extending from the cerebral cortex to the ventricles. Usually, more than one AVM is present. Males and females are affected equally, and some evidence exists that AVMs occur in families.

AGE ALERT
Most AVMs are present at birth; however, symptoms may occur at any time. Two-thirds of all cases occur before age 40.

Causes
- Congenital: hereditary defect
- Acquired: trauma such as penetrating injuries

Pathophysiology
AVMs lack the typical structural characteristics of the blood vessels. The vessel walls of an AVM are very thin; one or more arteries feed into the AVM, causing it to appear dilated and torturous. The typically high-pressured arterial flow moves into the venous system through the connecting channels to increase venous pressure, engorging and dilating the venous structures. An aneurysm may develop. If the AVM is large enough, the shunting can deprive the surrounding tissue of adequate blood flow. Additionally, the thin-walled vessels may ooze small amounts of blood or actually rupture, causing hemorrhage into the brain or subarachnoid space.

COMPLICATIONS
- Aneurysm and subsequent rupture
- Hemorrhage (intracranial, subarachnoid, subdural)
- Hydrocephalus

Signs and symptoms
Typically, few or none.
If AVM is large, leaks, or ruptures
- Chronic headache and confusion
- Seizures
- Systolic bruit over carotid artery, mastoid process, or orbit
- Focal neurologic deficits (depending on the location of the AVM)
- Hydrocephalus
- Paralysis
- Loss of speech, memory, or vision

CLINICAL TIP
Symptoms of intracranial hemorrhage, indicating AVM rupture, include sudden severe headache, seizures, confusion, lethargy, and meningeal irritation.

Diagnostic test results
- Cerebral arteriogram confirms the presence of AVMs and evaluates blood flow.
- Doppler ultrasonography of the cerebrovascular system indicates abnormal, turbulent blood flow.

Treatment
- Supportive measures, including aneurysm precautions
- Surgery, including block dissection, laser, or ligation
- Embolization or radiation therapy
- Radiosurgery

Cerebral cortex — Sagittal section

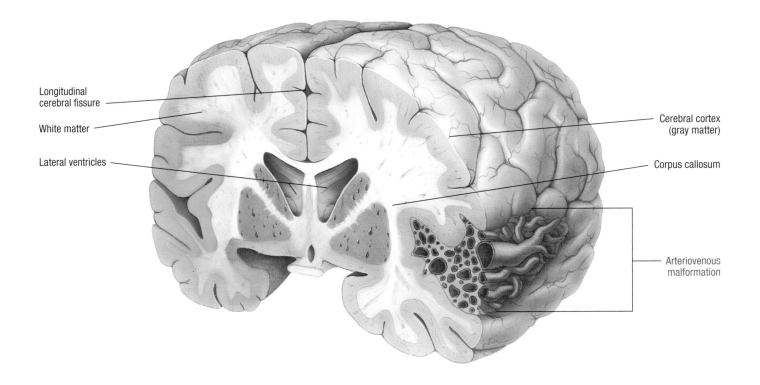

Longitudinal cerebral fissure

White matter

Lateral ventricles

Cerebral cortex (gray matter)

Corpus callosum

Arteriovenous malformation

BELL'S PALSY

Bell's palsy is a disease of the facial nerve (cranial nerve VII) that produces unilateral or bilateral facial weakness. Onset is rapid. In 80% to 90% of patients, it subsides spontaneously and recovery is complete in 1 to 8 weeks. If recovery is partial, contractures may develop on the paralyzed side of the face. Bell's palsy may recur on the same or opposite side of the face.

AGE ALERT
Although Bell's palsy affects all age-groups, it occurs most commonly in people between ages 20 to 60. Recovery may be slower in elderly patients.

Causes
- Infection such as herpes simplex virus
- Tumor
- Meningitis
- Local trauma
- Lyme disease
- Hypertension
- Sarcoidosis

Pathophysiology
Bell's palsy reflects an inflammatory reaction around the seventh cranial nerve, usually at the internal auditory meatus where the nerve leaves bony tissue. The characteristic unilateral or bilateral facial weakness results from the lack of appropriate neural stimulation to the muscle by the motor fibers of the facial nerve.

COMPLICATIONS
- Corneal ulceration and blindness
- Impaired nutrition
- Psychosocial problems due to altered body image

Signs and symptoms
- Unilateral face weakness
- Aching at jaw angle
- Drooping mouth
- Distorted taste or loss of taste
- Impaired ability to fully close the eye on the affected side
- Tinnitus
- Excessive or insufficient eye tearing on the affected side
- Hypersensitivity to sound on the affected side
- Headache

CLINICAL TIP
When the patient attempts to close the affected eye, it rolls upward (Bell's phenomenon) and shows excessive tearing.

Diagnostic test results
Diagnosis is based on clinical presentation. (See *Diagnosing Bell's Palsy.*) Other studies include:
- nerve conduction studies and electromyography to determine the extent of nerve damage
- blood tests to establish the presence of sarcoidosis or Lyme disease.

Treatment
- Oral corticosteroids such as prednisone
- Antivirals
- Analgesics
- Lubricating eyedrops or eye ointments
- Electrotherapy
- Surgery

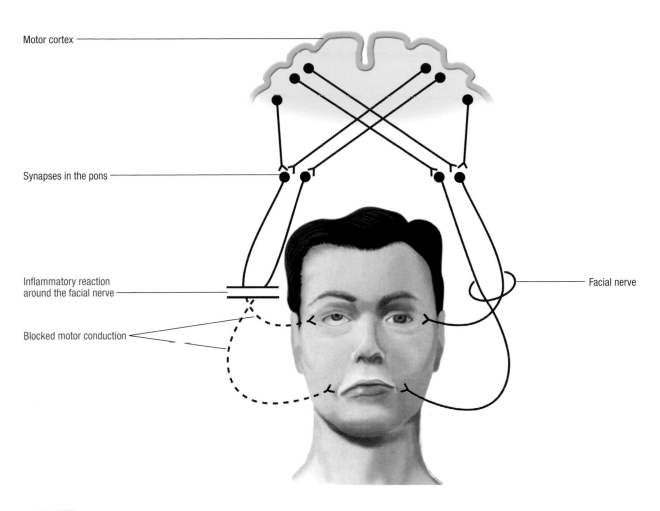

Motor cortex

Synapses in the pons

Inflammatory reaction around the facial nerve

Blocked motor conduction

Facial nerve

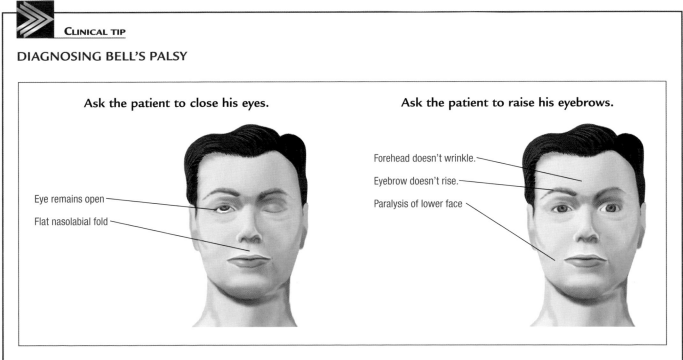

CLINICAL TIP

DIAGNOSING BELL'S PALSY

Ask the patient to close his eyes.

Eye remains open

Flat nasolabial fold

Ask the patient to raise his eyebrows.

Forehead doesn't wrinkle.

Eyebrow doesn't rise.

Paralysis of lower face

BRAIN TUMORS

Brain tumors are abnormal growths that develop after transformation of cells within the brain, cerebral vasculature, or meninges. They're usually referred to as *benign* or *malignant*. Malignancy in the brain is graded on the degree of cellularity, endothelial proliferation, nuclear atypia, and necrosis. Highly malignant brain tumors are aggressive tumors that grow and multiply rapidly. Survival and prognosis are directly related to tumor grade. However, even though benign tumors lack aggressiveness, they can be as devastating neurologically depending on their size and location. The most common types of primary brain tumors are gliomas, meningiomas, and pituitary adenomas.

AGE ALERT
Brain tumors are found in all age-groups, with peaks of incidence occurring in early childhood as well as in people ages 50 to 80.

Causes
- Unknown in most cases
- A genetic loss or mutation
- Prior cranial radiation exposure

Pathophysiology
At the level of the cell nucleus, both positive and negative regulators of growth are necessary for normal control of cell proliferation. The positive regulators, proto-oncogenes, have products that function as growth factors, growth factor receptors, and signaling enzymes. Excessive production may occur that converts proto-oncogenes into oncogenes, resulting in significant neoplastic growth.

Negative regulators of cell growth are called tumor suppressor genes. Suppressor genes inhibit cellular proliferation at the level of the nucleus. The loss of tumor suppressor genes by mutation, deletion, or reduced expression aids in the conversion of normal cells to malignant phenotypes. The excessive stimulation of proto-oncogenes and the lack of inhibition of tumor suppressor genes ultimately lead to neoplastic proliferation. As the tumor grows, edema develops in surrounding tissues and intracranial pressure (ICP) increases. As the tumor continues to grow, it may interfere with the normal flow and drainage of cerebrospinal fluid (CSF), causing an increase in ICP.

The brain compensates for increases by regulating the volume of the three substances in the following ways: limiting blood flow to the head, displacing CSF into the spinal canal, and increasing absorption or decreasing production of CSF.

COMPLICATIONS
- Coma
- Respiratory or cardiac arrest
- Brain herniation

Signs and symptoms
- Headache
- Decreased motor strength and coordination
- Seizures
- Altered vital signs
- Nausea and vomiting
- Increased ICP
- Neurologic deficits
- Diplopia
- Papilledema

Diagnostic test results
- Skull X-rays confirm the presence of the tumor.
- Computed tomography (CT) and magnetic resonance imaging (MRI) show changes in brain tissue density.
- Magnetic resonance spectroscopy evaluates the neurochemical changes in the bed of the tumor. Elevation in choline is noted in high-grade gliomas, as compared with elevated lactate levels in intracranial abscess.
- Positron emission tomography evaluates the blood flow patterns in the brain and the tumor, and differentiates normal brain tissue from the tumor.
- The MRI or CT angiogram evaluates the arterial and venous structures surrounding the tumor.
- Tissue biopsy confirms the presence of the tumor.
- Lumbar puncture shows increased CSF pressure, which reflects ICP, increased protein levels, decreased glucose levels and, occasionally, tumor cells in CSF.

Treatment
- Surgery
- Radiation
- Chemotherapy
- Corticosteroids such as dexamethasone
- Anticonvulsants such as phenytoin
- Ranitidine or famotidine
- Analgesics

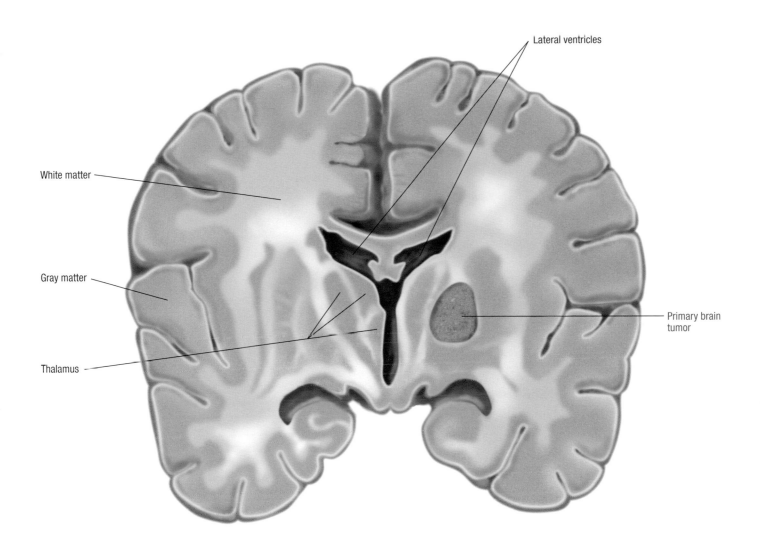

Lateral ventricles

White matter

Gray matter

Thalamus

Primary brain tumor

CEREBRAL ANEURYSM

In an intracranial, or cerebral, aneurysm, a weakness in the wall of a cerebral artery causes localized dilation. Cerebral aneurysms usually arise at an arterial junction in the circle of Willis, the circular anastomosis connecting the major cerebral arteries at the base of the brain. Many cerebral aneurysms rupture and cause subarachnoid hemorrhage.

AGE ALERT

Incidence is slightly higher in women than in men, especially those in their late 40s or early to mid-50s, but a cerebral aneurysm may occur at any age in either sex.

Causes

- Congenital defect
- Degenerative process such as atherosclerosis
- Hypertension
- Trauma
- Infection

Pathophysiology

Prolonged hemodynamic stress and local arterial degeneration at vessel bifurcations are believed to be a major contributing factor to the development and ultimate rupture of cerebral aneurysms. Bleeding spreads rapidly into the subarachnoid space and commonly into the intraventricular spaces and brain tissue, producing localized changes in the cerebral cortex and focal irritation of the cranial nerves and arteries. Increased intracranial pressure occurs, causing disruption of cerebral autoregulation and alterations in cerebral blood flow. Expanding intracranial hematomas may act as space-occupying lesions compressing or displacing brain tissue. Blockage of the ventricular system or decreased cerebrospinal fluid (CSF) absorption can result in hydrocephalus. Cerebral artery vasospasm occurs in the surrounding arteries and can further compromise cerebral blood flow, leading to cerebral ischemia and cerebral infarction.

COMPLICATIONS

- Subarachnoid hemorrhage
- Brain tissue infarction
- Cerebral vasospasm
- Hydrocephalus
- Rebleeding
- Meningeal irritation from blood in the sub-arachnoid space

Signs and symptoms

Cerebral aneurysms are generally asymptomatic until they rupture. Signs and symptoms of subarachnoid hemorrhage include:

- change in level of consciousness
- sudden severe headache
- photophobia
- nuchal rigidity
- lower back pain
- nausea and vomiting
- fever
- positive Kernig's sign
- positive Brudzinski's sign
- seizure
- cranial nerve deficits
- motor weakness.

Diagnostic test results

- Cerebral arteriogram shows the presence of a cerebral aneurysm.
- Head computed tomography scan reveals subarachnoid hemorrhage.
- Transcranial Doppler ultrasound study shows increased blood flow if vasospasm occurs.
- Examination of CSF confirms bleeding.
- Electrocardiogram changes reveal bradycardia, atrioventricular blocks, and premature ventricular contractions.
- Complete blood count shows elevated white blood cell count.

Treatment

- Bed rest in a quiet, darkened room with minimal stimulation
- Surgical repair by clipping, ligation, or wrapping
- Endovascular coiling
- Triple H therapy (hypervolemia, hypertension, hemodilution)
- Calcium channel blockers such as nimodipine
- Avoidance of caffeine or other stimulants; avoidance of aspirin
- Codeine or another analgesic as needed
- Antihypertensives
- Anticonvulsants
- Sedatives

Circle of Willis

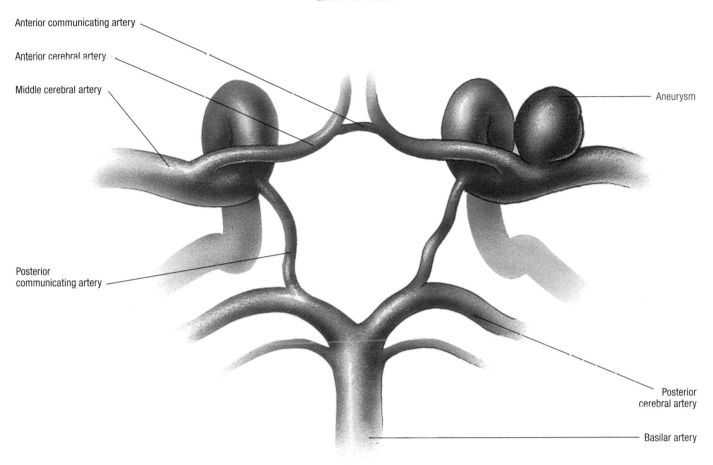

Anterior communicating artery

Anterior cerebral artery

Middle cerebral artery

Aneurysm

Posterior communicating artery

Posterior cerebral artery

Basilar artery

Vessels of the brain — Inferior view

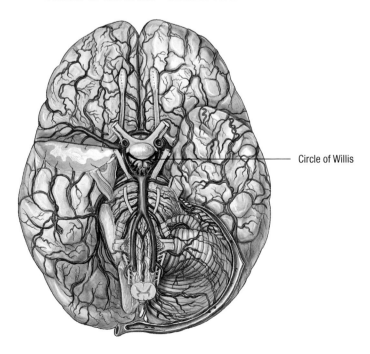

Circle of Willis

DEPRESSION

Depression is a chronic and recurrent mood disorder. Although many people may feel depressed at one time or another, clinical depression is defined when the symptoms interfere with everyday life for an extended period. It affects women twice as often as men, and it's reported to be significantly underdiagnosed and usually inadequately treated.

Forms of depression include major depression, dysthymia, postpartum depression, premenstrual dysphoric disorder, and seasonal affective disorder.

AGE ALERT
The peak age of depression onset is between 20 and 40.

Causes
Some people may have a genetic predisposition to developing depression.
Possible contributing factors
- Disappointment at home, work, or school
- Death of a friend or relative
- Prolonged pain or having a major illness
- Medical conditions, such as hypothyroidism, cancer, or hepatitis
- Drugs, such as sedatives and antihypertensives
- Alcohol or drug abuse
- Chronic stress
- Abuse or neglect
- Social isolation
- Nutritional deficiencies (such as folate and omega-3 fatty acids)
- Sleeping problems

Pathophysiology
An imbalance of the neurotransmitters is thought to be the underlying mechanism in depression. In a person with normal levels of neurotransmitters, serotonin and norepinephrine are released from one neuron and travel to another one, activating receptors. After the receptors are activated, the neurotransmitters are taken up by the presynaptic neuron. A patient with depression has inadequate levels of serotonin or norepinephrine, thus not allowing this smooth transmission of impulses.

COMPLICATIONS
- Suicide
- Altered social, family, and occupational functioning

Signs and symptoms

- Persistent sad, anxious, or "empty" mood
- Feelings of hopelessness and pessimism
- Feelings of guilt, worthlessness, and helplessness
- Loss of interest or pleasure in hobbies and activities that were once enjoyed

- Loss of energy or fatigue
- Unexplained pain
- GI symptoms
- Headache
- Insomnia
- Dizziness
- Palpitations
- Heartburn
- Numbness
- Loss of appetite
- Premenstrual syndrome

AGE ALERT
In children, symptoms of depression include hyperactivity, poor school performance, somatic complaints, sleeping and eating disturbances, lack of playfulness, and suicidal ideation or actions.

Diagnostic test results
Several screening questionnaires are used to detect depressive symptoms. They include:
- Beck Depression Inventory
- Center for Epidemiological Studies Depression Scale
- Zung Self-Rating Depression Scale.

CLINICAL TIP
To screen for depression, ask your patient these two questions:
- Have you felt down, depressed, or hopeless for most of the past 2 weeks?
- Have you felt little interest or pleasure in performing activities for most of the past 2 weeks?
If the patient answers yes to either question, further assessment is warranted.

Treatment
- Selective serotonin reuptake inhibitors, such as fluoxetine and sertraline
- Tricyclic antidepressants, such as nortriptyline and desipramine
- Venlafaxine
- Nefazodone
- Bupropion
- Monoamine oxidase inhibitors
- Psychotherapy
- Electroconvulsive therapy
- Exercise
- Support groups
- Self-help literature
- Light therapy

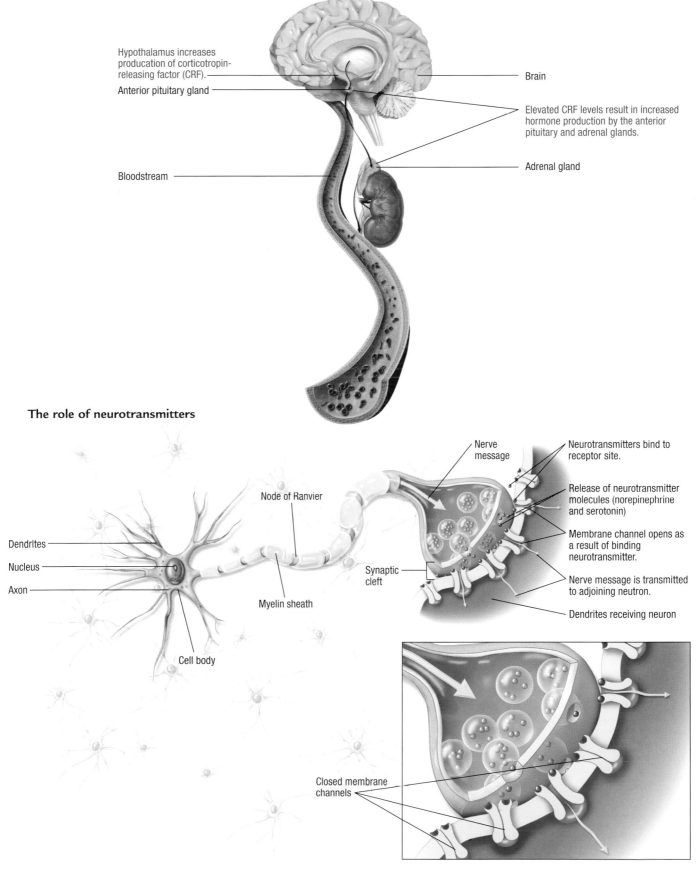

Hypothalamus increases producation of corticotropin-releasing factor (CRF).

Anterior pituitary gland

Brain

Elevated CRF levels result in increased hormone production by the anterior pituitary and adrenal glands.

Adrenal gland

Bloodstream

The role of neurotransmitters

Node of Ranvier

Nerve message

Neurotransmitters bind to receptor site.

Release of neurotransmitter molecules (norepinephrine and serotonin)

Dendrites

Nucleus

Axon

Synaptic cleft

Membrane channel opens as a result of binding neurotransmitter.

Nerve message is transmitted to adjoining neutron.

Dendrites receiving neuron

Myelin sheath

Cell body

Closed membrane channels

EPILEPSY

Epilepsy is a condition of the brain characterized by suscep-tibility to recurrent seizures — paroxysmal events associat-ed with abnormal electrical discharges of neurons in the brain.

Generalized seizures originate from multiple areas of the brain simultaneously. Partial seizures originate from a single focus but can spread or be generalized.

Causes
- Half of all cases are idiopathic
- Birth trauma
- Anoxia
- Perinatal infection
- Genetic abnormalities, such as tuberous sclerosis and phenylketonuria
- Perinatal injuries
- Metabolic abnormalities, such as hypoglycemia, pyridoxine deficiency, or hypoparathyroidism
- Brain tumors or other space-occupying lesions
- Meningitis, encephalitis, or brain abscess
- Traumatic injury
- Ingestion of toxins, such as mercury, lead, or carbon monox-ide
- Stroke
- Apparent familial incidence in some seizure disorders

Pathophysiology
Some neurons in the brain may depolarize easily or be hyperex-citable; this *epileptogenic focus* fires more readily than normal when stimulated. In these neurons, the membrane potential at rest is less negative or inhibitory connections are missing, pos-sibly because of decreased gamma-aminobutyric acid activity or localized shifts in electrolytes.

On stimulation, the epileptogenic focus fires and spreads electrical current toward the synapse and surrounding cells. These cells fire in turn, and the impulse cascades to one side of the brain (a partial seizure), both sides of the brain (a general-ized seizure), or cortical, subcortical, or brain stem areas.

The brain's metabolic demand for oxygen increases dramat-ically during a seizure. If this demand isn't met, hypoxia and brain damage ensue. Firing of inhibitory neurons causes the excitatory neurons to slow their firing and eventually stop.

If this inhibitory action doesn't occur, the result is status epilepticus: one prolonged seizure or one seizure occurring right after another and another. Without treatment, this may be fatal.

COMPLICATIONS
- Anoxia
- Traumatic injury
- Death from status epilepticus

Signs and symptoms
Generalized tonic-clonic seizures
- Altered consciousness
- Tonic stiffening followed by clonic muscular contractions
- Tongue biting
- Incontinence
- Labored breathing
- Apnea
- Cyanosis

Absence seizures
- Change in level of awareness
- Blank stare
- Automatisms (purposeless motor activity)

Atonic seizures
- Sudden loss of postural tone
- Temporary loss of alertness

Myoclonic seizures
- Brief muscle contractions that appear as jerks or twitching

Diagnostic test results
- EEG reveals paroxysmal abnormalities to confirm the diag-nosis and provide evidence of the continuing tendency to have seizures. In tonic-clonic seizures, high, fast voltage spikes are present in all leads; in absence seizures, rounded spike wave complexes are diagnostic. A negative EEG doesn't rule out epilepsy because the abnormalities occur intermittently.
- Computed tomography scan and magnetic resonance imag-ing show abnormalities in internal structures.
- Skull X-ray shows evidence of fractures or shifting of the pineal gland, bony erosion, or separated sutures.
- Brain scan reveals malignant lesions when X-ray findings are normal or questionable.
- Cerebral angiography shows cerebrovascular abnormalities, such as aneurysm or tumor.
- Serum chemistry blood studies show hypoglycemia, elec-trolyte imbalances, elevated liver enzymes, and elevated alcohol levels, providing clues to underlying conditions that increase the risk of seizure activity.

Treatment
- Drug therapy specific to the type of seizure, including pheny-toin, carbamazepine, phenobarbital, gabapentin, and primi-done for generalized tonic-clonic seizures and complex partial seizures
- Valproic acid, clonazepam, and ethosuximide for absence seizures
- Gabapentin and felbamate and other anticonvulsant drugs
- Surgical removal of a demonstrated focal lesion, if drug ther-apy is ineffective
- Surgery to remove the underlying cause, such as a tumor, ab-scess, or vascular problem
- Vagus nerve stimulator implant
- I.V. diazepam, lorazepam, phenytoin, or phenobarbital for status epilepticus
- Administration of dextrose (when seizures are secondary to hypoglycemia) or thiamine (in chronic alcoholism or with-drawal)

TYPES OF SEIZURES

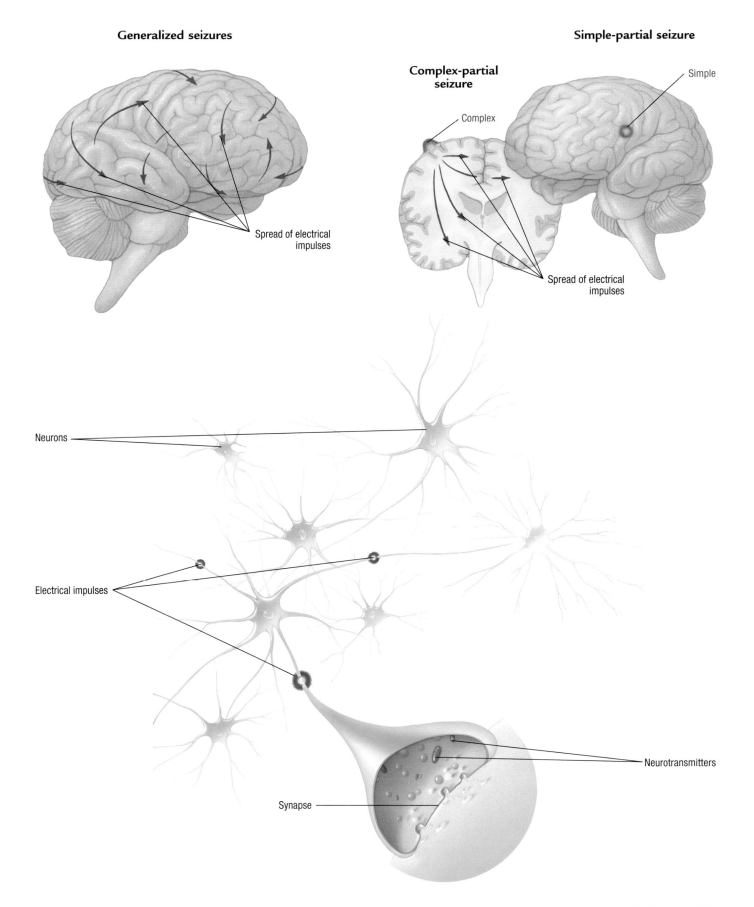

Generalized seizures

Spread of electrical impulses

Complex-partial seizure

Complex

Simple-partial seizure

Simple

Spread of electrical impulses

Neurons

Electrical impulses

Neurotransmitters

Synapse

GUILLAIN-BARRÉ SYNDROME

Also known as *infectious polyneuritis, Landry-Guillain-Barré syndrome,* or *acute idiopathic polyneuritis,* Guillain-Barré syndrome is a rapidly progressive and potentially fatal motor neuropathy of uncertain cause. Generally, the syndrome reaches its peak progress within 7 days to 4 weeks. Recovery occurs over weeks to months with approximately 10% to 25% of the population suffering with permanent weakness and disability.

AGE ALERT
The average age of onset of Guillain-Barré syndrome is 40.

Causes

An exact cause is unknown; however, in many cases, the syndrome is preceded by a viral infection that produces a cell-mediated immune reaction. The most common infection is *Campylobacter jejuni,* occurring in about 30% to 40% of the cases. Epstein-Barr virus, cytomegalovirus, human immunodeficiency virus, coxsackievirus, herpes simplex, hepatitis A virus, and *Mycoplasma* pneumonia have also been implicated.

Other precipitating factors
- Hematologic malignancies
- Hyperthyroidism
- Collagen vascular diseases
- Sarcoidosis
- Pregnancy
- Surgical procedures
- Transplants
- Immunizations (swine flu)
- Certain drugs (heroin)

Pathophysiology

Guillain-Barré syndrome is triggered by an autoimmune response in which the body's immune system starts to destroy the myelin sheath that surrounds the axons of many peripheral nerves, or even the axons themselves. It's possible that the virus changes the nature of the cells in the nervous system so that the immune system treats them as foreign cells. It's also possible that the virus makes the immune system itself less discriminating about what cells it recognizes, thereby allowing some of the immune cells, such as certain kinds of lymphocytes and macrophages, to attack the myelin. Sensitized T lymphocytes cooperate with B lymphocytes to produce antibodies against components of the myelin sheath and may contribute to destruction of the myelin as well.

Myelin destruction causes segmental demyelination of the peripheral nerves, preventing normal transmission of electrical impulses. Inflammation and degenerative changes in both the posterior (sensory) and anterior (motor) nerve roots result in

signs of sensory and motor losses simultaneously. The autonomic nervous system may also be impaired.

COMPLICATIONS
- Thrombophlebitis
- Pressure ulcers
- Contractures and muscle wasting
- Aspiration
- Respiratory tract infections
- Life-threatening respiratory and cardiac failure
- Paralysis

Signs and symptoms
- Symmetrical muscle weakness (major neurologic sign) appearing in the legs first (ascending type) and then extending to the arms and facial nerves within 24 to 72 hours
- Muscle weakness developing in the arms first (descending type) or in the arms and legs simultaneously
- Absent deep tendon reflexes
- Paresthesia, sometimes preceding muscle weakness but vanishing quickly
- Diplegia, possibly with ophthalmoplegia
- Dysphagia and dysarthria
- Hypotonia and areflexia

Diagnostic test results
- Cerebrospinal fluid (CSF) analysis by lumbar puncture reveals elevated protein levels, peaking in 4 to 6 weeks, probably as a result of widespread inflammation of the nerve roots; the CSF white blood cell count remains normal, but in severe disease, CSF pressure may rise above normal.
- Complete blood count shows leukocytosis with immature forms early in the illness, and then quickly returns to normal.
- Electromyography possibly shows repeated firing of the same motor unit instead of widespread sectional stimulation.
- Nerve conduction velocities show slowing soon after paralysis develops.
- Serum immunoglobulin measurements reveal elevated levels from inflammatory response.

Treatment
- Endotracheal intubation or tracheotomy, as indicated to clear secretions
- Plasmapheresis
- Continuous electrocardiogram monitoring
- I.V. immunoglobulin
- Pain management, with anti-inflammatories and opioids
- Rehabilitation

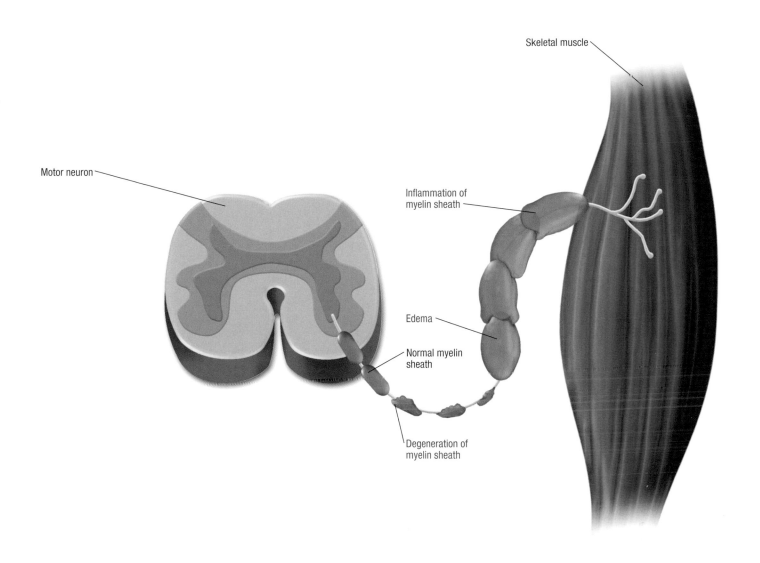

Skeletal muscle

Motor neuron

Inflammation of
myelin sheath

Edema

Normal myelin
sheath

Degeneration of
myelin sheath

HEADACHE

Headache, although usually benign, can be a serious and commonly disabling disorder. The International Headache Society identified a comprehensive classification system that includes more than 100 types of headaches, which are divided into 13 categories. Various processes may cause headache, and they range from benign to life-threatening.

Causes

Primary headaches are classified based on their symptom profiles and account for 90% to 98% of headaches. Primary headaches include migraines, tension-type, and cluster.

Acute and progressive, secondary headaches are the result of an identifiable structural or physiologic cause, including:
- head trauma
- vascular disorders
- nonvascular intracranial disorders
- substance abuse and substance withdrawal
- infections
- metabolic disorders
- disorders of the face and neck
- cranial neuralgias.

Pathophysiology

Primary headaches occur when pain-sensitive structures of the head, including the cerebral vasculature, musculature, and cranial or cervical nerves, are irritated. Vascular changes occur as follows:
- Stimulation of the trigeminal ganglion located in the midbrain releases substance P and calcitonin gene-related peptide.
- The release of substance P causes degranulation of mast cells. Mast cells release histamine, and platelets release serotonin.
- Vasodilation, plasma extravasation, and inflammation occur.
- Inflammation and release of substance P cause distention of cranial arteries and headache pain.
- Triggers either directly act on the vasomotor tone or mediate the neurochemical release of vasoactive substances.
- Vasoconstriction, platelet changes, and neurochemical mediators initiate cerebral ischemia and activate the trigeminal-vascular system.

COMPLICATIONS
- Rebound headaches
- Serotonin syndrome

Signs and symptoms

Migraine
- Commonly preceded by temporary focal neurologic signs known as *auras* (Auras are usually visual — scotomata, zigzag, flashing lights and colors, geometric shapes, jagged lines.)
- Unilateral in onset but may become generalized
- Begins as a dull ache that progressively worsens and develops into throbbing, pulsating pain
- Commonly associated with photophobia, nausea and vomiting, phonophobia, and paresthesia

Tension-type
- Gradual onset of bilateral bandlike pressure or tightening of mild to moderate intensity; usually doesn't prohibit daily activities
- Not aggravated by physical activity or accompanied by associated symptoms; may have phonophobia or photophobia
- May be triggered by stress, fatigue, loud noises, heat, or bright lights
- Chronic form possibly resembles depression or fibromyalgia syndrome

Cluster
- Acute onset of excruciating severe unilateral orbital pain lasting 15 to 180 minutes
- Episodic clusters; one every other day to eight per day; commonly nocturnal
- Accompanied by ipsilateral lacrimation, conjunctival injection, rhinorrhea, miosis, ptosis, and nasal congestion

CLINICAL TIP

The presence of one or more of these factors is an indication for further evaluation:
- first-onset headache that begins after age 50
- sudden-onset headache
- accelerating pattern of headaches
- new-onset headache in a patient with cancer or human immunodeficiency virus
- headache with systemic illness (fever, stiff neck, or rash)
- presence of focal neurologic symptoms (not typical aura)
- papilledema.

Diagnostic test results

- Skull X-rays identify skull fracture.
- Computed tomography scan shows tumor or subarachnoid hemorrhage or other intracranial pathology; reveals pathology of sinuses.
- Lumbar puncture shows increased intracranial pressure suggesting tumor, edema, or hemorrhage.
- EEG shows alterations in the brain's electrical activity, suggesting intracranial lesion, head injury, meningitis, or encephalitis.
- Sinus X-rays show sinusitis.

Treatment

- Beta-adrenergic blockers and calcium channel blockers to reduce frequency and severity of migraines
- Analgesics or combination analgesics
- Ergotamine tartrate, dihydroergotamine, butalbital combinations, and opiates
- Serotonin agonists, such as sumatriptan, naratriptan, rizatriptan, and zolmitriptan
- Antiemetics
- Tricyclic antidepressants (migraine)
- Antiseizure drugs (divalproex and topiramate) for migraine

VASCULAR CHANGES IN HEADACHE

Normal

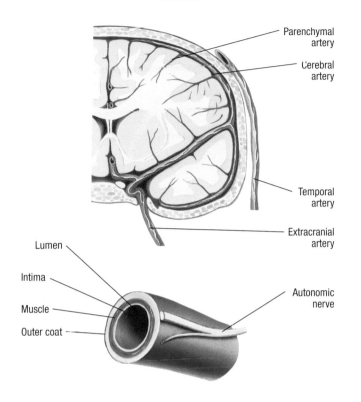

- Parenchymal artery
- Cerebral artery
- Temporal artery
- Extracranial artery

- Lumen
- Intima
- Muscle
- Outer coat
- Autonomic nerve

Vasoconstriction (aura) phase

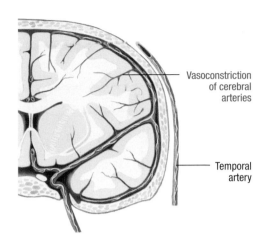

- Vasoconstriction of cerebral arteries
- Temporal artery

Platelet aggregation and release of serotonin granules

Parenchymal artery dilation

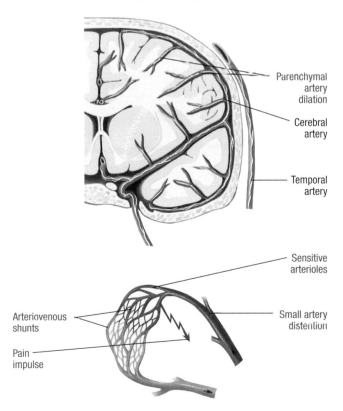

- Parenchymal artery dilation
- Cerebral artery
- Temporal artery

- Sensitive arterioles
- Arteriovenous shunts
- Small artery distention
- Pain impulse

Vasodilation (headache) phase

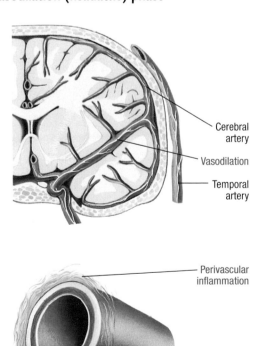

- Cerebral artery
- Vasodilation
- Temporal artery

- Perivascular inflammation

HERNIATED INTERVERTEBRAL DISK

A herniated disk, also called a *ruptured* or *slipped disk* or a *herniated nucleus pulposus,* occurs when all or part of the *nucleus pulposus* — the soft, gelatinous, central portion of an intervertebral disk — protrudes through the disk's weakened or torn outer ring (*anulus fibrosus*).

Herniated disks usually occur in adults (mostly men) older than age 45. About 90% of herniated disks are lumbar or lumbosacral; 8%, cervical; and 1% to 2%, thoracic. Patients with a congenitally small lumbar spinal canal or with osteophyte formation along the vertebrae may be more susceptible to nerve root compression and more likely to have neurologic symptoms.

AGE ALERT
A herniated disk occurs more frequently in middle-age and older men.

Causes
- Severe trauma or strain
- Intervertebral joint degeneration

AGE ALERT
In older patients whose vertebral disks have begun to degenerate, even minor trauma may cause herniation.

Pathophysiology
An intervertebral disk has two parts: the soft center called the *nucleus pulposus* and the tough, fibrous surrounding ring called the *anulus fibrosus.* The nucleus pulposus acts as a shock absorber, distributing the mechanical stress applied to the spine when the body moves.

Physical stress, usually a twisting motion, can tear or rupture the anulus fibrosus so that the nucleus pulposus herniates into the spinal canal. The vertebrae move closer together and in turn exert pressure on the nerve roots as they exit between the vertebrae.

Herniation occurs in three steps:
- *protrusion* — the nucleus pulposus presses against the anulus fibrosus
- *extrusion* — the nucleus pulposus bulges forcibly though the anulus fibrosus, pushing against the nerve root

- *sequestration* — the anulus gives way as the disk's core bursts and presses against the nerve root.

COMPLICATIONS
- Neurologic deficits
- Loss of bowel and bladder function

Signs and symptoms
- Severe lower back pain to the buttocks, legs, and feet; usually unilaterally
- Sudden pain after trauma, subsiding in a few days, and then recurring at shorter intervals and with progressive intensity
- Sciatic pain following trauma, beginning as a dull pain in the buttocks (Valsalva's maneuver, coughing, sneezing, and bending intensify the pain, which is commonly accompanied by muscle spasms)
- Sensory and motor loss in the area innervated by the compressed spinal nerve root and, in later stages, weakness and atrophy of leg muscles

Diagnostic test results
- Straight-leg raising test is positive only if the patient has posterior leg (sciatic) pain, not back pain.
- Lasègue's test reveals resistance and pain as well as loss of ankle or knee-jerk reflex, indicating spinal root compression.
- Myelogram, computed tomography scan, and magnetic resonance imaging show spinal canal compression as evidenced by herniated disk material.

Treatment
- Heat applications
- Exercise program
- Nonsteroidal anti-inflammatory drugs such as aspirin; rarely, corticosteroids such as dexamethasone; muscle relaxants, such as diazepam, methocarbamol, or cyclobenzaprine
- Surgery, including laminectomy to remove the protruding disk, spinal fusion to overcome segmental instability, or both to stabilize the spine

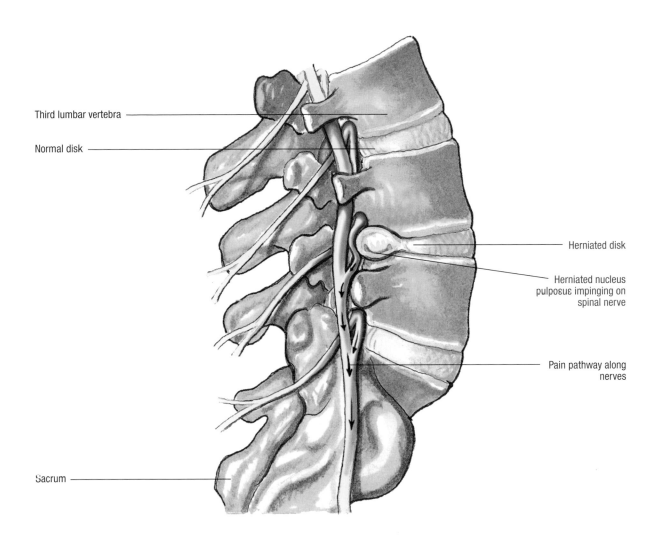

Third lumbar vertebra

Normal disk

Herniated disk

Herniated nucleus pulposus impinging on spinal nerve

Pain pathway along nerves

Sacrum

HYDROCEPHALUS

Hydrocephalus is a condition that results from an excessive accumulation of cerebrospinal fluid (CSF) in the brain. It results in an increase in intracranial pressure (ICP) with corresponding enlargement of the ventricular system. The condition is congenital or acquired, and communicating or noncommunicating (obstructive).

AGE ALERT
Hydrocephalus occurs most commonly in children but may also occur in adults and elderly people.

Causes
- Genetic inheritance (aqueductal stenosis)
- Developmental disorders such as those associated with neural tube defects, including spina bifida and encephalocele
- Complications of premature birth such as intraventricular hemorrhage
- Diseases (such as meningitis), tumors, traumatic head injury, or subarachnoid hemorrhage blocking the exit from the ventricles to the cisterns, thereby eliminating the cisterns

Pathophysiology
Ventricular dilation produces an increase in CSF pressure and volume, resulting in an increase in ICP. Compression of adjacent brain structures and cerebral blood vessels may lead to ischemia and, eventually, cell death.

COMPLICATIONS
- Mental retardation
- Impaired motor function
- Vision loss
- Death from increased ICP
- Death from infection and malnutrition (infants)

Signs and symptoms
In infants
- Rapid increase in head circumference or an unusually large head size
- Vomiting
- Sleepiness
- Irritability
- Downward deviation of the eyes (also called *sunsetting*)
- Seizures

In older children and adults
- Headache
- Vomiting
- Nausea
- Papilledema (swelling of the optic disk that's part of the optic nerve)
- Blurred vision
- Diplopia (double vision)
- Sunsetting of the eyes
- Problems with balance
- Poor coordination
- Gait disturbance
- Urinary incontinence
- Slowing or loss of development
- Lethargy
- Drowsiness
- Irritability
- Other changes in personality or cognition, including memory loss

Diagnostic test results
- Skull X-rays show thinning of the skull with separation of the sutures and widening of the fontanels.
- Angiography shows vessel abnormalities due to stretching.
- Computed tomography scan and magnetic resonance imaging reveal variations in tissue density and fluid in the ventricular system.
- Lumbar puncture reveals increased fluid pressure from communicating hydrocephalus.
- Ventriculography shows ventricular dilation with excess fluid.

CLINICAL TIP
In infants, abnormally large head size for the patient's age strongly suggests hydrocephalus. Measurement of the head circumference is the most important diagnostic technique.

Treatment
- Surgical correction by insertion of a ventriculoperitoneal or ventriculoatrial shunt
- Antibiotics
- Serial lumbar puncture
- Endoscopic third ventriculostomy

VENTRICLES OF THE BRAIN

Normal brain — Lateral view

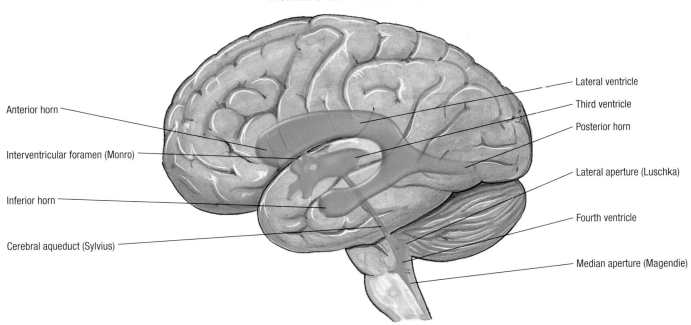

Anterior horn

Interventricular foramen (Monro)

Inferior horn

Cerebral aqueduct (Sylvius)

Lateral ventricle

Third ventricle

Posterior horn

Lateral aperture (Luschka)

Fourth ventricle

Median aperture (Magendie)

Ventricular enlargement

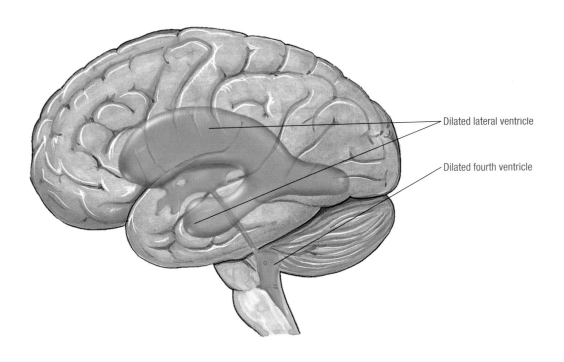

Dilated lateral ventricle

Dilated fourth ventricle

MENINGITIS

In meningitis, the brain and the spinal cord meninges become inflamed, usually because of bacterial infection. Such inflammation may involve all three meningeal membranes — the dura mater, arachnoid, and pia mater.

Causes

Meningitis is usually a complication of bacteremia, especially due to:
- pneumonia
- empyema
- osteomyelitis
- endocarditis.

Other infections associated with the development of meningitis include:
- sinusitis
- otitis media
- encephalitis
- myelitis
- brain abscess, usually caused by *Neisseria meningitidis, Haemophilus influenzae, Streptococcus pneumoniae*, and *Escherichia coli.*

Meningitis may follow trauma or invasive procedures, including:
- skull fracture
- penetrating head wound
- lumbar puncture
- ventricular shunting.

Aseptic meningitis may result from a virus or other organism. Sometimes no causative organism can be found.

Pathophysiology

Meningitis commonly begins as an inflammation of the pia-arachnoid, which may progress to congestion of adjacent tissues and destroy some nerve cells. The microorganism typically enters the central nervous system by way of blood; direct communication between cerebrospinal fluid (CSF) and the environment (trauma); along cranial or peripheral nerves; or through the mouth or nose. Microorganisms can reach a fetus through the intrauterine environment.

The invading organism triggers an inflammatory response in the meninges. In an attempt to ward off the invasion, neutrophils gather in the area and produce an exudate in the subarachnoid space, causing the CSF to thicken. The thickened CSF flows less readily around the brain and spinal cord, and it can block the arachnoid villi, causing hydrocephalus.

The exudate also:
- exacerbates the inflammatory response, increasing the pressure in the brain
- can extend to the cranial and peripheral nerves, triggering additional inflammation
- irritates the meninges, disrupting their cell membranes and causing edema.

The consequences are elevated intracranial pressure (ICP), engorged blood vessels, disrupted cerebral blood supply, possible thrombosis or rupture and, if ICP isn't reduced, cerebral infarction. Encephalitis may also ensue as a secondary infection of the brain tissue.

In aseptic meningitis, lymphocytes infiltrate the pia-arachnoid layers, but usually not as severely as in bacterial meningitis, and no exudate is formed. Thus, aseptic meningitis is self-limiting.

COMPLICATIONS
- Blindness
- Loss of speech
- Brain damage
- Deafness
- Paralysis

Signs and symptoms
- Fever, chills, and malaise
- Headache, vomiting and, rarely, papilledema
- Signs of meningeal irritation, including nuchal rigidity, positive Brudzinski's and Kernig's signs, exaggerated and symmetrical deep tendon reflexes, and opisthotonos
- Irritability, delirium, deep stupor, coma, and photophobia, diplopia, or other vision problems

Diagnostic test results
- Lumbar puncture shows elevated CSF pressure (from obstructed CSF outflow at the arachnoid villi), cloudy or milky-white CSF, high protein level, positive Gram stain and culture (unless a virus is responsible), and decreased glucose concentration.
- Cultures of blood, urine, and nose and throat secretions reveal the offending organism.
- Chest X-ray reveals pneumonitis or lung abscess, tubercular lesions, or granulomas secondary to a fungal infection.
- Sinus and skull X-rays identify cranial osteomyelitis or paranasal sinusitis as the underlying infectious process, or skull fracture as the mechanism for entrance of the microorganism.
- White blood cell count reveals leukocytosis.
- Computed tomography scan reveals hydrocephalus, cerebral hematoma, hemorrhage, or tumor.
- Electrocardiogram reveals sinus arrhythmia.

Treatment
- I.V. antibiotics for at least 2 weeks, followed by oral antibiotics selected by culture and sensitivity testing
- I.V. fluids
- Agents to control arrhythmias
- Mannitol
- Anticonvulsant (usually given I.V.) or a sedative
- Aspirin or acetaminophen

CLINICAL TIP
Health care workers should take droplet precautions (in addition to standard precautions) for meningitis caused by *H. influenzae* or *N. meningitidis,* until 24 hours after the start of effective therapy.

MENINGES AND CEREBROSPINAL FLUID FLOW

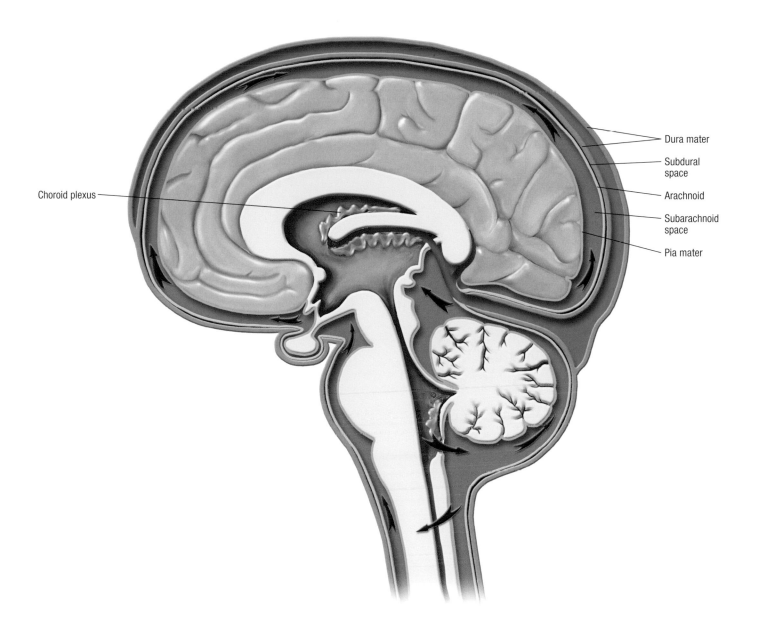

Choroid plexus

Dura mater

Subdural space

Arachnoid

Subarachnoid space

Pia mater

NORMAL MENINGES

Dura mater

Arachnoid

Pia mater

INFLAMMATION IN MENINGITIS

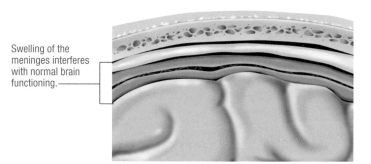

Swelling of the meninges interferes with normal brain functioning.

MULTIPLE SCLEROSIS

Multiple sclerosis (MS) causes demyelination of the white matter of the brain and spinal cord and damage to nerve fibers and their targets. Characterized by exacerbations and remissions, MS is a major cause of chronic disability in young adults and its prognosis varies. MS may progress rapidly, disabling the patient by early adulthood or causing death within months of onset. However, 70% of patients lead active, productive lives with prolonged remissions.

AGE ALERT
MS usually produces symptoms between ages 20 and 40 (the average age of onset is 27).

Types of MS include:
- *elapsing-remitting* — clear relapses (or acute attacks or exacerbations) with full recovery or partial recovery and lasting disability (The disease doesn't worsen between the attacks.)
- *primary progressive* — steady progression from the onset with minor recovery or plateaus (This form is uncommon and may involve different brain and spinal cord damage than other forms.)
- *secondary progressive* — begins as a pattern of clear-cut relapses and recovery (This form becomes steadily progressive and worsens between acute attacks.)
- *progressive relapsing* — steadily progressive from the onset, but also has clear acute attacks. (This form is rare.)

Causes
- Exact cause unknown

Possible causes
- Autoimmune response to a slow-acting or latent viral infection
- Environmental or genetic factors

Pathophysiology
Evidence suggests that activation of T lymphocytes against the myelin antigens, axons, and oligodendrocytes triggers an immunologic cascade. Recruitment of inflammatory cells and local release of lymphokines and cytokines results in injury to the myelin and the underlying axon. Axon demyelination and nerve fiber loss occur in patches throughout the central nervous system. The damaged myelin sheath can't conduct normally, and the partial loss or dispersion of the action potential causes neurologic dysfunction.

COMPLICATIONS
- Injuries from falls
- Urinary tract infections (UTIs)
- Constipation
- Joint contractures
- Pressure ulcers
- Rectal distention
- Pneumonia

Signs and symptoms
- Optic neuritis, diplopia, ophthalmoplegia, blurred vision, and nystagmus
- Sensory impairment, such as burning, pins and needles, and electrical sensations
- Fatigue (usually the most debilitating symptom)
- Weakness, paralysis ranging from monoplegia to quadriplegia, spasticity, hyperreflexia, intention tremor, and ataxia
- Incontinence, frequency, urgency, and frequent UTIs
- Involuntary evacuation or constipation
- Poorly articulated or scanning speech (syllables separated by pauses)
- Dysphagia

Diagnostic test results
Diagnosis of MS requires evidence of two or more neurologic attacks. These tests may also be useful:
- Magnetic resonance imaging reveals MS plaque or scarring.
- Lumbar puncture shows the elevation of certain immune system proteins (immunoglobulin [Ig] and IgG) and the presence of oligoclonal bands seen in 90% to 95% of people with MS.
- Evoked potential studies (visual, brain stem, auditory, and somatosensory) reveal slowed conduction of nerve impulses in most patients.
- Blood tests rule out other conditions.

Treatment
The aim of treatment is threefold: treat the acute exacerbation, treat the disease process, and treat the related signs and symptoms.
- I.V. methylprednisolone followed by oral therapy
- Interferon beta-1b and beta-1a or glatiramer
- Stretching and range-of-motion exercises, coupled with correct positioning, adaptive devices, and physical therapy
- Muscle relaxants, such as baclofen and tizanidine
- Frequent rest periods
- Natalizumab
- Speech and vision therapy
- Mitoxantrone

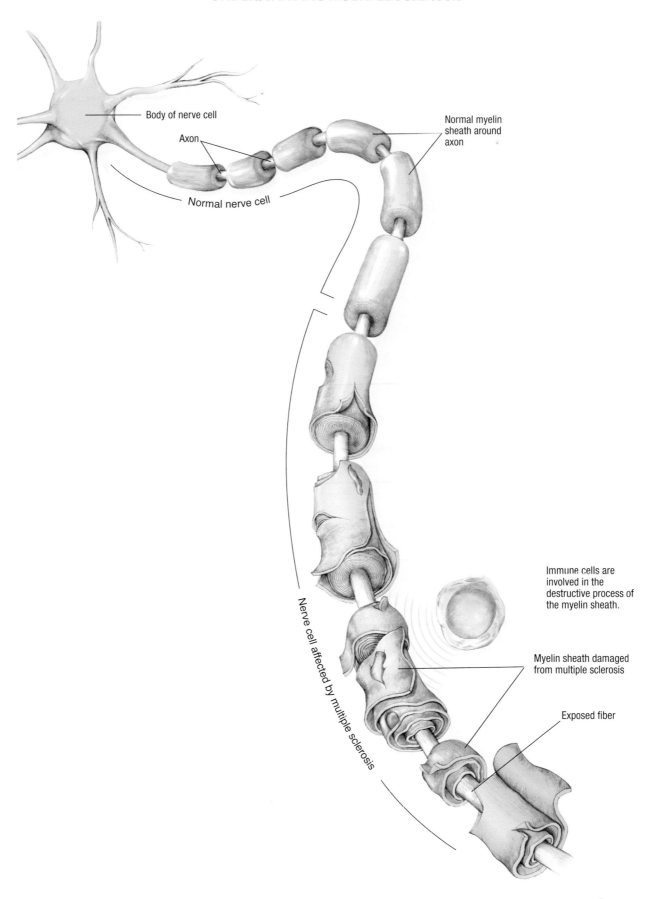

Body of nerve cell

Axon

Normal nerve cell

Normal myelin sheath around axon

Nerve cell affected by multiple sclerosis

Immune cells are involved in the destructive process of the myelin sheath.

Myelin sheath damaged from multiple sclerosis

Exposed fiber

MYASTHENIA GRAVIS

Myasthenia gravis is an autoimmune disorder that causes sporadic but progressive weakness and abnormal fatigability of striated (skeletal) muscles. Muscle weakness is exacerbated by continuing activity and repeated movement and is relieved by rest.

Myasthenia gravis follows an unpredictable course of periodic exacerbations and remissions. There's no known cure. Drug treatment has improved the prognosis and allows patients to lead relatively normal lives, except during exacerbations. When the disease involves the respiratory system, it may be life-threatening.

AGE ALERT
Women are most commonly affected in their 20s and 30s while men are usually affected in their 60s and 70s.

Causes
- Exact cause unknown

Possible causes
- Autoimmune response
- Ineffective acetylcholine release
- Inadequate muscle-fiber response to acetylcholine

Pathophysiology

Myasthenia gravis is an autoimmune disease of the neuromuscular junction resulting from the production of antibodies against the acetylcholine receptor protein of skeletal muscles. Musclelike (myoid) cells in the thymus gland bear surface acetylcholine receptors, and a break in immune regulation interferes with tolerance and initiates antibody production. The site of action is the postsynaptic membrane. The antibodies reduce the number of acetylcholine receptors available at each neuromuscular junction and thereby impair muscle depolarization necessary for movement.

Scientists believe the thymus gland may give incorrect instructions to developing immune cells, ultimately resulting in autoimmunity and the production of the acetylcholine receptor antibodies and thereby allowing for the attack on neuromuscular transmission.

COMPLICATIONS
- Respiratory distress
- Pneumonia
- Chewing and swallowing difficulties leading to choking and food aspiration

Signs and symptoms
- Weak eye closure, ptosis, and diplopia
- Skeletal muscle weakness and fatigue, increasing through the day but decreasing with rest (in the early stages, easy fatiga-

bility of certain muscles may appear with no other findings; later, it may be severe enough to cause paralysis)
- Progressive muscle weakness and accompanying loss of function depending on the muscle group affected; becoming more intense during menses and after emotional stress, prolonged exposure to sunlight or cold, or infections
- Blank, expressionless facial appearance and nasal vocal tones
- Frequent nasal regurgitation of fluids; difficulty chewing and swallowing
- Weak neck muscles (may become too weak to support the head without bobbing); patient must tilt head back to see
- Weak respiratory muscles; low tidal volume and vital capacity

CLINICAL TIP
Respiratory muscle weakness seen in myasthenic crisis may be severe enough to require emergency intubation and mechanical ventilation.

Diagnostic test results
- Tensilon test confirms diagnosis — temporarily improved muscle function within 30 to 60 seconds after I.V. injection of edrophonium or neostigmine and lasting up to 30 minutes.
- Electromyography with repeated neural stimulation shows progressive decrease in muscle-fiber contraction.
- Blood chemistry studies reveal elevated serum antiacetylcholine antibody titer.
- Chest X-ray reveals thymoma (in about 15% of patients).

Treatment
- Anticholinesterase drugs, such as neostigmine and pyridostigmine
- Immunosuppressant therapy with corticosteroids, azathioprine, cyclosporine, and cyclophosphamide used in a progressive fashion
- Immunoglobulin G during acute relapses or plasmapheresis in severe exacerbations
- Plasmapheresis
- Thymectomy
- Tracheotomy, positive-pressure ventilation, and vigorous suctioning
- Discontinuation of anticholinesterase drugs in myasthenic crisis until respiratory function improves

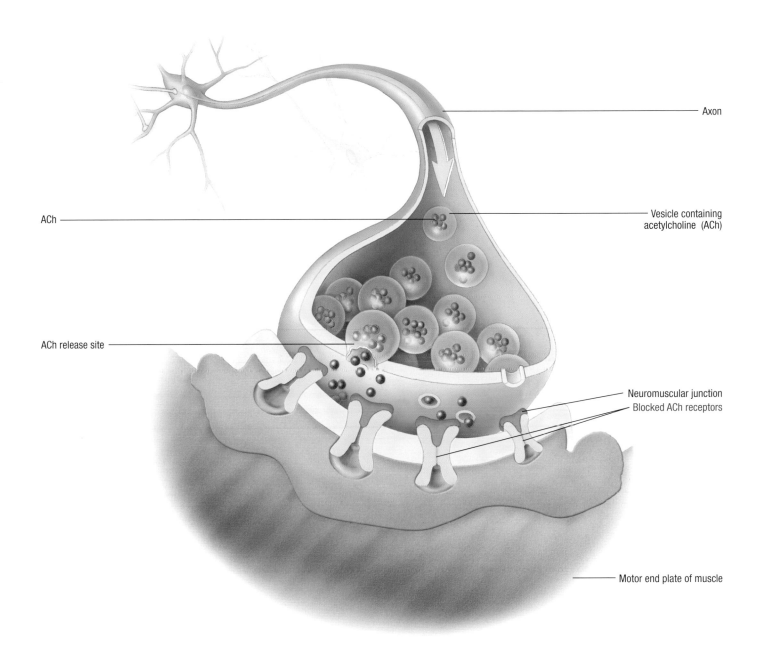

Axon

Vesicle containing
acetylcholine (ACh)

ACh

ACh release site

Neuromuscular junction
Blocked ACh receptors

Motor end plate of muscle

PARKINSON'S DISEASE

Parkinson's disease is a neurodegenerative disorder of the extrapyramidal system. It characteristically produces progressive muscle rigidity, akinesia, and involuntary tremor. Death may result from complications, such as aspiration pneumonia or other infection.

AGE ALERT

Parkinson's disease is one of the most common crippling diseases in the United States. It strikes 1 in every 100 people over age 60 and affects men more often than women.

Causes

Exact cause unknown

Possible contributing factors

- Advanced age
- Genetics
- Environment (rural residence with exposure to well water, herbicides, and pesticides)
- Industrial chemicals (such metals as manganese, iron, and steel alloys)

Pathophysiology

Parkinson's disease is a degenerative process involving the dopaminergic neurons in the substantia nigra (the area of the basal ganglia that produces and stores the neurotransmitter dopamine). This area plays an important role in the extrapyramidal system, which controls posture and coordination of voluntary motor movements.

Normally, stimulation of the basal ganglia results in refined motor movement because acetylcholine (excitatory) and dopamine (inhibitory) release is balanced. Degeneration of the dopaminergic neurons and loss of available dopamine lead to an excess of excitatory acetylcholine at the synapse and consequent rigidity, tremors, and bradykinesia. Other nondopaminergic neurons may be affected, possibly contributing to depression and the other nonmotor symptoms associated with this disease. Also, the basal ganglia are interconnected to the hypothalamus, potentially affecting autonomic and endocrine function as well.

Current research on the pathogenesis of Parkinson's disease focuses on damage to the substantia nigra from oxidative stress. Oxidative stress is believed to diminish brain iron content, impair mitochondrial function, inhibit antioxidant and protective systems, reduce glutathione secretion, and damage lipids, proteins, and deoxyribonucleic acid. Brain cells are less capable of repairing oxidative damage than are other tissues.

COMPLICATIONS

- Injury from falls
- Food aspiration
- Urinary tract infections
- Skin breakdown

Signs and symptoms

- Muscle rigidity, akinesia, and an insidious tremor beginning in the fingers (unilateral pill-roll tremor) that increases during stress or anxiety and decreases with purposeful movement and sleep
- Resistance to passive muscle stretching, which may be uniform (lead-pipe rigidity) or jerky (cogwheel rigidity)
- Akinesia causing difficulty walking (gait lacks normal parallel motion and may be retropulsive or propulsive)
- Loss of posture control
- Drooling and excessive sweating
- Masklike facial expression
- Dysarthria, dysphagia, or both
- Oculogyric crises or blepharospasm
- Decreased motility of GI and genitourinary smooth muscle
- Orthostatic hypotension
- Oily skin

Diagnostic test results

Generally, diagnostic tests are of little value in identifying Parkinson's disease. Diagnosis is based on the patient's age and history and on the characteristic clinical picture. However, urinalysis may support the diagnosis by revealing decreased dopamine levels.

A conclusive diagnosis is possible only after ruling out other causes of tremor, involutional depression, cerebral arteriosclerosis, intracranial tumors, Wilson's disease, or phenothiazine or other drug toxicity.

Treatment

- Levodopa, a dopamine replacement most effective during early stages and given in increasing doses until symptoms are relieved or adverse effects appear
- Drugs that enhance the therapeutic effect of levodopa— anticholinergics such as trihexyphenidyl; antihistamines such as diphenhydramine; amantidine, an antiviral agent; selegiline, an enzyme-inhibiting agent
- Deep brain stimulation surgery
- Physical therapy, including active and passive range-of-motion exercises, routine daily activities, walking, baths, and massage

NEUROTRANSMITTER ACTION IN PARKINSON'S DISEASE

Brain — Coronal section

Motor cortex
(gray matter)

Thalamus

Striatum

Subthalamic
nucleus

Globus pallidus
interna

Optic nerve

Substantia
nigra

Cerebellum

Spinal cord

Brain — Lateral view

Motor cortex

Parietal lobe

Frontal lobe

Occipital lobe

Temporal lobe

Cerebellum

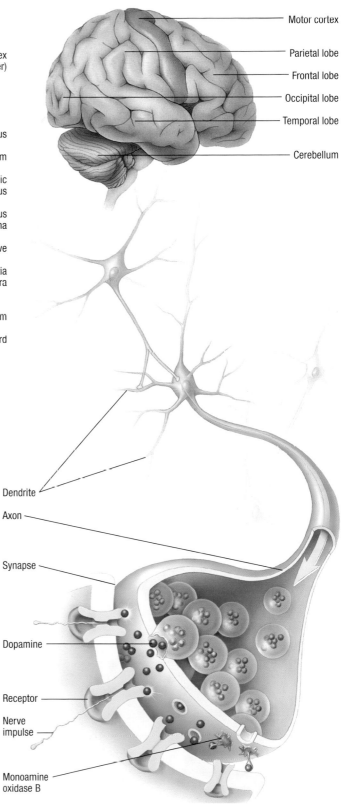

Dendrite

Axon

Synapse

Dopamine

Receptor

Nerve
impulse

Monoamine
oxidase B

Dopamine levels

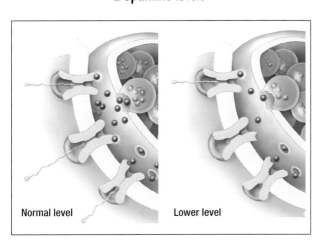

Normal level

Lower level

SPINA BIFIDA

Spina bifida and other neural tube defects (NTDs) are serious birth defects that involve the spine and spinal cord. In spina bifida, the neural tube fails to close at approximately 28 days after conception.

Causes

Exact cause and most of the specific environmental triggers unknown

Possible causes

- Maternal folic acid deficiency
- Fetal exposure to a teratogen such as valproic acid
- Multiple malformation syndrome (for example, chromosomal abnormalities such as trisomy 18 or 13 syndrome)
- Isolated NTDs (not due to a specific teratogen or associated with other malformations) believed to be caused by a combination of genetic and environmental factors

Pathophysiology

Spina bifida occulta is the most common and least severe spinal cord defect. It's characterized by incomplete closure of one or more vertebrae without protrusion of the spinal cord or meninges.

However, in more severe forms of spina bifida, the spinal contents protrude in an external sac or cystic lesion (spina bifida cystica). *Spina bifida cystica* has two forms: *myelomeningocele (meningomyelocele)* and *meningocele*. In myelomeningocele, the external sac contains meninges, cerebrospinal fluid (CSF), and a portion of the spinal cord or nerve roots distal to the conus medullaris. When the spinal nerve roots end at the sac, motor and sensory function below the sac is abolished. Arnold-Chiari syndrome is a form of meningomyelocele in which part of the brain protrudes into the spinal canal. Meningocele, in which the sac contains only meninges and CSF, is less severe and may not produce symptoms.

COMPLICATIONS
- Hydrocephalus
- Infection
- Paralysis
- Physical and mental disabilities

Signs and symptoms

Spina bifida occulta

- Depression or dimple, tuft of hair, soft fatty deposits, port-wine nevi, or a combination of these abnormalities on the skin over the spinal defect
- Occasionally associated with foot weakness or bowel and bladder disturbances

Meningocele

- Saclike structure protrudes over the spine
- Seldom causes neurologic deficit

Myelomeningocele (meningomyelocele)

- Saclike protrusion containing nerve tissue
- Depending on the level of the defect, causes permanent neurologic dysfunction

Associated disorders

- Trophic skin disturbances (ulcerations, cyanosis), clubfoot, knee contractures, curvature of the spine, hydrocephalus (in about 90% of patients) and, possibly, mental retardation

Diagnostic test results

- Amniocentesis detects elevated alpha fetoprotein (AFP) levels in amniotic fluid, which indicates the presence of an open NTD.
- Fetal karyotype detects chromosomal abnormalities.
- Maternal serum AFP screening is used in combination with other serum markers, such as human chorionic gonadotropin (HCG), free beta-HCG, or unconjugated estriol (for patients with a lower risk of NTDs and those who will be under age 34½ at the time of delivery) to estimate a fetus's risk of NTD as well as possible increased risk of perinatal complications, such as premature rupture of the membranes, abruptio placentae, or fetal death.
- Ultrasound is performed when increased risk of open NTD exists, based on family history or abnormal serum screening results (not conclusive for open NTDs or ventral wall defects).

If the NTD isn't diagnosed before birth, other tests are used to make the diagnosis, including:
- palpation and spinal X-ray for spina bifida occulta
- myelography to differentiate spina bifida occulta from other spinal abnormalities, especially spinal cord tumors
- transillumination of the protruding sac to distinguish between myelomeningocele (typically doesn't transilluminate) and meningocele (typically transilluminates)
- pinprick examination of the legs and trunk to show the level of sensory and motor involvement in myelomeningocele
- skull X-rays, cephalic measurements, and computed tomography scan to demonstrate associated hydrocephalus.

Treatment

- *Spina bifida occulta:* usually no treatment
- *Meningocele:* surgical closure of protruding sac
- *Myelomeningocele:* repair of the sac (doesn't reverse neurologic defects); shunt to relieve hydrocephalus if needed; supportive measures to promote independence and prevent further complications

Spina bifida occulta

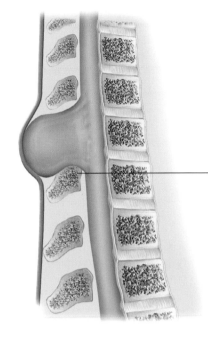

Vertebrae are incompletely fused; no external sac is present.

Meningocele

External sac contains meninges and cerebrospinal fluid (CSF).

Myelomeningocele

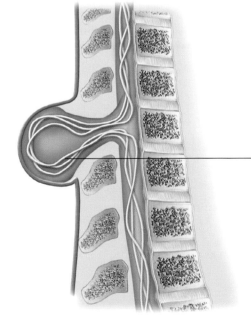

External sac contains meninges,CSF, peripheral nerves, and spinal cord tissue.

SPINAL CORD INJURY

Spinal injuries include fractures, contusions, and compressions of the vertebral column, usually as the result of trauma to the head or neck. The real danger lies in spinal cord damage — cutting, pulling, twisting, or compression. Damage may involve the entire spinal cord or be restricted to one-half, and it can occur at any level. Fractures of the C5, C6, C7, T12, and L1 vertebrae are most common.

Causes

Traumatic
- Motor vehicle accidents
- Falls
- Sports injuries or diving into shallow water
- Gunshot or stab wounds
- Lifting heavy objects

Nontraumatic
- Hyperparathyroidism
- Neoplastic lesions

Pathophysiology

Like head trauma, spinal cord trauma results from acceleration, deceleration, or other deforming forces usually applied from a distance.

Mechanisms triggered by spinal cord trauma include:
- *hyperextension* — acceleration-deceleration forces and sudden reduction in the anteroposterior diameter of the spinal cord
- *hyperflexion* — sudden and excessive force, propelling the neck forward or causing an exaggerated movement to one side
- *vertical compression* — upward or downward force along the vertical axis
- *rotation and shearing* — twisting.

Injury causes microscopic hemorrhages in the gray matter and pia-arachnoid. The hemorrhages gradually increase in size until all of the gray matter is filled with blood, which causes necrosis. From the gray matter, the blood enters the white matter, where it impedes the circulation within the spinal cord. Ensuing edema causes compression and decreases the blood supply. The edema and hemorrhage are greatest at the injury site and approximately two segments above and below it. The edema temporarily adds to the patient's dysfunction by increasing pressure and compressing the nerves. Edema near the C3 to C5 vertebrae may interfere with phrenic nerve-impulse transmission to the diaphragm and inhibit respiratory function.

In the white matter, circulation usually returns to normal in about 24 hours. However, in the gray matter, an inflammatory reaction prevents restoration of circulation. Phagocytes appear at the site within 36 to 48 hours after the injury, macrophages engulf degenerating axons, and collagen replaces the normal tissue. Scarring and meningeal thickening leave the nerves in the area blocked or tangled.

COMPLICATIONS
- Pressure ulcers
- Pulmonary embolism
- Autonomic dysreflexia
- Spinal shock
- Neurogenic shock
- Sexual dysfunction
- Deep vein thrombosis

Signs and symptoms

- Muscle spasm and back pain that worsens with movement:
- – In cervical fractures, pain may cause point tenderness.
- – In dorsal and lumbar fractures, pain may radiate to other body areas such as the legs.
- Mild paresthesia to quadriplegia and shock, if the injury damages the spinal cord (in milder injury, such symptoms may be delayed several days or weeks)

Specific to injury type or degree
- Loss of motor function; muscle flaccidity
- Loss of reflexes and sensory function below the level of injury
- Bladder and bowel atony
- Loss of perspiration below the level of injury
- Respiratory impairment

Diagnostic test results

- Spinal X-rays, the most important diagnostic measure, detect the fracture.
- Thorough neurologic evaluation locates the level of injury and detects cord damage.
- Lumbar puncture shows increased cerebrospinal fluid pressure from a lesion or trauma in spinal compression.
- Computed tomography scan or magnetic resonance imaging reveals spinal cord edema and compression and may reveal a spinal mass.

Treatment

- Immediate immobilization to stabilize the spine and prevent cord damage (primary treatment), including the use of sandbags on both sides of the patient's head, a hard cervical collar, or skeletal traction with skull tongs or a halo device for cervical spine injuries
- High doses of methylprednisolone
- Bed rest on firm support (such as a bed board), analgesics, and muscle relaxants
- Plaster cast or a turning frame
- Laminectomy and spinal fusion
- Neurosurgery
- Rehabilitation
- Medications, including analgesics, anticoagulants, antiulcer agents, antidepressants, anticholinergics, antispasmodics, and laxatives

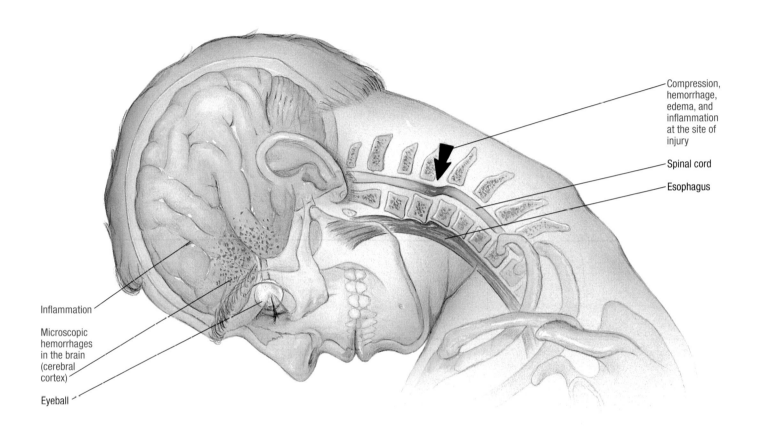

Compression, hemorrhage, edema, and inflammation at the site of injury

Spinal cord

Esophagus

Inflammation

Microscopic hemorrhages in the brain (cerebral cortex)

Eyeball

STROKE

Astroke is a sudden impairment of cerebral circulation in one or more blood vessels. Stroke interrupts or diminishes oxygen supply and commonly causes serious damage or necrosis in the brain tissues.

Causes
- Thrombosis of the cerebral arteries supplying the brain or of the intracranial vessels, occluding blood flow
- Embolism from thrombus outside the brain, such as in the heart, aorta, or common carotid artery
- Hemorrhage from an intracranial artery or vein, such as from hypertension, ruptured aneurysm, arteriovenous malformation trauma, hemorrhagic disorder, or septic embolism

Pathophysiology
Regardless of the cause, the underlying event is deprivation of oxygen and nutrients. Normally, if the arteries become blocked, autoregulatory mechanisms help maintain cerebral circulation until collateral circulation develops to deliver blood to the affected area. If the compensatory mechanisms become overworked, or if cerebral blood flow remains impaired for more than a few minutes, oxygen deprivation leads to infarction of brain tissue.

A thrombotic or embolic stroke causes ischemia. Some of the neurons served by the occluded vessel die from lack of oxygen and nutrients, resulting in cerebral infarction. Injury to surrounding cells disrupts metabolism and leads to changes in ionic transport, localized acidosis, and free radical formation. Calcium, sodium, and water accumulate in injured cells, and excitatory neurotransmitters are released. Consequent continued cellular injury and swelling may cause further damage.

When hemorrhage is the cause of stroke, impaired cerebral perfusion causes infarction, and the blood itself acts as a space-occupying mass. The brain's regulatory mechanisms attempt to maintain equilibrium by increasing blood pressure to maintain cerebral perfusion pressure. The increased intracranial pressure (ICP) forces cerebrospinal fluid out, thus restoring balance. If the hemorrhage is small, this may be enough to keep the patient alive with only minimal neurologic deficits. However, if bleeding is heavy, ICP increases rapidly and perfusion stops. Even if the pressure returns to normal, many brain cells die.

COMPLICATIONS
- Paralysis or loss of muscle movement
- Difficulty swallowing or talking
- Memory loss or trouble understanding
- Pain
- Pressure ulcers
- Infection

Signs and symptoms
The clinical features of stroke vary according to the affected artery and the region of the brain it supplies, the severity of damage, and the extent of collateral circulation developed. A stroke in one hemisphere causes signs and symptoms on the opposite side of the body. A stroke that damages cranial nerves affects structures on the same side. Symptoms include:
- hemiparesis
- hemisensory loss
- altered level of consciousness
- headache, dizziness, and anxiety
- visual field defects
- ataxia, vertigo, and incoordination
- dysphasia (expressive and receptive)
- dysarthria
- amaurosis fugax
- dysphagia.

Diagnostic test results
- Computed tomography scan identifies an ischemic stroke within the first 72 hours of symptom onset and evidence of a hemorrhagic stroke (lesions larger than 1 cm) immediately.
- Magnetic resonance imaging assists in identifying areas of ischemia or infarction and cerebral swelling.
- Arteriography reveals disruption of the cerebral circulation by occlusion, such as stenosis or acute thrombus, or by hemorrhage.
- Carotid duplex scan and transcranial Doppler identify the degree of stenosis.
- Echocardiography reveals thrombi within the atrium or ventricle.

Treatment
Ischemic stroke
- Thrombolytic therapy with tissue plasminogen activator within 3 hours after onset of symptoms
- Aspirin, warfarin, heparin
- Carotid endarterectomy
- Angioplasty and stents

Hemorrhagic stroke
- Aneurysm clipping
- Coiling (aneurysm embolization)

ISCHEMIC STROKE

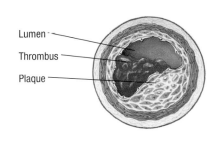

Lumen
Thrombus
Plaque

Common sites of plaque formation, embolism, and infarction

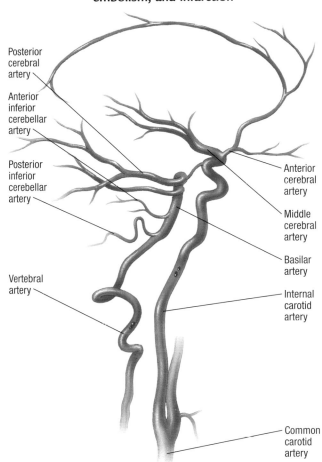

Posterior cerebral artery

Anterior inferior cerebellar artery

Posterior inferior cerebellar artery

Vertebral artery

Anterior cerebral artery

Middle cerebral artery

Basilar artery

Internal carotid artery

Common carotid artery

Common sites of cardiac thrombosis

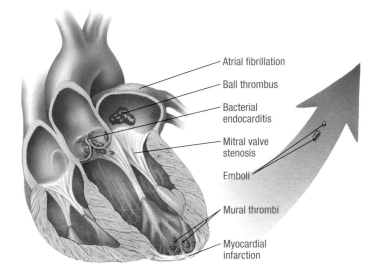

Atrial fibrillation

Ball thrombus

Bacterial endocarditis

Mitral valve stenosis

Emboli

Mural thrombi

Myocardial infarction

HEMORRHAGIC STROKE

Common sites of cerebral hemorrhage

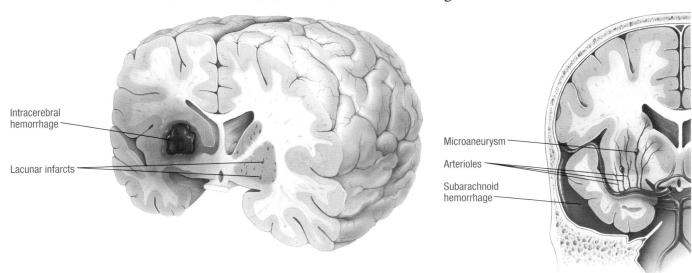

Intracerebral hemorrhage

Lacunar infarcts

Microaneurysm

Arterioles

Subarachnoid hemorrhage

WEST NILE VIRUS

West Nile is a virus transmitted by mosquitos that causes an illness that can range from mild to severe. Mild, flu-like illness is commonly called *West Nile fever*. In its most severe form, West Nile virus can infect the central nervous system and cause meningitis, encephalitis, and death.

Causes

Spreads when a mosquito bites an infected bird and then bites a person

Risk factors for developing a severe form of the disease

- Conditions that suppress the immune system, such as recent chemotherapy, recent organ transplantation, or human immunodeficiency virus
- Pregnancy
- Older age

The disease may also be spread through blood transfusions and organ transplantation. It's also possible for an infected mother to transmit the virus to her infant through breast milk.

Pathophysiology

West Nile virus is a type of organism called a flavivirus and is similar to many other mosquito-borne viruses. After infection, if encephalitis ensues, severe inflammation of the brain occurs. Intense lymphocytic infiltration of brain tissues and the leptomeninges causes cerebral edema, degeneration of the brain's ganglion cells, and diffuse nerve cell destruction.

COMPLICATIONS

- Coma
- Tremors
- Seizures
- Paralysis
- Death (rare)

Signs and symptoms

West Nile fever

- Fever
- Headache
- Back pain
- Muscle aches
- Lack of appetite
- Sore throat
- Nausea and vomiting
- Maculopapular or morbilliform rash on the neck
- Abdominal pain
- Diarrhea

Severe infection

- Fever
- Weakness
- Stiff neck
- Change in mental status
- Loss of consciousness

In addition, a patient with encephalitis may have paresis or paralysis, cranial nerve deficits, sensory deficits, abnormal reflexes, seizures, and involuntary jerks.

Diagnostic test results

- Serology reveals the presence of antibodies against West Nile virus in cerebrospinal fluid (CSF) or serum.
- Complete blood count shows a normal or elevated white blood cell count (WBC).
- Lumbar puncture and CSF testing show elevated WBC count (especially lymphocytes) and elevated protein level.
- Magnetic resonance imaging of the head shows evidence of inflammation.

Treatment

No specific treatment

Supportive treatment

- I.V. fluids
- Airway management
- Respiratory support
- Prevention of secondary infections
- Analgesics

Normal brain

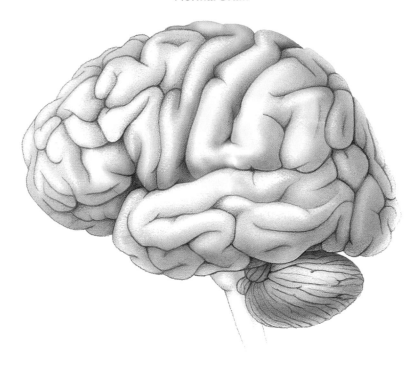

Edematous brain

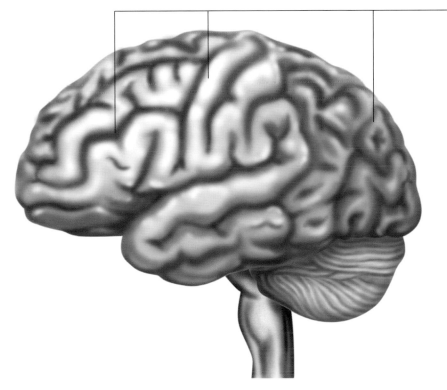

Intense lymphocytic infiltration causes cerebral edema.

ACHALASIA

Achalasia is a disease of the muscle of the esophagus. In achalasia, the lower esophageal sphincter (LES) "fails to relax" and open to allow food to pass into the stomach. As a result, patients with achalasia have difficulty swallowing food.

Causes

The exact cause is unknown, but theories include:
- heredity
- infection
- autoimmune disease.

Pathophysiology

In achalasia, the LES doesn't open properly to allow food to pass into the stomach and, in at least half of the patients with achalasia, the lower sphincter resting pressure also is abnormally high. The muscle of the lower half of the esophagus doesn't contract normally, and peristaltic waves don't occur. This results in food and saliva not being propelled down the esophagus and into the stomach.

Some patients with achalasia have high-pressure waves in the lower esophageal body following swallowing, but the waves aren't effective in pushing food into the stomach. This type of achalasia is called *vigorous achalasia*. These abnormalities of the lower sphincter and esophageal body are responsible for food sticking in the esophagus.

Early in achalasia, inflammation occurs in the muscle of the lower esophagus, especially around the nerves. As the disease progresses, the nerves (particularly the nerves that cause the LES to relax) begin to degenerate and ultimately disappear. This damage to the nerves may cause muscle cells to begin to degenerate as well. These changes result in a lower sphincter that can't relax and muscle in the lower esophageal body that can't support peristaltic waves. With time, the body of the esophagus stretches and becomes dilated.

COMPLICATIONS
- Aspiration
- Pneumonia
- Esophagitis
- Esophageal cancer

Signs and symptoms
- Consistent (occurring with every meal) dysphagia (with solids and liquids)
- Heavy sensation in the chest after eating
- Chest pain
- Regurgitation
- Weight loss

Diagnostic test results
- Video-esophagram shows esophageal dilation with a characteristic tapered narrowing of the lower end, sometimes likened to a "bird's beak." The barium also stays in the esophagus longer than normal before passing into the stomach.
- Esophageal manometry demonstrates the failure of the muscle of the esophageal body to contract with swallowing and the failure of the LES to relax.
- Endoscopy reveals high pressure in the LES, a dilated esophagus, and a lack of peristaltic waves. Endoscopy also excludes esophageal cancer.

Treatment
- Nitrates, such as isosorbide dinitrate, and calcium channel blockers, such as nifedipine and verapamil, to relax the LES
- Dilation of the LES
- Esophagomyotomy
- Endoscopic injection of botulinum toxin

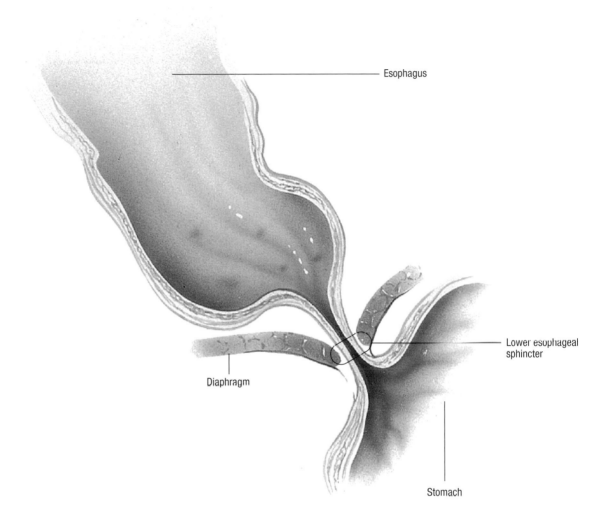

Esophagus

Lower esophageal sphincter

Diaphragm

Stomach

APPENDICITIS

The most common major surgical disease, appendicitis is inflammation and obstruction of the vermiform appendix. Since the advent of antibiotics, the incidence and the death rate of appendicitis have declined; if untreated, this disease is invariably fatal.

AGE ALERT
Appendicitis may occur at any age but the majority of cases occur between ages 11 and 20. It affects both sexes equally; however, between puberty and age 25, it's more prevalent in men.

Causes
- Mucosal ulceration
- Fecal mass (fecalith)
- Stricture
- Barium ingestion
- Viral infection
- Neoplasm
- Foreign body

Pathophysiology
Mucosal ulceration triggers inflammation, which temporarily obstructs the appendix. The obstruction blocks mucus outflow. Pressure in the now distended appendix increases, and the appendix contracts. Bacteria multiply, and inflammation and pressure continue to increase, restricting blood flow to the organ and causing severe abdominal pain.

Inflammation may lead to infection, clotting, and tissue decay.

COMPLICATIONS
- Rupture or perforation of the appendix
- Peritonitis
- Appendiceal abscess
- Pyelophlebitis

Signs and symptoms
Appendicitis
- Abdominal pain, which may become localized to the lower right quadrant (McBurney's point)

CLINICAL TIP
If a line is drawn from the umbilicus to the right superior iliac crest and divided into thirds, McBurney's point is two-thirds of the line from the umbilicus.

- Rebound tenderness
- Anorexia after the onset of pain
- Nausea or vomiting
- Low-grade fever

Rupture
- Pain
- Tenderness
- Spasm, followed by a brief cessation of abdominal pain

Diagnostic test results
- White blood cell count is moderately elevated with increased immature cells.
- Abdominal or transvaginal ultrasound shows inflammation of the appendix.
- Barium enema reveals a nonfilling appendix.
- Abdominal computed tomography scan shows perforation or abscess.

Treatment
- Nothing by mouth; parenteral fluids and electrolytes
- High Fowler's position
- Nasogastric intubation
- Appendectomy
- Antibiotics

Small and large intestines

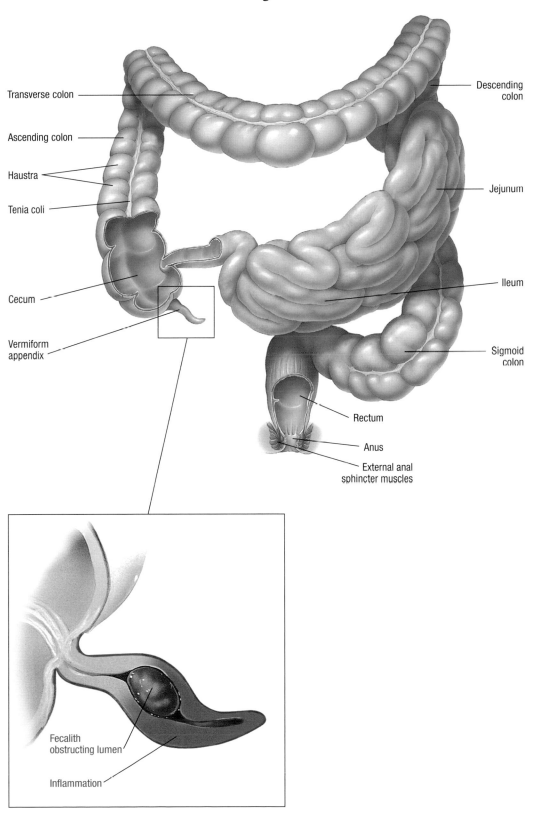

Transverse colon

Ascending colon

Haustra

Tenia coli

Cecum

Vermiform appendix

Descending colon

Jejunum

Ileum

Sigmoid colon

Rectum

Anus

External anal sphincter muscles

Fecalith obstructing lumen

Inflammation

CHOLECYSTITIS

Cholecystitis — acute or chronic inflammation causing painful distention of the gallbladder — is usually associated with a gallstone impacted in the cystic duct. Cholecystitis accounts for 10% to 25% of all gallbladder surgery. The acute form is most common among middle-aged women; the chronic form, among elderly people. The prognosis is good with treatment.

Causes
- Gallstones (the most common cause)
- Poor or absent blood flow to the gallbladder
- Abnormal metabolism of cholesterol and bile salts

Pathophysiology
In acute cholecystitis, inflammation of the gallbladder wall usually develops after a gallstone lodges in the cystic duct. Gallstones typically develop when metabolism of cholesterol and bile salts is abnormal. The liver usually makes bile continuously, and the gallbladder stores it until it's needed to help digest fat. Changes in the composition of bile may cause gallstones to form.

When gallstones block bile flow, the gallbladder becomes inflamed and distended. Growth of bacteria, usually *Escherichia coli,* may contribute to the inflammation and abscess formation or empyema.

Edema of the gallbladder (and sometimes the cystic duct) obstructs flow of bile, which chemically irritates the gallbladder. Cells in the gallbladder wall may become oxygen starved and die as the distended organ presses on vessels and impairs blood flow. The dead cells slough off, and an exudate covers ulcerated areas, causing the gallbladder to adhere to surrounding structures.

COMPLICATIONS
- Gangrene
- Perforation
- Peritonitis
- Fistula formation
- Pancreatitis

Signs and symptoms
- Acute abdominal pain in the right upper quadrant that may radiate to the back, between the shoulders, or to the front of the chest; typically occurs after a fatty meal
- Colic
- Nausea and vomiting
- Chills, low-grade fever
- Jaundice

Diagnostic test results
- X-ray reveals gallstones if they contain enough calcium to be radiopaque; also helps disclose porcelain gallbladder (hard, brittle gallbladder due to calcium deposited in wall), limy bile, and gallstone ileus.
- Computed tomography scan or magnetic resonance imaging show calcified gallbladder and the presence of stones.
- Ultrasonography detects gallstones as small as 2 mm and distinguishes between obstructive and nonobstructive jaundice.
- Technetium scan reveals cystic duct obstruction and acute or chronic cholecystitis if ultrasound doesn't visualize the gallbladder.
- Percutaneous transhepatic cholangiography supports the diagnosis of obstructive jaundice and reveals calculi in the ducts.
- Blood chemistry reveals elevated levels of serum alkaline phosphate, lactate dehydrogenase, aspartate aminotransferase, and total bilirubin; serum amylase level slightly elevated; and icteric index elevated.
- Blood studies reveal slightly elevated white blood cell counts during cholecystitis attack.

Treatment
- Cholecystectomy
- Choledochostomy
- Percutaneous transhepatic cholecystostomy
- Endoscopic retrograde cholangiopancreatography
- Lithotripsy
- Oral chenodeoxycholic acid or ursodeoxycholic acid
- Low-fat diet
- Vitamin K
- Antibiotics
- Nasogastric intubation

Liver and gallbladder

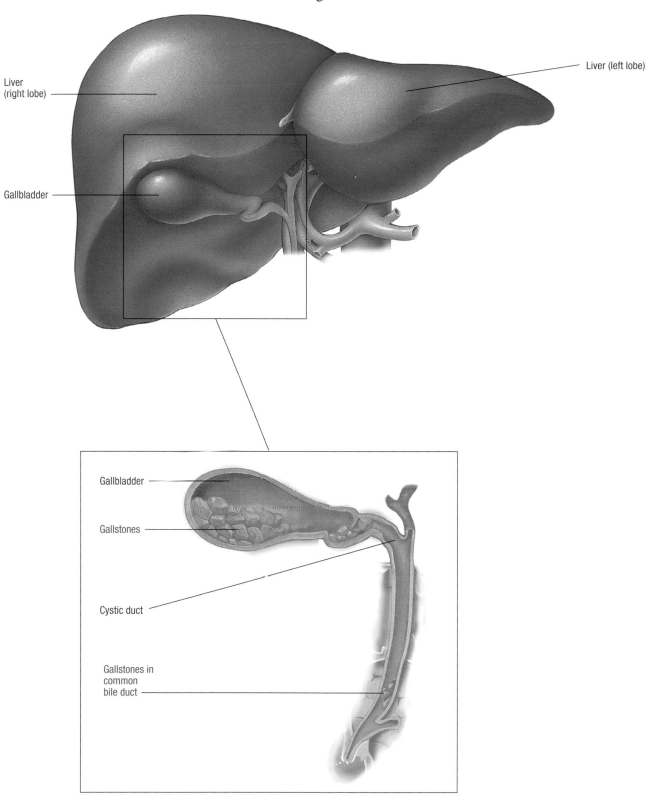

Liver (left lobe)

Liver
(right lobe)

Gallbladder

Gallbladder

Gallstones

Cystic duct

Gallstones in
common
bile duct

CIRRHOSIS

Cirrhosis is a chronic disease characterized by diffuse destruction and fibrotic regeneration of hepatic cells. Mortality is high; many patients die within 5 years of onset. As cirrhosis progresses, complications may occur; these include ascites, portal hypertension, jaundice, coagulopathy, hepatic encephalopathy, bleeding, esophageal varices, acute GI bleeding, liver failure, and renal failure.

AGE ALERT
Cirrhosis is especially prevalent among malnourished persons over age 50 with chronic alcoholism; it's also twice as common in men as in women.

Causes
- Hepatitis
- Alcoholism
- Malnutrition
- Autoimmune disease, such as sarcoidosis or chronic inflammatory bowel disease
- Diseases of the biliary tree
- Sclerosing cholangitis
- Wilson's disease
- Alpha$_1$ antitrypsin deficiency
- Hemochromatosis
- Hepatic vein obstruction
- Right-sided heart failure

Pathophysiology
The initial event in cirrhosis is hepatic scarring or fibrosis. The scar begins as an increase in extracellular matrix components — fibrin-forming collagens, proteoglycans, fibronectin, and hyaluronic acid. Hepatocyte function is eventually impaired as the matrix changes. Fat-storing cells are believed to be the source of the extracellular changes. Contraction of these cells may also contribute to disruption of the lobular architecture and obstruction of the flow of blood or bile. Cellular changes producing bands of scar tissue also disrupt the lobular structure.

COMPLICATIONS
- Portal hypertension
- Esophageal varices
- Ascites
- Hepatic encephalopathy
- Liver failure
- Death

Signs and symptoms
Early stage
- Anorexia; nausea and vomiting; diarrhea
- Dull abdominal ache

Late stage
- Respiratory — pleural effusion, limited thoracic expansion, impaired gas exchange
- Central nervous system — progressive signs or symptoms of hepatic encephalopathy, including lethargy, extreme obtundation, coma
- Hematologic — bleeding tendency, anemia, splenomegaly, portal hypertension
- Endocrine — testicular atrophy, menstrual irregularities, gynecomastia, loss of chest and axillary hair
- Skin — severe pruritus, extreme dryness and poor tissue turgor, spider angiomas, palmar erythema
- Hepatic — jaundice, hepatomegaly, ascites and edema of the legs, hepatorenal syndrome
- Miscellaneous — musty breath, enlarged superficial abdominal veins, pain in the right upper abdominal quadrant that worsens when patient sits up or leans forward, temperature of 101° to 103° F (38° to 39° C)
- Hemorrhage from esophageal varices

Diagnostic test results
- Liver biopsy reveals tissue destruction and fibrosis.
- Abdominal X-ray shows enlarged liver, cysts, or gas within the biliary tract or liver, liver calcification, and massive fluid accumulation (ascites).
- Computed tomography and liver scans show liver size, abnormal masses, and hepatic blood flow and obstruction.
- Esophagogastroduodenoscopy reveals bleeding esophageal varices, stomach irritation or ulceration, or duodenal bleeding and irritation.
- Blood studies reveal elevated levels of liver enzymes, total serum bilirubin, and indirect bilirubin; decreased levels of total serum albumin and protein; prolonged prothrombin time; decreased hemoglobin level, hematocrit, and serum electrolytes; and deficiency of vitamins A, C, and K.
- Urine studies show increased bilirubin and urobilirubinogen level.
- Fecal studies show decreased fecal urobilirubinogen level.

Treatment
- Vitamins and nutritional supplements
- Lactulose
- Beta-adrenergic blockers to treat portal hypertension
- Octreotide and other vasoconstrictors
- Endoscopic variceal ligation
- Surgical shunt placement
- Sclerosing agents
- Insertion of portosystemic shunts
- Liver transplantation
- Esophageal balloon tamponade

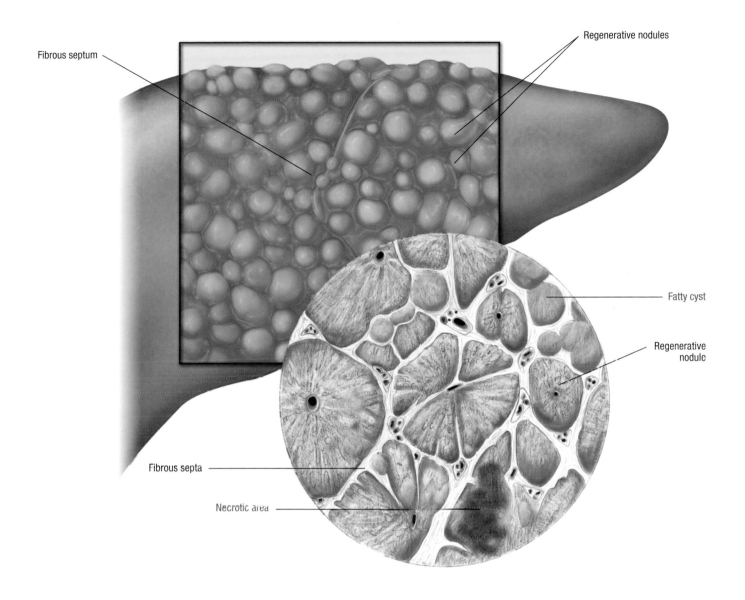

Fibrous septum

Regenerative nodules

Fatty cyst

Regenerative nodule

Fibrous septa

Necrotic area

COLONIC POLYPS

A polyp is a small tumorlike growth that projects from a mucous membrane surface. Types of polyps include common polypoid adenomas, villous adenomas, hereditary polyposis, focal polypoid hyperplasia, and juvenile polyps (hamartomas). Most rectal polyps are benign; however, villous and hereditary polyps tend to become malignant. Indeed, a striking feature of familial polyposis is its strong association with rectosigmoid adenocarcinoma.

AGE ALERT
Juvenile polyps, usually occurring among children under age 10, are characterized by rectal bleeding. Villous adenomas are most prevalent in men over age 55; common polypoid adenomas, in white women between ages 45 and 60. Incidence of nonjuvenile polyps rises after age 70 in both sexes.

Causes

Unknown
Predisposing factors
- Heredity
- Age
- Infection
- High-fat diet
- Sedentary lifestyle

Pathophysiology

Colonic polyps are masses of tissue resulting from unrestrained cell growth in the upper epithelium that rise above the mucosal membrane and protrude into the GI tract.

Polyps may be described by their appearance: pedunculated (attached by a stalk to the intestinal wall) or sessile (attached to the wall with a broad base and no stalk).

COMPLICATIONS
- Slow bleeding (can cause anemia)
- Bowel obstruction
- Gross rectal bleeding
- Intussusception
- Colorectal cancer

Signs and symptoms

- Usually asymptomatic; discovered incidentally during a digital examination or rectosigmoidoscopy
- Rectal bleeding (high rectal polyps leave a streak of blood on the stool, whereas low rectal polyps bleed freely)
- Painful defecation
- Diarrhea

CLINICAL TIP
Although most are asymptomatic, polyps may cause symptoms by virtue of their protrusion into the bowel lumen. They may bleed, cause abdominal pain, or actually obstruct the intestine.

Diagnostic test results

- Barium enema identifies polyps high in the colon.
- Fecal occult blood test is positive.
- Blood studies reveal decreased hemoglobin level and hematocrit.
- Proctosigmoidoscopy or colonoscopy and rectal biopsy confirm the presence of the polyps.
- Serum analysis reveals electrolyte imbalances (villous adenomas).

Treatment

Common polypoid adenomas
- Less than 1 cm in size — polypectomy, commonly by fulguration during endoscopy
- Over 4 cm — abdominoperineal resection or low anterior resection

Invasive villous adenomas
- Abdominoperineal resection
- Low anterior resection

Focal polypoid hyperplasia
- Obliterated by biopsy

Hereditary polyps
- Total abdominoperineal resection with permanent ileostomy
- Subtotal colectomy with ileoproctostomy
- Ileoanal anastomosis

Juvenile polyps
- Often autoamputate
- Snare removal during colonoscopy

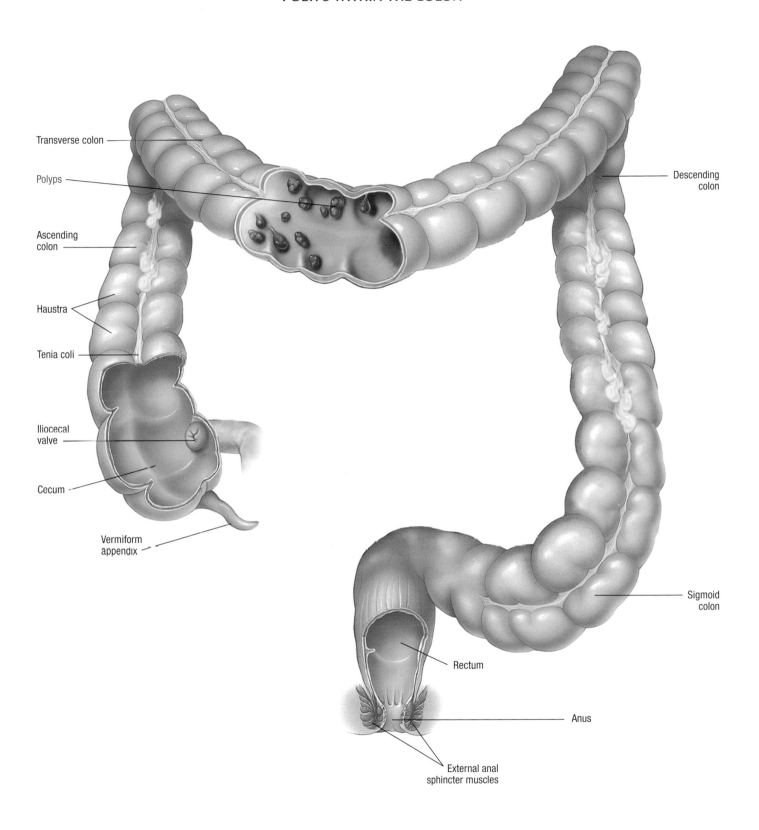

Transverse colon

Polyps

Ascending
colon

Haustra

Tenia coli

Iliocecal
valve

Cecum

Vermiform
appendix

Descending
colon

Sigmoid
colon

Rectum

Anus

External anal
sphincter muscles

COLORECTAL CANCER

Colorectal cancer is the second most common visceral malignant neoplasm in the United States and Europe. It tends to progress slowly and remains localized for a long time. Incidence is equally distributed between men and women. It's potentially curable in about 90% of patients if early diagnosis allows resection before nodal involvement.

Causes
Unknown

Risk factors
- Low-fiber, high-fat, high-calorie diet
- Other diseases of the digestive tract
- History of ulcerative colitis (average interval before onset of cancer 11 to 17 years), and Crohn's disease
- Familial polyposis (cancer usually develops by age 50)
- Sedentary lifestyle and obesity
- Smoking
- Alcohol abuse
- Diabetes
- Growth hormone disorder
- Radiation therapy or history of colorectal cancer or polyps
- Family history of colorectal cancer

AGE ALERT
Age over 40 is a risk factor for colorectal cancer.

Pathophysiology
Most lesions of the large bowel are moderately differentiated adenocarcinomas. These tumors tend to grow slowly and remain asymptomatic for long periods. Tumors in the sigmoid and descending colon grow circumferentially and constrict the intestinal lumen. At diagnosis, tumors in the ascending colon are usually large and are palpable on physical examination.

COMPLICATIONS
- Abdominal distention and intestinal obstruction
- Anemia
- Complications resulting from chemotherapy or radiation therapy

Signs and symptoms
- Changes in bowel habits, such as bleeding, pain, anemia, and anorexia
- Symptoms of local obstruction
- Symptoms of direct extension to adjacent organs (bladder, prostate, ureters, vagina, sacrum)
- Symptoms from distant metastasis (usually liver).

Signs specific to site of obstruction
- Right colon:
  - Black, tarry stools; anemia
  - Abdominal aching or pressure; dull cramps
  - Weakness, fatigue, exertional dyspnea
  - Vomiting

- Left colon:
  - Rectal bleeding; dark or bright red blood or mucus in stools
  - Abdominal fullness or cramping
  - Rectal pressure
  - Constipation
  - Diarrhea
  - Ribbon- or pencil-shaped stools
  - Pain relieved by flatus or bowel movement

Diagnostic test results
- Digital rectal examination detects almost 15% of colorectal cancers; specifically, it detects suspicious rectal and perianal lesions.
- Fecal occult blood test possibly shows blood in stool.
- Barium enema studies can determine the location of lesions that aren't normally detected manually or visually.

CLINICAL TIP
Barium examination shouldn't precede colonoscopy or excretory urography because barium sulfate interferes with these tests.

- Computed tomography scan allows better visualization if a barium enema yields inconclusive results or if metastasis to the pelvic lymph nodes is suspected.
- Proctoscopy or sigmoidoscopy permits visualization of the lower GI tract, which can detect up to 66% of colorectal cancers. Colonoscopy permits visual inspection and photography of the colon up to the ileocecal valve and provides access for polypectomies and biopsies of suspected lesions.
- Carcinoembryonic antigen permits patient monitoring before and after treatment to detect metastasis or recurrence.
- Excretory urography verifies bilateral renal function and allows inspection for displacement of the kidneys, ureters, or bladder from a tumor pressing against these structures.

Treatment
- Surgery to remove tumor plus adjacent tissues and any lymph nodes that may contain cancer cells
- Chemotherapy for patients with metastasis, residual disease, or a recurrent inoperable tumor
- Radiation therapy for tumor mass reduction, done before or after surgery or combined with chemotherapy
- High-fiber diet

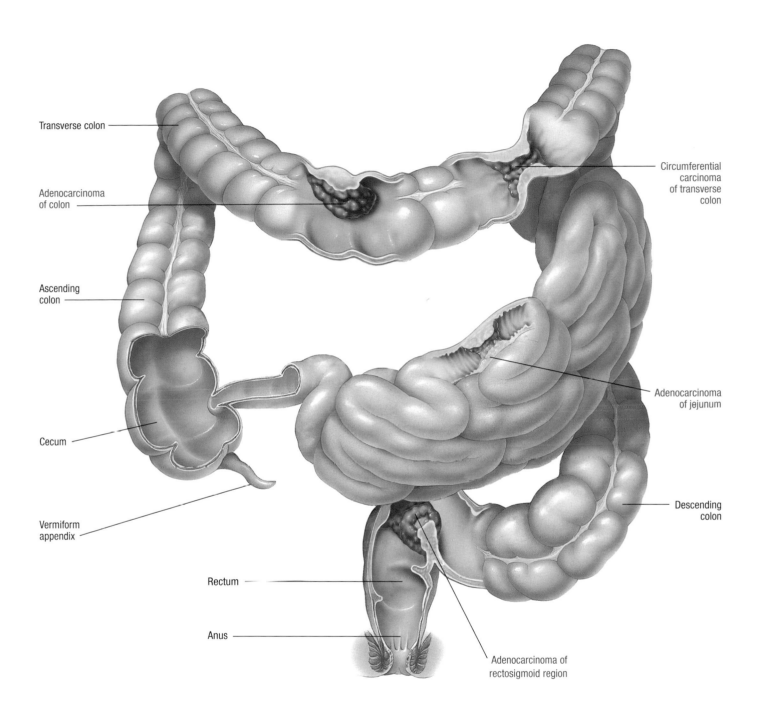

Transverse colon

Adenocarcinoma
of colon

Ascending
colon

Cecum

Vermiform
appendix

Rectum

Anus

Circumferential
carcinoma
of transverse
colon

Adenocarcinoma
of jejunum

Descending
colon

Adenocarcinoma of
rectosigmoid region

CROHN'S DISEASE

Crohn's disease, also known as *regional enteritis* or *granulomatous colitis,* is inflammation of any part of the GI tract (usually the terminal ileum), extending through all layers of the intestinal wall. It may also involve regional lymph nodes and the mesentery.

AGE ALERT
Crohn's disease is most prevalent in adults ages 20 to 40.

Causes

Unknown

Possible contributing conditions

- Lymphatic obstruction
- Allergies, immune disorders
- Infection
- Genetic predisposition

Pathophysiology

Whatever the cause of Crohn's disease, inflammation spreads slowly and progressively. Enlarged lymph nodes block lymph flow in the submucosa. Lymphatic obstruction leads to edema, mucosal ulceration and fissures, abscesses, and sometimes granulomas. Mucosal ulcerations are called *skipping lesions* because they aren't continuous, as in ulcerative colitis.

Oval, elevated patches of closely packed lymph follicles — called Peyer's patches — develop in the lining of the small intestine. Subsequent fibrosis thickens the bowel wall and causes stenosis, or narrowing of the lumen. The serous membrane becomes inflamed (serositis), inflamed bowel loops adhere to other diseased or normal loops, and diseased bowel segments become interspersed with healthy ones. Finally, diseased parts of the bowel become thicker, narrower, and shorter.

COMPLICATIONS

- Anal fistula
- Perineal abscess
- Fistulas to the bladder, vagina, or skin
- Intestinal obstruction
- Nutritional deficiencies
- Peritonitis

Signs and symptoms

- Steady, colicky pain in right lower quadrant
- Cramping, tenderness
- Weight loss
- Diarrhea, steatorrhea, bloody stools
- Low-grade fever
- Anal fistula
- Perineal abscess

Diagnostic test results

- Fecal occult blood test reveals minute amounts of blood in stools.
- Small bowel X-ray shows irregular mucosa, ulceration, and stiffening.
- Barium enema reveals the string sign (segments of stricture separated by normal bowel) and possibly fissures and narrowing of the bowel.
- Sigmoidoscopy and colonoscopy reveal patchy areas of inflammation (helps to rule out ulcerative colitis), with cobblestone-like mucosal surface. With colon involvement, ulcers may be seen.
- Biopsy reveals granulomas in up to one-half of all specimens.
- Blood tests reveal increased white blood cell count and erythrocyte sedimentation rate, and decreased potassium, calcium, magnesium, and hemoglobin levels.

Treatment

- Corticosteroids, immunosuppressants
- Aminosalicylates such as sulfasalazine
- Antidiarrheals (not in patients with significant bowel obstruction)
- Antibiotics, such as metronidazole and ampicillin
- Biologic therapies such as infliximab
- Stress reduction and reduced physical activity
- Vitamin supplements (iron supplements)
- Avoidance of fruits and vegetables; high-fiber, spicy, or fatty foods; dairy products; carbonated or caffeine-containing beverages; foods or liquids that stimulate intestinal activity
- Surgery, if necessary

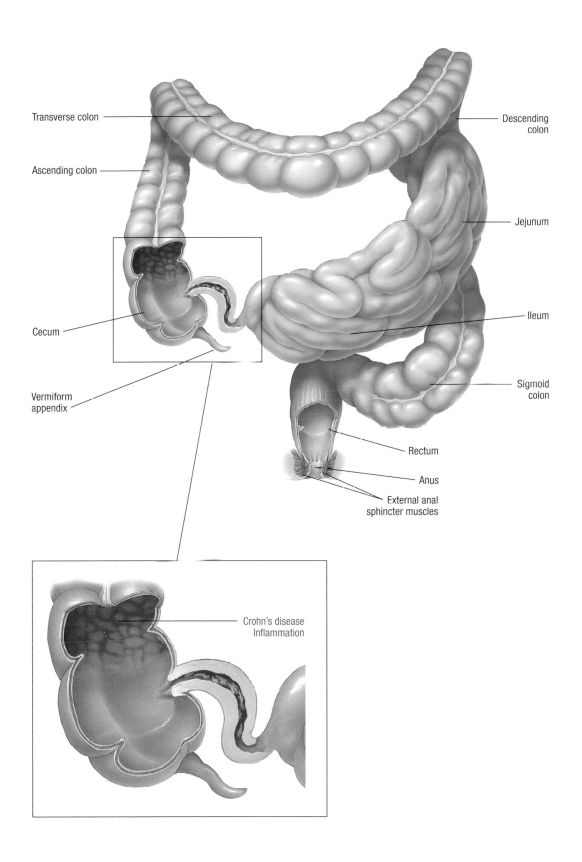

Transverse colon

Descending colon

Ascending colon

Jejunum

Cecum

Ileum

Vermiform appendix

Sigmoid colon

Rectum

Anus

External anal sphincter muscles

Crohn's disease Inflammation

DIVERTICULAR DISEASE

In diverticular disease, bulging pouches (diverticula) in the GI wall push the mucosal lining through the surrounding muscle. Although the most common site for diverticula is in the sigmoid colon, they may develop anywhere, from the proximal end of the pharynx to the anus. Common sites include the duodenum, near the pancreatic border or the ampulla of Vater, and the jejunum.

Diverticular disease of the stomach is rare and is usually a precursor of peptic or neoplastic disease. Diverticular disease of the ileum (Meckel's diverticulum) is the most common congenital anomaly of the GI tract.

Diverticular disease has two clinical forms:
- diverticulosis — diverticula present but asymptomatic
- diverticulitis — inflamed diverticula; may cause potentially fatal obstruction, infection, or hemorrhage.

AGE ALERT
Diverticular disease is most prevalent in men over age 40 and persons who eat a low-fiber diet. More than half of patients older than age 60 have colonic diverticula.

Causes
- Exact cause unknown
- Diminished colonic motility and increased intraluminal pressure
- Low-fiber diet
- Defects in colon wall strength

Pathophysiology
Diverticula probably result from high intraluminal pressure on an area of weakness in the GI wall where blood vessels enter. Diet may be a contributing factor, because insufficient fiber reduces fecal residue, narrows the bowel lumen, and leads to high intra-abdominal pressure during defecation.

In *diverticulitis,* undigested food and bacteria accumulate in the diverticular sac. This hard mass cuts off the blood supply to the thin walls of the sac, making them more susceptible to attack by colonic bacteria.

COMPLICATIONS
- Rectal hemorrhage
- Portal pyemia from artery or vein erosion
- Fistula
- Obstruction
- Perforation
- Abscess
- Peritonitis

Signs and symptoms
Diverticulosis
- Asymptomatic

Mild diverticulitis
- Moderate left lower abdominal pain
- Low-grade fever
- Leukocytosis
- Nausea and vomiting

Severe diverticulitis
- Nausea and vomiting
- Left lower quadrant pain; abdominal rigidity
- High fever, chills, hypotension, shock
- Microscopic to massive hemorrhage

Chronic diverticulitis
- Constipation, ribbonlike stools, intermittent diarrhea, abdominal distention
- Abdominal rigidity and pain, diminished or absent bowel sounds, nausea, and vomiting

Diagnostic test results
- Upper GI series reveals diverticulosis of the esophagus and upper bowel.
- Barium enema reveals filling of diverticula, which confirms diagnosis.
- Biopsy reveals evidence of benign disease, ruling out cancer.
- Blood studies show an elevated white blood cell count and elevated erythrocyte sedimentation rate in diverticulitis.

Treatment
- Liquid or bland diet, stool softeners, occasional doses of mineral oil
- Analgesics, such as meperidine or morphine
- Antispasmodics
- Antibiotics
- Exercise
- Colon resection with removal of involved segment
- Temporary colostomy if necessary
- Blood transfusions if necessary
- High-residue diet after pain has subsided

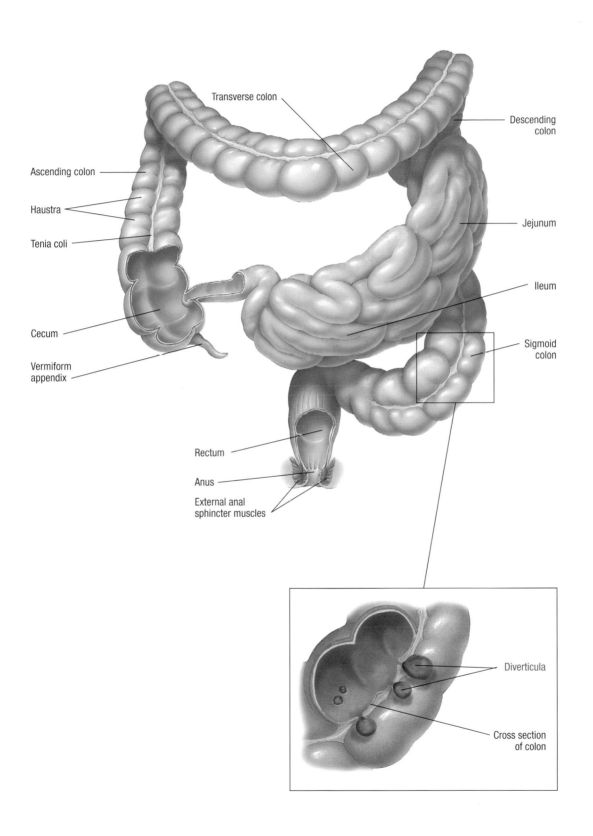

Transverse colon

Descending colon

Ascending colon

Haustra

Tenia coli

Jejunum

Ileum

Cecum

Sigmoid colon

Vermiform appendix

Rectum

Anus

External anal sphincter muscles

Diverticula

Cross section of colon

ESOPHAGEAL CANCER

Esophageal cancer is usually fatal. This disease occurs worldwide, but incidence varies geographically. It's most common in Japan, China, the Middle East, and parts of South Africa. Common sites of distant metastasis include the liver and lungs.

AGE ALERT
Esophageal cancer most commonly develops in men over age 60.

Causes
Unknown
Predisposing factors
- Chronic irritation by heavy smoking and excessive use of alcohol
- Stasis-induced inflammation as in achalasia or stricture
- Nutritional deficiency
- Diets high in nitrosamines
- Previous head and neck tumors

Pathophysiology
Esophageal cancer includes two types of malignant tumors: squamous cell carcinoma and adenocarcinoma. Most esophageal cancers are poorly differentiated squamous cell carcinomas. Adenocarcinomas are less frequent and are contained to the lower third of the esophagus. Esophageal tumors are usually fungating and infiltrating, and they partially constrict the lumen of the esophagus.

Regional metastasis occurs early by way of submucosal lymphatics, often fatally invading adjacent vital primary organs.

COMPLICATIONS
- Inability to control secretions
- Obstruction of the esophagus
- Loss of lower esophageal sphincter control
- Aspiration pneumonia
- Mediastinitis
- Tracheoesophageal or bronchoesophageal fistula
- Aortic perforation

Signs and symptoms
- Anorexia
- Vomiting
- Dehydration
- Regurgitation of food
- Dysphagia and weight loss (most common)
- Esophageal obstruction
- Pain
- Hoarseness, coughing
- Cachexia

Complications of metastasis
- Tracheoesophageal fistulas
- Mediastinitis
- Aortic perforation
- Aspiration pneumonia
- Inability to control secretions

Diagnostic test results
- X-rays of the esophagus, with barium swallow and motility studies, delineate structural and filling defects and reduced peristalsis.
- Computed tomography shows size and location of esophageal lesions.
- Magnetic resonance imaging permits evaluation of the esophagus and adjacent structures.
- Esophagoscopy, punch and brush biopsies, and exfoliative cytologic tests confirm esophageal tumors.
- Bronchoscopy, usually performed after an esophagoscopy, reveals tumor growth in the tracheobronchial tree.
- Endoscopic ultrasonography of the esophagus combines endoscopy and ultrasound technology and reveals the depth of penetration of the tumor.

Treatment
- Usually multimodal
- Resection to maintain a passageway for food
- Palliative treatments
- Feeding gastrostomy and chemotherapy
- Insertion of a prosthetic tube and chemotherapy
- Dilation of the esophagus
- Analgesics

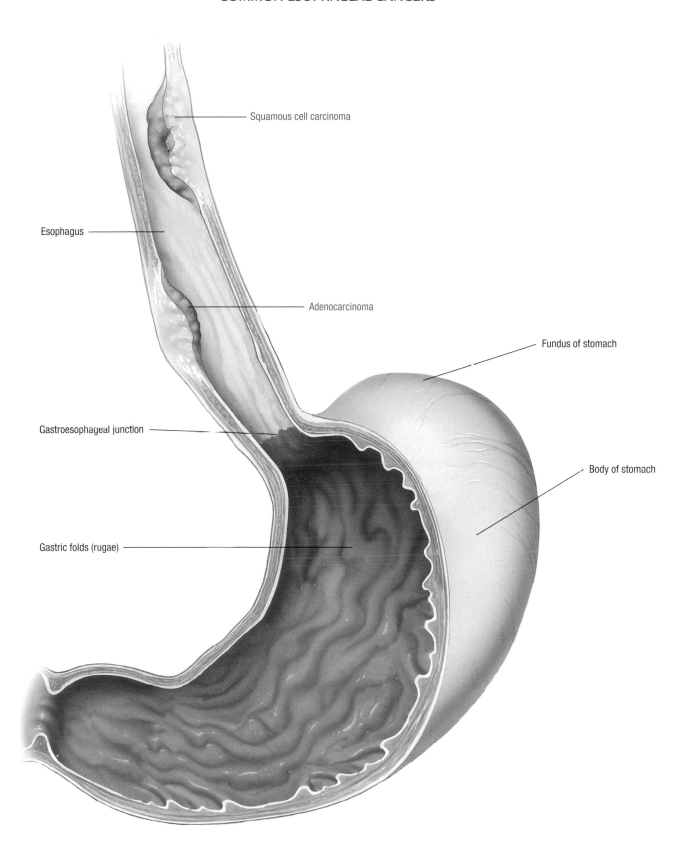

Squamous cell carcinoma

Esophagus

Adenocarcinoma

Fundus of stomach

Gastroesophageal junction

Body of stomach

Gastric folds (rugae)

GASTRIC CANCER

Gastric carcinoma is common throughout the world and affects all races; however, mortality is highest in Japan, Iceland, Chile, and Austria. In the United States, the incidence has decreased by 50% during the past 25 years and the resulting death rate is one-third of what it was 30 years ago.

 AGE ALERT
Incidence of gastric cancer is highest in men over age 40.

Causes
Unknown; commonly associated with atrophic gastritis
Predisposing factors
- Tobacco smoke
- Asbestos exposure
- High alcohol intake
- Intake of smoked, pickled, or salt-preserved foods, nitrates, and red meat
- Type A blood
- *Helicobacter pylori* infection (distal gastric cancer)
- Family history of gastric cancer
- Pernicious anemia

Pathophysiology
According to gross appearance, gastric carcinoma can be classified as polypoid, ulcerating, ulcerating and infiltrating, or diffuse. The parts of the stomach affected by gastric carcinoma, listed in order of decreasing frequency, are the pylorus and antrum, the lesser curvature, the cardia, the body of the stomach, and the greater curvature. Gastric carcinoma infiltrates rapidly to regional lymph nodes, omentum, liver, lungs, and bone.

 COMPLICATIONS
- Malnutrition
- GI obstruction
- Iron deficiency anemia

Signs and symptoms
Early clues
- Chronic dyspepsia, epigastric discomfort

Later clues
- Weight loss, anorexia
- Dysphagia, feeling of fullness after eating
- Anemia, fatigue
- Coffee-ground emesis
- Bloody stools

Diagnostic test results
- Barium X-rays of the GI tract with fluoroscopy show changes that suggest gastric cancer, including a tumor or filling defect in the outline of the stomach, loss of flexibility and distensibility; and abnormal gastric mucosa with or without ulceration.
- Gastroscopy with fiber-optic endoscope visualizes gastric mucosa including presence of gastric lesions for biopsy.
- Gastroscopic biopsy permits evaluation of gastric mucosal lesions.
- Gastric acid stimulation test discloses whether the stomach secretes acid properly.
- Complete blood count reveals anemia.
- Liver function studies possibly elevated with metastatic spread of tumor to liver.
- Radioimmunoassay reveals possibly elevated carcinoembryonic antigen.

Treatment
- Excision of lesion with appropriate margins (possible in more than one-third of patients) by subtotal or total gastrectomy or gastrojejunostomy
- Palliative surgery
- Radiation therapy with chemotherapy for patients with unresectable or partially resectable disease
- Antispasmodics, antacids for GI distress
- Antiemetics
- Opioid analgesics
- Proton pump inhibitors or histamine-2 blockers

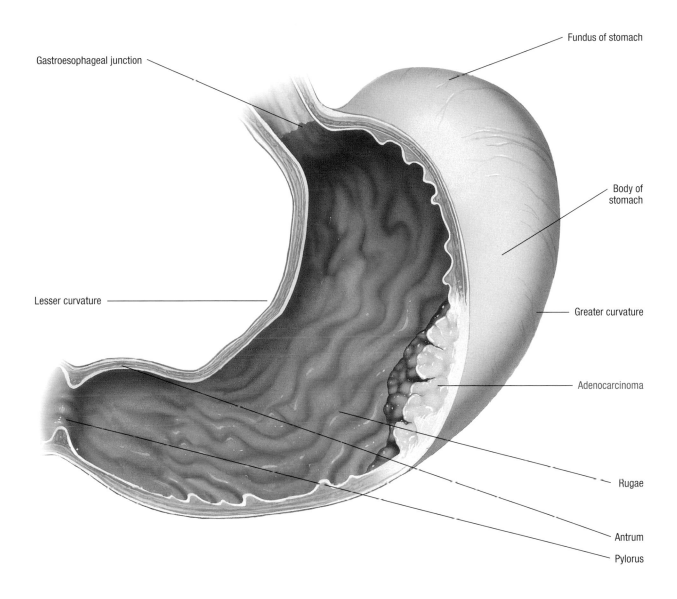

Gastroesophageal junction

Fundus of stomach

Body of stomach

Lesser curvature

Greater curvature

Adenocarcinoma

Rugae

Antrum

Pylorus

GASTRITIS

Gastritis, an inflammation of the gastric mucosa, may be acute or chronic. *Acute gastritis* produces mucosal reddening, edema, hemorrhage, and erosion; this benign, self-limiting disease is usually a response to local irritants. *Chronic gastritis* is common among elderly persons and those with pernicious anemia. It's characterized by progressive cell atrophy and commonly occurs as chronic atrophic gastritis (inflammation of all stomach mucosal layers and reduced numbers of chief and parietal cells). Acute or chronic gastritis can occur at any age.

Causes

Acute gastritis
- Habitually ingested irritants, such as hot peppers, alcohol
- Drugs, such as aspirin, other nonsteroidal anti-inflammatory agents, cytotoxic agents, caffeine, corticosteroids, antimetabolites, phenylbutazone
- Poisons, such as DDT, ammonia, mercury, carbon tetrachloride, corrosive substances
- Bacterial endotoxins, such as staphylococci, *Escherichia coli*, salmonella
- Physiological stress, such as surgery, head trauma, renal failure, hepatic failure, or respiratory failure

Chronic gastritis
- *Helicobacter pylori* infection
- Pernicious anemia
- Peptic ulcer disease
- Renal disease
- Diabetes mellitus

Pathophysiology

Gastritis is an inflammation of the lining of the stomach. In *acute gastritis,* the protective mucosal layer is altered. Acid secretion produces mucosal reddening, edema, and superficial surface erosion. *In chronic gastritis,* progressive thinning and degeneration of gastric mucosa occur. In either form, as mucus membranes become more eroded, gastric juices, containing pepsin and acid, come into contact with the erosion and an ulcer forms.

Pernicious anemia is often associated with atrophic gastritis, a chronic inflammation of the stomach resulting from degeneration of the gastric mucosa. In pernicious anemia, the stomach can no longer secrete intrinsic factor, which is needed for vitamin B_{12} absorption.

COMPLICATIONS
- Hemorrhage
- Shock
- Obstruction
- Perforation
- Peritonitis
- Gastric cancer

Signs and symptoms
- Epigastric discomfort
- Indigestion, cramping
- Anorexia
- Nausea, hematemesis, and vomiting
- Coffee-ground emesis or melena if GI bleeding present
- Grimacing
- Restlessness
- Pallor
- Tachycardia
- Hypotension
- Abdominal distention, tenderness, and guarding
- Normoactive to hyperactive bowel sounds

Diagnostic test results
- Occult blood tests reveal blood in vomitus or stools (or both) if the patient has gastric bleeding.
- Complete blood count shows decreased hemoglobin level and hematocrit.
- Urea breath test is positive for *H. pylori.*
- Upper GI endoscopy reveals gastritis when endoscopy is performed within 24 hours of bleeding.
- Biopsy reveals inflammatory process.

Treatment
- Elimination of the cause
- Bland diet
- Antacids, histamine antagonists, proton pump inhibitors
- Prostaglandins
- Vitamin B_{12}
- Antibiotics
- Blood replacement
- Iced saline lavage, possibly with norepinephrine
- Angiography with vasopressin
- Surgery — vagotomy, pyloroplasty, partial or total gastrectomy

CLINICAL TIP
Simply avoiding aspirin and spicy foods may relieve gastritis.

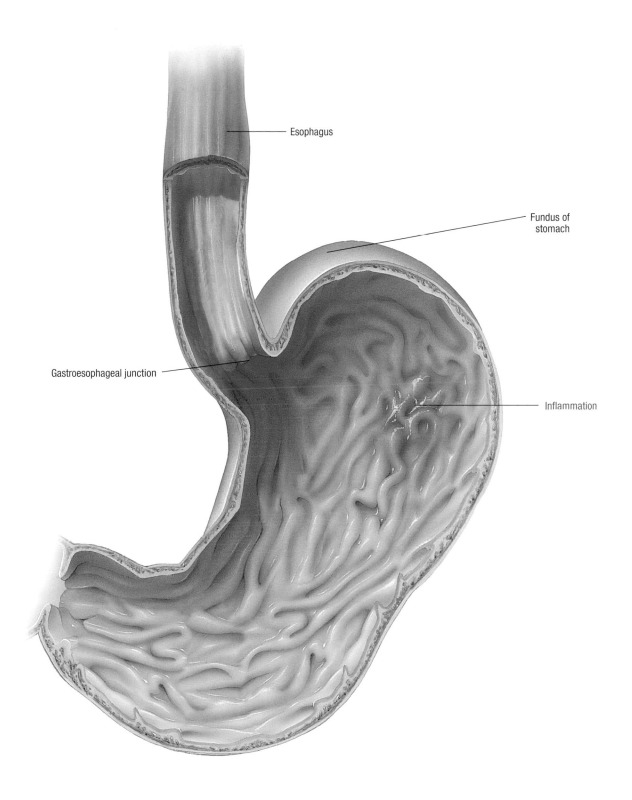

Esophagus

Fundus of
stomach

Gastroesophageal junction

Inflammation

GASTROESOPHAGEAL REFLUX DISEASE

Popularly known as *heartburn*, gastroesophageal disease (GERD) refers to backflow of gastric or duodenal contents or both into the esophagus and past the lower esophageal sphincter (LES), without associated belching or vomiting. The reflux of gastric contents causes acute epigastric pain, usually after a meal. The pain may radiate to the chest or arms. It commonly occurs in pregnant or obese persons. Lying down after a meal may also contribute to reflux.

Causes
- Weak esophageal sphincter
- Increased abdominal pressure, as in obesity or pregnancy
- Hiatal hernia
- Medications, such as morphine, meperidine, diazepam, calcium channel blockers, anticholinergic agents
- Alcohol, cigarette smoke
- Nasogastric intubation for longer than 4 days
- Pyloric surgery

Pathophysiology
Normally, the LES maintains enough pressure around the lower end of the esophagus to close it and prevent reflux. Typically, the sphincter relaxes after each swallow to allow food into the stomach. In GERD, the sphincter doesn't remain closed (usually due to deficient LES pressure or pressure within the stomach exceeding LES pressure) and stomach contents flow into the esophagus. The high acidity of the stomach contents causes pain and irritation in the esophagus, and stricture or ulceration may occur.

COMPLICATIONS
- Reflux esophagitis
- Esophageal stricture
- Esophageal ulcer
- Replacement of normal squamous epithelium with columnar epithelium (Barrett's syndrome)
- Anemia
- Pulmonary complications and reflux aspiration

Signs and symptoms
- Burning epigastric pain, possibly radiating to arms and chest, usually after a meal or when lying down
- Feeling of fluid accumulation in the throat without a sour or bitter taste
- Dyspepsia
- Chronic cough
- Laryngitis and morning hoarseness
- Wheezing
- Nausea and vomiting

Diagnostic test results
- Esophageal acidity test evaluates the competence of the LES and provides objective measure of reflux.
- Acid perfusion test confirms esophagitis and distinguishes it from cardiac disorders.
- Esophagoscopy allows visual examination of the lining of the esophagus to reveal the extent of the disease and confirm pathologic changes in mucosa.
- Barium swallow identifies hiatal hernia as the cause.
- Upper GI series detects hiatal hernia or motility problems.
- Esophageal manometry evaluates resting pressure of the LES and determines sphincter competence.

Treatment
- Frequent, small meals; avoidance of eating just before going to bed
- Sitting up during and after meals; sleeping with head of bed elevated
- Increased fluid intake
- Antacids, histamine-2 receptor antagonists
- Proton pump inhibitors
- Smoking cessation; reduction or cessation of alcohol intake
- Hiatal hernia repair
- Vagotomy or pyloroplasty

CLINICAL TIP
Advise patients with GERD to avoid foods that irritate the LES, such as caffeine, mint, and chocolate.

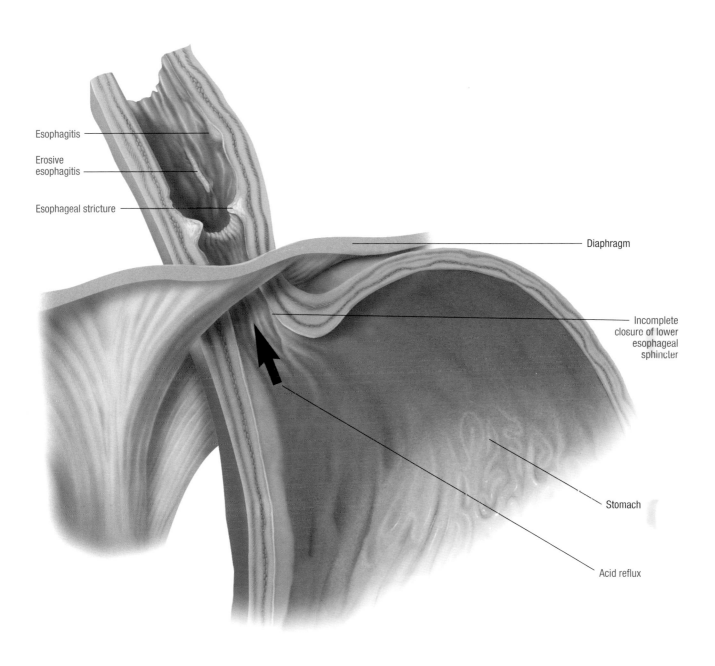

Esophagitis

Erosive esophagitis

Esophageal stricture

Diaphragm

Incomplete closure of lower esophageal sphincter

Stomach

Acid reflux

Hemorrhoids

Hemorrhoids are painful, swollen veins in the lower portion of the rectum or anus. They're very common, especially during pregnancy and after childbirth. They result from increased pressure in the veins of the anus, which causes the veins to bulge and expand, making them painful, especially while sitting.

AGE ALERT
Incidence of hemorrhoids is generally highest between ages 20 and 50.

Causes
- Straining at defecation, constipation, low-fiber diet
- Pregnancy
- Obesity
- Prolonged sitting

Predisposing factors
- Hepatic disease, such as amebic abscesses or hepatitis
- Alcoholism
- Anorectal infections

Pathophysiology
Hemorrhoids are varicosities in the superior or inferior hemorrhoidal venous plexus. Dilation and enlargement of the plexus of superior hemorrhoidal veins above the dentate line cause internal hemorrhoids. Enlargement of the plexus of inferior hemorrhoidal veins below the dentate line causes external hemorrhoids, which may protrude from the rectum.

Hemorrhoids result from activities that increase intravenous pressure, causing distention and engorgement. Hemorrhoids are classified according to severity.
- *First-degree* — confined to the anal canal
- *Second-degree* — prolapse during straining but reduce spontaneously
- *Third-degree* — prolapse and require manual reduction after each bowel movement
- *Fourth-degree* — irreducible

COMPLICATIONS
- Local infection
- Bleeding
- Anemia

Signs and symptoms
- Bright red blood on outside of the stool or on toilet tissue
- Painless, intermittent bleeding during defecation (internal hemorrhoids)
- Anal itching, vague anal discomfort
- Prolapse of rectal mucosa
- Pain
- Hard, tender lumps near anus

Diagnostic test results
- Physical examination confirms external hemorrhoids.
- Anoscopy shows internal hemorrhoids.
- Flexible sigmoidoscopy reveals internal hemorrhoids.
- Complete blood count shows decreased hemoglobin level and hematocrit.
- Fecal occult blood testing is positive for blood in stool.

Treatment
- High-fiber diet, increased fluid intake, bulking agents
- Avoidance of prolonged sitting on the toilet; avoidance of straining
- Local anesthetic agents, hydrocortisone cream, suppositories
- Warm sitz baths
- Injection sclerotherapy or rubber band ligation
- Hemorrhoidectomy

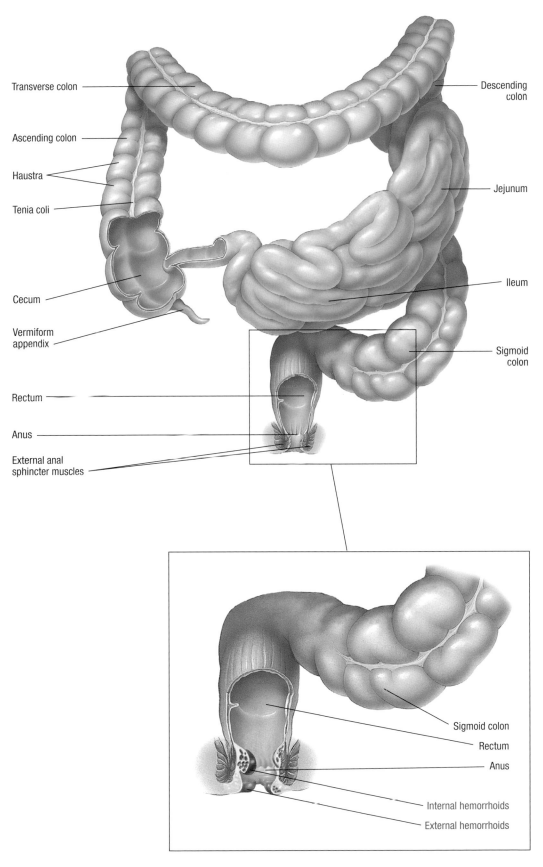

Transverse colon

Ascending colon

Haustra

Tenia coli

Cecum

Vermiform
appendix

Rectum

Anus

External anal
sphincter muscles

Descending
colon

Jejunum

Ileum

Sigmoid
colon

Sigmoid colon

Rectum

Anus

Internal hemorrhoids

External hemorrhoids

HEPATITIS

Nonviral hepatitis is an inflammation of the liver that usually results from exposure to certain chemicals or drugs. Most patients recover from this illness, although a few develop fulminating hepatitis, hepatic failure, or cirrhosis.

Viral hepatitis is a common infection, resulting in hepatic cell destruction, necrosis, and autolysis. In most patients, hepatic cells eventually regenerate with little or no residual damage. However, old age and serious underlying disorders make complications more likely. The prognosis is poor if edema and hepatic encephalopathy develop.

Causes
Nonviral
- Hepatotoxic chemicals, such as carbon tetrachloride, trichloroethylene, vinyl chloride
- Hepatotoxic drugs, such as acetaminophen
- Poisonous mushrooms
- Vinyl chloride

Viral
- Infection by hepatitis virus A, B, C, D, E, G, or transfusion transmissible virus

Pathophysiology
Nonviral
After exposure to a hepatotoxin, hepatic cellular necrosis, scarring, Kupffer cell hyperplasia, and infiltration by mononuclear phagocytes occur with varying severity. Alcohol, anoxia, and preexisting liver disease exacerbate the effects of some toxins.

Drug-induced hepatitis may begin with a hypersensitivity reaction unique to the individual, unlike toxic hepatitis, which appears to affect all exposed people indiscriminately. Symptoms usually manifest after 2 to 5 weeks of therapy.

Viral
Hepatic damage is usually similar in all types of viral hepatitis, but extent of cell injury or necrosis varies.

The virus causes hepatocyte injury and death, either by directly killing the cells or by activating inflammatory and immune reactions. The inflammatory and immune reactions, in turn, injure or destroy hepatocytes by lysing the infected or neighboring cells. Later, direct antibody attack against the viral antigens causes further destruction of the infected cells. Edema and swelling of the interstitium lead to collapse of capillaries, decreased blood flow, tissue hypoxia, scarring, and fibrosis.

COMPLICATIONS
- Chronic persistent hepatitis
- Chronic active hepatitis
- Cirrhosis
- Hepatic failure and death
- Primary hepatocellular carcinoma

Signs and symptoms
Nonviral
- Anorexia, nausea, vomiting
- Jaundice, dark urine, clay-colored stool
- Hepatomegaly
- Possible abdominal pain
- Pruritus

Viral, prodromal phase
- Easy fatigue, generalized malaise, anorexia, mild weight loss
- Arthralgia, myalgia
- Nausea, vomiting, changes in senses of taste and smell
- Fever
- Right upper quadrant tenderness
- Dark-colored urine, clay-colored stools

Viral, icteric phase
- Jaundice
- Worsening of prodromal symptoms
- Pruritus
- Abdominal pain or tenderness

Viral, recovery phase
- Symptoms subside and appetite returns

Diagnostic test results
- Hepatitis profile study identifies antibodies specific to the causative virus, establishing the type of hepatitis.
- Blood chemistry reveals elevated serum aspartate aminotransferase and serum alanine aminotransferase levels in the prodromal stage.
- Serum alkaline phosphatase level is slightly increased.
- Serum bilirubin level may remain high into late disease, especially in severe cases.
- Prothrombin time is prolonged (greater than 3 seconds longer than normal indicates severe liver damage).
- White blood cell counts reveal transient neutropenia and lymphopenia followed by lymphocytosis.
- Liver biopsy identifies underlying disease.

Treatment
Nonviral
- Lavage, catharsis, or hyperventilation, depending on the route of exposure — as soon as possible after exposure
- Acetylcysteine as antidote for acetaminophen poisoning
- Corticosteroids

Viral
- Rest to minimize energy demands
- Avoidance of alcohol or other hepatotoxic drugs
- Small, high-calorie meals
- Parenteral nutrition if patient can't eat
- Standard immunoglobulin
- Antiemetics
- Alfa-2B interferon
- Cholestyramine
- Liver transplantation

CLINICAL TIP
Vaccination against hepatitis A and B provides immunity to these viruses before transmission occurs.

Nonviral hepatitis

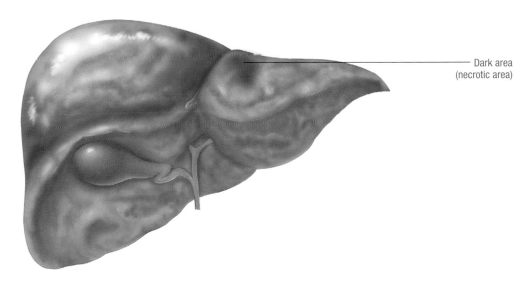

Dark area
(necrotic area)

Viral hepatitis

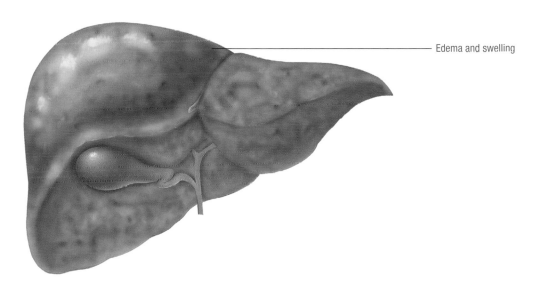

Edema and swelling

HIATAL HERNIA

Hiatal hernia is a defect in the diaphragm that permits a portion of the stomach to pass through the diaphragmatic opening into the chest. Hiatal hernia is the most common problem of the diaphragm affecting the alimentary canal. Treatment can prevent complications such as strangulation of the herniated intrathoracic portion of the stomach.

AGE ALERT
Hiatal hernias are common, especially in people over age 50.

Causes
- Esophageal carcinoma
- Kyphoscoliosis
- Trauma
- Congenital diaphragm malformations

Contributing factors
- Aging, obesity, trauma

Pathophysiology
Hernias typically result when an organ protrudes through an abnormal opening in the muscle wall of the cavity that surrounds it. In hiatal hernias, a portion of the stomach protrudes through the diaphragm.

Three types of hiatal hernia can occur: sliding, paraesophageal (rolling), or mixed, which include features of both. In a sliding hernia, both the stomach and the gastroesophageal junction slip up into the chest, so the gastroesophageal junction is above the diaphragmatic hiatus. In paraesophageal hernia, a part of the greater curvature of the stomach rolls through the diaphragmatic defect.

COMPLICATIONS
- Gastroesophageal reflux
- Esophagitis and esophageal ulcers
- Hemorrhage
- Respiratory distress
- Aspiration pneumonia
- Esophageal stricture
- Esophageal incarceration
- Gastric ulcer
- Peritonitis

Signs and symptoms
- Heartburn 1 to 4 hours after eating; aggravated by reclining, belching, or conditions that increase intra-abdominal pressure
- Regurgitation or vomiting
- Retrosternal or substernal chest pain (typically after meals or at bedtime)
- Feeling of fullness after eating
- Feeling of breathlessness or suffocation
- Chest pain resembling angina pectoris
- Dysphagia

Diagnostic test results
- Chest X-ray reveals an air shadow behind the heart in a large hernia; lower lobe infiltrates with aspiration.
- Barium swallow with fluoroscopy detects a hiatal hernia and diaphragmatic abnormalities.
- Endoscopy and biopsy results identify the mucosal junction and the edge of the diaphragm indenting the esophagus; differentiate hiatal hernia, varices, and other small gastroesophageal lesions; and rule out malignant tumors.
- Esophageal motility studies reveal esophageal motor or lower esophageal pressure abnormalities before surgical repair of the hernia.
- pH studies identify reflux of gastric contents.
- Acid perfusion (Bernstein) test identifies esophageal reflux.
- Blood chemistry reveals decreased serum hemoglobin level and hematocrit in patients with paraesophageal hernia, if bleeding from esophageal ulceration is present.
- Fecal occult blood test reveals presence of blood.
- Analysis of gastric contents possibly shows the presence of blood.

Treatment
- Restrict activities that raise intra-abdominal pressure (coughing, straining, bending)
- Pharmacologic agents: antiemetics, stool softeners, cough suppressants, antacids, and cholinergics
- Proton pump inhibitors
- Diet modifications: small, frequent, bland meals; not eating 2 hours prior to lying down; weight-loss programs
- Avoidance of foods that relax the lower esophageal sphincter, such as caffeine, mint, and chocolate
- Smoking cessation
- Surgical repair

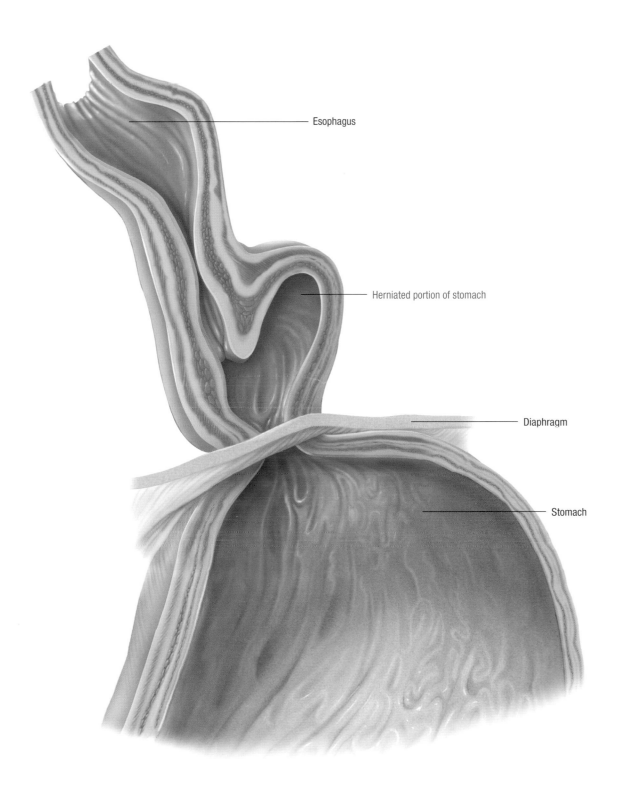

Esophagus

Herniated portion of stomach

Diaphragm

Stomach

HIRSCHSPRUNG'S DISEASE

Hirschsprung's disease, also called *congenital megacolon* or *congenital aganglionic megacolon,* is a congenital disorder of the large intestine, characterized by absence or marked reduction of parasympathetic ganglion cells in the colorectal wall. Hirschsprung's disease appears to be a familial, congenital defect, occurring in 1 in 5,000 to 1 in 8,000 live births. It's up to 7 times more common in males than in females (although the aganglionic segment is usually shorter in males) and is most prevalent in whites. Total aganglionosis affects both sexes equally. Females with Hirschsprung's disease are at higher risk for having affected children. This disease usually coexists with other congenital anomalies, particularly trisomy 21 and anomalies of the urinary tract such as megaloureter.

CLINICAL TIP

Without prompt treatment, an infant with colonic obstruction may die within 24 hours from enterocolitis that leads to severe diarrhea and hypovolemic shock. With prompt treatment, prognosis is good.

Causes

Familial congenital defect

Pathophysiology

In Hirschsprung's disease, parasympathetic ganglion cells in the colorectal wall are absent or markedly reduced in number. The aganglionic bowel segment contracts without the reciprocal relaxation needed to propel feces forward. Impaired intestinal motility causes severe, intractable constipation. Colonic obstruction can ensue, dilating the bowel and occluding surrounding blood and lymphatic vessels. The ensuing mucosal edema, ischemia, and infarction draw large amounts of fluid into the bowel, causing copious amounts of liquid stool. Continued infarction and destruction of the mucosa lead to infection and sepsis.

COMPLICATIONS

- Nutritional deficiencies
- Enterocolitis
- Hypovolemic shock

Signs and symptoms

In neonates

- Failure to pass meconium within 24 to 48 hours
- Bile-stained or fecal vomitus
- Constipation, overflow diarrhea
- Abdominal distention
- Dehydration, feeding difficulties, and failure to thrive

In children

- Intractable constipation
- Large protuberant abdomen, easily palpated fecal masses
- Wasted extremities (in severe cases)
- Loss of subcutaneous tissue (in severe cases)

In adults (rare)

- Abdominal distention
- Chronic intermittent constipation

Complications of Hirschsprung's disease include bowel perforation, electrolyte imbalances, nutritional deficiencies, enterocolitis, hypovolemic shock, and sepsis.

Diagnostic test results

- Rectal biopsy confirms diagnosis by showing the absence of ganglion cells.
- Barium enema, used in older infants, reveals a narrowed segment of distal colon with a saw-toothed appearance and a funnel-shaped segment above it. This confirms the diagnosis and assesses the extent of intestinal involvement.
- Rectal manometry detects failure of the internal anal sphincter to relax and contract.
- Upright plain abdominal X-rays show marked colonic distention.

Treatment

- Daily colonic lavage prior to surgery
- Temporary colostomy or ileostomy
- Corrective surgery
- Antibiotics
- Genetic counseling

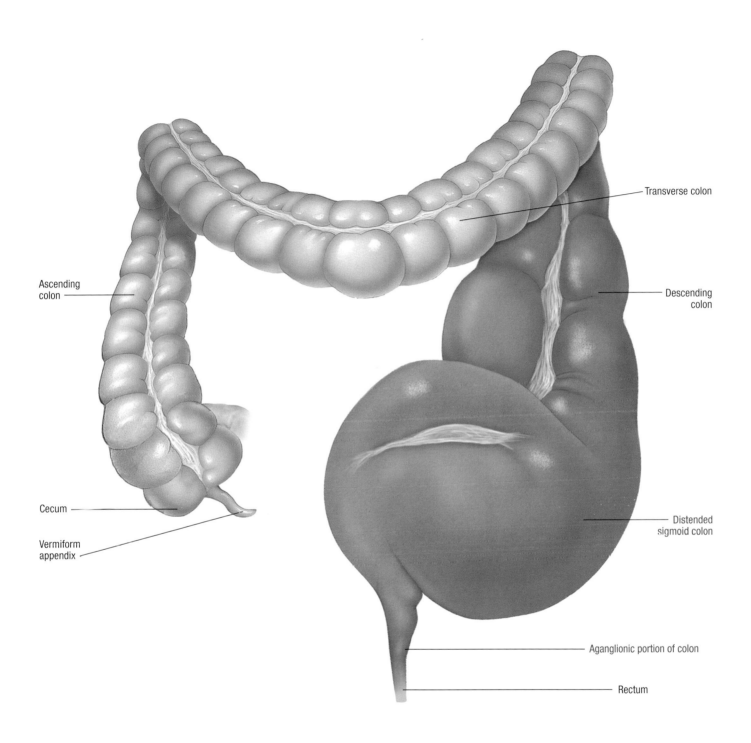

Transverse colon

Ascending colon

Descending colon

Cecum

Distended sigmoid colon

Vermiform appendix

Aganglionic portion of colon

Rectum

HYPERLIPIDEMIA

Hyperlipidemia, also called *hyperlipoproteinemia* or *lipid disorder,* occurs when excess cholesterol, triglycerides, and lipoproteins are present in the blood. The primary form includes at least five distinct and inherited metabolic disorders. Hyperlipidemia may also occur secondary to other conditions such as diabetes mellitus. It's an important risk factor in developing atherosclerosis and heart disease.

Causes
Primary hyperlipoproteinemia
- Types I and III transmitted as autosomal recessive traits
- Types II, IV, and V transmitted as autosomal dominant traits

Secondary hyperlipoproteinemia
- Diabetes mellitus
- Pancreatitis
- Hypothyroidism
- Renal disease
- Dietary fat intake greater than 40% of total calories; saturated fat intake greater than 10% of total calories; cholesterol intake greater than 300 mg/day
- Habitual excessive alcohol use
- Obesity

Pathophysiology
Lipids help in the production of energy, maintenance of body temperature, synthesis and repair of cell membranes, and production of steroid hormones. When lipid levels exceed what the body requires, the excess lipids form occlusive atherosclerotic plaques in blood vessels. These plaques obstruct normal blood flow, contribute to hypertension, and slow or decrease the transport of oxygen to the heart and other body organs.

COMPLICATIONS
- Coronary artery disease
- Pancreatitis
- Stroke
- Myocardial infarction
- Atherosclerosis

Signs and symptoms
Type I
- Recurrent attacks of severe abdominal pain, usually preceded by fat intake
- Malaise and anorexia
- Papular or eruptive xanthomas over pressure points and extensor surfaces
- Ophthalmoscopic examination revealing lipemia retinalis (reddish white retinal vessels)

- Abdominal spasm, rigidity, or rebound tenderness
- Hepatosplenomegaly, with liver or spleen tenderness
- Fever may be present

Type II
- History of premature and accelerated coronary atherosclerosis
- Tendinous xanthomas on the Achilles' tendon and tendons of the hands and feet
- Tuberous xanthomas, xanthelasma
- Juvenile corneal arcus

AGE ALERT
Symptoms of hyperlipidemia typically develop in people ages 20 to 30.

Type III
- Tuberoeruptive xanthomas over elbows and knees
- Palmar xanthomas on the hands, particularly the fingertips

Type IV
- Obesity
- Xanthomas may be noted during exacerbations

Type V
- Abdominal pain associated with pancreatitis
- Complaints related to peripheral neuropathy
- Eruptive xanthomas on extensor surface of arms and legs
- Ophthalmoscopic examination revealing lipemia retinalis
- Hepatosplenomegaly

Diagnostic test results
- Serum lipid profiles show elevated levels of total cholesterol, triglycerides, very low-density lipoproteins, low-density lipoproteins, or high-density lipoproteins.

Treatment
- Weight reduction
- Smoking cessation
- Treatment of hypertension, diabetes mellitus, and other secondary conditions
- Avoidance of hormonal contraceptives containing estrogen
- Restriction of cholesterol and saturated animal fat intake
- Avoidance of alcohol
- Diet high in polyunsaturated fats
- Exercise and physical fitness program
- Statins, bile acid resins, cholesterol absorption inhibitors, fibrates, or nicotinic acid
- Surgical creation of an ileal bypass
- Portacaval shunt

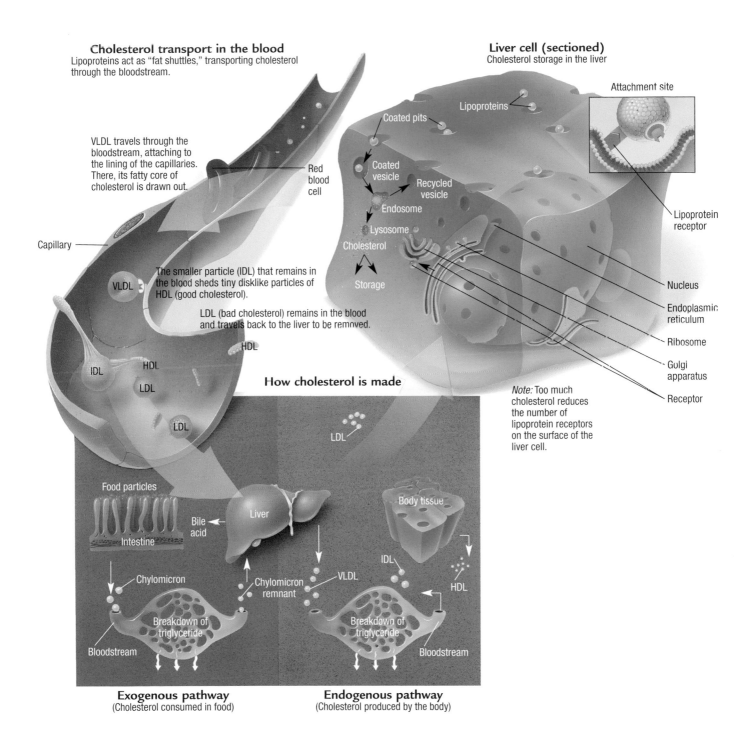

Cholesterol transport in the blood
Lipoproteins act as "fat shuttles," transporting cholesterol through the bloodstream.

VLDL travels through the bloodstream, attaching to the lining of the capillaries. There, its fatty core of cholesterol is drawn out.

Red blood cell

Capillary

The smaller particle (IDL) that remains in the blood sheds tiny disklike particles of HDL (good cholesterol).

LDL (bad cholesterol) remains in the blood and travels back to the liver to be removed.

VLDL

IDL

HDL

HDL

LDL

LDL

LDL

Liver cell (sectioned)
Cholesterol storage in the liver

Lipoproteins

Coated pits

Attachment site

Coated vesicle

Recycled vesicle

Endosome

Lysosome

Cholesterol

Storage

Lipoprotein receptor

Nucleus

Endoplasmic reticulum

Ribosome

Golgi apparatus

Receptor

Note: Too much cholesterol reduces the number of lipoprotein receptors on the surface of the liver cell.

How cholesterol is made

Food particles

Bile acid

Liver

Intestine

Chylomicron

Chylomicron remnant

VLDL

Breakdown of triglyceride

Bloodstream

LDL

Body tissue

IDL

HDL

Breakdown of triglyceride

Bloodstream

Exogenous pathway
(Cholesterol consumed in food)

Endogenous pathway
(Cholesterol produced by the body)

INGUINAL HERNIA

A hernia occurs when part of an internal organ protrudes through an abnormal opening in the wall of the cavity that surrounds it. Most hernias occur in the abdominal cavity. Although many kinds of abdominal hernias are possible, inguinal hernias (also called *ruptures*) are most common. Inguinal hernias may be direct or indirect. Indirect are more common; they may develop at any age, are three times more common in males, and are especially prevalent in infants.

Causes
- Weak fascial margin of internal inguinal ring
- Weak fascial floor of inguinal canal
- Weak abdominal muscles (caused by congenital malformation, trauma, or aging)
- Increased intra-abdominal pressure (due to heavy lifting, pregnancy, obesity, or straining)

Pathophysiology
In an inguinal hernia, the large or small intestine, omentum, or bladder protrudes into the inguinal canal. In an *indirect hernia,* abdominal viscera leave the abdomen through the inguinal ring and follow the spermatic cord (in males) or round ligament (in females); they emerge at the external ring and extend down into the inguinal canal, often into the scrotum or labia.

In a *direct inguinal hernia,* instead of entering the canal through the internal ring, the hernia passes through the posterior inguinal wall, protrudes directly through the transverse fascia of the canal (in an area known as Hesselbach's triangle), and comes out at the external ring.

In an infant, an inguinal hernia commonly coexists with an undescended testicle or hydrocele. In males, during the 7th month of gestation, the testicle normally descends into the scrotum, preceded by the peritoneal sac. If the sac closes improperly, it leaves an opening through which the intestine can slip.

Hernias can be reduced (if the hernia can be manipulated back into place with relative ease), incarcerated (if the hernia can't be reduced because adhesions have formed, obstructing the intestinal flow), or strangulated (part of the herniated intestine becomes twisted or edematous, seriously interfering with normal blood flow and peristalsis).

COMPLICATIONS
- Hernial strangulation
- Intestinal obstruction
- Necrosis

Signs and symptoms
Reduced or incarcerated hernia
- Lump over the herniated area; present when the patient stands or strains; absent when the patient is in a supine position

- Sharp, steady groin pain when tension is applied to herniated contents; fades when the hernia is reduced

Strangulated hernia
- Severe pain

Partial bowel obstruction
- Anorexia
- Vomiting
- Pain and tenderness in groin
- Irreducible mass
- Diminished bowel sounds

Complete bowel obstruction
- Shock
- High fever
- Absent bowel sounds
- Bloody stools

Diagnostic test results
- X-ray confirms suspected bowel obstruction.
- Complete blood count reveals elevated white blood cell count when bowel obstruction is present.

CLINICAL TIP
To detect a hernia in a male patient:
- Ask the patient to stand with his ipsilateral leg slightly flexed and his weight resting on the other leg.
- Insert an index finger into the lower part of the scrotum and invaginate the scrotal skin so the finger can advance through the external inguinal ring to the internal ring.
- Tell the patient to cough. If you feel pressure against the fingertip, an indirect hernia exists; pressure felt against the side of the finger indicates that a direct hernia exists.

Treatment
Temporary measures
- Reduction and a truss

In infants and otherwise healthy adults
- Herniorrhaphy or hernioplasty

For incarcerated or necrotic hernia
- Possibly, bowel resection
- Antibiotics
- Parenteral fluids
- Electrolyte replacement
- Analgesics

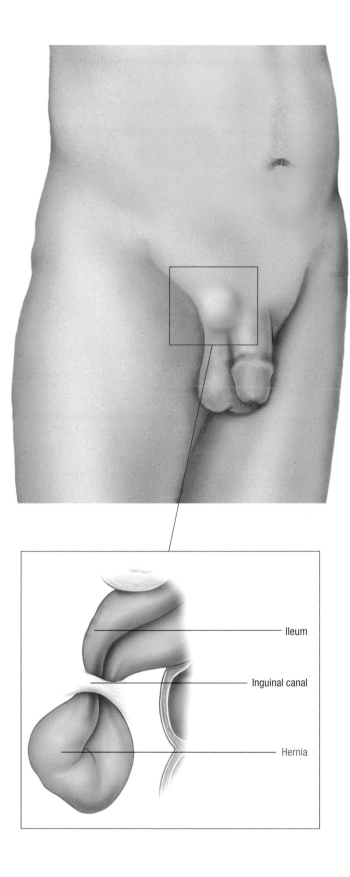

Ileum

Inguinal canal

Hernia

INTESTINAL OBSTRUCTION

Intestinal obstruction is the partial or complete blockage of the small or large bowel lumen. Small-bowel obstruction is far more common (90% of patients) and usually more serious. Complete obstruction in any part of the small or large bowel, if untreated, can cause death within hours due to shock and vascular collapse. Intestinal obstruction is most likely to occur after abdominal surgery or in persons with congenital bowel deformities.

Causes
- Adhesions and strangulated hernias usually causing small-bowel obstruction; large-bowel obstruction typically due to carcinoma
- Mechanical intestinal obstruction resulting from foreign bodies (fruit pits, gallstones, or worms) or compression of the bowel from intussusception, volvulus of the sigmoid or cecum, tumors, or atresia
- Nonmechanical obstruction resulting from physiologic disturbances, such as paralytic ileus, electrolyte imbalances, toxicity (uremia or generalized infection), neurogenic abnormalities (spinal cord lesions), and thrombosis or embolism of mesenteric vessels

Pathophysiology
Intestinal obstruction occurs in three forms:
- *Simple*—Blockage prevents intestinal contents from passing, with no other complications.
- *Strangulated*—Blood supply to part or all of the obstructed section is cut off, in addition to blockage of the lumen.
- *Close-looped*—Both ends of a bowel section are occluded, isolating it from the rest of the intestine.

The physiological effects are similar in all three forms of obstruction. When intestinal obstruction occurs, fluid, gas, and air collect near the obstruction. Peristalsis increases temporarily as the bowel tries to force the contents through the obstruction, injuring intestinal mucosa and causing distention at and above the site of the obstruction. Distention blocks the flow of venous blood and halts normal absorptive processes; as a result, the bowel wall becomes edematous and begins to secrete water, sodium, and potassium into fluid pooled in the ileum.

Obstruction in the small intestine results in metabolic alkalosis from dehydration and loss of gastric hydrochloric acid; lower bowel obstruction causes slower dehydration and loss of intestinal alkaline fluids, resulting in metabolic acidosis. Ultimately, intestinal obstruction may lead to ischemia, necrosis, and death.

AGE ALERT
Watch for air-fluid lock syndrome in older adults who remain recumbent for extended periods. In this syndrome, fluid collects in the dependent bowel loops. Then, peristalsis is too weak to push fluid "uphill." The resulting obstruction primarily occurs in the large bowel.

COMPLICATIONS
- Perforation
- Peritonitis
- Septicemia

- Secondary infection
- Metabolic acidosis or alkalosis
- Hypovolemia or septic shock

Signs and symptoms
Partial small-bowel obstruction
- Colicky pain
- Nausea
- Vomiting
- Constipation
- Abdominal distention
- Drowsiness
- Intense thirst
- Malaise
- Abdominal tenderness
- Borborygmi
- Rebound tenderness (strangulation with ischemia)

Complete small-bowel obstruction
- Spasms every 3 to 5 minutes and lasting for about 1 hour
- Epigastric or periumbilical pain
- Passage of small amounts of mucus and blood from the site of the obstruction
- Vomitus (may first contain gastric juices, bile, and then finally bowel contents)

Large-bowel obstruction
- Constipation
- Colicky abdominal pain
- Continuous hypogastric pain
- Nausea
- Dramatic abdominal distention with visible bowel loops on the abdomen
- Fecal vomitus

Diagnostic test results
- X-ray confirms the diagnosis and reveals the presence and location of intestinal gas or fluid. Small-bowel obstruction shows a characteristic "step-ladder" pattern.
- Barium enema reveals a distended, air-filled colon or a closed loop of sigmoid with extreme distention (in sigmoid volvulus) in large-bowel obstruction.
- Sodium, chloride, and potassium levels are decreased due to vomitus.
- White blood cell count is slightly elevated with necrosis, peritonitis, or strangulation.
- Serum amylase level is increased, possibly from irritation of the pancreas by a bowel loop.

Treatment
- Correction of fluid and electrolyte imbalances
- Decompression of the bowel to prevent vomiting
- Treatment of shock and peritonitis
- Passage of a nasogastric tube, followed by a weighted Miller-Abbott or Cantor tube for bowel decompression, especially in small-bowel obstruction
- Surgical resection with anastomosis, colostomy, or ileostomy in large-bowel obstruction
- Total parenteral nutrition

THREE CAUSES OF INTESTINAL OBSTRUCTION

Intussusception with invagination

The bowel is shortened by the involution of one segment of the bowel into another.

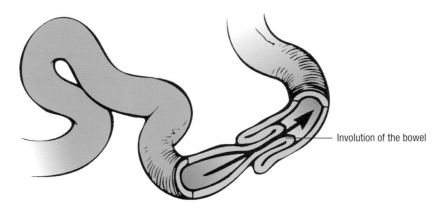

Involution of the bowel

Volvulus

In most cases, the bowel twists counterclockwise.

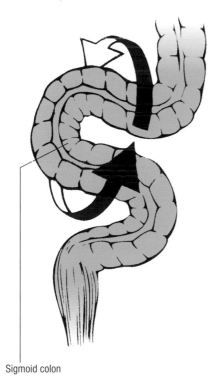

Sigmoid colon

Inguinal hernia

Intestine, omentum, and other abdominal contents pass through the hernia opening.

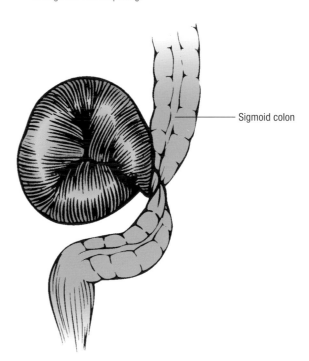

Sigmoid colon

IRRITABLE BOWEL SYNDROME

Also referred to as *spastic colon* or *spastic colitis,* irritable bowel syndrome (IBS) is marked by a group of GI symptoms often related to stress. About 20% of patients never seek medical attention for this benign condition that has no anatomical abnormality or inflammatory component. It's twice as common in women as in men.

AGE ALERT
IBS usually begins between ages 20 and 30.

Causes
- Psychological stress (most common)
- Ingested irritants (coffee, raw fruit, or vegetables)
- Lactose intolerance
- Abuse of laxatives
- Hormonal changes (menstruation)
- Allergy to certain foods or drugs

Pathophysiology
IBS appears to reflect motor disturbances of the entire colon in response to stimuli. Some muscles of the small bowel are particularly sensitive to motor abnormalities and distention; others are particularly sensitive to certain foods and drugs. The patient may be hypersensitive to the hormones gastrin and cholecystokinin. The pain of IBS seems to be caused by abnormally strong contractions of the intestinal smooth muscle as it reacts to distention, irritants, or stress.

COMPLICATIONS
- Diverticulitis
- Colon cancer
- Malnutrition

Signs and symptoms
- Nausea and vomiting
- Crampy lower abdominal pain, occurring during the day and relieved by defecation or passage of flatus
- Pain that intensifies 1 to 2 hours after a meal
- Constipation alternating with diarrhea, with one dominant
- Passage of mucus through the rectum
- Abdominal distention and bloating

Diagnostic test results
- Barium enema reveals colon spasm and tubular appearance of descending colon without evidence of cancer and diverticulosis.
- Sigmoidoscopy or colonoscopy reveals spastic contractions without evidence of colon cancer or inflammatory bowel disease.

Treatment
- Stress management measures, including counseling or mild antianxiety agents
- Identification and avoidance of food irritants
- Application of heat to abdomen
- Bulking agents such as fiber supplements
- Antispasmodics
- Possibly, loperamide or alosetron
- Bowel training (if cause is chronic laxative abuse) to regain muscle control
- Antidepressant medications, such as selective serotonin reuptake inhibitors and tricyclic antidepressants

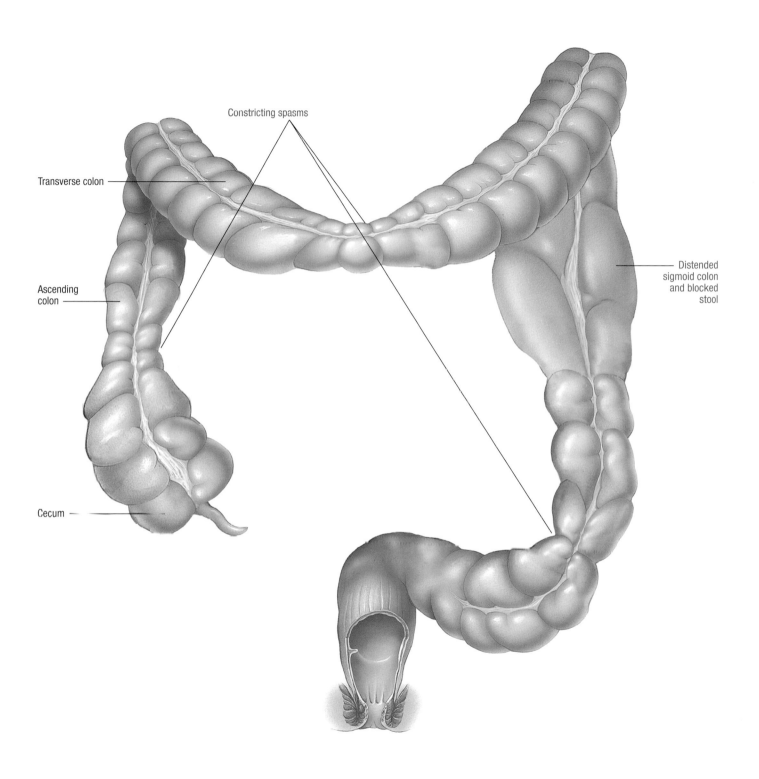

Constricting spasms

Transverse colon

Ascending colon

Cecum

Distended sigmoid colon and blocked stool

LIVER CANCER

Liver cancer, also known as *primary* or *metastatic hepatic carcinoma*, is a rare form of cancer in the United States. It's rapidly fatal, usually within 6 months, from GI hemorrhage, progressive cachexia, liver failure, or metastasis.

AGE ALERT
Liver cancer is most prevalent in men (particularly over age 60), and incidence increases with age.

It's common for patients with hepatomas to also have cirrhosis. (Hepatomas are 40 times more likely to develop in a cirrhotic liver than in a normal one.) Whether cirrhosis is a premalignant state or alcohol and malnutrition predispose the liver to develop hepatomas is still unclear. Other risk factors are exposure to the hepatitis C or hepatitis B virus.

CLINICAL TIP
The liver is one of the most common sites of metastasis from other primary cancers, particularly those of the colon, rectum, stomach, pancreas, esophagus, lung, breast, or melanoma. In the United States, metastatic carcinoma is more than 20 times more common than primary carcinoma and, after cirrhosis, is the leading cause of death related to liver disease. Liver metastasis may appear as a solitary lesion, the first sign of recurrence after a remission.

Causes
- Immediate cause unknown
- Possibly congenital in children
- Environmental exposure to carcinogens
- Androgens
- Oral estrogens
- Cirrhosis

Pathophysiology
Most primary liver tumors (90%) originate in the parenchymal cells and are *hepatomas* (hepatocellular carcinoma, primary lower-cell carcinoma). Primary tumors that originate in the intrahepatic bile ducts are known as *cholangiomas* (cholangiocarcinoma, cholangiocellular carcinoma). Rarer tumors include a mixed-cell type, Kupffer cell sarcoma, and hepatoblastomas (which occur almost exclusively in children and are usually resectable and curable).

COMPLICATIONS
- GI hemorrhage
- Cachexia
- Liver failure

Signs and symptoms
- Mass or enlargement in right upper quadrant
- Tender, nodular liver on palpation
- Severe epigastric or right upper quadrant pain
- Bruit, hum, or rubbing sound if tumor is large
- Weight loss, weakness, anorexia, fever
- Dependent edema
- Ascites
- Jaundice

Diagnostic test results
- Needle or open biopsy of the liver confirms cell type.
- Blood chemistry reveals elevated serum glutamic-oxaloacetic transaminase, serum glutamic-pyruvic transaminase, alkaline phosphatase, lactic dehydrogenase, and bilirubin, indicating abnormal liver function.
- Alpha-fetoprotein levels are elevated.
- Chest X-ray reveals possible metastasis.
- Liver scan shows filling defects.
- Serum electrolyte studies reveal hypernatremia and hypercalcemia; serum laboratory studies reveal hypoglycemia, leukocytosis, or hypocholesterolemia.

Treatment
- Resection if cancer is in early stage; few hepatic tumors are resectable
- Liver transplantation for a small subset of patients
- Palliative measures
- Radiation therapy, chemotherapy
- Controlling signs and symptoms of encephalopathy
- Caring for transhepatic catheters
- Hospice

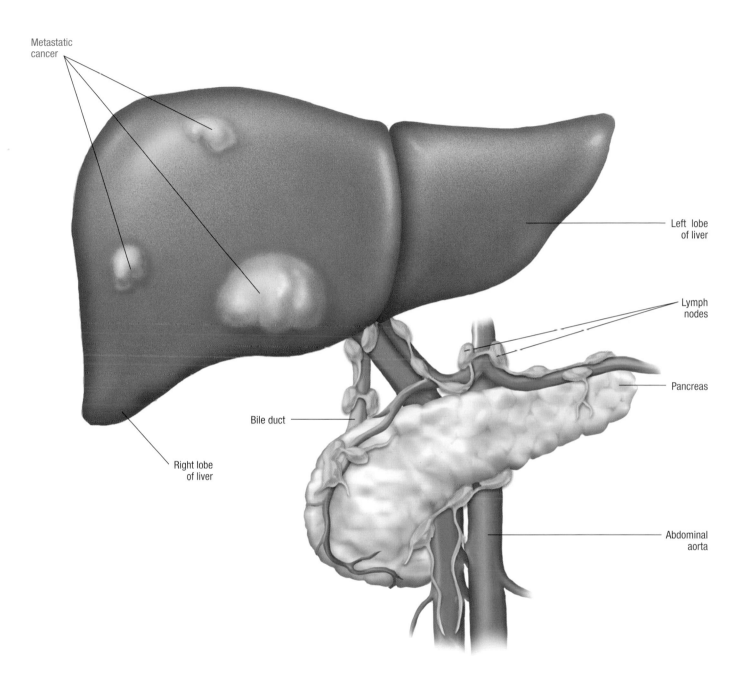

Metastatic cancer

Left lobe of liver

Lymph nodes

Pancreas

Bile duct

Right lobe of liver

Abdominal aorta

LIVER FAILURE

Any liver disease can end in organ failure. The liver performs more than 100 separate functions in the body. When it fails, a complex syndrome involving the impairment of many different organs and body functions ensues. The only cure for liver failure is liver transplantation.

Causes
- Viral or nonviral hepatitis
- Cirrhosis
- Liver cancer

Pathophysiology
Manifestations of liver failure include hepatic encephalopathy and hepatorenal syndrome.

Hepatic encephalopathy, a set of central nervous system disorders, results when the liver can no longer detoxify the blood. Liver dysfunction and collateral vessels that shunt blood around the liver to the systemic circulation permit toxins absorbed from the GI tract to circulate freely to the brain. Ammonia, a by-product of protein metabolism, is one of the main toxins causing hepatic encephalopathy. The normal liver transforms ammonia to urea, which the kidneys excrete. When the liver fails, ammonia is delivered to the brain. Short-chain fatty acids, serotonin, tryptophan, and false neurotransmitters may also accumulate in the blood and contribute to hepatic encephalopathy.

Hepatorenal syndrome is renal failure concurrent with liver disease. The kidneys appear to be normal but abruptly cease functioning. Blood volume expands, hydrogen ions accumulate, and electrolyte disturbances ensue. It's most common in patients with alcoholic cirrhosis or fulminating hepatitis. The cause may be the accumulation of vasoactive substances that cause inappropriate constriction of renal arterioles, leading to decreased glomerular filtration and oliguria. The vasoconstriction may also be a compensatory response to portal hypertension and the pooling of blood in the splenic circulation.

 COMPLICATIONS
- Coma
- Death

Signs and symptoms
- Jaundice
- Abdominal pain or tenderness
- Nausea, anorexia, weight loss
- Fetor hepaticus
- Fatigue
- Pruritus
- Oliguria
- Splenomegaly
- Ascites, peripheral edema
- Varices of esophagus, rectum, abdominal wall
- Bleeding tendencies from thrombocytopenia (secondary to blood accumulation in the spleen), prolonged prothrombin time (from the impaired production of coagulation factors), petechiae
- Amenorrhea, gynecomastia

    Complications of liver failure include variceal bleeding, GI hemorrhage, coma, and death.

Diagnostic test results
- Liver function tests reveal elevated levels of aspartate aminotransferase, alanine aminotransferase, alkaline phosphatase, and bilirubin.
- Blood studies reveal anemia, impaired red blood cell production, elevated bleeding and clotting times, low blood glucose levels, and increased serum ammonia levels.
- Urine analysis reveals increased urine osmolarity.

Treatment
- Liver transplantation
- Low-protein, high-carbohydrate diet
- Lactulose

For ascites
- Salt restriction, potassium-sparing diuretics, potassium supplements
- Eliminating alcohol intake
- Paracentesis, shunt placement

For portal hypertension
- Shunt placement between the portal vein and another systemic vein

For variceal bleeding
- Vasoconstrictor drugs
- Balloon tamponade
- Surgery
- Vitamin K

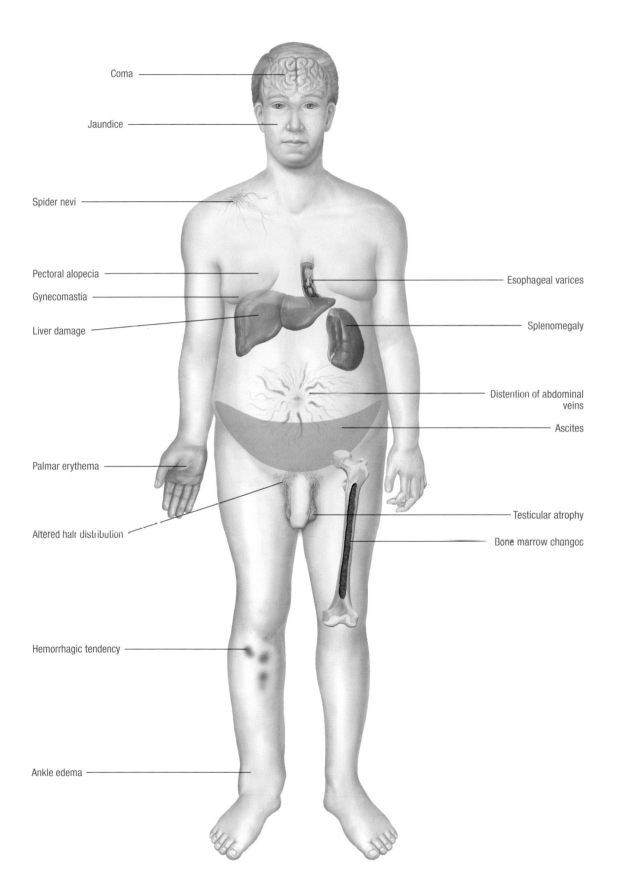

Coma

Jaundice

Spider nevi

Pectoral alopecia

Gynecomastia

Liver damage

Palmar erythema

Altered hair distribution

Hemorrhagic tendency

Ankle edema

Esophageal varices

Splenomegaly

Distention of abdominal veins

Ascites

Testicular atrophy

Bone marrow changes

ORAL CANCER

Oral cancer can occur anywhere in the mouth or throat but more than likely begins in the floor of the mouth. This includes the front two-thirds of the tongue, the upper and lower gums, the lining inside the cheeks and lips, the bottom of the mouth under the tongue, the bony top of the mouth, and the small area behind the wisdom teeth.

More than 34,000 Americans are diagnosed with oral or pharyngeal cancer each year. The death rate for oral cancer is higher than that of other cancers because it's hard to discover or diagnose. Commonly, it's only discovered when the cancer has metastasized to another location, most likely the lymph nodes of the neck. Men are affected twice as often as women, particularly men older than age 40.

Causes
- Tobacco use (smoking and smokeless)
- Alcohol use
- Poor dental and oral hygiene
- Chronic irritation from rough teeth or fillings and dentures
- Infection with human papillomavirus

Pathophysiology
Most oral cancers are caused by squamous cell carcinoma. Squamous cells normally form the lining of the mouth and throat. Squamous cell carcinoma begins as a collection of abnormal squamous cells.

Tobacco and other causative agents damage the lining of the oral cavity. The cells in this layer must grow more rapidly to repair the damage caused by tobacco and other causative agents. The more often cells need to divide, the more chances there are for them to make mistakes when copying their de-

oxyribonucleic acid (DNA), which may increase their chances of becoming cancerous.

Many of the chemicals found in tobacco can directly damage DNA. This direct damage to DNA can cause certain genes, such as those responsible for (starting or stopping cell growth), to malfunction. As the abnormal cells begin to build up, a tumor is formed.

COMPLICATIONS
- Disfigurement
- Metastasis

Signs and symptoms
- Painless, usually small and pale-colored skin lesion, lump, or ulcer on the tongue, lip or mouth area (but may be dark or discolored)
- Possible deep, hard-edged crack in the tissue
- Burning sensation or pain when the tumor is advanced
- Difficulty swallowing
- Abnormal taste

Diagnostic test results
- Tongue or gum biopsy confirms the presence of cancerous tissue.

Treatment
- Surgical excision of the tumor
- Radiation therapy
- Chemotherapy

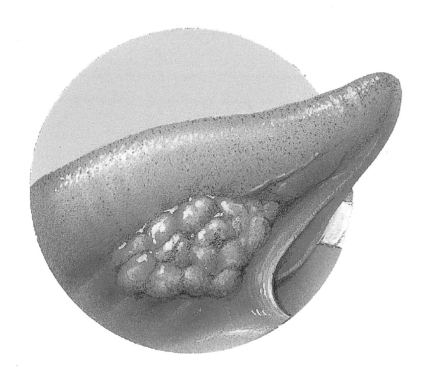

PANCREATIC CANCER

Pancreatic cancer is the fourth leading cause of cancer deaths in the United States. It occurs more frequently in Blacks than Whites. It occurs primarily in the head of the organ and progresses to death within 1 year of diagnosis. Rarer tumors are those of the body and tail of the pancreas and islet cell tumors.

AGE ALERT
The incidence of pancreatic cancer increases with age, peaking between ages 60 and 70.

Causes
- Inhalation or absorption of carcinogens, which are excreted by the pancreas
  - Cigarette smoke
  - Food additives
  - Industrial chemicals, such as beta-naphthalene, benzidine, and urea

Predisposing factors
- Family or personal history of chronic pancreatitis (may be early manifestation of disease)
- Diabetes mellitus (may be early manifestation of disease)
- Chronic alcohol abuse
- Family history of pancreatic cancer
- Obesity
- Diet rich in fat and protein

Pathophysiology
Most pancreatic tumors are adenocarcinomas that arise in the head of the pancreas. The two main tissue types are cylinder-cell and large, fatty, granular-cell tumors. Cancers of the pancreas progress insidiously and most have metastasized before diagnosis. Cancer cells may invade the stomach, duodenum, major blood vessels, bile duct, colon, spleen, and kidney, as well as the lymph nodes.

COMPLICATIONS
- Malabsorption of nutrients
- Type 1 diabetes mellitus
- Liver and GI problems
- Mental status changes
- Metastasis

Signs and symptoms
- Weight loss, anorexia, fatigue
- Pruritus, skin lesions (usually on the legs)
- Abdominal or low back pain
- Jaundice
- Diarrhea
- Fever
- Hyperglycemia, glucose intolerance
- Recurrent thrombophlebitis
- Clay-colored stools

Diagnostic test results
- Laparotomy with biopsy confirms cell type.
- Ultrasound identifies location of mass.
- Angiography reveals vascular supply of the tumor.
- Endoscopic retrograde cholangiopancreatography visualizes tumor area.
- Computed tomography scan and magnetic resonance imaging identify tumor location and size.
- Serum laboratory tests reveal increased serum bilirubin, serum amylase, and serum lipase.
- Prothrombin time is prolonged.
- Elevations of aspartate aminotransferase and alanine aminotransferase indicate necrosis of liver cells.
- Marked elevation of alkaline phosphatase indicates biliary obstruction.
- Plasma insulin immunoassay shows measurable serum insulin in the presence of islet cell tumors.
- Hemoglobin and hematocrit levels may show mild anemia.
- Fasting blood glucose reveals hypoglycemia or hyperglycemia.

Treatment
- Seldom successful because disease is usually metastatic at diagnosis
- Surgery including total pancreatectomy, cholecystojejunostomy, choledochoduodenostomy, choledochojejunostomy, pancreatoduodenectomy or Whipple's procedure, gastrojejunostomy
- Placement of a biliary stent
- Possibly, radiation therapy and chemotherapy
- Analgesics
- Antibiotics
- Anticholinergics
- Antacids
- Diuretics
- Insulin
- Pancreatic enzymes

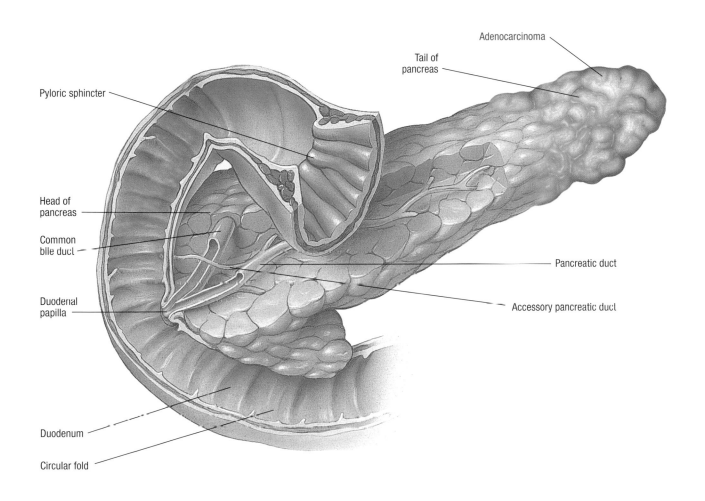

Adenocarcinoma

Tail of
pancreas

Pyloric sphincter

Head of
pancreas

Common
bile duct

Pancreatic duct

Accessory pancreatic duct

Duodenal
papilla

Duodenum

Circular fold

PANCREATITIS

Pancreatitis, inflammation of the pancreas, occurs in acute and chronic forms and may be due to edema, necrosis, or hemorrhage. In men, this disease is commonly associated with alcoholism, trauma, or peptic ulcer and carries a poor prognosis. In women, it's associated with biliary tract disease and has a good prognosis. Mortality in pancreatitis with necrosis and hemorrhage is as high as 60%.

Causes
- Biliary tract disease
- Alcoholism
- Abnormal organ structure
- Metabolic or endocrine disorders, such as high cholesterol levels or overactive thyroid
- Pancreatic cysts or tumors
- Penetrating peptic ulcers
- Blunt trauma, surgical trauma
- Drugs, such as glucocorticoids, sulfonamides, thiazides, hormonal contraceptives, nonsteroidal anti-inflammatory drugs
- Kidney failure or transplantation
- Endoscopic examination of bile ducts and pancreas
- Infection

Pathophysiology
Acute pancreatitis occurs in two forms: edematous (interstitial) and necrotizing. *Edematous* pancreatitis causes fluid accumulation and swelling. *Necrotizing* pancreatitis causes cell death and tissue damage. In both types, inappropriate activation of enzymes causes tissue damage.

Normally, the acini in the pancreas secrete enzymes in an inactive form. Two theories suggest why enzymes become prematurely activated:
- A toxic agent such as alcohol may alter the way the pancreas secretes enzymes. Alcohol probably increases pancreatic secretion, alters the metabolism of the acinar cells, and encourages duct obstruction by causing pancreatic secretory proteins to precipitate.
- *Autodigestion* may occur when duodenal contents containing activated enzymes reflux into the pancreatic duct, activating other enzymes and setting up a cycle of more pancreatic damage.

In chronic pancreatitis, persistent inflammation produces irreversible changes in the structure and function of the pancreas. It sometimes follows an episode of acute pancreatitis. Protein precipitates block the pancreatic duct and eventually harden or calcify. Structural changes lead to fibrosis and atrophy of the glands. Growths called pseudocysts contain pancreatic enzymes and tissue debris. An abscess results if pseudocysts become infected.

If pancreatitis damages the islets of Langerhans, diabetes mellitus may result. Sudden severe pancreatitis causes massive hemorrhage and total destruction of the pancreas, manifested as diabetic acidosis, shock, or coma.

COMPLICATIONS
- Diabetes mellitus
- Respiratory failure
- Pleural effusion
- GI bleeding
- Pancreatic abscess
- Pancreatic cancer

Signs and symptoms
- Epigastric pain
- Mottled skin
- Hypotension
- Tachycardia
- Left pleural effusion
- Basilar crackles
- Abdominal distention
- Nausea and vomiting
- Cullen's sign
- Turner's sign
- Steatorrhea
- In a severe attack: persistent vomiting, abdominal distention, diminished bowel activity, crackles at lung bases, left pleural effusion

Diagnostic test results
- Serum amylase and lipase levels are elevated.
- Blood and urine glucose tests reveal transient glucose in urine and hyperglycemia. In chronic pancreatitis, serum glucose levels may be transiently elevated.
- White blood cell count is elevated.
- Serum bilirubin levels are elevated in both acute and chronic pancreatitis.
- Blood calcium levels may be decreased.
- Stool analysis shows elevated lipid and trypsin levels in chronic pancreatitis.
- Abdominal and chest X-rays detect pleural effusions and differentiate pancreatitis from diseases that cause similar symptoms; may detect pancreatic calculi.
- Computed tomography scan and ultrasonography show enlarged pancreas with cysts and pseudocysts.
- Endoscopic retrograde cholangiopancreatography identifies ductal system abnormalities, such as calcification or strictures; helps differentiate pancreatitis from other disorders such as pancreatic cancer.

Treatment
- Nothing by mouth; I.V. fluids, protein, and electrolytes
- Blood transfusions
- Nasogastric suctioning
- Pain medication such as I.V. morphine
- Antacids, histamine antagonists
- Antibiotics
- Anticholinergics
- Insulin
- Surgical drainage
- Supplemental oxygen, mechanical ventilation
- Laparotomy if biliary tract obstruction causes acute pancreatitis

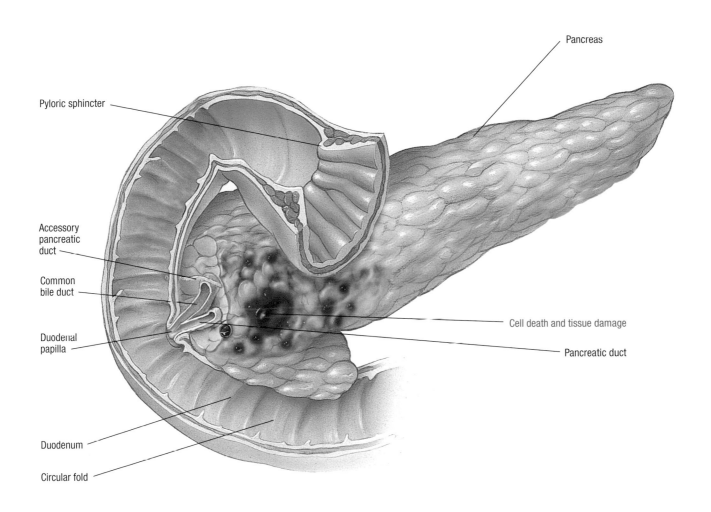

Pancreas

Pyloric sphincter

Accessory pancreatic duct

Common bile duct

Duodenal papilla

Cell death and tissue damage

Pancreatic duct

Duodenum

Circular fold

PERITONITIS

Peritonitis is an acute or chronic inflammation of the peritoneum, the membrane that lines the abdominal cavity and covers the visceral organs. Inflammation may extend throughout the peritoneum or be localized as an abscess. Peritonitis commonly decreases intestinal motility and causes intestinal distention with gas. With antibiotics, mortality is now 10%, and it's usually due to bowel obstruction.

Causes
- Chronic liver disease
- Renal failure
- Appendicitis, diverticulitis
- Chronic liver disease
- Renal failure
- Peptic ulcer, ulcerative colitis
- Volvulus, strangulated obstruction
- Abdominal neoplasm
- Penetrating trauma, such as a stab wound
- Rupture of a fallopian tube or the bladder
- Perforation of a gastric ulcer
- Released pancreatic enzymes

Pathophysiology
Although the GI tract normally contains bacteria, the peritoneum is sterile. When bacteria or chemical irritants invade the peritoneum due to inflammation and perforation of the GI tract, peritonitis is the result. Accumulated fluids containing protein and electrolytes make the transparent peritoneum opaque, red, inflamed, and edematous. Because the peritoneal cavity is so resistant to contamination, infection is commonly localized as an abscess.

COMPLICATIONS
- Abscess
- Septicemia
- Respiratory compromise
- Bowel obstruction
- Shock

Signs and symptoms
- Sudden, severe, and diffuse abdominal pain that tends to intensify and localize in the area of the underlying disorder, such as right lower quadrant in appendicitis
- Acutely tender, distended, rigid abdomen; rebound tenderness
- Pallor, excessive sweating, cold skin
- Absent or diminished bowel sounds
- Nausea, vomiting, abdominal rigidity
- Signs and symptoms of dehydration (oliguria, thirst, dry swollen tongue, and pinched skin)
- Temperature of 103° F (39.4° C) or higher
- Shoulder pain
- Hypotension
- Tachycardia
- Cloudy peritoneal dialysis fluid

CLINICAL TIP
Abdominal distention and resulting upward displacement of the diaphragm may decrease respiratory capacity. Typically, the patient with peritonitis tends to breathe shallowly and move as little as possible to minimize pain. He may lie on his back, with knees flexed, to relax abdominal muscles.

Diagnostic test results
- Abdominal X-ray shows edematous and gaseous distention of the small and large bowel or in the case of visceral organ perforation, air lying under the diaphragm.
- Chest X-ray shows elevation of the diaphragm.
- Blood studies show leukocytosis.
- Paracentesis reveals bacteria, exudate, blood, pus, or urine.
- Laparotomy identifies the underlying cause.

Treatment
Emergency treatment
- Nothing by mouth — to slow peristalsis and prevent perforation
- Nasogastric intubation
- Antibiotics, based on infecting organism
- Analgesics
- Parenteral fluids and electrolytes

When peritonitis results from perforation, surgery should be performed as soon as possible to eliminate the source of infection by evacuating the spilled contents and inserting drains.

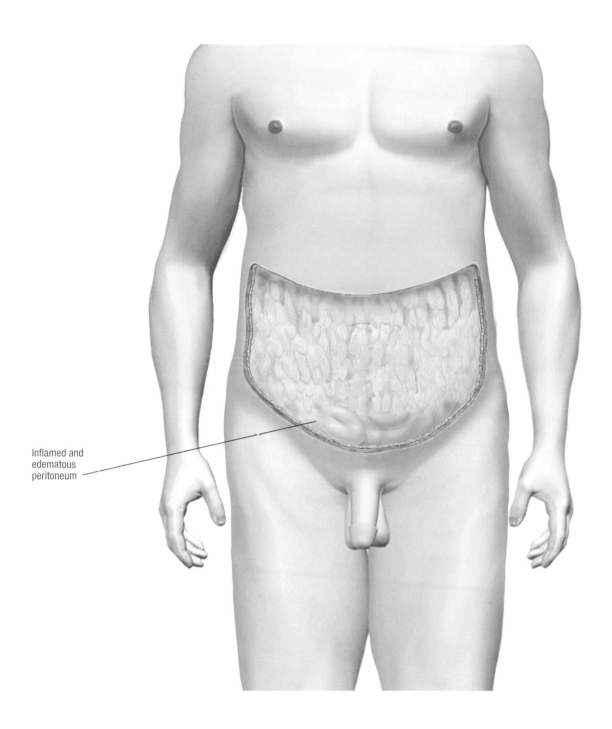

Inflamed and
edematous
peritoneum

PYLORIC STENOSIS

Pyloric stenosis is a narrowing of the pylorus — the outlet from the stomach to the small intestine. The incidence of pyloric stenosis is approximately 2 to 3 of every 1,000 infants. It occurs more frequently in Whites.

AGE ALERT
Pyloric stenosis primarily occurs in infants. It occurs more commonly in boys than in girls and is rare in patients older than age 6 months.

Causes
Unknown, possibly related to genetic factors

Pathophysiology
Pyloric stenosis is caused by hypertrophy and hyperplasia of the circular and longitudinal muscles of the pylorus. When the sphincter muscles thicken, they become inelastic and this leads to a narrowing of the opening. The pyloric canal becomes lengthened and the whole pylorus becomes thickened. The mucosa usually is edematous and thickened. The extra peristaltic effort needed to empty stomach contents into the small intestine leads to hypertrophied muscle layers of the stomach.

COMPLICATIONS
- Dehydration
- Electrolyte imbalance
- Jaundice

Signs and symptoms
- Vomiting, mild initially and then becoming projectile
- In infants: appearing hungry most of the time
- Diarrhea
- Dehydration (poor skin turgor, depressed fontanels, dry mucous membranes, decreased tearing)
- Failure to gain weight or weight loss
- Dyspepsia
- Abdominal pain
- Abdominal distension
- Visible gastric peristalsis
- Firm, nontender, and mobile 1 to 2 cm hard mass, known as an *olive*, present in the midepigastrium to the right of midline; best palpated after the infant has vomited and when calm
- Diminished stools
- Lethargy

Diagnostic test results
- Barium X-ray reveals a distended stomach and narrowed and elongated pylorus.
- Ultrasound shows thickened muscles of the pylorus.
- Chemistry panel often reveals hypochloremia, hypokalemia, and metabolic alkalosis. Hypernatremia or hyponatremia may also be present.

Treatment
- I.V. fluids
- Correction of electrolyte abnormalities
- Surgery
- Nothing by mouth before surgery; small frequent feedings after surgery

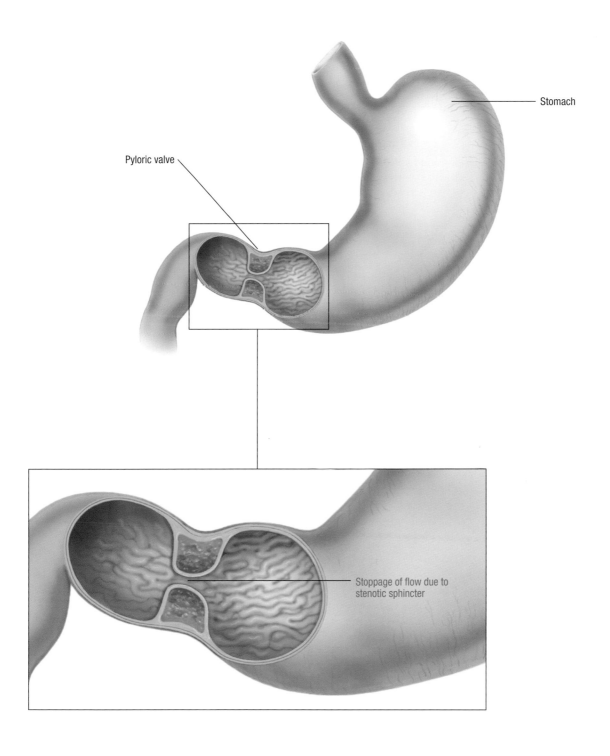

Stomach

Pyloric valve

Stoppage of flow due to stenotic sphincter

ULCERATIVE COLITIS

Ulcerative colitis is a continuous inflammatory disease that affects the mucosa of the colon and rectum. It invariably begins in the rectum and sigmoid colon, and commonly extends upward into the entire colon, rarely affecting the small intestine, except for the terminal ileum. Ulcerative colitis produces edema (leading to mucosal friability) and ulcerations. Severity ranges from a mild, localized disorder to a fulminant disease that may cause a perforated colon, progressing to potentially fatal peritonitis and toxemia. The disease cycles between exacerbation and remission.

AGE ALERT
Ulcerative colitis occurs primarily in young adults, especially women. Onset of symptoms seems to peak between ages 15 and 30 and between ages 55 and 65.

Causes
- Unknown
- May be related to abnormal immune response to food or bacteria such as *Escherichia coli*
- Heredity

Pathophysiology
Ulcerative colitis usually begins as inflammation in the base of the mucosal layer of the large intestine. The colon's mucosal surface becomes dark, red, and velvety. Inflammation leads to erosions that coalesce and form ulcers. The mucosa becomes diffusely ulcerated, with hemorrhage, congestion, edema, and exudative inflammation. Abscesses in the mucosa drain purulent pus, become necrotic, and ulcerate. Sloughing causes bloody, mucus-filled stools. As abscesses heal, scarring and thickening may appear in the bowel's inner muscle layer. As granulation tissue replaces the muscle layer, the colon narrows, shortens, and loses its characteristic pouches (hiatal folds).

COMPLICATIONS
- Nutritional deficiencies
- Anal fistula, abscess, and fissure
- Perforated colon
- Colon cancer
- Hemorrhage and toxic megacolon
- Liver disease
- Arthritis
- Coagulation defects
- Erythema nodosum of the face and arms
- Uveitis
- Pericholangitis, sclerosing cholangitis
- Cirrhosis
- Cholangiocarcinoma
- Ankylosing spondylitis
- Loss of muscle mass

Signs and symptoms
- Weight loss
- Foul-smelling stools
- Recurrent bloody diarrhea, often containing pus and mucus (hallmark sign)
- Abdominal cramping, fecal urgency
- Weakness

Diagnostic test results
- Sigmoidoscopy confirms rectal involvement, specifically, mucosal friability and flattening and thick, inflammatory exudate.
- Colonoscopy reveals extent of the disease, stricture areas, and pseudopolyps (not performed when the patient has active signs and symptoms).
- Biopsy with colonoscopy shows areas of inflammation.
- Barium enema reveals extent of the disease, detects complications, and identifies cancer (not performed when the patient has active signs and symptoms).
- Stool specimen analysis reveals blood, pus, and mucus but no disease-causing organisms.
- Serum potassium, magnesium, and albumin levels are decreased.
- White blood cell count is decreased.
- Hemoglobin level is decreased.
- Prothrombin time is prolonged.
- Elevated erythrocyte sedimentation rate correlates with severity of the attack.
- Abdominal X-ray may reveal loss of haustration, mucosal edema, and absence of formed stool in the diseased bowel.

Treatment
- Corticotropin and adrenal corticosteroids
- Sulfasalazine
- Antidiarrheals
- Iron supplements
- Liquid nutritional supplements

For severe disease
- Total parenteral nutrition and nothing by mouth
- I.V. fluids
- Proctocolectomy with ileostomy

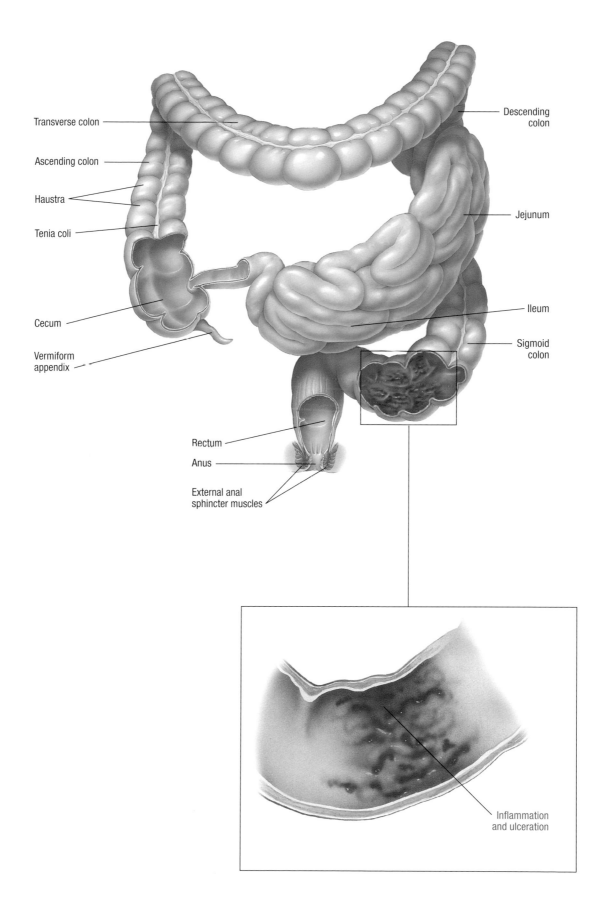

Transverse colon

Ascending colon

Haustra

Tenia coli

Cecum

Vermiform appendix

Rectum

Anus

External anal sphincter muscles

Descending colon

Jejunum

Ileum

Sigmoid colon

Inflammation and ulceration

ULCERS

Ulcers, circumscribed lesions in the mucosal membrane extending below the epithelium, can develop in the lower esophagus, stomach, pylorus, duodenum, or jejunum. Although erosions are often referred to as ulcers, erosions are breaks in the mucosal membranes that don't extend below the epithelium. Ulcers may be acute or chronic in nature. Acute ulcers are usually multiple and superficial. Chronic ulcers are identified by scar tissue at their base.

AGE ALERT
Gastric ulcers are most common in middle-age and elderly men, especially in chronic users of nonsteroidal anti-inflammatory drugs (NSAIDs), alcohol, or tobacco.

Causes
- *Helicobacter pylori* infection
- NSAIDs
- Inadequate protection of mucous membrane
- Pathologic hypersecretory disorders

Predisposing factors
- Blood type (gastric ulcers and type A; duodenal ulcers and type O)
- Other genetic factors
- Exposure to irritants, such as alcohol, coffee, tobacco
- Emotional stress
- Physical trauma and normal aging

Pathophysiology
Ulceration stems from inhibition of prostaglandin synthesis, increased gastric acid and pepsin secretion, reduced gastric mucosal blood flow, or decreased cytoprotective mucus production.

Although the stomach contains acidic secretions that can digest substances, intrinsic defenses protect the gastric mucosal membrane from injury. A thick, tenacious layer of gastric mucus protects the stomach from autodigestion, mechanical trauma, and chemical trauma. Prostaglandins provide another line of defense. Gastric ulcers may be a result of destruction of the mucosal barrier.

The duodenum is protected from ulceration by the function of Brunner's glands. These glands produce a viscid, mucoid, alkaline secretion that neutralizes the acid chyme. Duodenal ulcers appear to result from excessive acid production in the duodenum.

H. pylori release a toxin that destroys the gastric and duodenal mucosa, reducing the epithelium's resistance to acid digestion and causing gastritis and ulcer disease.

COMPLICATIONS
- GI hemorrhage
- Hypovolemic shock
- Perforation
- Penetration to attached structures

Signs and symptoms

Gastric ulcer
- Recent weight loss or loss of appetite
- Pain that worsens with eating
- Nausea and anorexia
- Pallor
- Epigastric tenderness
- Hyperactive bowel sounds

Duodenal ulcer
- Epigastric pain that's gnawing, sharp and burning, or dull; similar to hunger
- Pain relieved by food or antacids, but usually recurring 2 to 4 hours after ingestion
- Weight gain
- Pallor
- Epigastric tenderness
- Hyperactive bowel sounds

CLINICAL TIP
Complications may occur and include hemorrhage, shock, gastric perforation, and gastric outlet obstruction.

Diagnostic test results
- Barium swallow or upper GI and small bowel series reveal the presence of the ulcer.
- Esophagogastroduodenoscopy confirms the presence of an ulcer and permits cytologic studies and biopsy to rule out *H. pylori* or cancer.
- Upper GI tract X-rays reveal mucosal abnormalities.
- Stool analysis detects occult blood.
- White blood cell count is elevated.
- Gastric secretory studies show hyperchlorhydria.
- Urea breath test results reflect activity of *H. pylori*.

Treatment
- Physical and emotional rest
- For *H. pylori* infection: tetracycline, metronidazole, or clarithromycin; ranitidine, bismuth citrate, bismuth salicylate, or a proton pump inhibitor
- Misoprostol (a prostaglandin analog)
- Antacids
- Avoidance of caffeine, tobacco, and alcohol
- Anticholinergic drugs
- Histamine-2 antagonists
- Sucralfate
- Prostaglandin analogs
- Dietary therapy: small frequent meals and avoidance of eating before bedtime

Erosion — Penetration of only the superficial layer

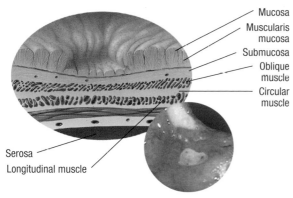

Mucosa
Muscularis mucosa
Submucosa
Oblique muscle
Circular muscle

Serosa
Longitudinal muscle

Acute ulcer — Penetration into muscle layer

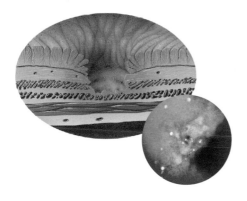

Perforating ulcer — Penetration of wall

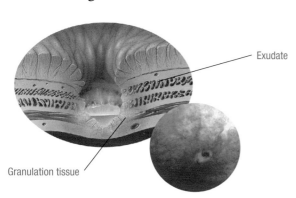

Exudate

Granulation tissue

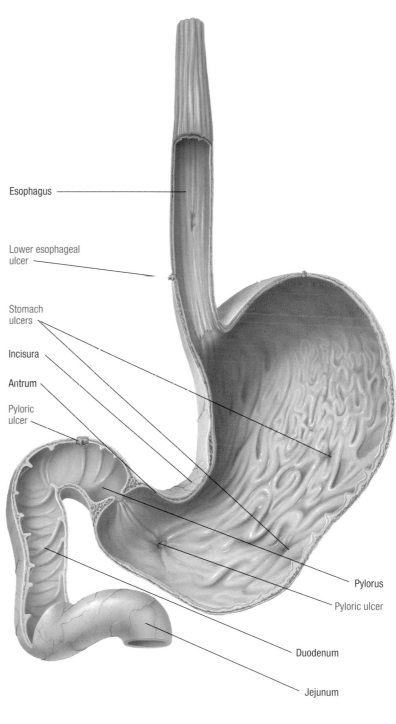

Esophagus

Lower esophageal ulcer

Stomach ulcers

Incisura

Antrum

Pyloric ulcer

Pylorus

Pyloric ulcer

Duodenum

Jejunum

BONE TUMORS

Primary malignant bone tumors (also called *sarcomas of the bone* and *bone cancer*) are rare, constituting less than 1% of all malignant tumors. Most bone tumors are secondary, caused by seeding from a primary site.

AGE ALERT
Primary malignant bone tumors are more common in males, especially in children and adolescents, although some types do occur in persons between ages 35 and 60.

Causes
Unknown
Suggested mechanisms
● Rapid bone growth — children and young adults with primary bone tumors are much taller than average
● Heredity
● Trauma
● Excessive radiotherapy

Pathophysiology
Bone tumors are growths of abnormal cells in bones. These abnormal cells divide uncontrollably and healthy tissue is replaced with unhealthy tissue. Bone tumors may originate in osseous or nonosseous tissue. *Osseous* bone tumors arise from the bony structure itself and include osteogenic sarcoma (the most common), parosteal osteogenic sarcoma, chondrosarcoma, and malignant giant cell tumor. *Nonosseous* tumors arise from hematopoietic, vascular, or neural tissues and include Ewing's sarcoma, fibrosarcoma, and chordoma.

COMPLICATIONS
● Hypercalcemia
● Reduced function of limb

Signs and symptoms
● Bone pain (most common indication of primary malignant bone tumors); characteristics include:
– greater intensity at night
– usually associated with movement
– dull and usually localized
– may be referred from hip or spine and result in weakness or a limp
● Tender, swollen, possibly palpable mass
● Pathologic fractures
● Cachexia, fever, impaired mobility in later stages

Diagnostic test results
● Incisional or aspiration biopsy confirms cell type.
● Bone X-rays, radioisotope bone scan, and computed tomography scan reveal tumor size.
● Blood studies reveal hypercalcemia and elevated alkaline phosphatase.

Treatment
● Excision of tumor with a 3″ (7.6 cm) margin
● Radiation therapy before or after surgery
● Preoperative chemotherapy
● Postoperative chemotherapy
● Radical surgery, such as hemipelvectomy or interscapulothoracic amputation, if necessary (seldom)
● Intensive chemotherapy

Musculoskeletal disorders

TYPES OF BONE TUMORS

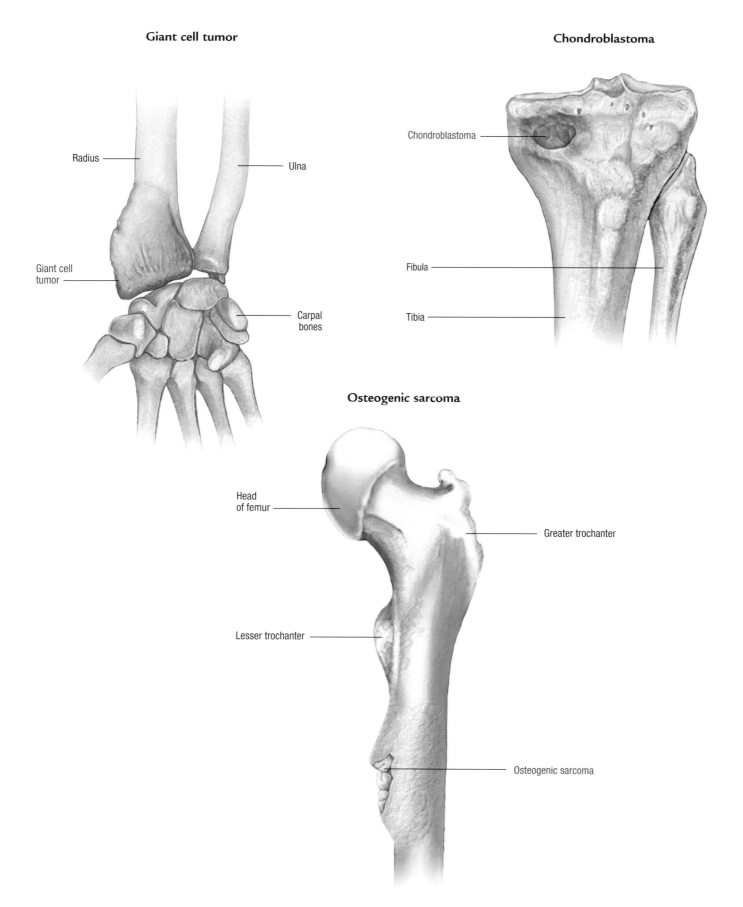

Giant cell tumor

Radius

Ulna

Giant cell
tumor

Carpal
bones

Chondroblastoma

Chondroblastoma

Fibula

Tibia

Osteogenic sarcoma

Head
of femur

Greater trochanter

Lesser trochanter

Osteogenic sarcoma

BURSITIS

Bursitis is a painful inflammation of one or more of the bursae — closed sacs lubricated with small amounts of synovial fluid that facilitate the motion of muscles and tendons over bony prominences. Bursitis usually occurs in the subdeltoid, olecranon, trochanteric, calcaneal, or prepatellar bursae.

Causes
- Recurring trauma that stresses or presses a joint
- Inflammatory joint disease, such as rheumatoid arthritis or gout
- Chronic bursitis — repeated attacks of acute bursitis, trauma, or infection
- Septic bursitis — wound infection; bacterial invasion of overlying skin

Pathophysiology
The role of the bursa is to act as a cushion and allow the tendon to move over bone as it contracts and relaxes. It's a fibrous sac lined with synovial fluid. Bursitis is an inflammation of the bursa. The inflammation leads to excessive production of fluid in the sac, which becomes distended and presses on sensory nerve endings, causing pain.

COMPLICATIONS
- Extreme pain
- Restricted joint movement

Signs and symptoms
- Irritation
- Inflammation
- Swelling
- Warmth over the affected joint
- Sudden or gradual onset of pain and limited movement

Site-specific
- Subdeltoid bursa — limited arm abduction
- Prepatellar bursa — so-called *housemaid's knee;* pain when climbing stairs
- Hip bursa — pain when climbing, squatting, crossing legs

Diagnostic test results
Bursitis typically occurs concurrently with tendinitis, and the two may be difficult to distinguish as discrete problems. X-rays are usually normal in the early stages. In calcific bursitis, they may show calcium deposits.

Treatment
- Resting joint by immobilization with a sling, splint, or cast
- Application of cold or heat
- Ultrasonography
- Mixture of a corticosteroid and an anesthetic such as lidocaine injected into bursal sac for immediate pain relief
- Nonsteroidal anti-inflammatory drugs until patient is free of pain and able to perform range-of-motion exercises easily
- Short-term analgesics, such as propoxyphene, codeine, acetaminophen with codeine, and, occasionally, oxycodone
- For chronic bursitis, lifestyle changes to prevent recurring joint irritation
- Antibiotics
- Surgical drainage of the bursa

Hip

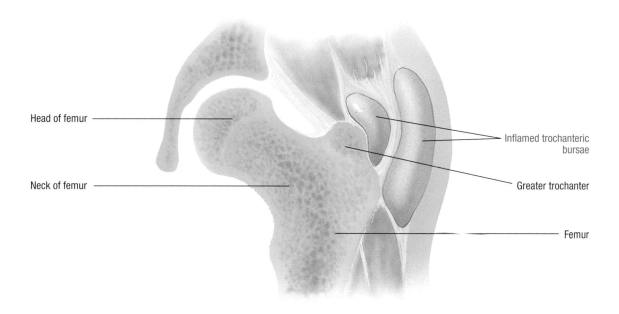

Head of femur

Neck of femur

Inflamed trochanteric bursae

Greater trochanter

Femur

Knee

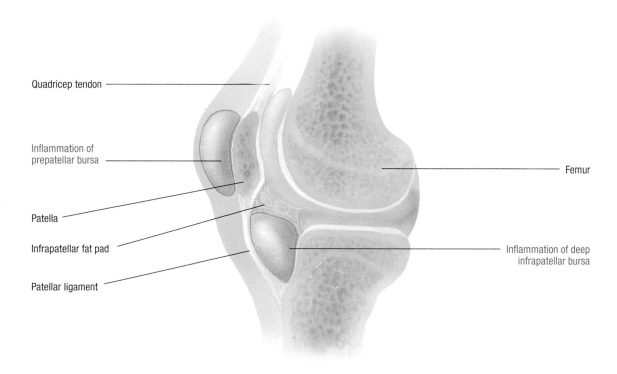

Quadricep tendon

Inflammation of prepatellar bursa

Patella

Infrapatellar fat pad

Patellar ligament

Femur

Inflammation of deep infrapatellar bursa

CARPAL TUNNEL SYNDROME

Carpal tunnel syndrome, a form of repetitive stress injury, is the most common of the nerve entrapment syndromes.

AGE ALERT
Carpal tunnel injury usually occurs in women between ages 30 and 60 and poses a serious occupational health problem.

Assembly-line workers and packers and people who repeatedly use poorly designed tools are also likely to develop this disorder. Computer keyboard and mouse users are also frequently affected. Any strenuous use of the hands — sustained grasping, twisting, or flexing — aggravates this condition.

Causes

Mostly idiopathic, or may result from:
- repetitive stress injury
- rheumatoid arthritis
- flexor tenosynovitis (commonly associated with rheumatic disease)
- nerve compression
- pregnancy
- multiple myeloma
- diabetes mellitus
- acromegaly
- hypothyroidism
- amyloidosis
- obesity
- benign tumor
- other conditions that increase fluid pressure in the wrist, including alterations in the endocrine or immune systems
- wrist dislocation or sprain, including Colles' fracture followed by edema.

Pathophysiology

The carpal bones and the transverse carpal ligament form the carpal tunnel. Inflammation or fibrosis of the tendon sheaths that pass through the carpal tunnel often cause edema and compression of the median nerve. This compression neuropathy causes sensory and motor changes in the median distribution of the hand, initially impairing sensory transmission to the thumb, index finger, second finger, and inner aspect of the third finger.

COMPLICATIONS
- Decrease in wrist function
- Permanent nerve damage with loss of movement and sensation

Signs and symptoms
- Weakness, pain, burning, numbness, or tingling in one or both hands

- Paresthesia in thumb, forefinger, middle finger, and half of the fourth finger
- Inability to clench fist
- Pain extending to forearm and, in severe cases, to shoulder
- Pain usually relieved by shaking or rubbing hands vigorously or dangling arms
- Symptoms typically worse at night and in the morning (Vasodilation, stasis, and prolonged wrist flexion during sleep may contribute to compression of the carpal tunnel.)
- Possibly, atrophic nails
- Dry, shiny skin

Diagnostic test results
- Electromyography shows a median-nerve motor conduction delay of more than 5 milliseconds.
- Digital electrical stimulation shows median nerve compression by measuring the length and intensity of stimulation from the fingers to the median nerve in the wrist.

CLINICAL TIP
These tests provide rapid diagnosis of carpal tunnel syndrome:
- Tinel's sign — tingling over the median nerve on light percussion
- Phalen's wrist-flexion test — holding the forearms vertically and allowing both hands to drop into complete flexion at the wrists for 1 minute reproduces symptoms of carpal tunnel syndrome
- Compression test — blood pressure cuff inflated above systolic pressure on the forearm for 1 to 2 minutes provokes pain and paresthesia along the distribution of the median nerve.

Treatment
- Conservative treatment — resting the hands by splinting the wrists in neutral extension for 1 to 2 weeks, along with gentle daily range-of-motion exercises
- Nonsteroidal anti-inflammatory drugs for symptomatic relief
- Injection of the carpal tunnel with hydrocortisone and lidocaine
- Treatment of any underlying disorder
- Surgical decompression of the nerve by resecting the entire transverse carpal tunnel ligament or by using endoscopic surgical techniques
- Possibly, neurolysis (freeing of the nerve fibers)
- Modification of the work area

Cross section of normal wrist

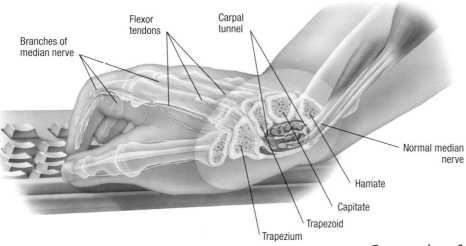

Branches of median nerve

Flexor tendons

Carpal tunnel

Normal median nerve

Hamate

Capitate

Trapezoid

Trapezium

HOW CARPAL TUNNEL SYNDROME OCCURS

Flexion

Compression of nerve between tendons and transverse carpal ligament

Tendon

Nerve

Transverse carpal ligament

Extension

Stretching of nerve over tendons and bones

Cross section of wrist with carpal tunnel syndrome

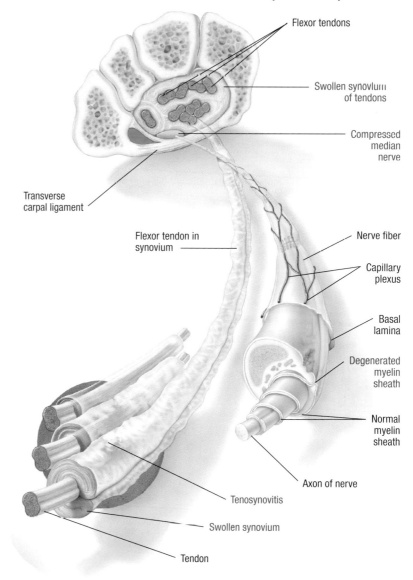

Flexor tendons

Swollen synovium of tendons

Compressed median nerve

Transverse carpal ligament

Flexor tendon in synovium

Nerve fiber

Capillary plexus

Basal lamina

Degenerated myelin sheath

Normal myelin sheath

Axon of nerve

Tenosynovitis

Swollen synovium

Tendon

Carpal tunnel syndrome   **223**

DEVELOPMENTAL DYSPLASIA OF THE HIP

Developmental dysplasia of the hip (DDH) is an abnormal development or dislocation of the hip joint present from birth.

DDH can be unilateral or bilateral. It affects the left hip more often (67%) than the right. This abnormality occurs in three degrees of severity:
- dislocatable — hip positioned normally but manipulation can cause dislocation
- subluxatable — femoral head rides on edge of acetabulum
- dislocated — femoral head totally outside the acetabulum.

Causes
Unknown, but genetic factors may play a role.

Risk factors
- Breech delivery (malposition in utero; DDH 10 times more common than after cephalic delivery)
- Elevated maternal relaxin
- Large neonates and twins (more common)

Pathophysiology
DDH may be related to trauma during birth, malposition in utero, or maternal hormonal factors. For example, the hormone relaxin, secreted by the corpus luteum during pregnancy, causes relaxation of pubic symphysis and cervical dilation; excessive levels may promote relaxation of the joint ligaments, predisposing the infant to DDH. Also, excessive or abnormal movement of the joint during a traumatic birth may cause dislocation. Displacement of the bones within the joint may damage joint structures, including articulating surfaces, blood vessels, tendons, ligaments, and nerves. This may lead to ischemic necrosis because of the disruption of blood flow to the joint.

COMPLICATIONS
- Degenerative hip changes
- Lordosis
- Joint malformation
- Soft-tissue damage
- Osteoarthritis
- Progressive limp

Signs and symptoms
- In neonates: no gross deformity or pain
- Complete dysplasia: hip rides above the acetabulum, causing the level of the knees to be uneven
- Limited abduction on the dislocated side as the growing child begins to walk
- Swaying from side to side ("duck waddle")
- Limp
- Asymmetry of the thigh fat folds
- Positive Ortolani's sign
- Positive Trendelenburg's sign

Eliciting Ortolani's sign
- Place infant on his back, with hip flexed and in abduction. Adduct the hip while pressing the femur downward. This will dislocate the hip.
- Then, abduct the hip while moving the femur upward. A click or a jerk (produced by the femoral head moving over the acetabular rim) indicates subluxation in a neonate younger than 1 month. The sign indicates subluxation or complete dislocation in an older infant.

Eliciting Trendelenburg's sign
- When the child rests his weight on the side of the dislocation and lifts his other knee, the pelvis drops on the normal side because abductor muscles in the affected hip are weak.
- However, when the child stands with his weight on the normal side and lifts the other knee, the pelvis remains horizontal.

Diagnostic test results
- X-rays show the location of the femur head and a shallow acetabulum (also to monitor disease or treatment progress).
- Sonography and magnetic resonance imaging assess reduction.

Treatment
Infants younger than age 3 months
- Reduce dislocation — gentle manipulation
- Maintain reduction — splint-brace or harness worn for 2 to 3 months to hold the hips in flexed and abducted position
- Tighten and stabilize joint capsule in correct alignment — night splint for another month

Beginning at ages 3 months to 2 years
- Try to reduce dislocation — gradual abduction of the hips with bilateral skin traction (in infant); or skeletal traction (in child who is walking)
- Maintain immobilization — Bryant's traction or divarication traction for 2 to 3 weeks (with both extremities in traction, even if only one is affected); for children weighing less than 35 lb (16 kg)
- If traction fails — gentle closed reduction under general anesthesia to further abduct the hips, followed by spica cast for 4 to 6 months
- If closed treatment fails — open reduction and immobilization in spica cast for an average of 6 months or surgical division and realignment of bone (osteotomy)

Beginning at ages 2 to 5
- Skeletal traction and subcutaneous adductor tenotomy (surgical cutting of the tendon)
- Osteotomy

Delayed until after age 5
- Restoration of satisfactory hip function is rare

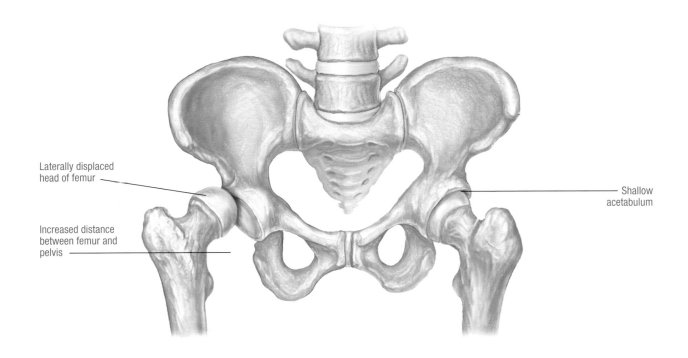

Laterally displaced head of femur

Increased distance between femur and pelvis

Shallow acetabulum

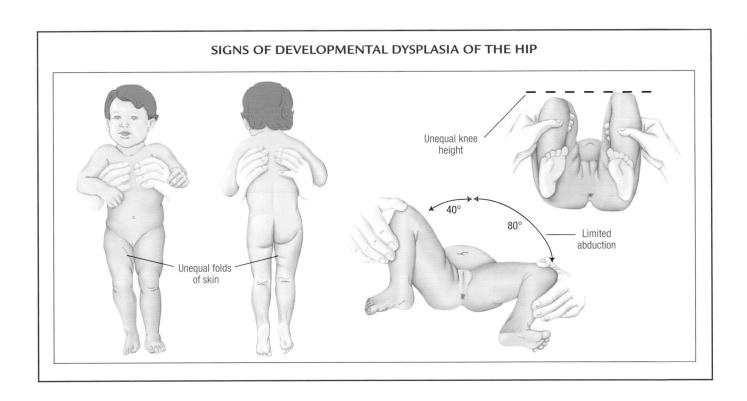

SIGNS OF DEVELOPMENTAL DYSPLASIA OF THE HIP

Unequal knee height

Unequal folds of skin

40°

80°

Limited abduction

FRACTURES

When a force exceeds the compressive or tensile strength of the bone, a fracture will occur. An estimated 25% of the population has traumatic musculoskeletal injury each year, and a significant number of these involve fractures. The prognosis varies with the extent of disability or deformity, amount of tissue and vascular damage, adequacy of reduction and immobilization, and patient's age, health, and nutritional status.

AGE ALERT
Children's bones usually heal rapidly and without deformity. However, epiphyseal plate fractures in children are likely to cause deformity because they interfere with normal bone growth. In elderly people, underlying systemic illness, impaired circulation, or poor nutrition may cause slow or poor healing.

Causes
- Falls, motor vehicle accidents, sports
- Drugs that impair judgment or mobility
- Young age (immaturity of bone)
- Bone tumors
- Metabolic illnesses (such as hypoparathyroidism or hyperparathyroidism)
- Medications that cause iatrogenic osteoporosis such as corticosteroids

AGE ALERT
The highest incidence of fractures occurs in young males between ages 15 and 24 (tibia, clavicle, and distal humerus); these fractures are usually the result of trauma. In elderly people, fractures of proximal femur, proximal humerus, vertebrae, distal radius, or pelvis are often associated with osteoporosis.

Pathophysiology
A fracture disrupts the periosteum and blood vessels in the cortex, marrow, and surrounding soft tissue. A hematoma forms between the broken ends of the bone and beneath the periosteum, and granulation tissue eventually replaces the hematoma.

Damage to bone tissue triggers an intense inflammatory response in which cells from surrounding soft tissue and the marrow cavity invade the fracture area, and blood flow to the entire bone increases. Osteoblasts in the periosteum, endosteum, and marrow produce osteoid (collagenous, young bone that hasn't yet calcified, also called callus). The osteoid hardens along the outer surface of the shaft and over the broken ends of the bone. Osteoclasts reabsorb material from previously formed bones and osteoblasts to rebuild bone. Osteoblasts then transform into osteocytes (mature bone cells).

COMPLICATIONS
- Arterial damage
- Nonunion
- Fat embolism
- Infection
- Shock
- Avascular necrosis
- Peripheral nerve damage

Signs and symptoms
- Pain
- Broken skin with bone protruding (open fracture)
- Deformity
- Swelling, muscle spasm, tenderness
- Ecchymosis
- Impaired sensation distal to fracture site
- Limited range of motion
- Crepitus or clicking sounds on movement

Diagnostic test results
- X-rays confirm the diagnosis and, after treatment, confirm alignment.

Treatment
Emergency treatment for arm or leg fractures
- Splinting the limb above and below the suspected fracture
- Applying a cold pack and elevating the limb

For severe fractures that cause blood loss
- Direct pressure to control bleeding
- Fluid replacement as soon as possible

Closed reduction
- Local anesthetic, analgesic, muscle relaxant, or a sedative
- Manual manipulation

Open reduction (if closed reduction is impossible or unsuccessful)
- Prophylactic tetanus immunization and antibiotics
- Surgery
- Thorough wound debridement
- Immobilization by rods, plates, screws, or external fixation device

FRACTURES OF THE ELBOW

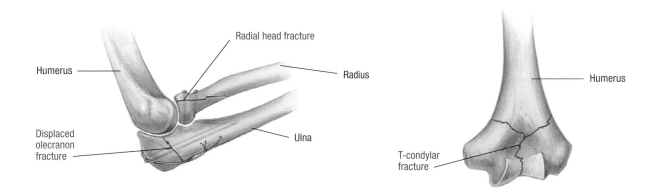

Humerus

Radial head fracture

Radius

Displaced olecranon fracture

Ulna

Humerus

T-condylar fracture

FRACTURES OF THE HAND AND WRIST

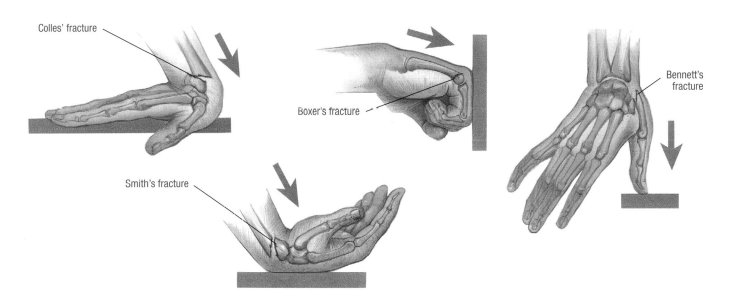

Colles' fracture

Boxer's fracture

Bennett's fracture

Smith's fracture

FRACTURES OF THE HIP

FRACTURES OF THE FOOT AND ANKLE

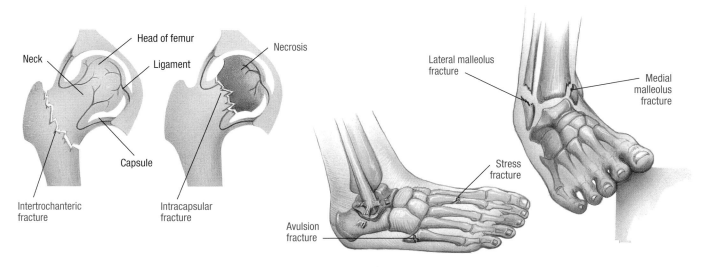

Neck

Head of femur

Ligament

Necrosis

Intertrochanteric fracture

Capsule

Intracapsular fracture

Lateral malleolus fracture

Medial malleolus fracture

Stress fracture

Avulsion fracture

GOUT

Primary gout is a metabolic disease marked by urate deposits that cause painfully arthritic joints. Secondary gout develops during the course of another disease. Gout most commonly affects the foot, especially the great toe, ankle, or midfoot, but it may affect any joint. Gout follows an intermittent course, and patients may be completely free of symptoms for years between attacks. The prognosis is good with treatment. However, renal-tubular damage by aggregates of urate crystals may result in progressively poorer excretion of uric acid and chronic renal dysfunction.

 AGE ALERT
Primary gout usually occurs in men after age 30 (95% of cases) and in postmenopausal women; secondary gout occurs in elderly people.

Causes

Primary gout
- Possibly genetic defect in purine metabolism, causing overproduction of uric acid (hyperuricemia), retention of uric acid, or both

Secondary gout
- Obesity, diabetes mellitus, hypertension, sickle cell anemia, renal disease
- Drug therapy, especially hydrochlorothiazide or pyrazinamide, which decrease excretion of urate (ionic form of uric acid)

Pathophysiology

When uric acid becomes supersaturated in blood and other body fluids, it crystallizes and forms tophi — accumulations of urate salts in connective tissue throughout the body. The presence of the crystals triggers an acute inflammatory response in which neutrophils begin to ingest the crystals. Tissue damage begins when the neutrophils release their lysosomes, which not only damage the tissues, but also perpetuate the inflammation.

 COMPLICATIONS
- Renal calculi
- Atherosclerotic disease
- Cardiovascular lesions
- Stroke
- Coronary thrombosis
- Hypertension
- Infection with tophi rupture and nerve entrapment

Signs and symptoms
- Joint pain, redness, swelling
- Tophi in great toe, ankle, pinna of ear
- Elevated skin temperature
- Hypertension
- Chills
- Fever

Diagnostic test results
- Needle aspiration of synovial fluid shows needlelike intracellular crystals.
- X-rays of the articular cartilage and subchondral bone shows evidence of chronic gout.
- Serum analysis reveals elevated uric acid levels and elevated white blood cell count.
- Urine analysis shows elevated uric acid levels.

Treatment

Acute gout
- Immobilization and protection of the inflamed, painful joints; local application of heat or cold
- Increased fluid intake to prevent kidney stone formation
- Colchicine (oral or I.V.) to inhibit phagocytosis of uric acid crystals by neutrophils (doesn't affect uric acid level)
- Nonsteroidal anti-inflammatory drugs for pain and inflammation.

Chronic gout
- Allopurinol to suppress uric acid formation or control uric acid levels, preventing further attacks (use cautiously in renal failure)
- Colchicine to prevent recurrent acute attacks until uric acid level subsides (doesn't affect uric acid level)
- Uricosuric agents (probenecid or sulfinpyrazone) to promote uric acid excretion and inhibit uric acid accumulation (of limited value in patients with renal impairment)
- Avoidance of alcohol and purine-rich foods (shellfish, liver, sardines, anchovies) that increase urate levels.

GOUT OF THE KNEE

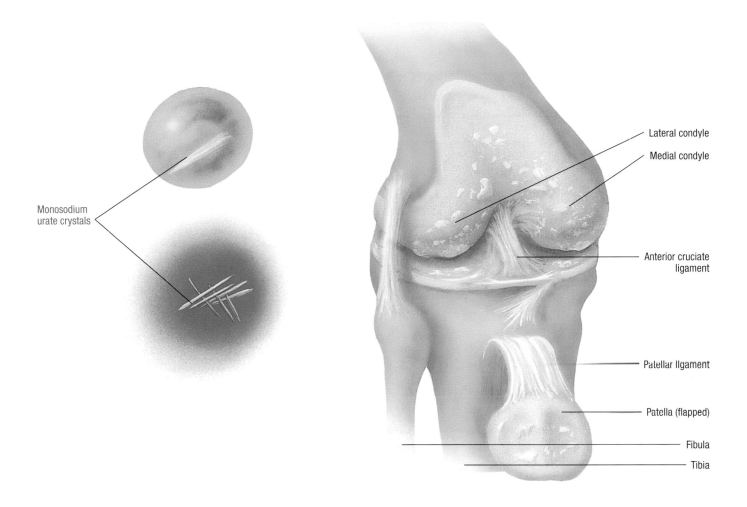

Monosodium urate crystals

Lateral condyle

Medial condyle

Anterior cruciate ligament

Patellar ligament

Patella (flapped)

Fibula

Tibia

GOUT OF THE FOOT

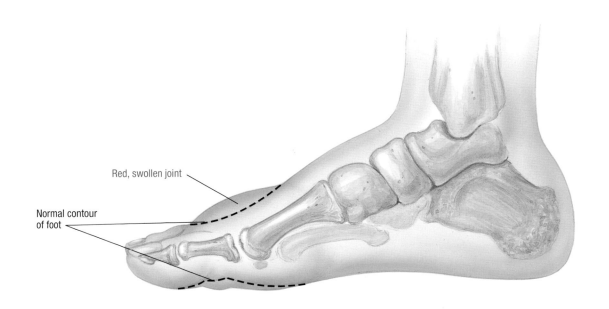

Red, swollen joint

Normal contour of foot

MUSCULAR DYSTROPHY

Muscular dystrophy is a group of congenital disorders characterized by progressive symmetric wasting of skeletal muscles without neural or sensory defects. Paradoxically, some wasted muscles tend to enlarge (pseudohypertrophy) because connective tissue and fat replace muscle tissue, giving a false impression of increased muscle mass. The prognosis varies with the form of disease. The four main types of muscular dystrophy include:

- *Duchenne's*, or *pseudohypertrophic* (50% of all cases) — strikes during early childhood, is usually fatal during the second decade of life, and affects 13 to 33 per 100,000 persons, mostly males
- *Becker's*, or *benign pseudohypertrophic* (milder form of Duchenne's) — becomes apparent between ages 5 and 15, is usually fatal by age 50, and affects 1 to 3 per 100,000 persons, mostly males
- *Facioscapulohumeral (Landouzy-Dejerine)* and *limb-girdle* — usually manifests in second to fourth decades of life, doesn't shorten life expectancy, and affects both sexes equally.

Causes

Genetic mechanisms, typically causing an enzymatic or metabolic defect
- Duchenne's or Becker's muscular dystrophy — X-linked recessive disorders; mapped to the Xp21 locus for the muscle protein dystrophin, which is essential for maintaining muscle cell membrane; muscle cells deteriorate or die without it
- Limb-girdle muscular dystrophy — autosomal recessive disorder
- Facioscapulohumeral muscular dystrophy — autosomal dominant disorder

Pathophysiology

Abnormally permeable cell membranes allow leakage of a variety of muscle enzymes, particularly creatine kinase. The metabolic defect that causes the muscle cells to die is present from fetal life onward. The absence of progressive muscle wasting at birth suggests that other factors compound the effect of dystrophin deficiency. The specific trigger is unknown, but phagocytosis of the muscle cells by inflammatory cells causes scarring and loss of muscle function.

As the disease progresses, skeletal muscle becomes almost totally replaced by fat and connective tissue. The skeleton eventually becomes deformed, causing progressive immobility. Cardiac muscle and smooth muscle of the GI tract typically become fibrotic. The brain exhibits no consistent structural abnormalities.

COMPLICATIONS
- Scoliosis
- Joint contractures
- Decreased mobility
- Cardiomyopathy
- Respiratory failure

Signs and symptoms

Duchenne's (pseudohypertrophic)
- Insidious onset between ages 3 and 5
- Initial effects on legs, pelvis, shoulders
- Enlarged, firm calf muscles
- Waddling gait, toe-walking, and lumbar lordosis
- Difficulty climbing stairs
- Frequent falls
- Positive Gower's sign — patient stands from a sitting position by "walking" hands up legs to compensate for pelvic and trunk weakness

Becker's (benign pseudohypertrophic)
- Similar to those of Duchenne's type but with slower progression

Facioscapulohumeral (Landouzy-Dejerine)
- Weak face, shoulder, and upper arm muscles (initial sign)
- Pendulous lip and absent nasolabial fold
- Abnormal facial movements; absence of facial movements when laughing or crying
- Masklike expression
- Inability to raise arms above head

Limb-girdle
- Weakness in upper arms and pelvis (initial sign)
- Lumbar lordosis, protruding abdomen
- Winging of scapulae
- Waddling gait, poor balance
- Inability to raise arms

Diagnostic test results

- Electromyography shows short, weak bursts of electrical activity in affected muscles.
- Muscle biopsy shows a combination of muscle cell degeneration and regeneration (in later stages, showing fat and connective tissue deposits).
- Immunologic and molecular biological techniques facilitate accurate prenatal and postnatal diagnosis of Duchenne's and Becker's muscular dystrophies.

Treatment

Supportive only
- Coughing and deep-breathing exercises
- Diaphragmatic breathing
- Teaching parents to recognize early signs of respiratory complications
- Orthopedic appliances, physical therapy
- Surgery to correct contractures
- Adequate fluid intake, increased dietary bulk, and stool softener
- Low-calorie, high-protein, high-fiber diet
- Genetic counseling

MUSCLES AFFECTED IN DIFFERENT TYPES OF MUSCULAR DYSTROPHY

Duchenne's

Limb-girdle

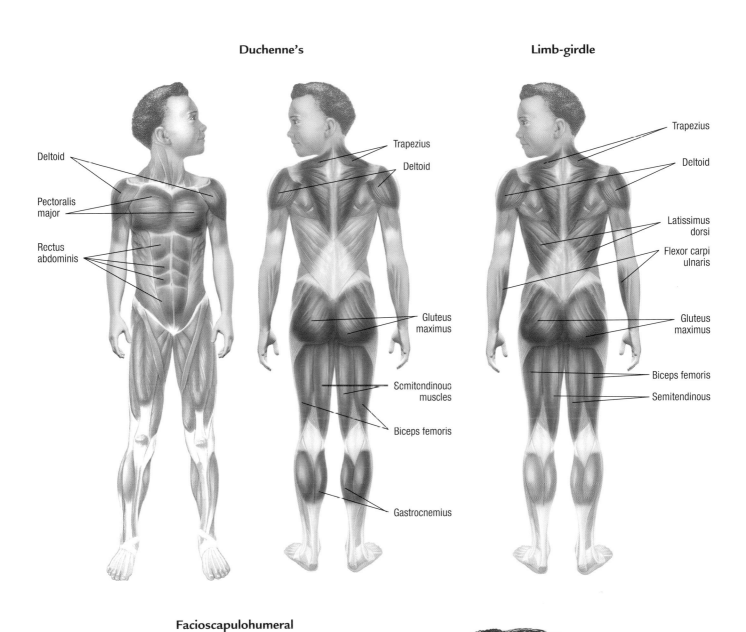

Deltoid

Pectoralis major

Rectus abdominis

Trapezius

Deltoid

Gluteus maximus

Semitendinous muscles

Biceps femoris

Gastrocnemius

Trapezius

Deltoid

Latissimus dorsi

Flexor carpi ulnaris

Gluteus maximus

Biceps femoris

Semitendinous

Facioscapulohumeral

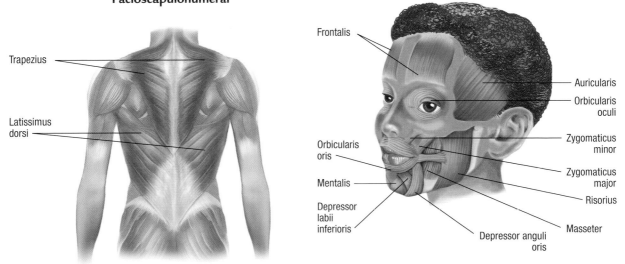

Trapezius

Latissimus dorsi

Frontalis

Orbicularis oris

Mentalis

Depressor labii inferioris

Depressor anguli oris

Auricularis

Orbicularis oculi

Zygomaticus minor

Zygomaticus major

Risorius

Masseter

OSTEOARTHRITIS

Osteoarthritis, the most common form of arthritis, is a chronic condition caused by deterioration of joint cartilage. It usually affects weight-bearing joints (knees, feet, hips, lumbar vertebrae). Osteoarthritis is widespread (affecting more than 20 million persons in the United States) and is more common in women. Typically, its earliest symptoms manifest in middle age and progress. Osteoarthritis may be secondary to the wear and tear of aging (idiopathic) or to some abnormal initiating event.

Osteoarthritis is the most common cause of disability in the United States. Disability depends on the site and severity of involvement and can range from minor limitation of finger movement to severe disability in persons with hip or knee involvement. The rate of progression varies, and joints may remain stable for years in an early stage of deterioration.

Causes

Idiopathic (contributing factors)
- Metabolic — endocrine disorders such as hyperparathyroidism
- Genetic — decreased collagen synthesis
- Chemical — drugs that stimulate collagen-digesting enzymes in synovial membranes, such as corticosteroids
- Mechanical factors — repeated stress

Secondary (identifiable predisposing event)
- Trauma (most common)
- Congenital deformity
- Obesity, poor posture
- Occupational stress

Pathophysiology

Osteoarthritis occurs in synovial joints. The joint cartilage deteriorates, and reactive new bone forms at the margins and subchondral areas of the joints. The degeneration results from damage to the chondrocytes. Cartilage softens with age, narrowing the joint space. Mechanical injury erodes articular cartilage, leaving the underlying bone unprotected. This causes sclerosis, or thickening and hardening of the bone underneath the cartilage.

Cartilage particles irritate the synovial lining, which becomes fibrotic and limits joint movement. Synovial fluid may be forced into defects in the bone, causing cysts. New bone, called *osteophyte* (bone spur), forms at joint margins as the articular cartilage erodes, causing gross alteration of the bony contours and enlargement of the joint.

COMPLICATIONS
- Flexion contractures
- Subluxation and deformity
- Ankylosis
- Bony cysts
- Gross bony overgrowth
- Central cord syndrome (with cervical spine osteoarthritis)
- Nerve root compression
- Cauda equina syndrome

Signs and symptoms
- Deep, aching joint pain
- Stiffness in the morning and after exercise (relieved by rest)
- Crepitus, or grating of the joint during motion
- Heberden's nodes (bony enlargements of distal interphalangeal joints)
- Altered gait from contractures
- Decreased range of motion
- Joint enlargement
- Localized headaches (may be direct result of cervical spine arthritis)
- Bouchard's nodes (bony enlargement of proximal interphalangeal joint)

Diagnostic test results
- Erythrocyte sedimentation rate is elevated.
- X-rays show:
- narrowing of joint space or margin
- cystlike bony deposits in joint space and margins, sclerosis of the subchondral space
- joint deformity
- bony growths
- joint fusion.
- Arthroscopy reveals bone spurs and narrowing of the joint space.

Treatment
- Weight loss to reduce stress on the joint
- Balanced rest and exercise
- Medications, including aspirin and other nonsteroidal anti-inflammatory drugs; propoxyphene, acetaminophen, glucosamine, celecoxib
- Support or stabilization of joint with crutches, braces, cane, walker, cervical collar, or traction
- Intra-articular injections of corticosteroids (every 4 to 6 months) to try to delay node formation in fingers.

Surgical treatment (for severe disability or uncontrollable pain)
- Arthroplasty — partial or total replacement of joint with prosthetic appliance
- Arthrodesis or laminectomy — fusion of bones, primarily in spine
- Osteoplasty — scraping and lavage of deteriorated bone
- Osteotomy — changing alignment of bone to relieve stress on joint

Hand

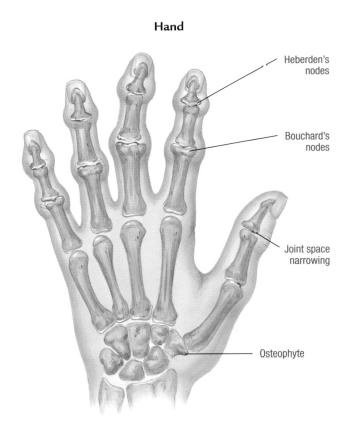

Heberden's nodes

Bouchard's nodes

Joint space narrowing

Osteophyte

Right knee

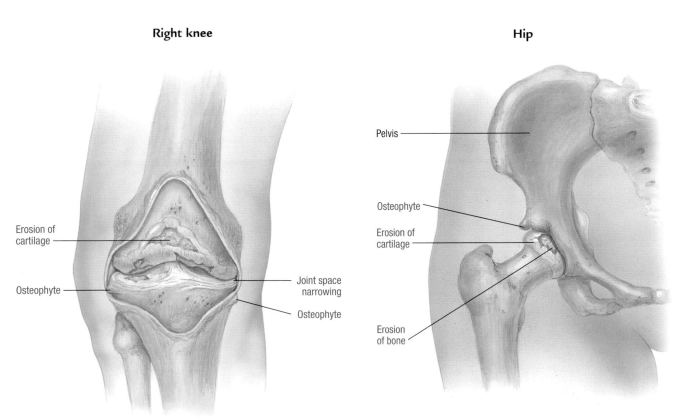

Erosion of cartilage

Osteophyte

Joint space narrowing

Osteophyte

Hip

Pelvis

Osteophyte

Erosion of cartilage

Erosion of bone

OSTEOMYELITIS

Osteomyelitis is a bone infection characterized by progressive inflammatory destruction after formation of new bone. It may be chronic or acute. It commonly results from a combination of local trauma — usually trivial but causing a hematoma — and an acute infection originating elsewhere in the body. Although osteomyelitis usually remains localized, it can spread through the bone to the marrow, cortex, and periosteum. Possible consequences include amputation of an arm or leg when resistant chronic osteomyelitis causes severe, unrelenting pain and decreased function due to weakened bone cortex. Acute osteomyelitis is usually a blood-borne disease and most commonly affects rapidly growing children. Draining sinus tracts and widespread lesions characterize chronic osteomyelitis, which is rare.

AGE ALERT
Osteomyelitis occurs more often in children (especially boys) than in adults — usually as a complication of an acute localized infection. The most common sites in children are the distal femur and the proximal tibia, humerus, and radius. The most common sites in adults are the pelvis and vertebrae, generally after surgery or trauma.

Incidence of osteomyelitis is declining, except in drug abusers. With prompt treatment, prognosis is good for acute osteomyelitis but remains poor for chronic osteomyelitis.

Causes
- Minor traumatic injury
- Acute infection originating elsewhere in the body
- *Staphylococcus aureus* (most common)
- *Streptococcus pyogenes*
- *Pneumococcus species*
- *Pseudomonas aeruginosa*
- *Escherichia coli*
- *Proteus vulgaris*
- *Pasteurella multocida* (part of normal mouth flora in cats and dogs)

Pathophysiology
Typically, a pathogen finds a culture site in a hematoma after recent trauma or in a weakened area, such as the site of local infection (for example, furunculosis), and travels through the bloodstream to the metaphysis, the section of a long bone that's continuous with the epiphysis plates, where the blood flows into sinusoids. Pus is produced and pressure builds in the rigid medullary cavity. An abscess forms and the bone is deprived of its blood supply. Necrosis results and new bone for-

mation is stimulated. Dead bone detaches and exits through an abscess of the sinuses and osteomyelitis becomes chronic.

COMPLICATIONS
- Chronic infection
- Skeletal and joint deformity
- Disturbed bone growth
- Differing leg lengths
- Impaired mobility

Signs and symptoms
- Sudden pain and tenderness in the affected bone
- Swelling, restricted movement of surrounding soft tissues
- Chronic infection presenting intermittently for years, flaring after minor trauma or persisting as drainage of pus from a pocket in a sinus tract
- Tachycardia
- Fever
- Chills, nausea, and malaise
- Drainage of pus

Diagnostic test results
- White blood cell count and erythrocyte sedimentation rate are elevated.
- Blood cultures show causative organism.
- X-ray may not show bone involvement until disease has been active for 2 to 3 weeks.
- Magnetic resonance imaging delineates bone marrow from soft tissue.
- Bone scans detect early infection.

Treatment
- Immobilization of affected body part by cast, traction, or bed rest
- Supportive measures, such as analgesics for pain and I.V. fluids to maintain hydration
- Incision, drainage, and culture of an abscess or sinus tract

Acute infection
- Systemic antibiotics
- Intracavitary instillation through closed-system continuous irrigation with low intermittent suction
- Limited irrigation; blood drainage system with suction (Hemovac)
- Packed, wet, antibiotic-soaked dressings

Chronic osteomyelitis
- Surgery to remove dead bone and promote drainage (prognosis remains poor even after surgery)
- Hyperbaric oxygen
- Skin, bone, and muscle grafts

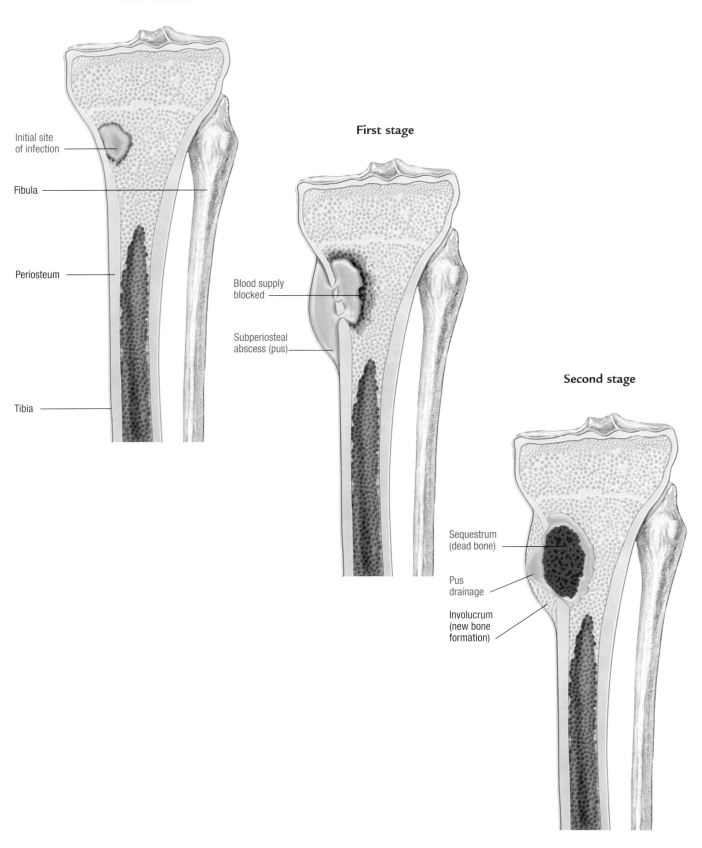

Initial infection

Initial site of infection

Fibula

Periosteum

Tibia

First stage

Blood supply blocked

Subperiosteal abscess (pus)

Second stage

Sequestrum (dead bone)

Pus drainage

Involucrum (new bone formation)

OSTEOPOROSIS

Osteoporosis is a metabolic bone disorder in which the rate of bone resorption accelerates while the rate of bone formation slows, causing a loss of bone mass. Bones affected by this disease lose calcium and phosphate salts and become porous, brittle, and abnormally vulnerable to fractures. Osteoporosis may be primary or secondary to an underlying disease, such as Cushing's syndrome or hyperthyroidism. It primarily affects the weight-bearing vertebrae. Only when the condition is advanced or severe, as in secondary disease, do similar changes occur in the skull, ribs, and long bones. Often, the femoral heads and pelvic acetabula are selectively affected.

AGE ALERT
Primary osteoporosis is often called senile or postmenopausal osteoporosis because it most commonly develops in postmenopausal women.

Causes

Primary osteoporosis
- Unknown
- Contributing factors:
- Mild but prolonged negative calcium balance
- Declining gonadal and adrenal function
- Relative or progressive estrogen deficiency
- Sedentary lifestyle
- Smoking

Secondary osteoporosis
- Prolonged therapy with corticosteroids, heparin, anticonvulsants
- Total immobilization or disuse of a bone (as in hemiplegia)
- Alcoholism, malnutrition, malabsorption, scurvy
- Lactose intolerance
- Endocrine disorders such as hyperthyroidism, hyperparathyroidism, Cushing's syndrome, diabetes mellitus
- Osteogenesis imperfecta
- Sudeck's atrophy (localized to hands and feet)

Pathophysiology

In normal bone, the rates of bone formation and resorption are constant; replacement follows resorption immediately, and the amount of bone replaced equals the amount of bone resorbed. The endocrine system maintains plasma and bone calcium and phosphate balance. Estrogen also supports normal bone metabolism by stimulating osteoblastic activity and limiting the osteoclastic-stimulating effects of parathyroid hormones. Osteoporosis develops when new bone formation falls behind resorption. For example, heparin promotes bone resorption by inhibiting collagen synthesis or enhancing collagen breakdown. Elevated levels of cortisone, either endogenous or exogenous, inhibit GI absorption of calcium.

COMPLICATIONS
- Compression fracture of the spine
- Hip and wrist fractures
- Loss of mobility

CLINICAL TIP
When the rate of bone resorption exceeds that of bone formation, the bone becomes less dense. Men have approximately 30% greater bone mass than women, which may explain why osteoporosis develops later in men.

Signs and symptoms
- Typically, asymptomatic until a fracture occurs
- Spontaneous fractures or those involving minimal trauma to vertebrae, distal radius, or femoral neck
- Progressive deformity — kyphosis, loss of height
- Decreased exercise tolerance
- Low back pain
- Neck pain

Diagnostic test results
- Dual energy X-ray absorptiometry test measures bone mass of the extremities, hips, and spine.
- X-rays show typical degeneration in the lower thoracic and lumbar vertebrae (vertebral bodies may appear flattened and may look denser than normal; bone mineral loss is evident only in later stages); also reveal fractures.
- Computed tomography scan detects spinal bone loss.
- Laboratory studies reveal elevated parathyroid hormone.
- Bone biopsy shows thin, porous, but otherwise normal-looking bone.

Treatment

Early prevention to control bone loss, prevent fractures, control pain
- Limited alcohol and tobacco use
- High-calcium diet
- Prevention of falls
- Early mobilization after surgery, trauma, or illness
- Identification and treatment of risk factors
- Physical therapy emphasizing regular, moderate weight-bearing exercise
- Supportive devices, such as a back brace
- Prompt, effective treatment of underlying disorder to prevent secondary osteoporosis

Pharmacotherapy
- Estrogen; selective estrogen-receptor modulators such as raloxifene; bisphosphonates, such as alendronate and risedronate
- Analgesics and local heat to relieve pain
- Calcium and vitamin D supplements
- Calcitonin

Normally, blood absorbs calcium from the digestive system and deposits it in the bones. In osteoporosis, blood levels of calcium are reduced. To maintain blood calcium levels as normal as possible, reabsorption from the bones increases.

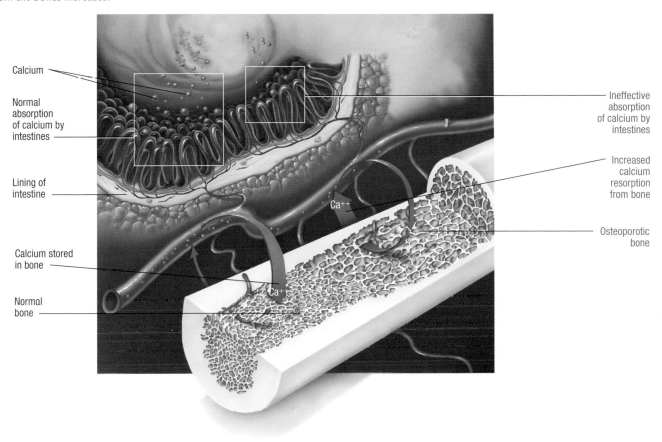

Bone formation and resorption

The organic portion of bone, called *osteoid*, acts as the matrix or framework for the mineral portion.

Bone cells called *osteoblasts* produce the osteoid matrix. The mineral portion, which consists of calcium and other minerals, hardens the osteoid matrix.

Large bone cells called *osteoclasts* reshape mature bone by resorbing the mineral and organic components. However, in osteoporosis, osteoblasts continue to produce bone, but resorption by osteoclasts exceeds bone formation.

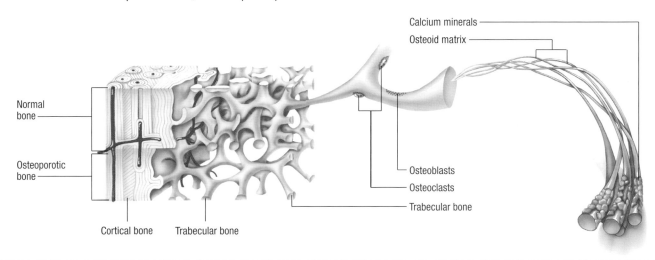

SCOLIOSIS

Scoliosis is a lateral curvature of the thoracic, lumbar, or thoracolumbar spine. The curve may be convex to the right (more common in thoracic curves) or to the left (more common in lumbar curves). Rotation of the vertebral column around its axis may cause rib cage deformity. Scoliosis may be associated with kyphosis (humpback) and lordosis (swayback).

AGE ALERT
About 2% to 3% of adolescents have scoliosis. In general, the greater the magnitude of the curve and the younger the child at the time of diagnosis, the greater the risk for progression of the spinal abnormality. Optimal treatment usually achieves favorable outcome.

Scoliosis may be functional, a reversible deformity, or structural (fixed deformity of spinal column). The most common curve in functional or structural scoliosis arises in the thoracic segment, with convexity to the right. As the spine curves laterally, compensatory curves (S curves) with convexity to the left develop in the cervical and lumbar segments to maintain body balance.

Idiopathic scoliosis, the most common type of structural scoliosis, varies according to age at onset, as follows:
• infantile — affects mostly male infants between birth and age 3; left thoracic and right lumbar curves
• juvenile — affects both sexes between ages 4 and 10; no typical curvature
• adolescent — generally affects girls between age 10 and skeletal maturity; no typical curvature.

Causes

Functional
• Poor posture
• Uneven leg length

Structural
• Congenital — wedge vertebrae, fused ribs or vertebrae, hemivertebrae
• Paralytic or musculoskeletal — asymmetric paralysis of trunk muscles due to polio, cerebral palsy, or muscular dystrophy
• Idiopathic — most common; appears in a previously straight spine during the growing years; may be transmitted as an autosomal dominant or multifactorial trait

Pathophysiology

Differential stress on vertebral bone causes an imbalance of osteoblastic activity. The vertebrae rotate, forming the convex part of the curve. The rotation causes rib prominence along the thoracic spine and waistline asymmetry in the lumbar spine.

COMPLICATIONS
• Severe deformity (if untreated)
• Reduced pulmonary function (curvature greater than 60 degrees)
• Cor pulmonale (curvature greater than 80 degrees)

Signs and symptoms
• Backache
• Lower back pain
• Fatigue
• Dyspnea
• Uneven hemlines or pant legs that appear unequal in length
• Apparent discrepancy in hip height
• Unequal shoulder heights, elbow levels, and heights of iliac crests
• Asymmetric thoracic cage and misalignment of the spinal vertebrae when patient bends forward
• Asymmetric paraspinal muscles, rounded on the convex side of the curve and flattened on the concave side
• Asymmetric gait

Diagnostic test results
• Anterior, posterior, and lateral spinal X-rays, taken with the patient standing upright and bending, confirm scoliosis and determine the degree of curvature and flexibility of the spine.
• Scoliosiometry measures the angle of trunk rotation.

Treatment

Mild scoliosis (less than 25 degrees)
• Observation — X-rays to monitor curve, examination every 3 months
• Exercise to strengthen torso muscles and prevent curve progression

Moderate scoliosis (30 to 50 degrees)
• Spinal exercises and a brace (may halt progression but doesn't correct established curvature); braces can be adjusted as the patient grows and worn until bone growth is complete
• Alternative therapy using transcutaneous electrical nerve stimulation

Severe scoliosis (50 degrees or more)
• Surgery — supportive instrumentation; spinal fusion in severe cases

NORMAL AND ABNORMAL CURVATURES OF THE SPINE

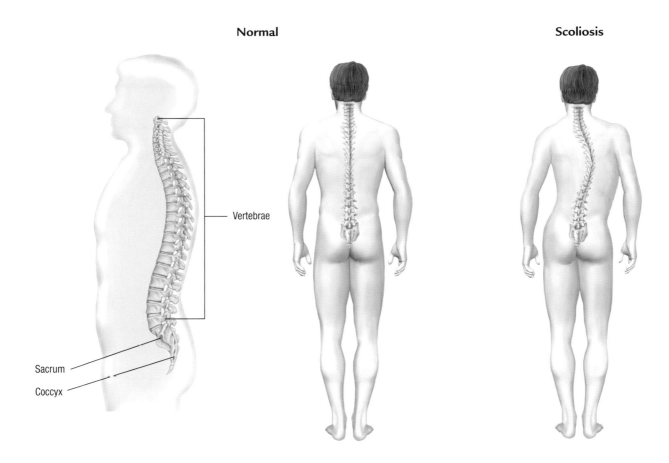

Normal

Vertebrae

Sacrum

Coccyx

Scoliosis

LORDOSIS

CAUSES OF KYPHOSIS

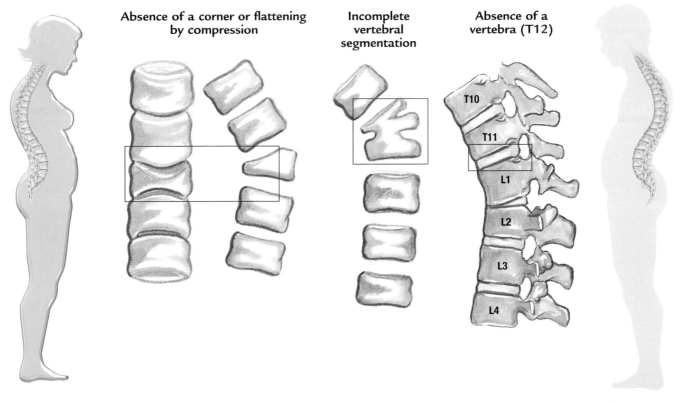

Absence of a corner or flattening by compression

Incomplete vertebral segmentation

Absence of a vertebra (T12)

T10

T11

L1

L2

L3

L4

SPRAINS

A sprain is a complete or incomplete tear of the supporting ligaments surrounding a joint when a joint is forced beyond its normal range of motion. Joint dislocations and fractures may accompany a severe sprain. The ankle is the most commonly sprained joint. Finger, wrist, knee, and shoulder sprains are also common.

Causes
- Falls
- Motor vehicle accidents
- Sports injuries

Pathophysiology
A ligament may tear at any point along the ligament itself or at its attachment to bone (with or without avulsion of bone). Bleeding and formation of hematoma are followed by formation of an inflammatory exudate and development of granulation tissue. Collagen formation begins 4 to 5 days after the injury, eventually organizing fibers parallel to the lines of stress. However, swelling, stretching, or impinging on nerves or vessels around the joint may cause neurovascular compromise. Further reorganization results in eventual strengthening of the damaged ligament, although persistent laxity may result in chronic joint instability.

COMPLICATIONS
- Avulsion fracture

Signs and symptoms
- Localized pain (especially during joint movement) and tenderness
- Swelling and warmth
- Progressive loss of motion
- Ecchymosis

CLINICAL TIP

Sprains are graded according to the degree of swelling and instability:
Grade I — stable, minimal swelling
Grade II — moderate instability and swelling
Grade III — gross instability, extensive swelling, and ecchymosis.

Diagnostic test results
- Stress radiography visualizes the injury in motion.
- X-ray confirms damage to ligaments.

Treatment
- Elevate the joint above the level of the heart for 48 to 72 hours (immediately after the injury)
- Intermittent ice packs for 12 to 48 hours
- Immobilizer or splint during acute phase (up to 1 week)
- Nonsteroidal anti-inflammatory drugs and analgesics
- Early range-of-motion exercise as tolerated
- Acute surgical repair if indicated — notably, for ulnar collateral ligament of thumb, multiple ligament injuries of the knee or elbow due to dislocation
- Late surgical reconstruction if indicated for chronic instability of shoulder, knee, ankle

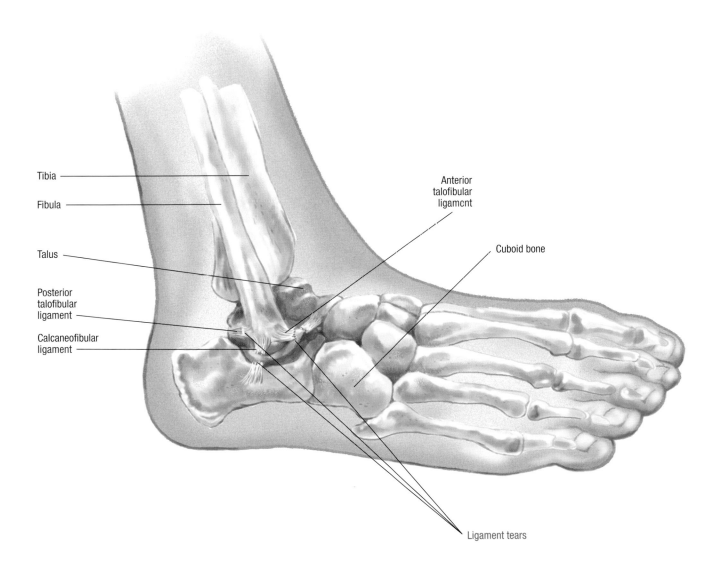

Tibia

Fibula

Talus

Posterior
talofibular
ligament

Calcaneofibular
ligament

Anterior
talofibular
ligament

Cuboid bone

Ligament tears

STRAINS

A strain is an injury to a muscle-tendon unit. Sudden forceful contraction of a muscle under stretch overloads its tensile strength, resulting in failure at the muscle-tendon junction. Muscles that cross two joints are most susceptible to strain. These include the hamstrings, rectus femoris of the thigh, gastrocnemius of the calf, and biceps brachialis of the upper arm.

Causes

- Sudden or unanticipated muscle contraction due to falling, sprinting, throwing, or other forceful activity
- Inadequate warm-ups and conditioning
- Degenerative changes in muscle-tendon units secondary to aging, or anabolic steroid use

Pathophysiology

Bleeding into the muscle and surrounding tissue occurs when a muscle is torn. When a tendon or muscle is torn, an inflammatory exudate develops between the torn ends. Granulation tissue grows inward from the surrounding soft tissue and cartilage. Collagen formation begins 4 to 5 days after the injury, eventually organizing fibers parallel to the lines of stress. With the aid of vascular fibrous tissue, the new tissue eventually fuses with surrounding tissues. As further reorganization takes place, the new tendon or muscle separates from the surrounding tissue and eventually becomes strong enough to withstand normal muscle strain.

COMPLICATIONS

- Calcium deposits in muscle (with repeated injury)
- Limited movement and stiffness
- Muscle fatigue

Signs and symptoms

- Pain
- Inflammation
- Erythema
- Ecchymosis
- Elevated skin temperature

Diagnostic test results

- Stress radiography visualizes the injury in motion.
- X-ray detects the presence of fracture.
- Muscle biopsy, which is rarely done, shows muscle regeneration and connective tissue repair.

Treatment

- Compression wrap
- Elevating injured part above the level of the heart
- Analgesics
- Application of ice for up to 48 hours, then application of heat
- Surgery to suture tendon or muscle ends in close approximation

Chronic strains

- Treatment usually unnecessary
- Heat, nonsteroidal anti-inflammatory drugs, analgesic muscle relaxants to relieve discomfort

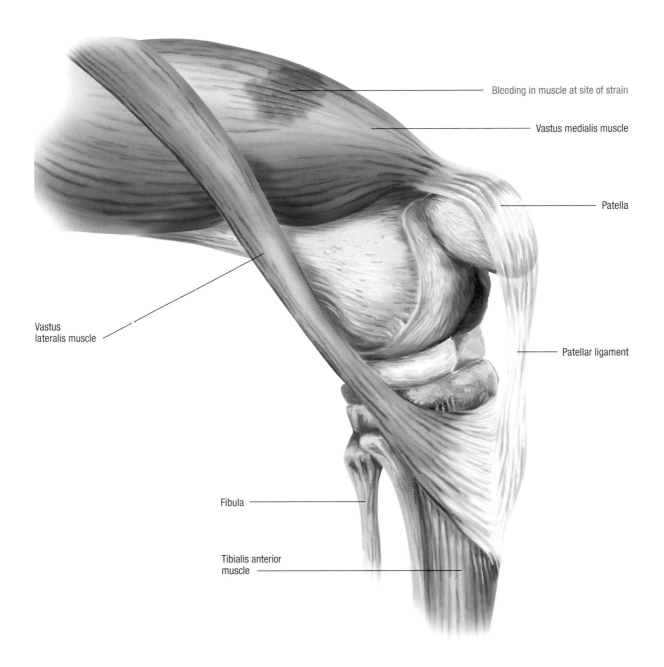

Bleeding in muscle at site of strain

Vastus medialis muscle

Patella

Patellar ligament

Vastus
lateralis muscle

Fibula

Tibialis anterior
muscle

TENDINITIS

Tendinitis is a painful inflammation of tendons and of tendon-muscle attachments to bone, especially in the shoulder rotator cuff, Achilles' tendon, or hamstring.

Causes
- Overuse, such as strain during sports activity
- Other musculoskeletal disorder, such as rheumatic diseases, congenital defects
- Postural misalignment
- Abnormal body development
- Hypermobility

Pathophysiology
A tendon is a band of dense fibrous connective tissue that attaches muscle to bone. Tendons are extremely strong, flexible, and inelastic. Tendinitis is an inflammation of the tendon, usually resulting from a strain.

AGE ALERT
Common forms of tendinitis in adolescents (both males and females) are patellar tendinitis associated with inflammation of the tibial apophysis (Osgood-Schlatter disease) and Achilles' tendinitis at the calcaneal apophysis (Sever's disease).

COMPLICATIONS
- Scar tissue
- Disability

Signs and symptoms
- Restricted range of motion
- Localized pain (most severe at night; commonly interferes with sleep)
- Swelling
- Crepitus
- Calcific tendinitis
  - Proximal weakness (due to calcium deposits in the tendon)
  - Calcium erosion into adjacent bursae (acute calcific bursitis)

Diagnostic test results
- X-rays may be normal at first but later show bony fragments, osteophyte sclerosis, or calcium deposits.
- Arthrography shows irregularities on the undersurface of the tendon.
- Computed tomography scan and magnetic resonance imaging identify tears, partial tears, and inflammation.

Treatment
- Immobilization with a sling, splint, or cast
- Systemic analgesics
- Application of cold or heat
- Injection of a corticosteroid and an anesthetic such as lidocaine into tendon sheath
- Oral nonsteroidal anti-inflammatory drugs until patient is free of pain and able to perform range-of-motion exercises easily
- Surgical debridement of degenerative tendon or excision of calcific deposits may be needed.

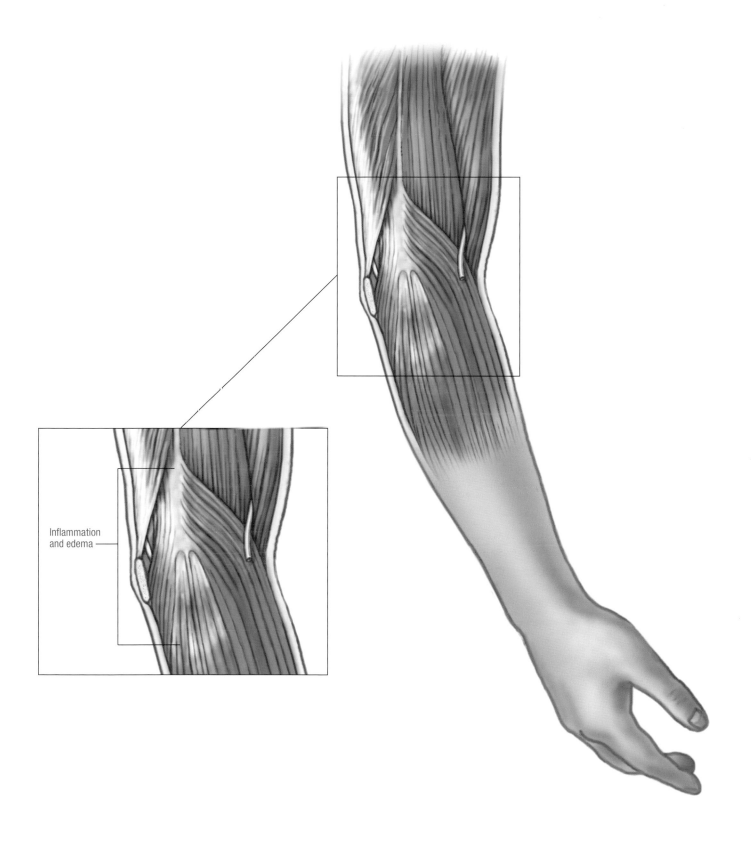

Inflammation
and edema

ANEMIA

Anemia causes lower than normal levels of erythrocytes in the blood. There are several types of anemia, including aplastic, iron deficiency, and pernicious.

Causes

Aplastic anemia
- Congenital
- Autoimmune reactions or other severe disease (hepatitis)
- Drugs, radiation, and toxic agents

Iron deficiency anemia
- Inadequate iron intake and iron malabsorption
- Blood loss
- Pregnancy, which diverts maternal iron to fetus
- Intravascular hemolysis-induced hemoglobinuria or paroxysmal nocturnal hemoglobinuria
- Trauma by prosthetic heart valve or vena cava filters

Pernicious anemia
- Genetic predisposition and age over 60
- Immunologically related disorder
- Partial gastrectomy

Pathophysiology

Aplastic anemia usually develops when damaged or destroyed stem cells inhibit blood cell production. Less commonly, damage to bone marrow microvasculature creates an unfavorable environment for cell growth and maturation.

Iron deficiency anemia occurs when the supply of iron is inadequate for optimal formation of red blood cells (RBCs); the result is microcytic cells with pale color (hypochromic) on staining. Body stores of iron, including plasma iron, become depleted, and the concentration of serum transferrin, which binds with and transports iron, decreases. Insufficient iron stores lead to a depleted RBC mass with low hemoglobin (Hb) concentration and impaired oxygen-carrying capacity.

Decreased production of hydrochloric acid in the stomach and a deficiency of intrinsic factor characterize pernicious anemia. The resulting vitamin B_{12} deficiency inhibits cell growth, leading to the production of scant, deformed, macrocytic RBCs having poor oxygen-carrying capacity.

COMPLICATIONS

Aplastic anemia
- Life-threatening hemorrhage

Iron deficiency anemia
- Infection and pneumonia
- Pica and lead poisoning in children
- Bleeding
- Hemochromatosis (from over-replacement of iron)

Pernicious anemia
- Psychotic behavior
- Neurologic disability

Signs and symptoms

Aplastic anemia
- Progressive weakness, fatigue, and altered level of consciousness
- Ecchymosis, pallor, petechiae, and hemorrhage from the mucous membranes or into the retina
- Fever, oral and rectal ulcers, and sore throat
- Bibasilar crackles and tachycardia

Iron deficiency anemia
- Tachycardia
- Spoon-shaped, brittle nails
- Glottitis

Pernicious anemia
- Weakness, numbness, and tingling of extremities
- Gingival bleeding and tongue inflammation
- Disturbed position sense, lack of coordination, impaired fine finger movement, and altered vision, taste, and hearing
- Irritability, poor memory, headache, depression, delirium, and ataxia; changes may have occurred before treatment
- Palpitations, tachycardia, and systolic murmur

Diagnostic test results

Aplastic anemia
- Laboratory studies show 1 million/mm³ or fewer RBCs of normal color and size with a very low absolute reticulocyte count, elevated serum iron level, normal or slightly reduced total iron-binding capacity, and decreased platelet, neutrophil, and lymphocyte counts.
- Bone marrow biopsy may show severely hypocellular or aplastic marrow and depression of RBCs and precursors.

Iron deficiency anemia
- Laboratory analysis reveals low hematocrit, low Hb, low serum ferritin and serum iron with high binding capacity, low RBC count with microcytic and hypochromic cells, decreased mean corpuscular Hb, and depleted or absent iron stores.
- Bone marrow studies show hyperplasia of precursor cells.

Pernicious anemia
- Schilling test shows excretion of radiolabeled vitamin B_{12}.
- Laboratory analysis shows Hb level 4 to 5 g/dl, low RBC count, mean corpuscular volume greater than 120 mm³, and serum vitamin B_{12} less than 0.1 mcg/ml.
- Bone marrow aspiration shows erythroid hyperplasia with increased megaloblasts but few normally developing RBCs.
- Gastric analysis shows the absence of free hydrochloric acid after histamine or pentagastrin injection.
- Antibody testing reveals intrinsic factor antibodies and antiparietal cell antibodies.

Treatment

Aplastic anemia
- RBC or platelet transfusion
- Bone marrow transplantation
- Measures to prevent infection and antibiotics
- Respiratory support with oxygen
- Corticosteroids, marrow-stimulating agents, immunosuppressive agents, and colony-stimulating factors

Iron deficiency anemia
- Oral or parenteral iron

Pernicious anemia
- Early parenteral vitamin B_{12} replacement
- After initial response, lifelong monthly dose of vitamin B_{12}
- Blood transfusions
- Digoxin, diuretic, and low-sodium diet (for heart failure)

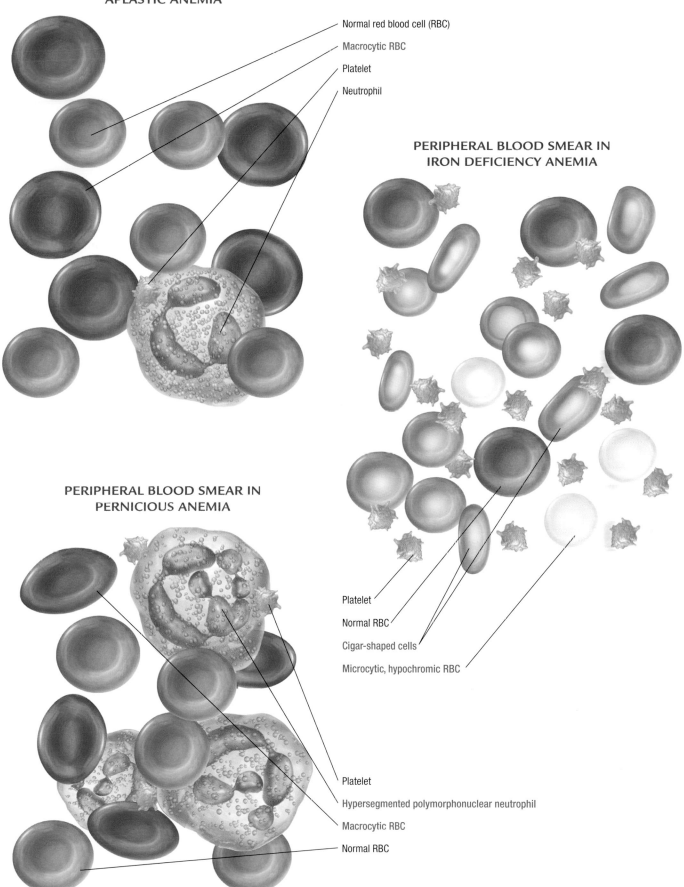

PERIPHERAL BLOOD SMEAR IN APLASTIC ANEMIA

Normal red blood cell (RBC)

Macrocytic RBC

Platelet

Neutrophil

PERIPHERAL BLOOD SMEAR IN IRON DEFICIENCY ANEMIA

Platelet

Normal RBC

Cigar-shaped cells

Microcytic, hypochromic RBC

PERIPHERAL BLOOD SMEAR IN PERNICIOUS ANEMIA

Platelet

Hypersegmented polymorphonuclear neutrophil

Macrocytic RBC

Normal RBC

DISSEMINATED INTRAVASCULAR COAGULATION

Disseminated intravascular coagulation (DIC) occurs as a complication of diseases and conditions that accelerate clotting. It causes small blood vessel occlusion, organ necrosis, depletion of circulating clotting factors and platelets, activation of the fibrinolytic system, and consequent severe hemorrhage. Clotting in the microcirculation usually affects the kidneys and extremities but may occur in the brain, lungs, pituitary and adrenal glands, and GI mucosa. DIC, also called *consumption coagulopathy* or *defibrination syndrome,* is generally an acute condition but may be chronic in cancer patients (Trousseau's syndrome). Prognosis depends on early detection and treatment, the severity of the hemorrhage, and treatment of the underlying disease.

Causes

Etiology unclear (however, in many patients, the triggering mechanisms may be the entrance of foreign protein into the circulation and vascular endothelial injury)

DIC may result from:
- Infections — gram-negative or gram-positive septicemia; viral, fungal, rickettsial, protozoal infection (malaria)
- Obstetric complications — abruptio placentae, amniotic fluid embolism, retained dead fetus, septic abortion, eclampsia
- Neoplasia — acute leukemia, metastatic carcinoma, especially adenocarcinoma
- Necrosis — extensive burns or trauma, brain tissue destruction, transplant rejection, hepatic necrosis
- Other causes — heatstroke, shock, poisonous snakebite, cirrhosis, fat embolism, incompatible blood transfusion, cardiac arrest, surgery necessitating cardiopulmonary bypass, giant hemangioma, severe venous thrombosis, purpura fulminans

Pathophysiology

Regardless of how DIC begins, the typical accelerated clotting results in generalized activation of prothrombin and a consequent excess of thrombin. The thrombin converts fibrinogen to fibrin, producing fibrin clots in the microcirculation. This process uses huge amounts of coagulation factors (especially fibrinogen, prothrombin, platelets, and factors V and VIII), causing hypofibrinogenemia, hypoprothrombinemia, thrombocytopenia, and deficiencies in factors V and VIII. Circulating thrombin also activates the fibrinolytic system, which dissolves fibrin clots into fibrin degradation products. Hemorrhage may be mostly the result of the anticoagulant activity of fibrin degradation products as well as depletion of plasma coagulation factors.

COMPLICATIONS
- Renal failure
- Hepatic damage
- Stroke
- Ischemic bowel
- Respiratory distress
- Hypoxia
- Anorexia
- Severe muscle pain
- Shock and coma

Signs and symptoms
- Abnormal bleeding:
- Cutaneous oozing of serum, bleeding from surgical or I.V. sites, bleeding from the GI tract
- Petechiae or blood blisters (purpura), epistaxis, hemoptysis
- Cyanosis; cold, mottled fingers and toes
- Severe muscle, back, abdominal, and chest pain
- Nausea and vomiting (may be a manifestation of GI bleeding)
- Shock
- Confusion
- Dyspnea
- Oliguria
- Hematuria

Diagnostic test results
Laboratory analysis reveals:
- decreased serum platelet count (less than 100,000/mm^3)
- decreased serum fibrinogen level (less than 150 mg/dl)
- prolonged prothrombin time (more than 15 seconds)
- prolonged partial thromboplastin time (more than 80 seconds)
- increased fibrin degradation products (commonly greater than 45 mcg/ml, or positive at less than 1:100 dilution)
- positive D-dimer test (specific fibrinogen test for DIC) at less than 1:8 dilution
- diminished blood clotting factors V and VIII
- complete blood count showing decreased hemoglobin levels (less than 10 g/dl)
- elevated blood urea nitrogen (greater than 25 mg/dl) and elevated serum creatinine levels (greater than 1.3 mg/dl).

Treatment
- Prompt recognition and treatment of underlying disorder
- Blood, fresh frozen plasma, platelet, packed red-blood-cell transfusions, or cryoprecipitate to support hemostasis in active bleeding
- I.V. fluids
- Vasopressors such as dopamine
- Inhibitors of fibrinolysis such as epsilon-aminocaproic acid
- Recombinant human activated protein C
- Unfractionated or low-molecular weight heparin in early stages to prevent microclotting and as a last resort in hemorrhage (controversial in acute DIC after sepsis)

NORMAL CLOTTING PROCESS

Blood vessel walls

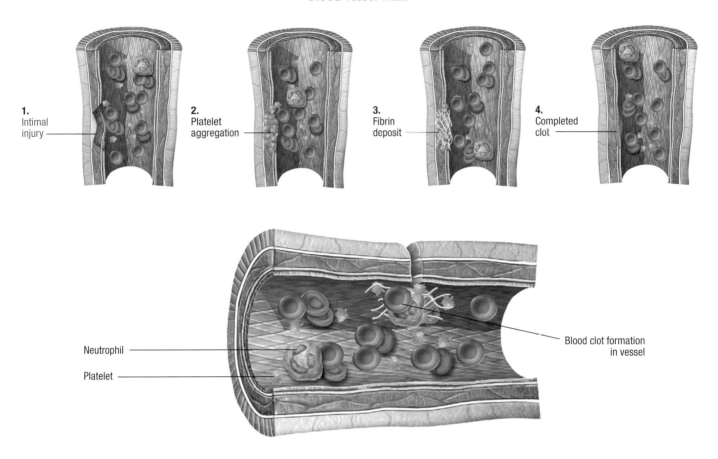

1.
Intimal injury

2.
Platelet aggregation

3.
Fibrin deposit

4.
Completed clot

Neutrophil

Platelet

Blood clot formation in vessel

UNDERSTANDING DISSEMINATED INTRAVASCULAR COAGULATION

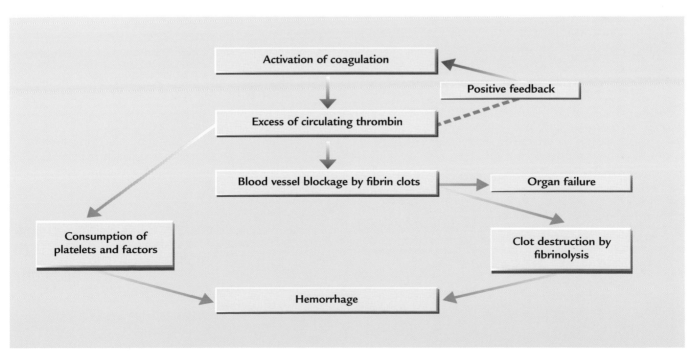

Activation of coagulation

Positive feedback

Excess of circulating thrombin

Blood vessel blockage by fibrin clots

Organ failure

Consumption of platelets and factors

Clot destruction by fibrinolysis

Hemorrhage

HEMOPHILIA

Hemophilia, a hereditary bleeding disorder, results from a deficiency of specific clotting factors. The severity of bleeding and the prognosis vary with the degree of deficiency, or nonfunction, and the site of bleeding. Hemophilia occurs in 20 of 100,000 male births.

Hemophilia A (classic hemophilia) results from a deficiency of factor VIII. More common than type B, it affects more than 80% of all hemophiliacs and is the most common X-linked genetic disease. Hemophilia B (Christmas disease) affects approximately 15% of all hemophiliacs and results from a deficiency of factor IX.

Advances in treatment have greatly improved the prognosis for hemophiliacs, many of whom live normal life spans. Surgical procedures can be done safely at special treatment centers under the guidance of a hematologist.

Causes

Hemophilia types A and B: X-linked recessive genetic traits

Pathophysiology

Hemophilia is an X-linked recessive genetic disease causing abnormal bleeding because of a specific clotting factor malfunction. Factors VIII and IX are components of the intrinsic clotting pathway; factor IX is an essential factor and factor VIII is a critical cofactor that accelerates the activation of factor X by several thousandfold. Excessive bleeding occurs when these clotting factors are reduced by more than 75%. A deficiency or nonfunction of factor VIII causes hemophilia A, and a deficiency or nonfunction of factor IX causes hemophilia B.

Hemophilia may be severe, moderate, or mild, depending on the degree of activation of clotting factors. Patients with severe disease have no detectable factor VIII or factor IX activity. Moderately afflicted patients have 1% to 4% of normal clotting activity, and mildly afflicted patients have 5% to 25% of normal clotting activity.

A patient with hemophilia forms a platelet plug at a bleeding site, but clotting factor deficiency impairs the ability to form a stable fibrin clot. Bleeding occurs primarily into large joints, especially after trauma or surgery. Delayed bleeding is more common than immediate hemorrhage.

COMPLICATIONS
- Intracranial bleeding, shock, and death
- Neuropathies
- Paresthesia
- Muscle atrophy
- Ischemia and gangrene of the major vessels

Signs and symptoms

- Spontaneous bleeding in severe hemophilia (prolonged or excessive bleeding after circumcision is often the first sign)
- Excessive or continued bleeding or bruising after minor trauma or surgery
- Large subcutaneous and deep I.M. hematomas due to mild trauma
- Prolonged bleeding in mild hemophilia after major trauma or surgery, but no spontaneous bleeding after minor trauma
- Pain, swelling, and tenderness due to bleeding into joints (especially weight-bearing joints)
- Internal bleeding, often manifested as abdominal, chest, or flank pain
- Hematuria
- Hematemesis or tarry stools

Diagnostic test results

- Specific coagulation factor assays show the type and severity of hemophilia.
- Laboratory analysis reveals low serum factor VIII activity of normal and prolonged activated partial thromboplastin time (hemophilia A).
- Laboratory analysis reveals deficient factor IX and normal factor VIII levels (hemophilia B).

Treatment

- Cryoprecipitate (for hemophilia A) or lyophilized factor VIII or IX to increase clotting factor levels and to permit normal hemostasis levels
- Factor IX concentrate during bleeding episodes (hemophilia B)
- Aminocaproic acid (Amicar) for oral bleeding (inhibits plasminogen activator substances)
- Prophylactic desmopressin before dental procedures or minor surgery to release stored von Willebrand's factor and factor VIII (to reduce bleeding)
- Fresh frozen plasma
- Immunization with hepatitis B vaccine

NORMAL CLOTTING AND CLOTTING IN HEMOPHILIA

Normal   **Hemophilia**

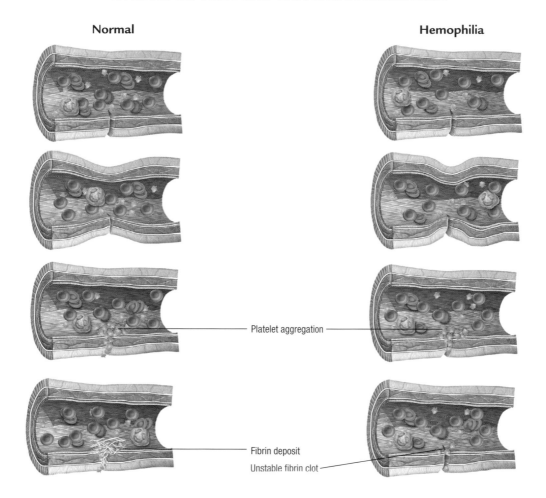

Platelet aggregation

Fibrin deposit

Unstable fibrin clot

 CLINICAL TIP

X-LINKED RECESSIVE INHERITANCE

The diagram shows the children of a normal parent and those of a parent with a recessive gene on the X chromosome (shown by an open dot). All daughters of an affected male will be carriers. The son of a female carrier may inherit a recessive gene on the X chromosome and be affected by the disease. Unaffected sons can't transmit the disorder.

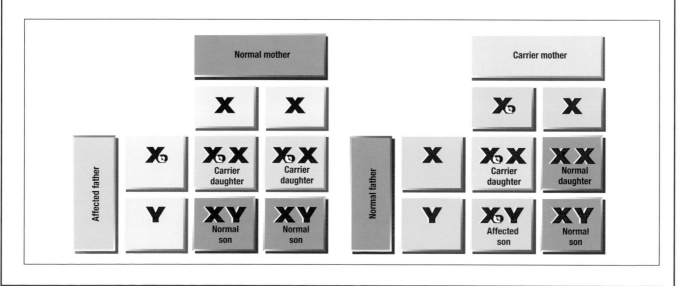

HODGKIN'S DISEASE

Hodgkin's disease is a neoplastic disease characterized by painless, progressive enlargement of lymph nodes, spleen, and other lymphoid tissue resulting from proliferation of lymphocytes, histiocytes, eosinophils, and Reed-Sternberg giant cells. Untreated, Hodgkin's disease follows a variable but relentlessly progressive and, ultimately, fatal course. With appropriate treatment, more than 80% of patients with stage I or II disease survive at least 10 years.

Causes
Unknown; however, viral etiology is suspected (Epstein-Barr virus is a leading candidate)

AGE ALERT
Hodgkin's disease is most common in young adults, and more common in males than in females. Incidence peaks in two age-groups: ages 15 to 38 and after age 50 — except in Japan, where it occurs exclusively among people over age 50.

Pathophysiology
Hodgkin's disease is characterized by proliferation of a tumor in which only a small proportion of the cells are malignant and most are normal lymphocytes. The characteristic malignant cells — called Reed-Sternberg cells — are most likely multinucleated, giant-cell mutations of the T-lymphocyte. Infiltration of the nodes with eosinophils and plasma cells is associated with lymph node necrosis and fibrosis.

COMPLICATIONS
- Secondary cancers
- Cardiac disease
- Liver failure
- Pulmonary disease

Signs and symptoms
- Painless swelling in one of lymph nodes (usually the cervical region) with a history of upper respiratory infection
- Persistent fever
- Night sweats
- Fatigue
- Weight loss
- Malaise
- Pruritus
- Extremity pain
- Nerve irritation
- Absence of pulse due to rapid enlargement of lymph nodes
- Pericardial friction rub
- Pericardial effusion
- Neck vein engorgement
- Enlargement of retroperitoneal nodes, spleen, and liver

Diagnostic test results
- Lymph node biopsy confirms presence of Reed-Sternberg cells, nodular fibrosis, and necrosis.
- Bone marrow, liver, mediastinal, lymph node, and spleen biopsies reveal histologic presence of cells.
- Chest X-ray, abdominal computed tomography scan, lung scan, bone scan, and lymphangiography detect lymph and organ involvement.
- Hematologic tests show:
  - mild to severe normocytic anemia
  - normochromic anemia
  - elevated, normal, or reduced white blood cell count
  - differential with any combination of neutrophilia, lymphocytopenia, monocytosis, and eosinophilia.
- Elevated serum alkaline phosphatase indicates bone or liver involvement.

Treatment
- Chemotherapy, radiation, or both, appropriate to stage of the disease — based on histologic interpretation and clinical staging
- Concomitant antiemetics, sedatives, or antidiarrheals to combat adverse GI effects
- Autologous bone marrow transplant
- Autologous peripheral blood sternal transfusions
- Immunotherapy

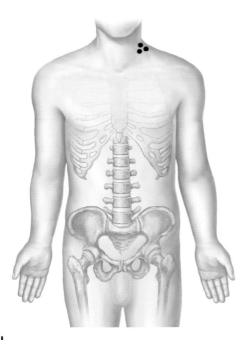

Stage I
- Involvement of single lymph node region
 or
- Involvement of single extralymphatic site (stage I$_E$)

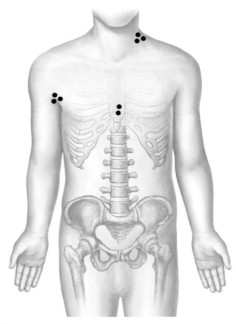

Stage II
- Involvement of 2 or more lymph node regions on same side of diaphragm
- May include localized extralymphatic involvement on same side of diaphragm (stage II$_E$)

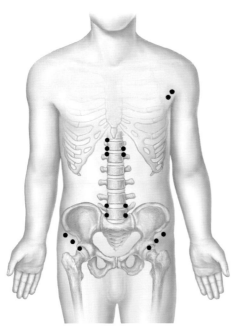

Stage III
- Involvement of lymph node regions on both sides of diaphragm
- May include involvement of spleen (stage III$_S$) or localized extranodal disease (stage III$_E$)
- Hodgkin's disease Stage III$_1$: disease limited to upper abdomen — spleen, splenic hilar, celiac, or portohepatic nodes
- Hodgkin's disease Stage III$_2$: disease limited to lower abdomen — periaortic, pelvic, or inguinal nodes

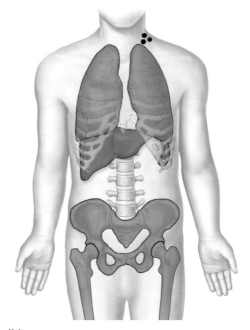

Stage IV
- Diffuse extralymphatic disease (for example, in liver, bone marrow, lung, skin)

LEUKEMIA

Leukemia is a group of diseases caused by malignant proliferation of white blood cells (WBCs); each is classified by the dominant cell type. The course of a leukemia may be acute or chronic.

• Acute — large numbers of immature leukocytes; rapid onset and progression

• Chronic — excessive mature leukocytes in the periphery and bone marrow; slower onset and progression.

AGE ALERT
Leukemias are the most common malignancies in children. Each specific type has its own prognosis, but generally, the prognosis in children is better than in adults.

Causes
No definitive cause identified
Possible risk factors
• Genetic predisposition
• Immunologic factors
• Environmental exposure to chemicals, radiation
• Predisposing disease
Chronic myeloid leukemia (CML)
• In almost 90% of patients, Philadelphia, or Ph[1] chromosome; translocated long arm of chromosome 22, usually to chromosome 9

Pathophysiology
Acute leukemia is characterized by malignant proliferation of WBC precursors (blasts) in bone marrow or lymph tissue and their accumulation in peripheral blood, bone marrow, and body tissues. Leukemic cells inhibit normal bone marrow production of erythrocytes, platelets, and immune function. Its most common forms and the characteristic cells include:
• acute lymphoblastic (or lymphocytic) leukemia (ALL) — lymphocyte precursors (lymphoblasts)
• acute myeloid leukemias (AMLs), known collectively as *acute non-lymphocytic leukemia:*
– acute myeloblastic (or myelogenous) leukemia — myeloid precursors (myeloblasts)
– acute monoblastic (monocytic) leukemia — monocyte precursors (monoblasts)
– other types — acute myelomonocytic leukemia, acute erythroleukemia.
• *CML* proceeds in two distinct phases:
– insidious chronic phase — anemia and bleeding disorders
– blastic crisis or acute phase — rapid proliferation of myeloblasts, the most primitive granulocyte precursors.
• *Chronic lymphocytic leukemia (CLL)* — abnormal small lymphocytes in lymphoid tissue, blood, and bone marrow.

COMPLICATIONS
• Infection
• Organ malfunction

Signs and symptoms
Acute leukemias
• Sudden high fever, thrombocytopenia, abnormal bleeding

• Nonspecific signs and symptoms, including weakness, pallor, chills
• Also, in ALL, AML, and acute monoblastic leukemia: possible dyspnea, anemia, fatigue, malaise, tachycardia, palpitations, systolic ejection murmur, abdominal and bone pain
CML
• Anemia, thrombocytopenia, hepatosplenomegaly
• Sternal and rib tenderness
• Low-grade fever
• Anorexia, weight loss
• Renal calculi or gouty arthritis
• Prolonged infection
• Ankle edema
CLL
• Early stages: fatigue, malaise, fever, nodular enlargement
• Late stages: severe fatigue, weight loss, liver or spleen enlargement, bone tenderness
• With disease progression and bone marrow involvement: anemia; pallor; weakness; dyspnea; tachycardia; palpitations; bleeding; opportunistic fungal, viral, and bacterial infections

Diagnostic test results
Acute leukemia
• Laboratory studies show thrombocytopenia and neutropenia. WBC differential shows cell type.
• Computed tomography (CT) scan shows affected organs.
• Bone marrow biopsy shows proliferation of immature WBCs.
CML
• Chromosomal studies of peripheral blood or bone marrow show the Philadelphia chromosome.
• Laboratory studies reveal low leukocyte alkaline phosphate, leukocytosis, leukopenia, neutropenia, decreased hemoglobin (Hb) and hematocrit, increased circulating myeloblasts, thrombocytosis, and increased serum uric acid level.
• CT scan shows affected organs.
• Bone marrow biopsy is hypercellular showing bone marrow infiltration by increased number of myeloid elements.
CLL
• Laboratory studies show increased WBC, granulocytopenia, decreased Hb, neutropenia, lymphocytosis, and thrombocytopenia.
• CT scan shows affected organs.
• Bone marrow biopsy shows lymphocytic invasion.
• Serum protein electrophoresis shows hypogammaglobulinemia.

Treatment
• Antibiotic, antifungal, antiviral drugs
• Systemic chemotherapy
• Granulocyte injections
• Transfusion of blood and blood products
• Bone marrow transplantation

Acute lymphocytic leukemia

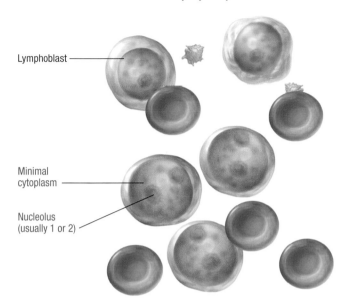

Lymphoblast

Minimal
cytoplasm

Nucleolus
(usually 1 or 2)

Acute myelogenous leukemia

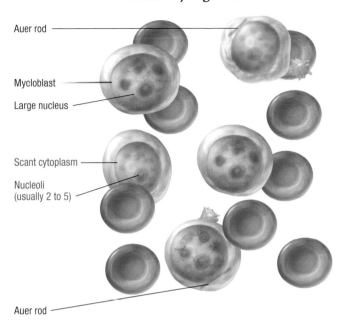

Auer rod

Mycloblast

Large nucleus

Scant cytoplasm

Nucleoli
(usually 2 to 5)

Auer rod

Chronic lymphocytic leukemia

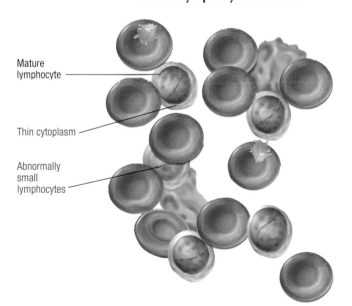

Mature
lymphocyte

Thin cytoplasm

Abnormally
small
lymphocytes

Chronic myeloid leukemia

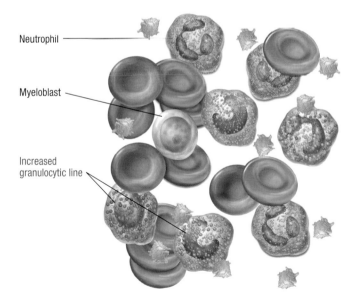

Neutrophil

Myeloblast

Increased
granulocytic line

MULTIPLE MYELOMA

Multiple myeloma, also known as *malignant plasmacytoma* or *plasma cell myeloma,* is a disseminated malignant neoplasia of marrow plasma cells that infiltrates bone to produce osteolytic lesions throughout the skeleton (flat bones, vertebrae, skull, pelvis, and ribs). It's a rare disease with only three new cases occurring per 100,000 people a year.

AGE ALERT
Multiple myeloma most commonly affects men over age 40.

Prognosis is usually poor because diagnosis is typically made after the disease has already infiltrated the vertebrae, pelvis, skull, ribs, clavicles, and sternum. By then, skeletal destruction is widespread and vertebral collapse is imminent. Without treatment, about half of all patients die within 6 months of diagnosis. Early diagnosis and treatment prolong the lives of many patients by 3 to 5 years. Death usually follows complications, such as infection, renal failure, hematologic imbalance, fractures, hypercalcemia, hyperuricemia, or dehydration.

Causes

Primary cause unknown
Possible links
- Genetic factors
- Autoimmune diseases or allergies
- Environmental toxins
- Chemicals in agricultural products or added during food processing

Pathophysiology

Plasma cells are normal leukocytes that secrete immunoglobulins. When plasma cells become malignant, they reproduce uncontrollably and create many abnormal immunoglobulins. During this process, they invade the bone marrow, then the bone matrix, causing osteolytic lesions of the bone. Myeloma cells then proliferate outside of the bone marrow in all lymphatic tissues where plasma cells are normally present. Because plasma cells exist in virtually all body organs, all body systems may be affected by this proliferation and abnormal immunoglobulin production. The severity of renal failure correlates with the amount of immunoglobulin protein found in the urine. Infiltration and precipitation of immunoglobulin light chains (Bence-Jones protein) in the distal tubules causes myeloma nephrosis.

COMPLICATIONS
- Infections
- Pyelonephritis
- Hematologic imbalance
- Fractures
- Hypercalcemia
- Hyperuricemia
- Dehydration
- Renal calculi
- Renal failure

Signs and symptoms

- Severe, constant back and rib pain that increases with exercise and may be worse at night
- Arthritic symptoms — achy pain; swollen, tender joints
- Fever, malaise
- Evidence of peripheral neuropathy (such as paresthesia)
- Evidence of diffuse osteoporosis and pathologic fractures

In advanced disease
- Acute symptoms of vertebral compression; loss of body height — 5″ (12.5 cm) or more
- Thoracic deformities (ballooning)
- Anemia
- Bleeding
- Weight loss
- Severe, recurrent infection, such as pneumonia, may follow damage to nerves associated with respiratory function

Diagnostic test results

- Complete blood count shows moderate to severe anemia; differential may show 40% to 50% lymphocytes but seldom more than 3% plasma cells.
- Differential smear reveals *rouleaux* formation from elevated erythrocyte sedimentation rate.
- Urine studies reveal Bence Jones protein and hypercalciuria.
- Bone marrow aspiration detects myelomatous cells (abnormal number of immature plasma cells).
- Serum electrophoresis shows elevated globulin spike that's electrophoretically and immunologically abnormal.
- Bone X-rays in early stages reveal diffuse osteoporosis; in later stages, they show multiple sharply circumscribed osteolytic lesions, particularly in the skull, pelvis, and spine.

Treatment

- Chemotherapy to suppress plasma cell growth and control pain
- Autologous hematopoietic blood cell transfusion
- Autologous bone marrow transplantation
- Adjuvant local radiation
- Melphalan-prednisone combination in high intermittent or low continuous daily doses
- Analgesics for pain
- Dialysis
- Plasmapheresis
- Immunotherapy

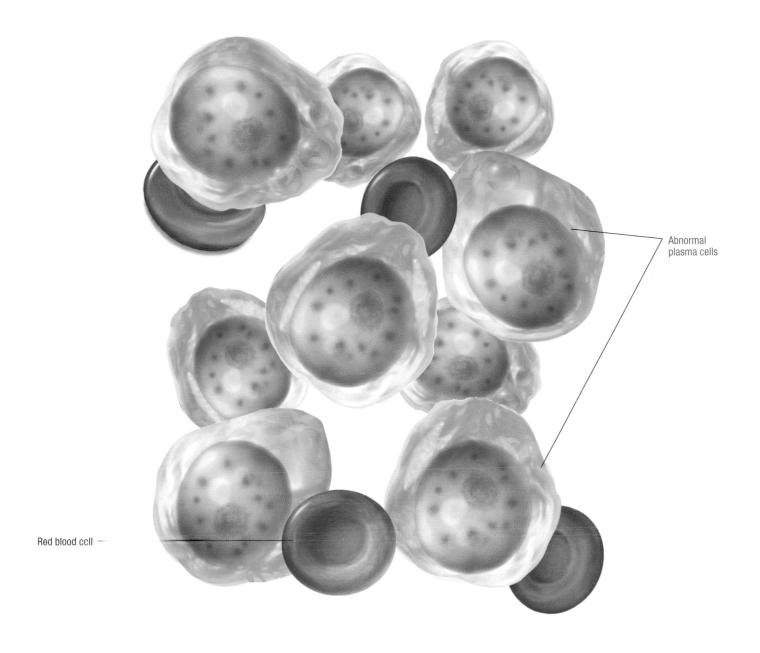

Abnormal
plasma cells

Red blood cell

NON-HODGKIN'S LYMPHOMAS

on-Hodgkin's lymphomas refer to a heterogeneous group of malignant diseases originating in lymph nodes and other lymphoid tissue. Non-Hodgkin's lymphomas are three times more common than Hodgkin's disease. The incidence is increasing, especially in patients with autoimmune disorders and those receiving immunosuppressant treatment.

Causes
- Direct cause unknown
- Possible viral etiology
- Exposure to toxins—benzene, gasoline, pesticides, herbicides

> **AGE ALERT**
> Malignant lymphomas occur in all age-groups, but incidence rises with age (median age is 50).

Pathophysiology
Non-Hodgkin's lymphoma is pathophysiologically similar to Hodgkin's disease, but Reed-Sternberg cells aren't present, and the specific mechanism of lymph node destruction is different. The abnormal lymphoid tissue is identified by its tissue architecture and patterns of infiltration. These lymphomas are defined as *follicular, interfollicular, mantle,* or *medullary,* depending on the distribution of malignant cells in specific regions of the lymph node. The tissue is then described by the pattern of infiltration as *diffuse* or *nodular.*

COMPLICATIONS
- Hypercalcemia
- Hyperuricemia
- Lymphomatosis
- Meningitis
- Anemia
- Increased intracranial pressure
- Respiratory problems
- Liver and kidney problems

Signs and symptoms
- Enlarged tonsils and adenoids
- Painless, rubbery enlargement of lymphatic tissue (lymphadenopathy), usually cervical or supraclavicular nodes

In children
- Cervical nodes usually affected first
- Dyspnea and coughing

In advancing disease
- Symptoms specific to involved structure
- Systemic complaints—fatigue, malaise, weight loss, fever, night sweats

Diagnostic test results
- Lymph node biopsy reveals cell type.
- Biopsy of tonsils, bone marrow, liver, bowel, or skin reveals malignant cells.
- Complete blood count detects anemia.
- Uric acid level is elevated or normal.
- Blood chemistry shows elevated serum calcium levels if bone lesions are present.
- Bone and chest X-rays, lymphangiography, liver and spleen scans, abdominal computed tomography scan, and excretory urography show evidence of metastasis.

Treatment
- Radiation therapy—mainly in the early, localized stage of disease
- Total nodal irradiation
- Chemotherapy with combinations of antineoplastic agents
- Autologous or allogeneic blood marrow transplantation

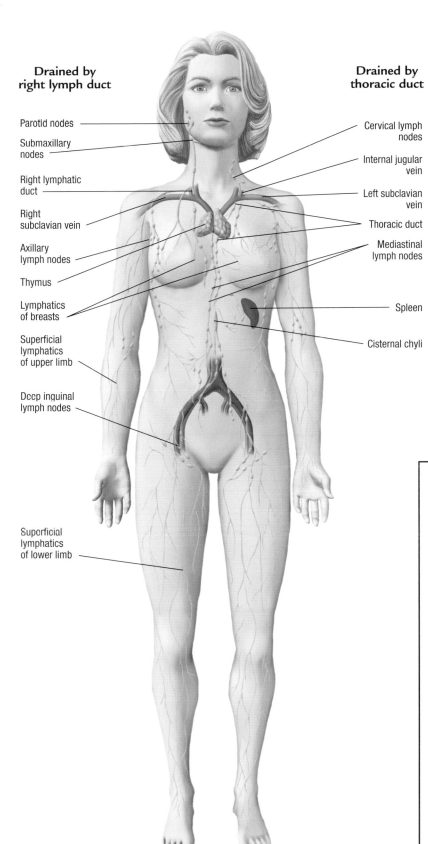

Drained by right lymph duct

Parotid nodes

Submaxillary nodes

Right lymphatic duct

Right subclavian vein

Axillary lymph nodes

Thymus

Lymphatics of breasts

Superficial lymphatics of upper limb

Deep inguinal lymph nodes

Superficial lymphatics of lower limb

Drained by thoracic duct

Cervical lymph nodes

Internal jugular vein

Left subclavian vein

Thoracic duct

Mediastinal lymph nodes

Spleen

Cisternal chyli

⫸ **CLINICAL TIP**

CERVICAL LYMPHADENOPATHY

This illustration shows a woman with characteristic lymphadenopathy (of the cervical lymph nodes) due to lymphoma.

POLYCYTHEMIA VERA

Polycythemia vera is a chronic disorder characterized by increased red blood cell (RBC) mass, erythrocytosis, leukocytosis, thrombocytosis, elevated hemoglobin level, and low or normal plasma volume. This disease is also known as *primary polycythemia, erythremia,* or *polycythemia rubra vera*. It occurs most commonly among Jewish males of European descent.

AGE ALERT
Polycythemia vera usually occurs between ages 40 and 60; it seldom affects children.

Prognosis depends on age at diagnosis, treatment, and complications. In untreated polycythemia, mortality is high and associated with thrombosis, hyperviscosity, or expanded blood volume. Additionally, myeloid metaplasia (ectopic hematopoiesis in the liver and spleen) with myelofibrosis (fibrous tissue in bone marrow) and acute leukemia may develop.

Causes
Unknown, but probably related to a clonal stem cell defect

Pathophysiology
In polycythemia vera, uncontrolled and rapid cellular reproduction and maturation cause proliferation or hyperplasia of all bone marrow cells (panmyelosis). Increased RBC mass makes the blood abnormally viscous and inhibits blood flow through the microcirculation. Diminished blood flow and thrombocytosis set the stage for intravascular thrombosis.

CLINICAL TIP
Secondary polycythemia is excessive production of circulating RBCs due to hypoxia, tumor, or disease. It occurs in approximately 2 of every 100,000 people living at or near sea level; the incidence increases among those living at high altitudes.

Spurious polycythemia is characterized by an increased hematocrit but decreased plasma volume. It usually affects the middle-aged population and is more common in men than in women. Causes include dehydration, hypertension, thromboembolic disease, or elevated serum cholesterol or uric acid.

COMPLICATIONS
- Renal calculi
- Abdominal thrombosis
- Hemorrhage
- Stroke or myocardial infarction
- Peptic ulcer disease
- Acute myelogenous leukemia

Signs and symptoms
- Feeling of fullness in the head, dizziness, headache
- Ruddy cyanosis (plethora) of nose
- Clubbing of digits
- Painful pruritus
- Ecchymosis
- Hepatosplenomegaly
- Alterations in vision
- Abdominal fullness

Diagnostic test results
- Laboratory studies reveal:
  - increased RBC mass
  - normal arterial oxygen saturation
  - increased uric acid level
  - increased blood histamine levels
  - decreased serum iron concentration
  - decreased or absent urinary erythropoietin.
- Bone marrow biopsy shows excess production of myeloid stem cells.

Treatment
- Phlebotomy to reduce RBC mass
- Myelosuppressive therapy with hydroxyurea or radioactive phosphorous
- Interferon alfa

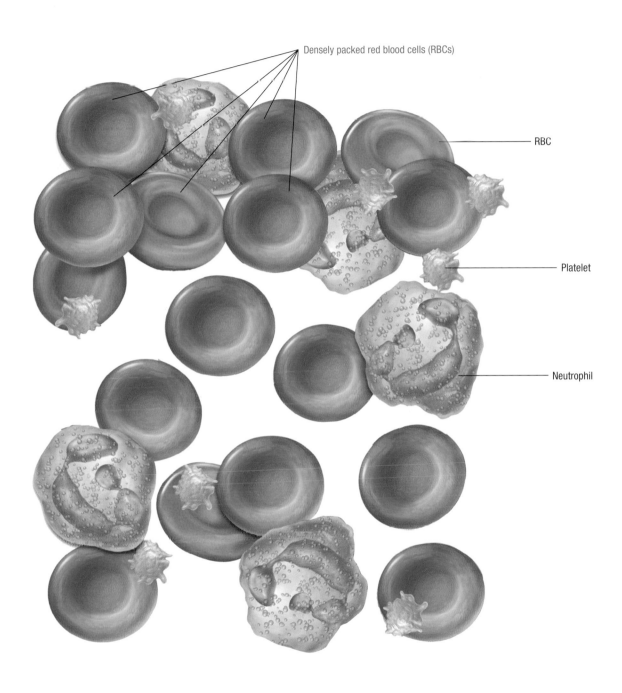

Densely packed red blood cells (RBCs)

RBC

Platelet

Neutrophil

Sickle cell anemia

A congenital hemolytic anemia that occurs primarily but not exclusively in blacks, sickle cell anemia results from a defective hemoglobin molecule (Hb S) that causes red blood cells (RBCs) to become sickle-shaped. Such cells clog capillaries and impair circulation, resulting in chronic ill health (fatigue, dyspnea on exertion, swollen joints), periodic crises, long-term complications, and early death.

If both parents are carriers of sickle cell trait (or another hemoglobinopathy), each child has a 25% chance of developing sickle cell anemia. Approximately one out of every 500 blacks has sickle cell anemia. The defective Hb S–producing gene may have persisted because, in areas where malaria is endemic, the heterozygous sickle cell trait provides resistance to malaria and is actually beneficial.

AGE ALERT
Half of patients with sickle cell anemia once died by their early 20s; few lived to middle age. Earlier diagnosis and more effective treatment have improved the prognosis of sickle cell anemia. Most patients now survive well into adulthood.

Causes
- Homozygous inheritance of the gene that produces Hb S
- Heterozygous inheritance of this gene results in sickle cell trait, which is usually asymptomatic

Pathophysiology
Hb S becomes insoluble whenever hypoxia occurs. As a result, these RBCs become rigid and elongated, forming a crescent or sickle shape. Such sickling can produce hemolysis (cell destruction). In addition, these altered cells make blood more viscous and tend to accumulate in smaller blood vessels and capillaries. The result is loss of normal circulation, swelling, tissue infarctions, and pain. Furthermore, the blockage causes anoxic changes that lead to further sickling and obstruction. Each patient with sickle cell anemia has a different hypoxic threshold and particular factors that trigger a sickle cell crisis. Illness, exposure to cold, stress, acidotic states, or a pathophysiologic process that pulls water out of the sickle cells precipitates a crisis in most patients. The blockages then cause anoxic changes that lead to further sickling and obstruction.

COMPLICATIONS
- Chronic obstructive pulmonary disease
- Heart failure and heart murmurs
- Splenic infarction and splenomegaly
- Retinopathy
- Nephropathy
- Major organ infarction

Signs and symptoms
- Tachycardia, cardiomegaly, systolic and diastolic murmurs
- Pulmonary infarctions, which may result in cor pulmonale
- Stroke
- Chronic fatigue, unexplained dyspnea or dyspnea on exertion
- Ischemic leg ulcers (especially around the ankles)
- Increased susceptibility to infection

Occlusive or infarctive crises
- Severe abdominal, thoracic, muscular, or bone pain
- Worsening jaundice, dark urine

Aplastic crisis
- Pallor
- Lethargy, sleepiness, coma
- Dyspnea
- Markedly decreased bone marrow activity, RBC hemolysis

Diagnostic test results
- Electrophoresis shows Hb S.
- Stained blood smear shows the presence of sickled cells.
- Laboratory studies show low RBC count, elevated white blood cell and platelet counts, decreased erythrocyte sedimentation rate, increased serum iron levels, decreased RBC survival, and reticulocytosis.
- Lateral chest X-ray shows "Lincoln log" deformity in the vertebrae of many adults and some adolescents.

Treatment
- Prophylactic penicillin before age 4 months
- Oral hydroxyurea to reduce the number of painful crises
- Packed RBC transfusions
- Sedation
- Analgesics
- Oxygen
- Oral or I.V. fluids
- Iron and folic acid supplements
- Antibiotics

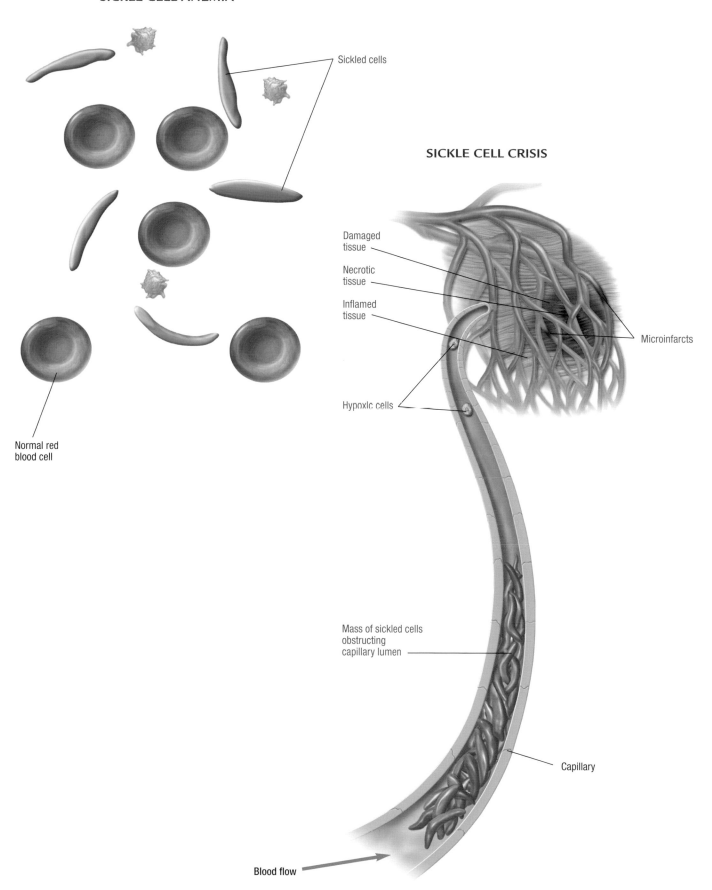

PERIPHERAL BLOOD SMEAR IN SICKLE CELL ANEMIA

Sickled cells

Normal red blood cell

SICKLE CELL CRISIS

Damaged tissue

Necrotic tissue

Inflamed tissue

Microinfarcts

Hypoxic cells

Mass of sickled cells obstructing capillary lumen

Capillary

Blood flow

Sickle cell anemia   **263**

THALASSEMIA

Thalassemia, a group of hereditary hemolytic anemias, is characterized by defective synthesis in the polypeptide chains of the protein component of hemoglobin (Hb). Red blood cell (RBC) synthesis is also impaired.

Thalassemias are most common in people of Mediterranean ancestry (especially Italian and Greek, who develop the form called *beta-thalassemia*). People whose ancestors originated in Africa, southern China, southeast Asia, and India develop the form called *alpha-thalassemia*, which reflects deletion of one or more of four Hb genes. Prognosis varies with the number of deleted genes.

In beta-thalassemia, the most common form of this disorder, synthesis of the beta-polypeptide chain is defective. It occurs in three clinical forms: *major, intermedia,* and *minor.* The severity of the resulting anemia depends on whether the patient is homozygous or heterozygous for the thalassemic trait. The prognosis varies:
- thalassemia major — patients seldom survive to adulthood
- thalassemia intermedia — children develop normally into adulthood; puberty usually delayed
- thalassemia minor — normal life span.

Causes
Beta-thalassemia
- Thalassemia major or intermedia — homozygous inheritance of a partially dominant autosomal gene
- Thalassemia minor — heterozygous inheritance of the same gene
Alpha-thalassemia
- Deletion of one or more of four genes

Pathophysiology
In beta-thalassemia, total or partial deficiency of beta-polypeptide chain production impairs Hb synthesis and results in continual production of fetal Hb beyond the neonatal period. Normally, immunoglobulin synthesis switches from gamma- to beta-polypeptides at the time of birth. This conversion doesn't happen in thalassemic infants. Their red cells are hypochromic and microcytic. In alpha-thalassemia, a much reduced quantity of alpha-globin chains is produced.

COMPLICATIONS
- Pathologic fractures
- Cardiac arrhythmias and heart failure

Signs and symptoms
Thalassemia major
- At birth — no symptoms
- Infants ages 3 to 6 months — pallor; yellow skin and sclera
- Infants ages 6 to 12 months — severe anemia, bone abnormalities, failure to thrive, and life-threatening complications
- Splenomegaly or hepatomegaly, with abdominal enlargement; frequent infections; bleeding tendencies (especially nose bleeds); anorexia

- Small body, large head (characteristic features); possible mental retardation
- Facial features similar to Down syndrome in infants, due to thickened bone at the base of the nose from bone marrow hyperactivity
Thalassemia intermedia
- Some degree of anemia, jaundice, and splenomegaly
- Signs of hemosiderosis, such as hemoptysis, iron deficiency anemia, or paroxysmal nocturnal hemoglobinemia — due to increased intestinal absorption of iron
Thalassemia minor
- Usually produces no symptoms
- Mild anemia, often overlooked
Alpha-thalassemia syndromes
- Reflect the number of gene deletions present
- Range from asymptomatic to incompatible with life

Diagnostic test results
- Laboratory analysis reveals low RBC and Hb level, microcytosis, and high reticulocyte count; elevated bilirubin and urinary and fecal urobilinogen levels; and low serum folate level.
- Peripheral blood smear shows target cells; microcytes; pale, nucleated RBCs; and marked anisocytosis.
- Skull and long bone X-rays show thinning and widening of the marrow space due to overactive bone marrow, granular appearance of bones of skull and vertebrae, areas of osteoporosis in long bones, and deformed (rectangular or biconvex) phalanges.
- Quantitative Hb studies reveal significantly increased fetal Hb level and slightly increased Hb A_2 level.
Thalassemia intermedia
- Peripheral blood smear shows hypochromic, microcytic RBCs (less severe than in thalassemia major).
Thalassemia minor
- Peripheral blood smear shows hypochromic microcytic RBCs.
- Quantitative Hb studies reveal significantly increased Hb A_2 level and moderately increased fetal Hb level.

Treatment
- Iron supplements contraindicated in all forms of thalassemia
Beta-thalassemia major — essentially supportive
- Prompt treatment with appropriate antibiotics for infections
- Folic acid supplements
- Transfusions of packed RBCs to increase Hb levels (used judiciously to minimize iron overload)
- Splenectomy and bone marrow transplantation (effectiveness hasn't been confirmed)
Beta-thalassemia intermedia and thalassemia minor
- No treatment
Alpha-thalassemia
- Blood transfusions
- In utero transfusion for hydrops fetalis

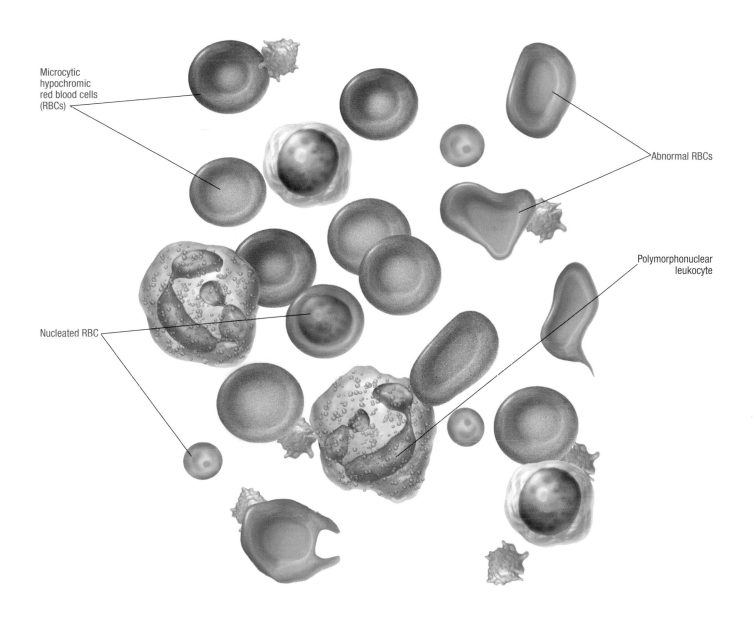

Microcytic
hypochromic
red blood cells
(RBCs)

Abnormal RBCs

Nucleated RBC

Polymorphonuclear
leukocyte

ACQUIRED IMMUNODEFICIENCY SYNDROME

Human immunodeficiency virus (HIV) infection may cause acquired immunodeficiency syndrome (AIDS). Although characterized by gradual destruction of cell-mediated (T cell) immunity, AIDS also affects humoral immunity and even autoimmunity through the central role of the CD4+ (helper) T lymphocyte in all immune reactions. The resulting immunodeficiency makes the patient susceptible to opportunistic infections, cancers, and other abnormalities that define AIDS.

Causes
- HIV-1 retrovirus transmitted by contact with infected blood or body fluids

High-risk populations
- Homosexual or bisexual men
- I.V. drug users
- Neonates of infected women
- Recipients of contaminated blood or blood products
- Heterosexual partners of persons in high-risk groups

Pathophysiology
The natural history of AIDS begins with infection by the HIV retrovirus, which is detectable only by laboratory tests, and ends with death. The HIV virus may enter the body by any of several routes involving the transmission of blood or body fluids; for example:
- direct inoculation during intimate sexual contact
- transfusion of contaminated blood or blood products
- use of contaminated needles
- transplacental or postpartum transmission.

HIV strikes helper T cells bearing the CD4+ antigen. Normally a receptor for major histocompatibility complex molecules, the antigen serves as a receptor for the retrovirus and allows it to enter the cell. Viral binding also requires the presence of a coreceptor on the cell surface. The virus may also infect CD4+ antigen-bearing cells of the GI tract, uterine cervix, and neuroglia.

Like other retroviruses, HIV copies its genetic material in a reverse manner compared with other viruses and cells. Through the action of reverse transcriptase, HIV produces deoxyribonucleic acid (DNA) from its viral ribonucleic acid (RNA). Transcription is often poor, leading to mutations, some of which make HIV resistant to antiviral drugs. The viral DNA enters the nucleus of the cell and is incorporated into the host cell's DNA, where it's transcribed into more viral RNA. If the host cell reproduces, it duplicates the HIV DNA along with its own and passes it on to the daughter cells. Thus, the host cell carries this information and, if activated, replicates the virus. Viral enzymes and proteases arrange the structural components and RNA into viral particles that move to the periphery of the host cell, where the virus buds and emerges from the host cell — free to infect other cells.

HIV replication may lead to cell death or the virus may become latent. HIV infection leads to profound pathology, either directly through destruction of CD4+ cells, other immune cells, and neuroglial cells, or indirectly through the secondary effects of CD4+ T-cell dysfunction and resulting immunosuppression.

COMPLICATIONS
- Opportunistic infections
- Wasting syndrome
- Kaposi's sarcoma and non-Hodgkin's lymphoma
- Lymphoid interstitial pneumonia
- Arthritis
- Hypergammaglobulinemia
- AIDS dementia complex
- HIV encephalopathy
- Peripheral neuropathy

Signs and symptoms
Latency
- Mononucleosis-like syndrome, which may be attributed to flu or another virus; may remain asymptomatic for years

Symptomatic phase
- Persistent generalized lymphadenopathy
- Nonspecific symptoms, including weight loss, fatigue, night sweats
- Fevers related to altered function of CD4+ cells, immunodeficiency, and infection of other CD4+ antigen-bearing cells
- Neurologic symptoms

Diagnostic test results
- Laboratory studies reveal CD4+ T-cell count less than 200 cells/µl and the presence of HIV antibodies.

Treatment
Antiretroviral agents
- Protease inhibitors
- Nucleoside reverse-transcriptase inhibitors
- Nonnucleoside reverse-transcriptase inhibitors

Additional treatment
- Immunomodulatory agents
- Human granulocyte colony-stimulating growth factor
- Anti-infective and antineoplastic agents
- Supportive therapy, including nutritional support, fluid and electrolyte replacement therapy, pain relief, and psychological support
- Treatment of opportunistic infections

MANIFESTATIONS OF HIV INFECTION AND AIDS

Symptoms of HIV infection

AIDS-related illnesses and opportunistic infections (OIs)

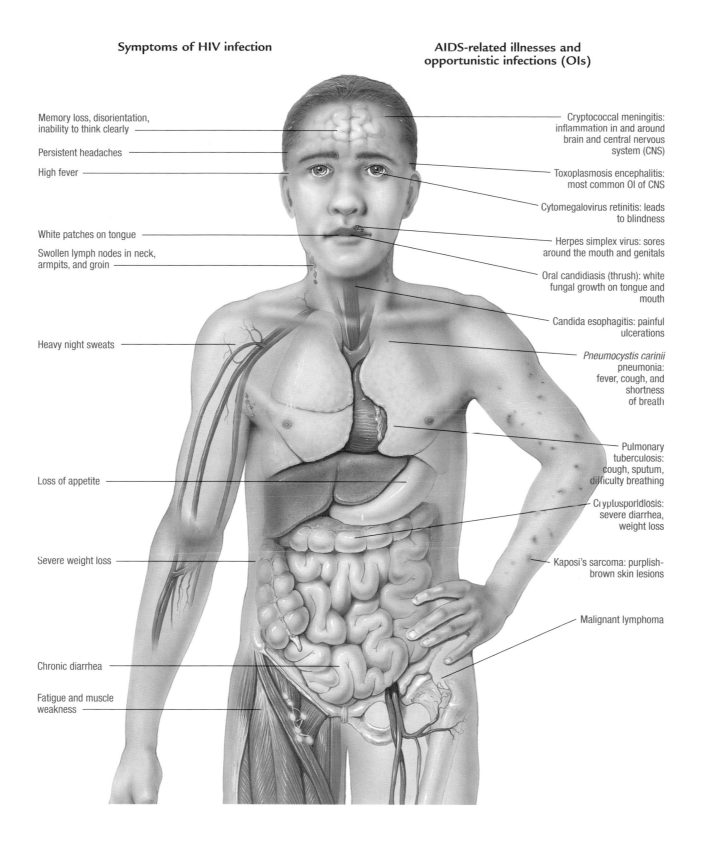

Memory loss, disorientation, inability to think clearly

Persistent headaches

High fever

White patches on tongue

Swollen lymph nodes in neck, armpits, and groin

Heavy night sweats

Loss of appetite

Severe weight loss

Chronic diarrhea

Fatigue and muscle weakness

Cryptococcal meningitis: inflammation in and around brain and central nervous system (CNS)

Toxoplasmosis encephalitis: most common OI of CNS

Cytomegalovirus retinitis: leads to blindness

Herpes simplex virus: sores around the mouth and genitals

Oral candidiasis (thrush): white fungal growth on tongue and mouth

Candida esophagitis: painful ulcerations

Pneumocystis carinii pneumonia: fever, cough, and shortness of breath

Pulmonary tuberculosis: cough, sputum, difficulty breathing

Cryptosporidiosis: severe diarrhea, weight loss

Kaposi's sarcoma: purplish-brown skin lesions

Malignant lymphoma

ALLERGIC RHINITIS

Allergic rhinitis is a reaction to airborne (inhaled) allergens. Depending on the allergen, the resulting rhinitis and conjunctivitis may occur seasonally (hay fever) or year-round (perennial allergic rhinitis). Allergic rhinitis is the most common atopic allergic reaction, affecting over 20 million U.S. residents.

AGE ALERT
Allergic rhinitis is most prevalent in young children and adolescents, but occurs in all age groups.

Causes
- Immunoglobulin (Ig) E-mediated type I hypersensitivity response to an environmental antigen (allergen) in a genetically susceptible person

Common triggers
- Wind-borne pollens:
  - Spring — oak, elm, maple, alder, birch, cottonwood
  - Summer — grasses, sheep sorrel, English plantain
  - Autumn — ragweed, other weeds
- Perennial allergens and irritants:
  - Dust mite excreta, fungal spores, molds
  - Feather pillows
  - Cigarette smoke
  - Animal dander

Pathophysiology
During primary exposure to an allergen, T cells recognize the foreign allergens and release chemicals that instruct B cells to produce specific antibodies called *IgE*. IgE antibodies attach themselves to mast cells. Mast cells with attached IgE can remain in the body for years, ready to react when they next encounter the same allergen.

The second time the allergen enters the body, it comes into direct contact with the IgE antibodies attached to the mast cells. This stimulates the mast cells to release chemicals, such as histamine, which initiate a response that causes tightening of the smooth muscles in the airways, dilation of small blood vessels, increased mucus secretion in the nasal cavity and airways, and itching.

COMPLICATIONS
- Secondary sinus and middle ear infections
- Nasal polyps

Signs and symptoms
Seasonal allergic rhinitis
- Paroxysmal sneezing
- Profuse watery rhinorrhea; nasal obstruction or congestion
- Pruritus of nose and eyes
- Pale, cyanotic, edematous nasal mucosa
- Red, edematous eyelids and conjunctivae
- Excessive lacrimation
- Headache or sinus pain
- Itching of the throat
- Malaise

Perennial allergic rhinitis
- Chronic nasal obstruction, commonly extending to eustachian tube
- Conjunctivitis and other extranasal effects rare

CLINICAL TIP
In both types of allergic rhinitis, dark circles may appear under the patient's eyes ("allergic shiners") because of venous congestion in the maxillary sinuses.

Diagnostic test results
A definitive diagnosis is based on the patient's personal and family history of allergies as well as physical findings during a symptomatic phase.
- Microscopic examination of sputum and nasal secretions reveals large numbers of eosinophils.
- Blood chemistry shows normal or elevated IgE.
- Skin testing paired with tested responses to environmental stimuli pinpoints the responsible allergens given the patient's history.

Treatment
- Antihistamines such as fexofenadine
- Inhaled intranasal steroids, such as beclomethasone, flunisolide, and fluticasone
- Immunotherapy or desensitization with injections of extracted allergens
- Nasal decongestants

REACTION TO ALLERGEN EXPOSURE

Primary exposure

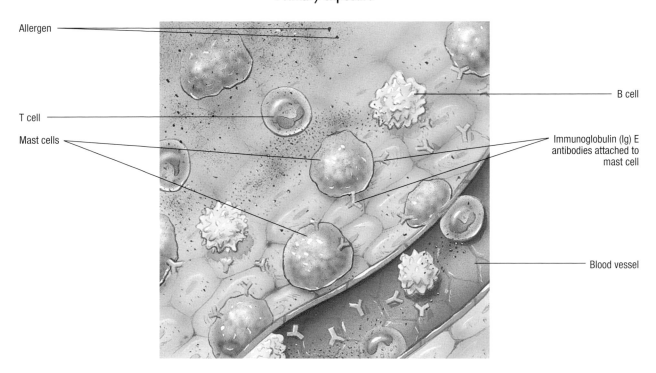

Allergen

T cell

Mast cells

B cell

Immunoglobulin (Ig) E antibodies attached to mast cell

Blood vessel

Reexposure

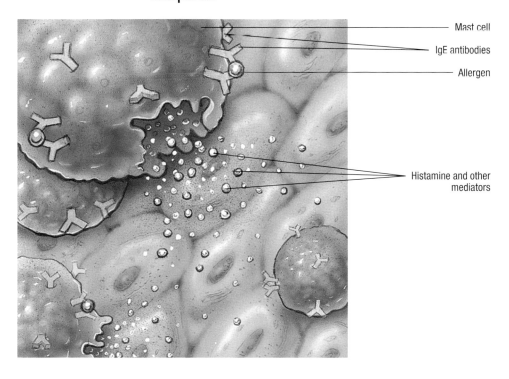

Mast cell

IgE antibodies

Allergen

Histamine and other mediators

ANAPHYLAXIS

Anaphylaxis is an acute, potentially life-threatening type I (immediate) hypersensitivity reaction marked by sudden onset of rapidly progressive urticaria (vascular swelling in skin, accompanied by itching) and respiratory distress. With prompt recognition and treatment, prognosis is good. Typically occurring within minutes, the reaction can occur up to 1 hour after reexposure to an antigen.

Causes

Ingestion of or other systemic exposure to sensitizing drugs or other substances, such as:
- serums (usually horse serum), vaccines, allergen extracts
- diagnostic chemicals, such as sulfobromophthalein, sodium dehydrocholate, radiographic contrast media
- enzymes such as L-asparaginase in chemotherapeutic regimens
- hormones such as insulin
- penicillin or other antibiotics, sulfonamides
- salicylates
- food proteins, as in legumes, nuts, berries, seafood, egg albumin
- sulfite food additives, common in dried fruits and vegetables, salad bars
- insect venom.

CLINICAL TIP

Latex allergy is a hypersensitivity reaction to products that contain natural latex derived from the sap of a rubber tree, not synthetic latex. Natural latex is increasingly present in products in the home and workplace. Hypersensitivity reactions can range from local dermatitis to a life-threatening anaphylactic reaction.

Pathophysiology

Anaphylaxis requires previous sensitization or exposure to the specific antigen, resulting in immunoglobulin (Ig) E production by plasma cells in the lymph nodes and enhancement by helper T cells. IgE antibodies then bind to membrane receptors on mast cells in connective tissue and basophils in the blood.

On reexposure, IgM and IgG recognize the antigen as foreign and bind to it. Destruction of the antigen by the complement cascade begins. Continued antigen presence activates IgE on basophils, which promotes the release of mediators, including histamine, serotonin, and eosinophil chemotactic factor of anaphylaxis (ECF-A) and platelet–activating factor. The sudden release of histamine causes vasodilation and increases capillary permeability.

Activated IgE also stimulates mast cells in connective tissue along the venule walls to release more histamine and ECF-A. These substances produce disruptive lesions that weaken the venules.

In the lungs, histamine causes endothelial cells to burst and endothelial tissue to tear away from surrounding tissue. Fluids leak into the alveoli, and leukotrienes prevent the alveoli from expanding, thus reducing pulmonary compliance.

At the same time, basophils and mast cells begin to release prostaglandins and bradykinin along with histamine and serotonin. These chemical mediators spread through the body in the circulation, triggering systemic responses: vasodilation, smooth muscle contraction, and increased mucus production. The mediators also induce vascular collapse by increasing vascular permeability, which leads to decreased peripheral resistance and plasma leakage from the vessels to the extravascular tissues.

COMPLICATIONS
- Hypovolemic shock
- Cardiac dysfunction
- Death

Signs and symptoms
- Sudden physical distress within seconds or minutes after exposure to an allergen
- Delayed or persistent reaction may occur up to 24 hours later (severity of the reaction relates inversely to the interval between exposure to the allergen and the onset of symptoms)

Usual initial symptoms
- Feeling of impending doom or fright
- Sweating
- Sneezing, shortness of breath, nasal pruritus, urticaria, angioedema

Systemic manifestations
- Hypotension, shock, cardiac arrhythmias
- Edema of the upper respiratory tract, resulting in hypopharyngeal and laryngeal obstruction
- Hoarseness, stridor, wheezing, and accessory muscle use
- Severe stomach cramps, nausea, diarrhea, and urinary urgency and incontinence

Diagnostic test results

No single diagnostic test can identify anaphylaxis. The following tests provide clues to the patient's risk of anaphylaxis:
- Skin tests show hypersensitivity to a certain allergen.
- Laboratory studies reveal elevated serum IgE levels.

Treatment
- Immediate administration of epinephrine to reverse bronchoconstriction and cause vasoconstriction
- Tracheostomy or endotracheal intubation and mechanical ventilation
- Oxygen therapy
- I.V. vasopressors, such as norepinephrine and dopamine
- Longer-acting epinephrine, corticosteroids, antihistamines, histamine-2 blocker
- Albuterol mini-nebulizer treatment
- Volume expanders
- Cardiopulmonary resuscitation

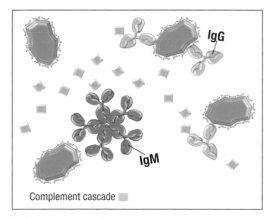

1. Response to antigen
Immunoglobulins (Ig) M and G recognize and bind the antigen. The patient has no signs or symptoms.

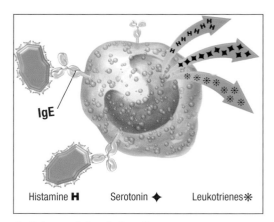

2. Release of chemical mediators
Activated IgE on basophils promotes the release of mediators: histamine, serotonin, and leukotrienes. The patient develops nasal congestion, itchy and watery eyes, flushing, weakness, and anxiety.

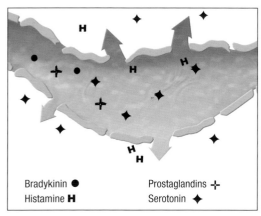

3. Intensified response
Mast cells release more histamine and eosinophil chemotactic factor of anaphylaxis (ECF-A), which create venule-weakening lesions. Signs and symptoms worsen; swelling and wheals appear.

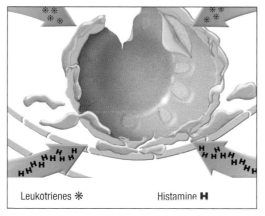

4. Respiratory distress
In the lungs, histamine causes endothelial cell destruction and fluid leak into alveoli. The patient develops changes in level of consciousness, respiratory distress and, possibly, seizures.

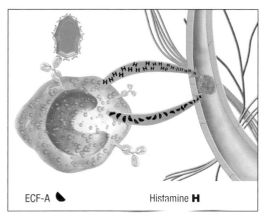

5. Deterioration
Meanwhile, mediators increase vascular permeability, causing fluid to leak from the vessels. Shock, confusion, tachycardia, and hypotension signal vascular collapse.

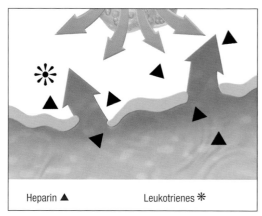

6. Failure of compensatory mechanisms
Endothelial cell damage causes basophils and mast cells to release heparin and mediator-neutralizing substances. However, anaphylaxis is now irreversible. Hemorrhage, disseminated intravascular coagulation, and cardiac arrest can occur.

ANKYLOSING SPONDYLITIS

A chronic, usually progressive inflammatory bone disease, ankylosing spondylitis primarily affects the sacroiliac, apophyseal, and costovertebral joints, along with adjacent soft tissue. The disease (also known as *rheumatoid spondylitis* and *Marie-Strümpell disease*) usually begins in the sacroiliac joints and gradually progresses to the lumbar, thoracic, and cervical regions of the spine. Deterioration of bone and cartilage can lead to formation of fibrous tissue and eventual fusion of the spine or peripheral joints.

Ankylosing spondylitis affects men 2 to 3 times more than it does women. Progressive disease is well recognized in men, but the diagnosis is commonly overlooked or missed in women, who tend to have more peripheral joint involvement.

Causes

- Direct cause unknown
- Familial tendency; more than 90% of patients are positive for human leukocyte antigen (HLA)-B27
- Presence of circulating immune complexes suggests immunologic activity

Pathophysiology

Spondylitis involves inflammation of one or more vertebrae. Ankylosing spondylitis is a chronic inflammatory disease that predominantly affects the joints between the vertebrae of the spine, and the joints between the spine and the pelvis. Fibrous tissue of the joint capsule is infiltrated by inflammatory cells that erode the bone and fibrocartilage. Repair of the cartilaginous structures begins with the proliferation of fibroblasts, which synthesize and secrete collagen. The collagen forms fibrous scar tissue that eventually undergoes calcification and ossification, causing the joint to fuse or lose flexibility.

Involvement of the peripheral joints or soft tissues is a rare occurrence. The disease waxes and wanes, it can go into remission, exacerbation, or arrest at any stage.

COMPLICATIONS
- Severe physical restrictions
- Inflammatory bowel disease
- Iritis

Signs and symptoms

- Intermittent low back pain most severe in the morning or after inactivity and relieved by exercise
- Mild fatigue, fever, anorexia, and weight loss
- Pain in shoulders, hips, knees, and ankles
- Pain over the symphysis pubis
- Stiffness or limited motion of the lumbar spine
- Pain and limited chest expansion
- Kyphosis
- Iritis
- Warmth, swelling, or tenderness of affected joints
- Small joints, such as toes, may become sausage-shaped
- Aortic murmur caused by regurgitation
- Cardiomegaly
- Upper lobe pulmonary fibrosis, which mimics tuberculosis, that may reduce vital capacity to 70% or less of predicted volume

Diagnostic test results

- HLA typing test shows serum findings that include HLA-B27 in about 95% of patients with primary ankylosing spondylitis and up to 80% of patients with secondary disease.
- Laboratory tests show slightly elevated erythrocyte sedimentation rate, serum alkaline phosphate levels, and creatine kinase levels in active disease.
- Serum immunoglobulin (Ig) profile shows elevated serum IgA levels.
- X-ray studies define characteristic changes, such as bilateral sacroiliac involvement (the hallmark of the disease), blurring of the joints' bony margins in early disease, patchy sclerosis with superficial bony erosions, eventual squaring of vertebral bodies, and "bamboo spine" with complete ankylosis.

Treatment

- No treatment that reliably halts progression
- Physical therapy to delay further deformity — good posture, stretching and deep-breathing exercises and, in some patients, braces and lightweight supports
- Heat, warm showers, baths, ice
- Nerve stimulation
- Nonsteroidal anti-inflammatory analgesics, such as aspirin, indomethacin, sulfasalazine
- Corticosteroids
- Tumor necrosis factor inhibitors
- Hip replacement
- Spinal wedge osteotomy

Lateral view

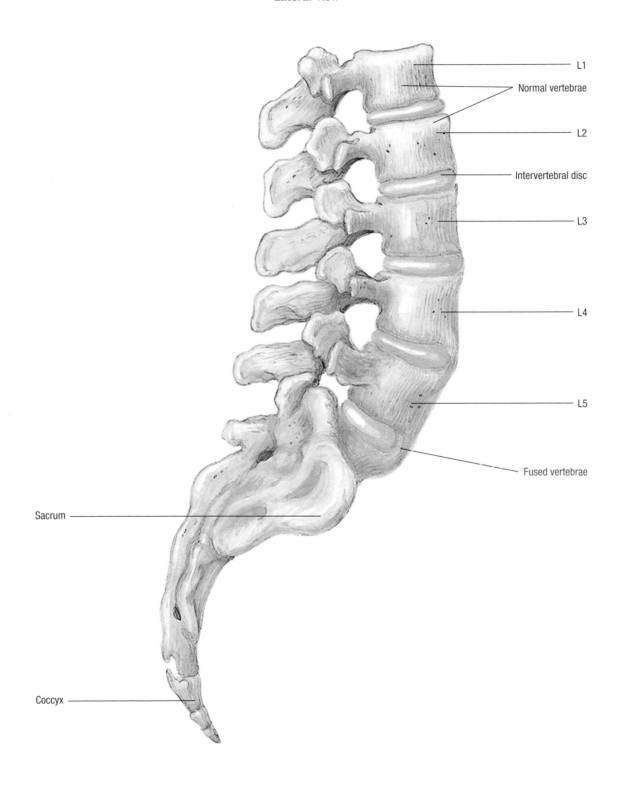

L1

Normal vertebrae

L2

Intervertebral disc

L3

L4

L5

Fused vertebrae

Sacrum

Coccyx

RHEUMATOID ARTHRITIS

Rheumatoid arthritis (RA) is a chronic, systemic inflammatory disease that primarily attacks peripheral joints and the surrounding muscles, tendons, ligaments, and blood vessels. Partial remissions and unpredictable exacerbations mark the course of this potentially crippling disease. RA strikes women three times more often than it does men.

 AGE ALERT
RA can occur at any age, but it begins most often between ages 25 and 55.

Causes
Direct cause unknown
Proposed mechanisms
- Abnormal immune activation (in a genetically susceptible person) leading to inflammation, complement activation, and cell proliferation in joints and tendon sheaths
- Infection (viral or bacterial), hormone action, or lifestyle factors

Pathophysiology
The body develops immunoglobulin (Ig) M antibody against the body's own IgG (also called *rheumatoid factor [RF]*). RF aggregates into complexes, generates inflammation, causing eventual cartilage damage and triggering other autoimmune responses.

If not arrested, the inflammatory process in the joints occurs in four stages:
- Congestion and edema of the synovial membrane and joint capsule cause synovitis. Infiltration by lymphocytes, macrophages, and neutrophils continues the local inflammatory response. These cells, as well as fibroblast-like synovial cells, produce enzymes that help to degrade bone and cartilage.
- Pannus — thickened layers of granulation tissue — covers and invades cartilage and eventually destroys the joint capsule and bone.
- Fibrous ankylosis — fibrous invasion of the pannus and scar formation — occludes the joint space. Bone atrophy and misalignment cause visible deformities and disrupt the articulation of opposing bones, causing muscle atrophy and imbalance and, possibly, partial dislocations (subluxations).
- Fibrous tissue calcifies, resulting in bony ankylosis and total immobility.

 COMPLICATIONS
- Joint deformities
- Vasculitis
- Pericarditis
- Peripheral neuropathy

Signs and symptoms
- Nonspecific symptoms (most likely related to the initial inflammatory reactions) precede inflammation of the synovium, including fever, weight loss, malaise, fatigue, and lymphadenopathy

As the disease progresses
- Specific localized, bilateral, and symmetric articular symptoms, frequently in the fingers at the proximal interphalangeal, metacarpophalangeal, and metatarsophalangeal joints, possibly extending to the wrists, knees, elbows, and ankles from inflammation of the synovium
- Stiffening of affected joints after inactivity, especially on arising in the morning
- Joint pain and tenderness, at first only with movement but eventually even at rest
- Gradual appearance of rheumatoid nodules — subcutaneous, round or oval, nontender masses (20% of RF-positive patients), usually on elbows, hands, or Achilles' tendon

Diagnostic test results
- X-rays show bone demineralization and soft-tissue swelling (early stages), cartilage loss and narrowed joint spaces and, finally, cartilage and bone destruction and erosion, subluxations, and deformities (later stages).
- RF titer is positive in 75% to 80% of patients (titer of 1:160 or higher).
- Synovial fluid analysis shows increased volume and turbidity but decreased viscosity and elevated white blood cell counts (usually greater than 10,000/µl).
- Serum protein electrophoresis shows elevated serum globulin levels.
- Erythrocyte sedimentation rate and C-reactive protein levels are elevated in 85% to 90% of patients (may be useful to monitor response to therapy because elevation frequently parallels disease activity).
- Complete blood count reveals moderate anemia, slight leukocytosis, and slight thrombocytosis.

Treatment
- Nonsteroidal anti-inflammatory agents
- Immunosuppressants
- Corticosteroids
- Disease-modifying anti-rheumatic drugs
- Anakinra
- Tumor necrosis factor inhibitors
- Abatacept
- Supportive measures, including rest, splinting to rest inflamed joints, range-of-motion exercises, physical therapy, heat applications for chronic disease and ice application for acute episodes
- Rituximab
- Synovectomy, osteotomy, and tendon repair
- Joint reconstruction or total joint replacement

THE EFFECTS OF RHEUMATOID ARTHRITIS ON CERTAIN JOINTS

Left knee
Patella removed to visualize

Erosion of bone

Erosion of cartilage

Pannus covers
synovial membrane

Hand and wrist

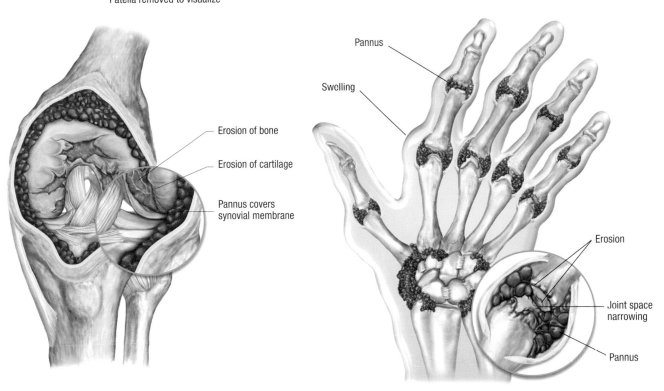

Pannus

Swelling

Erosion

Joint space
narrowing

Pannus

Left hip

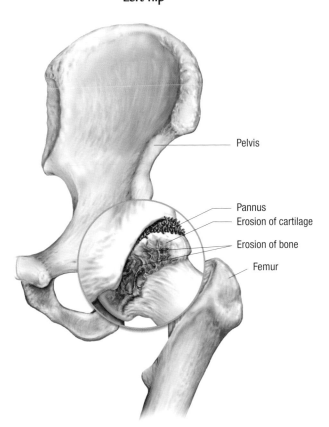

Pelvis

Pannus
Erosion of cartilage
Erosion of bone
Femur

SCLERODERMA

Scleroderma (also known as *systemic sclerosis*) is an uncommon disease of diffuse connective tissue. Degenerative and fibrotic changes in the skin, blood vessels, synovial membranes, skeletal muscles, and internal organs (especially the esophagus, intestinal tract, thyroid, heart, lungs, and kidneys) follow the initial inflammation. The seven forms of scleroderma are diffuse systemic sclerosis, localized, linear, chemically induced localized, eosinophilia myalgia syndrome, toxic oil syndrome, and graft-versus-host disease.

AGE ALERT
Scleroderma affects women 3 to 4 times more often than it does men, especially between ages 30 and 50. The peak incidence is in people ages 50 to 60.

Causes

Unknown

Possible causes
- Systemic exposure to silica dust or polyvinyl chloride
- Anticancer agents such as bleomycin; nonnarcotic analgesics such as pentazocine hydrochloride
- Abnormal immune response
- Underlying vascular cause with tissue changes initiated by persistent perfusion defect

Pathophysiology

Scleroderma usually begins in the fingers and extends proximally to the upper arms, shoulders, neck, and face. The skin atrophies, edema and infiltrates containing CD4⁺ T cells surround the blood vessels, and inflamed collagen fibers become edematous and degenerative, losing strength and elasticity. The dermis becomes tightly bound to the underlying structures, resulting in atrophy of the affected appendages and destruction of the distal phalanges by osteoporosis. As the disease progresses, the fibrosis and atrophy can affect other areas, including muscles and joints.

Signs and symptoms

- Skin thickening, commonly limited to the distal extremities and face, but possibly involving internal organs
- CREST syndrome (a benign subtype of limited systemic sclerosis): calcinosis, Raynaud's phenomenon, esophageal dysfunction, sclerodactyly, and telangiectasia
- Patchy skin changes with a teardrop-like appearance known as *morphea* (localized scleroderma)
- Band of thickened skin on the face or extremities that severely damages underlying tissues, causing atrophy and deformity (linear scleroderma)
- Raynaud's phenomenon (blanching, cyanosis, and erythema of the fingers and toes); progressive phalangeal resorption that may shorten the fingers (early symptoms)
- Taut, shiny skin over the entire hand and forearm due to skin thickening
- Tight and inelastic facial skin, causing a masklike appearance and "pinching" of the mouth

- Thickened skin over proximal limbs and trunk (diffuse systemic sclerosis)
- Abdominal distention
- Pain, stiffness, and swelling of fingers and joints (later symptoms)
- Frequent reflux, heartburn, dysphagia, and bloating after meals due to GI dysfunction
- Diarrhea, constipation, and malodorous floating stool

COMPLICATIONS
- Arrhythmias
- Dyspnea
- Malignant hypertension
- Renal failure
- Bowel obstruction
- Aspiration pneumonia
- Pulmonary hypertension
- Respiratory failure
- Cor pulmonale
- Heart failure
- Cardiomyopathy

Diagnostic test results

- Laboratory analysis reveals slightly elevated erythrocyte sedimentation rate, positive rheumatoid factor in 25% to 35% of patients, and positive antinuclear antibody.
- Urinalysis shows proteinuria, microscopic hematuria, and casts.
- Hand X-rays show terminal phalangeal tuft resorption, subcutaneous calcification, and joint space narrowing and erosion.
- Chest X-rays show bilateral basilar pulmonary fibrosis.
- GI X-rays show distal esophageal hypomotility and stricture, duodenal loop dilation, small-bowel malabsorption pattern, and large diverticula.
- Pulmonary function studies show decreased diffusion and vital capacity.
- Electrocardiogram reveals nonspecific abnormalities related to myocardial fibrosis and possible arrhythmias.
- Skin biopsy shows changes consistent with disease progression, such as marked thickening of the dermis and occlusive vessel changes.

Treatment

No cure

To preserve normal body functions and minimize complications
- Immunosuppressants, vasodilators, antihypertensives
- Digital sympathectomy, cervical sympathetic blockade
- Possible surgical debridement
- Antacids, soft, bland diet
- Angiotensin-converting enzyme inhibitors
- Physical therapy, heat therapy
- Broad-spectrum antibiotics

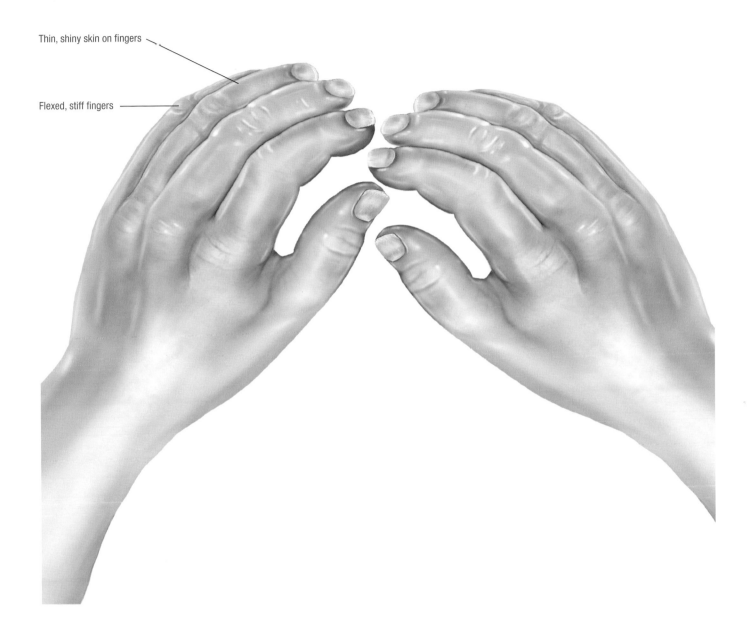

Thin, shiny skin on fingers

Flexed, stiff fingers

SYSTEMIC LUPUS ERYTHEMATOSUS

Systemic lupus erythematosus (SLE) is a chronic inflammatory autoimmune disorder that affects the connective tissues.

SLE is characterized by recurring remissions and exacerbations, which are especially common during the spring and summer. It strikes women 8 times as often as it does men, increasing to 15 times as often during childbearing years. The prognosis improves with early detection and treatment but remains poor for patients who develop cardiovascular, renal, or neurologic complications, or severe bacterial infections.

Causes

Direct cause unknown

Predisposing factors
- Physical or mental stress
- Streptococcal or viral infections
- Exposure to sunlight or ultraviolet light
- Immunization
- Pregnancy
- Abnormal estrogen metabolism
- Drugs, including procainamide, hydralazine, anticonvulsants; less commonly, penicillins, sulfa drugs, oral contraceptives

Pathophysiology

Autoimmunity is believed to be the prime mechanism in SLE. The body produces antibodies against components of its own cells, such as the antinuclear antibody (ANA), and immune complex disease follows. Patients with SLE may produce antibodies against many different tissue components, such as red blood cells (RBCs), neutrophils, platelets, lymphocytes, or almost any organ or tissue in the body.

COMPLICATIONS
- Pleurisy, pleural effusion, pneumonitis, pulmonary hypertension, and pulmonary infection
- Pericarditis, myocarditis, endocarditis, and coronary atherosclerosis
- Renal failure
- Seizures and mental dysfunction
- Infection
- Cancer
- Avascular necrosis

Signs and symptoms
- Joint pain
- Raynaud's phenomenon
- Photosensitivity
- Tachycardia, central cyanosis, and hypotension
- Altered level of consciousness, weakness of the extremities, and speech disturbances
- Skin lesions
- Malar rash
- Ulcers in the mouth or nose
- Patchy alopecia (common)
- Vasculitis
- Lymph node enlargement (diffuse or local and nontender)
- Fever
- Pericardial friction rub
- Irregular menstruation or amenorrhea, particularly during flare-ups
- Chest pain and dyspnea
- Emotional instability, psychosis, organic brain syndrome, headaches, irritability, and depression
- Oliguria, urinary frequency; dysuria, and bladder spasms

Diagnostic test results
- Complete blood count with differential reveals anemia and a reduced white blood cell (WBC) count; decreased platelet count; elevated erythrocyte sedimentation rate; and serum electrophoresis showing hypergammaglobulinemia.
- Positive ANA, deoxyribonucleic acid, and lupus erythematosus cell test findings in most patients with active SLE, but only slightly useful in diagnosing the disease (the ANA test is sensitive but not specific for SLE).
- Urine studies showing RBCs, WBCs, urine casts and sediment, and significant protein loss.
- Blood studies detect decreased serum complement (C3 and C4) levels, indicating active disease; increased C-reactive protein during flare-ups; and positive rheumatoid factor.
- Chest X-rays reveal pleurisy or lupus pneumonitis.
- Electrocardiogram reveals a conduction defect with cardiac involvement or pericarditis.
- Renal biopsy shows the progression of SLE and the extent of renal involvement.
- Skin biopsy shows immunoglobulin and complement deposition in the dermal-epidermal junction in 90% of patients.

Treatment
- Nonsteroidal anti-inflammatory compounds
- Topical corticosteroid creams
- Intralesional corticosteroids or antimalarials
- Systemic corticosteroids
- High-dose steroids and cytotoxic therapy
- Dialysis or renal transplant
- Antihypertensives
- Dietary changes
- Sunscreen use

ORGANS AFFECTED BY SYSTEMIC LUPUS ERYTHEMATOSUS

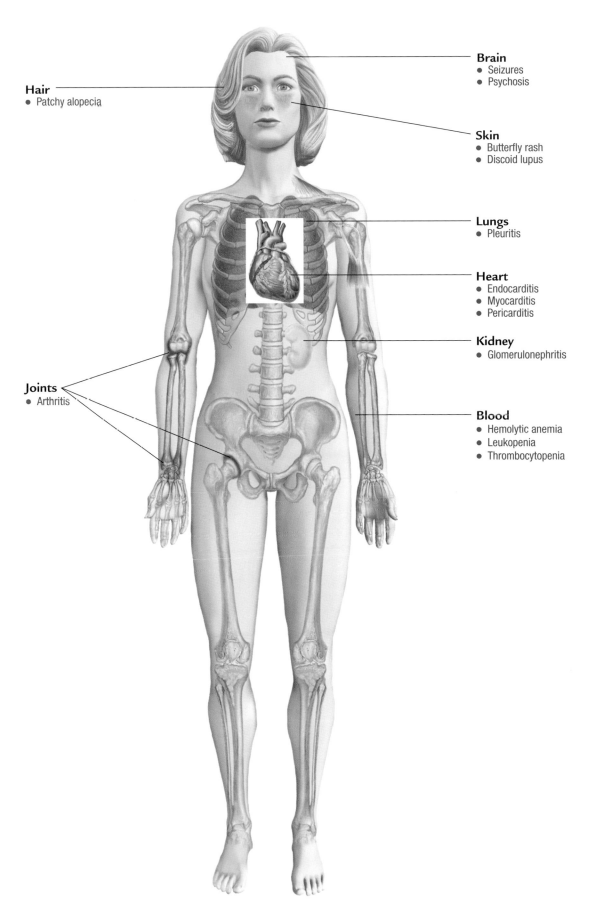

Hair
- Patchy alopecia

Brain
- Seizures
- Psychosis

Skin
- Butterfly rash
- Discoid lupus

Lungs
- Pleuritis

Heart
- Endocarditis
- Myocarditis
- Pericarditis

Kidney
- Glomerulonephritis

Joints
- Arthritis

Blood
- Hemolytic anemia
- Leukopenia
- Thrombocytopenia

ADRENAL HYPOFUNCTION

Adrenal hypofunction is classified as primary or secondary. *Primary* adrenal hypofunction or insufficiency (Addison's disease) originates within the adrenal gland and is characterized by the decreased secretion of mineralocorticoids, glucocorticoids, and androgens. It's defined as destruction of more than 90% of both adrenal glands and is usually caused by an autoimmune process. Addison's disease is relatively uncommon and can occur at any age and in both sexes. *Secondary* adrenal hypofunction is due to impaired pituitary secretion of adrenocorticotropin (ACTH) and is characterized by decreased glucocorticoid secretion.

With early diagnosis and adequate replacement therapy, the prognosis for adrenal hypofunction is good.

> ### CLINICAL TIP
> Adrenal crisis (Addisonian crisis) is a critical deficiency of mineralocorticoids and glucocorticoids that generally follows sepsis, trauma, surgery, omission of steroid therapy, or other acute physiologic stress. This medical emergency mandates immediate, vigorous treatment.

Causes
Primary hypofunction (Addison's disease)
- Bilateral adrenalectomy
- Hemorrhage into adrenal gland
- Neoplasms
- Tuberculosis, histoplasmosis, cytomegalovirus
- Family history of autoimmune disease

Secondary hypofunction (glucocorticoid deficiency)
- Hypopituitarism (causing decreased ACTH secretion)
- Abrupt withdrawal of long-term corticosteroid therapy
- Removal of an ACTH-secreting tumor
- Pituitary injury by tumor or infiltrative or autoimmune process

Pathophysiology
Addison's disease is a chronic condition that results from partial or complete adrenal destruction. In most cases, cellular atrophy is limited to the cortex, although medullary involvement may occur, resulting in catecholamine deficiency.

ACTH acts primarily to regulate the adrenal release of glucocorticoids (primarily cortisol); mineralocorticoids, including aldosterone; and sex steroids that supplement those produced by the gonads. ACTH secretion is controlled by corticotropin-releasing hormone from the hypothalamus and by negative feedback control by the glucocorticoids.

Cortisol deficiency causes decreased liver gluconeogenesis. Glucose levels of patients on insulin may be dangerously low.

Aldosterone deficiency causes increased renal sodium loss and enhances potassium reabsorption. Sodium excretion causes a reduction in water volume that leads to hypotension.

Androgen deficiency may result in decreased hair growth in axillary and pubic areas, loss of erectile function, or decreased libido.

Signs and symptoms
Primary hypofunction
- Weakness, fatigue
- Nausea, vomiting, anorexia, weight loss
- Conspicuous bronze color of the skin, especially on hands, elbows, and knees; darkening of scars
- Cardiovascular abnormalities, including orthostatic hypotension, decreased cardiac size and output, and weak, irregular pulse
- Decreased tolerance for even minor stress
- Fasting hypoglycemia
- Craving for salty food

Secondary hypofunction
- Similar to primary hypofunction; differences include:
  - hyperpigmentation absent because ACTH and melanocyte-stimulating hormone levels are low
  - possibly normal blood pressure and electrolyte balance because aldosterone secretion is near normal
  - usually normal androgen secretion.

> ### COMPLICATIONS
> - Adrenal crisis (profound weakness and fatigue, nausea, vomiting, dehydration, hypotension, confusion)

Diagnostic test results
- Blood test for plasma cortisol levels confirms adrenal insufficiency.
- Metyrapone test is used to detect secondary adrenal hypofunction.
- Rapid corticotropin stimulation test by I.V. or I.M. administration of cosyntropin, a synthetic form of corticotropin, after baseline sampling for cortisol and corticotropin (samples drawn for cortisol 30 and 60 minutes after injection), differentiates between primary and secondary adrenal hypofunction. A low corticotropin level indicates a secondary disorder. An elevated level is indicative of a primary disorder.
- Laboratory studies reveal decreased plasma cortisol level (less than 10 mcg/dl in the morning; less in the evening); decreased serum sodium and fasting blood glucose levels.
- Serum chemistry reveals increased serum potassium, calcium, and blood urea nitrogen levels.
- Complete blood count shows elevated hematocrit; and increased lymphocyte and eosinophil counts.
- X-rays show adrenal calcification if the cause is infectious.

Treatment
Primary or secondary adrenal hypofunction
- Lifelong corticosteroid replacement, usually with cortisone or hydrocortisone, which have a mineralocorticoid effect
- I.V. hydrocortisone

Primary adrenal hypofunction
- Oral fludrocortisone, a synthetic mineralocorticoid, to prevent dangerous dehydration, hypotension, hyponatremia, and hyperkalemia

ADRENAL HORMONE SECRETION

Adrenal hormones

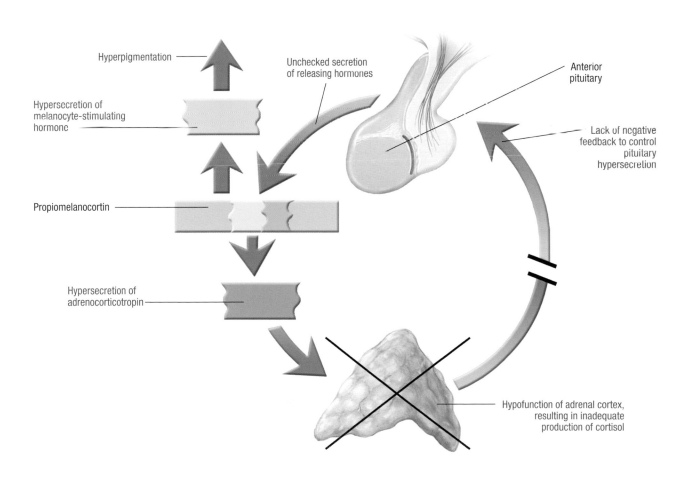

- Adrenal gland
- Adrenal gland cross section

Cortex
- Mineralocorticoids
- Glucocorticoids
- Androgens
- Estrogens

Medulla
- Norepinephrine
- Epinephrine

Blocked secretion of cortisol in primary adrenal hypofunction

Hyperpigmentation

Unchecked secretion of releasing hormones

Anterior pituitary

Hypersecretion of melanocyte-stimulating hormone

Lack of negative feedback to control pituitary hypersecretion

Propiomelanocortin

Hypersecretion of adrenocorticotropin

Hypofunction of adrenal cortex, resulting in inadequate production of cortisol

CUSHING'S SYNDROME

Cushing's syndrome is a cluster of clinical abnormalities caused by excessive adrenocortical hormones (particularly cortisol) or related corticosteroids and, to a lesser extent, androgens and aldosterone. Cushing's disease (adrenocorticotropin [ACTH] excess) accounts for about 70% of the cases of Cushing's syndrome.

AGE ALERT

Cushing's syndrome caused by ectopic corticotropin secretion is most common in adult men, with the peak incidence between ages 40 and 60. In 30% of patients, Cushing's syndrome results from a cortisol-secreting tumor. Adrenal tumors, rather than pituitary tumors, are more common in children, especially girls.

Causes
- Pituitary hypersecretion of ACTH
- Autonomous, ectopic ACTH secretion by a tumor outside the pituitary (usually malignant, frequently a pancreatic tumor or oat cell carcinoma of the lung)
- Administration of synthetic glucocorticoids or steroids
- Adrenal adenoma or a cancerous adrenal tumor

Pathophysiology
Cortisol excess results in anti-inflammatory effects and excessive catabolism of protein and peripheral fat to support hepatic glucose production. The mechanism may be ACTH-dependent, in which elevated plasma ACTH levels stimulate the adrenal cortex to produce excess cortisol, or ACTH-independent, in which excess cortisol is produced by the adrenal cortex or exogenously administered. This suppresses the hypothalamic-pituitary-adrenal axis, also present in ectopic ACTH-secreting tumors.

COMPLICATIONS
- Osteoporosis
- Peptic ulcer
- Diabetes mellitus or impaired glucose tolerance
- Ischemic heart disease and heart failure

Signs and symptoms
- Fat pads above the clavicles, over the upper back (buffalo hump), on the face (moon face), and throughout the trunk (truncal obesity); slender arms and legs
- Increased susceptibility to infection; decreased resistance to stress
- Hypertension, left ventricular hypertrophy, bleeding and ecchymosis, dyslipidemia
- Increased androgen production — clitoral hypertrophy, mild virilism, hirsutism, and amenorrhea or oligomenorrhea in women; sexual dysfunction
- Sodium and secondary fluid retention, increased potassium excretion, ureteral calculi
- Irritability and emotional lability
- Little or no scar formation; poor wound healing
- Purple striae, facial plethora, acne
- Muscle weakness
- Pathologic fractures; skeletal growth retardation in children

Diagnostic test results
- Laboratory studies reveal hyperglycemia, hypernatremia, glucosuria, hypokalemia, and metabolic acidosis; elevated urinary free cortisol levels; elevated salivary free cortisol; and elevated serum cortisol.
- Dexamethasone suppression test confirms the diagnosis and determines the cause, possibly an adrenal tumor or a nonendocrine, corticotropin-releasing tumor.
- Ultrasound, computed tomography scan, and magnetic resonance imaging detect the presence of a pituitary or adrenal tumor.

Treatment
- Specific for cause of hypercortisolism — pituitary, adrenal, ectopic
- Surgery for tumors of adrenal or pituitary glands or other tissue, such as lung
- Radiation therapy for tumor
- Cortisol replacement therapy after surgery
- Antihypertensives
- Potassium supplements
- Diuretics
- Antineoplastic, antihormone agents
- For inoperable tumor, drugs, such as mitotane or aminoglutethimide to block steroid synthesis

CLINICAL TIP

Most patients with Cushing's syndrome are treated with transphenoidal surgery, which has a high cure rate (80%). Pharmacotherapy is usually used as adjunctive rather than primary therapy.

MANIFESTATIONS OF CUSHING'S SYNDROME

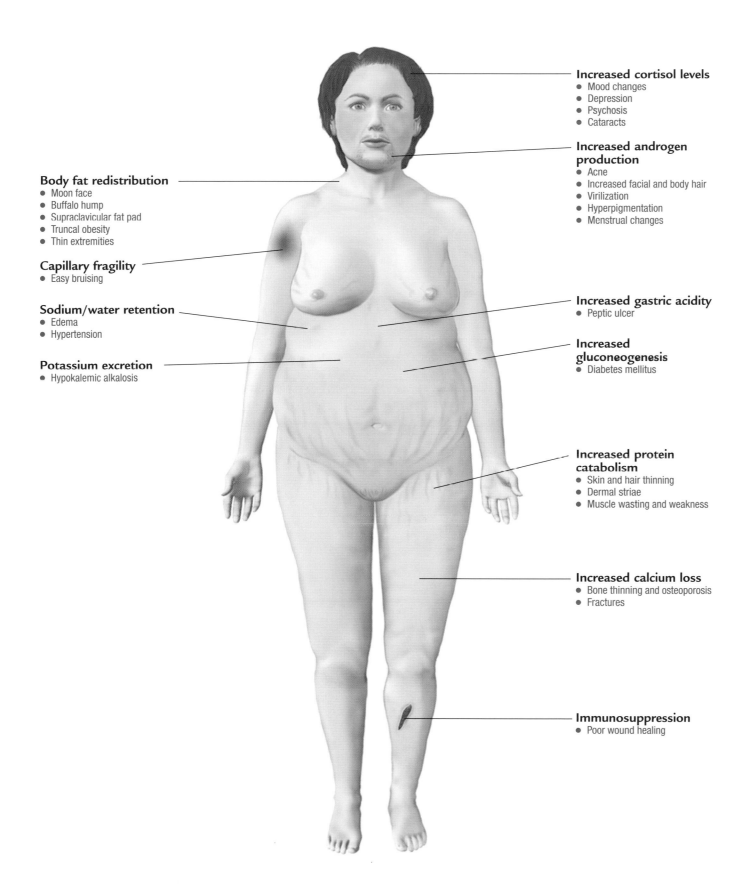

Increased cortisol levels
- Mood changes
- Depression
- Psychosis
- Cataracts

Increased androgen production
- Acne
- Increased facial and body hair
- Virilization
- Hyperpigmentation
- Menstrual changes

Body fat redistribution
- Moon face
- Buffalo hump
- Supraclavicular fat pad
- Truncal obesity
- Thin extremities

Capillary fragility
- Easy bruising

Sodium/water retention
- Edema
- Hypertension

Potassium excretion
- Hypokalemic alkalosis

Increased gastric acidity
- Peptic ulcer

Increased gluconeogenesis
- Diabetes mellitus

Increased protein catabolism
- Skin and hair thinning
- Dermal striae
- Muscle wasting and weakness

Increased calcium loss
- Bone thinning and osteoporosis
- Fractures

Immunosuppression
- Poor wound healing

DIABETES INSIPIDUS

A disorder of water metabolism, diabetes insipidus results from a deficiency of circulating vasopressin (also called *antidiuretic hormone,* or *ADH*) or from renal resistance to this hormone. The three forms of diabetes insipidus are neurogenic, nephrogenic, and psychogenic. Neurogenic diabetes insipidus is caused by a deficiency of ADH; nephrogenic diabetes insipidus, by the resistance of renal tubules to ADH. Diabetes insipidus is characterized by excessive fluid intake and hypotonic polyuria. A decrease in ADH levels leads to altered intracellular and extracellular fluid control, causing renal excretion of a large amount of urine.

 AGE ALERT
Diabetes insipidus may begin at any age and is slightly more common in men than in women.

In uncomplicated diabetes insipidus, the prognosis is good with adequate water replacement, and patients usually lead normal lives.

Causes
- Neurogenic: stroke, hypothalamic or pituitary tumor, cranial trauma, or surgery
- Nephrogenic: X-linked recessive trait, end-stage renal failure
- Psychogenic: primary polydipsia or sarcoidosis
- Transient diabetes insipidus: certain drugs, such as lithium, phenytoin, or alcohol

Pathophysiology
Diabetes insipidus is related to an insufficiency of ADH, leading to polydipsia and polyuria.

Neurogenic, or *central,* diabetes insipidus is an inadequate ADH response to changes in plasma osmolarity. A lesion of the hypothalamus, infundibular stem, or posterior pituitary partially or completely blocks ADH synthesis, transport, or release.

Neurogenic diabetes insipidus has an acute onset. A three-phase syndrome can occur, which involves:
- progressive loss of nerve tissue and increased diuresis
- normal diuresis
- polyuria and polydipsia, reflecting permanent loss of the ability to secrete adequate ADH.

Nephrogenic diabetes insipidus is caused by an inadequate renal response to ADH. The collecting duct's permeability to water doesn't increase in response to ADH. Nephrogenic diabetes insipidus is generally related to disorders and drugs that damage the renal tubules or inhibit the generation of cyclic adenosine monophosphate in the tubules. In addition, hy-

pokalemia or hypercalcemia impairs the renal response to ADH. A rare genetic form of nephrogenic diabetes insipidus is an X-linked recessive trait.

Psychogenic diabetes insipidus is caused by an extremely large fluid intake. This primary polydipsia may be idiopathic or reflect psychosis or sarcoidosis. The polydipsia and resultant polyuria wash out ADH more quickly than it can be replaced. Chronic polyuria may overwhelm the renal medullary concentration gradient, rendering the kidneys partially or totally unable to concentrate urine.

Regardless of the cause, insufficient ADH causes the immediate excretion of large volumes of dilute urine and consequent plasma hyperosmolality. In conscious individuals, the thirst mechanism is stimulated, usually for cold liquids.

 COMPLICATIONS
- Severe dehydration
- Shock
- Renal failure
- Central nervous system damage
- Bladder distention
- Hydronephrosis

Signs and symptoms
- Polydipsia and polyuria up to 20 L/day (cardinal symptoms)
- Nocturia
- Sleep disturbance and fatigue
- Headache and visual disturbance
- Abdominal fullness, anorexia, and weight loss
- Fever
- Changes in level of consciousness
- Hypotension
- Tachycardia

Diagnostic test results
- Urinalysis shows almost colorless urine of low osmolality and low specific gravity.
- Water deprivation test identifies vasopressin deficiency, resulting in renal inability to concentrate urine.

Treatment
- Vasopressin to control fluid balance and prevent dehydration until the cause of diabetes insipidus can be identified and eliminated
- Hydrochlorothiazide with potassium supplement
- Desmopressin acetate
- Chlorpropamide
- Fluid intake to match output

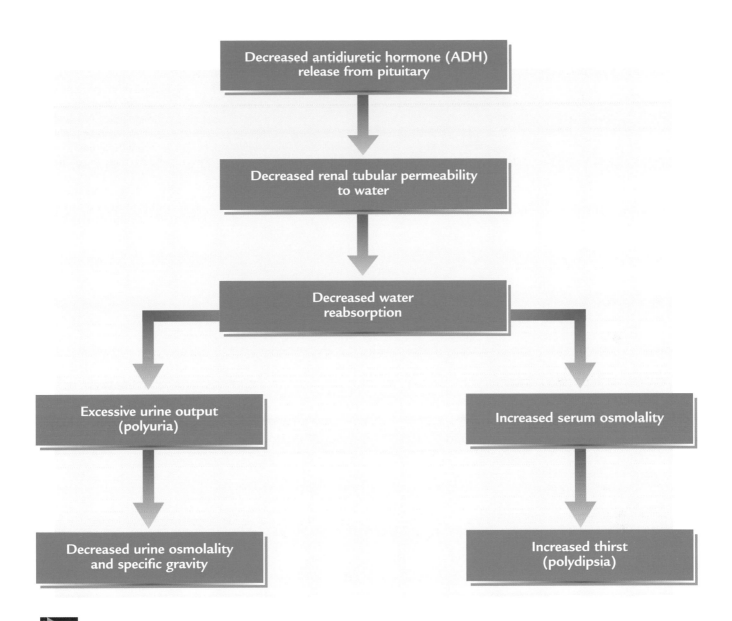

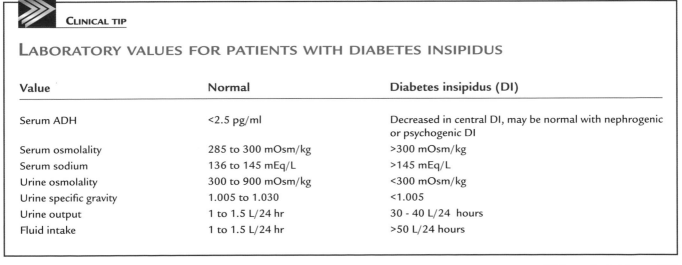

CLINICAL TIP

LABORATORY VALUES FOR PATIENTS WITH DIABETES INSIPIDUS

Value	Normal	Diabetes insipidus (DI)
Serum ADH	<2.5 pg/ml	Decreased in central DI, may be normal with nephrogenic or psychogenic DI
Serum osmolality	285 to 300 mOsm/kg	>300 mOsm/kg
Serum sodium	136 to 145 mEq/L	>145 mEq/L
Urine osmolality	300 to 900 mOsm/kg	<300 mOsm/kg
Urine specific gravity	1.005 to 1.030	<1.005
Urine output	1 to 1.5 L/24 hr	30 - 40 L/24 hours
Fluid intake	1 to 1.5 L/24 hr	>50 L/24 hours

DIABETES MELLITUS

Diabetes mellitus is a metabolic disorder characterized by hyperglycemia resulting from lack of insulin, lack of insulin effect, or both. Three general classifications are recognized:
- type 1 — absolute insulin insufficiency
- type 2 — insulin resistance with varying degrees of insulin secretory defects
- gestational diabetes — manifested during pregnancy.

AGE ALERT
Although possible at any age, type 1 usually manifests before age 30. Type 2 usually occurs in obese adults after age 40.

Causes
- Heredity
- Environment (infection, toxins)
- Stress, diet, lack of exercise in genetically susceptible persons
- Pregnancy

Pathophysiology

Type 1 and type 2 diabetes mellitus are two separate and distinct pathophysiological entities. In persons genetically susceptible to *type 1* diabetes, a triggering event, possibly a viral infection, causes production of autoantibodies which kill the beta cells of the pancreas. This leads to a decline in and an ultimate lack of insulin secretion. Insulin deficiency, when more than 90% of the beta cells have been destroyed, leads to hyperglycemia, enhanced lipolysis, and protein catabolism.

Type 2 diabetes mellitus is a chronic disease caused by one or more of the following factors: impaired insulin production, inappropriate hepatic glucose production, or peripheral insulin receptor insensitivity.

Gestational diabetes mellitus is glucose intolerance during pregnancy in a woman not previously diagnosed with diabetes. This may occur if placental hormones counteract insulin, causing insulin resistance.

COMPLICATIONS
- Cardiovascular disease
- Nephropathy
- Retinopathy
- Neuropathy
- Ketoacidosis and hyperosmolar coma
- Infections

Signs and symptoms
- Polyuria and polydipsia
- Nausea; anorexia (common) or polyphagia (occasional)
- Weight loss (usually 10% to 30%; persons with type 1 diabetes often have almost no body fat at diagnosis)
- Headaches, fatigue, lethargy, reduced energy levels, impaired school or work performance
- Muscle cramps, irritability, emotional lability
- Vision changes such as blurring
- Numbness and tingling
- Abdominal discomfort and pain; diarrhea or constipation
- Recurrent vaginal candidiasis

Diagnostic test results
In men and nonpregnant women
- Two of the following criteria obtained more than 24 hours apart, using the same test twice or any combination are indicators of the disease:
- fasting plasma glucose level of 126 mg/dl or more
- typical symptoms of uncontrolled diabetes and random blood glucose level of 200 mg/dl or more
- blood glucose level of 200 mg/dl or more 2 hours after ingesting 75 g of oral dextrose.
- Other criteria include:
- diabetic retinopathy on ophthalmologic examination
- other diagnostic and monitoring tests, including urinalysis for acetone and glycosylated hemoglobin (reflects glycemic control over the past 2 to 3 months).
In pregnant women
- Positive glucose tolerance test reveals high peak blood sugar levels after ingestion of glucose (1 g/kg body weight) and delayed return to fasting levels.

Treatment
Type 1 diabetes mellitus
- Insulin replacement, meal planning, and exercise (current forms of insulin replacement include mixed-dose, split mixed-dose, and multiple daily injection regimens and continuous subcutaneous insulin infusions)
- Pancreas transplantation (currently requires chronic immunosuppression)
Type 2 diabetes mellitus
- Oral antidiabetic drugs to stimulate endogenous insulin production, increase insulin sensitivity at the cellular level, suppress hepatic gluconeogenesis, and delay GI absorption of carbohydrates (drug combinations may be used)
- Exogenous insulin, alone or with oral antidiabetic drugs, to optimize glycemic control
Type 1 and type 2 diabetes mellitus
- Individualized meal plan designed to meet nutritional needs, control blood glucose and lipid levels, and reach and maintain appropriate body weight
- Weight reduction (obese patient with type 2 diabetes mellitus) or high calorie allotment, depending on growth stage and activity level (type 1 diabetes mellitus)
Gestational diabetes
- Medical nutrition therapy and exercise
- Alpha glucosidase inhibitors, injected insulin, or both (if euglycemia not achieved)
- Counseling on the high risk for gestational diabetes in subsequent pregnancies and type 2 diabetes later in life
- Exercise and weight control to help avert type 2 diabetes

Type 1 diabetes

Pancreas with no insulin production

Cell

Glucose

Closed glucose channel

Open glucose channel

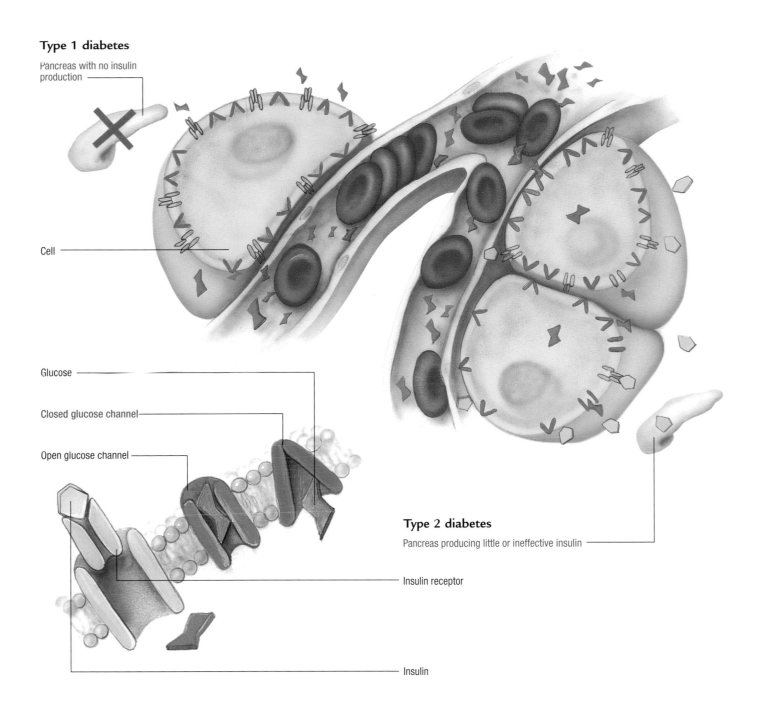

Type 2 diabetes

Pancreas producing little or ineffective insulin

Insulin receptor

Insulin

GROWTH HORMONE EXCESS

Growth hormone (GH) excess that begins in adulthood (after epiphyseal closure) is called *acromegaly*. GH excess that's present before closure of the epiphyseal growth plates of the long bones causes *pituitary gigantism*. In both cases, the result is increased growth of bone, cartilage, and other tissues, as well as increased carbohydrate catabolism and protein synthesis. In gigantism, a proportional overgrowth of all body tissues before epiphyseal closure causes remarkable height increases — as much as 6″ (15 cm) a year. Acromegaly is rare; its prevalence is about 70 people per million in the United States, affecting men and women equally. GH excess is a slow but progressive disease that shortens life if untreated. Morbidity and mortality tend to be related to coronary artery disease and hypertension secondary to prolonged exposure to excessive growth hormone.

AGE ALERT
Most cases of acromegaly are diagnosed in the fourth and fifth decades, but the disease is usually present for years before diagnosis. Gigantism affects infants and children, causing them to reach as much as three times the normal height for their age. Affected adults may reach a height of more than 7½′ (7.6 m).

Causes
Eosinophilic or mixed-cell adenomas of the anterior pituitary gland

Pathophysiology
A GH-secreting tumor creates an unpredictable GH secretion pattern, which replaces the usual peaks at 1 to 4 hours after the onset of sleep. Elevated GH and somatomedin levels stimulate growth of all tissues. In pituitary gigantism, the epiphyseal plates aren't closed, and so the excess GH stimulates linear growth. It also increases the bulk of bones and joints and causes enlargement of internal organs and metabolic abnormalities. In acromegaly, the excess GH increases bone density and width, and the proliferation of connective and soft tissues.

COMPLICATIONS
- Arthritis
- Carpal tunnel syndrome
- Osteoporosis
- Kyphosis
- Hypertension
- Diabetes mellitus
- Arteriosclerosis
- Heart enlargement
- Heart failure

Signs and symptoms
Acromegaly
- Soft-tissue thickening that causes enlargement of hands, feet, nose, mandible, supraorbital ridge, and ears
- Severe headache, central nervous system impairment, bitemporal hemianopia (defective vision) and loss of visual acuity
- Marked prognathism and malocclusion of teeth; may interfere with chewing
- Laryngeal hypertrophy, paranasal sinus enlargement, thickening of the tongue — causing the voice to sound deep and hollow
- Arrowhead appearance of distal phalanges on X-rays, thickened fingers
- Sweating, oily skin, hypertrichosis, new skin tags (typical)
- Irritability, hostility, various psychological disturbances
- Bow legs, barrel chest, arthritis, osteoporosis, kyphosis
- Glucose intolerance
- Hypertension and arteriosclerosis (effects of prolonged excessive GH secretion)
- Hypermetabolism
- Weakness, arthralgia

Gigantism
- Backache, arthralgia, arthritis
- Excessive height
- Headache, vomiting, seizure activity, visual disturbances, papilledema
- Deficiencies of other hormone systems if GH-producing tumor destroys other hormone-secreting cells
- Glucose intolerance

Diagnostic test results
- Laboratory studies reveal elevated plasma GH level measured by radioimmunoassay, the presence of somatomedin C, and elevated blood glucose levels.
- Glucose suppression test confirms hyperpituitarism.
- Skull X-rays, computed tomography scan, or magnetic resonance imaging show the presence and extent of pituitary lesion.
- Bone X-rays show a thickening of the cranium (especially frontal, occipital, and parietal bones) and long bones, and osteoarthritis in the spine.

Treatment
- Tumor removal by cranial or transphenoidal hypophysectomy or pituitary radiation therapy
- Mandatory surgery for a tumor causing blindness or other severe neurologic disturbances
- Postoperative replacement of thyroid, cortisone, and gonadal hormones
- Bromocriptine and octreotide to inhibit GH synthesis

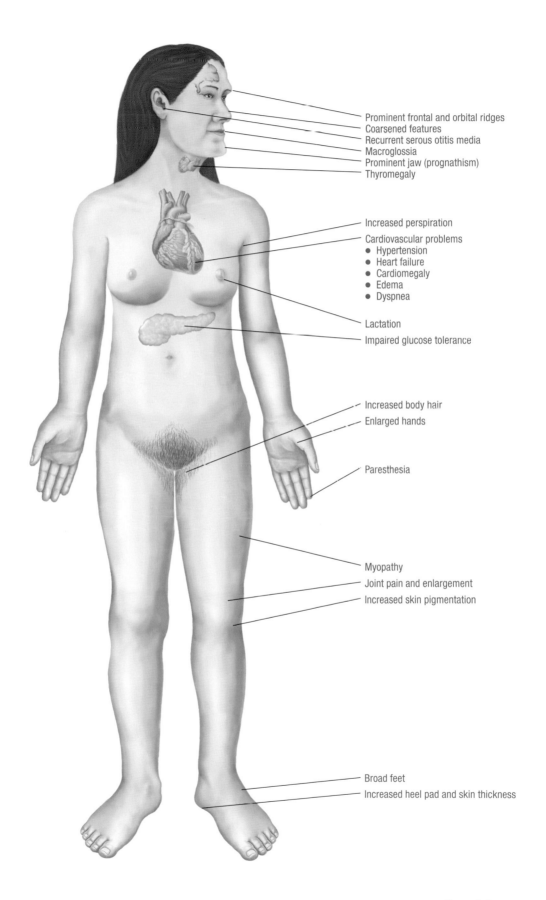

Prominent frontal and orbital ridges
Coarsened features
Recurrent serous otitis media
Macroglossia
Prominent jaw (prognathism)
Thyromegaly

Increased perspiration
Cardiovascular problems
- Hypertension
- Heart failure
- Cardiomegaly
- Edema
- Dyspnea

Lactation
Impaired glucose tolerance

Increased body hair
Enlarged hands

Paresthesia

Myopathy
Joint pain and enlargement
Increased skin pigmentation

Broad feet
Increased heel pad and skin thickness

HYPERPARATHYROIDISM

Hyperparathyroidism results from excessive secretion of parathyroid hormone (PTH) from one or more of the four parathyroid glands. PTH promotes bone resorption, and hypersecretion leads to hypercalcemia and hypophosphatemia. Renal and GI absorption of calcium increase. Primary hyperparathyroidism is commonly diagnosed when an asymptomatic patient has elevated calcium levels in routine laboratory tests.

AGE ALERT
Hyperparathyroidism affects women 2 to 3 times more frequently than it does men and is usually seen in women older than age 40.

Causes
Primary hyperparathyroidism
- Most commonly a single adenoma
- Multiple endocrine neoplasia (all four glands usually involved)

Secondary hyperparathyroidism
- Rickets, vitamin D deficiency, chronic renal failure, and osteomalacia due to phenytoin

Pathophysiology
Overproduction of PTH by a tumor or hyperplastic tissue increases intestinal calcium absorption, reduces renal calcium clearance, and increases bone calcium release. Response to this excess varies for each patient for unknown reasons.

Hypophosphatemia results when excessive PTH inhibits renal tubular phosphate reabsorption. It aggravates hypercalcemia by increasing the sensitivity of the bone to PTH. Pathologic fractures may be a presenting symptom.

A hypocalcemia-producing abnormality outside the parathyroids can cause excessive compensatory production of PTH, or secondary hyperparathyroidism.

COMPLICATIONS
- Renal calculi and renal failure
- Peptic ulcer
- Cholelithiasis
- Cardiac arrhythmias, vascular damage, and heart failure
- Central nervous system changes

Signs and symptoms
Primary hyperparathyroidism
- Polyuria, nephrocalcinosis, or recurring nephrolithiasis and consequent renal insufficiency
- Chronic low back pain and easy fracturing
- Bone tenderness, chondrocalcinosis
- Osteopenia and osteoporosis, especially of vertebrae
- Erosions of juxta-articular (adjoining joint) surface
- Subchondral fractures
- Traumatic synovitis
- Pseudogout
- Pancreatitis causing constant, severe epigastric pain that radiates to the back

- Peptic ulcers, causing abdominal pain, anorexia, nausea, and vomiting
- Muscle weakness and atrophy, particularly in the legs
- Psychomotor and personality disturbances, depression, overt psychosis
- Skin necrosis, cataracts, calcium microthrombi to lungs and pancreas, anemia, and subcutaneous calcification

Secondary hyperparathyroidism
- Same features of calcium imbalance as in primary hyperparathyroidism
- Skeletal deformities of the long bones (such as rickets)
- Symptoms of the underlying disease

Diagnostic test results
Primary hyperparathyroidism
- Hypercalcemia and high concentrations of serum PTH on radioimmunoassay (confirms the diagnosis).
- X-rays show diffuse demineralization of bones, bone cysts, outer cortical bone absorption, and subperiosteal erosion of the phalanges and distal clavicles.
- Microscopic bone examination by X-ray spectrophotometry typically shows increased bone turnover.
- Laboratory studies detect elevated urine and serum calcium, chloride, and alkaline phosphatase levels; decreased serum phosphorus levels; elevated uric acid and creatinine levels; increased serum amylase levels.

Secondary hyperparathyroidism
- Laboratory analysis reveals normal or slightly decreased serum calcium level, variable serum phosphorus level, especially when the cause is rickets, osteomalacia, or kidney disease.

Treatment
Primary hyperparathyroidism
- Surgery to remove the adenoma or, depending on the extent of hyperplasia, all but half of one gland, to provide normal PTH levels
- Treatments to decrease calcium levels — forcing fluids, limiting dietary intake of calcium, promoting sodium and calcium excretion through forced diuresis
- Oral sodium or potassium phosphate; subcutaneous calcitonin; I.V. mithramycin or biphosphonate
- I.V. magnesium and phosphate; sodium phosphate solution by mouth or retention enema; possibly supplemental calcium, vitamin D, or calcitrol

Secondary hyperparathyroidism
- Vitamin D to correct the underlying cause of parathyroid hyperplasia; oral calcium preparation to correct hyperphosphatemia in the patient with kidney disease
- Dialysis in patient with renal failure to decrease phosphorus levels
- Calcitonin
- Pamidronate

PATHOGENESIS OF HYPERPARATHYROIDISM

Tumor or hyperplastic tissue secretes excess parathyroid hormone

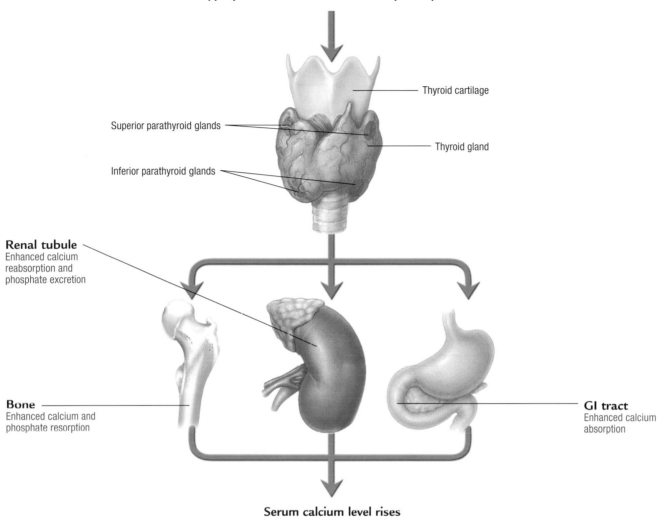

Thyroid cartilage

Superior parathyroid glands

Thyroid gland

Inferior parathyroid glands

Renal tubule
Enhanced calcium reabsorption and phosphate excretion

Bone
Enhanced calcium and phosphate resorption

GI tract
Enhanced calcium absorption

Serum calcium level rises

CLINICAL TIP

BONE RESORPTION IN PRIMARY HYPERPARATHYROIDISM

In hyperparathyroidism, body mechanisms sacrifice bone to preserve intracellular calcium levels. X-rays may show diffuse demineralization of bones, bone cysts, outer cortical bone absorption, and subperiosteal erosion of the phalanges and distal clavicles. Microscopic examination of the bone with tests — such as X-ray spectrophotometry — typically demonstrates increased bone turnover.

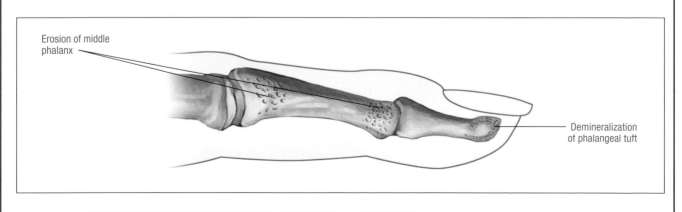

Erosion of middle phalanx

Demineralization of phalangeal tuft

HYPERTHYROIDISM

Hyperthyroidism, or thyrotoxicosis, is a metabolic imbalance that results from the overproduction of thyroid hormone. The most common form is Graves' disease, an autoimmune disorder that increases thyroxine (T_4) production, enlarges the thyroid gland (goiter), and causes multiple system changes.

AGE ALERT
Incidence of Graves' disease is greatest in women between ages 30 and 60, especially those with a family history of thyroid abnormalities; only 5% of patients are younger than age 15.

Causes
- Inherited predisposition, probably autosomal recessive gene
- Other endocrine abnormalities
- Defect in suppressor T-lymphocyte function and consequent production of autoantibodies
- Excessive dietary intake of iodine
- Stress, such as surgery, infection, toxemia of pregnancy, or diabetic ketoacidosis — can precipitate thyroid storm
- Medications, such as lithium and amiodarone
- Toxic nodules or tumors

Pathophysiology
The thyroid gland secretes the thyroid precursor T_4, the thyroid hormone triiodothyronine (T_3), and thyrocalcitonin. T_4 and T_3 stimulate protein, lipid, and carbohydrate metabolism primarily through catabolic pathways. Thyrocalcitonin removes calcium from the blood and incorporates it into bone. Biosynthesis, storage, and release of thyroid hormones are controlled by the hypothalamic-pituitary axis through a negative-feedback loop.

Thyrotropin-releasing hormone (TRH) from the hypothalamus stimulates the release of thyroid-stimulating-hormone (TSH) by the pituitary. Circulating T_3 levels provide negative feedback through the hypothalamus to decrease TRH levels, and through the pituitary to decrease TSH levels.

In Graves' disease, autoantibodies are produced that attach to and then stimulate TSH receptors on the thyroid gland. This process leads to increased stimulation of the gland and increased hormone production.

COMPLICATIONS
- Thyroid storm (extreme irritability, hypertension, tachycardia, vomiting, temperature up to 106°F [41.1°C], delirium, and coma)

Signs and symptoms
- Enlarged thyroid (goiter)
- Nervousness, tremor, and palpitations
- Heat intolerance, sweating
- Weight loss despite increased appetite
- Frequent bowel movements
- Exophthalmos (characteristic, but absent in many patients with thyrotoxicosis)

Other signs and symptoms, common because thyrotoxicosis profoundly affects virtually every body system
- Difficulty concentrating; fine tremor, shaky handwriting, and clumsiness; emotional instability and mood swings ranging from occasional outbursts to overt psychosis
- Moist, smooth, warm, flushed skin; fine, soft hair; premature patchy graying and increased hair loss in both sexes; friable nails and onycholysis; pretibial myxedema, producing thickened skin; accentuated hair follicles; sometimes itchy or painful raised red patches of skin with occasional nodule formation; microscopic examination showing increased mucin deposits
- Systolic hypertension, tachycardia, full bounding pulse, wide pulse pressure, cardiomegaly, increased cardiac output and blood volume, visible point of maximal impulse, paroxysmal supraventricular tachycardia and atrial fibrillation (especially in elderly people), and occasional systolic murmur at the left sternal border
- Increased respiratory rate, dyspnea on exertion and at rest; nausea and vomiting; soft stools or diarrhea; liver enlargement
- Weakness, fatigue, and muscle atrophy; rare coexistence with myasthenia gravis; possibly generalized or localized paralysis associated with hypokalemia and, rarely, acropachy
- Oligomenorrhea or amenorrhea, decreased fertility, increased incidence of spontaneous abortion (females), gynecomastia (males), diminished libido (both sexes)

Diagnostic test results
- Radioimmunoassay shows increased serum T_4 and T_3 levels.
- Laboratory studies reveal low TSH levels.
- Thyroid scan shows increased uptake of radioactive iodine (^{131}I) in Graves' disease and, usually, in toxic multinodular goiter and toxic adenoma; low radioactive uptake in thyroiditis and thyrotoxic factitia (test contraindicated in pregnancy).
- Ultrasonography confirms subclinical ophthalmopathy.

Treatment
- Antithyroid drugs — thyroid hormone antagonists, including propylthiouracil and methimazole, to block thyroid hormone synthesis; propranolol until antithyroid drugs reach their full effect — to manage tachycardia and other peripheral effects of excessive hypersympathetic activity
- Single oral dose of ^{131}I
- Surgery and lifelong regular medical supervision — most patients become hypothyroid, sometimes as long as several years after surgery

CLINICAL TIP
With treatment, most patients with hyperthyroidism can lead normal lives. However, thyroid storm — an acute, severe exacerbation of thyrotoxicosis — is a medical emergency that may have life-threatening cardiac, hepatic, or renal consequences.

THYROID GLAND AND ITS HORMONES

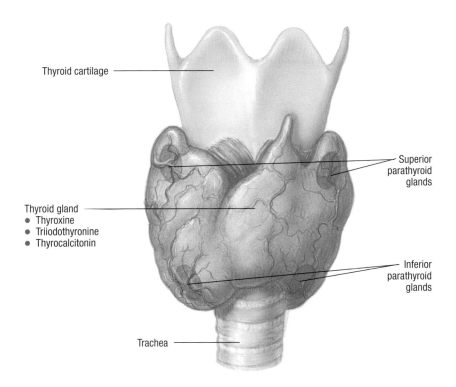

Thyroid cartilage

Superior parathyroid glands

Thyroid gland
- Thyroxine
- Triiodothyronine
- Thyrocalcitonin

Inferior parathyroid glands

Trachea

HISTOLOGIC CHANGES IN GRAVES' DISEASE

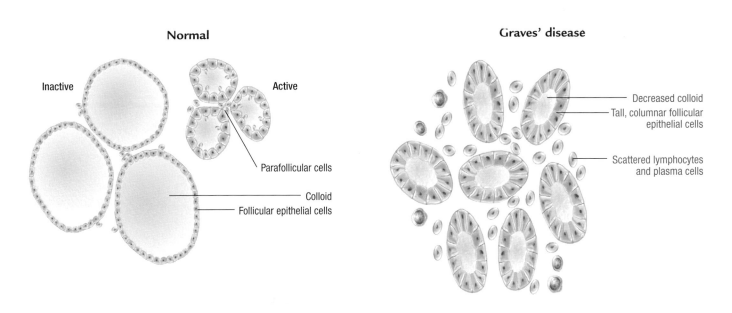

Normal

Inactive

Active

Parafollicular cells

Colloid

Follicular epithelial cells

Graves' disease

Decreased colloid

Tall, columnar follicular epithelial cells

Scattered lymphocytes and plasma cells

HYPOPITUITARISM

Hypopituitarism, also known as *panhypopituitarism,* is a complex syndrome marked by metabolic dysfunction, sexual immaturity, and growth retardation (when it occurs in childhood). The cause is a deficiency of the hormones secreted by the anterior pituitary gland. Panhypopituitarism is a partial or total failure of all six of this gland's vital hormones — adrenocorticotropin (ACTH), thyroid-stimulating hormone (TSH), luteinizing hormone (LH), follicle-stimulating hormone (FSH), growth hormone (GH), and prolactin.

AGE ALERT
Partial and complete forms of hypopituitarism affect adults and children; in children, these diseases may cause dwarfism and delayed puberty. The prognosis may be good with adequate replacement therapy and correction of the underlying causes.

Primary hypopituitarism usually develops in a predictable pattern. It generally begins with decreased gonadotropin (FSH and LH) levels and consequent hypogonadism, reflected by cessation of menses in women and impotence in men. GH deficiency follows, causing short stature, delayed growth, and delayed puberty in children. Subsequent decreased TSH levels cause hypothyroidism and, finally, decreased ACTH levels result in adrenal insufficiency, possibly leading to adrenal crisis. When hypopituitarism follows surgical ablation or trauma, the pattern of hormonal events may not necessarily follow that sequence. Damage to the hypothalamus or neurohypophysis may cause diabetes insipidus.

Causes
Primary hypopituitarism
- Tumor of the pituitary gland
- Congenital defect (hypoplasia or aplasia of the pituitary gland)
- Pituitary infarction (most often from postpartum hemorrhage)
- Partial or total hypophysectomy by surgery, irradiation, or chemical agents
- Granulomatous disease such as tuberculosis
- Idiopathic or autoimmune origin (occasionally)

Secondary hypopituitarism
- Deficiency of releasing hormones produced by the hypothalamus, either idiopathic or resulting from infection, trauma, or a tumor

Pathophysiology
The pituitary gland is highly vascular and therefore extremely vulnerable to ischemia and infarction. Any event that leads to circulatory collapse and compensatory vasospasm may result in gland ischemia, tissue necrosis, or edema. Expansion of the pituitary gland within the fixed compartment of the *sella turcica* further impedes its blood supply. An absence or decrease of one or more pituitary hormones leads to a loss of function in the gland or organ that it controls.

COMPLICATIONS
- Pituitary apoplexy
- Shock
- Coma
- Death

Signs and symptoms
- ACTH deficiency: weakness, fatigue, weight loss, fasting hypoglycemia, and altered mental function; loss of axillary and pubic hair; orthostatic hypotension and hyponatremia
- TSH deficiency: weight gain, constipation, cold intolerance, fatigue, and coarse hair
- Gonadotropin deficiency: sexual dysfunction, infertility
- Antidiuretic hormone deficiency: diabetes insipidus
- Prolactin deficiency: lactation dysfunction or gynecomastia

Diagnostic test results
- Blood test reveals decreased serum thyroxin levels in diminished thyroid gland function due to lack of TSH.
- Radioimmunoassay shows decreased plasma levels of some or all of the pituitary hormones.
- Increased prolactin levels possibly indicating a lesion in the hypothalamus or pituitary stalk.
- Computed tomography scans, magnetic resonance imaging, or cerebral angiography may show the presence of intrasellar or extrasellar tumors.
- Oral administration of metyrapone shows the source of low hydroxycorticosteroid levels.
- Insulin administration shows low levels of corticotropin, indicating pituitary or hypothalamic failure.
- Dopamine antagonist administration evaluates prolactin secretory reserve.
- I.V. administration of gonadotropin releasing hormone distinguishes pituitary and hypothalamic causes of gonadotropin deficiency.
- Provocative testing shows persistently low GH and insulin-like growth factor-1 levels confirming GH deficiency.

Treatment
- Replacement of hormones (cortisol, thyroxine, androgen or cyclic estrogen) secreted by the target glands; prolactin not replaced
- Clomiphene or cyclic gonadotropin-releasing hormone to induce ovulation in female patient of reproductive age
- Surgery for pituitary tumor

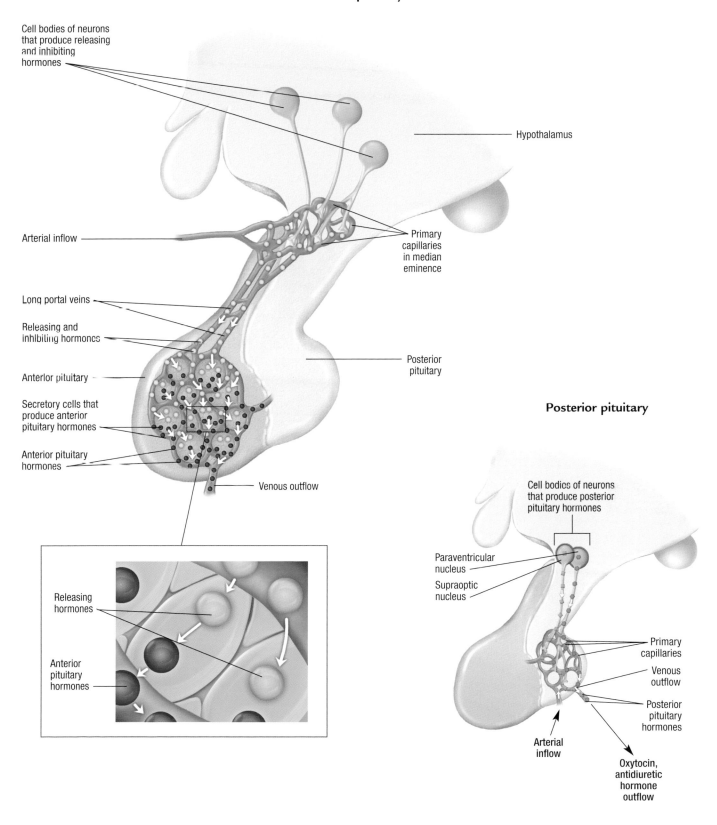

Anterior pituitary

Cell bodies of neurons that produce releasing and inhibiting hormones

Hypothalamus

Arterial inflow

Primary capillaries in median eminence

Long portal veins

Releasing and inhibiting hormones

Anterior pituitary

Posterior pituitary

Secretory cells that produce anterior pituitary hormones

Anterior pituitary hormones

Venous outflow

Posterior pituitary

Cell bodies of neurons that produce posterior pituitary hormones

Paraventricular nucleus

Supraoptic nucleus

Primary capillaries

Venous outflow

Posterior pituitary hormones

Arterial inflow

Oxytocin, antidiuretic hormone outflow

Releasing hormones

Anterior pituitary hormones

HYPOTHYROIDISM

Hypothyroidism results from hypothalamic, pituitary, or thyroid insufficiency or resistance to thyroid hormone. Hypothyroidism is more prevalent in women than men; in the United States, the incidence is increasing significantly in people ages 40 to 50.

AGE ALERT
Hypothyroidism occurs primarily after age 50 and is particularly underdiagnosed in elderly persons. After age 65, prevalence increases to as much as 10% in females and 3% in males.

A deficiency of thyroid hormone secretion during fetal development and early infancy results in infantile cretinism (congenital hypothyroidism). Subacute thyroiditis, painless thyroiditis, and postpartum thyroiditis are self-limited conditions that may follow an episode of hyperthyroidism.

Causes
Primary (disorder of thyroid gland)
- Thyroidectomy or radiation therapy (particularly with radioactive iodine)
- Inflammation, chronic autoimmune thyroiditis (Hashimoto's thyroiditis), or such conditions as amyloidosis and sarcoidosis (rare)
Secondary (failure to stimulate normal thyroid function)
- Inadequate production of thyroid hormone
- Use of such antithyroid medications as propylthiouracil
- Pituitary failure to produce thyroid-stimulating hormone (TSH)
- Inborn errors of thyroid hormone synthesis
- Iodine deficiency (usually dietary)
- Hypothalamic failure to produce thyrotropin-releasing hormone.

Pathophysiology
Hypothyroidism may reflect a malfunction of the hypothalamus, pituitary, or thyroid gland, all of which are part of the same negative-feedback mechanism. However, disorders of the hypothalamus and pituitary rarely cause hypothyroidism. Primary hypothyroidism is most common.

Chronic autoimmune thyroiditis, also called *chronic lymphocytic thyroiditis,* occurs when autoantibodies destroy thyroid gland tissue. Chronic autoimmune thyroiditis associated with goiter is called *Hashimoto's thyroiditis.* The cause of this autoimmune process is unknown, although heredity plays a role, and specific human leukocyte antigen subtypes are associated with greater risk.

Outside the thyroid, antibodies can reduce the effect of thyroid hormone in two ways. First, antibodies can block the TSH receptor and prevent the production of TSH. Second, cytotoxic antithyroid antibodies may trigger thyroid destruction.

COMPLICATIONS
- Myxedema coma
- Pernicious anemia
- Impaired fertility
- Achlorhydria
- Anemia
- Goiter
- Psychiatric disturbances

Signs and symptoms
- Typical, vague, early clinical features — weakness, fatigue, forgetfulness, sensitivity to cold, unexplained weight gain, constipation
- Myxedema — decreasing mental stability; coarse, dry, flaky, inelastic skin; puffy face, hands, and feet; hoarseness; periorbital edema; upper eyelid droop; dry, sparse hair; thick, brittle nails (as disorder progresses)
- Cardiovascular involvement — decreased cardiac output, slow pulse rate, signs of poor peripheral circulation, congestive heart failure, cardiomegaly (occasionally)
Other common effects
- Anorexia, abdominal distention, menorrhagia, decreased libido, infertility, ataxia, and nystagmus; reflexes with delayed relaxation time (especially Achilles' tendon)

Diagnostic test results
- Radioimmunoassay shows decreased serum levels of triiodothyronin (T_3) and thyroxine (T_4).
- Serum TSH level is increased with thyroid insufficiency; decreased with hypothalamic or pituitary insufficiency.
- Serum cholesterol, alkaline phosphatase, and triglycerides levels are elevated.
- Blood chemistry shows low serum sodium levels in myxedema coma.
- Arterial blood gases show decreased pH and increased partial pressure of carbon dioxide in myxedema coma.
- Skull X-ray, computed tomography scan, and magnetic resonance imaging may show pituitary or hypothalamic lesions.
- Chest X-ray detects cardiomegaly.

Treatment
- Gradual lifelong thyroid hormone replacement with T_4 and, occasionally, T_3
- Surgery for underlying cause such as pituitary tumor

AGE ALERT
Elderly patients should be started on a very low dose of T_4, such as 25 mcg every morning, to avoid cardiac problems. TSH levels guide gradual increases in the dosage.

HISTOLOGIC CHANGES IN HASHIMOTO'S THYROIDITIS

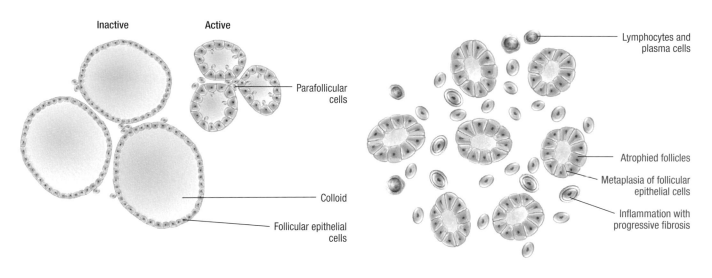

Normal

Inactive   Active

Parafollicular cells

Colloid

Follicular epithelial cells

Hashimoto's thyroiditis

Lymphocytes and plasma cells

Atrophied follicles

Metaplasia of follicular epithelial cells

Inflammation with progressive fibrosis

CLINICAL TIP

FACIAL MANIFESTATIONS OF MYXEDEMA

Before the era of rapid laboratory diagnosis and hormone replacement therapy, severe hypothyroidism was diagnosed by typical facial features.

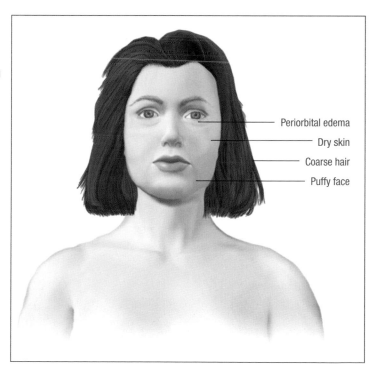

Periorbital edema

Dry skin

Coarse hair

Puffy face

METABOLIC SYNDROME

Metabolic syndrome is a common condition in which obesity, high blood pressure, high blood glucose, and an abnormal cholesterol profile cluster together in one person. When these risk factors occur together, the chance of developing heart disease, stroke, and diabetes is much greater than when these risk factors develop independently. According to the American Heart Association, almost 25% of U.S. residents are affected by metabolic syndrome.

Causes

Some studies suggest that metabolic syndrome is closely tied to an individual's metabolism. Normally food is absorbed into the bloodstream in the form of glucose, and other basic substances. When glucose levels in the bloodstream rise, the pancreas releases insulin. Insulin attaches to the body's cells, allowing glucose to enter, where it's used for energy. In some people, the body's cells aren't able to respond to insulin. As suggested by recent studies, this insulin resistance is behind the development of metabolic syndrome.

Pathophysiology

When insulin resistance occurs, the body is unable to process glucose and the pancreas responds by creating more insulin. This cycle leads to high glucose levels and hyperinsulinemia. The increase in circulating insulin causes hypertrophy and vascular remodeling. It also leads to increased cholesterol and triglyceride levels, increased serum uric acid, increased platelet adhesion, increased response to angiotensin II, and decreased amounts of nitric oxide.

COMPLICATIONS
- Coronary artery disease
- Stroke
- Peripheral vascular disease
- Type 2 diabetes mellitus

Signs and symptoms
- Abdominal obesity
- *Acanthosis nigricans* (darkening of the skin on the neck or under the arms)
- Irregular or absent menstrual periods
- Ovarian cysts
- Infertility
- Acne
- Hirsutism
- Alopecia

Diagnostic test results
- Measurement of waist circumference is greater than 35″ in females or greater than 40″ in males.
- Blood tests reveal triglyceride levels that are greater than or equal to 150 mg/dl.
- Blood tests reveal fasting blood glucose that's greater than or equal to 100 mg/dl.
- Blood test reveals high-density lipoprotein level that's less than 50 mg/dl in females and less than 40 mg/dl in males.
- Blood pressure 130 mm Hg/85 mm Hg or greater suggests disorder.

Treatment
- Weight loss through diet and exercise, or if needed, weight loss drugs, such as sibutramine or orlistat
- Exercise
- Antihypertensive medications such as diuretics, angiotensin-converting enzyme inhibitors, calcium channel blockers, or beta-adrenergic blockers
- Cholesterol-lowering medications, such as statins, fibrates, or niacin
- Thiazolinediones or metformin to decrease insulin resistance
- Aspirin
- Smoking cessation
- Reduction of saturated fats, cholesterol, and salt intake
- Increase of high fiber foods like fruits, vegetables, and grains

METABOLIC SYNDROME

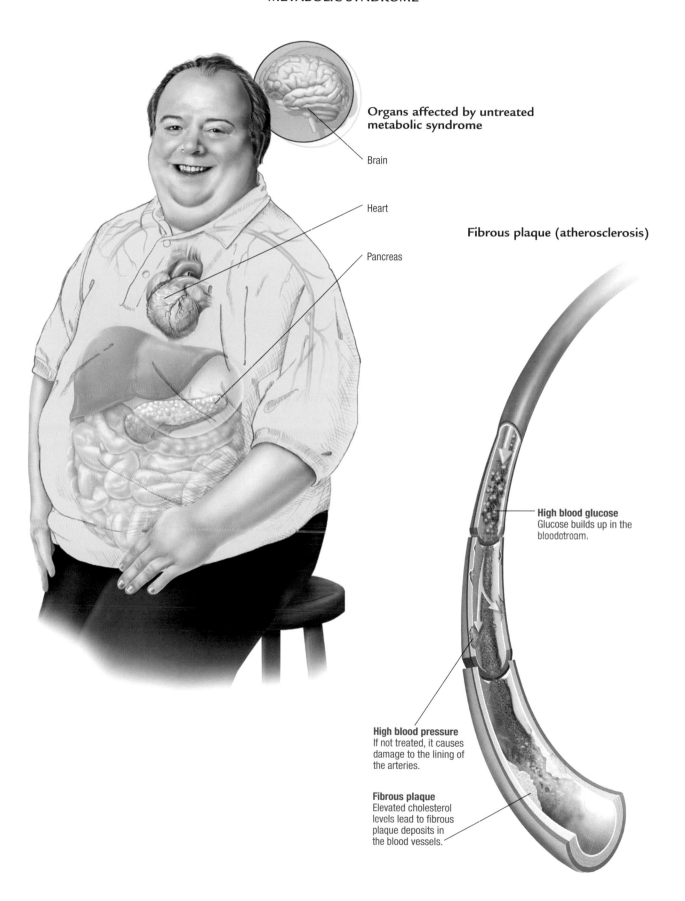

Organs affected by untreated metabolic syndrome

Brain

Heart

Pancreas

Fibrous plaque (atherosclerosis)

High blood glucose
Glucose builds up in the bloodstream.

High blood pressure
If not treated, it causes damage to the lining of the arteries.

Fibrous plaque
Elevated cholesterol levels lead to fibrous plaque deposits in the blood vessels.

SIMPLE GOITER

Simple (or nontoxic) goiter is a thyroid gland enlargement that isn't caused by inflammation or a neoplasm, and is commonly classified as endemic or sporadic. Inherited defects may be responsible for insufficient thyroxine (T_4) synthesis or impaired iodine metabolism. Because families tend to congregate in a single geographic area, this familial factor may contribute to the incidence of both endemic and sporadic goiters.

Causes

Endemic goiter
- Inadequate dietary iodine

Sporadic goiter
- Large amounts of foods containing agents that inhibit T_4 production, such as rutabagas, cabbage, soybeans, peanuts, peaches, peas, strawberries, spinach, radishes
- Drugs, such as propylthiouracil, iodides, phenylbutazone, para-aminosalicylic acid, cobalt, lithium; may cross placenta and affect fetus

Pathophysiology

Goiters can occur in the presence of hypothyroidism, hyperthyroidism, or normal levels of thyroid hormone. In the presence of a severe underlying disorder, compensatory responses may cause both thyroid enlargement (goiter) and hypothyroidism. Simple goiter occurs when the thyroid gland can't secrete enough thyroid hormone to meet metabolic requirements. As a result, the thyroid gland enlarges to compensate for inadequate hormone synthesis, a compensation that usually overcomes mild to moderate hormonal impairment.

COMPLICATIONS
- Respiratory distress
- Hypothyroidism
- Hyperthyroidism
- Thyroid cancer

Signs and symptoms

- Enlarged thyroid
- Dysphagia
- Venous engorgement; development of collateral venous circulation in the chest
- Dizziness or syncope (Pemberton's sign) when the patient raises her arms above her head

Diagnostic test results

Laboratory tests reveal:
- normal serum thyroid levels
- high or normal thyroid-stimulating hormone (TSH) levels
- low-normal or normal T_4 concentrations
- normal or increased radioactive iodine uptake.

Treatment

- Exogenous thyroid hormone replacement with levothyroxine (treatment of choice) — inhibits TSH secretion and allows gland to rest
- Small doses of iodide (Lugol's iodine or potassium iodide solution) — commonly relieves goiter due to iodine deficiency
- Avoidance of known goitrogenic drugs and foods
- For large goiter that's unresponsive to treatment — subtotal thyroidectomy

RECOGNIZING TYPES OF GOITERS

Toxic goiter (Graves' disease)

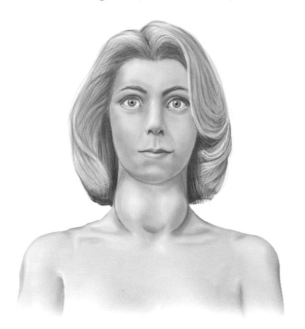

Simple (nontoxic) goiter

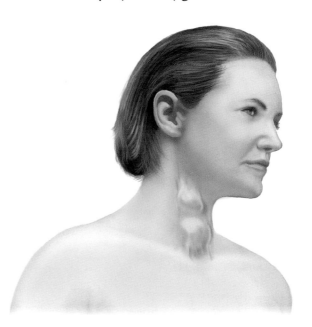

Nodular goiter

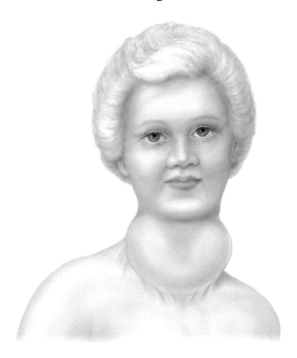

THYROID CANCER

Thyroid carcinoma is the most common endocrine malignancy. It occurs in all age groups, especially in people who have had radiation treatment of the neck area.

Causes

Direct cause unknown

Predisposing factors
- Prolonged thyroid-stimulating hormone stimulation due to radiation exposure or heredity
- Familial predisposition
- Chronic goiter

Pathophysiology

Papillary carcinoma accounts for half of all thyroid cancers in adults. Most common in young adult females, it's the least virulent form of thyroid cancer and metastasizes slowly. *Follicular carcinoma* is less common but more likely to recur and metastasize to the regional nodes and through blood vessels into the bones, liver, and lungs. *Medullary carcinoma* originates in the parafollicular cells derived from the last branchial pouch and contains amyloid and calcium deposits. It can produce thyrocalcitonin, histaminase, adrenocorticotropin (producing Cushing's syndrome), and prostaglandin E_2 and F_3 (producing diarrhea). This rare form of thyroid cancer is familial, associated with pheochromocytoma, and completely curable when detected before it causes symptoms. Untreated, it progresses rapidly. Seldom curable by resection, anaplastic tumors resist radiation and metastasize rapidly.

COMPLICATIONS
- Metastasis
- Stridor

Signs and symptoms

- Painless nodule; hard nodule in an enlarged thyroid gland; or palpable lymph nodes and thyroid enlargement
- Hoarseness, dysphagia, dyspnea, pain on palpation
- Cough
- Hypothyroidism (low metabolism, mental apathy, sensitivity to cold) or hyperthyroidism (hyperactivity, restlessness, sensitivity to heat)
- Diarrhea, anorexia, irritability, vocal cord paralysis

Diagnostic test results

- Calcitonin assay identifies silent medullary carcinoma; calcitonin level measuring during a resting state and during a calcium infusion (15 mg/kg over a 4-hour period) showing an elevated fasting calcitonin level and an abnormal response to calcium stimulation — a high release of calcitonin from the node in comparison with the rest of the gland — indicates medullary cancer.
- Thyroid scan differentiates functional nodes, which are rarely malignant, from hypofunctional nodes, which are commonly malignant.
- Ultrasonography shows changes in the size of thyroid nodules after thyroxine suppression therapy and is used to guide fine-needle aspiration and to detect recurrent disease.
- Magnetic resonance imaging and computed tomography scans provide a basis for treatment planning because they establish the extent of the disease within the thyroid and in surrounding structures.
- Fine-needle aspiration biopsy differentiates benign from malignant thyroid nodules.
- Histologic analysis stages the disease and guides treatment plans.

Treatment

- Papillary or follicular cancer — total or subtotal thyroidectomy; modified node dissection (bilateral or unilateral) on the side of the primary cancer

CLINICAL TIP
Before surgery, tell the patient to expect temporary voice loss or hoarseness lasting several days after surgery.

- Medullary, giant, or spindle cell cancer — total thyroidectomy and radical neck excision
- Inoperable cancer or postoperatively in lieu of radical neck excision — radiation (^{131}I) or external radiation
- To increase tolerance to surgery and radiation — adjunctive thyroid suppression with exogenous thyroid hormones and simultaneous administration of an adrenergic blocking agent such as propranolol
- Metastasis — ^{131}I; chemotherapy for symptomatic, widespread metastasis is rare

CLINICAL TIP
Hypocalcemia may develop if parathyroid glands are removed during surgery.

- Thyroid hormone replacement after surgeries

Anterior view

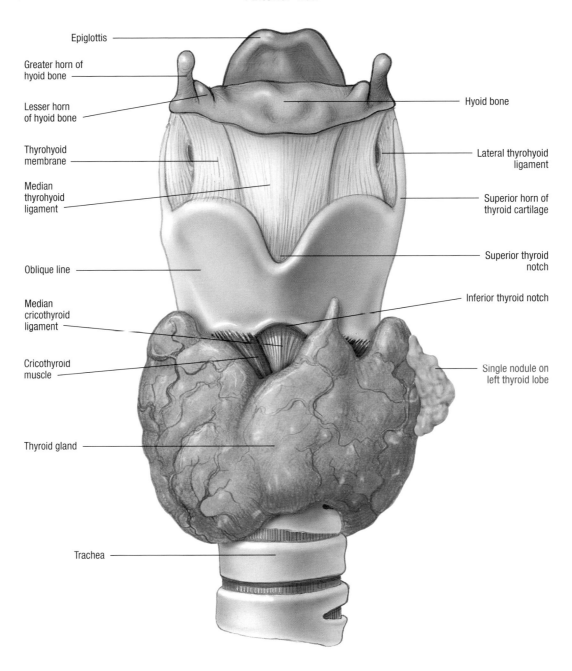

Epiglottis

Greater horn of
hyoid bone

Lesser horn
of hyoid bone

Thyrohyoid
membrane

Median
thyrohyoid
ligament

Oblique line

Median
cricothyroid
ligament

Cricothyroid
muscle

Thyroid gland

Trachea

Hyoid bone

Lateral thyrohyoid
ligament

Superior horn of
thyroid cartilage

Superior thyroid
notch

Inferior thyroid notch

Single nodule on
left thyroid lobe

AMENORRHEA

Amenorrhea is the *abnormal* absence of menstruation. Absence of menstruation is normal before puberty, after menopause, or during pregnancy and lactation; it's pathologic at any other time. Primary amenorrhea is the absence of menarche in an adolescent by age 14 without the development of secondary sex characteristics or by age 16 with normal development of secondary sex characteristics. Secondary amenorrhea is the absence of menstruation for at least 6 months after the normal onset of menarche. Primary amenorrhea occurs in 0.3% of women; secondary amenorrhea, in about 4% of women. Prognosis is variable, depending on the specific cause. Surgical correction of outflow tract obstruction is usually curative.

Causes
- Anovulation due to deficient secretion of:
- estrogen
- gonadotropins
- luteinizing hormone
- follicle-stimulating hormone (FSH)
- Lack of ovarian response to gonadotropins
- Constant presence of progesterone or other endocrine abnormalities
- Endometrial adhesions (Asherman syndrome)
- Ovarian, adrenal, or pituitary tumor
- Emotional disorders — common in patients with depression or anorexia nervosa:
- mild emotional disturbances tend to distort the ovulatory cycle
- severe psychic trauma may abruptly change the bleeding pattern or completely suppress one or more full ovulatory cycles
- Malnutrition or intense exercise — suppresses hormonal changes initiated by the hypothalamus
- Pregnancy
- Weight loss
- Thyroid disorder
- Ovarian or adrenal tumor
- Anatomic defects

Pathophysiology
The mechanism varies depending on the cause and whether the defect is structural, hormonal, or both. Women who have adequate estrogen levels but a progesterone deficiency don't ovulate and are thus infertile. In primary amenorrhea, the hypothalamic-pituitary-ovarian axis is dysfunctional. Because of anatomic defects of the central nervous system, the ovary doesn't receive the hormonal signals that normally initiate the development of secondary sex characteristics and the beginning of menstruation.

Secondary amenorrhea can result from any of several mechanisms, including:
- central — hypogonadotropic hypoestrogenic anovulation
- uterine — such as Asherman syndrome, in which severe scarring has replaced functional endometrium
- premature ovarian failure.

COMPLICATIONS
- Infertility

Signs and symptoms
- Absence of menstruation
- Vasomotor flushes
- Vaginal atrophy
- Hirsutism
- Acne (secondary amenorrhea)

Diagnostic test results
- Physical and pelvic examination and sensitive pregnancy test rule out pregnancy as well as anatomic abnormalities (such as cervical stenosis) that may cause false amenorrhea (cryptomenorrhea), in which menstruation occurs without external bleeding.
- Onset of menstruation (spotting) within 1 week after giving pure progestational agents such as medroxyprogesterone (Provera) indicate enough estrogen to stimulate the lining of the uterus (if menstruation doesn't occur, special diagnostic studies such as gonadotropin levels are indicated).
- Blood and urine studies show hormonal imbalances, such as elevated pituitary gonadotropin levels. low pituitary gonadotropin levels, and abnormal thyroid levels (without suspicion of premature ovarian failure or central hypogonadotropism, gonadotropin levels aren't clinically meaningful because they're released in a pulsatile fashion).
- Complete medical workup, including appropriate X-rays, computed tomography scans, or magnetic resonance imaging; laparoscopy; and a biopsy, identify ovarian, adrenal, and pituitary tumors.
- Tests to identify dominant or missing hormones include:
- "ferning" of cervical mucus on microscopic examination (an estrogen effect)
- vaginal cytologic examination
- endometrial biopsy
- serum progesterone level
- serum androgen levels
- elevated urinary 17-ketosteroid levels with excessive androgen secretions
- plasma FSH level more than 50 International Units/L, depending on the laboratory (suggests primary ovarian failure); or normal or low FSH level (possible hypothalamic or pituitary abnormality, depending on the clinical situation).

Treatment
- Appropriate hormone replacement to reestablish menstruation
- Treatment of the cause of amenorrhea not related to hormone deficiency — for example, surgery for amenorrhea due to a tumor
- Inducing ovulation — for example, with clomiphene citrate in women with intact pituitary gland and amenorrhea secondary to gonadotropin deficiency, polycystic ovarian disease, or excessive weight loss or gain
- FSH and human menopausal gonadotropins for women with pituitary disease
- Reassurance and emotional support (psychiatric counseling if amenorrhea results from emotional disturbances)
- Teaching the patient how to keep an accurate record of her menstrual cycles

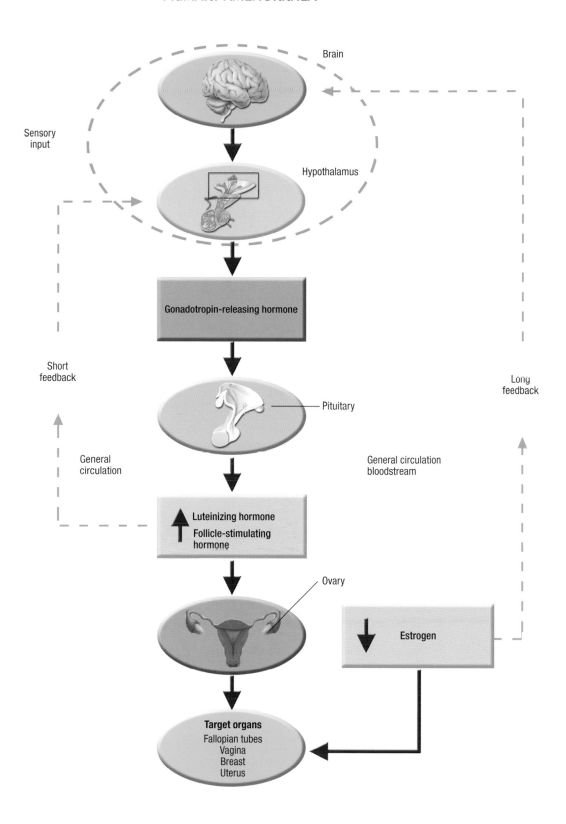

Brain

Sensory input

Hypothalamus

Gonadotropin-releasing hormone

Short feedback

Pituitary

General circulation

Long feedback

General circulation bloodstream

Luteinizing hormone
Follicle-stimulating hormone

Ovary

Estrogen

Target organs
Fallopian tubes
Vagina
Breast
Uterus

BENIGN BREAST CONDITIONS

Also incorrectly known as *fibrocystic disease of the breast,* this disorder of benign changes in breast tissue is usually bilateral.

AGE ALERT
Fibrocystic change is the most common benign breast disorder, affecting an estimated 10% of women ages 21 and younger, 25% of women ages 22 and older, and 50% of postmenopausal women.

Although most lesions are benign, some may proliferate and show atypical cellular growth. Fibrocystic change by itself isn't a precursor to breast cancer, but if atypical hyperplasia is present, the risk for breast carcinoma increases.

Causes
Exact cause unknown
Proposed causes
● Estrogen excess and progesterone deficiency during luteal phase of menstrual cycle
● Environmental toxins that inhibit cyclic guanosine monophosphate enzymes:
– Methylxanthines — caffeine (coffee), theophylline (tea), theobromine (chocolate)
– Tyramine — in cheese, wine, nuts
– Tobacco

Pathophysiology
Breast tissue appears to respond to hormonal stimulation, although the exact mechanism is unknown. Fibrocystic breast changes involve three types: cystic, fibrous, and epithelial proliferation. Cysts, fluid-filled sacs, are the most common feature, and are easily treated. Fibrous tissue increases progressively until menopause and regresses thereafter. Epithelial prolifera-tion diseases include structurally diverse lesions, such as sclerosing adenosis and the lobular and ductal hyperplasias.

COMPLICATIONS
● Possible increased risk of breast cancer

Signs and symptoms
● Breast pain due to inflammation and nerve root stimulation (most common symptom), beginning 4 to 7 days into the luteal phase of the menstrual cycle and continuing until the onset of menstruation
● Pain in the upper outer quadrant of both breasts (common site)
● Palpable lumps that increase in size premenstrually and are freely moveable (about 50% of all menstruating women)
● Granular feeling of breasts on palpation
● Occasional greenish-brown to black nipple discharge that contains fat, proteins, ductal cells, and erythrocytes (ductal hyperplasia)

Diagnostic test results
● Ultrasonography distinguishes cystic (fluid-filled) from solid masses.
● Tissue biopsy distinguishes benign from malignant changes.
● Cytologic analysis of bloody aspirate rules out malignancy.

Treatment
● Symptomatic to relieve pain, including:
– diet low in caffeine and fat and high in fruits and vegetables
– support bra.
● Draining of painful cysts under local anesthesia
● Synthetic androgens (danazol) for severe pain (occasionally)
● Oral contraceptives

BENIGN BREAST CONDITIONS

Fibrocystic changes

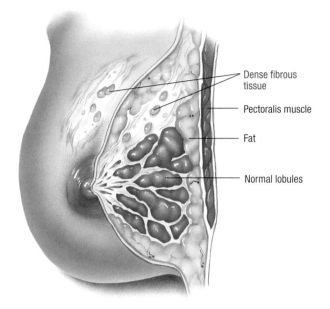

Dense fibrous tissue

Pectoralis muscle

Fat

Normal lobules

Breast cyst

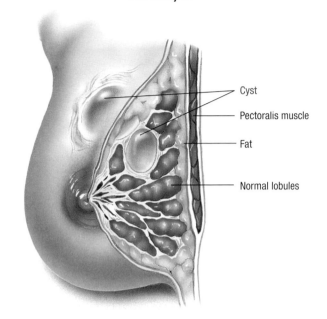

Cyst

Pectoralis muscle

Fat

Normal lobules

BENIGN BREAST TUMORS

Intraductal papilloma

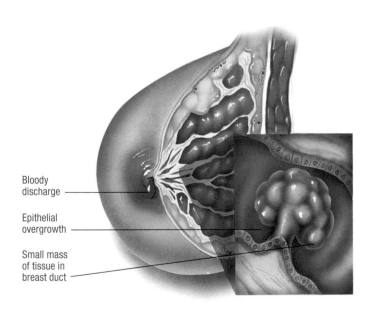

Bloody discharge

Epithelial overgrowth

Small mass of tissue in breast duct

Fibroadenoma

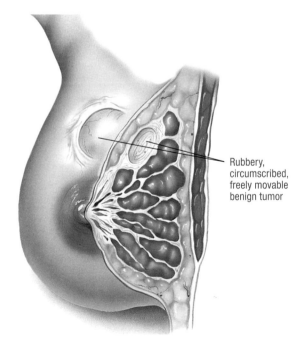

Rubbery, circumscribed, freely movable benign tumor

BENIGN PROSTATIC HYPERPLASIA

In benign prostatic hyperplasia (BPH), also known as *benign prostatic hypertrophy*, the prostate gland enlarges enough to compress the urethra and cause overt urinary obstruction. Depending on the size of the enlarged prostate, the age and health of the patient, and the extent of obstruction, BPH is treated symptomatically or surgically.

AGE ALERT

BPH is common, affecting more than 90% of men over age 80.

Causes
- Age-associated changes in hormone activity
- Arteriosclerosis
- Inflammation
- Metabolic or nutritional disturbances

Pathophysiology
Androgenic hormone production decreases with age, causing imbalance in androgen and estrogen levels and high levels of dihydrotestosterone, the main prostatic intracellular androgen. The shift in hormone balance induces the early, nonmalignant changes of BPH in periurethral glandular tissue. The growth of the fibroadenomatous nodules (masses of fibrous glandular tissue) progresses to compress the remaining normal gland (nodular hyperplasia). The hyperplastic tissue is mostly glandular, with some fibrous stroma and smooth muscle. As the prostate enlarges, it may extend into the bladder and obstruct urinary outflow by compressing or distorting the prostatic urethra. Progressive bladder distention may lead to formation of a pouch that retains urine when the rest of the bladder empties. This retained urine may lead to calculus formation or cystitis.

COMPLICATIONS
- Urinary stasis, urinary tract infection (UTI), or calculi
- Bladder wall trabeculation
- Detrusor muscle hypertrophy
- Bladder diverticula and saccules
- Urethral stenosis
- Hydronephrosis
- Paradoxical (overflow) incontinence
- Acute or chronic renal failure
- Acute postobstructive diuresis

Signs and symptoms
Presenting signs and symptoms
- Reduced urinary stream caliber and force
- Urinary hesitancy
- Feeling of incomplete voiding, interrupted stream

As obstruction increases
- Frequent urination with nocturia
- Sense of urgency
- Retention, dribbling, incontinence
- Possible hematuria

Diagnostic test results
- Excretory urography rules out urinary tract obstruction, hydronephrosis (distention of the renal pelvis and calices due to obstruction of the ureter and consequent retention of urine), calculi or tumors, and filling and emptying defects in the bladder.
- Cystoscopy rules out other causes of urinary tract obstruction (neoplasm, calculi).
- Elevated blood urea nitrogen and serum creatinine levels (suggest renal dysfunction).
- Laboratory studies reveal elevated prostate-specific antigen; however, prostatic carcinoma must be ruled out.
- Urinalysis and urine cultures show hematuria, pyuria, and, with bacterial count more than $100,000/\mu l$, revealing UTI.
- Cystourethroscopy for severe symptoms (definitive diagnosis) shows prostate enlargement, bladder-wall changes, and a raised bladder. (Cystourethroscopy is only done immediately before surgery to determine the next course of therapy.)

Treatment
Conservative therapy
- Prostate massages
- Sitz baths
- Fluid restriction for bladder distention
- Antimicrobials for infection
- Regular ejaculation
- Alpha-adrenergic blockers (terazosin, prazosin)
- Medical management to reduce risk of urinary retention (finasteride)
- Continuous drainage with a urinary catheter to alleviate urine retention (high-risk patients)

Surgical procedures (to relieve intolerable symptoms)
- Suprapubic (transvesical) resection
- Transurethral resection
- Retropubic (extravesical) resection allowing direct visualization; usually maintains potency and continence
- Suprapubic cystostomy under local anesthetic if indwelling urinary catheter can't be passed transurethrally
- Laser excision to relieve prostatic enlargement
- Nerve-sparing surgery to reduce common complications
- Indwelling urinary catheter for urine retention
- Balloon dilation of urethra and prostatic stents to maintain urethral patency

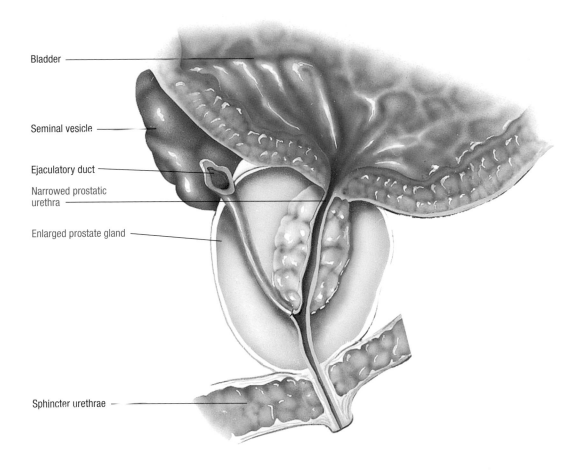

Bladder

Seminal vesicle

Ejaculatory duct

Narrowed prostatic
urethra

Enlarged prostate gland

Sphincter urethrae

 CLINICAL TIP

PALPATING THE PROSTATE GLAND

To detect early signs of prostate enlargement, follow these steps:
- Have the patient stand and lean over the examination table; if he can't do this, have him lie on his left side with his right knee and hip flexed or with both knees drawn to his chest.
- Inspect the skin of the perineal, anal, and posterior scrotal walls.
- Insert a lubricated gloved finger into the rectum.
- Palpate the prostate through the anterior rectal wall.
- The gland should feel smooth and rubbery, about the size of a walnut.

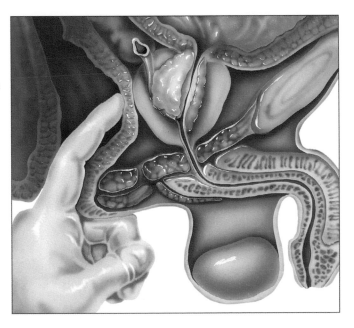

BREAST CANCER

Breast cancer is the most common cancer affecting women. It's estimated that 1 in 8 women in the United States will develop breast cancer during her lifetime. Male breast cancer accounts for 1% of all male cancers and less than 1% of all breast cancers. The 5-year survival rate for localized breast cancer is 98% because of early diagnosis and a variety of treatments. Lymph node involvement is the most valuable prognostic predictor. With adjuvant therapy, 70% to 75% of women with negative nodes will survive 10 years or more, compared with 20% to 25% of women with positive nodes.

AGE ALERT
Breast cancer may develop any time after puberty but is most common after age 50.

Causes

High risk factors

- Family history of breast cancer, particularly first-degree relatives (mother, sister, and/or maternal aunt)
- Positive tests for genetic mutations (BRCA 1 and BRCA 2)
- Long menstrual cycles, early menarche, late menopause
- Nulliparous or first pregnancy after age 30
- History of unilateral breast cancer or ovarian cancer
- Exposure to low-level radiation

Low risk factors

- Pregnancy before age 20, history of multiple pregnancies
- Native American or Asian ancestry

Pathophysiology

Breast cancer occurs more commonly in the left breast than the right and more commonly in the outer upper quadrant. Slow-growing breast cancer spreads by way of the lymphatic system and the bloodstream, through the right side of the heart to the lungs, and eventually to the other breast, the chest wall, liver, bone, and brain.

Most breast cancers arise from the ductal epithelium. Tumors of the infiltrating ductal type don't grow to a large size, but metastasize early (70% of breast cancers).

Breast cancer is classified by histologic appearance and location of the lesion, as follows:

- adenocarcinoma — arising from the epithelium
- intraductal — within the ducts (includes Paget's disease)
- infiltrating — in parenchymal tissue of the breast
- inflammatory (rare) — overlying skin becomes edematous, inflamed, and indurated; reflects rapid tumor growth
- lobular carcinoma in situ — involves glandular lobes
- medullary or circumscribed — large tumor, rapid growth rate.

The descriptive terms should be coupled with a staging or nodal status classification system. The most commonly used staging system is the TNM (tumor size, nodal involvement, metastatic progress).

COMPLICATIONS

- Infection
- Decreased mobility with bone metastasis
- Central nervous system effects with brain metastasis
- Respiratory difficulty with lung involvement

Signs and symptoms

- Painless lump or mass in the breast, breast pain
- Change in symmetry or size of the breast
- Change in skin — thickening, scaly skin around the nipple, dimpling, edema (peau d'orange), ulceration, or temperature
- Unusual drainage or discharge
- Change in nipple (itching, burning, erosion, or retraction)
- Pathologic bone fractures, hypercalcemia
- Edema of the arm, axillary node enlargement
- Dilated blood vessels visible through the skin of the breast
- Bone pain

Diagnostic test results

- Alkaline phosphatase levels and liver function tests uncover distant metastases.
- Hormonal receptor assay determines whether the tumor is estrogen- or progesterone-dependent.
- Mammography reveals a tumor that's too small to palpate.
- Ultrasonography distinguishes between a fluid-filled cyst and solid mass.
- Chest X-rays pinpoint metastases in the chest.
- Scans of the bone, brain, liver, and other organs detect distant metastases.
- Fine-needle aspiration and excisional biopsy provide cells for histologic examination may confirm the diagnosis.

Treatment

Surgical

- Lumpectomy — in many cases, radiation therapy is combined with this surgery
- Lumpectomy and dissection of axillary lymph nodes
- Quadrant excision
- Simple mastectomy — removes breast but not lymph nodes or pectoral muscles
- Modified radical mastectomy — removes breast and axillary lymph nodes
- Radical mastectomy (now seldom used) — removes breast, axillary lymph nodes, and pectoralis major and minor muscles

Other treatments

- Reconstructive surgery if no advanced disease
- Chemotherapy — adjuvant or primary therapy
- Selective estrogen receptor modulators such as tamoxifen
- Aromatase inhibitors, such as anastrozole and letrozole
- Peripheral stem cell therapy for advanced disease
- Primary radiation therapy before or after tumor removal:
- effective for small tumors in early stages
- helps make inflammatory breast tumors more surgically manageable
- also used to prevent or treat local recurrence
- Biotherapy with such drugs as trastuzumab, bevacizumab, and lapatinib

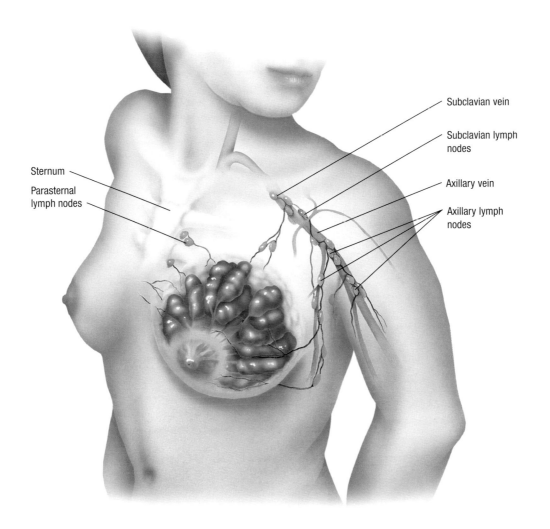

Sternum

Parasternal
lymph nodes

Subclavian vein

Subclavian lymph
nodes

Axillary vein

Axillary lymph
nodes

Ductal carcinoma in situ

Infiltrating (invasive) ductal carcinoma

CERVICAL CANCER

The third most common cancer of the female reproductive system, cervical cancer is classified as either microinvasive or invasive. Precancerous dysplasia, also called *cervical intraepithelial carcinoma* or *cervical carcinoma in situ*, is more frequent than invasive cancer and occurs more often in younger women.

Causes
- Human papillomavirus (HPV)

Predisposing factors
- Frequent intercourse at a young age (under age 16)
- Multiple sexual partners
- Multiple pregnancies
- Sexually transmitted diseases
- Smoking

Pathophysiology
Preinvasive disease ranges from mild cervical dysplasia, in which the lower third of the epithelium contains abnormal cells, to carcinoma in situ, in which the full thickness of epithelium contains abnormally proliferating cells. Other names for carcinoma in situ include *cervical intraepithelial neoplasia* and *squamous intraepithelial lesion.* Preinvasive disease detected early and properly treated is curable in 75% to 90% of cases. If preinvasive disease remains untreated (and depending on the form in which it appears), it may progress to invasive cervical cancer.

In invasive carcinoma, cancer cells penetrate the basement membrane and can spread directly to contiguous pelvic structures or disseminate to distant sites by lymphatic routes.

In almost all cases of cervical cancer (95%), the histologic type is squamous cell carcinoma, which varies from well-differentiated cells to highly anaplastic spindle cells. Only 5% are adenocarcinomas.

AGE ALERT
Usually, invasive carcinoma occurs in women between ages 30 and 50; rarely, in those under age 25.

COMPLICATIONS
- Hematuria
- Renal failure

Signs and symptoms
Preinvasive disease
- Often produces no symptoms or other clinically apparent changes

Early invasive cervical cancer
- Abnormal vaginal bleeding
- Persistent vaginal discharge
- Postcoital pain and bleeding

Advanced disease
- Pelvic pain
- Vaginal leakage of urine and stool from a fistula
- Anorexia, weight loss, and anemia

Diagnostic test results
- Papanicolaou (Pap) test screens for abnormal cells.
- Colposcopy shows the source of the abnormal cells seen on the Pap test.
- Cone biopsy is performed if endocervical curettage is positive.
- Vira-Pap test permits examination of the specimen's deoxyribonucleic acid structure to detect HPV.
- Lymphangiography and cystography detect metastasis.
- Organ and bone scans show metastasis.

Treatment
Preinvasive lesions
- Loop electrosurgical excision procedure
- Cryosurgery
- Laser destruction
- Conization (with frequent Pap smear follow-up)
- Hysterectomy

Invasive carcinoma
- Radical hysterectomy
- Radiation therapy (internal, external, or both)
- Chemotherapy
- Combination of the above procedures

Carcinoma in situ

Squamous cell carcinoma

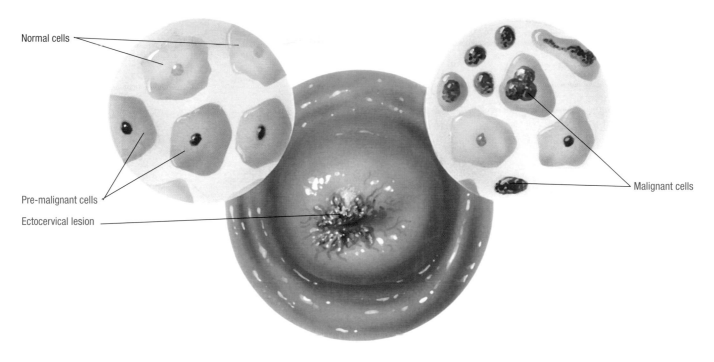

Normal cells

Pre-malignant cells

Ectocervical lesion

Malignant cells

CLINICAL TIP

PAP SMEAR FINDINGS

Normal
- Large, surface-type squamous cells
- Small, pyknotic nuclei

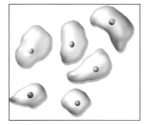

Invasive carcinoma
- Marked pleomorphism
- Irregular nuclei
- Clumped chromatin
- Prominent nucleoli

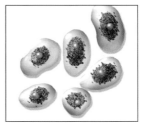

Mild dysplasia
- Mild increase in nuclear:cyto-plasmic ratio
- Hyperchromasia
- Abnormal chromatin pattern

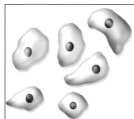

Severe dysplasia, carcinoma in situ
- Basal type cells
- Very high nuclear:cytoplasmic ratio
- Marked hyperchromasia
- Abnormal chromatin

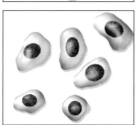

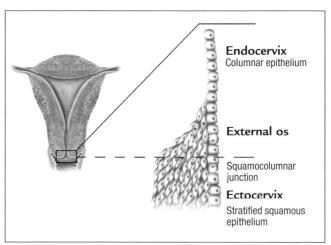

Endocervix
Columnar epithelium

External os

Squamocolumnar junction

Ectocervix
Stratified squamous epithelium

CRYPTORCHIDISM

Cryptorchidism is a congenital disorder in which one or both testes fail to descend into the scrotum, remaining in the abdomen or inguinal canal or at the external ring. Although this condition may be bilateral, it more commonly affects the right testis. True undescended testes remain along the path of normal descent; ectopic testis deviate from that path.

Undescended testes are susceptible to neoplastic changes. The risk of testicular cancer is greater for men with cryptorchidism than for the general male population.

AGE ALERT
Cryptorchidism occurs in 30% of premature male neonates but in only 3% of those born at term. In about 80% of affected infants, the testes descend spontaneously during the first year; in the rest, the testes may descend later. If indicated, surgical therapy is successful in up to 95% of the cases if the infant is treated early enough.

Causes
Primary cause unknown
Possible causes
- Testosterone deficiency resulting in a defect in the hypothalamic-pituitary-gonadal axis, causing failure of gonadal differentiation and gonadal descent
- Structural factors impeding gonadal descent, such as ectopic testis or short spermatic cord
- Genetic predisposition in a small number of cases; greater incidence of cryptorchidism in infants with neural tube defects
- In premature neonates — early gestational age; normal descent of testes into the scrotum is in seventh month of gestation

Pathophysiology
A prevalent but still unsubstantiated theory links undescended testes to the development of the gubernaculum, a fibromuscular band that connects the testes to the scrotal floor and probably helps pull the testes into the scrotum by shortening as the fetus grows. Normally in the male fetus, testosterone stimulates the formation of the gubernaculum. Thus, cryptorchi-

dism may result from inadequate testosterone levels or a defect in the testes or the gubernaculum. Because the undescended testis is maintained at a higher temperature, spermatogenesis is impaired, leading to reduced fertility.

COMPLICATIONS
- Sterility
- Testicular cancer
- Testicular trauma

Signs and symptoms
Unilateral cryptorchidism
- Testis on affected side not palpable in scrotum; scrotum underdeveloped
- Enlarged scrotum on unaffected side due to compensatory hypertrophy (occasionally)
Uncorrected bilateral cryptorchidism
- Infertility after puberty despite normal testosterone levels

Diagnostic test results
Physical examination confirms cryptorchidism after sex is determined by these laboratory tests:
- Buccal smear (cells from oral mucosa) determines genetic sex (a male sex chromatin pattern).
- Blood test of serum gonadotropin level confirms the presence of testes by showing presence of circulating hormone.

Treatment

AGE ALERT
If the testes don't descend spontaneously by age 1, surgical correction is generally indicated. Surgery should be performed before age 2; by this time about 40% of undescended testes can no longer produce viable sperm.

- Orchiopexy to secure the testes in the scrotum and prevent sterility, excessive trauma from abnormal positioning, and harmful psychological effects (usually before age 4 years; optimum age, 1 to 2 years)
- Human chorionic gonadotropin I.M. to stimulate descent (rarely); ineffective for testes located in the abdomen

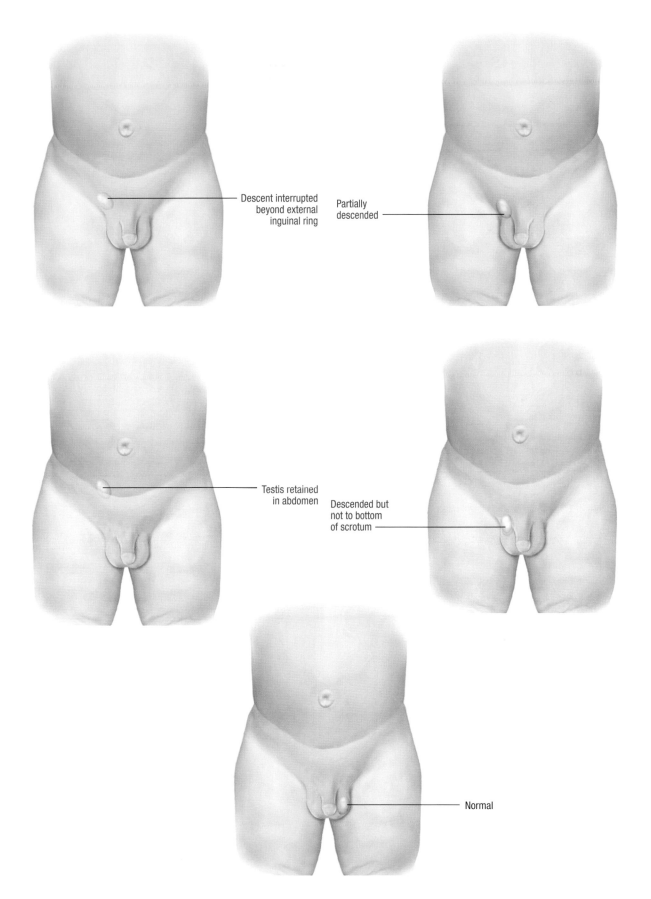

Descent interrupted
beyond external
inguinal ring

Partially
descended

Testis retained
in abdomen

Descended but
not to bottom
of scrotum

Normal

DYSFUNCTIONAL UTERINE BLEEDING

Dysfunctional uterine bleeding refers to endometrial bleeding without recognizable organic lesions. It's the indication for almost 25% of gynecologic surgical procedures. The prognosis varies with the cause. Correction of hormonal imbalance or structural abnormality yields a good prognosis.

AGE ALERT
Approximately 20% of dysfunctional uterine bleeding cases occur in adolescents and 40% in women over age 40.

Causes
● Polycystic ovarian syndrome
● Obesity — enzymes in peripheral adipose tissue convert the androgen androstenedione to estrogens
● Immaturity of the hypothalamic-pituitary-ovarian mechanism (postpubertal teenagers)
● Anovulation (women in their late 30s or early 40s)
● Hormone-producing ovarian tumor
● Endometriosis
● Sexual assault
● Trauma
● Pelvic inflammatory disease
● Coagulopathy

Pathophysiology
Irregular bleeding is associated with hormonal imbalance and absence of ovulation (anovulation). When progesterone secretion is absent but estrogen secretion continues, the endometrium proliferates and become hypervascular. When ovulation doesn't occur, the endometrium randomly breaks down, and exposed vascular channels cause prolonged and excessive bleeding. In the absence of adequate progesterone levels, the usual endometrial control mechanisms are missing, such as vasoconstrictive rhythmicity, tight coiling of spiral vessels, and orderly collapse, and stasis doesn't occur. Unopposed estrogen induces a progression of endometrial responses beginning with proliferation, hyperplasia, and adenomatous hyperplasia; over a course of years, unopposed estrogen may lead to atypia and carcinoma.

COMPLICATIONS
● Anemia
● Atypia
● Carcinoma

Signs and symptoms
● Metrorrhagia — episodes of vaginal bleeding between menses
● Hypermenorrhea — heavy or prolonged menses, longer than 8 days
● Chronic polymenorrhea (menstrual cycle less than 18 days) or oligomenorrhea (infrequent menses)
● Fatigue due to anemia
● Oligomenorrhea and infertility due to anovulation

Diagnostic test results
● Laboratory studies reveal decreased progesterone levels.
● Complete blood count test reveals anemia if excessive bleeding is present.
● Coagulation profile detects prolonged bleeding times in the presence of a coagulation disorder.
● Thyroid studies detect abnormal thyroid hormone levels.
● Dilation and curettage and endometrial biopsy detect endometrial hyperplasia or carcinoma.

Treatment
● High-dose estrogen-progestogen combination therapy (oral contraceptives) to control endometrial growth and reestablish a normal cyclic pattern of menstruation (usually given four times daily for 5 to 7 days even though bleeding usually stops in 12 to 24 hours; drug choice and dosage determined by patient's age and cause of bleeding); maintenance therapy with lower dose combination oral contraceptives
● Progestogen therapy — alternative in many women, especially those susceptible to adverse effects of estrogen such as thrombophlebitis
● I.V. estrogen followed by progesterone or combination oral contraceptives if the patient is young (more likely to be anovulatory) and severely anemic (if oral drug therapy is ineffective)
● Iron replacement or transfusions of packed cells or whole blood, as indicated, due to anemia caused by recurrent bleeding
● Dilatation and curettage
● Endometrial oblation
● Hysterectomy

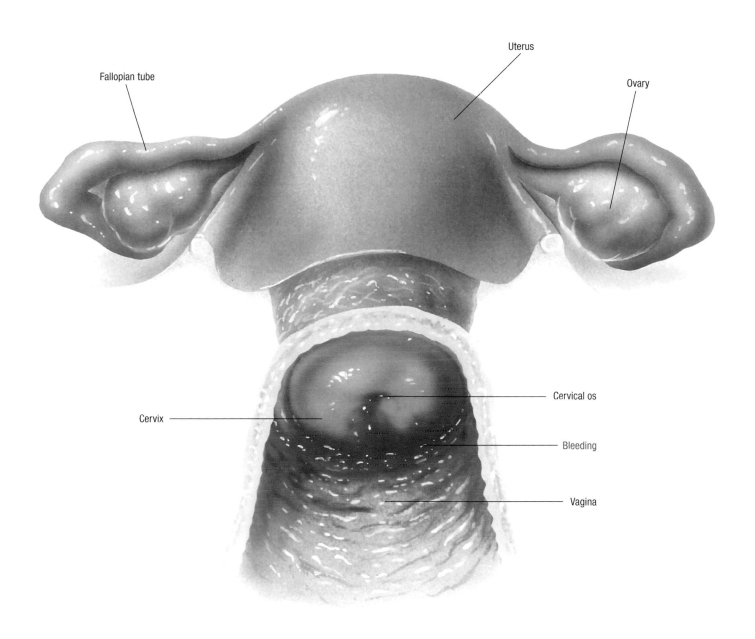

Fallopian tube

Uterus

Ovary

Cervix

Cervical os

Bleeding

Vagina

ECTOPIC PREGNANCY

An ectopic pregnancy occurs when a fertilized ovum implants outside the uterine cavity, most commonly in the fallopian tube. Prognosis is good with prompt diagnosis, appropriate surgical intervention, and control of bleeding. Few ectopic pregnancies are carried to term; rarely, with abdominal implantation, the fetus survives to term.

In whites, ectopic pregnancy occurs in about 1 of 200 pregnancies. In non-whites, the incidence is about 1 of 120 pregnancies.

Causes
- Endosalpingitis
- Diverticula
- Tumors pressing against the tube
- Previous surgery, such as tubal ligation or resection
- Transmigration of the ovum
- Congenital defects in reproductive tract
- Ectopic endometrial implants in the tubal mucosa
- Sexually transmitted tubal infection
- Intrauterine device

Pathophysiology
In ectopic pregnancy, transport of a blastocyst to the uterus is delayed and the blastocyst implants at another available vascularized site, usually the fallopian tube lining. Normal signs of pregnancy are initially present and uterine enlargement occurs in about 25% of cases. Human chorionic gonadotropin (HCG) hormonal levels are lower than in uterine pregnancies.

COMPLICATIONS
- Rupture of fallopian tube
- Internal hemorrhage
- Shock
- Peritonitis
- Infertility

Signs and symptoms
- Abdominal tenderness and discomfort
- Amenorrhea
- Abnormal menses (after fallopian tube implantation)
- Slight vaginal bleeding
- Unilateral pelvic pain over the mass
- If fallopian tube ruptures, sharp lower abdominal pain, possibly radiating to the shoulders and neck

CLINICAL TIP
Ectopic pregnancy sometimes produces symptoms of normal pregnancy or no symptoms other than mild abdominal pain (especially in abdominal pregnancy).

- Possible extreme pain when cervix is moved and adnexa palpated
- Boggy and tender uterus
- Adnexa may be enlarged

Diagnostic tests
- Blood test reveals abnormally low serum HCG; when repeated in 48 hours, level remains lower than levels found in a normal intrauterine pregnancy.
- Real-time ultrasonography shows intrauterine pregnancy or ovarian cyst.
- Culdocentesis shows free blood in the peritoneum.
- Laparoscopy reveals pregnancy outside the uterus.

Treatment
- Transfusion with whole blood or packed red blood cells
- Broad-spectrum I.V. antibiotics
- Supplemental iron
- Methotrexate
- Analgesics
- Rh$_O$ immune globulin if the patient is Rh negative
- Laparotomy and salpingectomy if culdocentesis shows blood in the peritoneum; possibly after laparoscopy to remove affected fallopian tube and control bleeding
- Microsurgical repair of the fallopian tube for patients who wish to have children
- Oophorectomy for ovarian pregnancy
- Hysterectomy for interstitial pregnancy
- Laparotomy to remove the fetus for abdominal pregnancy

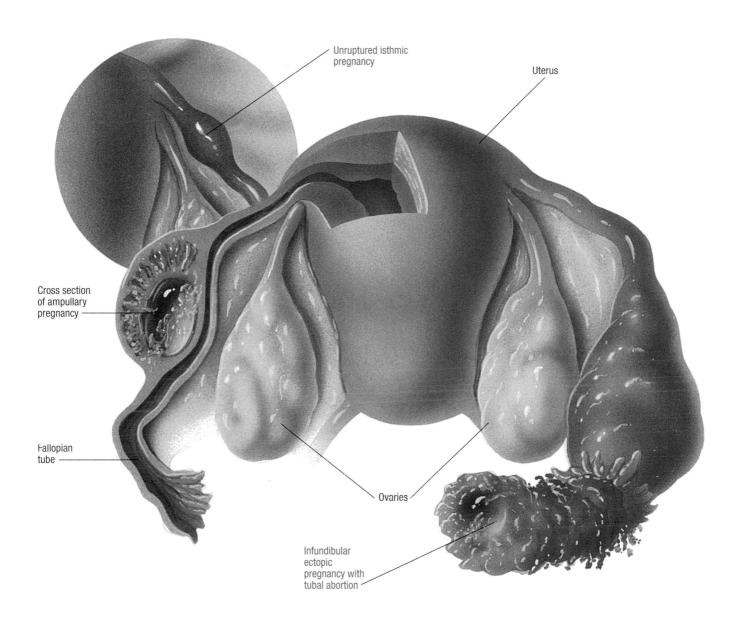

Unruptured isthmic pregnancy

Uterus

Cross section of ampullary pregnancy

Fallopian tube

Ovaries

Infundibular ectopic pregnancy with tubal abortion

ENDOMETRIAL CANCER

Also known as *uterine cancer* (cancer of the endometrium), endometrial cancer is the most common gynecologic cancer.

AGE ALERT
Uterine cancer usually affects postmenopausal women between ages 50 and 60; it's uncommon between ages 30 and 40 and extremely rare before age 30. Most premenopausal women who develop uterine cancer have a history of anovulatory menstrual cycles or other hormonal imbalance.

Causes
Primary cause unknown
Predisposing factors
- Anovulation, abnormal uterine bleeding
- History of atypical endometrial hyperplasia
- Unopposed estrogen stimulation
- Nulliparity
- Polycystic ovarian syndrome
- Familial tendency
- Obesity, hypertension, diabetes

Pathophysiology
In most cases, uterine cancer is an adenocarcinoma that metastasizes late, usually from the endometrium to the cervix, ovaries, fallopian tubes, and other peritoneal structures. It may spread to distant organs, such as the lungs and the brain, through the blood or the lymphatic system. Lymph node involvement can also occur. Less common are adenoacanthoma, endometrial stromal sarcoma, lymphosarcoma, mixed mesodermal tumors (including carcinosarcoma), and leiomyosarcoma.

COMPLICATIONS
- Intestinal obstruction
- Ascites
- Hemorrhage

Signs and symptoms
- Uterine enlargement
- Persistent and unusual premenopausal bleeding
- Any postmenopausal bleeding
- Other signs or symptoms, such as pain and weight loss, don't appear until the cancer is well advanced

Diagnostic test results
- Endometrial, cervical, or endocervical biopsy confirms the presence of cancer cells.
- Fractional dilation and curettage identifies cancer when biopsy is negative.
- Cervical biopsies and endocervical curettage pinpoint cervical involvement.

Treatment
- Surgery — generally total abdominal hysterectomy, bilateral salpingo-oophorectomy, or possibly omentectomy with or without pelvic or para-aortic lymphadenectomy
- Radiation therapy — intracavitary or external (or both):
- if tumor is poorly differentiated or histology is unfavorable
- if tumor has deeply invaded uterus or spread to extrauterine sites
- may be curative in some patients
- Hormonal therapy:
- synthetic progesterones, such as medroxyprogesterone or megestrol, for recurrent disease
- tamoxifen as a second-line treatment; 20% to 40% response rate
- Chemotherapy — usually tried when other treatments have failed:
- varying combinations of cisplatin, doxorubicin, etoposide, dactinomycin
- no evidence that they're curative.

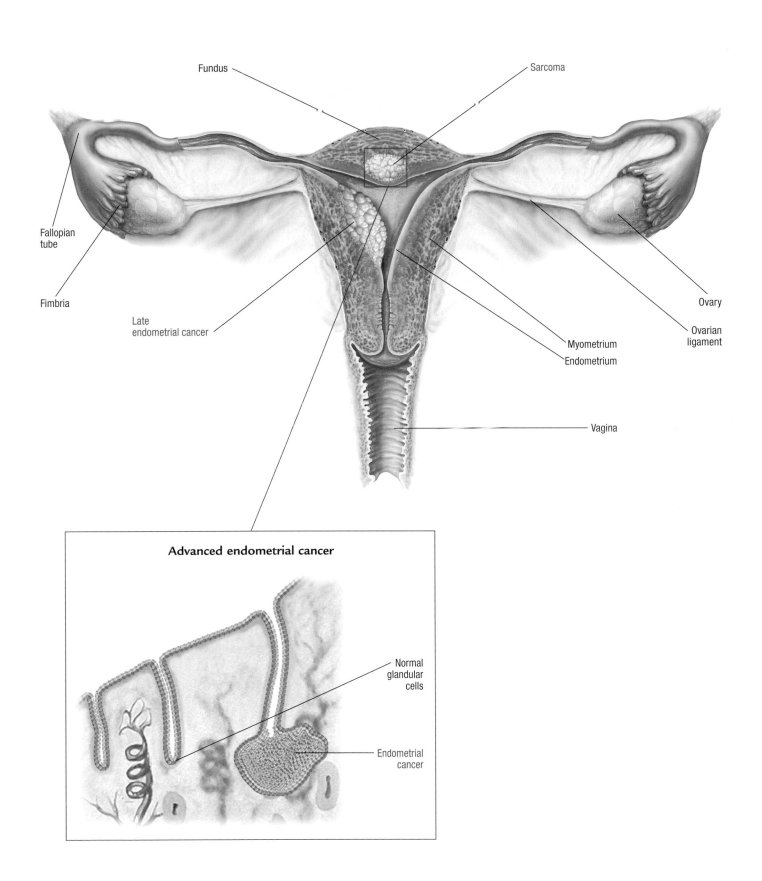

Fundus

Sarcoma

Fallopian tube

Fimbria

Late endometrial cancer

Myometrium

Endometrium

Ovary

Ovarian ligament

Vagina

Advanced endometrial cancer

Normal glandular cells

Endometrial cancer

ENDOMETRIOSIS

Endometriosis is the presence of endometrial tissue outside the lining of the uterine cavity. Ectopic tissue is generally confined to the pelvic area, usually around the ovaries, uterovesical peritoneum, uterosacral ligaments, and cul de sac, but it can appear anywhere in the body.

Active endometriosis may occur at any age, including adolescence. As many as 50% of infertile women may have endometriosis, although the true incidence in both fertile and infertile women remains unknown.

Severe symptoms of endometriosis may have an abrupt onset or may develop over many years. Of women with endometriosis, 30% to 40% become infertile. Endometriosis usually manifests during the menstrual years; after menopause, it tends to subside.

Causes
Primary cause unknown
Suggested causes (one or more may be true in different women)
- Retrograde menstruation with implantation at ectopic sites; may not be causative alone; occurs in women with no clinical evidence of endometriosis
- Genetic predisposition and depressed immune system
- Coelomic metaplasia (metaplasia of mesothelial cells to the endometrial epithelium caused by repeated inflammation)
- Lymphatic or hematogenous spread to extraperitoneal sites

Pathophysiology
The ectopic endometrial tissue responds to normal stimulation in the same way as the endometrium, but less predictably. The endometrial cells respond to estrogen and progesterone with proliferation and secretion. During menstruation, the ectopic tissue bleeds, which causes inflammation of the surrounding tissues. This inflammation causes fibrosis, leading to adhesions that produce pain and infertility.

COMPLICATIONS
- Infertility
- Spontaneous abortion
- Anemia
- Emotional problems

Signs and symptoms
- Classic symptoms – dysmenorrhea, abnormal uterine bleeding, infertility
- Pain – begins 5 to 7 days before menses, peaks, and lasts for 2 to 3 days; severity doesn't reflect extent of disease
- Depending on site of ectopic tissue:
- ovaries and oviducts: infertility, profuse menses
- ovaries or cul de sac: deep-thrust dyspareunia
- bladder: suprapubic pain, dysuria, hematuria
  large bowel, appendix: abdominal cramps, pain on defecation, constipation, bloody stools
- cervix, vagina, perineum: bleeding from endometrial deposits, painful intercourse

Diagnostic test results
- Laparoscopy or laparotomy reveal multiple tender nodules on uterosacral ligaments or in the rectovaginal septum, and ovarian enlargement in the presence of endometrial cysts on the ovaries.
- A pelvic ultrasound test detects an endometrial tissue on an ovary.
- Empiric trial of gonadotropin-releasing hormone (Gn-RH) agonist therapy confirms or refutes the impression of endometriosis before resorting to laparoscopy.
- Biopsy at the time of laparoscopy may be helpful to confirm the diagnosis.

Treatment
Conservative therapy for young women who want to have children
- Androgens such as danazol
- Progestins and continuous combined oral contraceptives (pseudopregnancy regimen) to relieve symptoms by causing regression of endometrial tissue
- Gn-RH agonists to induce pseudomenopause (medical oophorectomy), causing remission of the disease (commonly used)
- Analgesics
- Antigonadotropin drugs
To rule out cancer, when ovarian masses are present
- Laparoscopic removal of endometrial implants
Treatment of last resort for women who don't want to bear children or with extensive disease
- Total abdominal hysterectomy with or without bilateral salpingo-oophorectomy; success rates vary; unclear whether ovarian conservation is appropriate

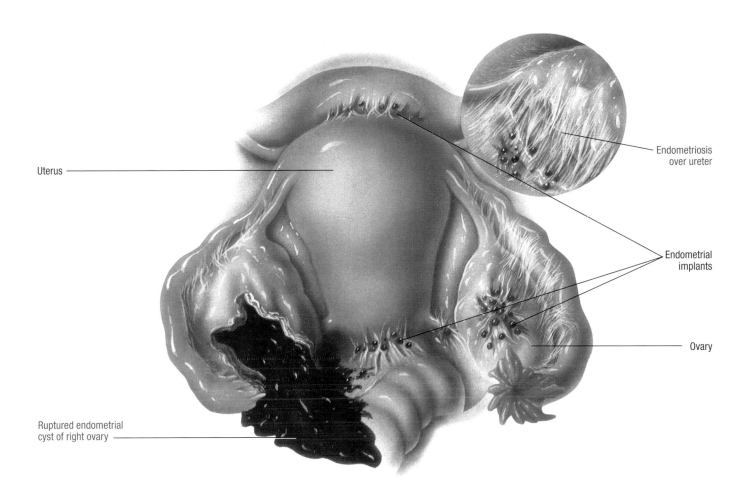

Uterus

Endometriosis over ureter

Endometrial implants

Ovary

Ruptured endometrial cyst of right ovary

 CLINICAL TIP

COMMON SITES OF ENDOMETRIOSIS

Ectopic endometrial tissue can implant almost anywhere in the pelvic peritoneum. It can even invade distant sites such as the lungs.

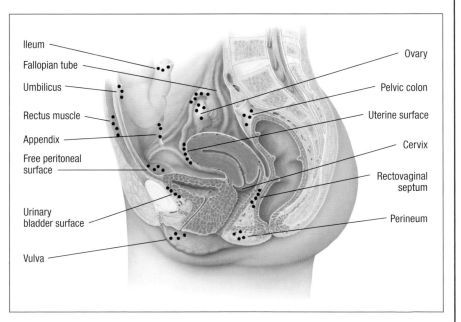

Ileum

Fallopian tube

Umbilicus

Rectus muscle

Appendix

Free peritoneal surface

Urinary bladder surface

Vulva

Ovary

Pelvic colon

Uterine surface

Cervix

Rectovaginal septum

Perineum

ERECTILE DYSFUNCTION

Erectile dysfunction, or impotence, refers to a male's inability to attain or maintain penile erection sufficient to complete intercourse. The patient with primary impotence has never achieved a sufficient erection. Secondary impotence is more common but no less disturbing than the primary form, and implies that the patient has succeeded in completing intercourse in the past.

Transient periods of impotence aren't considered dysfunction and probably occur in half of adult males. The prognosis for erectile dysfunction patients depends on the severity and duration of their impotence and the underlying causes.

AGE ALERT
Erectile dysfunction affects men of all age groups but increases in frequency with age.

Causes
Psychogenic
- Personal sexual anxieties that generally involving guilt, fear, depression, or feelings of inadequacy resulting from previous traumatic sexual experience, rejection by parents or peers, exaggerated religious orthodoxy; abnormal mother-son intimacy, or homosexual experiences
- Disturbed sexual relationship, possibly stemming from differences in sexual preferences between partners, lack of communication, insufficient knowledge of sexual function, or nonsexual personal conflicts
- Situational impotence, a temporary condition in response to stress

Organic
- Chronic diseases that cause neurologic and vascular impairment, such as cardiopulmonary disease, diabetes, multiple sclerosis, or renal failure
- Liver cirrhosis causing increased circulating estrogen due to reduced hepatic inactivation
- Spinal cord trauma
- Complications of surgery, particularly radical prostatectomy
- Drug- or alcohol-induced dysfunction
- Genital anomalies or central nervous system defects

Pathophysiology
Upon stimulation, chemicals are released in the brain that cause signals to pass down the spinal cord and outward through special nerves into the penis. These nerves release another chemical (nitric oxide) that causes the smooth muscles of the penis to relax and blood to rush into the erectile bodies, causing erection. Neurologic dysfunction results in lack of the autonomic signal and, in combination with vascular disease, interferes with arteriolar dilation. The blood is shunted around the sacs of the corpus cavernosum into medium-sized veins, which prevents the sacs from filling completely. Also, perfusion of the corpus cavernosum is initially compromised because of partial obstruction of small arteries, leading to loss of erection before ejaculation.

Anxiety or fear can prevent the brain signals from reaching the level required to induce erection. Medical conditions can block the erection arteries or cause scarring of the spongy erection tissue and prevent proper blood flow or trapping of blood and, therefore, limit the erection.

COMPLICATIONS
- Disruption of sexual relationships
- Depression

Signs and symptoms
- Inability to achieve or sustain a full erection
- Anxiety
- Perspiration
- Palpitations
- Loss of interest in sexual activity
- Depression

Diagnostic test results
- A detailed sexual history helps differentiate between organic and psychogenic factors and primary and secondary impotence.
- Fulfilling the diagnostic criteria for the *Diagnostic and Statistical Manual of Mental Disorders*, Fourth edition, Text Revision by meeting either of two criteria:
  – persistent or recurrent partial or complete failure to attain or maintain erection until completion of sexual activity
  – marked distress or interpersonal difficulty occurs as a result of erectile dysfunction.

Treatment
Psychogenic impotence
- Sex therapy including both partners (course and content of therapy depend on the specific cause of dysfunction and nature of the partner relationship)
- Teaching or helping the patient to improve verbal communication skills, eliminate unreasonable guilt, or reevaluate attitudes toward sex and sexual roles

Organic impotence
- Reversing the cause if possible
- Psychological counseling to help the couple deal realistically with their situation and explore alternatives for sexual expression if reversing the cause isn't possible
- Sildenafil, tadalafil, or vardenafil to cause vasodilatation within the penis
- Adrenergic antagonist, yohimbine, to enhance parasympathetic neurotransmission
- Testosterone supplementation for hypogonadal men (not for men with prostate cancer)
- Prostaglandin E injected directly into the corpus cavernosum (may induce an erection for 30 to 60 minutes in some men)
- Surgically inserted inflatable or noninflatable penile implants

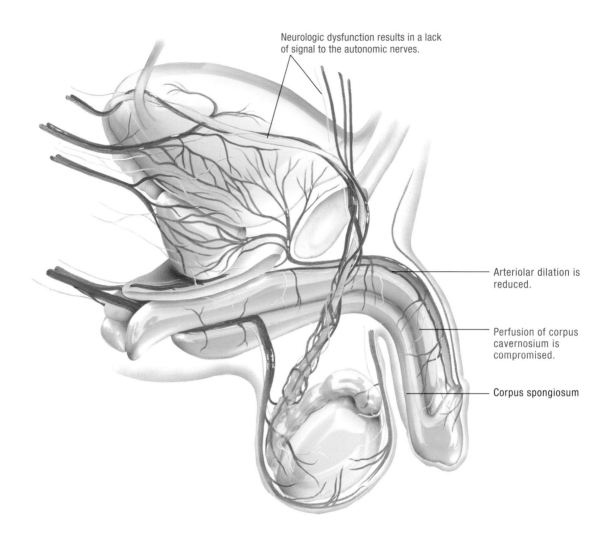

Neurologic dysfunction results in a lack of signal to the autonomic nerves.

Arteriolar dilation is reduced.

Perfusion of corpus cavernosium is compromised.

Corpus spongiosum

FIBROID DISEASE OF UTERUS

Uterine leiomyomas, also known as *myomas, fibromyomas,* or *fibroids,* are the most common benign tumors in women. They're most common in the uterine corpus, although they may appear on the cervix or on the round or broad ligament.

The tumors become malignant (leiomyosarcoma) in less than 0.1% of patients, which should serve to comfort women concerned with the possibility of a uterine malignancy in association with a fibroid.

AGE ALERT
Fibroids of the uterus may be present in 15% to 20% of reproductive age women and 30% to 40% of women over age 30.

Causes
Primary cause unknown
Implicated regulators of leiomyoma growth
- Several growth factors, including epidermal growth factor
- Steroid hormones, including estrogen and progesterone

Pathophysiology
Leiomyomas are masses of smooth muscle and fibrous connective tissue. They're classified according to location: in the uterine wall (intramural), protruding into the endometrial cavity (submucous), or protruding from the serosal surface of the uterus (subserous). Their size varies greatly. They're usually firm and surrounded by a pseudocapsule composed of compressed but otherwise normal uterine myometrium. The uterine cavity may become larger, increasing the endometrial surface area and causing increased uterine bleeding.

COMPLICATIONS
- Infertility
- Anemia
- Intestinal obstruction
- During pregnancy: spontaneous abortion, premature labor, dystocia

Signs and symptoms
- Mostly asymptomatic
- Abnormal bleeding, typically menorrhagia with disrupted submucosal vessels (most common symptom)
- Pain only with:
  - torsion of a pedunculated (stemmed) subserous tumor
  - degenerating leiomyomas (fibroid outgrows its blood supply and shrinks down in size; after myolysis, a laparoscopic procedure to shrink fibroids; after uterine artery embolization)
- Pelvic pressure and impingement on adjacent viscera leads to mild hydronephrosis

Diagnostic test results
- Blood studies show anemia from abnormal bleeding.
- Bimanual examination reveals enlarged, firm, nontender, and irregularly contoured uterus.
- Ultrasound and magnetic resonance imaging accurately assess the dimension, number, and location of tumors.

Treatment
Nonsurgical
- Gonadotropin-releasing hormone agonists (not a cure, as tumors increase in size after cessation of therapy)
- Nonsteroidal anti-inflammatory drugs

Surgical
- Hysteroscopic resection of fibroids
- Abdominal, laparoscopic, or hysteroscopic myomectomy (removal of tumors in the uterine muscle)
- Myolysis (a laparoscopic procedure, performed on an outpatient basis); contraindicated in women who desire fertility
- Uterine artery embolization (a promising alternative to surgery, but no existing long-term studies confirm effect on fertility or establish long-term success)
- Hysterectomy (usually isn't the only available option)
- Blood transfusions for severe anemia due to excessive bleeding

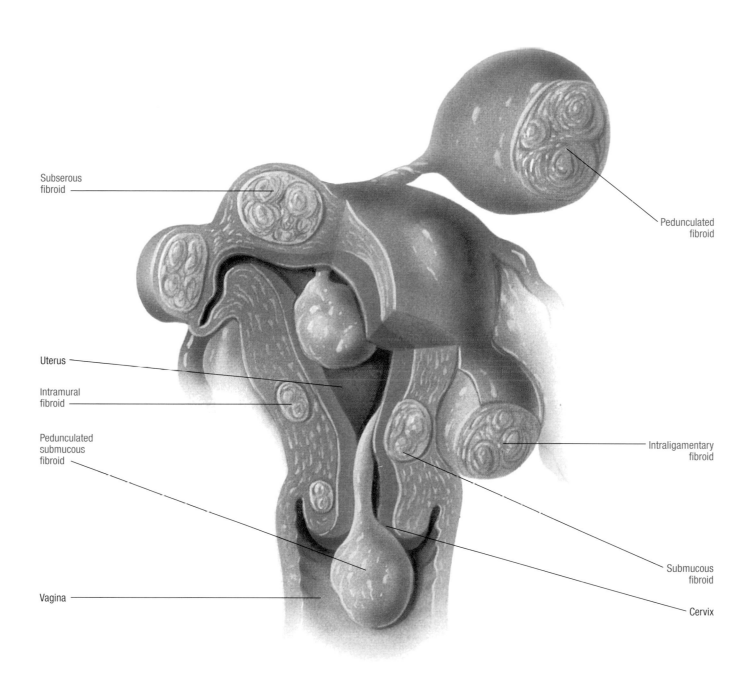

Subserous
fibroid

Pedunculated
fibroid

Uterus

Intramural
fibroid

Pedunculated
submucous
fibroid

Intraligamentary
fibroid

Submucous
fibroid

Vagina

Cervix

HYDROCELE

A hydrocele is a collection of fluid between the visceral and parietal layers of the tunica vaginalis of the testicle or along the spermatic cord. It's the most common cause of scrotal swelling.

AGE ALERT
Congenital hydrocele commonly resolves spontaneously during the first year of life. Usually, no treatment is indicated.

Causes
- Congenital malformation (infants)
- Trauma to the testes or epididymis
- Infection of the testes or epididymis
- Testicular tumor

Pathophysiology
Congenital hydrocele occurs when an opening between the scrotal sac and the peritoneal cavity allows peritoneal fluids to collect in the scrotum. The exact mechanism is unknown.

In adults, the fluid accumulation may be caused by infection, trauma, tumor, an imbalance between the secreting and absorptive capacities of scrotal tissue, or an obstruction of lymphatic or venous drainage in the spermatic cord. Consequent swelling obstructs blood flow to the testes.

COMPLICATIONS
- Infection
- Inguinal hernia
- Tumor

Signs and symptoms
- Scrotal swelling and feeling of heaviness
- Inguinal hernia (commonly accompanies congenital hydrocele)
- Fluid collection, presenting as flaccid or tense mass
- Pain with acute epididymal infection or testicular torsion
- Scrotal tenderness due to severe swelling

Diagnostic test results
- Transillumination distinguishes fluid-filled from solid mass; tumor doesn't transilluminate.
- Ultrasonography visualizes the testes and the presence of fluid.
- Tissue biopsy differentiates between normal cells and malignancy.

Treatment
- Inguinal hernia with bowel present in the sac: surgical repair
- Tense hydrocele that impedes blood circulation or causes pain: aspiration of fluid and injection of sclerosing drug
- Recurrent hydroceles: excision of tunica vaginalis
- Testicular tumor detected by ultrasound: suprainguinal excision

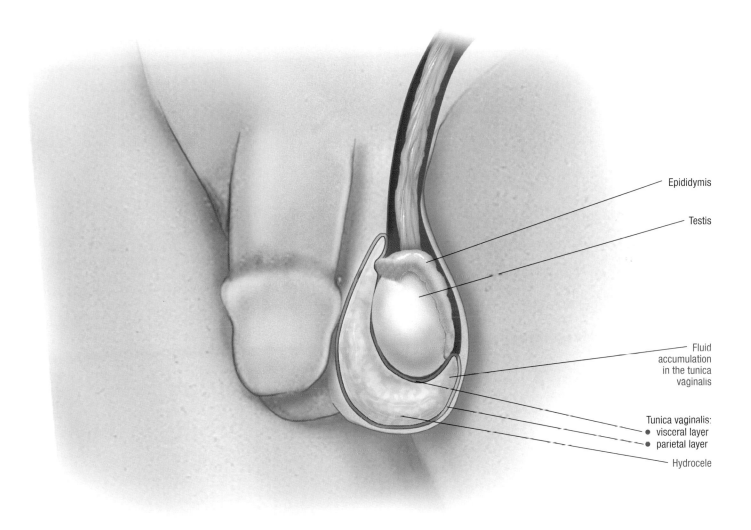

Epididymis

Testis

Fluid accumulation in the tunica vaginalis

Tunica vaginalis:
● visceral layer
● parietal layer

Hydrocele

HYPOSPADIAS AND EPISPADIAS

Among the most common birth defects, congenital anomalies of the ureter, bladder, and urethra occur in about 5% of all births. The abnormality may be obvious at birth or may go unrecognized until symptoms appear.

Hypospadias is a congenital abnormality in which the urethral meatus is located on the ventral side, or undersurface of the penis. It may be on the glans, the base of the penis, the penoscrotal sac, or the perineum. The defect may be slight to extreme, and it occurs in 1 of 300 live male births. Epispadias occurs in 1 in 200,000 infant boys and 1 in 400,000 infant girls. In males, the urethral opening is on the dorsal aspect of the penis; in females, a cleft along the ventral urethral opening extends to the bladder neck.

Causes
- Congenital malformation
- Genetic factors
- Hormonal variations

Pathophysiology
In *hypospadias*, the urethral opening is on the ventral surface of the penis. A genetic factor is suspected in less severe cases. It's usually associated with a downward bowing of the penis (chordee), making normal urination with the penis elevated impossible. The ventral prepuce may be absent or defective, and the genitalia may be ambiguous. In the rare case of hypospadias in a female, the urethral opening is in the vagina, and vaginal discharge may be present.

Epispadias occurs more commonly in males than in females and often accompanies bladder exstrophy, in which a portion of posterior bladder wall protrudes through a defect in the lower abdominal and anterior bladder wall. In mild cases, the orifice is on the dorsum of the glans; in severe cases, on the dorsum of the penis. Affected females have a bifid (cleft into two parts) clitoris and a short, wide urethra. Total urinary incontinence occurs when the urethral opening is proximal to the sphincter.

COMPLICATIONS
- Infections
- Hematuria
- Calculi

Signs and symptoms
- Displaced urethral opening
- Altered voiding patterns due to displaced opening of the urethra
- Chordee, or bending of the penis (in hypospadias)
- Ejaculatory dysfunction due to displaced penile opening

Diagnostic test results
- None are necessary if sexual identification is clear.
- If sexual identification is unclear, buccal smears or karyotyping determines gender.

Treatment
- Mild, asymptomatic hypospadias: no treatment
- Severe hypospadias: surgery, preferably before child reaches school age
- Epispadias: multistage surgical repair, almost always necessary

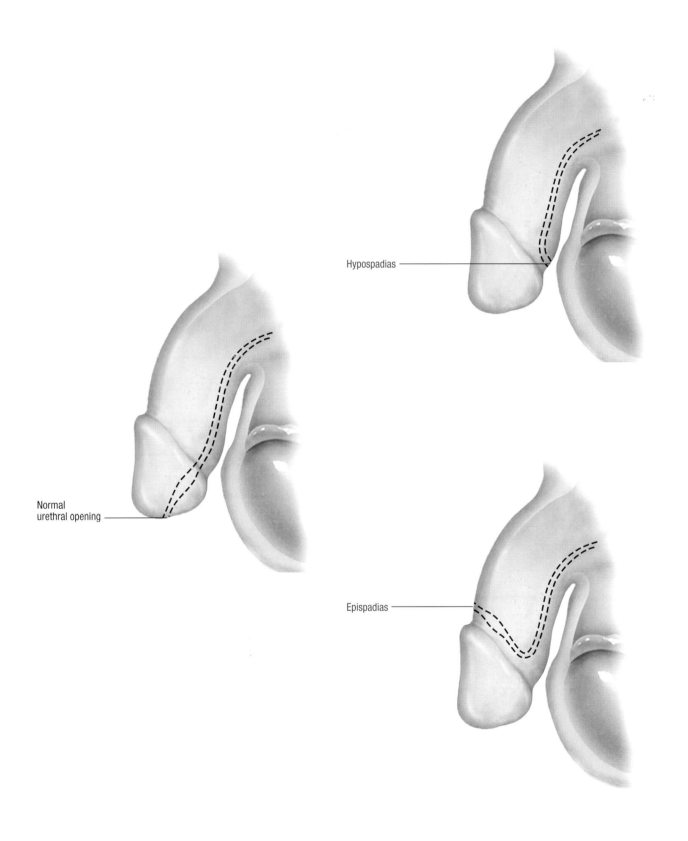

Hypospadias

Normal
urethral opening

Epispadias

OVARIAN CANCER

Ovarian cancer is the fifth leading cause of cancer death among U.S. women and has the highest mortality rate of all gynecologic cancers. In women with previously treated breast cancer, metastatic ovarian cancer is more common than cancer at any other site.

AGE ALERT
More than half of all deaths from ovarian cancer occur in women between ages 65 and 84, and more than one-quarter of ovarian cancer deaths occur between ages 45 and 64.

The prognosis varies with the histologic type and stage of the disease. It's generally poor because ovarian tumors produce few early signs and are usually advanced at diagnosis. With early detection, about 90% of women with ovarian cancer at the localized stage survive for 5 years. The overall survival rate is about 45%.

Causes
Exact cause unknown
Associated factors
- Infertility, nulliparity
- Familial tendency
- Ovarian dysfunction, irregular menses, ovarian cysts
- Exposure to asbestos, talc, industrial pollutants
- Fertility drugs
- Diet high in saturated fat, obesity by age 18
- Hormone replacement therapy
- Breast cancer genes (BRCA1 or BRCA2)

Pathophysiology
Primary epithelial tumors (account for 90% of all ovarian cancers) arise in the Müllerian epithelium; germ cell tumors, in the ovum itself; and sex cord tumors, in the ovarian stroma. Ovarian tumors spread rapidly intraperitoneally by local extension or surface seeding and, occasionally, through the lymphatics and the bloodstream. Generally, extraperitoneal spread travels through the diaphragm into the chest cavity, where the tumor may cause pleural effusions. Other metastasis is rare.

COMPLICATIONS
- Fluid and electrolyte imbalances
- Leg edema
- Intestinal obstruction
- Cachexia
- Malignant effusions

Signs and symptoms
- May grow to considerable size before overt symptoms appear
Occasionally, in the early stages
- Vague abdominal discomfort, distention
- Mild GI discomfort (nausea, vomiting, bloating)
- Urinary frequency, pelvic discomfort
- Constipation
- Vaginal bleeding
- Weight loss
Later stages
- Tumor rupture, torsion, or infection — pain, which, in young patients, may mimic appendicitis
- Granulosa cell tumors — effects of estrogen excess such as bleeding between periods in premenopausal women
- Arrhenoblastomas (seen rarely) — virilizing effects
Advanced ovarian cancer
- Ascites
- Postmenopausal bleeding and pain (rarely)
- Symptoms of metastatic tumors, most commonly pleural effusion

Diagnostic test results
- Exploratory laparotomy, including lymph node evaluation and tumor resection, is required for accurate diagnosis and staging.
- Laboratory tumor marker studies (such as ovarian carcinoma antigen, carcinoembryonic antigen, and human chorionic gonadotropin) show abnormalities that may indicate complications.
- Abdominal ultrasonography, computed tomography scan, or X-rays delineate tumor size.
- Aspiration of ascitic fluid reveals atypical cells.

Treatment
- Varying combinations of surgery, chemotherapy, and radiation
Conservative treatment for unilateral encapsulated tumor in young girl or young woman
- Resection of the involved ovary
- Careful follow-up, including periodic chest X-rays to rule out lung metastasis
More aggressive treatment
- Total abdominal hysterectomy and bilateral salpingo-oophorectomy with tumor resection, omentectomy, possible appendectomy, lymphadenectomy, tissue biopsies, and peritoneal washings
If tumor has matted around other organs or involves organs that can't be resected
- Surgically debulk tumor implants to less than 2 cm (or smaller) in greatest diameter
Chemotherapy
- May be curative; extends survival time in most patients; largely palliative in advanced disease
- Current standard is combination paclitaxel and platinum-based chemotherapy

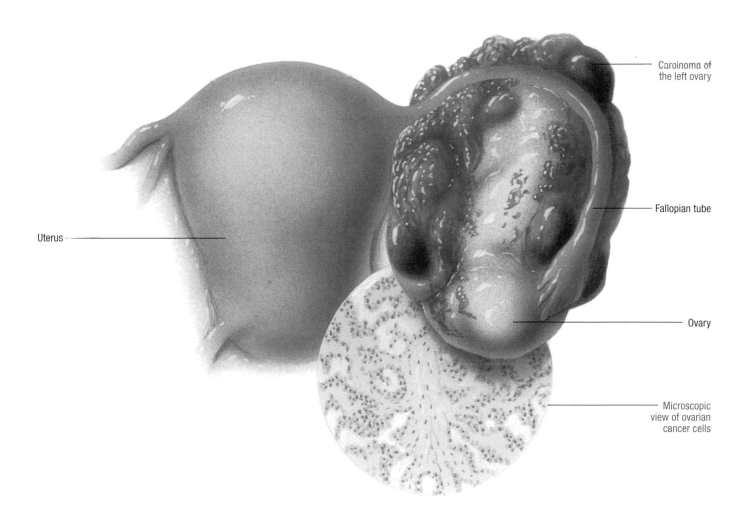

Carcinoma of
the left ovary

Fallopian tube

Uterus

Ovary

Microscopic
view of ovarian
cancer cells

CLINICAL TIP

METASTATIC SITES FOR OVARIAN CANCER

Ovarian cancer can metastasize to almost any site. Illustrated here are the most common sites.

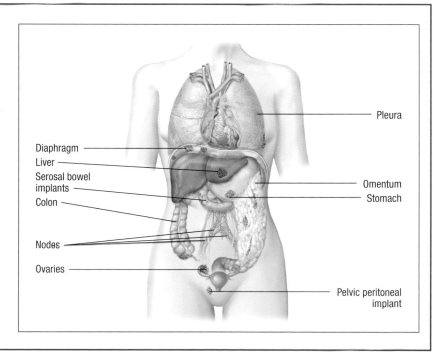

Pleura

Diaphragm

Liver

Serosal bowel
implants

Omentum

Colon

Stomach

Nodes

Ovaries

Pelvic peritoneal
implant

OVARIAN CYSTS

Ovarian cysts are usually benign sacs that contain fluid or semisolid material. Although these cysts are usually small and produce no symptoms, they may require thorough investigation as possible sites of malignant change. Cysts may be single or multiple (polycystic ovarian disease). Most ovarian cysts are physiologic, or functional; that is, they arise during the normal ovulatory process. Physiologic ovarian cysts include *follicular* cysts, *theca-lutein* cysts, which are commonly bilateral and filled with clear, straw-colored liquid, and *corpus luteum* cysts. Ovarian cysts can develop any time between puberty and menopause, including during pregnancy. The prognosis for benign ovarian cysts is excellent. The presence of a functional ovarian cyst doesn't increase the risk for malignancy.

CLINICAL TIP
Polycystic ovarian syndrome is a metabolic disorder characterized by multiple ovarian cysts. About 22% of the women in the United States have the disorder, and about 50% to 80% of these women are obese. Among those who seek treatment for infertility, more than 75% have some degree of polycystic ovarian syndrome, usually manifested by anovulation alone.

Causes
- Granulosa-lutein cysts (occur within the corpus luteum): excessive accumulation of blood during hemorrhagic phase of menstrual cycle
- Theca-lutein cysts:
- hydatidiform mole, choriocarcinoma
- hormone therapy (human chorionic gonadotropin [HCG] or clomiphene citrate)

Pathophysiology
Follicular cysts are generally very small and arise from follicles that either haven't ruptured or have ruptured and resealed before their fluid is reabsorbed. *Luteal cysts* develop if a mature corpus luteum persists abnormally and continues to secrete progesterone. They consist of blood or fluid that accumulates in the cavity of the corpus luteum and are typically more symptomatic than follicular cysts. When such cysts persist into menopause, they secrete excessive amounts of estrogen in response to the hypersecretion of follicle-stimulating hormone and luteinizing hormone that normally occurs during menopause.

Dermoid cysts are tumors of developmental origin that consist of a fibrous wall lined with stratified epithelium and may contain hair follicles, sweat glands, sebaceous glands, nerve elements, and teeth.

COMPLICATIONS
- Amenorrhea
- Oligomenorrhea
- Secondary dysmenorrhea
- Infertility
- Rupture of the cyst, peritonitis, intraperitoneal hemorrhage, shock, and death

Signs and symptoms
- Large or multiple cysts:
- mild pelvic discomfort, low back pain, dyspareunia
- abnormal uterine bleeding
- Ovarian cysts with torsion: acute abdominal pain similar to that of appendicitis
- Granulosa-lutein cysts:
- in pregnancy: unilateral pelvic discomfort
- in nonpregnant women: delayed menses, followed by prolonged or irregular bleeding

Diagnostic test results
Ultrasound, laparoscopy, or surgery confirm the presence of ovarian cysts.

Treatment
- If cyst disappears spontaneously within one to two menstrual cycles — no treatment
- Persisting cyst indicates excision to rule out malignancy
- Functional cysts that appear during pregnancy — analgesics
- Theca-lutein cysts:
- elimination of hydatidiform mole
- destruction of choriocarcinoma
- discontinuation of HCG or clomiphene therapy
- Persistent or suspicious ovarian cyst:
- laparoscopy or exploratory laparotomy with possible ovarian cystectomy or oophorectomy
- if necessary during pregnancy, optimal time is second trimester
- Ruptured corpus luteum cyst:
- culdocentesis to drain intraperitoneal fluid
- surgery for ongoing hemorrhage

Follicular cyst

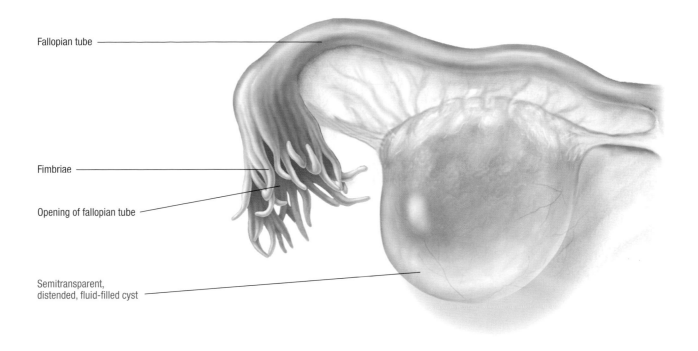

Fallopian tube

Fimbriae

Opening of fallopian tube

Semitransparent, distended, fluid-filled cyst

Dermoid cyst

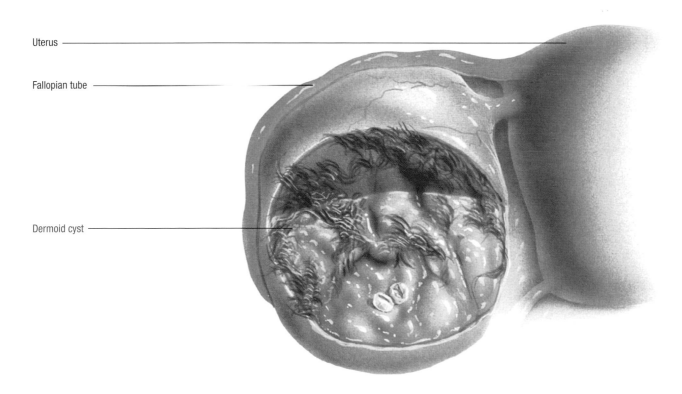

Uterus

Fallopian tube

Dermoid cyst

PELVIC INFLAMMATORY DISEASE

Pelvic inflammatory disease (PID) is infection of the uterus, fallopian tubes, or ovaries. About 1 million women are treated for PID each year in the United States and about 1 in 7 women are treated for the disease at some point in their lives. Early diagnosis and treatment prevent damage to the reproductive system. Untreated PID may cause infertility and may lead to potentially fatal septicemia and shock.

Causes
- Infection with aerobic or anaerobic organisms, such as:
- *Neisseria gonorrhoeae* and *Chlamydia trachomatis* (most common)
- staphylococci, streptococci, diphtheroids, *Pseudomonas, Escherichia coli*

Predisposing conditions
- Conization or cauterization of the cervix
- Insertion of an intrauterine device
- Use of a biopsy curette or an irrigation catheter
- Tubal insufflation
- Abortion, pelvic surgery, infection during or after pregnancy

Pathophysiology
Normally, cervical secretions have a protective and defensive function. Conditions or procedures that alter or destroy cervical mucus impair this bacteriostatic mechanism and allow bacteria present in the cervix or vagina to ascend into the uterine cavity. Uterine infection can also follow the transfer of contaminated cervical mucus into the endometrial cavity by instrumentation. Bacteria may also enter the uterine cavity through the bloodstream or from drainage from a chronically infected fallopian tube, a pelvic abscess, a ruptured appendix, diverticulitis of the sigmoid colon, or other infectious focus.

Uterine infection can result from contamination by one or several common pathogens or may follow the multiplication of normally nonpathogenic bacteria in an altered endometrial environment. Bacterial multiplication is most common during parturition because the endometrium is atrophic, quiescent, and not stimulated by estrogen.

COMPLICATIONS
- Chronic pelvic pain
- Formation of adhesions
- Septicemia
- Pulmonary emboli
- Infertility
- Shock

Signs and symptoms
- Profuse, purulent vaginal discharge
- Low-grade fever, malaise
- Lower abdominal pain
- Severe pain on movement of cervix or palpation of adnexa
- Vaginal bleeding
- Chills
- Nausea and vomiting
- Dysuria

Diagnostic test results
- Culture and sensitivity and Gram stain testing of endocervix or cul-de-sac secretions show the causative agent.
- Urethral and rectal secretions reveal the causative agent.
- Blood test reveals elevated C-reactive protein level.
- Transvaginal ultrasonography shows the presence of thickened, fluid-filled fallopian tubes.
- Computed tomography scan shows complex tubo-ovarian abscesses.
- Magnetic resonance imaging provides images of soft tissue; useful not only for establishing the diagnosis of PID, but also for detecting other processes responsible for symptoms.
- Culdocentesis obtains peritoneal fluid or pus for culture and sensitivity testing.
- Diagnostic laparoscopy identifies cul de-sac fluid, tubal distention, and masses in pelvic abscess.

Treatment
- Antibiotic therapy beginning immediately after culture specimens are obtained and reevaluated as soon as laboratory results are available (usually after 24 to 48 hours); infection may become chronic if treated inadequately; PID therapy regimens should provide broad-spectrum coverage of likely etiologic pathogens: *C. trachomatis, N. gonorrhoeae,* anaerobes, gram-negative rods, and streptococci
- Analgesics
- I.V. fluids
- Adequate drainage if pelvic abscess forms
- Ruptured abscess (life-threatening complication):
- total abdominal hysterectomy with bilateral salpingo-oophorectomy
- laparoscopic drainage with preservation of the ovaries and uterus appears to hold promise

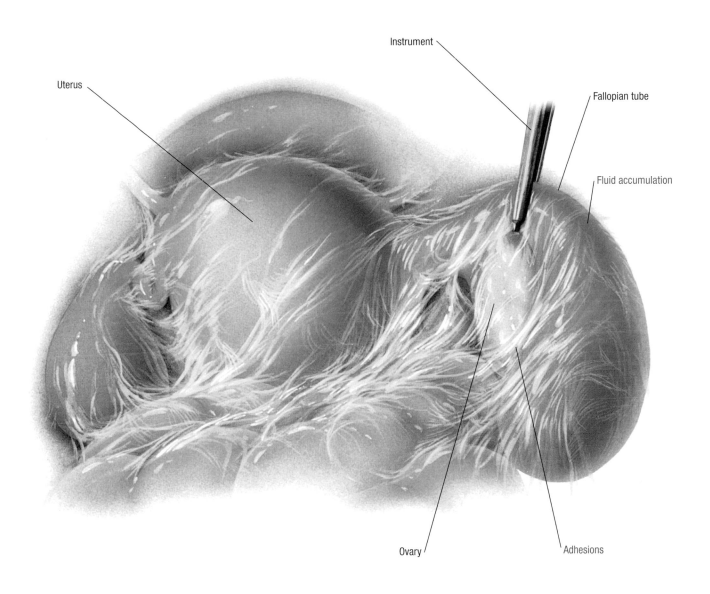

PROSTATE CANCER

Prostate cancer is the most common cancer in men over age 50. Adenocarcinoma is its most common form; sarcoma occurs only rarely. Most prostatic carcinomas originate in the posterior prostate gland; the rest originate near the urethra. Malignant prostatic tumors seldom result from the benign hyperplastic enlargement that commonly develops around the prostatic urethra in elderly men. Prostatic cancer seldom produces symptoms until it's advanced.

AGE ALERT
Incidence of prostate cancer increases with age more rapidly than that of any other cancer.

Causes
Exact cause unknown
Implicated contributing factors
- Familial or ethnic predisposition
- Exposure to environmental toxins (radiation, air pollution: arsenic, benzene, hydrocarbons, polyvinyl chlorides)
- Sexually transmitted diseases
- Endogenous hormonal influence
- Diet containing fat from animal products

Pathophysiology
Typically, when a primary prostatic lesion spreads beyond the prostate gland, it invades the prostatic capsule and spreads along ejaculatory ducts in the space between the seminal vesicles or perivesicular fascia. Endocrine factors may play a role, leading researchers to suspect that androgens speed tumor growth.

COMPLICATIONS
- Spinal cord compression
- Deep vein thrombosis
- Pulmonary emboli
- Myelophthisis

Signs and symptoms
Early stages
- Nonraised, firm, nodular mass with a sharp cage
Advanced disease
- Difficulty initiating a urine stream
- Dribbling, urine retention
- Unexplained cystitis
- Hematuria
- Edema of the scrotum or leg
- Hard lump in the prostate region
- Pain

Diagnostic test results
- Serum prostate-specific antigen test reveals elevated levels indicating cancer with or without metastases.
- Transrectal prostatic ultrasonography shows prostate size and presence of abnormal growths.
- Bone scan and excretory urography determine the extent of disease.
- Magnetic resonance imaging and computed tomography scan define the extent of the tumor.
- Standard screening test, digital rectal examination, is recommended yearly by the American Cancer Society for men over age 40.

Treatment
- Prostatectomy
- Orchiectomy
- Radiation by external beam radiation or radioactive implants
- Hormonal manipulation
- Luteinizing hormone-releasing hormone agonists, such as Lupron or Zoladex
- Androgen blocking agents
- Chemotherapy

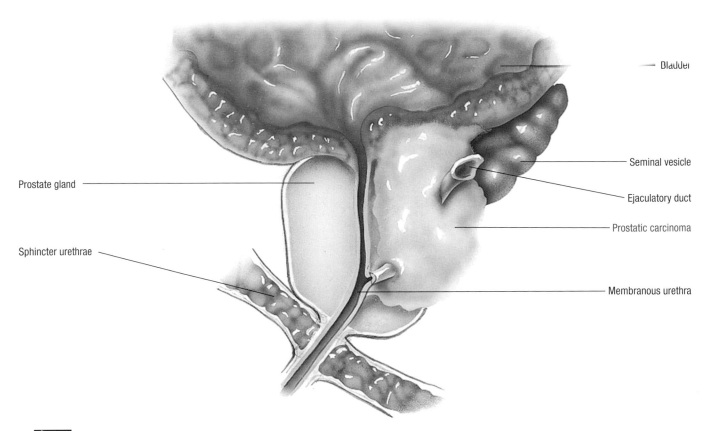

Prostate gland

Sphincter urethrae

Bladder

Seminal vesicle

Ejaculatory duct

Prostatic carcinoma

Membranous urethra

 CLINICAL TIP

PATHWAY FOR METASTASIS OF PROSTATE CANCER

When primary prostatic lesions metastasize, they typically invade the prostatic capsule, spreading along the ejaculatory ducts in the space between the seminal vesicles or perivesicular fascia.

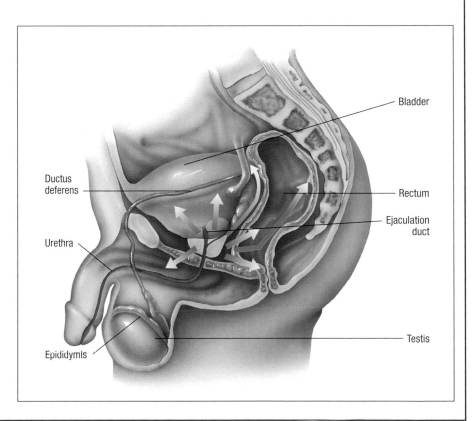

Ductus deferens

Urethra

Epididymis

Bladder

Rectum

Ejaculation duct

Testis

PROSTATITIS

Prostatitis, or inflammation of the prostate gland, may be classified according to four categories:
- acute bacterial prostatitis
- chronic bacterial prostatitis
- chronic nonbacterial prostatitis and chronic pelvic pain syndrome
- asymptomatic inflammatory prostatitis.

Causes

Acute bacterial
- Previous bladder or urethral infection
- Gram-negative organisms, such as *Escherichia coli*; *Enterobacter, Serratia, Pseudomonas,* and *Proteus* species, and enterococci (account for 80% of cases)

Chronic bacterial
- Cytomegalovirus
- Human immunodeficiency virus
- Urinary catheter tube use
- Acute prostatitis

Chronic nonbacterial
- Ejaculatory duct obstruction
- Interstitial cystitis and other infectious agents
- Pelvic muscle spasm
- Structural abnormalities of the urinary tract such as strictures
- Heavy lifting when the bladder is full

Asymptomatic inflammatory
- Similar to chronic inflammatory form but without symptoms

Pathophysiology

Spasms in the genitourinary tract or tension in the pelvic floor muscles may cause inflammation in nonbacterial prostatitis.

Bacterial prostatitic infection can be a result of previous or recurrent infection, which stimulates an inflammatory response in the prostate. Inflammation is usually limited to a few of the gland's ducts.

 COMPLICATIONS
- Infertility
- Bacteremia
- Pyelonephritis
- Prostatic abscess
- Epididymitis

Signs and symptoms

Acute bacterial
- Fever, chills
- Low back pain, especially when standing
- Frequent and urgent urination
- Dysuria, nocturia, urinary obstruction, blood-tinged urine

Chronic bacterial
- Same urinary symptoms as in acute form but to a lesser degree
- Painful ejaculation
- Recurrent symptomatic cystitis

Chronic nonbacterial
- Same as chronic bacterial form but afebrile
- Pelvic pain
- Painful ejaculation
- Erectile dysfunction
- Incomplete voiding

Diagnostic test results

- Elevated PSA level supports diagnosis of chronic bacterial prostatitis.
- Transrectal ultrasound reveals enlarged, thickened seminal vesicles.
- Computed tomography scan of the prostate may reveal abscess or a suspected neoplasm.
- Urine culture identifies the causative agent; must be performed when the patient starts voiding, then during midstream, after the patient stops voiding, and after the physician massages the prostate to express prostate secretions along with the voiding.

Treatment

General
- Muscle relaxants to relieve muscle spasms
- Alpha-adrenergic blockers (terazosin, tamsulosin) to relax the bladder
- Pain relievers
- Finasteride
- Limiting alcohol and caffeine and increasing water intake
- Regular ejaculation and urination (helps promote drainage of prostate secretions) and careful massage of the prostate (to relieve discomfort); vigorous massage may cause secondary epididymitis or septicemia

Acute bacterial
- Broad-spectrum antibiotics

Chronic bacterial
- Antibiotics (such as co-trimethoprim), fluoroquinolones (such as ofloxacin, ciprofloxacin, or levofloxacin), alpha-adrenergic blockers, or diazepam
- Sitz baths

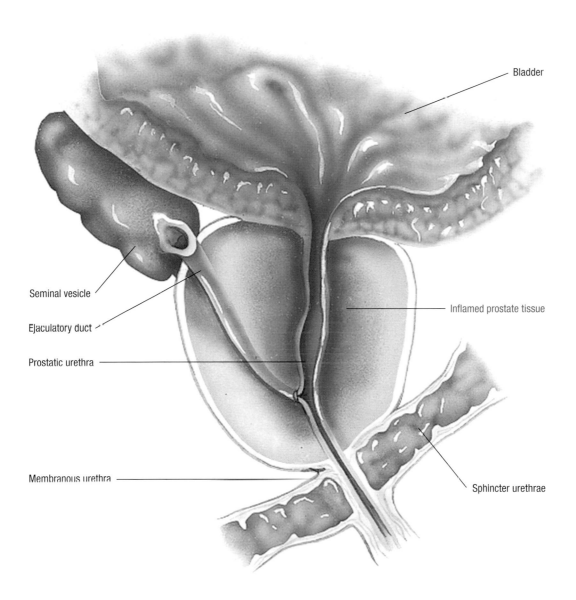

Bladder

Seminal vesicle

Ejaculatory duct

Prostatic urethra

Inflamed prostate tissue

Membranous urethra

Sphincter urethrae

Sexually transmitted infections

Chlamydia

Chlamydial infections are transmitted by orogenital contact or vaginal or rectal intercourse with an infected person. They're the most common sexually transmitted diseases in the United States.

COMPLICATIONS
- Epididymitis and prostatitis
- Salpingitis, pelvic inflammatory disease (PID), and sterility
- Spontaneous abortion, premature delivery, and neonatal death

Causes
Chlamydia trachomatis

Signs and symptoms
- Commonly asymptomatic
- Dysuria, urinary frequency, pyuria, pelvic or abdominal pain
- Chills, fever
- Genital discharge, genital pain
- Vaginal bleeding after intercourse; painful scrotal swelling

Diagnostic test results
- Swab culture of the infection site shows *C. trachomatis.*
- Serologic studies reveal previous exposure.
- Enzyme-linked immunosorbent assay shows *C. trachomatis* antibody.

Treatment
- Azithromycin, erythromycin, or doxycycline

Gonorrhea

Gonorrhea of the genitourinary tract (most commonly the urethra or cervix), or, occasionally, the rectum, pharynx, or eyes, almost always follows sexual contact with an infected person. An infected mother can transmit it during delivery.

COMPLICATIONS
- Epididymitis and prostatitis
- PID and salpingitis
- Septic arthritis, dermatitis, and perihepatitis
- Conjunctivitis, corneal ulceration, and blindness

Causes
Neisseria gonorrhoeae

Signs and symptoms
- May be asymptomatic
- In males, 3 to 6 days after contact, urethritis, dysuria, purulent discharge, redness, and swelling at the site
- Occasionally, vaginal inflammation, burning, itching, or greenish-yellow vaginal discharge
- Urinary frequency, incontinence, pelvic and lower abdominal pain or distention
- Nausea, vomiting, fever, tachycardia, polyarthritis (advanced disease)

Gonococcal ophthalmia neonatorum
- Lid edema, redness, abundant purulent discharge appearing 2 or 3 days postpartum

Diagnostic test results
- Positive culture of *N. gonorrhoeae* from site confirms infection.
- Conjunctival scrapings confirm gonococcal conjunctivitis.
- Gonococcal arthritis is confirmed by Gram stain of smears from joint fluid and skin lesions.

Treatment
- Ceftriaxone plus doxycycline
- Alternative agents given with doxycycline: cefixime, ofloxacin, spectinomycin, ciprofloxacin, erythromycin

Genital herpes

Genital herpes is an acute inflammatory disease of the genitalia. It's typically transmitted through sexual intercourse, orogenital sexual activity, kissing, and hand-to-body contact. Pregnant women may transmit the infection to neonates during vaginal delivery if an active infection is present.

COMPLICATIONS
- Neonatal infections

Causes
- Herpes simplex virus (HSV) type 2 — most common
- HSV type 1 — increasing incidence

Signs and symptoms
After a 3- to 7-day incubation period
- Appearance of genital vesicles
- Fever, malaise, dysuria, possible lesions on mouth or anus
- Leukorrhea

Diagnostic test results
- Staining of lesion scrapings shows characteristic giant cells or intranuclear inclusion of herpes virus infection.
- Tissue culture shows isolation of virus.
- Tissue analysis shows HSV antigens or deoxyribonucleic acid.

Treatment
- Acyclovir or other antiviral agents

Genital warts

Genital warts, also known as *venereal warts* or *condylomata acuminata,* grow rapidly in the presence of immune suppression or pregnancy and can accompany other genital infections.

COMPLICATIONS
- Genital tract dysplasia or cancer
- Vaginal delivery problems

Causes
Human papillomavirus

Genital herpes

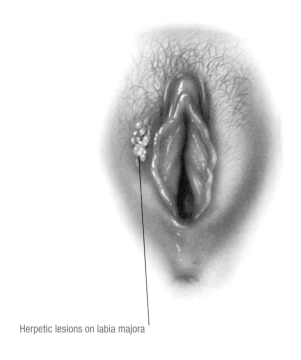

Herpetic lesions on labia majora

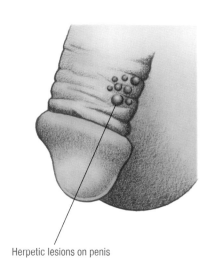

Herpetic lesions on penis

Genital warts

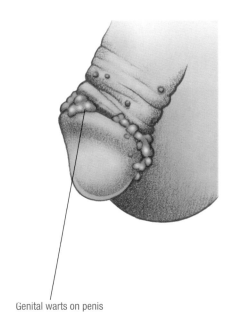

Genital warts on penis

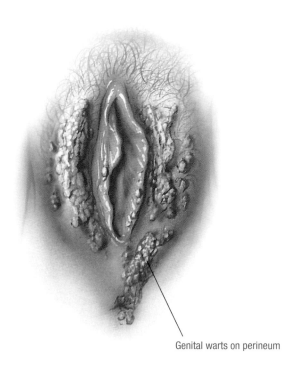

Genital warts on perineum

Signs and symptoms

- After a 1- to 6-month incubation period (usually 2 months), tiny, red or pink, painless swellings on moist surfaces:
  – subpreputial sac, in urethral meatus and, less commonly, on penile shaft
  – vulva and on vaginal and cervical walls
- Progressive disease:
  – spread to perineum and perianal area
  – large warts up to about 4″ (10 cm) in diameter
  – pedunculated; typical cauliflower-like appearance

Diagnostic test results

- Dark-field microscopy of wart-cell scrapings show marked epidermal cell vascularization.
- Application of 5% acetic acid turns warts white if they're papillomas.

Treatment

- None to eradicate virus; relapse is common
- Small warts: topical 10% to 25% podophyllum in tincture of benzoin, trichloroacetic acid, or bichloroacetic acid
- Warts larger than 1″ (2.5 cm): carbon dioxide laser treatment, cryosurgery, or electrocautery
- Podofilox, imiquimod, interferon, combined laser and interferon therapy

SYPHILIS

Syphilis is a contagious, systemic venereal or congenital disease caused by a spirochete. It begins in the mucous membranes and quickly spreads to nearby lymph nodes and the bloodstream. Transmission occurs primarily through sexual contact during the primary, secondary, and early latent stages of infection. Transmission from a mother to her fetus is possible.

COMPLICATIONS
- Aortic regurgitation or aneurysm
- Meningitis and central nervous system damage

Causes

The spirochete *Treponema pallidum*

Signs and symptoms

Primary syphilis
- Develops after a 3-week incubation period
- One or more chancres erupt at site of infection, usually genitalia or, possibly, on anus, fingers, lips, tongue, nipples, tonsils, eyelids

Secondary syphilis
- Symptoms develop within a few days or up to 8 weeks after onset of primary chancres
- Symmetrical mucocutaneous lesions – of uniform size; well defined; macular, papular, pustular, or nodular:
  – commonly between rolls of fat on the trunk and, proximally, on the arms, palms, soles, face, and scalp
  – in warm, moist areas, lesions enlarge and erode, becoming highly contagious, pink or grayish white lesions (*condylomata lata*)
- Headache, malaise, anorexia, weight loss, nausea, vomiting, sore throat and, possibly, slight fever, lymphadenopathy

- Alopecia, usually temporary; brittle, pitted nails

Latent tertiary syphilis
- Absence of clinical symptoms
- Reactive serologic test for syphilis

Late syphilis
- Final, destructive but noninfectious stage of the disease
- Any or all of three subtypes: late benign syphilis, cardiovascular syphilis, and neurosyphilis

Diagnostic test results

- Dark-field microscopy identifies *T. pallidum* from lesion exudate.
- Non-treponemal serologic tests include the Venereal Disease Research Laboratory (VDRL) slide test, the rapid plasma reagin test, and the automated reagin test, detecting nonspecific antibodies.
- Treponemal serologic studies include the fluorescent treponemal antibody absorption test, the *T. pallidum* hemagglutination assay, and the microhemagglutination assay that detect the specific antitreponemal antibody and confirm positive screening results.
- Cerebrospinal fluid examination identifies neurosyphilis when the total protein level is above 40 mg/dl, the VDRL slide test is reactive, and the white blood cell count exceeds 5 mononuclear cells/mm.

Treatment

- Penicillin G benzathine I.M.
- Nonpregnant patients allergic to penicillin: oral tetracycline or doxycycline

TRICHOMONIASIS

A protozoal infection, trichomoniasis affects about 15% of sexually active females and 10% of sexually active males. Common sites of infection in females include the vagina, urethra and, possibly, the endocervix, bladder, Bartholin's glands, or Skene's glands; in males, the lower urethra and, possibly, the prostate gland, seminal vesicles, or epididymis.

COMPLICATIONS
- Vaginal infection and PID

Causes

Trichomonas vaginalis, a tetraflagellated, motile protozoan

Signs and symptoms

- None in approximately 70% of females and most males
- In females; gray or greenish-yellow and possibly profuse and frothy, malodorous vaginal discharge; severe itching, redness, swelling, dyspareunia, dysuria; occasionally, postcoital spotting, menorrhagia, dysmenorrhea

Diagnostic tests

- Microscopic examination of vaginal or seminal discharge or urine specimen is positive for *T. vaginalis.*

Treatment

- Metronidazole

Syphilis

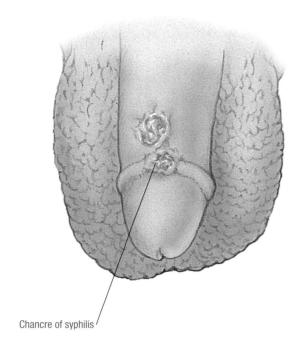

Chancre of syphilis

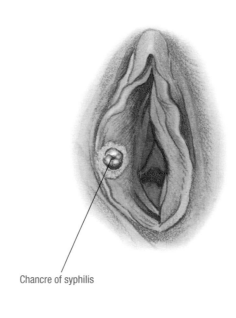

Chancre of syphilis

Mucopurulent cervicitis with chlamydia and gonorrhea

Trichomoniasis

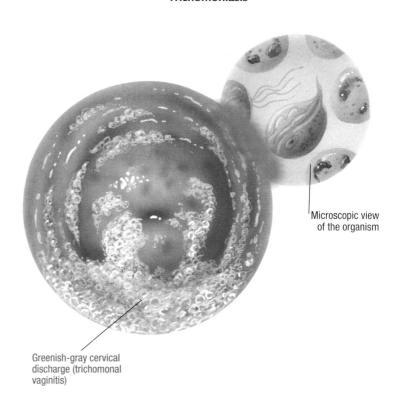

Microscopic view of the organism

Greenish-gray cervical discharge (trichomonal vaginitis)

TESTICULAR CANCER

Most testicular tumors originate in gonadal cells. About 40% are seminomas — uniform, undifferentiated cells resembling primitive gonadal cells. The remainder are nonseminomas — tumor cells showing various degrees of differentiation. The prognosis varies with the cell type and disease stage. When treated with surgery and radiation, almost all patients with localized disease survive beyond 5 years.

AGE ALERT
Malignant testicular tumors primarily affect young to middle-aged men and are the most common solid tumor in these age-groups. Incidence peaks between ages 20 and 40. Testicular tumors seldom occur in children.

Testicular cancer is rare in nonwhite males and accounts for fewer than 1% of male cancer deaths.

Causes
Primary cause unknown
Associated conditions
- Cryptorchidism (even if surgically corrected)
- Maternal use of diethylstilbestrol during pregnancy

Pathophysiology
Testicular cancer may metastasize to the lungs, liver, viscera, or bone. It spreads through the lymphatic system to the iliac, para-aortic, and mediastinal lymph nodes.

COMPLICATIONS
- Back or abdominal pain
- Lung metastasis
- Ureteral obstruction

Signs and symptoms
- Firm, painless, smooth testicular mass, varying in size and sometimes producing a sense of testicular heaviness
- Gynecomastia and nipple tenderness may result if tumor produces chorionic gonadotropin or estrogen may result
- Dull ache in the lower abdomen or back
- Lump or swelling in either testicle

In advanced stages
- Ureteral obstruction
- Abdominal mass
- Cough, hemoptysis, shortness of breath
- Weight loss
- Fatigue, pallor, lethargy

Diagnostic test results
- Scrotal ultrasound confirms the presence of a solid mass.
- Laboratory studies show elevated human corticotropin, human chorionic gonadotropin (HCG), and alfa fetoprotein (AFP) (nonseminoma) or elevated HCG and normal AFP (seminoma).
- Tissue biopsy confirms the diagnosis and stages the disease.

Treatment
Surgery
- Orchiectomy and retroperitoneal node dissection
- Hormone replacement therapy after bilateral orchiectomy
Postoperative radiation
- Seminoma — retroperitoneal and homolateral iliac nodes
- Nonseminoma — all positive nodes
- Retroperitoneal extension — mediastinal and supraclavicular nodes prophylactically
Combination chemotherapy
- Essential for tumors beyond stage 0
- Agents include bleomycin, etoposide, and cisplatin; cisplatin, vindesine, and bleomycin; cisplatin, vinblastine, and bleomycin; cisplatin, vincristine, methotrexate, bleomycin, and leucovorin
Unresponsive malignancy
- Chemotherapy and radiation
- Autologous bone marrow transplantation

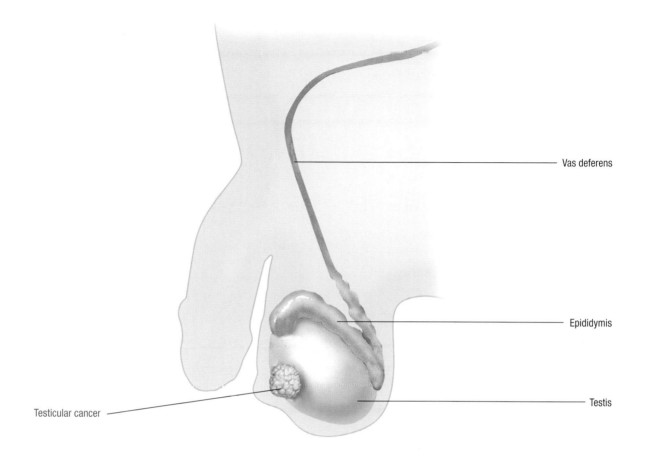

Vas deferens

Epididymis

Testis

Testicular cancer

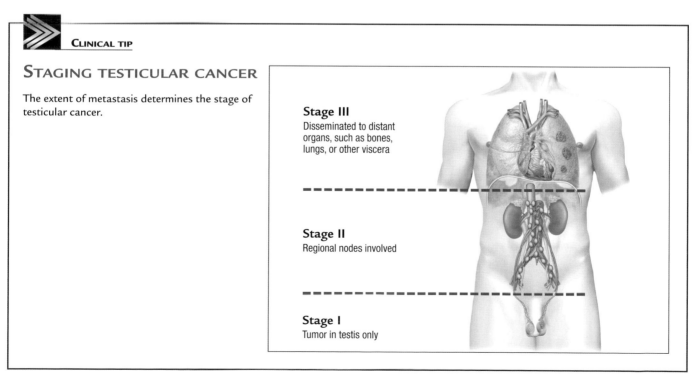

CLINICAL TIP

STAGING TESTICULAR CANCER

The extent of metastasis determines the stage of testicular cancer.

Stage III
Disseminated to distant organs, such as bones, lungs, or other viscera

Stage II
Regional nodes involved

Stage I
Tumor in testis only

TESTICULAR TORSION

Testicular torsion is an abnormal twisting of the spermatic cord due to rotation of a testis or the mesorchium; it may occur inside or outside the tunica vaginalis. Intravaginal torsion is most common in adolescents, extravaginal, in neonates. Onset may be spontaneous or follow physical exertion or trauma. Potential outcomes range from strangulation to eventual infarction of the testis without treatment. This condition is almost always (90%) unilateral.

AGE ALERT
The greatest risk of testicular torsion occurs during the neonatal period and again between ages 12 and 18 (puberty), but it may occur at any age. Infants with torsion of one testis have a greater incidence of torsion of the other testis later in life than do males in the general population. The prognosis is good with early detection and prompt treatment.

Causes
Intravaginal torsion
- Abnormality of the coverings of the testis and abnormally positioned testis
- Incomplete attachment of the testis and spermatic fascia to the scrotal wall, leaving the testis free to rotate around its vascular pedicle

Extravaginal torsion
- Loose attachment of the tunica vaginalis to the scrotal lining causing spermatic cord rotation above the testis
- Sudden forceful contraction of the cremaster muscle due to physical exertion or irritation of the muscle

Pathophysiology
Normally, the tunica vaginalis envelops the testis and attaches to the epididymis and spermatic cord. Normal contraction of the cremaster muscle causes the left testis to rotate counterclockwise, and the right, clockwise. In testicular torsion, the testis rotates on its vascular pedicle and twists the arteries and vein in the spermatic cord, interrupting blood flow to the testis. Vascular engorgement and ischemia ensue, causing scrotal swelling unrelieved by rest or elevation of the scrotum. If manual reduction is unsuccessful, torsion must be surgically corrected within 6 hours after the onset of symptoms to preserve testicular function (70% salvage rate). After 12 hours, the testis becomes dysfunctional and necrotic.

COMPLICATIONS
- Complete testicular infarction
- Testicular atrophy

Signs and symptoms
- Excruciating pain in the affected testis or iliac fossa of the pelvis
- Edematous, elevated, and ecchymotic scrotum
- Loss of the cremasteric reflex (stimulation of the skin on the inner thigh retracts the testis on the same side) on the affected side
- Abdominal pain; nausea and vomiting
- Lightheadedness

Diagnostic test results
Doppler ultrasonography distinguishes testicular torsion from strangulated hernia, undescended testes, or epididymitis (absent blood flow and avascular testis in torsion).

Treatment
- Manual manipulation of the testis counterclockwise to improve blood flow before surgery (not always possible)
- Immediate surgical repair by:
– *orchiopexy* — fixation of a viable testis to the scrotum and prophylactic fixation of the contralateral testis
– *orchiectomy* — excision of a nonviable testis to limit risk for autoimmune response to necrotic testis and its contents, damage to unaffected testis, and subsequent infertility.

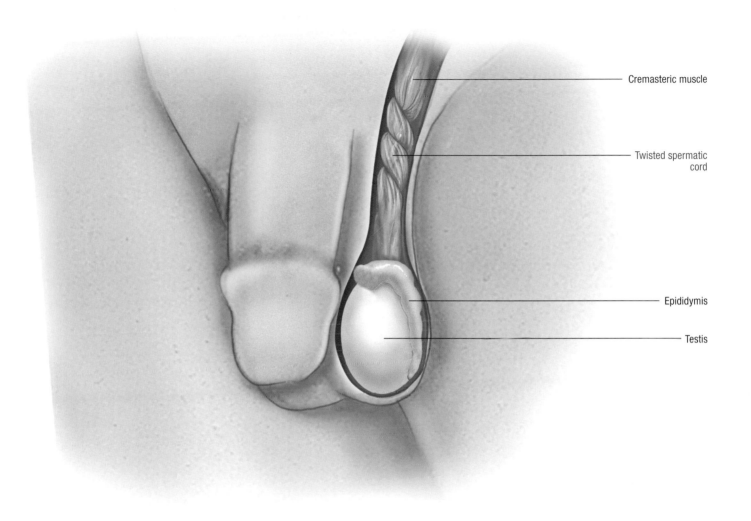

Cremasteric muscle

Twisted spermatic cord

Epididymis

Testis

VAGINITIS

Vaginitis is inflammation of the vulva (vulvitis) and vagina (vaginitis). Because of the proximity of these two structures, inflammation of one occasionally causes inflammation of the other. Vaginitis may occur at any age and affects most females at some time. The prognosis is excellent with treatment.

Causes

Vaginitis (with or without consequent vulvitis)
- *Trichomonas vaginalis*, a protozoan flagellate, usually transmitted through sexual intercourse
- *Candida albicans*, a fungus that requires glucose for growth

CLINICAL TIP
Some women are at particular risk of infection with *C. albicans*. The incidence of candidal vaginitis rises during the secretory phase of the menstrual cycle and doubles during pregnancy. The infection is also common in women with diabetes and in those who use oral contraceptives. Incidence may reach 75% in patients receiving systemic therapy with broad-spectrum antibiotics.

- *Gardnerella vaginalis*, a gram-negative bacillus

Vulvitis
- Parasite infestation, as with *Phthirus pubis* (crab louse)
- Trauma
- Poor personal hygiene
- Chemical irritants, or allergic reactions to hygiene sprays, douches, detergents, clothing, or toilet paper
- Vulvar atrophy in menopausal women due to decreasing estrogen levels
- Retention of a foreign body, such as a tampon or diaphragm

Pathophysiology

Bacterial vaginosis is caused by a disturbance of the normal vaginal flora. There's an overgrowth of anaerobic bacteria and of an organism, *Gardnerella*, with an associated loss of the normally dominant *Lactobacillus* species.

Candida albicans is normally found in small amounts in the vagina, mouth, digestive tract, and on the skin, without causing disease or symptoms. Symptoms appear when the balance between normal micro-organisms of the vagina is lost; the *C. albicans* population then becomes larger in relation to other micro-organism populations. This happens when the environment (vagina) has certain favorable conditions that allow for growth and nourishment of *C. albicans*. An environment that makes it difficult for other micro-organisms to survive may also cause an imbalance and lead to yeast infection.

Yeast infection may develop in reaction to antibiotics prescribed for another purpose. The antibiotics change the nor-

mal flora in the vagina and suppress the growth of the protective bacteria, *Lactobacillus*. Infection is common among women who use estrogen-containing birth control pills and among women who are pregnant. This is due to the increased level of estrogen in the body, causing changes in the environment that make it perfect for fungal growth and nourishment.

COMPLICATIONS
- Secondary infections
- Skin breakdown
- Edema of the perineum
- Preterm delivery and low-birth-weight babies

Signs and symptoms

T. vaginitis
- Thin, bubbly, green-tinged, malodorous discharge
- Irritation, itching; urinary symptoms, such as burning and frequency

C. albicans
- Thick, white, cottage cheese–like discharge
- Red, edematous mucous membranes, with white flecks adhering to the vaginal wall
- Intense itching

G. vaginalis
- Gray, foul, "fishy" smelling discharge

Acute vulvitis
- Mild to severe inflammatory reaction, including edema, erythema, burning, and pruritus
- Severe pain on urination, dyspareunia

Chronic vulvitis
- Relatively mild inflammation

Diagnostic test results

Microscopic examination of vaginal exudate on a wet slide preparation (a drop of vaginal exudate placed in normal saline solution) reveals the infectious organism.

Treatment

- Trichomonal vaginitis: oral metronidazole
- Candidal infection:
- topical miconazole or clotrimazole
- single dose of oral fluconazole
- *Gardnerella* infection: oral or vaginal metronidazole
- Acute vulvitis:
- cold compresses or cool sitz baths for pruritus
- warm compresses for severe inflammation
- topical corticosteroids to reduce inflammation
- Chronic vulvitis:
- topical hydrocortisone or antipruritics
- good hygiene, especially in elderly or incontinent patients
- Atrophic vulvovaginitis: topical estrogen ointment

Candida infection

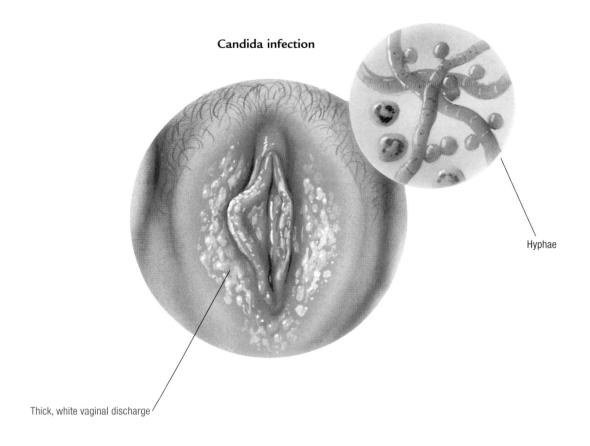

Hyphae

Thick, white vaginal discharge

Bacterial vaginosis

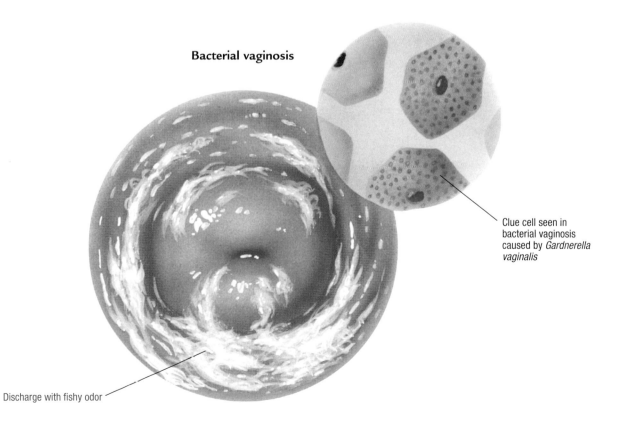

Clue cell seen in bacterial vaginosis caused by *Gardnerella vaginalis*

Discharge with fishy odor

VARICOCELE

A mass of dilated and tortuous varicose veins in the spermatic cord is called a *varicocele*. It's classically described as a "bag of worms." Thirty percent of all men diagnosed with infertility have a varicocele; 95% of cases affect the left spermatic cord.

AGE ALERT
Varicoceles are more common in men between ages 15 and 25.

Causes
● Incompetent or congenitally absent valves in spermatic veins
● Tumor or thrombus obstructing inferior vena cava (unilateral left-sided varicocele)

CLINICAL TIP
Sudden development of a varicocele in an older man may be caused by a renal tumor that has affected the renal vein and altered blood flow into the spermatic vein.

Pathophysiology
As a result of a valvular disorder in the spermatic vein, blood pools in the pampiniform plexus of veins that drain each testis rather than flowing into the venous system. One function of the pampiniform plexus is to keep the testes slightly cooler than the body temperature, which is the optimum temperature for sperm production.

COMPLICATIONS
● Testicular atrophy
● Infertility

Signs and symptoms
● Usually asymptomatic
● Feeling of heaviness on the affected side
● Testicular pain and tenderness on palpation

Diagnostic test results
None exist. A physical examination is performed.

Treatment
● Mild varicocele (fertility not a concern): scrotal support to relieve discomfort
● To retain or restore fertility, surgical repair or removal by ligation of the spermatic cord at the internal inguinal ring

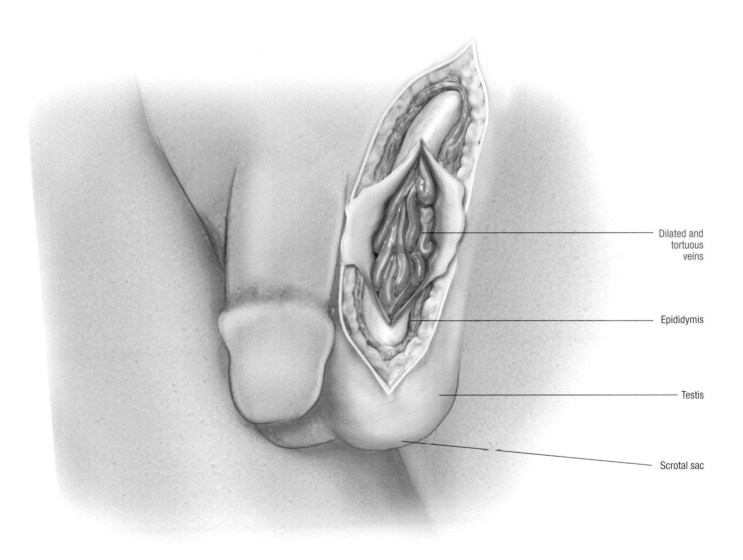

Dilated and tortuous veins

Epididymis

Testis

Scrotal sac

Vulvar cancer

Cancer of the vulva accounts for approximately 4% of all gynecologic malignancies.

AGE ALERT
Vulvar cancer can occur at any age, even in infants, but its peak incidence is after age 60.

The most common vulvar cancer is squamous cell carcinoma. Early diagnosis increases the chance of effective treatment and survival. If lymph node dissection reveals no positive nodes, 5-year survival rate is 90%; otherwise, 50% to 60%.

Causes

Primary cause unknown

Predisposing factors
- Leukoplakia (white epithelial hyperplasia), in about 25% of patients
- Chronic vulvar granulomatous disease
- Chronic pruritus of the vulva, with friction, swelling, and dryness
- Pigmented moles that are constantly irritated by clothing or perineal pads
- Irradiation of the skin such as nonspecific treatment for pelvic cancer
- Infection with human papilloma virus
- Obesity, hypertension, diabetes

Pathophysiology

Vulvar neoplasms may arise from varying cell origins. Because much of the vulva is made of skin, any type of skin cancer can develop there. The majority of vulvar cancers arise from squamous epithelial cells.

COMPLICATIONS
- Metastasis

Signs and symptoms

In 50% of patients
- Vulvar pruritus, bleeding
- Small vulvar mass — may begin as small ulcer on the surface, which eventually becomes infected and painful

Less common
- Mass in the groin
- Abnormal urination or defecation

Diagnostic test results

- Colposcopy and toluidine-blue staining identify biopsy sites.
- Histologic examination of biopsy samples confirm diagnosis and identify the type of cancer.

Treatment

Small, confined lesions with no lymph node involvement
- Simple vulvectomy or hemivulvectomy (without pelvic node dissection):
  - Personal considerations (young age of patient, active sexual life) may mandate such conservative management
  - Requires careful postoperative follow-up because it leaves the patient at risk for developing a new lesion

For widespread tumor
- Radical vulvectomy
- Radical wide local excision — can be as effective as more radical resection, but with much less morbidity
- Depending on extent of metastasis, resection may include the urethra, vagina, and bowel, leaving an open perineal wound until healing — about 2 to 3 months
- Plastic surgery, including mucocutaneous graft to reconstruct pelvic structures
- Radiation therapy

Extensive metastasis, advanced age, or fragile health
- Rules out surgery
- Palliative treatment with irradiation of the primary lesion or chemotherapy

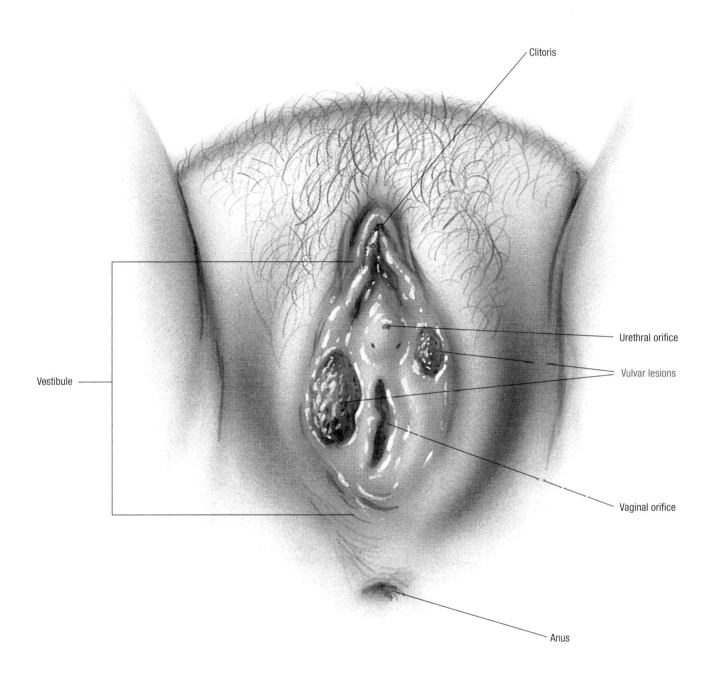

Clitoris

Urethral orifice

Vulvar lesions

Vestibule

Vaginal orifice

Anus

ACUTE RENAL FAILURE

Acute renal failure, the sudden interruption of renal function, can be caused by obstruction, poor circulation, or underlying kidney disease. It may be prerenal, intrarenal, or postrenal in origin; it usually passes through three distinct phases: oliguric, diuretic, and recovery.

Causes

Prerenal failure
- Arrhythmias, cardiac tamponade, cardiogenic shock, heart failure, myocardial infarction
- Burns, trauma, sepsis, tumor
- Dehydration, hypovolemic shock
- Diuretic overuse, antihypertensive drugs
- Hemorrhage, arterial embolism, arterial or venous thrombosis, vasculitis
- Disseminated intravascular coagulation
- Eclampsia, malignant hypertension

Intrarenal failure
- Poorly treated prerenal failure
- Nephrotoxins
- Obstetric complications
- Crush injuries
- Myopathy
- Transfusion reaction
- Acute glomerulonephritis, acute interstitial nephritis, acute pyelonephritis, bilateral renal vein thrombosis, malignant nephrosclerosis, papillary necrosis
- Polyarteritis nodosa
- Renal myeloma
- Sickle cell disease
- Systemic lupus erythematosus
- Vasculitis

Postrenal failure
- Bladder, ureteral, or urethral obstruction

Pathophysiology

Prerenal failure is caused by a condition that diminishes blood flow to the kidneys, leading to hypoperfusion. Hypoperfusion leads to hypoxemia, which can rapidly damage the kidney. The tubules are most susceptible to hypoxemia's effect. The impaired blood flow results in decreased glomerular filtration rate (GFR) and increased tubular reabsorption of sodium and water. Electrolye imbalances and metabolic acidosis result.

   Intrarenal failure, also called *intrinsic* or *parenchymal renal failure,* results from damage to the filtering structures of the kidneys. Nephrotoxicity or inflammation irreparibly damages the delicate layer under the epithelium (basement membrane). Use of nephrotoxins also causes acute renal failure because they accumulate in the renal cortex.

   Postrenal failure is a consequence of bilateral obstruction of urine outflow. The cause may be in the bladder, ureters, or urethra.

COMPLICATIONS
- Volume overload
- Acute pulmonary edema
- Hypertensive crisis
- Hyperkalemia
- Infection

Signs and symptoms
- Oliguria or anuria
- Tachycardia and hypotension
- Dry mucous membranes and flat neck veins
- Lethargy
- Cool, clammy skin

Progressive disease
- Edema
- Confusion
- GI symptoms
- Crackles
- Infection
- Seizures and coma
- Hematuria, petechiae, ecchymosis

Diagnostic test results
- Blood studies show elevated blood urea nitrogen, serum creatinine, and potassium levels; decreased bicarbonate level, hematocrit, and hemoglobin levels; and low blood pH.
- Urine studies show casts, cellular debris, and decreased specific gravity; in glomerular diseases, proteinuria and urine osmolality close to serum osmolality; urine sodium level less than 20 mEq/L if oliguria results from decreased perfusion and more than 40 mEq/L if the cause is intrarenal.
- Creatinine clearance test measures GFR and reflects the number of remaining functioning nephrons.
- Electrocardiogram (ECG) shows tall, peaked T waves; widening QRS complex; and disappearing P waves if hyperkalemia is present.
- Ultrasonography, plain films of the abdomen, kidney-ureterbladder radiography, excretory urography, renal scan, retrograde pyelography, computed tomography scans, and nephrotomography are used to investigate the cause of renal failure.

Treatment
- High-calorie diet low in protein, sodium, and potassium
- Electrolyte imbalance: I.V. fluids and electrolytes; hemodialysis or peritoneal dialysis if needed; continuous renal replacement therapies
- Edema: fluid restriction
- Oliguria: diuretic therapy
- With mild hyperkalemic symptoms (malaise, anorexia, muscle weakness): sodium polystyrene sulfonate by mouth or enema
- With severe hyperkalemic symptoms (numbness and tingling and ECG changes): hypertonic glucose, insulin, and sodium bicarbonate I.V.
- Short-term dialysis

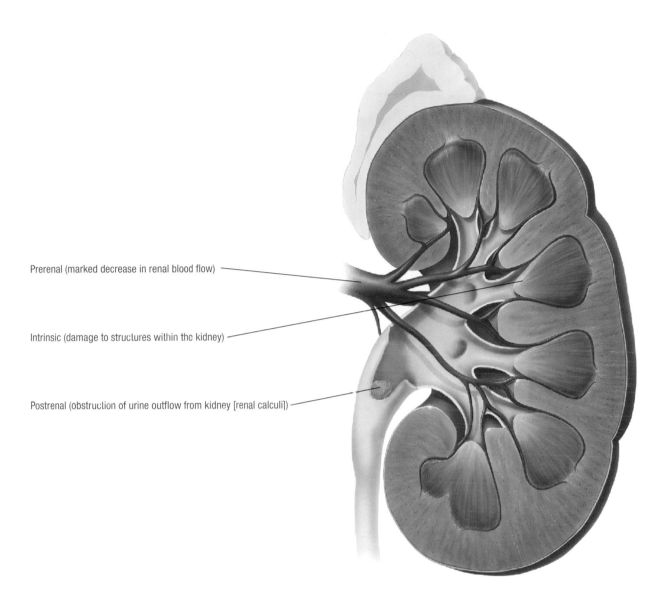

Prerenal (marked decrease in renal blood flow)

Intrinsic (damage to structures within the kidney)

Postrenal (obstruction of urine outflow from kidney [renal calculi])

ACUTE TUBULAR NECROSIS

Acute tubular necrosis, also known as *acute tubulointerstitial nephritis,* accounts for about 75% of all cases of acute renal failure and is the most common cause of acute renal failure in hospitalized patients. Acute tubular necrosis injures the tubular segment of the nephron, causing renal failure and uremic syndrome. Mortality ranges from 40% to 70%, depending on complications from underlying diseases. Nonoliguric forms of acute tubular necrosis have a better prognosis.

Causes

Acute tubular necrosis results from ischemic or nephrotoxic injury, most commonly in debilitated patients, such as the critically ill or those who have undergone extensive surgery.

Ischemic injury
- Sepsis
- Severe hypotension
- Dehydration
- Heart failure
- Surgery
- Anesthetics
- Transfusion reactions
- Burns

Nephrotoxic injury
- Certain medications such as aminoglycosides
- Contrast media

Pathophysiology

When ischemic injury occurs, the tubular cells of the kidney suffer from cellular energy depletion, intracellular accumulation of calcium, and damage to the cell membranes. Patch necrosis results at multiple points in the tubules, the basement membrane may be ruptured, and the tubular lumen may become occluded by casts and debris. If the episode of acute tubular necrosis isn't fatal, regeneration eventually will completely reverse the damage.

When nephrotoxic injury occurs, hemoglobin or myoglobin precipitates in the urine. Tubular cells are destroyed by direct toxic effects, lysis of red blood cells (RBCs), intravascular coagulation, occlusion of tubules, and tissue hypoxia. In this form of acute tubular necrosis, most necrosis occurs in the proximal tubules.

COMPLICATIONS
- Infections
- GI hemorrhage
- Fluid and electrolyte imbalances
- Cardiovascular dysfunction
- Neurologic complications

Signs and symptoms

- Early stages: effects of primary disease may mask symptoms of acute tubular necrosis
- Decreased urine output may be first recognizable effect
- Hyperkalemia
- Uremic syndrome, with oliguria (or, rarely, anuria) and confusion, which may progress to uremic coma
- Heart failure, uremic pericarditis
- Pulmonary edema, uremic lung
- Anemia
- Anorexia
- Intractable vomiting
- Poor wound healing

CLINICAL TIP

Fever and chills may signal the onset of an infection, the leading cause of death in acute tubular necrosis.

Diagnostic test results

- Urine analysis shows sediment containing RBCs and casts, low specific gravity (1.010), osmolality less than 400 mOsm/kg, and high sodium level (40 to 60 mEq/L).
- Blood studies reveal elevated blood urea nitrogen and creatinine levels, anemia, defects in platelet adherence, metabolic acidosis, and hyperkalemia.
- Electrocardiogram shows arrhythmias and, with hyperkalemia, widening QRS segment, disappearing P waves, and tall, peaked T waves.

Treatment

Acute phase
- Vigorous supportive measures until normal kidney function resumes; initial treatment may include:
  - diuretics
  - I.V. fluids to flush tubules of cellular casts and debris and to replace fluid loss

Long-term fluid management
- Daily replacement of projected and calculated losses (including insensible loss)

Other measures to control complications
- Epoetin alfa to stimulate RBC production; packed RBCs for anemia
- Antibiotics for infection
- Emergency I.V. administration of 50% glucose, regular insulin, and sodium bicarbonate for hyperkalemia
- Sodium polystyrene sulfonate with sorbitol by mouth or by enema to reduce extracellular potassium levels
- Hemodialysis
- Continuous renal replacement therapies

ISCHEMIC NECROSIS

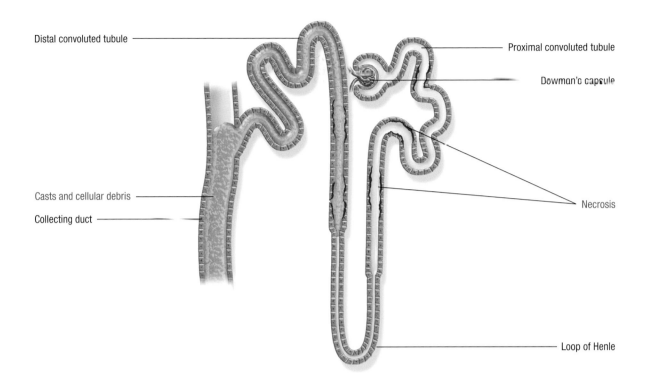

Distal convoluted tubule

Proximal convoluted tubule

Bowman's capsule

Casts and cellular debris

Collecting duct

Necrosis

Loop of Henle

NEPHROTOXIC INJURY

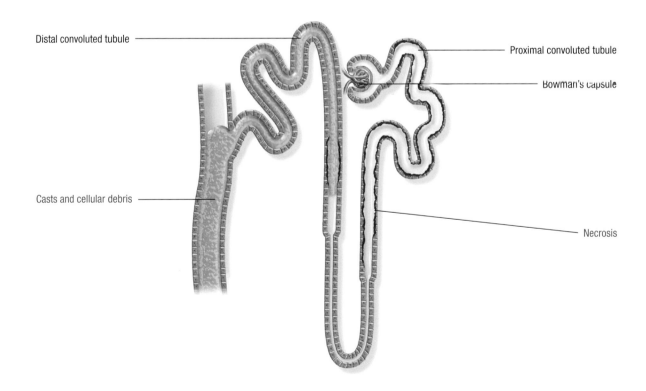

Distal convoluted tubule

Proximal convoluted tubule

Bowman's capsule

Casts and cellular debris

Necrosis

Acute tubular necrosis   **359**

BLADDER CANCER

Cancer of the bladder is the most common cancer of the urinary tract.

Workers in certain industries (rubber workers, weavers and leather finishers, aniline dye workers, hairdressers, petroleum workers, and spray painters) are at high risk for bladder cancer. The period between exposure to the carcinogen and development of symptoms is about 18 years.

AGE ALERT
Bladder tumors are most prevalent in men over age 50 and are most common in densely populated industrial areas.

Causes
Primary cause unknown
Predisposing factors
- Transitional cell tumors — certain environmental carcinogens, including 2-naphthylamine, benzidine, tobacco, nitrates
- Squamous cell carcinoma of the bladder:
– chronic bladder irritation or infection; for example, from kidney stones, indwelling urinary catheters, cystitis from cyclophosphamide
– schistosomiasis

Pathophysiology
Bladder tumors can develop on the surface of the bladder wall (benign or malignant papillomas) or grow within the bladder wall (generally more virulent) and quickly invade underlying muscles. Ninety percent of bladder tumors are transitional cell carcinomas, arising from the transitional epithelium of mucous membranes. Less common are adenocarcinomas, epidermoid carcinomas, squamous cell carcinomas, sarcomas, tumors in bladder diverticula, and carcinoma in situ.

COMPLICATIONS
- Metastasis to the bone
- Tumor invasion of contiguous viscera

Signs and symptoms
- In early stages, no symptoms in approximately 25% of patients
- First sign: gross, painless, intermittent hematuria (in many cases with clots in the urine)
- Invasive lesions: suprapubic pain after voiding
- Other signs and symptoms:
– bladder irritability, urinary frequency
– nocturia
– dribbling

Diagnostic test results
- Cystoscopy and biopsy confirm bladder cancer diagnosis.
- Excretory urography identifies a large, early-stage tumor or an infiltrating tumor; delineates functional problems in the upper urinary tract; assesses hydronephrosis; and detects rigid deformity of the bladder wall.
- Retrograde cystography evaluates bladder structure and integrity and also helps confirm bladder cancer diagnosis.
- Bone scan detects metastases.
- Computed tomography scan defines the thickness of the involved bladder wall and discloses enlarged retroperitoneal lymph nodes.
- Ultrasonography finds metastases in tissues beyond the bladder and distinguishes a bladder cyst from a bladder tumor.
- Complete blood count detects anemia.
- Urinalysis detects blood and malignant cells in the urine.

Treatment
Superficial bladder tumors
- Transurethral cystoscopic resection and fulguration (electrical destruction); adequate when the tumor hasn't invaded the muscle
- Intravesicular chemotherapy; useful for multiple tumors (especially those that occur in many sites) and to prevent tumor recurrence
- If additional tumors develop:
– fulguration every 3 months
– more radical therapy if tumors penetrate the muscle layer or recur frequently
Larger tumors
- Segmental bladder resection to remove a full-thickness section of the bladder; only if tumor isn't near the bladder neck or ureteral orifices
- Instillation of thiotepa after transurethral resection
Infiltrating bladder tumors
- Radical cystectomy — removal of the bladder with perivesical fat, lymph nodes, urethra, and prostate and seminal vesicles or uterus and adnexa
- Possibly, preoperative external beam therapy to bladder
- Urinary diversion, usually an ileal conduit (patient must then wear an external pouch continuously)
- Possible later penile implant
Advanced bladder cancer
- Cystectomy to remove tumor
- Radiation therapy
- Systemic chemotherapy:
– cyclophosphamide, fluorouracil, doxorubicin, cisplatin combination may arrest bladder cancer
– cisplatin most effective single agent
Investigational treatments
- Photodynamic therapy:
– I.V. injection of a photosensitizing agent such as hematoporphyrin ether, which malignant cells readily absorb, followed by cystoscopic laser treatment to kill malignant cells
– treatment also renders normal cells photosensitive (patient must totally avoid sunlight for about 30 days)
- Intravesicular administration of interferon alfa and tumor necrosis factor

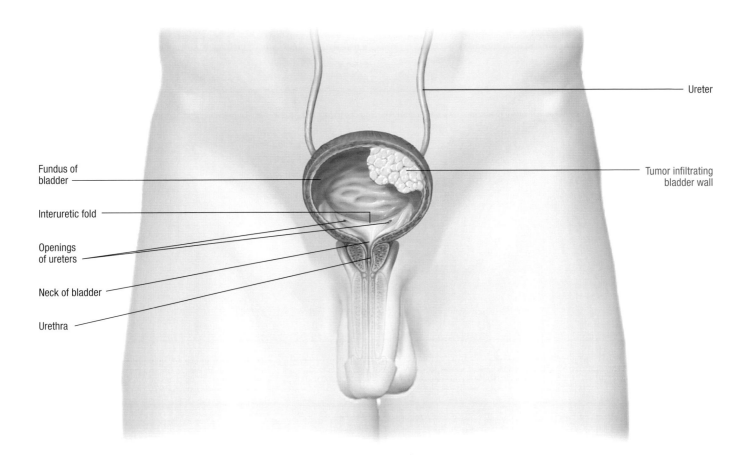

Ureter

Tumor infiltrating
bladder wall

Fundus of
bladder

Interuretic fold

Openings
of ureters

Neck of bladder

Urethra

CYSTITIS

Cystitis and urethritis, the two forms of lower urinary tract infection (UTI), are nearly 10 times more common in women than in men and affect about 10% to 20% of all women at least once. Lower UTI is also a prevalent bacterial disease in children, most commonly in girls. Men are less vulnerable because their urethras are longer and their prostatic fluid serves as an antibacterial shield. In both men and women, infection usually ascends from the urethra to the bladder. UTIs generally respond readily to treatment, but recurrence and resistant bacterial flare-up during therapy are possible.

CLINICAL TIP

All children with a proven UTI should receive a workup to exclude an abnormality of the urinary tract that would predispose them to renal damage.

Causes

Ascending infection by a single, gram-negative, enteric species of bacteria, such as *Escherichia* (commonly *E. coli*), *Klebsiella*, *Proteus, Enterobacter, Pseudomonas*, or *Serratia*

In women
● Predisposition to infection by bacteria from vagina, perineum, rectum, or a sexual partner, a possible result of a short urethra.

In men and children
● Commonly related to anatomic or physiologic abnormalities

Recurrence
● In 99% of patients, reinfection by the same organism or a new pathogen
● Persistent infection — usually from renal calculi, chronic bacterial prostatitis, or a structural anomaly that harbors bacteria

AGE ALERT

As a person ages, progressive weakening of bladder muscles may result in incomplete bladder emptying and chronic urine retention — factors that predispose the older person to bladder infections.

Pathophysiology

Infection results from a breakdown in local defense mechanisms in the bladder that allow bacteria to invade the bladder mucosa and multiply. These bacteria can't be readily eliminated by normal micturition.

COMPLICATIONS

● Chronic UTIs
● Damage to the urinary tract lining
● Infection of adjacent organs such as the kidneys (pyelonephritis)

Signs and symptoms

● Urgency, frequency, dysuria
● Cramps or spasms of the bladder
● Itching, feeling of warmth or burning during urination
● Nocturia
● Urethral discharge in males
● Hematuria
● Fever, chills
● Other common features:
– malaise
– nausea, vomiting
– low back pain, flank pain
– abdominal pain, tenderness over the bladder area

Diagnostic test results

● Microscopic urinalysis is positive for pyuria, hematuria, or bacteriuria.
● Bacterial count in clean-catch midstream urine specimen reveals more than 100,000 bacteria per milliliter.
● Sensitivity testing determines the appropriate therapeutic antimicrobial agent.
● Blood test or stained smear of the discharge rules out sexually transmitted disease.
● Voiding cystoureterography or excretory urography detects congenital anomalies that predispose the patient to recurrent UTIs.

Treatment

● Appropriate antimicrobials:
– single-dose therapy with amoxicillin or co-trimoxazole may be effective in women with acute noncomplicated UTI
● If urine isn't sterile after 3 days:
– bacterial resistance likely
– use of a different antimicrobial necessary
● Sitz baths or warm compresses
● Increased fluid intake
● Phenazopyridine hydrochloride (Pyridium)

Recurrent infections
● Infected renal calculi, chronic prostatitis, or structural abnormality — possible surgery
● Prostatitis — long-term antibiotic therapy
● In absence of predisposing conditions — long-term, low-dose antibiotic therapy

Bladder

Cystitis

Urethra

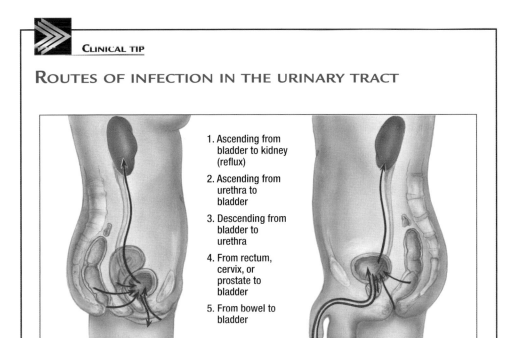

CLINICAL TIP

ROUTES OF INFECTION IN THE URINARY TRACT

1. Ascending from bladder to kidney (reflux)

2. Ascending from urethra to bladder

3. Descending from bladder to urethra

4. From rectum, cervix, or prostate to bladder

5. From bowel to bladder

Bladder wall — Endoscopic view

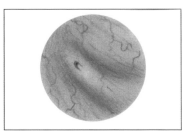

Normal wall

Acute cystitis

GLOMERULONEPHRITIS

Glomerulonephritis is a bilateral inflammation of the glomeruli, commonly following a streptococcal infection. Acute glomerulonephritis is also called *acute poststreptococcal glomerulonephritis.*

AGE ALERT

Acute glomerulonephritis is most common in boys ages 3 to 7 but can occur at any age. Rapidly progressive glomerulonephritis most commonly occurs between ages 50 and 60. Up to 95% of children and 70% of adults recover fully. Elderly patients may progress to chronic renal failure within months.

Rapidly progressive glomerulonephritis — also called subacute, crescentic, or extracapillary glomerulonephritis — may be idiopathic or associated with a proliferative glomerular disease such as poststreptococcal glomerulonephritis.

Chronic glomerulonephritis is a slowly progressive disease characterized by inflammation, sclerosis, scarring and, eventually, renal failure. It usually remains undetected until the progressive (irreversible) phase.

Causes

Acute or rapidly progressive glomerulonephritis
- Streptococcal infection of the respiratory tract
- Immunoglobulin A nephropathy (Berger's disease)
- Impetigo
- Lipoid nephrosis

Chronic glomerulonephritis
- Membranoproliferative glomerulonephritis
- Membranous glomerulopathy
- Focal glomerulosclerosis
- Rapidly progressive glomerulonephritis, poststreptococcal glomerulonephritis
- Systemic lupus erythematosus, Goodpasture's syndrome
- Hemolytic uremic syndrome

Pathophysiology

In nearly all types of glomerulonephritis, the epithelial or podocyte layer of the glomerular membrane is damaged.

Acute poststreptococcal glomerulonephritis results from the entrapment and collection of antigen-antibody complexes, also known as immune complexes, in the glomerular capillary membranes, after infection with a group A beta-hemolytic streptococcus. The antigens, which are endogenous or exogenous, stimulate the formation of antibodies, which form immune complexes. Circulating immune complexes become lodged in the glomerular capillaries. The severity of glomerular damage and consequent renal insufficiency is related to the size, number, location (focal or diffuse), duration of exposure, and type of immune complexes.

In the glomerular capillary wall, immune complexes activate biochemical mediators of inflammation — complement, leukocytes, and fibrin. Activated complement attracts neutrophils and monocytes, which release lysosomal enzymes that damage the cell walls and cause a proliferation of the extracellular matrix, affecting glomerular blood flow. Those events in-

crease membrane permeability, which causes a loss of negative charge across the glomerular membrane and enhanced protein filtration. Membrane damage also leads to platelet aggregation, and platelet degranulation releases substances that increase glomerular permeability.

Protein molecules and red blood cells (RBCs) can now pass into the urine, resulting in proteinuria or hematuria. Activation of the coagulation system leads to fibrin deposits in Bowman's space. The result is formation of crescent-shaped blood cells and diminished renal blood flow and glomerular filtration rate. The presence of crescents signifies severe, often irreversible kidney damage. Glomerular bleeding acidifies the urine and thereby transforms hemoglobin to methemoglobin; the result is brown urine without clots.

COMPLICATIONS
- End-stage renal failure
- Cardiac hypertrophy
- Heart failure

Signs and symptoms
- Decreased urination; smoky or coffee-colored urine
- Shortness of breath, dyspnea, orthopnea, bibasilar crackles
- Periorbital and peripheral edema
- Mild to severe hypertension

Diagnostic test results
- Blood studies reveal elevated blood urea nitrogen and creatinine levels; decreased serum protein levels; decreased hemoglobin; elevated antistreptolysin-O titers in 80% of patients; elevated streptozyme (a hemagglutination test that detects antibodies to several streptococcal antigens) and anti-DNase B (a test to determine a previous infection of group A beta-hemolytic streptococcus) titers; and low serum complement levels indicate recent streptococcal infection.
- Urinalysis reveals RBCs, white blood cells, mixed cells casts, and protein.
- Throat culture detects group A beta-hemolytic streptococcus.
- Kidney-ureter-bladder X-ray shows bilateral kidney enlargement (acute glomerulonephritis).
- Renal biopsy confirms the diagnosis or assesses renal tissue.

Treatment
- Treatment for primary disease, antibiotics for infections
- Bed rest to reduce metabolic demands
- Fluid and dietary sodium restriction, correction of electrolyte imbalances
- Loop diuretics for extracellular fluid overload
- Vasodilators (hydralazine or nifedipine) for hypertension
- Corticosteroids to decrease antibody synthesis and suppress inflammatory response
- In rapidly progressive glomerulonephritis, plasmapheresis to suppress rebound antibody production, possibly combined with corticosteroids and cyclophosphamide
- In chronic glomerulonephritis, dialysis or kidney transplantation

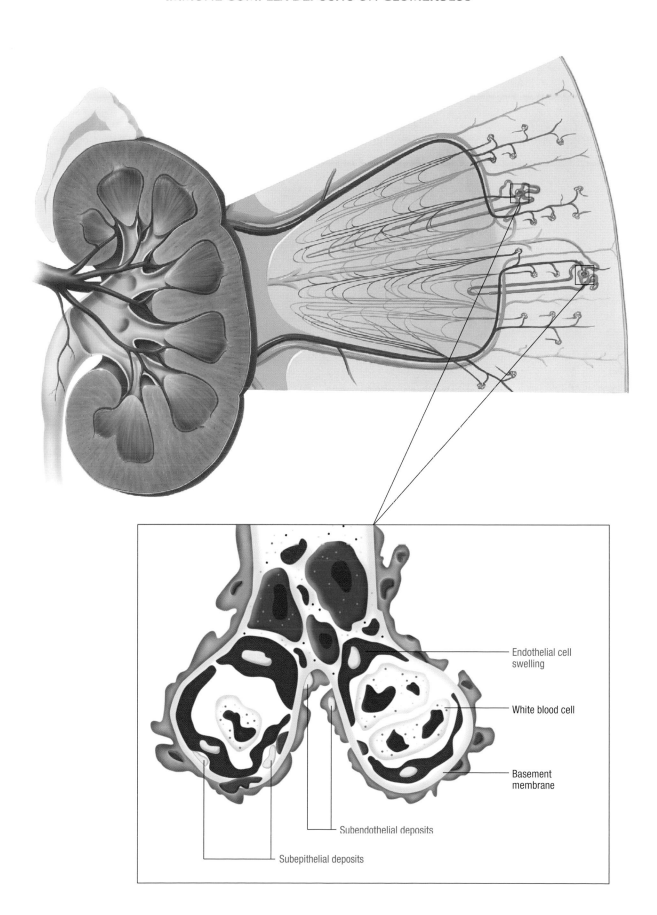

Endothelial cell swelling

White blood cell

Basement membrane

Subendothelial deposits

Subepithelial deposits

HYDRONEPHROSIS

Hydronephrosis is an abnormal dilation of the renal pelvis and the calyces of one or both kidneys, caused by an obstruction of urine flow in the genitourinary tract. Although partial obstruction and hydronephrosis may not produce symptoms initially, the pressure built up behind the area of obstruction eventually results in symptomatic renal dysfunction.

 AGE ALERT
Hydronephrosis may be detected by prenatal ultrasound. Postnatal follow-up is critical.

Causes
- Obstructive uropathy
- Most common:
- benign prostatic hyperplasia
- urethral strictures
- calculi
- Less common:
- strictures or stenosis of the ureter or bladder outlet
- congenital abnormalities
- trauma
- abdominal tumors
- blood clots
- neurogenic bladder

Pathophysiology
If obstruction is in the urethra or bladder, hydronephrosis is usually bilateral; if obstruction is in a ureter, it's usually unilateral. Obstructions distal to the bladder cause the bladder to dilate and act as a buffer zone, delaying hydronephrosis. Total obstruction of urine flow with dilation of the collecting system ultimately causes complete cortical atrophy and cessation of glomerular filtration.

 COMPLICATIONS
- Pyelonephritis
- Paralytic ileus
- Renal failure

Signs and symptoms
Clinical features of hydronephrosis vary with the cause of the obstruction.
- No symptoms, or mild pain and slightly decreased urinary flow
- Severe, colicky renal pain or dull flank pain that may radiate to the groin
- Gross urinary abnormalities, such as hematuria, pyuria, dysuria, alternating oliguria and polyuria, or complete anuria
- Nausea, vomiting, abdominal fullness, pain on urination, dribbling, hesitancy

Diagnostic test results
- Renal function blood studies are abnormal.
- Urine studies confirm the inability to concentrate urine, decreased glomerular filtration rate, and pyuria if infection is present.
- Excretory urography, retrograde pyelography, and renal ultrasound confirm the diagnosis.
- I.V. urogram detects the site of obstruction.
- Nephrogram shows delayed appearance time.
- Radionuclide scan shows the site of obstruction.

Treatment
- Ureteral stent or nephrostomy tube
- Surgical removal of the obstruction:
- dilation for stricture of the urethra
- prostatectomy for benign prostatic hyperplasia
- With renal damage: diet low in protein, sodium, and potassium to slow progression before surgery
- Inoperable obstructions: decompression and drainage of kidney through temporary or permanent nephrostomy tube in the renal pelvis
- Concurrent infection: appropriate antibiotic therapy

Hydronephrotic kidney

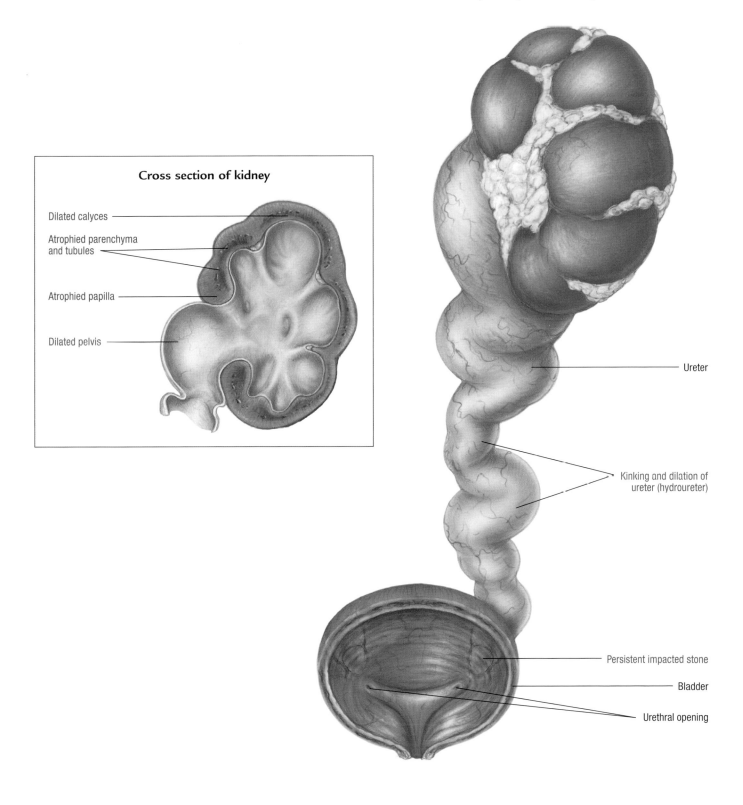

Cross section of kidney

Dilated calyces

Atrophied parenchyma and tubules

Atrophied papilla

Dilated pelvis

Ureter

Kinking and dilation of ureter (hydroureter)

Persistent impacted stone

Bladder

Urethral opening

NEUROGENIC BLADDER

Neurogenic bladder is any type of bladder dysfunction caused by an interruption of normal bladder innervation by the nervous system. It can be hyperreflexic (hypertonic, spastic, or automatic) or flaccid (hypotonic, atonic, or autonomous).

Causes

Once thought to result primarily from spinal cord injury; now appears to stem from several underlying conditions:
- cerebral disorders, such as stroke, brain tumor, Parkinson's disease, multiple sclerosis, dementia, and incontinence associated with aging
- spinal cord disease or trauma, such as spinal stenosis or arachnoiditis
- disorders of peripheral innervation, including autonomic neuropathies resulting from endocrine disturbances such as diabetes mellitus
- metabolic disturbances such as hypothyroidism
- acute inflammatory demyelinating diseases such as Guillain-Barré syndrome
- heavy metal toxicity
- chronic alcoholism
- collagen diseases such as systemic lupus erythematosus
- vascular diseases such as atherosclerosis
- distant effects of certain cancers such as primary oat cell carcinoma of the lung
- herpes zoster
- sacral agenesis.

Pathophysiology

An upper motor neuron lesion (at or above T12) causes spastic neurogenic bladder, with spontaneous contraction of the detrusor muscles, increased intravesical voiding pressure, bladder wall hypertrophy with trabeculation, and urinary sphincter spasms. The patient may experience incomplete emptying and loss of voluntary control of voiding. Urine retention can also lead to urinary tract infection (UTI).

A lower motor neuron lesion (at or below S2 to S4) affects the spinal reflex that controls micturition. The result is a flaccid neurogenic bladder with decreased intravesical pressure, increased bladder capacity and residual urine retention, and poor detrusor contraction. The bladder may not empty spontaneously. The patient experiences loss of voluntary and involuntary control of urination. Lower motor neuron lesions lead to overflow incontinence. When sensory neurons are interrupted, the patient can't perceive the need to void.

Interruption of the efferent nerves at the cortical or upper motor neuron level results in loss of voluntary control. Higher centers also control micturition, resulting in incomplete voiding. Sensory neuron interruption leads to dribbling and overflow incontinence, and altered bladder sensation often makes symptoms difficult to discern.

Urine retention contributes to renal calculi and infection. If not promptly diagnosed and treated, neurogenic bladder can lead to the deterioration of renal function.

COMPLICATIONS
- Incontinence
- Residual urine retention
- UTI
- Calculus formation
- Renal failure

Signs and symptoms

General
- Some degree of incontinence
- Interruption or changes in initiation of micturition
- Inability to completely empty the bladder
- History of frequent UTIs
- Vesicoureteral reflux
- Hydroureteral nephrosis

Spastic neurogenic bladder
- Involuntary or frequent scanty urination without a feeling of bladder fullness
- Increased anal sphincter tone
- Increased tactile stimulation of the abdomen, thighs, or genitalia possibly precipitating voiding

Flaccid neurogenic bladder
- Overflow incontinence
- Diminished anal sphincter tone
- Greatly distended bladder (evident on palpation or percussion) but with the patient possibly not experiencing the feeling of bladder fullness because of sensory impairment

Diagnostic test results
- Uroflow shows diminished or impaired flow.
- Cystometry evaluates the bladder's nerve supply, detrusor muscle tone, and intravesical pressures during bladder filling and contraction.
- Urethral pressure profile determines urethral function by examining urethral length and outlet pressure resistance.
- Sphincter electromyography correlates the neuromuscular function of the external sphincter with bladder muscle function during bladder filling and contraction, indicating how well the bladder and urinary sphincter muscles work together.
- Videourodynamic studies correlate visual documentation of bladder function with pressure studies.

Treatment
- Treatment goals: maintain the integrity of the upper urinary tract, control infection, and prevent urinary incontinence through evacuation of the bladder, drug therapy, surgery or, less often, nerve blocks and electrical stimulation
- Bladder evacuation techniques, such as Credé's method, Valsalva's maneuver, and intermittent self-catheterization
- Bethanechol or phenoxybenzamine to promote bladder emptying; propantheline, methantheline, flavoxate, dicyclomine, imipramine, or pseudoephedrine to aid urine storage
- When conservative treatment fails, surgery to correct structural impairment: transurethral resection of the bladder neck, urethral dilation, external sphincterotomy, or urinary diversion procedures; if permanent incontinence follows surgery, possible implantation of an artificial urinary sphincter

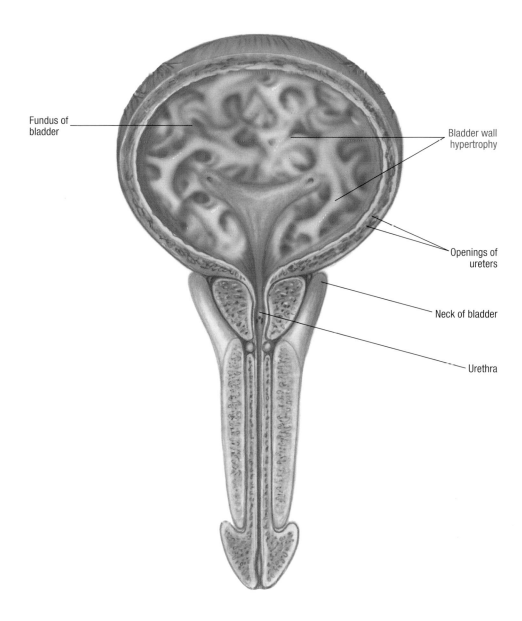

Fundus of bladder

Bladder wall hypertrophy

Openings of ureters

Neck of bladder

Urethra

Polycystic kidney disease

Polycystic kidney disease is an inherited disorder characterized by multiple, bilateral, grapelike clusters of fluid-filled cysts that enlarge the kidneys, compressing and eventually replacing functioning renal tissue. The disease affects males and females equally and appears in distinct infantile and adult-onset forms. The adult form, autosomal dominant polycystic kidney disease, occurs in nearly 1 in 1,000 persons and accounts for about 10% of end-stage renal disease in the United States. Autosomal recessive polycystic kidney disease occurs in 1 in 10,000 to 1 in 40,000 live births. Renal deterioration is more gradual in adults than infants, but in both age-groups, the disease progresses relentlessly to fatal uremia.

AGE ALERT
The rare infantile form of polycystic kidney disease causes stillbirth or early neonatal death due to pulmonary hypoplasia. The adult form has an insidious onset. It usually becomes obvious between ages 30 and 50; rarely, it remains asymptomatic until the patient is in his 70s.

The prognosis in adults is extremely variable. Progression may be slow, even after symptoms of renal insufficiency appear. After uremia symptoms develop, polycystic disease usually is fatal within 4 years, unless the patient receives dialysis.

Causes
- Autosomal dominant trait (adult type); three genetic variants identified
- Autosomal recessive trait (infantile type)

Pathophysiology
Grossly enlarged kidneys are caused by multiple spherical cysts, a few millimeters to centimeters in diameter, that contain straw-colored or hemorrhagic fluid. The cysts are distributed evenly throughout the cortex and medulla. Hyperplastic polyps and renal adenomas are common. Renal parenchyma may have varying degrees of tubular atrophy, interstitial fibrosis, and nephrosclerosis. The cysts cause elongation of the pelvis, flattening of the calyces, and indentations in the kidney.

Accompanying hepatic fibrosis and intrahepatic bile duct abnormalities may cause portal hypertension and bleeding varices. In most cases, about 10 years after symptoms appear, progressive compression of kidney structures by the enlarging mass causes renal failure.

Cysts also form on the liver, spleen, pancreas, or ovaries. Intracranial aneurysms, colonic diverticula, and mitral valve prolapse also occur.

COMPLICATIONS
In neonates
- Renal failure
- Respiratory failure
- Heart failure

In adults
- Hematuria
- Retroperitoneal bleeding from cyst rupture
- Proteinuria
- Abdominal pain from passage of clots or calculi
- Mitral valve prolapse
- Colonic diverticuli
- Subarachnoid hemorrhage

Signs and symptoms
In neonates
- Potter facies — pronounced epicanthic folds; pointed nose; small chin; floppy, low-set ears
- Huge, bilateral, symmetrical masses on the flanks that are tense and can't be transilluminated
- Signs of respiratory distress, heart failure and, eventually, uremia and renal failure

In adults
- Hypertension
- Headache
- Lumbar pain
- Widening abdominal girth
- Swollen or tender abdomen, worsened by exertion and relieved by lying down
- Grossly enlarged kidneys on palpation

Diagnostic test results
- Excretory or retrograde urography shows enlarged kidneys, with elongation of the pelvis, flattening of the calyces, and indentations in the kidney caused by cysts.
- Excretory urography of the neonate shows poor excretion of contrast medium.
- Ultrasonography, tomography, and radioisotope scans show kidney enlargement and cysts; tomography, computed tomography, and magnetic resonance imaging show multiple areas of cystic damage.
- Urinalysis detects hematuria, bacteriuria, or proteinuria.
- Creatinine clearance tests show renal insufficiency or failure.

Treatment
- Antibiotics for infections
- Analgesics for abdominal pain
- Adequate hydration to maintain fluid balance
- Antihypertensives, diuretics to control blood pressure
- Changes in diet and exercise
- Surgical drainage of cystic abscess or retroperitoneal bleeding
- Nephrectomy not recommended (polycystic kidney disease occurs bilaterally, and infection could recur in the remaining kidney)
- Dialysis or kidney transplantation for progressive renal failure

Cross section

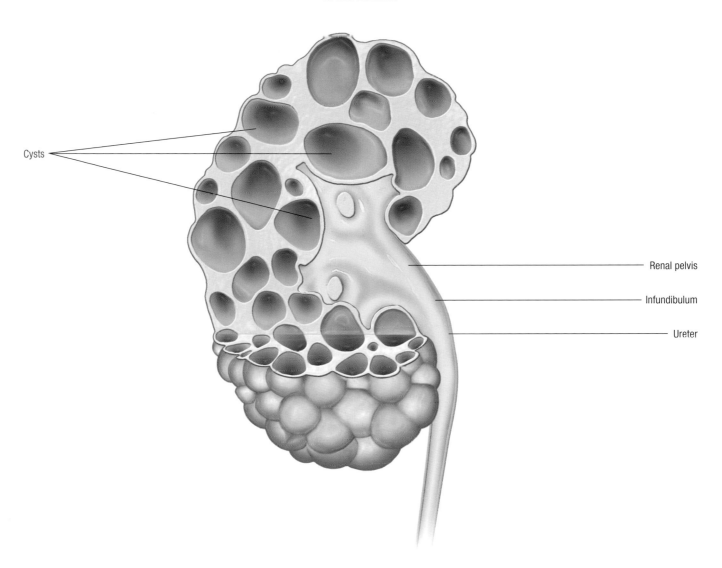

Cysts

Renal pelvis

Infundibulum

Ureter

PYELONEPHRITIS

Acute pyelonephritis (also known as *acute infective tubulointerstitial nephritis*) is a sudden inflammation caused by bacterial infection; it primarily affects the interstitial area and the renal pelvis or, less often, the renal tubules. It's one of the most common renal diseases. Symptoms characteristically develop rapidly over a few hours or days and may disappear within days, even without treatment. However, residual bacterial infection is likely and may cause symptoms to recur later. With treatment and continued follow-up care, the prognosis is good and extensive permanent damage is rare.

Causes

Acute pyelonephritis results from bacterial infection of the kidneys. Infecting bacteria usually are normal intestinal and fecal flora that grow readily in urine. The most common causative organism is *Escherichia coli*, but *Proteus* or *Pseudomonas* species, *Staphylococcus aureus*, or *Enterococcus faecalis* (formerly *Streptococcus faecalis*) may also cause this infection.

CLINICAL TIP
Emphysematous pyelonephritis is an uncommon disorder seen in patients with diabetes or those who are immunocompromised. It's caused by a gas-forming organism such as *E. coli*, which produces gas that forms in the renal parenchyma or perirenal space. This life-threatening condition requires aggressive medical management or nephrectomy.

CLINICAL TIP
Pyelonephritis occurs more commonly in females, probably because bacteria reach the bladder more easily through the short female urethra; the urinary meatus is in close proximity to the vagina and the rectum, and women lack the male's antibacterial prostatic secretions.

Pathophysiology

Typically, the infection spreads from the bladder to the ureters, then to the kidneys, as in vesicoureteral reflux. Vesicoureteral reflux may result from congenital weakness at the junction of the ureter and the bladder. Bacteria refluxed to intrarenal tissues may create colonies of infection within 24 to 48 hours. Infection may also result from instrumentation (such as catheterization, cystoscopy, or urologic surgery), a hematogenic infection (as in septicemia or endocarditis), or possibly lymphatic infection.

Pyelonephritis may also result from an inability to empty the bladder (for example, in patients with neurogenic bladder), urinary stasis, or urinary obstruction due to tumors, strictures, or benign prostatic hyperplasia.

COMPLICATIONS
- Chronic pyelonephritis
- Acute renal failure
- Sepsis

Signs and symptoms
- Urgency, frequency, nocturia
- Burning during urination, dysuria
- Hematuria, usually microscopic but may be gross
- Cloudy urine, ammonia-like or fishy odor
- Fever of 102° F (38.9° C) or higher, shaking chills
- Flank pain
- Anorexia
- General fatigue

AGE ALERT
Elderly patients may exhibit GI or pulmonary symptoms rather than the usual febrile responses to pyelonephritis.
In children younger than age 2, fever, vomiting, nonspecific abdominal complaints, or failure to thrive may be the only signs of acute pyelonephritis.

Diagnostic test results
- Urine sediment reveals the presence of leukocytes singly, in clumps, and in casts and, possibly, a few red blood cells.
- Urine culture reveals more than 100,000 organisms/μl of urine.
- Urinalysis reveals low specific gravity and osmolality, proteinuria, glycosuria, and ketonuria.
- Urine pH testing shows a slightly alkaline pH.
- Computed tomography scan of the kidneys, ureters, and bladder reveals calculi, tumors, or cysts in the kidneys and the urinary tract.
- Excretory urography shows asymmetrical kidneys.

Treatment
Antibiotic therapy appropriate to the specific infecting organism after identification by urine culture and sensitivity studies:
- *Enterococcus* — ampicillin, penicillin G, vancomycin
- *Staphylococcus* — penicillin G; if resistance develops, a semisynthetic penicillin, such as nafcillin, or a cephalosporin
- *E. coli* — sulfisoxazole, nalidixic acid, nitrofurantoin
- *Proteus* — ampicillin, sulfisoxazole, nalidixic acid, a cephalosporin
- *Pseudomonas* — gentamicin, tobramycin, carbenicillin
- Not identified — broad-spectrum antibiotic, such as ampicillin or cephalexin
- Pregnancy or renal insufficiency — antibiotics prescribed cautiously

Follow-up
- Urine culture repeated 1 week after drug therapy stops, then periodically for the next year

Infection from obstruction or vesicoureteral reflux
- Antibiotics possibly less effective
- Surgery to relieve the obstruction or correct the anomaly

Patients at high risk for recurring urinary tract and kidney infections
- Prolonged use of an indwelling catheter or maintenance antibiotic therapy
- Long-term follow-up to prevent chronic pyelonephritis

3. End phase

2. Progressive phase

Progressive
scarring

Atrophied
parenchyma

**Acute pyelonephritis
and progressive scarring
from repeated infection**

Focal
parenchyma
scarring

Narrowed
calyx neck

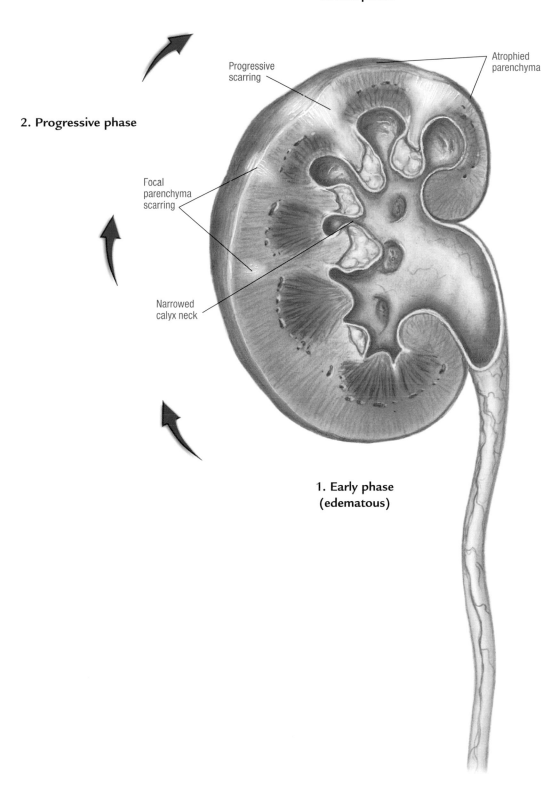

**1. Early phase
(edematous)**

RENAL CALCULI

Renal calculi, or stones (nephrolithiasis), can form anywhere in the urinary tract, although they most commonly develop on the renal pelves or calyces. They may vary in size and may be single or multiple.

AGE ALERT
Renal calculi are more common in men than women and rarely occur in children. Calcium stones generally occur in middle-aged men with a familial history of stone formation.

Causes
Exact cause unknown
Predisposing factors
- Dehydration
- Infection
- Changes in urine pH (calcium carbonate stones, high pH; uric acid stones, lower pH)
- Obstruction to urine flow leading to stasis in the urinary tract
- Immobilization causing bone reabsorption
- Metabolic factors, such as hyperparathyroidism, renal tubular acidosis, elevated uric acid, defective oxalate metabolism
- Dietary factors such as increased intake of calcium or of oxalate-rich foods
- Renal disease

Pathophysiology
Calculi form when substances that are normally dissolved in the urine, such as calcium oxalate and calcium phosphate, precipitate. Dehydration may lead to renal calculi as calculus-forming substances concentrate in urine.

Stones form around a nucleus or nidus in the appropriate environment. A stone-forming substance (calcium oxalate, calcium carbonate, magnesium, ammonium, phosphate, uric acid, or cystine) forms a crystal that becomes trapped in the urinary tract, where it attracts other crystals to form a stone. A high urine saturation of these substances encourages crystal formation and results in stone growth. The pH of the urine affects the solubility of many stone-forming substances. Formation of calcium oxalate and cystine stones is independent of urine pH. Most stones are calcium oxalate or a combination of oxalate and phosphate.

Stones may form in the papillae, renal tubules, calyces, renal pelves, ureter, or bladder. Most are less than 5 mm in diameter and are usually passed in the urine. Staghorn calculi (casts of the calyceal and pelvic collecting system) can continue to grow in the pelvis, extending to the calyces, forming a branching stone, and ultimately resulting in renal failure if not surgically removed.

Calcium stones are the smallest. Although 80% are idiopathic, they frequently occur in patients with hyperuricosuria. Prolonged immobilization can lead to bone demineralization, hypercalciuria, and stone formation. In addition, hyperparathyroidism, renal tubular acidosis, and excessive intake of vitamin D or dietary calcium may predispose a person to renal calculi.

Struvite (magnesium, ammonium, and phosphate) stones are often precipitated by an infection, particularly with *Pseudomonas* or *Proteus* species. These urea-splitting organisms are more common in women. Struvite calculi can destroy renal parenchyma.

COMPLICATIONS
- Hydronephrosis
- Damage to renal parenchyma

Signs and symptoms
- Severe pain from obstruction
- Nausea and vomiting
- Fever and chills from infection
- Hematuria when calculi abrade a ureter
- Abdominal distention
- Anuria from bilateral obstruction or obstruction of only kidney

Diagnostic test results
- Kidney-ureter-bladder (KUB) radiography shows most renal calculi.
- Excretory urography confirms the diagnosis and determines the size and location of calculi.
- Kidney ultrasonography detects such obstructive changes as unilateral or bilateral hydronephrosis and radiolucent calculi not seen on KUB radiography.
- Urine culture shows pyuria.
- A 24-hour urine collection determines levels of calcium oxalate, phosphorus, and uric acid excretion.
- Calculus analysis determines mineral content.
- Serial blood calcium and phosphorus levels diagnose hyperparathyroidism.
- Blood protein levels determine the level of free calcium unbound to protein.

Treatment
- Fluid intake greater than 3 L/day to promote hydration
- Antimicrobial agents; vary with the cultured organism
- Narcotic analgesics or nonsteroidal anti-inflammatory drugs
- Diuretics to prevent urinary stasis and further calculus formation; thiazides to decrease calcium excretion
- Acetohydroxamic acid to suppress calculus formation when infection is present
- Cystoscopy and manipulation of calculus to remove stones too large for natural passage
- Percutaneous ultrasonic lithotripsy and extracorporeal shock wave lithotripsy or laser therapy to shatter the calculus into fragments for removal by suction or natural passage
- Surgical removal of cystine calculi or large stones
- Placement of urinary diversion around the stone
Type-specific treatment
- Low-calcium diet
- Oxalate-binding cholestyramine
- Allopurinol for uric acid calculi
- Daily small doses of ascorbic acid to acidify urine

Uric acid stones

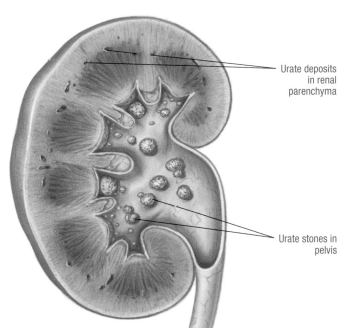

Urate deposits
in renal
parenchyma

Urate stones in
pelvis

Ammoniomagnesium phosphate (struvite) stones

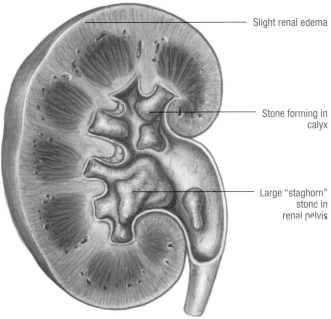

Slight renal edema

Stone forming in
calyx

Large "staghorn"
stone in
renal pelvis

Calcium stones

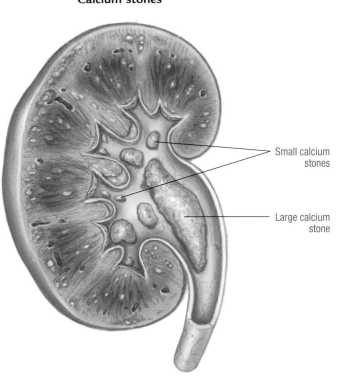

Small calcium
stones

Large calcium
stone

RENAL CANCER

Renal cancer (nephrocarcinoma, renal cell carcinoma, hypernephroma, or Grawitz's tumor) usually occurs in older adults. Although the incidence of this malignancy is rising, it accounts for only about 2% of all adult cancers. Most renal tumors are metastases from primary cancer sites. Renal pelvic tumors and Wilms' tumor occur primarily in children. Kidney tumors are large, firm, nodular, encapsulated, unilateral, and solitary; they're classified histologically as clear-cell, granular, or spindle-cell tumors.

Causes

Primary cause unknown

Predisposing factors

- Tobacco use
- Environmental toxins
- Analgesic abuse
- Advancing age

AGE ALERT
Renal cancer is more common in men than in women and peaks in incidence between ages 50 and 70.

Pathophysiology

Renal cancers arise from tubular epithelium and can occur anywhere in the kidney. The tumor margins are usually clearly defined, and the tumors can include areas of ischemia, necrosis, and focal hemorrhage. Tumor cells vary from well differentiated to very anaplastic.

COMPLICATIONS
- Hemorrhage
- Metastases to the lungs, brain, and liver

Signs and symptoms

Classic clinical triad

- Hematuria — microscopic or gross; may be intermittent; suggests spread to renal pelvis
- Pain — constant abdominal or flank pain (may be dull); if cancer causes bleeding or blood clots, acute and colicky

- Palpable mass — generally smooth, firm, and nontender
- All three present in only about 10% of patients

Other signs

- Fever
- Hypertension
- Rapidly progressing hypercalcemia
- Urine retention, edema in the legs
- Nausea, vomiting, weight loss

Diagnostic test results

- Computed tomography scan, I.V. and retrograde pyelography, ultrasound, cystoscopy (to rule out associated bladder cancer) and nephrotomography, and renal angiography identify the presence of the tumor and help differentiate it from a cyst.
- Liver function tests show increased levels of alkaline phosphatase, bilirubin, alanine aminotransferase, and aspartate aminotransferase.
- Prothrombin time is prolonged.
- Urinalysis reveals gross or microscopic hematuria.
- Complete blood count shows anemia, polycythemia, and increased erythrocyte sedimentation rate.
- Serum calcium levels are elevated.

Treatment

- Radical nephrectomy, with or without regional lymph node dissection — the only chance of cure
- High-dose radiation — used only if the cancer spreads to the perinephric region or the lymph nodes or if the primary tumor or metastatic sites can't be fully excised
- Chemotherapy — results usually poor against kidney cancer
- Biotherapy (interferon and interleukins) — commonly used in advanced disease; has produced few durable remissions
- Hormone therapy
- Pain control (analgesics)

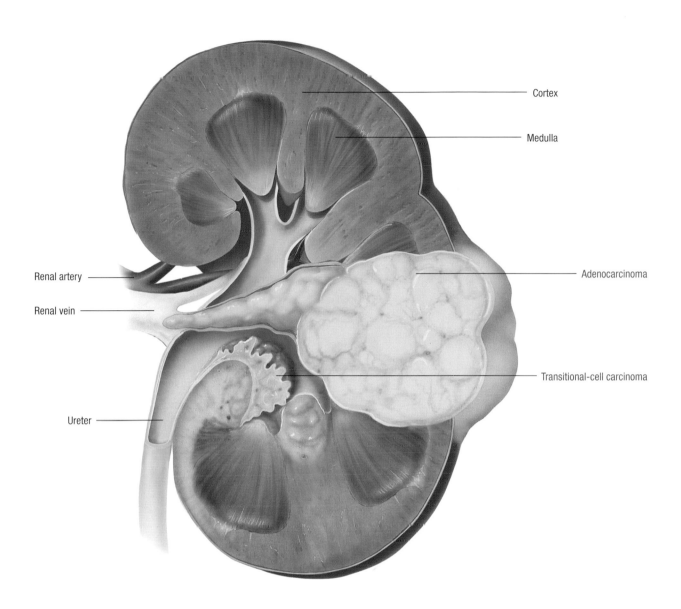

Cortex

Medulla

Renal artery

Renal vein

Adenocarcinoma

Transitional-cell carcinoma

Ureter

RENOVASCULAR HYPERTENSION

Renovascular hypertension is a rise in systemic blood pressure resulting from stenosis of the major renal arteries or their branches or from intrarenal atherosclerosis. The narrowing or sclerosis may be partial or complete, and the resulting blood pressure elevation may be benign or malignant. Approximately 5% to 10% of patients with high blood pressure display renovascular hypertension.

AGE ALERT
Renovascular hypertension is most common in persons under age 30 or over age 50.

Causes
In 95% of all patients with renovascular hypertension
- Atherosclerosis (especially in older men)
- Fibromuscular diseases of the renal artery wall layers, such as medial fibroplasia and, less commonly, intimal or subadventitial fibroplasia

Other causes
- Arteritis
- Anomalies of renal arteries
- Embolism
- Trauma
- Tumor
- Dissecting aneurysm

Pathophysiology
Stenosis or occlusion of the renal artery stimulates the affected kidney to release the enzyme renin, which converts the plasma protein angiotensinogen to angiotensin I. As angiotensin I circulates through the lungs and liver, it's converted to angiotensin II, which causes peripheral vasoconstriction, increased arterial pressure and aldosterone secretion and, eventually, hypertension.

COMPLICATIONS
- Heart failure
- Myocardial infarction
- Stroke
- Renal failure

Signs and symptoms
- Elevated systemic blood pressure
- Headache, light-headedness
- Palpitations, tachycardia
- Anxiety, mental sluggishness
- Decreased tolerance of temperature extremes
- Retinopathy
- Significant complications: heart failure, myocardial infarction, stroke, renal failure

Diagnostic test results
- Renal scan testing that includes administration of an angiotensin-converting enzyme inhibitor such as captopril, *renal angiography*, and renal ultrasound with Doppler evaluation shows evidence of renal stenosis.
- Excretory urography shows slow uptake in one or both kidneys.
- Complete blood count reveals anemia.
- Blood chemistries show abnormal electrolyte levels and elevated blood urea nitrogen and creatinine.

Treatment
- Symptomatic measures: antihypertensives, diuretics, sodium-restricted diet
- Balloon catheter renal artery dilation in selected cases to correct renal artery stenosis without risks and morbidity of surgery
- Insertion of renal artery stents
- Surgery to restore adequate circulation and to control severe hypertension or severely impaired renal function:
  - renal artery bypass, endarterectomy, arterioplasty
  - as a last resort, nephrectomy

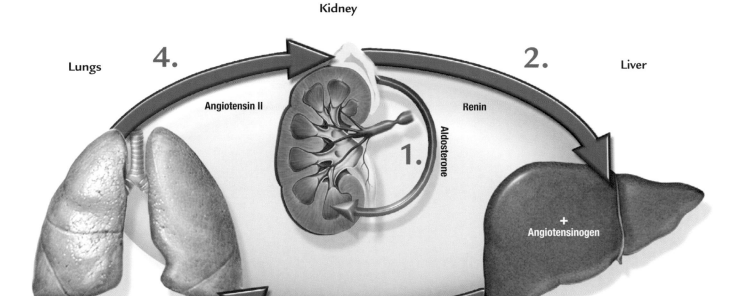

Kidney

Lungs **4.** **2.** **Liver**

Angiotensin II Renin

Aldosterone

1.

+
Angiotensinogen

Angiotensin I **3.**

Mechanism of renovascular hypertension

1. Renal artery stenosis causes reduction of blood flow to the kidneys.
2. Kidneys secrete renin in response.
3. Renin combines with angiotensinogen in the liver to form angiotensin I.
4. In the lungs, angiotensin I is converted to angiotensin II, a vasoconstrictor.

ACNE

Acne is an inflammatory disease of the pilosebaceous units (hair follicles). It occurs on areas of the body that have sebaceous glands, such as the face, neck, chest, back, and shoulders, and is associated with a high rate of sebum secretion. When sebum blocks a hair follicle, one of two types of acne ensues. In inflammatory acne, bacterial growth in the blocked follicle leads to inflammation and eventual rupture of the follicle; in noninflammatory acne, the follicle remains dilated by accumulating secretions but doesn't rupture.

AGE ALERT
Acne occurs in both males and females. Acne vulgaris develops in 80% to 90% of adolescents or young adults, primarily between ages 15 and 18, although the lesions can appear as early as age 8 or into the late 20s.

Causes
- Multifactorial; diet not believed to be a factor

Predisposing factors
- Heredity
- Androgen stimulation
- Certain drugs, including corticosteroids, corticotropin, androgens, iodides, bromides, trimethadione, phenytoin, isoniazid, lithium, halothane
- Exposure to heavy oils, greases, tars, cosmetics
- Cobalt irradiation
- Hyperalimentation
- Trauma; skin occlusion or pressure
- Emotional stress
- Hormonal contraceptive use (may exacerbate acne in some women)

Pathophysiology
Androgens stimulate sebaceous gland growth, sebum production, and shedding of the epithelial cells that line sebaceous follicles. The stimulated follicles become dilated, and sebum and keratin from the epithelial cells form a plug that seals the follicle, creating a favorable environment for bacterial growth. The bacteria, usually *Propionibacterium acnes* or *Staphylococcus epidermidis,* are normal skin flora that secrete lipase. This enzyme converts sebum to free fatty acids, which provoke inflammation and formation of open or closed comedones that may rupture and cause a foreign body response resulting in the formation of papules, nodules, or pustules. Rupture and inflammation may lead to scarring.

COMPLICATIONS
- Infection
- Gross inflammation
- Abscess
- Scars
- Hyperpigmentation

Signs and symptoms
- Closed comedo, or whitehead; doesn't protrude from follicle, covered by epidermis
- Open comedo, or blackhead; protrudes from the follicle, not covered by epidermis; black color caused by melanin or pigment of the follicle
- Rupture or leakage of comedo into the epidermis:
  - inflammation
  - pustules, papules
  - in severe forms, cysts or abscesses (chronic, recurring lesions producing acne scars)

Diagnostic test results
No test for acne vulgaris exists other than visualization of acne lesions to confirm diagnosis.

Treatment
- Gentle cleaning with a sponge to dislodge superficial comedones

Topical agents for mild acne
- Antibacterial agents, such as benzoyl peroxide gels (2%, 5% or 10%), clindamycin, or erythromycin

Keratolytic agents
- Dry and peel the skin to open blocked follicles and release sebum
- Benzoyl peroxide, tretinoin

Systemic therapy for moderate to severe acne
- Tetracycline or minocycline
- Oral isotretinoin to inhibit sebaceous gland function and abnormal keratinization; has severe adverse effects, which limit its use to patients with severe papulopustular or cystic acne not responding to conventional therapy
- For females, antiandrogens—birth control pills, such as norgestimate and ethinyl estradiol, or spironolactone

For severe acne
- For severe scarring—dermabrasion or laser resurfacing to smooth the skin
- Bovine collagen injections into dermis beneath scarred area to fill in pitted areas and smooth skin surface (not recommended by all dermatologists)

HOW ACNE DEVELOPS

Excessive sebum production

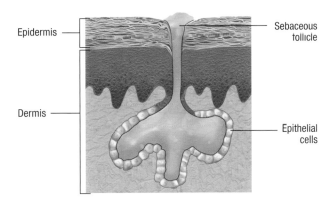

Epidermis

Dermis

Sebaceous follicle

Epithelial cells

Increased shedding of epithelial cells

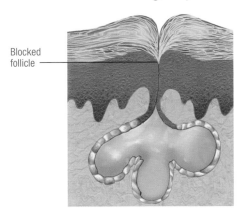

Blocked follicle

Inflammatory response in follicle

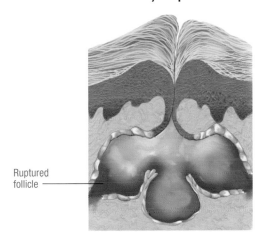

Ruptured follicle

COMEDONES OF ACNE

Closed comedo (whitehead)   **Open comedo (blackhead)**

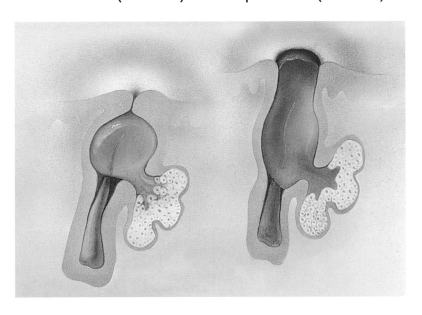

ATOPIC DERMATITIS

Atopic (allergic) dermatitis (also called *atopic* or *infantile eczema*) is a chronic or recurrent inflammatory response commonly associated with other atopic diseases, such as bronchial asthma and allergic rhinitis.

AGE ALERT
Atopic dermatitis commonly develops in infants and toddlers between ages 1 month and 1 year, usually in those with a strong family history of atopic disease. These children commonly develop other atopic disorders as they grow older.

Typically, this form of dermatitis flares and subsides repeatedly before finally resolving during adolescence, but it can persist into adulthood.

Causes
Exact etiology unknown; genetic predisposition likely
Possible contributing factors
- Food allergy, especially eggs, peanuts, milk, or wheat
- Infection
- Chemical irritants
- Extremes of temperature and humidity
- Psychological stress or strong emotions

Pathophysiology
The allergic mechanism of hypersensitivity results in a release of inflammatory mediators through sensitized antibodies of the immunoglobulin (Ig) E class. Histamine and other cytokines induce acute inflammation. Abnormally dry skin and a decreased threshold for itching set up the "itch-scratch-itch" cycle, which eventually causes lesions (excoriations, lichenification).

COMPLICATIONS
- Sleep difficulties
- Secondary infection
- Scars

Signs and symptoms
- Erythematous areas on excessively dry skin; in children, typically on the forehead, cheeks, and extensor surfaces of the arms and legs; in adults, at flexion points (antecubital fossa, popliteal area, and neck)
- Edema, crusting, scaling caused by pruritus and scratching
- Multiple areas of dry, scaly skin, with white dermatographism, blanching, and lichenification with chronic atrophic lesions
- Infantile form presents as red skin with tiny vesicles, especially on the face (sparing the mouth); possible development of wet crusts and fissures
- In blacks, follicular eczema common, appearing as discrete follicular papules involving hair follicles in the affected area
- Pinkish, swollen upper eyelid and double fold under lower lid
- Viral, fungal, or bacterial infections and ocular disorders possible secondary conditions

Diagnostic test results
Blood tests reveal eosinophilia and elevated IgE levels.

Treatment
- Eliminating allergens and avoiding irritants (strong soaps, cleansers, and other chemicals), extreme temperature changes, and other precipitating factors
- Preventing excessive dryness of the skin (critical to successful therapy) by maintaining adequate fluid intake, taking tepid baths, and humidifying air
- Topical tar preparations in a lubricating base (contraindicated for intensely inflamed or open lesions)
- Topical corticosteroid ointment, especially after bathing, to alleviate inflammation; moisturizing cream between steroid doses to help retain moisture
- Topical doxepin hydrochloride
- Topical immunomodulators, such as tacrolimus and pimecrolimus
- Systemic antihistamines such as diphenhydramine
- Systemic corticosteroid therapy for severe disease only
- Ultraviolet B or psoralens plus ultraviolet A therapy
- In severe adult-onset disease, cyclosporine A, if other treatments fail
- Antibiotics, if skin culture positive for bacteria

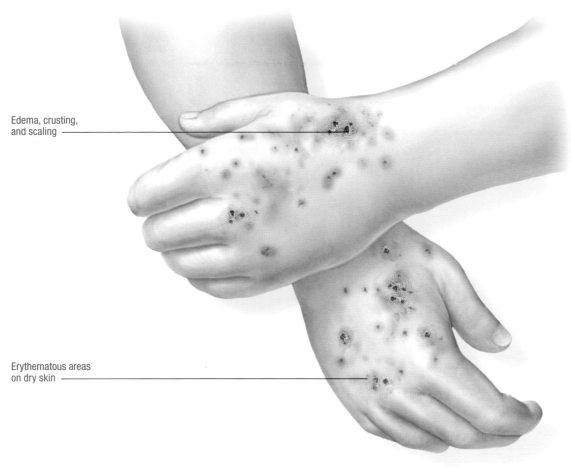

Edema, crusting, and scaling

Erythematous areas on dry skin

CLINICAL TIP

MORGAN'S LINE

In children with atopic dermatitis, severe pruritus with recurrent rubbing leads to characteristic pink pigmentation and swelling of the upper eyelid and a double fold under the lower lid (Morgan's line, Dennie's sign, or mongolian fold).

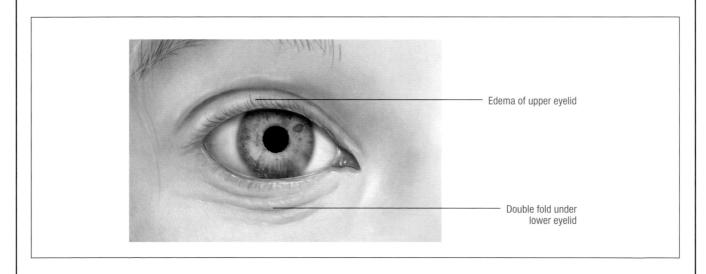

Edema of upper eyelid

Double fold under lower eyelid

BURNS

Burns are the third leading cause of accidental death in the United States.

Causes
- Thermal: residential fires, automobile accidents, playing with matches, improper handling of firecrackers, scalds caused by kitchen or bathroom accidents
- Chemical: contact, ingestion, inhalation, or injection of acids, alkalis, or vesicants
- Electrical: contact with faulty electrical wiring, electrical cords, or high-voltage power lines
- Friction or abrasion
- Ultraviolet radiation: sunburn

Pathophysiology
The injuring agent denatures all cellular proteins. Some cells die because of traumatic or ischemic necrosis. Denaturation disrupts collagen cross-links in connective tissue. The consequent abnormal osmotic and hydrostatic pressure gradients force intravascular fluid into interstitial spaces. Cellular injury triggers the release of mediators of inflammation, further contributing to local or systemic increases in capillary permeability.

First-degree burns. Localized injury to or destruction of epidermis by direct or indirect contact. The barrier function of the skin remains intact.

Second-degree superficial partial-thickness burns. Destruction of epidermis and some of the upper area of the dermis. The barrier function of the skin is lost.

Second-degree deep partial-thickness burns. Destruction of epidermis and more of the dermis.

Third- and fourth-degree burns. Affect every body system and organ. A third-degree burn extends through the epidermis and dermis and into the subcutaneous tissue layer; a fourth-degree burn damages muscle, bone, and interstitial tissues. Within hours, fluids and protein shift from capillary to interstitial spaces, causing edema.

COMPLICATIONS
- Sepsis
- Respiratory complications
- Hypovolemic shock and multisystem organ dysfunction
- Anemia
- Malnutrition

Signs and symptoms
- First-degree burn: localized pain and erythema, usually without blisters in the first 24 hours
- More severe first-degree burn: chills, headache, localized edema, nausea, vomiting
- Second-degree superficial partial-thickness burn: thin-walled, fluid-filled blisters that appear within minutes of injury; mild to moderate edema; pain
- Second-degree deep partial-thickness burn: white, waxy appearance of damaged area, edema, pain (or may be nonpainful)
- Third- and fourth-degree burns: white, brown, or black leathery tissue; visible thrombosed vessels; no blisters

- Electrical burn: silver-colored, raised area, usually at the site of electrical contact (damage to underlying tissue can occur even with intact epidermis)
- Smoke inhalation and pulmonary damage: singed nasal hairs, mucosal burns, voice changes, coughing, wheezing, soot in mouth or nose, darkened sputum

Total burn surface area (BSA) may be estimated quickly using the Rule of Nines, in which an adult patient's body parts are assigned percentages based on the number 9. The Lund-Browder classification allows more precise assessment by assigning specific percentages to an infant or child's body parts and accounts for burn thickness and age differences.

Minor burns
- Third-degree burns on less than 2% of BSA
- Second-degree burns on less than 15% of adult BSA (less than 10% in children)
- All first-degree burns

Moderate burns
- Third-degree burns on 2% to 10% of BSA
- Second-degree burns on 15% to 25% of adult BSA (10% to 20% in children)

Major burns
- Third-degree burns on more than 10% of BSA
- Second-degree burns on more than 25% of adult BSA (more than 20% in children)
- Burns of hands, face, feet, or genitalia
- Burns complicated by fractures or respiratory damage
- Electrical burns and burns in poor-risk patients

Diagnostic test results
- Arterial blood gas levels show evidence of smoke inhalation; they may also show decreased alveolar function and hypoxia.
- Complete blood count reveals decreased hemoglobin level and hematocrit if blood loss occurs.
- Blood chemistries show abnormal electrolytes from fluid loss and shifts, increased blood urea nitrogen with fluid loss, and decreased glucose in children due to limited glycogen storage.
- Urinalysis shows myoglobinuria and hemoglobinuria.
- Other blood tests detect increased carboxyhemoglobin.
- Electrocardiogram shows ischemia, injury, or arrhythmias, especially in electrical burns.
- Fiber-optic bronchoscopy reveals edema of the airways.

Treatment
- Minor burns: immersion of burned area in cool water (55° F [12.8° C]) or application of cool compresses
- Immediate treatment for moderate and major burns: maintain an open airway, endotracheal intubation, 100% oxygen
- Immediate I.V. therapy to prevent hypovolemic shock and maintain cardiac output (lactated Ringer's solution or a fluid replacement formula; additional I.V. lines may be needed)
- Partial-thickness burns over 30% of BSA or full-thickness burns over 5% of BSA: cover patient with a clean, dry, sterile bed sheet to help preserve body temperature; don't cover large burns with saline-soaked dressings
- Debridement followed by application of antimicrobial and nonstick bulky dressing; tetanus prophylaxis if needed
- Pain or anti-inflammatory medication as needed
- Major burns: systemic antimicrobial therapy

CLASSIFICATION OF BURNS BY DEPTH OF INJURY

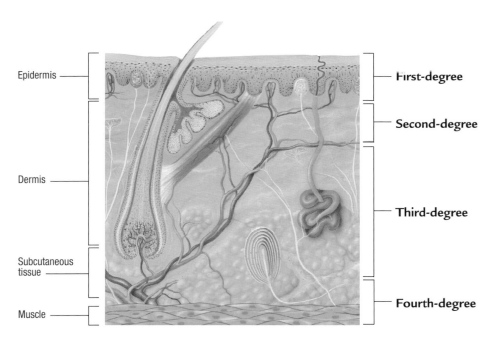

Epidermis — First-degree

Dermis — Second-degree

— Third-degree

Subcutaneous tissue —

Muscle — Fourth-degree

CLINICAL TIP

ESTIMATING THE EXTENT OF BURNS

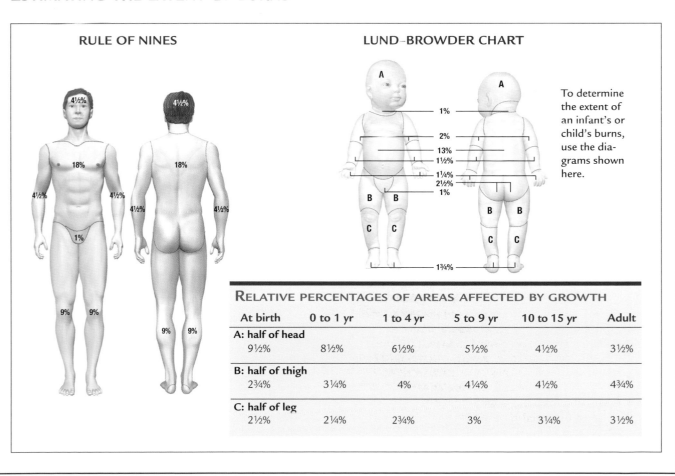

RULE OF NINES

4½% 4½%

18% 18%

4½% 4½% 4½% 4½%

1%

9% 9% 9% 9%

LUND–BROWDER CHART

A   A

1%

2%

13%

1½%

1¼%

2½%

1%

B B   B B

C C   C C

1¾%

To determine the extent of an infant's or child's burns, use the diagrams shown here.

RELATIVE PERCENTAGES OF AREAS AFFECTED BY GROWTH

	At birth	0 to 1 yr	1 to 4 yr	5 to 9 yr	10 to 15 yr	Adult
A: half of head	9½%	8½%	6½%	5½%	4½%	3½%
B: half of thigh	2¾%	3¼%	4%	4¼%	4½%	4¾%
C: half of leg	2½%	2¼%	2¾%	3%	3¼%	3½%

CELLULITIS

Cellulitis is an acute, spreading infection of the dermis or subcutaneous layer of the skin. It may follow damage to the skin, such as a bite or wound. As the cellulitis spreads, fever, erythema, and lymphangitis may occur. Persons with contributing health problems, such as diabetes, immunodeficiency, or impaired circulation, have an increased risk. If treated promptly, the prognosis is usually good.

AGE ALERT
Cellulitis of the lower extremity is more likely to develop into thrombophlebitis in an elderly patient. Orbital cellulitis, especially in children, may require hospitalization and I.V. antibiotics because of the increased risk of spread to intracranial structures, such as in thin bones and numerous openings in the bone.

Causes
- Bacterial infections, commonly with group A beta-hemolytic streptococcus or *Staphylococcus aureus*
- In patients with diabetes or decreased immune function: *Escherichia coli, Proteus mirabilis, Acinetobacter, Enterobacter, Pseudomonas aeruginosa, Pasteurella multocida, Vibrio vulnificus, Mycobacterium fortuitum complex,* and *Cryptococcus neoformans*
- In children, less commonly caused by pneumococci and *Neisseria meningitidis* group B (periorbital)

Pathophysiology
After the organisms enter the tissue spaces and planes of cleavage, hyaluronidases break down the ground substances composed of polysaccharides while fibrinolysins digest fibrin barriers and lecithinases destroy cell membranes. This overwhelms the normal cells of defense (neutrophils, eosinophils, basophils, and mast cells) that normally contain and localize inflammation, and cellular debris accumulates.

COMPLICATIONS
- Bacteremia
- Necrotizing fasciitis
- Lymphangitis
- Meningitis (in facial cellulitis)

Signs and symptoms
- Classic signs: erythema and edema due to inflammatory response, usually well-demarcated
- Pain at site and possibly in surrounding area
- Fever and warmth
- Regional lymphadenopathy or lymphangitis

Diagnostic test results
- White blood cell count shows mild leukocytosis with a shift to the left.
- Erythrocyte sedimentation rate is mildly elevated.
- Culture and gram stain results of fluid from abscesses and bulla are positive for the offending organism.
- Using the "Touch" preparation, potassium hydroxide is applied to a microscope slide containing a skin lesion specimen that detects the presence of yeast or mycelial forms of fungus.

Treatment
- Oral or I.V. penicillinase-resistant penicillin (drug of choice for initial treatment) unless patient has known penicillin allergy; antifungal medications if needed
- Alternative antibiotics based on culture and sensitivity results
- Warm soaks to the site to help relieve pain and decrease edema by increasing vasodilation
- Pain medication as needed
- Elevation of infected extremity
- Surgical drainage or debridement for abscess formation

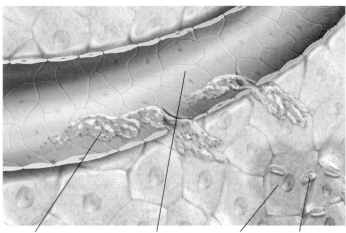

Increased blood flow carrying plasma proteins and fluid to injured tissue

Blood vessel Wound Bacterium

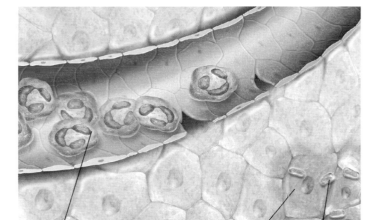

Movement of defensive white blood cells to injured tissue

Wound Bacterium

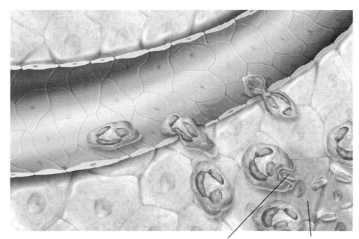

Phagocyte engulfing bacterium

Wound

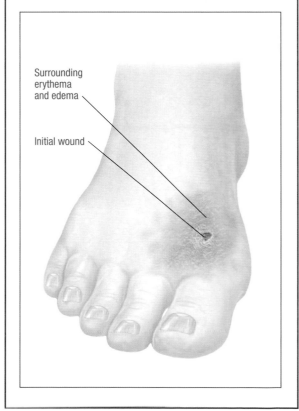

CLINICAL TIP

RECOGNIZING CELLULITIS

The classic signs of cellulitis, a spreading soft tissue infection, are erythema and edema surrounding the initial wound. The tissue is warm to the touch.

Surrounding erythema and edema

Initial wound

Cellulitis **387**

CONTACT DERMATITIS

Contact dermatitis commonly appears as a sharply demarcated inflammation of the skin that results from contact with an irritating chemical or atopic allergen (a substance that produces an allergic reaction in the skin). It can also appear as an irritation of the skin that results from contact with concentrated substances to which the skin is sensitized, such as perfumes, soaps, chemicals, or metals and alloys (such as nickel used in jewelry).

Causes

Mild irritants
- Chronic exposure to detergents or solvents

Strong irritants
- Damage on contact with acids or alkalis

Allergens
- Sensitization after repeated exposure

Pathophysiology

The allergic mechanism of hypersensitivity results in a release of inflammatory mediators through sensitized antibodies of immunoglobulin E. Histamine and other cytokines induce an inflammatory response, resulting in edema, skin breakdown, and pruritus.

COMPLICATIONS
- Altered pigmentation
- Lichenification
- Scarring

Signs and symptoms

Mild irritants and allergens
- Erythema
- Small vesicles that ooze, scale, and itch

Strong irritants
- Blisters
- Ulcerations

Classic allergic response
- Clearly defined lesions with straight lines following points of contact

Severe allergic reaction
- Marked erythema
- Blistering
- Edema of the affected site

Diagnostic test results

- Patch test identifies allergens.

Treatment

- Eliminating known allergens
- Decreasing exposure to irritants
- Wearing protective clothing such as gloves
- Washing immediately after contact with irritants or allergens
- Topical anti-inflammatory (including a corticosteroid)
- Systemic corticosteroids for edema and bullae
- Antihistamine
- Local application of Burrow's solution (for blisters)

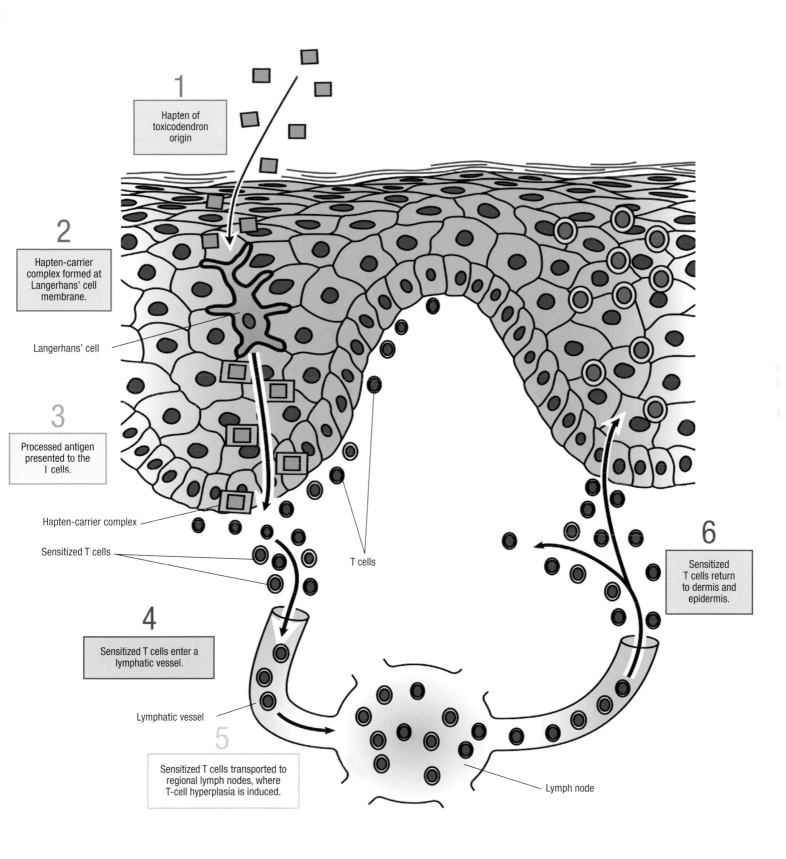

1

Hapten of toxicodendron origin

2

Hapten-carrier complex formed at Langerhans' cell membrane.

Langerhans' cell

3

Processed antigen presented to the T cells.

Hapten-carrier complex

Sensitized T cells

T cells

4

Sensitized T cells enter a lymphatic vessel.

Lymphatic vessel

5

Sensitized T cells transported to regional lymph nodes, where T-cell hyperplasia is induced.

Lymph node

6

Sensitized T cells return to dermis and epidermis.

FOLLICULITIS, FURUNCLES, CARBUNCLES

Folliculitis is a bacterial infection in the upper portion of a hair follicle that causes a papule, pustule, or erosion. The infection can be superficial (follicular impetigo or Bockhart's impetigo) or deep (sycosis barbae). Furuncles, also known as *boils,* affect the entire hair follicle and the adjacent subcutaneous tissue. Carbuncles are a group of interconnected furuncles.

With appropriate treatment, the prognosis for patients with folliculitis is good. The disorder usually resolves within 2 to 3 weeks. The prognosis for patients with carbuncles depends on the severity of the infection and the patient's physical condition and ability to resist infection.

Causes
- Coagulase-positive *Staphylococcus aureus* (most common)
- *Klebsiella, Enterobacter,* or *Proteus* organisms (gram-negative folliculitis in patients on long-term antibiotic therapy such as for acne)
- *Pseudomonas aeruginosa* (thrives in warm environment with high pH and low chlorine content — "hot-tub folliculitis")

Predisposing risk factors
- Shaving, plucking, or waxing
- Infected wound, poor hygiene
- Chronic staphylococcus carrier state in nares, axillae, perineum, or bowel
- Diabetes
- Debilitation
- Immunosuppressive therapy, defects in chemotaxis, hyper-immunoglobulinemia E syndrome
- Tight clothes, friction
- Living in a tropical climate

Pathophysiology
The affecting organism enters the body, usually at a break in the skin barrier such as a wound site. The organism then causes an inflammatory reaction within the hair follicle.

Staphylococcal infection commonly causes the abscess, which consists of a fibrin wall with surrounding inflamed tissues. This encloses a core of pus containing organisms and leukocytes.

Hematologic spread of infection is possible even from the smallest abscess and is enhanced by proteolytic enzymes produced by the staphylococcal organisms.

 COMPLICATIONS
- Sepsis
- Cellulitis
- Scarring
- Pneumonia
- Endocarditis
- Infection of bones and joints

Signs and symptoms
Folliculitis
- In children — papule or pustules on scalp, arms, or legs
- In adults — papule or pustules on trunk, buttocks, legs, or face

Furuncles
- Firm or fluctuant, painful nodules, commonly on neck, face, axillae, or buttocks
- Nodules enlarge for several days, then rupture, discharging pus and necrotic material
- After rupture, pain subsides (erythema and edema persist for days or weeks)

Carbuncles
- Extremely painful, deep abscesses draining through multiple openings onto the skin surface, around several hair follicles
- Fever and malaise

Diagnostic test results
- Wound culture and sensitivity test results show the offending organism.
- Blood chemistry reveals elevated white blood cell count.

Treatment
- Thorough cleaning of the infected area with antibacterial soap and water several times per day
- Warm, wet compresses to promote vasodilation and drainage
- Topical antibiotics, such as mupirocin ointment or clindamycin or erythromycin solution

Specific treatments
- Extensive folliculitis: systemic antibiotics, such as a cephalosporin or dicloxacillin
- Furuncles (ripe lesions):
- warm, wet compresses
- incision and drainage
- systemic antibiotic therapy
- Carbuncles:
- incision and drainage
- systemic antibiotic therapy

Superficial folliculitis
- Erythema
- Pustule
- Single-follicle involvement

Deep folliculitis
- Extensive follicular involvement

Furuncle
- Red, tender nodule surrounding a follicle
- Single draining point

Carbuncle
- Deep follicular abscesses of several follicles
- Several draining points

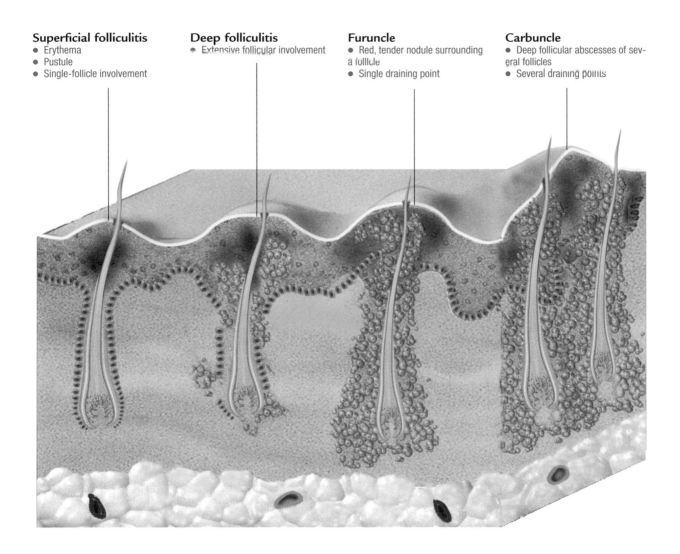

FUNGAL INFECTIONS

Fungal infections of the skin are often regarded as superficial infections affecting the hair, nails, and stratum corneum (the dead top layer of the skin). Fungi infect and survive only on the nonviable keratin within these structures. The most common fungal infections are dermatophyte infections (tineas) and candidiasis (moniliasis).

Tinea infections are classified by the body location in which they occur — for example:
- *capitis,* scalp
- *corporis,* body
- *pedis,* foot
- *cruris,* groin.

Some forms infect one gender more commonly than the other. For example, tinea cruris is more common in males. Obesity and diabetes predispose to tinea and candida infection.

AGE ALERT
Children develop tinea scalp infections, young adults more commonly develop infection in the interiginous areas, and older adults develop onchomycosis.

Candidiasis of the skin or mucous membranes is also classified according to the infected site or area:
- intertrigo — axilla or inner aspect of thigh
- balanoposthitis — glans penis and prepuce
- vulvitis
- diaper dermatitis
- paronychia — folds of skin at the margin of a nail
- onychia — nail bed
- thrush — mouth.

Candida organisms may be normal flora of the skin, mouth, GI tract, or genitalia.

Causes
Tinea infection
- *Microsporum, Trichophyton,* or *Epidermophyton* organisms
- Contact with contaminated objects or surfaces
Risk factors for tinea infection
- Obesity
- Atopy, immunosuppression
- Antibiotic therapy with suppression of normal flora
- Softened skin from prolonged water contact, such as with water sports or diaphoresis
Candidiasis
- Overgrowth of *Candida* organisms and infection due to depletion of the normal flora (such as with antibiotic therapy)
- Neutropenia and bone marrow suppression in immunocompromised patients (at greater risk for the disseminating form)
- *Candida albicans,* normal GI flora (causes candidiasis in susceptible patients)
- *Candida* overgrowth in the mouth (thrush)

Pathophysiology
Dermatophytes, which grow only on or within keratinized structures, make keratinases that digest keratin and maintain the existence of fungi in keratinized tissue. The pathogenicity of dermatophytes is restricted by the cell-mediated immunity and antimicrobial activity of the polymorphonuclear leukocytes. Clinical presentation depends on fungal species, site of infection, and host susceptibility and immune response.

In candidiasis, the organism penetrates the epidermis after binding to integrin receptors and adhesion molecules and then secretes proteolytic enzymes, which facilitate tissue invasion. An inflammatory response results from the attraction of neutrophils to the area and from activation of the complement cascade.

COMPLICATIONS
Tinea infection
- Hair or nail loss
- Secondary bacterial or candidal infection
Candidiasis
- *Candida* dissemination
- Organ failure: kidneys, brain, GI tract, eyes, lungs, heart

Signs and symptoms
Tinea infection
- Erythema, scaling, pustules, vesicles, bullae, maceration
- Itching, stinging, burning
- Circular lesions with erythema and a collarette of scale (central clearing)
Candidiasis
- Superficial papules and pustules; later, erosions
- Erythema and edema of epidermis or mucous membrane
- As inflammation progresses, a white-yellow, curdlike material over the infected area
- In thrush — white coating of tongue, buccal mucosa, and lips, which can be wiped off to reveal a red base
- Severe pruritus and pain at the lesion sites (common)

Diagnostic test results
- Microscopic examination of a potassium hydroxide-treated skin scraping reveals the offending organism.
- Culture determines the causative organism and suggests the mode of transmission.
- Wood's lamp examination in a darkened room demonstrates fluorescence.

Treatment
Tinea infection
- Topical fungicidal agents, such as imidazole or an allylamine product
- If no response to topical treatment — oral agents, such as allylamines or azoles
Candidiasis
- Intertrigo, balanitis, vulvitis, diaper dermatitis, paronychia — nystatin or imidazoles
- Oral candidiasis (thrush) — azoles, imidazoles
- Systemic infections — I.V. amphotericin B or oral ketonazole

SKIN SCRAPINGS FROM FUNGAL SKIN INFECTION

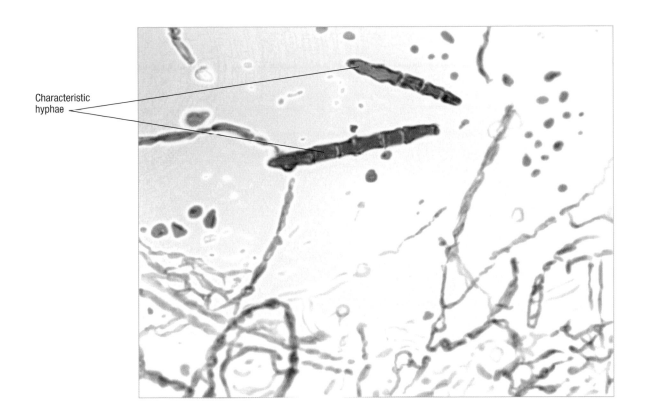

Characteristic
hyphae

FUNGAL INFECTION OF NAIL

Onycholysis

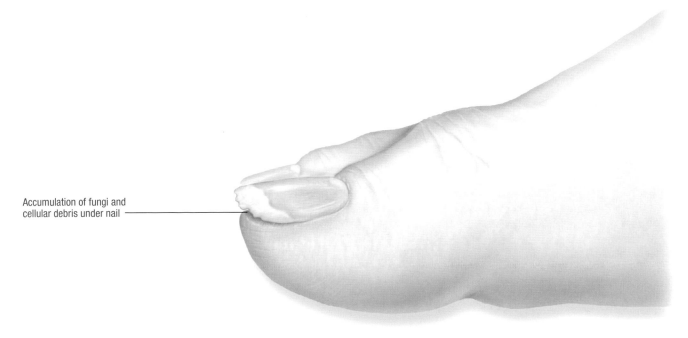

Accumulation of fungi and
cellular debris under nail

LYME DISEASE

A multisystemic disorder, Lyme disease is caused by the spirochete *Borrelia burgdorferi,* which is carried by the minute tick *Ixodes dammini* (also known as *I. scapularis*) or another tick in the Ixodidae family. It commonly begins in the summer months with a papule that becomes red and warm but isn't painful. This classic skin lesion is called erythema migrans. Weeks or months later, cardiac or neurologic abnormalities sometimes develop, possibly followed by arthritis of the large joints.

Causes

B. burgdorferi

Pathophysiology

Lyme disease begins when a tick injects spirochete-laden saliva into the bloodstream or deposits fecal matter on the skin. After incubating for 3 to 32 days, the spirochetes migrate out to the skin, causing erythema migrans. Then they disseminate to other skin sites or organs by the bloodstream or lymph system. The spirochetes' life cycle isn't completely clear. They may survive for years in the joints, or they may trigger an inflammatory response in the host and then die.

COMPLICATIONS
- Myocarditis
- Pericarditis
- Arrhythmias
- Heart block
- Meningitis
- Encephalitis
- Cranial or peripheral neuropathies
- Arthritis
- Memory loss
- Difficulty concentrating

Signs and symptoms
Prodrome
- Malaise
- Fatigue
- Headache
- Fever
- Lethargy
- Chills
- Arthralgia
- Myalgia
- Anorexia
- Sore throat
- Nausea
- Vomiting
- Abdominal pain
- Photophobia

Stage I
- Initial red macule or papule that enlarges within days, forming an expanding annular lesion with a well-defined red border and central clearing (erythema migrans) with an average maximum diameter of 15 to 20 cm; center of lesion may become vesicular, indurated, or necrotic, or concentric rings may occur (when occurring on the face, neck, or scalp, only a linear streak may be noted)
- Multiple tick bites producing multiple erythema migrans lesions
- Erythema migrans lesions most commonly occurring in the proximal extremities, especially the axillae and groin
- As erythema migrans lesion evolves, possible development of postinflammatory erythema or hyperpigmentation, alopecia, or desquamation
- Additionally, a malar rash, diffuse urticaria, or subcutaneous nodules possible

Stage II
- Low-grade fever in adults, high persistent fever in children; adenopathy
- Neurologic involvement occurs in up to 20% of untreated cases — meningitis, encephalitic signs (poor concentration, memory, and sleep, or irritability), cranial neuritis, radiculoneuropathy, and myelitis
- Cardiac involvement in up to 10% of untreated cases — atrioventricular block, myopericarditis, left ventricular dysfunction
- Migratory pain in joints, bursae, tendons, bones, or muscles

Stage III
- Fever and adenopathy
- Arthritis
- Chronic neurologic involvement

Diagnostic test results
- Assays for anti–*B. burgdorferi* show evidence of previous or current infection.
- Enzyme-linked immunosorbent technology or indirect immunofluorescence microscopy shows immunoglobulin (Ig) M levels that peak 3 to 6 weeks after infection; IgG antibodies detected several weeks after infection may continue to develop for several months and generally persist for years.
- Positive Western blot assay shows serologic evidence of past or current infection with *B. burgdorferi.*
- Lumbar puncture with analysis of cerebrospinal fluid reveals antibodies to *B. burgdorferi.*

Treatment
- Antibiotics, such as doxycycline, tetracycline, cefuroxime, ceftriaxone, and penicillin
- Anti-inflammatory medications such as ibuprofen

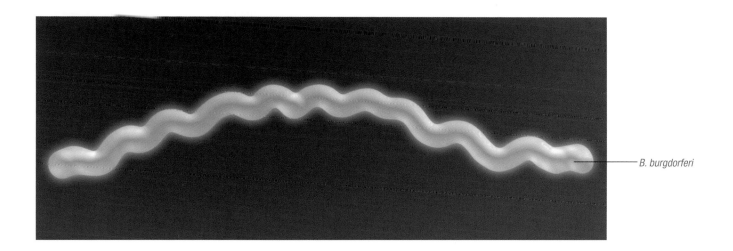

B. burgdorferi

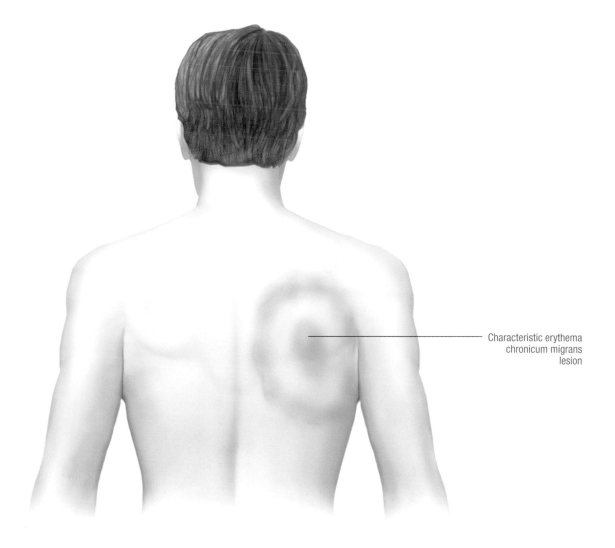

Characteristic erythema chronicum migrans lesion

PRESSURE ULCERS

Pressure ulcers are localized areas of cellular necrosis that occur most commonly in the skin and subcutaneous tissue over bony prominences. These ulcers may be superficial, caused by local skin irritation with subsequent surface maceration, or deep, originating in underlying tissue. Deep lesions commonly go undetected until they penetrate the skin; by then, they have usually caused subcutaneous damage.

Five body locations together account for 95% of all pressure ulcer sites: sacral area, greater trochanter, ischial tuberosity, heel, and lateral malleolus. Patients who have contractures are at an increased risk for developing pressure ulcers because the abnormal position adds pressure on the tissue and the alignment of the bones.

AGE ALERT
Age also has a role in the incidence of pressure ulcers. Muscle and subcutaneous tissue is lost with aging, and skin elasticity decreases. Both factors increase the risk of developing pressure ulcers.

A *stage I* pressure ulcer is characterized by intact skin with nonblanchable redness of a localized area, usually over a bony prominence. In darker skin, the ulcer may appear with persistent red, blue, or purple hues.

A *suspected deep tissue injury* is characterized by a purple or maroon localized intact area or blood-filled blister caused by damage to underlying soft tissue from pressure or shear. Preceding the injury, the tissue may be painful, firm, mushy, boggy, or warm or cool compared to adjacent tissue. It may be hard to detect in dark-skinned patients.

A *stage II* pressure ulcer is characterized by partial-thickness skin loss involving the dermis. The ulcer is shallow and has a red-pink wound bed without slough. It may also appear as an intact or open serum-filled blister.

A *stage III* pressure ulcer is characterized by full-thickness skin loss involving damage or necrosis of subcutaneous tissue, which may extend down to, but not through, the underlying fascia. The ulcer appears as a deep crater with or without undermining of adjacent tissue.

Full-thickness skin loss with extensive destruction, tissue necrosis, or damage to muscle, bone, or support structures (for example, tendon or joint capsule) characterizes a *stage IV* pressure ulcer. Tunneling and sinus tracts may also occur.

An *unstageable* ulcer is characterized by full-thickness tissue loss in which the base of the ulcer in the wound bed is covered by slough (yellow, tan, gray, green, or brown) or eschar (tan, brown, or black), or both. Until enough slough is removed to expose the base of the wound, the true depth — and therefore, stage — can't be determined.

Causes
- Immobility and decreased level of activity
- Friction and shear, causing damage to the epidermal and upper dermal skin layers
- Tissue maceration
- Skin breakdown

Contributing conditions
- Malnutrition, hypoalbuminemia
- Medical conditions such as diabetes; orthopedic injuries
- Depression, chronic emotional stress

Pathophysiology
A pressure ulcer is caused by an injury to the skin and its underlying tissues. The pressure exerted on the area restricts blood flow to the site and causes ischemia and hypoxemia. As the capillaries collapse, thrombosis occurs and leads to tissue edema and necrosis. Ischemia also contributes to an accumulation of toxins. The toxins further break down the tissue and also contribute to tissue necrosis.

COMPLICATIONS
- Bacteremia and septicemia
- Necrotizing fasciitis
- Osteomyelitis

Signs and symptoms
- First clinical sign: blanching erythema, varying from pink to bright red depending on the patient's skin color; in dark skin, purple discoloration or a darkening of normal skin color
- Pain at the site and surrounding area
- Localized edema and increased body temperature due to initial inflammatory response; in more severe cases, cool skin due to severe damage or necrosis
- In more severe cases with deeper dermal involvement: nonblanching erythema, ranging from dark red to cyanotic
- As ulcer progresses: skin deterioration, blisters, crusts, or scaling
- Deep ulcer originating at or extending to the bony prominence below the skin surface: usually dusky red, possibly mottled appearance, doesn't bleed easily, warm to the touch

Diagnostic test results
- Wound culture and sensitivity tests detect infectious organisms.
- Blood testing reveals elevated white blood cells, elevated erythrocyte sedimentation rate, and hypoproteinemia.

Treatment
Treatment is based on the stage and may include the following:
- For immobile patients, repositioning at least every 2 hours with support of pillows; for those able to move, a pillow and encouragement to change position
- Foam, gel, or air mattress to aid in healing by reducing pressure on the ulcer site and reducing the risk of more ulcers
- Nutritional supplements, such as vitamin C and zinc, for the malnourished patient; adequate protein intake
- Adequate fluid intake to prevent dehydration
- Meticulous skin care and hygiene practices, particularly for incontinent patients
- Transparent film, polyurethane foam, or hydrocolloid dressing
- Wound loosely filled with saline- or gel-moistened gauze; exudate managed with absorbent dressing (moist gauze or foam); covered with secondary dressing
- Surgical debridement

Stage I

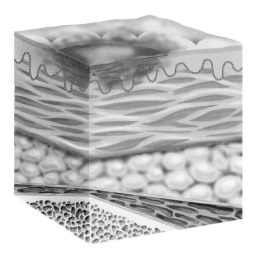

Suspected deep tissue injury

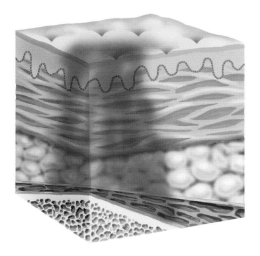

Stage II

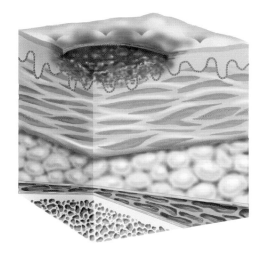

Stage III

Stage IV

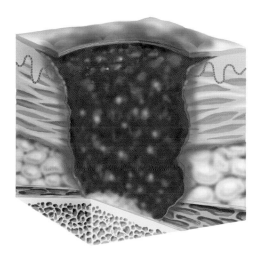

Unstageable

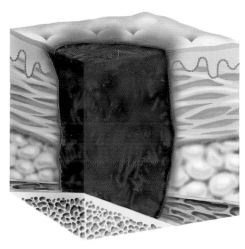

PSORIASIS

Psoriasis is a chronic, recurrent disease marked by epidermal proliferation and characterized by remissions and exacerbations. Flare-ups are commonly related to specific systemic and environmental factors but may be unpredictable. Widespread involvement is called *exfoliative* or *erythrodermic psoriasis*.

Although this disorder commonly affects young adults, it may strike at any age, including infancy. Genetic factors predetermine the incidence of psoriasis; affected families have a significantly greater incidence of human leukocyte antigens (HLA) B13, B17, and CW6.

Flare-ups can usually be controlled with therapy. Appropriate treatment depends on the type of psoriasis, the extent of the disease, the patient's response, and the effect of the disease on the patient's lifestyle. No permanent cure exists, and all methods of treatment are palliative.

Causes

- Genetically determined tendency to develop psoriasis
- Possible immune disorder, as suggested by HLA type in families
- Flare-up of guttate (drop-shaped) lesions from infections, especially beta-hemolytic streptococci

Other contributing factors

- Pregnancy
- Endocrine changes
- Climate (cold weather tends to exacerbate psoriasis)
- Emotional stress or physical illness
- Infection
- Certain medications, such as systemic glucocorticoids and lithium

Pathophysiology

A skin cell normally takes 14 days to move from the basal layer to the stratum corneum, where it's sloughed off after 14 days of normal wear and tear. Thus, the life cycle of a normal skin cell is 28 days.

In psoriasis, the immune system sends signals that speed up the normal process from 28 days to just 4 days. This markedly shortened cycle doesn't allow time for the cell to mature. Consequently, the stratum corneum becomes thick with extra skin cells. On the surface, the skin cells pile up and the dead cells create a white, flaky layer, the cardinal manifestation of psoriasis.

COMPLICATIONS

- Infection
- Altered self-image, depression, and isolation

Signs and symptoms

- Erythematous papules and plaques with thick silver scales, most commonly on the scalp, chest, elbows, knees, back, buttocks
- Plaques with characteristic silver scales that either flake off easily or thicken, covering the lesion (scale removal can produce fine bleeding [Auspitz's sign])
- Itching and occasional pain from dry, cracked, encrusted lesions
- Occasional small guttate lesions (usually thin and erythematous, with few scales), either alone or with plaques

Diagnostic test results

Diagnosis is based on patient history, appearance of the lesions and, if needed, the results of skin biopsy. Blood chemistry reveals elevated serum uric acid level.

Treatment

- Topical fluorinated glucocorticoids
- Low-dose antihistamines, oatmeal baths, emollients, and open wet dressings to help relieve pruritus
- Aspirin and local heat to help alleviate the pain of psoriatic arthritis; nonsteroidal anti-inflammatory drugs in severe cases
- Ultraviolet B (UVB) or natural sunlight exposure to retard rapid cell production to the point of minimal erythema
- Tar preparations or crude coal tar applications to the affected areas about 15 minutes before exposure to UVB or at bedtime and wiped off the next morning
- Intralesional steroid injection for small, stubborn plaques
- Anthralin ointment or paste mixture for well-defined plaques (because anthralin injures and stains normal skin, apply petroleum jelly around the affected skin before applying it)
- Calcipotriene ointment, a vitamin D analogue; best when alternated with a topical steroid
- Tazarotene, a topical retinoid
- Topical administration of psoralens (plant extracts that accelerate exfoliation) followed by exposure to high-intensity UVA
- Extensive psoriasis: acitretin, a retinoid compound
- Resistant disease: cyclosporine
- Last-resort treatment for refractory psoriasis: cytotoxin, usually methotrexate
- Psoriasis of scalp: tar shampoo followed by a steroid lotion

PSORIATIC LESION

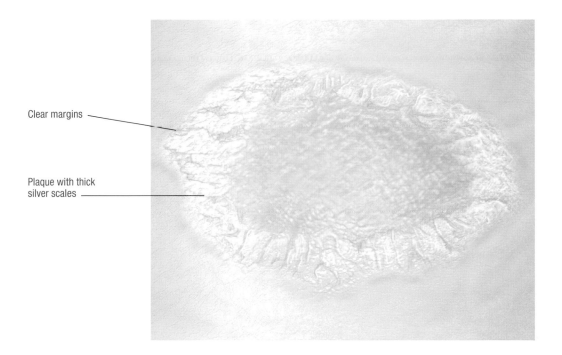

Clear margins

Plaque with thick
silver scales

DIFFUSE PSORIATIC PLAQUES

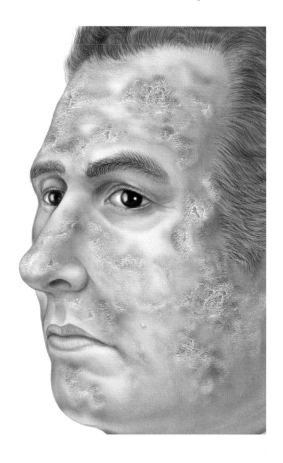

SKIN CANCERS

BASAL CELL CARCINOMA

Basal cell carcinoma, also known as *basal cell epithelioma,* is a slow-growing, destructive skin tumor. The most common form of skin cancer, it rarely metastasizes.

Causes
- Prolonged sun exposure (most common)
- Extensive sunburns or sun exposure in childhood
- Arsenic, radiation, burns, immunosuppression
- Previous X-ray therapy for acne

Pathophysiology
The pathogenesis is uncertain, but it's thought to originate when undifferentiated basal cells become carcinomatous instead of differentiating into sweat glands, sebum, and hair.

COMPLICATIONS
- Disfiguring lesions

Signs and symptoms
Noduloulcerative lesions
- Usually occur on the face, particularly the forehead, eyelid margins, nasolabial folds
- Lesions small, smooth, pinkish, and translucent papules with telangiectatic vessels crossing the surface; occasionally pigmented
- When lesions enlarge, centers possibly depressed and borders firm and elevated
- Eventual local invasion and ulceration, or "rodent ulcers" (these rarely metastasize but can spread to vital areas and become infected or cause massive hemorrhage)

Superficial basal cell carcinoma
- Commonly multiple; usually occur on the chest and back
- Oval or irregularly shaped, lightly pigmented plaques, with sharply defined, slightly elevated threadlike borders:
  – superficial erosion scaly in appearance; small, atrophic areas in center resembling psoriasis or eczema
  – usually chronic and *unlikely* to invade other areas

Sclerosing basal cell carcinoma (morphea-like carcinoma)
- Waxy, sclerotic, yellow to white plaques; no distinct borders
- Occur on the head and neck

Diagnostic test results
Incisional or excisional biopsy and histologic study determine the tumor type.

Treatment
- Surgical excision
- Curettage and electrodesiccation
- Topical 5-fluorouracil, imiquimod
- Microscopically controlled surgical excision (Mohs' surgery)
- Irradiation
- Cryotherapy with liquid nitrogen
- Chemosurgery: for persistent or recurrent lesions

SQUAMOUS CELL CARCINOMA

Squamous cell carcinoma of the skin is an invasive tumor with metastatic potential. It usually occurs on sun-exposed areas but can occur elsewhere.

Causes
- Overexposure to the sun's ultraviolet rays
- Premalignant lesions, such as actinic keratosis or leukoplakia
- X-ray therapy
- Ingested herbicides, medications, or waxes containing arsenic
- Chronic skin irritation and inflammation
- Local carcinogens, such as tar and oil
- Hereditary diseases, such as xeroderma pigmentosum and albinism

Pathophysiology
Squamous cell carcinoma arises from keratinizing epidermal cells.

COMPLICATIONS
- Lymph node and visceral metastases
- Respiratory problems

Signs and symptoms
- Induration and inflammation of a preexisting lesion
- Slowly growing nodule on a firm, indurated base; eventual ulceration and invasion of underlying tissues
- Metastasis to regional lymph nodes: characteristic systemic symptoms of pain, malaise, fatigue, weakness, anorexia

Diagnostic test results
Excisional biopsy determines the tumor type.

Treatment
- Surgical excision
- Electrodesiccation and curettage
- Radiation therapy
- Chemosurgery

MALIGNANT MELANOMA

A malignant neoplasm that arises from melanocytes, malignant melanoma is relatively rare and accounts for only 1% to 2% of all malignancies. However, the incidence is rapidly increasing, by 300% in the past 40 years. The four types of melanomas are *superficial spreading, nodular malignant, lentigo maligna,* and *acral lentiginous.*

Melanoma spreads through the lymphatic and vascular systems and metastasizes to the regional lymph nodes, skin, liver, lungs, and central nervous system. Its course is unpredictable, and recurrence and metastases may not appear for more than 5 years after resection of the primary lesion. The prognosis varies with tumor thickness. Generally, superficial lesions are curable, whereas deeper lesions tend to metastasize.

SKIN RESPONSE TO ULTRAVIOLET RADIATION

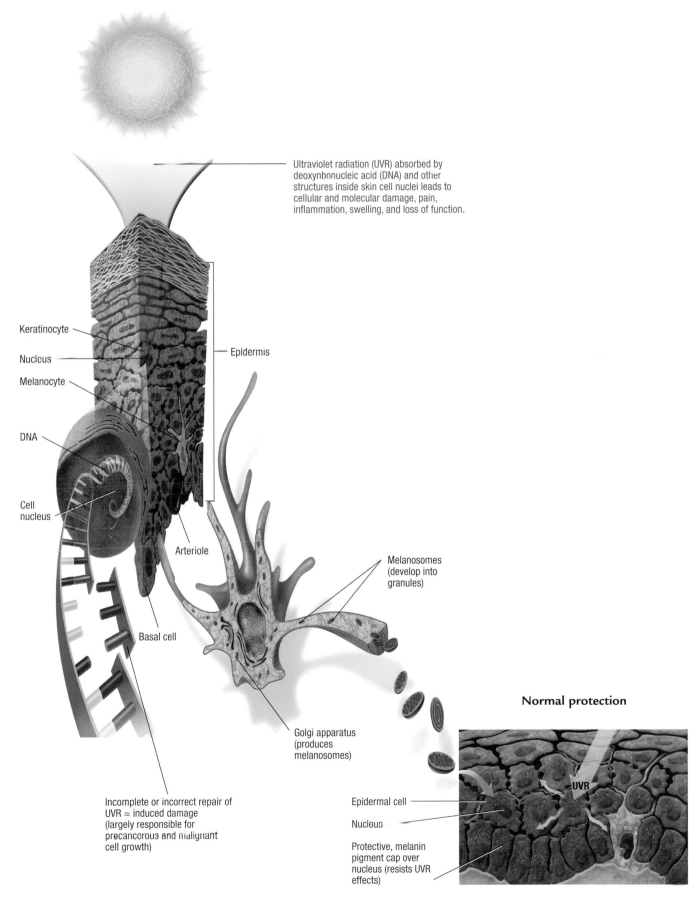

Ultraviolet radiation (UVR) absorbed by deoxynbonucleic acid (DNA) and other structures inside skin cell nuclei leads to cellular and molecular damage, pain, inflammation, swelling, and loss of function.

Keratinocyte

Nucleus

Melanocyte

DNA

Cell nucleus

Epidermis

Arteriole

Basal cell

Melanosomes (develop into granules)

Golgi apparatus (produces melanosomes)

Incomplete or incorrect repair of UVR = induced damage (largely responsible for precancerous and malignant cell growth)

Normal protection

Epidermal cell

Nucleus

Protective, melanin pigment cap over nucleus (resists UVR effects)

UVR

Causes

- Excessive exposure to sunlight

Contributing factors

- Skin type: most common in persons with blonde or red hair, fair skin, and blue eyes; who are prone to sunburn; and who are of Celtic or Scandinavian ancestry; rare among people of African ancestry
- Hormonal factors: growth possibly exacerbated by pregnancy
- Family history: slightly more common within families
- Past history of melanoma

Pathophysiology

Malignant melanoma arises from melanocytes, the pigment-producing cells of the skin.

Up to 70% of patients with melanoma have a preexisting nevus (mole) at the tumor site.

COMPLICATIONS

- Metastases to the lungs, liver, or brain

Signs and symptoms

Melanoma (if any skin lesion or nevus)

- Enlarges, becomes inflamed or sore, itches, ulcerates, bleeds, undergoes textural changes
- Changes color or shows signs of surrounding pigment regression (halo nevus or vitiligo)

Superficial spreading melanoma

- Arises on an area of chronic irritation
- In women, most common between the knees and ankles; in Blacks and Asians, on the toe webs and soles — lightly pigmented areas subject to trauma
- Red, white, and blue color over a brown or black background and an irregular, notched margin
- Irregular surface with small elevated tumor nodules that may ulcerate and bleed

Nodular melanoma

- Usually a polypoidal nodule, with uniformly dark or grayish coloration — resembles a blackberry
- Occasionally, flesh-colored, with flecks of pigment around its base; possibly inflamed

Lentigo maligna melanoma

- Resembles a large (3- to 6-cm) flat freckle of tan, brown, black, whitish, or slate color
- Irregularly scattered black nodules on the surface
- Develops slowly, usually over many years, and eventually may ulcerate
- Commonly develops under fingernail, on face, or on back of hand

CLINICAL TIP

Remember the ABCDEs of malignant melanoma when examining skin lesions:

- A: ASYMMETRICAL lesion
- B: BORDER is irregular
- C: COLORS of lesion are multiple types
- D: DIAMETER of the lesion is > 0.5 cm
- E: ELEVATED or ENLARGING lesion

Diagnostic test results

- Excisional biopsy and full-depth punch biopsy with histologic examination shows tumor thickness and disease stage.
- Complete blood count with differential reveals anemia.
- Other blood tests show elevated erythrocyte sedimentation rate, abnormal platelet count, and abnormal liver function tests.
- Chest X-ray assists with staging.
- Computed tomography scan of abdomen, pelvis, and neck; magnetic resonance imaging of the eye and brain; and bone scan detect metastasis.

Treatment

- Surgical resection to remove the tumor
- Regional lymphadenectomy
- Adjuvant chemotherapy and biotherapy
- Radiation therapy

CLINICAL TIP

Regardless of the treatment method, melanomas require close long-term follow-up to detect metastasis and recurrences. Statistics show that 13% of recurrences develop more than 5 years after primary surgery.

TYPES OF SKIN CANCER

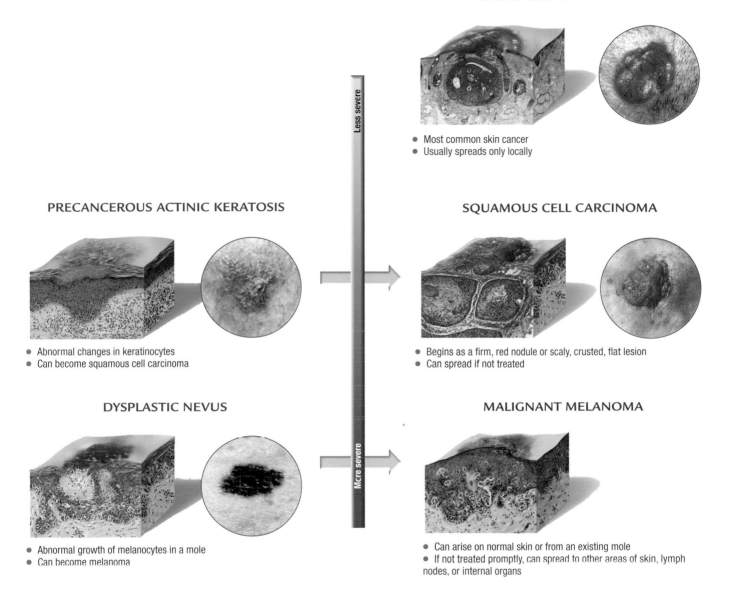

BASAL CELL CARCINOMA

- Most common skin cancer
- Usually spreads only locally

PRECANCEROUS ACTINIC KERATOSIS

- Abnormal changes in keratinocytes
- Can become squamous cell carcinoma

SQUAMOUS CELL CARCINOMA

- Begins as a firm, red nodule or scaly, crusted, flat lesion
- Can spread if not treated

DYSPLASTIC NEVUS

- Abnormal growth of melanocytes in a mole
- Can become melanoma

MALIGNANT MELANOMA

- Can arise on normal skin or from an existing mole
- If not treated promptly, can spread to other areas of skin, lymph nodes, or internal organs

Less severe

Mcre severe

ABCDEs OF MALIGNANT MELANOMA

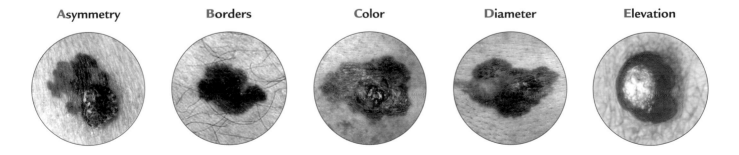

Asymmetry

Borders

Color

Diameter

Elevation

WARTS

Warts, also known as *verrucae*, are common, benign, viral infections of the skin and adjacent mucous membranes. The prognosis varies; some warts disappear spontaneously, some readily with treatment, and others need vigorous and prolonged treatment.

AGE ALERT
Although their incidence is highest in children and young adults, warts may occur at any age.

Causes
- Human papilloma virus (HPV)
- Probably transmitted through direct contact; autoinoculation

Pathophysiology
HPV replicates in the epidermal cells, causing irregular thickening of the stratum corneum in the infected areas. People who lack virus-specific immunity are susceptible.

COMPLICATIONS
- Secondary infection
- Scarring

Signs and symptoms

- Common (*verruca vulgaris*): rough, elevated, rounded surface; appears most frequently on extremities, particularly hands and fingers; most prevalent in children and young adults
- Filiform: single, thin, threadlike projection; commonly occurs around the face and neck
- Periungual: rough, irregularly shaped, elevated surface; occurs around edges of fingernails and toenails; when severe, may extend under the nail and lift it off the nail bed, causing pain
- Flat (juvenile): multiple groupings of up to several hundred slightly raised lesions with smooth, flat, or slightly rounded tops; common on the face, neck, chest, knees, dorsa of hands, wrists, and flexor surfaces of the forearms; usually occurs in children but can affect adults; distribution is often linear because these can spread from scratching or shaving
- Plantar: slightly elevated or flat; occurs singly or in large clusters (mosaic warts), primarily at pressure points of the feet; typically cause pain with weight bearing
- Digitate: fingerlike, horny projection arising from a pea-shaped base; occurs on scalp or near hairline

- Condyloma acuminatum (moist wart): usually small, flesh-colored pink to red, moist, soft; may occur singly or in large cauliflower-like clusters on penis, scrotum, vulva, or anus; may be transmitted through sexual contact; not always venereal in origin

Diagnostic test results
- Sigmoidoscopy when anal warts are recurrent rules out internal involvement necessitating surgery.
- Application of 5% acetic acid turns warts white if they're papillomas.

Treatment
Electrodesiccation and curettage
- High-frequency electric current to destroy the wart, surgical removal of dead tissue at the base
- Effective for common, filiform and, occasionally, plantar warts
- More effective than cryosurgery

Cryotherapy
- Liquid nitrogen kills the wart; resulting dried blister peeled off several days later
- If initial treatment unsuccessful, can be repeated at 2- to 4-week intervals
- Useful for periungual warts or for common warts on face, extremities, penis, vagina, or anus

Acid therapy (primary or adjunctive)
- Applications of plaster patches impregnated with acid (such as 40% salicylic acid plasters) or acid drops (such as 5% to 16.7% salicylic acid in flexible collodion) every 12 to 24 hours for 2 to 4 weeks
- Hyperthermia for *verruca plantaris*

For genital warts
- Cryotherapy
- Podophyllin in tincture of benzoin; may be repeated every 3 to 4 days (avoid using this drug on pregnant patients)
- 25% to 50% trichloroacetic acid applied to wart and neutralized with baking soda or water when wart turns white
- Carbon dioxide laser therapy

Other
- Antiviral drugs under investigation
- If immunity develops, possible resolution without treatment
- Imiquimod ointment

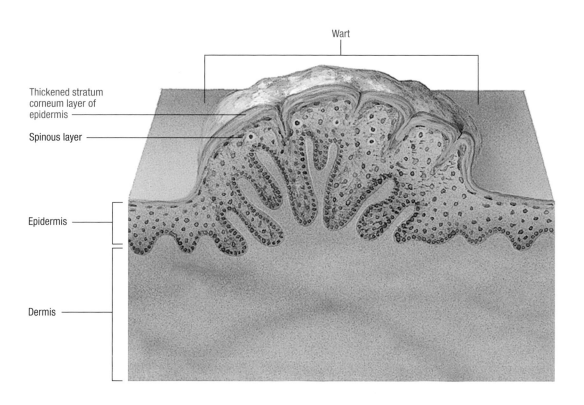

Wart

Thickened stratum corneum layer of epidermis

Spinous layer

Epidermis

Dermis

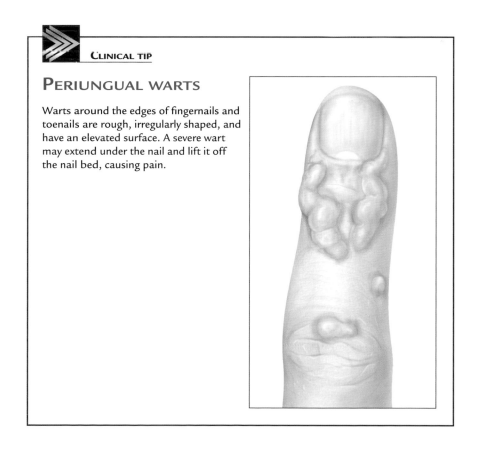

CLINICAL TIP

PERIUNGUAL WARTS

Warts around the edges of fingernails and toenails are rough, irregularly shaped, and have an elevated surface. A severe wart may extend under the nail and lift it off the nail bed, causing pain.

CATARACT

A cataract is a gradually developing opacity of the lens or lens capsule. Light shining through the cornea is blocked by this opacity, and a blurred image is cast onto the retina. As a result, the brain interprets a hazy image. Cataracts commonly occur bilaterally, and each progresses independently. Exceptions are traumatic cataracts, which are usually unilateral, and congenital cataracts, which may remain stationary.

AGE ALERT
Cataracts are most prevalent in people older than age 70. The prognosis is generally good; surgery improves vision in 95% of affected people.

Causes
- Aging
- Trauma, foreign body injury
- Exposure to ionizing radiation or infrared rays
- Exposure to ultraviolet radiation
- Drugs that are toxic to the lens, such as prednisone, ergot alkaloids, dinitrophenol, naphthalene, phenothiazines, pilocarpine
- Genetic abnormalities
- Infection such as maternal rubella during the first trimester of pregnancy
- Maternal malnutrition
- Metabolic disease, such as diabetes mellitus or hypothyroidism
- Myotonic dystrophy
- Uveitis, glaucoma, retinitis pigmentosa, retinal detachment
- Atopic dermatitis

Pathophysiology
Pathophysiology may vary with each form of cataract. Congenital cataracts are particularly challenging. They may result from chromosomal abnormalities, metabolic disease, intrauterine nutritional deficiencies, or infection during pregnancy (such as rubella). Senile cataracts show evidence of protein aggregation, oxidative injury, and increased pigmentation in the center of the lens. In traumatic cataracts, phagocytosis of the lens or inflammation may occur when a lens ruptures. The mechanism of a complicated cataract varies with the disease process — for example, in diabetes, increased glucose in the lens causes it to absorb water.

Typically, cataract development goes through these four stages:
- *immature* — partially opaque lens
- *mature* — completely opaque lens; significant vision loss
- *tumescent* — water-filled lens; may lead to glaucoma
- *hypermature* — lens proteins deteriorate; peptides leak through the lens capsule; glaucoma may develop if intraocular fluid outflow is obstructed.

COMPLICATIONS
- Vision loss

Signs and symptoms
- Gradual painless blurring and loss of vision
- Milky white pupil
- Blinding glare from headlights at night
- Poor reading vision caused by reduced clarity of images
- In central opacity — vision improves in dim light; as pupils dilate, patients able to see around the opacity

AGE ALERT
Elderly patients with reduced vision may become depressed and withdraw from social activities rather than complain about reduced vision.

Diagnostic test results
- Indirect ophthalmoscopy and slit-lamp examination show a dark area in the normally homogeneous red reflex.
- Visual acuity test confirms vision loss.

Treatment
- Phacoemulsification cataract extraction to remove lens but leave capsule in place:
- phacoemulsification to fragment the lens with ultrasonic vibrations
- aspiration of pieces
- implantation of intraocular lens
- Extracapsular cataract extraction:
- lens removed in one piece, capsule left intact
- implantation of intraocular lens
- Intracapsular cataract extraction of entire lens and capsule:
- rarely performed; may be necessary in trauma cases
- intraocular lens placed in front of iris
- Laser surgery to restore visual acuity if a secondary membrane forms in the intact posterior lens capsule after an extracapsular cataract extraction
- Discission (an incision) and aspiration possibly still used in children with soft cataracts
- Contact lenses or lens implantation after surgery to improve visual acuity, binocular vision, and depth perception

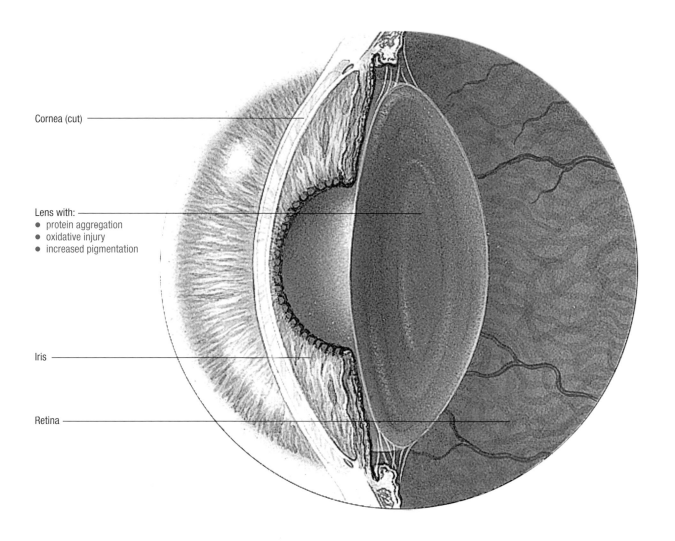

Cornea (cut)

Lens with:
- protein aggregation
- oxidative injury
- increased pigmentation

Iris

Retina

CLEFT LIP AND CLEFT PALATE

Cleft lip and cleft palate — an opening in the lip or palate — may occur separately or in combination. Cleft lip and cleft palate are twice as common in males as in females; isolated cleft palate is more common in females.

Causes
- Isolated birth defect: normal development of orofacial structures disrupted by a combination of genetic and environmental factors
- Part of a chromosomal or mendelian syndrome (cleft defects are associated with over 300 syndromes)
- Exposures to specific teratogens during fetal development

CLINICAL TIP
A family history of cleft defects increases the risk that a couple may have a child with a cleft defect. Likewise, an individual with a cleft defect is at an increased risk to have a child with a cleft defect. Children with cleft defects and their parents or adult individuals should be referred for genetic counseling for accurate diagnosis of cleft type and recurrence-risk counseling. Recurrence-risk is based on family history, the presence or absence of other physical or cognitive traits within a family, and prenatal exposure information.

Pathophysiology
Cleft deformities originate in the 2nd month of pregnancy, when the front and sides of the face and the palatine shelves fuse imperfectly. Cleft deformities usually occur unilaterally or bilaterally, rarely midline.

COMPLICATIONS
- Speech difficulties
- Failure to thrive
- Dentition problems
- Otitis media
- Hearing defects
- Physical deformity and self-image issues

Signs and symptoms
- *Cleft lip* may range from a simple notch in the upper lip to a complete cleft from the lip edge through the floor of the nostril.
- *Cleft palate* may be partial or complete, involving only the soft palate or extending from the soft palate completely through the hard palate into the upper jaw or nasal cavity.

CLINICAL TIP
The constellation of U-shaped cleft palate, mandibular hypoplasia, and glossoptosis (downward displacement and retraction of the tongue) is known as Pierre Robin sequence, or Robin sequence. It can occur as an isolated defect or one feature of many different syndromes; therefore, a comprehensive genetic evaluation is suggested for infants with Robin sequence. Because of the mandibular hypoplasia and glossoptosis, careful evaluation and management of the airway are mandatory for infants with Robin sequence.

Diagnostic test results
Prenatal ultrasonography reveals the defect.

Treatment
Surgical correction (timing varies)
- Cleft lip:
- within the first few days of life to make feeding easier
- or, delay lip repairs for 2 to 8 months to minimize surgical and anesthesia risks, rule out associated congenital anomalies, and allow time for parental bonding
- Cleft palate:
- performed only after the infant is gaining weight and is infection-free
- usually completed by age 12 to 18 months
- two steps: soft palate between ages 6 and 18 months; hard palate as late as age 5 years

Speech therapy
- Palate essential to speech formation (structural changes, even in a repaired cleft, can permanently affect speech patterns)
- Hearing difficulties common in children with cleft palate because of middle ear damage or infections

Other
- Orthodontic prosthesis
- Adequate nutrition
- Use of a large soft nipple with large holes

VARIATIONS OF CLEFT DEFORMITY

Cleft lip

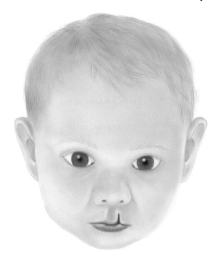

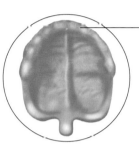

Front of palate

Unilateral cleft lip and cleft palate

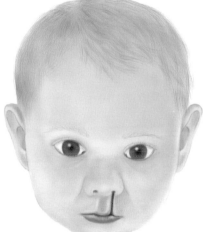

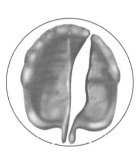

Bilateral cleft lip and cleft palate

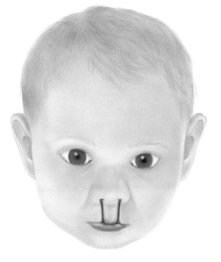

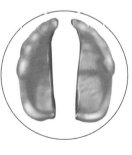

Cleft palate

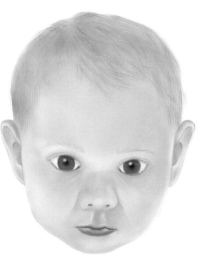

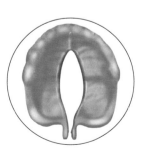

CONJUNCTIVITIS

Conjunctivitis is characterized by hyperemia of the conjunctiva. The three main types of conjunctivitis are infectious (called *pinkeye*), allergic, and chemical. This disorder usually occurs as benign, self-limiting pinkeye; it may also be chronic, possibly indicating degenerative changes or damage from repeated acute attacks. Epidemic keratoconjunctivitis is an acute, highly contagious viral conjunctivitis. Careful hand washing is essential to prevent the spread of conjunctivitis.

Causes

Infectious conjunctivitis
Most commonly by:
● Bacterial—*Staphylococcus aureus, Streptococcus pneumoniae, Neisseria gonorrhoeae, Neisseria meningitidis*
● Chlamydial—*Chlamydia trachomatis* (inclusion conjunctivitis)
● Viral—adenovirus types 3, 7, and 8; herpes simplex 1
Allergic conjunctivitis
Hypersensitivity to:
● Pollen, grass, unknown seasonal allergens (vernal conjunctivitis), animals
● Topical medications, cosmetics, fabrics
● Air pollutants, smoke
● Contact lenses or solutions
Chemical conjunctivitis
Chemical reaction to:
● Environmental irritants (wind, dust, smoke, swimming pool chlorine)
● Occupational irritants (acids, alkalies)

Pathophysiology

Conjunctivitis is an inflammation of the conjunctiva, the transparent layer covering the surfaces in the inner eyelid and the front of the eyeball. It usually begins in one eye and rapidly spreads to the other by contamination of towels, washcloths, or the patient's own hands.

Vernal conjunctivitis (so called because symptoms tend to be worse in the spring) is a severe form of immunoglobulin E–mediated mast cell hypersensitivity reaction. This form of conjunctivitis is bilateral. It usually begins between ages 3 and 5 and persists for about 10 years. It's sometimes associated with other signs of allergy commonly related to pollens, asthma, or allergic rhinitis.

COMPLICATIONS
● Corneal infiltrates
● Corneal ulcers

Signs and symptoms
● Hyperemia of the conjunctiva
● Discharge, tearing
● Pain, photophobia
Acute bacterial conjunctivitis (pinkeye)
● Usually lasts only 2 weeks
● Itching, burning, and the sensation of a foreign body in the eye
● Crust of sticky, mucopurulent discharge on the eyelids
N. gonorrhoeae conjunctivitis
● Itching, burning, foreign body sensation
● Profuse, purulent discharge
Viral conjunctivitis
● Copious tearing, minimal exudate
● Enlargement of the preauricular lymph node
● In children, sore throat or fever if the cause is an adenovirus
● Variable time course, depending on the virus:
– some self-limiting, lasting 2 to 3 weeks
– others chronic, producing a severe disabling disease

Diagnostic test results
● In stained smears of conjunctival scrapings, the predominance of lymphocytes indicates viral infection; of neutrophils, bacterial infection; of eosinophils, allergy-related infection.
● Culture and sensitivity tests identify the causative organism.

Treatment
● Bacterial conjunctivitis: topical appropriate broad-spectrum antibiotic
● Viral conjunctivitis:
– resists treatment; most important aspect of treatment is preventing transmission
– herpes simplex infection generally responsive to treatment with trifluridine drops, vidarabine ointment, oral acyclovir
– secondary infection possibly prevented by sulfonamide or broad-spectrum antibiotic eyedrops
● Vernal (allergic) conjunctivitis:
– corticosteroid drops followed by cromolyn sodium
– cold compresses to relieve itching
– occasionally, oral antihistamines

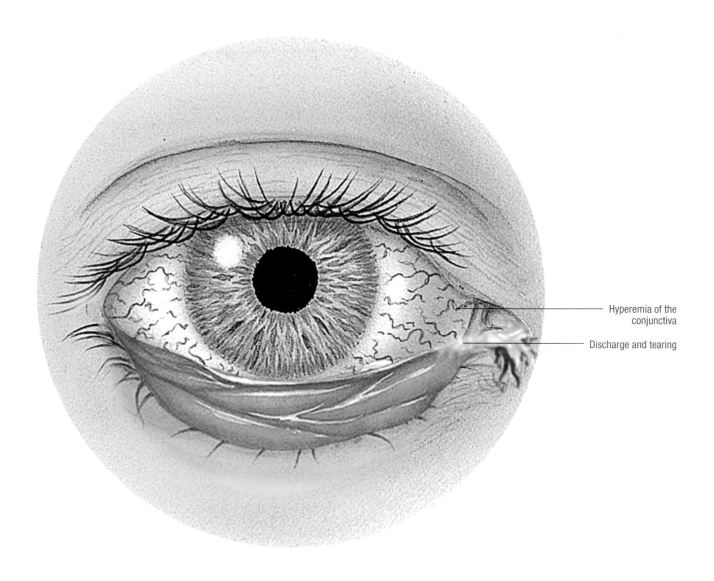

Hyperemia of the conjunctiva

Discharge and tearing

CORNEAL ULCER

Corneal ulcers produce corneal scarring or perforation and are a major cause of blindness worldwide. They occur in the central or marginal areas of the cornea, vary in shape and size, and may be singular or multiple. Marginal ulcers are the most common form. Prompt treatment (within hours of onset) can prevent visual impairment.

Causes

Protozoan infection
- Acanthamoeba

Bacterial infections
- *Staphylococcus aureus*
- *Pseudomonas aeruginosa*
- *Streptococcus viridans*
- *Streptococcus (Diplococcus) pneumoniae*
- *Moraxella liquefaciens*

Viral infections
- Herpes simplex 1
- Variola
- Vaccinia
- Varicella zoster

Fungal infections
- *Candida*
- *Fusarium*
- *Acremonium*

Other
- Trauma
- Exposure reactions to bacterial infections, toxins, trichiasis, entropion, allergens, or contact lenses
- Vitamin A deficiency (xerophthalmia)
- Fifth cranial nerve lesions (neurotropic ulcers)

Pathophysiology

The introduction of a causative factor, such as bacterial or herpes virus infection, trauma, or misuse of contact lenses, starts the process. This leads to epithelial destruction of the stoma with inflammation and tearing. Superficial ulceration results in photophobia, discomfort, and decreased visual acuity.

Deep ulcerations penetrate the epithelial layers of the eye, leading to perforation and allowing infection of deeper eye structures and extrusion of eye contents. Fibrous tissue can form during healing of deep ulcerations, leading to scarring and eventual opacity of the cornea. These processes can lead to partial or total vision loss.

COMPLICATIONS
- Corneal scarring
- Loss of the eye
- Vision loss

Signs and symptoms
- Pain aggravated by blinking
- Increased tearing
- Pronounced visual blurring
- Purulent discharge (with bacterial ulcer)

Diagnostic test results
- Flashlight examination reveals an irregular corneal surface.
- Fluorescein dye instilled in the conjunctival sac stains the outline of the ulcer and confirms the diagnosis.
- Culture and sensitivity testing of corneal scrapings may identify the causative bacteria or fungus.

Treatment

All corneal ulcers
- Prompt treatment to prevent complications and permanent visual impairment
- Systemic and topical broad-spectrum antibiotics until culture results identify the causative organism
- Measures to eliminate the underlying cause of the ulcer and relieve pain

Fungal infection
- Topical instillation of natamycin for *Fusarium, Acremonium,* and *Candida* infections

Infection with herpes simplex 1
- Topical application of trifluridine drops or vidarabine ointment
- Trifluridine for recurrence

Vitamin A deficiency
- Correction of dietary deficiency or GI malabsorption of vitamin A

Infection with **P. aeruginosa**
- Polymyxin B and gentamicin administered topically and by subconjunctival injection
- Hospitalization and isolation and I.V. carbenicillin and tobramycin to stop the rapid spread of infection and prevent corneal perforation, which can occur within 48 hours

CLINICAL TIP

Treatment for a corneal ulcer caused by bacterial infection should never include an eye patch. Use of an eye patch creates the dark, warm, moist environment ideal for bacterial growth.

Neurotropic ulcers or exposure keratitis
- Frequent instillation of artificial tears or lubricating ointments and use of a plastic bubble eye shield

Infection with varicella zoster
- Topical sulfonamide ointment applied three to four times daily to prevent secondary infection
- Analgesics for pain
- Cycloplegic eyedrops for associated anterior uveitis

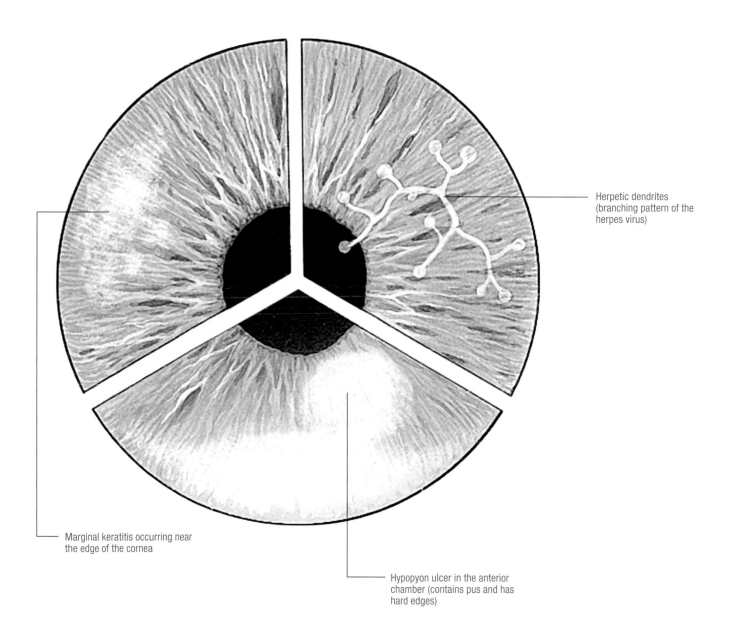

Herpetic dendrites
(branching pattern of the
herpes virus)

Marginal keratitis occurring near
the edge of the cornea

Hypopyon ulcer in the anterior
chamber (contains pus and has
hard edges)

ECTROPION AND ENTROPION

Ectropion, the outward turning or eversion of the eyelid, may be congenital or acquired. Acquired ectropion may be involutional, paralytic, cicatricial, or mechanical. Involutional ectropion is the most common form and usually stems from age-related weakness in the lid. Paralytic ectropion may occur with seventh nerve palsy from diverse causes, such as Bell's palsy, tumors, herpes zoster oticus, and infiltrations or tumors of the parotid gland. Cicatricial ectropion results from scarring of the anterior lamella from facial burns, trauma, chronic dermatitis, or excessive skin excision with blepharoplasty. Mechanical ectropion can occur with lid tumors that cause the lower eyelid to evert.

Entropion is the inward turning or inversion of the eyelid. It can be unilateral or bilateral and can occur in the upper or lower eyelid, although it occurs more commonly in the lower lid. Entropion can be congenital (rare), acute spastic, involutional, or cicatricial.

Although both ectropion and entropion can occur at any age, they're more common in adults over age 60.

Causes

Ectropion
● Deficiency of the anterior lamella (congenital)
● Genetic ocular syndromes
● Lack of tone of muscles that hold the eyelid taut (acquired)

Entropion
● Dysgenesis of the lower eyelid retractors (congenital)
● Ocular irritation from infection, inflammation, or trauma (acute spastic)
● Scarring of the palpebral conjunctiva and rotation of the eyelid margin (cicatricial)

Pathophysiology

Ectropion
Poor insertion of the muscles that pull the eyelid downward along with contraction of the orbicularis muscle allows the eyelid to turn one way or the other. Laxity of the canthal tendon can aggravate the problem. If both tendons become significantly lax, all of the horizontal support of the eyelid is weakened, resulting in an ectropion or eversion of the eyelid.

Entropion
In acute spastic entropion, the spastic closing of the orbicularis oculi muscle overtakes the opposing action of the lower eyelid retraction, resulting in an inward turning of the eyelid.

In acquired entropion, the brow and lower facial muscles are weak, which results in a drooping of the lower eyelid.

In involutional entropion, dehiscence of the lower lid retractors allows the inferior tarsal margin to move anteriorly. Horizontal eyelid laxity and overriding of the pretarsal and preseptal orbicularis muscles add to this, resulting in involutional entropion. Cicatricial entropion results from scarring of the palpebral conjunctiva and subsequent inward rotation of the eyelid margin.

COMPLICATIONS
● Corneal abrasions
● Corneal scarring
● Tearing
● Keratinization of the palpebral conjunctiva
● Vision loss

Signs and symptoms
● Irritated or red eyes
● Tearing
● Watery eyes
● Discharge
● Crusting of the eyelid
● A sensation of something in the eye

Diagnostic test results
● Although laboratory studies don't show entropion, biopsy may help rule out anti–basement membrane antibodies in cicatricial entropion.
● Exophthalmometry readings may reveal the presence of exophthalmos in involutional ectropion.
● Distraction and snap-back tests reveal abnormal horizontal lid laxity in ectropion.

Treatment
● Ocular lubrication and artificial tear preparations for spastic entropion resulting from dry eye syndrome
● Antibiotics and corticosteroids for spastic entropion caused by blepharitis
● Botulinum (Botox) injection in small amounts for spastic entropion to weaken the pretarsal orbicularis oculi muscle
● Chemotherapy (Dapsone) for cicatricial entropion secondary to pemphigus
● Surgical repair

ECTROPION

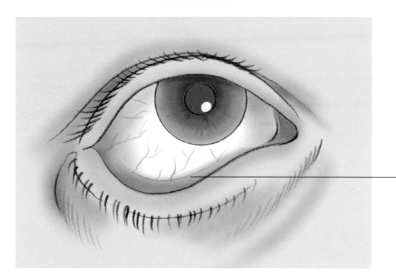

Weakness in the eyelid causes the outward turning of the eyelid.

ENTROPION

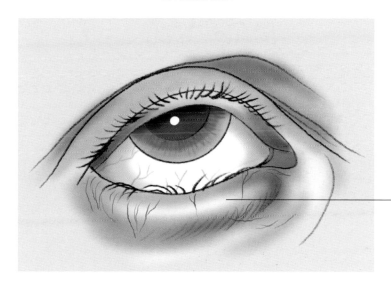

The eyelid turns inward.

GLAUCOMA

Glaucoma is a group of disorders characterized by an abnormally high intraocular pressure (IOP) that damages the optic nerve and other intraocular structures. Glaucoma occurs in several forms: chronic open-angle (primary), acute angle-closure, congenital (inherited as an autosomal recessive trait), and secondary to other causes. Chronic open-angle glaucoma is usually bilateral, with insidious onset and a slowly progressive course. Acute angle-closure glaucoma typically has a rapid onset, constituting an ophthalmic emergency. Unless treated promptly, this acute form of glaucoma causes blindness in 3 to 5 days.

Causes
Chronic open-angle glaucoma
- Genetics
- Hypertension
- Diabetes mellitus
- Aging
- Black ethnicity
- Severe myopia

Acute angle-closure glaucoma
- Drug-induced mydriasis (extreme dilation of the pupil)
- Excitement or stress, which can lead to hypertension

Secondary glaucoma
- Uveitis
- Trauma
- Steroids
- Diabetes
- Infections
- Surgery

Pathophysiology
Chronic open-angle glaucoma results from overproduction or obstruction of the outflow of aqueous humor through the trabecular meshwork or the canal of Schlemm, causing increased IOP and damage to the optic nerve. In secondary glaucoma, conditions such as trauma and surgery increase the risk of obstruction of intraocular fluid outflow caused by edema or other abnormal processes.

Acute angle-closure glaucoma results from obstruction to the outflow of aqueous humor. Obstruction may be caused by anatomically narrow angles between the anterior iris and the posterior corneal surface, shallow anterior chambers, a thickened iris that causes angle closure on pupil dilation, or a bulging iris that presses on the trabeculae, closing the angle (peripheral anterior synechiae). Any of these may cause IOP to increase suddenly.

AGE ALERT
In older patients, partial closure of the angle also may occur, so that two forms of glaucoma may coexist.

COMPLICATIONS
- Vision loss and blindness

Signs and symptoms
Chronic open-angle glaucoma
- Typically bilateral
- Mild aching in the eyes
- Loss of peripheral vision
- Images of halos around lights
- Reduced visual acuity, especially at night, not correctable with glasses

Acute angle-closure glaucoma
- Rapid onset; usually unilateral
- Inflammation; red, painful eye
- Sensation of pressure over the eye
- Moderate papillary dilation nonreactive to light
- Cloudy cornea
- Blurring and decreased visual acuity; halos around lights
- Photophobia
- Nausea and vomiting

Diagnostic test results
- Tonometry measurement shows increased IOP.
- Slit-lamp examination shows effects of glaucoma on anterior eye structures.
- Gonioscopy shows the angle of the eye's anterior chamber.
- Ophthalmoscopy aids visualization of the fundus.
- Perimetry or visual field tests show the extent of peripheral vision loss.
- Fundus photography shows optic disk changes.

Treatment
Chronic open-angle glaucoma
- Beta-adrenergic blockers, such as timolol or betaxolol (a beta$_1$-receptor antagonist)
- Alpha agonists, such as brimonidine or apraclonidine
- Carbonic anhydrase inhibitors, such as dorzolamide or acetazolamide
- Epinephrine
- Prostaglandins such as latanoprost
- Miotic eyedrops such as pilocarpine
- Surgical procedures if medical therapy fails to reduce IOP:
  - argon laser trabeculoplasty of the trabecular meshwork of an open angle, to produce a thermal burn that changes the surface of the meshwork and increases the outflow of aqueous humor
  - trabeculectomy, to remove scleral tissue, followed by a peripheral iridectomy, to produce an opening for aqueous outflow under the conjunctiva, creating a filtering bleb

Acute angle-closure glaucoma
- Ocular emergency, requiring immediate intervention, including:
  - I.V. mannitol (20%) or oral glycerin (50%)
  - steroid drops
  - acetazolamide, a carbonic anhydrase inhibitor
  - pilocarpine, to constrict the pupil, forcing the iris away from the trabeculae and allowing fluid to escape
  - timolol, a beta-adrenergic blocker
  - opioid analgesics
  - laser iridotomy or surgical peripheral iridectomy
  - cycloplegic drops, such as apraclonidine, in the affected eye (only after laser peripheral iridectomy)

Normal optic disk

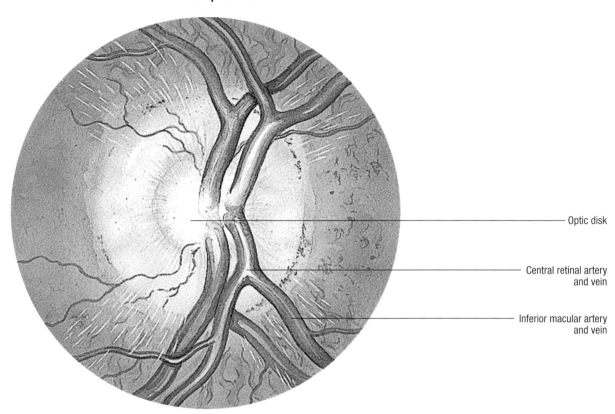

Optic disk

Central retinal artery and vein

Inferior macular artery and vein

Disk changes

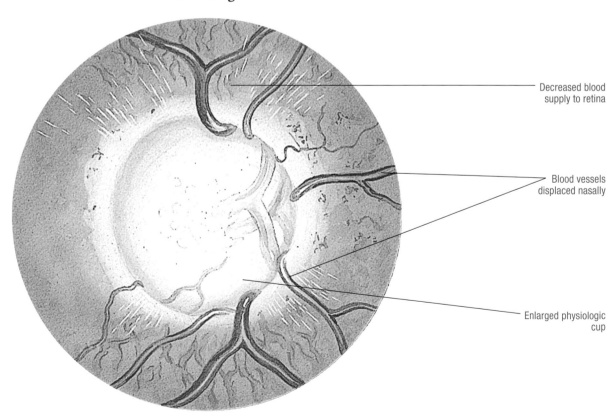

Decreased blood supply to retina

Blood vessels displaced nasally

Enlarged physiologic cup

HEARING LOSS

Hearing loss, or deafness, results from a mechanical or nervous impediment to the transmission of sound waves and is the most common pathologic process associated with hearing alteration. Hearing loss is further defined as an inability to perceive the normal range of sounds audible to an individual with normal hearing. Types of hearing loss include congenital hearing loss, sudden deafness, noise-induced hearing loss, and presbycusis.

Causes

Congenital hearing loss
- Dominant, autosomal dominant, autosomal recessive, or sex-linked recessive trait
- Maternal exposure to rubella or syphilis during pregnancy
- Use of ototoxic drugs during pregnancy
- Trauma or prolonged fetal anoxia during delivery
- Congenital abnormalities of ears, nose, or throat
- Prematurity or low birth weight
- Serum bilirubin levels above 20 mg/dl

Sudden deafness
- Mumps — most common cause of unilateral sensorineural hearing loss in children
- Other bacterial and viral infections — rubella, rubeola, influenza, herpes zoster, infectious mononucleosis, mycoplasma
- Metabolic disorders — diabetes mellitus, hypothyroidism, hyperlipoproteinemia
- Vascular disorders — hypertension, arteriosclerosis
- Head trauma or brain tumors
- Ototoxic drugs — tobramycin, streptomycin, quinine, gentamicin, furosemide, ethacrynic acid
- Neurologic disorders — multiple sclerosis, neurosyphilis
- Blood dyscrasias — leukemia, hypercoagulation

Noise-induced hearing loss
- Prolonged exposure to loud noise (85 to 90 dB)
- Brief exposure to extremely loud noise (greater than 90 dB)

Presbycusis
- Loss of hair cells in the organ of Corti

Pathophysiology

The major forms of hearing loss are classified as conductive loss, interrupted passage of sound from the external ear to the junction of the stapes and oval window; sensorineural loss, impaired cochlea or acoustic (eighth cranial) nerve dysfunction, causing failure of transmission of sound impulses within the inner ear or brain; or mixed loss, combined dysfunction of conduction and sensorineural transmission.

COMPLICATIONS
- Difficulty communicating

Signs and symptoms
- Deficient response to auditory stimuli
- Impaired speech development
- Loss of perception of certain frequencies (around 4,000 Hz)
- Tinnitus
- Inability to understand the spoken word

AGE ALERT
A deaf infant's behavior can appear normal and mislead the parents as well as the health care professional, especially if the infant has autosomal recessive deafness and is the first child of carrier parents.

Diagnostic test results
- Computed tomography scan shows vestibular and auditory pathways.
- Magnetic resonance imaging reveals acoustic tumors and brain lesions.
- Auditory brain response shows activity in auditory nerve and brain stem.
- Pure tone audiometry reveals presence and degree of hearing loss.
- Electronystagmography shows vestibular function.
- Otoscopic or microscopic examination reveals middle ear disorders and removes debris.
- Rinne and Weber's tests show whether hearing loss is conductive or sensorineural.

Treatment

Congenital hearing loss
- Surgery, if correctable
- Sign language, speech reading, or other effective means of developing communication
- Phototherapy and exchange transfusions for hyperbilirubinemia
- Appropriate childhood immunizations

Sudden deafness
- Prompt identification of underlying cause, such as acoustic neuroma or noise, and appropriate treatment

Noise-induced hearing loss
- Normal hearing usually restored by overnight rest after several hours' exposure to noise levels greater than 90 dB
- High-frequency hearing loss generally prevented by reducing exposure to loud noises
- Speech and hearing rehabilitation possibly required after repeated exposure to such noise, because hearing aids are seldom helpful

Presbycusis
- Amplifying sound, as with a hearing aid, helpful to some patients
- Hearing aid no help for many patients who are intolerant of loud noise

Other
- Antibiotics
- Agents to dissolve cerumen
- Decongestants
- Analgesics

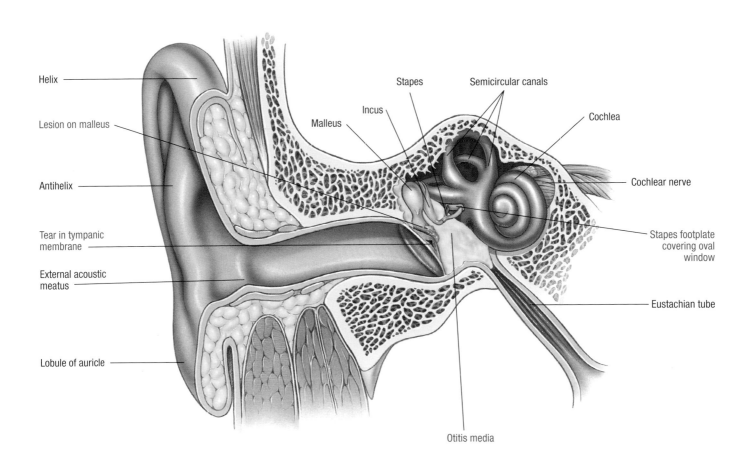

Helix

Lesion on malleus

Antihelix

Tear in tympanic membrane

External acoustic meatus

Lobule of auricle

Stapes

Incus

Malleus

Semicircular canals

Cochlea

Cochlear nerve

Stapes footplate covering oval window

Eustachian tube

Otitis media

 CLINICAL TIP

HOW HEARING OCCURS

- Sound vibrations strike the tympanic membrane (eardrum).
- The auditory ossicles vibrate, and the footplate of the stapes moves at the oval window.
- Movement of the oval window causes the fluid inside the scala vestibuli and scala tympani to move.
- Fluid movement against the cochlear duct sets off nerve impulses, which are carried to the brain via the cochlear nerve.

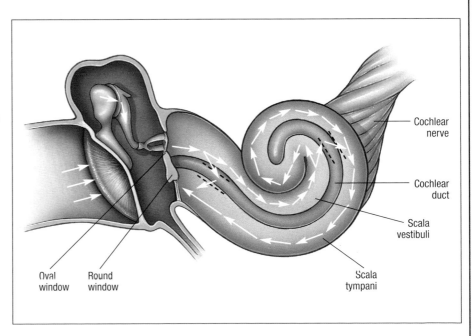

Cochlear nerve

Cochlear duct

Scala vestibuli

Scala tympani

Oval window

Round window

Hearing loss **419**

Laryngeal cancer

Laryngeal cancer is cancer of the larynx or voice box in which malignant cells are found in the tissue of the larynx. The most common form of laryngeal cancer is squamous cell carcinoma (95%); rare forms include adenocarcinoma, sarcoma, and others.

Causes

Unknown

Risk factors

- Smoking
- Alcoholism
- Chronic inhalation of noxious fumes
- Familial tendency
- History of gastroesophageal reflux disease

Pathophysiology

Laryngeal cancer may be intrinsic or extrinsic. An intrinsic tumor is on the true vocal cord and doesn't tend to spread because underlying connective tissues lack lymph nodes. An extrinsic tumor is on some other part of the larynx and tends to spread early. Laryngeal cancer is further classified according to these locations:

- *supraglottis* (false vocal cords)
- *glottis* (true vocal cords)
- *subglottis* (downward extension from vocal cords [rare]).

COMPLICATIONS
- Swallowing difficulty

Signs and symptoms

Intrinsic laryngeal cancer

- Hoarseness that persists longer than 3 weeks

Extrinsic cancer

- Lump in the throat
- Pain or burning in the throat when drinking citrus juice or hot liquid

Later clinical effects of metastases

- Dysphagia
- Dyspnea
- Cough
- Enlarged cervical lymph nodes
- Pain radiating to the ear

Diagnostic test results

- Xeroradiography, laryngeal tomography, computed tomography scan, and laryngography confirm the presence of a mass.
- Chest X-ray identifies metastasis.
- Laryngoscopy allows definitive staging by obtaining multiple biopsy specimens to establish a primary diagnosis, to determine the extent of disease, and to identify additional premalignant lesions or second primary lesions.
- Biopsy identifies cancer cells.

Treatment

Precancerous lesions

- Laser surgery

Early lesions

- Surgery or radiation

Advanced lesions

- Surgery; procedures vary with tumor size and can include cordectomy, partial or total laryngectomy, supraglottic laryngectomy, or total laryngectomy with laryngoplasty
- Laser surgery to help relieve obstruction caused by tumor growth
- Radiation and chemotherapy

Speech rehabilitation

- If speech preservation isn't possible, may include:
- esophageal speech
- prosthetic devices
- experimental surgical techniques to construct a new voice box

Mirror view

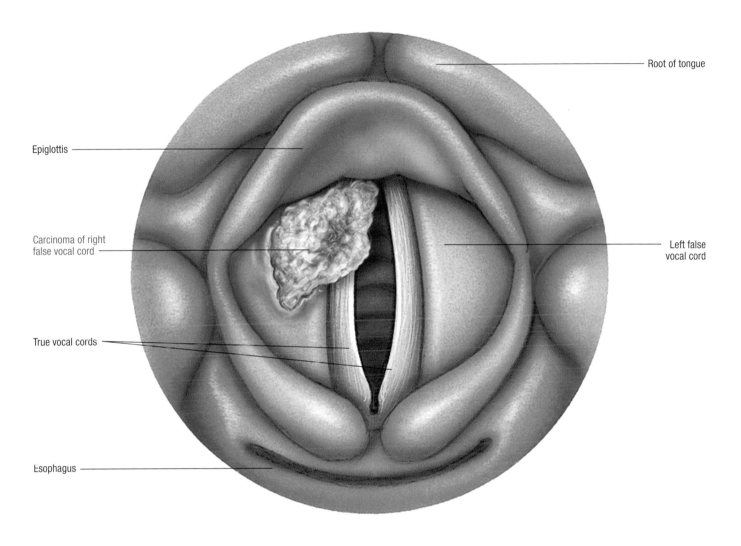

Root of tongue

Epiglottis

Carcinoma of right
false vocal cord

Left false
vocal cord

True vocal cords

Esophagus

MACULAR DEGENERATION

Macular degeneration — atrophy or degeneration of the macular disk — is the most common cause of legal blindness in adults. Commonly affecting both eyes, it accounts for about 12% of blindness in the United States and for about 17% of new blindness. It's one cause of severe, irreversible, and unpreventable loss of central vision in elderly patients.

AGE ALERT
Two types of age-related macular degeneration occur:
- dry, or atrophic — characterized by atrophic pigment epithelial changes; most commonly causes mild, gradual visual loss
- wet, or exudative — characterized by subretinal formation of new blood vessels (neovascularization) that cause leakage, hemorrhage, and fibrovascular scar formation; causes severe, rapid vision loss.

Causes
Primary cause unknown
Possible contributing factors
- Aging
- Inflammation
- Trauma
- Infection
- Poor nutrition
- Family history
- Smoking
- Cardiovascular disease

Pathophysiology
Age-related macular degeneration results from hardening and obstruction of retinal arteries, which probably reflect normal degenerative changes. The formation of new blood vessels in the macular area obscures central vision. Underlying pathologic changes occur primarily in the retinal pigment epithelium, Bruch's membrane, and choriocapillaries in the macular region.

The dry form develops as yellow extracellular deposits, or drusen, accumulate beneath the pigment epithelium of the retina; they may be prominent in the macula. Drusen are common in elderly patients. Over time, drusen grow and become more numerous. Visual loss occurs as the retinal pigment epithelium detaches and becomes atrophic.

Exudative macular degeneration develops as new blood vessels in the choroid project through abnormalities in Bruch's membrane and invade the potential space underneath the retinal pigment epithelium. As these vessels leak, fluid in the retinal pigment epithelium is increased, causing blurry vision.

COMPLICATIONS
- Blindness
- Macular lesions
- Nystagmus

Signs and symptoms
- Changes in central vision due to neovascularization, such as a blank spot (scotoma) in the center of a page when reading
- Distorted appearance of straight lines caused by relocation of retinal receptors

Diagnostic test results
- Indirect ophthalmoscopy shows gross macular changes, opacities, hemorrhage, neovascularization, retinal pallor, or retinal detachment.
- I.V. fluorescein angiography sequential photographs show leaking vessels as fluorescein dye flows into the tissues from the subretinal neovascular net.
- Amsler's grid test reveals central visual field loss.

Treatment
- Exudative form (subretinal neovascularization): laser photocoagulation
- Atrophic form: currently no cure

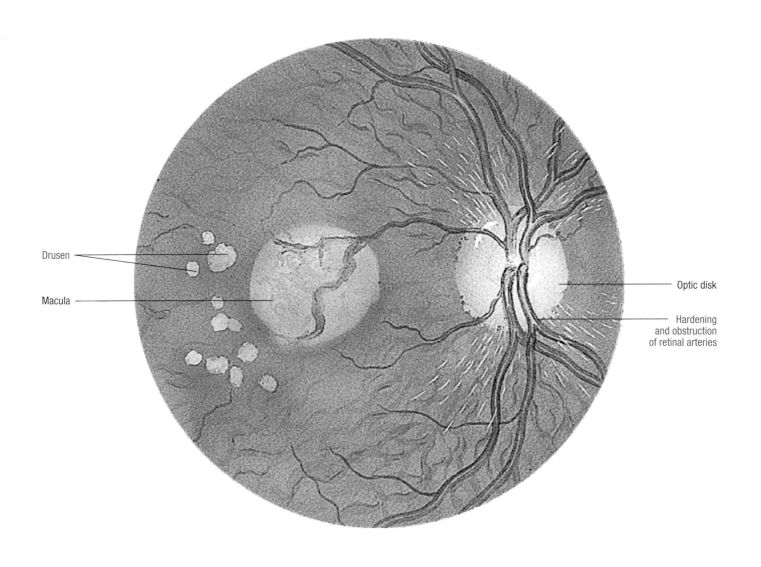

Drusen

Macula

Optic disk

Hardening
and obstruction
of retinal arteries

MÉNIÈRE'S DISEASE

Ménière's disease, a labyrinthine dysfunction also known as *endolymphatic hydrops,* causes severe vertigo, sensorineural hearing loss, and tinnitus.

AGE ALERT
Ménière's disease usually affects adults between ages 30 and 60, men slightly more often than women. It rarely occurs in children.

Usually, only one ear is involved. After multiple attacks over several years, residual tinnitus and hearing loss can be incapacitating.

Causes
Unknown
Possible associations
- Positive family history
- Immune disorder
- Migraine headaches
- Middle ear infection
- Head trauma
- Autonomic nervous system dysfunction
- Premenstrual edema

Pathophysiology
Ménière's disease may result from overproduction or decreased absorption of endolymph — the fluid contained in the labyrinth of the ear. Accumulated endolymph dilates the saccule and cochlear duct. Dilation of the endolymphatic system occurs and the Reissner membrane often tears. When rupture of the membrane causes endolymph to escape into the perilymph, the symptoms of Ménière's occurs.

COMPLICATIONS
- Trauma from falls
- Dehydration
- Decreased quality of life

Signs and symptoms
- Sudden, severe spinning, whirling vertigo, lasting from 10 minutes to several hours, because of increased endolymph (attacks may occur several times a year, or remissions may last as long as several years)
- Tinnitus caused by altered firing of sensory auditory neurons; possibly, residual tinnitus between attacks
- Hearing impairment due to sensorineural loss:
- hearing possibly normal between attacks
- repeated attacks possible progressive cause of permanent hearing loss
- Feeling of fullness or blockage in the ear before an attack, a result of changing sensitivity of pressure receptors
- Severe nausea, vomiting, sweating, and pallor during an acute attack because of autonomic dysfunction
- Nystagmus due to asymmetry and intensity of impulses reaching the brain stem
- Loss of balance and falling to the affected side due to vertigo

Diagnostic test results
- Audiometric testing shows a sensorineural hearing loss and loss of discrimination and recruitment.
- Electronystagmography reveals normal or reduced vestibular response on the affected side.
- Cold caloric testing shows impairment of oculovestibular reflex.
- Electrocochleography reveals increased ratio of summating potential to action potential.
- Brain stem-evoked response audiometry test evaluates for acoustic neuroma, brain tumor, and vascular lesions in the brain stem.
- Computed tomography scan and magnetic resonance imaging detects acoustic neuroma as a cause of symptoms.

Treatment
During an acute attack
- Lying down to minimize head movement
- Avoiding sudden movements and glaring lights to reduce dizziness
- Promethazine or prochlorperazine to relieve nausea and vomiting
- Atropine to control an attack by reducing autonomic nervous system function
- Dimenhydrinate to control vertigo and nausea
- Central nervous system depressants, such as lorazepam or diazepam, to reduce excitability of vestibular nuclei
- Antihistamines, such as meclizine or diphenhydramine, to reduce dizziness and vomiting
Long-term management
- Diuretics, such as triamterene or acetazolamide, to reduce endolymph pressure
- Betahistine, to alleviate vertigo, hearing loss, and tinnitus
- Vasodilators, to dilate blood vessels supplying the inner ear
- Sodium restriction, to reduce endolymphatic hydrops
- Antihistamines or mild sedatives, to prevent attacks
- Systemic streptomycin, to produce chemical ablation of the sensory neuroepithelium of the inner ear and thereby control vertigo in patients with bilateral disease for whom no other treatment can be considered
Disease that persists despite medical treatment or produces incapacitating vertigo
- Endolymphatic drainage and shunt placement, to reduce pressure on the hair cells of the cochlea and prevent further sensorineural hearing loss
- Vestibular nerve resection in patients with intact hearing, to reduce vertigo and prevent further hearing loss
- Labyrinthectomy to relieve vertigo in patients with incapacitating symptoms and poor or no hearing (destruction of the cochlea results in a total loss of hearing in the affected ear)
- Cochlear implantation, to improve hearing in patients with profound deafness

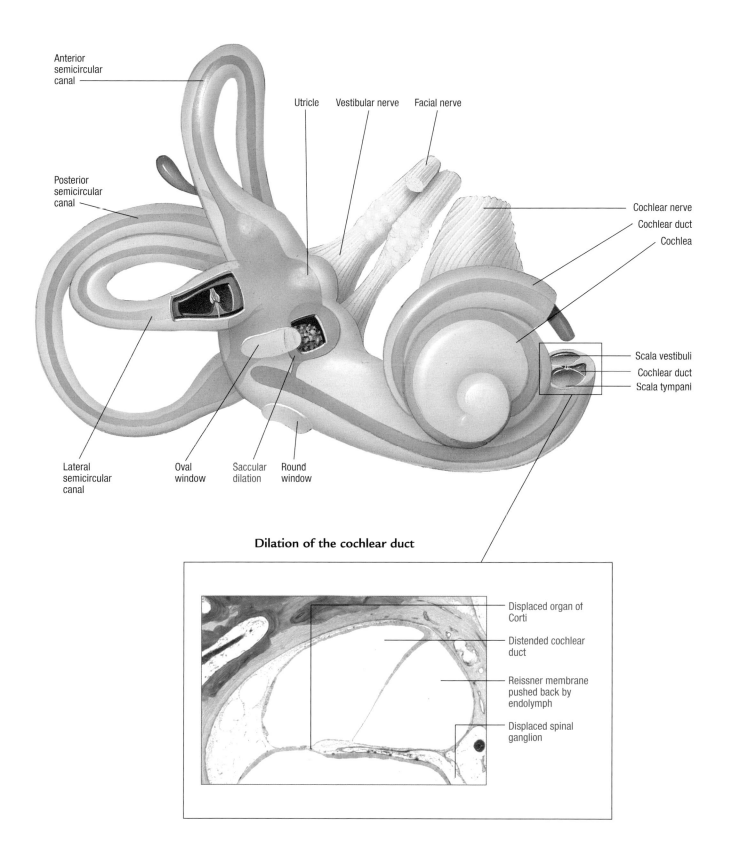

Anterior semicircular canal

Posterior semicircular canal

Utricle

Vestibular nerve

Facial nerve

Cochlear nerve

Cochlear duct

Cochlea

Scala vestibuli

Cochlear duct

Scala tympani

Lateral semicircular canal

Oval window

Saccular dilation

Round window

Dilation of the cochlear duct

Displaced organ of Corti

Distended cochlear duct

Reissner membrane pushed back by endolymph

Displaced spinal ganglion

OCULAR MELANOMA

Although melanoma typically develops in areas of the body that contain cells that produce melanin such as the skin, it can also occur in the pigmented area of the eye. Ocular melanoma most commonly occurs in the vascular layer of the eye called the uvea, the area between the retina and the sclera. It can occur in the iris and ciliary body (the front part of the uvea) or in the choroid layer (the back part of the uvea).

Melanoma that originates in the eye is a primary cancer, the most common primary cancer of the eye in adults. Melanoma that appears elsewhere first and then spreads to the eye is a secondary cancer. Both types of ocular melanoma are rare.

Causes
- Exact cause unknown
- Blue eye color (increased risk)
- Dysplastic nevus syndrome (possible increased risk)

Pathophysiology
Primary melanoma originates in the melanocytes of the choroid or back part of the uvea and typically begins as preexisting melanocytic nevi. Choroidal melanoma impedes circulation to the pigmented retinal epithelium. The tumors can become large before noticeable vision loss occurs, depending on the distance from the optic nerve and fovea where they originate. Seepage of fluid into the subretinal space can lead to total retinal detachment.

Choroidal melanomas ultimately result in death because of metastasis. Unfortunately, this cancer metastasizes before diagnosis. Because there are no lymphatic vessels in the eye, the cancer can only spread through the hematologic system and most often metastasizes to the liver. Other organs of metastasis include the lungs, bone, skin, and central nervous system.

COMPLICATIONS
- Metastasis
- Blindness

Signs and symptoms
- Light flashes
- Visual blurring
- Dark spot in the visual field
- Change in the color of the iris
- Growing dark spot on the iris
- Loss of peripheral vision in the affected eye
- Visual floaters
- Red, painful eye

Diagnostic test results
- Ultrasound of the eye shows the tumor and helps to evaluate size and thickness to determine appropriate treatment.
- Blood tests, radiography, ultrasonography, magnetic resonance imaging, or computerized tomography scanning detects metastasis to the liver and lungs.

Treatment
- Surgery (iridectomy, iridotrabeculectomy, iridocyclectomy, choroidectomy, or enucleation)
- Radiation therapy (teletherapy or brachytherapy)
- Chemotherapy
- Interferon
- Cryotherapy or transpupillary thermotherapy (for small tumors)

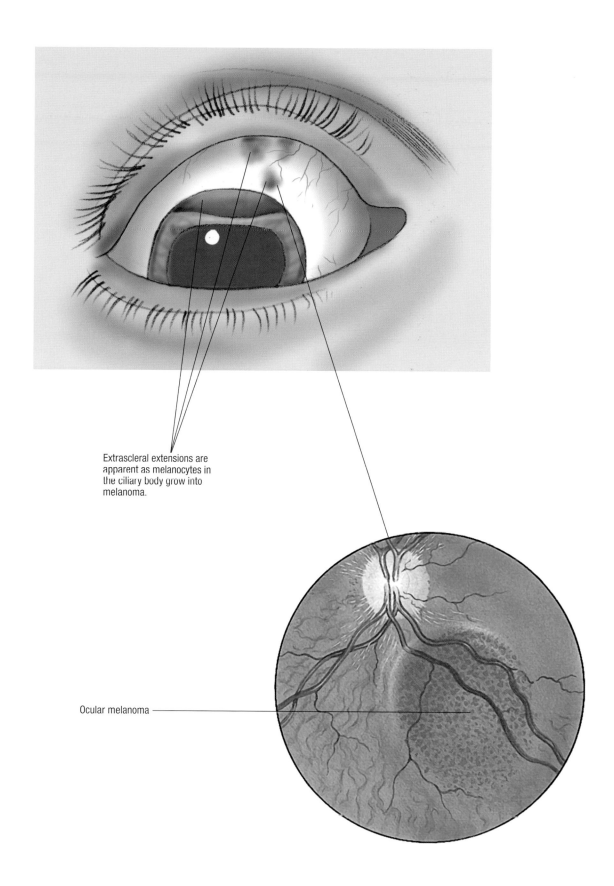

Extrascleral extensions are apparent as melanocytes in the ciliary body grow into melanoma.

Ocular melanoma

OTITIS MEDIA

Otitis media — inflammation of the middle ear — may be suppurative or secretory and acute, persistent, unresponsive, or chronic.

Acute otitis media is common in children; its incidence rises during the winter months, paralleling the seasonal rise in nonbacterial respiratory tract infections. Prolonged accumulation of fluid within the middle ear cavity causes chronic otitis media.

Chronic suppurative otitis media may lead to scarring, adhesions, and severe structural or functional ear damage. Chronic secretory otitis media, with its persistent inflammation and pressure, may cause conductive hearing loss. It most commonly occurs in children with tympanostomy tubes or those with a perforated tympanic membrane.

Recurrent otitis media is defined as three near-acute otitis media episodes within 6 months or four episodes of acute otitis media within 1 year.

Causes

Suppurative otitis media (bacterial infection)
- Pneumococci
- *Haemophilus influenzae,* most common cause in children under age 6
- *Moraxella catarrhalis*
- *Beta-hemolytic streptococci*
- Staphylococci, most common cause in children age 6 or older
- Gram-negative bacteria

Chronic suppurative otitis media
- Inadequate treatment of acute otitis episodes
- Infection by resistant strains of bacteria
- Tuberculosis (rare)

Secretory otitis media
- Obstruction of the eustachian tube secondary to eustachian tube dysfunction from viral infection or allergy
- Barotrauma — pressure injury caused by inability to equalize pressures between the environment and the middle ear during aircraft descent or underwater ascent

Chronic secretory otitis media
- Mechanical obstruction — adenoidal tissue overgrowth, tumors
- Edema — allergic rhinitis, chronic sinus infection
- Inadequate treatment of acute suppurative otitis media

Pathophysiology

Otitis media results from disruption of eustachian tube patency. In the suppurative form, respiratory tract infection, allergic reaction, nasotracheal intubation, or positional changes allow nasopharyngeal flora to reflux through the eustachian tube and colonize the middle ear.

In the secretory form, obstruction of the eustachian tube promotes transudation of sterile serous fluid from blood vessels in the middle ear membrane.

COMPLICATIONS
- Mastoiditis
- Meningitis
- Permanent hearing loss
- Septicemia
- Abscesses
- Vertigo
- Lymphadenopathy
- Damage to middle ear structures
- Perforation of the tympanic membrane

Signs and symptoms

Acute suppurative otitis media
- Severe, deep, throbbing pain from pressure behind the tympanic membrane
- Signs of upper respiratory tract infection (sneezing, coughing)
- Mild to very high fever
- Hearing loss, usually mild and conductive
- Tinnitus, dizziness, nausea, vomiting
- Bulging, erythematous tympanic membrane; purulent drainage in the ear canal if the tympanic membrane ruptures

Acute secretory otitis media
- Severe conductive hearing loss — varies from 15 to 35 dB, depending on the thickness and amount of fluid in the middle ear cavity
- Sensation of fullness in the ear
- Popping, crackling, or clicking sounds on swallowing or with jaw movement
- Echo during speech
- Vague feeling of top-heaviness

Chronic otitis media
- Thickening and scarring of the tympanic membrane
- Decreased or absent tympanic membrane mobility
- Cholesteatoma (cystlike mass in middle ear)
- Painless, purulent discharge

Diagnostic test results

- Culture and sensitivity tests of exudate show the causative organism.
- Complete blood count reveals leukocytosis.
- Radiographic studies demonstrate mastoid involvement.
- Tympanometry detects hearing loss and evaluates the condition of the middle ear.
- Audiometry shows degree of hearing loss.
- Pneumatic otoscopy reveals decreased tympanic membrane mobility.

Treatment

- Antibiotic therapy
- Myringotomy — insertion of polyethylene tube into tympanic membrane
- Inflation of eustachian tube by performing Valsalva's maneuver several times per day
- Nasopharyngeal decongestant
- Aspiration of middle ear fluid
- Concomitant treatment of underlying cause, such as elimination of allergens, or adenoidectomy for hypertrophied adenoids
- Myringoplasty, tympanoplasty, or mastoidectomy

Classifications

Otoscopic view

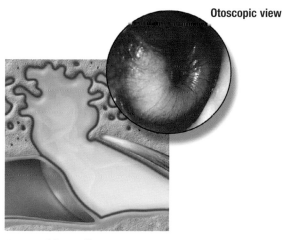

Acute otitis media
- Infected fluid in middle ear
- Rapid onset and short duration

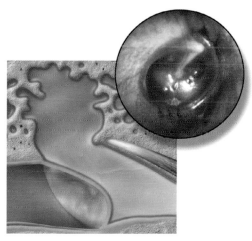

Otitis media with effusion
- Relatively asymptomatic fluid in middle ear
- May be acute, subacute, or chronic in nature

Complications

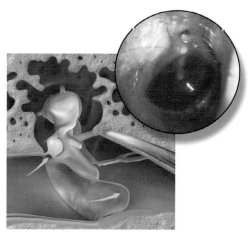

Atelectasis
- Thinning and potential collapse of tympanic membrane

Perforation
- Hole in tympanic membrane caused by chronic negative middle ear pressure, inflammation, or trauma

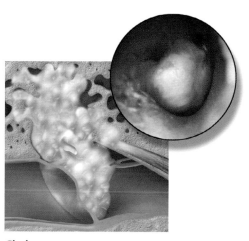

Cholesteatoma
- Mass of entrapped skin in middle ear or temporal lobe

APPENDIX, GLOSSARY, SELECTED REFERENCES, AND INDEX

TYPES OF CARDIAC ARRHYTHMIAS

ARRHYTHMIA AND FEATURES	CAUSES

Sinus tachycardia

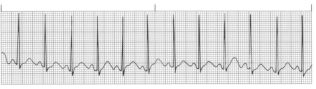

- Rhythm: atrial and ventricular regular; rate >100 beats/minute
- Normal P wave preceding each QRS complex

- May be a normal physiologic response
- Left ventricular failure, cardiac tamponade, hyperthyroidism, anemia, hypovolemia, pulmonary embolism (PE), anterior wall myocardial infarction (MI), cardiogenic shock, pericarditis, anemia, hemorrhage
- Atropine, epinephrine, isoproterenol, quinidine, caffeine, alcohol, amphetamines, dobutamine, dopamine, or nicotine

Sinus bradycardia

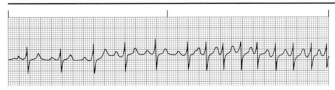

- Rhythm: atrial and ventricular regular; rate <60 beats/minute
- Normal P waves preceding each QRS complex

- Normal in well-conditioned heart
- Increased intracranial pressure
- Increased vagal tone
- Hypothermia
- Hyperkalemia
- Hypothyroidism
- Anticholinesterase, beta blocker, calcium channel blocker, digoxin, lithium, antiarrhythmics, or morphine

Supraventricular tachycardia (SVT)

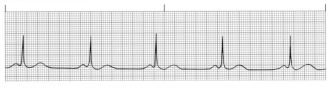

- Rhythm: atrial and ventricular regular; rate > 160 beats/minute; rarely exceeds 250 beats/minute
- P waves regular but aberrant; difficult to differentiate from preceding T wave; P waves proceed each QRS complex
- If the arrhythmia starts and stops suddenly, it's called *paroxysmal SVT.*

- Intrinsic abnormality of atrioventricular (AV) conduction
- Physical or psychological stress, hypoxia, hypokalemia, cardiomyopathy, congenital heart disease, MI, valvular disease, Wolff-Parkinson-White syndrome, cor pulmonale, hyperthyroidism, or systemic hypertension
- Digoxin toxicity; use of caffeine, marijuana, or central nervous system stimulants

Atrial flutter

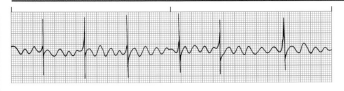

- Heart failure, tricuspid or mitral valve disease, PE, cor pulmonale, inferior wall MI, sick sinus syndrome, or pericarditis
- Digoxin toxicity

- Atrial rhythm regular; rate 250 to 400 beats/minute
- Ventricular rate variable, depending on degree of AV block
- No P waves; atrial activity appears as flutter waves (F waves); sawtooth P wave configuration common in Lead II.
- QRS complexes uniform in shape, but often irregular in rate

ARRHYTHMIA AND FEATURES	CAUSES

Atrial fibrillation

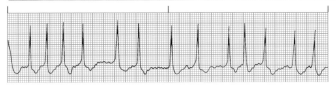

- Atrial rhythm grossly irregular; rate >400 beats/minute
- Ventricular rate grossly irregular
- QRS complexes of uniform configuration and duration
- PR interval indiscernible
- No P waves; atrial activity appear as erratic, irregular, baseline fibrillatory waves (f waves)

- Heart failure, chronic obstructive pulmonary disease, thyrotoxicosis, constrictive pericarditis, ischemic heart disease, sepsis, PE, rheumatic heart disease, hypertension, mitral stenosis, atrial irritation, or complication of coronary bypass or valve replacement surgery
- Nifedipine and digoxin use

Junctional rhythm

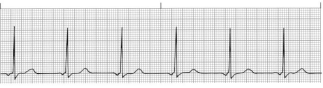

- Rhythm: regular; atrial rate 40 to 60 beats/minute; ventricular rate usually 40 to 60 beats/minute (60 to 100 beats/minute is called *accelerated junctional rhythm*)
- P waves preceding, hidden within, or after QRS complex; may be inverted if visible
- PR interval (when present) <0.12 second
- QRS complex configuration and duration normal, except in aberrant conduction

- Inferior wall MI or ischemia, hypoxia, vagal stimulation, or sick sinus syndrome
- Acute rheumatic fever
- Valve surgery
- Digoxin toxicity

First-degree atrioventricular (AV) block

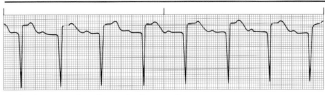

- Rhythm: atrial and ventricular regular
- PR interval > 0.20 second
- P wave precedes QRS complex
- QRS complex normal

- May occur in healthy persons
- Inferior wall MI or ischemia, hypothyroidism, hypokalemia, or hyperkalemia
- Digoxin toxicity; quinidine, procainamide, amiodarone, propranolol, beta blocker, or calcium channel blocker

Second-degree AV block

Mobitz I (Wenckebach)

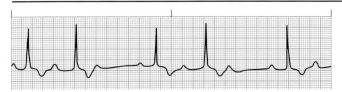

- Rhythm: atrial regular, ventricular irregular; atrial rate exceeds ventricular rate
- PR interval progressively, but only slightly, longer with each cycle until QRS complex disappears (dropped beat); PR interval shorter after dropped beat

- Inferior wall MI, cardiac surgery, acute rheumatic fever, or vagal stimulation
- Digoxin toxicity
- Propranolol, quinidine, or procainamide

(continued)

Second-degree AV block

Mobitz II

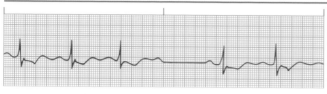

- Severe coronary artery disease (CAD), anterior wall MI, or acute myocarditis
- Digoxin toxicity

- Rhythm: atrial regular, ventricular irregular
- P-P interval constant for conducted beats
- P waves normal size and shape; some not followed by a QRS complex

Third-degree AV block

(Complete heart block)

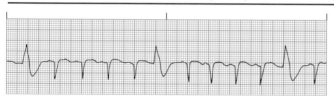

- Inferior or anterior wall MI, congenital abnormality, rheumatic fever, hypoxia, postoperative complication of mitral valve replacement, postprocedure complication of radiofrequency ablation in or near AV nodal tissue, Lev's disease (fibrosis and calcification that spreads from cardiac structures to the conductive tissue), or Lenègre's disease (conductive tissue fibrosis)
- Digoxin toxicity

- Rhythm: atrial and ventricular regular; ventricular rate slower than atrial
- No relation between P waves and QRS complexes
- No constant PR interval
- QRS duration normal (junctional pacemaker) or wide and bizarre (ventricular pacemaker)

Premature ventricular contractions (PVCs)

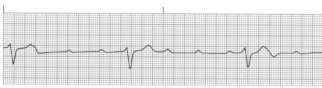

- Heart failure; old or acute MI, ischemia, or contusion; myocardial irritation by ventricular catheter or pacemaker; hypercapnia; hypokalemia; hypocalcemia; or hypomagnesemia
- Drug toxicity: digoxin, aminophylline, tricyclic antidepressants, beta blockers, isoproterenol, or dopamine
- Caffeine, tobacco, or alcohol use
- Psychological stress, anxiety, pain, or exercise

- Rhythm: atrial regular, ventricular irregular
- QRS complex premature, usually followed by a compensatory pause
- QRS complex wide and distorted, usually >0.12 second
- Premature QRS complexes occurring singly, in pairs, or in threes, alternating with normal beats; focus from one or more sites
- Ominous when clustered, multifocal, or with R wave on T pattern

Ventricular tachycardia

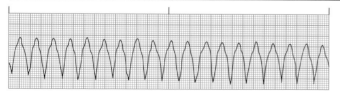

- Myocardial ischemia, MI, or aneurysm; CAD; rheumatic heart disease; mitral valve prolapse; heart failure; cardiomyopathy; ventricular catheters; hypokalemia; hypercalcemia; hypomagnesemia; or PE
- Drug toxicity: digoxin, procainamide, epinephrine, or quinidine
- Anxiety

- Ventricular rate 100 to 220 beats/minute, rhythm usually regular
- QRS complexes wide, bizarre, and independent of P waves
- P waves not discernible
- May start and stop suddenly

ARRHYTHMIA AND FEATURES	CAUSES

Ventricular fibrillation

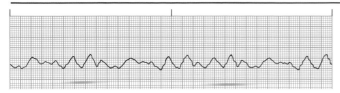

- Ventricular rhythm and rate rapid and chaotic
- QRS complexes wide and irregular; no visible P waves

- Myocardial ischemia, MI, untreated ventricular tachycardia, R-on-T phenomenon, hypokalemia, hyperkalemia, hypercalcemia, alkalosis, electric shock, or hypothermia
- Drug toxicity: digoxin, epinephrine, or quinidine

Asystole

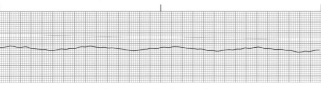

- No atrial or ventricular rate or rhythm
- No discernible P waves, QRS complexes, or T waves

- Myocardial ischemia, MI, aortic valve disease, heart failure, hypoxia, hypokalemia, severe acidosis, electric shock, ventricular arrhythmia, AV block, PE, heart rupture, cardiac tamponade, hyperkalemia, or electromechanical dissociation
- Cocaine overdose

GLOSSARY

Acanthosis nigrans Darkening of the skin on the neck or under the arms

Acidemia Abnormal acidity, or low pH, of the blood

Acidosis Condition caused by accumulation of acid or depletion of the alkaline reserve in the blood and body tissues

Acinus Any of the smallest lobules of a gland

Acromegaly Abnormal enlargement of the extremities of the skeleton caused by hypersecretion of growth hormone from the pituitary gland

Acropachy Soft tissue swelling accompanied by underlying bone changes where new bone formation occurs

Acyanotic Not characterized by or accompanied by cyanosis

Adenomyosis Invasion of the muscular wall of the uterus by glandular tissue

Afterload The force opposing ventricular contraction

Agranulocyte Leukocyte (white blood cell) not containing granules or grains; includes lymphocytes, monocytes, and plasma cells

Akinesia Absence or loss of power of voluntary movement

Alkalemia Abnormal alkalinity, or high pH, of the blood

Alkalosis Abnormal condition of body fluids resulting from accumulation of base or from loss of acid without comparable loss of base

Allele One of two or more different genes that occupy a corresponding position (locus) on matched chromosomes; allows for different forms of the same inherited characteristic

Alopecia Hair loss

Amyloidosis Disorder of unknown cause, in which insoluble protein fibers become deposited in tissues and organs, impairing their function

Anaphase Third stage of division of the nucleus in meiosis or mitosis

Anaplasia Loss of differentiation of cells; a characteristic of tumor cells

Aneurysm Sac formed by localized vasodilation of the wall of an artery or vein

Angioedema Localized edematous reaction of the dermis or subcutaneous or submucosal tissues

Angiography Radiographic examination of vessels of the body

Anion Ion carrying a negative charge

Anisocytosis Presence of erythrocytes with abnormal variations in size

Ankylosis Immobility and consolidation of a joint, often in an abnormal position; caused by disease, trauma, or surgical procedure

Anorexia Lack of or loss of appetite for food

Anovulation Absence of ovulation

Anoxia Absence of oxygen in the tissues

Antibody Immunoglobulin molecule that reacts only with the specific antigen that induced its formation in the lymph system

Antigen Foreign substance, such as a bacteria or toxin, that induces antibody formation

Anuria Complete cessation of urine formation by the kidney

Areflexia Absence of reflexes

Arnold-Chiari syndrome Congenital anomaly in which the cerebellum and medulla protrude through the foramen magnum into the spinal canal

Arousal State of being ready to respond to sensory stimulation

Arteriosclerosis Group of diseases characterized by thickening and loss of elasticity of the arterial walls

Arthralgia Pain in a joint

Arthrodesis Surgical fusion of a joint

Ascites Abnormal accumulation of serous fluid in the peritoneal cavity

Aspiration Inhalation of mucus or vomitus into the respiratory tract; suctioning of fluid or gas from a body cavity

Asterixis Motor disturbance marked by intermittent lapses of assumed posture; also known as *liver flap*

Atelectasis Collapsed or airless state of the lung; may involve all or part of the lung

Atopy Clinical hypersensitivity or allergy with a hereditary predisposition

Atrophy Decrease in size or wasting away of a cell, tissue, organ, or body part

Autoimmune disorder Disorder in which the body launches an immunologic response against itself

Autoinoculation Inoculation with microorganisms from one's own body

Autosome Any of the 22 pairs of chromosomes not concerned with determination of gender

Azotemia Excess nitrogenous waste products in the blood

Babinski's reflex Reflex action of the toes, normal during infancy, elicited by rubbing a firm substance on the sole of the foot, which results in dorsiflexion (upward bending) of the great toe and fanning of the smaller toes; after infancy, normal response is downward bending of all toes on the foot

Bacteria One-celled microorganisms that have no true nucleus and reproduce by cell division

Bactericidal Destructive to bacteria

Bacteriostatic Preventing bacteria from multiplying or growing

Bacteriuria Bacteria in the urine

Balanoposthitis Inflammation of the glans penis and prepuce

Barotrauma Injury caused by pressure

Benign Not malignant or recurrent; favorable for recovery

Biopsy Examination, usually microscopic, of tissue removed from the living body

Blepharospasm Spasm of the orbicular muscle of the eyelid that completely closes eyelids

Bone Hard, rigid form of connective tissue constituting most of the skeleton

Bone marrow Soft organic material filling the cavities of bones

Bradykinin Nonpeptide kinin formed from a plasma protein; a powerful vasodilator that increases capillary permeability, constricts smooth muscle, and stimulates pain receptors

Bronchiectasis Chronic dilation of the bronchi and bronchioles with secondary infection, usually of the lower lung lobes

Bronchiolitis Inflammation of the bronchioles

Bruch's membrane Support structure on the inner side of the choroid

Brudzinski's sign In meningitis, bending the patient's neck usually produces flexion of the knee and hip

Bulla Space filled with air or fluid

Bursa Fluid-filled sac or cavity in connective tissue near a joint; acts as a cushion

Cachexia State of marked ill health and malnutrition

Carcinogen Any substance that causes cancer

Carcinoma Malignant growth made of epithelial cells; tends to infiltrate surrounding tissues and metastasize

Cardiac output Volume of blood ejected by the heart per minute

Carphology Involuntary picking at the bedclothes; seen in states of great exhaustion and high fevers

Cartilage Dense connective tissue consisting of fibers embedded in a strong, gel-like substance; supports, cushions, and shapes body structures

Cation Ion carrying a positive charge

Cell-mediated immunity Immune response that involves effector T lymphocytes and not the production of humoral antibody

Cercaria Final, free-swimming stage of a trematode larva

Chemonucleolysis Injection of the enzyme chymopapain (a chemolytic agent) into a herniated intervertebral disk

Chemotaxis Response of leukocytes to products formed in immunologic reactions, wherein leukocytes are attracted to and accumulate at the site of the reaction

Cholangioma Tumor of the bile ducts

Cholangitis Inflammation of a bile duct

Cholecystectomy Excision of the gallbladder

Choledochostomy Creation of an opening into the common bile duct for drainage

Cholestasis Stopped or decreased bile flow

Cholesteatoma Cystlike mass filled with desquamating debris frequently including cholesterol, which occurs most commonly in the middle ear and mastoid region

Chondrocalcinosis Deposition of calcium salts in the cartilage of joints

Chorea Rapid, jerky involuntary movements

Choriocapillaries Capillary layer of the choroid

Choroid Thin membrane that covers the eyeball and supplies blood to the retina

Chromatin The substance of chromosomes, composed of deoxyribonucleic acid and basic proteins

Chvostek's sign Spasm of a hyperirritable facial nerve induced by tapping the facial nerve in the region of the parotid gland

Claudication Pain in the calves caused by reduced blood flow to the legs

Cognition Process by which a person becomes aware of objects; includes all aspects of perception, thought, and memory

Commissurotomy Surgical separation of adherent, thickened leaflets of the mitral valve

Complement system Major mediator of inflammatory response; a functionally related system of 20 proteins circulating as inactive molecules

Congenital Present at birth

Constipation Condition in which feces in the bowel are too hard to pass easily

Cor pulmonale Right ventricular hypertrophy with right-sided heart failure caused by pulmonary hypertension

Corrigan's pulse Jerky pulse with full expansion and sudden collapse

Cremasteric reflex Stimulation of the skin on the inner thigh retracts the testis on the same side

Crepitus Crackling sound in the joints, skin, or lungs

Curettage Scraping or collecting tissue from the wall of a body cavity

Cyanosis Bluish discoloration of the skin and mucous membranes caused by reduced hemoglobin in the blood

Cystitis Inflammation of the urinary bladder

Cytokines Nonantibody proteins, secreted by inflammatory leukocytes and some nonleukocytic cells, that act as intercellular mediators

Cytology The study of cells, their origin, structure, function, and pathology

Cytotoxic Destructive to cells

Debridement Removal of all foreign material and diseased and devitalized tissue from or adjacent to a traumatic or infected lesion until surrounding healthy tissue is exposed

Decortication Surgical removal of the thick coating over an organ, such as the lung or kidney

Demyelination Destruction of a nerve's myelin sheath; prevents normal conduction

Diabetic ketoacidosis Complication of diabetes mellitus that results from by-products of fat metabolism (ketones) when glucose isn't available as a fuel source in the body

Diaphoresis Perspiration, especially profuse perspiration

Diarrhea Frequent evacuation of watery stools caused by rapid movement of intestinal contents; results in poor absorption of water, nutritive elements, and electrolytes

Differentiation Process of cells maturing into specific types

Diffusion Spontaneous movement of molecules or other particles in a solution

Diplegia Paralysis of like parts on either side of the body

Diploid Cell with a full set of genetic material; a human diploid cell has 46 chromosomes

Diplopia Double vision

Disjunction Separation of chromosomes during cell division

Divarication Separation into two parts or branches; bifurcation

Diverticula Pockets of tissue that push out from the colon walls

Dominant gene Gene that produces an effect in an organism regardless of the state of the corresponding allele

Dressler's syndrome Pericarditis that develops weeks to several months after myocardial infarction or open heart surgery

Dysarthria Imperfect articulation of speech caused by disturbances of muscular control

Dyscrasia Condition related to a disease, usually referring to an imbalance of component elements

Dysphagia Difficulty swallowing

Dysplasia Alteration in size, shape, and organization of adult cells

Dyspnea Labored or difficult breathing

Dysthymia Depression

Dysuria Painful or difficult urination

Eclampsia Potentially life-threatening disorder of pregnancy characterized by seizures, hypertension, generalized edema, and proteinuria

Ejection fraction Measure of ventricular contractility

Embolism Sudden obstruction of a blood vessel by a foreign substance or a blood clot

Empyema Accumulation of pus in a body cavity

Endocrine Pertaining to internal hormone secretion by glands

Endogenous Occurring inside the body

Endolymph Fluid within the membranous labyrinth of the ear

Endotoxin Toxin associated with the outer membranes of certain gram-negative bacteria

Epistaxis Hemorrhage from the nose, usually caused by rupture of small vessels

Erythema marginatum Nonpruritic, macular, transient rash on the trunk or inner aspects of the upper arms or thighs, that gives rise to red lesions with blanched centers

Erythrocyte Red blood cell; carries oxygen to the tissues and removes carbon dioxide from them

Erythropoiesis Production of red blood cells or erythrocytes

Estrogen Female sex hormone

Exacerbation Increase in the severity of a disease or any of its symptoms

Exanthem Rash or skin eruption

Exocrine External or outward secretion of a gland

Exogenous Occurring outside the body

Exotoxin Potent toxin formed and excreted by a bacterial cell and found in the surrounding medium

Extracellular fluid Fluid in the spaces outside the cells

Fetor hepaticus Musty, sweetish breath characteristic of hepatic disease

Fubernaculum Fibromuscular band that connects the testes to the scrotal floor

Fulguration Destruction of tissue by high-frequency electricity

Fungate Funguslike growth; growing rapidly like a fungus

Fungus Nonphotosynthetic microorganism that reproduces asexually by cell division

Furunculosis Occurrence of furuncles serially over weeks or months

Gait ataxia Unsteady, uncoordinated walk, with a wide base and the feet turned out, coming down first on the heel and then on the toes with a double tap

Gap junctions Channels through which ions and other small molecules pass

Gastrectomy Excision of the stomach or a portion of it

Gastrostomy Creation of an opening into the stomach for the purpose of administering food or fluids

Genome Total of all genetic information included in a set of unreplicated chromosomes

Gibson murmur Continuous murmur heard throughout systole and diastole in older children and adults caused by shunting of blood from the aorta to the pulmonary artery

Gland Organ composed of specialized cells that produce a secretion used in some other body part

Glomerulopathy Any disease of the renal glomeruli

Glomerulosclerosis Glomerular disease characterized by hardening of focal and segmental areas of the glomerulus

Glomerulus Network of twisted capillaries in the nephron, the basic unit of the kidney; brings blood and waste products carried by blood to the nephron

Glucagon Hormone released during the fasting state that increases blood glucose concentration

Gluconeogenesis Formation of glucose from molecules that aren't carbohydrates, such as amino acids and glycerol

Glycogenolysis Splitting of glycogen in the liver, yielding glucose

Glycosuria Presence of glucose in the urine

Goblet cells Mucus-secreting cells of the epithelial lining of the small intestine and respiratory passages

Granulocyte Any cell containing granules, especially a granular leukocyte (white blood cell)

Granuloma Any small nodular aggregation of mononuclear inflammatory cells or a similar collection of modified macrophages resembling endothelial cells, usually surrounded by lymphocytes, often with multinucleated giant cells

Hamartoma Benign tumorlike nodule composed of an overgrowth of mature cells and tissues normally present in the affected part

Haploid Having half the normal number of chromosomes

Heberden's nodules Small, hard nodules on the distal interphalangeal joints of the fingers in osteoarthritis

Hematemesis Vomiting of blood

Hematoma Localized collection of blood, usually clotted, in an organ, space, or tissue

Hematopoiesis Production of red blood cells in the bone marrow

Hematuria Blood in the urine

Hemochromatosis Disorder of iron metabolism with excess deposition of iron in the tissues, bronze skin pigmentation, cirrhosis, and diabetes mellitus

Hemoglobin Protein in erythrocytes that transports oxygen

Hemolysis Red blood cell destruction

Hemostasis Complex process whereby platelets, plasma, and coagulation factors interact to control bleeding

Hepatojugular reflux Distention of the jugular vein induced by manual pressure over the liver

Hepatoma Any tumor of the liver

Heterozygous Genes having different alleles at the same site (locus)

Hirsutism Abnormal hairiness

Histamine An amine found in all body tissues that induces capillary dilation, which increases capillary permeability, lowers blood pressure, and causes contraction of most smooth muscle tissue, increased gastric acid secretion, and increased heart rate; also a mediator of immediate hypersensitivity

Homeostasis Dynamic, steady state of internal balance in the body

Homologous genes Gene pairs sharing a corresponding structure and position

Homozygous Genes that have identical alleles for a given trait

Hormone Chemical substance produced in the body that has a specific regulatory effect on the activity of specific cells or organs

Humoral immunity Form of immunity in which B lymphocytes and plasma cells produce antibodies to foreign agents (antigens) and stimulate T lymphocytes to attack them (cellular immunity)

Hyperplasia Excessive growth of normal cells that causes an increase in the volume of a tissue or organ

Hyperpnea Increase in depth of breathing, which may be accompanied by an increased respiratory rate

Hyperreflexia Exaggeration of reflexes

Hypertonic Having an osmotic pressure greater than that of the solution with which it's compared

Hypertrichosis Excessive hair growth

Hypertrophy Increase in volume of tissue or organ caused by enlargement of existing cells

Hypervolemia Abnormal increase in the volume of circulating fluid in the body

Hypoplasia Incomplete development or underdevelopment of an organ or tissue

Hypotonia Abnormally low tonicity or strength

Hypotonic Having an osmotic pressure lower than that of the solution with which it's compared

Hypovolemia Abnormally low volume of circulating fluid in the body

Hypoxia Reduction of oxygen in body tissues to below normal levels

Idiopathic Occurring without known cause

Ileal conduit Use of a segment of the ileum for the diversion of urinary flow from the ureters

Ileus Failure of appropriate forward movement of bowel contents

Immunodeficiency Disorder caused by inadequate immune response; caused by hypoactivity or decreased numbers of lymphoid cells

Immunoglobulin Serum protein synthesized by lymphocytes and plasma cells that has known antibody activity

Intention tremor Tremor occurring when one attempts voluntary movement

Interphase Interval between two successive cell divisions

Interstitial fluid Fluid between cells in tissues

Intertrigo Erythematous skin eruption in such areas as the creases of the neck, folds of the groin and axillae, and beneath pendulous breasts

Intracellular fluid Fluid inside each cell

Intrapleural Within the pleura

Ion Atom or group of atoms having a positive or negative electric charge

Ischemia Decreased blood supply to a body organ or tissue

Isotonic Solution having the same tonicity as another solution with which it's compared

Jaundice Yellow discoloration of skin, sclerae, mucous membranes, and excretions caused by hyperbilirubinemia and deposition of bile pigments

Joint Intersection of two or more bones; most provide motion and flexibility

Karyotype Chromosomal arrangement of the cell nucleus

Kernig's sign Sign of meningitis in which a patient in supine position can easily and completely extend the leg; patient in sitting position or lying with the thigh flexed upon the abdomen can't completely extend leg

Ketones By-products of fat metabolism when glucose isn't available

Ketonuria Excess of ketones in the urine

Koilonchyia Abnormally thin nails that are concave from side to side, with the edges turned up

Korotkoff sound Sound heard during auscultation of blood pressure

Kupffer's cells Large, phagocytic cells lining the walls of the hepatic sinusoids

Kussmaul's respirations Dyspnea characterized by increased rate and depth of respirations, panting, and labored respiration; seen in metabolic acidosis

Kussmaul's sign Increased jugular vein distention on inspiration; caused by restricted right-sided filling

Kyphoscoliosis Forward and lateral curvature of the spine

Lasègue's sign In sciatica, pain in the back and leg elicited by passive raising of the heel from the bed with the knee straight

Leukapheresis Selective removal of leukocytes from withdrawn blood, which is then retransfused into the donor

Leukocyte White blood cell that protects the body against microorganisms causing disease

Leukocytosis Increase in the number of leukocytes in the blood; generally caused by infection

Leukopenia Reduction in the number of leukocytes in the blood

Leukotrienes Group of compounds derived from unsaturated fatty acids; extremely potent mediators of immediate hypersensitivity reactions and inflammation

Lichenification Thickening and hardening of the skin

Ligament Band of fibrous tissue that connects bones or cartilage, provides stability, strengthens joints, and limits or facilitates movement

Locus Location on a chromosome

Lymph node Structure that filters the lymphatic fluid that drains from body tissue and is later returned to the plasma

Lymphadenitis Inflammation of one or more lymph nodes

Lymphedema Chronic swelling of a body part from accumulation of interstitial fluid secondary to obstruction or surgical removal of lymphatic vessels or lymph nodes

Lymphocytes Leukocytes produced by lymphoid tissue that participate in immunity

Lysozyme Enzyme that can kill microorganisms or microbes

Macroglossia
Excessive size of the tongue

Macrophages Highly phagocytic cells that are stimulated by inflammation

Malignant Condition that becomes progressively worse and results in death

Megakaryocyte Platelet precursor; the giant cell of bone marrow

Megaloureter Congenital ureteral dilation without demonstrable cause

Meiosis Process of cell division by which reproductive cells are formed

Menorrhagia Heavy or prolonged menses

Merozoite Stage in the life cycle of the malaria parasite

Mesorchium Fold in the tissue between the testis and epididymis

Metabolic acidosis Acidosis resulting from accumulation of keto acids in the blood at the expense of bicarbonate

Metabolic alkalosis Disturbance in which the acid-base status shifts toward the alkaline because of uncompensated loss of acids, ingestion or retention of excess base, or potassium depletion

Metaphase Stage of cell division in which the chromosomes, each consisting of two chromatids, are arranged in the equatorial plane of the spindle

Metaplasia Change in adult cells to a form abnormal for that tissue

Metastasis Transfer of disease via pathogenic microorganisms or cells from one organ or body part to another not directly associated with it

Metrorrhagia Episodes of vaginal bleeding between menses

Microembolus Embolus of microscopic size

Micturition Urination

Mitosis Ordinary process of cell division in which each chromosome with all its genes reproduces itself exactly

Monocyte Mononuclear, phagocytic leukocyte

Monoplegia Paralysis of a single part

Monosomy Presence of one chromosome less than the normal number

Morbidity Condition of having a disease

Morphea Condition in which connective tissue replaces skin and sometimes subcutaneous tissues

Mortality Ratio of the total number of deaths to the total population

Mucolytic Agent that acts by destroying mucus

Muscle Bundle of long slender cells, or fibers, that has the power to contract and produce movement

Mutation Permanent change in genetic material

Myalgia Muscle pain

Myectomy Excision of a muscle

Myelomatous cells Increased number of immature plasma cells

Myolysis Degeneration of muscle tissue

Myomectomy Removal of tumors in the uterine muscle

Myotomy Cutting or dissection of a muscle

Myxedema Condition resulting from advanced hypothyroidism or defiency of thyroxine

Nausea
Unpleasant sensation with the tendency to vomit

Necrosis Cell or tissue death

Neoplasm Abnormal growth in which cell multiplication is uncontrolled and progressive

Nephrolithiasis Condition marked by the presence of renal calculi

Nephron Structural and functional unit of the kidney that forms urine

Neuritis Inflammation of a nerve

Neurolysis Freeing of nerve fibers by cutting the nerve sheath longitudinally

Neuron Highly specialized conductor cell that receives and transmits electrochemical nerve impulses

Neutropenia Neutrophil deficiency in the blood

Neutrophil Granular leukocyte

Nevus Circumscribed, stable malformation of the skin and oral mucosa

Nondisjunction Failure of chromosomes to separate properly during cell division; causes an unequal distribution of chromosomes between the two resulting cells

Nystagmus Involuntary, rapid, rhythmic movement of the eyeball

Obstipation
Intractable constipation

Oculogyric crises Eyelids are fixed upward with involuntary tonic movements

Oligomenorrhea Abnormally infrequent menses

Oliguria Diminished urine secretion

Omentum Fold of the peritoneum between the stomach and adjacent abdominal organs

Onychia Inflammation of the nail bed

Onycholysis Distal nail separated from the bed

Oophoritis Inflammation of the ovary

Opisthotonos Spasm in which the head and heels arch backward and the body bows forward

Opportunistic infection Infection striking people with altered, weakened immune systems; caused by microorganism that doesn't ordinarily cause disease but becomes pathogenic under certain conditions

Opthalmoplegia Ocular paralysis

Optic neuritis Inflammation of the optic nerve

Orchiectomy Excision of a testis

Orchiopexy Surgical fixation of an undescended testis in the scrotum

Organelle Structure in the cytoplasm that performs a specific function

Orthopnea Ability to breathe easily only in the upright position

Orthostatic hypotension Fall in blood pressure that occurs upon standing or when standing motionless in a fixed position

Osmolality Concentration of a solution expressed in terms of osmoles of solute per kilogram of solvent

Osmolarity Concentration of a solution expressed in terms of osmoles of solute per liter of solution

Osseous Of the nature or quality of bone

Osteoblasts Bone-forming cells

Osteoclasts Giant, multinuclear cells that reabsorb material from previously formed bones, tear down old or excess bone structure, and allow osteoblasts to rebuild new bone

Osteotomy Surgical division and realignment of bone

Ostium primium Opening in the lower portion of the membrane dividing the embryonic heart into right and left sides

Pancarditis Concurrent myocarditis, pericarditis, and endocarditis

Pancytopenia Abnormal depression of all the cellular elements of blood

Panmyelosis Proliferation of all the elements of the bone marrow

Papilledema Inflammation and edema of the optic nerve; associated with increased intracranial pressure

Paracentesis Surgical puncture of a cavity for the aspiration of fluid

Parametritis Inflammation of the parametrium

Paresthesia Abnormal burning or prickling sensation

Paronchyia Inflammation of the folds of tissue around the fingernail

Paroxysmal nocturnal dyspnea Respiratory distress related to posture (reclining at night) usually associated with heart failure and pulmonary edema

Pericardectomy Surgical creation of an opening to remove accumulated fluid from the pericardial sac

Pericardiocentesis Needle aspiration of the pericardial cavity

Perilymph Fluid in the space separating the membranous and osseus labyrinths of the ear

Periosteum Specialized connective tissue covering all bones and possessing bone-forming potential

Perseveration Abnormally persistent replies to questions

Petechiae Minute, round purplish red spots caused by intradermal or submucosal hemorrhage

Phagocyte Cell that ingests microorganisms, other cells, and foreign materials

Phagocytosis Engulfing of microorganisms, other cells, and foreign material by a phagocyte

Phlebectomy Removing a varicose vein through small incisions in the skin

Phlebography Radiographic examination of a vein

Photoplethysmography Plethysmographic determination in which the intensity of light reflected from the skin surface and the red cells below is measured to determine the blood volume of the respective area

Pilosebaceous Pertaining to the hair follicles and sebaceous glands

Plasmapheresis Removal of plasma from withdrawn blood and retransfusion of the formed elements into the donor

Plethora Edema and blood vessel distention

Polycythemia Increase in the total red cell mass of the blood

Polydipsia Excessive thirst

Polygenic traits Determined by several different genes

Polymenorrhea Menstrual cycle of less than eighteen days

Polyphagia Excessive ingestion of food

Polyuria Excessive excretion of urine

Preload Volume of blood in the ventricle at the end of diastole

Presbycusis Progressive, symmetrical, bilateral sensorineural hearing loss, usually of high frequency tones, caused by loss of hair cells in the organ of Corti

Pretibial edema Nonpitting edema of the anterior surface of the legs, dermopathy

Prognathism Projection of the jaw

Prophase First stage of cell replication in meiosis or mitosis

Prostaglandins Group of fatty acids that stimulate contractility of the uterine and other smooth muscle and have the ability to lower blood pressure, regulate acid secretion in the stomach, regulate body temperature and platelet aggregation, and control inflammation and vascular permeability

Protease inhibitor Drug that binds to and blocks the action of the human immunodeficiency virus protease enzyme

Proteinuria Excess of serum proteins in the urine

Pruritus Itching

Ptosis Paralytic drooping of the upper eyelid

Pulsus biferiens Peripheral pulse with a characteristic double impulse

Pulsus paradoxus Drop in systemic blood pressure that's greater than 15 mm Hg and coincides with inspiration

Pyloroplasty Plastic surgery of the pylorus to create larger communication between the stomach and duodenum

Pyrosis Heartburn

Pyuria Pus in urine

Quadriplegia Paralysis of all four limbs

Quincke's sign Alternate blanching and flushing of the skin

Recessive gene Gene that doesn't express itself in the presence of its dominant allele

Red blood cell Erythrocyte

Remission Abatement of a disease's symptoms

Remyelination Healing of demyelinated nerves

Renin Enzyme produced by the kidneys in response to an actual decline in extracellular fluid volume

Resistance Opposition to airflow in the lung tissue, chest wall, or airways; opposition to blood flow in the circulatory system

Respiratory acidosis Acidosis resulting from impaired ventilation and retention of carbon dioxide

Respiratory alkalosis Alkalosis caused by excessive excretion of carbon dioxide through the lungs

Romberg's sign Tendency of a patient to sway while standing still with feet close together and eyes closed

Rubella syndrome Exposure of a nonimmune mother to rubella during the first trimester of pregnancy

Salpingitis Inflammation of the fallopian tubes

Sclerodactyly Scleroderma of the fingers and toes

Sebum Oily secretion of the sebaceous glands

Sepsis Pathologic state resulting from microorganisms or their poisonous products in the bloodstream

Serositis Inflammation of a serous membrane

Serotonin Hormone and neurotransmitter that inhibits gastric acid secretion, stimulates smooth muscle, and produces vasoconstriction

Shunt Passage or anastomosis between two natural channels

Specific gravity Weight of a substance compared with the weight of an equal amount of water

Status asthmaticus Particularly severe episode of asthma

Steatorrhea Excess fat in the feces caused by a malabsorption syndrome

Stenosis Constriction or narrowing of a passage or orifice

Stratum corneum epidermidis Dead top layer of skin

Stroke volume Amount of blood pumped out of the heart in a single contraction

Subcutaneous emphysema Crackling beneath the skin on palpation

Subluxation Incomplete or partial dislocation

Surfactant Mixture of phospholipids that reduces the surface tension of pulmonary fluids and contributes to the elastic properties of pulmonary tissue

Sympathectomy Excision or interruption of some portion of the sympathetic nervous pathway

Synovectomy Removal of destructive, proliferating synovium, usually, in the wrists, knees, and fingers

Synovial fluid Viscous, lubricating substance secreted by the synovial membrane, which lines the cavity between the bones of free-moving joints

Telophase Last of the four stages of mitosis or of the two divisions of meiosis

Tendon Fibrous cord of connective tissue that attaches the muscle to bone or cartilage and enables bones to move when skeletal muscles contract

Tenotomy Surgical cutting of the tendon

Teratogens Agents or factors that can harm the developing fetus by causing congenital structural or functional defects

Thoracentesis Surgical puncture and drainage of the thoracic cavity

Thrombocytopenia Decreased number of platelets in circulating blood

Thrombocytosis Excessive number of platelets in circulating blood

Thrombus Blood clot

Thymoma Tumor on the thymus gland

Tinea cruris Fungal infection of the groin

Tinel's sign Tingling over the median nerve on light percussion

Tophi Accumulations of urate salts; occur throughout the body in gout

Torticollis Abnormal contraction of the cervical muscles, producing torsion of the neck

Transcription Synthesis of ribonucleic acid using a deoxyribonucleic acid template

Transient ischemic attack Brief episode of neurologic deficit resulting from cerebral ischemia

Translocation Alteration of a chromosome by attachment of a fragment to another chromosome or a different portion of the same chromosome

Trisomy Presence of an extra chromosome

Trousseau's sign Carpal spasm

Truss Elastic, canvas, or metallic device for retaining a reduced hernia within the abdominal cavity

Vagotomy Surgical interruption of the impulses carried by the vagus nerve or nerves

Vasculitis Inflammation of a vessel

Ventriculatrial shunt Drains fluid from the brain's lateral ventricle into the right atrium of the heart, where the fluid enters the venous circulation

Ventriculoperitoneal shunt Transports excess fluid from the lateral ventricle into the peritoneal cavity

Virus Microscopic, infectious parasite that contains genetic material and needs a host to replicate

Vitiligo Absence of pigmentation

Wilms' tumor Rapidly developing malignant mixed tumor of the kidneys, made up of embryonal elements; occurs mainly in children before age five

X-linked Inheritance pattern in which single gene disorders are passed through sex chromosomes

Xanthoma A papule, nodule, or plaque in the skin caused by lipid deposits

SELECTED REFERENCES

Alió, J.L., et al. "Ten-Year Follow-up of Photorefractive Keratectomy for Myopia of Less Than -6 Diopters," *American Journal of Ophthalmology* 145(1):29–36, January 2008.

Campbell, S., et al. "A Clinical Investigation to Determine the Effect of Pressure Injection on the Penetration of Topical Methyl Aminolevulinate into Nodular Basal Cell Carcinoma of the Skin," *Journal of Environmental Pathology, Toxicology and Oncology* 26(4):295–303, 2007.

Geere, J., et al. "Power Grip, Pinch Grip, Manual Muscle Testing or Thenar Atrophy—Which Should be Assessed as a Motor Outcome after Carpal Tunnel Decompression? A Systematic Review," *BMC Musculoskeletal Disorders* 8:114, November 2007.

Hall, J.C. *Sauer's Manual of Skin Diseases*, 9th ed. Philadelphia: Lippincott Williams & Wilkins, 2006.

Honein, M.A., et al. "Maternal Smoking and Environmental Tobacco Smoke Exposure and the Risk of Orofacial Clefts," *Epidemiology* 18(2):226–33, March 2007.

Hosokawa, K., and Nakajima, Y. "An Evaluation of Acute Cardiac Tamponade by Transesophageal Echocardiography," *Anesthesia Analgesia* 106(1):61 62, January 2008.

Kaukiainen, A., et al. "Work Tasks, Chemical Exposure and Respiratory Health in Construction Painting," *American Journal of Industrial Medicine* 51(1):1–8, January 2008.

Lawrence, R.C., et al. "Estimates of the Prevalence of Arthritis and Other Rheumatic Conditions in the United States: Part II," *Arthritis and Rheumatology* 58(1):26–35, January 2008.

Mitchell, S.Y., et al. "Venous Thromboembolism in Patients with Primary Bone or Soft-Tissue Sarcomas," *Journal of Bone and Joint Surgery* 89(11):2433–439, November 2007.

Porth, C.M. *Essentials of Pathophysiology: Concepts of Altered Health States,* 2nd ed. Philadelphia: Lippincott Williams & Wilkins, 2007.

Roehrborn, C.G., et al. "The Effects of Dutasteride, Tamsulosin and Combination Therapy on Lower Urinary Tract Symptoms in Men with Benign Prostatic Hyperplasia and Prostatic Enlargement: 2-Year Results from the CombAT Study," *Journal of Urology* 179(2):616–21, February 2008.

Smeltzer, S.C., et al. *Brunner and Suddarth's Textbook of Medical-Surgical Nursing,* 11th ed. Philadelphia: Lippincott Williams & Wilkins, 2008.

van Iterson, V., et al. "VEGF-D in Association with VEGFR-3 Promotes Nodal Metastasis in Human Invasive Lobular Breast Cancer," *American Journal of Clinical Pathology* 128(5):759–66, November 2007.

Welters, M.J., et al. "Induction of Tumor-Specific CD4+ and CD8+ T-Cell Immunity in Cervical Cancer Patients by a Human Papillomavirus Type 16 E6 and E7 Long Peptides Vaccine," *Clinical Cancer Research* 14:178–87, January 2008.

INDEX

A

Abdominal aortic aneurysm, 38
Abdominal hernia. *See* Inguinal hernia
Absence seizures, 135
Absorption, as cell function, 2
Acceleration-deceleration injuries, 118–119
  types of, 119
Achalasia, 160–161
Achilles' tendonitis, 244
Acid-base balance, 28–29
  buffer systems in, 33
  compensation in, 33
  disorders related to, 34–35t
  pulmonary mechanisms in, 33
  renal mechanisms in, 33
  types of, 31, 33
Acidemia, 31, 33
Acid-fast stain, 16
Acidosis, 31, 33
  metabolic, 35t
  respiratory, 34t
Acne, 380–381
  development of, 381
Acquired immunodeficiency syndrome (AIDS), 266–267
  manifestations of, 267
  opportunistic infections related to, 267
Acral lentiginous melanoma, 400
Acromegaly, 288
Acute angle-closure glaucoma, 414
Acute coryza, 116–117
Acute erythroleukemia, 254
Acute idiopathic polyneuritis, 136–137
Acute illness, as infection stage, 15t
Acute infective tubulointerstitial nephritis, 372–373
Acute lymphoblastic leukemia (ALL), 254–255
Acute lymphocytic leukemia (ALL), 254–255
Acute monoblastic leukemia, 254
Acute myeloblastic leukemia, 254–255
Acute myelogenous leukemia, 254–255
Acute myeloid leukemia (AML), 254
Acute myelomonocytic leukemia, 254
Acute non-lymphocytic leukemias, 254
Acute otitis media, 117
Acute phase, of disease, 5

Acute poststreptococcal glomerulonephritis, 364–365
Acute renal failure, 356–357
Acute respiratory distress syndrome (ARDS), 80–83
  phases of, 80–81, 83
Acute tubular necrosis, 358–359
Acute tubulointerstitial nephritis, 358–359
Adaptation, 3–4
Addisonian crisis, 280
Addison's disease, 280–281
Adenocarcinoma
  of colon, 171
  of endometrium, 320–321
  of esophagus, 176
  gastric, 178–179
  of lung, 96
  of pancreas, 206–207, 207
  of prostate gland, 339t
Adenomatous polyposis coli (APC) suppressor gene, 7
Adhesions, in pelvic inflammatory disease, 337
Adhesiveness, pathogenicity and, 14
Adrenal crisis, 280
Adrenal hormones, secretion of, 281
Adrenal hypofunction, 280–281
Adrenocorticotropin (ACTH)
  in adrenal hypofunction, 281
  in Cushing's syndrome, 282
Adult respiratory distress syndrome, 80–83
Age considerations
  in acne, 380
  in allergic rhinitis, 268
  in Alzheimer's disease, 120
  in amyotrophic lateral sclerosis, 122
  in aortic aneurysm, 38
  in appendicitis, 162
  in arteriovenous malformation, 124
  in atopic eczema, 382
  in Bell's palsy, 126
  in benign breast conditions, 306
  in benign prostatic hyperplasia, 308
  in bladder cancer, 360
  in bone tumors, 218
  in brain tumors, 128
  in breast cancer, 310
  in cancer, 7
  in cardiac arrhythmias, 40
  in carpal tunnel syndrome, 222

  in cataract, 406
  in cellulitis, 386
  in cerebral aneurysm, 130
  in cervical cancer, 312
  in cirrhosis, 166
  in colonic polyps, 168
  in colorectal cancer, 170
  in coronary artery disease, 50
  in Crohn's disease, 172
  in cryptorchidism, 314
  in Cushing's syndrome, 282–283
  in cystic fibrosis, 88
  in cystitis, 362
  in depression, 132
  in diabetes insipidus, 284
  in diabetes mellitus, 286
  in diverticular disease, 174
  in dysfunctional uterine bleeding, 316
  in emphysema, 90
  in endometrial cancer, 320
  in erectile dysfunction, 324
  in esophageal cancer, 176
  in fat embolism syndrome, 92
  in fibroid disease of uterus, 326
  in fractures, 226
  in fungal infections of skin, 392
  in gastric cancer, 178
  in glaucoma, 414
  in gout, 228
  in growth hormone excess, 288
  in Guillain-Barré syndrome, 136
  in hearing loss, 418
  in hemorrhoids, 184
  in herniated intervertebral disk, 140
  in hiatal hernia, 188
  in Hodgkin's disease, 252
  in hydrocele, 328
  in hydrocephalus, 142
  in hydronephrosis, 366
  in hyperlipidemia, 192
  in hyperthyroidism, 292
  in hypopituitarism, 294
  in hypothyroidism, 296
  in idiopathic pulmonary fibrosis, 94
  in infection, 14
  in intestinal obstruction, 196
  in irritable bowel syndrome, 198
  in leukemia, 254
  in liver cancer, 200
  in lung cancer, 97
  in macular degeneration, 422

t refers to table.

Age considerations (*continued*)
in Ménière's disease, 424
in multiple myeloma, 256
in multiple sclerosis, 146
in muscle cells, 3
in myasthenia gravis, 148
in nonHodgkin's lymphoma, 258
in osteomyelitis, 234
in osteoporosis, 236
in ovarian cancer, 332
in pancreatic cancer, 206
in Parkinson's disease, 150
in pericarditis, 66
in pneumonia, 100
in polycystic kidney disease, 370
in pressure ulcers, 396
in prostate cancer, 338–339
in pulmonary hypertension, 108
in pyelonephritis, 372
in Raynaud's disease, 68
in renal calculi, 374
in renal cancer, 376
in renovascular hypertension, 378
in rheumatoid arthritis, 274
in sarcoidosis, 110
in scleroderma, 276
in scoliosis, 238
in sickle cell anemia, 262
in tendonitis, 244
in testicular cancer, 346
in testicular torsion, 348
in tumor development, 9
in ulcerative colitis, 214
in ulcers, 216
in varicocele, 352
in varicose veins, 78
in vulvar cancer, 354
in warts, 404
Age-related macular degeneration, 422
Aging, of cells, 5
Air-fluid lock syndrome, 196
Air pollution, as cancer risk factor, 6
Alcohol, as cancer risk factor, 6
Aldosterone deficiency, in adrenal
hypofunction, 280
Alkalemia, 31, 33
Alkalosis, 33
metabolic, 35t
respiratory, 34t
Alleles, 22
Allergens
in asthma, 84
in contact dermatitis, 388
Allergic conjunctivitis, 410
Allergic rhinitis, 268–269
primary exposure, 269
reexposure, 269
Alpha-thalassemia, 264
Alveolar duct, 105
Alveolar pores, 105

Alveolar sac, 105
Alveoli
in asthma, 85
in chronic bronchitis, 87
in emphysema, 90–91, 91
normal, 105
in pneumonia, 101
in pulmonary edema, 105
in sarcoidosis, 111
in severe acute respiratory syndrome,
113
Alveolitis, 111
Alzheimer's disease, 120–121
tissue changes in, 121
Amenorrhea, 304–305
Ammoniomagnesium phosphate renal
calculi, 375
Amyotrophic lateral sclerosis, 122–123
motor neuron changes in, 123
Anaphylaxis, 270–271
development of, 271
Anaplasia, 8
Androgen deficiency, in adrenal
hypofunction, 280
Anemia, 246–247
blood smears in, 247
sickle cell, 24t, 262–263
Aneurysm
aortic, 38–39
cerebral, 130–131
Angle-closure glaucoma, acute, 414
Ankle
fractures of, 227
sprain of, 241
Ankylosing spondylitis, 272–273
Ann Arbor staging system, for
Hodgkin's disease, 253
Anovulation, 304, 316
Anthrax, 17t
Antibiotics, in infection
treatment, 16
Antidiuretic hormone (ADH), in
diabetes insipidus, 284–285
Antifungals, in infection
treatment, 16
Antigenicity, pathogenicity and, 14
Antivirals, in infection treatment, 16
Anulus fibrosus, 140
Aorta, 51
aneurysm of, 38–39
in atrial septal defect, 47
coarctation of, 46–47
in myocardial infarction, 62
in rheumatic heart disease, 71
in tetralogy of Fallot, 49
in transposition of the great
arteries, 49
Aortic aneurysm, 38–39
Aortic insufficiency, 74, 76
Aortic stenosis, 74, 76

Aortic valve, 75
in mitral valve prolapse, 61
in rheumatic heart disease, 71
Aplastic anemia, 246–247
Aplastic crisis, 262
Apoptosis, 5
Appendicitis, 162–163
Arrhythmias, cardiac, 40–41
Arterial septal defect, 46–47
Arteriovenous malformation, 124–125
Arthritis
osteoarthritis, 232–233
rheumatoid, 274–275
Ascending aortic aneurysm, 38
Aspiration pneumonia, 100
Asthma, 84–85
Asthmatic bronchus, 85
Astrocytes, 3
Atelectasis, in otitis media, 429
Atherosclerosis, 50–51, 299
Atonic seizures, 135
Atopic dermatitis, 382–383
appearance of, 383
Morgan's line in, 383t
Atopic eczema, 382–383
Atria
in atrial septal defect, 47
in cardiac circulation, 61
in cardiomyopathy, 45
in mitral valve prolapse, 61
in myocardial infarction, 62
in rheumatic heart disease, 71
in tetralogy of Fallot, 49
Atrial arrhythmias, 41
Atrial fibrillation, 41
Atrial flutter, 41
Atrial septal defect, 47
Atrioventricular block, 41
Atrioventricular heart valve, 75, 77
defects in, 77
Atrioventricular valve, 77
Atrophy, 3–4
Auras, 138
Autodigestion, 208
Automaticity, in cardiac arrhythmias, 40
Autonomy, cell growth and, 8
Autosomal disorders, 22
dominant, 22, 25t
recessive, 22, 24t
Autosomal inheritance, 22
Autosomes, 21
Avian influenza, 18t
Avulsion fracture, 227

B

Bacteria, in infection, 13
Bacterial endocarditis, 54–55
Bacterial infections, 17–18t

t refers to table.

Bacterial pneumonia, 100
Bacterial vaginosis, 351
Barrett's syndrome, 182
Basal cell carcinoma, 400, 403
Becker's muscular dystrophy, 230
Beck's triad, 42
Bed sores, 396–397
Bell's palsy, 126–127
   neurologic dysfunction in, 127
Bell's phenomenon, 126
Benign breast conditions, 306–307
Benign prostatic hyperplasia (BPH),
    308–309
   prostatic enlargement, 309
Bennett's fracture, 227
Berger's disease, 364
Bernstein test, 188
Beta-thalassemia, 264
Bile duct, gallstones in, 165
Biologic markers, in cancer diagnosis, 12
Biologic response modifiers, in cancer
    treatment, 12
Biopsy, in cancer diagnosis, 12
Biotherapy, in cancer treatment, 12
Blackhead, 380–381
Bladder
   cancer of, 360–361
   cystitis, 362–363
   neurogenic, 368–369
Blood clotting
   in disseminated intravascular
     coagulation, 248–249
   in hemophilia, 250–251
   normal, 249, 251
Blood pressure, high, 58–59
Blood supply
   to brain, 157
   to heart, 51
Bockhart's impetigo, 390
Boils, 390–391
Bone
   cancer of, 218–219
   formation of, 237
Bone resorption
   in hyperparathyroidism, 291t
   in osteoporosis, 236–237
Bone spur, 232
Bone tumors, 218–219
   types of, 219
Bowel. See Intestines
Boxer's fracture, 227
Brain
   arteries of, 131, 157
   cerebral aneurysm, 130–131
   cerebral cortex, 125
   changes in Alzheimer's disease, 121
   changes in arteriovenous
     malformation, 125
   changes in depression, 133
   changes in headache, 139

changes in hydrocephalus, 143
changes in meningitis, 145
changes in Parkinson's disease, 151
changes in West Nile virus, 159
coronal section, 151
inferior view, 131
lateral view, 143, 151
meninges and cerebrospinal fluid
   flow in, 145
sagittal section of, 125
during seizures, 135
stroke, 156–157
tumors of, 128–129
BRCA 1 gene, 8
Breast
   benign conditions, 306–307
   cancer of, 310–311
   cyst of, 307
Bronchi
   in asthma, 84–85
   in lung cancer, 97
   in pneumonia, 101
   in severe acute respiratory syndrome,
    113
Bronchioles, 105
   in chronic bronchitis, 87
   in emphysema, 90–91
   in pulmonary edema, 105
   in severe acute respiratory syndrome,
    113
Bronchitis, 117
   chronic, 86–87
Bronchopneumonia, 100–101
Bronchospasm, 85
Buffer systems, 33
Burns, 384–385
   classification of, 384–385
   estimating extent of, 385t
Bursitis, 220–221

C

Calcium
   electrolyte characteristics of, 29t
   metabolism in osteoporosis, 237
   normal values for, 29t
Calcium renal calculi, 374–375
Callus, 226
Cancer, 6–12. See also specific type
   of bladder, 360–361
   bone tumors, 218–219
   brain tumors, 128–129
   breast, 310–311
   causes of, 6
   cell differentiation in, 8–9
   cell growth in, 8
   cell histology, 8
   cervical, 312–313
   colorectal, 170–171

diagnostic testing for, 11–12
endometrial, 320–321
of esophagus, 176–177
gastric, 178–179
intracellular changes, 9
laryngeal, 420–421
of liver, 200–201
of lung, 96–97
metastasis, 9–11
oral, 204–205
ovarian, 332–333
pancreatic, 206–207
prostate, 338–339
renal, 376–377
risk factors for, 6–8
signs and symptoms, 11
of skin, 400–403
testicular, 346–347
of thyroid gland, 302–303
treatment, 12
tumor classification in, 12
tumor development, 9
tumor types in, 9–11
vulvar, 354–355
warning signs of, 11
Candida albicans, in vaginitis, 350–351
Candidiasis, of skin, 392–393
Capillary changes
   in acute respiratory distress
    syndrome, 80–81, 83
   in fat embolism syndrome, 93
   in pleural effusion, 98
   in pulmonary edema, 104–105
Carbuncles, 390–391
Carcinogens, 22
Carcinoma. See Cancer
Carcinoma in situ
   cervical, 313
   ductal, 311
Cardiac arrhythmias, 40–41
   sites of common, 41
Cardiac circulation, normal, 57
Cardiac muscle cells, 3
Cardiac tamponade, 42–43
Cardiac thrombosis, 157
Cardiogenic shock, 73
Cardiomyopathy, 44–45
   types of, 45
Carpal tunnel syndrome, 222–223
Caseous necrosis, 5
Cataract, 406–407
Cell cycle, 8
Cell membrane, 2
   in cancer, 9
Cells
   aging of, 5
   components of, 2–3
   death of, 5
   degeneration of, 4
   division of, 2–3

t refers to table.

Cells (*continued*)
functions of, 2
injury to, 4
types of, 2–3
Cellulitis, 386–387
recognizing, 387t
Central diabetes insipidus, 284
Central nervous system (CNS), control
center, homeostasis and, 5
Centrosomes, 2
Cerebral aneurysm, 130–131
Cerebral hemorrhage, 156–157
sites of, 157
Cerebrospinal fluid
flow of, 145
in hydrocephalus, 142–143
in meningitis, 144–145
Cerebrovascular accident. *See* Stroke
Cervical cancer, 312–313
human papilloma virus and, 7
Cervical intraepithelial neoplasia, 312
Cervical lymphadenopathy, 259
Chemical burn, 384
Chemical conjunctivitis, 410
Chemotherapy, in cancer treatment, 12
Chickenpox, 20t
Chlamydia, 13, 17t, 342, 345
Chloride
electrolyte characteristics of, 29t
normal values for, 29t
Cholangiocarcinoma, 200
Cholangiocellular carcinoma, 200
Cholangiomas, 200
Cholecystitis, 164–165
Cholesteatoma, in otitis media, 429
Cholesterol
high, 192–193
production of, 193
transport of, 193
Chondroblastoma, 219
Chondrosarcoma, 218
Chordoma, 218
Choroidal melanoma, 426
Christmas disease, 250
Chromosomes defects, 23, 27t
Chronic bronchitis, 86–87
mucus buildup in, 87
Chronic glomerulonephritis, 364–365
Chronic inflammation, in infection,
15–16
Chronic lymphocytic leukemia (CLL),
254–255
Chronic lymphocytic thyroiditis, 296
Chronic myeloid leukemia (CML),
254–255
Chronic open-angle glaucoma, 414
Circle of Willis, 131
Circumflex artery, 51, 63
Cirrhosis, 166–167
Cleft lip/palate, 26t, 408–409

Closed pneumothorax, 102
Cluster headache, 138
Coagulative necrosis, 5
Coarctation of the aorta, 46–47
Cochlear duct, in Ménière's disease, 425
Codons, 21
Cold, common, 116–117
Colitis
granulomatous, 172–173
spastic, 198–199
ulcerative, 214–215
Colles' fracture, 227
Colonic polyps, 168–169
Colorectal cancer, 170–171
Comedones, of acne, 381
Common cold, 116–117
complications of, 116–117
Compensation, in acid-base imbalance,
33
Compensatory hyperplasia, 4
Compensatory stage, of shock, 72
Complex-partial seizures, 136
Compression test
for carpal tunnel syndrome, 222
manual, for varicose veins, 78
Computed tomography (CT) scan, in
cancer diagnosis, 11
Conduction, as cell function, 2
Conductive hearing loss, 419
Condyloma acuminatum, 404
Condylomata acuminata, 342–344
Congenital anomalies, 23
Congenital defects, of heart, 46–49
Congenital hearing loss, 418
Congenital hydrocele, 328–329
Congenital megacolon, 190–191
Conjunctivitis, 17t, 410–411
manifestations of, 411
Connective tissue cells, 3
Consumption coagulopathy, 248–249
Contact dermatitis, 388–389
Convalescence
as disease stage, 5
as infection stage, 15t
Corneal ulcer, 412–413
Coronary arteries, 51
atherosclerosis and, 50–51
in myocardial infarction, 62–63
Coronary artery disease, 50–51
Coronavirus, 112
Corpus luteum cysts, ovarian, 334
Cortisol
deficiency, in adrenal hypofunction,
280–281
excess, in Cushing's syndrome,
282–283
Coryza, acute, 116–117
Coup/contrecoup injury, 118
Crescentic glomerulonephritis, 364–365
Cretinism, infantile, 296

Crohn's disease, 172–173
bowel changes in, 173
Cryptogenic fibrosing alveolitis, 94–95
Cryptorchidism, 314–315
Cushing's disease, 282
Cushing's syndrome, 282–283
manifestations of, 283
Cystic fibrosis, 24t, 88–89
systemic changes in, 89
Cystic fibrosis transmembrane regulator,
88
Cystitis, 362–363
Cysts
breast, 307
ovarian, 334–335
Cytomegalovirus, 19t
Cytoplasm, 2
in cancer, 9
Cytoskeleton, 2
in cancer, 9

D

Da Nang lung, 80–83
Deafness, 418–419
Deep veins, of leg, 53
Deep vein thrombosis, 52–53, 106
Defense mechanisms, weakened, as
infection risk factor, 14
Defibrination syndrome, 248–249
Deficit injury, cell, 4
Dementia, Alzheimer's, 120–121
Demyelination
in multiple sclerosis, 146–147
peripheral nerve, 136–137
Deoxyribonucleic acid (DNA), 2, 21
Depression, 132–133
brain changes in, 133
pediatric symptoms, 132
Dermatitis
atopic, 382–383
contact, 388–389
Dermoid cysts, ovarian, 334–335
Descending aortic aneurysm, 38
Developmental dysplasia of hip,
224–225
signs of, 225
Developmental factors, in infection, 14
Diabetes insipidus, 284–285
laboratory values for, 285t
mechanism of deficiency, 285
Diabetes mellitus, 286–287
type 1, 286–287
type 2, 286–287
Diagonal artery, 51
Diaphoresis, 15
Diaphragm, in hiatal hernia, 188–189
Diastolic dysfunction, in heart failure,
56

t refers to table.

Diet, as cancer risk factor, 7
Differentiation, cancer cells and, 8–9
Diffuse interstitial fibrosis, 94–95
Digitate wart, 404
Dilated cardiomyopathy, 44–45
Diploid cells, 21
Disease
    defined, 5
    illness vs., 5
    stages of, 5
Disjunction, 23
Dissecting aortic aneurysm, 38–39
Disseminated intravascular
        coagulation, 248–249
Diverticular disease, 174–175
Diverticulitis, 174
Diverticulosis, 174–175
Dominant gene, 22
Dopamine levels, in Parkinson's disease,
        150–151
Down syndrome, 27t
Dry gangrene, 5
Dry macular degeneration, 422
Duchenne's muscular dystrophy,
        230–231
Ductal carcinoma
    infiltrating, 311
    in situ, 311
Dysfunctional uterine bleeding,
        316–317
Dysplasia, 4
    in cancer, 9

E

Ectopic pregnancy, 318–319
Ectropion, 416–417
Eczema, atopic, 382–383
Edema
    fluid balance and, 29
    pulmonary, 104–105
Edematous pancreatitis, 208
Edward's syndrome, 27t
Effector, homeostasis and, 5
Elbow
    fracture of, 227
    tendonitis of, 245
Electrical burn, 384
Electrolyte balance, 30–31
    disorders of, 32–33t
    pathophysiologic concepts, 29–33
Electrolytes, 28
    characteristics of major, 29t
    normal values for, 29t
Embolism
    pulmonary, 106–107
    in stroke, 156–157
Emphysema, 90–91
    lung changes in, 91

Emphysematous pyelonephritis, 372
Empyema, 99
Encephalopathy, hepatic, 202
Endemic goiter, 300
Endocarditis, 54–55
Endolymphatic hydrops, 424–425
Endometrial cancer, 320–321
        progress of, 321
Endometriosis, 322–323
        common sites of, 323
Endoplasmic reticulum, 2
Endoscopy, in cancer diagnosis, 11
Enteritis, regional, 172–173
Entropion, 416–417
Environmental factors, in infection, 14
Environmental teratogens, 22
Ependymal cells, 3
Epilepsy, 134–135
        types of seizures, 135
Epileptogenic focus, 134
Epispadias, 330–331
Epithelial cells, 3
Erectile dysfunction, 324–325
Erythema migrans, 394–395
Erythrocyte sedimentation rate, in
        infection diagnosis, 16
Erythrodermic psoriasis, 398
Esophageal stricture, 182–183
Esophagitis, 182–183
Esophagus
    in achalasia, 160–161
    cancer of, 176–177
    in gastroesophageal reflux disease,
        182–183
Estrogen, in dysfunctional uterine
        bleeding, 316
Ewing's sarcoma, 218
Excretion, as cell function, 2
Exfoliative psoriasis, 398
Extracapillary glomerulonephritis,
        364–365
Extracellular fluid, 28
Extrinsic allergens, in asthma, 84
Exudative macular degeneration, 422
Exudative pleural effusion, 99

F

Facial cellulitis, 386
Facial nerve, in Bell's palsy, 126–127
Facioscapulohumeral muscular
        dystrophy, 230–231
Factor IX deficiency, 250
Factor VIII deficiency, 250
False aortic aneurysm, 38–39
Familial adenomatous polyposis
        (FAP), 7
Familial cutaneous malignant
        melanoma gene, 7

Fat embolism syndrome, 92–93
    pulmonary circulation and, 93
Fat necrosis, 5
Feedback mechanisms, in homeo-
        stasis, 5
Fever, in infection, 15
Fibroadenoma, breast, 307
Fibrocystic disease of breast, 306–307
Fibroid disease of uterus, 326–327
Fibromyoma, uterine, 326
Fibrosarcoma, 218
Fibrosis, idiopathic pulmonary,
        94–95
Fibrous ankylosis, 274
Fibrous plaque, 299
Filiform wart, 404
First-degree atrioventricular block,
        41
First-degree burns, 384–385
Flaccid neurogenic bladder, 368
Flat wart, 404
Floppy mitral valve prolapse, 60–61
Fluid
    extracellular, 28
    intracellular, 28
Fluid balance, 28–29
    acid-base balance and, 28–29, 31, 33
    electrolyte balance and, 30–31
    hypervolemia, 31t
    hypovolemia, 30t
    pathophysiologic concepts, 29–33
Fluid exchange, 28
Focal polypoid hyperplasia, 168
Follicular carcinoma, thyroid, 302
Follicular cysts, ovarian, 334–335
Follicular impetigo, 390
Folliculitis, 390–391
Foot
    fractures of, 227
    gout of, 229
Fourth-degree burns, 384–385
Fractures, 226–227
    locations of, 227
Fragile X syndrome, 25t
Fungal infections, 20t
    of nail, 393
    of skin, 392–393
Fungi, in infection, 13
Furuncles, 390–391
Fusiform aortic aneurysm, 38–39

G

Gallbladder
    anatomical considerations, 165
    cholecystitis, 164–165
Gallstones, 164–165
Gangrene, forms of, 5
Gangrenous necrosis, 5

t refers to table.

Gas gangrene, 5
Gastric cancer, 178–179
Gastric ulcers, 216–217
Gastritis, 180–181
Gastroesophageal reflux disease
    (GERD), 182–183
Gene mutations
    in cancer, 8
    causes of, 22
Generalized tonic-clonic seizures,
    135–136
Genes, 21
Genetics, 21–23, 24–27t
    as cancer risk factor, 7
    common disorders, 24–27t
    defined, 21
    deoxyribonucleic acid (DNA) in, 21
    pathophysiologic concepts, 22–23
    trait dominance in, 22
    transmission traits, 21
Genital herpes, 342, 345
Genital warts, 342–344
Genome sequence, 21
Germ cells, 21
Gestational diabetes, 286
Giant cell tumor, 218–219
Gigantism, 288
Glaucoma, 414–415
    optic disk changes in, 415
    types of, 414
Gliomas, 128–129
Glomerulonephritis, 364–365
    immune complex deposits on
        glomerulus, 364–365
Glomerulus, in glomerulonephritis,
    364–365
Glucocorticoid deficiency, 280
GM$_2$ gangliosidosis, 24t
Goiter, 292, 300–301
    simple, 300–301
    types of, 301
Golgi apparatus, 2
Gonorrhea, 17t, 342, 345
Gout, 228–229
Gram stain, 16
Granulomatous colitis, 172–173
Granulomatous tissue formation, in
    sarcoidosis, 111
Granulovascular degeneration, in
    Alzheimer's disease, 121
Graves' disease, 292–293, 301
    histologic changes in, 293
Grawitz's tumor, 376
Growth hormone excess, 288–289
    effects of, 289
Guillain-Barré syndrome, 136–137
    peripheral nerve demyelination
        in, 137
Gurd's criteria, for fat embolism
    syndrome, 92

H

Hamman-Rich syndrome, 94–95
Hand
    fracture of, 227
    osteoarthritis of, 233
    rheumatoid arthritis of, 275
Haploid number, 21
Hashimoto's thyroiditis, 296–297
Hay fever, 268
Head, whiplash injury of, 118–119
Headache, 138–139
    vascular changes in, 139
Hearing, process of, 419t
Hearing loss, 418–419
Heart
    blood supply to, 51
    normal cardiac circulation, 57
    normal valves, 75, 77
Heartburn, 182–183
Heart failure, 56–57
    left-sided, 56–57
    right-sided, 56–57
Heart valves
    endocarditis and, 54
    mitral valve prolapse, 60–61
    normal, 75, 77
    rheumatic heart disease and, 70–71
Heart wall
    in cardiac tamponade, 43
    in endocarditis, 55
    in myocarditis, 65
    normal cross section of, 43, 55,
        65, 67
    in pericarditis, 67
Helicobacter pylori infection, 216
Hemophilia, 25t, 250–251
Hemorrhagic stroke, 156–157
Hemorrhoids, 184–185
Hepatic carcinoma, 200–201
Hepatic encephalopathy, 202
Hepatitis, 186–187
Hepatocellular carcinoma, 200
Hepatomas, 200
Hepatorenal syndrome, 202
Hereditary genes, as cancer risk factor,
    7–8
Hereditary polyps, 168
Hernia
    hiatal, 188–189
    inguinal, 194–195, 197
Herniated intervertebral disk,
    140–141
Herniated nucleus pulposus, 140–141
Herpes, genital, 342, 345
Herpes simplex virus (HSV), 19t
Herpes zoster, 19t
Heterozygous, 22
Hiatal hernia, 188–189

Hip
    bursitis of, 221
    developmental dysplasia of, 224–225
    fractures of, 227
    osteoarthritis of, 233
    rheumatoid arthritis of, 275
Hirschsprung's disease, 190–191
Histamine, role in asthma, 84
Histoplasmosis, 20t
HIV infection. *See* Human
    immunodeficiency virus (HIV)
    infection
Hodgkin's disease, 252–253
    stages of, 253
Homeostasis, 5
Homozygous, 22
Hormonal therapy, in cancer treatment,
    12
Human epidermal growth factor
    receptor-2 (HER-2)/neu
    proto-oncogene, 7–8
Human genome, 21
Human immunodeficiency virus (HIV)
    infection, 19t, 266–267
    symptoms of, 267
Human papillomavirus (HPV)
    cervical cancer and, 7
    in warts, 404
Hydrocele, 328–329
Hydrocephalus, 142–143
    brain changes in, 143
Hydronephrosis, 366–367
Hydrostatic pressure
    in fluid balance, 28
    in pulmonary edema, 104–105
Hypercalcemia, 32t
    in hyperparathyroidism, 290
Hyperchloremia, 32t
Hyperextension, spinal injury, 119, 154
Hyperflexion, spinal injury, 119, 154
Hyperkalemia, 32t
Hyperlipidemia, 192–193
Hyperlipoproteinemia, 192–193
Hypermagnesemia, 33t
Hypermenorrhea, 316
Hypernatremia, 32t
Hypernephroma, 376
Hyperparathyroidism, 290–291
    bone resorption in, 291t
    pathogenesis of, 291
Hyperphosphatemia, 33t
Hyperplasia, 3–4
Hypertension, 58–59
    blood vessel damage in, 59
    primary, 58
    pulmonary, 108–109
    renovascular, 378–379
    secondary, 58
Hyperthyroidism, 292–293
    histologic changes in, 293

t refers to table.

Hypertonic solutions, 30
Hypertonic tonicity, 28
Hypertrophic cardiomyopathy, 44–45
Hypertrophy, 3–4
Hypervolemia, 31t
Hypocalcemia, 32t
Hypochloremia, 32t
Hypokalemia, 32t
Hypomagnesemia, 32t
Hyponatremia, 32t
Hypophosphatemia, 33t, 290
Hypopituitarism, 294–295
Hypospadias, 330–331
Hypothyroidism, 296–297
Hypotonic solutions, 30
Hypotonic tonicity, 28
Hypovolemia, 30t
Hypovolemic shock, 73

I

Idiopathic disease, 5
Idiopathic interstitial pneumonitis,
    94–95
Idiopathic pulmonary fibrosis, 94–95
    end-stage, 95
Illness *vs.* disease, 5
Immune complex deposits, in
    glomerulonephritis, 364–365
Immunodeficiency
    acquired, 14
    as infection risk factor, 14
Immunotherapy, in cancer treatment, 12
Impotence, 324–325
Incubation
    as disease stage, 5
    as infection stage, 15t
Infantile eczema, 382–383
Infection, 13–20
    bacterial, 17–18t
    causes of, 13
    in cell injury, 4
    common disorders, 17–20t
    diagnostic testing for, 16
    fungal, 20t
    pathogen characteristics, 14–15
    pathophysiologic concepts, 15
    protozoal, 20t
    risk factors for, 14
    signs and symptoms, 15–16
    stages of, 14–15
    treatment, 16
    upper respiratory tract, 116–117
    viral, 18–20t
Infectious conjunctivitis, 410
Infectious mononucleosis, 19t
Infectious polyneuritis, 136–137
Infective endocarditis, 54–55
Infectivity, pathogenicity and, 14

Inferior vena cava, in cardiac
    circulation, 61
Inflammation
    in acne, 380–381
    acute, 15
    in ankylosing spondylitis, 272
    in appendicitis, 162–163
    in bursitis, 220–221
    in carpal tunnel syndrome, 222
    in cholecystitis, 164
    chronic, 15–16
    in Crohn's disease, 172–173
    in gastritis, 180–181
    in idiopathic pulmonary fibrosis, 94
    in meningitis, 144–145
    in osteomyelitis, 234
    in otitis media, 428–429
    in peritonitis, 210–211
    in prostatitis, 340–341
    in pyelonephritis, 372
    in rheumatoid arthritis, 274–275
    in spinal cord injury, 154–155
    in systemic lupus erythematosus,
        278–279
    in tendonitis, 244–245
    in ulcerative colitis, 214–215
    in vaginitis, 350
    in West Nile virus, 158–159
Inflammatory response, 15
    in fractures, 226
Inguinal hernia, 194–195, 197
    direct, 194
    indirect, 194–195
Inheritance
    autosomal, 22
    multifactorial, 22
    sex-linked, 22
Injury
    acceleration-deceleration, 118–119
    cell, 4
    as disease stage, 5
Insulin resistance, in metabolic
    syndrome, 298–299
Intertrochanteric fracture, 227
Interventricular arteries, 51
Intervertebral disk, herniated, 140–141
Intestines
    anatomy of, 163
    changes in colorectal cancer, 171
    changes in Crohn's disease, 173
    changes in diverticular disease,
        174–175
    changes in Hirschsprung's disease,
        191
    changes in irritable bowel syndrome,
        198–199
    changes in polyps, 171
    changes in ulcerative colitis, 215
    obstruction of, 196–197
Intracapsular fracture, 227

Intracellular fluid, 28
Intracranial aneurysm, 130–131
Intracranial hemorrhage, 156–157
Intraocular pressure, in glaucoma, 414
Intrarenal failure, 356–357
Intrinsic allergens, in asthma, 84
Intrinsic renal failure, 356–357
Intussusception, with invagination, 197
Invasiveness, pathogenicity and, 14
Ionizing radiation, as cancer risk factor,
    6–7
Iron deficiency anemia, 246–247
Irreversible stage, of shock, 72
Irritable bowel syndrome, 198–199
Ischemia, in myocardial infarction,
    62–63
Ischemic stroke, 156–157
Ischemic tubular necrosis, 358–359
Isotonic solutions, 30
Isotonic tonicity, 28

J

Jejunum, adenocarcinoma of, 171
Jones criteria, for rheumatic heart
    disease, 70
Junctional arrhythmia, 41
Junctional rhythm, 41
Juvenile polyps, 168
Juvenile wart, 404

K

Karyotype, 21
Kidneys
    in acid-base imbalance, 33
    cancer of, 376–377
    in fluid balance, 28
    glomerulonephritis, 364–365
    hydronephrosis, 366–367
    polycystic kidney disease, 370–371
    pyelonephritis, 372–373
    renal calculi, 374–375
    renovascular hypertension,
        378–379
Knee
    bursitis of, 221
    gout of, 229
    osteoarthritis of, 233
    rheumatoid arthritis of, 275
Kveim-Stilzbach skin test, 110
Kyphosis, 239

L

Landouzy-Dejerine muscular dystrophy,
    230–231

t refers to table.

Landry-Guillain-Barré syndrome, 136–137
Large-cell undifferentiated carcinoma, of lung, 96
Large intestines. *See also* Intestines
  anatomy of, 163
  obstruction of, 196–197
Laryngeal cancer, 420–421
Latency period, of disease, 5
Lateral malleolus fracture, 227
Latex allergy, 270–271
Left-sided heart failure, 56–57
Leg, deep veins of, 53
Leiomyoma, uterine, 326
Lentigo maligna melanoma, 400, 402
Leukemia, 254–255
Leukocytosis
  defined, 15
  in infection, 15
Ligament sprains, 240–241
Limb-girdle muscular dystrophy, 230–231
Linear scleroderma, 276
Lip, cleft, 26t, 408–409
Lipid disorder, 192–193
Lipoproteins, in hyperlipidemia, 192–193
Liquefactive necrosis, 5
Listeriosis, 17t
Liver
  anatomical considerations, 165
  cancer of, 200–201
  cirrhosis of, 167
  in cystic fibrosis, 89
  in hepatitis, 187
  in hyperlipidemia, 193
Liver failure, 202–203
  signs of, 203
Lobular pneumonia, 100–101
Lordosis, 239
Lou Gehrig's disease, 122–123
Lower esophageal sphincter, in gastroesophageal reflux disease, 182–183
Lund-Browder chart, for burn extent, 385t
Lung cancer, 96–97
  tumor infiltration in, 97
Lungs
  acute injury, 82
  in cystic fibrosis, 89
  in emphysema, 91
  in fat embolism syndrome, 92–93
  in idiopathic pulmonary fibrosis, 95
  normal alveoli, 105
  normal pulmonary arteries, 109
  in pleural effusion, 99
  in pneumonia, 100–101
  in pneumothorax, 102–103
  in sarcoidosis, 111

in severe acute respiratory syndrome, 113
  in tuberculosis, 115
Lupus erythematosus, 278–279
Luteal cysts, ovarian, 334
Lyme disease, 17t, 394–395
Lymphadenopathy, cervical, 259
Lymphatic system, 259
Lysosomes, 2

M

Macrophages, 15
Macular degeneration, 422–423
  retinal changes in, 423
Magnesium
  electrolyte characteristics of, 29t
  normal values for, 29t
Malignant hypertension, 58
Malignant melanoma, 400, 402–403
  ABCDEs of, 402–403
Malignant plasmacytoma, 256–257
Malleolus fractures, 227
Manual compression test, for varicose veins, 78
Marfan syndrome, 25t
Marginal arteries, 51
Marie-Strümpell disease, 272–273
McBurney's point, 162
Medial malleolus fracture, 227
Medulla oblongata, in homeostasis, 5
Medullary carcinoma, thyroid, 302
Meiosis, 21
Melanoma
  malignant, 400, 402–403
  ocular, 426–427
Membrane, cell, 2
  in cancer, 9
Ménière's disease, 424–425
Meninges, cerebrospinal fluid flow and, 145
Meningiomas, 128–129
Meningitis, 17t, 144–145
  inflammation in, 145
Meningocele, 152–153
Meningomyelocele, 152–153
Merkel's diverticulum, 174
Metabolic acidosis, 35t
Metabolic alkalosis, 35t
Metabolic syndrome, 298–299
  organs affected by, 299
Metaplasia, 4
Metastasis, 9–11
  to liver, 200
  ovarian cancer and, 333t
  prostate cancer and, 339t
Metastatic hepatic carcinoma, 200
Metrorrhagia, 316
Microfilaments, 2

Microglia, 3
Microtubules, 2
Migraine headache, 138
Mitochondria, 2
Mitosis
  defined, 21
  phases of, 21
Mitral insufficiency, 74, 76
Mitral stenosis, 74, 76
Mitral valve, 75
  in rheumatic heart disease, 71
Mitral valve prolapse, 60–61
  valve position in, 61
Moist gangrene, 5
Moist wart, 404
Monkeypox, 19t
Monocytes, 15
Mononucleosis, 19t
Monosomy, 23
Morgan's line, in atopic dermatitis, 383t
Morphea, 276
Mosaicism, 23
Motor neurons, in amyotrophic lateral sclerosis, 123
Movement, as cell function, 2
Mucus buildup
  in asthma, 84–85
  in chronic bronchitis, 86–87
  in cystic fibrosis, 88
Mucus plug, in asthma, 85
Multifactorial inheritance, 22
  disorders due to, 23, 26t
Multiple myeloma, 256–257
Multiple sclerosis, 146–147
Multisystem effects
  in cystic fibrosis, 89
  in liver failure, 203
  in sarcoidosis, 110
  in shock, 73
  in systemic lupus erythematosus, 279
Mumps, 19t
Muscle cells
  normal, 123
  types of, 3
Muscle strains, 242–243
Muscular dystrophy, 230–231
  muscles affected in various types of, 231
Mutations, gene
  in cancer, 8
  causes of, 22
  defined, 22
Myasthenia gravis, 148–149
  nerve impulse transmission failure in, 149
Myasthenic crisis, 148
Mycoplasmas, in infection, 13
Myelin sheath, degeneration of
  in multiple sclerosis, 146–147
  peripheral nerve, 136–137

t refers to table.

Myelomeningocele, 152–153
Myobacterium tuberculosis, 114
Myocardial infarction, 62–63
   tissue destruction in, 63
   zones of, 63
Myocarditis, 64–65
Myoclonic seizures, 135
Myoma, uterine, 326
Myxedema, 296–297

N

Nail, fungal infection of, 393
Native valve endocarditis, 54
Neck
   ligaments of, 119
   whiplash injury of, 118–119
Necrosis
   acute tubular, 358–359
   in myocardial infarction, 62–63
   types of, 5
Necrotizing pancreatitis, 208–209
Nephritis
   acute infective tubulointerstitial,
      372–373
   acute tubulointerstitial, 358–359
Nephrocarcinoma, 376
Nephrogenic diabetes insipidus, 284
Nephrolithiasis, 374–375
Nephrotoxic injury, in acute tubular
      necrosis, 358–359
Nerve cells, 3
   in Alzheimer's disease, 121
   in amyotrophic lateral sclerosis, 123
   in depression, 133
   in multiple sclerosis, 147
   in myasthenia gravis, 149
   normal, 123
   in Parkinson's disease, 151
   in seizures, 135
Neural tube defects, 26t
Neuritic plaques, 120–121
Neurofibrillary tangles, 120–121
Neurogenic bladder, 368–369
Neurogenic diabetes insipidus, 284
Neurogenic shock, 73
Neuroglial cells, 3
Neuronal loss, 120
Neurons, 3
Neurotransmission
   in depression, 132–133
   in myasthenia gravis, 148–149
   in Parkinson's disease, 151
Neurotransmitters, 133
Neutrophils, 15
N-myc-oncogene expression, 7
Nodular goiter, 301
Nodular malignant melanoma, 400, 402
Noise-induced hearing loss, 418

Nondisjunction, 23
NonHodgkin's lymphomas, 258–259
Nonosseous bone tumors, 218
Non-small-cell lung cancer, 96
Nonstriated muscle cells, 3
Nontoxic goiter, 300–301
Nonviral hepatitis, 186–187
Nucleus, cell, 2
   in cancer, 9
Nucleus pulposus, herniated, 140–141

O

Occupation, as cancer risk factor, 6
Ocular melanoma, 426–427
Olecranon fracture, displaced, 227
Oligodendroglia, 3
Oligomenorrhea, 316
Oncogenes, 6
Oncotic pressure
   in fluid balance, 28–29
   in pulmonary edema, 105
Open-angle glaucoma, chronic, 414
Open pneumothorax, 102
Opportunistic infections, related to
      AIDS, 267
Optic disk changes, in glaucoma,
   415
Oral cancer, 204–205
Orbital cellulitis, 386
Orchiectomy, 348
Orchiopexy, 348
Organelles, 2
Organic erectile dysfunction, 324
Ortolani's sign, 224
Osgood-Schlatter disease, 244
Osmotic pressure
   in fluid balance, 28
   in pulmonary edema, 104–105
Osseous bone tumors, 218
Osteoarthritis, 232–233
Osteoblasts, 226, 237
Osteoclasts, 226, 237
Osteocytes, 226
Osteogenic sarcoma, 218–219
Osteoid, 237
Osteomyelitis, 234–235
   stages of, 235
Osteophyte, 232
Osteoporosis, 236–237
   calcium metabolism in, 237
Otitis media, 17t, 428–429
   acute, 117, 429
   classification of, 429
   complications of, 429
   with effusion, 117, 429
Ovarian cancer, 332–333
   metastatic sites for, 333t
Ovarian cysts, 334–335

PQ

Pain, as inflammation sign, 15
Palate, cleft, 26t, 408–409
Pancreas
   cancer of, 206–207
   in cystic fibrosis, 89
   pancreatitis, 208–209
Pancreatitis, 208–209
Panhypopituitarism, 294–295
Pannus, 274
Papillary carcinoma, thyroid,
   302–303
Papillary muscle, 63
Papilloma, intraductal, 307
Pap smear findings, 313
Paraesophageal hernia, 188
Parasites, in infection, 13
Parathyroid hormone (PTH), in
      hyperparathyroidism, 290–291
Parenchymal renal failure, 356–357
Parkinson's disease, 150–151
   neurotransmitter action in, 151
Parosteal osteogenic sarcoma, 218
Patau's syndrome, 27t
Patellar tendonitis, 244
Patent ductus arteriosus, 46–47
Pathogenesis, 5
Pathogenicity, factors in, 14
Pathologic hyperplasia, 4
Pathologic hypertrophy, 3
Pathologic metaplasia, 4
Pelvic inflammatory disease, 336–337
   adhesions in, 337
Perennial allergic rhinitis, 268
Perforation, in otitis media, 429
Pericardial effusion, in cardiac
      tamponade, 42
Pericardial friction rub, auscultation of,
   64
Pericarditis, 66–67
Peripheral nerve demyelination,
   136–137
Peritonitis, 17t, 210–211
   generalized, 211
Periungual wart, 404–405
Pernicious anemia, 246–247
Peroxisomes, 2
Pertussis, 17t
P53 gene, 7
pH, blood, 29
Phagocytosis, 2, 15
Phalen's wrist test, 222
Phenylketonuria (PKU), 24t
Phosphate
   electrolyte characteristics of, 29t
   normal values for, 29t
Physical injury, cell, 4
Physiologic hyperplasia, 3

t refers to table.

Physiologic hypertrophy, 3
Physiologic metaplasia, 4
Pinkeye, 410
Pituitary adenomas, 128–129
Pituitary gigantism, 288
Pituitary gland
    anatomical considerations, 295
    in homeostasis, 5
    hypopituitarism, 294–295
Plantar wart, 404
Plasma cell myeloma, 256–257
Pleural effusion, 98–99
    lung compression in, 99
Pneumonia, 100–101
    bacterial, 18t
    types of, 101
    viral, 20t
Pneumothorax, 102–103
    effects of, 103
    tension, 103
Polycystic kidney disease, 370–371
Polycystic ovarian syndrome, 334
Polycythemia vera, 260–261
    blood smear in, 261
Polygenic disorders, 22–23, 26t
Polymenorrhea, 316
Polypoid adenomas, 168
Polyps, colonic, 168–169
Positron emission tomography (PET)
    scan, in cancer diagnosis, 11
Postrenal failure, 356–357
Poststreptococcal glomerulonephritis,
    364
Potassium
    electrolyte characteristics of, 29t
    normal values for, 29t
Pregnancy, ectopic, 318–319
Premature atrial contractions, 41
Premature ventricular contractions, 41
Prerenal failure, 356–357
Presbycusis, 418
Pressure ulcers, 396–397
    staging of, 397
Primary polycythemia, 260–261
Prodromal stage
    of disease, 5
    of infection, 15t
Progesterone, in dysfunctional uterine
    bleeding, 316
Progressive stage, of shock, 72
Prostate cancer, 338–339
    metastatic sites for, 339t
Prostate gland
    benign prostatic hyperplasia (BPH),
        308–309
    enlargement of, 309
    palpation of, 309t
Prostatitis, 340–341
Prosthetic valve endocarditis, 54
Proto-oncogenes, 6

Protozoal infections, 20t
Pseudohypertrophic muscular
    dystrophy, 230–231
Psoriasis, 398–399
Psychogenic diabetes insipidus, 284
Psychogenic erectile dysfunction, 324
Pulmonary artery
    in atrial septal defect, 47
    in cardiac circulation, 61
    emboli in, 106–107
    normal, 109
    in patent ductus arteriosus, 46–47
    in pulmonary hypertension,
        108–109
    in tetralogy of Fallot, 49
    in transposition of the great arteries,
        49
Pulmonary edema, 104–105
    development of, 105
    fat embolism syndrome in, 92–93
Pulmonary embolism, 106–107
Pulmonary fibrosis, idiopathic, 94–95
Pulmonary hypertension, 108–109
    early, 109
    late, 109
Pulmonary mechanisms, in acid-base
    imbalance, 33
Pulmonary veins, 105
    in atrial septal defect, 47
    in cardiac circulation, 61
    in tetralogy of Fallot, 49
Pulmonic stenosis, 74, 76
Pulmonic valve, 75
Pyelonephritis, 372–373
    phases of, 373
Pyloric stenosis, 212–213

R

Rabies, 19t
Radial head fracture, 227
Radiation, as cancer risk factor,
    6–7
Radiation therapy, in cancer treatment,
    12
Radioactive isotope scanning, in cancer
    diagnosis, 11
Rapidly progressive glomerulonephritis,
    364–365
Raynaud's disease, 68–69
    progressive changes in, 69
Raynaud's phenomenon, 69, 276
Recessive gene, 22
Recovery, as disease stage, 5
Redness, as inflammation sign, 15
Refractory stage, of shock, 72
Regional enteritis, 172–173
Remission, as disease stage, 5
Remodeling, 62

Renal calculi, 374–375
    calcium, 374–375
    struvite, 375
    uric acid, 375
Renal cancer, 376–377
Renal cell carcinoma, 376
Renal failure
    acute, 356–357
    acute tubular necrosis in, 358–359
Renal mechanisms, in acid-base
    imbalance, 33
Renovascular hypertension, 378–379
    mechanism of, 379
Reproductive tract, in cystic fibrosis, 89
Respiratory acidosis, 34t
Respiratory alkalosis, 34t
Respiratory syncytial virus, 19t
Restrictive cardiomyopathy, 44–45
Reticular formation, in homeostasis, 5
Retina, changes in macular
    degeneration, 423
Retrograde refilling test, 78
Rheumatic fever, 70
    sequelae of, 71
Rheumatic heart disease, 70–71
Rheumatoid arthritis, 274–275
Rheumatoid factor, 274
Rheumatoid spondylitis, 272–273
Rhinitis, 117
    allergic, 268–269
Ribonucleic acid (RNA), 2
Ribosomes, 2
Rickettsia, in infection, 13
Right-sided heart failure, 56–57
Rolling hernia, 188
Rubella, 20t
Rubeola, 20t
Rule of nines, for burns, 385t
Ruptured disk, 140–141
Ruptures, 194–195

S

Saccular aortic aneurysm, 38–39
Salmonellosis, 18t
Sarcoidosis, 110–111
    lung changes in, 111
Sarcomas, of bone, 218–219
Sclerodactyly, 277
Scleroderma, 276–277
Scoliosis, 238–239
Screening tests, for cancer, 11
Secondary polycythemia, 260
Second-degree atrioventricular
    block, 41
Second-degree burns, 384–385
Secretion, as cell function, 2
Secretory otitis media, 428
Seizures, types of, 135

t refers to table.

Semilunar heart valves, 75, 77
  defects in, 77
Sensorineural hearing loss, 419
Sensors, homeostasis and, 5
Septic shock, 73
Severe acute respiratory syndrome,
  112–113
  lung changes in, 113
Sever's disease, 244
Sex chromosomes, 21
Sex-linked inheritance, 22
  disorders due to, 22–23
Sexually transmitted infections (STIs),
  342–345
Sexual practices, as cancer risk factor, 7
Shigellosis, 18t
Shock, 72–73
  multiorgan system effects of, 73
Shock lung, 80–83
Sickle cell anemia, 24t, 262–263
  blood smear in, 263
Sickle cell crisis, 24t, 263
Silver stain, 16
Simple goiter, 300–301
Simple-partial seizures, 136
Sinoatrial block, 41
Sinus bradycardia, 41
Sinusitis, 117
Sinus node arrhythmias, 41
Sinus tachycardia, 41
Skeletal muscle cells, 3
Skin, in cystic fibrosis, 89
Skin cancer, 400–403
  ultraviolet radiation in, 401
Sliding hernia, 188
Slipped disk, 140–141
Small-cell lung cancer, 96
Small intestines. See also Intestines
  anatomy of, 163
  in cystic fibrosis, 89
  obstruction of, 196–197
Smallpox, 20t
Smith's fracture, 227
Smoking, as cancer risk factor, 6
Smooth muscle cells, 3
Sodium
  electrolyte characteristics of, 29t
  normal values for, 29t
Spastic colitis, 198–199
Spastic colon, 198–199
Spastic neurogenic bladder, 368
Specificity, pathogenicity and, 14
Spina bifida, 152–153
Spinal cord injury, 154–155
  acceleration-deceleration, 118–119
  effects of, 155
  herniated intervertebral disk, 140–141
  suspected, 118
Spine curvature
  kyphosis, 239

lordosis, 239
  normal, 239
  scoliosis, 238–239
Spirochetes, in infection, 13
Sporadic goiter, 300
Sprains, 240–241
Spurious polycythemia, 260
Squamous cell carcinoma
  of bladder, 360
  of cervix, 312–313
  of esophagus, 176
  of larynx, 420–421
  of lung, 96
  of oral cavity, 204
  of skin, 400, 403
  of vulva, 354
Squamous intraepithelial lesion, 312–313
Stains, in infection diagnosis, 16
Status asthmaticus, 84
Stiff lung, 80–83
Stomach
  cancer of, 178–179
  gastric ulcers, 216–217
  gastritis, 180–181
  herniation of, 188–189
Strains, 242–243
Stress fracture, 227
Striated cardiac muscle cells, 3
Striated muscle cells, 3
Stroke, 156–157
Struvite renal calculi, 375
Subacute glomerulonephritis, 364–365
Subarachnoid hemorrhage, 130
Sudden deafness, 418
Sunburn, 384
Superficial spreading melanoma, 400
Superior vena cava
  in cardiac circulation, 61
  in myocardial infarction, 62
  in rheumatic heart disease, 71
Suppurative otitis media, 428
Sweating, 15
Sweat test, 88
Sycosis barbae, 390
Syphilis, 343–344
Systemic lupus erythematosus, 278–279
  organs affected by, 279
Systemic sclerosis, 276–277
Systolic click-murmur syndrome, 60–61
Systolic dysfunction, in heart failure, 56

Testes
  cryptorchidism, 314–315
  testicular torsion, 348–349
Testicular cancer, 346–347
  staging of, 347t
Testicular torsion, 348–349
Tetanus, 18t
Tetralogy of Fallot, 48–49
Thalassemia, 264–265
Theca-lutein cysts, ovarian, 334
Thermal burn, 384
Third-degree atrioventricular block, 41
Third-degree burns, 384–385
Third space, defined, 28
Thrombosis
  cardiac, 157
  deep vein, 52–53
  in pulmonary embolism, 106
  in stroke, 156–157
Thyroid gland
  anatomy of, 293
  cancer of, 302–303
  goiter, 300–301
  hormones of, 292–293
  hyperthyroidism, 292–293
  hypothyroidism, 296–297
Thyroiditis, Hashimoto's, 296–297
Thyroid-stimulating hormone (TSH),
  292
Thyroid storm, 292
Thyrotoxicosis, 292
Thyrotropin-releasing hormone (TRH),
  292
Tinea infection, 392
Tinel's sign, 222
Tobacco, as cancer risk factor, 6
Tongue, cancer of, 204–205
Tonicity
  alterations in, 28t
  defined, 29–30
  fluid balance and, 29–30
Toxic shock syndrome, 18t
Toxigenicity, pathogenicity and, 14
Toxins, in cell injury, 4
Toxoplasmosis, 20t
Trait dominance, 22
Transitional cell carcinoma, of bladder,
  360
Transmission traits, 21
Transposition of the great arteries,
  48–49
Transudative pleural effusion, 99
Traumatic pneumothorax, 102
Trendelenburg's test
  in developmental dysplasia of hip, 224
  in varicose veins, 78
Trichinosis, 20t
Trichomoniasis, 344–345
Tricuspid valve, 75
  in rheumatic heart disease, 71

T

Tay-Sachs disease, 24t
T-condylar fracture, 227
Tendonitis, 244–245
Tension pneumothorax, 102–103
Tension-type headache, 138
Teratogens, 22

t refers to table.

Triiodothyronine (T_3), 292
Trisomy, 23
Trisomy 13 syndrome, 27t
Trisomy 18 syndrome, 27t
Trisomy 21 syndrome, 27t
Trousseau's syndrome, 248
Tuberculosis, 18t, 114–115
    lung tissue appearance in, 115
Tubular necrosis, acute, 358–359
Tumor markers, in cancer
      diagnosis, 12
Tumors. *See also* Cancer
    bone, 218–219
    brain, 128–129
    classification of, 12
    development of, 9
    invasive, 10
    localized, 9
    metastatic, 10–11
Tumor suppressor genes, 6
Type 1 diabetes mellitus, 286–287
Type 2 diabetes mellitus, 286–287

U

Ulcerative colitis, 214–215
Ulcers
    corneal, 412–413
    gastric, 216–217
Ultrasonography, in cancer diagnosis,
    11–12
Ultraviolet radiation
    burn due to, 384
    as cancer risk factor, 6
Undescended testes, 314–315
Upper respiratory tract infection,
    116–117
Urethritis, 362–363
Uric acid calculi, 375
Urinary tract infection (UTI), 18t
    cystitis, 362–363
    routes of infection, 363t
Uterus
    dysfunctional uterine bleeding,
      316–317
    endometrial cancer, 320–321
    endometriosis, 322–323

fibroid disease of, 326–327
pelvic inflammatory disease,
    336–337

V

Vaginitis, 350–351
    Candida albicans, 350–351
    trichomonal, 345, 350
Vaginosis, 351
Valvular heart disease, 74–77
    rheumatic heart disease and, 70–71
Varicella, 20t
Varicocele, 352–353
Varicose veins, 78–79
Vascular changes
    in headache, 138–139
    in Raynaud's disease, 68–69
Veins
    deep, of leg, 53
    normal, 79
    varicose, 78–79
Venereal warts, 342–344
Venous thrombosis, 53
    deep vein thrombosis, 52–53
Ventricles
    in atrial septal defect, 47
    in cardiac circulation, 61
    in cardiomyopathy, 45
    in mitral valve prolapse, 61
    in rheumatic heart disease, 71
    in tetralogy of Fallot, 49
    in transposition of the great arteries,
      49
Ventricular arrhythmias, 41
Ventricular fibrillation, 41
Ventricular septal defect, 48–49
Ventricular tachycardia, 41
Vermiform appendix, inflammation and
      obstruction of, 162–163
Vernal conjunctivitis, 410
Verrucae, 404–405
Vertical compression spinal injury, 119,
    154
Viability, pathogenicity and, 14
Vigorous achalasia, 160
Villous adenomas, 168
Viral conjunctivitis, 410

Viral hepatitis, 186–187
Viral infections, 18–20t
Viral pneumonia, 20t, 100
Virulence, pathogenicity and, 14
Viruses, in infection, 13
Vulvar cancer, 354–355
Vulvitis, 350

W

Warts, 404–405
    genital, 342–344
West Nile virus, 158–159
Wet gangrene, 5
Wet lung, 80–83
Whiplash, 118–119
White blood cell count, in infection
      diagnosis, 16
Whitehead, 380–381
White lung, 80–83
Whooping cough, 17t
Wrist
    anatomy of, 223
    carpal tunnel syndrome,
      222–223
    fracture of, 227
    rheumatoid arthritis of, 275

X

X inactivation, 22
X-linked disorders, 22–23
    recessive, 23, 25t
X-linked hemophilia, 250–251
X-rays
    in cancer diagnosis, 11
    as cancer risk factor, 6–7

Y

Yeast infection, vaginal, 350–351

Z

Zygote, 21